# TEST CRICKET LISTS

# TEST CRICKET LISTS

## THE ULTIMATE GUIDE TO INTERNATIONAL TEST CRICKET

GRAHAM DAWSON & CHARLIE WAT
INTRODUCTION BY
CHRISTOPHER MARTIN-JENKINS

Robinson
LONDON

Robinson Publishing Ltd
7 Kensington Church Court
London W8 4SP

First published in the UK by Robinson Publishing Ltd 1998
This edition first published in Australia by The Five Mile Press Pty Ltd 1998



A copy of the British Library Cataloguing in Publication Data
for this title is available from the British Library.

ISBN 1-85487-582-5

Printed and bound in the EC

# Introduction

For a part of the 1998 season it was possible to make a list of exactly eleven English cricketers who were still playing regularly as professionals and had each represented their country in a Test match once and only once. No other country came remotely close to that. If in nothing else England leads the world, it seems, in investing hope in some bright new talent, only to cast him off as inadequate for the supreme test of a player's worth.

Talent and worth are on trial almost from the moment a child picks up a bat and in a sense this book is a collection of those who fulfilled their talent and those who did not. It is good that it has its genesis in Australia because the majority of record books of one kind and another emanate from England and the Mother Country long ago had to admit that the rest of the world has produced more tough competitors than she has. One of the more interesting lists outside these pages, indeed, would be an eleven of cussed Aussies.

Warwick Armstrong would be a suitable captain. He was one of those who went on strike and refused to tour England in 1912 because the terms for touring were too mean. It was he, too, who picked up an evening newspaper and began reading it in the outfield after taking off his regular bowlers and posting himself in the deep when England were playing for a draw during the Oval Test of 1921 because, he said with calculating insult, he 'wanted to find out who he was playing against'.

Dennis Lillee would certainly be one of the fast bowlers, assured of selection not just for his deliberate belligerence and a memorable eyeball-to-eyeball confrontation with Pakistan's equally irascible Javed Miandad, but also for being the only man to start an innings in a Test match with a bat made of aluminium. Ian Chappell, at least during his rebellious era, would get a place too, as would gum-chewing Slasher Mackay with his knees-bent walk, determined to defend his wicket till the cows came home and to hell with entertainment.

One could carry on quite easily with Australian cricketers hewn from that sort of rock, but who could England put against them? Trevor Bailey and Michael Atherton might vie for the captaincy and Fred Trueman, too, would be on the list. So would David Steele, the 'bank clerk who went to war', as John Arlott called him: grey-haired, bespectacled, defiant and believing with a wonderful certainty in his ability to put Lillee and Jeff Thomson in their places. There were plenty of professionals of old with the same streak of stubbornness, Herbert Sutcliffe being first amongst them. Ken Barrington was another: whereas Englishmen saw him as staunch and full of humour, Australians considered him only to be a damned nuisance, all too ready to bat for long, defiant hours. Cussedness is in the eye of the beholder.

Nevertheless, for sheer competitiveness, England struggles to compare with Australia—and with South Africa too; as indeed it has in technical correctness over recent years at least. Bad habits starting at the top and trickling down to the bottom of the game by imitation? Or simply a lack of decent coaching at the bottom? The debate continues.

Technique is one thing, disposition another. Cricket is a tough game, requiring more guts and bloody-mindedness the higher a player climbs, and whatever the reason for the technical shortcomings which have been exposed in national teams of recent vintage, one convincing theory is that the cause of the brittleness of English batting and the lack of venom in their bowling probably has much to do with the softness of the national character generally since affluence began to spread. There are not enough hungry fighters in England, it seems, partly because the hungriest have not seen cricket as a route to a full stomach, as they do in the West Indies and, if they are lucky enough to get a break, in India, Pakistan and Sri Lanka too.

In Australia it is not so much poverty as out-and-out patriotism, and a desire to make a name in the city which has been the motivation for success. Many of the toughest Australian competitors have come from the outback. Not that all Australians are dour or fierce or ruthless. On the contrary, they are well versed in the game's conventions and ethics. Two of the most charming men who ever graced a cricket field were the post-war heroes Keith Miller and Lindsay Hassett. I cannot believe Miller was ever rude or graceless to anyone while Hassett's poker-faced mischievousness was legendary. When one of his team in India lost his temper and let the side down on a matter of cricketing etiquette, Hassett asked him to field in the deep and then began fastidiously directing his position, taking him nearer and ever nearer to the pavilion steps before ushering him up the steps themselves and finally commanding him to 'go inside and cool off for a while'.

A list of cricketing charmers would also be a nice selection: genuine charmers, as opposed to smoothies—although a list of smoothies would produce another interesting test of opinion and judgement. Both would probably have to be selected by women. One or two of those merry cricketers who survived the Second World War and therefore seemed to get more fun out of the game than the players of any other era would probably make both these teams. Keith Miller, Denis Compton, Godfrey Evans and Bill Edrich all come to mind. Of all the impromptu witticisms ever made, John Warr's at Bill Edrich's fourth wedding must surely come close to winning the gold medal: asked by an usher at the door of the church whether he was a friend of the bride or the groom, he replied: 'Season Ticket'.

There is no end to cricket lists once you start. A friend of mine with a very good mind, is also a near insomniac. In order to lull himself into at least a brief sleep some time after midnight, his latest ruse is to select cricket elevens not, as in this book, from players whose names begin with A, B, C, etc. but whose names end with these letters. Less flexible minds than his might be stumped quickly enough by having to produce rival elevens from the first letters of famous players' christian names, or teams of players with the same first names. Start with Peter and John and, if you are still awake, see how you get on with Gary and Wayne.

One of the most enjoyable selections has always been an eleven of cricketing epithets: the likes of Thomas Box (Sussex, Surrey and Hampshire), Frank Bale of Leicestershire or any one of the various cricketing Balls. A young left-arm over bowler called Chris Batt made his County Championship debut for Middlesex in 1998 and it could only be a matter of time, surely, before he dismissed the Somerset captain, Peter Bowler, thus producing some such scorecard entry as 'Bowler caught and bowled Batt, 24'. (Could we arrange a game in which it would be possible for Bowler to be caught Ball bowled Batt?)

Talking of nomenclature, I was once caught and bowled in a match at Horsham by a bowler called Charlie Oliphant-Cullum and much mirth was caused by the reaction of the wicket-keeper: 'Blimey, how's the bloomin' scorer going to fit that one in?'

Why are wicket-keepers invariably so talkative? A Loquacious versus Silent cricketers match would make intriguing watching and listening. And, on the subject of double-barrelled folk (they would make an interesting eleven in themselves) the late Raymond Robertson-Glasgow (Oxford and Somerset) once sat down with the playwright Ben Travers to choose an eleven from the most famous men in history. They had plumped for Ludwig van Beethoven and John the Baptist as openers until they realised that there would inevitably be a run-out. Beethoven, of course, was deaf.

But, I want to conclude on a serious note. Cricket writing of recent vintage has tended to be critical to the point of cruelty whenever a prominent team is defeated. Everyone who plays sports seriously has to accept that it is the winner who gains all the glory, but it is too easily forgotten by those whose privilege it is to report cricket how very good the players are and how many hurdles they have crossed to get to a professional standard.

It starts in childhood:

*Where else, you ask, can England's game be seen*
*Rooted so deep as on the village green?*
*Here, in the slum, where doubtful sunlight falls*
*To gild three stumps chalked on decaying walls.*

Too much traffic and too much football has killed off street cricket in England, but certainly not on the sub-continent. There may be fewer who get the chance to play cricket in Britain these days but of those who do the naturally gifted soon emerge and, with luck, their innate skill is spotted and nurtured by an adult. The promising youngster starts to play in matches, at school or a local club, and if he does well he is brought to the notice of those running county sides at junior level.

These are still only small steps towards the top but they are achievements in themselves. Only the winter before writing this I was hailed by a complete stranger in a restaurant in Barbados and given the lengthy story of a school match in which he had played. Frequently I am told with quiet pride by strangers that they once represented Essex under 12s or had a trial for Cheshire under 15s.

The sifting process continues further still. If the growing youngster shines at county level as well as in school or club colts games, the proud day comes when he is offered the chance to play for his county second eleven, or, if he lives and plays outside one of the 18 first-class counties, in a Minor County Championship match. By now the physical characteristics of the young cricketer will have taken their final shape more or less. If he is tall and reasonably strong the chances are he will be bowling somewhere above medium pace, but if he begins to think that a professional career is beckoning, that burgeoning strength has to be honed and preserved. So no more over-indulging in beer or the wrong kind of food. Now the ambitious youngster has to spend much of his time weight-training and running, stretching and twisting: lonely hours devoted to building up the muscles needed for prolonged hard work or hot afternoons. Long hours in the nets, too: practising the Trueman maxims of line and length before buckling on the pads and preparing to face a hard leather ball hurled faster than anything previously encountered. Bowlers at the level to which our ambitious youngster is now beginning to aspire are intent on testing not just technique, but courage too.

Along with physical courage and stamina, the would-be professional cricketer has to learn necessary mental disciplines. Concentration for long periods is required of batsmen who know that one moment of carelessness will almost certainly waste hours of practice. When Robert Croft, the Glamorgan all-rounder, was battling to save the third Test for England against South Africa at Old Trafford in 1998 he made himself think between each ball he received of all sorts of matters unrelated to the fierce challenge confronting him. Where would he eat in the evening? What would he say to the boys in the pub when he got home to Wales about his country's latest humiliating defeat on the rugby field? Then, as soon as Allan Donald, with sunblock splodged like warpaint on his nose and cheeks, began his long, athletic, magnificent sprint to the crease, Croft's attention snapped back to the ball about to be received.

The bowler has to concentrate all the time too. While Croft was clearing his mind by a process of distraction and relaxation, Donald had to be thinking on the walk back to his mark. Should it be the bouncer now, or possibly the yorker? An away-swinger on a length just outside the off-stump, to invite the unwary drive and an edge to the slips; or an inswinger darting back into the pads?

If a cricketer can thus train his body and mind, harness his talent, retain his will to succeed through days of disappointment, the rising youngster may succeed in minor county or first-class second eleven cricket and get his chance in first-class cricket itself. Then he has to find the consistency which will persuade the committee to offer him a professional contract; but it may be years before the England selection committee start to take an interest and the longed-for telephone call from the chairman himself.

The list of the eleven current players who, by August 1998, had had that sort of call, is mingled in this book with those who have had a similar experience for other countries. For the record, therefore, England's eleven, top heavy with fastish bowlers but in some sort of batting order, is:

Steve James (Glamorgan)
John Stephenson (Essex and Hampshire)
James Whitaker (Leicestershire)
Alan Wells (Sussex and Kent)
Ben Hollioake (Surrey)
Ashley Giles (Warwickshire)
Neil Williams (Middlesex and Essex)
Chris Silverwood (Yorkshire)
Mike Smith (Gloucestershire)
Joey Benjamin (Warwickshire and Surrey)
Simon Brown (Durham)

Failures to a man, judged by the highest standard—but each a brilliant cricketer who outstripped his rivals all the way along the nettle-strewn path to the summit. We should lay a stone on the cairn for them all.

It is with a plea for sympathy when a cricketer 'fails' that I hand over to you the useful and diverting collection of Cricket Lists which follows. Also with a word of congratulation to the compilers. Charlie Wat has long been respected as a thorough cricket statistician of independent mind, whose figures on Test Cricketers have been gratefully carried by many cricket correspondents, myself included. I must also offer belated public acknowledgement to Graham Dawson. When in the Centenary Test at Melbourne in 1977 I found myself by sheer good fortune at the microphone as Australia completed their 45 run win over England, it was Graham who whispered in my ear that the margin of victory was precisely the same as it had been in the first Test ever played. For the next edition, gentlemen, how about a list of remarkable cricketing coincidences?

*Christopher Martin-Jenkins*

# Acknowledgements

It has been a great pleasure to have been involved in another edition of *Test Cricket Lists*.

Since the previous publication, there has been a new Test record score of 6 for 952 — declared by Sri Lanka against India — and for the first time in 1345 Test matches, the scores between Zimbabwe and England at Bulawayo in December 1996 were tied, but the match ended in a draw. How would you explain that scenario to someone from a non-cricket playing country? These, and many more magnificent contests appear in the considerably expanded 'Famous Test Match' section of this edition.

Once again, statistician Charlie Wat has been magnificent. His attention to detail and presentation of the statistics are matched only by his great knowledge, understanding and love of the game — all of which have proved to be a constant source of strength.

In compiling this volume, I am again indebted to the works of some far more knowledgable students of the game than me. In particular, I acknowledge my debt to the *Wisden Book of Test Cricket*, compiled and edited by Bill Findall; the *Wisden Cricketers' Almanack*, edited by Matthew Engel; and *The Complete Who's Who of Test Cricketers* by Christopher Martin-Jenkins.

I would also like to thank David Horgan, Emma Borghesi and Emma Short from The Five Mile Press for their continued support, encouragement and patience.

In order to meet the publication deadlines, figures and statistics are current up to and including the fifth Test between England and South Africa in August 1998.

Graham Dawson

Graham Dawson
September, 1998

# Contents

# PART 1

# FAMOUS TEST MATCHES

## A Guide to the Symbols

Throughout this book we have used asterisks (*) alongside individual scores to indicate that the player was not out.

In the score cards, we have used an asterisk after a player's name to indicate the captain of the team, and a dagger (†) to indicate the wicketkeeper.

All other symbols are explained where they occur.

## Spelling

Players' names have been spelt as they appear in the cricketing records of their own country.

## Ground names

'Bombay' became known as 'Mumbai' in November 1995 and 'Madras' became known as 'Chennai' in June 1996. The new names have been used for matches played at these grounds since the changes.

## AUSTRALIA v ENGLAND 1876-77

Melbourne Cricket Ground, Melbourne
15, 16, 17, 19 March 1877
Australia won by 45 runs

Australia 245 (C. Bannerman 165 retired hurt) and 104; England 196 (H. Jupp 63, W.E. Midwinter 5 for 78) and 108 (T. Kendall 7 for 55)

This is regarded as the first official Test match. England was represented by professional players who had been touring Australia during the 1876-77 season, but it would have been a stronger team had it included the leading amateur cricketers of the day.

Australia won the toss and batted first. Charles Bannerman dominated the innings and, after receiving the first ball in Test cricket, went on to score the first Test century. He eventually retired hurt after making 165 in an Australian total of 245. Surrey opener Harry Jupp top-scored in England's first innings with a patient knock of 63.

Shaw and Ulyett combined to bowl Australia out for 104, but the target of 154 proved too much for the England batsmen. The Victorian Kendall captured seven wickets for 55 runs as England was dismissed for 208; Australia won by 45 runs.

A collection at the ground for the injured Bannerman raised £165. (See scorecard on page 12.)

## ENGLAND v AUSTRALIA 1882

The Ashes match
The Oval, London
28, 29 August 1882
Australia won by seven runs

Australia 63 (R.G. Barlow 5 for 19) and 122 (H.H. Massie 55); England 101 (F.R. Spofforth 7 for 46) and 77 (F.R. Spofforth 7 for 44)

This most remarkable and exciting match will be remembered for as long as cricket history exists. The Ashes match was Australia's first Test victory in England. The win was set up by Spofforth's magnificent bowling, and his figures of 14 for 90 enhanced his reputation as the finest bowler in the world.

Australia was bundled out for 63 after winning the toss. England's reply was not much better, and the team was dismissed for 101. Australia's second innings was an improvement on the first, and Massie led the way with 55 in an opening stand of 66 with Bannerman, but the rest struggled. By mid-afternoon on the second day, Australia had been dismissed for 122, with a lead of just 84 runs. England looked comfortable in the second innings when W.G. Grace and Ulyett took the score to 51 after the early loss of Hornby and Barlow, but inspired bowling by 'the Demon' (Spofforth) and Boyle, supported by magnificent fielding, carried Australia to a thrilling victory. See page 14 for the complete scoreboard.

The day after the match, the *Sporting Times* carried an 'In Memoriam' announcement as follows:

'IN AFFECTIONATE REMEMBERANCE
OF
ENGLISH CRICKET
which died at the Oval on 29th August 1882.
Deeply lamented by a large circle
of sorrowing friends and
acquaintances.
R.I.P.
N.B. — The body will be cremated and
the ashes taken to Australia.'

## AUSTRALIA v ENGLAND 1884-85

Sydney Cricket Ground, Sydney
20, 21, 23, 24 February 1885
Australia won by six runs

Australia 181 (T.W. Garrett 51 not out, W. Flowers 5 for 46) and 165 (W. Bates 5 for 24); England 133 (T.P. Horan 6 for 40) and 207 (W. Fellows 56, J.M. Reid 56, F.R. Spofforth 6 for 90)

Australia crawled to 0 for 40 at lunch before a violent storm hit the ground. When play finally resumed on the damp pitch Australia collapsed, finishing the day at 8 for 97. When Spofforth went at 101 Australia was in real trouble. But fortunately Garrett, 51, and Evans, 33, added 80 runs for the last wicket in a match-winning partnership. Barnes — the leading wicket-taker on the tour — refused to bowl after a disagreement with his captain, Shrewsbury.

The England innings finished quickly as Horan and Spofforth bundled out the visitors for 133, Flowers top-scoring with 24. Australia then built on its first-innings lead of 48 before Bates struck. England's target was now 214. At 5 for 61 and then 6 for 92 the game appeared lost. It was Flowers and Reid who combined for a 102-run partnership that turned the game the visitors' way, before Australia's great bowlers, Spofforth and Trumble, wrapped up the England tail. 'The Demon' Spofforth captured ten wickets in a match for the third time.

## AUSTRALIA v ENGLAND 1894-95

Sydney Cricket Ground, Sydney
14, 15, 17, 18, 19, 20 December 1895
England won by ten runs

Australia 586 (S.E. Gregory 201, G. Giffen 161, F.A. Iredale 81, J. Blackham 74, T. Richardson 5 for 181) and 166 (J. Darling 53, R. Peel 6 for 67); England 325 (A. Ward 75, J. Briggs 57) and 437 (A. Ward 117, J.T. Brown 53)

## AUSTRALIA v ENGLAND 1876-77 (First Test)

Melbourne Cricket Ground, 15, 16, 17, 19 March. Australia won by 45 runs

**AUSTRALIA**

| | | | | | |
|---|---|---|---|---|---|
| C. Bannerman | retired hurt | 165 | | b Ulyett | 4 |
| N.Thompson | b Hill | 1 | | c Emmett b Shaw | 7 |
| T.P.Horan | c Hill b Shaw | 12 | | c Selby b Hill | 20 |
| D.W. Gregory* | run out | 1 | (9) | b Shaw | 3 |
| B.B.Cooper | b Southerton | 15 | | b Shaw | 3 |
| W.E.Midwinter | c Ulyett b Southerton | 5 | | c Southerton b Ulyett | 17 |
| E.J. Gregory | c Greenwood b Lillywhite | 0 | | c Emmett b Ulyett | 11 |
| J.M.Blackham† | b Southerton | 17 | | lbw b Shaw | 6 |
| T.W.Garrett | not out | 18 | (4) | c Emmett b Shaw | 0 |
| T.K.Kendall | c Southerton b Shaw | 3 | | not out | 17 |
| J.Hodges | b Shaw | 0 | | b Lillywhite | 8 |
| Extras | (B 4, LB 2, W 2) | 8 | | (B 5, LB 3) | 8 |
| Total | | 245 | | | 104 |

**ENGLAND**

| | | | | | |
|---|---|---|---|---|---|
| H.Jupp | lbw b Garrett | 63 | (3) | lbw b Midwinter | 4 |
| J.Selby† | c Cooper b Hodges | 7 | (5) | c Horan b Hodges | 38 |
| H.R.J.Charlwood | c Blackham b Midwinter | 36 | (4) | b Kendall | 13 |
| G.Ulyett | lbw b Thompson | 10 | (6) | b Kendall | 24 |
| A.Greenwood | c E.J. Gregory b Midwinter | 1 | (2) | c Midwinter b Kendall | 5 |
| T.Armitage | c Blackham b Midwinter | 9 | (8) | c Blackham b Kendall | 3 |
| A.Shaw | b Midwinter | 10 | | st Blackham b Kendall | 2 |
| T.Emmett | b Midwinter | 8 | (9) | b Kendall | 9 |
| A.Hill | not out | 35 | (1) | c Thompson b Kendall | 0 |
| J.Lillywhite* | c and b Kendall | 10 | | b Hodges | 4 |
| J.Southerton | c Cooper b Garrett | 6 | | not out | 1 |
| Extras | (LB 1) | 1 | | (B 4, LB 1) | 5 |
| **Total** | | **196** | | | **108** |

| **ENGLAND** | O | M | R | W | | O | M | R | W |
|---|---|---|---|---|---|---|---|---|---|
| Shaw | 55.3 | 34 | 51 | 3 | Shaw | 34 | 16 | 38 | 5 |
| Hill | 23 | 10 | 42 | 1 | Ulyett | 19 | 7 | 39 | 3 |
| Ulyett | 25 | 12 | 36 | 0 | Hill | 14 | 6 | 18 | 1 |
| Southerton | 37 | 17 | 61 | 3 | Lillywhite | 1 | 0 | 1 | 1 |
| Armitage | 3 | 0 | 15 | 0 | | | | | |
| Lillywhite | 14 | 5 | 19 | 1 | | | | | |
| Emmett | 12 | 7 | 13 | 0 | | | | | |

| **AUSTRALIA** | O | M | R | W | | O | M | R | W |
|---|---|---|---|---|---|---|---|---|---|
| Hodges | 9 | 0 | 27 | 1 | Kendall | 33.1 | 12 | 55 | 7 |
| Garrett | 18.1 | 10 | 22 | 2 | Midwinter | 19 | 7 | 23 | 1 |
| Kendall | 38 | 16 | 54 | 1 | D.W.Gregory | 5 | 1 | 9 | 0 |
| Midwinter | 54 | 23 | 78 | 5 | Garrett | 2 | 0 | 9 | 0 |
| Thompson | 17 | 10 | 14 | 1 | Hodges | 7 | 5 | 7 | 2 |

FALL OF WICKETS

| | A | E | A | E |
|---|---|---|---|---|
| Wkt | 1st | 1st | 2nd | 2nd |
| 1st | 2 | 23 | 7 | 0 |
| 2nd | 40 | 79 | 27 | 7 |
| 3rd | 41 | 98 | 31 | 20 |
| 4th | 118 | 109 | 31 | 22 |
| 5th | 142 | 121 | 35 | 62 |
| 6th | 143 | 135 | 58 | 68 |
| 7th | 197 | 145 | 71 | 92 |
| 8th | 243 | 145 | 75 | 93 |
| 9th | 245 | 168 | 75 | 100 |
| 10th | 245 | 196 | 104 | 108 |

Umpires: C.A.Reid and R.B.Terry

This high-scoring match was one of many highlights and records: the aggregate of 1514 runs was a new mark, Australia's score of 586 remained an Australian record for 30 years, the ninth-wicket partnership of 154 by Gregory and Blackham still remains Australia's best and, for the first time, a team won after following-on. Giffen produced an outstanding all-round performance for Australia: 161 and 41 with the bat, and 8 for 238 from 118 overs with the ball. But luck went against the Australians. First, Blackham sustained a severe thumb injury and couldn't keep wicket in England's second innings. Then after five days' play, with Australia needing just 64 runs with eight wickets in hand to win, the heavens opened and the rain tumbled down. The next day followed with blazing sunshine, and Australia was caught on a classic 'sticky' wicket. Briggs and Peel took full advantage of the conditions to bowl England to a memorable victory. The details of this absorbing Test are set out on page 16.

## ENGLAND v AUSTRALIA 1902

Old Trafford, Manchester
24, 25, 26 July 1902
Australia won by three runs

Australia 299 (V.T. Trumper 104, C. Hill 65, R.A. Duff 54, J. Darling 51, W.H. Lockwood 6 for 48); and 86 (W.H. Lockwood 5 for 28); England 262 (Hon. F.S. Jackson 128, L.C. Braund 65) and 120 (H. Trumble 6 for 53)

---

Australia went into this vital Test one up with two matches to play, and England had made four changes to the team that had lost the previous Test at Sheffield. Significantly, Jessop and Hirst were left out of the team, and F.W. Tate, a bowler with no batting ability, was included for his first Test. Trumper played a magnificent innings for Australia and posted his century before lunch. With Hill, 65, Duff, 54, and Darling, 51, making useful contributions, Australia posted 299, a somewhat disappointing total after the opening stand of 135. England's reply was dominated by Jackson, 128, and Braund, 65, who scored 193 out of 262. With a lead of 37, Australia collapsed in its second innings and was dismissed for a paltry 86. Only Darling, 37, and Gregory, 24, reached double figures. Tate dropped Darling early in his innings. If the catch had been taken, Australia would have struggled to reach 50.

With light rain falling, England needed 124 to square the series. After a steady start, the wickets began to tumble — 15 runs were needed with two wickets to fall when Rhodes joined Lilley. But shortly afterwards Lilley fell to a magnificent outfield catch by Hill.

With eight runs required, Tate was the last man, and the rain was coming down in torrents. After delay of 45 minutes, play resumed. Rhodes calmly played three balls from Trumble, then Tate faced Saunders. The first ball was snicked for four; Tate survived the next two and was then clean-bowled by the fourth ball of the over.

Australia had snatched victory by three runs. Both Lockwood and Trumble bowled superbly: Lockwood claimed eleven wickets and Trumble claimed ten.

## ENGLAND v AUSTRALIA 1902

The Oval, London
11, 12, 13 August 1902
England won by one wicket

Australia 324 (H. Trumble 64 not out, M.A. Noble 52, G.H. Hirst 5 for 77) and 121 (W.H. Lockwood 5 for 45); England 183 (H. Trumble 8 for 65) and 9 wickets for 263 (G.L. Jessop 104, G.H. Hirst 58 not out)

---

The classic contest is always referred to as 'Jessop's match' for it was Jessop (known as 'the Croucher') who eventually won the game for England.

Darling called correctly, and Australia took advantage of the good weather and pitch to compile 324. Trumble's 64 not out proved his all-round ability.

England made a modest reply, scoring 183 with Trumble claiming 8 for 65.

Australia's second innings started disastrously with Thrumper being run out for 2. After this early setback, the Australia batsmen struggled and only Hill, 34, Armstrong, 21, were able to score more than 20. Australia was all out for 121, for a lead of 262.

England collapsed and was at one point only 5 for 48. The match looked to be over. Then 'the Croucher' joined Jackson, and the pair turned the game around for the home team. In 75 minutes Jessop smashed 104 runs with 17 boundaries and a five. But 15 runs were still required when the last man, Rhodes, joined Hirst.

Legend has it that Hirst said to Rhodes, "We'll get them in singles." However, although these men of Yorkshire did manage to score the runs needed to record a famous victory, they did not do it in singles.

## SOUTH AFRICA v ENGLAND 1905-06

Old Wanderers, Johannesburg
2, 3, 4 January 1906
South Africa won by one wicket

England 184 and 190 (P.F. Warner 51); South Africa 91 (W. Lees 5 for 34) and 9 wickets for 287 (A.W. Nourse 93 not out, G.C. White 81)

---

In this low-scoring match, England gained a first innings lead of 93. Faulkner bowled superbly to capture 4 for 26 and restrict England's second innings to 190. Crawford batted well in both innings, scoring 44 and 43.

When Nourse joined White, the home team was struggling at 6 for 105 and England appeared likely to win. Nourse played with remarkable maturity as he and White carried the score to 226. After White's departure, Vogler and Schwarz fell at 230 and 239 respectively. The last

## ENGLAND v AUSTRALIA 1882 (Only Test)

Kennington Oval, London, 28, 29 August. Australia won by 7 runs

**AUSTRALIA**

| | | | | | |
|---|---|---|---|---|---|
| A.C.Bannerman | c Grace b Peate | 9 | | c Studd b Barnes | 13 |
| H.H.Massie | b Ulyett | 1 | | b Steel | 55 |
| W.L.Murdoch* | b Peate | 13 | (4) | run out | 29 |
| G.J.Bonnor | b Barlow | 1 | (3) | b Ulyett | 2 |
| T.P.Horan | b Barlow | 3 | | c Grace b Peate | 2 |
| G.Giffen | b Peate | 2 | | c Grace b Peate | 0 |
| J.M.Blackham† | c Grace b Barlow | 17 | | c Lyttelton b Peate | 7 |
| T.W.Garrett | c Read b Peate | 10 | (10) | not out | 2 |
| H.F.Boyle | b Barlow | 2 | (11) | b Steel | 0 |
| S.P.Jones | c Barnes b Barlow | 0 | (8) | run out | 6 |
| F.R.Spofforth | not out | 4 | (9) | b Peate | 0 |
| Extras | (B 1) | 1 | | (B 6) | 6 |
| **Total** | | **63** | | | **122** |

**ENGLAND**

| | | | | | |
|---|---|---|---|---|---|
| R.G.Barlow | c Bannerman b Spofforth | 11 | (3) | b Spofforth | 0 |
| W.G.Grace | b Spofforth | 4 | (1) | c Bannerman b Boyle | 32 |
| G.Ulyett | st Blackham b Spofforth | 26 | (4) | c Blackham b Spofforth | 11 |
| A.P.Lucas | c Blackham b Boyle | 9 | (5) | b Spofforth | 5 |
| Hon.A.Lyttelton† | c Blackham b Spofforth | 2 | (6) | b Spofforth | 12 |
| C.T.Studd | b Spofforth | 0 | (10) | not out | 0 |
| J.M.Read | not out | 19 | (8) | b Spofforth | 0 |
| W.Barnes | b Boyle | 5 | (9) | c Murdoch b Boyle | 2 |
| A.G.Steel | b Garrett | 14 | (7) | c and b Spofforth | 0 |
| A.N.Hornby* | b Spofforth | 2 | (2) | b Spofforth | 9 |
| E.Peate | c Boyle b Spofforth | 0 | | b Boyle | 2 |
| Extras | (B 6, LB 2, NB 1) | 9 | | (B 3, LB 1) | 4 |
| **Total** | | **101** | | | **77** |

| **ENGLAND** | O | M | R | W | | O | M | R | W |
|---|---|---|---|---|---|---|---|---|---|
| Peate | 38 | 24 | 31 | 4 | Peate | 21 | 9 | 40 | 4 |
| Ulyett | 9 | 5 | 11 | 1 | Ulyett | 6 | 2 | 10 | 1 |
| Barlow | 31 | 22 | 19 | 5 | Barlow | 13 | 5 | 27 | 0 |
| Steel | 2 | 1 | 1 | 0 | Steel | 7 | 0 | 15 | 2 |
| | | | | | Barnes | 12 | 5 | 15 | 1 |
| | | | | | Studd | 4 | 1 | 9 | 0 |
| **AUSTRALIA** | O | M | R | W | | O | M | R | W |
| Spofforth | 36.3 | 18 | 46 | 7 | Spofforth | 28 | 15 | 44 | 7 |
| Garrett | 16 | 7 | 22 | 1 | Garrett | 7 | 2 | 10 | 0 |
| Boyle | 19 | 7 | 24 | 2 | Boyle | 20 | 11 | 19 | 3 |

FALL OF WICKETS

| | A | E | A | E |
|---|---|---|---|---|
| Wkt | 1st | 1st | 2nd | 2nd |
| 1st | 6 | 13 | 66 | 15 |
| 2nd | 21 | 18 | 70 | 15 |
| 3rd | 22 | 57 | 70 | 51 |
| 4th | 26 | 59 | 79 | 53 |
| 5th | 30 | 60 | 79 | 66 |
| 6th | 30 | 63 | 99 | 70 |
| 7th | 48 | 70 | 114 | 70 |
| 8th | 53 | 96 | 117 | 75 |
| 9th | 59 | 101 | 122 | 75 |
| 10th | 63 | 101 | 122 | 77 |

Umpires: L.Greenwood and R.Thoms

man in was South Africa's captain Sherwell; when he arrived at the crease, 45 runs were still required for victory. Amid great excitement Nourse and Sherwell hit the runs needed to win. It was South Africa's first Test victory.

## AUSTRALIA v ENGLAND 1907-08

Melbourne Cricket Ground, Melbourne
1, 2, 3, 4, 6, 7 January 1908
England won by one wicket

Australia 266 (M.A. Noble 61, J.N. Crawford 5 for 79) and 397 (W.W. Armstrong 77, M.A. Noble 64, V.T. Trumper 63, C.G. Macartney 54, H. Carter 53, S.F. Barnes 5 for 72); England 382 (K.L. Hutchings 126, J.B. Hobbs 83, A. Cotter 5 for 142) and 9 wickets for 282 (F.L. Fane 50)

---

The first Test in Sydney was close, but this one was even closer.

Australia's 266 was a modest effort after an 84-run opening stand by Trumper and Macartney. The skipper, Noble, top-scored with 61.

This match saw the test debut of J.B. Hobbs. He made 83 and paved the way for Hutchings to smash 126 with 25 fours and a six. England finished with 382 for a lead of 116.

Five batsmen scored half-centuries as Australia compiled a second innings total of 397, despite the untiring effort of S.F. Barnes who captured 5 for 72 from 27.4 overs.

England needed to score 282 to win the match and level the series. After the fifth day, it was 4 for 159 and anyone's game. When Rhodes was run out, it was 8 for 209 with 73 runs still required. Barnes and Humphries added 34, but 39 were still needed when the last pair was at the crease.

Finally, with one run needed, the batsmen went for a suicidal single. But Hazlitt's throw was wild and England scored a thrilling victory.

## AUSTRALIA v SOUTH AFRICA 1912

Old Trafford, Manchester
27, 28 May 1912
Australia won by an innings and 88 runs

Australia 448 (W. Bardsley 121, C. Kelleway 114, S.J. Pegler 6 for 105); South Africa 265 (G.A. Faulkner 122 not out, W.J. Whitty 5 for 55) and 95 (C. Kelleway 5 for 33)

---

This was the first match in the triangular tournament of 1912. The Australians started confidently as Kelleway and Bardsley scored freely, compiling a 202-run partnership for the third wicket. Low-order batsmen Matthews and Whitty hit lustily in a last-wicket stand of 63.

Faulkner played a lone hand for South Africa. Dropped at 36, he carried his bat for 122. Whitty had broken the back of the batting with a fiery spell before Matthews ended the innings with the first of his two hat-tricks for the day. Beaumont was bowled, and both Pegler and Ward were trapped lbw.

Forced to follow-on, South Africa's second innings was a dismal effort. At 5 for 70 Matthews bowled Taylor and then caught and bowled both Schwarz and Ward, capturing his second hat-trick. Ward bagged a 'king pair', being the third victim of both hat-tricks.

## ENGLAND v AUSTRALIA 1928-29

Exhibition Ground, Brisbane
30 November 1928 1, 3, 4, 5 December 1928
England won by 675 runs

England 521 (E.H. Hendren 169, H. Larwood 70, A.P.F. Chapman 50) and 8 for 342 dec. (C.P. Mead 72, D.R. Jardine 65 not out, C.V. Grimmett 6 for 131); Australia 122 (H. Larwood 6 for 32) and 66

---

This was Brisbane's first Test match and one of only two to be played at the Exhibition Ground. The 675-run winning margin is the largest Test match victory, by runs, ever recorded.

Under Chapman, who had regained the Ashes at the Oval in 1926, England had one of its strongest teams. But many of the Australian stalwarts, including Collins, Bardsley, Macartney, Andrews, Taylor and Mailey, had retired after the last tour of England.

Hendren, playing perhaps his finest innings against Australia, scored a masterly 169 as England reached 521. Towards the end of the innings, Gregory injured his knee attempting to take a return catch and was told by the doctor that he would never play again.

It was in this match that Bradman made his debut, although he failed, scoring only 18 and 1. He was subsequently left out of the team for the second test.

Larwood crashed through Australia's batting. He captured 6 for 32, and, with Tate claiming 3 for 50, the home team was bundled out for 122.

With Kelleway indisposed with food poisioning and Gregory out of the match, Chapman decided to bat again. He eventually made the first declaration in a Test in Australia at 8 for 342.

Australia's target: just 742 runs! On a difficult pitch, the effort put up by the home team was abysmal: all out for 66 in just 25.3 overs. Woodfull carried his bat in making 30.

Larwood had an outstanding match: he scored 70 and 37 and took 6 for 32 and 2 for 30. And, to round it off, he took four catches in Australia's second innings.

## AUSTRALIA v ENGLAND 1894-95 (First Test)

Sydney Cricket Ground, 14, 15, 17, 18, 19, 20 December. England won by 10 runs

**AUSTRALIA**

| | | | | | |
|---|---|---|---|---|---|
| J.J.Lyons | b Richardson | 1 | | b Richardson | 25 |
| G.H.S.Trott | b Richardson | 12 | | c Gay b Peel | 8 |
| G.Giffen | c Ford b Brockwell | 161 | | lbw b Briggs | 41 |
| J.Darling | b Richardson | 0 | | c Brockwell b Peel | 53 |
| F.A.Iredale | c Stoddart b Ford | 81 | (6) | c and b Briggs | 5 |
| S.E.Gregory | c Peel b Stoddart | 201 | (5) | c Gay b Peel | 16 |
| J.C.Reedman | c Ford b Peel | 17 | | st Gay b Peel | 4 |
| C.E.McLeod | b Richardson | 15 | | not out | 2 |
| C.T.B.Turner | c Gay b Peel | 1 | | c Briggs b Peel | 2 |
| J.M.Blackham*† | b Richardson | 74 | (11) | c and b Peel | 2 |
| E.Jones | not out | 11 | (10) | c MacLaren b Briggs | 1 |
| Extras | (B 8, LB 3, W 1) | 12 | | (B 2, LB 1, NB 4) | 7 |
| **Total** | | **586** | | | **166** |

**ENGLAND**

| | | | | |
|---|---|---|---|---|
| A.C.MacLaren | c Reedman b Turner | 4 | b Giffen | 20 |
| A.Ward | c Iredale b Turner | 75 | b Giffen | 117 |
| A.E.Stoddart* | c Jones b Giffen | 12 | c Giffen b Turner | 36 |
| J.T.Brown | run out | 22 | c Jones b Giffen | 53 |
| W.Brockwell | c Blackham b Jones | 49 | b Jones | 37 |
| R.Peel | c Gregory b Giffen | 4 | b Giffen | 17 |
| F.G.J.Ford | st Blackham b Giffen | 30 | c and b McLeod | 48 |
| J.Briggs | b Griffen | 57 | b McLeod | 42 |
| W.H.Lockwood | c Giffen b Trott | 18 | b Trott | 29 |
| L.H.Gay† | c Gregory b Reedman | 33 | b Trott | 4 |
| T.Richardson | not out | 0 | not out | 12 |
| Extras | (B 17, LB 3, W 1) | 21 | (B 14, LB 8) | 22 |
| **Total** | | **325** | | **437** |

| **ENGLAND** | O | M | R | W | | O | M | R | W |
|---|---|---|---|---|---|---|---|---|---|
| Richardson | 55.3 | 13 | 181 | 5 | Richardson | 11 | 3 | 27 | 1 |
| Peel | 53 | 14 | 140 | 2 | Peel | 30 | 9 | 67 | 6 |
| Briggs | 25 | 4 | 96 | 0 | Lockwood | 16 | 3 | 40 | 0 |
| Brockwell | 22 | 7 | 78 | 1 | Briggs | 11 | 2 | 25 | 3 |
| Ford | 11 | 2 | 47 | 1 | | | | | |
| Stoddart | 3 | 0 | 31 | 1 | | | | | |
| Lockwood | 3 | 2 | 1 | 0 | | | | | |

| **AUSTRALIA** | O | M | R | W | | O | M | R | W |
|---|---|---|---|---|---|---|---|---|---|
| Jones | 19 | 7 | 44 | 1 | Jones | 19 | 0 | 57 | 1 |
| Turner | 44 | 16 | 89 | 2 | Turner | 35 | 14 | 78 | 1 |
| Giffen | 43 | 17 | 75 | 4 | Giffen | 75 | 25 | 164 | 4 |
| Trott | 15 | 4 | 59 | 1 | Trott | 12.4 | 2 | 22 | 2 |
| McLeod | 14 | 2 | 25 | 0 | McLeod | 30 | 7 | 67 | 2 |
| Reedman | 3.3 | 1 | 12 | 1 | Reedman | 6 | 1 | 12 | 0 |
| Lyons | 2 | 2 | 0 | 0 | Lyons | 2 | 0 | 12 | 0 |
| | | | | | Iredale | 2 | 1 | 3 | 0 |

FALL OF WICKETS

| | A | E | E | A |
|---|---|---|---|---|
| Wkt | 1st | 1st | 2nd | 2nd |
| 1st | 10 | 14 | 44 | 26 |
| 2nd | 21 | 43 | 115 | 45 |
| 3rd | 21 | 78 | 217 | 130 |
| 4th | 192 | 149 | 245 | 135 |
| 5th | 331 | 155 | 290 | 147 |
| 6th | 379 | 211 | 296 | 158 |
| 7th | 400 | 211 | 385 | 159 |
| 8th | 409 | 252 | 398 | 161 |
| 9th | 563 | 325 | 420 | 162 |
| 10th | 586 | 325 | 437 | 166 |

Umpires: C.Bannerman and J.Phillips

## ENGLAND v AUSTRALIA 1930

Lord's Cricket Ground, London
27, 28, 30 June, 1 July 1930
Australia won by seven wickets

England 425 (K.S. Duleepsinhji 173, M.W. Tate 54) and 375 (A.P.F. Chapman 121, G.O.B. Allen 57, C.V. Grimmett 6 for 167); Australia 6 wickets for 729 dec. (D.G. Bradman 254, W.M. Woodfull 155, A.F. Kippax 83, W.H. Ponsford 81) and 3 for 72

This was the match in which Bradman played the innings he considered to be (technically) the best in his life.

Australia had gone to Lord's one down, but determined to square the series. Duleepsinhji contributed a century, 173, in his first Test against Australia to England's total of 425.

Woodfull and Ponsford gave Australia a flying start and posted 162 for the first wicket. With Bradman's arrival, the scoring rate increased. At stumps, 'the Don' was 155 not out, with Australia 2 for 404 — 829 runs had been scored in two days' play. On the third day, Bradman and Kippax continued on to post a 192-run partnership. Woodfull declared at tea with a new record score for Australia of 729 (since broken). Bradman's chanceless 254 had taken just five and a half hours to compile.

Grimmett struck early in England's second innings, dismissing Hobbs and Woolley. And when he removed Hammond just after play resumed on the final day, Australia knew victory was a distinct possibility. Chapman scored a fine century, but it wasn't enough to save the match. Australia's target was 72, and they had plenty of time to polish off the runs. The Bradman era had dawned!

## AUSTRALIA v ENGLAND 1932-33

Sydney Cricket Ground, Sydney
2, 3, 5, 6, 7, December 1932
England won by ten wickets

Australia 360 (S.J. McCabe 187 not out, J. Larwood 5 for 96) and 164 (H. Larwood 5 for 28); England 524 (H. Sutcliff 194, W.R. Hammond 112, Nawab of Pataudi, Sr. 102) and 0 for 1

This was the first test of the infamous 'Bodyline Series', but unfortunately illness prevented 'the Don' from taking part in the game.

McCabe played one of the truly great Test innings. He hit 25 boundaries in his four-hour stay at the crease and scored 51 of a 55-run last-wicket partnership in just 33 minutes. In a sign of what was to come throughout the series, Larwood and Voce did the damage for England with five and four wickets respectively.

The Nawab of Pataudi, snr, playing for England, became the third Indian prince after 'Ranji' and 'Duleep' to score a century in his first Test against Australia. Sutcliffe and Hammond were the other century-makers as England gained a lead of 164. Then Larwood, bowling with great pace, ripped the heart out of the Australian batting. Only Fingleton, 40, and McCabe, 32, offered any resistance, and England wrapped up the match.

## AUSTRALIA v ENGLAND 1932-33

Melbourne Cricket Ground, Melbourne
30, 31 December 1932, 2, 3, January 1933
Australia won by 111 runs

Australia 228 (J.H.W. Fingleton 83) and 191 (D.G. Bradman 103 not out); England 169 (H Sutcliffe 52, W.J. O'Reilly 5 for 63) and 139 (W.J. O'Reilly 5 for 66)

The great Don Bradman returned to the Australian line-up after missing the first Test in Sydney. Woodfull elected to bat first and was quickly back in the pavilion. When O'Brien went shortly afterwards 'the Don' strode out to join Fingleton. On his first ball he attempted to hook Bowes but only succeeded in edging it onto his stumps.

Fingleton was the mainstay of Australia's innings, top-scoring with a patient 83, and England could not match the home side's modest total of 228. Wall and O'Reilly were the chief destroyers for Australia.

The third day crowd of 70 000 was a record and the patrons did not go home disappointed as their hero Bradman scored a superb 103 not out in a total of 191.

England's target was 251 runs. When the fourth day began this had been reduced to 208 with all wickets in hand. Once again it was O'Reilly, this time with the assistance of Ironmonger, who proved to be damaging on the responsive pitch. O'Reilly's match-winning ten-wicket haul was the first of three he was to claim in Test cricket.

## AUSTRALIA v ENGLAND 1932-33

Adelaide Oval, Adelaide
13, 14, 16, 17, 18, 19 January 1933
England won by 338 runs

England 341 (M. Leyland 83, R.E.S. Wyatt 78, E. Paynter 77, T.W. Wall 5 for 72) and 412 (W.R. Hammond 85, L.E.G. Ames 69) D.R. Jardine 56); Australia 222 (W.H. Ponsford 85) and 193 (W.M. Woodfull 73 not out, D.G. Bradman 66)

This must have been one of the most unpleasant Test matches ever played. The 'Bodyline' controversy had reached its ugliest; in fact, ill-feeling was so great that Jardine had to persuade local officials to close while the England team had its final practice session the day before the match.

Jardine elected to bat first, but his team was soon in desperate trouble with the score at 4 for 30. Leyland, 83, and Wyatt, 78, added 156 for the fifth wicket before Verity helped Paynter carry the total beyond 300.

The crowd became hostile early in Australia's innings when Woodfull was struck a painful blow above the heart by a Larwood thunderbolt. Later in the innings, Oldfield went down after misjudging a Larwood delivery. This incident stirred the crowd to fever pitch, and they began to count the England team 'out' — 'one, two, three, four, five, six, seven, eight, nine, ten, out!'. Australia was dismissed for 222 with Ponsford, 85, top-scoring. England produced an even team performance in its second innings. With six batsmen reaching 40, the total climbed to 412. Australia's target was 532, which proved far too difficult a task. Only Bradman, 66, and Woodfull, who carried his bat for 73, offered any resistance.

It was during this match that the Australian captain, Woodfull, made his famous utterance to the MCC tour management, Sir Pelham Warner and Lionel Palairet: 'There are two teams out there and one of them is trying to play cricket.'

## AUSTRALIA v ENGLAND 1932-33

Woolloongabba, Brisbane
10, 11, 13, 14, 15, 16 February 1933
England won by six wickets

Australia 340 (V.Y. Richardson 83, D.G. Bradman 79, W.M. Woodfull 67) and 175; England 356 (H. Sutcliffe 86, E. Paynter 83) and 4 for 162 (M. Leyland 86)

England regained the Ashes with their third win of the 'Bodyline' series on the day that Archie Jackson died. Woodfull took Richardson in with him first and they posted Australia's best opening partnership of the series. Bradman built on the solid foundation and, along with Woodfull, carried the total to 200. However, the middle and lower order failed to capitalise on the home team's promising start.

In reply, England really struggled after a painstaking opening partnership between Jardine and Sutcliffe had realised 114. Paynter was the English hero. Suffering from acute tonsillitis he left a nursing home sick-bed to play a match-winning innings of 83. He added 92 with Verity for the ninth wicket, to gain a 16-run lead for the visitors.

Australia's top order failed in the second innings. A mix-up between debutants Darling and Bromley saw Darling run out, and the innings quickly folded. Leyland played one of his finest knocks to take England within sight of victory before the first-innings hero Paynter won the match by hitting McCabe for six.

## ENGLAND v AUSTRALIA 1934

The Oval, London
18, 20, 21, 22 August 1934
Australia won by 562 runs

Australia 701 (W.H. Ponsford 266, D.G. Bradman 244) and 327 (D.G. Bradman 77, S.J. McCabe 70, W.E. Bowes 5 for 55, E.W. Clark 5 for 98); England 321 (M. Leyland 110, C.F. Walters 64) and 145 (C.V. Grimmet 5 for 64)

This was the final Test of the summer and with the series tied at one apiece, there was no restriction on the number of days' play to get a result. England recalled Woolley at the age of 47 to make the last Test appearance by a pre-1914 Test player, but this move backfired. Woolley scored 4 and 0 and while deputising for the injured Ames in Australia's second innings, conceded a record number of byes (37) for a Test innings.

After Brown had fallen cheaply, Ponsford and Bradman combined to create one of the greatest partnerships in the game's history. Australia's champion batsmen added 451 for the second wicket in five and a quarter hours. Bradman's classic knock included one six and 32 fours; while Ponsford hit a five and 27 boundaries in his highest ever Test innings.

After an opening stand of 104 between the English batsmen Walters and Sutcliffe, only Leyland provided resistance against the Australians. In a superb knock he added 110 of 185 runs to the score. Despite leading by 380, Woodfull did not enforce the follow-on. England, left to make 708 for victory, were bundled out for just 145 with Grimmet doing most of the damage. For the second time in four years, Australia regained the Ashes on the captain's birthday.

## SOUTH AFRICA v ENGLAND 1938-39

Kingsmead, Durban
3, 4, 6, 7, 8, 9, 10, 11, 13, 14 March 1939
Match drawn

South Africa 530 (P.G.V Van der Bijl 125, A.D. Nourse 103, A. Melville 78, R.E. Grieveson 75, E.L. Dalton 57, R.T.D. Perks 5 for 100) and 481 (A. Melville 103, P.G.V. Van der Bijl 97, B. Mitchell 89, K.G. Viljoen 74); England 316 (L.E.G Ames 84, E. Paynter 62) and 5 for 654 (W.J. Edrich 219, W.R. Hamond 140, P.A. Gibb 120, E. Paynter 75, L. Hutton 55)

This was the famous 'timeless' Test. There was play on nine out of ten possible days, and the game only ended because the ship that was to take the England team home could wait no longer. After the tenth day, England was just 40 runs away from achieving an amazing victory.

Details of the close-of-play scores on each day were as follows:

Day 1: South Africa 2 for 229
Day 2: South Africa 6 for 423
Day 3: South Africa all out 530
England 1 for 35 (rain stopped play)
Day 4: England 7 for 268 (bad light stopped play)
Day 5: England all out 316
South Africa 3 for 193
Day 6: South Africa all out 481
England 0 for 0 (bad light stopped play)
Day 7: England 1 for 253 (bad light)
Day 8: Rain

Day 9: England 3 for 496
Day 10: England 5 for 654
(interruptions because of rain)

## NEW ZEALAND v AUSTRALIA 1945-46

Basin Reserve, Wellington
29, 30 March 1946
Australia won by an innings and 103 runs
New Zealand 42 (W.J. O'Reilly 5 for 14) and 54; Australia 9 for 199 dec. (W.A. Brown 67, S.G. Barnes 54, J. Cowie 6 for 40)

This was the first Test to be played between the countries and the first for Lindwall, Miller and Tallon — who were to become three of Australia's finest Test players. New Zealand batted first on a rain-affected pitch. The Kiwis lost their last eight wickets for just five runs as O'Reilly, playing his final Test, captured five wickets in an innings for the eleventh time.

The match ended on the second afternoon after eight and a half hours of play. New Zealand's aggregate of 96 was their lowest score in all Tests, and the match aggregate of 295 was the third lowest of any completed Test. Australia and New Zealand would not meet again in a Test until 1973-74.

## ENGLAND v AUSTRALIA 1948

Headingley, Leeds
22, 23, 24, 26, 27 July 1948
Australia won by seven wickets
England 496 (C. Washbrook 143, W.J. Edrich 111, L. Hutton 81, A.V. Bedser 79) and 8 for 365 dec. (D.C.S. Compton 66, C. Washbrook 65, L. Hutton 57, W.J. Edrich 54); Australia 458 (R.N. Harvey 112, S.J.E Loxton 93, R.R. Lidwall 77, K.R. Miller 58) and 3 for 404 (A.R. Morris 182, D.G. Bradman 173 not out)

This was a memorable match with many highlights. England batted better than at any other stage in the series, and was content to have scored 496. But it should have been more, for at one stage on the second day they were 2 for 423. Australia started poorly and lost Morris, Hassett and Bradman cheaply (3 for 68). Then Harvey, in his first Test against England, joined Miller, and they proceeded to hit themselves out of trouble. After Miller departed, Loxton took over and he smashed five sixes and eight fours in an innings of 93. The 19-year-old Harvey reached his century; then Lindwall added 77 and Australia trailed by only 38 runs. England again batted soundly in the second innings and, by the end of the fourth day, was 8 for 362 (a lead of 400). Yardley batted on for five minutes the following morning, so he could use the heavy roller in the hope that it would further break up the pitch.

Australia only needed to draw the match to retain the Ashes, but when Bradman joined Morris they went for victory. They got there with less than fifteen minutes remaining. Bradman fed the strike to Harvey to allow him to hit the winning runs.

It was 'the Don's' last innings at Leeds. In four Tests at the ground he scored 963 runs at an average of 192.6.

## SOUTH AFRICA v ENGLAND 1948-49

Kingsmead, Durban
16, 17, 18, 20 December 1948
England won by two wickets
South Africa 161 and 219 (W.W. Wade 63) England 253 (L. Hutton 83, D.C.S. Compton 72, N.B.F Mann 6 for 59) and 8 for 128 (C.N. McCarthy 6 for 43)

This match was played on the same pitch as the 'timeless' Test ten years before.

However, this time the pitch played at varying heights and with the ball swinging late in the humid atmosphere, conditions were not easy for batting. Bedser and Gladwin utilised the conditions beautifully and with the support of some magnificent fielding, the South Africans were dismissed for a disappointing 161.

England's batsmen, apart from Hutton and Compton, struggled against the South African spinners Mann and A.M.B. Rowan. The pitch started turning appreciably on the second day and they were able to take advantage of the conditions. Two and a quarter hours were left for play when South Africa's second innings ended — England's target for victory was 128 runs.

England's final innings was played in drizzling rain and poor light but both teams were determined to play on. McCarthy, in his first Test, claimed 6 for 33 in a devastating spell that gave South Africa a winning chance.

Compton and Jenkins added 45 for the seventh wicket to stem the tide for England.

Bedser and Gladwin were at the crease with Tuckett to bowl the last over.

Eight runs were required from the eight-ball over. With three balls left, any one of four results (a win, loss, draw or tie) was possible. Bedser levelled the scores with a single from the sixth delivery, then Gladwin missed the seventh, and after a mid-pitch conference, the batsmen decided to run whatever happened on the final ball. Gladwin swung at the last ball, missed, but then ran the leg bye that gave England the most narrow and exciting of victories.

## SOUTH AFRICA v ENGLAND 1948-49

St George's Park, Port Elizabeth
5, 7, 8, 9 March 1949
England won by three wickets
South Africa 379 (W.W. Wade 125, B. Mitchell 99, A.D. Nourse 73) and 3 for 189 dec. (B. Mitchell 56); England 395 (F.G. Mann 136 not out, A.M.B. Rown 5 for 167) and 7 for 174

South Africa recovered from yet another bad start but as had been the case throughout the series, there was never any urgency about their batting. Mitchell's 99 was scored in over six and a half hours of an innings that lasted more than nine hours.

England was in trouble with the top five batsmen out and only 168 runs on the board. The captain, F.G. Mann, played his finest innings to save the side. With the support of the tail he carried England to a 16-run lead.

When Nourse declared South Africa's second innings, he left England needing 172 in 95 minutes to win. Hutton hit the first ball of the innings for four and Washbrook smacked his first ball for six — their opening stand of 58 in 27 minutes set the visitors on the road for victory. Compton and Washbrook carried the total to 104 in 53 minutes. Six wickets fell for 49 and the run chase was on in earnest! In the final over of the match, Crapp made ten runs from three successive balls bowled by Mann to get England home with just one minute of the match remaining. England won the series 2-0, both matches coming down to the wire in the final over.

## SOUTH AFRICA v AUSTRALIA 1949-50

Kingsmead, Durban
20, 21, 23, 24 January 1950
Australia won by five wickets

South Africa 311 (E.A.B. Rowan 143, A.D. Nourse 66) and 99 (I.W. Johnson 5 for 34); Australia 75 (H.J. Tayfield 7 for 23) and 5 for 101 (R.N. Harvey 151 not out, S.J.E. Loxton 54)

This was a truly remarkable victory by Australia after South Africa gained a first-innings lead of 236 runs. Rowan's patient knock of 143 was the backbone of the Springboks' innings which carried on well into the second day. It is contended that Hassett, the Australian captain, in conjunction with his bowlers, Miller and Johnson, did not attempt to take South African wickets on the second day. The South African innings eventually finished on 311. By stumps, Australia was dismissed for a paltry 75, with ten wickets falling for 44. Tayfield, the off-spinner, claimed 7 for 23. Nourse, South Africa's skipper, had the weekend to decide whether he should enforce the follow-on. With rain threatening, he decided to bat again. South Africa's collapse was worse than Australia's, with the last eight wickets falling for just 14 runs. South Africa was dismissed for 99 — and Australia needed 336 to win.

On a wearing, turning pitch, Harvey proceeded to play possibly his finest Test innings, He finished on 151 not out and was involved in match-winning partnerships with Loxton (135 for the fifth wicket), and McCool (106 unbroken for the sixth).

Australia got home by five wickets to be 2-0 up in the series.

## AUSTRALIA v ENGLAND 1950-51

Woolloongabba, Brisbane
1, 2, 4, 5 December 1950
Australia won by 70 runs

Australia 228 (R.N. Harvey 74) and 7 for 32 dec.; England 7 for 62 dec. (W.A. Johnston 5 for 35) and 122 (L. Hutton 62 not out)

Hassett won the toss for Australia and decided to take advantage of the near-perfect batting conditions.

England did remarkably well to bowl out the home team on the first day for 228. Only Harvey, 74, and Lindwall, with a patient 41, took advantage of the conditions. Bedser and Bailey were the pick of the English bowlers.

A typical Brisbane thunderstorm washed out play on Saturday and rain delayed the start until half an hour before lunch on Monday. What followed was one of the most amazing day's play in Test cricket history — 20 wickets fell for just 102 runs!

Brown declared England's innings while still 160 runs behind in the hope that his bowlers would also be able to take advantage of the conditions. They were — and Australia was soon 3 for 0. Hassett declared the innings at 7 for 32 for an overall lead of 192 runs. Bedser and Bailey were the only two bowlers used in the innings, both finishing with seven wickets for the match.

With a target of 193, England's innings started disastrously with Lindwall bowling Simpson first ball. Brown shuffled his order with his finest batsmen, Hutton and Compton, coming in at eight and nine respectively. Hassett's bold declaration was vindicated as England crashed to 6 for 30 at stumps.

On the fourth day, Hutton played one of the great Test innings. He made 62 not out while 92 runs were added on the treacherous pitch. Unorthodox spinner Iverson claimed four wickets in his first Test to seal the Australia victory.

## AUSTRALIA v ENGLAND 1950-51

Melbourne Cricket Ground, Melbourne
22, 23, 26, 27 December 1950
Australia won by 28 runs

Australia 194 (A.L. Hassett 52) and 181; England 197 (F.R. Brown 62) and 150

Hassett won the toss as he had done in the first match of the series. However, this time Brown may not have been sorry to lose — the square had been completely covered for several days to protect it from heavy rain and this had made the pitch green and fast.

Morris fell cheaply as Australia's top order struggled for runs. The home team owed much to the captain Hassett and Loxton who added 84 for the fifth wicket. This was the best partnership of the match and contributed greatly to Australia's success. The last four wickets of the innings fell for just two runs.

On the second day, with conditions more favourable for batting, England struggled against the Australian pace attack of Lindwall, Miller, Johnston and the 'mystery' spin of Iverson. At 6 for 61 the visitors were in desperate trouble. The fightback was again led by the captain who received admirable support from Evans and Bailey. England gained a three-run lead. A two-day break followed for Sunday and Christmas Day and when play resumed on Boxing Day cracks had appeared in the pitch — the result of scorching sunshine on the two rest days.

Australia batted poorly again, debutant K.A. Archer top-scoring with 46. England was left with more than three days to score 179 required for victory. However, more poor batting and sustained hostile bowling by the Australia attack saw then fall short of the target. Compton's absence from the match because of injury may have proved crucial to the result.

## AUSTRALIA v WEST INDIES 1951-52

Melbourne Cricket Ground, Melbourne
31 December 1951, 1, 2, 3 January 1952
Australia won by one wicket

West Indies 272 (F.M.M. Worrell 108, K.R. Miller 5 for 60) and 203 (J.B. Stollmeyer 54, G.E. Gomez 52); Australia 216 (R.N. Harvey 83, J. Trim 5 for 34) and 9 for 260 (A.L. Hassett 102, A.L. Valentine 5 for 88)

The injured Worrell scored a superb century in the first innings to carry the West Indies to 272, but Miller captured 5 for 60 to spearhead Australia's attack. The visitors, however, gained a first-innings lead of 56 after a disappointing reply from Australia. Only Harvey, 83, mastered the attack of which Trim, with 5 for 34, was the star.

Despite half-centuries by Stollmeyer and Gomez, the West Indies could only manage 203 in the second innings for a lead of 259. The captain, Hassett, scored a superb 102, but, despite his efforts, Australia looked beaten when the ninth wicket fell at 222. With 38 runs needed, Johnson joined Ring at the crease. As they crept closer to the target, confusion became evident in the West Indies team: Ring and Johnson took 13 off a Valentine over, and seven off the next by Ramadhin. Then Ramadhin limped off and nearly everyone was trying to set the field.

Johnson deflected Worrell to fine leg for the single that won an unlikely victory. Later, Johnson was reported to have said: "I was never worried. I knew we couldn't make the runs."

## INDIA v ENGLAND 1951-52

Chepauk (Chidambaram Stadium), Madras
6, 8, 9, 10 February 1952
India won by an innings and eight runs

England 266 (J.D.B. Robertson 77, R.T. Spooner 66, M.H. Mankad 8 for 55) and 183 (J.D.B. Robertson 56); India 9 for 457 dec. (P.R. Umrigar 130 not out, Pankaj Roy 111, D.G. Phadkar 61)

This was India's first Test victory after almost 20 years and 24 previous matches. Carr, deputising for the ill Howard, won the toss and made first use of the excellent batting conditions.

Robertson, Spooner and Graveney gave England a sound start until Mankad produced his match-winning spell — his figures of 38.5-15-55-8 are the best by an Indian bowler in all Tests against England — and wicketkeeper Sen assisted with four stumpings.

The death of King George VI was announced during the first day's play and arrangements were changed to make the following day the rest day. India batted far more positively than in the previous matches of the series. Umrigar, who had originally been left out of the team, led the way with an unbeaten 130 — his maiden Test century. (Umrigar gained his reprieve when Adhikari sustained a wrist injury just before the game.) Pankaj Roy scored the second century of his series and this got the home team's innings away to a flying start.

Trailing by 191 runs and with the pitch deteriorating, England struggled in the second innings. Robertson top-scored again but the consistent Watkins was the only other batsman to offer any real resistance to the Indian spinners, Mankad and Ghulam Ahmed.

Both bowlers collected four wickets, giving Mankad a total of twelve for the match. The Indian players and officials were jubilant at the victory after such a long wait for success.

## WEST INDIES v ENGLAND 1953-54

Bourda, Georgetown, British Guiana
24, 25, 26, 27 February, 1,2, March 1954
England won by nine wickets

England 435 (L. Hutton 169, D.C.S. Compton 64, S. Ramadhin 6 for 113) and 1 for 75; West Indies 251 (E.deC. Weekes 94, C.A. McWatt 54) and 256 (J.K. Holt 64)

There was controversy before the match when the Englishman Hutton objected to the appointed umpires standing in the Test. Inter-island jealousies meant that two other Georgetown umpires had to be used. Hutton won the toss but the advantage seemed lost with the early dismissal of Watson and May. Hutton then proceeded to play one of his best Test innings. His knock of 169 was the foundation of the sizeable England total and the innings lasted until early on the third day. Then in the thirty-five minutes before lunch Statham, bowling with great hostility, removed Worrell, Stollmeyer and Walcott. Rain washed out play for the rest of the day.

The batting collapse continued the next morning until seven wickets were down for 139. Of these runs, Week had made a memorable 94. McWatt and Holt set about restoring the West Indies' innings. Holt, batting with a runner because of a pulled leg muscle, went in at number nine rather than opening as usual. Ninety-nine had been added by this pair before McWatt was run out by May. Sections of the crowd disagreed with Umpire Menzies' decision and started hurling bottles and wooden packing-cases on to the field. It was an ugly scene with several players lucky to escape injury. The British Guiana Cricket Association officials suggested to Hutton that he takes his players from the field, but Hutton wanted to remain on the ground to press home his team's advantage.

England enforced the follow-on and although several of the West Indian batsmen got a reasonable start, no-one played the big innings that was required to save the game.

In England's final innings, Watson completed the visitors' victory by hitting a six.

## ENGLAND v PAKISTAN 1954

The Oval, London
12, 13, 14, 16, 17 August 1954
Pakistan won by 24 runs

Pakistan 133 and 164 (J.H. Wardle 7 for 56); England 130 (D.C.S Compton 53, Fazal Mahmood 6 for 53) and 143 (P.B.H. May 53, Fazal Mahmood 6 for 46)

England rested Bailey and Bedser from the game and included Loader and Tyson to boost their Test match experience. This pair had been selected for the MCC tour to Australia later in the year, but Bailey's omission left England with a long 'tail'.

Rain prevented play starting until 2.30 pm and Pakistan, after winning the toss, soon found themselves in trouble. The debutants, Loader and Tyson, had the visitors reeling at 7 for 51. Kardar led the fightback with a patient 36 before 56 was added for the last two wickets.

Further rain washed out play on the second day. When play resumed, conditions were difficult for batting with the ball rising awkwardly from a good length. Fazal Mahmood and Mahmood Hussain exploited the conditions superbly with Fazal bowling 30 overs unchanged throughout the innings.

With the pitch drying out in Pakistan's second innings, the English spinners came into their own. It was Wardle who looked likely to spin the home side to victory as the visitors slimped to 8 for 82. But once again the tail wagged — Wazir Mohammad and Zulfiqar Ahmed posting 58 for the ninth wicket.

England needed 168 for victory and looked likely to score the runs on the fourth afternoon. Simpson and May added 51 in forty minutes for the second wicket; but the aggressive approach and the absence of Bailey's steadiness from the middle order saw the wickets tumble. When the final day began, England required 43 for victory with four wickets in hand. Fazal captured six wickets for the second tine in the match to bowl Pakistan to a memorable win. It was their first victory over England and the first time a visiting country had won a Test match on their first tour of England.

## AUSTRALIA v ENGLAND 1954-55

Sydney Cricket Ground, Sydney
17, 18, 20, 21, 22 December 1954
England won by 38 runs

England 154 and 296 (P.B.H. May 104, M.C. Cowdrey 54); Australia 228 and 84 (R.N. Harvey 92 not out, F.H. Tyson 6 for 85)

Morris, capturing Australia in the absence of the injured Johnson, invited England to bat first. The decision was vindicated with the visitors bowled out for a modest total of 154. The Australian pace quartet of Lindwall, Archer, Davidson and Johnson shared the wickets with two, three, two and three respectively. Wardle, coming in at number nine, top scored with an invaluable 35.

Australia's reply was disappointing. They gained a lead of only 74 runs despite the fact that six batsmen 'got a start' — Archer led the way with a hard-hitting 49. England's speedsters did the damage. Bailey and Tyson captured four wickets each while Statham picked up the other two.

England then looked to be in real trouble with Hutton, Bailey and Graveney out and only 55 runs on the board. However, May and Cowdrey gave the visitors some hope with a partnership of 116.

May went on to compile his first century against Australia in just under five hours. Again the England tail wagged, and this time Appleyard and Statham put on 46 for the last wicket. Tyson had been knocked out when he turned his back on a Lindwall bouncer and was struck on the back of the head.

Australia required 223 for victory and Tyson bowled with great pace and hostility despite his painful blow. He was superbly supported by Statham who operated into a strong wind. Only Harvey offered any resistance to the pace of the English pair. He played one of his finest innings to remain 92 not out and almost single-handedly pulled off an Australia victory. However, Tyson's six wickets gave him ten for the match, spearheading England to victory.

## ENGLAND v AUSTRALIA 1956

Old Trafford, Manchester
26, 27, 28, 30, 31, July 1956

England won by an innings and 170 runs
England 459 (Rev. D.S. Sheppard 113, P.E. Richardson 104, M.C. Cowdrey 80); Australia 84 (J.C. Laker 9 for 37) and 205 (C.C. McDonald 89, J.C. Laker 10 for 53)

This was 'Laker's Match' on a dust bowl of an Old Trafford pitch. Groundsman Bert Stack as good as admitted he was instructed to prepare the wicket to suit the England spinners, Laker and Lock. (See scoreboard on page 24.)

There were no problems for Richardson and Cowdrey. They compiled 174 for the first wicket and, with Sheppard scoring a century, England posted a daunting 459. McDonald and Burke started Australia's innings steadily, scoring 48 for the first wicket. But after McDonald's dismissal, the rest capitulated, and Australia was all out for 84. After tea on the second day, Laker had taken seven wickets for eight runs from 22 balls. Laker's first nine overs had yielded 0 for 21; his next 7.4 returned 9 for 16.

Australia followed-on, 375 runs behind. McDonald was soon to retire hurt and out came Harvey who was dismissed on his first ball, a full toss from Laker to Cowdrey (the great left-hander made a pair on the same day!). Rain permitted only 49 minutes of play on the third day (Saturday) when Burke was dismissed. On Monday, there was more rain, and only 19 overs of play were possible, but McDonald and Craig survived on the soft, rain-affected pitch. On the final day, they continued until lunch to give the visitors some hope of survival.

Sunshine ended Australia's hopes. Laker utilised the sticky wicket to spin a web over the batsmen. Craig went just after lunch after almost four and a half hours of defiant defence. Mackay, Miller and Archer followed in quick succession. When McDonald went for 89 after more than five and a half resolute hours at the crease, it was all but over. Maddocks was trapped in front to give Laker 'all ten'. All hell erupted, the result and retention of the Ashes forgotten in the thrill of Laker's historic achievement. His figures were 16.4-4-39-9 and 51.2-23-53-10.

## SOUTH AFRICA v ENGLAND 1956-57

Old Wanderers, Johannesburg
15, 16, 18, 19, 20 February 1957
South Africa won by 17 runs
South Africa 340 (R.A. McLean 93, T.L. Goddard 67, J.H.B. Waite 61) and 142; England 251 (P.B.H. May 61) and 214 (D.J. Insole 68, M.C. Cowdrey 55, H.J. Tayfield 9 for 113)

South Africa won the toss for the first time in the series and decided to adopt a more positive approach to its batting. Goddard and Waite set up the innings with a 112-run partnership for the second wicket. McLean, who top-scored with a hard-hitting 93, was dropped at slip on 3. South Africa's total of 340 was their highest score of the series in a rubber dominated by the bowlers of both sides.

England were making reasonable progress at 2 for 131, with May and Insole having added 71 for the third wicket, when Insole was run out in unusual circumstances. Tayfield unsuccessfully appealed for lbw. The ball flew to Goddard at slip, but Insole thought the ball had gone through the slips and started for a run — Goddard ran in and easily removed the bails. Compton, with the support of the tail-enders, struggled to take England's total to 251.

South Africa's 89-run lead proved decisive, although a lion-hearted effort by the England attack restricted the Springboks' second innings to 142. Goddard completed a fine double, top-scoring with 49.

The visitors needed 232 for victory. They lost Bailey late on the fourth afternoon and started the final day requiring 213 to win. Tayfield bowled unchanged for four hours and fifty minutes sending down 35 eight-ball overs. He was to bowl South Africa to its first win at home on a turf pitch. Tayfield was the first South African bowler to take nine wickets in an innings and 13 in a match. Loader, the last wicket to fall was caught by Tayfield's brother Arthur who was substituting for Funston.

## WEST INDIES v PAKISTAN 1957-58

Kensington Oval, Bridgetown, Barbados
17, 18, 20, 21, 22, 23 January 1958
Match drawn
West Indies 9 for 579 declared (E.deC. Weekes 197, C.C. Hunte 142, O.G. Smith 78, G.St.A. Sobers 52) and 0 for 28; Pakistan 106 and 8 for 657 declared (Hanif Mohammad 337, Imtiaz Ahmed 91, Saeed Ahmed 65)

This was the first Test to be played between the two countries and it was a match of many records. Nasim-Ul-Ghani, aged 16 years and 248 days, became the youngest Test player ever. On the first day of the game, Hunte scored a brilliant century on debut to set up a sizeable West Indies total. Weekes then proceeded to blast the Pakistani attack all over the ground.

Pakistan followed on 473 runs behind after a miserable display with the bat realised only 106. Hanif then proceeded to play the longest innings in Test history — he batted for 16 hours and 53 minutes, hitting 24 boundaries in a great knock of 337. He shared in century partnerships with Imtiaz Ahmed (152), Alimuddin (112), Saeed Ahmed (154) and his brother Wazir (121).

Hanif was finally dismissed after tea on the final (sixth) day, having started his innings mid-afternoon on the third day. Although the match resulted in a draw, Pakistan's 8 for 657 will be remembered as the highest total after following-on in all Tests.

## ENGLAND v AUSTRALIA 1956 (Fourth Test)

Old Trafford, Manchester, 26, 27, 28, 30, 31 July. England won by an innings and 170 runs

**ENGLAND**

| | | |
|---|---|---|
| P.E.Richardson | c Maddocks b Benaud | 104 |
| M.C.Cowdrey | c Maddocks b Lindwall | 80 |
| Rev.D.S.Sheppard | b Archer | 113 |
| P.B.H.May* | c Archer b Benaud | 43 |
| T.E.Bailey | b Johnson | 20 |
| C.Washbrook | lbw b Johnson | 6 |
| A.S.M.Oakman | c Archer b Johnson | 10 |
| T.G.Evans† | st Maddocks b Johnson | 47 |
| J.C.Laker | run out | 3 |
| G.A.R.Lock | not out | 25 |
| J.B.Stratham | c Maddocks b Lindwall | 0 |
| Extras | (B 2, LB 5, W 1) | 8 |
| **Total** | | **459** |

**AUSTRALIA**

| | | | | | |
|---|---|---|---|---|---|
| C.C.McDonald | c Lock b Laker | 32 | | c Oakman b Laker | 89 |
| J.W.Burke | c Cowdrey b Lock | 22 | | c Lock b Laker | 33 |
| R.Nharvey | b Laker | 0 | | c Cowdrey B Laker | 0 |
| I.D.Craig | lbw b Laker | 8 | | lbw b Laker | 38 |
| K.R.Miller | c Oakman b Laker | 6 | (6) | b Laker | 0 |
| K.D.Mackay | c Oakman b Laker | 0 | (5) | c Oakman b Laker | 0 |
| R.G.Archer | st Evans b Laker | 6 | | c Oakman b Laker | 0 |
| R.Benaud | c Stratham b Laker | 0 | | b Laker | 18 |
| R.R.Lindwall | not out | 6 | | c Lock bLaker | 8 |
| L.V.Maddocks† | b Laker | 4 | (11) | lbw b Laker | 2 |
| I.W.Johnson* | b Laker | 0 | (10) | not out | 1 |
| Extras | | - | | (B 12, LB 4) | 16 |
| **Total** | | **84** | | | **205** |

| **AUSTRALIA** | O | M | R | W | | O | M | R | W |
|---|---|---|---|---|---|---|---|---|---|
| Lindwall | 21.3 | 6 | 63 | 2 | | | | | |
| Miller | 21 | 6 | 41 | 0 | | | | | |
| Archer | 22 | 6 | 73 | 1 | | | | | |
| Johnson | 47 | 10 | 151 | 4 | | | | | |
| Benaud | 47 | 17 | 123 | 2 | | | | | |
| **ENGLAND** | O | M | R | W | | O | M | R | W |
| Statham | 6 | 3 | 6 | 0 | Statham | 16 | 10 | 15 | 0 |
| Bailey | 4 | 3 | 4 | 0 | Bailey | 20 | 8 | 31 | 0 |
| Laker | 16.4 | 4 | 37 | 9 | Laker | 51.2 | 23 | 53 | 10 |
| Lock | 14 | 3 | 37 | 1 | Lock | 55 | 30 | 69 | 0 |
| | | | | | Oakman | 8 | 3 | 21 | 0 |

FALL OF WICKETS

| | E | A | A |
|---|---|---|---|
| 1st | 174 | 48 | 28 |
| 2nd | 195 | 48 | 55 |
| 3rd | 288 | 62 | 114 |
| 4th | 321 | 62 | 124 |
| 5th | 327 | 62 | 130 |
| 6th | 339 | 73 | 130 |
| 7th | 401 | 73 | 181 |
| 8th | 417 | 78 | 198 |
| 9th | 458 | 84 | 203 |
| 10th | 459 | 84 | 205 |

Umpires: D.E.Davies and F.S.Lee

## WEST INDIES v PAKISTAN 1957-58

Sabina Park, Kingston, Jamaica
26, 27, 28 February, 1, 3, 4, March
West Indies won by an innings and 174 runs

Pakistan 328 (Imtiaz Ahmed 122, W.Mathias 77, Saeed Ahmed 52, E.St.E. Atkinson 5 for 42) and 228 (Wazir Mohammad 106, A.H. Kardar 57); West Indies 3 for 790 dec. (G.St.A. Sobers 365 not out, C.C. Hunte 260, C.L. Walcott 88 not out)

---

This crushing win by the West Indies was dominated by Sobers' great innings. The 21-year-old left-hander broke the Test record individual score of 364, set by Hutton for England against Australia at the Oval in 1938.

Sobers batted for just over ten hours, which was three hours less than Hutton. He received grand support from Hunte — their partnership was worth 446 and was only broken by the run-out of Hunte for 260. They became only the fourth pair to bat through a whole day's play and it was also Sobers' first century in Test cricket.

Pakistan was limited to two fit bowlers after the first five balls with Nasim-Ul-Ghani (fractured thumb) and Mahmood Hussain (pulled thigh muscle) unable to bowl. The captain Kardar went into the match with a broken finger on his left hand yet he bowled 37 overs of left-arm spinners.

Because of these injuries, Pakistan batted two men short in the second innings and despite a determined rearguard action by Wazir Mohammad and Karder, the match finished early on the final day with victory going to the West Indies.

## AUSTRALIA v WEST INDIES 1960-61

Woolloongabba, Brisbane
9, 10, 12, 13, 14 December 1960
Match tied

West Indies 453 (G.S. Sobers 132, F.M.M. Worrell 65, J.S. Solomon 65, F.C.M. Alexander 60, W.W. Hall 50, A.K. Davidson 5 for 135) and 284 (F.M.M. Worrell 65, R.B. Kanhai 54, A.K. Davidson 6 for 87); Australia 505 (N.C. O'Neill 181, R.B. Simpson 92, C.C. McDonald 57) and 232 (A.K. Davidson 80, R. Benaud 52, W.W. Hall 5 for 63)

---

This Test will live forever in cricket history. It was the first tie in almost 500 matches, and was truly one of the great games highlighted by many outstanding individual efforts.

Sobers, 132 with 21 fours, played one of the greatest innings ever, according to the Australia Captain, Benaud. The grace of Worrell (who scored 65 in each innings), the 181 runs scored by O'Neill, the fast bowling of Hall and the magnificent all-round performance of Davidson (who scored 44 and 80 and captured 5 for 135 and 6 for 87) also contributed to the memorable impact of this match. So to the final day: Hall and Valentine added 25 valuable runs to the West Indies tally, leaving Australia 233 to win in just over five hours. Midway through the afternoon session, all looked lost as Simpson, Harvey, McDonald, O'Neill, Favell and Mackay were back in the pavilion with only 92 on the board. But Davidson and Benaud staged a tremendous fightback, adding 134 for the seventh wicket before Solomon threw Davidson out.

Grout joined his captain with seven runs needed to win. He took a single and faced the last over which was to be bowled by Hall (at this time they were still bowling eight-ball overs). The first ball took Grout on the thigh for one leg-bye so now five were needed. The next delivery was a bouncer; Benaud swung, got a faint edge, and was caught behind by Alexander.

Meckiff was the new batsman. He played his first ball defensively, then Grout called him for a bye from the next. Four were now needed to win from four balls, with two wickets in hand. Grout skied the next ball towards square leg; Kanhai was waiting to take the catch, but Hall charged towards the ball, causing his team-mates to scatter. The big fast bowler, however, muffed the chance, and the batsmen ran a single.

Three balls to go, three runs to win. Meckiff swung the next ball towards the mid-wicket boundary, and the game looked over as the batsmen turned to complete the third run. But Conrad Hunte returned fast and flat to Alexander beside the balls, with Grout just short of his crease.

The scores were tied as the last man, Kline, joined Meckiff with two balls left. He pushed the first ball to square leg, and Meckiff called for the single. Jo Solomon gathered, and from 20 metres and with one stump at which to aim, ran Meckiff out — a thrilling finish to a magnificent game of cricket and the first tie in Test match history. See the final scoreboard on page 26.

## AUSTRALIA v WEST INDIES 1960-61

Adelaide Oval, Adelaide
27, 28, 30, 31 January, 1 February 1961
Match drawn

West Indies 393 (R.B. Kanhai 117, F.M.M. Worrell 71, F.C.M. Alexander 63 not out, R.Benaud 5 for 96) and 6 for 432 dec. (R.B. Kanhai 115, F.C.M. Alexander 87 not out, C.C. Hunte 79, F.M.M. Worrell 53); Australia 366 (R.B. Simpson 85, R. Benaud 77, C.C. McDonald 71, L.R. Gibbs 5 for 97) and 9 for 273 (N.C. O'Neill 65, K.D. Mackay 62 not out)

---

This match produced an even longer period of suspense than did the tied Test in Brisbane. Kanhai produced his best batting of the series, ripping a century off Australia's attack in each innings. The West Indian wicketkeeper Alexander added great depth to his team's batting, scoring 63 not out and 87 not out from the lower order.

Worrell was again among the run-scorers with 71 and 53. Australia sorely missed the injured Davidson on a belter of an Adelaide pitch.

## AUSTRALIA v WEST INDIES 1960-61 (First Test)

Wolloongabba, Brisbane, 9, 10, 12, 13,14 December. Match tied

**WEST INDIES**

| | | | | |
|---|---|---|---|---|
| C.C.Hunte | c Benaud b Davidson | 24 | c Simpson b Mackay | 39 |
| C.W.Smith | c Grout b Davidson | 7 | c O'Neill b Davidson | 6 |
| R.B.Kanhai | c Grout b Davidson | 15 | c Grout b Davidson | 54 |
| G.S.Sobers | c Kline b Meckiff | 132 | b Davidson | 14 |
| F.M.M.Worrell* | c Grout b Davidson | 65 | c Grout b Davidson | 65 |
| J.S.Solomon | hit wkt b Simpson | 65 | lbw b Simpson | 47 |
| P.D.Lashley | c Grout b Kline | 19 | b Davidson | 0 |
| F.C.M.Alexander† | c Davidson b Kline | 60 | b Benaud | 5 |
| S.Ramadhin | c Harvey b Davidson | 12 | c Harvey b Simpson | 6 |
| W.W.Hall | st Grout b Kline | 50 | b Davidson | 18 |
| A.L.Valentine | not out | 0 | not out | 7 |
| Extras | (LB 3, W 1) | 4 | (B 14, LB 7, W 2) | 23 |
| **Total** | | **453** | | **284** |

**AUSTRALIA**

| | | | | |
|---|---|---|---|---|
| C.C.McDonald | c Hunte b Sobers | 57 | b Worrell | 16 |
| R.B.Simpson | b Ramadhin | 92 | c sub (L.R.Gibbs) b Hall | 0 |
| R.N.Harvey | b Valentine | 15 | c Sobers b Hall | 5 |
| N.C.O'Neill | c Valentine b Hall | 181 | c Alexander b Hall | 26 |
| L.E.Favell | run out | 45 | c Solomon b Hall | 7 |
| K.D.Mackay | b Sobers | 35 | b Ramadhin | 28 |
| A.K.Davidson | c Alexander b Hall | 44 | run out | 80 |
| R.Benaud* | lbw b Hall | 10 | c Alexander b Hall | 52 |
| A.T.W.Grout† | lbw b Hall | 4 | run out | 2 |
| I.Meckiff | run out | 4 | run out | 2 |
| L.F.Kline | not out | 3 | not out | 0 |
| Extras | (B 2, LB 8, NB 4, W 1) | 15 | (B2, LB 9, NB 3) | 14 |
| **Total** | | **505** | | **232** |

| **AUSTRALIA** | O | M | R | W | | O | M | R | W |
|---|---|---|---|---|---|---|---|---|---|
| Davidson | 30 | 2 | 135 | 5 | Davidson | 24.6 | 4 | 87 | 6 |
| Meckiff | 18 | 0 | 129 | 1 | Meckiff | 4 | 1 | 19 | 0 |
| Mackay | 3 | 0 | 15 | 0 | Benaud | 31 | 6 | 69 | 1 |
| Benaud | 24 | 3 | 93 | 0 | Mackay | 21 | 7 | 52 | 1 |
| Simpson | 8 | 0 | 25 | 1 | Kline | 4 | 0 | 14 | 0 |
| Kline | 17.6 | 6 | 52 | 3 | Simpson | 7 | 2 | 18 | 2 |
| | | | | | O'Neill | 1 | 0 | 2 | 0 |

| **WEST INDIES** | O | M | R | W | | O | M | R | W |
|---|---|---|---|---|---|---|---|---|---|
| Hall | 29.3 | 1 | 140 | 4 | Hall | 17.7 | 3 | 63 | 5 |
| Worrell | 30 | 0 | 93 | 0 | Worrell | 16 | 3 | 41 | 1 |
| Sobers | 32 | 0 | 115 | 2 | Sobers | 8 | 0 | 30 | 0 |
| Valentine | 24 | 6 | 82 | 1 | Valentine | 10 | 4 | 27 | 0 |
| Ramadhin | 15 | 1 | 60 | 1 | Ramadhin | 17 | 3 | 57 | 1 |

FALL OF WICKETS

| | W | A | W | A |
|---|---|---|---|---|
| Wkt | 1st | 1st | 2nd | 2nd |
| 1st | 23 | 84 | 13 | 1 |
| 2nd | 42 | 138 | 88 | 7 |
| 3rd | 65 | 194 | 114 | 49 |
| 4th | 239 | 278 | 127 | 49 |
| 5th | 243 | 381 | 210 | 57 |
| 6th | 283 | 469 | 210 | 92 |
| 7th | 347 | 484 | 241 | 226 |
| 8th | 366 | 489 | 250 | 228 |
| 9th | 452 | 496 | 253 | 232 |
| 10th | 453 | 505 | 284 | 232 |

Umpires: C.J.Egar and C.Hoy

The highlight of Australia's first innings was the hat-trick taken by Gibbs. The victims were Mackay, Grout and Misson. It was the first hat-trick in Australia — West Indies Tests, and the first to be taken in Australia for 57 years.

Worrell's declaration left Australia 460 to score in about six and a half hours. When McDonald, Favell and Simpson fell before stumps on the fourth day, things were serious.

O'Neill, 65, Burge, 49, and Grount, 42, batted well. But the match seemed over just after tea when Australia was 9 for 207 with 110 minutes still to play. The last man, Kline (who had been dismissed repeatedly in the nets), walked out to join Mackay. The pair remained calm in the crisis as Worrell continually changed his bowlers. The new ball was seen off and the spinners kept out. Mackay faced the last over from Hall and was so determined to save the game that he took several deliveries on the body. His courage was rewarded! The last pair saved the day for Australia.

## AUSTRALIA v WEST INDIES 1960-61

Melbourne Cricket Ground, Melbourne
10, 11, 13, 14, 15 February 1961
Australia won by two wickets

West Indies 292 (G.St.A. Sobers 64) and 321 (F.C.M. Alexander 73, C.C. Hunte 52, A.K. Davidson 5 for 84); Australia 356 (C.C. McDonald 91, R.B. Simpson 75, P.J.P. Burge 68, G.St.A. Sobers 5 for 120) and 8 for 258 (R.B. Simpson 92, P.J.P. Burge 53)

This was the deciding match of one of the most exciting series ever played. Both teams agreed to play a sixth day, if required, to obtain a result. Benaud surprised most people when he invited the West Indian visitors to bat. However, it was not the spearhead Davidson who did the damage but Mission and the spinners who claimed most of the wickets. Six of the West Indies batsmen reached 30 but no-one was able to play the commanding innings required to lay the foundation for a sizeable total.

Before a world-record MCG crowd of 90 800 on the second day, Simpson and McDonald posted the highest opening partnership of the series (146) to place the home team in a sound position. The middle order, apart from Burge, failed to capitalise on the excellent start and at the end of the innings Australia's lead was just 64 runs.

Once again the West Indies' batsmen made a reasonable start but only Alexander and Hunte reached 50. Simpson dismissed the dangerous Sobers — caught at the wicket for the second time in the match — while tragically for the visitors, Solomon was run out again after being well set.

Simpson started the chase for victory at breakneck speed. Eighteen runs came from the first over and 24 from the first ten balls he received. The innings ebbed the flowed until Grout, with Australia 7 for 254, late-cut Valentine. The off-bail fell to the ground and wicketkeeper Alexander pointed to the bail, while the batsmen ran two. Umpire Egar conferred with square leg umpire Hoy and they decided that Grout was not out. Ironically, Grout was then dismissed without further addition to the score.

Mackay and Martin ran a bye to win a thrilling Test and thousands from the final-day crowd of 41 186 swarmed on to the ground to celebrate the climax of a memorable series. The teams were given a ticker-tape parade through the streets of Melbourne two days later.

## ENGLAND v AUSTRALIA 1961

Old Trafford, Manchester
27, 28, 29, 31 July, 1 August 1961
Australia won by 54 runs

Australia 190 (W.M. Lawry 74, J.B. Statham 5 for 53) and 432 (W.M. Lawry 102, A.K. Davidson 77 not out, N.C. O'Neill 67, R.B. Simpson 51); England 367 (P.B.H. May 95, K.F. Barrington 78, G.Pullar 63) and 201 (E.R. Dexter 76, R.Benaud 6 for 70)

It was one test apiece when the English and Australian teams arrived in Manchester for the fourth match of the series. The pitch was the complete opposite to the 'dust bowl' of 1956. Once again, Australia's innings was held together by Lawry, who scored 74 in a disappointing total of just 190. Statham exploited the conditions and bowled superbly, returning five wickets for 53 from 21 overs.

England reached 6 for 358 before Simpson crashed through the English lower order, capturing 4 for 2 off just 26 balls. Simpson was bowling because Benaud was still struggling with the shoulder injury which caused him to miss the second Test at Lord's.

The Ashes were at stake, and Australia's batsmen put their heads down. Lawry scored his second century of the series, and with O'Neill, 67, and Simpson, 51, gave Australia a lead of 154 runs with four wickets in hand at the start of the final day's play.

Mackay, Benaud and Grout fell for the addition of three runs when the No. 11 batsman, McKenzie, joined Davidson. The pair produced one of the finest last-wicket partnerships seen, so that when Flavell bowled the 19-year-old McKenzie, 98 runs had been added. The home team was left with 256 to score at 67 per hour. After a steady start by Pullar and Subba Row that realised 40, 'Lord Ted' Dexter accepted the challenge. He hammered the Australian attack to score 75 in 84 minutes, before Benaud switched to bowl around the wicket. The change worked! Dexter was caught behind, with England 2 for 150, England crashed to 9 for 193, with Australia's captain producing a match-winning spell at the crease. Benaud's return — injured shoulder and all — was 6 for 70 from 32 overs. When Davidson captured the last wicket Australia had won by 54 runs and, more importantly, they had retained the Ashes.

## ENGLAND v AUSTRALIA 1964

Headingley, Leeds
2, 3, 4, 6 July 1964
Australia won by seven wickets

England 268 (J.M. Parks 68, E.R. Dexter 66, N.J.N. Hawke 5 for 75) and 229 (K.F. Barrington 89); Australia 389 (P.J.P Burge 160, W.M. Lawry 78) and 3 for 111 (I.R. Redpath 58 not out)

Australia did well to bowl England out on the first day. Hawke and McKenzie were in fine form as they restricted the home team to 268 — Dexter and Parks played many handsome strokes but neither were able to get through the sixties.

Berge joined Lawry with Australia in a comfortable position at 2 for 124. Lawry was run out five runs later and the middle order collapsed, leaving the visitors 7 for 178 and struggling against the English spinners, Titmus and Gifford. Burge was 38 not out when Dexter decided to take the new ball with Australia 7 for 187.

Forty-two runs came from the first seven overs bowled by Trueman and Flavell. Burge and Hawke added 105 for the eight wicket, in better than even time. Burge reached his century just before stumps.

The following morning, Grout assisted Burge in compiling an 89-run partnership for the ninth wicket. The last three wickets had realised 221 runs and Burge had played one of the great innings in Anglo-Australian Tests, batting for five and a quarter hours and hitting 24 boundaries.

Apart from Barrington, England's batsmen struggled against the Australian attack which was supported by superb fielding. Australia was never troubled to make the 109 required for victory.

The win in this match was the only result in the series and enabled Australia to retain the Ashes. It will always be remembered as 'Burge's Match'.

## SOUTH AFRICA v AUSTRALIA 1966-67

Old Wanderers, Johannesburg
23, 24, 26, 27, 28 December 1966
South Africa won by 233 runs

South Africa 199 (J.D. Lindsay 69, G.D. McKenzie 5 for 46) and 620 (J.D. Lindsay 182, R.G. Pollock 90, P.L. Van der Merwe 76, H.R. Lance 70, A. Bacher 63, E.J. Barlow 50); Australia 325 (W.M. Lawry 98, R.B. Simpson 65) and 261 (T.R. Veivers 55, T.L. Goddard 6 for 53)

This was Australia's first defeat in a Test match on South African soil. Although the ground had been saturated by days of rain, Van der Merwe put South Africa in first after winning the toss. It certainly looked like he had made a grave mistake when the score stood at 5 for 41. Lindsay and Lance added some respectability with a stand of 110, but 199 looked anything but a winning total. Simpson and Lawry posted 118 before the captain was dismissed for 65. Australia passed South Africa's total with the loss of just one wicket but then Australia collapsed losing 9 for 121, resulting in a lead of 126.

Lindsay made a match-winning century in his maiden Test and R.G. Pollock also produced a classic innings of 90. The Australians put down some vital chances, the most crucial when Lindsay was 10 and Van der Merwe 2 — this pair shared a record seventh-wicket partnership of 221. South Africa's score proved to be way beyond the visitors, with Goddard returning career-best figures of 6 for 53 to bowl his team to a historic victory.

## INDIA v WEST INDIES 1966-67

Eden Gardens, Calcutta
31 December 1966, 1, 3, 4, 5 January 19676
West Indies won by an innings and 45 runs

West Indies 390 (R.B. Kanhai 90, G.St.A. Sobers 70, S.M. Nurse 56); India 167 (L.R. Gibbs 5 for 51) and 178 runs.

This match will be remembered not for the cricket but for the riot that caused the second day's play to be abandoned. The authorities had sold more tickets than there were seats so the disappointed Indian spectators invaded the ground, clashed with police and set fire to several of the stands. The players, naturally concerned for their own safety, were reluctant to continue the match. It came close to being abandoned until assurances were received from important government officials that there would be no further trouble.

The game was played on an under-prepared pitch so the toss virtually decided the outcome. After both openers were run out, cautious batting placed the visitors in a match-winning position. With the ball spinning viciously and coming off the pitch at an uneven height, Sobers and Gibbs triumphed, leading the West Indies to a comprehensive victory.

## WEST INDIES v ENGLAND 1967-68

Queen's Park Oval, Port-of-Spain, Trinidad
14, 15, 16, 18, 19 March 1968
England won by 78 wickets

West Indies 7 for 526 dec. (R.B. Kanhai 153, S.M. Nurse 136, S. Camacho 87) and 2 for 92 dec.; England 414 (M.C. Cowdrey 148, A.P.E. Knott 69 not out, G. Boycott 62, B.F. Butcher 5 for 34) and 3 for 215 (G. Boycott 80 nt out, M.C. Cowdrey 71)

This was the fourth match of the series and the only one in which a result was obtained. England had had the better of the first three matches but this time the West Indies dominated proceedings until the final day.

An aggressive start by Camancho laid the foundation for Nurse and Kanhai to plunder the bowling. This pair added 273 for the third wicket to leave the home side in a seemingly impregnable position.

Cowdrey played a superb captain's knock to lead the fightback until the part-time spinner Butcher ran through the lower middle order to record career-best figures of 5 for 34. With a lead of 112 and the success of the leg spinners, Rodriguez and Butcher, Sobers gambled and declared for the West Indies at 2 for 92 — leaving England to reach 215 in two and three quarter hours. Again it was Cowdrey and Boycott who led the way for the visiting team. They paced the innings perfectly after Edrich, 29, had laid the foundation for an improbable victory. Boycott was there when the match was won with three minutes and eight balls remaining. The West Indian captain Sobers was severely criticised in the Caribbean for the generosity of his declaration.

## ENGLAND v AUSTRALIA 1968

Kennington Oval, London
22, 23, 24, 26, 27, August 1968
England won by 226 runs

England 494 (J.H. Edrich 164, B.L. D'Olivera 158, T.W. Graveney 63) and 181; Australia 324 (W.M. Lawry 135, I.R. Redpath 67) and 125 (R.J. Inverarity 56, D.L. Underwood 7 for 50)

England was to win this memorable match with just five minutes of the match remaining.

Rain sent the players from the field one minute before lunch on the last day with Australia in real trouble at 5 for 86. Then a freak storm flooded the ground during the interval and looked likely to prevent the English victory. However, the ground staff mopped up — assisted by volunteers from the crowd — to enable play to resume at 4.45 pm with just 75 minutes of the match remaining. Rain had played havoc with earlier matches in the rubber and again looked likely to deprive England of a win. No-one will ever forget the sight of hundreds of people mopping up pools of water on the Oval!

Inverarity and Jarman continued to defend stoutly on the deadened pitch. Cowdrey tried his front-line bowlers — Snow, Brown, Illingworth and Underwood — then introduced D'Oliveira who bowled Jarman with the last ball of his second over. Cowdrey immediately recalled Underwood to the attack and the left-armer found the pitch more to his liking as it dried out in the afternoon sun. He removed Mallett and McKenzie in his first over, Gleeson survived until twelve minutes to six, and Inverarity — who had batted for over four hours since the start of the innings — was the last man out at five to six. England thoroughly deserved the victory to square the series.

Of the four centuries scored in the series, three were made in this match — Edrich and D'Oliveira for England, and Lawry for Australia.

## AUSTRALIA v WEST INDIES 1968-69

Adelaide Oval, Adelaide
24, 25, 27, 28, 29 January 1969
Match drawn

West Indies 276 (G.St.A. Sobers 110, B.F. Butcher 52) and 616 (B.F. Butcher 118, M.C. Carew 90, R.B. Kanhai 80, D.A.J. Holford 80, G.St.A. Sobers 52, A.N. Connolly 5 for 122); Australia 533 (K.D. Walters 110, I.M. Chappell 76, W.M. Lawry 62, K.R. Stackpole 62, G.D. McKenzie 59, A.P. Sheahan 51) and 9 for 339 (I.M. Chappell 96, W.M. Lawry 89, K.R. Stackpole 50, K.D. Walters 50)

Despite the fact that the match ended in a draw it was a dramatic and exciting finish. The West Indies batted poorly on the first day after winning the toss, with most of the visitors' batsmen throwing their wickets away on the easy-paced pitch. Sober's 110 came in just over two hours but apart from Butcher, the skipper lacked support. It was also a surprise to many of the pundits that Sobers continued to bat down the order at number six or seven.

Australia replied aggressively with Redpath's 45 the lowest score from the top six. The West Indies' attack was undermanned, and Hall had been left out of the line-up for the first time in many years. The home team had a lead of 257 and it looked only a matter of time before another comfortable victory was achieved.

However, the West Indies batsmen clicked and played with a determination that had been missing since the first Test of the series. Carew and Kanhai launched an assault on 'mystery' spinner Gleeson and hit him out of the attack. Shortly before tea on the fourth day, the visitors' lead was 235 with two wickets in hand. Hendriks joined Holford in a ninth-wicket stand of 122 which carried West Indies past 600 and to relative safety.

Australia's target on the last day was 360 in five and three-quarter hours. Positive batting by Lawry, Stackpole, Chappell and Walters, who were scoring at more than four runs per over, had the home team 3 for 298 with the last 15 overs to be bowled. Along the way there was some drama when Redpath, the non-striker, was run out by the bowler, Griffith, without a warning for backing-up before the ball had been bowled.

The final 15 overs produced a nerve-tingling finish. Chappell went lbw to Griffith and then Walters, Freeman and Jarman were run out by a mixture of good fielding and poor calling by Sheahan. When McKenzie swept Gibbs to square leg and Gleeson was lbw to Griffith,

Sheahan and Connolly had 26 balls to face. Sobers took the new ball against Connolly but he was able to survive, leaving Australia 21 runs down and West Indies one wicket short of victory.

## AUSTRALIA v ENGLAND 1970-71

Sydney Cricket Ground, Sydney
12, 13, 14, 16, 17 February 1971
England won by 62 runs
England 184 and 302 (B.W. Luckhurst 59, J.H. Edrich 57); Australia 264 (G.S. Chappell 65, I.R. Redpath 59) and 160 (K.R. Stackpole 67)

This was the seventh and final Test with Australia needing to win to level the series and retain the Ashes. Ian Chappell replaced Lawry as captain but the former skipper's batting would be sorely missed.

Chappell invited England to bat in his first Test as captain. The gamble paid off with the visitors dismissed for a modest 184. Interestingly, it was the spinners Jenner and O'Keeffe who did the damage claiming three wickets apiece.

Australia struggled in reply and at 4 for 66 looked likely to trail on the first innings. However, stubborn resistance from Redpath, Greg Chappell and Walters, 42, carried Australia to a lead of 80. There was some high drama late on the second day when Jenner ducked into a short-pitched ball from Snow, who was then warned by umpire Rowan for the persistent use of bouncers, which in turn led to a protest from the England captain, Illingworth. The crowd demonstrated against Snow and Illingworth, Snow being assaulted by a spectator who had lent over the boundary fence. Illingworth led his side from the field and only returned after being warned by the umpires that his team could forfeit the game.

A timely opening partnership of 94 by Edrich and Luckhurst restored the balance England's way and with useful contributions from the rest of the top order, Australia was set 223 to win.

After dismissing Eastwood in the first over of the home team's second innings, England's spearhead Snow, broke his hand on the boundary fence when going for a catch. It mattered not as Illingworth and Underwood mesmerised Australia's batsmen with their wily spin. Only Stackpole and Greg Chappell offered any resistance as the home team surrendered meekly.

England had regained the Ashes for the first time since 1958-59.

## WEST INDIES v INDIA 1970-71

Queen's Park Oval, Port-of-Spain
6, 7, 9, 10 March 1971
India won by seven wickets
West Indies 214 (C.A. Davis 71 not out) and 261 (R.C. Fredericks 80, C.A. Davis 74 not out, S. Venkataraghavan 5 for 95); India 352 (D.N. Sardesai 112, S.M. Gavaskar 65, E.D. Solkar 55, J.M. Noreiga 9 for 95) and 3 for 125 (S.M. Gavaskar 67 not out)

This was a memorable match on many counts. It was India's first victory against West Indies and it saw the debut of India's greatest batsman, Gavaskar, who had the honour of hitting the winning run.

The West Indies batted first on a sub-standard pitch and could not have had a worse start, losing Fredericks from the first ball of the match. The home team slumped to 4 for 62 before Sobers joined Davis and attempted to hit his way out of trouble. At the end of the innings the bowlers, Holder and Shillingford, added some valuable runs with Davis. However, 214 was a disappointing total.

Gavaskar and Mankad gave India a sound start, although they did have their share of good fortune. Sardesai provided the big score from the middle order that was to guarantee a sizeable first innings lead for the visitors. At the same time, the 34-year-old off-spinner Noreiga became the first bowler to take nine wickets in an innings for West Indies, playing in only his second Test.

After trailing by 138 the home team adopted a positive approach to wipe off the deficit. By stumps on the third day they had gone twelve runs ahead with only one wicket lost. An unfortunate accident before the start of the fourth day turned the wheel India's way. Davis, who was 33 not out, was struck over the eye while practising and had to go to hospital for stitches. He returned to find four wickets had fallen for only 19 runs. Davis carried his bat again but this time the wily Indian spinners were too crafty for the West Indies tail.

The visitors had more than eight hours in which to score the 124 needed for victory. With Gavaskar in full cry they wasted no time and completed the historic victory on the fourth day.

## ENGLAND v PAKISTAN 1971

Headingley, Leeds
8, 9, 10, 12, 13 July 1971
England won by 25 runs
England 316 (G. Boycott 112, B.L. D'Oliveira 74) and 264 (B.L. D'Oliveira 72, D.L. Amiss 56); Pakistan 350 (Zaheer Abbas 72, Wasim Bari 63, Mushtaq Mohammad 57) and 205 (Sadiq Mohammad 91)

England won the deciding Test on the final day in a match that could have gone either way.

Illingworth won the toss but the home team got away to a poor start with Luckhurst and Edrich out cheaply. Boycott's third century in successive innings was the backbone of England's effort. He put on 135 in an enterprising stand with D'Oliveira, with Illingworth, Hutton and Lever all adding valuable runs in the lower order.

When Pakistan reached 2 for 198 shortly before stumps on the second day, with Zaheer Abbas and Mushtaq Mohammad in full flight, the visitors looked likely to gain a commanding lead. Lever and Hutton broke through with the new ball to tip the scales England's way. The third day's play was the slowest in England's Test history, seven wickets falling for just 159 runs. Wasim Bari laboured for more than four hours to record his highest Test score and build a Pakistani lead of 34.

Despite Luckhurst 'bagging a pair' and Boycott failing, the home team gave themselves a chance with some resolute batting from Edrich, Amiss, D'Oliveira and Illingworth. Salim Altaf crashed through the tail taking 4 for 9, the last five wickets falling for 16.

Aftab Gul and Sadiq Mohammad had wiped 25 runs off the target of 231 by stumps on the fourth day. The final day started disastrously for Pakistan with Aftab Gul out third ball and Zaheer Abbas caught from the next. Sadiq Mohammad looked the likely match-winner as he defended resolutely against the good balls and smashed the loose deliveries to the boundary. With Asif Iqbal, Sadiq took the score to 160 before Gifford had Asif Iqbal stumped. D'Oliveira swung the game England's way by removing Sadiq and Intikhab Alam for three runs. Lever ended the match taking three wickets in four balls. Wasim Bari equalled the Test record by holding eight catches.

## ENGLAND v INDIA 1971

Kennington Oval, London
19, 20, 21, 23, 24 August 1971
India won by four wickets

England 355 (A.P.E. Knott 90, J.A. Jameson 82, R.A. Hutton 81) and 101 (B.S. Chandrasekhar 6 for 38); India 284 (F.M. Engineer 59, D.N. Sardesai 54, R. Illingworth 5 for 70) and 6 for 174

This was India's first Test win in England and the victory brought to an end England's record run of 26 Tests without defeat.

After winning the toss the home team scored 355 on the first day at nearly three and a half runs per over. Jameson smashed an aggressive 82 at the top of the order before Knott and Hutton established a record seventh-wicket partnership of 103 in just over an hour, Knott's 90 coming from only 117 deliveries.

Rain prevented play on the second day and when it started fifteen minutes late on the third India got away to a poor start, Gavaskar and Mankad falling cheaply. In a welcome return to form, Sardesai with skipper Wadekar, 48, put on 93 for the third wicket to restore the balance. Illingworth did his best to upset India's plans by removing Wadekar, Sardesai and Viswanath in 23 balls without conceding a run. Then Solkar, 44, and Engineer hit back with an attractive 97-run stand for the sixth wicket. Abid Ali, 26, and Venkataraghavan, 24, took India to within 71 runs of the home team.

It was expected that England would set the visitors a sizeable target on the final day. However, Wadekar attacked with his spinners and in just 45.1 overs the home team was bundled out for 101. Chandrasekhar produced a match-winning spell of 6 for 38 to give him eight wickets for the match.

Illingworth was not going to give up the match without a great fight. He bowled superbly, but without luck, conceding only 40 runs from 36 overs, and operating in tandem with Underwood. Again Wadekar and Sardesai held the top order together as the visitors crawled ever so carefully to victory, Engineer's experience proving invaluable as the final 40 runs were scored.

The win was greeted with unbridled joy by millions of supporters across India.

## WEST INDIES v NEW ZEALAND 1971-72

Sabina Park, Kingston, Jamaica
16, 17, 18, 19, 21 February 1972
Match drawn

West Indies 4 for 508 dec. (L.G. Rowe 214, R.C. Fredericks 163) and 3 for 218 dec. (L.G. Rowe 100 not out); New Zealand 386 (G.M. Turner 223 not out, K.J. Wadsworth 78) and 6 for 236 (M.G. Burgess 101)

This was New Zealand's first Test match in the Caribbean and it was an amazing game of cricket.

Sobers won the toss and Fredericks and Rowe proceeded to put the game out of New Zealand's reach on the first day. Their partnership realised 269 before Fredericks was finally dismissed for 163. In his first Test innings, the local hero Rowe finished on 214 not out.

When the visitors had slumped to 5 for 108 shortly before lunch on the third day they looked headed for an overwhelming defeat. Wadsworth, whose previous highest score had been 21, joined Turner in a match-saving partnership of 220. Wadsworth, who had played the support role to perfection, was finally dismissed for 78. Turner, New Zealand's premier batsman, carried his bat for the second time. His innings of 223 was the highest score by any batsman carrying his bat in Tests.

The West Indies declaration was delayed until Rowe had reached his second hundred of the match. Perhaps Sobers waited too long, as New Zealand required 341 in 310 minutes for victory. When Holford dismissed Dowling and Turner shortly after lunch the home team had a glimmer of hope. However, a fighting century by Burgess enabled New Zealand to save the game.

Rowe became the first player to score hundreds in both innings of his first Test and was the third, after Walters and Gavaskar to score a century and a double-century in the same match. His aggregate of 314 was a record for any debutant.

## ENGLAND v AUSTRALIA 1972

Lord's Cricket Ground, London
22, 23, 24, 26 June 1971
Australia won by eight wickets

England 272 (A.W. Greig 54, R.A.L. Massie 8 for 84) and 116 (R.A.L. Massie 8 for 53); Australia 308 (G.S. Chappell 131, I.M. Chappell 56, R.W. Marsh 50, J.A. Snow 5 for 57) and 2 for 81 (K.R. Stackpole 57 not out)

Australia won what has become known as 'Massie's match' on the fourth afternoon to maintain its fine record at the 'home of cricket'.

England batted first on a hard fast pitch that was ideal for pace bowling while for the first three days the atmosphere was heavy and suited to swing. Boycott, Luckhurst and Edrich fell cheaply before the middle order dug in to retrieve the situation.

The next six batsmen all got set but only Greig reached fifty. Knott, 43, Snow, 37, Smith, 34, D'Oliveira, 32, and Illingworth, 30, failed to capitalise on their start. Lillee bowled with great pace and hostility to capture two early wickets but it was his Western Australian team-mate, Massie, who did the damage. In his first Test, the fast-medium swing bowler captured 8 for 84 from 32.5 overs. Only Trott, for Australia against England in 1894/95, and Valentine, for West Indies against England in 1950, had previously taken eight wickets in an innings on debut.

Francis and Stackpole fell cheaply before the Chappell brothers combined in a 75-run partnership for the third wicket. Ian, the more aggressive, fell to a suspect outfield catch by Smith for an attractive 56. When Walters was dismissed for 1 the visitors were again in trouble at 4 for 84. Greg then received valuable support from another Western Australian debutant, Edwards. This pair added 106 for the fifth wicket before Edwards fell to another splendid outfield catch by Smith. Greg Chappell, who brought up his century shortly before stumps on the second day, was finally dismissed for a magnificent 131. Hard hitting by Marsh and Colley gave the visitors a slender lead of 36. Snow bowled superbly finishing with 5 for 57 from 32 overs.

The capacity Saturday crowd did not know what was in store as England started its second innings. A short ball from Lillee struck Boycott on the body before dropping onto the off-bail. Luckhurst was next to go, caught Marsh bowled Lillee for four. Under cloudy skies the England batsmen had no answer to the superb swing bowling of Massie. The last pair of Gifford and Price put on 35 which was the best stand of the innings. Massie's second innings figures 8 for 53 from 27.2 overs were even better than his first. His match return of 16 for 137 was a record on debut until Hirwani of India captured 16 for 136 against the West Indies in 1987/88.

With only 81 required for victory, Australia wrapped up the match on the fourth afternoon by eight wickets. The match-winner, Massie, had made one of the greatest debuts in the game's long history.

## AUSTRALIA v PAKISTAN 1972-73

Sydney Cricket Ground, Sydney
6, 7, 8, 10, 11 January 1973
Australia won by 52 runs

Australia 334 (I.R. Redpath 79, R. Edwards 69) and 184; Pakistan 360 (Mushtaq Mohammad 121, Asif Iqbal 65, Nasim-ul-Ghani 64, G.S. Chappell 5 for 61) and 106 (M.H.N. Walker 6 for 15)

Pakistan won the toss and sent Australia in to bat on a green and responsive pitch. However, the pace trio of Asif Masood, Salim Altaf and Sarfraz Nawaz failed to take advantage of the favourable conditions. Redpath's patient innings of 79 was the cornerstone of Australia's total of 334. Sarfraz with 4 for 53 was the best of the visitors' bowlers.

Mushtaq Mohammad and Asif Iqbal, who came together with the score at 131, added 139 for the fifth wicket. The home team's premier bowler, Lillee, sent down only ten overs before a back problem caused him to leave the field. Greg Chappell exploited the conditions with his lively medium-pace deliveries to return 5 for 61.

With Pakistan leading by 26 the game was wide open. In the final session of the third day, Salim Altaf and Sarfraz Nawaz bowled the visitors to the edge of victory. Walker's dismissal early on the fourth morning left Australia 75 runs in front with just two wickets in hand. Massie joined the debutant Watkins in a match-winning 83-run partnership for the ninth wicket. It wasn't a swashbuckling affair as the pair occupied the crease for two and a half hours. Both Salim and Sarfraz claimed four wickets apiece, giving Sarfraz eight for the match and Salim seven.

The target for Pakistan was 159 with more than a day to play. Lillee bowled Nasim-ul-Ghani, 5, with the score on seven then Edwards took one of the great catches at cover point to remove Sadiq for 6. Zaheer Abbas, 26, and Majid Khan, 11, resumed on the final morning with only 111 required. However, the batsmen were overwhelmed by the occasion and the superb bowling of Lillee and Walker. Lillee reduced his pace because of the back problem while Walker, in only his second Test, captured 6 for 15 from 16 overs to win the match.

## WEST INDIES v AUSTRALIA 1973

Queen's Park Oval, Port-of-Spain, Trinidad
23, 24, 25, 27, 28 March 1973
Australia won by 44 runs

Australia 332 (K.D. Walters 112, I.R. Redpath 66, G.S. Chappell 56) and 281 (I.M. Chappell 97, L.R. Gibbs 5 for 102); West Indies 280 (R.B. Kanhai 56, A.I. Kallicharran 53) and 289 (A.I. Kallicharran 91, R.C. Fredericks 76)

Australia pulled off a fighting victory on a turning pitch in Trinidad. Walters played one of his great Test innings. He scored 100 between lunch and tea on the first day (Later, in December 1974 in Perth he was to score 100 between tea and stumps against England.)

The West Indies replied with 280 to trail by 52 runs in the first innings. They were disadvantaged by the fact that their number three batsman, Rowe, tore the ligaments in his right ankle on the first day and was therefore unable to bat in either innings of the match.

Ian Chappell's gutsy 97 was the foundation of Australia's second effort with the bat. He was seventh out at 231, and then some strange bowling by Gibbs allowed the last three wickets to add 50 (including 33 for the last wicket between Walker and Hammond).

The home team's target was 334. At lunch on the final day, an improbable victory seemed likely when Kallicharran and Foster were together with the score at 4 for 268. The tireless Walker snared 'Kalli' on the first ball after lunch and then O'Keeffe removed Foster. The rout continued with O'Keeffe picking up one of his best returns in the Test arena taking 4 for 57 from 24.1 overs.

## INDIA v ENGLAND 1972-73

Eden Gardens, Calcutta
30, 31 December, 1, 3, 4 January
India won by 28 runs

India 210 (F.M. Engineer 75) and 155 (A.S. Durani 53, A.W. Greig 5 for 24); England 173 (B.S. Chandrasekhar 5 for 65) and 163 (A.W. Greig 67, B.S. Bedi 5 for 63)

Almost 70,000 spectators packed the famous Eden Gardens stadium each day of the match, which fluctuated throughout every session.

India batted first after winning the toss. Tight English bowling supported by splendid fielding restricted the home team to 5 for 148 on the first day. Skipper Wadekar held the top order together with a patient 44 before he was tragically run out. Wicketkeeper Engineer played with his customary bravado. Coming in at number seven he scored 75 out of 110 runs while he was at the crease.

England struggled in reply. The Indian spinners Bedi, Chandrasekhar and Prasanna were able to weave their spell over the visitors' batsmen. Greig, 29, Knott, 35, and Old, 33 not out, bolstered the middle order but they fell 36 runs short on the first innings.

Hostile bowling by debutant Old put India on the back foot at the start of their second innings. Durani (batting with a runner) and Viswanath put on 71 for the third wicket in what proved to be a match-winning partnership. Greig, bowling a mixture of medium-pace cutters and fast off-spinners, captured 5 for 24 from 19.5 overs to give England some hope of victory.

Greig followed up his superb spell with the ball with a fine knock. He joined Denness with the visitors in desperate trouble at 4 for 17, but by stumps it was 4 for 105. The final day started with England needing a further 86 for victory with six wickets in hand. However, when Chandrasekhar removed Greig, Knott and Denness the balance had returned to India. Cottam was the batsman out in the first over after lunch as India scored a thoroughly-deserved win in a stirring low-scoring contest.

## NEW ZEALAND v ENGLAND 1974-75

Eden Park, Auckland
20, 21, 22, 23, 25 February 1975
England won by an innings and 83 runs

England 6 for 593 dec. (K.W.R. Fletcher 216, M.H. Denness 181, J.H. Edrich 64, A.W. Greig 51); New Zealand 326 (J.M. Parker 121, J.F.M. Morrison 58, K.J. Wadsworth 58, A.W. Greig 5 for 98) and 184 (J.F.M. Morrison 58, G.P. Howarth 51 not out, A.W. Greig 5 for 51)

The match ended amid great drama when the New Zealand number eleven, Chatfield, deflected a bouncer from Lever into his temple and collapsed with a hairline fracture of the skull. Chatfield's heart stopped beating for several seconds and only heart massage and mouth-to-mouth resuscitation by Bernard Thomas, the England physiotherapist, saved his life. Lever, who was visibly distressed by the incident, was reassured by Chatfield that the accident was his fault.

The dramatic finish to the match diverted attention from the excellent cricket that had been played on the first four days of the game. England had made a shaky start before Denness added 117 for the third wicket with Edrich and 266 for the fourth with Fletcher, who batted for seven hours to record his highest Test score of 216.

Despite a splendid century from Parker and half-centuries from Morrison and Wadsworth, New Zealand followed on 267 runs behind. By the fourth day the pitch had bare patches and the ball turned with uneven bounce, bringing Greig and Underwood into their own. During the match Greig took his 100th wicket, becoming the fourth English all-rounder to score 2000 runs and take 100 wickets. Underwood became the fourth English bowler to take 200 wickets when he dismissed Congdon in New Zealand's second innings.

While Chatfield will always remember his first Test with mixed emotions, he recovered to play a further 42 times for his country and take 123 wickets.

## WEST INDIES v INDIA 1975-76

Queens Park Oval, Port-of-Spain, Trinidad
7, 8, 10, 11, 12 April 1976
India won by six wickets

West Indies 359 (I.V.A Richards 177, C.J. Lloyd 68, B.S. Chandrasekhar 6 for 120) and 6 for 271 dec. (A.I.

Kallicharran 103 not out); India 228 (M.A. Holding 6 for 65) and 4 for 406 (G.R. Viswanath 112, S.M. Gavaskar 102, M. Amarnath 85)

In this match, India scored over 400 in the fourth innings to win. The only previous occasion had been at Headingley in 1948 (see page 19). Richards, with 177, mastered the Indian spinners, and made nearly half of the West Indies first-innings total of 359. The youthful Holding ripped through the visitors, who were bowled out for 228, leaving a deficit of 131. The home team built on the first-innings lead and, after Kallicharran reached his century, Lloyd declared. India needed 403 in a day and a half. (Australia's target at Leeds had been 404.)

Gavaskar, at his best, smashed 86 with twelve fours before stumps were drawn at 1 for 134. India needed 269 runs in six hours. After Gavaskar's early departure, Viswanath took over and, with Amarnath as the sheet anchor, they progressed steadily towards an improbable victory. The West Indian spinners bowled poorly and without the skill of their opposite numbers. Even though 'Vishy' and Amarnath were run out, Patel took over and India was home with seven overs to spare.

## AUSTRALIA v ENGLAND 1976-77

The Centenary Test
Melbourne Cricket Ground, Melbourne
12, 13, 14, 16, 17 March 1977
Australia won by 45 runs

Australia 138 and 9 for 419 dec. (R.W. Marsh 110 not out, I.C. Davis 68, K.D. Walters 66, D.W. Hookes 56); England 95 (D.K. Lillee 6 for 26) and 417 (D.W. Randall 174, D.L. Amiss 64, D.K. Lillee 5 for 139)

The Centenary of Test cricket was celebrated with a special match at Melbourne 100 years after that first match in March 1877. Australia, sent in on a lively pitch, was bundled out for just 138. The huge Sunday crowd roared as Lillee and Walker crashed through England's batting. England was all out for 95 as a result of the onslaught. Lillee took 6 for 26 and Walker took 4 for 54.

The MCC officials were concerned; the match seemed certain to be over by the fourth day of play. However, the Queen and Duke of Edinburgh were not due to attend until the afternoon of the fifth day.

The pitch was now favouring the batsmen. Although the homeside was in trouble at 3 for 53 in the second innings, they were able to turn that situation around. Rodney Marsh reached his first Test century against England, and the 21-year-old Hookes, on debut, hit Greig for five successive fours. The gutsy McCosker (who had his jaw fractured in the first innings) batted at number ten and scored 25 in an invaluable partnership of 54 with Marsh. Chappell declared Australia's innings with his team leading by 462.

Randall and Amiss gave England a glimmer of hope with a third-wicket stand of 166. O'Keeffe had both Randall and Greig caught at short leg by Cosier, then Lillee trapped Knott in front.

The result was an Australian victory by 45 runs — the same margin by which they had won the first match 100 years earlier. See page 35 for final scoreboard.

## NEW ZEALAND v ENGLAND 1977-78

Basin Reserve, Wellington
10, 11, 12, 14, 15 February 1978
New Zealand won by 72 runs

New Zealand 228 (J.G. Wright 55, C.M. Old 6 for 54) and 123 (R.G.D. Willis 5 for 32); England 215 (G. Boycott 77) and 64 (R.J. Hadlee 6 for 26)

This was the 48th match in 48 years between the two countries. Wright, playing his first Test, laid the foundation for New Zealand's innings. His 55 was scored in almost six hours and, with Congdon, 44, the home team reached a modest 228. Old bowled into the howling gale and finished with 6 for 54 from 30 overs. If Wright was laborious, then Boycott was, too. His 77 took almost seven and a half hours to compile. England lost its last six wickets for 32 runs to trail by 13 runs on the first innings. New Zealand's second-innings collapse was just as dramatic. The home team went from 1 for 82 to be all out for 123, with the last nine wickets falling for 41 runs. Willis was the destroyer, taking 5 for 32. England's target was 137, but by the end of the fourth day the innings was in tatters: eight wickets had fallen for 53 runs. Rain delayed the inevitable on the final morning for 40 minutes. It then took the Kiwis 49 minutes to claim the last two wickets, both falling to Richard Hadlee, who finished with 6 for 26. England was all out for 64.

New Zealand defeated England for the first time amid chaotic scenes at the Basin Reserve.

## WEST INDIES v AUSTRALIA 1977-78

Bourda, Georgetown, Guyana
31 March, 1, 2, 4, 5 April 1978
Australia won by three wickets

West Indies 205 (A.E. Greenidge 56, S. Shivnarine 53) and 439 (H.A. Gomes 101, A.B. Williams 100, S. Shivnarine 63, D.R. Parry 51); Australia 286 (R.B. Simpson 67, S.J. Rixon 54, G.M. Wood 50) and 7 for 362 (G.M. Wood 126, C.S. Serjeant 124)

A pre-match dispute between the West Indies Board and their captain, Lloyd, over team selection resulted in all the players contracted to World Series Cricket withdrawing from the team. As a result of this action, Kallicharran was named captain and the team comprised six new caps. It was hardly the perfect preparation for an important Test match for the West Indies.

## AUSTRALIA v ENGLAND 1976-77 (Centenary Test)

Melbourne Cricket Ground, 12, 13, 14, 16, 17 March. Australia won by 45 runs

**AUSTRALIA**

| | | | | | |
|---|---|---|---|---|---|
| I.C.Davis | lbw b Lever | 5 | | c Knott b Greig | 68 |
| R.B.McCosker | b Willis | 4 | (10) | c Greig b Old | 25 |
| G.J.Cosier | c Fletcher b Lever | 10 | (4) | c Knott b Lever | 4 |
| G.S.Chappell* | b Underwood | 40 | (3) | b Old | 2 |
| D.W.Hookes | c Greig b Old | 17 | (6) | c Fletcher b Underwood | 56 |
| K.D.Walters | c Greig b Willis | 4 | (5) | c Knott b Greig | 66 |
| R.W.Marsh† | c Knott b Old | 28 | | not out | 110 |
| G.J.Gilmour | c Greig b Old | 4 | | c Knott b Greig | 16 |
| K.J.O'Keeffe | c Brearley b Underwood | 0 | (2) | c Willis b Old | 14 |
| D.K.Lillee | not out | 10 | (9) | c Amiss b Old | 25 |
| M.H.N.Walker | b Underwood | 2 | | not out | 8 |
| Extras | (B 4, LB 2, NB 8) | 14 | | (LB 10, NB 15) | 25 |
| **Total** | | **138** | | **(9wkts dec.)** | **419** |

**ENGLAND**

| | | | | | |
|---|---|---|---|---|---|
| R.A.Woolmer | c Chappell b Lillee | 9 | | lbw b Walker | 12 |
| J.M.Brearley | c Hookes b Lillee | 12 | | lbw b Lillee | 43 |
| D.L.Underwood | c Chappell b Walker | 7 | (10) | b Lillee | 7 |
| D.W.Randall | c Marsh b Lillee | 4 | (3) | c Cosier b O'Keeffe | 174 |
| D.L.Amiss | c O'Keeffe b Walker | 4 | (4) | b Chappell | 64 |
| K.W.R.Fletcher | c Marsh b Walker | 4 | (5) | c Marsh b Lillee | 1 |
| A.W.Greig* | b Walker | 18 | (6) | c Cosier b O'Keeffe | 41 |
| A.P.E.Knott† | lbw b Lillee | 15 | (7) | lbw b Lillee | 42 |
| C.M.Old | c Marsh b Lillee | 3 | (8) | c Chappell b Lillee | 2 |
| J.K.Lever | c Marsh b Lillee | 11 | (9) | not out | 4 |
| R.G.D.Willis | not out | 1 | | not out | 5 |
| Extras | (B 2, LB 2, NB 2, W 1) | 7 | | (B 8, LB 4, NB 7, W 3) | 22 |
| **Total** | | **95** | | | **417** |

| **ENGLAND** | O | M | R | W | | O | M | R | W |
|---|---|---|---|---|---|---|---|---|---|
| Lever | 12 | 1 | 36 | 2 | Lever | 21 | 1 | 95 | 2 |
| Willis | 8 | 0 | 33 | 2 | Willis | 22 | 0 | 91 | 0 |
| Old | 12 | 4 | 39 | 3 | Old | 27.6 | 2 | 104 | 4 |
| Underwood | 11.6 | 2 | 16 | 3 | Greig | 14 | 3 | 66 | 2 |
| | | | | | Underwood | 12 | 2 | 38 | 1 |

| **AUSTRALIA** | O | M | R | W | | O | M | R | W |
|---|---|---|---|---|---|---|---|---|---|
| Lillee | 13.3 | 2 | 26 | 6 | Lillee | 34.4 | 7 | 139 | 5 |
| Walker | 15 | 3 | 54 | 4 | Walker | 22 | 4 | 83 | 1 |
| O'Keeffe | 1 | 0 | 4 | 0 | Gilmour | 4 | 0 | 29 | 0 |
| Gilmour | 5 | 3 | 4 | 0 | Chappel | 16 | 7 | 29 | 1 |
| | | | | | O'Keeffe | 33 | 6 | 108 | 3 |
| | | | | | Walters | 3 | 2 | 7 | 0 |

FALL OF WICKETS

| | A | E | A | E |
|---|---|---|---|---|
| Wkt | 1st | 1st | 2nd | 2nd |
| 1st | 11 | 19 | 33 | 28 |
| 2nd | 13 | 30 | 40 | 113 |
| 3rd | 23 | 34 | 53 | 279 |
| 4th | 45 | 40 | 132 | 290 |
| 5th | 51 | 40 | 187 | 346 |
| 6th | 102 | 61 | 244 | 369 |
| 7th | 114 | 65 | 277 | 380 |
| 8th | 117 | 78 | 353 | 385 |
| 9th | 136 | 86 | 407 | 410 |
| 10th | 138 | 95 | - | 417 |

Umpires: T.F.Brooks and M.G.O'Connell

Hostile bowling by Thomson and Clark restricted the inexperienced line-up to 205 with two of the debutants, A.E. Greenidge and Shivnarine scoring half-centuries. Australia lost Darling and Ogilvie before the close and by lunch on the second day were 6 for 146. Simpson, Rixon and Yardley retrieved the situation for the visitors with some splendid batting which saw Australia gain a lead of 81. Two of the new caps, Phillip with four and Clarke with three, were amongst the wickets and they both bowled with good pace and hostility. Another of the debutants, Williams, turned the game for the West Indies with a cavalier knock. He raced to his century from just 118 deliveries and then departed next ball. Williams received excellent support from nightwatchman Parry in a third-wicket partnership of 77. Gomes, who took over from Williams, was less aggressive but equally effective. Gomes reached his century in three hours and 25 minutes with eleven boundaries and, like Williams, was dismissed next ball after completing his hundred. Shivnarine again played a vital role with the bat, putting on 70 with Gomes for the seventh wicket and 62 with Holder for the ninth. Australia had two days in which to score 359 for victory.

After forty minutes on the fourth day it looked like a certain West Indies win. Darling, Ogilvie and Simpson had been dismissed by Clarke with only 22 runs on the board. However, Wood and Serjeant played with great determination in a stand of 251 to give the visitors some hope of pulling off a memorable victory. When the century-makers and Cosier fell in the final session it was again anyone's match.

Australia started the fifth day needing a further 69 with four wickets in hand. Wicketkeeper Rixon with 39 not out, Laughlin with 24, and Yardley with 15 not out, saw the visitors home.

The total of 7 for 362 remains the third-highest fourth innings score to win a Test.

## WEST INDIES v AUSTRALIA 1977-78

Sabina Park, Kingston, Jamaica
28, 29, 30 April, 2, 3, May 1978
Match drawn

Australia 343 (P.M. Toohey 122, G.N. Yallop 57) and 3 for 305 dec. (P.M. Toohey 97, G.M. Wood 90); West Indies 280 (H.A. Gomes 115, S. Shivnarine 53, T.J. Laughlin 5 for 101) and 9 for 258 (A.I. Kallicharran 126)

Australia was denied an almost certain victory when spectators rioted and invaded the ground after Holder had been given out caught behind by Umpire Malcolm. Thirty-eight balls of the mandatory final 20 overs remained when the incident occurred. Officials of both teams had decided to extend the match into a sixth day but had not consulted nor informed the umpires of this decision. One of them, Gosein, was adamant there was no provision in the laws or playing conditions for the match to be extended so he refused to continue, as did the third umpire, John Gayle. Although Malcolm was prepared to stand, no other official of first-class status was available so the match was abandoned as a draw.

The visitors had held sway from the start with Toohey's maiden century making up the cornerstone of Australia's total of 343. Left-arm spinner Jumadeen polished off the tail, taking the last four wickets in 28 balls. Gomes' splendid hundred held the West Indies innings together after they had slumped to be 5 for 63. He shared stands of 96 with Shivnarine, 46 with Phillip, and 57 with Holder.

Aggressive batting by Australia in its second innings gave the visitors the opportunity to declare late on the fourth day, leaving the home team 369 for victory with Toohey and Wood both just missing out on well-deserved centuries.

Skipper Kallicharran held the West Indies innings together with a determined century but it was problematical that Parry and Jumadeen would have been able to survive against the Australian spinners, Yardley and Higgs, on a turning pitch.

## AUSTRALIA v PAKISTAN 1978-79

Melbourne Cricket Ground, Melbourne
10, 11, 12, 14, 15 March 1979
Pakistan won by 71 runs

Pakistan 196 and 353 (Majid Khan 108, Zaheer Abbas 59); Australia 168 and 310 (A.R. Border 105, K.J. Hughes 84, A.M.J. Hilditch 62, Sarfraz Nawaz 9 for 86)

This Test was the first of a two-match series and came at the end of an Australian season in which six Tests had been played in an Ashes series and Pakistan had completed a successful tour of New Zealand.

Yallop sent Pakistan in after winning the toss. Hogg responded with a fiery opening spell which reduced the visitors to 4 for 40. The situation became even worse after Javed Miandad and Wasim Raja had been removed, with Pakistan in real trouble at 6 for 99. Mushtaq Mohammad played a gritty captain's knock, top-scoring with 36. He received valuable support from Imran Khan, 33, and Sarfraz Nawaz, 35, which carried Pakistan to a modest 196. Hogg was the pick of the bowlers finishing with 4 for 49.

Australia's reply was poor. Openers Wood and Hilditch collided while running which forced Wood to retire hurt. Apart from new cap Whatmore, who top-scored with a patient 43, the home team struggled. Imran bowled superbly taking 4 for 26 from 18 overs. There was a stir when Hogg was run out after leaving the crease before the ball was 'dead'. Mushtaq asked umpire Harvey to reverse his decision, but the request was denied. Umpire Harvey, standing in his first Test, was the elder brother of Neil, the celebrated Australian left-hand batsman.

Pakistan consolidated its position with some aggressive batting. Majid Khan led the way with his seventh century, his 108 featuring sixteen majestic boundaries. The declaration was made mid-afternoon on the fourth day with Australia set 382 for victory.

With Wood inconvenienced, Whatmore opened and put on 49 with Hilditch who fell just before stumps for 62. Australia started the final day needing 265 to win with eight wickets in hand. Within half an hour, Yallop was foolishly run out. Border and Hughes, with a mixture of splendid batting and good fortune, carried Australia to 3 for 305 by half past four. Seventy-seven runs were needed with seven wickets in hand. Sarfraz Nawaz then produced one of the greatest spells in Test history. In 65 balls the home team was dismissed for 310. Sarfraz had taken 7 for 1 from 33 deliveries to finish with 9 for 86 and the other dismissal had been a run-out. Pakistan had pulled off a great victory, as a result of the inspired bowling by Sarfraz.

## NEW ZEALAND v WEST INDIES 1979-80

Carisbrook, Dunedin
8, 9, 10, 12, 13 February 1980
New Zealand won by 1 wicket

West Indies 140 (D.L. Haynes 55, R.J. Hadlee 5 for 34) and 212 (D.L. Haynes 105, R.J. Hadlee 6 for 68); New Zealand 249 (B.A. Edgar 65, R.J. Hadlee 51) and 9 for 104

After Lloyd called correctly, Hadlee tore the heart out of the visitors' innings. They were 3 for 4 after Hadlee had bowled 13 deliveries. Haynes with 55 played a lone hand, as the West Indies were bowled out for 140.

Against hostile fast bowling, Edgar and Howarth played with great courage and determination for New Zealand, with Edgar taking almost five hours to score 65. After a middle-order collapse, Hadlee and Cairns added 64 in 34 minutes for the eighth wicket. Cairns hit Parry for 3 sixes in one over, and Hadlee's 51 runs included nine fours.

New Zealand's lead was a valuable 109 runs. Again it was Haynes who held the visitors innings together. He scored 105 out of 212, and added 88 for the fifth wicket with King and 63 for the sixth with Murray to save the side.

New Zealand needed 104 to win. By lunch on the final day they had reached 2 for 33. Under intense pressure from the pace battery (Holding, Croft and Garner), they crashed to be 7 for 54 and appeared to be beaten.

Again Hadlee and Cairns came to the rescue. They added 19 for the eighth wicket before Cairns and Troup put on 27 for the ninth. At tea it was 9 for 95. With one run added, Holding hit Cairns' off-stump without dislodging the bail. Cairns went when the score reached 100. Boock, the No.11 batsman, joined Troup. He survived the last five balls of Holding's over. Garner continued the attack. The first ball produced a bye. On the second ball, Boock survived an appeal for lbw. He defended the next two before pushing the fifth ball behind point for two runs. With scores level, the batsmen scampered a leg bye to produce a thrilling New Zealand victory.

Hadlee's eleven wickets included a Test record of eight lbw decisions (of the total twelve lbw decisions made in the match).

## ENGLAND v WEST INDIES 1980

Trent Bridge, Nottingham
5, 6, 7, 9, 10 June 1980
West Indies won by two wickets

England 263 (I.T. Botham 57, A.M.E. Roberts 5 for 72) and 252 (G. Boycott 75); West Indies 308 (I.V.A. Richards 64, D.L. Murray 64, C.G. Greenidge 53) and 8 for 209 (D.L. Haynes 62, R.G.D Willis 5 for 65)

This was Botham's first Test as captain. He decided to bat on a pitch that offered considerable movement off the seam and conditions conducive to swing bowling. England was aided by some shoddy fielding. Their three top-scorers (Botham, 57, Woolmer, 46, and Boycott, 36) were all given a life. Botham's innings was his only half-century in twelve Tests as captain. Roberts was outstanding for the visitors with 5 for 72. Garner provided great support taking 3 for 44 from 21 overs.

A whirlwind second-wicket partnership of 88 in only 91 minutes by Greenidge and Richards rested the initiative with the West Indies, but Willis and Botham exploited the favourable conditions and restricted the lead to 45. Wicketkeeper Murray, producing a belligerent knock of 64 in the lower order, was mainly responsible for the visitors' lead.

England had just wiped off the deficit without loss when Gooch was superbly run out by Bacchus. Missed chances again assisted Boycott and Woolmer who added 106 for the third wicket. Only Willey with 38 made a contribution from the lower order and 'extras' with 52 was the second-top score of the innings.

The West Indies' target was 208 in more than eight hours. It was never going to be easy under difficult conditions, especially after Greenidge fell cheaply. Richards proceeded to rip into the bowling. In a cavalier stay of 56 minutes he scored 48 with eight boundaries. Haynes and Bacchus consolidated the position late on the fourth afternoon so that when the final day started the West Indies required 99 with eight wickets in hand. Hendrick removed Bacchus with the first ball of the day to give England some hope. Willis, maintaining his pace and hostility in a long spell, continued to remove the visitors with Kallicharran, 9, Lloyd, 6, Murray, 16, and Marshall, 7, among his victims. It was 7 for 180 when Roberts joined the sheet-anchor, Haynes, who had been there since the start of the innings. A direct hit from Willey ran Haynes out after a marathon stay of more than five hours. With three runs required, Haynes ran off the ground in tears believing that the game would be lost. However, Roberts hit Botham to the long-on boundary to record a nail-biting victory.

This was to be the only result in a rain-marred series.

## ENGLAND v AUSTRALIA 1981

Headingley, Leeds
16, 17, 18, 20, 21 July 1981
England won by 18 runs
Australia 9 for 401 dec. (J. Dyson 102, K.J. Hughes 89, G.N. Yallop 58, I.T. Botham 6 for 95) and 111 (R.G.D. Willis 8 for 43); England 174 (I.T. Botham 50) and 356 (I.T. Botham 149 not out, G.R. Dilley 56, T.M. Alderman 6 for 135)

For this third Test of the series, Brearley replaced Botham as England's captain. Hughes won the toss for the third time in succession for Australia, and batted first. Dyson's solid century and the skipper's 89 steered Australia to the relative safety of 401 before declaring.

Australia's pace bowlers, Lillee, Alderman and Lawson, bundled England out for 174. The deposed Botham, who had taken six wickets in Australia's innings, top-scored with 50.

England followed on, 227 runs behind, but the second innings proceeded along similar lines to the first. Taylor became Alderman's fourth victim for the innings, and England's score was 7 for 135.

Botham proceeded to play one of the great Test hands and, with admirable support from the tail, at least avoided the innings defeat and gave his team a glimmer of hope. With Dilley, 56, he added 117 for the eighth wicket in 80 minutes; with Old, 29, it was 67 for the ninth; and with Willis, 2, it was 37 for the last. Botham finished with 149 not out and posted his century from 87 balls. (Jessop had smashed 104 in 75 minutes at The Oval in 1902 — see page 13.)

Australia had almost the entire final day to score 130 to win. With the score at 1 for 56, Willis changed ends to bowl with the wind. He proceeded to take eight of the last nine wickets to fall and, in a career-best performance, returned 8 for 43 from 15.1 overs as England snatched a dramatic 18-run victory.

This was only the second time that a team following-on had won a Test match. The previous occasion was in Sydney on December 1894 (see pages 11 and 13).

Early in England's second innings, odds of 500 to 1 for an England victory were posted in the betting tents at Headingley.

## ENGLAND v AUSTRALIA 1981

Edgbaston, Birmingham
30, 31 July, 1, 2 August 1981
England won by 29 runs
England 189 (T.M. Alderman 5 for 42) and 219 (R.J. Bright 5 for 68); Australia 258 and 121 (I.T. Botham 5 for 11)

Less than two weeks after England's unbelievable win at Headingley, they did it again at Edgbaston. The ball dominated to the extent that no batsman scored 50. This had not happened since January 1935 when the West Indies played England on a rain-affected pitch at Bridgetown.

Despite some concern about the wicket, Brearley chose to bat after winning the toss. The skipper top-scored with a patient 48, and next best was Botham who made 26. For the third time in the series, Alderman claimed five wickets in an innings. By stumps on the first day England had struck back with Old removing Dyson and Border.

Tight bowling and alert fielding by the home team restricted Australia's lead to 69 runs. Hughes top-scored with 47, debutant Kent made 46 and Yallop, 30. Emburey bowled his off-spinners with great control, finishing with 4 for 43 from 26 overs.

When Bright, bowling his left-arm orthodox into the bowler's footmarks, had dismissed Gower, Boycott, Gooch and Willey, and Lillee had Botham caught behind, England's lead was just 46 with only four wickets in hand. Gatting, who top-scored with 39, kept the game alive with valuable support from the bowlers. Emburey remained 37 not out while Old made 23.

Australia's target was 151, 21 more than was required at Headingley. Old struck before stumps on the third day, trapping Wood in front. The visitors required 142 with two days to play.

Willis gave England some hope by removing Dyson and Hughes within forty minutes on the fourth morning. Yallop, who made 30 for the second time in the match, and Border carefully took the score to 87. Australia still looked likely winners as Border, with Kent's assistance, moved the total to 105.

With just 46 needed, Emburey dismissed Australia's sheet-anchor and with Border gone the brittleness of the visitors' batting was exposed. Botham, who had been reluctant to bowl, destroyed the lower order taking 5 for 1 in 28 balls to end the match.

On only the second Sunday during which there had been Test cricket played in England, the home team had scored a remarkable victory to the delight of the capacity crowd.

## AUSTRALIA v PAKISTAN 1981-82

W.A.C.A. Ground, Perth
13, 14, 15, 16, 17 November 1981
Australia won by 286 runs

Australia 180 and 424 (K.J. Hughes 106, B.M. Laird 85); Pakistan 62 (D.K. Lillee 5 for 18) and 256 (Javed Miandad 79, B. Yardley 6 for 84)

This was another incident-filled match. On the previous occasion these teams played in Perth, in March 1979, Sikander Bakht had been run out by the bowler while he was backing up and Hilditch was given out 'handled the ball'.

There were to be no such controversial dismissals in this game but Pakistan was bowled out in just 21.2 overs for its lowest Test score of 62. Alderman, who had taken 42 wickets in his first series in England earlier in the year, captured the wicket of Riswan-Uz-Zaman with his first ball in a Test on home soil. Lillee became the third bowler, after S.F. Barnes and Grimmett, to take five wickets in an innings 20 times.

The low point of the match came on the fourth afternoon when there was an ugly confrontation between the Pakistan captain, Javed Miandad, and Australia's premier fast bowler. Lillee, who claimed that he had been provoked by abuse from Javed, deliberately impeded and then aimed a kick at the visiting captain. It was left to Umpire Crafter to separate the combatants as Javed aimed to hit Lillee with his bat.

Despite a disappointing first innings total of 180, Australia comprehensively outplayed the visitors, highlights being a controlled century from Hughes and six second innings wickets to the off-spinner Yardley.

## AUSTRALIA v WEST INDIES 1981-82

Melbourne Cricket Ground, Melbourne
26, 27, 28, 29, 30 December 1981
Australia won by 58 runs

Australia 198 (K.J. Hughes 100 not out, M.A. Holding 5 for 45) and 222 (A.R. Border 66, B.M. Laird 64, M.A. Holding 6 for 62); West Indies 201 (H.A. Gomes 55, D.K. Lillee 7 for 83) and 161

Australia won a memorable Test that ended the West Indies' sequence of 15 matches without defeat.

Chappell somewhat surprisingly decided to bat on a damp pitch and when Holding removed Laird and the skipper with successive balls in the fifth over, it looked as if the Australian captain had made a mistake. The situation got progressively worse as 2 for 4 became 3 for 8, then 4 for 26 and 5 for 59. Hughes proceeded to play one of the great innings. With a mixture of resolute defence and scorching strokes he remained 100 not out in a total of 198. When the number eleven Alderman joined him, Hughes was on 71. Their 43-run partnership was the second best of the innings. Holding was easily the pick of the four-pronged pace battery and thoroughly deserved his five-wicket haul.

The West Indies were left with 35 minutes to bat on the first day, and this produced some more dramatic cricket. Alderman had Bacchus caught at fourth slip then Lillee had Haynes caught by Border at second slip and the visitors were 2 for 5. Nightwatchman Croft was trapped in front by Lillee and it was 3 for 6. The big crowd roared like it was a football match when Lillee bowled Richards with the last ball of the day's play, leaving West Indies 4 for 10.

Lillee started the second day needing two wickets to break Gibb's world record of 309. Dujon, on debut as a specialist batsman, was the first, caught at deep backward square after an impressive innings of 41. Gomes was next, caught at slip by Chappell. West Indies finished with a lead of three runs. On an improving pitch, Australia's openers Wood and Laird produced the best partnership of the match, Wood contributing 46 in a stand of 82. Border then held the innings together with another pugnacious knock. He top-scored with 66 after Laird had made 64. The only other batsman to reach double figures was Yardley with 13. Holding was once again magnificent taking 6 for 62. His match figures of 11 for 107 still remain the best for a West Indies bowler against Australia. Wicketkeeper David Murray took nine catches for the match to establish another West Indian record.

The target for victory was 220 but when Alderman removed Bacchus and Richards in the second over Australia held the whip hand. Dujon played another fine knock but he lacked support. Yardley with 4 for 38 and Lillee with 3 for 44 were the pick of Australia's bowlers, the record-breaking fast bowler claiming 10 for 127 for the match.

## AUSTRALIA v ENGLAND 1982-83

Melbourne Cricket Ground, Melbourne
26, 27, 28, 29, 30 December 1982
England won by three runs

England 284 (C.J. Tavare 89, A.J. Lamb 83) and 294 (G.Fowler 65); Australia 287 (K.J. Hughes 66, D.W. Hookes 53, R.W. Marsh 53) and 288 (D.W. Hookes 68, A.R. Border 62 not out, N.G. Cowans 6 for 77)

This was one of the great Test matches. In terms of runs, the only closer Tests were a tie between Australia and the West Indies in Brisbane, 1960-61 (page 25); a tie between India and Australia in Madras, 1986-87 (page 40); and the West Indies' one run win over Australia in Adelaide, 1992-93 (page 43).

Chappell sent England in on a slightly damp pitch. The visitors were soon struggling at 3 for 56 before Tavare and Lamb added 161 for the fourth wicket in sparkling fashion. England's tail failed to wag, and the innings ended at 284.

On the second day, Australia was bowled out for 287. After Cowans dismissed Dyson and Chappell with successive deliveries, Hughes grafted a patient 66 to hold the Australian innings together. Both Hookes and Marsh, with a mixture of aggression and good fortune, scored half-centuries.

The pattern continued on the third day with England being dismissed for 294. This time, it was the lower order that held the innings together. Botham scored his 46 at a run a ball before Pringle and Taylor realised 61 in an eighth-wicket partnership.

Australia's target was 292. An occasional ball was keeping low on the relaid pitch, but the outfield was usually fast (the result of a prolonged drought that had restricted the watering of the ground).

Fortunes fluctuated throughout Australia's innings. Early on, England was on top. Chappell fell cheaply, again to Cowans, and when Dyson was brilliantly caught by Tavare at Slip it was 3 for 71. Australia regained the initiative when Hughes and Hookes posted a century partnership for the fourth wicket.

Then the inspired spell from Cowans tipped the scales England's way. He captured 4 for 19 in seven overs to have the home team in desperate trouble at 9 for 218. Thomson joined Border with 74 runs still required. By stumps, the last pair had taken the score to 255 — they were half-way there. On the final morning 18 000 spectators turned up for the climax to what had been the most enthralling Test since the tie at the Gabba 22 years earlier.

Willis kept the field back for Border to enable him to take singles. The pugnacious left-hander had been out of touch, and the lack of pressure helped play him back to form. The new ball had been taken early on the final morning with the score at 259, but still the last pair defied the England team. Botham started the eighteenth over of the day with four runs needed for an improbable victory. Thomson fended at the first ball, edging it to Tavare at second slip. The straightforward catch bounced out, but within reach of Miller at first slip. He completed the catch, and England won the titanic struggle by three runs. With that final wicket, Botham became only the second English Test player (Rhodes being the other) to score 1000 runs and take 100 wickets against Australia.

## ENGLAND v WEST INDIES 1984

Lord's Cricket Ground, London
28, 29, 30 June, 2, 3 July 1984
West Indies won by nine wickets

England 286 (G.Fowler 106, B.C Broad 55, M.D. Marshall 6 for 85) and 9 for 300 dec. (A.J. Lamb 110, I.T. Botham 81); West Indies 245 (I.V.A. Richards 72, I.T. Botham 8 for 103) and 1 for 344 (C.G. Greenidge 214 not out, H.A. Gomes 92 not out)

England controlled the match for four of the five days, only to be convincingly defeated at the end. Fowler and Broad, on debut, scored a rare century opening stand against the West Indies pace battery. Fowler applied himself for over six hours to post his second Test century. The last six English wickets fell for only 43 as Marshall cleaned up the tail to finish with 6 for 70.

Botham knocked over the top order to have the West Indies in trouble at 3 for 35. Richards and Lloyd dug in until Botham trapped Richards in front for 72.

Umpire Barry Meyer later admitted that he had considered recalling Richards, fearing he may have made a mistake. Botham was magnificent and finished with 8 for 103 as England gained first innings lead of 41 runs.

This advantage was quickly lost as the home team slumped to 3 for 36. Lamb, with support from Gatting and Botham, turned the innings around. The irrepressible Botham hammered 81, while Lamb finished with 110.

When Gower declared early on the final morning the West Indies required 342 to win in five and a half hours.

Greenidge proceeded to play a superb innings. He made the England attack look pedestrian as he plundered 29 boundaries in compiling a brilliant double-century. Greenidge and Gomes added an unbroken 287 for the second wicket to bring the West Indies home with almost twelve overs to spare.

For the first time, a 'Man of the Match' award was shared — Botham joined Greenidge for the honour.

Finally, of the 30 dismissals in the match, twelve were lbw, thereby equalling the record set at Dunedin in 1979-80.

## INDIA v AUSTRALIA 1986-87

Chepauk (Chidambaram Stadium), Madras
18, 19, 20, 21, 22 September 1986
Match tied

Australia 7 for 574 dec. (D.M. Jones 210, D.C. Boon 122, A.R. Border 106) and 5 for 170 dec.; India 397 (Kapil Dev 119, R.J. Shastri 62, K.R. Srikkanth 53, M. Azharuddin 50, G.R.J. Matthews 5 for 103) and 347 (S.M. Gavaskar 90, M. Amarnath 51, G.R.J. Matthews 5 for 146, R.J. Bright 5 for 94)

This match resulted in the second tie in Test history. (Australia was also involved in the first tie — against the West Indies — in 1960-61. See page 25. At the finish, it was Australia who managed to avoid defeat, even though they had dominated proceedings for the first four days' play. Australia declared both its innings, and lost only twelve wickets in the match.

## INDIA v AUSTRALIA 1986-87 (First Test)

Chidambaram Stadium, Chepauk, Madras, 18, 19, 20, 21, 22 September. A tie

**AUSTRALIA**

| | | | | | |
|---|---|---|---|---|---|
| D.C.Boon | c Kapil Dev b Sharma | 122 | (2) | lbw b Maninder Singh | 49 |
| G.R.Marsh | c Kapil Dev b Yadav | 22 | (1) | b Shastri | 11 |
| D.M.Jones | b Yadav | 210 | | c Azharuddin b Maninder Singh | 24 |
| R.J.Bright | c Shastri b Yadav | 30 | | | |
| A.R.Border* | c Gavaskar b Shastri | 106 | (4) | b Maninder Singh | 27 |
| G.M.Ritchie | run out | 13 | (5) | c Pandit b Shastri | 28 |
| G.R.J.Matthews | c Pandit b Yadav | 44 | (6) | not out | 27 |
| S.R.Waugh | not out | 12 | (7) | not out | 2 |
| T.J.Zoehrer† | | | | | |
| C.J.McDermott | | | | | |
| B.A.Reid | | | | | |
| Extras | (B 1, LB 7, NB 6, W 1) | 15 | | (LB 1, NB 1) | 2 |
| **Total** | **(7 wkts dec.)** | **574** | | **(5 wkts dec.)** | **170** |

**INDIA**

| | | | | | |
|---|---|---|---|---|---|
| S.M.Gavaskar | c and b Matthews | 8 | | c Jones b Bright | 90 |
| K. Srikkanth | c Ritchie b Matthews | 53 | | c Waugh b Matthews | 39 |
| M.Amarnath | run out | 1 | | c Boon b Matthews | 51 |
| M.Azharuddin | c and b Bright | 50 | | c Ritchie b Bright | 42 |
| R.J.Shastri | c Zoehrer b Matthews | 62 | (7) | not out | 48 |
| C.S.Pandit | c Waugh b Matthews | 35 | (5) | b Matthews | 39 |
| Kapil Dev* | c Border b Matthews | 119 | (6) | C Bright b Matthews | 1 |
| K.S.More† | c Zoehrer b Waugh | 4 | (9) | lbw b Bright | 0 |
| C.Sharma | c Zoehrer b Reid | 30 | (8) | c McDermott b Bright | 23 |
| N.S.Yadav | c Border b Bright | 19 | | b Bright | 8 |
| Maninder Singh | not out | 0 | | lbw b Matthews | 0 |
| Extras | (B 1, LB 9, NB 6) | 16 | | (B 1, LB 3, NB 2) | 6 |
| **Total** | | **397** | | | **347** |

| **INDIA** | O | M | R | W | | O | M | R | W |
|---|---|---|---|---|---|---|---|---|---|
| Kapil Dev | 18 | 5 | 52 | 0 | Sharma | 6 | 0 | 19 | 0 |
| Sharma | 16 | 1 | 70 | 1 | Kapil Dev | 1 | 0 | 5 | 0 |
| ManinderSingh | 39 | 8 | 135 | 0 | Shastri | 14 | 2 | 50 | 2 |
| Yadav | 49.5 | 9 | 142 | 4 | M. Signh | 19 | 2 | 60 | 3 |
| Shastri | 47 | 8 | 161 | 1 | Yadav | 9 | 0 | 35 | 0 |
| Srikkanth | 1 | 0 | 6 | 0 | | | | | |
| **AUSTRALIA** | O | M | R | W | | O | M | R | W |
| McDermott | 14 | 2 | 59 | 0 | McDermott | 5 | 0 | 27 | 0 |
| Reid | 18 | 4 | 93 | 1 | Reid | 10 | 2 | 48 | 0 |
| Matthews | 28.2 | 3 | 103 | 5 | Matthews | 39.5 | 7 | 146 | 5 |
| Bright | 23 | 3 | 88 | 2 | Bright | 25 | 3 | 94 | 5 |
| Waugh | 11 | 2 | 44 | 1 | Border | 3 | 0 | 12 | 0 |
| | | | | | Waugh | 4 | 1 | 16 | 0 |

FALL OF WICKETS

| | A | I | A | I |
|---|---|---|---|---|
| Wkt | 1st | 1st | 2nd | 2nd |
| 1st | 48 | 62 | 31 | 55 |
| 2nd | 206 | 65 | 81 | 158 |
| 3rd | 282 | 65 | 94 | 204 |
| 4th | 460 | 142 | 125 | 251 |
| 5th | 481 | 206 | 165 | 253 |
| 6th | 544 | 220 | - | 291 |
| 7th | 573 | 245 | - | 331 |
| 8th | - | 330 | - | 334 |
| 9th | - | 334 | - | 344 |
| 10th | - | 397 | - | 347 |

Umpires: D.N.Dotiwalla and V.Vikramraju

Australia's first innings continued until early on the third day. Jones' double-century was the cornerstone of the visitors' highest Test score in India, and Boon and Border were the other centurions. However, the Indian skipper, Kapil Dev, made sure that Australia batted again by blasting a century off 109 balls with 21 fours.

The off-spinner Matthews picked up five wickets in an innings for the first time. From the 49 overs remaining on the fourth day, Australia scored 170. This allowed Border to declare on the final morning, setting India 348 to win from a minimum of 87 overs.

After a steady start, Gavaskar and Amarnath picked up the batting tempo and, when they went to tea at 2 for 190, India had a realistic chance of winning the match. The target for the final session was 158 runs from 30 overs. At the start of the final 20 overs, 118 runs were needed with seven wickets in hand.

Gavaskar, 90, went out at 251; when Kapil Dev was out two runs later, Australia again had a chance. Shastri, Pandit and Chetan Sharma turned the game India's way until only 18 runs were needed from 30 balls. The situation changed again when Sharma and More were dismissed in an over by Bright. Yadav, who had hit Matthews for six, was ninth out at 344, bowled by Bright.

With just eight balls remaining, Maninder Singh joined Shastri and defended two balls from Bright, giving Shastri the strike for the last over from Matthews. The first ball was blocked. He went for a big hit off the second ball and mistimed the stroke. But after a misfield he was able to take two runs.

The third ball was pushed to mid-wicket for a single and the scores were tied. Maninder defended the fourth, but from the fifth delivery he was trapped lbw. The match ended in a thrilling tie before 30 000 excited fans. Matthews picked up his second five-wicket haul, and the left-armer Bright gained the other five. All ten wickets in India's second innings had fallen to spin. See page 41 for the final scoreboard.

## INDIA v WEST INDIES 1987-88

Chepauk (Chidambaram Stadium), Madras
11, 12, 14, 15 January 1988
India won by 255 runs

India 382 (Kapil Dev 109, Arun Lal 69) and 8 for 217 dec. (W.V. Raman 83); West Indies 184 (I.V.A. Richards 68, N.D. Hirwani 8 for 61) and 160 (A.L. logie 67, N.D. Hirwani 8 for 75).

In this match India recorded the most convincing of its six victories over the West Indies. The player mainly responsible was a new cap, the 19-year-old leg spinner Hirwani. He captured eight wickets in each innings, which equalled the performance of Australia's Massie at Lord's in 1972. Coincidentally, Hirwani returned match figures of 16 for 136 — Massie's were an almost identical 16 for 137. Shastri was captaining India for the first time. He won the toss and batted first on what was an under-prepared pitch. The home team was struggling at 6 for 156 but then the former captain, Kapil Dev, joined another new cap, Ajay Sharma, at the crease. This pair added 113 runs for the sixth wicket, and Kapil Dev's contribution was a match-winning 109 runs from 119 balls. Given the difficult batting conditions, 382 was a most respectable score.

The West Indies struggled from the start of its innings, and certainly missed the experienced opener Greenidge. Richardson batted for two hours at the crease to make 36, and Richards produced some amazing strokes in compiling 68. The follow-on was avoided on the third morning as Hirwani, on debut, finished with 8 for 61 from 18.3 overs.

With time on its side, India steadily increased its lead. Raman, yet another new cap, showed considerable maturity in making 83. Walsh was again the pick of the West Indies bowlers, toiling manfully to finish with 4 for 55.

The West Indies required 416 to win, or more realistically, to bat for one and a half days to save the game. Their batsmen played as if it were limited overs match, and the Test was over on the fourth day.

This time, Hirwani finished with 8 for 75 from 15.2 overs, and India's wicketkeeper, More, excelled in the difficult conditions. He stumped six batsmen in the match, five of them in the second innings and in doing so made two Test records.

## NEW ZEALAND v SRI LANKA 1990-91

Basin Reserve, Wellington
31 January, 1, 2, 3, 4, February 1991
Match Drawn

New Zealand 174 and 4 for 671 (M.D. Crowe 299, A.H. Jones 186, J.G. Wright 88); Sri Lank 497 (P.A. de Silva 267, A.P. Gurusinha 70, A. Ranatunga 55, D.K. Morrison 5 for 153)

This match will be remembered forever as the Test in which a new world Test record partnership for any wicket was established. Sri Lanka dominated the first half of the match and had played itself into a winning position before New Zealand produced a superb fightback to save the game. Ratnayake and Labrooy, with four wickets apiece, combined on the opening day to bowl the home team out for 174. Aravinda de Silva then hammered the New Zealand bowlers to all parts of the ground as he posted his country's highest Test score. His 267 contained 40 fours, and was scored from 376 balls. Sri Lanka declared on the third day with a lead of 323. New Zealand had the task of batting for 15 hours to save the game. Wright and Franklin posted 134 for the opening stand, but then both batsmen were out within 14 runs. This set the stage for the highest partnership in test history. The New Zealand captain, Martin Crowe, joined Jones and in just over nine hours together added 467, surpassing the previous best of 451. (Ponsford and Bradman scored 451 for the second test wicket against England in 1934, and Mudassar Nazar and Javed Miandad made their partnership of 451 against India in 1982-83).

Jones was out for 186, and Crowe was dismissed in the final over of the match for 299.

## AUSTRALIA v WEST INDIES 1992-93

Adelaide Oval, Adelaide
23, 24, 25, 26 January 1993
West Indies won by one run
West Indies 252 (B.C. Lara 52, M.G. Hughes 5 for 64) and 146 (R.B. Richardson 72, T.B.A. May 5 for 9); Australia 213 (C.E.L. Ambrose 6 for 74) and 184 (J.L. Langer 54)

This was one of the greatest Test matches ever played and the closest of all Tests decided on a run basis. (See scoreboard on page 44).

Haynes, 45, and Simmons, 46, got the West Indies off to a flying start with an opening stand of 84 but the visitors failed to capitalise on this foundation. On a pitch that offered more assistance to the bowlers than normal, only Lara and Murray — apart from the openers — played an innings of consequence. The lion-hearted Hughes was rewarded for his persistence with another five-wicket haul for the Australians.

Australia had a taste of what was in store for them when Taylor fell on the first evening and the debutant Langer had his helmet split by some fierce bowling from the West Indies. Australia's woes continued on the rain-shortened second day when Boon was forced to retire hurt after being struck on the arm.

Ambrose was at the peak of his form and bowled the visitors to a 39-run first innings lead.

The third day of this fluctuating match saw 17 wickets fall for 259 runs. A hostile spell of fast-bowling from McDermott reduced the visitors to 4 for 65 before Richardson and Hooper addd 59 for the fifth wicket. However, careless batting then saw the West Indies lose their last six wickets for only 22 runs. May, playing his first Test for almost four years, captured 5 for 5 from 32 deliveries.

Australia had two days in which to score 186 and thus regain the Frank Worrell Trophy. The openers went cheaply but Langer and M. Waugh carefully carried the score beyond fifty. Waugh went out for 26 with the total on 54. Shortly after lunch Ambrose removed S. Waugh, Border and Hughes with Walsh chipping in to dismiss Healy — Australia had lost 4 for 10 and the team was now reeling at 7 for 74.

Langer's determined resistance continued and 28 more runs were added before Warne fell to Bishop. May — on his 31st birthday and with a fractured finger — valiantly continued the struggle.

It was Bishop who finally removed the doughty Langer — his great effort of four and a quarter hours at the crease had yielded the home team's only half-century of the match.

McDermott, at number eleven, supported May bravely. They carried Australia to within two runs of victory before a lifting delivery from Walsh brushed McDermott's glove and Umpire Hair upheld the West Indies appeal. So it was the visitors who were celebrating on Australia Day, winning a thrilling match by the narrowest of possible margins.

## AUSTRALIA v SOUTH AFRICA 1993-94

Sydney Cricket Ground, Sydney
2, 3, 4, 5, 6 January 1994
South Africa won by five runs
South Africa 169 (G. Kirsten 67, S.K. Warne 7 for 56) and 239 (J.N. Rhodes 76 not out, S.K. Warne 5 for 72); Australia 292 (M.J. Allater 92, D.R. Martyn 59) and 111 (P.S. De Villiers 6 for 43)

South Africa scored a thrilling victory after Australia had held control for most of the match.

The visitors were bowled out on a suspect pitch for a disappointing 169. Hudson fell cheaply before F. Kirsten and Cronje added 90 for the second wicket. Warne ripped through the middle and lower order — in one spell he claimed 5 for 5 in 22 balls — while his figures of 7 for 56 are the best for Australia against South Africa at home. Apart from Kirsten and Cronje, only De Villiers reached double figures.

Michael Slater, playing with unusual caution, guided Australia to a 123-run lead. The other major contributions came from Martyn and the captain Border. The Australian supporters may have been concerned that the lead wasn't greater as the team had to bat last in the match and the Australians had a poor record when chasing a target. South Africa's opening bowlers, Donald and De Villiers, stuck to their task and claimed four wickets apiece.

When the fifth wicket of the South African second innings had fallen for 110, the match looked lost for the Springboks. However, Rhodes played superbly and with the assistance of Richardson and Donald, South Africa gained a lead of 116. Rhodes and Richardson put on 72 for the sixth wicket while 36 was added for the last by Rhodes and Donald.

The brilliant Warne once again mesmerised the South African batsmen as he claimed his first ten-wicket haul in Test cricket. Australia needed 117 to win its first Test against South Africa for 27 years. Shortly before stumps

## AUSTRALIA v WEST INDIES 1992-93 (Fourth Test)

Adelaide Oval, 23, 24, 25, 26, 27 January. West Indies won by 1 run

**WEST INDIES**

| | | | | |
|---|---|---|---|---|
| D.L.Haynes | st Healy b May | 45 | c Healy b McDermott | 11 |
| P.V.Simmons | c Hughes b S.R.Waugh | 46 | b McDermott | 10 |
| R.B.Richardson* | lbw b Hughes | 2 | c Healy b Warne | 72 |
| B.C.Lara | c Healy b McDermott | 52 | c S.R.Waugh b Hughes | 7 |
| K.L.T.Arthurton | c S.R.Waugh b May | 0 | c Healy b McDermott | 0 |
| C.L.Hooper | c Healy b Hughes | 2 | c Hughes b May | 25 |
| J.R.Murray† | not out | 49 | c M.E.Waugh b May | 0 |
| I.R.Bishop | c M.E.Waugh b Hughes | 13 | c M.E.Waugh b May | 6 |
| C.E.L.Ambrose | c Healy b Hughes | 0 | st Healy b May | 1 |
| K.C.G.Benjamin | b M.E.Waugh | 15 | c Warne b May | 0 |
| C.A.Walsh | lbw b Hughes | 5 | not out | 0 |
| Extras | (LB 11, NB 12) | 23 | (LB 2, NB 12) | 14 |
| **Total** | | **252** | | **146** |

**AUSTRALIA**

| | | | | | |
|---|---|---|---|---|---|
| M.A.Taylor | c Hooper b Bishop | 1 | (2) | Murray b Benjamin | 7 |
| D.C.Boon | not out | 39 | (1) | lbw b Ambrose | 0 |
| J.L.Langer | c Murray b Benjamin | 20 | | c Murray b Bishop | 54 |
| M.E.Waugh | c Simmons b Ambrose | 0 | | c Hooper b Walsh | 26 |
| S.R.Waugh | c Murray b Ambrose | 42 | | c Arthurton b Ambrose | 4 |
| A.R.Border* | c Hooper b Ambrose | 19 | | c Haynes b Ambrose | 1 |
| I.A.Healy† | c Hooper b Ambrose | 0 | | b Walsh | 0 |
| M.G.Hughes | c Murray b Hooper | 43 | | lbw b Ambrose | 1 |
| S.K.Warne | lbw b Hooper | 0 | | lbw b Bishop | 9 |
| T.B.A.May | c Murray b Ambrose | 6 | | not out | 42 |
| C.J.McDermott | b Ambrose | 14 | | c Murray b Walsh | 18 |
| Extras | (B7, LB 3, NB 19) | 29 | | (B1, LB8 NB 13) | 22 |
| **Total** | | **213** | | | **184** |

| **AUSTRALIA** | O | M | R | W | | O | M | R | W |
|---|---|---|---|---|---|---|---|---|---|
| McDermott | 16 | 1 | 85 | 1 | McDermott | 11 | 0 | 66 | 3 |
| Hughes | 21.3 | 3 | 64 | 5 | Hughes | 13 | 1 | 43 | 1 |
| S.R.Waugh | 13 | 4 | 37 | 1 | S.R.Waugh | 5 | 1 | 8 | 0 |
| May | 14 | 1 | 41 | 2 | May | 6.5 | 3 | 9 | 5 |
| Warne | 2 | 0 | 11 | 0 | Warne | 6 | 2 | 18 | 1 |
| M.E.Waugh | 1 | 0 | 3 | 1 | | | | | |

| **WEST INDIES** | O | M | R | W | | O | M | R | W |
|---|---|---|---|---|---|---|---|---|---|
| Ambrose | 28.2 | 6 | 74 | 6 | Ambrose | 26 | 5 | 46 | 4 |
| Bishop | 18 | 3 | 48 | 1 | Bishop | 17 | 3 | 41 | 2 |
| Benjamin | 6 | 0 | 22 | 1 | Benjamin | 12 | 2 | 32 | 1 |
| Walsh | 10 | 3 | 34 | 0 | Walsh | 19 | 4 | 44 | 3 |
| Hooper | 13 | 4 | 25 | 2 | Hooper | 5 | 1 | 12 | 0 |

FALL OF WICKETS

| | W | A | W | A |
|---|---|---|---|---|
| Wkt | 1st | 1st | 2nd | 2nd |
| 1st | 84 | 1 | 14 | 5 |
| 2nd | 99 | 16 | 49 | 16 |
| 3rd | 129 | 46 | 63 | 54 |
| 4th | 130 | 108 | 65 | 64 |
| 5th | 134 | 108 | 124 | 72 |
| 6th | 189 | 112 | 137 | 73 |
| 7th | 206 | 181 | 145 | 74 |
| 8th | 206 | 181 | 146 | 102 |
| 9th | 247 | 197 | 146 | 144 |
| 10th | 252 | 213 | 146 | 184 |

Umpires: D.B.Hair and L.J.King

on the penultimate day, the home team was cruising at 1 for 51. Then De Villiers removed Taylor, Boon and nightwatchman May to set the stage for an exciting finish to what had been a truly absorbing match.

With free admission, an estimated crowd of 12 000 turned up on the final morning. When Donald bowled Border in the very first over of the day the game had swung South Africa's way. Then Donald struck again, removing M. Waugh with a fast yorker, and when the acting captain Cronje threw down the stumps to run out Warne, the Australian team was on the ropes at 8 for 75.

McDermott made some telling blows and while he and Martyn were together the Australians still had some hope. After 35 had been added for the ninth wicket, Martyn holed out to cover and was caught. McGrath was dismissed in the next over and South Africa had pulled off a stunning victory. The Australian score of 111 was the same as that recorded in 'Botham's match' at Headingley in 1981.

## SOUTH AFRICA v PAKISTAN 1994-95

Wanderers, Johannesburg
19, 20, 21, 22, 23 January 1994
South Africa won by 324 runs

South Africa 460 (B.M. McMillan 113, J.N. Rhodes 72, P.S. De Villiers 66 not out, G. Kirsten) and 7 for 259 dec. (D.J. Cullinan 69 not out); Pakistan 230 (Salim Malik 99, P.S. De Villiers 6 for 81) and 165 (Inzamam-Ul-Haq 95)

This was the first Test to be played between the two countries and resulted in South Africa's biggest ever home victory.

Positive batting on the first day saw South Africa score at almost four runs an over. McMillan completed his maiden Test century from 146 balls while he and Rhodes added 157 for the sixth wicket. On the second morning, De Villiers and Donald realised 71 for the last wicket in just 35 minutes.

Pakistan's reply was a disappointing 230 with only skipper Salim Malik taking the attack to the home team. He struck 16 boundaries before falling one short of a third hundred in successive Tests.

Cronje did not enforce the follow-on as he was concerned about the deteriorating state of the pitch. He declared South Africa's second innings at lunch on the fourth day leaving Pakistan five sessions to score 490.

Donald and De Villiers soon had the visitors 3 for 5 with the match as good as over. This time, only Inzamam-Ul-Haq played an innings of any substance. His 95 was like an oasis in the desert. Man-of-the-match De Villiers became the first South African to take ten wickets and score 50 in a Test match.

This game was also notable because it was played amidst alleged rumours of match-fixing by certain members of the Pakistan team.

## PAKISTAN v AUSTRALIA 1994-95

National Stadium, Karachi
28, 29, 30 September, 1, 2 October 1994
Pakistan won by one wicket

Australia 337 (M.G. Bevan 82, S.R. Waugh 73, I.A. Healy 57) and 232 (D.C. Boon 114 not out, M.E. Waugh 61, Wasim Akram 5 for 63); Pakistan 256 (Saeed Anwar 85) and 9 for 315 (Saeed Anwar 77, Inzamamul Haq 58 not out, S.K. Warne 5 for 89)

This was the seventh Test to be decided by a margin of one wicket. It was the first Test Australia had played since the retirement of former captain Allan Border, who had appeared in 153 successive matches. Mark Taylor, the new captain, did win the toss but unfortunately he became the first player to mark his first Test as captain by 'bagging a pair'.

Australia took the honours on the opening day compiling 7 for 325. Bevan, on debut, scored a stylish 82. He added 121 in better than even time with S. Waugh, whose 73 included 13 boundaries. Keeper Healy contributed yet another useful half-century.

The last three wickets fell for just twelve runs on the second morning. Pakistan started brightly with Saeed Anwar and Aamir Sohail posting 90 for the first wicket in even time. A middle-order collapse left the home side struggling at 7 for 209 at stumps on the second day. A breezy 39 from Wasim Akram carried the Pakistan total to 256.

Despite Taylor going cheaply again, the visitors built on the 81-run lead, with Boon and M. Waugh pushing the score to 2 for 171 shortly before the close of the day's play. Pakistan then struck back with Waqar Younis removing M. Waugh for 61 and Wasim Akram dismissing both Bevan and S. Waugh first ball. The determined Tasmanian Boon posted his nineteenth Test century, which was his first against Pakistan, but the Australian tail failed to wag.

The home team's target was 314 with almost two full days' play remaining. Saeed Anwar again batted positively giving his side a good start for the second time in the match. However, when Saleem Malik fell for 43 runs just before stumps the game was evenly balanced with the home team at 3 for 155.

The spinner Warne ripped out the Pakistan middle order on the final morning to set up what looked a certain Australian victory. When the last man in for the home side, Mushtaq, joined Inzamamul Haq, 56 runs were still needed. Some brave batting brought the scores closer until just three were required.

Warne bowled to Inzamamul Haq who went down the pitch to a ball pitched outside the leg stump. It missed the bat, flicked the pad and sped away for four leg byes. Pakistan had won a thrilling match to retain its unbeaten record in Karachi. (See final scoreboard on page 48.)

## INDIA v WEST INDIES 1994-95

Wankhede Stadium, Bombay
18, 19, 20, 21, 22 November 1994
India won by 96 runs

India 272 (N.R. Mongia 80, S.V. Manjrekar 51, C.A. Walsh 6 for 79) and 333 (S.R. Tendulkar 85, S.V. Manjrekar 66, J Srinath 60); West Indies 243 (S.L.V. Raju 5 for 60) and 266 (J.R. Murray 85, J.C. Adams 81)

Azharuddin won an important toss on a pitch that was grossly under-prepared. Walsh dismissed Prabhakar with the second ball of the match and then removed Sidhu for 18, Kambli on 40 and Tendulkar on 34, to have the home team in trouble at 5 for 99. Manjrekar and Mongia's 136-run partnership for the sixth wicket was a vital contribution that turned the game India's way. Walsh carried the West Indies' attack and picked up six wickets in an innings for the first time in India.

The visitors reply stuttered along with five of the top seven passing twenty but with not one of those batsmen reaching fifty. Williams top-scored with 49, Arthurton made 42 and Adams, 39. As usual, it was the spinners who did the damage, taking nine of the ten wickets to fall.

India's lead of 29 did not seem enough after K. Benjamin had removed Prabhakar, Kambli and Mongia for 11 by stumps on the second day. Damp foot holes delayed the start of the third day by 45 minutes. This was crucial as it allowed the pitch time to dry. India's star batsman, Tendulkar, helped play his team into a winning position. However, when he was sixth out the home team's lead was still only 191. Manjrekar's second half-century of the match together with valuable contributions from tail-ender Srinath with 60 and Kumble with 42 took India's score to 333.

Prabhakar snuffed out the West Indies' hopes when he removed Simmons and Lara in his first over. The visitors recovered from 5 for 82 as a result of a 162-run partnership for the sixth wicket by Adams and Murray. But after Murray's dismissal, the tail quickly succumbed and Azharuddin had won a record tenth Test match as captain of India.

## SOUTH AFRICA v NEW ZEALAND 1994-95

Wanderers, Johannesburg
25, 26, 27, 28, 29 November 1994
New Zealand won by 137 runs

New Zealand 411 (S.A. Thomson 84, M.D. Crowe 83, K.R. Rutherford 68) and 194 (C.R. Matthews 5 for 42); South Africa 279 (D.J. Richardson 93, D.J. Cullinan 58) and 189 (W.J. Cronje 62, M.N. Hart 5 for 77)

New Zealand surprised the confident South Africans with the ease of their win. M.D. Crowe and Rutherford batted with calm assurance through most of the first day to leave the visitors soundly placed. However, when three quick wickets fell on the second morning the home team was back in the match. Thomson, who top-scored in the innings, held the lower order together before Doull, 31 not out, and De Groen, 26, added 57 for the last wicket.

South Africa was soon in trouble and were 3 for 38 within an hour. Wicketkeeper Richardson, batting with a guard on his broken right thumb, led the recovery that saw the home team avoid the follow-on. He scored 93 out of the 132 runs added in the three hours that he was at the crease.

De Villiers then produced a superb spell of bowling to remove Murray, Young, Crowe and Rutherford while Matthews picked up Fleming to have the Kiwis reeling at 5 for 34. However, Parore, 49, Hart, 34, Thomson, 29, and Nash, 20, dug in to carry New Zealand to 194, leaving South Africa with 327 to score on a wearing pitch.

They started the final day needing 198 to win with eight wickets in hand. The match was all over before lunch, the last seven wickets falling for 39 runs. Doull captured 4 for 33 to support Hart, the left-arm orthodox spinner, who exploited the bowlers' foot-marks for a career best 5 for 77.

## INDIA v WEST INDIES 1994-95

Punjab Cricket Association Stadium, Mohali,
10, 11, 12, 13, 14 December 1994
West Indies won by 243 runs

West Indies 443 (J.C. Adams 174 not out, A.C. Cummings 50) and 3 for 301 dec. (B.C. Lara 91, J.C. Adams 78 not out, K.L.T. Arthurton 70 not out); India 387 (M. Prabhakar 120, J. Srinath 52 not out) and 114 (K.C.G. Benjamin 5 for 65)

Once again, West Indies had to win the final match of the series to maintain their unbeaten run, which had begun in March 1980.

The pitch was the best of the series, which enabled the West Indies to revert to an attack of four fast bowlers. Adams' highest Test score, 174 not out, was the cornerstone of the visitors' innings. His batting with the tail was outstanding, 174 runs being added for the last four wickets.

India's determined reply was built around a patient maiden century by Prabhakar and a record last-wicket partnership of 64 between Srinath and Raju.

With a lead of just 56 runs and less than two days to play, a West Indies victory looked unlikely. The visitors then seized the initiative and scored 301 from only 56.3 overs. Lara was promoted to open and proceeded to hammer 91 from just 104 balls. Walsh declared, leaving India 358 to win.

The innings started badly with Prabhakar having his nose broken by a ball from Walsh that burst through his helmet grille. Hostile fast bowling on the final morning by Benjamin and Walsh reduced the home team to 8 for 68 before Srinath and Raju put on 46 for the last wicket. Cuffy removed Raju to end the match before lunch, thus maintaining the West Indies' unbeaten series run.

## AUSTRALIA v ENGLAND 1994-95

Melbourne Cricket Ground, Melbourne
24, 26, 27, 28, 29 December 1994
Australia won by 295 runs

Australia 279 (S.R. Waugh 94 not out, M.E. Waugh 71) and 7 for 320 dec. (D.C. Boon 131); England 212 (G.P. Thorpe 51, S.K. Warne 6 for 64) and 92 (C.J. McDermott 5 for 42)

Atherton invited Australia to bat on a damp pitch that offered the England bowlers considerable encouragement. However, they failed to take full advantage of the conditions, with the Waugh twins providing the backbone of the home team's total of 279. S.R. Waugh was left unconquered on 94. He held the lower order together, as he had done so often in the past.

Luck was against the visitors as Stewart had his right index finger broken by the first ball after lunch on the second day. Resolute batting by Atherton and Thorpe then carried England to 1 for 119, and a position of comparative safety, before Warne struck with his lethal leg-spinners. When Gooch hit a return catch to McDermott from the first ball of the third day's play, the visitors' hopes had all but disappeared.

Australia built on its lead of 67 runs, and with Boon occupying the crease for more than six hours to compile his first Test century at the Melbourne Cricket Ground, Taylor was able to declare, leaving England with 388 needed for victory.

After Fleming removed Gooch and Hick with only ten runs on the board, the visitors were in desperate trouble. McDermott crashed through the middle-order before Warne removed De Freitas, Gough and Malcolm with successive deliveries. De Freitas was lbw, Gough caught behind and Malcolm was snapped up by Boon at short-leg. It was the first hat-trick in Ashes Tests since Trumble at Melbourne in 1903-04.

Australia's trump cards, McDermott with eight wickets and Warne with nine, had bowled the home team to a comprehensive victory.

## AUSTRALIA v ENGLAND 1994-95

Sydney Cricket Ground, Sydney
1, 2, 3, 4, 5 January 1995
Match drawn

England 309 (M.A. Atherton 88, J.P. Crawley 72, D. Gough 51, C.J. McDermott 5 for 101) and 2 for 255 dec. (G.A. Hick 98 not out, M.A. Atherton 67); Australia 116 (D. Gough 6 for 49) and 7 for 344 (M.A. Taylor 113, M.J. Slater 103, A.R.C. Fraser 5 for 73)

England was denied an improbable victory by the intervention of rain on the second and final days of the match.

The visitors were quickly in trouble after Atherton decided to bat first on a pitch that had pace and bounce. Gooch, Hick and Thorpe were dismissed within the first hour with only 20 runs on the board. Crawley, in his first Ashes Test, then combined with Atherton in a determined stand of 174. However, Australia struck back with the new ball to claim four late wickets and the honours for the first day.

Belligerent batting by the England tail regained the initiative for the visitors. Gough's 51 came from just 56 balls while Malcolm's highest Test score, 29, came from only 18 deliveries.

Slater and Taylor faced only a handful of overs before rain washed out the remainder of the second day. When they resumed the next morning conditions were ideal for England's seamers. Taylor, who was second last out for 49, and McDermott, 21, took the home team past the follow-on figure. Had this not been achieved the result may have been different.

Although England's lead was 193, they batted too cautiously in the second innings. It wasn't until Thorpe joined Hick that the scoring rate reached four an over. Atherton denied Hick his century by declaring with the batsman on 98 not out.

Australia's target was 449 but Taylor and Slater took up the challenge and by lunch on the final day the home team was 0 for 206. Rain intervened and although only seven overs were officially lost, the batsmen had lost momentum after taking an early tea. After the openers had scored hundreds, Fraser ripped out the middle order to give England an outside chance of victory. Warne and May defended stoutly in the gloom, and because the light was so poor Atherton was not able to bowl his seamers. The spinners, too, were unable to get assistance from the pitch. Play continued until nearly half past seven.

## AUSTRALIA v ENGLAND 1994-95

Adelaide Oval, Adelaide
26, 27, 28, 29, 30 January 1995
England won by 106 runs

England 353 (M.W. Gatting 117, M.A. Atherton 80) and 328 (P.A.J. De Freitas 88, G.P. Thorpe 83, J.P. Crawley 71, M.E. Waugh 5 for 40); Australia 419 (G.S. Blewett 102 not out, M.A. Taylor 90, I.A. Healy 74, M.J. Slater 67) and 156 (I.A. Healy 51 not out)

An under-manned England team surprised with its first Test win in Australia for eight years.

Gatting's painstaking knock was the basis of the visitors' innings. He was at the crease for nearly seven hours scoring 117, including 77 minutes in the 90s and 31 minutes on 99.

## PAKISTAN v AUSTRALIA 1994-95 (First Test)

National Stadium, Karachi, 28, 29, 30 September, 1, 2 October. Pakistan won by 1 wicket

**AUSTRALIA**

| | | | | |
|---|---|---|---|---|
| M.J.Slater | lbw b Wasim Akram | 36 | lbw b Mushtaq Ahmed | 23 |
| M.A.Taylor* | c and b Wasim Akram | 0 | c Rashid Latif b Waqar Younis | 0 |
| D.C.Boon | b Mushtaq Ahmed | 19 | not out | 114 |
| M.E.Waugh | c Zahid Fazal b Mushtaq Ahmed | 20 | b Waqar Younis | 61 |
| M.G.Bevan | c Aamer Sohial b Mushtaq Ahmed | 82 | b Wasim Akram | 0 |
| S.R.Waugh | b Waqar Younis | 73 | lbw b Wasim Akram | 0 |
| I.A.Healy† | c Rashid Latif b Waqar Younis | 57 | c Rashid Latif b Wasim Akram | 9 |
| S.K.Warne | c Rashid Latif b Aamer Sohail | 22 | lbw b Waqar Younis | 0 |
| J.Angel | b Wasim Akram | 5 | c Rashid Latif b Wasim Akram | 8 |
| T.B.A.May | not out | 1 | b Wasim Akram | 1 |
| G.D.McGrath | b Waqar Younis | 0 | b Waqar Younis | 1 |
| Extras | (B 2, LB 12, NB 8) | 22 | (B 6, LB 4, NB 5) | 15 |
| **Total** | | **337** | | **232** |

**PAKISTAN**

| | | | | | |
|---|---|---|---|---|---|
| Saeed Anwar | c M.E.Waugh b May | 85 | | c and b Angel | 77 |
| Aamer Sohail | c Bevan b Warne | 36 | | run out | 34 |
| Zahid Fazal | c Boon b May | 27 | | c Boon b Warne | 3 |
| Saleem Malik* | lbw b Angel | 26 | | c Taylor b Angel | 43 |
| Basit Ali | c Bevan b McGrath | 0 | (6) | lbw b Warne | 12 |
| Inzamamul Haq | c Taylor b Warne | 9 | (8) | not out | 58 |
| Rashid Latif† | c Taylor b Warne | 2 | (9) | lbw S.R.Waugh | 35 |
| Wasim Akram | c Healy b Angel | 39 | (7) | c and b Warne | 4 |
| Akram Raza | b McGarth | 13 | (5) | lbw b Warne | 2 |
| Waqar Younis | c Healy b Angel | 6 | | c Healy b Warne | 7 |
| Mushtaq Ahmed | not out | 2 | | not out | 20 |
| Extras | (LB 7, NB 4) | 11 | | (B 4, LB 13, NB 3) | 20 |
| **Total** | | **256** | | **(9 wkts)** | **315** |

| **PAKISTAN** | O | M | R | W | | O | M | R | W |
|---|---|---|---|---|---|---|---|---|---|
| Wasim Akram | 25 | 4 | 75 | 3 | Wasim Akram | 22 | 3 | 64 | 5 |
| Waqar Younis | 19.2 | 2 | 75 | 3 | Waqar Younis | 18 | 2 | 69 | 4 |
| Mushtaq Ahmed | 24 | 2 | 97 | 3 | Mushtaq Ahmed | 21 | 3 | 51 | 1 |
| Akram Raza | 14 | 1 | 50 | 0 | Akram Raza | 10 | 1 | 19 | 0 |
| Aamer Sohail | 5 | 0 | 19 | 1 | Aamer Sohail | 7 | 0 | 19 | 0 |
| Saleem Malik | 1 | 0 | 7 | 0 | | | | | |

| **AUSTRALIA** | O | M | R | W | | O | M | R | W |
|---|---|---|---|---|---|---|---|---|---|
| McGarth | 25 | 6 | 70 | 2 | McGarth | 6 | 2 | 18 | 0 |
| Angel | 13.1 | 0 | 54 | 3 | Angel | 28 | 8 | 92 | 2 |
| May | 20 | 5 | 55 | 2 | S.R.Waugh | 15 | 3 | 28 | 1 |
| Warne | 27 | 10 | 61 | 3 | Warne | 36.1 | 12 | 89 | 5 |
| S.R.Waugh | 2 | 0 | 9 | 0 | May | 18 | 4 | 67 | 0 |
| | | | | | M.E.Waugh | 3 | 1 | 4 | 0 |

FALL OF WICKETS

| | A | P | A | P |
|---|---|---|---|---|
| Wkt | 1st | 1st | 2nd | 2nd |
| 1st | 12 | 90 | 1 | 45 |
| 2nd | 41 | 153 | 49 | 64 |
| 3rd | 75 | 154 | 171 | 148 |
| 4th | 95 | 157 | 174 | 157 |
| 5th | 216 | 175 | 174 | 174 |
| 6th | 281 | 181 | 213 | 179 |
| 7th | 325 | 200 | 218 | 184 |
| 8th | 335 | 234 | 227 | 236 |
| 9th | 335 | 253 | 229 | 258 |
| 10th | 337 | 256 | 232 | - |

Umpires: H.D.Bird and Khizer Hayat

The home team gained a first innings lead of 66 by adopting a far more positive approach. The local hero, Blewett, became the 16th Australian to score a hundred on debut, he and Healy adding 164 runs for the sixth wicket. Taylor and Slater had scored another opening partnership before a slump left Australia 5 for 232. A further collapse saw the home team lose its last five wickets for just 23 runs.

Encouraged by the bowler's efforts to wrap up the tail, Thorpe led the England counter-attack with an aggressive 83. However, wickets continued to fall and when Lewis was bowled by Fleming, the visitors were 6 for 181. Crawley and De Freitas carried the total to 220 by stumps on the fourth day but with a lead of only 154, England's prospects of saving the game looked remote. De Freitas turned the match with his bold innings. He scored 88 from just 95 balls in a two-hour stay at the crease.

Australia had 67 overs to score 263 and took unnecessary risks in chasing the victory target. On a superb pitch, saving the game should not have presented the home team with any problems at all. Malcolm and Lewis bowled with tremendous hostility to reduce Australia to 8 for 83 before Healy and Fleming survived for nearly two hours. But it was in vain, as the last wicket fell with 35 balls remaining.

## ZIMBABWE v PAKISTAN 1994-95

Harare Sports Club, Harare
15, 16, 18, 19 February 1995
Pakistan won by 99 runs

Pakistan 231 (Inzamam-Ul-Haq 101) and 250 (Inzamam-Ul-Haq 83, Ijaz Ahmed 55); Zimbabwe 243 and 139 (Aamir Nazir 5 for 46)

Pakistan joined England (against Australia in 1888) and South Africa (against New Zealand in 1995) as one of very few teams to come from behind and win a three-Test series. They were the first to do so away from home.

Fortunes fluctuated constantly in this low-scoring match. Streak bowled with pace and hostility to have the visitors 4 for 83 before Ijaz Ahmed, 41, and Inzamam-Ul-Haq retrieved the situation with a stand of 76. Aamir Nazir, 0 not out, was there while 27 runs were added for the last wicket which enabled Inzamam to score his fourth century.

Zimbabwe's reply was disappointing. The home team gained a twelve-run lead, but it should have been more as six batsmen passed 20. A. Flower top-scored with 37, and Aaqib Javed, with 4 for 64, was the pick of the visitors' bowlers.

Once again, Inzamam-Ul-Haq and Ijaz Ahmed held the Pakistan batting together with a stand of 116 for the fourth wicket before the last six fell for 20. Streak, who needed cortisone injections to overcome a side strain, picked up another four-wicket haul. Zimbabwe had nearly two days to score 239 for their first series win. However, the Pakistan pace trio bowled with sustained hostility to rout the home team. Aamir Nazir took five wickets in an innings for the first time, in only his fifth Test.

## NEW ZEALAND v SOUTH AFRICA 1994-95

Eden Park, Auckland
4, 5, 6, 7, 8 March 1995
South Africa won by 93 runs

South Africa 294 (D.J. Cullinan 96) and 6 for 308 dec. (W.J. Cronje 101, G. Kirsten 76, A.C. Hudson 64); New Zealand 328 (A.C Parore 89, B.A. Young 74) and 181 (K.R. Rutherford 56)

South Africa was invited to play this one-off match, known as the Centenary Test, to mark the 100th anniversary of the New Zealand Cricket Council.

After the first session was lost to rain, South Africa struggled to score 294. Cullinan's 96 was the major contribution as New Zealand's seamers, with steady bowling, restricted the visitors to a modest total. Nash claimed four wickets while Morrison and Larsen picked up three apiece.

The home team's response was built on the back of Young's cautious 74 and Parore's aggressive 89. However, with the prospect of batting last, a lead of 34 runs hardly seemed enough.

South Africa's second innings started early on the fourth day and after the foundation had been laid by Kirsten and Hudson, Cronje launched into the New Zealand attack, posting his 50 off 67 balls with three sixes. The skipper declared the innings on the final morning, after he had reached his century, leaving the home team a target of 275 for victory.

The challenge was accepted. At tea, 161 runs were still needed from 35 overs with seven wickets in hand. Fleming's dismissal off the third ball after the interval set the chase back and when Rutherford fell shortly afterwards, South Africa had grasped the initiative. Matthews trapped Nash lbw to end the match with 7.1 overs remaining.

## WEST INDIES v AUSTRALIA 1994-95

Kensington Oval, Bridgetown, Barbados
31 March, 1, 2 April 1995
Australia won by ten wickets

West Indies 195 (B.C. Lara 65, C.L. Hooper 60) and 189 (G.D. McGrath 5 for 68); Australia 346 (I.A. Healy 74 not out, S.R. Waugh 65, M.A. Taylor 55) and 0 for 39

Richardson returned to lead his country in Test cricket after an illness had kept him out of the game. Australia had lost both its opening bowlers, McDermott and Fleming, to injury before a ball was bowled in the series.

Reiffel and Julian reduced the West Indies to 3 for 6 before Lara and Hooper proceeded to smash the visitors' attack. A breathtaking opening session saw the home team at 3 for 116 at lunch. Hooper and then Adams fell shortly after the break before S. Waugh claimed a juggling catch in the gully to dismiss Lara. Television replays confirmed that the ball hit the ground. This dismissal may have been pivotal in deciding the test, as the lower order offered little resistance. Julian was Australia's surprise packet, picking up four top-order wickets.

The visitors had the opportunity to put the match out of the West Indies' reach but until Healy and Julian added 60 for the seventh wicket, the innings had stuttered along. The top six batsmen all reached double figures with only Taylor and S. Waugh posting half-centuries.

The West Indies' second effort with the bat was even more disappointing than the first. Adams, 39 not out, and Richardson, 36, were the only batsmen to show any resistance. McGrath seized the opportunity to spearhead Australia's attack with his first five-wicket haul in Tests.

It was the first time for thirty years that West Indies had lost in three days and only their third defeat at Bridgetown.

## WEST INDIES v AUSTRALIA 1994-95

Sabina Park, Kingston, Jamaica
29, 30 April, 1, 2 May 1995
Australia won by an innings and 53 runs

West Indies 265 (R.B. Richardson 100, B.C. Lara 65) and 213 (W.K.M. Benjamin 51); Australia 531 (S.R. Waugh 200, M.E. Waugh 126, G.S. Blewett 69)

Richardson won his fourth consecutive toss and took first use of the magnificent batting pitch. Williams fell without a run on the board before the skipper and Lara posted a century in only 20 overs. Lara's dismissal at 103, caught behind off Warne, turned the game Australia's way. Richardson was eighth out with the score at 251, after posting his first hundred of the series. The West Indies' total of 265 was their best effort in four Tests, but it was well short of what should have been scored under the conditions.

When S. Waugh joined his twin brother at the crease, Australia was 3 for 73 and the game was in the balance. Shortly before stumps, M. Waugh departed but the pair had put on 231 from 57 overs in a match-winning partnership. It was the eighth Test century for both, Mark's coming from 146 balls and Steve's from 183. The longer the partnership continued the more dispirited West Indies became. With splendid support from Blewett and Reiffel, S. Waugh reached his maiden double-century before being last man out after a stay of nearly ten hours at the crease.

With their spirit broken and facing a deficit of 266, the home team was soon in more trouble as Reiffel removed Richardson, Williams and Lara with only 46 runs on the board. Warne dismissed the last four batsmen to inflict a shattering defeat on the West Indies.

Australia regained the Sir Frank Worrell Trophy, last held in 1975-76. The West Indies had lost a series for the first time since New Zealand in 1979-80 and they had been beaten in the Caribbean for the first time since I. Chappell's team in 1972-73.

It was a truly significant Australian victory.

## ENGLAND v WEST INDIES 1995

Lord's Cricket Ground, London
22, 23, 24, 25, 26 June 1995
England won by 72 runs

England 283 (R.A. Smith 61, G.P. Thorpe 52) and 336 (R.A. Smith 90, G.A. Hick 67); West Indies 324 (K.L.T. Arthurton 75, J.C. Adams 54, A.R.C. Fraser 5 for 66) and 223 (S.L. Campbell 93, B.C. Lara 54, D.G. Cork 7 for 43)

After being soundly defeated in the first Test of the series, England played with great character to win a match that could have gone either way.

Atherton chose to bat on a pitch that provided some movement and bounce for the West Indies' pace-bowling quartet. England's innings was held together by a partnership of 111 for the fourth wicket by Thorpe and Hick, and 50 for the eighth by Cork and Martin. The home team's total of 283 left the game wide open.

The visitors' reply followed a similar path to England's innings and there is no doubt the West Indies missed a golden opportunity to wrest the initiative. Four of the recognised batsmen reached forty but no-one went on to play the big innings that was required. The lion-hearted Fraser was at his miserly best, taking 5 for 66 from 33 overs.

Trailing by 41 on the first innings, England was in real trouble with both openers back in the pavilion and a lead of only ten runs. Their position became worse when Thorpe was struck in the head and forced to retire. However, resolute batting by Smith for 90, Hick for 67 and Thorpe for 42 on his return, gave the home team a glimmer of hope.

Needing only 296 to win this see-sawing Test, the West Indies started the final day at 1 for 68 with their leading batsman Lara, on 38, the key to victory. When Gough had the talented batsman caught behind, he opened the door for England. It was Cork, playing in his first Test, who proved to be the match-winner. His figures of 7 for 43 were the best on debut for an England bowler in Test history, as the home team pulled off a memorable win.

## ENGLAND v WEST INDIES 1995

Edgbasten, Birmingham
6, 7, 8 July 1995
West Indies won by an innings and 64 runs
England 147 and 89 (C.A. Walsh 5 for 54); West Indies 300 (S.L. Campbell 79, R.B. Richardson 69)

With the series level at one-all, England's hopes of gaining the ascendancy were shattered before lunch on the third day, with the West Indies winning by an innings and 64 runs.

After winning the toss, Atherton decided to bat first on a pitch that came in for considerable criticism. Only three English batsmen (Smith with 46, Stewart with 37 and Thorpe with 30) reached double figures, as the home team was bundled out for 147 in the 45th over. This was after Ambrose had broken down with a groin strain in his eighth over and couldn't bowl again in the match.

With half the visitors' side out and the lead only 24 runs, the home team was back in the match. However, the skipper Richardson, playing an uncharacteristically patient innings, stretched the margin to 153. He received valuable support from J.R. Murray, Bishop and K. Benjamin.

England's second innings effort was abysmal with Walsh and Bishop bowling the home team out in 30 overs. Only Smith with 41 made more than sixteen in a disappointing display.

## PAKISTAN v SRI LANKA 1995-96

Jinnah Stadium, Sialkot
22, 23, 24, 25, 26 September 1995
Sri Lanka won by 144 runs
Sri Lanka 232 (H.D.P.K. Dharmasena 62 not out) and 9 for 338 dec. (A Ranatunga 87, U.S. Hathurusinghe 73, H.P. Tillekeratne 50); Pakistan 214 and 212 (Moin Khan 117 not out)

With the series tied at one-all Sri Lanka won a valuable toss. The home team was weakened by the absence of its opening bowlers Wasim Akram and Waqar Younis. Despite the relative inexperience of Pakistan's attack, the visitors were restricted to a moderate total of 232. Dharmasena, batting at number seven, top-scored with a patient 62 not out.

The home team struggled against the Sri Lankan off-spinners Muralitharan, Dharmasena and De Silva and was bowled out early on the third day for 214. Opener Aamir Sohail top-scored with 48.

With a lead of only 18 runs and both the match and series in the balance, the visitors seized control on the back of some resolute batting by opener Hathurusinghe and the more aggressive Ranatunga.

When the declaration was made just before tea on the fourth day, Pakistan required 357 to win in four sessions.

Total humiliation was on the cards when Vaas and Wickremasinghe reduced the home team to 5 for 15. However, a determined century from wicketkeeper Moin Khan took the match into the final afternoon and saved Pakistan some face.

The victory gave Sri Lanka their first series win over Pakistan and only their second series success away from home. It was Pakistan's first series loss at home since 1980-81.

## ZIMBABWE v SOUTH AFRICA 1995-96

Harare Sports Club, Harare
13, 14, 15, 16 October 1995
South Africa won by seven wickets
Zimbabwe 170 (H.H. Streak 53) and 283 (A. Flower 63, A.A. Donald 8 for 71); South Africa 346 (A.C. Hudson 135, B.M. McMillan 98 not out, B.C. Strang 5 for 101) and 3 for 105 (W.J. Cronje 56 not out)

This was the first Test played between these neighbouring countries. Zimbabwe won the toss but did not capitalise on the advantage of batting first. The home team never recovered from a poor start and 4 for 23 became 7 for 84 before Streak added some respectability, batting at number nine for an aggressive half-century.

Schultz, 4 for 54, and Donald, 3 for 42, were outstanding for South Africa. It was Schultz's first Test for two years because of a knee injury.

The visitors' innings got off to a shaky start and at 4 for 85 the game was in the balance. Hudson marked his return to the team with a stylish century while the pugnacious McMillan played another valuable innings only to be denied his century when he ran out of partners.

Trailing by 176 runs with more than three days to play, Zimbabwe was always going to struggle to save the game. Donald proved to be the match-winner. Bowling off a shortened run but with little loss of pace he captured 8 for 71, the best figures by any South African since their return to Test cricket. Seven of the home team's batsmen passed 20 but only the skipper, Andy Flower, reached 50.

After another shaky start, Cronje and McMillan scored the required runs, the match finishing shortly after lunch on the fourth day.

## AUSTRALIA v PAKISTAN 1995-96

Sydney Cricket Ground, Sydney
30 November, 1, 2, 3, 4 December 1995
Pakistan won by 74 runs

Pakistan 299 (Ijaz Ahmed 137) and 204 (Inzamam-Ul-Haq 59, C.J. McDermott 5 for 49); Australia 257 (M.E. Waugh 116, Mushtaq Ahmed 5 for 95) and 172 (M.A. Taylor 59)

Pakistan entered the match two-nil down in a three-Test series, but were able to salvage some prestige with a determined effort and some fine spin bowling by Mushtaq Ahmed.

Wasim Akram's correct call was a good toss to win and the pitch was a typical Sydney slow-turner. The visitors' first innings total of 299 was the highest score of the match and was built on Ijaz Ahmed's patient 137. His third Test century occupied more than seven and a half hours at the crease. Warne was once again the pick of Australia's bowlers claiming 4 for 55 from 34 overs.

By stumps on the second day the home team was well placed at 3 for 151 with the Waugh twins at the crease. Mushtaq Ahmed and Wasim Akram bowled Pakistan back into the match with five and four wickets respectively. M. Waugh's 116 was his first Test century on his home ground. Fine bowling from Warne, again, and McDermott restricted the visitors to 204 and a lead of 246. A target of 247 should have been well within Australia's reach. Instead, the home team was bowled out for a modest 172. Mushtaq Ahmed picked up four wickets to give him nine for the match while Waqar Younis polished off the tail with some hostile bowling. It was a disappointing capitulation by the Australians.

## SOUTH AFRICA v ENGLAND 1995-96

Wanderers, Johannesburg
30 November, 1, 2, 3, 4 December 1995
Match drawn

South Africa 332 (G. Kirsten 110, D.J. Cullinan 69, D.G. Cork 5 for 84) and 9 for 346 dec. (B.M. McMillan 100 not out, D.J. Cullinan 61, J.N. Rhodes 57); England 200 (R.A. Smith 52) and 5 for 351 (M.A. Atherton 185 not out)

Atherton played one of the great innings to save the match for his team after a South African victory looked certain on the fourth day.

England's attack bowled poorly and failed to take advantage of the favourable conditions after Atherton had sent the home team in to bat. Positive batting and aggressive running by Kirsten placed the momentum with South Africa. The left-handed opener was rewarded with his maiden century. Apart from Cullinan's 69, there were useful contributions from Cronje, 35, McMillan, 35, and Pollock, 33, that lifted the home team to a respectable 332.

The visitors were bundled out for a disappointing total of 200 on the second day. Only Smith, 52, Stewart, 45, and Thorpe, 34, offered any resistance to the South African bowlers. With a lead of 122, the home team pushed on for victory, Cullinan again producing a dazzling array of strokes. Inexplicably the South African batsmen came off for bad light with 7.3 overs remaining on the third day with the lead at 428. Somewhat surprisingly the innings continued for another 92 minutes to allow McMillan to complete his second Test century.

England was left with just five sessions to survive. After Stewart, Ramprakash, Thorpe and Hick had fallen on the fourth day, the visitors' prospects of saving the game looked remote. Atherton had a life on 99 when he forced Donald into the hands of Kirsten at short-leg and the ball popped straight out again. Wicketkeeper Russell joined his skipper with over four and a half hours to play. Russell had already broken the world record for dismissals in a Test by taking eleven catches. He had a life on five when Pringle dropped a return catch. Russell batted for 277 minutes while Atherton played the fourth-longest innings for England. His 643 minutes was bettered by only Hutton (797) against Australia at the Oval in 1938, Barrington (683) against Australia at Old Trafford in 1964 and Radly (648) against New Zealand at Auckland in 1977-78. It was a great captain's knock.

## SOUTH AFRICA v ENGLAND 1995-96

Newlands, Capetown
2, 3, 4 January 1996
South Africa won by ten wickets

England 153 (R.A. Smith 66, A.A. Donald 5 for 46) and 157 (G.P. Thorpe 59, S.M. Pollock 5 for 32); South Africa 244 (D.J. Cullinan 62, D.J. Richardson 54 not out) and 0 for 70

This was the fifth and final match of the series in which the previous four Tests had been drawn. England batted first after winning the toss on what was the fastest pitch of the series. Donald was at his most hostile and quickly had the visitors on the back foot. Smith, the only batsman to provide any resistance, batted patiently for more than four hours after being promoted in the order from number six to three.

After a reasonably promising start, South Africa lost 7 for 92 to be 9 for 171 on the second afternoon when Adams joined Richardson. In the previous match, at 18 years and 340 days, Adams became South Africa's youngest Test player. Before this match-winning partnership he had faced only 16 balls in his first class career. Adams scored 29 as he and Richardson realised 73 for the last wicket.

Trailing by 91, England's second innings was no better than the first. This time it was Pollock who was the chief destroyer. Thorpe, who top-scored with 59, was run out in unusual circumstances. Umpire Orchard, the local official, turned down the appeal after a direct hit by

Hudson. Spectators with access to the television replay, which indicated Thorpe may have been out, shouted for Orchard to change his mind. Cronje, the South African captain, approached the umpire who consulted his colleague, umpire Randall from the international panel, and then called for the replay.

Kirsten and Hudson reached the target, scoring at better than four runs per over, with the match finishing on the third day.

## NEW ZEALAND v ZIMBABWE 1995-96

Eden Park, Auckland
20, 21, 22, 23, 24 January 1996
Match drawn

New Zealand 251 (S.P. Fleming 84, C.L. Cairns 57) and 5 for 441 dec. (C.L. Cairns 120, C.M. Spearman 112, R.G. Twose 94, A.C. Parore 76 not out); Zimbabwe 326 (D.L. Houghton 104 retired hurt) and 4 for 246 (G.W. Flower 71, S.V. Carlisle 58)

This was the second match in a two-Test series. Although it finished in a tame draw the game will be remembered for some swashbuckling hitting by Cairns.

Zimbabwe gained a lead of 75 after a brave century by the experienced Houghton. On 55, he had his left foot broken by a delivery from home team paceman Kennedy, but he continued at the crease despite the obvious discomfort.

Spearman and Twose posted New Zealand's third double-century in an opening partnership and with further support from Parore, laid the foundation for the onslaught by Cairns. He hit nine sixes, one short of Hammond's Test record on the same ground in 1932-33. He reached 100 from 86 balls and scored 120 from 96 with ten fours as well as the sixes. New Zealand went from 350 to 400 in 26 balls.

Zimbabwe didn't accept the challenge of scoring 367 from 109 overs for victory; however, the visitors were not threatened by the pedestrian New Zealand attack. G. Flower and Carlisle's opening stand of 120 was a Zimbabwe record.

## PAKISTAN v ZIMBABWE 1996-97

Sheikhupura Cricket Stadium
17, 18, 19, 20, 21 October 1996
Match drawn

Zimbabwe 375 (G.W. Flower 110, P.A. Strang 106 not out, Shahid Nazir 5 for 54) and 7 for 241 (D.L. Houghton 65); Pakistan 553 (Wasim Akram 257 not out, Saqlain Mushtaq 79, Salim Malik 52, P.A. Strang 5 for 212)

This was the first match played at Test cricket's newest ground. The ground was given a remarkable baptism. On a grassless pitch the Pakistan captain, Wasim Akram, played a record-breaking innings while the Zimbabwean leg spinner P.A. Strang produced an outstanding all-round performance.

Strang joined G.W. Flower with Zimbabwe in desperate trouble at 6 for 142. Their partnership realised 131 before the Strang brothers put on 87 for the ninth wicket. Paul Strang posted his maiden first class century in just under five hours.

The home team found themselves in a similar predicament when Saqlain Mushtaq joined his skipper with Pakistan at 7 for 237. They proceeded to post a new world record of 313 for the eighth wicket in a Test match, easily passing the 246 set by Ames and Allen for England against New Zealand in 1931. Wasim Akram's 257 not out was the highest Test score returned by a number eight batsman, exceeding Imitaz Ahmed's 209 for Pakistan against New Zealand in 1955-56. Akram smashed twelve sixes in his innings, breaking the previous best in Tests (Hammond's 10 against New Zealand in 1932-33).

P.A. Strang finished with 5 for 212 from 69 overs to become the 18th player to score a century and take five wickets in an innings in the same Test. He also had the dubious 'honour' of becoming the 13th bowler in Test history to concede 200 runs in an innings.

## INDIA v SOUTH AFRICA 1996-97

Gujarat Stadium, Ahmedabad
20, 21, 22, 23 November 1996
India won by 64 runs

India 223 and 190 (V.V.S. Laxman 51); South Africa 244 (P.S. DeVilliers 67 not out) and 105 (J. Srinath 6 for 21)

Tendulkar won a crucial toss to give the home team the advantage of batting first. Although it was to be the pace bowling of Srinath, not the spinners, that was to win the Test for India.

South Africa's fine fast bowler Donald showed what could be done on the docile pitch. He led the way for the visitors with 4 for 37 as India was dismissed for 223. However, the home team was able to restrict South Africa's lead to just 21 runs. This was hardly likely to be enough on a deteriorating pitch.

With batting becoming more difficult, India could manage only 190 in its second innings, with Laxman and Kumble adding 66 priceless runs for the eighth wicket.

South Africa's target of 170 for victory was always going to be a difficult proposition. It became more so after Srinath had removed both Hudson and Cullinan in his first over. He came back to finish off the innings with the visitors crashing from 4 for 96 to be all out for 105. Only the skipper Cronje, who remained 48 not out, offered any resistance to the pace of Srinath and the spin of Kumble.

## PAKISTAN v NEW ZEALAND 1996-97

Gaddafi Stadium, Lahore
21, 22, 23, 24 November 1996
New Zealand won by 44 runs

New Zealand 155 and 311 (C.L. Cairns 93, S.P. Fleming 92 not out, Mushtaq Ahmed 6 for 84); Pakistan 191 (Moin Khan 59, S.B. Doull 5 for 46) and 231 (Mohammad Wasim 109 not out)

This was only New Zealand's second win in Pakistan and it came after a break of 27 years. However, the home team was without its dynamic skipper, Wasim Akram, who withdrew on the morning of the match with a shoulder injury.

Despite having the advantage of winning the toss, New Zealand was bundled out for a modest 155, Waqar Younis and Mushtaq Ahmed claiming four wickets each.

The visitors struck back, Doull ripping the heart out of the Pakistan top order to have the home team reeling at 5 for 37. However, resolute batting by the bottom half of the order gave Pakistan a lead of 36 runs.

New Zealand slumped to 5 for 101 on the third morning before Cairns joined Fleming. Cairns, in the manner of his father before him, carved 93 from 89 balls in a 141-run partnership. Doull then assisted Fleming to add 49 for the last wicket, which left Pakistan with a target of 276 for victory.

Again the home team's top order failed, with 6 for 60 being the tale of woe. Debutant Mohammad Wasim restored some respectability with an elegant century. But only Moin Khan provided any worthwhile support as the veteran off-spinner, Patel, wrapped up the innings claiming 4 for 36.

## INDIA v SOUTH AFRICA 1996-97

Eden Gardens, Calcutta
27, 28, 29, 30 November, 1 December 1996
South Africa won by 329 runs

South Africa 428 (A.C. Hudson 146, G. Kirsten 102, B.K.V. Prasad 6 for 104) and 3 for 367 dec. (D.J. Cullinan 153 not out, G. Kirsten 133); India 329 (M. Azharuddin 109, Kumble 88) and 137 (M. Azharuddin 52, L. Klusener 8 for 64)

This time Cronje won the toss to give the visitors the vital first use of the pitch. By the time openers Hudson and Kirsten had both posted centuries on the way to an opening partnership of 236, the match was out of India's reach. That South Africa did not score more than 428 was due almost entirely to the home team's opening bowler, Prasad, who returned career-best figures of 6 for 104 from 35 overs.

India was struggling with the bat and when former captain Azharuddin was forced to retire after being struck on the elbow, it seemed unlikely they would avoid the follow-on. Azharuddin returned to join Kumble at the fall of the seventh wicket for 161. He then proceeded to smash the South African bowlers all over Eden Gardens, with his 50 coming from 35 balls and his century from just 74. All the bowlers suffered, none more so than the debutant Klusener, whose 14 overs cost 75 runs.

Kirsten and Cullinan proceeded to take the game out of India's reach with a record partnership of 212 for the second wicket. In the process, Kirsten became only the third South African batsman to score a century in each innings of a Test.

Despite the absence of Donald, who had a severely bruised heel, 467 was always going to be beyond India's reach. Klusener responded magnificently to the challenge and captured 8 for 64 to become only the fifth bowler ever to claim eight wickets on debut.

## PAKISTAN v NEW ZEALAND 1996-97

Rawalpindi Cricket Stadium, Rawalpindi
28, 29, 30 November, 1 December 1996
Pakistan won by an innings and 13 runs

New Zealand 249 (S.P. Fleming 67, L.K. Germon 55, Mushtaq Ahmed 6 for 87) and 168 (B.A. Young 61, Mohammad Zahid 7 for 66); Pakistan 430 (Saeed Anwar 149, Ijaz Ahmed 125, Salim Mailk 78, C.L. Cairns 5 for 137)

This second Test in a two-match series was most notable for the debut of 20-year-old Pakistan fast bowler Mohammad Zahid, who was called up to play after Waqar Younis joined Wasim Akram on the injured list.

Mohammad Zahid's figures of 11 for 130 placed him seventh on the all-time list and were the best by a Pakistan bowler on debut. Of his eleven wickets, eight came from lbw decisions.

## ZIMBABWE v ENGLAND 1996-97

Queen's Club, Bulawayo
18, 19, 20, 21, 22 December 1996
Match drawn

Zimbabwe 376 (A. Flower 112, A.D.R. Campbell 84) and 234 (G.J. Whittall 56, A.C. Waller 50); England 406 (N. Hussain 113, J.P. Crawley 112, N.V. Knight 56, P.A. Strang 5 for 123) and 6 for 204 (N.V. Knight 96, A.J. Stewart 73)

After 1345 Test matches in 119 years, this was the first ever game that was drawn with the scores level. It was also the first Test played between the two countries, the home team having the added incentive of knowing the Test and County Cricket Board had opposed their application for Test status in 1992.

New skipper Campbell and A. Flower, who had recently relinquished the position, were the backbone of Zimbabwe's competitive first innings total. Flower posted his third Test century in a stay of just over six hours, while Campbell had scored 50 for the ninth time without reaching three figures.

## ZIMBABWE v ENGLAND 1996-97 (First Test)

Queens Sport Oval, Bulawayo, December 18, 19, 20, 21, 22, 1996. Match drawn

**ZIMBABWE**

| | | | | | |
|---|---|---|---|---|---|
| G.W.Flower | c Hussain b Silverwood | 43 | | lbw b Gough | 0 |
| S.V.Carlisle | c Crawley b Gough | 0 | | c Atherton b Mullally | 4 |
| A.D.R.Campbell* | c Silverwood b Croft | 84 | | b Croft | 29 |
| D.L.Houghton | c Stewart b Croft | 34 | | c Croft b Tufnell | 37 |
| A.Flower† | c Stewart b Tufnell | 112 | | c Crawley b Tufnell | 14 |
| A.C.Waller | c Crawley b Croft | 15 | | c Knight b Gough | 50 |
| G.J.Whittall | c Atherton b Silverwood | 7 | (8) | c Croft b Tufnell | 56 |
| P.A.Strang | c Tufnell b Silverwood | 38 | (9) | c Crawley b Croft | 19 |
| H.H.Streak | b Mullally | 19 | (10) | not out | 8 |
| B.C.Strang | not out | 4 | (7) | c Mullally b Tufnell | 3 |
| H.K.Olonga | c Knight b Tufnel | 0 | | c Stewart b Silverwood | 0 |
| Extras | LB 4, NB 13, W 3 | 20 | | B 4, LB 6, NB 2, W 2 | 14 |
| **Total** | **376** | | | | **234** |

**ENGLAND**

| | | | | | |
|---|---|---|---|---|---|
| N.V.Knight | lbw b Olonga | 56 | | run out (B.C.Strang/A.Flower) | 96 |
| M.A.Atherton* | lbw b P.A.Strang | 16 | | b Ologna | 4 |
| A.J.Stewart† | lbw b P.A.Strang | 48 | | c Campbell b P.A.Strang | 73 |
| N.Hussain | c B.C.Strang b Streak | 113 | | c Carlisle b P.A.Strang | 0 |
| G.P.Thorpe | c Campbell b P.A.Strang | 13 | (6) | c Campbell b Streak | 2 |
| J.P.Crawley | c A.Flower b P.A.Strang | 112 | (5) | c Carlisle b Whittall | 7 |
| R.D.B.Croft | lbw b Olonga | 7 | | | |
| D.Gough | c G.W.Flower b Olonga | 2 | (7) | not out | 3 |
| C.E.W.Silverwood | c Houghton b P.A.Strang | 0 | | | |
| A.D.Mullally | c Waller b Streak | 4 | | | |
| P.C.R.Tufnell | not out | 2 | | | |
| Extras | B 4, LB 4, NB 24, W 1 | 33 | | B 2, LB 13, Nb 1, W 3 | 19 |
| **Total** | | **406** | | **6 wickets** | **204** |

| **ENGLAND** | O | M | R | W | | O | M | R | W |
|---|---|---|---|---|---|---|---|---|---|
| Mullally | 23 | 4 | 69 | 1 | Gough | 12 | 2 | 44 | 2 |
| Gough | 26 | 4 | 87 | 1 | Mullally | 18 | 5 | 49 | 1 |
| Silverwood | 18 | 5 | 63 | 3 | Croft | 33 | 9 | 62 | 2 |
| Croft | 44 | 15 | 77 | 3 | Silverwood | 7 | 3 | 8 | 1 |
| Tufnell | 26.5 | 4 | 76 | 2 | Tufnell | 31 | 12 | 61 | 4 |

| **ZIMBABWE** | O | M | R | W | | O | M | R | W |
|---|---|---|---|---|---|---|---|---|---|
| Streak | 36 | 8 | 86 | 2 | Streak | 11 | 0 | 64 | 1 |
| B.C.Strang | 17 | 5 | 54 | 0 | Olonga | 2 | 0 | 16 | 1 |
| P.A.Strang | 58.4 | 14 | 123 | 5 | P.A.Strang | 14 | 0 | 63 | 2 |
| Olonga | 23 | 2 | 90 | 3 | G.W.Flower | 8 | 0 | 36 | 0 |
| Whittall | 10 | 2 | 25 | 0 | Whittall | 2 | 0 | 10 | 1 |
| G.W.Flower | 7 | 3 | 20 | 0 | | | | | |

FALL OF WICKETS

| Wkt | Z | E | Z | E |
|---|---|---|---|---|
| 1st | 3 | 48 | 6 | 17 |
| 2nd | 129 | 92 | 6 | 154 |
| 3rd | 135 | 160 | 57 | 156 |
| 4th | 205 | 180 | 82 | 178 |
| 5th | 235 | 328 | 103 | 182 |
| 6th | 252 | 340 | 111 | 204 |
| 7th | 331 | 344 | 178 | - |
| 8th | 372 | 353 | 209 | - |
| 9th | 376 | 378 | 233 | - |
| 10th | 376 | 406 | 234 | - |

Umpires: R.S. Dunne and I.D.Robinson

Centuries by Hussain and Crawley gave the visitors a 30-run lead. Their fifth-wicket partnership realised 148 runs, however the England batsman should have adopted a more positive approach to gain ascendancy. But when the home team lost five wickets for 107 with one day to play, the visitors still looked likely winners.

Positive batting, which produced half-centuries to Waller and Whittall, left England with 205 needed for victory in 37 overs. After Atherton's early departure, Knight and Stewart took up the challenge. Eighty-seven runs were needed with 15 overs remaining. However, this was not a one-day game so there was no 30-yard circle or fielding restrictions.

Fifty-nine runs from ten overs became 33 from five but Stewart, Hussain, Crawley and Thorpe had been dismissed in the chase for victory. Finally, 13 was required from the last over with Streak bowling to Knight. All nine fieldsmen were on the boundary. The first ball was down leg-side, and splendid running by Gough scored two from the second. Knight lifted England's hopes with a six over square leg, leaving five runs needed from three balls. The fourth delivery was well wide of the off-stump but not called by Umpire Robinson. Two more runs came from the fifth ball of the over. Streak then fired in the perfect yorker which Knight played into the covers. Flower removed the bails after a fine throw from B. Strang, before the batsmen had crossed for the winning run. (See final score on page 55.)

## SOUTH AFRICA v INDIA 1996-97

Wanderers, Johannesburg
16, 17, 18, 19, 20 January 1997
Match drawn

India 410 (R.S. Dravid 148, S.C. Ganguly 73) and 8 for 266 dec. (R.S. Dravid 81, S.C. Ganguly 60, N.R. Mongia 50); South Africa 321 (S.M. Pollock 79, J. Srinath 5 for 104) and 8 for 228 (D.J. Cullinan 122 not out)

After being soundly defeated in the first two Tests of the series, India nearly pulled off an unexpected victory. A thunderstorm on the final day caused a 152-minute delay that went a long way in assisting the home team to save the match.

A patient century by Dravid, who received admirable support from Ganguly in their 145-run partnership for the fourth wicket, was the anchor of the visitors' innings. Kumble, 29, and Srinath, 41, added valuable runs in the lower order. South Africa's pace bowlers failed to exploit the conditions with some wayward bowling, particularly on the first morning.

The home team replied in a most positive manner, scoring at four runs an over despite losing wickets regularly along the way. McMillan, 47, and Pollock retrieved the situation with a 112-run partnership for the sixth wicket. During his innings, Pollock passed his father Peter's highest Test score of 75. Pollock senior was now chairman of the National Selection Panel.

With a lead of 89, India adopted a more positive approach to its second innings and scored at more than three an over. Once again, Dravid and Ganguly were the principal scorers after Rathore and Mongia had produced an opening stand of 90. The declaration was made late on the fourth day, leaving South Africa a target of 375 from 95 overs.

India got the breakthrough they were looking for when Hudson was bowled by Kumble before the close of play. One for 4 overnight soon became 5 for 76 with the home side staring at defeat. Then the heavens opened, the deluge delaying play for nearly three hours. On resumption, Pollock and then Richardson departed quickly, Klusener joining Cullinan with South Africa at 7 for 95. No grim defence here as Klusener scored 49 from 77 balls in a 127-run stand that lasted two hours. Donald survived 16 deliveries before the umpires abandoned play because of poor light. Cullinan had been his side's saviour. He occupied the crease for more than four hours in his match-saving innings.

## NEW ZEALAND v ENGLAND 1996-97

Eden Park, Auckland
24, 25, 26, 27, 28 January 1997
Match drawn

New Zealand 390 (S.P. Fleming 129, B.A. Pocock 70, C.L. Cairns 67) and 9 for 248 (N.P. Astle 102 not out); England 521 (A.J. Stewart 173, G.P. Thorpe 119, M.A. Atherton 83, D.G. Cork 59)

New Zealand found an unlikely batting hero in their number eleven, Morrison, who survived for 165 minutes to hold England out. The same batsman has a record of 24 test ducks!

Atherton sent the Kiwis in but his pace bowlers wasted the conditions with their inaccuracy. Fleming's maiden century and aggressive batting by Cairns carried New Zealand to a respectable total of 390.

England replied with 521. Stewart's 173, the highest score by an English wicketkeeper, beat the previous best of 149 by Ames at Kingston in 1930. Thorpe produced another solid if unspectacular century, while Atherton returned to form with an elegant 83.

By lunch on the final day, England had the game as good as won, with New Zealand 8 for 105 and only Doull and Morrison to support Astle. Doull made 26, hitting lustily to avoid the innings defeat before Morrison and Astle produced their superb rear-guard effort.

## NEW ZEALAND v ENGLAND 1996-97

Lancaster Park, Christchurch
14, 15, 16, 17, 18 February 1997
England won by four wickets
New Zealand 346 (S.P. Fleming 62, A.C. Parore 59, C.L. Cairns 57, R.D.B. Croft 5 for 95) and 186 (C.L. Cairns 52); England 228 (M.A. Atherton 94 not out) and 6 for 307 (M.A. Atherton 118)

This was a remarkable victory for England as only once before, at Melbourne in January 1929, had they scored more than 300 in the fourth innings to win a Test.

With Germon injured, Fleming became New Zealand's youngest skipper. He lost the toss and then proceeded to top-score with 62 in an innings of 346 that took almost nine hours to complete. It was an innings of missed opportunities as six batsmen passed 20.

England's reply was disappointing, falling 118 runs short of the home team's total. Atherton played a lone hand for the visitors, carrying his bat for 94 in a patient knock that took almost six hours to compile. Allott marked his return to Test cricket with four wickets, including three of the first five to fall.

New Zealand failed to drive home its advantage and by lunch on the fourth day had been dismissed for 186. This left the visitors with ample time to reach the target of 305.

Once again, the sheet anchor of England's innings was skipper Atherton who was at the crease for 399 minutes making 118. Until his dismissal, he had been on the field for the first 26 and a half hours of the match. Hussain and Thorpe fell in quick succession, leaving England 6 for 231 and still 74 runs short of the victory target. However, there was to be no further success for New Zealand as Crawley and Cork steered the visitors to victory. The match was won with just 12.2 overs remaining. The 18-year-old Vettori bowled with maturity beyond his years to claim 4 for 97 from 57 overs.

## SOUTH AFRICA v AUSTRALIA 1996-97

Wanderers, Johannesburg
28 February, 1, 2, 3, 4 March 1997
Australia won by an innings and 196 runs
South Africa 302 (W.J. Cronje 76, D.J. Richardson 72 not out) and 130; Australia 8 for 628 dec. (G.S. Blewett 214, S.R. Waugh 160, M.T.G. Elliot 85)

This was the first match in a three Test series that was billed as the world championship decider.

The South Africans were in trouble early as McGrath exploited the conditions superbly to remove Hudson, Kallis and Kirsten in his first ten-over spell. Only the skipper Cronje made a worthwhile contribution in the top order. Late on the first day, wicketkeeper Richardson hit lustily to add respectability to the home team's score. Australia's reply was dominated by a record fifth-wicket partnership of 385 by S. Waugh and Blewett. (Waugh was playing with his twin brother for the 44th time, breaking the record of Ian and Greg Chappell). During the partnership, Waugh and Blewett became the ninth pair to bat through a day's play, and it was the twelfth time in Test history that a full day's play had failed to produce a wicket. The partnership was the best ever against South Africa while Blewett's 214 was the highest score by an Australian in South Africa.

On a wearing pitch, Australian spinners Warne and Bevan bowled the visitors to a commanding victory before lunch on the final day, Bevan ending the match with four wickets for two runs from twelve deliveries.

## SOUTH AFRICA v AUSTRALIA 1996-97

St. George's Park, Port Elizabeth
14, 15, 16, 17 March 1997
Australia won by two wickets
South Africa 209 (B.M. McMillan 55, J.N. Gillespie 5 for 54) and 168; Australia 108 and 8 for 271 (M.E. Waugh 116)

Taylor sent Australia in on a pitch that the Australian captain labelled 'under-prepared'. Hostile fast bowling by both McGrath and Gillespie had the home team reeling at 4 for 22 within the first hour's play. The experienced pair of McMillan and Richardson added 85 runs for the eighth wicket to restore some credibility to the innings.

Australia's batsmen failed to come to terms with the difficult conditions and were dismissed for 108, their second lowest total in South Africa. Elliott top-scored with a painstaking 23, and only four Australian batsmen reached double figures. South Africa suffered a telling blow when their opening bowler Pollock was forced from the field with a hamstring injury.

When the home team reached 0 for 83 by stumps on the second day, Australia looked a beaten side. However, the match was turned upside-down by a mixture of high-quality bowling and poor batting on the third morning. Apart from the openers, Bacher with 49 and Kirsten with 43, only Cronje and Pollock (batting with a runner) reached double figures. Gillespie and Bevan claimed three wickets apiece to spearhead Australia's fight-back.

The target of 270 was a testing one on a difficult pitch. Taylor went cheaply and when Hayden was run out in a mix-up with Elliott, the visitors were in trouble at 2 for 30. M. Waugh, playing in his 100th Test innings, then carried Australia to within twelve runs of victory. Waugh's 116 was one of the finest centuries in Test history and certainly his most valuable in an illustrious career. With his dismissal and those of Bevan and Warne, Australia still required five runs with two wickets in hand.

Healy ended the match triumphantly swinging Cronje over backward square leg for six.

## WEST INDIES v INDIA 1996-97

Kensington Oval, Bridgetown, Barbados
27, 29, 30, 31 March 1997
West Indies won by 38 runs

West Indies 298 (S. Chanderpaul 137 not out, B.K.V. Prasad 5 for 82) and 140 (A. Kuruvilla 5 for 68); India 319 (S.R. Tendulkar 92, R.S. Dravid 78) and 81

Brian Lara captained the West Indies for the first time in the absence of the injured Walsh. Tendulkar sent the home team in on a pitch that was going to favour the pace bowlers for the duration of the match. After 13 half-centuries in 18 Tests, Chanderpaul finally reached the three figures, with his 137 not out forming the backbone of the West Indies innings.

Tendulkar and Dravid produced the best batting of the match in their 170-run partnership for the third wicket. The West Indies fast bowlers delivered 30 no-balls in India's innings and perhaps it should have been more, with video replay suggesting that Bishop overstepped the line when he had Tendulkar caught in the gully. To its credit the home team fought back to claim the last six wickets for 66 and restrict the visitors' lead to just 21 runs.

India's pace trio of Prasad, Kuruvilla and Ganesh, bowling a fuller length than their West Indian counterparts, had the home team in desperate trouble at 9 for 107 when Dillon joined Ambrose. Their 33-run partnership was the highest of the innings and left the visitors needing 120 for victory.

On a pitch that was becoming increasingly difficult, this was never going to be an easy target. Sustained hostile bowling by Ambrose, Bishop and Rose dismissed India for 81 (their lowest score in the West Indies) and the home team had snatched yet another victory from 'the jaws of defeat'.

## SRI LANKA v INDIA 1997-98

Premadasa Stadium, Colombo
2, 3, 4, 5, 6 August 1997
Match drawn

India 8 for 537 dec. (S.R. Tendulkar 143, M. Azharuddin 126, N.S. Sidhu 111, R.S. Dravid 69); Sri Lanka 6 for 952 dec. (S.T. Jayasuriya 340, R.S. Mahanama 225, P.A. De Silva 126, A. Ranatunga 86, Drmjayawardene 66

Two of cricket's most imposing records were broken on a docile pitch in Colombo.

Sri Lanka's total of 6 for 952 easily surpassed England's 7 for 903 declared at the Oval in 1938. Jayasuriya and Mahanama added 576 for the second wicket. They cruised past the previous highest Test partnership of 467 set by Crowe and Jones of New Zealand against Sri Lanka at Wellington in 1990-91. Jayasuriya's score of 340 was the fourth highest in Test history. The three higher scores were Lara's 375, Sobers' 365 not out and Hutton's 364.

Jayasuriya started the final day requiring 50 runs to break the record. Local officials let the public in free with the prospect of a new record score but many in the crowd of more than 30000 were still finding their vantage point when Jayasuriya was dismissed, caught at silly point by Ganguly off Chauhan. Kulkarni became the twelfth bowler to take a wicket with his first ball in Test cricket when he had Atapattu caught behind by Mongia.

The Sri Lankan run feast had come after India had plundered the home team's attack, scoring 537 at better than three runs per over. Centuries were scored by Sidhu, Tendulkar and Azahruddin who put on 221 for the fourth wicket. India's captain, Tendulkar, claimed that his team had only lost wickets because they took chances trying to score runs. (See final score on page 59.)

## ENGLAND v AUSTRALIA 1997

The Oval, London
21, 22, 23 August 1997
England won by 19 runs

England 180 (G.D. McGrath 7 for 76) and 163 (G.P. Thorpe 62, M.S. Kasprowicz 7 for 36); Australia 220 (P.C.R. Tufnell 7 for 66) and 104 (A.R. Caddick 5 for 42)

This was the final Test of a six-match series. Australia had retained the Ashes and won the rubber by the time this game was played but England was able to salvage much lost pride with a memorable win inside three days.

The match was played on a dry pitch that was crumbling by the second day. Luck was with England as Taylor called incorrectly for the first time in the series although it appeared as if the home team may have squandered that advantage with another inept batting display. McGrath, bowling fast and straight, followed his eight-wicket haul at Lords with 7 for 76. Stewart, 36, Hussain, 35, and Thorpe, 27, all got a start but were unable to convert that into the big total the home team was looking for. By stumps on the first day, Australia had reached 2 for 77 in reply to England's 180.

Although the visitors finished with a lead of 40 it should have been more, as all the recognised batsmen reached double figures yet no one scored a half-century. Blewett top-scored with 47, Ponting made 40 and Taylor, 38. Tufnell, playing in his first match of the series, bowled unchanged for 35 overs to reap the splendid reward of 7 for 66. England made another poor start losing Atherton, Butcher and Stewart with only 26 on the board. However, Warne was struggling with a groin strain and was only able to bowl off three paces. When he removed Hussain with the third ball of the third day the home team was

## SRI LANKA v INDIA 1997-98 (First Test)

R.Premadasa (Khettarama) Stadium, Colombo, August 2, 3, 4, 5, 6, 1997 — Match drawn

**INDIA**

| | | |
|---|---|---|
| N.R.Mongia† | c Jayawardene b Pushpakumara | 7 |
| N.S.Sidhu | c Kaluwitharana b Vaas | 111 |
| R.S.Dravid | c and b Jayasurija | 69 |
| S.R.Tendulkar* | c Jayawardene b Muralidaran | 143 |
| M.Azharuddin | c and b Muralidaran | 126 |
| S.C.Ganguly | c Mahanama b Jayasuriya | 0 |
| A.R.Kumble | not out | 27 |
| R.K.Chauhan | c Vaas b Jayasuriya | 23 |
| A.Kuruvilla | c Atapattu b Pushpakumara | 9 |
| N.M.Kulkarni | | |
| B.K.Venkatesh Prasad | | |
| Extras | B 10, NB 12 | 22 |
| **Total** | **8 wickets declared** | **537** |

**SRI LANKA**

| | | |
|---|---|---|
| S.T. Jayasuriya | c Ganguly b Chauhan | 340 |
| M.S.Atapattu | cw Mongia b Kulkarni | 26 |
| R.S.Mahanama | lbw b Kumble | 225 |
| P.A.de Silva | c Venkatesh Prasad b Ganguly | 126 |
| A.Ranatunga* | run out (sub Jadeja/Mongia) | 86 |
| D.R.M.Jayawardene | c Kulkarni b Ganguly | 66 |
| R.S.Kaluwitharana† | not out | 14 |
| W.P.U.J.C.Vaas | not out | 11 |
| K.R.Pushpakumara | | |
| M.Muralidaran | | |
| K.J.Silva | | |
| Extras | B 27, LB 10, NB 14, W 7 | 58 |
| **Total** | **6 wickets declared** | **952** |

| **SRI LANKA** | O | M | R | W | O | M | R | W |
|---|---|---|---|---|---|---|---|---|
| Vaas | 23 | 5 | 80 | 1 | | | | |
| Pushpakumara | 19.3 | 2 | 97 | 2 | | | | |
| Jayawardene | 2 | 0 | 6 | 0 | | | | |
| Muralidaran | 65 | 9 | 174 | 2 | | | | |
| Silva | 39 | 3 | 122 | 0 | | | | |
| Jayasuriya | 18 | 3 | 45 | 3 | | | | |
| Atapattu | 1 | 0 | 3 | 0 | | | | |
| **INDIA** | O | M | R | W | O | M | R | W |
| Venkatesh Prasad | 24 | 1 | 88 | 0 | | | | |
| Kuruvilla | 14 | 2 | 74 | 0 | | | | |
| Chauhan | 78 | 8 | 276 | 1 | | | | |
| Kumble | 72 | 7 | 223 | 1 | | | | |
| Kulkarni | 70 | 12 | 195 | 1 | | | | |
| Ganguly | 9 | 0 | 53 | 2 | | | | |
| Tendulkar | 2 | 1 | 2 | 0 | | | | |
| Dravid | 2 | 0 | 4 | 0 | | | | |

FALL OF WICKETS

| Wkt | I | SL | I | SL |
|---|---|---|---|---|
| 1st | 36 | 39 | - | - |
| 2nd | 183 | 615 | - | - |
| 3rd | 230 | 615 | - | - |
| 4th | 451 | 790 | - | - |
| 5th | 451 | 921 | - | - |
| 6th | 479 | 924 | - | - |
| 7th | 516 | - | - | - |
| 8th | 537 | - | - | - |
| 9th | - | - | - | - |
| 10th | - | - | - | - |

Umpires: K.T.Francis and S.R.Randell

effectively 4 for 12. Thorpe and Ramprakash gave England just a glimmer of hope with a 69-run partnership for the fifth wicket, Thorpe scoring the only half-century of the match and Ramprakash falling two runs short. Kasprowicz joined McGrath and Tufnell in taking seven wickets in an innings, the first time three bowlers had done this in the same Test.

Australia required 124 to win. As had been the case in the recent past, the chase was deplorable with a lack of application that went with the dead rubber status of the match.

Caddick finished the innings with a five-wicket haul but it was Tufnell who created the uncertainty in the batsmen's minds and fittingly he claimed the last wicket, McGrath, at 24 minutes past five on the Saturday afternoon to give him eleven for the game in a match-winning performance.

## PAKISTAN v WEST INDIES 1997-98

Arbab Niaz, Peshawar
17, 18, 19, 20 November 1997
Pakistan won by an innings and 19 runs
West Indies 151 (Mushtaq Ahmed 5 for 35) and 211 (S.L. Campbell 66, Mushtaq Ahmed 5 for 71); Pakistan 381 (Inzamam-Ul-Haq 92 not out, Saeed Anwar 65, Ijaz Ahmed 65, Moin Khan 58, C.A. Walsh 5 for 78)

This was the first Test of a three-match series played in the volatile North West Frontier Province city of Peshawar, only 20 kilometres from the Khyber Pass.

Despite winning the toss, the West Indies were always on the back foot going to lunch at 4 for 29 on the first morning. The situation got worse with the visitors crashing to 7 for 58 before wicketkeeper David Williams, 31, and bowlers Ambrose, 30, and Bishop, 20, took the score to 151. Mushtaq Ahmed's wily spinners proved too much for the West Indies' batsmen.

A 133-run partnership for the second wicket by Saeed Anwar and Ijaz Ahmed was the launching pad for Pakistan's reply with both batsmen scoring 65. However, it was Inzamam-Ul-Haq who top-scored with 92 not out. Inzamam was forced to bat with a runner throughout his innings after injuring his foot while fielding on the first day.

With a deficit of 230, it was always going to be difficult for West Indies to save the match and although the batting in the second innings was an improvement to that of the first day, only Campbell played with the concentration and application required. Pakistan's premier bowlers Wasim Akram and Mushtaq Ahmed were in top form, Mushtaq claiming 5 for 71 for his best match return of 10 for 106.

It was Pakistan's biggest ever win against West Indies.

## PAKISTAN v WEST INDIES 1997-98

Rawalpindi Cricket Stadium, Rawalpindi
29, 30 November, 1, 2, 3 December 1997
Pakistan won by an innings and 29 runs
West Indies 303 (S. Chanderpaul 95, S.L. Campbell 78) and 139 (C.L. Hooper 73 not out); Pakistan 471 (Inzamam-Ul-Haq 177, Aamir Sohail 160, C.A. Walsh 5 for 143)

The Rawalpindi pitch, unlike the one at Peshawar, was green and lively and gave the West Indies some encouragement. However, Wasim Akram won the toss and sent the visitors in to bat. Waqar Younis and Wasim Akram soon made inroads into the West Indies batting, the visitors in trouble at 4 for 58 before Campbell and Chanderpaul added 147 for the fifth wicket. The batting was disappointing apart from this pair and wicketkeeper Williams, who made 48.

The turning point of the match came when Lara, at first slip, dropped a straightforward catch from Aamir Sohail who was 38 at the time. Aamir and Inzamam-Ul-Haq went on to add 323, the highest third-wicket stand for any country against the West Indies. Apart from the tireless Walsh and the enthusiastic Rose, the visitors' bowling was lamentable.

On what was now an excellent pitch, the West Indies were expected to save the match. Their effort was disgraceful with the game over less than an hour into the final day and only Hooper, 73 not out, and Campbell, 34, reaching double figures, the winning margin even bigger than in the previous Test.

## PAKISTAN v WEST INDIES 1997-98

National Stadium, Karachi
6, 7, 8, 9 December 1997
Pakistan won by ten wickets
West Indies 216 (S.L. Campbell 50, Saqlain Mushtaq 5 for 54) and 212 (C.L. Hooper 106); Pakistan 417 (Aamir Sohail 160, Ijaz Ahmed 151, M.V. Dillon 5 for 111) and 0 for 15.

After losing the first two Tests of the series by an innings West Indies were hoping to salvage some wounded pride in this final Test.

The visitors batted first on the best pitch produced for the series and at lunch were 1 for 94 with the only wicket to fall, S. Williams, being run out. The situation changed dramatically during the remainder of the day, as reckless West Indies batting saw the last nine wickets fall for 107 runs. It was a disappointing effort as Chanderpaul, Holder and D. Williams passed 20, and S. Williams and Lara passed 30, with only Campbell going on to score a half-century. Saqlain Mushtaq, who was surprisingly left out of the Pakistan team for the first two Tests, bowled superbly in taking 5 for 54 from 24 overs. Saqlain received splendid support from his skipper, Wasim Akram, who picked up 3 for 76.

Aamir Sohail and Ijaz Ahmed proceeded to put the game out of the visitors' reach with a record opening stand of 298, Aamir Sohail scoring 160 for the second successive Test and Ijaz Ahmed 151. The West Indies did fight back splendidly on the third day, as ten wickets fell for 119. Skipper Walsh turned in another lionhearted performance to claim 4 for 74 while rookie speedster Dillon captured 5 for 111.

The West Indies' second innings was more dismal than their first. Only a belligerent 80-ball century by Hooper added respectability to the score. Once again, Saqlain Mushtaq and Wasim Akram did the damage, Saqlain taking 4 for 24 for match figures of 9 for 80 and Wasim Akram 4 for 42 for an analysis of 7 for 118. Pakistan needed only five overs to reach the target and inflict one of the worst series defeats in the otherwise illustrious history of West Indies' cricket.

## AUSTRALIA v SOUTH AFRICA 1997-98

Sydney Cricket Ground, Sydney
2, 3, 4, 5 January 1998
Australia won by an innings and 21 runs
South Africa 287 (W.J. Cronje 88, H.H. Gibbs 54, S.K. Warne 5 for 75) and 113 (S.K. Warne 6 for 34); Australia 421 (M.E. Waugh 100, S.R. Waugh 85, R.T. Ponting 62)

Australia's champion leg-spinner, Warne, captured his 300th Test wicket on the way to another match-winning performance. It was exactly six years to the day since he had captured his first victim at the highest level.

South Africa batted first on the best Sydney pitch for many years. The visitors' lack of initiative on the opening day went a long way to deciding the result. Only 197 runs were scored from 97 overs for the loss of five wickets. Cronje was uncharacteristically restrained with a patient 88. Gibbs, with a maiden half-century, added 97 for the fourth wicket with his captain. Warne, wicketless on the first day, returned to top form on the second morning taking the last five wickets for 29 as South Africa slumped from 5 for 228 to be all out for 287.

On such a good pitch the home team set about gaining a sizeable lead. With Taylor, Elliott and Blewett out and only 103 on the board, the visitors had a chance to fight their way back into the match. However, the Waugh twins produced another memorable partnership despite some of the most hostile bowling seen in Sydney for years. With the second new ball, Donald was at his fiery best but was not able to make the vital breakthrough. Ponting and Healy, who finished 46 not out, gave Australia a 134-run advantage.

After McGrath and Reiffel had picked up an early wicket, Warne was at his brilliant best as he reduced South Africa to 7 for 55. A storm delayed play for three hours, but the hardy souls who stayed at the ground were not disappointed as Warne bowled Kallis for wicket number 300 to produce scenes of great jubilation. Reiffel dismissed Symcox and Donald to end the match at nine minutes past seven in the gloomy weather with the SCG lights blazing.

## WEST INDIES v ENGLAND 1997-98

Sabina Park, Kingston
29 January 1998
Match abandoned
England 3 for 17

The first Test of the series was abandoned after just 56 minutes and 10.1 overs. It was the first Test to have been called off because of a dangerous pitch. Umpire Venkataraghavan had contacted match referee Jarman as early as the third over expressing his concern about the state of the pitch.

Physiotherapist Wayne Morton had been called upon to treat England's batsmen six times in less than an hour's play. Opener Stewart called his captain Atherton on to the field at the drinks break and after consultation with West Indies' captain Lara and Jarman, the umpires suspended play and later decided to abandon the match.

It was deemed that the results of the 10.1 overs play would count in the players' career statistics.

## AUSTRALIA v SOUTH AFRICA 1997-98

Adelaide Oval, Adelaide
30, 31 January, 1, 2, 3 February 1998
Match drawn
South Africa 517 (B.M. McMillan 87 not out, G. Kirsten 77, W.J. Cronje 73, A.M. Bacher 64, P.L. Symcox 54) and 6 for 193 dec. (G. Kirsten 108 not out); Australia 350 (M.A. Taylor 169 not out, M.E. Waugh 63, S.M. Pollock 7 for 87) and 7 for 227 (M.E. Waugh 115 not out)

South Africa, who needed to win the match to square the series, was unable to select its pace-bowling spearhead Donald while Australia was without its three leading fast bowlers, McGrath, Gillespie and Reiffel.

Cronje won the toss again and batted on a typical Adelaide 'belter'. Against the inexperienced new-ball attack of Kasprowicz and Bichel, Bacher and Kirsten added 140 for the first wicket. Cronje, playing with more purpose than in Sydney then scored 73 in just under three hours. With the visitors at 7 for 305, the home team had fought back well before McMillan, in a return to form, realised 214 for the last three wickets with Pollock, who scored 40 from 67 deliveries; Klusener, 38 off 59; and Symcox, 54 from just 42 balls.

Australia's reply was built around the captain's gutsy innings. Taylor had not played in the one-day series so was fresher than most of his teammates. In extremely hot conditions, he batted for over eight hours to become the ninth Australian to carry his bat.

In a game of many individual highlights, Pollock's 7 for 87 from 41 overs in the searing heat was an outstanding performance. Pollock's magnificent bowling had given South Africa a realistic chance of winning the match and levelling the series.

Kirsten played another splendid innings to compile his sixth century and allow Cronje to declare at 6 for 193, leaving Australia 361 to win from 109 overs. This was never going to be an attainable target and was even less likely after both Taylor and Elliott were out with only 17 on the board.

M. Waugh was then to play one of his most responsible knocks for his country. Even though he was dropped four times, his patient century was to save the side. There was a moment of high drama in the seventh over of the final hour. Waugh was hit on the elbow by Pollock, the ball carrying to Symcox in the gully, who appealed for the catch. As Waugh turned, he lost control of his arm and his bat broke the wicket. An appeal for hit-wicket followed. Third umpire Davis was consulted and correctly ruled in the batsman's favour as the bails were not dislodged in the act of facing the ball or in taking a run.

It was a tense end to a wonderful match.

## WEST INDIES v ENGLAND 1997-98

Queen's Park Oval, Port of Spain
5, 6, 7, 8, 9 February 1998
West Indies won by three wickets

England 214 (N. Hussain 61 not out, A.J. Stewart 50) and 258 (A.J. Stewart 73, C.E.L. Ambrose 5 for 52); West Indies 191 (B.C. Lara 55, A.R.C. Fraser 8 for 53) and 7 for 282 (C.L. Hooper 94 not out, D. Williams 65, S.C. Williams 62)

This Test was added to the England tour itinerary after the match in Kingston had been abandoned on the first day.

The game was played on a mediocre pitch which produced slow uneven bounce and where patience was a real virtue. Atherton won the toss and decided to bat first. Stewart played stylishly before his half-century, but only Hussain batted with the resolve required in the difficult conditions, Fraser staying with him for 90 minutes on the second morning while 42 runs were added for the ninth wicket.

Fraser then dominated proceedings with the ball as he returned career-best figures of 8 for 53. New skipper Lara top-scored for the home team with 55 but only Chanderpaul, 34, and Ambrose, 31, offered any real support. With a lead of 23, England had an opportunity to press home the advantage and received an added bonus when Lara used Benjamin and McLean to open the bowling and not the experienced Ambrose and Walsh. Stewart was again the pick of England's batsmen, but this time he received more support so that by the end of the third day the visitors were 4 for 219, leading by 242.

On the fourth morning, Ambrose produced one of his great spells taking 5 for 16 from 7.5 overs as the last six wickets fell for 30 runs. West Indies required 282 to record an amazing victory. S. Williams, 62, held the top order together with one of his most responsible knocks but when half the team was out for 121 it was England who looked likely to win.

The little wicketkeeper D. Williams joined the enigmatic Hooper and they added 57 before stumps, so 101 was still required when the final day started. Fraser dropped a return catch from Williams from the first ball of the day and from that moment the home team looked more likely to succeed. Williams was dismissed after a 129-run partnership but by then only 29 was required for victory. Ambrose fell cheaply but Hooper found a capable partner in Benjamin and they carried the West Indies to a memorable win. In a match in which there were many outstanding individual performances, Hooper was a worthy man-of-the-match.

## WEST INDIES v ENGLAND 1997-98

Queen's Park Oval, Port of Spain
13, 14, 15, 16, 17 February 1998
England won by three wickets

West Indies 159 (A.R.C. Fraser 5 for 40, A.R. Caddick 5 for 67) and 210 (J.C. Adams 53); England 145 (C.E.L. Ambrose 5 for 25) and 7 for 225 (A.J. Stewart 83)

Because of the farce in Jamaica when the Test was abandoned after just 56 minutes of play, back-to-back matches were played in Trinidad. A different pitch was used for this match than for the game the West Indies had won three days earlier.

Atherton invited the West Indies to bat but the decision looked likely to back-fire with the home team at 1 for 72 just after lunch and Lara in dominant form. Accurate bowling from Caddick and Fraser supported by excellent catching turned the match, reducing the West Indies from 1 for 93 to be all out for a modest 159. Nine wickets had fallen for 66 in 40 overs.

England's reply was no better despite reasonable contributions from Stewart, 44, Thorpe, 32, Butcher, 28, and Russel, 20 not out. No other batsman reached double figures as Ambrose, revelling in the conditions, claimed another five-wicket haul.

The West Indies, after leading by 14 runs, had increased their advantage to 85 with eight wickets in hand at the end of the second day. Lara, who was on 30, again loomed as England's danger man. When Fraser trapped him in front for 47 the visitors had regained the initiative. Chanderpaul and Adams, with a 56-run partnership for the sixth wicket, went some way to restoring the West Indies' ascendancy. However, when three wickets fell for just one run, England was again in the driver's seat. Adams then managed to eke out 51 valuable runs with McLean and Walsh. Fraser and Headley both picked up four wickets, Fraser finishing with nine for the match.

The visitors had more than two days to score the 225 required for victory. Atherton and Stewart had polished 52 off the target by the end of the third day. Unseasonal rain frustrated both teams on the fourth day as England laboured towards victory. Atherton and Stewart had scored more than half the runs required with their 129-run opening stand.

The final day started with the visitors still needing to score 38 with six wickets in hand. Rain delayed play for 45 minutes and then Thorpe, Russel and Caddick fell in quick succession before Butcher and Headley took England to a nail-biting victory.

## WEST INDIES v PAKISTAN 1997-98

Kingsmead, Durban
26, 27, 28 February, 1, 2 March 1998
Pakistan won by 29 runs

Pakistan 259 (Azhar Mahmood 132, A.A. Donald 5 for 79) and 226 (Saeed Anwar 118, S.M. Pollock 6 for 50); South Africa 231 (S.M. Pollock 70 not out, H.D. Ackerman 57, Shoaib Akhtar 5 for 43) and 225 (M.V. Boucher 52, Mushtaq Ahmed 6 for 78)

This was the second Test of a three-match series. South Africa gambled by not including a spinner in its line-up. The selection of four pace bowlers no doubt prompted Cronje to field after winning the toss. He was not let down as Donald and Pollock ripped through Pakistan's top order. It was Azhar Mahmood who again came to the visitors' rescue. Coming in at 5 for 89, he scored his second consecutive century, making 132 from 163 balls with 24 boundaries. With the help of Shoaib Akhtar, 6, and Fazl-E-Akbar, 0 not out, 106 runs were added for the last two wickets.

South Africa's reply was disappointing. Ackerman, on debut, posted a stylish half-century but it was the aggressive Pollock who held the innings together. He finished unbeaten on 70 as the home team trailed by 28 on the first innings. Shoaib Akhtar, bowling at a brisk pace, was able to get reverse-swing which caused no end of trouble for the home team's batsmen. The South African batsmen also had difficulty picking the deliveries of the wily Mushtaq Ahmed.

Saeed Anwar and Aamir Sohail then posted the first opening stand century against South Africa. Saeed Anwar returned to form with an authoritative hundred. Pollock produced an inspired spell claiming five wickets in 43 balls as Pakistan lost its last nine wickets for 67 runs, leaving the home team 255 for victory. A difficult task on a wearing pitch.

Difficult became almost impossible when eight wickets had fallen for 133. However, Boucher and De Villiers offered a glimmer of hope with an 86-run partnership for the ninth wicket. Waqar Younis came back to remove Boucher and Donald, leaving De Villiers 46 not out. Mushtaq Ahmed's six wicket haul took him past 150 Test wickets in his 36th match.

## INDIA v AUSTRALIA 1997-98

Chinambaram Stadium, Madras
6, 7, 8, 9, 10 March 1998
India won by 179 runs

India 257 (N.S. Sidhu 62, N.R. Mongia 58, R.S. Dravid 52) and 4 for 418 dec. (S.R. Tendulkar 155 not out, N.S. Sidhu 64, M. Azharuddin 64, R.S. Dravid 56); Australia 328 (I.A. Healy 90, M.E. Waugh 66, G.R. Robertson 57) and 168

In the end India scored a resounding win but it was not before Australia had gained a first-innings lead of 70 runs in a match that ebbed and flowed constantly.

Azharuddin won the toss and batted on a pitch that looked likely to favour the spinners late in the match. Mongia and Sidhu took full advantage of the conditions to post a century for the opening partnership. Mongia went at 122 and when Mark Waugh ran Sidhu out four runs later, the stage was set for the classic confrontation with the world's premier batsman, Tendulkar, to face the best leg-spinner of this era and perhaps any era, Warne. After one slashing boundary, Tendulkar went for an extravagant drive and was superbly held by Taylor at slip. First round to Warne.

Apart from a patient fifty by Dravid, 26 from Azharuddin and Kumble's 30, the Indian total of 257 was disappointing after the fine start. Warne and the off-spinner Robertson picked up four wickets apiece.

Australia struggled in reply. Slater, in his first Test for eighteen months, fell cheaply as did the captain Taylor. Of the top order only Mark Waugh, promoted to number three because of an injury to Blewett, played to his best form. The visitors' handy lead resulted from a determined eighth-wicket partnership of 90 by Healy and debutant Robertson. Kumble returned to his best with a four-wicket haul while the left-arm orthodox spinner Raju provided steady support to claim 3 for 54 from 32 overs.

Sidhu's positive approach soon had the Indian deficit wiped out and his dismissal for 64 with the score 2 for 115 set the stage for round two of the classic confrontation. This time it was the bat's turn to take the honours. Tendulkar played one of the great innings, and his fifteenth Test century included 14 fours and four sixes. Tendulkar's superb knock allowed Azharuddin to declare late on the fourth day, leaving Australia 348 to win from a minimum of 105 overs.

Slater and Taylor both fell cheaply so Australia's task of saving the game on the final day was always going to be difficult. The cause was not helped by some doubtful umpiring decisions. Mark Waugh, Reiffel, Steve Waugh and Ponting could all consider themselves unlucky. The final three had been given out by English umpire George Sharp. Warne hit lustily at the end for 35 while Healy defended doggedly and finished unbeaten on 32. The Indian spinners claimed nine of the ten wickets. Kumble was again the best with 4 for 51. Raju captured 3 for 26 and Chauhan 2 for 66.

## WEST INDIES v ENGLAND 1997-98

Kensington Oval, Bridgetown, Barbados
12, 13, 14, 15, 16 March 1998
Match drawn

England 403 (M.R. Ramprakash 154, G.P. Thorpe 103, C.L. Hooper 5 for 80) and 3 for 233 dec. (M.A. Atherton 64); West Indies 262 (C.B. Lambert 55) and 2 for 112 (P.A. Wallace 61)

This match proved to be one of the most exciting draws of recent years. West Indies selected a pair of unconventional openers, Wallace and Lambert, and included Holder to bat in the middle order, leaving out Campbell, Williams and Adams from the top six that had played in the first four Tests.

Lara sent England in to bat and almost immediately the visitors were on the back foot as they went to lunch at 4 for 55. It could have been worse as Ambrose had dropped a return catch from Ramprakash. Back spasms prevented Thorpe from continuing after the interval but a positive approach from his replacement, Russell, slowly turned the game England's way. Thorpe returned after Russell's dismissal and with Ramprakash continued to restore the visitors' position. Both batsmen scored centuries, a maiden Test hundred for Ramprakash being one of the most emotional moments in recent history.

The West Indies started their innings at breakneck speed with Wallace smashing nine boundaries from 51 balls in a knock of 45. On the third day England played tight intelligent cricket to restrict the free-scoring Caribbean batsmen. After the flying start and an 82-run opening partnership, the West Indies trailed by 141 runs.

The visitors consolidated their position on the fourth day, allowing Atherton to declare at 3 for 233. The West Indies' target was 375 from 109 overs. Lambert and Wallace scored 71 from 19 overs on the fourth evening which set up the intriguing scenario of 304 from 90 overs on the final day.

Unfortunately, rain restricted play to just 18.3 overs with both teams claiming they could have won the match.

## SOUTH AFRICA v SRI LANKA 1997-98

Newlands, Capetown
18, 19, 20, 21, 22 March 1998
South Africa won by 70 runs

South Africa 418 (D.J. Cullinan 113, S.M. Pollock 92, G. Kirsten 62) and 264 (W.J. Cronje 74 and D.J. Cullinan 68); Sri Lanka 306 (P.A. De Silva 77, M.S. Atapattu 60) and 306 (M.S. Atapattu 71, G.P. Wickremasinghe 51)

This was the first Test in a two-match series and offered a number of significant highlights including the Test match debut of Makhaya Ntini, the first black African to represent South Africa at this level.

Cullinan returned to the South African line-up and compiled an attractive century that was to be the backbone of the home team's first innings. Pollock proved his worth as an all-rounder by holding the lower order together with an aggressive 92. He added 95 for the seventh wicket with the dependable Boucher.

Atapattu and De Silva, both playing at their best, added 129 for the third wicket to dominate the visitors' reply. Perhaps Sri Lanka should have made more than 306 as all but two batsmen reached double figures. Pollock with four wickets and Donald with three were the pick of the home team's bowlers.

South Africa, with a lead of 112, consolidated its position on the back of some excellent batting by Cullinan, Cronje and Kallis. They were pinned down for long spells by accurate bowling from the Sri Lankan spinners, Muralitharan and Jayasuriya. Both bowlers claimed four wickets giving Muralitharan eight for the match.

Chasing 377, the visitors made a bold attempt at victory after losing the aggressive opener Jayasuriya for a duck. Atapattu again played stylishly while Wickremasinghe smashed a half-century off just 39 balls. Fittingly, Ntini bowled Wickremasinghe to end the match.

For the second Test in a row, the South African keeper Boucher took six dismissals in an innings.

## WEST INDIES v ENGLAND 1997-98

Recreation Ground, St John's, Antigua
20, 21, 22, 23, 24 March 1998
West Indies won by an innings and 52 runs

England 127 and 321 (N. Hussain 106, G.P. Thorpe 84 not out, A.J. Stewart 79); West Indies 7 for 500 dec. (C.L. Hooper 108 not out, C.B. Lambert 104, P.A. Wallace 92, B.C. Lara 89)

England had a chance to level the series by winning this final match. However, luck was with the home team as Lara won another vital toss and invited England to bat on a wet wicket that would only get better as the match progressed.

Rain restricted play to less than 21 overs on the first day as England lost Atherton and Butcher in the difficult conditions. There was a general consensus that the covers at the Recreation Ground were inadequate for a Test venue and that spectators in attendance should have seen more cricket on the opening day.

Two for 35 overnight became all out for 127 as the visitors capitulated in a most disappointing performance. The little Trinidad leg spinner, Ramnarine captured four wickets while Ambrose claimed three and Walsh two.

Once again Lambert and Wallace smashed the England attack, putting on 167 for the first wicket. The run feast continued as first Lara and then Hooper helped themselves to big scores on the ever-improving pitch. The declaration was made when the score reached 500.

Ambrose removed Atherton and Butcher cheaply but Stewart and Hussain set about restoring some pride into the visitor's batting. Stewart, in particular, was in majestic form. Poor weather prevented play until after lunch on the final day then Hussain and Thorpe carried on until after tea. The partnership ended with a disastrous misunderstanding that saw Hussain run out for 106. The dark clouds hovering over the ground produced no rain as Walsh and Ramnarine finished off the match with England losing its last six wickets for 26.

The West Indies had retained the Wisden Trophy, winning the series three to one.

## ZIMBABWE v PAKISTAN 1997-98

Harare Sports Club, Harare
21, 22, 23, 24, 25 March 1998
Pakistan won by three wickets

Zimbabwe 277 (G.J. Whittall 62, M.W. Goodwin 53, B.C. Strang 53) and 268 (M.W. Goodwin 81); Pakistan 354 (Mohammad Wasim 192, Mushtaq Ahmed 57) and 7 for 192 (Saeed Anwar 65, Yousuf Youhana 52)

This was the second of back-to-back Tests in a two-match series that produced plenty of interesting cricket. Both teams had their chances to win the first match at Bulawayo while this second Test fluctuated in a similar way.

After winning the toss, Zimbabwe appeared to be cruising at 2 for 141 just before tea. Five wickets fell for twelve runs as Pakistan gained the ascendancy. Whittal and Bryan Strang, scoring at four runs an over, restored the innings with a partnership of 110. Waqar Younis was the pick of the visitors' bowlers taking 4 for 47 from 20 hostile overs.

Zimbabwe's seamers frustrated Pakistan's batsmen to the extent that the visitors were reduced to 8 for 187 before Mohammad Wasim and Mushtaq Ahmed added a match-winning 147-run partnership for the ninth wicket. The home team had only themselves to blame as Mohammad Wasim was dropped on 81 and 125.

Goodwin and Andy Flower rescued Zimbabwe from 3 for 38 with a 95-run partnership to once again give the home team some hope of victory. Streak and Strang hit lustily towards the end of the innings to leave Pakistan a target of 192. Saeed Anwar and the inexperienced Yousef Youhana steered the visitors to a hard fought but well-earned victory. Zimbabwe lacked the confidence, and the belief in themselves, to win at this highest level.

## INDIA v AUSTRALIA 1997-98

Chinnaswamy Stadium, Bangalore
25, 26, 27, 28 March 1998
Australia won by eight wickets

India 424 (S.R. Tendulkar 177, N.S. Sidhu 74) and 169 (M.S. Kasprowicz 5 for 28); Australia 400 (M.E. Waugh 153 not out, M.J. Slater 91, D.S. Lehmann 52, A. Kumble 6 for 98) and 2 for 195 (M.A. Taylor 102 not out)

Australia had lost the rubber by the time the teams had assembled in Bangalore for the third and final Test but they were able to salvage some pride with an eight-wicket victory in a match that fluctuated throughout.

India batted after winning the toss and once again Sidhu gave them a flying start. He set the stage for another Tendulkar masterpiece. Tendulkar's innings of 177 rivalled the 155 not-out in the first Test for its majestic strokeplay. His blazing innings carried the home team to an imposing total of 424. Warne and the new ball bowler Dale, in his first Test, finished with three wickets apiece.

With a positive approach, Australia was able to get within 24 runs of India's score. Slater led the way with a stylish 91 but it was Mark Waugh who was outstanding. With a mixture of deadbat defence and slashing strokes he posted his highest Test score of 153 not out. Lehmann, with 52 in his first Test innings, and Warne with 33 provided valuable support. Kumble was again the outstanding bowler for India and he finished with 6 for 98 from 41.3 overs. At the end of the third day India was 123 runs ahead with seven wickets in hand and Tendulkar and Azharuddin at the crease. A tight finish was expected although the home side had a slight advantage. Kasprowicz turned the game Australia's way with some magnificent bowling. He caught and bowled Tendulkar with a slower ball then yorked Azharuddin with a fast inswinger. The tail offered little resistance as Kasprowicz finished with a match-winning 5 for 28 from 18 overs.

The target was 194 for an Australian victory. Taylor and Slater began aggressively and a 91-run opening stand just about made the game safe for the visitors. Taylor posted his 18th century as Australia cruised to an eight-wicket win to salvage something from another disappointing series on the sub-continent.

# PART 2

# TEST CRICKET LISTS

## NOTABLE DEBUTS

1. G. Gunn (England), on holidays in Australia for health reasons in 1907-08, was called into the injury-hit England side for the Sydney Test. Playing his very first innings on Australian soil — and his first Test match innings — Gunn hit a brilliant 119 in two and a half hours and followed up with 74 in the second innings.
2. H.L. Collins (Australia) began his Test career with consecutive scores of 70 and 104 (Sydney), 64 (Melbourne) and 162 (Adelaide) against England 1920-21.
3. A.L. Valentine (West Indies) making his debut in the match against England at Manchester in 1950, took the first eight wickets to fall.
4. L.G. Rowe (West Indies) made history by scoring 214 and 100* in his first Test match against New Zealand at Kingston in 1971-72. Rowe is the only batsman to make 100 in each innings on his Test debut, and only one of three players — R.E. Foster, (England) and D.S.B.P. Kuruppu, (Sri Lanka) being the others to make a double-century on debut.
5. R.E. Foster (England) making his debut against Australia at Melbourne 1903-04, after an uncertain start, helped himself to a glorious 287, with 38 boundaries in 420 minutes. Foster added 192 for the fifth wicket with G.H. Hirst, 115 for the ninth with R.E. Relf, and 130 for the tenth with W. Rhodes, the latter being scored in an amazing 66 minutes.
6. D.S.B.P.Kuruppu (Sri Lanka), achieved a rare feat by being on the field throughout his maiden Test. He took 776 minutes to reach his double-century — the slowest 200 in first class cricket — and batted for 777 minutes for his 201* v New Zealand at Colombo in 1986-87.
7. R.A.L. Massie (Australia), confounding the opposition batsmen with an astonishing display of swing-bowling in overcast conditions, demolished England in the Lord's Test of 1972, taking 8 for 53 and 8 for 84 for an Australian record Test match 'bag' of 16 wickets.
8. N.D. Hirwani (India), exacting great turn on an under-prepared pitch, exploited the weakness of the West Indies' batsmen to take 8 for 61 and 8 for 75 at Madras in 1987-88 to establish an Indian record for wickets in a Test.
9. H.B. Taber (Australia), playing against South Africa at Johannesburg in 1966-67, caught seven and stumped one, a 'bag' never equalled by a wicket-keeper in his first Test. *Note:* A.T.W. Grout (Australia) caught six in an innings in his first Test, against South Africa in 1957-58.
10. J.E. Barrett became the first Australian player to carry his bat through a completed innings in a Test against England. Barrett scored 67* in Australia's second innings at Lord's in 1890 — his first Test match.
11. F. Martin (England) took twelve wickets in his first Test appearance against Australia at the Oval in 1890. His figures were 6 for 50 and 6 for 52.
12. A.E. Trott (Australia) in his first Test, played against England at the Adelaide Oval in January 1895, scored 110 runs (38* and 72*) without being dismissed and bowled unchanged throughout the second innings taking eight wickets for 43 runs.
13. E.G. Arnold (England) took the wicket of the great Victor Trumper with his first delivery in a Test match.
14. A. Warren (England) took five wickets for 57 against Australia at Leeds in 1905 in his only Test match.
15. G.M. Parker, a South African cricketer playing Bradford League cricket during the South African tour of England in 1924, was called up to play for his country in the first Test at Birmingham although not a member of the touring party. He took six wickets for 152 in England's only innings.
16. W.R. Hammond (England) scored 51 runs and took five wickets in his first Test — against South Africa at Johannesburg 1927-28.
17. M.J.C. Allom (England), in his first Test against New Zealand in 1930, took four wickets in five balls, including the hat-trick.
18. H.D. Smith (New Zealand) bowled E. Paynter (England) with his first ball in Test cricket — his only wicket in his only Test.
19. C.S. Marriott (England) took eleven wickets in his first and only Test against the West Indies at the Oval in 1933.
20. J.C. Laker (England), playing against West Indies at Bridgetown during the 1947-48 season, took 7 for 103 in his first Test innings.
21. H.H.H. Johnson (West Indies) played in his first Test at the age of 37 when he appeared against England at Kingston during 1947-48. He took 5 for 41 in the first innings and 5 for 55 in the second.
22. A.T.W. Grout (Australia) keeping wickets against South Africa in his first Test (1957-58) set a then world Test record of six catches in an innings.
23. C.A. Milton (England) played his first Test against New Zealand at Leeds in 1958. He scored 104* in England's only innings and became the first English player to be on the ground throughout an entire Test match — although there was no play on the first two days.

24. J.D.F. Larter (England) against Pakistan at The Oval, 1962 took nine wickets in his first Test.

25. P.J. Petherick (New Zealand) took a hat-trick in his first Test against Pakistan at Lahore in October 1976. In the same match, Javed Miandad scored 163 and 25* in his first Test.

26. Yajurvindra Singh (India) equalled two Test records in his first Test. Playing against England in Bangalore in the fourth Test of the 1976-77 season, he took five catches in the first innings and a total of seven for the match — records for non-wicket-keepers.

27. R.A. Duff (Australia), in his first Test, played against England at Melbourne during 1901-02, top-scored in the first innings with 32 and again in the second with 104. He also shared in the first hundred partnership for the tenth wicket with W.W. Armstrong who was playing in his first Test.

28. C.V. Grimmett (Australia) took eleven wickets in his first Test (England v Sydney in 1924-25). He took 5 for 45 in the first innings and 6 for 37 in the second.

29. B.R. Taylor (New Zealand), is the only Test match cricketer to make 100 and take five wickets in an innings on debut. He scored 105 and took 5 for 86 against India at Calcutta in 1964-65.

30. A.V. Bedser (England) took eleven wickets in each of his first two Test matches. In his first, against India at Lord's in June 1946, he took 7 for 49 and 4 for 96. In his second appearance the following month at Manchester, he captured 4 for 41 and 7 for 52.

31. J.K. Lever (England) scored 53 and took 7 for 46 and 3 for 24 in his first Test (v India at Delhi in 1976-77.

32. M. Azharuddin (India) began his Test career with 110 at Calcutta, 48 and 105 at Madras, and 122 and 54* at Kanpur — all against England in 1984-85.

33. A.I.C. Dodemaide (Australia), a late replacement for the injured B.A. Reid, scored 50 in his first innings and took 6 for 58 in the second innings against New Zealand at Melbourne in 1987-88.

34. When A.C. Hudson scored 163 and 0 against the West Indies at Bridgetown in 1991-92, he became the first South African to score a century on Test debut and the first player to score a 'ton' and a 'duck' in his first Test.

35. D.L. Houghton (Zimbabwe) emulated the feat of C.Bannerman (Australia v England at Melbourne 1876-77) by scoring a century in his country's inaugural Test.

36. D.W. Fleming (Australia) captured 4 for 75 and 3 for 86, including the hat-trick, against Pakistan at Rawalpindi.

37. G.S. Blewett (Australia) followed his 102* and 12 against England at Adelaide in 1994-95 with 20 and 115 at Perth.

38. C.I. Dunusinghe (Sri Lanka) scored 11 and 91 against New Zealand at Napier in 1994-95 as well as taking seven catches behind the stumps.

39. D.G. Cork (England) captured 7 for 43 against the West Indies at Lord's in 1995.

40. S. Ganguly (India) became the third player to score a century in his first two Test innings, when he scored 131 at Lord's and 136 and 48 at Nottingham, against England in 1996.

41. Ali Naqvi (115) and Azhar Mahmood (128*) playing for Pakistan against South Africa at Rawalpindi[2] in 1997-98, provided the first instance that two players scored centuries on debut in the same Test.

## INGLORIOUS DEBUTS

1. M. Leyland was dismissed for a 'duck' during England's only innings in the third Test against West Indies at The Oval in 1928 — his first appearance for his country.

2. D.G. Bradman scored only 18 and 1 in his debut in the first Test against England at Brisbane in the 1928-29 season. He was subsequently dropped from the team for the second Test but reinstated for the third, scoring 79 and 112.

3. L. Hutton (England) scored a 'duck' and 1 in his debut Test match, against New Zealand at Lord's in 1937. In his second match, at Manchester, he made 100 and 14.

4. I.M. Chappell (Australia) made a modest eleven runs and bowled 26 overs without a wicket in his debut Test against Pakistan at Melbourne in 1964-65.

5. New Zealand batsman J.M. Parker fractured a bone in his hand whilst fielding against Pakistan at Wellington in 1973 and was unable to bat in his debut match.

6. G.A. Gooch (England) recorded a pair of 'ducks' in his first Test which was against Australia at Birmingham in 1975.

7. In 1991-92, S.K. Warne (Australia) took 1 for 150 against India at Sydney on his Test debut.

## A NOTABLE UMPIRING DEBUT

Umpire W.E. Alley, standing in his first Test match — England against India at Birmingham 1974 — was given little time to settle in. He was required to make a decision about the first ball of the match. His verdict? S.M.Gavaskar, out, caught behind by Knott, bowled Arnold.

## RAPID RISES

1. In the first-ever Test at Melbourne in 1876-77, J.R. Hodges and T.K. Kendall made their first-class debuts in their first Test appearance.

2. Joseph Emile Patrick McMaster (England) deserves his spot in the record books. His Test appearance for England (v South Africa in 1888-89) was his only match in first-class cricket. As he scored a 'duck', he must be the only cricketer of Test match status who never scored a run in his entire first-class career.

2. L. Hone of Ireland kept wicket for England against Australia in 1878-79 but never appeared in English county cricket. (This was his third first-class match.)

3. B.A.F. Grieve (England) appeared in only three first-class matches, of which two (against South Africa in 1888-89) were Test matches.

4. Edric Leadbeater (England) was flown out to India as a replacement for A.E.G. Rhodes during the 1951-52 season. He played his first Test before being capped for his county.

5. G.M. Parker (South Africa) came into the South African Test side (against England at Birmingham in 1924) from the Bradford League for only his second first-class match. He later played in another Test that year — his entire first-class career comprised three games, two of which were Tests.

6. D.W. Carr (England) played his first first-class game for Kent on May 27 1909, aged 37. He was chosen for Gentlemen v Players on July 8, made his debut in county cricket on July 29, and appeared for England against Australia on August 9. It was his seventh first-class game and he had risen to Test honours within ten weeks of his first-class debut.

7. A.L. Valentine and S. Ramadhin (West Indies) were selected to tour England in 1950 after each had played in only two first-class games.

8. S.F. Barnes (England) was selected to tour Australia in 1901-02 after only six first-class games and 13 first-class wickets.

9. I.A.R. Peebles (England) played for his country against South Africa at Johannesburg 1927-28, before he had made his debut in county cricket.

10. A.G. Chipperfield (Australia) was selected to tour England in 1934 after only three first-class games.

11. T.R. McKibbin (Australia) played against England in 1894-95 in his sixth first-class match. J.J.Ferris, J. Darling, A.G. Fairfax, E.L. a'Beckett, D.G. Bradman, W.J. O'Reilly, J.R. Thomson, I.C. Davis and G.M. Wood were other Australians to make their Test debuts within ten matches of their first-class debut.

12. G.N. Francis (West Indies) had never played a first-class game before touring England in 1923. (No Tests were played that year).

13. G.J. Bonnor (Australia) was selected to tour England in 1880 without ever having played a first-class game.

14. G.E. Vivian (New Zealand) was selected to tour India, Pakistan and England in 1965 without having appeared in a first-class match. He made his Test debut in the against India at Calcutta in 1964-65.

15. C.C. Griffith (West Indies) was chosen for his first Test against England in Port-of-Spain in 1959-60, after only one first-class match.

16. M.D. Marshall (West Indies) was selected for the tour of India 1978-79 after only one first-class appearance and played in his first Test (against India in Bombay) after only three matches.

17. J.E.F. Beck (South Africa 1953-54) and J.C.Alabaster (India 1955-56) were chosen for New Zealand tours without having made a first-class appearance and made their Test debuts after five and one match respectively.

18. Wasim Akram (Pakistan) was selected to tour New Zealand in 1984-85 after two first-class games and made his Test debut in Auckland in his fourth match.

19. A. Ranatunga (Sri Lanka) made his first-class debut against the touring English team in 1982 and made his Test debut in his next game a week later.

20. G.F. Labrooy (Sri Lanka) was chosen to tour India in 1986-87 without any first-class experience and made his Test debut in only his second game.

21. Saleem Elahi (Pakistan) made his first-class debut on the tour of Australia in 1995-96 and his Test debut in his third first-class match. He had made his Limited Over International debut two months earlier (scoring a century).

## RELATED TEST PLAYERS

### Father and Son and Grandson

G.A. and R.G.A. Headley (West Indies) and D.W. Headley (England)

### Father and Two Sons

N.B. Amarnath and his sons M. and S. Amarnath (India)

W.A.Hadlee and his sons D.R. and R.J.(New Zealand)

### Fathers and Sons

N.B. and M. S.Amarnath (India)

W.M. and R.W. Anderson (New Zealand)

W.P. and G.E. Bradburn (New Zealand)

A.R. and M.A. Butcher (England)

B.L. and C.L. Cairns (New Zealand)

M.C. and C.S. Cowdrey (England)

D.K. and A.D. Gaekwad (India)

E.J. and S.E. Gregory (Australia)

W.A. and D.R., R.J.Hadlee (New Zealand)

J. Hardstaff, snr and J. Hardstaff, jnr (England)

P.G.Z. and C.Z. Harris (New Zealand)

G.A. and R.G.A. Headley (West Indies)

F. Hearne (England and South Africa) and G.A.L. Hearne (South Africa)

L. and R.A. Hutton (England)

M. Jahangir Khan (India) and Majid Khan (Pakistan)

J.D. and D.T. Lindsay (South Africa)

V.L. and S.V. Manjrekar (India)

M.H. and A.V. Mankad (India)

F.T. and F.G. Mann (England)

Hanif Mohammad and Shoaib Mohammad (Pakistan)

Nazar Mohammad and Mudassar Nazar (Pakistan)

A.W. and A.D. Nourse (South Africa)

J.H. and J.M. Parks (England)

Nawab of Pataudi, snr (England and India) and Nawab of Pataudi, jnr (India)

P.M. and S.M. Pollock (South Africa)

Pankaj and Pranab Roy (India)

O.C. and A.P.H. Scott (West Indies)

M.J. and A.J. Stewart (England)

F.W. and M.W. Tate (England)

C.L. and D.C.H.Townsend (England)

L.R. and L. Tuckett (South Africa)

H.G. and G.E. Vivian (New Zealand)

S. Wazir Ali (India) and Khalid Wazir (Pakistan)

## Four Brothers

Hanif, Mushtaq, Sadiq and Wazir Mohammad (Pakistan)

*Hanif, Mushtaq and Sadiq all played against New Zealand at Karachi[1] in 1969-70*

## Three Brothers

G.S., I.M. and T.M. Chappell (Australia)

E.M., G.F. and W.G. Grace (England)

Manzoor Elahi, Saleem Elahi and Zahoor Elahi (Pakistan)

A., F. and G.G. Hearne (England) — F. Hearne also played for South Africa

A., D. and S. Ranatunga (Sri Lanka)

A.B., L.J. and V.M. Tancred (South Africa)

All three Grace brothers played against Australia at The Oval in 1880.

A. and G.G. Hearne (E) and F. Hearne (SA) all played in the match between South Africa and England at Cape Town in 1891-92.

## Two Brothers

### Australia

K.A. and R.G. Archer

A.C. and C. Bannerman

J. and R. Benaud

G. and W.F. Giffen

D.W. and E. Gregory

M.R. and R.N. Harvey

C.E. and R.W. McLeod

A.E. and G.H.S. Trott

H. and J.W. Trumble

M.E. and S.R. Waugh

### England

A.E.R. and A.H.H. Gilligan

A.W. and I.A. Greig

G. and J.R. Gunn

D.W. and P.E. Richardson

C.L. and R.A. Smith

C.T. and G.B. Studd

G.E. and J.T. Tyldesley

C.E.M. and E.R. Wilson

A.J. and B.C. Hollioake

### South Africa

P.A.M. and R.H.M. Hands

G. and P.N. Kirsten

A.J. and D.B. Pithey

P.M. and R.G. Pollock

A.R. and W.H.M. Richards

A.M.B. and E.A.B. Rowan

S.D. and S.J. Snooke

G.L. and L.E. Tapscott

D. and H.W. Taylor

H.F. and W.W. Wade

### West Indies

D.S. and E.S. Atkinson

F.J. and J.H. Cameron

C.M. and R.J. Christiani
B.A. and C.A. Davis
G.C. and R.S. Grant
N.E. and R.E. Marshall
E.L. and W.H. St Hill
J.B. and V.H. Stollmeyer

## New Zealand

B.P. and J.G. Bracewell
J.J. and M.D. Crowe
D.R. and R.J. Hadlee
G.P. and H.J.Howarth
J.M. and N. M. Parker
P.A. and M.J. Horne

## India

M. and S. Amarnath
L. Amar Singh and L. Ramji
A.L. and M.L. Apte
B. P. and S.P. Gupte
A. G. Kripal Singh and A. G. Milkha Singh
C.K. and C.S. Nayudu
S. Nazir Ali and S. Wazir Ali

## Pakistan

Rameez Raja and Wasim Raja
Azmat Rana and Shafqat Rana
Pervez Sajjad and Waqar Hassan
Saeed Ahmed and Younis Ahmed
Moin Khan and Nadeem Khan

## Sri Lanka

M.S. and S. Wettimuny

## Zimbabwe

A. and G.W. Flower
G.J. and J.A. Rennie
B.C. and P.A. Strang

*The Flower, Rennie and Strang brothers played for Zimbabwe against New Zealand at Harare in 1997-98.*

# GREAT CRICKETING FAMILIES

1. Gregory (Australia). The family produced four Test cricketers, two of whom (Dave and Syd) captained Australia. Father of the clan was Edward William who played in Sydney in the 1820s. Four of his children played cricket for NSW — Dave (Australia's first captain), Ned, Charlie and Arthur. Ned's sons were Syd and Charles (who scored the first triple-century in a first-class game in Australia). Jack, who arrived on the scene in the 1920s, was the grandson of Edward William — a cricket star a century after his grandfather.

2. Mohammad (Pakistan). At least one Mohammad brother represented Pakistan in 100 of that country's first 101 Tests in 27 years of Test cricket between 1952-80. A fifth brother, Raees, was once Pakistan's twelfth man against India (1954-55). Three brothers — Hanif, Mushtaq and Sadiq — all played together in one Test against New Zealand in 1969 and all batted and bowled during the match. Between them Hanif, Mushtaq, Sadiq and Wazir aggregated almost 11,000 Test runs with 29 centuries. They have also held 115 catches and taken 80 wickets.

3. Amarnath (India). Father Lala and son Surinder are the only father-son combination to record centuries on debut. Second son Mohinder narrowly missed becoming one of the few to score a century in each innings when he made 90 and 100 against Australia in Perth in 1977-78.

4. Bannerman (Australia). Elder brother Charles faced the first ball bowled in Test cricket, scored the first run, the first 50 and the first 100. He was also the first Australian to make a century in England, New Zealand and Canada. Younger brother Alec scored the first run in a Test on English soil.

5. Chappell (Australia). Grandsons of Victor Richardson, Ian, Greg and Trevor represent only the fourth set of three brothers to appear in Test cricket. Ian and Greg captained Australia more than 50 times, are the only brothers to score centuries in each innings of a Test, and were the first brothers to score a century in the same Test. They were the first set of brothers who each scored over 5000 Test runs.

6. Waugh (Australia). Steve and Mark — the first set of twins to play Test cricket — became the first set of brothers to play together in more than 50 Tests and the second set of brothers to each score over 5000 Test runs.

## TEST CRICKETERS WHO BATTED RIGHT-HANDED AND BOWLED LEFT-ARMED

### *Australia*

M.J. Bennett
R.J. Bright
H.L. Collins
A.R. Dell
L.O. Fleetwood-Smith
J.B. Gannon
T.G. Hogan
R.J. Inverarity
B.P. Julian
C.G. Macartney
I. Meckiff
D.J. Sincock
E.R.H. Toshack
M.R. Whitney
W.J. Whitty

### *England*

J.C. Balderstone
R.G. Barlow
C. Blythe
J.B. Bolus
J. Briggs
H.R. Bromley-Davenport
S.J.E. Brown
D.B. Carr
D.C.S. Compton
C. Cook
G. Cook
N.G.B. Cook
P.H. Edmonds
P.R. Foster
A.F. Giles
M.J. Hilton
G.H. Hirst
J.L. Hopwood
J. Iddon
R.K. Illingworth
I.J. Jones
J.K. Lever
G.A.R. Lock
B.W. Luckhurst
A.D. Mullally
G.A.E. Paine
C.W.L. Parker
M.M. Patel
W. Rhodes
F.E. Rumsey
A.M. Smith
D.S. Steele
P.C.R. Tufnell
D.L. Underwood
H. Verity
W. Voce
A. Waddington
P.M. Walker
J.C. White
H.I. Young
J.A. Young

### *South Africa*

P.R. Adams
W.H. Ashley
C.P. Carter
G.A. Chevalier
M.K. Elgie
A.E. Hall
G.A. Kempis
M.J. Macaulay
A.H. McKinnon
Q. McMillan
J.B. Plimsoll
N.A. Quinn
A. Rose-Innes
G.A. Rowe
P.L. van der Merwe

### *West Indies*

M.R. Bynoe
G.M. Carew
B.D. Julien
R.R. Jumadeen
C.B. Lambert
S. Shivnarine
A.L. Valentine
F.M.M. Worrell

### New Zealand

G.I. Allott
S.L. Boock
T.B. Burtt
M.E. Chapple
R.O. Collinge
F.E. Fisher
N. Gallichan
E.J. Gray
A.F. Lissette
J.F. M.Morrison
D.R. O'Sullivan
M.W. Priest
D.G. Sewell
G.B. Troup
B.W. Yuile

### India

B.S. Bedi
R.J.D. Jamshedji
Maninder Singh
M.H. Mankad
Mushtaq Ali
R.G. Patel
A.K. Sharma
R.J. Shastri
K.K. Tarapore
S.L. Venkatapathy Raju

### Pakistan

Inzamamul Haq
Kabir Khan
Liaqat Ali
Mufasir-ul-Haq
Nadeem Ghauri
Nadeem Khan
Pervez Sajjad
Saleem Jaffer
Shujauddin

### Sri Lanka

S.D. Anurasiri
M.L.C.N. Bandaratilleke
S. Jeganathan
A.K. Kuruppuarachchi
A.N. Ranasinghe
K.J. Silva
R.G.C.E. Wijesuriya
P.K. Wijetunge

### Zimbabwe

M.H. Dekker
G.W. Flower
M.P. Jarvis
B.C. Strang

## TEST CRICKETERS WHO BATTED LEFT-ARMED AND BOWLED RIGHT-HANDED

### Australia

J. Angel
D.D. Blackie
I.W. Callen
S.H. Cook
R.M. Cowper
A.C. Dale
L.S. Darling
R.A. Gaunt
J.M. Gregory
R.N. Harvey
T.V. Hohns
W.P. Howell
J.L. Langer
T.J. Laughlin
E.L. McCormick
K.D. Mackay
T.R. McKibbin
R.W. McLeod
A.L. Mann
R.W. Marsh
R.L.A. Massie
G.R.J. Matthews
L.C. Mayne
J.D.A. O'Connor
W.J. O'Reilly
G.F. Rorke
B.K. Shepherd
P.L. Taylor
T.R. Veivers
K.C. Wessels
S. Young

## England

R.W. Barber
J. Birkenshaw
B.C. Broad
M.A. Butcher
D.B. Close
G.R. Dilley
J.H. Edrich
R.M. Ellison
J.A. Flavell
G. Fowler
D.I. Gower
K. Higgs
J.T. Ikin
H. Morris
M.S. Nichols
C.M. Old
P.H. Parfitt
R.T.D. Perks
J.S.E. Price
G. Pullar
P.E. Richardson
T.F. Smailes
J.B. Statham
R. Subba Row
R. Tattersall
G.P. Thorpe
C.L. Townsend
D.W. White

## South Africa

D.J. Cullinan
G. Kirsten
J.F.W. Nicolson
A.W. Nourse
R.G. Pollock
K.C. Wessels

## West Indies

C.E.L. Ambrose
M.C. Carew
S. Chanderpaul
J.D.C. Goddard
H.A. Gomes
A.F.G. Griffith
A.B. Howard
A.I. Kallicharran
B.C. Lara
P.D. Lashley
C.H. Lloyd
N.A.M. McLean
C.A. McWatt
F.L. Reifer
G.C. Shillingford

## New Zealand

V.R. Brown
D.C. Cleverley
G.F. Cresswell
B.A. Edgar
S.P. Fleming
R.J. Hadlee
C.Z. Harris
E.G. McLeod
L.S.M. Miller
B.D. Morrison
G.W.F. Overton
J.F. Reid
I.M. Sinclair
M.C. Snedden
B.R. Taylor
R.G. Twose
J.T.C. Vaughan
G.E. Vivian
J.G. Wright

## India

S. Amarnath
N.J. Contractor
S.C. Ganguly
V.G. Kambli
A.G. Milka Singh
S.V. Nayak
A.M. Pai

## Pakistan

Sadiq Mohammad
Shadab Kabir
Wasim Raja

### Sri Lanka

F.S. Ahangama
R.P. Arnold
E.A.R. de Silva
A.P. Gurusinha
R.S. Kalpage
M.A.W.R. Madurasinghe
A. Ranatunga
S. Ranatunga
J.R. Ratnayeke
C.P. Senanayake
H.P. Tillekeratne
K.P.J. Warnaweera

### Zimbabwe

A. Flower
S.G. Peall
A.H. Shah

## COMPLETE SIDE DISMISSED TWICE IN A DAY

| | | | | | |
|---|---|---|---|---|---|
| India | (58 + 82) | v | England Manchester | 3rd day | 1952 |

## HIGHEST SCORES FOR EACH BATTING POSITION

| No. | | | | | | | |
|---|---|---|---|---|---|---|---|
| 1 | 364 | L. Hutton | England | v | Australia | The Oval | 1938 |
| 2 | 325 | A. Sandham | England | v | West Indies | Kingston | 1929-30 |
| 3 | 375 | B. C.Lara | West Indies | v | England | St John's | 1993-94 |
| 4 | 307 | R.M. Cowper | Australia | v | England | Melbourne | 1965-66 |
| 5 | 304 | D.G. Bradman | Australia | v | England | Leeds | 1934 |
| 6 | 250 | K.D. Walters | Australia | v | New Zealand | Christchurch | 1976-77 |
| 7 | 270 | D.G. Bradman | Australia | v | England | Melbourne | 1936-37 |
| 8 | 257* | Wasim Akram | Pakistan | v | Zimbabwe | Sheikhupura | 1996-97 |
| 9 | 173 | I.D.S. Smith | New Zealand | v | India | Auckland | 1989-90 |
| 10 | 117 | W.W. Read | England | v | Australia | The Oval | 1884 |
| 11 | 68* | R.O. Collinge | New Zealand | v | Pakistan | Auckland | 1972-73 |

## HIGHEST SCORE AT THE FALL OF EACH WICKET

| | | | | | | |
|---|---|---|---|---|---|---|
| 1st | 413 | India (3d-537) | v | New Zealand | Chennai[2] | 1955-56 |
| 2nd | 615 | Sri Lanka (6d-952) | v | India | Colombo (PIS) | 1997-98 |
| 3rd | 615 | New Zealand (4-671) | v | Sri Lanka | Wellington | 1990-91 |
| 3rd | 615 | Sri Lanka (6d-952) | v | India | Colombo (PIS) | 1997-98 |
| 4th | 790 | Sri Lanka (6d-952) | v | India | Colombo (PIS) | 1997-98 |
| 5th | 921 | Sri Lanka (6d-952) | v | India | Colombo (PIS) | 1997-98 |
| 6th | 924 | Sri Lanka (6d-952) | v | India | Colombo (PIS) | 1997-98 |
| 7th | 876 | England (7d-903) | v | Australia | The Oval | 1938 |
| 8th | 813 | England (849) | v | West Indies | Kingston | 1929-30 |
| 9th | 821 | England (849) | v | West Indies | Kingston | 1929-30 |
| 10th | 849 | England (849) | v | West Indies | Kingston | 1929-30 |

## LOWEST SCORE AT THE FALL OF EACH WICKET

| | | | | | | |
|---|---|---|---|---|---|---|
| 1st | 0 | Numerous instances | | | | |
| 2nd | 0 | Numerous instances | | | | |
| 3rd | 0 | {Australia(7d-32) | v | England | Brisbane[2] | 1950-51 |
| | | {India (165) | v | England | Leeds | 1952 |
| 4th | 0 | India (165) | v | England | Leeds | 1952 |
| 5th | 6 | India (98) | v | England | The Oval | 1952 |
| 6th | 7 | Australia (70) | v | England | Manchester | 1888 |
| 7th | 14 | Australia (44) | v | England | The Oval | 1896 |
| 8th | 19 | Australia (44) | v | England | The Oval | 1896 |
| 9th | 25 | Australia (44) | v | England | The Oval | 1896 |
| 10th | 26 | New Zealand (26) | v | England | Auckland | 1954-55 |

## LONGEST MATCHES

| | | | | | |
|---|---|---|---|---|---|
| 10 days | South Africa | v | England | Durban[2] | 1938-39 |
| 9 days | West Indies | v | England | Kingston | 1929-30 |
| 8 days | Australia | v | England | Melbourne | 1928-29 |

## MATCHES COMPLETED IN TWO DAYS

| | | | | | | |
|---|---|---|---|---|---|---|
| England | (101 + 77) | v | Australia | (63 + 122) | The Oval | 1882 |
| England | (53 + 62) | v | Australia | (116 + 60) | Lord's | 1888 |
| England | (317) | v | Australia | (80 + 100) | The Oval | 1888 |
| England | (172) | v | Australia | (81 + 70) | Manchester | 1888 |
| South Africa | (84 + 129) | v | England | (148 + 2-67) | Port Elizabeth | 1888-89 |
| South Africa | (47 + 43) | v | England | (292) | Cape Town | 1888-89 |
| England | (100 + 8-95) | v | Australia | (92 + 102) | The Oval | 1890 |
| South Africa | (93 + 30) | v | England | (185 + 226) | Port Elizabeth | 1895-96 |
| South Africa | (115 + 117) | v | England | (265) | Cape Town | 1895-96 |
| England | (176 + 0-14) | v | South Africa | (95 + 93) | The Oval | 1912 |
| Australia | (448) | v | South Africa | (265 + 95) | Manchester | 1912 |
| England | (112 + 147) | v | Australia | (232 + 0-30) | Nottingham | 1921 |
| Australia | (8d-328) | v | West Indies | (99 + 107) | Melbourne | 1930-31 |
| South Africa | (157 + 98) | v | Australia | (439) | Johannesburg[1] | 1935-36 |
| New Zealand | (42 + 54) | v | Australia | (8d-199) | Wellington | 1945-46 |

## TEST CRICKETERS WHO HAVE BEEN KNIGHTED

### *Australia*

D.G. Bradman

### *England*

Sir George Oswald Browning Allen

Sir Alec Victor Bedser

Sir Michael Colin Cowdrey

Sir John Berry Hobbs

Sir Leonard Hutton

Sir Francis Stanley Jackson

Sir Henry Dudley Gresham Leveson Gower

Sir Timothy Carew O'Brien

Sir Charles Aubrey Smith

Sir Pelham Francis Warner

### *South Africa*

Sir Murray Bissett

Sir William Henry Milton

### *West Indies*

Sir Learie Nicholas Constantine

Sir Garfield St Aubrun Sobers

Sir Clyde Leopold Walcott

Sir Everton de Courcy Weekes

Sir Frank Mortimor Maglinne Worrell

### *New Zealand*

Sir Richard John Hadlee

Sir Jack Newman

### *India*

Sir Gajapatairaj Vijaya Anada, the Maharajkumar of Vizianagram.

### *The following were made life peers:*

Baron Constantine of Maraval and Nelson

Baron Cowdrey of Tonbridge

Lord Harris

Lord Hawke

Baron David Stuart Sheppard (Bishop of Liverpool)

## TWENTY BOWLERS IN A MATCH

South Africa (7d-501 + 346) v England (442 + 0-15) Cape Town 1964-65

## ELEVEN BOWLERS IN AN INNINGS

| | | | | |
|---|---|---|---|---|
| England | v | Australia (551) | The Oval | 1884 |
| Australia | v | Pakistan (2-382) | Faisalabad | 1979-80 |

## TEST CAREERS WHICH ENDED IN TRAGEDY

1. K.J. Wadsworth (New Zealand). One of his country's finest wicketkeepers, Ken Wadsworth died of cancer at the age of 29, at the peak of his career.
2. O.G. Smith (West Indies). 'Collie' Smith was a versatile all rounder who died of injuries received in a car accident in England in 1959.
3. G.B. Street (England). A good county wicket-keeper and useful tail-end batsmen, Street played one Test for England against South Africa in 1922-23. Tragically he was killed in a motorcycle accident just before the 1924 season.
4. F. Morley (England). A left-arm fast bowler Morley was a member of Hon. Ivo Bligh's team that sailed to Australia for the 1882-83 season. Morley was apparently hurt in a collision at sea on the voyage out but carried on throughout the tour nursing a broken rib. Upon his return to England his health deteriorated and he died the following year.
5. H.B. Cameron (South Africa). 'Jock' Cameron was a wicket-keeper and gifted batsman who captained his country in nine Tests. He contracted enteric fever on the voyage home from the 1935 tour of England and died at the age of 30, ten weeks after playing in his final Test.
6. N.B.F. Mann (South Africa). 'Tufty' Mann was a versatile middle-order batsman and left-arm spinner who died aged 31, after an abdominal operation.

## CRICKETERS ROLL OF HONOUR TEST CRICKETERS KILLED IN THE BOER WAR, WORLD WAR I and WORLD WAR II

### *Boer War*

J.J. Ferris (Australia/England)

### *World War I*

A. Cotter (Australia)

C. Blythe (England)

K.L. Hutchings (England)

R.M.H. Hands (South Africa)

E.B. Lundie (South Africa)

R.O. Schwarz (South Africa)

G.C. White (South Africa)

### *World War II*

R.G. Gregory (Australia)

K. Farnes (England)

G.B. Legge (England)

G.G. Macaulay (England)

M.J.L. Turnbull (England)

H. Verity (England)

A.W. Briscoe (South Africa)

A.B.C. Langton (South Africa)

D.A.R. Moloney (New ZealandVenue

## TEAM UNCHANGED THROUGHOUT A SERIES

| | | | Venue | | Tests |
|---|---|---|---|---|---|
| England | v | Australia | Australia | 1884-85 | 5 |
| South Africa | v | England | South Africa | 1905-06 | 5 |
| West Indies | v | Australia | West Indies | 1990-91 | 5 |
| England | v | Australia | Australia | 1881-82 | 4 |
| Australia | v | England | England | 1884 | 3 |
| Australia | v | England | England | 1893 | 3 |
| Pakistan | v | New Zealand | Pakistan | 1964-65 | 3 |
| India | v | England | England | 1971 | 3 |
| Australia | v | New Zealand | New Zealand | 1981-82 | 3 |
| India | v | England | India | 1992-93 | 3 |
| India | v | Sri Lanka | India | 1993-94 | 3 |
| South Africa | v | Australia | South Africa | 1993-94 | 3 |
| Australia | v | West Indies | West Indies | 1994-95 | 4 |
| Australia | v | Pakistan | Australia | 1995-96 | 3 |
| Australia | v | South Africa | South Africa | 1996-97 | 3 |

## MOST PLAYERS ENGAGED BY ONE SIDE IN A SERIES

| | | | | | |
|---|---|---|---|---|---|
| 30 in 5 Tests | England | v | Australia | England | 1921 |
| 29 in 6 Tests | England | v | Australia | England | 1989 |
| 28 in 5 Tests | Australia | v | England | Australia | 1884-85 |
| 27 in 4 Tests | West Indies | v | England | West Indies | 1929-30 |
| 26 in 5 Tests | India | v | Pakistan | India | 1952-53 |
| 25 in 4 Tests | England | v | West Indies | England | 1950 |
| 25 in 5 Tests | England | v | Australia | England | 1909 |
| 25 in 5 Tests | England | v | South Africa | England | 1935 |
| 25 in 5 Tests | England | v | South Africa | England | 1955 |

*South Africa used 20 players in the 3-match rubber of 1895-96 against England in South Africa.*

## NO BATSMAN REACHING DOUBLE FIGURES IN A COMPLETED INNINGS

| | | | | |
|---|---|---|---|---|
| South Africa (30 - highest score 7) | v | England | Birmingham | 1924 |

## ELEVEN BATSMEN REACHING DOUBLE FIGURES IN AN INNINGS

| | | | | Venue | Lowest Score |
|---|---|---|---|---|---|
| 1894-95 | England (475) | v | Australia | Melbourne | 11 |
| 1905-06 | South Africa (385) | v | England | Johannesburg[2] | 10 |
| 1928-29 | England (636) | v | Australia | Sydney | 11 |
| 1931-32 | South Africa (358) | v | Australia | Melbourne | 10* |
| 1947-48 | Australia (8d-575) | v | India | Melbourne | 11 |
| 1952-53 | India (397) | v | Pakistan | Calcutta | 11 |
| 1967-68 | India (359) | v | New Zealand | Dunedin | 12 |
| 1976-77 | India (9d-524) | v | New Zealand | Kanpur | 10* |
| 1992-93 | Australia (471) | v | Sri Lanka | Colombo (SSC) | 10* |

## ONLY FOUR BOWLERS IN AN INNINGS OF OVER 400 RUNS

| | | | | |
|---|---|---|---|---|
| Australia | v | England (8d-403) | The Oval | 1921 |
| South Africa | v | England (8-421) | The Oval | 1924 |
| New Zealand | v | England (482) | The Oval | 1949 |
| England | v | Australia (426) | Sydney | 1950-51 |
| India | v | England (9d-419) | Lord's | 1979 |
| India | v | Australia (528) | Adelaide | 1980-81 |
| Australia | v | England (404) | Manchester | 1981 |
| England | v | India (428) | Bangalore | 1981-82 |
| Sri Lanka | v | Pakistan (7d-500) | Lahore[2] | 1981-82 |
| Pakistan | v | Australia (6d-454) | Sydney | 1983-84 |
| Australia | v | West Indies (8d-468) | Port-of-Spain | 1983-84 |
| Australia | v | West Indies (498) | St John's | 1983-84 |
| Australia | v | West Indies (416) | Perth | 1984-85 |
| Australia | v | England (456) | Nottingham | 1985 |
| Pakistan | v | England (447) | Manchester | 1987 |
| New Zealand | v | India (482) | Auckland | 1989-90 |
| England | v | West Indies (446) | Bridgetown | 1989-90 |
| England | v | West Indies (446) | St John's | 1989-90 |
| England | v | Australia (408) | Birmingham | 1993 |
| Pakistan | v | Australia (455) | Lahore[2] | 1994-95 |

## MOST WICKETS IN ONE DAY

| | | | | | | |
|---|---|---|---|---|---|---|
| 27-157 | England (3-18 to 53 + 62) | v | Australia (60) | Lord's | 1888 | 2nd |
| 25-221 | Australia (112 + 5-48) | v | England (61) | Melbourne | 1901-02 | 1st |
| 24-255 | England (1-69 to 145 + 5-60) | v | Australia (61) | The Oval | 1896 | 2nd |
| 22-197 | Australia (92 + 2-5) | v | England (100) | The Oval | 1890 | 1st |
| 22-207 | Australia (82 + 2-0) | v | West Indies (105) | Adelaide | 1951-52 | 1st |
| 22-195 | England (7-292 to 9d-347) | v | India (58 + 82) | Manchester | 1952 | 3rd |
| 21-278 | England (185 + 1-0) | v | South Africa (93) | Port Elizabeth | 1895-96 | 1st |

## MOST WICKETS BEFORE LUNCH

| | | | | | |
|---|---|---|---|---|---|
| 18 | Australia (2-32 to 81 + 70) | v England | Manchester | 1888 | 2nd |

## NO WICKETS IN A FULL DAY'S PLAY

| | | | | |
|---|---|---|---|---|
| England (0-283) | v Australia | Melbourne | 3rd | 1924-25 |
| West Indies (6-187 to 6-494) | v Australia | Bridgetown | 4th | 1954-55 |
| India (0-234) | v New Zealand | Chennai² | 1st | 1955-56 |
| West Indies (1-147 to 1-504) | v Pakistan | Kingston | 3rd | 1957-58 |
| West Indies (3-279 to 3-486) | v England § | Bridgetown | 5th | 1959-60 |
| West Indies (2-81 to 2-291) | v England | Kingston | 3rd | 1959-60 |
| Australia (0-263) | v West Indies | Bridgetown | 1st | 1964-65 |
| West Indies (7-310 to 7d-365) | v New Zealand (0-163) | Georgetown | 3rd | 1971-72 |
| India (1-70 to 1d-361) | v West Indies 0-15) | Calcutta | 4th | 1978-79 |
| India (2-178 to 395-2) | v England | Chennai² | 2nd | 1981-82 |
| Sri Lanka (3-83 to 3-323) | v Pakistan | Colombo (PSS) | 5th | 1985-86 |
| India (5-291 to 5-517) | v Australia (0-9) | Bombay³ | 4th | 1986-87 |
| Australia (0-301) | v England | Nottingham | 1st | 1989 |
| Australia (4-191 to 4-479) | v South Africa | Johannesburg³ | 3rd | 1996-97 |
| Sri Lanka (1-39 to 1-322) | v India † | Colombo (PIS) | 3rd | 1997-98 |
| Sri Lanka (1-322 to 1-587) | v India † | Colombo (PIS) | 4th | 1997-98 |

*† S.T. Jayasuriya (340) and R.S. Mahanama (225) added 576 for the second wicket in the longest partnership in Test cricket (753 minutes) and remain the only pair of batsmen to bat throughout two consecutive days of Test cricket, although § G.S. Sobers (226) and F.M.M. Worrell (197*) also batted throughout two consecutive days, the final hour of the fourth day was lost to rain and a rest day intervened.*
*The following pairs of batsmen also batted throughout one full day's play in the above matches: J.B. Hobbs and H. Sutcliffe (1924-25), D.S. Atkinson and C.C. Depeiza (1954-55), M.H. Mankad and Pankaj Roy (1955-56), C.C. Hunte and G.S. Sobers (1957-58) W.M. Lawry and R.B. Simpson (1964-65), G.R. Viswanath and Yashpal Sharma (1981-82), A.P. Gurusinha and A. Ranatunga (1985-86), G.R. Marsh and M.A. Taylor (1989), and S.R. Waugh and G.S.Blewett (1996-97).*

## SIMILARITY OF DISMISSAL — TEN BATSMEN CAUGHT IN AN INNINGS

| | | | |
|---|---|---|---|
| Australia | v England | Melbourne | 1903-04 |
| South Africa | v Australia | Melbourne | 1931-32 |
| England | v South Africa | Durban² | 1948-49 |
| New Zealand | v England | Leeds | 1949 |
| England | v Pakistan | The Oval | 1954 |
| England | v Australia | Melbourne | 1958-59 |
| West Indies | v Australia | Sydney | 1960-61 |
| New Zealand | v India | Wellington | 1967-68 |
| New Zealand | v West Indies | Auckland | 1968-69 |
| New Zealand | v India | Mumbai² | 1969-70 |
| India | v West Indies | Port-of-Spain | 1970-71 |
| India | v England | Lord's | 1971 |
| Australia | v England | Nottingham | 1972 |
| England | v India | Chennai¹ | 1972-73 |
| England | v West Indies | Lord's | 1973 |
| Australia | v New Zealand | Auckland | 1973-74 |
| New Zealand | v Pakistan | Auckland | 1978-79 |
| § England | v Australia | Brisbane² | 1982-83 |
| England | v Australia | Melbourne | 1982-83 |
| India | v West Indies | Bridgetown | 1982-83 |
| West Indies | v India | Bridgetown | 1982-83 |
| Sri Lanka | v Australia | Kandy | 1982-83 |
| England | v New Zealand | Christchurch | 1987-88 |
| England | v West Indies | The Oval | 1988 |

| | | | |
|---|---|---|---|
| India | v New Zealand | Hyderabad | 1988-89 |
| Pakistan | v India | Karachi[1] | 1989-90 |
| West Indies | v Australia | Bridgetown | 1990-91 |
| Australia | v India | Perth | 1991-92 |
| India | v Australia | Perth | 1991-92 |
| India | v South Africa | Port Elizabeth | 1992-93 |
| West Indies | v England | Bridgetown | 1993-94 |
| Sri Lanka | v Zimbabwe | Harare | 1994-95 |
| Pakistan | v Zimbabwe | Harare | 1994-95 |
| New Zealand | v Sri Lanka | Napier | 1994-95 |
| West Indies | v Australia | Bridgetown | 1994-95 |
| West Indies | v Australia | Port-of-Spain | 1994-95 |
| New Zealand | v England | Wellington | 1996-97 |
| India | v West Indies | Georgetown | 1996-97 |
| West Indies | v England | Bridgetown | 1997-98 |

*§ Australia held nine catches in England's second innings. This is the only occasion where a side has held 19 catches in a Test.*

## MOST BATSMEN CAUGHT IN A MATCH

| | | | | |
|---|---|---|---|---|
| 33 | Australia | v India | Perth | 1991-92 |

*(of the 36 batsmen dismissed not one was bowled - a unique feat for a completed Test match)*

| | | | | |
|---|---|---|---|---|
| 32 | England | v Pakistan | Leeds | 1971 |
| 32 | New Zealand | v Pakistan | Auckland | 1993-94 |
| 32 | Zimbabwe | v Pakistan | Harare | 1994-95 |
| 31 | West Indies | v England | Bridgetown | 1993-94 |
| 30 | India | v West Indies | Mumbai[3] | 1994-95 |

## MOST BATSMEN CAUGHT AND BOWLED IN AN INNINGS

| | | | | |
|---|---|---|---|---|
| 4 | Australia | v England | Lord's | 1890 |
| 4 | Australia | v New Zealand | Sydney | 1985-86 |

## MOST BATSMEN CAUGHT AND BOWLED IN A MATCH

| | | | | |
|---|---|---|---|---|
| 6 | Australia | v England | Lord's | 1890 |

## MOST BATSMEN BOWLED IN AN INNINGS

| | | | | |
|---|---|---|---|---|
| 9 | South Africa | v England | Cape Town | 1888-89 |

## MOST BATSMEN BOWLED IN A MATCH

| | | | | |
|---|---|---|---|---|
| 23 | South Africa | v England | Port Elizabeth | 1895-96 |

## MOST BATSMEN LBW IN AN INNINGS

| | | | | |
|---|---|---|---|---|
| 6 | England | v South Africa | Leeds | 1955 |
| 6 | England | v West Indies | Kingston | 1959-60 |
| 6 | England | v Pakistan | Karachi[1] | 1977-78 |
| 6 | West Indies | v England | Kingston | 1985-86 |
| 6 | Pakistan | v Australia | Melbourne | 1989-90 |
| 6 | India | v Sri Lanka | Chandigarh | 1990-91 |
| 6 | Pakistan | v Sri Lanka | Faisalabad | 1991-92 |
| 6 | New Zealand | v Pakistan | Hamilton | 1992-93 |
| 6 | South Africa | v Australia | Durban[2] | 1993-94 |
| 6 | West Indies | v India | Mohali | 1994-95 |

## MOST BATSMEN LBW IN A MATCH

| | | | | |
|---|---|---|---|---|
| 17 | West Indies (8) | v Pakistan (9) | Port-of-Spain | 1992-93 |
| 15 | Pakistan (5) | v New Zealand (10) | Lahore[2] | 1996-97 |
| 14 | Pakistan (8) | v Sri Lanka (6) | Faisalabad | 1991-92 |

| | | | | | |
|---|---|---|---|---|---|
| 13 | New Zealand (8) | v | England (5) | Auckland | 1991-92 |
| 13 | Pakistan (4) | v | New Zealand (9) | Rawalpindi[2] | 1996-97 |
| 12 | New Zealand (5) | v | West Indies (7) | Dunedin | 1979-80 |
| 12 | England (9) | v | West Indies (3) | Lord's | 1984 |
| 12 | Pakistan (5) | v | West Indies (7) | Faisalabad | 1986-87 |
| 12 | New Zealand (8) | v | Pakistan (4) | Hamilton | 1992-93 |
| 12 | Pakistan (8) | v | Zimbabwe (4) | Rawalpindi[2] | 1993-94 |

## MOST BATSMEN RUN OUT IN AN INNINGS

| | | | | | |
|---|---|---|---|---|---|
| 4 | India | v | Pakistan | Peshawar[1] | 1954-55 |
| 4 | Australia | v | West Indies | Adelaide | 1968-69 |

## MOST BATSMEN RUN OUT IN A MATCH

| | | | | | |
|---|---|---|---|---|---|
| 7 | Australia (3) | v | Pakistan (4) | Melbourne | 1972-73 |
| 6 | Australia (2) | v | England (4) | Adelaide | 1901-02 |
| 6 | Australia (4) | v | South Africa (2) | Melbourne | 1910-11 |
| 6 | Australia (5) | v | England (1) | Sydney | 1920-21 |
| 6 | England (2) | v | South Africa (4) | Leeds | 1924 |
| 6 | West Indies (3) | v | India (3) | Georgetown | 1970-71 |
| 6 | England (3) | v | New Zealand (3) | The Oval | 1983 |
| 6 | England (4) | v | Pakistan (2) | Birmingham | 1987 |

## MOST BATSMEN STUMPED IN AN INNINGS

| | | | | | |
|---|---|---|---|---|---|
| 5 | West Indies | v | India (K.S.More) | Chennai[1] | 1987-88 |
| 4 | England | v | Australia (W.A.S.Oldfield) | Melbourne | 1924-25 |
| 4 | England | v | India (P.Sen) | Chennai[1] | 1951-52 |

## MOST BATSMEN STUMPED IN A MATCH

| | | | | | |
|---|---|---|---|---|---|
| 6 | Australia | v | England | Sydney | 1894-95 |
| 6 | India | v | England | Chennai[1] | 1951-52 |
| 6 | West Indies | v | India (all by K.S.More) | Chennai[1] | 1987-88 |

## TEST CRICKETERS WHO WERE RHODES SCHOLARS

| | |
|---|---|
| C.B. Van Ryneveld | South Africa |
| J.P. Duminy | South Africa |
| P.A.M. Hands | South Africa |
| R.H.M. Hands | South Africa |
| H.G. Owen-Smith | South Africa |
| D.B. Pithey | South Africa |
| J.A. Dunning | New Zealand |

## TEST CRICKET CAPTAINS BORN ABROAD

### Australia

| | |
|---|---|
| T.P. Horan | Ireland |
| P.S. McDonnell | England |

### England

| | |
|---|---|
| Lord Harris | West Indies |
| P.F. Warner | West Indies |
| F.L. Fane | Ireland |
| D.R. Jardine | India |
| G.O.B. Allen | Australia |
| F.R. Brown | Peru |
| M.C. Cowdrey | India |
| E.R. Dexter | Italy |
| A.R. Lewis | Wales |
| M.H. Denness | Scotland |
| A.W. Greig | South Africa |
| A.J. Lamb | South Africa |

### South Africa

| | |
|---|---|
| W.H. Milton | England |
| E.A. Halliwell | England |
| F. Mitchell | England |

### West Indies

| | |
|---|---|
| G.A. Headley | Panama |

### Pakistan

| | |
|---|---|
| A.H. Kardar | India |
| Fazal Mahmood | India |
| Imtiaz Ahmed | India |
| Javed Burki | India |
| Hanif Mohammad | India |

| | |
|---|---|
| Saeed Ahmed | India |
| Intikhab Alam | India |
| Majid J. Khan | India |
| Mushtaq Mohammad | India |
| Asif Iqbal | India |

### Zimbabwe

| | |
|---|---|
| A. Flower | South Africa |

## RETIRED HURT

J.J. Kelly (Australia). A useful batsman and outstanding wicketkeeper, Kelly played 36 Tests for Australia around the turn of the century. He retired from first-class cricket after his last tour of England because of the effects of a damaged finger and a blow over the heart by a ball in a Test at Manchester.

C. Milburn (England). One of the most punishing batsmen seen on the Test arena for many years, Colin Milburn was involved in a car accident in 1969 which cost him his left eye. He attempted a county come-back in 1973 but to all intents and purposes his career was finished by the crash.

R.K. Oxenham (Australia). An excellent all-rounder, Oxenham represented his country in seven Tests in the late 1920s and '30s. He was seriously injured in a car accident in 1937, never fully recovered, and died in 1939.

N.J. Contractor (India). An opening bat and occasional medium-pace bowler Contractor captained India on twelve occasions. During a match against Barbados, on the 1961-62 tour of the West Indies, Contractor was hit on the head by a ball from C.C. Griffith. His skull was fractured and he remained gravely ill for some days. Fortunately he recovered but never again played international cricket.

G.F. Rorke (Australia). A big man, Gordon Rorke played four Tests for Australia and was a very effective fast bowler in Sheffield Shield cricket. His Test career was unfortunately cut short in 1959-60 when he contracted hepatitis on tour of India.

G.B. Stevens (Australia). An opening batsman Gavin Stevens played four Tests for Australia in 1959-60. He dehydrated badly from the same strain of hepatitis that G.F.Rorke picked up. He lost two stone in weight and was sent home early from the sub-continent and never played first-class cricket again.

R.C. Motz (New Zealand). One of New Zealand's most successful Test bowlers — taking 100 Test wickets — Motz was forced to retire from first-class cricket when it was discovered he had been bowling for some time with a displaced vertabra.

I.J. Jones (England). A Welshman, Jones represented England on 15 occasions taking 44 wickets as a left-arm fast bowler. In May 1968, yet to reach his peak, he tore the ligaments in his elbow and from then on was a spent force in top cricket.

W. Bates (England). In a short but brilliant career, Billy Bates represented England 15 times scoring 656 runs and taking 50 wickets in the late 1880s. His career came to an abrupt end in Melbourne in 1887 when struck in the eye at net practice. He suffered permanent damage to his sight, forcing his retirement.

J. Briggs (England). A regular member of the England team during the late 1880s, Briggs scored over 800 runs and took 118 wickets. During a Test against Australia in 1899 he was struck over the heart by a ball while fielding, and suffered what was believed to be an epileptic fit. He retired from the game and although he attempted a first-class come-back the following year, his Test career was over.

M.F. Kent (Australia). Kent opened the batting for Australia on the 1981 tour of England. He suffered a back strain which degenerated so badly that he was forced to retire from all grades of cricket.

## TEST CRICKETERS WHO WERE TEST UMPIRES

### Australia

C. Bannerman

G. Coulthard

T.W. Garrett *

P.G. McShane #

H.H. Massie ¶

A.J. Richardson

J.P.F. Travers

* T.W. Garrett, who was playing in the game, replaced umpire J.H. Hodges after tea on the last day (Australia v England, Melbourne 1884-85).

# P.G. McShane played and umpired in the same series (Australia v England 1884-85).

¶ H.H. Massie substituted for E.H. Elliott (Australia v England, Sydney 1884-85).

### England

R.G. Barlow

J. Birkenshaw

L.C. Braund

H.R. Butt

J.F. Crapp

A. Dolphin

H. Elliott

A.E. Fagg

W. Gunn †

J.H. Hampshire

J. Hardstaff sr

F. Hearne

A. Hill

J.W. Hitch

J. Lillywhite

A.S.M. Oakman §

N. Oldfield

K.E. Palmer

W.F.F. Price

M. Sherwin

E.J. Smith

G.J. Thompson

P. Willey

H. Young

† W. Gunn replaced umpire Swift, injured in the England v Australia Test at (Sydney) 1886-87. (He was playing in the Test.)

§ A.S.M. Oakman deputised for H.D. Bird (injured back) after tea on the third day of the first Test (England v Australia, Birmingham, 1975).

### *West Indies*

E.E. Achong

G.E. Gomez

### *South Africa*

W.W. Wade

### *New Zealand*

J.A. Cowie

E.W.T. Tindill

### *India*

S. Venkataraghavan

### *Pakistan*

Javed Akhtar

Mohammad Aslam

## PLAYERS WHO HAVE OPENED THE BATTING AND BOWLING IN SAME MATCH (FIRST INNINGS ONLY APPLIES IN THIS RECORD)

### *Australia*

| | |
|---|---|
| G. Giffen | v England, Sydney 1882-83 |
| G.E. Palmer | v England, Sydney 1884-85 |
| W. Bruce | v England, Melbourne 1884-85 |
| C.T.B. Turner | v England, Lord's 1890 |
| C.T.B. Turner | v England, The Oval 1890 |
| G.H.S. Trott | v England, Sydney 1894-95 |
| G.H.S. Trott | v England, Melbourne 1894-95 |
| W.W. Armstrong | v South Africa, Johannesburg 1902-03 |
| V.T. Trumper | v South Africa, Johannesburg, 1902-03 |
| M.A.Noble | v England, Sydney 1907-08 |
| F.J. Laver | v England, Lord's 1909 |
| C. Kelleway | v England, Melbourne 1911-12 |
| J.M. Gregory | v South Africa, Durban 1921-22 |

### *England*

| | |
|---|---|
| A. Shaw | v Australia, Melbourne 1876-77 |
| G. Ulyett | v Australia, Melbourne 1878-79 |
| C.T. Studd | v Australia, Melbourne 1882-83 |
| R.G. Barlow | v Australia, Sydney 1882-83 (3rd Test) |
| R.G. Barlow | v Australia, Sydney 1882-83 (4th Test) |
| G. Ulyett | v Australia, Sydney 1884-85 |
| G. Ulyett | v South Africa, Cape Town 1888-89 |
| G.A. Lohmann | v South Africa, Port Elizabeth 1895-96 |
| G.L. Jessop | v Australia, Melbourne 1901-02 |
| J.B. Hobbs | v South Africa, Johannesburg 1909-10 |
| J.B. Hobbs | v South Africa, Durban 1909-10 |
| J.B. Hobbs | v South Africa, Cape Town 1909-10 |
| M.W. Tate | v Australia, Adelaide 1924-25 |
| W.R. Hammond | v South Africa, Cape Town 1930-31 |
| W.R. Hammond | v South Africa, Durban 1930-31 |
| R.E.S. Wyatt | v West Indies, Port-of-Spain 1934-35 |
| R.E.S. Wyatt | v West Indies, Georgetown 1934-35 |
| R.E.S. Wyatt | v South Africa, Lord's 1935 |
| W.J. Edrich | v South Africa, Johannesburg 1938-39 |
| T.E. Bailey | v West Indies, Kingston 1953-54 |
| T.E. Bailey | v Australia, Sydney 1954-55 |
| T.E. Bailey | v South Africa, Port Elizabeth 1956-57 |

### *South Africa*

| | |
|---|---|
| A. Rose-Innes | v England, Cape Town 1888-89 |
| J.H. Sinclair | v England, Johannesburg 1895-96 |
| G.A. Faulkner | v England, The Oval 1907 |
| D.J. Meintjes | v England, Johannesburg 1922-23 |
| T.L. Goddard | v England, Nottingham 1955 |
| T.L. Goddard | v England, The Oval 1955 |
| T.L. Goddard | v Australia, Cape Town 1957-58 |

### *West Indies*

| | |
|---|---|
| M. Prabhakar | v England, Bombay, 1992-93 |
| M. Prabhakar | v Zimbabwe, Delhi, 1992-93 |
| M. Prabhakar | v Sri Lanka, Colombo (SSC), 1993-94 |
| M. Prabhakar | v Sri Lanka, Colombo (PSS), 1993-94 |
| M. Prabhakar | v Sri Lanka, Lucknow, 1993-94 |
| M. Prabhakar | v Sri Lanka, Bangalore, 1993-94 |
| M. Prabhakar | v Sri Lanka, Motera, 1993-94 |
| M. Prabhakar | v West Indies, Bombay, 1994-95 |
| M. Prabhakar | v West Indies, Nagpur, 1994-95 |
| M. Prabhakar | v West Indies, Mohali, 1994-95 |
| M. Prabhakar | v New Zealand, Bangalore, 1994-95 |
| M. Prabhakar | v New Zealand, Cuttack, 1994-95 |

### Pakistan

Mudassar Nazar v New Zealand, Lahore 1984-85
Mudassar Nazar v New Zealand, Hyderabad 1984-85
Mudassar Nazar v New Zealand, Karachi 1984-85
Mudassar Nazar v New Zealand, Wellington 1984-85
Mudassar Nazar v England, Lahore 1987-88
Mudassar Nazar v England, Faisalabad 1987-88
Mudassar Nazar v Australia, Karachi 1988-89
Mudassar Nazar v Australia, Faisalabad 1988-89
Mudassar Nazar v Australia, Lahore 1988-89

### Sri Lanka

B.Warnapura v England, Colombo 1981-82
J.R.Ratnayeke v India, Nagpur 1986-87
J.R.Ratnayeke v India, Calcutta 1986-87

## CALENDAR YEAR TEST RECORDS

## BATSMEN WITH 1000 RUNS IN THE CALENDAR YEAR

| Player (Country) | Year | Tests | I | NO | Runs | HS | Avge | 100 | 50 |
|---|---|---|---|---|---|---|---|---|---|
| I.V.A. Richards (W) | 1976 | 11 | 19 | 0 | 1710 | 291 | 90.00 | 7 | 5 |
| S.M. Gavaskar (I) | 1979 | 18 | 27 | 1 | 1555 | 221 | 59.80 | 5 | 8 |
| G.R. Viswanath (I) | 1979 | 17 | 26 | 3 | 1388 | 179 | 60.34 | 5 | 6 |
| R.B. Simpson (A) | 1964 | 14 | 26 | 3 | 1381 | 311 | 60.04 | 3 | 7 |
| D.L. Amiss (E) | 1974 | 13 | 22 | 2 | 1379 | 262* | 68.95 | 5 | 3 |
| S.M. Gavaskar (I) | 1983 | 18 | 32 | 4 | 1310 | 236* | 46.78 | 5 | 5 |
| S.T. Jayasuriya (SL) | 1997 | 11 | 19 | 0 | 1271 | 340 | 66.89 | 3 | 7 |
| G.A. Gooch (E) | 1990 | 9 | 17 | 1 | 1264 | 333 | 79.00 | 4 | 5 |
| D.C. Boon (A) | 1993 | 16 | 25 | 5 | 1241 | 164* | 62.05 | 4 | 7 |
| B.C. Lara (W) | 1995 | 12 | 20 | 2 | 1222 | 179 | 67.88 | 4 | 6 |
| P.A. de Silva (SL) | 1997 | 11 | 19 | 3 | 1220 | 168 | 76.25 | 7 | 2 |
| M.A. Taylor (A) | 1989 | 11 | 20 | 1 | 1219 | 219 | 64.15 | 4 | 5 # |
| G.S. Sobers (W) | 1958 | 7 | 12 | 3 | 1193 | 365* | 132.55 | 5 | 3 |
| D.B. Vengsarkar (I) | 1979 | 18 | 27 | 4 | 1174 | 146* | 51.04 | 5 | 6 |
| K.J. Hughes (A) | 1979 | 15 | 28 | 4 | 1163 | 130* | 48.45 | 2 | 8 |
| D.C.S. Compton (E) | 1947 | 9 | 15 | 1 | 1159 | 208 | 82.78 | 6 | 3 |
| C.G. Greenidge (W) | 1984 | 14 | 22 | 4 | 1149 | 223 | 63.83 | 4 | 3 |
| M.A. Atherton (E) | 1995 | 13 | 24 | 1 | 1129 | 185* | 49.08 | 2 | 7 |
| M.A.Taylor (A) | 1993 | 15 | 23 | 2 | 1106 | 170 | 52.66 | 4 | 4 |
| A.R. Border (A) | 1985 | 11 | 20 | 3 | 1099 | 196 | 64.64 | 4 | 2 |
| D.M. Jones (A) | 1989 | 11 | 18 | 3 | 1099 | 216 | 73.26 | 4 | 4 |
| I.T. Botham (E) | 1982 | 14 | 22 | 0 | 1095 | 208 | 49.77 | 3 | 6 |
| K.W.R. Fletcher (E) | 1973 | 13 | 22 | 4 | 1090 | 178 | 60.55 | 2 | 9 |
| M. Amarnath (I) | 1983 | 14 | 24 | 1 | 1077 | 120 | 46.82 | 4 | 7 |
| A.R. Border (A) | 1979 | 14 | 27 | 3 | 1073 | 162 | 44.70 | 3 | 6 |
| G.S. Blewett (A) | 1997 | 15 | 25 | 0 | 1067 | 214 | 42.68 | 2 | 6 |
| C. Hill (A) | 1902 | 12 | 21 | 2 | 1061 | 142 | 55.78 | 2 | 7 |
| D.I. Gower (E) | 1982 | 14 | 25 | 2 | 1061 | 114 | 46.13 | 1 | 8 |
| D.I. Gower (E) | 1986 | 14 | 25 | 1 | 1059 | 136 | 44.12 | 2 | 6 |
| W.M. Lawry (A) | 1964 | 14 | 27 | 2 | 1056 | 157 | 42.24 | 2 | 6 |
| S.M. Gavaskar (I) | 1978 | 9 | 15 | 2 | 1044 | 205 | 80.30 | 4 | 4 |
| G.A. Gooch (E) | 1991 | 9 | 17 | 1 | 1040 | 174 | 65.00 | 3 | 5 |
| K.F. Barrington (E) | 1963 | 12 | 22 | 2 | 1039 | 132* | 51.95 | 3 | 5 |
| E.R. Dexter (E) | 1962 | 11 | 15 | 1 | 1038 | 205 | 74.14 | 2 | 6 |
| K.F. Barrington (E) | 1961 | 10 | 17 | 4 | 1032 | 172 | 79.38 | 4 | 5 |
| Mohsin Khan (P) | 1982 | 10 | 17 | 3 | 1029 | 200 | 73.50 | 4 | 4 |
| D.G. Bradman (A) | 1948 | 8 | 13 | 4 | 1025 | 201 | 113.88 | 5 | 2 |
| S.M. Gavaskar (I) | 1976 | 11 | 20 | 1 | 1024 | 156 | 53.89 | 4 | 4 |
| A.R. Border (A) | 1986 | 11 | 19 | 3 | 1000 | 140 | 62.50 | 5 | 3 |
| S.R. Tendulkar (I) | 1997 | 12 | 17 | 1 | 1000 | 169 | 62.50 | 4 | 3 |

*# Taylor achieved the feat in his debut calendar year.*

## 50 WICKETS IN THE CALENDAR YEAR

*# includes one match in which player did not bowl.*

| Player (Country) | Year | Tests | Balls | Mdns | Runs | Wkts | Avge | 5w | 10w | Best |
|---|---|---|---|---|---|---|---|---|---|---|
| D.K. Lillee (A) | 1981 | 13 | 3710 | 162 | 1781 | 85 | 20.95 | 5 | 2 | 7/83 |
| J. Garner (W) | 1984 | 15 | 3620 | 149 | 1603 | 77 | 20.81 | 4 | 0 | 6/60 |
| Kapil Dev (I) | 1983 | 18 | 3469 | 112 | 1738 | 75 | 23.17 | 5 | 1 | 9/83 |
| Kapil Dev (I) | 1979 | 18 | 3651 | 147 | 1720 | 74 | 23.24 | 5 | 0 | 6/63 |
| M.D. Marshall (W) | 1984 | 13 | 3251 | 121 | 1471 | 73 | 20.15 | 9 | 1 | 7/53 |
| S.K. Warne (A) | 1993 | 16 | 5054 | 316 | 1697 | 72 | 23.56 | 2 | 0 | 6/31 |
| G.D. McKenzie (A) | 1964 | 14 | 4106 | 119 | 1737 | 71 | 24.46 | 4 | 1 | 7/153 |
| S.K. Warne (A) | 1997 | 15 | 4091 | 194 | 1661 | 68 | 24.42 | 2 | 0 | 6/48 |
| A.A. Donald (SA) | 1998 | 10 | 2664 | 115 | 1253 | 66 | 18.98 | 6 | 0 | 6/88 |
| S.F. Barnes (E) | 1912 | 10 | 2394 | 106 | 959 | 64 | 14.98 | 8 | 3 | 8/29 # |
| R.J. Hadlee (N) | 1985 | 10 | 2588 | 102 | 1116 | 64 | 17.43 | 6 | 2 | 9/52 |
| I.T. Botham (E) | 1978 | 12 | 2757 | 91 | 1160 | 63 | 18.41 | 6 | 1 | 8/34 |
| G.D. McGrath (A) | 1997 | 13 | 3113 | 151 | 1347 | 63 | 21.38 | 4 | 0 | 8/38 |
| F.S. Trueman (E) | 1963 | 11 | 2563 | 90 | 1061 | 62 | 17.11 | 6 | 2 | 7/44 |
| I.T. Botham (E) | 1981 | 12 | 3338 | 136 | 1590 | 62 | 25.64 | 4 | 1 | 6/95 |
| Imran Khan (P) | 1982 | 9 | 2359 | 112 | 824 | 62 | 13.29 | 5 | 2 | 8/58 |
| C.A. Walsh (W) | 1995 | 12 | 3051 | 111 | 1347 | 62 | 21.72 | 4 | 1 | 7/37 |
| M.D. Marshall (W) | 1988 | 10 | 2477 | 83 | 1072 | 60 | 17.86 | 4 | 1 | 7/22 |
| R.G.D. Willis (E) | 1978 | 14 | 2921 | 94 | 1056 | 57 | 18.52 | 4 | 0 | 5/32 |
| M.G. Hughes (A) | 1993 | 12 | 3033 | 127 | 1448 | 57 | 25.40 | 2 | 0 | 5/64 |
| C.J. McDermott (A) | 1991 | 9 | 2416 | 84 | 1188 | 56 | 21.21 | 4 | 1 | 8/97 |
| A.A. Mailey (A) | 1921 | 10 | 2849 | 63 | 1567 | 55 | 28.49 | 4 | 2 | 9/121 # |
| R. Benaud (A) | 1959 | 9 | 3248 | 177 | 1031 | 55 | 18.74 | 4 | 0 | 5/76 |
| Waqar Younis (P) | 1993 | 7 | 1626 | 59 | 838 | 55 | 15.23 | 6 | 1 | 7/91 |
| T.M. Alderman (A) | 1981 | 9 | 2672 | 105 | 1222 | 54 | 22.62 | 4 | 0 | 6/135 |
| M.D. Marshall (W) | 1983 | 11 | 2371 | 99 | 1119 | 54 | 20.72 | 2 | 0 | 6/37 |
| H. Trumble (A) | 1902 | 8 | 2520 | 140 | 994 | 53 | 18.75 | 4 | 2 | 8/65 |
| M.H. Mankad (I) | 1952 | 10 | 3512 | 218 | 1170 | 53 | 22.07 | 5 | 2 | 8/52 |
| M.A. Holding (W) | 1976 | 11 | 2305 | 88 | 1080 | 53 | 20.37 | 4 | 1 | 8/92 |
| B.S. Chandrasekhar (I) | 1976 | 11 | 3139 | 108 | 1458 | 52 | 28.03 | 3 | 0 | 6/94 |
| J. Garner (W) | 1980 | 13 | 2758 | 139 | 897 | 52 | 17.25 | 1 | 0 | 6/56 |
| R.G.D.Willis (E) | 1982 | 13 | 2428 | 72 | 1236 | 52 | 23.76 | 2 | 0 | 6/101 |
| G.D. McGrath (A) | 1995 | 10 | 2319 | 92 | 1138 | 52 | 21.88 | 4 | 0 | 6/47 |
| S.K. Warne (A) | 1995 | 12 | 3051 | 156 | 1254 | 52 | 24.11 | 1 | 1 | 7/23 |
| A.A. Donald (SA) | 1998 | 8 | 2032 | 84 | 973 | 52 | 18.71 | 4 | 0 | 6/88 |
| M. Muralidaran (SL) | 1998 | 7 | 2618 | 121 | 1038 | 52 | 19.96 | 5 | 1 | 7/94 |
| M.A. Noble (A) | 1902 | 12 | 2208 | 100 | 989 | 51 | 19.39 | 6 | 2 | 7/17 |
| J.M. Gregory (A) | 1921 | 12 | 2702 | 84 | 1292 | 51 | 25.33 | 3 | 0 | 7/69 |
| A.R.C Fraser (E) | 1998 | 11 | 2345 | 105 | 984 | 51 | 19.29 | 5 | 2 | 8/53 |
| R.G.D. Willis (E) | 1977 | 11 | 2146 | 58 | 1108 | 50 | 22.16 | 5 | 0 | 7/78 |
| T.M. Alderman (A) | 1989 | 10 | 2414 | 106 | 1019 | 50 | 20.38 | 6 | 1 | 6/128 |
| S.K. Warne (A) | 1994 | 8 | 3099 | 174 | 1084 | 50 | 21.68 | 4 | 1 | 7/56 |

## WICKETKEEPERS WITH 30 DISMISSALS IN THE CALENDAR YEAR

| Player | Country | Year | Tests | C | S | Dismissals |
|---|---|---|---|---|---|---|
| I.A. Healy | Australia | 1993 | 15 | 57 | 9 | 66 |
| I.A. Healy | Australia | 1997 | 15 | 55 | 4 | 59 |
| M.V. Boucher | South Africa | 1998 | 10 | 55 | 2 | 57 |
| P.J.L. Dujon | West Indies | 1984 | 15 | 54 | 1 | 55 |
| R.W. Marsh | Australia | 1981 | 13 | 52 | 1 | 53 |
| M.V. Boucher | South Africa | 1998 | 8 | 44 | 2 | 46 |
| R.W. Taylor | England | 1978 | 14 | 43 | 1 | 44 |

| | | | | | | |
|---|---|---|---|---|---|---|
| R.W. Marsh | Australia | 1982 | 12 | 42 | 1 | 43 |
| R.W. Marsh | Australia | 1975 | 10 | 38 | 2 | 40 |
| R.C. Russell | England | 1990 | 12 | 39 | 1 | 40 |
| P.J.L. Dujon | West Indies | 1991 | 10 | 40 | 0 | 40 |
| A.P.E. Knott | England | 1974 | 14 | 37 | 2 | 39 |
| D.L. Murray | West Indies | 1976 | 12 | 37 | 2 | 39 |
| A.J. Stewart | England | 1997 | 9 | 37 | 2 | 39 |
| A.P.E. Knott | England | 1971 | 11 | 34 | 4 | 38 |
| S.M.H. Kirmani | India | 1983 | 18 | 35 | 3 | 38 |
| P.J.L. Dujon | West Indies | 1988 | 12 | 37 | 1 | 38 |
| R.W. Marsh | Australia | 1974 | 9 | 36 | 1 | 37 |
| A.T.W. Grout | Australia | 1961 | 9 | 33 | 3 | 36 |
| I.A. Healy | Australia | 1995 | 12 | 32 | 4 | 36 |
| K.J. Wright | Australia | 1979 | 10 | 31 | 4 | 35 |
| R.W. Taylor | England | 1982 | 14 | 35 | 0 | 35 |
| P.J.L. Dujon | West Indies | 1983 | 11 | 34 | 1 | 35 |
| Wasim Bari | Pakistan | 1983 | 11 | 32 | 3 | 35 |
| A.T.W. Grout | Australia | 1964 | 10 | 33 | 1 | 34 |
| I.A. Healy | Australia | 1991 | 10 | 34 | 0 | 34 |
| M.V. Boucher | South Africa | 1998 | 6 | 32 | 2 | 34 |
| R.W. Marsh | Australia | 1977 | 10 | 33 | 0 | 33 |
| Wasim Bari | Pakistan | 1979 | 9 | 31 | 2 | 33 |
| J.R. Murray | West Indies | 1995 | 9 | 33 | 0 | 33 |
| R.C. Russell | England | 1995 | 7 | 30 | 3 | 33 |
| J.R. Murray | West Indies | 1995 | 9 | 33 | 0 | 33 |
| P.R. Downton | England | 1985 | 9 | 31 | 1 | 32 |
| T.G. Evans | England | 1957 | 9 | 29 | 2 | 31 |
| J.M. Parks | England | 1966 | 10 | 28 | 3 | 31 |
| S.M.H. Kirmani | India | 1979 | 14 | 27 | 4 | 31 |
| D.J. Richardson | South Africa | 1997 | 8 | 29 | 2 | 31 |
| A.T.W. Grout | Australia | 1959 | 8 | 24 | 6 | 30 |
| A.P.E. Knott | England | 1973 | 13 | 30 | 0 | 30 |
| I.A. Healy | Australia | 1995 | 11 | 28 | 2 | 30 |
| D.J. Richardson | South Africa | 1995 | 8 | 30 | 0 | 30 |

## PLAYERS WITH 15 CATCHES IN THE CALENDAR YEAR

| Player | Country | Year | Tests | C |
|---|---|---|---|---|
| S.P. Fleming | New Zealand | 1997 | 10 | 28 |
| J.M. Gregory | Australia | 1921 | 12 | 27 |
| M.A. Taylor | Australia | 1997 | 15 | 27 |
| R.B. Simpson | Australia | 1964 | 14 | 26 |
| M.A. Taylor | Australia | 1993 | 15 | 25 |
| M.A. Taylor | Australia | 1995 | 12 | 24 |
| A.W. Greig | England | 1974 | 13 | 23 |
| I.M. Chappell | Australia | 1974 | 9 | 21 |
| I.T. Botham | England | 1979 | 9 | 20 |
| G.S. Chappell | Australia | 1974 | 9 | 19 |
| G.R.J. Roope | England | 1978 | 9 | 19 |
| M.D. Crowe | New Zealand | 1985 | 10 | 19 |
| A.L. Logie | West Indies | 1988 | 12 | 19 |
| M. Azharuddin | India | 1997 | 12 | 19 |
| G.S. Blewett | Australia | 1997 | 15 | 19 |
| L.C. Braund | England | 1902 | 9 | 18 |
| W.R. Endean | South Africa | 1953 | 7 | 18 |
| R.N. Harvey | Australia | 1959 | 9 | 18 |
| R.B. Simpson | Australia | 1961 | 9 | 18 |

| | | | | |
|---|---|---|---|---|
| G.R.J. Roope | England | 1973 | 8 | 18 |
| A.R. Border | Australia | 1980 | 10 | 18 |
| A.R. Border | Australia | 1981 | 10 | 18 |
| I.M. Chappell | Australia | 1969 | 8 | 17 |
| J.M. Brearley | England | 1977 | 10 | 17 |
| A.W. Greig | England | 1977 | 10 | 17 |
| J.M. Brearley | England | 1978 | 10 | 17 |
| I.T. Botham | England | 1981 | 13 | 17 |
| C.H. Lloyd | West Indies | 1984 | 14 | 17 |
| G.A. Gooch | England | 1986 | 11 | 17 |
| D.C. Boon | Australia | 1989 | 11 | 17 |
| G.B. Hole | Australia | 1953 | 7 | 16 |
| G.S. Chappell | Australia | 1975 | 10 | 16 |
| I.V.A. Richards | West Indies | 1980 | 11 | 16 |
| D.B. Vengsarkar | India | 1979 | 18 | 16 |
| G.S. Chappell | Australia | 1980 | 10 | 16 |
| I.V.A. Richards | West Indies | 1981 | 11 | 16 |
| M.E. Waugh | Australia | 1991 | 9 | 16 # |
| A.R. Border | Australia | 1985 | 12 | 16 |
| M.E. Waugh | Australia | 1993 | 15 | 16 |
| R.S. Mahanama | Sri Lanka | 1997 | 9 | 16 |
| W.R. Hammond | England | 1928 | 10 | 15 |
| M.C. Cowdrey | England | 1957 | 9 | 15 |
| A.L. Wadekar | India | 1968 | 7 | 15 |
| K.R. Stackpole | Australia | 1969 | 8 | 15 |
| M.H. Denness | England | 1974 | 14 | 15 |
| J.J. Crowe | New Zealand | 1985 | 10 | 15 |
| C.L. Hooper | West Indies | 1991 | 10 | 15 |
| A.R. Border | Australia | 1993 | 16 | 15 |
| J.H. Kallis | South Africa | 1998 | 12 | 15 |

*# Waugh achieved the feat in his debut calendar year.*

## SOME NOTABLE 'FIRSTS' AND 'LASTS'

L. Hone was the first player to represent England in a Test without playing for a county. (England v Australia, 1878-79.)

D.C.H. Townsend was the last player to represent England in a Test match without having played for a first-class county. (England v West Indies, 1934-35.)

Rt. Rev. D.S. Sheppard (later Baron Sheppard, Bishop of Liverpool) was the first ordained minister to play Test Cricket.

A. Sandham (England) was the first batsman to score 300 in a Test innings. (325, England v West Indies at Kingston,1929-30.)

W. Bardsley (Australia) was the first batsman to score a century in each innings of a Test match. (136 and 130, Australia v England at The Oval 1909.)

A.K. Davison (Australia) was the first male player to complete the match double of 100 runs and ten wickets in a Test. (44 and 80 runs; 30-2-135-5 and 24.6-4-87-6; Australia v West Indies, Brisbane, 1960-61). E.R. Wilson had performed the feat with eleven wickets and 100 runs (10:3-4-7-7, including the hat-trick, and 19-14-9-4, Australia v England at St Kilda in a women's Test in 1957-58.)

S. Morris (Australia) was the first black man to play in a Test match. (Australia v England at Melbourne, 1884-85.) Morris was born in Hobart of West Indian parents and when the eleven players from the first Test at Adelaide demanded 50% of the gate money for the second Test and were refused by officials, Morris got his chance — he scored 4 and 10* and took 2 for 73 in his only Test.

Gloucestershire-born W.E. Midwinter was the first cricketer to have played for and against Australia in Test matches. Midwinter played eight times for Australia against England 1876-77 (2), 1882-83 (1), 1884 (3), 1886-87 (2). He played four times for England against Australia in 1881-82.

K.C. Wessels is the last player to play for and against Australia in Test cricket. He represented Australia in 24 Tests between 1982-83 and 1985-86, and represented South Africa in 16 Tests between 1991-92 and 1994.

In the second Test at Melbourne in 1882-83, W. Bates achieved the first hat-trick for England when he dismissed P.S. McDonnell, G. Giffen and G.J. Bonnor in Australia's first innings. He became the first player to score a fifty and take ten or more wickets in the same Test. (55 runs; 26.2-14-28-7 and 33-14-74-7) — this was the first Test to be won by an innings.

The first double-century in Test cricket was scored by the Australian captain W.L. Murdoch (211) against England at The Oval in 1884.

P.S. McDonnell (Australia) was the first batsman to score two centuries in successive Test innings. (103 against England at The Oval in 1884 and 124 against England at Adelaide in 1884-85.)

A.Shrewsbury (England) became the first batsman to score 1000 runs in Test cricket, at Lord's in 1893.

J. Briggs (England) became the first player to take 100 Test wickets, at the fourth Test in Sydney, in 1894-95. In the same match, C.T.B. Turner became the first Australian bowler to capture 100 Test wickets.

The first bowler to take nine wickets in a Test innings was G.A. Lohmann for England against South Africa at Johannesburg in 1895-96. (14.2-6-28-9.)

J. Darling (Australia) was the first left-hander to score a hundred in a Test match with 101 against England at Sydney in 1897-98. In the 1897-98 series, Darling became the first batsman to score three hundreds in the same series and the first to aggregate 500 runs in the same series.

## FIRSTS

Australia defeated England three matches to two in 1936-37. This was the first time a country had won a Test series after losing the first two matches.

The third Test at Melbourne in 1946-47 between Australia and England was the first drawn match in Australia since 1881-82.

The first time an extra day was added to a Test match was at Christchurch, in 1946-47 (New Zealand v England) after the third had been washed out but rain prevented play on the extra day also.

The first time Test cricket was played on Christmas Day was in the third Test between Australia and the West Indies at Adelaide in 1951-52.

## A FEW MORE FIRSTS

First ball bowled in Test cricket — by A. Shaw (England) against Australia from eastern end at Melbourne 1876-77.

First run in Test cricket — C. Bannerman (Australia) from the second ball of A. Shaw's first over (above).

First wicket taken in Test cricket — by A. Hill (England) when he clean-bowled N. Thompson (Australia) in Melbourne in 1876-77. (The fourth over bowled in Test cricket).

First five-wickets-in-an-innings haul — W.E. Midwinter (Australia) 5 for 78 against England, in Melbourne, 1876-77.

First ten-wickets-in-match-haul — F.R. Spofforth (Australia) 6 for 48 and 7 for 62 against England, in Melbourne, 1878-79.

First catch taken in Test cricket — A. Hill (England) caught Australian batsman T.P. Horan at third man (England v Australia, Melbourne 1876-77).

First stumping completed in Test cricket — J.M. Blackham (Australia) stumped England's A. Shaw for 2 in the second innings of the first-ever Test match, Melbourne 1876-77.

First boundary hit — by T.P. Horan (Australia) against England at Melbourne 1876-77 (a snick through slips).

First 100-run partnership — W.G. Grace (152) and A.P. Lucas (55) put on 120 for England's second wicket against Australia at The Oval, 1880.

First century — C. Bannerman (Australia), 165 retired hurt, against England at Melbourne 1876-77.

First to score fifty in each innings — 52 and 63, G. Ulyett (England) against Australia, in Melbourne, 1876-77. (In 1881-82, Ulyett became the first to score a century and a 50 in the same Test.)

First hat-trick in Test cricket — F.R. Spofforth (Australia) in dismissing England batsmen V.P.F.A. Royle (bowled), F.A. McKinnon (bowled) and T. Emmett (caught by T.P. Horan) in Melbourne, 1878-79.

First declaration in Test cricket — A.E. Stoddart (England), 8 for 234 against Australia at Lord's, 1893. Match drawn.

First six (without overthrows) in a Test — J. Darling (Australia) against England at Adelaide 1897-98. (To be a six in those early days the ball had to be hit out of the ground and not merely over the boundary.)

First bowler to be 'no-balled' for throwing — E. Jones (Australia) called by umpire J. Phillips in the match against England played at Melbourne, 1897-98.

First century before lunch — K.S. Ranjitsinhji (England) against Australia at Manchester in 1896. 'Ranji' the first Indian to play Test cricket finished not out on 154 in his first Test.

First batsman to carry his bat through a completed innings — A.B. Tancred (South Africa) 26* from a team total of 47 against England at Cape Town in 1888-89.

First Sunday Test match played — India v England, 1933-34, at Bombay (first Test).

First Test match streaker — Michael Angelow on the fourth day of the second test between England and Australia at Lord's, August 1975. He did it to win a bet but lost the proceeds to the magistrate in court the next day.

First U.S. President to watch a Test match — Dwight D. Eisenhower (Pakistan v Australia, Karachi, 1959-60.)

First batsman to wear a protective helmet in a Test — D.L. Amiss (England v West Indies, The Oval in 1976.)

## ATTENDANCE RECORDS

Single day — 90,800 spectators watched the second day (February 11) of the fifth Test between Australia and the West Indies at Melbourne, in 1960-61.

Match - the third Test at Melbourne in 1936-37 attracted 350,534 spectators, the record confirmed crowd for any cricket match. The Test was played on January 1, 2, 4, 5, 6, 7. (*Note:* At the fourth Test at Calcutta in 1981-82, it was *estimated* that about 394,000 attended the five days of the match. However, no official crowd fiigures were kept.)

Series — The five matches in the 1936-37 series between Australia and England attracted 943,000 spectators, the biggest attendance for any Test rubber.

## MOST RUNS OFF ONE BALL

8 E.H. Hendren (169), England v Australia, Brisbane, 1928-29 (four boundary overthrows).

8 J.G. Wright (44), New Zealand v Australia, Melbourne, 1980-81 (four boundary overthrows).

7 A. Sandham (325), England v West Indies, Kingston, 1929-30 (four boundary overthrows).

7 A.P.E. Knott (116), England v West Indies, Leeds, 1976 (one, plus two overthrows, plus four boundary overthrows).

7 Majid Khan (74), Pakistan v Australia, Melbourne, 1981-82 (ran four plus three overthows).

## GAMES ABANDONED WITHOUT A BALL BEING BOWLED

England v Australia, Manchester, 1890 — Rain washed out play on each day.

England v Australia, Manchester, 1938 — Rain washed out play on each day.

Australia v England, Melbourne, 1970-71 — This game, originally scheduled as the Third Test of the series, was abandoned after solid rain on the first three days. A replacement Test, becoming a historic seventh Test of the series, was arranged to replace the washed-out game.

West Indies v England, Georgetown, 1980-81 — Two days before this match was due to start, England bowler Robin Jackman (who had been flown out to replace the injured Bob Willis) had his visitor's permit revoked by the Guyanese Government, and was ordered to leave the country. This was because he had spent several English winters in South Africa (as, incidentally, had several other members of the English team). M.C.C. Manager Alan Smith then issued a statement saying that England would not play this second Test of the series "as it is no longer possible for the Test team to be chosen without restrictions being imposed". The game was then abandoned.

New Zealand v Pakistan, Dunedin, 1988-89 — Heavy sweeping rain caused the match to be called off on the third day.

West Indies v England, Georgetown, 1989-90 — Torrential rain, falling nightly for five days, left the ground under water, and a contentiously early decision to abandon the match was made on the rest day.

Sri Lanka v Pakistan, Sinhalese Sports Club Ground, Colombo, 1994-95 — Cancelled due to post-election curfew.

## FAVOURITE GROUNDS

1. J.B. Hobbs (England) scored 1178 runs avge. 69.29 at Melbourne - 83 and 28; 57 and 0 (1907-08); 6 and 126*; 178 (1911-12); 122 and 20; 27 and 13 (1920-21); 154 and 22; 66 (1924-25); 20 and 49; 142 and 65 (1928-29).
2. H. Sutcliffe (England) scored 724 runs avge 103.50 at Melbourne - 176 and 127; 143 (1924-25); 58 and 135 (1928-29); 52 and 33 (1932-33).
3. W.R. Hammond (England) scored 808 runs avge. 161.60 at Sydney - 251 (1928-29); 112; 101 and 75* (1932-33); 231* (1936-37); 1 and 37 (1946-47).
4. D.G. Bradman (Australia) scored 1671 runs avge. 128.53 at Melbourne - 79 and 112; 123 and 37* (1928-29); 152 (1930-31); 2 and 167 (1931-32); 0 and 103* (1932-33); 13 and 270; 169 (1936-37); 79 and 49 (1946-47); 132 and 127*; 57 retired hurt (1947-48).
5. D.G. Bradman (Australia) scored 963 runs avge. 192.60 at Leeds - 334 (1930); 304 (1934); 103 and 16 (1938); 33 and 173* (1948).
6. L. Hutton (England) scored 1521 runs avge. 89.47 at The Oval - 12 (1937); 364 (1938); 73 and 165* (1939); 25 (1946); 83 and 36 (1947); 30 and 64 (1948); 206 (1949); 20* and 2 (1950); 28 and 27 (1951); 86 (1952); 82 and 17 (1953); 14 and 5 (1954).
7. D.C.S. Compton (England) scored 955 runs avge. 95.50 at Nottingham - 102 (1938); 65 and 163 (1947); 19 and 184 (1948); 112 and 5 (1951); 0 (1953); 278 (1954); 27 (1955).

8. E.D. Weekes (West Indies) scored 1074 runs avge. 97.63 at Port-of-Spain - 30 and 20 (1947-48); 207; 161 and 55*(1952-53); 206 and 1 (1953-54); 139 and 87* (1954-55); 78 and 24; 51 and 9 (1957-58).

9. G.S. Sobers (West Indies) scored 1354 runs avge. 104.15 at Kingston - 14* and 26 (1953-54); 35* and 64 (1954-55); 365* (1957-58); 147 and 19 (1959-60); 153; 104 and 50 (1961-62); 30 and 27 (1964-65); 0 and 113* (1967-68); 44 and 93 (1967-68); 44 and 93 (1970-71); 13* (1971-72); 57 (1973-74).

10. W.M. Lawry (Australia) scored 1023 runs avge. 78.69 at Melbourne - 52 and 57 (1962-63); 157 and 20 (1963-64); 41 and 19 (1964-65); 88 and 78; 108 (1965-66); 100 (1967-68); 205 (1968-69); 56 and 42 (1970-71).

11. S.M. Gavaskar (India) scored 793 runs avge 113.28 at Port-of-Spain - 64 and 67*; 124 and 220 (1970-71); 156; 26 and 10 (1975-76); 1 and 32 (1982-83).

12. G.S. Chappell (Australia) scored 1006 runs avge. 111.78 at Brisbane (Woolloongabba) - 58 and 71 (1974-75); 123 and 109* (1975-76); 74 and 124 (1979-80); 35 (1980-81); 201 (1981-82); 53 and 8 (1982-83); 150* (1983-84).

13. Zaheer Abbas (Pakistan) scored 1093 runs avge. 99.36 at Lahore - 18 and 33 (1974-75); 15 and 15 (1976-77); 235* and 34* (1978-79); 134 (1981-82); 52 (v Australia 1982-83); 215; 13 (v India 1982-83); 82* and 5 (1983-84); 168* (v India 1984-85); 43 and 31 (v New Zealand 1984-85).

14. Javed Miandad (Pakistan) scored 1068 runs avge. 56.21 at Faisalabad - 154* and 6* (1978-79); 106* (1979-80); 50 and 22 (1980-81); 18 and 36 (1981-82); 6 (v Australia 1982-83); 126; 16 (v India 1982-83); 203* (1985-86); 1 and 30 (1986-87); 19 (1987-88); 43 and 107 (1988-89); 13 (1989-90); 25 and 55 (v New Zealand 1990-91); 7 and 9 (v West Indies 1990-91); 14 and 2 (1991-92).

15. A.R. Border (Australia) scored 1415 runs avge. 58.95 at Adelaide - 11 and 1 (1978-79); 54 and 24 (1979-80); 57 and 7 (1980-81); 78 and 126 (1981-82); 26 (1982-83); 117* and 66 (1983-84); 21 and 18 (1984-85); 49 (1985-86); 70 and 100* (1986-87); 205 (1987-88); 64 and 6* (1988-89); 13 and 8 (1989-90); 12 and 83* (1990-91); 0 and 91* (1991-92); 19 + 1 (1992-93); 84 + 4 (1993-94).

16. M.D. Crowe (New Zealand) scored 1123 runs avge. 70.18 at Wellington - 9 (1981-82); 13 and 100 (1983-84); 37 and 33 (1984-85); 19 (1985-86); 3 and 119 (1986-87); 143 (1987-88); 174 and 0 (1988-89); 30 and 299 (1989-90); 30 and 13* (1991-92); 98 + 3 (1992-93).

17. D.C. Boon (Australia) scored 1127 runs avge. 62.61 at Sydney - 49 (1984-85); 0 and 81 (v New Zealand 1985-86); 131 and 25 (v India 1985-86); 12 and 184* v England (1987-88); 149 and 10 (1988-89); 97 and 29 (1990-91); 129* and 7 (1991-92); 76 + 63* (1992-93); 50 + 38 (1993-94); 3 + 17 (1994-95); 16 + 6 (1995-96).

## 1000 RUNS AT A TEST GROUND

| Player | Country | Ground | M | I | NO | Runs | HS | Avge | 100's | 50's | 0's |
|---|---|---|---|---|---|---|---|---|---|---|---|
| G.A. Gooch | Eng | Lord's | 21 | 39 | 1 | 2015 | 333 | 53.02 | 6 | 5 | 2 |
| D.G. Bradman | Aust | Melbourne | 11 | 17 | 4 | 1671 | 270 | 128.53 | 9 | 3 | 1 |
| L. Hutton | Eng | The Oval | 12 | 19 | 2 | 1521 | 364 | 89.47 | 4 | 5 | 0 |
| A.R. Border | Aust | Adelaide | 16 | 29 | 5 | 1415 | 205 | 58.95 | 4 | 9 | 1 |
| Javed Miandad | Pak | Karachi[1] | 17 | 25 | 1 | 1393 | 211 | 58.04 | 3 | 8 | 0 |
| G.S. Sobers | WI | Kingston | 11 | 18 | 5 | 1354 | 365* | 104.15 | 5 | 4 | 0 |
| A.R. Border | Aust | Melbourne | 20 | 36 | 3 | 1272 | 163 | 38.54 | 4 | 5 | 3 |
| G.S. Chappell | Aust | Melbourne | 17 | 31 | 4 | 1257 | 121 | 46.55 | 4 | 9 | 4 |
| D.I. Gower | Eng | Lord's | 17 | 30 | 2 | 1241 | 108 | 44.32 | 2 | 8 | 1 |
| R.B. Kanhai | WI | Port-of-Spain | 16 | 31 | 3 | 1212 | 153 | 43.28 | 4 | 4 | 1 |
| D.L. Haynes | WI | Bridgetown | 13 | 25 | 5 | 1210 | 145 | 60.50 | 4 | 6 | 1 |
| G. Boycott | Eng | Lord's | 16 | 29 | 3 | 1189 | 128* | 45.73 | 3 | 6 | 1 |
| J.B. Hobbs | Eng | Melbourne | 10 | 18 | 1 | 1178 | 178 | 69.29 | 5 | 4 | 1 |
| A.R. Border | Aust | Sydney | 17 | 29 | 8 | 1177 | 89 | 56.04 | 0 | 11 | 0 |
| G.S. Chappell | Aust | Sydney | 12 | 22 | 4 | 1150 | 204 | 63.88 | 4 | 3 | 2 |
| M.D. Crowe | NZ | Wellington | 10 | 17 | 1 | 1123 | 299 | 70.18 | 5 | 1 | 1 |
| S.M. Gavaskar | India | Mumbai[3] | 11 | 20 | 0 | 1122 | 205 | 56.10 | 5 | 3 | 0 |
| Javed Miandad | Pak | Lahore[2] | 17 | 23 | 3 | 1122 | 163 | 56.10 | 3 | 3 | 0 |
| G.A. Gooch | Eng | The Oval | 12 | 22 | 1 | 1097 | 196 | 52.23 | 1 | 9 | 3 |
| Zaheer Abbas | Pak | Lahore[2] | 10 | 15 | 4 | 1093 | 235* | 99.36 | 4 | 2 | 0 |

| | | | | | | | | | | | |
|---|---|---|---|---|---|---|---|---|---|---|---|
| D.C. Boon | Aust | Sydney | 11 | 21 | 3 | 1127 | 184* | 62.61 | 4 | 4 | 1 |
| E.D. Weekes | WI | Port-of-Spain | 7 | 13 | 2 | 1074 | 207 | 97.63 | 4 | 4 | 0 |
| Javed Miandad | Pak | Faisalabad | 15 | 23 | 4 | 1068 | 203* | 56.21 | 5 | 2 | 0 |
| P.A. de Silva | SL | Colombo,SSC | 11 | 20 | 3 | 1060 | 146 | 62.35 | 5 | 2 | 0 |
| J.G. Wright, | NZ | Auckland | 15 | 29 | 2 | 1060 | 130 | 39.25 | 3 | 5 | 1 |
| C.H. Lloyd | WI | Port-of-Spain | 16 | 28 | 2 | 1035 | 143 | 39.80 | 2 | 1 | 0 |
| A.J. Stewart | Eng | Lord's | 11 | 22 | 2 | 1031 | 119 | 51.55 | 2 | 7 | 0 |
| W.M. Lawry | Aust | Melbourne | 8 | 13 | 0 | 1023 | 205 | 78.69 | 4 | 5 | 0 |
| S.M. Gavaskar | India | Chennai[1] | 12 | 21 | 4 | 1018 | 236* | 59.88 | 3 | 3 | 1 |
| I.V.A. Richards | WI | Port-of-Spain | 14 | 21 | 0 | 1015 | 177 | 48.33 | 3 | 4 | 1 |
| G.S. Chappell | Aust | Brisbane[2] | 7 | 11 | 2 | 1006 | 201 | 111.77 | 5 | 4 | 0 |
| J.G. Wright | NZ | Wellington | 13 | 23 | 2 | 1005 | 138 | 47.85 | 3 | 4 | 1 |

## FIFTY WICKETS AT A TEST GROUND

| Player | Country | Ground | M | Balls | Mdns | Runs | Wkts | Avge | 5w | 10w | Best |
|---|---|---|---|---|---|---|---|---|---|---|---|
| D.K. Lillee | Aust | Melbourne | 14 | 3833 | 105 | 1798 | 82 | 21.92 | 7 | 4 | 7/83 |
| R.J. Hadlee | NZ | Christchurch | 14 | 3679 | 112 | 1635 | 76 | 21.51 | 6 | 0 | 7/116 |
| I.T. Botham | Eng | Lord's | 15 | 3194 | 125 | 1693 | 69 | 24.53 | 8 | 1 | 8/34 |
| F.S. Trueman | Eng | Lord's | 12 | 3087 | 113 | 1394 | 63 | 22.12 | 5 | 1 | 6/31 |
| Abdul Qadir | Pak | Karachi[1] | 13 | 3655 | 128 | 1571 | 59 | 26.62 | 5 | 1 | 5/44 |
| Imran Khan | Pak | Lahore[2] | 11 | 2443 | 93 | 937 | 56 | 16.73 | 3 | 1 | 8/58 |
| C.E.L. Ambrose | WI | Port-of-Spain | 10 | 2284 | 100 | 767 | 54 | 14.20 | 6 | 1 | 6/24 |
| R.J. Hadlee | NZ | Wellington | 12 | 2623 | 90 | 1075 | 53 | 20.28 | 3 | 2 | 7/23 |
| I.T. Botham | Eng | The Oval | 11 | 2615 | 90 | 1379 | 52 | 26.51 | 2 | 1 | 6/125 |
| L.R. Gibbs | WI | Port-of-Spain | 13 | 4754 | 239 | 1646 | 52 | 31.65 | 2 | 0 | 6/108 |
| A.V. Bedser | Eng | Manchester | 7 | 1816 | 88 | 686 | 51 | 13.45 | 5 | 2 | 7/52 |
| Imran Khan | Pak | Karachi[1] | 11 | 2406 | 100 | 938 | 51 | 18.39 | 2 | 1 | 8/60 |
| Abdul Qadir | Pak | Lahore[2] | 12 | 3099 | 105 | 1348 | 51 | 26.43 | 3 | 2 | 9/56 |

## BATTING CURIOSITIES

1. A.C. Bannerman (Australia v England, Sydney 1891-92) scored off only five of 208 balls bowled to him by W. Attewell. Attewell bowled 46 overs (6-ball), 24 of which were maidens, for figures of 1 for 43. Bannerman batted 421 minutes for his 91.

2. C.F. Root (England) played in three Test matches during his career and failed to get a hit in any of them. (All v Australia 1926.)

3. C.S. Nayudu (India v England, Calcutta 1933-34) played only four scoring strokes in a stay of 145 minutes — a six, two fours and a single.

4. W.J. Edrich (England) played two innings before lunch on the third day of the Test against South Africa at Nottingham in 1947. Edrich had been not out at the start of play, and came in at number three when England followed-on.

5. R.A. Duff and W.H. Ponsford (Australia) scored a century in their first and last Tests against England.

6. M. Leyland and R. Subba Row (England) scored a century in their first and last Tests against Australia.

7. A.R. Morris (Australia) batted at one end and D.G. Bradman and I.W. Johnson at the other for 100 minutes against England at The Oval in1948 before the first single was scored and the batsmen changed ends.

8. Three batsmen in the Australian team against England at Nottingham in 1953 scored 237 out of 244 runs from the bat in Australia's first innings of 249. A.R. Morris hit 67, A.L. Hassett 115, and K.R. Miller 55, Morris and Hassett sharing a stand of 122 for the second wicket and Hassett and Miller one of 109 for the fourth. The next highest score was 4.

9. Each batsman to go to the crease in the test between India and New Zealand at Delhi in 1955-56 reached double figures. Highest of the 15 who batted was 230*, lowest 10*.

10. There have been nine instances of all eleven batsmen reaching double figures in an innings of a Test match. On each occasion a team score of over 350 has been recorded. The most recent instance was for Australia against Sri Lanka at Colombo in 1992-93.

11. Only once has an innings been completed without a single batsman reaching double figures. This was when South Africa was all out for 30 against England at Birmingham in 1924 — the highest score was 7 and there were eleven extras.

12. In 1932 the Nawab of Pataudi snr scored a century in his first Test against Australia. Thirty-two years later his son achieved the same distinction.

13. W.J. Edrich (England) who batted on 63 occasions for his country at an average of 40.00 had an incredible run of failures during 1938 and 1939. In consecutive innings, he scored 5, 0, 10, 12, 28, 12, 4, 10, 0, 6 and 1. In his next he notched up 219.

14. In the second Test between South Africa and New Zealand in 1953-54, two New Zealand batsmen retired hurt before scoring. Both had been hit by balls from N.A.T. Adcock — B. Sutcliffe on the head and L.S.M. Miller on the chest. Both returned later — Sutcliffe scoring 80*, including seven sixes, and Miller 14.

15. In the first Test of the 1957-58 rubber between West Indies and Pakistan played at Bridgetown, Pakistan scored 106 in its first innings and 8d-657 in its second — a difference of 551 between the two innings.

16. R.E. Foster's score of 287 at Sydney in the first Test of the 1903-04 series is the highest score by any player in his first Test. He was the first player to share in three century partnerships in the same innings.

17. In the first Test of the triangular Tournament at Manchester in 1912, T.A.Ward, South Africa, bagged a 'king pair'. He was the third victim of T.J. Matthews's two hat-tricks and was dismissed twice on the one day (May 28).

18. In the second Test between South Africa and Australia at Johannesburg[1] in 1921-22, A.W. Nourse (South Africa) became the oldest player to score a maiden Test century at 43 years and 294 days.

19. At Lord's in 1926, W. Bardsley carried his bat in scoring 193*. At 42 years and 201 days he is the oldest to score a century for Australia against England.

20. G.A. Headley (West Indies) with scores of 176, 114, 112, and 223 was the first batsman to score four Test hundreds before turning 21. S.R.Tendulkar (India) passed this record by scoring seven Test centuries before his 21st birthday.

21. G.C. Grant (West Indies) against Australia at Adelaide in 1930-31 with scores of 53* and 71*, was the first batsman to score a not-out fifty in each innings of a Test.

22. A.G. Ganteaume (West Indies) scored 112 in his only Test innings at Port-of-Spain against England, 1947-48.

23. At Durban in 1964-65, K.F. Barrington (England) became the first batsman to score a Test hundred in all seven Test-playing countries. (Since Barrington's retirement, Sri Lanka played its first Test in 1982 and Zimbabwe played its first Test in 1992-93.)

24. At Bridgetown in 1964-65, Australia's W.M. Lawry (210) and R.B. Simpson (201) became the first opening pair to score double-centuries in the same Test innings.

25. I.M. Chappell (Australia) with 165 scored the 1000th Test hundred, against the West Indies at Melbourne in 1968-69. It was scored in the 643rd Test match.

26. G.M. Turner (New Zealand) became the youngest player to carry his bat through a completed Test innings. Turner was 22 years and 63 days when he scored scored 43* at Lord's in 1969.

27. In South Africa's last official Test series against Australia before their 22 year isolation, B.A. Richards became the only batsman to score 500 runs in his first rubber for South Africa (508 runs, average 72.57).

28. The record aggregate for a batsman playing in his first rubber is 774 (average 154.80) scored by S.M. Gavaskar (India v West Indies 1970-71).

29. The highest aggregate by a batsman in his debut calendar year is 1219 (average 64.15) by M.A. Taylor (Australia) in 1989.

30. The first time brothers scored centuries in the same innings of a Test was at The Oval in 1972. I.M.Chappell (118) and G.S.Chappell (113), Australia v England.

31. R.E. Redmond (New Zealand) scored 107 and 56 in his only Test match at Auckland against Pakistan in 1972-73. (see also A.G. Ganteaume.)

32. The first time brothers scored centuries in each innings of the same Test was at Wellington in 1973-74. I.M.Chappell (145 and 121) and G.S. Chappell (247* and 133) against New Zealand.

33. M.E. Waugh and S.R. Waugh (Australia) provided the first instance in Test cricket of twins playing in the same Test — against West Indies at Port-of-Spain in 1990-91.

34. G.S. Chappell (Australia) became the first player to score centuries in each innings of his first Test as captain, with 123 and 109* against West Indies at Brisbane in 1975-76.

35. When S. Amarnath (India) scored 124 against New Zealand at Auckland in 1975-76, he became the first player to emulate his father by scoring a century in his first Test. (*Note:* 'Lala' Amarnath, 118, against England in 1933-34.)

36. The record number of runs scored in Tests in a calendar year was achieved by I.V.A. Richards (West Indies) in 1976 with 1710 runs (average 90.00).

37. In the second Test at Kanpur in 1976-77, India scored 524 against New Zealand. This is the highest total in Test cricket in which no batsman has scored a century.

38. At Leeds in 1977, G. Boycott (England) became the first batsman to score his 100th first-class century in a Test match when he scored 191 against Australia.

39. C. Hill (Australia) became the only batsman to be dismissed for three consecutive nineties: 99 (second innings, second Test) 98 and 97 (third Test) against England in 1901-02. In this series, Hill also became the first player to score 500 runs in a series without making a century. In his career, Hill made the following nervous nineties scores: 96, 99, 98, 97, 91*, 98.

    The only other batsmen to score 500 runs in a series without making a century are: C.C. Hunte, (West Indies v Australia 1964-65); M.A. Atherton, (England v Australia 1993); G.P. Thorpe, (England v West Indies 1995).

40. F.C.M. Alexander (West Indies) who went in at the fall of the seventh wicket, was not called upon to face a single ball in the first innings of the fourth Test against England played at Leeds in 1957. F.S. Trueman took a wicket with the last ball of the over and in the next, P.J. Loader took a hat-trick to dismiss the last three batsmen and end the innings. Four wickets fell in consecutive balls.

41. M.C. Cowdrey (England) became the first cricketer to play 100 Tests (England v Australia, Birmingham, 1968). He duly celebrated this feat by scoring 104.

## SIXES TO WIN TEST MATCHES

At Brisbane, (fourth Test 1932-33) E. Paynter won the match, and the Ashes, for England by hitting a six.

At Sydney, (fifth Test 1932-33) W.R. Hammond (England) won the match by hitting a six.

At Bridgetown, (first Test 1934-35) W.R. Hammond (England) won the match by hitting a six. (This was the only Test that the West Indies lost at Bridgetown until 1994-95.)

At Georgetown, (third Test 1953-54) W. Watson (England) won the match by hitting a six.

At Port Elizabeth, (fifth Test 1966-67) H.R. Lance (South Africa v Australia) won the match by hitting a six.

At Lahore, (first Test 1976-77) Javed Miandad (Pakistan v New Zealand) won the match by hitting a six.

At Auckland, (second Test 1976-77) A. Turner (Australia) won the match by hitting a six.

At Lahore, (second Test 1978-79) Zaheer Abbas (Pakistan v India) won the match by hitting a six.

At Auckland, (first Test 1981-82) R.J. Hadlee (New Zealand v Australia) won the match by hitting a six.

At Karachi, (first Test 1982-83) Mohsin Khan (Pakistan v Australia) won the match by hitting a six.

At Kingston, (first Test 1982-83) P.J.L. Dujon (West Indies v India) won the match by hitting a six.

At Wellington, (second Test 1982-83) R.J. Hadlee (New Zealand v Sri Lanka) won the match by hitting a six.

At Lord's, (first Test 1986) Kapil Dev (India) won the match by hitting a six.

At Kingston, (fourth Test 1988-89) A.L. Logie (West Indies v India) won the match by hitting a six.

At Birmingham, (fourth Test 1991) I.V.A. Richards (West Indies) won the match by hitting a six.

At Colombo, (only Test 1992-93) S.T. Jayasuriya (Sri Lanka v England) won the match by hitting the first ball he faced for six.

At Auckland, (first Test 1993-94) Rashid Latif (Pakistan) won the match by hitting a six.

At Port Elizabeth, (second Test 1996-97) I.A. Healy (Australia) won the match by hitting a six.

At St John's, (second Test 1996-97) C.L. Hooper (West Indies v Sri Lanka) won the match by hitting a six.

## REACHING CENTURY WITH A SIX

| Batsman | Bowler | | | | | |
|---|---|---|---|---|---|---|
| J. Darling (178) | J. Briggs | Australia | v | England | Adelaide | 1897-98 |
| E.H. Bowley (109) | W.E. Merritt | England | v | New Zealand | Auckland | 1929-30 |
| P.R. Umrigar (130) | S. Ramadhin | India | v | West Indies | Port-of-Spain | 1952-53 |
| P.L. Winslow (108) | G.A.R. Lock | South Africa | v | England | Manchester | 1955 |
| K.F. Barrington (132*) | R.B. Simpson | England | v | Australia | Adelaide | 1962-63 |
| K.F. Barrington (121) | M.A. Seymour | England | v | South Africa | Johannesburg[3] | 1964-65 |
| J.H. Edrich (103) | P.I. Philpott | England | v | Australia | Sydney | 1965-66 |
| K.F. Barrington (115) | T.R. Veivers | England | v | Australia | Melbourne | 1965-66 |
| D.T. Lindsay (131) | D.A. Renneberg | South Africa | v | Australia | Johannesburg[3] | 1966-67 |
| K.F. Barrington (143) | L.R. Gibbs | England | v | West Indies | Port-of-Spain | 1967-68 |
| B.R. Taylor (124) | R.M. Edwards | New Zealand | v | West Indies | Auckland | 1968-69 |
| J. Benaud (142) | Intikhab Alam | Australia | v | Pakistan | Melbourne | 1972-73 |

| | | | | | | |
|---|---|---|---|---|---|---|
| K.R.Stackpole (142) | M.L.C. Foster | Australia | v | West Indies | Kingston | 1972-73 |
| K.D. Walters (103) | R.G.D. Willis | Australia | v | England | Perth | 1974-75 |
| D.L. Amiss (179) | B.S. Chandrasekhar | England | v | India | Delhi | 1976-77 |
| I.C. Davis (105) | Salim Altaf | Australia | v | Pakistan | Adelaide | 1976-77 |
| R.B. McCosker (107) | R.G.D. Willis | Australia | v | England | Nottingham | 1977 |
| Haroon Rashid (108) | G. Miller | Pakistan | v | England | Hyderabad | 1977-78 |
| Javed Miandad (154*) | B.S. Bedi | Pakistan | v | India | Faisalabad | 1978-79 |
| Kapil Dev (126*) | N. Phillip | India | v | West Indies | Delhi | 1978-79 |
| I.T. Botham (137) | Kapil Dev | England | v | India | Leeds | 1979 |
| C.L. King (100*) | G.P. Howarth | West Indies | v | New Zealand | Christchurch | 1979-80 |
| J.G. Wright (110) | R.J. Shastri | New Zealand | v | India | Auckland | 1980-81 |
| I.T. Botham (118) | M.R. Whitney | England | v | Australia | Manchester | 1981 |
| L.R.D. Mendis (105) | D.R. Doshi | Sri Lanka | v | India | Madras | 1982-83 |
| Imran Khan (117) | Kapil Dev | Pakistan | v | India | Faisalabad | 1982-83 |
| P.A. de Silva (122) | Imran Khan | Sri Lanka | v | Pakistan | Faisalabad | 1985-86 |
| G.R.J. Matthews (115) | V.R. Brown | Australia | v | New Zealand | Brisbane[2] | 1985-86 |
| Imran Khan (135*) | N.S. Yadav | Pakistan | v | India | Madras | 1986-87 |
| M.D. Crowe (104) | C.G. Butts | New Zealand | v | West Indies | Auckland | 1986-87 |
| Ijaz Faqih (105) | Maninder Singh | Pakistan | v | India | Ahmedabad | 1986-87 |
| D.L. Haynes (112*) | N.D. Hirwani | West Indies | v | India | Bridgetown | 1988-89 |
| C.C. Lewis (117) | S.L. Venkatapathy Raju | England | v | India | Madras | 1992-93 |
| D.L. Haynes (125) | Asif Mujtaba | West Indies | v | Pakistan | Bridgetown | 1992-93 |
| C.L. Hooper (178*) | Nadeem Khan | West Indies | v | Pakistan | St John's | 1992-93 |
| P.A. de Silva (148) | A.R. Kumble | Sri Lanka | v | India | Colombo (PSS) | 1993-94 |
| P.A. de Silva (127) | Mushtaq Ahmed | Sri Lanka | v | Pakistan | Colombo (PSS) | 1994-95 |
| S.R. Tendulkar (179) | C.A. Walsh | India | v | West Indies | Nagpur | 1994-95 |
| R.G. Samuels (125) | D.N. Patel | West Indies | v | New Zealand | St John's | 1995-96 |
| S.R. Tendulkar (122) | M.M. Patel | India | v | England | Birmingham | 1996 |
| Inzamamul Haq (148) | G.A. Hick | Pakistan | v | England | Lord's | 1996 |
| Wasim Akram (257*) | A.R. Whittall | Pakistan | v | Zimbabwe | Sheikhupura | 1996-97 |
| J.P. Crawley (112) | H.H. Streak | England | v | Zimbabwe | Bulawayo[2] | 1996-97 |
| B.C. Lara (103) | A.R. Kumble | West Indies | v | India | St John's | 1996-97 |
| G.W. Flower (150) | C.L. Cairns | Zimbabwe | v | New Zealand | Harare | 1997-98 |
| C.D. McMillan (139) | A.R. Whittall | New Zealand | v | Zimbabwe | Wellington | 1997-98 |
| M. Azharuddin (163*) | G.R. Robertson | India | v | Australia | Calcutta | 1997-98 |

*R.N. Harvey (153) reached his 100 with an all-run five from the bowling of N.B.Amarnath - Australia v India at Melbourne 1947-78.*

## BOUNDARY CURIOSITIES

1. E.H. Hendren (England) v Australia at Brisbane in 1928-29 scored an eight (including four overthrows) from the bowling of P.M. Hornibrook.

2. G.S. Sobers (West Indies) v Australia at Bridgetown 1954-55 hit ten fours in an innings of 43, his other scoring shots consisting of three singles.

3. J.H. Edrich (England) v New Zealand at Leeds 1965 scored 238 in boundary hits (five sixes and 52 fours) in an innings of 310*. Edrich is the only batsman to accumulate more than 200 runs through boundaries in a Test innings.

4. K.H. Weekes (West Indies) v England at The Oval, 1939, scored four successive fours from the bowling of R.T.D. Perks.

5. D.T. Lindsay (South Africa) v Australia at Port Elizabeth in 1969-70 scored five consecutive fours from the bowling of J.W.Gleeson.

6. R.E. Redmond (New Zealand) v Pakistan at Auckland 1972-73 scored five consecutive fours from the bowling of Majid J.Khan.

7. D.W. Hookes (Australia) v England at Melbourne 1976-77 hit five successive fours from the bowling of A.W. Greig.

8. S.M. Patil (India) v England at Manchester 1982 scored six successive boundaries from the bowling of R.G.D. Willis.

9. B. Sutcliffe (New Zealand) v South Africa at Johannesburg 1953-54 hit four sixes (three in four balls) from one eight-ball over bowled by H.J. Tayfield.

10. F.S. Trueman (England) v West Indies at Lord's 1957 hit three sixes from one six-ball over bowled by S. Ramadhin.

11. W.R. Hammond (England) v New Zealand at Auckland 1932-33 hit three successive sixes from the bowling of J. Newman.

12. W. Voce (England) v South Africa at Johannesburg 1930-31 hit three sixes from four balls bowled by A.E. Hall.

13. R.C. Motz (New Zealand) v England at Dunedin 1965-66 hit three sixes from five balls bowled by D.A. Allen.

14. A.M.E. Roberts (West Indies) v England at Port-of-Spain 1980-81 hit three sixes and a four from five balls bowled by I.T. Botham.

15. S.T. Clarke (West Indies) v Pakistan at Faisalabad 1980-81 hit three sixes from three successive balls bowled by Mohammad Nazir.

16. I.V.A. Richards (West Indies) in making 145 v England at Lord's 1980 hit 106 runs in boundaries — 25 four and one six.

17. B.L. Cairns (New Zealand) hit three sixes in one over from the bowling of D.R. Parry v West Indies at Dunedin 1979-80.

18. Intikhab Alam (Pakistan ) hit eleven fours in his score of 48 v Australia at Melbourne 1972-73.

19. Kapil Dev (India) at Lord's v England in 1982 scored 70 runs from boundaries in an innings of 89. He hit 13 fours and three sixes.

20. Kapil Dev (India) at Lord's v England in 1990 hit four successive sixes off the last four balls of an over from E.E. Hemmings to avoid the follow-on.

## MOST RUNS FROM STROKES WORTH FOUR OR MORE IN AN INNINGS

| | 6's | 5's | 4's | | | | | | | |
|---|---|---|---|---|---|---|---|---|---|---|
| 238 | 5 | - | 52 | J.H. Edrich | 310* | England | v | New Zealand | Leeds | 1965 |
| 196 | 10 | - | 34 | W.R. Hammond | 336* | England | v | New Zealand | Auckland | 1932-33 |
| 190 | 3 | - | 43 | G.A. Gooch | 333 | England | v | India | The Oval | 1990 |
| 184 | - | - | 46 | D.G. Bradman | 334 | Australia | v | England | Leeds | 1930 |
| 184 | 2 | - | 43 | D.G. Bradman | 304 | Australia | v | England | Leeds | 1934 |
| 180 | - | - | 45 | B.C. Lara | 375 | West Indies | v | England | St John's | 1993-94 |
| 177 | - | 1 | 43 | R.G. Pollock | 274 | South Africa | v | Australia | Durban[2] | 1969-70 |
| 168 | - | - | 42 | R.B. Kanhai | 256 | West Indies | v | India | Calcutta | 1958-59 |
| 166 | 1 | - | 40 | D.L. Amiss | 262* | England | v | West Indies | Kingston | 1973-74 |
| 160 | - | - | 40 | P.A. de Silva | 267 | Sri Lanka | v | New Zealand | Wellington | 1990-91 |
| 160 | 12 | - | 22 | Wasim Akram | 257* | Pakistan | v | Sri Lanka | Sheikhupura | 1996-97 |
| 158 | 3 | - | 35 | D.L. Houghton | 266 | Zimbabwe | v | Sri Lanka | Bulawayo[2] | 1994-95 |
| 157 | - | 1 | 38 | G.S. Sobers | 365* | West Indies | v | Pakistan | Kingston | 1957-58 |
| 156 | 2 | - | 36 | S.T. Jayasuriya | 340 | Sri Lanka | v | India | Colombo (PIS) | 1997-98 |
| 152 | 2 | - | 35 | F.M.M. Worrell | 261 | West Indies | v | England | Nottingham | 1957 |
| 152 | - | - | 38 | Zaheer Abbas | 274 | Pakistan | v | England | Birmingham | 1971 |
| 152 | - | - | 38 | I.V.A. Richards | 291 | West Indies | v | England | The Oval | 1976 |
| 152 | - | - | 38 | B.C. Lara | 277 | West Indies | v | Australia | Sydney | 1992-93 |
| 152 | - | - | 38 | N. Hussain | 207 | England | v | Australia | Birmingham | 1997 |
| 150 | 1 | - | 36 | L.G. Rowe | 302 | West Indies | v | England | Bridgetown | 1973-74 |

## MOST SIXES IN AN INNINGS

| | | | | | | |
|---|---|---|---|---|---|---|
| **TWELVE** | Wasim Akram (257*) | Pakistan | v | Sri Lanka | Sheikhupura | 1996-97 |
| **TEN** | W.R. Hammond (336*) | England | v | New Zealand | Auckland | 1932-33 |
| **NINE** | C.L. Cairns (120) | New Zealand | v | Zimbabwe | Auckland | 1995-96 |
| **EIGHT** | N.S. Sidhu (124) | India | v | Sri Lanka | Lucknow[2] | 1993-94 |
| **SEVEN** | B. Sutcliffe (80*) | New Zealand | v | South Africa | Johannesburg[2] | 1953-54 |
| | I.V.A. Richards (110*) | West Indies | v | England | St John's | 1985-86 |
| | C G. Greenidge (213) | West Indies | v | New Zealand | Auckland | 1986-87 |
| **SIX** | J.H. Sinclair (104) | South Africa | v | Australia | Cape Town | 1902-03 |
| | I.V.A. Richards (192*) | West Indies | v | India | Delhi | 1974-75 |
| | Haroon Rashid (108) | Pakistan | v | England | Hyderabad | 1977-78 |

| | | | | | |
|---|---|---|---|---|---|
| I.T. Botham (118) | England | v | Australia | Manchester | 1981 |
| R.J. Shastri (121*) | India | v | Australia | Mumbai[3] | 1986-87 |
| W.J. Cronje (82) | South Africa | v | Sri Lanka | Centurion | 1997-98 |
| C.D. McMillan (142) | New Zealand | v | Sri Lanka | Colombo (PIS) | 1997-98 |

## MOST SIXES OFF CONSECUTIVE BALLS

| | | | | | | |
|---|---|---|---|---|---|---|
| **FOUR** | Kapil Dev (77*) off E.E.Hemmings | India | v | England | Lord's | 1990 |
| **THREE** | W.R. Hammond (336*) off J.Newman | England | v | New Zealand | Auckland | 1932-33 |
| | S.T. Clarke (35*) off Mohammad Nazir | West Indies | v | Pakistan | Faisalabad | 1980-81 |
| | W.J. Cronje (82) off M.Muralidaran | South Africa | v | Sri Lanka | Centurion | 1997-98 |

## MOST FOURS OFF CONSECUTIVE BALLS

| | | | | | | |
|---|---|---|---|---|---|---|
| **FIVE** | D.T. Lindsay (60) off J.W.Gleeson | South Africa | v | Australia | Port Elizabeth | 1969-70 |
| | R.E. Redmond (107) off Majid Khan | New Zealand | v | Pakistan | Auckland | 1972-73 |
| | D.W. Hookes (56) off A.W.Greig | Australia | v | England | Melbourne | 1976-77 |
| | M. Azharuddin (109) off L.Klusener | India | v | South Africa | Calcutta | 1996-97 |

## MOST RUNS OFF ONE OVER

**EIGHT-BALLS** (L 1 leg-bye) (**bold** no-ball)

| | | | | |
|---|---|---|---|---|
| 25 (66061600) | B. Sutcliffe/R.W. Blair (off H.J. Tayfield) | New Zealand v South Africa | Johannesburg[2] | 1953-54 |
| 24 (2x6, 3x4) | J.F.M. Morrison (off Imran Khan) | New Zealand v Pakistan | Karachi[1] | 1976-77 |
| 22 (42444004) | P.G. van der Bijl (off D.P.V. Wright) | South Africa v England | Durban[2] | 1938-39 |
| 22 (44422204) | R.C. Fredericks (off G.J. Gilmour) | West Indies v Australia | Perth | 1975-76 |
| 22 (?) | Javed Miandad/Wasim Raja (off B.P. Bracewell) | Pakistan v New Zealand | Christchurch | 1978-79 |
| 21 (44442300) | V.Y. Richardson (off J.W.H.T. Douglas) | Australia v England | Melbourne | 1924-25 |
| 21 (34144104) | R.N. Harvey/C.L. McCool (off J.C. Watkins) | Australia v South Africa | Cape Town | 1949-50 |
| 21 (10206444) | K.R. Miller/R.R. Lindwall (off S. Ramadhin) | Australia v West Indies | Brisbane[2] | 1951-52 |
| 21 (14466000) | E.J. Barlow/R.G. Pollock (off R.B. Simpson) | South Africa v Australia | Adelaide | 1963-64 |
| 21 (3x6?) | I.M. Chappell of Intikhab Alam | Australia v Pakistan | Adelaide | 1972-73 |
| 21 (34200444) | G.J.Cosier/G.S.Chappell (off Saleem Altaf) | Australia v Pakistan | Melbourne | 1976-77 |
| 21 (04614222) | J.R.Thomson/A.G.Hurst (off S.Madan Lal) | Australia v India | Brisbane[2] | 1977-78 |
| 20 (66422000) | G.D. McKenzie (off G.S. Sobers) | Australia v West Indies | Sydney | 1968-69 |
| 20 (?) | I.M. Chappell/R. Edwards (off Intikhab Alam) | Australia v Pakistan | Adelaide | 1972-73 |
| 20 (?) | R.W. Marsh (off Asif Iqbal) | Australia v Pakistan | Adelaide | 1972-73 |
| 20 (44444?) | R.E. Redmond (off Majid Khan) | New Zealand v Pakistan | Auckland | 1972-73 |
| 20 (044440400) | A.I. Kallicharran (off Asif Masood) | West Indies v Pakistan | Karachi[1] | 1974-75 |
| 20 (20**4**404402) | R.C. Fredericks (off J.R. Thomson) | West Indies v Australia | Perth | 1975-76 |
| 20 (64442000) | Zaheer Abbas (off K.J. O'Keeffe) | Pakistan v Australia | Adelaide | 1976-77 |
| 20 (00444440) | D.W. Hookes (off A.W. Greig) | Australia v England | Melbourne | 1976-77 |

**SIX-BALLS**

| | | | | |
|---|---|---|---|---|
| 25 (462660L) | A.M.E. Roberts (off I.T. Botham) | West Indies v England | Port-Of-Spain | 1980-81 |
| 24 (44**4**0444) | S.M. Patil (off R.G.D. Willis) | India v England | Manchester | 1982 |
| 24 (464604) | I.T. Botham (off D.A. Stirling) | England v New Zealand | The Oval | 1986 |
| 24 (244266) | I.D.S. Smith (off A.S. Wassan) | New Zealand v India | Auckland | 1989-90 |
| 24 (006666) | Kapil Dev (off E.E. Hemmings) | India v England | Lord's | 1990 |

| | | | | |
|---|---|---|---|---|
| 23 (106646) | Azhar Mahmood/Mushtaq Ahmed (off P.L. Symcox) | Pakistan v South Africa | Rawalpindi[2] | 1997-98 |
| 22 (116626) | M.W.T ate/W. Voce (off A.E. Hall) | England v South Africa | Johannesburg[1] | 1930-31 |
| 22 (064066) | R.C. Motz (off D.A. Allen) | New Zealand v England | Dunedin | 1965-66 |
| 22 (664420) | R.C. Motz (off E.A.S. Prasanna) | New Zealand v India | Dunedin | 1967-68 |
| 22 (006664) | S.T. Clarke (off Mohammad Nazir) | West Indies v Pakistan | Faisalabad | 1979-80 |
| 22 (613642) | I.T. Botham/C.J. Tavare (off D.K. Lillee) | England v Australia | Manchester | 1981 |
| 22 (046444) | K. Srikkanth (off R.G. Holland) | India v Australia | Sydney | 1985-86 |
| 22 (224644) | I.T. Botham (off M.G. Hughes) | England v Australia | Brisbane[2] | 1986-87 |
| 22 (440446) | P.A.J. DeFreitas (off C.J. McDermott) | England v Australia | Adelaide | 1994-95 |
| 22 (4444nn04) | Aamer Sohail (off D.H. Brain) | Pakistan v Zimbabwe | Bulawayo[2] | 1994-95 |
| 22 (040666) | W.J. Cronje (off M. Muralidaran) | South Africa v Sri Lanka | Centurion | 1997-98 |
| 21 (124464) | J.H. Sinclair/C.M.H. Hathorn (off A.J.Y. Hopkins) | South Africa v Australia | Cape Town | 1902-03 |
| 21 (122466) | D.G. Bradman/S.G. Barnes (off J.C. Laker) | Australia v England | Lord's | 1948 |
| 21 (660612) | B.S. Bedi/B.S. Chandrasekhar (off P.J. Petherick) | India v New Zealand | Kanpur | 1976-77 |
| 21 (4144044) | M. Amarnath/S.M. Gavaskar (off Sikander Bakht) | India v Pakistan | Karachi[1] | 1978-79 |
| 21 (640461) | Imran Khan (off Kapil Dev) | Pakistan v India | Faisalabad | 1982-83 |
| 21 (144444) | A.R. Kumble/M. Azharuddin (off L. Klusener) | India v South Africa | Calcutta | 1996-97 |
| 20 (664400) | E.A.V. Williams (off J.C. Laker) | West Indies v England | Bridgetown | 1947-48 |
| 20 (604046) | A.K. Davidson (off D.A. Allen) | Australia v England | Manchester | 1961 |
| 20 (44444?) | D.T. Lindsay (off J.W. Gleeson) | South Africa v Australia | Port Elizabeth | 1969-70 |
| 20 (444620) | D.L. Haynes (off J.R. Thomson) | West Indies v Australia | Port-of-Spain | 1977-78 |
| 20 (460406) | Yashpal Sharma (off P.R. Sleep) | India v Australia | New Delhi | 1979-80 |
| 20 (446420) | S.M. Patil (off Jalaluddin) | India v Pakistan | Lahore[2] | 1982-83 |
| 20 (?) | N.S. Sidhu (off E.J. Gray) | India v New Zealand | Bangalore | 1988-89 |
| 20 (1nn0nn13n30nn41) | (off C.E.L. Ambrose) | Australia v West Indies | Perth | 1996-97 |
| 20 (044 624) | M. Muralidaran (off H.T. Davis) | Sri Lanka v New Zealand | Dunedin | 1996-97 |

## BATSMEN WHO SCORED THEIR ONE AND ONLY TEST CENTURY IN THEIR DEBUT MATCH (§ to date)

| | | | | |
|---|---|---|---|---|
| C. Bannerman | Australia | 165* | v England | 1876-77 |
| P.F. Warner | England | 132* | v South Africa | 1898-99 |
| R.E. Foster | England | 287 | v Australia | 1903-04 |
| R.J. Hartigan | Australia | 116 | v England | 1907-08 |
| A. Jackson | Australia | 164 | v England | 1928-29 |
| J.E. Mills | New Zealand | 117 | v England | 1929-30 |
| Nawab of Pataudi sr | England | 102 | v Australia | 1932-33 |
| N.B. Amarnath | India | 118 | v England | 1933-34 |
| S.C. Griffith | England | 140 | v West Indies | 1947-48 |
| A.G. Ganteaume | West Indies | 112 | v England | 1947-48 |
| R.H. Shodhan | India | 110 | v Pakistan | 1952-53 |
| B.H. Pairaudeau | West Indies | 115 | v India | 1952-53 |
| A.G. Kripal Singh | India | 100* | v New Zealand | 1955-56 |
| C.A. Milton | England | 104* | New Zealand | 1958 |
| A.A. Baig | India | 112 | v England | 1959 |
| Hanumant Singh | India | 105 | v England | 1963-64 |
| Khalid Ibadulla | Pakistan | 166 | v Australia | 1964-65 |
| J.H. Hampshire | England | 107 | v West Indies | 1969 |
| R.E. Redmond | New Zealand | 107 | v Pakistan | 1973 |
| F.C. Hayes | England | 106* | v West Indies | 1973 |

| | | | | |
|---|---|---|---|---|
| L. Baichan | West Indies | 105* | v Pakistan | 1974-75 |
| S. Amarnath | India | 124 | v New Zealand | 1975-76 |
| A.B. Williams | West Indies | 100 | v Australia | 1977-78 |
| D.M. Wellham | Australia | 103 | v England | 1981 |
| D.S.B.P. Kuruppu | Sri Lanka | 201* | v New Zealand | 1986-87 |
| P.K. Amre § | India | 103 | v South Africa | 1992-93 |
| Ali Naqvi § | Pakistan | 115 | v South Africa | 1997-98 |

## MOST RUNS IN A MATCH

| | | | | | |
|---|---|---|---|---|---|
| 456 | G.A. Gooch (333 + 123) | England | v India | Lord's | 1990 |
| 380 | G.S. Chappell (247* + 133) | Australia | v New Zealand | Wellington | 1973-74 |
| 375 | A. Sandham (325 + 50) | England | v West Indies | Kingston | 1929-30 |
| 375 | B.C. Lara (375) | West Indies | v England | Bridgetown | 1993-94 |
| 365 | G.S. Sobers (365*) | West Indies | v Pakistan | Kingston | 1957-58 |
| 364 | L. Hutton (364) | England | v Australia | The Oval | 1938 |
| 354 | Hanif Mohammad (17 + 337) | Pakistan | v West Indies | Bridgetown | 1957-58 |

The most for the other countries are as follows:

| | | | | | |
|---|---|---|---|---|---|
| 344 | S.M. Gavaskar (124 + 220) | India | v West Indies | Port-of-Spain | 1970-71 |
| 340 | S.T. Jayssuriya (340) | Sri Lanka | v India | Colombo (PIS) | 1997-98 |
| 329 | M.D. Crowe (30 + 299) | New Zealand | v Sri Lanka | Wellington | 1990-91 |
| 309 | B. Mitchell (120 + 189*) | South Africa | v England | The Oval | 1947 |
| 266 | D.L. Houghton (266) | Zimbabwe | v Sri Lanka | Bulawayo[2] | 1994-95 |

## FEWEST RUNS IN A DAY

| | | | | | | |
|---|---|---|---|---|---|---|
| 49 | (5*-54*) | M.L. Jaisimha (99) | India | v Pakistan | Kanpur | 1960-61 |
| 52 | (52*) | Mudassar Nazar(114) | Pakistan | v England | Lahore[2] | 1977-78 |
| 56 | (1*-57*) | D.J. McGlew (70) | South Africa | v Australia | Johannesburg[3] | 1957-58 |
| 59 | (0*-59*) | M.L. Jaisimha (74) | India | v Australia | Calcutta | 1959-60 |

## FEWEST BOUNDARIES IN AN INNINGS

| Runs | Fours | | | | | |
|---|---|---|---|---|---|---|
| 84 | 0 | W.M. Lawry | Australia | v England | Brisbane[2] | 1970-71 |
| 77 | 0 | G. Boycott | England | v Australia | Perth | 1978-79 |
| 67 | 0 | E.A.B. Rowan | South Africa | v England | Durban[2] | 1938-39 |
| 120 | 2 | P.A. Gibb | England | v South Africa | Durban[2] | 1938-39 |
| 94 | 2 | K.F. Barrington | England | v Australia | Sydney | 1962-63 |
| 102 | 3 | W.M. Woodfull | Australia | v England | Melbourne | 1928-29 |
| 144* | 5 | D.G. Bradman | Australia | v England | Nottingham | 1938 |
| 161 | 5 | W.M. Woodfull | Australia | v South Africa | Melbourne | 1931-32 |

*G. Boycott's innings included one four but it was all-run and included two runs from an overthrow.*

## OVER 60% OF A COMPLETED INNINGS TOTAL

| | | | | | | |
|---|---|---|---|---|---|---|
| 67.34 | C. Bannerman | 165*/245 | Australia | v England | Melbourne | 1876-77 |
| 63.50 | C.G. Greenidge | 134/211 | West Indies | v England | Manchester | 1976 |
| 63.41 | A.P. Gurusinha5 | 2*/82 | Sri Lanka | v India | Chandigarh | 1990-91 |
| 62 89 | J.R. Reid | 100/159 | New Zealand | v England | Christchurch | 1962-63 |
| 61 87 | S.M. Nurse | 258/417 | West Indies | v New Zealand | Christchurch | 1968-69 |
| 61.85 | M. Amarnath | 60/97† | India | v West Indies | Kingston | 1975-76 |
| 61.11 | G.N. Yallop | 121/198 | Australia | v England | Sydney | 1978-79 |
| 61.11 | G.A. Gooch | 154*/252 | England | v West Indies | Leeds | 1991 |
| 60.65 | V.T. Trumper | 74/122 | Australia | v England | Melbourne | 1903-04 |
| 60.26 | H.A. Gomes | 91/151 | West Indies | v India | Chennai[1] | 1978-79 |
| 60.19 | J.T. Tyldesley | 62/103 | England | v Australia | Melbourne | 1903-04 |
| 60.00 | Kapil Dev | 129/215 | India | v South Africa | Port Elizabeth | 1992-93 |

*† Five men were absent hurt.*

*D.L. Houghton (266) scored 62.29% of Zimbabwe's total of 462 for 9 dec. against Sri Lanka at Bulawayo[2] in 1994-95.*

*D.L. Amiss (262*) scored 60.64% of England 's total of 432 for 9 against West Indies at Kingston in 1973-74)*

## BATTED ON EACH DAY OF A FIVE-DAY MATCH

| | Scores | | | | | |
|---|---|---|---|---|---|---|
| M.L. Jaisimha | 20* | 74 | India | v Australia | Calcutta | 1959-60 |
| G. Boycott | 107 | 80* | England | v Australia | Nottingham | 1977 |
| K.J. Hughes | 117 | 84 | Australia | v England | Lord's | 1980 |
| A.J. Lamb | 23 | 110 | England | v West Indies | Lord's | 1984 |
| R.J. Shastri | 111 | 7* | India | v England | Calcutta | 1984-85 |

## BATSMAN RUN OUT IN EACH INNINGS OF A TEST

| | | | | | |
|---|---|---|---|---|---|
| P.A. McAlister | Australia | v | England | Melbourne | 1907-08 |
| C. Kelleway | Australia | v | South Africa | Melbourne | 1910-11 |
| J. Ryder | Australia | v | England | Sydney | 1920-21 |
| J. Trim | West Indies | v | Australia | Melbourne | 1951-52 |
| J.B. Stollmeyer | West Indies | v | England | Bridgetown | 1953-54 |
| I. Meckiff | Australia | v | West Indies | Brisbane[2] | 1960-61 |
| J.S. Solomon | West Indies | v | Australia | Melbourne | 1960-61 |
| S.N. McGregor | New Zealand | v | South Africa | Dunedin | 1963-64 |
| R.M. Edwards | West Indies | v | New Zealand | Wellington | 1968-69 |
| C.H. Lloyd | West Indies | v | India | Kingston | 1970-71 |
| J.A. Jameson | England | v | India | The Oval | 1971 |
| Zaheer Abbas | Pakistan | v | Australia | Melbourne | 1972-73 |
| A.R. Border | Australia | v | Pakistan | Melbourne | 1981-82 |
| M.A. Taylor | Australia | v | West Indies | Adelaide | 1988-89 |
| Wasim Akram | Pakistan | v | West Indies | Faisalabad | 1990-91 |
| M.A. Taylor | Australia | v | England | Adelaide | 1990-91 |
| I.A. Healy | Australia | v | West Indies | Georgetown | 1990-91 |
| A.H. Jones | New Zealand | v | Pakistan | Christchurch | 1993-94 |
| J. Angel | Australia | v | England | Perth | 1994-95 |
| A.C. Parore | New Zealand | v | Sri Lanka | Hamilton | 1996-97 |

## FAMOUS BATSMEN WHO SCORED A 'DUCK' IN FIRST TEST INNINGS

It's been said of some cricketers, "...he batted so badly he was lucky to make a 'duck'" and, on occasions, this applies equally to batsmen of proven ability as to their less-accomplished colleagues.

One occasion which seems to have overawed a number of otherwise reliable batters is their first Test innings and below is a list of some who failed this, their first big test. Their second appearance is shown in brackets.

| | | | | | |
|---|---|---|---|---|---|
| Hon. I.F.W. Bligh § | England | v Australia | Melbourne | 1882-83 | (3) |
| S.E. Gregory | Australia | v England | Lord's | 1890 | (9) |
| J. Darling | Australia | v England | Sydney | 1894-95 | (53) |
| V.T. Trumper | Australia | v England | Nottingham | 1899 | (11) |
| G.E. Tyldesley | England | v Australia | Nottingham | 1921 | (7) |
| R.E.S. Wyatt | England | v South Africa | Johannesburg | 1927-28 | (2)† |
| M. Leyland | England | v West Indies | The Oval | 1928 | (137)† |
| L. Hutton | England | v New Zealand | Lord's | 1937 | (1) |
| G.E. Gomez | West Indies | v England | Manchester | 1939 | (11) |
| D.B. Close | England | v New Zealand | Manchester | 1949 | (0)† |
| J.G. Leggatt | New Zealand | v West Indies | Auckland | 1951-52 | (6*) |
| K.F. Barrington | England | v South Africa | Nottingham | 1955 | (34)† |
| M.J.K. Smith | England | v New Zealand | Birmingham | 1958 | (7) |
| C. Milburn | England | v West Indies | Manchester | 1966 | (94) |
| A.P.E. Knott | England | v Pakistan | Nottingham | 1967 | (28)† |
| K.W.R. Fletcher | England | v Australia | Leeds | 1968 | (23*) |
| G.M. Turner | New Zealand | v West Indies | Auckland | 1968-69 | (40) |
| G.R. Viswanath | India | v Australia | Kanpur | 1969-70 | (137) |
| A.R. Lewis § | England | v India | Delhi | 1972-73 | (70*) |

| | | | | | |
|---|---|---|---|---|---|
| G.A. Gooch | England | v Australia | Birmingham | 1975 | (0) |
| J.M. Brearley | England | v West Indies | Nottingham | 1976 | (17) |
| R.B. Richardson | West Indies | v India | Bombay | 1983-84 | (26) |
| Saeed Anwar | Pakistan | v West Indies | Faisalabad | 1990-91 | (0) |

§ Captained England on first Test appearance; † not in the same match

## NOUGHT AND A CENTURY IN THE SAME MATCH (§ in first Test)

| AUSTRALIA | Scores | | Opponents | | |
|---|---|---|---|---|---|
| W.L. Murdoch | 0 | 153* | England | The Oval | 1880 |
| G.H.S. Trott | 0 | 143 | England | Lord's | 1896 |
| C. Hill | 188 | 0 | England | Melbourne | 1897-98 |
| D.G. Bradman | 0 | 103* | England | Melbourne | 1932-33 |
| J.H.W. Fingleton | 100 | 0 | England | Brisbane[2] | 1936-37 |
| D.G. Bradman | 138 | 0 | England | Nottingham | 1948 |
| S.G. Barnes | 0 | 141 | England | Lord's | 1948 |
| R.N. Harvey | 122 | 0 | England | Manchester | 1953 |
| I.R. Redpath | 0 | 132 | West Indies | Sydney | 1968-69 |
| I.M. Chappell | 138 | 0 | India | Delhi | 1969-70 |
| I.C. Davis | 105 | 0 | Pakistan | Adelaide | 1976-77 |
| R.B. McCosker | 0 | 105 | Pakistan | Melbourne | 1976-77 |
| C.S. Serjeant | 0 | 124 | West Indies | Georgetown | 1977-78 |
| G.N. Yallop | 0 | 114 | England | Manchester | 1981 |
| G.R. Marsh | 118 | 0 | New Zealand | Auckland | 1985-86 |
| D.C. Boon | 103 | 0 | England | Adelaide | 1986-87 |
| M.E. Waugh | 139* | 0 | West Indies | St John's | 1990-91 |

| ENGLAND | Scores | | Opponents | | |
|---|---|---|---|---|---|
| L.C. Braund | 102 | 0 | Australia | Sydney | 1903-04 |
| J.T. Tyldesley | 0 | 100 | Australia | Leeds | 1905 |
| G. Gunn | 122* | 0 | Australia | Sydney | 1907-08 |
| F.E. Woolley | 0 | 123 | Australia | Sydney | 1924-25 |
| G.B. Legge | 196 | 0 | New Zealand | Auckland | 1929-30 |
| D.C.S. Compton | 145* | 0 | Australia | Manchester | 1948 |
| L. Hutton | 101 | 0 | New Zealand | Leeds | 1949 |
| P.B.H. May | 0 | 112 | South Africa | Lord's | 1955 |
| M.C. Cowdrey | 119 | 0 | West Indies | Port-of-Spain | 1959-60 |
| Rev. D.S. Sheppard | 0 | 113 | Australia | Melbourne | 1962-63 |
| M.C. Cowdrey | 101 | 0 | West Indies | Kingston | 1967-68 |
| D.L. Amiss | 158 | 0 | Pakistan | Hyderabad | 1972-73 |
| D.W. Randall | 0 | 150 | Australia | Sydney | 1978-79 |
| I.T. Botham | 0 | 118 | Australia | Manchester | 1981 |
| G. Boycott | 137 | 0 | Australia | The Oval | 1981 |
| M.W. Gatting | 100 | 0 | Australia | Adelaide | 1986-87 |
| D.I. Gower | 100 | 0 | Australia | Melbourne | 1990-91 |
| C.C. Lewis | 0 | 117 | India | Chennai[1] | 1992-93 |
| M.A. Atherton | 144 | 0 | West Indies | Georgetown | 1993-94 |
| M.W. Gatting | 117 | 0 | Australia | Adelaide | 1994-95 |
| G.P. Thorpe | 123 | 0 | Australia | Perth | 1994-95 |
| N. Hussain | 113 | 0 | Zimbabwe | Bulawayo[2] | 1996-97 |

| SOUTH AFRICA | Scores | | Opponents | | |
|---|---|---|---|---|---|
| J.H. Sinclair | 0 | 104 | Australia | Cape Town | 1902-03 |
| G.A. Faulkner | 122* | 0 | Australia | Manchester | 1912 |
| R.H. Catterall | 0 | 120 | England | Birmingham | 1924 |
| A.D. Nourse | 0 | 231 | Australia | Johannesburg[1] | 1935-36 |
| E.J. Barlow | 114 | 0 | Australia | Brisbane[2] | 1963-64 |
| A.C. Hudson § | 163 | 0 | West Indies | Bridgetown | 1991-92 |

| | | | | | |
|---|---|---|---|---|---|
| G. Kirsten | 103 | 0 | India | Cape Town | 1996-97 |
| D.J. Cullinan | 103 | 0 | Sri Lanka | Centurion | 1997-98 |

| **WEST INDIES** | Scores | | Opponents | | |
|---|---|---|---|---|---|
| I. Barrow | 105 | 0 | England | Manchester | 1933 |
| F.C.M. Alexander | 0 | 108 | Australia | Sydney | 1960-61 |
| S.M. Nurse | 201 | 0 | Australia | Bridgetown | 1964-65 |
| G.S. Sobers | 0 | 113* | England | Kingston | 1967-68 |
| C.A. Davis | 103 | 0 | England | Lord's | 1969 |
| G.S. Sobers | 132 | 0 | India | Port-of-Spain | 1970-71 |
| A.I. Kallicharran | 0 | 103* | India | Port-of-Spain | 1975-76 |
| R.C. Fredericks | 0 | 138 | England | Lord's | 1976 |
| D.L. Haynes | 0 | 122 | New Zealand | Christchurch | 1979-80 |
| C.L. King | 0 | 100* | New Zealand | Christchurch | 1979-80 |
| I.V.A. Richards | 0 | 182* | England | Bridgetown | 1980-81 |
| I.V.A. Richards | 208 | 0 | Australia | Melbourne | 1984-85 |
| D.L. Haynes | 0 | 109 | England | Bridgetown | 1989-90 |
| R.B. Richardson | 104 | 0 | England | Birmingham | 1991 |
| K.L.T. Arthurton | 157* | 0 | Australia | Brisbane[2] | 1992-93 |
| C.L. Hooper | 0 | 106 | Pakistan | Karachi[1] | 1997-98 |
| S. Chanderpaul | 118 | 0 | England | Georgetown | 1997-98 |

| **NEW ZEALAND** | Scores | | Opponents | | |
|---|---|---|---|---|---|
| G.T. Dowling | 129 | 0 | India | Mumbai[2] | 1964-65 |
| B.F. Hastings | 0 | 117* | West Indies | Christchurch | 1968-69 |
| M.D. Crowe | 174 | 0 | Pakistan | Wellington | 1988-89 |
| J.G. Wright | 116 | 0 | England | Wellington | 1991-92 |
| M.D. Crowe | 0 | 107 | Sri Lanka | Colombo (SSC) | 1992-93 |
| C.D. McMillan | 0 | 142 | Sri Lanka | Colombo (PIS) | 1997-98 |

| **INDIA** | Scores | | Opponents | | |
|---|---|---|---|---|---|
| M.H. Mankad | 111 | 0 | Australia | Melbourne | 1947-48 |
| Pankaj Roy | 140 | 0 | England | Bombai | 1951-52 |
| V.L. Manjrekar | 133 | 0 | England | Leeds | 1952 |
| M.L. Apte | 0 | 163* | West Indies | Port-of-Spain | 1952-53 |
| V.L. Manjrekar | 108 | 0 | England | Madras | 1963-64 |
| G.R. Viswanath § | 0 | 137 | Australia | Kanpur | 1969-70 |
| S.M. Gavaskar | 0 | 118 | Australia | Melbourne | 1977-78 |
| D.B. Vengsarkar | 0 | 103 | England | Lord's | 1979 |
| N.S. Sidhu | 116 | 0 | West Indies | Kingston | 1988-89 |
| M. Azharuddin | 0 | 109 | Pakistan | Faisalabad | 1989-90 |
| N.R. Mongia | 152 | 0 | Audtralia | Delhi | 1996-97 |

| **PAKISTAN** | Scores | | Opponents | | |
|---|---|---|---|---|---|
| Imtiaz Ahmed | 209 | 0 | New Zealand | Lahore[1] | 1955-56 |
| Imtiaz Ahmed | 122 | 0 | West Indies | Kingston | 1957-58 |
| Hanif Mohammad | 160 | 0 | India | Mumbai[2] | 1960-61 |
| Javed Burki | 140 | 0 | England | Dacca | 1961-62 |
| Asif Iqbal | 0 | 152* | Australia | Adelaide | 1976-77 |
| Sadiq Mohammad | 105 | 0 | Australia | Melbourne | 1976-77 |
| Asif Iqbal | 0 | 104 | India | Faisalabad | 1978-79 |
| Ijaz Ahmed | 122 | 0 | Australia | Faisalabad | 1988-89 |
| Mohammad Wasim § | 0 | 109* | New Zealand | Lahore[2] | 1996-97 |

| **SRI LANKA** | Scores | | Opponents | | |
|---|---|---|---|---|---|
| A. Ranatunga | 127 | 0 | Australia | Colombo (SSC) | 1992-93 |
| P.A.de Silva | 0 | 105 | Pakistan | Faisalabad | 1994-95 |
| H.P.Tillakaratne | 115 | 0 | Pakistan | Faisalabad | 1994-95 |

## FIRST THREE BATSMEN SCORING CENTURIES

| | | | |
|---|---|---|---|
| England (2d-531) | v South Africa | Lord's | 1924 |
| | (J.B. Hobbs 211; H. Sutcliffe 122; F.E. Woolley 134*) | | |
| Australia (9d-600) | v West Indies | Port-of-Spain | 1954-55 |
| | (C.C. McDonald 110; A.R. Morris 111; R.N. Harvey 133) | | |
| Australia (6d-650) | v West Indies | Bridgetown | 1964-65 |
| | (W.M. Lawry 210; R.B. Simpson 201; R.M. Cowper 102) | | |
| India (4d-600) | v Australia | Sydney | 1985-86 |
| | (S.M. Gavaskar 172; K. Srikkanth 116; M. Amarnath 138) | | |
| Australia (4d-632) | v England | Lord's | 1993 |
| | (M.A. Taylor 111; M.J. Slater 152; D.C. Boon 164*) | | |

## PLAYER DISMISSED FROM THE FIRST BALL OF A TEST

| Batsman | Bowler | († on debut. § in his last Test.) | | | | |
|---|---|---|---|---|---|---|
| A.C. MacLaren | A. Coningham † | England | v | Australia | Melbourne | 1894-95 |
| T.W. Hayward | A.E.E. Vogler | England | v | South Africa | The Oval | 1907 |
| W. Bardsley | M.W. Tate | Australia | v | England | Leeds | 1926 |
| H. Sutcliffe | F.T. Badcock | England | v | New Zealand | Christchurch | 1932-33 |
| T.S. Worthington | E.L. McCormick | England | v | Australia | Brisbane[2] | 1936-37 |
| C.C. Hunte | Fazal Mahmood | West Indies | v | Pakistan | Port-of-Spain | 1957-58 |
| E.J. Barlow | G.D. McKenzie | South Africa | v | Australia | Durban[2] | 1966-67 |
| R.C. Fredericks | S. Abid Ali | West Indies | v | India | Port-of-Spain | 1970-71 |
| K.R. Stackpole § | R.J. Hadlee | Australia | v | New Zealand | Auckland | 1973-74 |
| S.M. Gavaskar | G.G. Arnold | India | v | England | Birmingham | 1974 |
| S.S. Naik § | A.M.E. Roberts | India | v | West Indies | Calcutta | 1974-75 |
| J.F.M.Morrison | G.G. Arnold | New Zealand | v | England | Christchurch | 1974-75 |
| Mohsin Khan | Kapil Dev | Pakistan | v | India | Jullundur | 1983-84 |
| S.M. Gavaskar | M.D. Marshall | India | v | West Indies | Calcutta | 1983-84 |
| S.M. Gavaskar | Imran Khan | India | v | Pakistan | Jaipur | 1986-87 |
| W.V. Raman | R.J. Hadlee | India | v | New Zealand | Napier | 1989-90 |
| S.J. Cook † | Kapil Dev | South Africa | v | India | Durban[2] | 1992-93 |

## LONGEST INNINGS FOR EACH COUNTRY

| For | Min | | Opponents | | |
|---|---|---|---|---|---|
| Australia | 762 | R.B. Simpson (311) | England | Manchester | 1964 |
| England | 797 | L. Hutton (364) | Australia | The Oval | 1938 |
| South Africa | 652 | G. Kirsten (210) | England | Manchester | 1998 |
| West Indies | 682 | F.M.M. Worrell (197*) | England | Bridgetown | 1959-60 |
| New Zealand | 704 | G.M. Turner (259) | West Indies | Georgetown | 1971-72 |
| India | 708 | S.M. Gavaskar (172) | England | Bangalore | 1981-82 |
| Pakistan | 970 | Hanif Mohammad(337) | West Indies | Bridgetown | 1957-58 |
| Sri Lanka | 799 | S.T. Jayasuriya (340) | India | Colombo (PIS) | 1997-98 |
| Zimbabwe | 675 | D.L. Houghton (266) | Sri Lanka | Bulawayo[2] | 1994-95 |

## FAMOUS BATSMEN WHO BAGGED A TEST MATCH 'PAIR'

| | Career Test Runs | Career Average | HS | 100's |
|---|---|---|---|---|
| ***Australia*** | | | | |
| A.C. Bannerman | 1108 | 23.08 | 94 | - |
| R. Benaud | 2201 | 24.45 | 122 | 3 |
| A.R. Border | 11174 | 50.56 | 205 | 27 |
| J. Darling | 1657 | 28.56 | 178 | 3 |
| R. Edwards | 1171 | 40.37 | 170* | 2 |
| J.H.W. Fingleton | 1189 | 42.46 | 136 | 5 |
| S.E. Gregory | 2282 | 24.53 | 201 | 4 |
| R.N. Harvey | 6149 | 48.41 | 205 | 21 |
| I.A. Healy | 3906 | 28.72 | 161* | 3 |
| D.W. Hookes | 1306 | 34.36 | 143* | 1 |
| K.J. Hughes | 4415 | 37.41 | 213 | 9 |
| D.M. Jones | 3631 | 46.55 | 216 | 11 |
| P.S. McDonnell | 950 | 28.78 | 147 | 3 |
| R.W. Marsh | 3633 | 26.51 | 132 | 3 |
| M.A. Noble | 1997 | 30.25 | 133 | 1 |
| V.Y. Richardson | 706 | 23.53 | 138 | 1 |
| K.R. Stackpole | 2807 | 37.42 | 207 | 7 |
| M.A. Taylor | 6784 | 42.66 | 219 | 18 |
| V.T. Trumper (3 'ducks' in a row) | 3163 | 39.04 | 214* | 8 |
| M.E. Waugh (twice) | 3627 | 44.23 | 140 | 10 |
| G.M. Wood | 3374 | 31.83 | 172 | 9 |
| ***England*** | | | | |
| D.L. Amiss (twice) | 3612 | 46.30 | 262* | 11 |
| T.E. Bailey | 2290 | 29.74 | 134* | 1 |
| I.T. Botham | 5200 | 33.54 | 208 | 14 |
| G.A. Gooch | 7571 | 43.76 | 333 | 17 |
| A.P.E. Knott | 4389 | 32.75 | 135 | 5 |
| B.W. Luckhurst | 1298 | 36.05 | 131 | 4 |
| G. Pullar | 1974 | 43.86 | 175 | 4 |
| M.J.K. Smith | 2278 | 31.61 | 121 | 3 |
| G.P. Thorpe | 3366 | 40.07 | 138 | 6 |
| R.A. Woolmer | 1059 | 33.09 | 149 | 3 |
| ***South Africa*** | | | | |
| W.R. Endean | 1630 | 33.95 | 162* | 3 |
| D.J. McGlew | 2440 | 42.06 | 255* | 7 |
| ***West Indies*** | | | | |
| F.C.M. Alexander | 961 | 30.03 | 108 | 1 |
| K.L.T. Arthurton | 1382 | 30.71 | 157* | 2 |
| P.J.L. Dujon | 3322 | 31.94 | 139 | 5 |
| C.G. Greenidge | 7558 | 44.72 | 226 | 19 |
| A.I. Kallicharran (twice) | 4399 | 44.43 | 187 | 12 |
| A.L. Logie | 2470 | 35.79 | 130 | 2 |
| D.L. Murray | 1993 | 22.90 | 91 | - |
| C.A. Roach (twice) | 952 | 30.70 | 209 | 2 |
| O.G. Smith | 1331 | 31.69 | 168 | 4 |
| J.S. Solomon | 1326 | 34.00 | 100* | 1 |
| E.D. Weekes | 4455 | 58.61 | 207 | 15 |
| F.M.M. Worrell | 3860 | 49.48 | 261 | 9 |
| ***New Zealand*** | | | | |
| J.V. Coney | 2668 | 37.57 | 174* | 3 |
| S.P. Fleming | 2349 | 37.88 | 176* | 2 |
| T.W. Jarvis | 625 | 29.76 | 182 | 1 |
| I.D.S. Smith | 1815 | 25.56 | 173 | 2 |
| J.G. Wright | 4964 | 37.61 | 185 | 12 |
| ***India*** | | | | |
| M. Amarnath (twice in run of 0 + 0, 1 + 0, 0 + 0) | 4378 | 42.50 | 138 | 11 |
| F.M. Engineer | 2611 | 31.08 | 121 | 2 |
| V.S. Hazare | 2192 | 47.65 | 164* | 7 |
| M.L. Jaisimha | 2056 | 30.68 | 129 | 3 |
| Pankaj Roy | 2442 | 32.56 | 173 | 5 |
| G.S. Ramchand | 1180 | 24.58 | 109 | 2 |
| D.N. Sardesai | 2001 | 39.23 | 212 | 5 |
| D.B. Vengsarkar | 6868 | 42.13 | 166 | 17 |
| Yashpal Sharma | 1606 | 33.45 | 140 | 2 |
| ***Pakistan*** | | | | |
| Aamer Sohail | 1960 | 35.63 | 205 | 2 |
| Imtiaz Ahmed | 2079 | 29.28 | 209 | 3 |
| Javed Burki | 1341 | 30.47 | 140 | 3 |
| Majid J. Khan | 3930 | 38.91 | 167 | 8 |
| Mudassar Nazar | 4114 | 38.09 | 231 | 10 |
| Saeed Anwar | 1038 | 41.52 | 169 | 2 |
| Wazir Mohammad | 801 | 27.62 | 189 | 2 |
| ***Sri Lanka*** | | | | |
| A. Ranatunga | 2023 | 34.87 | 135* | 3 |
| ***Zimbabwe*** | | | | |
| G.W. Flower | 1991 | 38.28 | 201* | 5 |

## PARTNERSHIP FEATS

1. H. Sutcliffe (England) v Australia at Sydney 1932-33 shared in century stands for the first three wickets.
2. J.B. Hobbs & H. Sutcliffe (England) shared four century opening stands v Australia in 1924-25. Three of these were recorded in the first three innings in which they partnered each other.
3. L. Hutton & C. Washbrook (England) shared three consecutive opening stands of over 100 v Australia 1946-47.
4. R.S. Modi & V.S. Hazare (India) shared three consecutive century stands for the third wicket v West Indies 1948-49.
5. C.G. Greenidge partnered D.L. Haynes in sixteen century opening stands for the West Indies.

6. J.B. Hobbs (England) shared in 24 century opening stands (15 with H. Sutcliffe, 8 with W. Rhodes and one with C.B. Fry). S.M. Gavaskar (India) and C.G. Greenidge (West Indies) in 22; H. Sutcliffe (England) 21 ; G. Boycott (England) 20.

7. G. Boycott, B.W. Luckhurst and J.H. Edrich (England) figured in four successive opening stands of more than 100 v Australia in 1970-71. In eight successive innings these pairs registered six century opening stands.

8. I.M. Chappell (Australia) and S.M. Gavaskar (India) figured in 18 century partnerships for the second wicket.

9. Batsmen who have featured in the most century partnerships are A.R. Border (Australia) 62; S.M. Gavaskar (India) with 58; Javed Miandad (Pakistan) 50; G. Boycott (England) 47; C.G. Greenidge (West Indies) 46; G.S. Chappell (Australia) and I.V.A. Richards (West Indies) 44; G.S. Sobers (West Indies) 43; D.C. Boon (Australia) and M.C. Cowdrey (England) 42; G.A. Gooch (England), L. Hutton (England) and C.H. Lloyd (West Indies) 41.

## CENTURIES BY TAIL-ENDERS (lower than No. 8 in order)

1. W.W. Read (England). Read batted No.10 in the match v Australia at The Oval in 1884, and in the second innings came in with England facing defeat at 8 for 181. It was said that Read was in a towering rage at his captain's decision to place him so low in the order, and he made his point with a brilliant 117 in two hours, during which time he added 151 with W.H. Scotton (90 in 5¾ hours).

2. R.A. Duff (Australia). Batted at No.6 in the first innings of the second Test against England at Melbourne in 1901-02 but was held back to No.10 in the second innings. Duff scored 104 and shared in a tenth wicket partnership of 120 with fellow debutant W.W. Armstrong.

3. R.J. Hartigan (Australia). Hartigan, batting at No. 9 in his Test debut v England at Adelaide in 1907-08, came in when Australia in their second innings led by only 102 with seven wickets down. He joined C. Hill, who was suffering a bout of influenza, but the two defied the English bowling and the 107°F heat to put on 243 for the eighth wicket, of which Hartigan's share was 116. Their record stand enabled Australia to win the match. (Due to business commitments Hartigan was unavailable for the next Test.)

4. J.M. Gregory (Australia). After taking 7 for 69 earlier in the match v England at Melbourne in 1920-21, Gregory, batting at No. 9, joined C.E. Pellew with Australia 7 for 282 in their second innings. Together they put on 173, Gregory's share being exactly 100.

5. G.O.B. Allen (England). Batting at No. 9, Allen joined wicketkeeper L.E.G. Ames with England 7 for 190 in their first innings v New Zealand at Lord's in 1931. The two added 246 runs, with Allen making 122.

6. R.R. Lindwall (Australia). Batting at No. 9 in Australia's second innings v England at Melbourne 1946-47, Lindwall joined wicketkeeper D. Tallon with Australia 7 for 341. These two then shared a blistering partnership, adding 154 in 88 minutes of brilliant hitting, Lindwall making 100 (one six and 13 fours) in 109 minutes.

7. J.T. Murray (England). Batting at No. 9 in England's only innings v West Indies at The Oval 1966, Murray joined T.W. Graveney with England 7 for 166 in reply to West Indies's 268. This pair then added 217 for the eighth wicket to take England to the lead. Murray scored 112 — his only Test century. Then a tenth wicket stand of 128 by K. Higgs and J.A. Snow helped gain an innings victory.

8. Asif Iqbal (Pakistan). Batting at No. 9 in Pakistan's second innings, Asif was joined by Intikhab Alam with Pakistan 8 for 65 and still 139 in arrears. They added 190 for a new Test record ninth wicket as Asif Iqbal made his maiden Test century — 146.

9. I.D.S. Smith (New Zealand). Batting at No. 9 in New Zealand's first innings v India at Auckland 1989-90, Smith joined R.J. Hadlee with the score 7 for 131. He then added 101 with Hadlee for the eighth wicket and 136 for the ninth wicket with M.C. Snedden. His innings of 173 included 24 (244266) of an over from A.S. Wassan.

10. D.J. Richardson (South Africa). Batting at No. 8 in South Africa's first innings v New Zealand at Cape Town 1994-95, Richardson came in at 6 for 271 and scored 109 out of a total of 440.

11. Moin Khan (Pakistan). Batting at No. 8 in Pakistan's first innings at Leeds 1996, he joined Asif Mujtaba with the score 6 for 266. Moin Khan scored 105 as they added 122 for the seventh wicket.

12. P.A. Strang (Zimbabwe). Batting at No. 8 in Zimbabwe's first innings at Sheikhupura in 1996-97 came in with the score at 6 for 142. He scored 106 not out as he added 131 for the seventh wicket with G.W. Flower and 87 for the ninth wicket with his brother B.C. Strang.

13. Wasim Akram (Pakistan). Batting at No. 8 in Pakistan's only innings at Sheikhupura in 1996-97, he came in with the score at 6 for 183 and played a captain's innings in scoring 257 not out as he added a record 313 for the eighth wicket with Saqlain Mushtaq.

14. L. Klusener (South Africa). Batting at No. 8 in South Africa's first innings v India at Cape Town 1996-97 joined B.M. McMillan with the score 7 for 382. They then shared an unbroken partnership of 143 as Klusener scored 102 not out in 143 minutes from 100 balls.

15. Azhar Mahmood (Pakistan). Batting at No. 8 in his debut Test v South Africa at Rawalpindi in 1997-98 came to the wicket with the score 6 for 206 and proceeded to score 128 not out and added 74 for the ninth wicket with Waqar Younis and a record equalling 151 for the tenth wicket with Mushtaq Ahmed.

16. P.L. Symcox (South Africa). Batting at No. 9 in South Africa's first innings v Pakistan in 1997-98 at Johannesburg, joined M.V. Boucher with the score on 8 for 166. He scored his maiden Test century (108) as they then proceeded to add a record 195 runs for the ninth wicket to break the previous record held by Asif Iqbal and Intikhab Alam (see above). Symocx was relegated to twelfth man for the next Test and has not been chosen again since that effort.

## GOOD EFFORTS BY 'NIGHT-WATCHMEN'

1. H. Carter (Australia) v England at Adelaide 1911-12 went in to bat late on the third day with Australia 1 for 86 in the second innings. He scored 71 and shared in a 124 run-stand for the fourth wicket with C. Hill.

2. H. Larwood (England) v Australia at Sydney 1932-33 went in to bat late on the second evening when England were 2 for 153. The Australian bowlers did not see his back until the score had reached 310, of which Larwood's share in 135 minutes was a grand 98. His innings was ended by a catch to Bert Ironmonger, not noted as a safe catcher — he held only three in 14 Test matches.

3. A.V. Bedser (England) v Australia at Leeds 1948 came in late on the first day with England 2 for 268. The following morning he defied the Australian attack of R.R. Lindwall, K.R. Miller, W.A. Johnston, E.R.H. Toshack and I.W. Johnson to make his highest Test score of 79 and help add 155 for the third wicket with W.J. Edrich.

4. Nasim-ul-Ghani (Pakistan) v England at Lord's 1962. Normally batting at No. 8, Nasim was promoted two places and sent in as night-watchman when Pakistan were 4 for 77 in their second innings. He stayed to score 101 and shared in a Pakistan record fifth-wicket partnership of 197 with Javed Burki — a record which still stands. Nasim's century was his first in first-class cricket and the first by a Pakistan batsman in England.

5. A.P.E. Knott (England) v Australia at Brisbane 1970-71 was sent in as 'night-watchman' with England 1 for 92 late on the second day. He stayed long enough to score 73.

6. A.L. Mann (Australia) v India at Perth 1977-78, came in with the score at 1 for 13 late on the fourth day, having batted at No. 8 in the first innings. The following day Mann proceeded to score 105 out of a total of 8 for 342, sharing a partnership of 139 for the third wicket with P.M. Toohey. Mann's other seven Test innings in a four Test career netted a mere 84 runs. (In the first innings wicketkeeper S.J. Rixon was sent in as 'night-watchman' with Australia 4 for 149 and scored 50 while sharing a fifth wicket stand of 101 with R.B. Simpson).

7. D.R. Parry (West Indies) v Australia at Georgetown 1977-78 was sent in with West Indies 2 for 95 in their second innings. He went on to score 51 — his only Test fifty.

8. Wasim Bari (Pakistan) v India at Lahore 1978-79 was sent in as night-watchman when the score was 1 for 19. He scored a Test career highest score of 85 sharing in a second wicket stand of 115 with Majid J.Khan and was dismissed when the score was 3 for 161.

9. R.R. Jumadeen (West Indies) v India at Kanpur 1978-79 came in late on the third day when the score was 2 for 134 and stayed long enough to score his only Test half-century (56) and share a third wicket stand of 129 with S.F.A.F. Bacchus.

10. S.M.H. Kirmani (India) v Australia at Bombay 1979-80 (sixth Test) came in late on the first day to act as 'night-watchman' when India was 3 for 231. Overnight, Kirmani (in the side as a wicketkeeper) batted for the remainder of the innings until India declared at 8 for 458. He scored 101* in 5 hours, adding 127 with K.D. Ghavri for the eighth wicket. (In the first Test at Madras Kirmani had been sent in late on the second day with India 1 for 80 and scored 57, adding 99 for the fourth wicket with D.B. Vengsarkar.)

11. Iqbal Qasim (Pakistan) v Sri Lanka at Karachi 1981-82 came in late on the third day to act as 'night-watchman' with Pakistan 1 for 16 in the second innings. He scored his highest Test score of 56 before he was dismissed at 3 for 107.

12. E.E. Hemmings (England) v Australia at Sydney 1982-83 came in late on the fourth day at 1 for 3 in the second innings. He batted for 226 minutes to record his highest Test score of 95.

13. W.W. Davis (West Indies) v England at Manchester 1984 came in late on the first day when the score was 5 for 267. He scored 77 sharing in a sixth wicket stand of 170 with C.G. Greenidge.

14. C. Sharma (India) v Australia at Adelaide 1985-86 came in late on the second day with India 1 for 97 scored 54 as 'night-watchman'.

15. Saleem Yousuf (Pakistan) v West Indies at Faisalabad 1986-87 came in late on the second day with Pakistan 2 for 19 in the second innings. He scored 61 adding 94 for the third wicket with Qasim Omar.

16. B.N. French (England) v Pakistan at Manchester 1987 came in late on the first day with the score 3 for 133. He scored 59 whilst adding 113 for the fourth wicket with R.T. Robinson.

17. R.C. Russell (England) v Sri Lanka at Lord's 1988, making his Test debut, was sent in late on the first day as 'night-watchman' with the score at 1 for 40. He scored 94 and shared in a second wicket stand of 131 with G.A. Gooch.

18. R.C. Russell (England) v West Indies at Bridgetown 1989-90, was sent in late on the fourth day with the score at 3 for 10 in England's second innings. He was sixth out for 55 when the score was 166.

19. P.L. Taylor (Australia) v New Zealand at Wellington 1989-90, was sent in as 'night-watchman' late on the third day with Australia 2 for 54. He top-scored with 87 and added 103 for the fourth wicket with A.R. Border.

20. I.A. Healy (Australia) v England at Sydney 1990-91, came in as 'night-watchman' late on the fourth day with Australia 1 for 21 in the second innings. He went on to top-score in the innings with 69.

21. W.K.M. Benjamin (West Indies) v Australia at Kingston 1994-95, came in as 'night-watchman' late on the third day with the score 3 for 46 in the second innings. He went on to top-score with 51.

22. P.L. Symcox (South Africa) v Pakistan at Faisalabad 1997-98, came in as 'night-watchman' late on the second day with the score 2 for 21 in the second innings. He went on to top-score in the innings with 55.

## HIGHEST SCORES BY A No. 11

68* R.O. Collinge (New Zealand) v Pakistan at Auckland 1972-73. (Added 151 for the 10th wicket with B.F. Hastings, 110, a record for Test cricket.)

62* A.E.E. Vogler (South Africa) v England, Cape Town 1905-06.

60* Wasim Bari (Pakistan) v West Indies, Bridgetown 1976-77

59* J.A. Snow (England) v West Indies, The Oval 1966.

59 Mushtaq Ahmed (Pakistan) v South Africa at Rawalpindi 1997-98. (Added 151 for the 10th wicket with Azhar Mahmood,128*, equal record for Test cricket.)

54 P.L. Symcox (South Africa) v Australia, Adelaide 1997-98.

52 R.M. Hogg (Australia) v West Indies, Georgetown 1984-85.

50* W.W. Hall (West Indies) v India, Port-of-Spain 1961-62.

50 F.R. Spofforth (Australia) v England, Melbourne 1884-85.

50 Ghulam Ahmed (India) v Pakistan, Delhi 1952-53.

## SLOW SCORING MEMORABILIA

- Fourteen consecutive (four-ball) maiden overs were bowled to A.C. Bannerman and W.L. Murdoch (Australia) during their second wicket partnership v England at Melbourne 1882-83.
- A.C. Bannerman (Australia) scored 19 runs in 200 minutes during the match v England at Sydney 1886-87. Bannerman made 15* in two hours in the first innings and 4 in 80 minutes in the second.
- Fifty-eight maiden overs were included in Australia's total of 175 in 325 minutes v England at Manchester, 1921.
- B. Mitchell, on debut for South Africa v England at Birmingham in 1929 made a combined total of 149 in 575 minutes — 88 in 420 minutes and 61* in 155 minutes.
- England scored only 37 runs in the pre-lunch session v Australia at Adelaide 1932-33.
- I.D. Craig (Australia) scored 38 in $4^1/_2$ hours spread over 4 days v England, Manchester 1956.
- P.G. van der Bijl (125) for South Africa v England at Durban in 1938-39 did not hit his first boundary until he had been at the wicket for three hours. The first four of the South African innings came after 130 minutes.
- England took 972 minutes and 1723 balls to score 442 runs v Australia at Leeds in 1953 — 167 in 386 minutes (658 balls) and 275 in 586 minutes (1065 balls).
- England scored only 27 (39 overs) before lunch on the third day v West Indies at Bridgetown 1953-54. The new ball (then taken after 65 overs) arrived with the score at 77.

- Hanif Mohammad scored 59 runs in 337 minutes for the match v England at Lord's 1954 — 20 in 197 minutes and 39 in 140 minutes.
- New Zealand had scored only 24 at lunch (after 90 minutes) on the first day of the match v England at Dunedin 1954-55. The total for the day was 125 in 292 minutes.
- New Zealand scored only 69 off 90 six-ball overs (56 maidens) v Pakistan at Dacca 1955-56.
- New Zealand scored 6 for 32 and 3 for 37 in two pre-lunch sessions v England at Birmingham 1958.
- England scored only 19 runs before lunch (90 minutes) v Australia at Brisbane 1958-59, taking an overnight score of 2 for 92 to 4 for 114. T.E. Bailey scored 8 of the 19 runs in the session.
- Pakistan scored 24 before lunch v Australia at Karachi 1959-60. The innings of 8 (dec.) for 194 lasted eight hours.
- M.L. Jaisimha (India) v Australia at Calcutta 1959-60 batted through a whole day's play, taking his overnight score of 0* to 59*.
- T.E. Bailey (England) in the first Test v Australia, Brisbane 1958-59 scored 68 runs in 458 minutes — less than nine runs an hour. He took 357 minutes to reach fifty and scored off only 40 of the 425 balls bowled to him.

## SHORTEST TEAM TEST MATCH INNINGS

1. 50 minutes — South Africa, all out for 30 in 12.3 overs (6-ball) v England at Birmingham 1924.
2. 80 minutes — England, all out for 45 in 35.3 overs (4-ball) v Australia at Sydney 1886-87.
3. 90 minutes — Australia, all out for 30 in 23 overs (6-ball) v England at Birmingham 1902.
4. $3^3/_4$ hours — India, all out twice in one day for 58 (21.4 6-ball overs) and 82 (37.3 overs) v England at Manchester 1952.

## COURAGEOUS PERFORMANCES

1. During the second Test of the 1970-71 Australia v England rubber at Perth, English batsman B.W. Luckhurst damaged his thumb early in his innings but carried on to score 131 runs. In the fifth Test, played a little over a month later at Melbourne, Luckhurst's left little finger was fractured early in his innings and on this occasion he scored 109 runs.
2. During the first Test at Dunedin, of the 1967-68 New Zealand v India series R.B. Desai (India) had his jaw fractured by a rising ball from R.C. Motz but went on to score 32* in a tenth-wicket partnership of 57 with B.S. Bedi.
3. A.R. Border (Australia), despite batting in considerable pain from a broken finger during the 1981 series v England, scored in succession 123*, 106* and 84, batting in all for 15 hours and two minutes before losing his wicket.
4. E. Paynter (England) hospitalised with acute tonsillitis during the fourth Test against Australia in 1932-33, insisted on taking his place at the crease where he stayed for four hours scoring 83 runs. In the second innings he struck a six which won the match and regained the Ashes for England.
5. A.D. Nourse (South Africa) batted for 550 minutes to score 208 in the first Test v England at Nottingham in 1951 — with a broken thumb.
6. W.M. Lawry (Australia) had ten stitches inserted in a head wound caused by a fast rising ball from P.M.Pollock in the third Test against South Africa at Durban in 1966-67. He returned to the crease and top-scored with 44 out of the first innings total of 147.
7. R.B. McCosker (Australia). In the Centenary Test between Australia and England played at Melbourne in March 1977 McCosker suffered a fractured jaw whilst batting in the first innings. He returned to the crease, however, his face swathed in bandages to help Australia to a second innings total of 9 (dec.) for 419.
8. S.M. Patil (India). Playing in the first Test against Australia 1980-81, Patil was knocked unconscious by a 'bouncer' from L.S. Pascoe. Three weeks later at Adelaide in the second Test he scored 174 in 301 minutes.

## UNUSUAL DISMISSALS

1. S.P. Jones (Australia) playing against England in the 1882 'Ashes' Test at The Oval was run out by W.G. Grace when, after completing a run, he left his crease to pat the pitch down. This was said to so infuriate F.R. Spofforth, that he bowled like a man possessed, and taking 7 for 44 in England's second innings was instrumental in gaining Australia's first-ever win in a Test on English soil.
2. S.J. Snooke for South Africa v England at Durban in 1909-10 was stumped for 53 by N.C. Tufnell, who was keeping wicket as a substitute in place of H. Strudwick (injured).
3. A. Ducat had scored 3 for England v Australia at Leeds 1921 when the shoulder of his bat was broken by an express delivery from E.A. McDonald, the broken piece of the bat knocking off a bail and the ball being

caught by J.M. Gregory. (The umpire's decision, incidentally, was 'out caught'.)

4. J.W. Zulch (South Africa) in the second Test against Australia played at Johannesburg in 1921-22 was given out 'hit wicket' when a splinter of wood from his bat, dislodged by a ball from E.A. McDonald removed the bails.

5. W.H. Brann for South Africa v England at Cape Town in 1922-23 was given 'not out' for a catch at the wicket from the bowling of G.G. Macauley — who then appealed for lbw and had the appeal granted.

6. Mushtaq Ali, batting for India v England at Manchester in 1936, was run out when a ball hit by his partner, V.M. Merchant, hit the back of Mushtaq Ali's bat and deflected to mid-off where A.E.Fagg fielded and threw down the non-striker's wicket with Mushtaq Ali out of his ground.

7. D.G.Bradman (Australia) was batting against India at Brisbane in 1947-48 when he played back so far to N.B.Amarnath that the downward swing of his bat broke the wicket from behind. Bradman was out "hit wicket" to Amarnath for 185.

8. W.A.Brown (Australia) was run out by the bowler, M.H.Mankad, when batting for Australia v India at Sydney 1947-48. Brown had been backing up too far and Mankad removed the bails as he ran in to bowl. Mankad did not deliver a warning as he had been involved in a similar incident with Brown only four weeks before in the match between an Australian XI and the touring Indian team.

9. L.Hutton (England) was dismissed for "obstructing the field" v South Africa at The Oval, 1951. A delivery hit Hutton's bat handle or hand and lobbed into the air where wicket-keeper W.R.Endean prepared to take the catch. Hutton, however, hit the ball away as it fell (with the intention of preventing it hitting his wicket) and upon appeal was given out.

10. Ironically, W.R.Endean (South Africa) became the first batsman to be given out "handled the ball" v England at Cape Town in 1956-57, when a ball from J.C.Laker rose sharply and Endean palmed it away with his hand in hockey goalkeeper style.

11. West Indian batsman J.S.Solomon was adjudged out "hit wicket" when his cap fell off dislodging the bails during the Second Test of the 1960-61 series against Australia at Melbourne.

12. Pervez Sajjad (Pakistan) was stumped by B.E.Congdon (New Zealand) at Lahore 1964-65. Congdon was substituting as wicket-keeper for A.E.Dick, who had been injured.

13. B.L.d'Oliveira (England). In the Second Test v West Indies played at Lord's in 1966 England's J.M.Parks and B.L.d'Oliveira were batting together in the first innings. Parks, facing W.W.Hall, drove a ball back down the pitch which rebounded off d'Oliveira's boot onto the stumps whilst he was out of his crease. Thinking he was run out d'Oliveira 'walked' whereupon Hall picked up the ball and removed a stump with the hand holding the ball, thus correctly completing the dismissal. Had the batsman stood his ground he would not have been out as no fielder had touched the ball when the wicket was first broken.

14. I.R.Redpath (Australia) was run out, when backing-up too far, by bowler C.C.Griffith (West Indies) at Adelaide 1968-69. Redpath had been involved in a similar incident some time before. (Interestingly, I.M.Chappell was caught out of his ground in the same way by bowler D.A.J.Holford only minutes later, but in this instance the bowler refrained from removing the bails.)

15. D.W.Randall (England) was run out by bowler E.J.Chatfield (New Zealand) in the Test at Christchurch 1977-78.

16. R.M.Hogg (Australia) when batting against Pakistan at Melbourne 1978-79, had run a single and then, between deliveries, walked up the pitch to prod down some loose turf. However, the ball was still in the possession of a fielder, Javed Miandad, who put down the stumps with Hogg yards down the wicket to run the batsman out for 9.

17. Sikander Bakht (Pakistan) was similarly dismissed by bowler A.G.Hurst (Australia) at Perth 1978-79.

18. A.M.J.Hilditch (Australia) when batting against Pakistan at Perth, 1978-79, took pity on the perspiring fast bowler Sarfraz Nawaz and bent down and collected the ball by his feet at the bowler's end, and handed it to Sarfraz. Instead of thanking Hilditch, the bowler appealed for "handled the ball" and the umpire had no option but to uphold the appeal.

19. Moin Khan (Pakistan) when batting against Australia at Karachi, 1982-83 defended a ball from J.R.Thomson and instinctively knocked it away with his hand when it rebounded towards his stumps and became the third player to be given out "handled the ball".

20. D.L.Haynes (West Indies) when batting against India at Bombay, 1983-84 played a ball from Kapil Dev, which took and inside edge hit his pads and rolled slowly towards the stumps. He brushed it away with his glove to become the fourth player to be dismissed "handled the ball".

21. D.M.Jones (Australia) v West Indies at Georgetown 1990-91 was bowled by a no-ball from C.A.Walsh. Because of his helmet and the noise from the crowd, he did not hear the umpire's call and started to walk

off the field. C.L.Hooper grabbed the ball and snatched up a stump with the hand holding the ball. The umpire then, incorrectly, gave the batsman out. The laws of cricket had been changed in 1980 so that the umpire can call back a batsman leaving the ground under a misapprehension that he had been dismissed. [It should be noted that at Port-of-Spain in 1973-74 A.W.Greig (England) ran out I.A.Kallicharran when, B.D.Julien played the last ball of the second day's play down the pitch, Greig picked up the ball and, seeing Kallicharran out of his ground, threw down the non-striker's wicket and appealed. Umpire D.Sang Hue ruled Kallicharran "run out". That evening lengthy off-field discussions between the captains, officials and umpires led to the appeal being withdrawn in the interests of cricket.]

22. G.A. Gooch (England v Australia, Manchester 1993) became the fifth batsman to be out 'handled the ball' when, after playing a ball from M.G.Hughes down into his crease, he knocked it away with his right glove when it bounced up and was about to fall on his stumps.

## A FEW SURPRISE SELECTIONS

1. E.J.K. Burn (Australia) was selected in the 1890 Australian team to England as the second wicketkeeper. It was only when the team was assembled in Adelaide that it became known that Burn had never kept wickets in his life!

2. S.F. Barnes (England) was selected to tour Australia in 1901-02, mainly at the instigation of A.C. McLaren. Barnes, then a professional with Burnley in the Lancashire League, had taken only nine wickets in first-class cricket — but then proceeded to take 19 wickets in his first two Tests on the way to becoming recognised as one of the greatest bowlers the world has ever seen.

3. Australian selectors had a 'double' selection bonanza in 1907-08 when they brought J.D.A. O'Connor and R.J. Hartigan into the side for the Adelaide Test against England. Hartigan scored 48 and 116 (sharing in a record stand of 243 with C. Hill after Australia had been 7 for 180) and O'Connor bowled Australia to victory with 5 for 40 in the vital fourth innings of the match.

4. W. Rhodes (England) was brought back into the England team for the vital fifth Test of the 1926 series against Australia aged 48! With England needing a win to regain the 'Ashes', Rhodes bowled them to victory with 2 for 35 and 4 for 44.

5. A.L. Valentine (West Indies) was taken to England in 1950 after only two first-class matches in which he had taken two wickets for 190 runs.

6. S. Ramadhin (West Indies) was pulled out of Trinidad club cricket to tour England in 1950, a tour on which he and A.L. Valentine mystified the best batsmen in England, on the way to becoming Test 'greats'. Ramadhin, like Valentine, had played only two games of first-class cricket — both on matting.

7. J.E.F. Beck (New Zealand) played only club cricket and never appeared in a first-class match when chosen to tour South Africa in 1953-54. He was run out for 99 at Cape Town in his second Test match.

8. G.S. Sobers (West Indies) was called into the Test side (to replace the injured A.L. Valentine) v England at Kingston in 1953-54 after playing in only two first-class matches.

9. The English selectors in 1956 for the series against Australia pulled off three of the most amazing selections in history — and all worked!

   For the third Test at Leeds, they included 41-year-old C. Washbrook, who had not played Test cricket for five years. Coming in to bat with the score at 3 for 17, Washbrook made 98 and shared in a stand of 177 with P.B.H. May.

   For the next Test at Manchester, the Rev. David Sheppard was included. Because of clerical duties, he had played only four innings that year for Sussex — but promptly made 113 to help England win the Test.

   For The Oval Test, the selectors brought in Denis Compton — 18 years after he had played his first Test and not long after he had undergone an operation for the removal of a knee-cap. Compton completed the 'hat-trick' for the selectors with scores of 94 and 35*.

10. J.R. Watkins (Australia) — After A.A. Mallett had announced his unavailability for the forthcoming tour of the West Indies the Australian selectors chose Watkins for the Test against Pakistan at Sydney in 1972-73, although his first-class record for New South Wales was not particularly distinguished. In the second innings he made a fine 36 and shared in a stand of 83 with R.A.L. Massie after Australia had collapsed to 8 for 101 — but with the ball, delivered probably the six most inaccurate overs ever bowled at Sydney.

11. M.R. Whitney (Australia) was in England to play League cricket, and appear occasionally for Gloucestershire, when he was brought into the Australian Test team in 1981 after injuries to G.F. Lawson and R.M.Hogg. Whitney had previously made four appearances for NSW.)

12. P.L. Taylor (Australia) was selected for the fifth Test against England at Sydney 1986-87 after only six first-class matches — only one of them during the

season. There was speculation in the media whether the selectors had chosen the wrong Taylor — M.A. Taylor, an opening batsmen for New South Wales having experienced a successful debut in first-class cricket the previous season. P.L. Taylor, bowling off-spin, took a career-best 6 for 78 and 2 for 76 as well as scoring a crucial 42 runs in Australia's second innings as Australia won their first Test against England since June 1985.

## UNUSUAL INCIDENTS

1. G.J. Bonnor (Australia) in making 87 v England at Sydney 1882-83 was dropped eight (!) times. A.G.Steel dropped four of the chances, when Bonnor was 2, 17, 24 and 80. When England batted, Steel himself was dropped 4 times – but went on to make 135*.

2. In the England v Australia series= in Australia in 1936-37, Middlesex captain R.W.V.Robins played under the leadership of his county vice-captain, G.O.B.Allen. A similar situation occurred in 1980 when Somerset captain B.C.Rose played under the leadership of Somerset vice-captain I.T.Botham for England v West Indies and 1995 when Lancashire captain M.Watkinson played under the leadership of his county colleague M.A.Atherton v West Indies and v South Africa.

3. In the Seventh Test Australia v England at Sydney 1970-71, England nearly became the first team to forfeit a Test. England paceman J.A.Snow felled Australian tail-ender T.J.Jenner with a 'bouncer', and became involved in a war of words with umpire L.P.Rowan when warned for "intimidatory" bowling. R.Illingworth, England's captain, joined in, and the crowd began to boo and hiss. Cans came flying onto the field and, when Snow was sent to field right on the fine-leg boundary, a drunken spectator leaned over the fence and grabbed his arm.

   Illingworth immediately motioned his team from the ground, and it was only the umpires's advice that if they did not return they would forfeit the match that persuaded Illingworth to resume.

4. In the India v Australia Test at Bangalore 1979-80, Australian pace-bowler R.M.Hogg, becoming upset with the feather-bed pitch and with his own spate of no-balls (7 in 5 overs), kicked down the stumps at the bowler's end. His captain, K.J.Hughes tendered an immediate apology to the umpire, an action which Hogg duplicated at the end of play.

5. In the Australia v England Test at Perth in 1979-80, Australian batsman D.K.Lillee, not out overnight, continued his innings the next morning using an aluminium bat, (which he had used once previously). After two balls had been played (rather noisily), England captain J.M.Brearley complained to the umpires that the aluminium bat was damaging the ball! The umpires therefore requested that Lillee change his bat, but Lillee, quite within his rights, refused, arguing heatedly with Brearley. Finally, the umpires ordered him off for a replacement, but after stalking from the ground, Lillee re-appeared — still carrying his aluminium bat. Still more argument ensued, and eventually Lillee threw the bat away in disgust, accepted a willow replacement, and the game was allowed to continue.

6. In the New Zealand v West Indies Test at Christchurch 1979-80, West Indian fast-bowler C.E.H.Croft took bad sportsmanship to the brink. After being no-balled and showing his displeasure several times, Croft ran in very close to the umpire (F.R.Goodall) — so close that the batsman could not see him — and shouldered Goodall heavily. Croft was later suspended for his actions, but the West Indians were so upset about Goodall's umpiring that they refused to take the field after tea on the third day unless he was replaced. They were finally persuaded to resume, 12 minutes late.

7. M.A.Holding, West Indies v New Zealand, Dunedin 1979-80, duplicated the behaviour of R.M.Hogg (above) by kicking down the stumps at the batsman's end after having an appeal disallowed.

8. The start of the Pakistan v West Indies Test at Multan in 1980-81 was delayed because of the late arrival of one of the umpires.

9. In the match West Indies v Pakistan at Multan in 1980-81, bowler S.T.Clarke (West Indies) was bombarded by a shower of oranges, and a brick, thrown from the crowd as he fielded on the fine-leg fence. Enraged, Clarke picked up the brick and threw it back into the crowd, injuring a young student. Play was immediately held up, and only West Indies vice-captain A.I.Kallicharran's calming plea, on bended knee in front of the grandstand, restored order in the angry crowd. Clarke was later suspended for three matches by the West Indies Cricket Board of Control.

10. When given out lbw v Australia at Melbourne 1980-81, Indian captain S.M.Gavaskar indicated that the ball had hit his pad and was so angry at the decision that he ordered his batting partner, C.P.S.Chauhan, to accompany him from the field of play and forfeit the match! Both players were only metres inside the boundary when India's manager, Wing-Commander Durani, intervened and ordered Chauhan back to the crease. The following day Kapil Dev and D.R.Doshi bowled India to victory as Australia was dismissed for 83 chasing a target of 143.

11. West Indies v England at St John's 1980-81 opened the Test by scoring 45 from the first seven overs — made up of 11 fours and a single.

## CAPTAINCY CURIOSITIES

H.M.Taberer captained South Africa in his one and only Test match appearance when he led his country against England at Johannesburg in the 1st Test of 1902-03. For the 2nd Test less than a week later J.H.Anderson led South Africa in his only Test appearance.

N.Betancourt captained West Indies in his only Test match played against England in the 1929-30.

In the 4th Test between West Indies and England played at Kingston in 1934-35 both captains were forced off the field through injury. England's R.E.S. Wyatt suffered a broken jaw and West Indies's C.G. Grant retired with an ankle injury.

C.A. Smith (England) captained his country at his only appearance in a Test match — against South Africa 1888-89. Smith, later knighted, was afterwards famous as an Hollywood film actor.

P.W. Sherwell (South Africa) captained his country in his first Test appearance, against England at Johannesburg, 1905-06.

During his period as captain of England (twelve matches from June 1980 to July 1981) I.T. Botham scored 276 runs at an average of 13.80 and took 35 wickets at 32.00 average. Compare these figures to his overall career-to-date statistics of 33.54 runs per innings and 28.40 for each wicket.

## ODDMENTS

1. In the second Test match between Australia played at the Melbourne Cricket Ground in 1877, Australian batsman T.J.D. Kelly hit eight consecutive fours in the second innings and C. Bannerman scored 30 in 15 minutes. Despite these spirited efforts Australia lost by four wickets.

2. An Australian team advertised for opponents. This unique event occurred during the visit of the Australians to England in 1880. Apparently, it was not certain until the late spring of that year that the Australians would be touring and consequently the county programmes had already been drawn up. The Australians therefore found the large part of their tour consisted of fixtures with local clubs in the North and Midlands, usually against odds. It was during this period that the team took out newspaper advertisements for opponents.

   Finally, at the end of August, and mainly through the efforts of one man, C.W. Alcock, a match against a representative English team was organised — this became the first of all Test matches on English soil.

3. In the first Test of the 1881-82 season between Australia and England, played at Melbourne, W.E. Midwinter made his debut for England having played for Australia in the first two Tests between the two countries. (In the same match T.P. Horan and G. Giffen scored Australia's first-ever century partnership: 107 for the fifth wicket.)

4. W.L. Murdoch of Australia scored the first double-century in Test cricket when he knocked up 211 against England at The Oval during the Third Test in 1884. In the same match all eleven English players were called upon to bowl whilst Australia scored 551 runs. The match was drawn.

5. In the fifth Test between Australia and England at Melbourne during the 1884-85 season umpire J. Hodges refused to take the field after tea on the third day because of complaints made by some English players about his decisions. Australian player T.W. Garrett deputised for Hodges during the last session and the English manager J. Lillywhite took over on the last day. There is nothing in the records to indicate how Garrett performed in this unusual role.

6. Four players with the same surname played in the South Africa v England Test at Cape Town in 1891-92 - A., G.E., and J.T. Hearne for England, F. Hearne for South Africa.

7. In his debut Test match (v South Africa at Cape Town in 1922-23) G.G. Macaulay (England) took a wicket with his first ball, and made the winning hit when England won the match by one wicket.

8. M.H. Mankad (India) in 72 innings and W. Rhodes (England) in 98 innings in Test match cricket are the only two batsmen to bat in every position from one to eleven in their Test match careers.

9. The only occasion when one country has simultaneously played official Test matches in two different countries was in 1929-30 when England played New Zealand at Christchurch on 10, 11, 13 January and West Indies at Bridgetown on 11, 13, 14, 15, 16 January.

10. The most expensive miss? B.A. Barnett when keeping wicket for Australia v England at The Oval, 1938, missed stumping L. Hutton off L.O. Fleetwood-Smith when the batsman was 40. Hutton went on to make 364.

11. The appearance of a mouse on the field held up play for several minutes during the England v Pakistan Test at Birmingham in 1962.

12. In the Pakistan v England Test at Lahore in 1977-78, England off-spinner G.A. Cope dismissed Abdul Qadir lbw and bowled Sarfraz Nawaz first ball. Iqbal Qasim then snicked the next delivery to J.M.Brearley, the English captain, at slip and the umpire confirmed

the catch and Copes's hat-trick. However, Brearley indicated that the 'catch' had been taken on the bounce and Qasim was allowed to bat on. It would be difficult to get much closer to a Test hat-trick than Cope did on that day.

13. Australia's first seven batsmen in the batting order: A.M.J. Hilditch, G.M. Wood, A.R. Border, K.J. Hughes, G.N.Yallop, D.F.Whatmore and K.J.Wright opened their score with a boundary in the first Test v India at Madras 1979-90.

14. The only other instance of all eleven players bowling in an innings occurred at Faisalabad in 1979-80 during the 2nd Test between Pakistan and Australia. The entire Australian team, including wicket-keeper R.W.Marsh, had a spell at the bowling crease during Pakistan's only innings. The match was drawn. Australia made 617 and Pakistan 2 for 382.

## BOWLERS NO-BALLED FOR THROWING IN TEST MATCHES

The following bowlers have been no-balled for throwing:

1. E. Jones, Australia, once by umpire J. Phillips in the second Test against England at Melbourne in 1897-98.
2. G.A.R. Lock, England, in the first Test against West Indies at Kingston in 1953-54.
3. G.M. Griffin, South Africa, eleven times by umpire F.S. Lee in the second Test against England at Lord's in 1960. In England's only innings Griffin claimed the only Test hat-trick achieved for South Africa when he took the wickets of M.J.K. Smith, P.M. Walker and F.S. Trueman.
4. Haseeb Ahsan, Pakistan, in the first Test against India at Bombay 1960-61.
5. I. Meckiff, Australia, four times by umpire C.J. Egar in his only over in the first Test against South Africa at Brisbane 1963-64.
6. S. Abid Ali, India, once by umpire F.R. Goodall in the second Test against New Zealand at Christchurch in 1967-68. He deliberately threw the ball in protest at the action of G.A. Bartlett who had not been 'called'.
7. D.I. Gower, England, deliberately threw the only ball he 'bowled' in the second Test against New Zealand at Nottingham in 1986. The scores were level and New Zealand had eight wickets in hand.
8. H.R. Olonga, Zimbabwe, celebrated his Test debut by dismissing Saeed Anwar with his third ball, Zimbabwe v Pakistan, Harare 1994-95. However, his celebrations were short-lived as he was no-balled for throwing in his fifth over.
9. M. Muralidaran, Sri Lanka, was no-balled seven times by umpire D.B. Hair in the 2nd Test against Australia at Melbourne in 1995-96. This is the only instance of a player being 'called' by the umpire at the bowler's end.

## MOST WICKETS BY A BOWLER IN ONE DAY

| | | | | | | | |
|---|---|---|---|---|---|---|---|
| 15 | J. Briggs | 15-28 | England | v | South Africa | Cape Town | 1888-89 |
| 14 | H. Verity | 14-80 | England | v | Australia | Lord's | 1934 |

## WICKET WITH FIRST BALL IN TEST CRICKET

| Bowler | Batsman dismissed | | | | | |
|---|---|---|---|---|---|---|
| A. Coningham | A.C. MacLaren | Australia | v | England | Melbourne | 1894-95 |
| W.M. Bradley | F.J. Laver | England | v | Australia | Manchester | 1899 |
| E.G. Arnold | V.T. Trumper | England | v | Australia | Sydney | 1903-04 |
| G.G. Macaulay | G.A.L. Hearne | England | v | South Africa | Cape Town | 1922-23 |
| M.W. Tate | M.J. Susskind | England | v | South Africa | Birmingham | 1924 |
| M. Henderson | E.W. Dawson | New Zealand | v | England | Christchurch | 1929-30 |
| H.D. Smith | E. Paynter | New Zealand | v | England | Christchurch | 1932-33 |
| T.F. Johnson | W.W. Keeton | West Indies | v | England | The Oval | 1939 |
| R. Howorth | D.V. Dyer | England | v | South Africa | The Oval | 1947 |
| Intikhab Alam | C.C. McDonald | Pakistan | v | Australia | Karachi[1] | 1959-60 |
| R.K. Illingworth | P.V. Simmons | England | v | West Indies | Nottingham | 1991 |
| N.M. Kulkarni | M.S. Atapattu | India | v | Sri Lanka | Colombo (PIS) | 1997-98 |

## WICKET IN FIRST OVER IN TEST CRICKET

| Ball | Bowler | Batsman dismissed | | | | |
|---|---|---|---|---|---|---|
| 1st | A. Coningham | A.C. MacLaren | Australia | v England | Melbourne | 1894-95 |
| 1st | W.M. Bradley | F.J. Laver | England | v Australia | Manchester | 1899 |
| 1st | E.G. Arnold | V.T. Trumper | England | v Australia | Sydney | 1903-04 |
| 1st | G.G. Macaulay | G.A.L. Hearne | England | v South Africa | Cape Town | 1922-23 |
| 1st | M.W. Tate | M.J. Susskind | England | v South Africa | Birmingham | 1924 |
| 1st | M. Henderson | E.W. Dawson | New Zealand | v England | Christchurch | 1929-30 |
| 1st | H.D. Smith | E. Paynter | New Zealand | v England | Christchurch | 1932-33 |
| 1st | T.F. Johnson | W.W. Keeton | West Indies | v England | The Oval | 1939 |
| 1st | R. Howorth | D.V. Dyer | England | v South Africa | The Oval | 1947 |
| 1st | Intikhab Alam | C.C. McDonald | Pakistan | v Australia | Karachi[1] | 1959-60 |
| 1st | R.K.I llingworth | P.V. Simmons | England | v West Indies | Nottingham | 1991 |
| 1st | N.M. Kulkarni | M.S. Atapattu | India | v Sri Lanka | Colombo (PIS) | 1997-98 |
| 2nd | G.A. Rowe | T.C. O'Brien | South Africa | v England | Johannesburg[1] | 1895-96 |
| 2nd | W. Barber | H.B. Cameron | England | v South Africa | Leeds | 1935 |
| 2nd | J.H. Cameron | H. Gimblett | West Indies | v England | Lord's | 1939 |
| 2nd | C.L. McCool | D.A.N. McRae | Australia | v New Zealand | Wellington | 1945-46 |
| 2nd | G.W.A. Chubb | J.T. Ikin | South Africa | v England | Nottingham | 1951 |
| 2nd | R. Appleyard | Hanif Mohammad | England | v Pakistan | Nottingham | 1954 |
| 2nd | F.M. Misson | C.C. Hunte | Australia | v West Indies | Melbourne | 1960-61 |
| 2nd | P.I. Philpott | C.C. Hunte | Australia | v West Indies | Kingston | 1964-65 |
| 2nd | B.A.G. Murray | S. Abid Ali | New Zealand | v India | Wellington | 1967-68 |
| 2nd | G. Dymock | J.M. Parker | Australia | v New Zealand | Adelaide | 1973-74 |
| 3rd | I.W. Johnson | L. Hutton | Australia | v England | Sydney | 1946-47 |
| 3rd | R.O. Jenkins | E.A.B. Rowan | England | v South Africa | Durban[2] | 1948-49 |
| 3rd | M.S. Hardikar | R.B. Kanhai | India | v West Indies | Bombay | 1958-59 |
| 3rd | P.D. Lashley | G. Boycott | West Indies | v England | Leeds | 1966 |
| 3rd | E.W. Freeman | S. Abid Ali | Australia | v India | Brisbane[2] | 1967-68 |
| 3rd | K.Thompson | F.M. Engineer | New Zealand | v India | Wellington | 1967-68 |
| 3rd | M.Hendrick | E.D. Solkar | England | v India | Manchester | 1974 |
| 3rd | B.P. Bracewell | G.A. Gooch | New Zealand | v England | The Oval | 1978 |
| 3rd | A.K. Kuruppuarachchi | Mudassar Nazar | Sri Lanka | v Pakistan | Colombo (CCC) | 1985-86 |
| 3rd | G.A. Hick | P.V. Simmons | England | v West Indies | Lord's | 1991 |
| 3rd | C.B. Lambert | M.R. Ramprakash | West Indies | v England | The Oval | 1991 |
| 3rd | D.K. Liyanage | T.M. Moody | Sri Lanka | v Australia | Colombo (PIS) | 1992-93 |
| 3rd | H.R. Olonga | Saeed Anwar | Zimbabwe | v Pakistan | Harare | 1994-95 |
| 4th | G.L. Weir | G.B. Legge | New Zealand | v England | Wellington | 1929-30 |
| 4th | D.V.P. Wright | J.H.W. Fingleton | England | v Australia | Nottingham | 1938 |
| 4th | F.W. Freer | C. Washbrook | Australia | v England | Sydney | 1946-47 |
| 4th | A.M.B. Rowan | L. Hutton | South Africa | v England | Nottingham | 1947 |
| 4th | J.C. Laker | C.L. Walcott | England | v West Indies | Bridgetown | 1947-48 |
| 4th | H.J. Rhodes | Pankaj Roy | England | v India | Leeds | 1959 |
| 4th | D.A.J. Holford | F.J. Titmus | West Indies | v England | Manchester | 1966 |
| 4th | D.S. Steele | A.A. Mallett | England | v Australia | Lord's | 1975 |
| 4th | J.E. Emburey | B.A. Edgar | England | v New Zealand | Lord's | 1978 |
| 4th | E.E. Hemmings | Javed Miandad | England | v Pakistan | Birmingham | 1982 |
| 4th | C.S. Cowdrey | Kapil Dev | England | v India | Bombay | 1984-85 |
| 4th | F.S. Ahangama | M. Azharuddin | Sri Lanka | v India | Colombo (SSC) | 1985-86 |
| 4th | W.V. Raman | C.A. Walsh | India | v West Indies | Madras | 1987-88 |
| 4th | J.C. Adams | W.J.Cronje | West Indies | v South Africa | Bridgetown | 1991-92 |
| 4th | S.G. Peall | Aamer Sohail | Zimbabwe | v Pakistan | Karachi[2] | 1993-94 |
| 4th | Shahid Nazir | A.D.R. Campbell | Pakistan | v Zimbabwe | Sheikhupura | 1996-97 |
| 5th | G.H.T. Simpson-Hayward | J.W. Zulch | England | v South Africa | Johannesburg[1] | 1909-10 |
| 5th | S.A. Banerjee | D.S. Atkinson | India | v West Indies | Calcutta | 1948-49 |
| 5th | L.J. Coldwell | Imtiaz Ahmed | England | v Pakistan | Lord's | 1962 |
| 5th | B.W. Yuile | E.R. Dexter | New Zealand | v England | Auckland | 1962-63 |

| | | | | | | |
|---|---|---|---|---|---|---|
| 5th | A.A. Mallett | M.C. Cowdrey | Australia | v England | The Oval | 1968 |
| 5th | G.A. Chevalier | A.P. Sheahan | South Africa | v Australia | Cape Town | 1969-70 |
| 5th | R.D. Jackman | C.G. Greenidge | England | v West Indies | Bridgetown | 1980-81 |
| 5th | C. Sharma | Mohsin Khan | India | v Pakistan | Lahore[2] | 1984-85 |
| 5th | D. Gough | M.J. Greatbatch | England | v New Zealand | Manchester | 1994 |
| 5th | R.C. Irani | M. Azharuddin | England | v India | Birmingham | 1996 |
| 6th | D.P.B. Morkel | P. Holmes | South Africa | v England | Johannesburg[1] | 1927-28 |
| 6th | E.W. Clark | R.H. Catterall | England | v South Africa | The Oval | 1929 |
| 6th | L.O. Fleetwood-Smith | K.G. Viljoen | Australia | v South Africa | Durban[2] | 1949-50 |
| 6th | V.V. Kumar | Imtiaz Ahmed | India | v Pakistan | Delhi | 1960-61 |
| 6th | M.W.W. Selvey | R.C. Fredericks | England | v West Indies | Manchester | 1976 |
| 6th | D.R. Pringle | Yashpal Sharma | England | v India | Lord's | 1982 |
| 6th | Fazl-e-Akbar | G. Kirsten | Pakistan | v South Africa | Durban[2] | 1997-98 |
| 7th | R.A. Gaunt | R.J. Westcott | Australia | v South Africa | Durban[2] | 1957-58 |
| 7th | A.L. Mann | G.R. Viswanath | Australia | v India | Brisbane[2] | 1977-78 |
| | M. Leyland | G. Challenor | England | v West Indies | The Oval | 1928 |
| | B. Sutcliffe | A. Wharton | New Zealand | v England | Leeds | 1949 |
| | E.W. Dempster | D.J. McGlew | New Zealand | v South Africa | Auckland | 1952-53 |
| | A.F. Lissette | A.P. Binns | New Zealand | v West Indies | Dunedin | 1955-56 |
| | L.A. King | M.L. Jaisimha | West Indies | v India | Kingston | 1961-62 |

## LONG BOWLING SPELLS

1. G.E. Palmer (53-36-68-7) and E. Evans (57-32-64-3) (Australia) together bowled unchanged for the entire English innings of 133 scored in 190 minutes — at Sydney 1881-82.
2. T. Richardson, for England v Australia at Manchester in 1896, bowled unchanged for three hours in the second innings to try and stave off an England defeat. Richardson, a pace bowler, delivered 42.3 overs, 16 maidens and took 6 for 76.
3. A.M.B. Rowan (South Africa) bowled unchanged for 46 six-ball overs v England at Leeds, 1947 for figures of 46-12-89-1.
4. Ghulam Ahmed, for India v Pakistan at Dacca 1954-55, bowled 40 overs unchanged on the first day, his figures being 40-8-84-4.
5. T.L. Goddard (South Africa) bowled 46 overs unchanged on the last day of the match v England at Leeds in 1955. His spell resulted in figures of 46-27-45-4.
6. H.J. Tayfield (South Africa) had an unchanged spell of 53.4-29-60-5 in the second English innings at The Oval in 1955.
7. T.R. Veivers (Australia) sent down 55 consecutive overs v England at Manchester in 1964. Veivers bowled 75 of the last 80 overs sent down from the City end.

## 500 BALLS IN AN INNINGS

| Balls | Player | O | M | R | W | | | | | |
|---|---|---|---|---|---|---|---|---|---|---|
| 588 | S. Ramadhin | 98 | 35 | 179 | 2 | West Indies | v | England | Birmingham | 1957 |
| 571 | T.R. Veivers | 95.1 | 36 | 155 | 3 | Australia | v | England | Manchester | 1964 |
| 552 | A.L. Valentine | 92 | 49 | 140 | 3 | West Indies | v | England | Nottingham | 1950 |
| 522 | L.O. Fleetwood-Smith | 87 | 11 | 298 | 1 | Australia | v | England | The Oval | 1938 |
| 512 | Fazal Mahmood | 85.2 | 20 | 247 | 2 | Pakistan | v | West Indies | Kingston | 1957-58 |
| 510 | W.J. O'Reilly | 85 | 26 | 178 | 3 | Australia | v | England | The Oval | 1938 |
| 504 | Haseeb Ahsan | 84 | 19 | 202 | 6 | Pakistan | v | India | Madras | 1960-61 |

## 700 BALLS IN A MATCH

| Balls | Player | O | M | R | W | | | | | |
|---|---|---|---|---|---|---|---|---|---|---|
| 774 | S. Ramadhin | 129 | 51 | 228 | 9 | West Indies | v | England | Birmingham | 1957 |
| 766 | H. Verity | 95.6 | 23 | 184 | 4 | England | v | South Africa | Durban[2] | 1938-39 |
| 749 | J.C. White | 124.5 | 37 | 256 | 13 | England | v | Australia | Adelaide | 1928-29 |
| 738 | N. Gordon | 92.2 | 17 | 256 | 1 | South Africa | v | England | Durban[2] | 1938-39 |
| 728 | A.B.C. Langton | 91 | 24 | 203 | 4 | South Africa | v | England | Durban[2] | 1938-39 |
| 712 | M.W. Tate | 89 | 19 | 228 | 11 | England | v | Australia | Sydney | 1924-25 |
| 708 | G. Giffen | 118 | 42 | 239 | 8 | Australia | v | England | Sydney | 1894-95 |

## GOOD BOWLING SPELLS

7 wickets for 1 run in 26 balls - Sarfraz Nawaz Pakistan v Australia, Melbourne 1978-79.

7 wickets for 1 run in 32 balls - C.E.L. Ambrose West Indies v Australia, Perth 1992-93.

7 wickets for 8 runs in 22 balls - J.C. Laker England v Australia, Manchester 1956.

6 wickets for 6 runs in 45 balls - S. Haigh England v South Africa, Cape Town 1898-99.

7 wickets for 17 runs in 46 balls - M.A. Noble Australia v England, Melbourne 1901-02.

8 wickets for 7 runs in 49 balls - G.A. Lohmann England v South Africa, Johannesburg 1895-96.

6 wickets for 7 runs in 29 balls - S.J. Pegler South Africa v England, Lord's 1912.

5 wickets for 1 run in 17 balls - G.R. Hazlitt Australia v England, The Oval 1912.

5 wickets for 7 runs in 31 balls - E.P. Nupen South Africa v England, Durban 1927-28.

6 wickets for 11 runs in 24 balls - E.P. Nupen South Africa v England, Johannesburg 1930-31.

6 wickets for 8 runs in 36 balls - H. Ironmonger Australia v South Africa, Melbourne 1931-32.

6 wickets for 9 runs in 56 balls - C.V. Grimmett Australia v South Africa, Adelaide 1931-32.

5 wickets for 1 run in 28 balls - I.T. Botham England v Australia, Birmingham 1981.

5 wickets for 2 runs in 19 balls - E.R.H. Toshack Australia v India, Brisbane 1947-48.

## INEXPENSIVE ANALYSES

| | |
|---|---|
| 25-19-18-0 | Fazal Mahmood Pakistan v India, Dacca, 1954-55 |
| 28-17-21-2 | A.H. Kardar Pakistan v New Zealand Dacca, 1955-56 |
| 30-19-20-2 | Khan Mohammad Pakistan v New Zealand, Dacca 1955-56 |
| 32-27-5-0 | R.G. Nadkarni India v England, Madras 1963-64 |
| 32-23-24-4 | J.H. Wardle England v South Africa, Nottingham 1955 |
| 36-23-27-3 | J.C. Laker England v New Zealand, Leeds 1958 |
| 45-28-48-4 | A.L. Valentine West Indies v England, Lord's 1950 |
| 45-26-42-6 | K.D. Mackay Australia v Pakistan, Dacca 1959-60 |
| 46-24-43-1 | W. Attewell England v Australia, Sydney 1891-92 |
| 46.1-20-42-1 | G.E. Gomez West Indies v India, Port-of-Spain 1952-53 |
| 46.3-24-42-6 | Zulfiqar Ahmed Pakistan v New Zealand, Karachi 1955-56 |
| 47-29-42-5 | H. Ironmonger Australia v South Africa, Brisbane 1931-32 |
| 47-28-39-3 | C.V. Grimmett Australia v England, Nottingham 1934 |
| 53-30-50-4 | S. Ramadhin West Indies v England, Bridgetown 1953-54 |
| 53.3-37-38-8 | L.R. Gibbs West Indies v India, Bridgetown 1961-62 |
| 54-38-43-4 | B.W. Yuile New Zealand v Pakistan, Auckland 1964-65 |
| 57-30-64-1 | J.C. White England v Australia, Melbourne 1928-29 |
| 61-34-71-1 | M.H. Mankad India v Pakistan, Peshawar 1954-55 |
| 61-32-51-3 | W. Attewell England v Australia, Melbourne 1891-92 |
| 62-37-69-4 | T.L. Goddard South Africa v England, Leeds 1955 |
| 62-35-61-1 | D.S. Atkinson West Indies v Pakistan, Bridgetown 1957-58 |
| 69-34-79-2 | D.R. Doshi India v New Zealand, Auckland 1980-81 |
| 71-47-79-3 | A.L. Valentine West Indies v England, Lord's 1950 |
| 72-43-86-6 | S. Ramadhin West Indies v England, Lord's 1950 |
| 76-47-58-4 | M.H. Mankad India v England, Delhi 1951-52 |
| 81-36-105-5 | G. Geary England v Australia, Melbourne 1928-29 |

All of the above instances were 6-ball overs.

## OUTSTANDING ANALYSES IN A TEST INNINGS

| O | M | R | W | | | | | | |
|---|---|---|---|---|---|---|---|---|---|
| 51.2 | 23 | 53 | 10 | J.C. Laker | England | v | Australia | Manchester | 1956 |
| 14.2 | 6 | 28 | 9 | G.A. Lohmann | England | v | South Africa | Johannesburg[1] | 1895-96 |
| 16.4 | 4 | 37 | 9 | J.C. Laker | England | v | Australia | Manchester | 1956 |
| 9.4 | 5 | 7 | 8 | G.A. Lohmann | England | v | South Africa | Port Elizabeth | 1895-96 |
| 14.2 | 5 | 11 | 8 | J. Briggs | England | v | South Africa | Cape Town | 1888-89 |
| 19.1 | 11 | 17 | 7 | J. Briggs | England | v | South Africa | Cape Town | 1888-89 |

| | | | | | | | | | |
|---|---|---|---|---|---|---|---|---|---|
| 7.4 | 2 | 17 | 7 | M.A. Noble | Australia | v | England | Melbourne | 1901-02 |
| 11 | 3 | 17 | 7 | W. Rhodes | England | v | Australia | Birmingham | 1902 |
| 6.3 | 4 | 7 | 6 | A.E.R. Gilligan | England | v | South Africa | Birmingham | 1924 |
| 11.4 | 6 | 11 | 6 | S. Haigh | England | v | South Africa | Cape Town | 1898-99 |
| 11.6 | 7 | 12 | 6 | D.L. Underwood | England | v | New Zealand | Christchurch | 1970-71 |
| 17.5 | 13 | 12 | 6 | S.L. Venkatapathy Raju | India | v | Sri Lanka | Chandigarh | 1990-91 |
| 14 | 7 | 13 | 6 | H.J. Tayfield | South Africa | v | New Zealand | Johannesburg[2] | 1953-54 |
| 18 1 | 1 | 15 | 6 | C.T.B. Turner | Australia | v | England | Sydney | 1886-87 |
| 16 | 8 | 15 | 6 | M.H.N .Walker | Australia | v | Pakistan | Sydney | 1972-73 |
| 2.3 | 1 | 2 | 5 | E.R.H.T oshack | Australia | v | India | Brisbane[2] | 1947-48 |
| 7.2 | 5 | 6 | 5 | H. Ironmonger | Australia | v | South Africa | Melbourne | 1931-32 |
| 12 | 8 | 5 | 4 | Pervez Sajjad | Pakistan | v | New Zealand | Rawalpindi[1] | 1964-65 |
| 9 | 7 | 5 | 4 | K. Higgs | England | v | New Zealand | Christchurch | 1965-66 |
| 8 | 6 | 6 | 4 | P.H. Edmonds | England | v | Pakistan | Lord's | 1978 |
| 6.3 | 2 | 7 | 4 | J.C. White | England | v | Australia | Brisbane[1] | 1928-29 |
| 5 | 2 | 7 | 4 | J.H. Wardle | England | v | Australia | Manchester | 1953 |
| 6 | 3 | 7 | 4 | R. Appleyard | England | v | New Zealand | Auckland | 1954-55 |
| 3.4 | 3 | 0 | 3 | R. Benaud | Australia | v | India | Delhi | 1959-60 |

## MOST ECONOMICAL CAREER BOWLING (Qualification: 2000 balls)

| Player | Country | Runs/100 balls | Tests | Balls | Runs | Wkts | Avge |
|---|---|---|---|---|---|---|---|
| W. Attewell | England | **21.96** | 10 | 2850 | 626 | 28 | 22.35 |
| C. Gladwin | England | **26.82** | 8 | 2129 | 571 | 15 | 38.06 |
| T.L. Goddard | South Africa | **27.48** | 41 | 11736 | 3226 | 123 | 26.22 |
| R.G. Nadkarni | India | **27.92** | 41 | 9165 | 2559 | 88 | 29.07 |
| H. Ironmonger | Australia | **28.32** | 14 | 4695 | 1330 | 74 | 17.97 |
| J.C. Watkins | South Africa | **29.09** | 15 | 2805 | 816 | 29 | 28.13 |
| K.D. Mackay | Australia | **29.71** | 37 | 5792 | 1721 | 50 | 34.42 |
| A.R.A. Murray | South Africa | **29.90** | 10 | 2374 | 710 | 18 | 39.44 |

## DISMISSING ALL ELEVEN BATSMEN IN A MATCH

| | | | | | | |
|---|---|---|---|---|---|---|
| J.C. Laker | 19-90 | England | v | Australia | Manchester | 1956 |
| S. Venkataraghavan | 12-152 | India | v | New Zealand | Delhi | 1964-65 |
| G. Dymock | 12-166 | Australia | v | India | Kanpur | 1979-80 |
| Abdul Qadir | 13-101 | Pakistan | v | England | Lahore[2] | 1987-88 |
| Waqar Younis | 12-130 | Pakistan | v | New Zealand | Faisalabad | 1990-91 |

## OVER 200 RUNS CONCEDED IN AN INNINGS

| O | M | R | W | | | | | | |
|---|---|---|---|---|---|---|---|---|---|
| 87 | 11 | 298 | 1 | L.O. Fleetwood-Smith | Australia | v | England | The Oval | 1938 |
| 78 | 8 | 276 | 1 | R.K. Chauhan | India | v | Sri Lanka | Colombo (PIS) | 1997-98 |
| 80.2 | 13 | 266 | 5 | O.C. Scott | West Indies | v | England | Kingston | 1929-30 |
| 54 | 5 | 259 | 0 | Khan Mohammad | Pakistan | v | West Indies | Kingston | 1957-58 |
| 85.2 | 20 | 247 | 2 | Fazal Mahmood | Pakistan | v | West Indies | Kingston | 1957-58 |
| 70 | 10 | 229 | 1 | S.L. Boock | New Zealand | v | Pakistan | Auckland | 1988-89 |
| 82 | 17 | 228 | 5 | M.H. Mankad | India | v | West Indies | Kingston | 1952-53 |
| 64.2 | 8 | 226 | 6 | B.S. Bedi | India | v | England | Lord's | 1974 |
| 54 | 3 | 224 | 2 | M. Muralidaran | Sri Lanka | v | Australia | Perth | 1995-96 |
| 72 | 7 | 223 | 1 | A.R. Kumble | India | v | Sri Lanka | Colombo (PIS) | 1997-98 |
| 38.4 | 3 | 220 | 7 | Kapil Dev | India | v | Pakistan | Faisalabad | 1982-83 |
| 52 | 7 | 217 | 3 | I.T. Botham | England | v | Pakistan | The Oval | 1987 |
| 69 | 12 | 212 | 5 | P.A. Strang | Zimbabwe | v | Pakistan | Sheikhupura | 1996-97 |
| 71 | 8 | 204 | 6 | I.A.R. Peebles | England | v | Australia | The Oval | 1930 |
| 75 | 16 | 202 | 3 | M.H. Mankad | India | v | West Indies | Bombay | 1948-49 |
| 84 | 19 | 202 | 6 | Haseeb Ahsan | Pakistan | v | India | Madras | 1960-61 |

## OVER 300 RUNS CONCEDED IN A MATCH

| O | M | R | W | | | | | | |
|---|---|---|---|---|---|---|---|---|---|
| 105.2 | 13 | 374 | 9 | O.C. Scott | West Indies | v | England | Kingston | 1929-30 |
| 63 | 3 | 308 | 7 | A.A. Mailey | Australia | v | England | Sydney | 1924-25 |
| 61.3 | 6 | 302 | 10 | A.A. Mailey | Australia | v | England | Adelaide | 1920-21 |

## HAT-TRICKS TO END A TEST

1. Australia v England second Test at Melbourne 1901-02. H. Trumble completed Australia's win by taking a hat-trick in dismissing A.O. Jones, J.R. Gunn and S.F. Barnes. Australia won by 229 runs.

2. South Africa v Australia second Test at Cape Town 1957-58. L.F. Kline completed Australia's win when he did the hat-trick, dismissing E.R.H. Fuller, H.J. Tayfield and N.A.T. Adcock. Australia won by an innings and 141 runs.

   England v Pakistan third Test at Leeds 1971. P. Lever completed England's win by taking three wickets in four balls. He dismissed Wasim Bari, Asif Masood and Pervez Sajjad. England won by 25 runs.

## BOWLING CURIOSITIES

1. J. Briggs (7 for 17 and 8 for 11) for England v South Africa at Cape Town in 1888-89 took all of his wickets unaided, bowling 14 and trapping one lbw.

2. W.W. Armstrong for Australia v England at Nottingham in 1905 bowled off-breaks wide outside leg stump in an attempt to slow the scoring. From 204 consecutive balls, the England batsmen scored from only 25. Of the remaining 179 balls, 19 only were played by the batsmen, the other 160 being allowed to go through to the wicketkeeper.

3. T.J. Matthews (Australia) took a hat-trick in each innings of the match Australia v South Africa at Manchester in 1912, the only instance of this type in all Test cricket history. These six wickets were the only ones taken by Matthews in the match, and constituted over one-third of his Test career 'bag'.

4. W.W. Armstrong (Armstrong) became the first man in Test history to bowl two consecutive overs when he did so against England at Manchester in 1921. England closed its innings on the second day but as the first day had been washed out, it was discovered that Australia was not left with sufficient batting time under the Laws as they then stood. After some confusion, the England innings was resumed and Armstrong, who had bowled the last over before the break, bowled the first one after it.

5. G.O.B. Allen (England) opened the bowling v Australia at Manchester in 1934 with a 13-ball over — three wides and four no-balls.

6. England's score of 7 (dec.) for 469 v South Africa at Durban in 1938-39 did not include a single maiden over (8-ball overs).

7. N.B.F. Mann (South Africa) — making his debut v England at Nottingham in 1947, bowled eight consecutive maiden overs before giving up his first run in Test cricket.

8. A.M. Moir (New Zealand) equalled the record of W.W.Armstrong by sending down two consecutive overs. Moir bowled the last over before tea in the Test v England at Wellington in 1950-51, and then the first over after tea.

9. H.J. Tayfield (South Africa) v New Zealand at Johannesburg in 1953-54 bowled 14 eight-ball overs, 7 of which were maidens, for figures of 6 for 13. There were only nine scoring shots made from 112 balls.

10. H.J. Tayfield (South Africa) v England at Durban 1956-57 bowled 16 consecutive (8-ball) maiden overs — he delivered 137 successive balls all told from which no runs were scored.

11. K.R. Miller (Australia) bowled unchanged before lunch on the first day v England at Melbourne 1954-55 for figures of 9-8-5-3. All five runs scored from Miller came in his fourth over.

12. S. Ramadhin (West Indies) v England at Lord's, 1950 bowled ten consecutive maidens in the first innings and eleven consecutive in the second.

13. In the England v Australia Test at The Oval in 1882, English bowlers E. Peate and R.G. Barlow delivered 14 consecutive maidens in Australia's first innings of 63. Peate's return for the innings was 24 maidens in 38 overs, whilst Barlow's 31 overs included 22 maidens.

14. In the third Test between West Indies and England played at Bridgetown in 1973-74 a total of 79 no-balls were bowled. With 20 runs scored off them the bowlers had given away almost a century.

15. In the six-match Test series between Australia and England played in Australia in 1970-71 not one lbw appeal was upheld against an Australian batsman.

16. L.R. Gibbs (West Indies) v India 1961-62 at Bridgetown. His second innings figures of 53.3 overs 37 maidens 38 runs 8 wickets included 15.3-4-14-6-8 in the final session of the match.

17. In the India v England Test played at Madras in 1963-64 R.G. Nadkarni bowled 21 consecutive maiden overs in the first innings but didn't take a wicket. His first innings figures were 32-27-5-0. In the second he took 2 for 6 off 6 overs (four maidens).

18. H.Verity (England) bowled a Chinaman when he dismissed E.E. Achong (West Indies) in the second Test at Manchester in 1933.

19. Because of an umpiring error, J.T. Sparling, New Zealand, bowled an 11-ball over (excluding no-balls and wides) in England's innings of the 1st Test at Auckland 1962-63.

20. At Lord's 1972, R.A.L. Massie, Australia, returned match figures of 16 for 137. 32.5-7-84-8 and 27.2-9-53-8. At Madras 1987-88, N.D.Hirwani equalled this feat by taking 16 for 136. 18.3-3-61-8 and 15.2-3-75-8. This is the record for any bowler in his first Test. A.E. Trott and A.L. Valentine are the only other bowlers to have taken eight wickets in an innings in their first Test.

## MOST CONSECUTIVE MAIDENS

### 6-ball overs

21 R.G. Nadkarni, India v England, Madras 1963-64. (bowled 131 consecutive balls not scored from.)

15 M.C. Carew, West Indies v England, Port-of-Spain 1967-68. (90 consecutive balls not scored from.)

13 J.H. Wardle, England v South Africa, Nottingham 1955.

11 J.A. Young, England v Australia, Nottingham, 1948.

11 S. Ramadhin, West Indies v England, Lord's 1950.

10 S. Ramadhin, West Indies v England, Lord's 1950.

### 8-ball overs

16 H.J. Tayfield, South Africa v England, Durban 1956-57. (137 consecutive balls not scored from.)

9 H.J. Tayfield, South Africa v Australia, Melbourne 1952-53.

## WIDES

Most by one bowler

9 Kabir Khan Pakistan v South Africa, Johannesburg 1994-95 (also bowled 5 wides in 1st innings!).

8 B.J.T. Bosanquet England v Australia, Leeds 1905.

8 M.B. Owens New Zealand v Sri Lanka, Moratuwa 1992-93.

8 A.D. Mullally England v India, Lord's 1996.

6 M.A. Noble Australia v England, Leeds 1905.

6 J.R. Watkins Australia v Pakistan, Sydney 1972-73.

## WICKETKEEPING CURIOSITIES

In the first-ever Test between England and South Africa played at Port Elizabeth in March 1889 both wicketkeepers were at one stage off the field.

South Africa's W.H. Milton deputised for regular keeper F.W. Smith in the England second innings whilst M.P. Bowden filled in for H.Wood when the England keeper was unavailable.

Ironically deputy Milton was caught behind by deputy Bowden.

In the first Test England v New Zealand at Lord's 1986 four different players shared the wicketkeeping duties for England in the New Zealand first innings. The selected 'keeper, B.N. French was injured whilst batting. C.W.J. Athey kept wickets for the first two overs before handing over the gloves to R.W. Taylor (substitute). After a further 74 overs, R.J. Parks (substitute) took over the gloves until the end of the 140th over of the innings. B.N.French then returned and kept wicket for the remainder of the innings — viz one ball!

## WICKETKEEPERS WHO HAVE OPENED THE BOWLING IN A TEST MATCH

C.L. Walcott (West Indies) opened the bowling in England's second innings at Manchester in 1950 replacing the injured H.H.H.Johnson. R.J. Christiani deputised behind the stumps whilst Walcott bowled four overs without success.

## OLD AND YOUNG PLAYERS APPEARING TOGETHER IN TESTS

This list shows those cricketers who have played in Tests with others who were born after their Test debuts. The dates after the names are the dates of birth. When the players have appeared together more than once, only the first instance is listed.

*D.B.CLOSE (England); Test Debut - 23 Jul 1949*

| | | | | | |
|---|---|---|---|---|---|
| Opponents - | W.W.Daniels | 16 Jan 1956 | v West Indies | Nottingham | 1976 |
| | H.A.Gomes | 13 Jul 1953 | v West Indies | Nottingham | 1976 |
| | C.G.Greenidge | 1 May 1951 | v West Indies | Nottingham | 1976 |

| | | | | | |
|---|---|---|---|---|---|
| | B.D.Julien | 13 Mar 1950 | v West Indies | Nottingham | 1976 |
| | I.V.A.Richards | 7 May 1952 | v West Indies | Nottingham | 1976 |
| | A.M.E.Roberts | 29 Jan 1954 | v West Indies | Nottingham | 1976 |
| | M.A.Holding | 16 Feb 1954 | v West Indies | Lord's | 1976 |
| | C.L.King | 1 Jun 1951 | v West Indies | Manchester | 1976 |

*G.GUNN (England); Test Debut - 13 Dec 1907*

| | | | | | |
|---|---|---|---|---|---|
| Teammate - | W.Voce | 8 Aug 1909 | v West Indies | Bridgetown | 1929-30 |
| Opponents - | G.A.Headley | 30 May 1909 | v West Indies | Bridgetown | 1929-30 |
| | J.E.D.Sealy | 11 Sep 1912 | v West Indies | Bridgetown | 1929-30 |
| | I.Barrow | 6 Jan 1911 | v West Indies | Kingston | 1929-30 |

*J.B.HOBBS (England); Test Debut - 1 Jan 1908*

| | | | | | |
|---|---|---|---|---|---|
| Teammate - | I.A.R.Peebles | 20 Jan 1908 | v Australia | Manchester | 1930 |
| Opponents - | D.G.Bradman | 27 Aug 1908 | v Australia | Brisbane | 1928-29 |
| | A.A.Jackson | 5 Sep 1909 | v Australia | Adelaide | 1928-29 |
| | B.Mitchell | 8 Jan 1909 | v South Africa | The Oval | 1929 |
| | H.G.Owen-Smith | 18 Feb 1909 | v South Africa | The Oval | 1929 |
| | N.A.Quinn | 21 Feb 1908 | v South Africa | The Oval | 1929 |
| | S.J.McCabe | 16 Jul 1910 | v Australia | Nottingham | 1930 |

*W.RHODES (England); Test Debut - 1 Jun 1899*

| | | | | | |
|---|---|---|---|---|---|
| Teammates - | A.P.F.Chapman | 3 Sep 1900 | v Australia | The Oval | 1926 |
| | H.Larwood | 14 Nov 1904 | v Australia | The Oval | 1926 |
| | G.T.S.Stevens | 7 Jan 1901 | v Australia | The Oval | 1926 |
| | L.E.G.Ames | 3 Dec 1905 | v West Indies | Bridgetown | 1929-30 |
| | W.Voce | 8 Aug 1909 | v West Indies | Bridgetown | 1929-30 |
| | L.F.Townsend | 8 Jun 1903 | v West Indies | Georgetown | 1929-30 |
| | R.E.S.Wyatt | 2 May 1901 | v West Indies | Georgetown | 1929-30 |
| Opponents - | W.H.Ponsford | 19 Oct 1900 | v Australia | The Oval | 1926 |
| | L.N.Constantine | 21 Sep 1901 | v West Indies | Bridgetown | 1929-30 |
| | F.I.de Caires | 12 May 1909 | v West Indies | Bridgetown | 1929-30 |
| | G.A.Headley | 30 May 1909 | v West Indies | Bridgetown | 1929-30 |
| | C.A.Roach | 13 Mar 1904 | v West Indies | Bridgetown | 1929-30 |
| | E.L.St Hill | 9 Mar 1904 | v West Indies | Bridgetown | 1929-30 |
| | J.E.D.Sealy | 11 Sep 1912 | v West Indies | Bridgetown | 1929-30 |
| | E.A.C.Hunte | 3 Oct 1905 | v West Indies | Bridgetown | 1929-30 |
| | E.E.Achong | 16 Feb 1904 | v West Indies | Port-of-Spain | 1929-30 |
| | M.G.Grell | 18 Dec 1899 | v West Indies | Port-of-Spain | 1929-30 |
| | C.E.L.Jones | 3 Nov 1902 | v West Indies | Port-of-Spain | 1929-30 |
| | C.V.Wright | 28 Jul 1902 | v West Indies | Georgetown | 1929-30 |
| | I.Barrow | 6 Jan 1911 | v West Indies | Kingston | 1929-30 |
| | O.C.da Costa | 11 Sep 1907 | v West Indies | Kingston | 1929-30 |
| | G.Gladstone | 14 Jan 1901 | v West Indies | Kingston | 1929-30 |
| | C.C.Passailaigue | 7 Aug 1902 | v West Indies | Kingston | 1929-30 |

*F.E.WOOLEY (England); Test Debut - 9 Aug 1909*

| | | | | | |
|---|---|---|---|---|---|
| Teammate - | F.R.Brown | 16 Dec 1910 | v India | Lord's | 1929 |
| Opponents - | L.Amar Singh | 4 Dec 1910 | v India | Lord's | 1929 |
| | M.Jahangir Khan | 1 Feb 1910 | v India | Lord's | 1929 |
| | Lall Singh | 16 Dec 1909 | v India | Lord's | 1929 |
| | Mohammad Nissar | 1 Aug 1910 | v India | Lord's | 1929 |
| | P.E.Palia | 5 Sep 1910 | v India | Lord's | 1929 |
| | S.J.McCabe | 16 Jul 1910 | v Australia | Nottingham | 1930 |
| | J.L.Kerr | 28 Dec 1910 | v New Zealand | Lord's | 1931 |
| | W.A.Brown | 31 Jul 1912 | v Australia | The Oval | 1934 |

*S.E.GREGORY (Australia); Test Debut - 21 Jul 1890*

| | | | | | |
|---|---|---|---|---|---|
| Opponent - | J.W.Hearne | 11 Feb 1891 | v England | Sydney | 1911-12 |

*G.A.HEADLEY (West Indies); Test Debut - 11 Jan 1930*

| | | | | | |
|---|---|---|---|---|---|
| Teammate - | A.L.Valentine | 29 Apr 1930 | v England | Kingston | 1953-54 |
| Opponents - | A.E.Moss | 14 Nov 1930 | v England | Kingston | 1953-54 |
| | J.B.Statham | 17 Jun 1930 | v England | Kingston | 1953-54 |
| | F.R.Trueman | 6 Feb 1931 | v England | Kingston | 1953-54 |

*R.J.HADLEE (New Zealand); Test Debut - 2 Feb 1973*

| | | | | | |
|---|---|---|---|---|---|
| Opponent - | S.R.Tendulkar | 24 Apr 1973 | v India | Christchurch | 1989-90 |

*N.B.AMARNATH (India); Test Debut - 15 Dec 1933*

| | | | | | |
|---|---|---|---|---|---|
| Opponent - | Hanif Mohammad | 21 Dec 1934 | v Pakistan | Delhi | 1952-53 |

*S.VENKATARAGHAVAN (India); Test Debut - 27 Feb 1965*

| | | | | | |
|---|---|---|---|---|---|
| Teammate - | L.Shivaramakrishnan | 31 Dec 1965 | v West Indies | St John's | 1982-83 |

*IMRAN KHAN (Pakistan); Test Debut - 3 Jun 1971*

| | | | | | |
|---|---|---|---|---|---|
| Teammate - | Aaqib Javed | 5 Aug 1972 | v New Zealand | Wellington | 1988-89 |
| Opponent - | S.R.Tendulkar | 24 Apr 1973 | v India | Karachi | 1989-90 |

*MAJID KHAN (Pakistan); Test Debut - 24 Oct 1964*

| | | | | | |
|---|---|---|---|---|---|
| Opponent - | Maninder Signh | 13 Jun 1965 | v India | Lahore | 1982-83 |

*MUSHTAQ MOHAMMAD (Pakistan); Test Debut - 26 Mar 1959*

| | | | | | |
|---|---|---|---|---|---|
| Opponent - | B.P.Bracewell | 14 Sep1959 | v New Zealand | Christchurch | 1978-79 |

*A.J.TRAICOS (South Africa/Zimbabwe); Test Debut - 5 Feb 1970*

| | | | | | |
|---|---|---|---|---|---|
| Teammates - | A.DR.Campbell | 23 Sep 1972 | v India | Harare | 1992-93 |
| | G.W.Flower | 20 Dec 1970 | v India | Harare | 1992-93 |
| Opponents - | A.R.Kumble | 17 Oct 1970 | v India | Harare | 1992-93 |
| | S.R.Tendulkar | 24 Apr 1973 | v India | Harare | 1992-93 |
| | M.J.Haslam | 26 Sep 1972 | v New Zealand | Bulawayo | 1992-93 |
| | A.C.Parore | 23 Jan 1971 | v New Zealand | Bulawayo | 1992-93 |
| | D.J.Nash | 20 Nov 1971 | v New Zealand | Harare | 1992-93 |
| | V.G.Kambli | 18 Jan 1972 | v India | Delhi | 1992-93 |

## MOST STUMPINGS IN A SERIES

| | | | | | | |
|---|---|---|---|---|---|---|
| 9 | P.W. Sherwell | South Africa | v | Australia | in Australia | 1910-11 |

## MOST STUMPINGS IN A MATCH

| | | | | | | |
|---|---|---|---|---|---|---|
| 6 | K.S. More | India | v | West Indies | Chennai[1] | 1987-88 |

## MOST STUMPINGS IN AN INNINGS

| | | | | | | |
|---|---|---|---|---|---|---|
| 5 | K.S. More | India | v | West Indies | Chennai[1] | 1987-88 |

## MOST BYES CONCEDED IN AN INNINGS

| | | | | | | |
|---|---|---|---|---|---|---|
| 37 | F.E. Woolley | England | v | Australia | The Oval | 1934 |

(At the age of 47, standing-in for the injured L.E.G.Ames).

| | | | | | | |
|---|---|---|---|---|---|---|
| 33 | J.T. Murray | England | v | India | Mumbai[2] | 1961-62 |
| 33 | J.M. Parks | England | v | West Indies | Kingston | 1967-68 |

## MOST SUBSTITUTE CATCHES BY ONE FIELDER IN A MATCH

### Four

| | | | | | |
|---|---|---|---|---|---|
| Gursharan Singh | India | v | West Indies | Ahmedabad | 1983-84 |

### Three

| | | | | | |
|---|---|---|---|---|---|
| H. Strudwick | England | v | Australia | Melbourne | 1903-04 |
| J.E.D. Sealy | West Indies | v | England | Port-of-Spain | 1929-30 |
| W.V. Rodriguez | West Indies | v | India | Port-of-Spain | 1961-62 |
| Yajurvindra Singh | India | v | West Indies | Chennai[1] | 1978-79 |
| Haroon Rashid | Pakistan | v | England | Leeds | 1982 |
| M.J. Greatbatch | New Zealand | v | England | Christchurch | 1987-88 |
| W.V. Raman | India | v | England | Chennai[1] | 1992-93 |

## SOME OF CRICKET'S DOUBLE INTERNATIONALS

E = England  A = Australia
SA = South Africa  NZ = New Zealand
W = Wales  WI = West Indies
Sc = Scotland  An = Antigua

| | Cricket | Rugby | Soccer |
|---|---|---|---|
| A.N. Hornby | E | E | - |
| S.M.J. Woods | A/E | E | - |
| G. McGregor | E | Sc | - |
| A. E. Stoddart | E | E | - |
| C.B. Fry | E | - | E |
| (Missed at rugby due to injury) | | | |
| F. Mitchell | E/SA | E | - |
| L.B. Fishlock | E | - | E |
| J.H. Sinclair | SA | SA/E | E |
| R.O. Schwarz | SA | E | - |
| L.H. Gay | E | - | E |
| R.H. Spooner | E | E | - |
| R.E. Foster | E | - | E |
| (Only man to captain England at cricket and soccer) | | | |
| A. Ducat | E | - | E |
| H.T.W. Hardinge | E | - | E |
| J.W.H. Makepeace | E | - | E |
| K.W. Hough | NZ | - | NZ/A |
| A.E. Knight | E | - | E |
| M.J. Turnbull | E | W | - |
| (Also played hockey for Wales) | | | |
| J. Arnold | E | - | E |
| W. Gunn | E | - | E |
| G.C. White | SA | - | SA |
| J. Sharp | E | - | E |
| R.S. Grant | WI | - | E |
| J.M.M. Commaille | SA | - | SA |
| M.K. Elgie | SA | Sc | - |
| S. O'Linn | SA | - | SA |
| C.A. Smith | E | - | E |
| Hon. A. Lyttelton | E | - | E |
| G.F. Vernon | E | E | - |
| H.G. Owen-Smith | SA | E | - |
| D.C.S. Compton | E | - | E |
| J.H. Anderson | SA | SA | - |
| G.R. Dickinson | NZ | NZ | - |
| M.P. Donnelly | NZ | E | - |
| T.A. Harris | SA | SA | - |
| R.M.H. Hands | SA | E | - |
| P.S. Twentyman-Jones | SA | SA | - |
| W. Watson | E | - | E |
| W.H. Milton | SA | E | - |
| C.A. Milton | E | - | E |
| O.E. Nothling | A | A | - |
| M.L. Page | NZ | NZ | - |
| A.W. Powell | SA | SA | - |
| A.R. Richards | SA | SA | - |
| M.J.K. Smith | E | E | - |
| E.W.T. Tindill* | NZ | NZ | - |
| C.B. van Ryneveld | SA | E | - |
| F.C.M. Alexander | WI | - | E |
| (Amateur International) | | | |
| I.V.A. Richards | WI | - | An |
| R.B. Richardson | WI | - | An |

* also a Test umpire and international rugby referee

## TEST CRICKETERS WHO WON F.A. CUP WINNERS' MEDALS

E.G. Wynyard — with Old Carthusians 1880-81
J. Sharp — with Everton 1905-06
J.W.H. Makepeace — with Everton 1905-06
A. Ducat — with Aston Villa 1919-20
D.C.S. Compton — with Arsenal 1949-50

Other Test cricketers who were well-known soccer players in England include:
I.T. Botham (Scunthorpe United)
D.B. Close (Leeds United, Bradford City, Arsenal)
J.G. Dewes (Middlesborough, Plymouth Argyle, Walsall)
S. O'Linn (Charlton Athletic)
C.J. Poole (Gillingham, Mansfield Town)
D.R. Smith (Bristol City, Millwall)
F. Sugg (Sheffield Wednesday, Derby County, Burnley)
K. Taylor (Huddersfield Town, Bradford City, Plymouth Argyle)
F.J. Titmus (Watford)
A.J. Watkins (Plymouth Argyle, Cardiff City)
E.G. Wynyard (Old Carthusians)
D.L. Bairstow (Bradford City)
R.W.V. Robins (Nottingham Forest)
M. Sherwin (Notts County)
M.J. Stewart (Charlton Athletic)
L.E.G. Ames (Clapton Orient, Gillingham)
J.C. Balderstone (Huddersfield Town, Carlisle United, Doncaster Rovers)
H.E. Dollery (Reading)
W.J. Edrich (Tottenham Hotspurs)
J.A. Flavell (Walsall)
W. Gunn (Notts County)
W.R. Hammond (Bristol Rovers)
J. Hardstaff sr (Nottingham Forest)
E.H. Hendren (Manchester City, Brentford)
H. Howell (Wolverhampton Wanderers, Accrington Stanley)
W.W. Keeton (Sunderland, Nottingham Forest)
J.W. Sharpe (Notts County)
A. Sidebottom (Manchester United, Huddersfield Town, Halifax)
W. Storer (Derby County)
A. Waddington (Halifax Town)
F.J. Barratt (Aston Villa, Sheffield Wednesday)

## TEST CRICKETERS WHO PLAYED OTHER SPORTS AT INTERNATIONAL LEVEL

B.C. Booth (Australia — Hockey
(1956 Olympics)
V.Y. Richardson (Australia) — Baseball
B. Dooland (Australia) — Baseball
C.B. Fry (England) — Athletics
(Fry held the world Long-jump record for 21 years)
D.C. Cleverley (New Zealand) — Boxing
J.W.H.T. Douglas (England) — Boxing
(Douglaswon the gold medal in the middleweight boxing in the 1908 London Olympics and also represented England in amateur soccer)
R.C. Grant (West Indies) — Boxing
M.L.C. Foster (West Indies) — Table tennis
(Jamacian champion)
E.M. Grace (England) — Triple jump
(world record 1866)
W.G. Grace (England) — Athletics
(was the national champion of 400 yard hurdles)
P.A. Horne (New Zealand) — Badminton
(Commonwealth Games)
E.L. Dalton (South Africa) — Golf
(South African Amateur Golf Champion 1950)
Farooq Hamid (Pakistan) — Athletics
(Olympics level)
P.W. Sherwell (South Africa) — Tennis
(national champion in 1904)
C. Ramaswami (India) — Tennis
(Davis Cup 1922)
G. Miller (England) played table tennis for Derbyshire.
A.D.G. Matthews (England) — Table tennis
(for Wales)
K. Thomson (New Zealand) — Hockey
E.G. McLeod (New Zealand) — Hockey
Nawab of Pataudi sr (India) — Hockey
M.J. Gopalan (India) — Hockey
W.R. Endean (South Africa) — Hockey
J.N. Rhodes (South Africa) — Hockey
D.L. Houghton (Zimbabwe) — Hockey
T.J. Laughlin (Australia) — Hockey

## 'GREATEST EVER' TEAMS

For this edition of *Test Cricket Lists* I decided to pick each country's best ever line-up instead of the Alphaetical Teams that have appeared in previous editions.

I have no doubt that these teams will provoke animated discussion wherever the great game is played.

The teams have been selected to play against the best opposition under all conditions.

**AUSTRALIA**: Miller was the pivotal player in this selection. Acknowledged as the leading all-rounder he has been picked to bat at six so that a second spinner could be selected. With Miller batting at number six Morris was squeezed out of the line-up. A considerable amount of agonising took place before Tallon was named as wicketkeeper.

**ENGLAND**: Not too many options with this team. The famous opening pair were retained with Hutton named at three. A third pace bowler was preferred to a second spinner, although Laker came close to selection as did Knott and Trueman.

**SOUTH AFRICA**: This team just about picked itself. Donald is one of the few current players to be picked in any team and his selection completes an extremely potent pace-bowling battery.

**WEST INDIES**: With so many magnificent players this was the most difficult team to select. It is the one team where I selected batsmen on their ability and record rather than on their normal position in the batting order. Then there was the fast-bowling talent!

**NEW ZEALAND**: A highly competitive team from limited resources.

**INDIA**: Rich in talent in the batting and spin-bowling departments but lacking in fast bowling. Two outstanding all-rounders, Mankad and Umrigar, give the side bowling depth while Prasanna and Gupte were unlucky to miss selection.

**PAKISTAN**: Another powerful team with attractive stroke-playing batsmen and an outstanding attack.

**SRI LANKA**: The gloves have been given to Tillakaratne so that an extra bowler could be picked. D.S. de Silva and Muralidaran provide the attack with excellent variety.

**ZIMBABWE**: The newest Test-playing nation does not have a lot of depth but does have a highly competitive outfit.

## THE TEAMS

**AUSTRALIA**
1. W.H. Ponsford
2. V.T. Trumper
3. D.G. Bradman (c)
4. S.J. McCabe
5. R.N. Harvey
6. K.R. Miller
7. R.R. Lindwall
8. D. Tallon (wk)
9. S.K. Warne
10. D.K. Lillee
11. W.J. O'Reilly

**ENGLAND**
1. J.B. Hobbs
2. H. Sutcliffe
3. L. Hutton
4. W.G. Grace (c)
5. W.R. Hammond
6. I.T. Botham
7. W. Rhodes
8. T.G. Evans (wk)
9. H. Larwood
10. A.V. Bedser
11. S.F. Barnes

**SOUTH AFRICA**
1. B.A. Richards
2. B. Mitchell
3. A.D. Nourse (c)
4. R.G. Pollock
5. E.J. Barlow
6. J.H.B. Waite (wk)
7. M.J. Procter
8. P.M. Pollock
9. H.J. Tayfield
10. A.A. Donald
11. N.A.T. Adcock

**WEST INDIES**
1. F.M.M. Worrell (c)
2. R.B. Kanhai
3. G.A. Headley
4. E.D. Weekes
5. I.V.A. Richards
6. G.S. Sobers
7. C.L. Walcott (wk)
8. M.A. Holding
9. W.W. Hall
10. J. Garner
11. L.R. Gibbs

**NEW ZEALAND**
1. G.M. Turner
2. C.S. Dempster
3. B. Sutcliffe
4. M.P. Donnelly
5. M.D. Crowe
6. J.R. Reid (c)
7. B.R. Taylor
8. R.J. Hadlee
9. I.D.S. Smith (wk)
10. J.G. Bracewell
11. J. Cowie

**PAKISTAN**
1. Hanif Mohammad (c)
2. Majid Khan
3. Zaheer Abbas
4. Javed Miandad
5. Mushtaq Mohammad
6. Asif Iqbal
7. Imran Khan
8. Wasim Akram
9. Wasim Bari (wk)
10. Abdul Qadir
11. Fazal Mahmood

**ZIMBABWE**
1. G.W. Flower
2. K.J. Arnott
3. M.W. Goodwin
4. D.L. Houghton (c)
5. A. Flower (wk)
6. A.D.R. Campbell
7. G.J. Whittall
8. P.A. Strang
9. H.H. Streak
10. D.H. Brain
11. B.C. Strang

**INDIA**
1. S.M. Gavaskar (c)
2. V.M. Merchant
3. V.S. Hazare
4. S.R. Tendulkar
5. M. Azharuddin
6. M.H. Mankad
7. P.R. Umrigar
8. Kapil Dev
9. S.M.H. Kirmani (wk)
10. B.S. Bedi
11. B.S. Chandrasekhar

**SRI LANKA**
1. S.T. Jayasuriya
2. R.L. Dias
3. A.P. Gurusinha
4. P.A. de Silva
5. A. Ranatunga (c)
6. H.P. Tillakaratne (wk)
7. J.R. Ratnayeke
8. D.S. de Silva
9. R.J. Ratnayake
10. W.P.J.U.C. Vaas
11. M. Muralidaran

## PART 3

# TEST MATCH RESULTS & RECORDS

## Summary of Tests

### SUMMARY OF ALL TEST MATCHES 1876-77 TO 1998

| | | | won by | | | | | | | | | | |
|---|---|---|---|---|---|---|---|---|---|---|---|---|---|
| | Opponent | Tests | A | E | SA | WI | NZ | I | P | SL | Z | Tied | Draw |
| Australia | v England | 291 | 114 | 92 | - | - | - | - | - | - | - | - | 85 |
| | v South Africa | 65 | 34 | - | 14 | - | - | - | - | - | - | - | 17 |
| | v West Indies | 86 | 35 | - | - | 29 | - | - | - | - | - | 1 | 21 |
| | v New Zealand | 35 | 15 | - | - | - | 7 | - | - | - | - | - | 13 |
| | v India | 54 | 25 | - | - | - | - | 11 | - | - | - | 1 | 17 |
| | v Pakistan | 40 | 14 | - | - | - | - | - | 11 | - | - | - | 15 |
| | v Sri Lanka | 10 | 7 | - | - | - | - | - | - | 0 | - | - | 3 |
| | v Zimbabwe | 0 | - | - | - | - | - | - | - | - | - | - | 0 |
| England | v South Africa | 115 | - | 49 | 21 | - | - | - | - | - | - | - | 45 |
| | v West Indies | 121 | - | 27 | - | 51 | - | - | - | - | - | - | 42 |
| | v New Zealand | 78 | - | 36 | - | - | 4 | - | - | - | - | - | 38 |
| | v India | 84 | - | 32 | - | - | - | 14 | - | - | - | - | 38 |
| | v Pakistan | 55 | - | 14 | - | - | - | - | 9 | - | - | - | 32 |
| | v Sri Lanka | 5 | - | 3 | - | - | - | - | - | 1 | - | - | 1 |
| | v Zimbabwe | 2 | - | 0 | - | - | - | - | - | - | 0 | - | 2 |
| South Africa | v New Zealand | 21 | - | - | 12 | - | 3 | - | - | - | - | - | 6 |
| | v West Indies | 1 | - | - | 0 | 1 | - | - | - | - | - | - | 0 |
| | v India | 10 | - | - | 4 | - | - | 2 | - | - | - | - | 4 |
| | v Sri Lanka | 5 | - | - | 3 | - | - | - | - | 0 | - | - | 2 |
| | v Pakistan | 7 | - | - | 3 | - | - | - | 1 | - | - | - | 3 |
| | v Zimbabwe | 1 | - | - | 1 | - | - | - | - | - | 0 | - | 0 |
| West Indies | v New Zealand | 28 | - | - | - | 10 | 4 | - | - | - | - | - | 14 |
| | v India | 70 | - | - | - | 28 | - | 7 | - | - | - | - | 35 |
| | v Pakistan | 34 | - | - | - | 12 | - | - | 10 | - | - | - | 12 |
| | v Sri Lanka | 3 | - | - | - | 1 | - | - | - | 0 | - | - | 2 |
| | v Zimbabwe | 0 | - | - | - | - | - | - | - | - | - | - | 0 |
| New Zealand | v India | 35 | - | - | - | - | 6 | 13 | - | - | - | - | 16 |
| | v Pakistan | 39 | - | - | - | - | 5 | - | 18 | - | - | - | 16 |
| | v Sri Lanka | 18 | - | - | - | - | 7 | - | - | 4 | - | - | 7 |
| | v Zimbabwe | 8 | - | - | - | - | 3 | - | - | - | 0 | - | 5 |
| India | v Pakistan | 44 | - | - | - | - | - | 4 | 7 | - | - | - | 33 |
| | v Sri Lanka | 19 | - | - | - | - | - | 7 | - | 1 | - | - | 11 |
| | v Zimbabwe | 2 | - | - | - | - | - | 1 | - | - | 0 | - | 1 |
| Pakistan | v Sri Lanka | 19 | - | - | - | - | - | - | 9 | 3 | - | - | 7 |
| | v Zimbabwe | 10 | - | - | - | - | - | - | 6 | - | 1 | - | 3 |
| Sri Lanka | v Zimbabwe | 7 | - | - | - | - | - | - | - | 4 | 0 | - | 3 |
| | | 1422 | 244 | 254 | 55 | 132 | 39 | 59 | 71 | 13 | 1 | 2 | 549 |

| | Tests | Won | Lost | Drawn | Tied | Toss Won |
|---|---|---|---|---|---|---|
| Australia | 581 | 244 | 164 | 171 | 2 | 290 |
| England | 751 | 254 | 214 | 283 | - | 367 |
| South Africa | 225 | 58 | 90 | 77 | - | 108 |
| West Indies | 343 | 132 | 84 | 126 | 1 | 179 |
| New Zealand | 262 | 39 | 108 | 115 | - | 133 |
| India | 318 | 59 | 103 | 155 | 1 | 163 |
| Pakistan | 248 | 71 | 56 | 121 | - | 120 |
| Sri Lanka | 86 | 13 | 37 | 36 | - | 42 |
| Zimbabwe | 30 | 1 | 15 | 14 | - | 19 |
| | 1422 | 871 | 871 | 1098 | 4 | 1422 |

## The Grounds

### TEST MATCH GROUNDS

The Test played at Galle has lifted the number of Test match grounds to 79. Colombo has now used four grounds, Johannesburg and Mumbai three apiece, whilst Brisbane, Bulawayo, Chennai, Durban, Karachi, Lahore, Lucknow, Peshawar and Rawalpindi have each played Test matches on two different grounds. For these eleven cities the exact ground is denoted by a superscript numeral (e.g. Brisbane[1]) except for Colombo, where the ground is shown in brackets. This key to this numeral is given in the tables below. The tables show the full title, date of the first day's play and number of Tests staged for each ground.

*Note: Where the name of a centre has been changed — Madras to Chennai and Bombay to Mumbai — the name in use at the time, has been listed.*

| Test Match Centres | Grounds | First Test Match Day | No.of Tests |
|---|---|---|---|
| **AUSTRALIA** | | | (301) |
| Adelaide | Adelaide Oval | 12 Dec 1884 | 56 |
| Brisbane | [1]Exhibition Ground (1928-29 to 1930-31) | 30 Nov 1928 | 2 |
| | [2]Woolloongabba | 27 Nov 1931 | 40 |
| Hobart | Bellerive Oval | 16 Dec 1989 | 4 |
| Melbourne | Melbourne Cricket Ground | 15 Mar 1877 | 90 |
| Perth | Western Australia Cricket Association (W.A.C.A.) Ground | 11 Dec 1970 | 25 |
| Sydney | Sydney Cricket Ground (No.1) | 17 Feb 1882 | 84 |
| **ENGLAND** | | | (382) |
| Birmingham | Edgbaston | 29 May 1902 | 34 |
| Leeds | Headingley | 29 Jun 1899 | 60 |
| Lord's, London | Lord's Cricket Ground | 21 Jul 1884 | 97 |
| Manchester | Old Trafford | †10 Jul 1884 | 64 |
| Nottingham | Trent Bridge | 1 Jun 1899 | 46 |
| The Oval, London | Kennington Oval | 6 Sep 1880 | 80 |
| Sheffield | Bramall Lane | 3 Jul 1902 | 1 |
| **SOUTH AFRICA** | | | (125) |
| Cape Town | Newlands | 25 Mar 1889 | 30 |
| Durban | [1]Lord's (1909-10 to 1921-22) | 21 Jan 1910 | 4 |
| | [2]Kingsmead | 18 Jan 1923 | 25 |
| Johannesburg | [1]Old Wanderers (1895-96 to 1938-39) | 2 Mar 1896 | 22 |
| | [2]Ellis Park (1948-49 to 1953-54) | 27 Dec 1948 | 6 |
| | [3]Wanderers Stadium | 24 Dec 1956 | 19 |
| Port Elizabeth | St George's Park | 12 Mar 1889 | 16 |
| Centurion (formerly Verwoerdburg) | Centurion Park | 16 Nov 1995 | 3 |
| **WEST INDIES** | | | (153) |
| Bridgetown, Barbados | Kensington Oval | 11 Jan 1930 | 34 |
| Georgetown, Guyana | Bourda | 21 Feb 1930 | 25 |
| Kingston, Jamaica | Sabina Park | 3 Apr 1930 | 33 |
| Kingstown, St Vincent | Arnos Vale | 20 Jun 1997 | 1 |
| Port-of-Spain, Trinidad | Queen's Park Oval | 1 Feb 1930 | 47 |
| St John's, Antigua | Recreation Ground | 27 Mar 1981 | 13 |
| **NEW ZEALAND** | | | (125) |
| Auckland | Eden Park | #14 Feb 1930 | 40 |
| Christchurch | Lancaster Park | 10 Jan 1930 | 35 |
| Dunedin | Carisbrook | 11 Mar 1955 | 10 |
| Hamilton | Trust Bank Park | 22 Feb 1991 | 5 |
| Napier | McLean Park | 16 Feb 1979 | 3 |
| Wellington | Basin Reserve | 24 Jan 1930 | 32 |

| | | | |
|---|---|---|---|
| **INDIA** | | | (169) |
| Ahmedabad | Gujarat Stadium, Motera | 12 Nov 1983 | 4 |
| Bangalore | M.Chinnaswamy Stadium (Karnataka State Cricket Association Stadium) | 22 Nov 1974 | 12 |
| Calcutta | Eden Gardens | 5 Jan 1934 | 29 |
| Chandigarh | Sector 16 Stadium | 23 Nov 1990 | 1 |
| Chennai | [1]M.A.Chidambaram Stadium (Chepauk) | 10 Feb 1934 | 23 |
| (formerly Madras) | [2]Nehru (Corporation) Stadium (1955-56 to 1964-65) | 6 Jan 1956 | 9 |
| Cuttack | Barabati Stadium | 4 Jan 1987 | 2 |
| Delhi | Feroz Shah Kotla (Willingdon Pavillion) | 10 Nov 1948 | 24 |
| Hyderabad (Deccan) | Lal Bahadur Shastri Stadium (Fateh Maidan) | 19 Nov 1955 | 3 |
| Jaipur | Sawai Mansingh Stadium (Chogan Stadium) | 21 Feb 1987 | 1 |
| Jullundur | Burlton Park (B.S.Bedi Stadium) | 24 Sep 1983 | 1 |
| Kanpur | Green Park (Modi Stadium) | 12 Jan 1952 | 17 |
| Lucknow | [1]University Ground (1952-53 only) | 23 Oct 1952 | 1 |
| | [2]K.D.Singh Babu Stadium (Central Sports Stadium) | 19 Jan 1994 | 1 |
| Mohali | Punjab Cricket Association Stadium | 10 Dec 1994 | 2 |
| Mumbai | [1]Gymkhana (1933-34 Only) | 15 Dec 1933 | 1 |
| (formerly | [2]Brabourne Stadium (1948-49 to 1972-73) | 9 Dec 1948 | 17 |
| Bombay) | [3]Wankhede Stadium | 23 Jan 1975 | 16 |
| Nagpur | Vidarbha Cricket Association Ground | 3 Oct 1969 | 5 |
| **PAKISTAN** | | | (113) |
| Bahawalpur | Bahawal Stadium (Dring Stadium) | 15 Jan 1955 | 1 |
| Dacca | Dacca Stadium | 1 Jan 1955 | 7 |
| Faisalabad | Iqbal Stadium (Lyallpur Stadium) | 16 Oct 1978 | 19 |
| Gujranwala | Municipal Stadium | 20 Dec 1991 | 1 |
| Hyderabad (Sind) | Niaz Stadium | 16 Mar 1973 | 5 |
| Karachi | [1]National Stadium | 26 Feb 1955 | 32 |
| | [2]Defence Stadium | 1 Dec 1993 | 1 |
| Lahore | [1]Bagh-e-Jinnah (Lawrence Gardens) (1954-55 to 1958-59) | 29 Jan 1955 | 3 |
| | [2]Gaddafi Stadium (Lahore Stadium) | 21 Nov 1959 | 28 |
| Multan | Ibn-e-Qasim Bagh Stadium (Old Fort) | 30 Dec 1980 | 1 |
| Peshawar | [1]Services Club Ground (Peshawar Club Ground)(1954-55 only) | 13 Feb 1955 | 1 |
| | [2]Arbab Niaz Stadium | 8 Sep 1995 | 2 |
| Rawalpindi | [1]Army Sports Stadium (Pindi Club Ground) (1964-65 only) | 27 Mar 1965 | 1 |
| | [2]Pindi Cricket Stadium | 9 Dec 1993 | 5 |
| Sheikhupura | Sheikhupura Cricket Stadium | 17 Oct 1996 | 2 |
| Sialkot | Jinnah (Park) Stadium | 27 Oct 1985 | 4 |
| **SRI LANKA** | | | (38) |
| Colombo | P.Saravanamuttu Stadium (PSS) | 17 Feb 1982 | 6 |
| | Sinhalese Sports Club Ground (SSC) | 16 Mar 1984 | 12 |
| | Colombo Cricket Club Ground (CCC) | 24 Mar 1984 | 3 |
| | Premadasa (Khettamara)International Stadium (PIS) | 28 Aug 1992 | 5 |
| Galle | Galle International Stadium, The Esplanade | 3 Jun 98 | 1 |
| Kandy | Asgiriya Stadium | 22 Apr 1983 | 7 |
| Moratuwa | Tyrone Fernando Stadium | 8 Sep 1992 | 4 |
| **ZIMBABWE** | | | (16) |
| Bulawayo | [1]Bulawayo Athletic Club Ground (1992-93 only) | 1 Nov 1992 | 1 |
| | [2]Queens Sports Oval | § 18 Oct 1994 | 5 |
| Harare | Harare (Salisbury) Sports Club Ground | 18 Oct 1992 | 10 |

*† Rain prevented play until 11 Jul 1884. # Rain prevented play until 17 Feb 1930. § Rain prevented play until 20 Oct 1994.*

*The 1890 and 1938 Tests at Manchester, the 1970-71 Third Test at Melbourne, the 1988-89 Test at Dunedin and the 1989-90 Test at Georgetown, all abandoned without a ball being bowled, plus the cancelled 1980-81 second Test at Georgetown and 1994-95 Second Test at Kandy are excluded from these figures.*

# RECORD TOTALS FOR EACH TEST MATCH GROUND

## AUSTRALIA

| Centre | | Highest Total | | | Lowest Total | |
|---|---|---|---|---|---|---|
| Adelaide | 674 | Australia v India | 1947-48 | 82 | Australia v West Indies | 1951-52 |
| Brisbane[1] | 558 | Australia v West Indies | 1930-31 | 66 | Australia v England | 1928-29 |
| Brisbane[2] | 645 | Australia v England | 1946-47 | 58 | Australia v England | 1936-37 |
| | | | | 58 | India v Australia | 1947-48 |
| Hobart | 544-6d | Australia v New Zealand | 1993-94 | 161 | New Zealand v Australia | 1993-94 |
| Melbourne | 604 | Australia v England | 1936-37 | 36 | South Africa v Australia | 1931-32 |
| Perth | 617-5d | Australia v Sri Lanka | 1995-96 | 62 | Pakistan v Australia | 1981-82 |
| Sydney | 659-8d | Australia v England | 1946-47 | 42 | Australia v England | 1887-88 |

## ENGLAND

| Centre | | Highest Total | | | Lowest Total | |
|---|---|---|---|---|---|---|
| Birmingham | 633-5d | England v India | 1979 | 30 | South Africa v England | 1924 |
| Leeds | 653-4d | Australia v England | 1993 | 67 | New Zealand v England | 1958 |
| Lord's | 729-6d | Australia v England | 1930 | 42 | India v England | 1974 |
| Manchester | 656-8d | Australia v England | 1964 | 58 | India v England | 1952 |
| Nottingham | 658-8d | England v Australia | 1938 | 88 | South Africa v England | 1960 |
| The Oval | 903-7d | England v Australia | 1938 | 44 | Australia v England | 1896 |
| Sheffield | 289 | Australia v England | 1902 | 145 | England v Australia | 1902 |

## SOUTH AFRICA

| Centre | | Highest Total | | | Lowest Total | |
|---|---|---|---|---|---|---|
| Cape Town | 559-9d | England v South Africa | 1938-39 | 35 | South Africa v England | 1898-99 |
| Centurion | 384 | South Africa v Australia | 1996-97 | 122 | Sri Lanka v South Africa | 1997-98 |
| Durban[1] | 450 | England v South Africa | 1913-14 | 111 | South Africa v England | 1913-14 |
| Durban[2] | 654-5 | England v South Africa | 1938-39 | 66 | India v South Africa | 1996-97 |
| Johannesburg[1] | 491 | England v South Africa | 1193-36 | 85 | South Africa v Australia | 1902-03 |
| Johannesburg[2] | 608 | England v South Africa | 1948-49 | 79 | New Zealand v South Africa | 1953-54 |
| Johannesburg[3] | 628-8d | Australia v South Africa | 1996-97 | 72 | South Africa v England | 1956-57 |
| Port Elizabeth | 549-7d | Australia v South Africa | 1949-50 | 30 | South Africa v England | 1895-96 |

## WEST INDIES

| Centre | | Highest Total | | | Lowest Total | |
|---|---|---|---|---|---|---|
| Bridgetown | 668 | Australia v West Indies | 1954-55 | 81 | India v West Indies | 1996-97 |
| Georgetown | 569 | West Indies v Australia | 1990-91 | 109 | West Indies v Australia | 1972-73 |
| Kingston | 849 | England v West Indies | 1929-30 | 97† | India v West Indies | 1975-76 |
| Kingstown | 343 | West Indies v Sri Lanka | 1996-97 | 147 | West Indies v Sri Lanka | 1996-97 |
| Port-of-Spain | 681-8d | West Indies v England | 1953-54 | 46 | England v West Indies | 1993-94 |
| St John's | 593-5d | West Indies v England | 1993-94 | 127 | England v West Indies | 1997-98 |
| | 593 | England v West Indies | 1993-94 | | | |

## NEW ZEALAND

| Centre | | Highest Total | | | Lowest Total | |
|---|---|---|---|---|---|---|
| Auckland | 616-5d | Pakistan v New Zealand | 1988-89 | 26 | New Zealand v England | 1954-55 |
| Christchurch | 560-8d | England v New Zealand | 1932-33 | 65 | New Zealand v England | 1970-71 |
| Dunedin | 586-7d | New Zealand v Sri Lanka | 1996-97 | 74 | New Zealand v West Indies | 1955-56 |
| Hamilton | 374-6d | New Zealand v Sri Lanka | 1990-91 | 93 | New Zealand v Pakistan | 1992-93 |
| Napier | 402 | New Zealand v Pakistan | 1978-79 | 129 | New Zealand v Sri Lanka | 1994-95 |
| Wellington | 671-4 | New Zealand v Sri Lanka | 1990-91 | 42 | New Zealand v Australia | 1945-46 |

## INDIA

| Centre | | Highest Total | | | Lowest Total | |
|---|---|---|---|---|---|---|
| Ahmedabad | 395 | Pakistan v India | 1986-87 | 103 | India v West Indies | 1983-84 |
| Bangalore | 541-6d | India v Sri Lanka | 1993-94 | 116 | Pakistan v India | 1986-87 |
| Calcutta | 633-5d | India v Australia | 1958-59 | 90 | India v West Indies | 1997-98 |
| Chandigarh | 288 | India v Sri Lanka | 1990-91 | 82 | Sri Lanka v India | 1990-91 |
| Chennai[1] | 652-7d | England v India | 1984-85 | 83 | India v England | 1976-77 |

| | | | | | | |
|---|---|---|---|---|---|---|
| Madras[2] | 539-9d | India v Pakistan | 1960-61 | 138 | India v Australia | 1959-60 |
| Cuttack | 400 | India v Sri Lanka | 1986-87 | 142 | Sri Lanka v India | 1986-87 |
| Delhi | 644-8d | West Indies v India | 1958-59 | 75 | India v West Indies | 1987-88 |
| Hyderabad | 498-4d | India v New Zealand | 1955-56 | 89 | India v New Zealand | 1969-70 |
| Jaipur | 465-8d | India v Pakistan | 1986-87 | 341 | Pakistan v India | 1986-87 |
| Jullundur | 374 | India v Pakistan | 1983-84 | 337 | Pakistan v India | 1983-84 |
| Kanpur | 676-7 | India v Sri Lanka | 1986-87 | 105 | Australia v India | 1959-60 |
| Lucknow[1] | 331 | Pakistan v India | 1952-53 | 106 | India v Pakistan | 1952-53 |
| Lucknow[2] | 511 | India v Sri Lanka | 1993-94 | 174 | Sri Lanka v India | 1993-94 |
| Mohali | 515-9d | India v Sri Lanka | 1994-95 | 114 | India v West Indies | 1997-98 |
| Bombay[1] | 438 | England v India | 1933-34 | 219 | India v England | 1933-34 |
| Bombay[2] | 629-6d | West Indies v India | 1948-49 | 88 | India v New Zealand | 1964-65 |
| Mumbai[3] | 604-6d | West Indies v India | 1974-75 | 102 | England v India | 1981-82 |
| Nagpur | 546-9d | India v Sri Lanka | 1994-95 | 109 | India v New Zealand | 1969-70 |

**PAKISTAN**

| Centre | | Highest Total | | | Lowest Total | |
|---|---|---|---|---|---|---|
| Bahawalpur | 312-9d | Pakistan v India | 1954-55 | 235 | India v Pakistan | 1954-55 |
| Dacca | 439 | England v Pakistan | 1961-62 | 70 | New Zealand v Pakistan | 1955-56 |
| Faisalabad | 674-6 | Pakistan v India | 1984-85 | 53 | West Indies v Pakistan | 1986-87 |
| Gujranwala | 109-2 | Pakistan v Sri Lanka | 1991-92 | | no instance | |
| Hyderabad | 581-3d | Pakistan v India | 1982-83 | 189 | India v Pakistan | 1982-83 |
| | | | | 189 | New Zealand v Pakistan | 1984-85 |
| Karachi[1] | 565-9d | Pakistan v New Zealand | 1976-77 | 80 | Australia v Pakistan | 1956-57 |
| Karachi[2] | 423 | Pakistan v Zimbabwe | 1993-94 | 134 | Zimbabwe v Pakistan | 1993-94 |
| Lahore[1] | 561 | Pakistan v New Zealand | 1955-56 | 104 | Pakistan v West Indies | 1958-59 |
| Lahore[2] | 699-5 | Pakistan v India | 1989-90 | 77 | Pakistan v West Indies | 1986-87 |
| Multan | 249 | West Indies v Pakistan | 1980-81 | 166 | Pakistan v West Indies | 1980-81 |
| Peshawar[1] | 245 | India v Pakistan | 1954-55 | 182 | Pakistan v India | 1954-55 |
| Peshawar[2] | 459-9d | Pakistan v Sri Lanka | 1995-96 | 151 | West Indies v Pakistan | 1997-98 |
| Rawalpindi[1] | 318 | Pakistan v New Zealand | 1964-65 | 79 | New Zealand v Pakistan | 1964-65 |
| Rawalpindi[2] | 537 | Pakistan v Australia | 1996-97 | 139 | West Indies v Pakistan | 1997-98 |
| Sheikhupura | 553 | Pakistan v Zimbabwe | 1996-97 | 375 | Zimbabwe v Pakistan | 1996-97 |
| Sialkot | 423-5d | Pakistan v Sri Lanka | 1991-92 | 157 | Sri Lanka v Pakistan | 1985-86 |

**SRI LANKA**

| Centre | | Highest Total | | | Lowest Total | |
|---|---|---|---|---|---|---|
| Colombo (CCC) | 459 | New Zealand v Sri Lanka | 1983-84 | 132 | Pakistan v Sri Lanka | 1985-86 |
| Colombo (PIS) | 952-6d | Sri Lanka v India | 1996-97 | 127 | Zimbabwe v Sri Lanka | 1996-97 |
| Colombo (PSS) | 446 | India v Sri Lanka | 1993-94 | 175 | Sri Lanka v England | 1981-82 |
| Colombo (SSC) | 547-8d | Sri Lanka v Australia | 1992-93 | 102 | New Zealand v Sri Lanka | 1992-93 |
| Galle | 323 | Sri Lanka v New Zealand | 1997-98 | 114 | New Zealand v Sri Lanka | 1997-98 |
| Kandy | 514-4d | Australia v Sri Lanka | 1982-83 | 71 | Sri Lanka v Pakistan | 1994-95 |
| Moratuwa | 337 | Australia v Sri Lanka | 1992-93 | 190 | Sri Lanka v West Indies | 1993-94 |

**ZIMBABWE**

| Centre | | Highest Total | | | Lowest Total | |
|---|---|---|---|---|---|---|
| Bulawayo[1] | 325-3d | New Zealand v Zimbabwe | 1992-93 | 219 | Zimbabwe v New Zealand | 1992-93 |
| Bulawayo[2] | 462-9d | Zimbabwe v Sri Lanka | 1994-95 | 146 | Zimbabwe v Pakistan | 1994-95 |
| Harare | 544-4d | Zimbabwe v Pakistan | 1994-95 | 137 | Zimbabwe v New Zealand | 1992-93 |

*†Five men were absent hurt. The second lowest total at Kingston is 103 by England in 1934-35.*

## HIGHEST INDIVIDUAL SCORE FOR EACH TEST MATCH GROUND

**AUSTRALIA**

| | | | | |
|---|---|---|---|---|
| Adelaide | 299* | D.G.Bradman | Australia v South Africa | 1931-32 |
| Brisbane[1] | 223 | D.G.Bradman | Australia v West Indies | 1930-31 |
| Brisbane[2] | 226 | D.G.Bradman | Australia v South Africa | 1931-32 |
| Hobart | 168 | M.J.Slater | Australia v New Zealand | 1993-94 |

| | | | | |
|---|---|---|---|---|
| Melbourne | 307 | R.M.Cowper | Australia v England | 1965-66 |
| Perth | 219 | M.J.Slater | Australia v Sri Lanka | 1995-96 |
| Sydney | 287 | R.E.Foster | England v Australia | 1903-04 |
| **ENGLAND** | | | | |
| Birmingham | 285* | P.B.H.May | England v West Indies | 1957 |
| Leeds | 334 | D.G.Bradman | Australia v England | 1930 |
| Lord's | 333 | G.A.Gooch | England v India | 1990 |
| Manchester | 311 | R.B.Simpson | Australia v England | 1964 |
| Nottingham | 278 | D.C.S.Compton | England v Pakistan | 1954 |
| The Oval | 364 | L.Hutton | England v Australia | 1938 |
| Sheffield | 119 | C.Hill | Australia v England | 1902 |
| **SOUTH AFRICA** | | | | |
| Cape Town | 209 | R.G.Pollock | South Africa v Australia | 1966-67 |
| Centurion | 141 | G.A.Hick | England v South Africa | 1995-96 |
| Durban[1] | 119 | J.W.H.T.Douglas | England v South Africa | 1913-14 |
| Durban[2] | 274 | R.G.Pollock | South Africa v Australia | 1969-70 |
| Johannesburg[1] | 231 | A.D.Nourse | South Africa v Australia | 1935-36 |
| Johannesburg[2] | 195 | C.Washbrook | England v South Africa | 1948-49 |
| Johannesburg[3] | 214 | G.S.Blewett | Australia v South Africa | 1996-97 |
| Port Elizabeth | 167 | A.L.Hassett | Australia v South Africa | 1949-50 |
| **WEST INDIES** | | | | |
| Bridgetown | 337 | Hanif Mohammad | Pakistan v West Indies | 1957-58 |
| Georgetown | 259 | G.M.Turner | New Zealand v West Indies | 1971-72 |
| Kingston | 365* | G.S.Sobers | West Indies v Pakistan | 1957-58 |
| Kingstown | 115 | B.C.Lara | West Indies v Sri Lanka | 1996-97 |
| Port-of-Spain | 220 | S.M.Gavaskar | India v West Indies | 1970-71 |
| St John's | 375 | B.C.Lara | West indies v England | 1993-94 |
| **NEW ZEALAND** | | | | |
| Auckland | 336* | W.R.Hammond | England v New Zealand | 1932-33 |
| Christchurch | 258 | S.M.Nurse | West Indies v New Zealand | 1968-69 |
| Dunedin | 267* | B.A.Young | New Zealand v Sri Lanka | 1996-97 |
| Hamilton | 133 | M.J.Greatbatch | New Zealand v Pakistan | 1992-93 |
| Napier | 119* | Majid Khan | Pakistan v New Zealand | 1978-79 |
| Wellington | 299 | M.D.Crowe | New Zealand v Sri Lanka | 1990-91 |
| **INDIA** | | | | |
| Ahmedabad | 152 | M.Azharuddin | India v Sri Lanka | 1993-94 |
| Bangalore | 177 | S.R.Tendulkar | India v Australia | 1997-98 |
| Calcutta | 256 | R.B.Kanhai | West Indies v India | 1958-59 |
| Chandigarh | 88 | R.J.Shastri | India v Sri Lanka | 1990-91 |
| Chennai[1] | 236* | S.M.Gavaskar | India v West Indies | 1983-84 |
| Madras[2] | 231 | M.H.Mankad | India v New Zealand | 1955-56 |
| Cuttack | 166 | D.B.Vengsarkar | India v Sri Lanka | 1986-87 |
| Delhi | 230* | B.Sutcliffe | New Zealand v India | 1955-56 |
| Hyderabad | 223 | P.R.Umrigar | India v New Zealand | 1955-56 |
| Jaipur | 125 | R.J.Shastri | India v Pakistan | 1986-87 |
| Jullundur | 201 | A.D.Gaekwad | India v Pakistan | 1983-84 |
| Kanpur | 250 | S.F.A.F.Bacchus | West Indies v India | 1978-79 |
| Lucknow[1] | 124* | Nazar Mohammad | Pakistan v India | 1952-53 |
| Lucknow[2] | 142 | S.R.Tendulkar | India v Sri Lanka | 1993-94 |
| Mohali | 174* | J.C.Adams | West Indies v India | 1994-95 |
| Bombay[1] | 136 | B.H.Valentine | England v India | 1933-34 |
| Bombay[2] | 223 | M.H.Mankad | India v New Zealand | 1955-56 |
| Mumbai[3] | 242* | C.H.Lloyd | West Indies v India | 1974-75 |
| Nagpur | 179 | S.R.Tendulkar | India v West Indies | 1994-95 |

| **PAKISTAN** | | | | |
|---|---|---|---|---|
| Bahawalpur | 142 | Hanif Mohammad | Pakistan v India | 1954-55 |
| Dacca | 165 | G.Pullar | England v Pakistan | 1961-62 |
| Faisalabad | 235 | G.S.Chappell | Australia v Pakistan | 1979-80 |
| Gujranwala | 51* | Rameez Raja | Pakistan v Sri Lanka | 1991-92 |
| Hyderabad | 280* | Javed Miandad | Pakistan v India | 1982-83 |
| Karachi[1] | 211 | Javed Miandad | Pakistan v Australia | 1988-89 |
| Karachi[2] | 81 | Shoaib Mohammad | Pakistan v Zimbabwe | 1993-94 |
| Lahore[1] | 217 | R.B.Kanhai | Pakistan v India | 1978-79 |
| Lahore[2] | 235* | Zaheer Abbas | Pakistan v India | 1978-79 |
| Multan | 120* | I.V.A.Richards | West Indies v Pakistan | 1980-81 |
| Peshawar[1] | 108 | P.R.Umrigar | India v Pakistan | 1954-55 |
| Peshawar[2] | 95 | Inzamamul Haq | Pakistan v Sri Lanka | 1995-96 |
| Rawalpindi[1] | 76 | B.R.Taylor | New Zealand v Pakistan | 1964-65 |
| Rawalpindi[2] | 237 | Saleem Malik | Pakistan v Australia | 1994-95 |
| Sheikhupura | 257* | Wasim Akram | Pakistan v New Zealand | 1996-97 |
| Sialkot | 117* | Moin Khan | Pakistan v Sri Lanka | 1995-96 |
| **SRI LANKA** | | | | |
| Colombo (CCC) | 201* | D.S.B.P.Kuruppu | Sri Lanka v New Zealand | 1986-87 |
| Colombo (PIS) | 340 | S.T.Jayasuriya | Sri Lanka v India | 1996-97 |
| Colombo (PSS) | 151 | R.S.Mahanama | Sri Lanka v India | 1993-94 |
| Colombo (SSC) | 199 | S.T.Jayasuriya | Sri Lanka v India | 1996-97 |
| Galle | 167 | D.P.M.Jayawardene | Sri Lanka v New Zealand | 1997-98 |
| Kandy | 223 | M.S.Atapattu | Sri Lanka v Zimbabwe | 1997-98 |
| Moratuwa | 153 | R.S.Mahanama | Sri Lanka v New Zealand | 1992-93 |
| **ZIMBABWE** | | | | |
| Bulawayo[1] | 119 | R.T.Latham | New Zealand v Zimbabwe | 1992-93 |
| Bulawayo[2] | 266 | D.L.Houghton | Zimbabwe v Sri Lanka | 1994-95 |
| Harare | 201* | G.W.Flower | Zimbabwe v Pakistan | 1994-95 |

## HIGHEST WICKET PARTNERSHIPS FOR EACH TEST GROUND

| | Runs | Wkt | | | |
|---|---|---|---|---|---|
| **AUSTRALIA** | | | | | |
| Adelaide | 341 | 3rd | E.J.Barlow, R.G.Pollock | South Africa v Australia | 1963-64 |
| Brisbane[1] | 229 | 2nd | W.H.Ponsford D.G.Bradman | Australia v West Indies | 1930-31 |
| Brisbane[2] | 276 | 3rd | D.G.Bradman, A.L.Hassett | Australia v England | 1946-47 |
| Hobart | 260* | 6th | D.M.Jones, S.R.Waugh | Australia v Sri Lanka | 1989-90 |
| Melbourne | 346 | 6th | J.H.W.Fingleton, D.G.Bradman | Australia v England | 1936-37 |
| Perth | 259 | 2nd | W.B.Phillips, G.N.Yallop | Australia v Pakistan | 1983-84 |
| Sydney | 405 | 5th | S.G.Barnes, D.G.Bradman | Australia v England | 1946-47 |
| **ENGLAND** | | | | | |
| Birmingham | 411 | 4th | P.B.H.May, M.C.Cowdrey | England v West Indies | 1957 |
| Leeds | 388 | 4th | W.H.Ponsford, D.G.Bradman | Australia v England | 1934 |
| Lord's | 370 | 3rd | W.J.Edrich, D.C.S.Compton | England v South Africa | 1947 |
| Manchester | 246 | 3rd | E.R.Dexter, K.F.Barrington | England v Australia | 1964 |
| Nottingham | 329 | 1st | G.R.Marsh, M.A.Taylor | Australia v England | 1989 |
| The Oval | 451 | 2nd | W.H.Ponsford, D.G.Bradman | Australia v England | 1934 |
| Sheffield | 107 | 4th | C.Hill, S.E.Gregory | Australia v England | 1902 |
| **SOUTH AFRICA** | | | | | |
| Cape Town | 260 | 1st | B.Mitchell, I.J.Siedle | South Africa v England | 1930-31 |
| Centurion | 142 | 4th | M.A.Atherton, G.A.Hick | England v South Africa | 1995-96 |
| Durban[1] | 143 | 4th | G.C.White, A.W.Nourse | South Africa v England | 1909-10 |
| Durban[2] | 280 | 2nd | P.A.Gibb, W.J.Edrich | England v South Africa | 1938-39 |
| Johannesburg[1] | 230 | 2nd | H.Sutcliffe, G.E.Tyldesley | England v South Africa | 1927-28 |
| Johannesburg[2] | 359 | 1st | L.Hutton, C.Washbrook | England v South Africa | 1948-49 |

| | | | | | |
|---|---|---|---|---|---|
| Johannesburg[3] | 385 | 5th | S.R.Waugh, G.S.Blewett | Australia v South Africa | 1996-97 |
| Port Elizabeth | 187 | 3rd | A.R.Morris, R.N.Harvey | Australia v South Africa | 1949-50 |

**WEST INDIES**

| | | | | | |
|---|---|---|---|---|---|
| Bridgetown | 399 | 4th | G.S.Sobers.F.M.M.Worrell | West Indies v England | 1959-60 |
| Georgetown | 387 | 1st | G.M.Turner, T.W.Jarvis | New Zealand v West Indies | 1971-72 |
| Kingston | 446 | 2nd | C.C.Hunte, G.S.Sobers | West Indies v Pakistan | 1957-58 |
| Kingstown | 97 | 4th | B.C.Lara, C.L.Hooper | West Indies v Sri Lanka | 1996-97 |
| Port-of-Spain | 338 | 3rd | E.D.Weekes, F.M.M.Worrell | West Indies v England | 1953-54 |
| St John's | 308 | 3rd | R.B.Richardson, I.V.A.Richards | West Indies v Australia | 1983-84 |

**NEW ZEALAND**

| | | | | | |
|---|---|---|---|---|---|
| Auckland | 266 | 4th | M.H.Denness, K.W.R.Fletcher | England v New Zealand | 1974-75 |
| Christchurch | 242 | 5th | W.R.Hammond, L.E.G.Ames | England v New Zealand | 1932-33 |
| Dunedin | 350 | 4th | Mushtaq Mohammad, Asif Iqbal | Pakistan v New Zealand | 1972-73 |
| Hamilton | 161 | 1st | T.J.Franklin, J.G.Wright | New Zealand v Sri Lanka | 1990-91 |
| Napier | 195 | 2nd | J.G.Wright, G.P.Howarth | New Zealand v Pakistan | 1978-79 |
| Wellington | 467 | 3rd | M.D.Crowe, A.H.Jones | New Zealand v Sri Lanka | 1990-91 |

**INDIA**

| | | | | | |
|---|---|---|---|---|---|
| Ahmedabad | 154 | 7th | Imran Khan, Ijaz Faqih | Pakistan v India | 1986-87 |
| Bangalore | 207 | 4th | C.G.Greenidge, C.H.Lloyd | West Indies v India | 1974-75 |
| Calcutta | 344* | 2nd | S.M.Gavaskar, D.B.Vengsarkar | India v West Indies | 1978-79 |
| Chandigarh | 76 | 2nd | R.J.Shastri, S.V.Manjrekar | India v Sri Lanka | 1990-91 |
| Chennai[1] | 316 | 3rd | G.R.Viswanath, Yashpal Sharma | India v England | 1981-82 |
| Madras[2] | 413 | 1st | M.H.Mankad, P.Roy | India v New Zealand | 1955-56 |
| Cuttack | 111 | 6th | D.B.Vengsarkar, Kapil Dev | India v Sri Lanka | 1986-87 |
| Delhi | 267 | 4th | C.L.Walcott, G.E.Gomez | West Indies v India | 1948-49 |
| Hyderabad | 238 | 3rd | P.R.Umrigar, V.L.Manjrekar | India v New Zealand | 1955-56 |
| Jaipur | 130 | 5th | M.Azharuddin, R.J.Shastri | India v Pakistan | 1986-87 |
| Jullundur | 121 | 6th | A.D.Gaekwad, R.M.H.Binny | India v Pakistan | 1983-84 |
| Kanpur | 272 | 6th | M.Azharuddin, Kapil Dev | India v Sri Lanka | 1986-87 |
| Lucknow[1] | 63 | 8th | Nazar Mohammad, Zulfiqar Ahmed | Pakistan v India | 1952-53 |
| Lucknow[2] | 142 | 4th | S.R.Tendulkar, M.Azharuddin | India v Sri Lanka | 1993-94 |
| Mohali | 145* | 4th | J.C.Adams, K.L.T.Arthurton | West Indies v India | 1994-95 |
| Bombay[1] | 186 | 3rd | N.B.Amarnath, C.K.Nayudu | India v England | 1933-34 |
| Bombay[2] | 254 | 5th | K.W.R.Fletcher, A.W.Greig | England v India | 1972-73 |
| Mumbai[3] | 298* | 6th | D.B.Vengsarkar, R.J.Shastri | India v Australia | 1986-87 |
| Nagpur | 202 | 5th | S.R.Tendulkar, M.Azharuddin | India v West Indies | 1994-95 |

**PAKISTAN**

| | | | | | |
|---|---|---|---|---|---|
| Bahawalpur | 127 | 1st | Hanif Mohammad, Alimuddin | Pakistan v India | 1954-55 |
| Dacca | 198 | 1st | G.Pullar, R.W.Barber | England v Pakistan | 1961-62 |
| Faisalabad | 397 | 3rd | Qasim Omar, Javed Miandad | Pakistan v Sri Lanka | 1985-86 |
| Gujranwala | 59 | 2nd | Rameez Raja, Zahid Fazal | Pakistan v Sri Lanka | 1991-92 |
| Hyderabad | 451 | 3rd | Mudassar Nazar, Javed Miandad | Pakistan v India | 1982-83 |
| Karachi[1] | 298 | 1st | Saeed Anwar, Ijaz Ahmed | Pakistan v West Indies | 1997-98 |
| Karachi[2] | 95 | 1st | Aamer Sohail, Shoaib Mohammad | Pakistan v Zimbabwe | 1993-94 |
| Lahore[1] | 308 | 7th | Waqar Hassan, Imtiaz Ahmed | Pakistan v New Zealand | 1955-56 |
| Lahore[2] | 281 | 5th | Javed Miandad, Asif Iqbal | Pakistan v New Zealand | 1976-77 |
| Multan | 100 | 3rd | Majid Khan, Javed Miandad | Pakistan v West Indies | 1980-81 |
| Peshawar[1] | 91 | 3rd | P.R.Umrigar, V.L.Manjrekar | India v Pakistan | 1954-55 |
| Peshawar[2] | 133 | 2nd | Aamer Sohail, Inzamamul Haq | Pakistan v West Indies | 1997-98 |
| Rawalpindi[1] | 114 | 2nd | Mohammad Ilyas, Saeed Ahmed | Pakistan v New Zealand | 1964-65 |
| Rawalpindi[2] | 323 | 3rd | Aamer Sohail, Ijaz Ahmed | Pakistan v West Indies | 1997-98 |
| Sheikhupura | 313 | 8th | Wasim Akram, Saqlain Mushtaq | Pakistan v Sri Lanka | 1996-97 |
| Sialkot | 128 | 3rd | S.V.Manjrekar, M.Azharuddin | India v Pakistan | 1985-86 |

**SRI LANKA**

| | | | | | |
|---|---|---|---|---|---|
| Colombo (CCC) | 246* | 6th | J.J.Crowe, R.J.Hadlee | New Zealand v Sri Lanka | 1986-87 |
| Colombo (PIS) | 576 | 1st | S.T.Jayasuriya, R.S.Mahanama | Sri Lanka v India | 1996-97 |
| Colombo (PSS) | 240* | 4th | A.P.Gurusinha, A.Ranatunga | Sri Lanka v Pakistan | 1985-86 |
| Colombo (SSC) | 230 | 4th | A.P.Gurusinha, A.Ranatunga | Sri Lanka v Australia | 1992-93 |
| Galle | 74 | 4th | D.P.M.Jayawardene, A.Ranatunga | Sri Lanka v New Zealand | 1997-98 |
| Kandy | 216 | 4th | R.L.Dias, L.R.D.Mendis | Sri Lanka v India | 1985-86 |
| Moratuwa | 151 | 5th | K.R.Rutherford, C.Z.Harris | New Zealand v Sri Lanka | 1992-93 |

**ZIMBABWE**

| | | | | | |
|---|---|---|---|---|---|
| Bulawayo[1] | 127 | 2nd | R.T.Latham, A.H.Jones | New Zealand v Zimbabwe | 1992-93 |
| Bulawayo[2] | 277* | 5th | M.W.Goodwin, A.Flower | Zimbabwe vPakistan | 1997-98 |
| Harare | 269 | 3rd | G.W.Flower, A.Flower | Zimbabwe v Pakistan | 1994-95 |

## BEST INNINGS BOWLING ANALYSIS FOR EACH TEST GROUND

**AUSTRALIA**

| | | | | |
|---|---|---|---|---|
| Adelaide | 8-43 | A.E.Trott | Australia v England | 1894-95 |
| Brisbane[1] | 6-32 | H.Larwood | England v Australia | 1928-29 |
| Brisbane[2] | 9-52 | R.J.Hadlee | New Zealand v Australia | 1985-86 |
| Hobart | 6-31 | S.K.Warne | Australia v New Zealand | 1993-94 |
| Melbourne | 9-86 | Sarfraz Nawaz | Pakistan v Australia | 1978-79 |
| Perth | 8-87 | M.G.Hughes | Australia v West Indies | 1988-89 |
| Sydney | 8-35 | G.A.Lohmann | England v Australia | 1886-87 |

**ENGLAND**

| | | | | |
|---|---|---|---|---|
| Birmingham | 7-17 | W.Rhodes | England v Australia | 1902 |
| Leeds | 8-43 | R.G.D.Willis | England v Australia | 1981 |
| Lord's | 8-34 | I.T.Botham | England v Pakistan | 1978 |
| Manchester | 10-53 | J.C.Laker | England v Australia | 1956 |
| Nottingham | 8-107 | B.J.T.Bosanquet | England v Australia | 1905 |
| The Oval | 9-57 | D.E.Malcolm | England v South Africa | 1994 |
| Sheffield | 6-49 | S.F.Barnes | England v Australia | 1902 |

**SOUTH AFRICA**

| | | | | |
|---|---|---|---|---|
| Cape Town | 8-11 | J.Briggs | England v South Africa | 1888-89 |
| Centurion | 6-86 | G.D.McGrath | Australia v England | 1996-97 |
| Durban[1] | 7-56 | S.F.Barnes | England v South Africa | 1913-14 |
| Durban[2] | 8-69 | H.J Tayfield | South Africa v England | 1956-57 |
| Johannesburg[1] | 9-28 | G.A.Lohmann | England v South Africa | 1895-96 |
| Johannesburg[2] | 6-13 | H.J.Tayfield | South Africa v New Zealand | 1953-54 |
| Johannesburg[3] | 9-113 | H.J.Tayfield | South Africa v England | 1956-57 |
| Port Elizabeth | 8-7 | G.A.Lohmann | England v South Africa | 1895-96 |

**WEST INDIES**

| | | | | |
|---|---|---|---|---|
| Bridgetown | 8-38 | L.R.Gibbs | West Indies v India | 1961-62 |
| Georgetown | 7-44 | I.W.Johnson | Australia v West Indies | 1954-55 |
| Kingston | 7-34 | T.E.Bailey | England v West Indies | 1953-54 |
| Kingstown | 5-26 | C.L.Hooper | West Indies v Sri Lanka | 1996-97 |
| Port-of-Spain | 9-95 | J.M.Noreiga | West Indies v India | 1970-71 |
| St John's | 6-54 | C.A.Walsh | West Indies v Australia | 1994-95 |

**NEW ZEALAND**

| | | | | |
|---|---|---|---|---|
| Auckland | 8-76 | E.A.S.Prasanna | India v New Zealand | 1975-76 |
| Christchurch | 7-47 | P.C.R. Tufnell | England v New Zealand | 1991-92 |
| Dunedin | 7-52 | Intikhab Alam | Pakistan v New Zealand | 1972-73 |
| Hamilton | 5-22 | Waqar Younis | Pakistan v New Zealand | 1992-93 |
| Napier | 5-43 | W.P.U.J.C.Vaas | Sri Lanka v New Zealand | 1994-95 |
| Wellington | 7-23 | R.J.Hadlee | New Zealand v India | 1975-76 |

**INDIA**

| | | | | |
|---|---|---|---|---|
| Ahmedabad | 9-83 | Kapil Dev | India v West Indies | 1983-84 |
| Bangalore | 7-27 | Maninder Singh | India v Pakistan | 1986-87 |
| Calcutta | 8-64 | L.Klusener | South Africa v India | 1996-97 |
| Chandigarh | 6-12 | S.L.Venkatapathy Raju | India v Sri Lanka | 1990-91 |
| Chennai[1] | 8-55 | M.H.Mankad | India v England | 1951-52 |
| Madras[2] | 7-43 | R.R.Lindwall | Australia v India | 1956-57 |
| Cuttack | 6-59 | N.D.Hirwani | India v New Zealand | 1995-96 |
| Delhi | 8-52 | M.H.Mankad | India v Pakistan | 1952-53 |
| Hyderabad | 7-128 | S.P.Gupte | India v New Zealand | 1955-56 |
| Jaipur | 4-88 | G.Sharma | India v Pakistan | 1986-87 |
| Jullundur | 4-50 | Wasim Raja | Pakistan v India | 1983-84 |
| Kanpur | 9-69 | J.M.Patel | India v Australia | 1959-60 |
| Lucknow[1] | 7-42 | Fazal Mahmood | Pakistan v India | 1952-53 |
| Lucknow[2] | 7-59 | A.R.Kumble | India v Sri Lanka | 1993-94 |
| Mohali | 5-65 | K.C.G.Benjamin | West Indies v India | 1994-95 |
| Bombay[1] | 5-55 | M.S.Nichols | England v India | 1933-34 |
| Bombay[2] | 7-157 | B.S.Chandrasekhar | India v West Indies | 1966-67 |
| Mumbai[3] | 7-48 | I.T.Botham | England v India | 1979-80 |
| Nagpur | 7-51 | Maninder Singh | India v Sri Lanka | 1986-87 |

**PAKISTAN**

| | | | | |
|---|---|---|---|---|
| Bahawalpur | 6-74 | P.R.Umrigar | India v Pakistan | 1954-55 |
| Dacca | 6-21 | Khan Mohammad | Pakistan v New Zealand | 1955-56 |
| Faisalabad | 7-52 | C.Pringle | New Zealand v Pakistan | 1990-91 |
| Gujranwala | 1-27 | G.P.Wickramasinghe | Sri Lanka v Pakistan | 1991-92 |
| Hyderabad | 7-87 | S.L.Boock | New Zealand v Pakistan | 1984-85 |
| Karachi[1] | 8-60 | Imran Khan | Pakistan v India | 1982-83 |
| Karachi[2] | 7-91 | Waqar Younis | Pakistan v Zimbabwe | 1993-94 |
| Lahore[1] | 5-87 | W.W.Hall | West Indies v Pakistan | 1958-59 |
| Lahore[2] | 9-56 | Abdul Qadir | Pakistan v England | 1987-88 |
| Multan | 5-62 | Imran Khan | Pakistan v West Indies | 1980-81 |
| Peshawar[1] | 5-63 | S.P.Gupte | India v Pakistan | 1954-55 |
| Peshawar[2] | 5-35 | Mushtaq Ahmed | Pakistan v West Indies | 1997-98 |
| Rawalpindi[1] | 4-5 | Pervez Sajjad | Pakistan v New Zealand | 1964-65 |
| Rawalpindi[2] | 7-66 | Mohammad Zahid | Pakistan v New Zealand | 1996-97 |
| Sheikhupura | 5-53 | Shahid Nazir | Pakistan v Zimbabwe | 1996-97 |
| Sialkot | 8-83 | J.R.Ratnayeke | Sri Lanka v Pakistan | 1985-86 |

**SRI LANKA**

| | | | | |
|---|---|---|---|---|
| Colombo (CCC) | 5-29 | R.I.Hadlee | New Zealand v Sri Lanka | 1983-84 |
| Colombo (PIS) | 6-98 | M.Muralidaran | Sri Lanka v Pakistan | 1996-97 |
| Colombo (PSS) | 6-33 | J.E.Emburey | England v Sri Lanka | 1981-82 |
| Colombo (SSC) | 6-64 | D.L. Vettori | New Zealand v Sri Lanka | 1997-98 |
| Galle | 6-72 | H.D.P.K.Dharmasena | Sri Lanka v New Zealand | 1997-98 |
| Kandy | 7-94 | M.Muralidaran | Sri Lanka v Zimbabwe | 1997-98 |
| Moratuwa | 5-69 | A.A.Donald | South Africa v Sri Lanka | 1993-94 |

**ZIMBABWE**

| | | | | |
|---|---|---|---|---|
| Bulawayo[1] | 6-113 | D.N.Patel | New Zealand v Zimbabwe | 1992-93 |
| Bulawayo[2] | 6-109 | A.G.Huckle | Zimbabwe v New Zealand | 1997-98 |
| Harare | 8-71 | A.A.Donald | South Africa v Zimbabwe | 1995-96 |

## BEST MATCH BOWLING ANALYSIS FOR EACH TEST GROUND

| Ground | Analysis | Bowler | Match | Season |
|---|---|---|---|---|
| **AUSTRALIA** | | | | |
| Adelaide | 14-199 | C.V.Grimmett | Australia v South Africa | 1931-32 |
| Brisbane[1] | 9-144 | C.V.Grimmett | Australia v West Indies | 1930-31 |
| Brisbane[2] | 15-123 | R.J.Hadlee | New Zealand v Australia | 1985-86 |
| Hobart | 9-67 | S.K.Warne | Australia v New Zealand | 1993-94 |
| Melbourne | 15-124 | W.Rhodes | England v Australia | 1903-04 |
| Perth | 13-217 | M.G.Hughes | Australia v West Indies | 1988-89 |
| Sydney | 12-87 | C.T.B.Turner | Australia v England | 1887-88 |
| **ENGLAND** | | | | |
| Birmingham | 12-119 | F.S.Trueman | England v West Indies | 1963 |
| Leeds | 15-99 | C.Blythe | England v South Africa | 1907 |
| Lord's | 16-137 | R.A.L.Massie | Australia v England | 1972 |
| Manchester | 19-90 | J.C.Laker | England v Australia | 1956 |
| Nottingham | 14-99 | A.V.Bedser | England v Australia | 1953 |
| The Oval | 14-90 | F.R.Spofforth | Australia v England | 1882 |
| Sheffield | 11-103 | M.A.Noble | Australia v England | 1902 |
| **SOUTH AFRICA** | | | | |
| Cape Town | 15-28 | J.Briggs | England v South Africa | 1888-89 |
| Centurion | 8-96 | A.A.Donald | South Africa v Australia | 1996-97 |
| Durban[1] | 14-144 | S.F.Barnes | England v South Africa | 1913-14 |
| Durban[2] | 13-173 | C.V.Grimmett | Australia v South Africa | 1935-36 |
| Johannesburg[1] | 17-159 | S.F.Barnes | England v South Africa | 1913-14 |
| Johannesburg[2] | 8-61 | H.J.Tayfield | South Africa v New Zealand | 1953-54 |
| Johannesburg[3] | 13-192 | H.J.Tayfield | South Africa v England | 1956-57 |
| Port Elizabeth | 15-45 | G.A.Lohmann | England v South Africa | 1895-96 |
| **WEST INDIES** | | | | |
| Bridgetown | 11-120 | M.D.Marshall | West Indies v New Zealand | 1984-85 |
| Georgetown | 11-121 | Imran Khan | Pakistan v West Indies | 1987-88 |
| Kingston | 10-96 | H.H.H.Johnson | West Indies v England | 1947-48 |
| Kingstown | 8-139 | M.Muralidaran | Sri Lanka v West Indies | 1996-97 |
| Port-of-Spain | 13-156 | A.W.Greig | England v West Indies | 1973-74 |
| St John's | 9-127 | Wagar Younis | Pakistan v West Indies | 1992-93 |
| **NEW ZEALAND** | | | | |
| Auckland | 11-123 | D.K.Lillee | Australia v New Zealand | 1976-77 |
| Christchurch | 12-97 | D.L.Underwood | England v New Zealand | 1970-71 |
| Dunedin | 11-102 | R.J.Hadlee | New Zealand v West Indies | 1979-80 |
| Hamilton | 9-81 | Waqar Younis | Pakistan v New Zealand | 1992-93 |
| Napier | 10-90 | W.P.J.U.C.Vaas | Sri Lanka v New Zealand | 1994-95 |
| Wellington | 13-55 | C.A.Walsh | West Indies v New Zealand | 1994-95 |
| **INDIA** | | | | |
| Ahmedabad | 11-125 | S.L.Venkatapathy Raju | India v Sri Lanka | 1993-94 |
| Bangalore | 10-126 | Maninder Singh | India v Pakistan | 1986-87 |
| Calcutta | 11-105 | R.Benaud | Australia v India | 1956-57 |
| Chandigarh | 8-37 | S.L.Venkatapathy Raju | India v Sri Lanka | 1990-91 |
| Chennai[1] | 16-136 | N.D.Hirwani | India v West Indies | 1987-88 |
| Madras[2] | 11-122 | R.G.Nadkarni | India v Australia | 1964-65 |
| Cuttack | 6-83 | Maninder Singh | India v Sri Lanka | 1986-87 |
| Delhi | 13-131 | M.H.Mankad | India v Pakistan | 1952-53 |
| Hyderabad | 8-109 | E.A.S.Prasanna | India v New Zealand | 1969-70 |
| Jaipur | 4-88 | G.Sharma | India v Pakistan | 1986-87 |
| Jullundur | 4-50 | Wasim Raja | Pakistan v India | 1983-84 |

| | | | | |
|---|---|---|---|---|
| Kanpur | 14-124 | J.M.Patel | India v Australia | 1959-60 |
| Lucknow[1] | 12-94 | Fazal Mahmood | Pakistan v India | 1952-53 |
| Lucknow[2] | 11-128 | A.R.Kumble | India v Sri Lanka | 1993-94 |
| Mohali | 8-171 | K.C.G.Benjamin | West Indies v India | 1994-95 |
| Bombay[1] | 8-108 | M.S.Nichols | England v India | 1933-34 |
| Bombay[2] | 11-235 | B.S.Chandrasekhar | India v West Indies | 1966-67 |
| Mumbai[3] | 13-106 | I.T.Botham | England v India | 1979-80 |
| Nagpur | 10-107 | Maninder Singh | India v Sri Lanka | 1986-87 |
| **PAKISTAN** | | | | |
| Bahawalpur | 7-124 | Khan Mohammad | Pakistan v India | 1954-55 |
| Dacca | 12-100 | Fazal Mahmood | Pakistan v West Indies | 1958-59 |
| Faisalabad | 12-130 | Waqar Younis | Pakistan v New Zealand | 1990-91 |
| Gujranwala | 1-27 | G.P.Wickramasinghe | Sri Lanka v Pakistan | 1991-92 |
| Hyderabad | 8-80 | Imran Khan | Pakistan v India | 1982-83 |
| Karachi[1] | 13-114 | Fazal Mahmood | Pakistan v Australia | 1956-57 |
| Karachi[2] | 13-135 | Waqar Younis | Pakistan v Zimbabwe | 1993-94 |
| Lahore[1] | 7-167 | S.P.Gupte | India v Pakistan | 1954-55 |
| Lahore[2] | 14-116 | Imran Khan | Pakistan v Sri Lanka | 1981-82 |
| Multan | 5-89 | Imran Khan | Pakistan v West Indies | 1980-81 |
| Peshawar[1] | 6-115 | S.P.Gupte | India v Pakistan | 1954-55 |
| Peshawar[2] | 10-106 | Mushtaq Ahmed | Pakistan v West Indies | 1997-98 |
| Rawalpindi[1] | 8-47 | Pervez Sajjad | Pakistan v New Zealand | 1964-65 |
| Rawalpindi[2] | 11-130 | Mohammad Zahid | Pakistan v New Zealand | 1996-97 |
| Sheikhupura | 7-98 | Shahid Nazir | Pakistan v Zimbabwe | 1996-97 |
| Sialkot | 9-95 | Imran Khan | Pakistan v Sri Lanka | 1985-86 |
| **SRI LANKA** | | | | |
| Colombo (CCC) | 10-102 | R.J.Hadlee | New Zealand v Sri Lanka | 1983-84 |
| Colombo (PIS) | 9-226 | Saqlain Mushtaq | Pakistan v Sri Lanka | 1996-97 |
| Colombo (PSS) | 9-125 | R.J.Ratnayake | Sri Lanka v India | 1985-86 |
| Colombo (SSC) | 9-106 | B.N.Schultz | South Africa v Sri Lanka | 1993-94 |
| Galle | 9-83 | M.L.C.N.Bandaratilleke | Sri Lanka v New Zealand | 1997-98 |
| Kandy | 12-117 | M.Muralidaran | Sri Lanka v Zimbabwe | 1997-98 |
| Moratuwa | 8-157 | C.P.H.Ramanayake | Sri Lanka v Australia | 1992-93 |
| **ZIMBABWE** | | | | |
| Bulawayo[1] | 7-173 | D.N.Patel | New Zealand v Zimbabwe | 1992-93 |
| Bulawayo[2] | 11-257 | A.G.Huckle | Zimbabwe v New Zealand | 1997-98 |
| Harare | 11-113 | A.A.Donald | South Africa v Zimbabwe | 1995-96 |

## SERIES BY SERIES RECORDS

*• denotes batted first (Where a captain's name appears only once he was captain throughout the entire series).*

| **AUSTRALIA v ENGLAND** | Australia | | England | | Captains | |
|---|---|---|---|---|---|---|
| Venue and Result | 1st | 2nd | 1st | 2nd | Australia | England |
| **1876-77 in AUSTRALIA** | | | | | | |
| Melbourne-Australia 45 runs | •245 | 104 | 196 | 108 | D.W.Gregory | J.Lillywhite |
| Melbourne-England 4 wkts | •122 | 259 | 261 | 6-122 | | |
| **1878-79 in AUSTRALIA** | | | | | | |
| Melbourne-Australia 10 wkts | 256 | 0-19 | •113 | 160 | D.W.Gregory | Lord Harris |
| **1880 in ENGLAND** | | | | | | |
| The Oval-England 5 wkts | 149 | 327 | •420 | 5-57 | W.L.Murdoch | Lord Harris |
| **1881-82 in AUSTRALIA** | | | | | | |
| Melbourne-Drawn | 320 | 3-127 | •294 | 308 | W.L.Murdoch | A.Shaw |
| Sydney-Australia 5 wkts | 197 | 5-169 | •133 | 232 | | |
| Sydney-Australia 6 wkts | 260 | 4-66 | •188 | 134 | | |
| Melbourne-Drawn | 300 | - | •309 | 2-234 | | |
| **1882 in ENGLAND** | | | | | | |
| The Oval-Australia 7 runs | •63 | 122 | 101 | 77 | W.L.Murdoch | A.N.Hornby |
| **1882-83 in AUSTRALIA** | | | | | | |
| Melbourne-Australia 9 wkts | •291 | 1-58 | 177 | 169 | W.L.Murdoch | Hon.I.F.W.Bligh |
| Melbourne-England inns & 27 runs | 114 | 153 | •294 | - | | |
| Sydney-England 69 runs | 218 | 83 | •247 | 123 | | |
| Sydney-Australia 4 wkts | 262 | 6-199 | •263 | 197 | | |
| **1884 in ENGLAND** | | | | | | |
| Manchester-Drawn | 182 | - | •95 | 9-180 | W.L.Murdoch | A.N.Hornby |
| Lord's-England inns & 5 runs | •229 | 145 | 379 | - | | Lord Harris |
| The Oval-Drawn | •551 | - | 346 | 2-85 | | Lord Harris |
| **1884-85 in AUSTRALIA** | | | | | | |
| Adelaide-England 8 wkts | •243 | 191 | 369 | 2-67 | W.L.Murdoch | A.Shrewsbury |
| Melbourne-England 10 wkts | 279 | 126 | •401 | 0-7 | T.P.Horan | |
| Sydney-Australia 6 runs | •181 | 165 | 133 | 207 | H.H.Massie | |
| Sydney-Australia 8 wkts | 309 | 2-40 | •269 | 77 | J.M.Blackham | |
| Melbourne-England inns & 98 runs | •163 | 125 | 386 | - | T.P.Horan | |
| **1886 in ENGLAND** | | | | | | |
| Manchester-England 4 wkts | •205 | 123 | 223 | 6-107 | H.J.H.Scott | A.G.Steel |
| Lord's-England inns & 106 runs | 121 | 126 | •353 | - | | |
| The Oval-England inns & 217 runs | 68 | 149 | •434 | - | | |
| **1886-87 in AUSTRALIA** | | | | | | |
| Sydney-England 13 runs | 119 | 97 | •45 | 184 | P.S.McDonnell | A.Shrewsbury |
| Sydney-England 71 runs | 84 | 150 | •151 | 154 | | |
| **1887-88 in AUSTRALIA** | | | | | | |
| Sydney-England 126 runs | 42 | 82 | •113 | 137 | P.S.McDonnell | W.W.Read |
| **1888 in ENGLAND** | | | | | | |
| Lord's-Australia 61 runs | •116 | 60 | 53 | 62 | P.S.McDonnell | A.G.Steel |
| The Oval-England inns & 137 runs | •80 | 100 | 317 | - | | W.G.Grace |
| Manchester-England inns & 21 runs | 81 | 70 | •172 | - | | W.G.Grace |

| AUSTRALIA v ENGLAND (cont.) | Australia | | England | | Captains | |
|---|---|---|---|---|---|---|
| Venue and Result | 1st | 2nd | 1st | 2nd | Australia | England |
| **1890 in ENGLAND** | | | | | | |
| Lord's-England 7 wkts | •132 | 176 | 173 | 3-137 | W.L.Murdoch | W.G.Grace |
| The Oval-England 2 wkts | •92 | 102 | 100 | 8-95 | | |
| Manchester-Abandoned | - | - | - | - | | |
| **1891-92 in AUSTRALIA** | | | | | | |
| Melbourne-Australia 54 runs | •240 | 236 | 264 | 158 | J.M.Blackham | W.G.Grace |
| Sydney-Australia 72 runs | •145 | 391 | 307 | 157 | | |
| Adelaide-England inns & 230 runs | 100 | 169 | •499 | | | |
| **1893 in ENGLAND** | | | | | | |
| Lord's-Drawn | 269 | - | •334 | 8d-234 | J.M.Blackham | A.E.Stoddart |
| The Oval-England inns & 43 runs | 91 | 349 | •483 | - | | W.G.Grace |
| Manchester-Drawn | •240 | 236 | 243 | 4-118 | | W.G.Grace |
| **1894-95 in AUSTRALIA** | | | | | | |
| Sydney-England 10 runs | •586 | 166 | 325 | 437 | J.M.Blackham | A.E.Stoddart |
| Melbourne-England 94 runs | 123 | 333 | •75 | 475 | G.Giffen | |
| Adelaide-Australia 382 runs | •238 | 411 | 124 | 143 | G.Giffen | |
| Sydney-Australia inns & 147 runs | •284 | - | 65 | 72 | G.Giffen | |
| Melbourne-England 6 wkts | •414 | 267 | 385 | 4-298 | G.Giffen | |
| **1896 in ENGLAND** | | | | | | |
| Lord's-England 6 wkts | •53 | 347 | 292 | 4-111 | G.H.S.Trott | W.G.Grace |
| Manchester-Australia 3 wkts | •412 | 7-125 | 231 | 305 | | |
| The Oval-England 66 runs | 119 | 44 | •145 | 84 | | |
| **1897-98 in AUSTRALIA** | | | | | | |
| Sydney-England 9 wkts | 237 | 408 | •551 | 1-96 | G.H.S.Trott | A.C.MacLaren |
| Melbourne-Australia inns & 55 runs | •520 | - | 315 | 150 | | A.C.MacLaren |
| Adelaide-Australia inns & 13 runs | •573 | - | 278 | 282 | | A.E.Stoddart |
| Melbourne-Australia 8 wkts | •323 | 2-115 | 174 | 263 | | A.E.Stoddart |
| Sydney-Australia 6 wkts | 239 | 4-276 | •335 | 178 | | A.C.MacLaren |
| **1899 in ENGLAND** | | | | | | |
| Nottingham-Drawn | •252 | 8d-230 | 193 | 7-155 | J.Darling | W.G.Grace |
| Lord's-Australia 10 wkts | 421 | 0-28 | •206 | 240 | | A.C.MacLaren |
| Leeds-Drawn | •172 | 224 | 220 | 0-19 | | A.C.MacLaren |
| Manchester-Drawn | 196 | 7d-346 | •372 | 3-94 | | A.C.MacLaren |
| The Oval-Drawn | 352 | 5-254 | •576 | - | | A.C.MacLaren |
| **1901-02 in AUSTRALIA** | | | | | | |
| Sydney-England inns & 124 runs | 168 | 172 | •464 | - | J.Darling | A.C.MacLaren |
| Melbourne-Australia 229 runs | •112 | 353 | 61 | 175 | J.Darling | |
| Adelaide-Australia 4 wkts | 321 | 6-315 | •388 | 247 | J.Darling | |
| Sydney-Australia 7 wkts | 299 | 3-121 | •317 | 99 | H.Trumble | |
| Melbourne-Australia 32 runs | •144 | 255 | 189 | 178 | H.Trumble | |
| **1902 in ENGLAND** | | | | | | |
| Birmingham-Drawn | 36 | 2-46 | •9d-376 | - | J.Darling | A.C.MacLaren |
| Lord's-Drawn | - | - | •2-102 | - | | |
| Sheffield-Australia 143 runs | •194 | 289 | 145 | 195 | | |
| Manchester-Australia 3 runs | •299 | 86 | 262 | 120 | | |
| The Oval-England 1 wkt | •324 | 121 | 183 | 9-263 | | |

| **AUSTRALIA v ENGLAND** (cont.) | Australia | | England | | Captains | |
|---|---|---|---|---|---|---|
| Venue and Result | 1st | 2nd | 1st | 2nd | Australia | England |
| **1903-04 in AUSTRALIA** | | | | | | |
| Sydney-England 5 wkts | •285 | 485 | 577 | 5-194 | M.A.Noble | P.F.Warner |
| Melbourne-England 185 runs | 122 | 111 | •315 | 103 | | |
| Adelaide-Australia 216 runs | •388 | 351 | 245 | 278 | | |
| Sydney-England 157 runs | 131 | 171 | •249 | 210 | | |
| Melbourne-Australia 218 runs | •247 | 133 | 61 | 101 | | |
| **1905 in ENGLAND** | | | | | | |
| Nottingham-England 213 runs | 221 | 188 | •196 | 5d-426 | J.Darling | Hon.F.S.Jackson |
| Lord's-Drawn | 181 | - | •282 | 5-151 | | |
| Leeds-Drawn | 195 | 7-224 | •301 | 5d-295 | | |
| Manchester-England inns & 80 runs | 197 | 169 | •446 | - | | |
| The Oval-Drawn | 363 | 4-124 | •430 | 6d-261 | | |
| **1907-08 in AUSTRALIA** | | | | | | |
| Sydney-Australia 2 wkts | 300 | 8-275 | •273 | 300 | M.A.Noble | F.L.Fane |
| Melbourne-England 1 wkt | •266 | 397 | 382 | 9-282 | | F.L.Fane |
| Adelaide-Australia 245 runs | •285 | 506 | 363 | 183 | | F.L.Fane |
| Melbourne-Australia 308 runs | •214 | 385 | 105 | 186 | | A.O.Jones |
| Sydney-Australia 49 runs | •137 | 422 | 281 | 229 | | A.O.Jones |
| **1909 in ENGLAND** | | | | | | |
| Birmingham-England 10 wkts | •74 | 151 | 121 | 0-105 | M.A.Noble | A.C.MacLaren |
| Lord's-Australia 9 wkts | 350 | 1-41 | •269 | 121 | | |
| Leeds-Australia 126 runs | •188 | 207 | 182 | 87 | | |
| Manchester-Drawn | •147 | 9d-279 | 119 | 3-108 | | |
| The Oval-Drawn | •325 | 5d-339 | 352 | 3-104 | | |
| **1911-12 in AUSTRALIA** | | | | | | |
| Sydney-Australia 146 runs | •447 | 308 | 318 | 291 | C.Hill | J.W.H.T.Douglas |
| Melbourne-England 8 wkts | •184 | 299 | 265 | 2-219 | | |
| Adelaide-England 7 wkts | •133 | 476 | 501 | 3-112 | | |
| Melbourne-England inns & 225 runs | •191 | 173 | 589 | - | | |
| Sydney-England 70 runs | 176 | 292 | •324 | 214 | | |
| **1912 in ENGLAND** | | | | | | |
| Lord's-Drawn | 7-282 | - | •7d-310 | - | S.E.Gregory | C.B.Fry |
| Manchester-Drawn | 0-14 | - | •203 | - | | |
| The Oval-England 244 runs | 111 | 65 | •245 | 175 | | |
| **1920-21 in AUSTRALIA** | | | | | | |
| Sydney-Australia 377 runs | •267 | 581 | 190 | 281 | W.W.Armstrong | J.W.H.T.Douglas |
| Melbourne-Australia inns & 91 runs | •499 | - | 251 | 157 | | |
| Adelaide-Australia 119 runs | •354 | 582 | 447 | 370 | | |
| Melbourne-Australia 8 wkts | 389 | 2-211 | •284 | 315 | | |
| Sydney-Australia 9 wkts | 392 | 1-93 | •204 | 280 | | |
| **1921 in ENGLAND** | | | | | | |
| Nottingham-Australia 10 wkts | 232 | 0-30 | •112 | 147 | W.W.Armstrong | J.W.H.T.Douglas |
| Lord's-Australia 8 wkts | 342 | 2-131 | •187 | 283 | | J.W.H.T Douglas |
| Leeds-Australia 219 runs | •407 | 7d-273 | 259 | 202 | | Hon.L.H.Tennyson |
| Manchester-Drawn | 175 | - | •4d-362 | 1-44 | | Hon.L.H.Tennyson |
| The Oval-Drawn | 389 | - | •8d-403 | 2-244 | | Hon.L.H.Tennyson |

| **AUSTRALIA v ENGLAND** (cont.) | Australia | | England | | Captains | |
|---|---|---|---|---|---|---|
| Venue and Result | 1st | 2nd | 1st | 2nd | Australia | England |
| **1924-25 in AUSTRALIA** | | | | | | |
| Sydney-Australia 193 runs | •450 | 452 | 298 | 411 | H.L.Collins | A.E.R.Gilligan |
| Melbourne-Australia 81 runs | •600 | 250 | 479 | 290 | | |
| Adelaide-Australia 11 runs | •489 | 250 | 365 | 363 | | |
| Melbourne-England inns & 29 runs | 269 | 250 | •548 | - | | |
| Sydney-Australia 307 runs | •295 | 325 | 167 | 146 | | |
| **1926 in ENGLAND** | | | | | | |
| Nottingham-Drawn | - | - | •0-32 | - | H.L.Collins | A.W.Carr |
| Lord's-Drawn | •383 | 5-194 | 3d-475 | - | H.L.Collins | A.W.Carr |
| Leeds-Drawn | •494 | - | 294 | 3-254 | W.Bardsley | A.W.Carr |
| Manchester-Drawn | •335 | - | 5-305 | - | W.Bardsley | A.W.Carr |
| The Oval-England 289 runs | 302 | 125 | •280 | 436 | H.L.Collins | A.P.F.Chapman |
| **1928-29 in AUSTRALIA** | | | | | | |
| Brisbane[1]-England 675 runs | 122 | 66 | •521 | 8d-342 | J.Ryder | A.P.F.Chapman |
| Sydney-England 8 wkts | •253 | 397 | 636 | 2-16 | | A.P.F.Chapman |
| Melbourne-England 3 wkts | •397 | 351 | 417 | 7-332 | | A.P.F.Chapman |
| Adelaide-England 12 runs | 369 | 336 | •334 | 383 | | A.P.F.Chapman |
| Melbourne-Australia 5 wkts | 491 | 5-287 | •519 | 257 | | J.C.White |
| **1930 in ENGLAND** | | | | | | |
| Nottingham-England 93 runs | 144 | 335 | •270 | 302 | W.M.Woodfull | A.P.F.Chapman |
| Lord's-Australia 7 wkts | 6d-729 | 3-72 | •425 | 375 | | A.P.F.Chapman |
| Leeds-Drawn | •566 | - | 391 | 3-95 | | A.P.F.Chapman |
| Manchester-Drawn | •345 | - | 8-251 | - | | A.P.F.Chapman |
| The Oval-Australia inns & 39 runs | 695 | - | •405 | 251 | | R.E.S.Wyatt |
| **1932-33 in AUSTRALIA** | | | | | | |
| Sydney-England 10 wkts | •360 | 164 | 524 | 0-1 | W.M.Woodfull | D.R.Jardine |
| Melbourne-Australia 111 runs | •228 | 191 | 169 | 139 | | |
| Adelaide-England 338 runs | 222 | 193 | •341 | 412 | | |
| Brisbane[2]-England 6 wkts | •340 | 175 | 356 | 4-162 | | |
| Sydney-England 8 wkts | •435 | 182 | 454 | 2-168 | | |
| **1934 in ENGLAND** | | | | | | |
| Nottingham-Australia 238 runs | •374 | 8d-273 | 268 | 141 | W.M.Woodfull | C.F.Walters |
| Lord's-England inns & 38 runs | 284 | 118 | •440 | - | | R.E.S.Wyatt |
| Manchester-Drawn | 491 | 1-66 | •9d-627 | 0d-123 | | R.E.S.Wyatt |
| Leeds-Drawn | 584 | - | •200 | 6-229 | | R.E.S.Wyatt |
| The Oval-Australia 562 runs | •701 | 327 | 321 | 145 | | R.E.S.Wyatt |
| **1936-37 in AUSTRALIA** | | | | | | |
| Brisbane[2]-England 322 runs | 234 | 58 | •358 | 256 | D.G.Bradman | G.O.B.Allen |
| Sydney-England inns & 22 runs | 80 | 324 | •6d-426 | - | | |
| Melbourne-Australia 365 runs | •9d-200 | 564 | 9d-76 | 323 | | |
| Adelaide-Australia 148 runs | •288 | 433 | 330 | 243 | | |
| Melbourne-Australia inns & 200 runs | •604 | - | 239 | 165 | | |
| **1938 in ENGLAND** | | | | | | |
| Nottingham-Drawn | 411 | 6-427 | •8d-658 | - | D.G.Bradman | W.R.Hammond |
| Lord's-Drawn | 422 | 6-204 | •494 | 8d-242 | | |
| Manchester-Abandoned | - | - | - | - | | |
| Leeds-Australia 5 wkts | 242 | 5-107 | •223 | 123 | | |
| The Oval-England inns & 579 runs | 201 | 123 | •7d-903 | - | | |

| **AUSTRALIA v ENGLAND** (cont.) | Australia | | England | | Captains | |
|---|---|---|---|---|---|---|
| Venue and Result | 1st | 2nd | 1st | 2nd | Australia | England |
| **1946-47 in AUSTRALIA** | | | | | | |
| Brisbane[2]-Australia inns & 332 runs | •645 | - | 141 | 172 | D.G.Bradman | W.R.Hammond |
| Sydney-Australia inns & 33 runs | 8d-659 | - | •255 | 371 | | W.R.Hammond |
| Melbourne-Drawn | •365 | 536 | 351 | 7-310 | | W.R.Hammond |
| Adelaide-Drawn | 487 | 1-215 | •460 | 8d-340 | | W.R.Hammond |
| Sydney-Australia 5 wkts | 253 | 5-214 | •280 | 186 | | N.W.D.Yardley |
| **1948 in ENGLAND** | | | | | | |
| Nottingham-Australia 8 wkts | 509 | 2-98 | •165 | 441 | D.G.Bradman | N.W.D.Yardley |
| Lord's-Australia 409 runs | •350 | 7d-460 | 215 | 186 | | |
| Manchester-Drawn | 221 | 1-92 | •363 | 3d-174 | | |
| Leeds-Australia 7 wkts | 458 | 3-404 | •496 | 8d-365 | | |
| The Oval-Australia inns & 149 runs | 389 | - | •52 | 188 | | |
| **1950-51 in AUSTRALIA** | | | | | | |
| Brisbane[2]-Australia 70 runs | •228 | 7d-32 | 7d-68 | 122 | A.L.Hassett | F.R.Brown |
| Melbourne-Australia 28 runs | •194 | 181 | 197 | 150 | | |
| Sydney-Australia inns &13 runs | 426 | - | •290 | 123 | | |
| Adelaide-Australia 274 runs | •371 | 8d-403 | 272 | 228 | | |
| Melbourne-England 8 wkts | •217 | 197 | 320 | 2-95 | | |
| **1953 in ENGLAND** | | | | | | |
| Nottingham-Drawn | •249 | 123 | 144 | 1-120 | A.L.Hassett | L.Hutton |
| Lord's-Drawn | •346 | 368 | 372 | 7-282 | | |
| Manchester-Drawn | •318 | 8-35 | 276 | - | | |
| Leeds-Drawn | 266 | 4-147 | •167 | 275 | | |
| The Oval-England 8 wkts | •275 | 162 | 306 | 2-132 | | |
| **1954-55 in AUSTRALIA** | | | | | | |
| Brisbane[2]-Australia inns & 154 runs | •8d-601 | - | 190 | 257 | I.W.Johnson | L.Hutton |
| Sydney-England 38 runs | 228 | 184 | •154 | 296 | A.R.Morris | |
| Melbourne-England 128 runs | 231 | 111 | •191 | 279 | I.W.Johnson | |
| Adelaide-England 5 wkts | •323 | 111 | 341 | 5-97 | I.W.Johnson | |
| Sydney-Drawn | 221 | 6-118 | •7d-371 | - | I.W.Johnson | |
| **1956 In ENGLAND** | | | | | | |
| Nottingham-Drawn | 148 | 3-120 | •8d-217 | 3d-188 | I.W.Johnson | P.B.H.May |
| Lord's-Australia 185 runs | •285 | 257 | 171 | 186 | | |
| Leeds-England inns & 42 runs | 143 | 140 | •325 | - | | |
| Manchester-England inns & 170 runs | 84 | 205 | •459 | - | | |
| The Oval-Drawn | 202 | 5-27 | •247 | 3d-182 | | |
| **1958-59 In AUSTRALIA** | | | | | | |
| Brisbane[2]-Australia 8 wkts | 186 | 2-147 | •134 | 198 | R.Benaud | P.B.H.May |
| Melbourne-Australia 8 wkts | 308 | 2-42 | •259 | 87 | | |
| Sydney-Drawn | 357 | 2-54 | •219 | 7d-287 | | |
| Adelaide-Australia 10 wkts | •476 | 0-36 | 240 | 270 | | |
| Melbourne-Australia 9 wkts | 351 | 1-69 | •205 | 214 | | |
| **1961 In ENGLAND** | | | | | | |
| Birmingham-Drawn | 9d-516 | - | •195 | 4-401 | R.Benaud | M.C.Cowdrey |
| Lord's-Australia 5 wkts | 340 | 5-71 | •206 | 202 | R.N.Harvey | M.C.Cowdrey |
| Leeds-England 8 wkts | •237 | 120 | 299 | 2-62 | R.Benaud | P.B.H.May |
| Manchester-Australia 54 runs | •190 | 432 | 367 | 201 | R.Benaud | P.B.H.May |
| The Oval-Drawn | 494 | - | •256 | 8-370 | R.Benaud | P.B.H.May |

| AUSTRALIA v ENGLAND (cont.) | Australia | | England | | Captains | |
|---|---|---|---|---|---|---|
| Venue and Result | 1st | 2nd | 1st | 2nd | Australia | England |
| **1962-63 in AUSTRALIA** | | | | | | |
| Brisbane[2]-Drawn | •404 | 4d-362 | 389 | 6-278 | R.Benaud | E.R.Dexter |
| Melbourne-England 7 wkts | •316 | 248 | 331 | 3-237 | | |
| Sydney-Australia 8 wkts | 319 | 2-67 | •279 | 104 | | |
| Adelaide-Drawn | •393 | 293 | 331 | 4-223 | | |
| Sydney-Drawn | 349 | 4-152 | •321 | 8d-268 | | |
| **1964 in ENGLAND** | | | | | | |
| Nottingham-Drawn | 168 | 2-40 | •8d-216 | 9d-193 | R.B.Simpson | E.R.Dexter |
| Lord's-Drawn | •176 | 4-168 | 246 | - | | |
| Leeds-Australia 7 wkts | 389 | 3-111 | •268 | 229 | | |
| Manchester-Drawn | •8d-656 | 0-4 | 611 | - | | |
| The Oval-Drawn | 379 | - | •182 | 4-381 | | |
| **1965-66 in AUSTRALIA** | | | | | | |
| Brisbane[2]-Drawn | •6d-443 | - | 280 | 3-186 | B.C.Booth | M.J K.Smith |
| Melbourne-Drawn | •358 | 426 | 558 | 0-5 | R.B.Simpson | |
| Sydney-England inns & 93 runs | 221 | 174 | •488 | - | B.C.Booth | |
| Adelaide-Australia inns & 9 runs | 516 | - | •241 | 266 | R.B.Simpson | |
| Melbourne-Drawn | 8d-543 | - | •9d-485 | 3-69 | R.B Simpson | |
| **1968 in ENGLAND** | | | | | | |
| Manchester-Australia 159 runs | •357 | 220 | 165 | 253 | W.M.Lawry | M.C.Cowdrey |
| Lord's-Drawn | 78 | 4-127 | •7d-351 | - | W.M.Lawry | M.C.Cowdrey |
| Birmingham-Drawn | 222 | 1-68 | •409 | 3d-142 | W.M.Lawry | M.C.Cowdrey |
| Leeds-Drawn | •315 | 312 | 302 | 4-230 | B.N.Jarman | T.W.Graveney |
| The Oval-England 226 runs | 324 | 125 | •494 | 181 | W.M.Lawry | M.C.Cowdrey |
| **1970-71 in AUSTRALIA** | | | | | | |
| Brisbane[2]-Drawn | •433 | 214 | 464 | 1-39 | W.M.Lawry | R.Illingworth |
| Perth-Drawn | 440 | 3-100 | •397 | 6d-287 | W.M.Lawry | |
| Melbourne-Abandoned | - | - | - | - | W.M.Lawry | |
| Sydney-England 299 runs | 236 | 116 | •332 | 5d-319 | W.M.Lawry | |
| Melbourne-Drawn | •9d-493 | 4d-169 | 392 | 0-161 | W.M.Lawry | |
| Adelaide-Drawn | 235 | 3-328 | •470 | 4d-233 | W.M.Lawry | |
| Sydney-England 62 runs | 264 | 160 | •184 | 302 | I.M.Chappell | |
| **1972 in ENGLAND** | | | | | | |
| Manchester-England 89 runs | 142 | 252 | •249 | 234 | I.M.Chappell | R.Illingworth |
| Lord's-Australia 8 wkts | 308 | 2-81 | •272 | 116 | | |
| Nottingham-Drawn | •315 | 4d-324 | 189 | 4-290 | | |
| Leeds-England 9 wkts | •146 | 136 | 263 | 1-21 | | |
| The Oval-Australia 5 wkts | 399 | 5-242 | •284 | 356 | | |
| **1974-75 in AUSTRALIA** | | | | | | |
| Brisbane[2]-Australia 166 runs | •309 | 5d-288 | 265 | 166 | I.M.Chappell | M.H.Denness |
| Perth-Australia 9 wkts | 481 | 1-23 | •208 | 293 | | M.H.Denness |
| Melbourne-Drawn | 241 | 8-238 | •242 | 244 | | M.H.Denness |
| Sydney-Australia 171 runs | •405 | 4d-289 | 295 | 228 | | J.H.Edrich |
| Adelaide-Australia 163 runs | 304 | 5d-272 | 172 | 241 | | M.H.Denness |
| Melbourne-England inns & 4 runs | •152 | 373 | 529 | - | | M.H.Denness |
| **1975 in ENGLAND** | | | | | | |
| Birmingham-Australia inns & 85 runs | •359 | - | 101 | 173 | I.M.Chappell | M.H.Denness |
| Lord's-Drawn | 268 | 3-329 | •315 | 7d-436 | | A.W.Greig |
| Leeds-Drawn | 135 | 3-220 | •288 | 291 | | A.W.Greig |
| The Oval-Drawn | •9d-532 | 2-40 | 191 | 538 | | A.W.Greig |

| **AUSTRALIA v ENGLAND** (cont.) | Australia | | England | | Captains | |
|---|---|---|---|---|---|---|
| Venue and Result | 1st | 2nd | 1st | 2nd | Australia | England |
| **1976-77 in AUSTRALIA (CENTENARY TEST)** | | | | | | |
| Melbourne-Australia 45 runs | •138 | 9d-419 | 95 | 417 | G.S.Chappell | A.W.Greig |
| **1977 in ENGLAND** | | | | | | |
| Lord's-Drawn | 296 | 6-114 | •216 | 305 | G.S.Chappell | J.M.Brearley |
| Manchester-England 9 wkts | •297 | 218 | 437 | 1-82 | | |
| Nottingham-England 7 wkts | •243 | 309 | 364 | 3-189 | | |
| Leeds-England inns & 85 runs | 103 | 248 | •436 | - | | |
| The Oval-Drawn | 385 | - | •214 | 2-57 | | |
| **1978-79 in AUSTRALIA** | | | | | | |
| Brisbane[2]-England 7 wkts | •116 | 339 | 286 | 3-170 | G.N.Yallop | J.M.Brearley |
| Perth-England 166 runs | 190 | 161 | •309 | 208 | | |
| Melbourne-Australia 103 runs | •258 | 167 | 143 | 179 | | |
| Sydney-England 93 runs | 294 | 111 | •152 | 346 | | |
| Adelaide-England 205 runs | 164 | 160 | •169 | 360 | | |
| Sydney-England 9 wkts | 198 | 143 | 308 | 1-35 | | |
| **1979-80 in AUSTRALIA** | | | | | | |
| Perth-Australia 138 runs | •244 | 337 | 228 | 215 | G.S.Chappell | J.M.Brearley |
| Sydney-Australia 6 wkts | 145 | 4-219 | •123 | 237 | | |
| Melbourne-Australia 8 wkts | 477 | 2-103 | •306 | 273 | | |
| **1980 in ENGLAND (CENTENARY TEST)** | | | | | | |
| Lord's-Drawn | •5d-385 | 4d-189 | 205 | 3-244 | G.S.Chappell | I.T.Botham |
| **1981 in ENGLAND** | | | | | | |
| Nottingham-Australia 4 wkts | 179 | 6-132 | •185 | 125 | K.J.Hughes | I.T.Botham |
| Lord's-Drawn | 345 | 4-90 | •311 | 8-265 | | I.T.Botham |
| Leeds-England 18 runs | •9-401 | 111 | 174 | 356 | | J.M.Brearley |
| Birmingham-England 29 runs | 258 | 121 | •189 | 219 | | J.M.Brearley |
| Manchester-England 103 runs | 130 | 402 | •231 | 404 | | J.M.Brearley |
| The Oval-Drawn | •352 | 9d-344 | 314 | 7-261 | | J.M.Brearley |
| **1982-83 in AUSTRALIA** | | | | | | |
| Perth-Drawn | 9d-424 | 2-73 | •411 | 358 | K.J.Hughes | R.G.D.Willis |
| Brisbane[2]-Australia 7 wkts | 341 | 3-190 | •219 | 309 | | |
| Adelaide-Australia 8 wkts | •438 | 2-83 | 216 | 304 | | |
| Melbourne-England 3 runs | 287 | 288 | •284 | 294 | | |
| Sydney-Drawn | •314 | 382 | 237 | 7-314 | | |
| **1985 in ENGLAND** | | | | | | |
| Leeds-England 5 wkts | •331 | 324 | 533 | 5-123 | A.R.Border | D.I.Gower |
| Lord's-Australia 4 wkts | 425 | 6-127 | •290 | 261 | | |
| Nottingham-Drawn | 539 | - | •456 | 2-196 | | |
| Manchester-Drawn | •257 | 5-340 | 9d-482 | - | | |
| Birmingham-England inns & 118 runs | •335 | 142 | 5d-595 | - | | |
| The Oval-England inns & 94 runs | 241 | 129 | •464 | - | | |
| **1986-87 in AUSTRALIA** | | | | | | |
| Brisbane[2]-England 7 wkts | 248 | 282 | •456 | 3-77 | A.R.Border | M.W.Gatting |
| Perth-Drawn | 401 | 4-197 | •8d-592 | 8d-199 | | |
| Adelaide-Drawn | •5d-514 | 3d-201 | 455 | 2-39 | | |
| Melbourne-England inns & 14 runs | •141 | 194 | 349 | - | | |
| Sydney-Australia 55 runs | •343 | 251 | 275 | 264 | | |

| **AUSTRALIA v ENGLAND** (cont.) | Australia | | England | | Captains | |
|---|---|---|---|---|---|---|
| Venue and Result | 1st | 2nd | 1st | 2nd | Australia | England |
| **1987-88 in AUSTRALIA (BICENTENNIAL TEST)** | | | | | | |
| Sydney-Drawn | 214 | 2-328 | •425 | - | A.R.Border | M.W.Gatting |
| **1989 in ENGLAND** | | | | | | |
| Leeds-Australia 210 runs | •7d-601 | 3d-230 | 430 | 191 | A.R.Border | D.I.Gower |
| Lord's-Australia 6 wkts | 528 | 4-119 | •286 | 359 | | |
| Birmingham-Drawn | •424 | 2-158 | 242 | - | | |
| Manchester-Australia 9 wkts | 447 | 1-81 | •260 | 264 | | |
| Nottingham-Australia inns & 180 runs | •6d-602 | - | 255 | 167 | | |
| The Oval-Drawn | •468 | 4d-219 | 285 | 5-143 | | |
| **1990-91 in AUSTRALIA** | | | | | | |
| Brisbane[2]-Australia 10 wkts | 152 | 0-157 | •194 | 114 | A.R.Border | A.J.Lamb |
| Melbourne-Australia 8 wkts | 306 | 2-197 | •352 | 150 | | G.A.Gooch |
| Sydney-Drawn | •518 | 205 | 8d-469 | 4-113 | | G.A.Gooch |
| Adelaide-Drawn | •386 | 6d-314 | 229 | 5-335 | | G.A.Gooch |
| Perth-Australia 9 wkts | 307 | 1-120 | •244 | 182 | | G.A.Gooch |
| **1993 in ENGLAND** | | | | | | |
| Manchester-Australia 179 runs | •289 | 5d-432 | 210 | 332 | A.R.Border | G.A.Gooch |
| Lord's-Australia inns & 62 runs | •4d-632 | - | 205 | 365 | | G.A.Gooch |
| Nottingham-Drawn | 373 | 6-202 | •321 | 422 | | G.A.Gooch |
| Leeds-Australia inns & 148 runs | •4d-653 | - | 200 | 305 | | G.A.Gooch |
| Birmingham-Australia 8 wkts | 408 | 2-120 | •276 | 251 | | M.A.Atherton |
| The Oval-England 161 runs | 303 | 229 | •380 | 313 | | M.A.Atherton |
| **1994-95 in AUSTRALIA** | | | | | | |
| Brisbane[2]-Australia 184 runs | •426 | 8d-248 | 167 | 323 | M.A.Taylor | M.A.Atherton |
| Melbourne-Australia 295 runs | •279 | 7d-320 | 212 | 92 | | |
| Sydney-Drawn | 116 | 7-344 | •309 | 2d-255 | | |
| Adelaide-England 106 runs | 419 | 156 | •353 | 328 | | |
| Perth-Australia 329 runs | •402 | 8d-345 | 295 | 123 | | |
| **1997 in ENGLAND** | | | | | | |
| Manchester-England 9 wkts | •118 | 477 | 9d-478 | 1-119 | M.A.Taylor | M.A.Atherton |
| Lord's-drawn | 7d-213 | - | •77 | 4d-266 | | |
| Nottingham-Australia 268 runs | •235 | 8d-395 | 162 | 200 | | |
| Leeds-Australia inns & 61 runs | 9d-501 | - | •172 | 268 | | |
| Birmingham-Australia 264 runs | •427 | 336 | 313 | 186 | | |
| The Oval-England 19 runs | 220 | 104 | •180 | 163 | | |

## Test Match Results Summary

**AUSTRALIA v ENGLAND-IN AUSTRALIA**

| | | Result | | | Melbourne | | | Sydney | | | Adelaide | | | Brisbane[1] | | | Brisbane[2] | | | Perth | | |
|---|---|---|---|---|---|---|---|---|---|---|---|---|---|---|---|---|---|---|---|---|---|---|
| | Tests | A | E | D | A | E | D | A | E | D | A | E | D | A | E | D | A | E | D | A | E | D |
| 1876-77 | 2 | 1 | 1 | - | 1 | 1 | - | - | - | - | - | - | - | - | - | - | - | - | - | - | - | - |
| 1878-79 | 1 | 1 | - | - | 1 | - | - | - | - | - | - | - | - | - | - | - | - | - | - | - | - | - |
| 1881-82 | 4 | 2 | - | 2 | - | - | 2 | 2 | - | - | - | - | - | - | - | - | - | - | - | - | - | - |
| 1882-83 | 4 | 2 | 2 | - | 1 | 1 | - | 1 | 1 | - | - | - | - | - | - | - | - | - | - | - | - | - |
| 1884-85 | 5 | 2 | 3 | - | - | 2 | - | 2 | - | - | - | 1 | - | - | - | - | - | - | - | - | - | - |
| 1886-87 | 2 | - | 2 | - | - | - | - | - | 2 | - | - | - | - | - | - | - | - | - | - | - | - | - |
| 1887-88 | 1 | - | 1 | - | - | - | - | - | 1 | - | - | - | - | - | - | - | - | - | - | - | - | - |
| 1891-92 | 3 | 2 | 1 | - | 1 | - | - | 1 | - | - | - | 1 | - | - | - | - | - | - | - | - | - | - |
| 1894-95 | 5 | 2 | 3 | - | - | 2 | - | 1 | 1 | - | 1 | - | - | - | - | - | - | - | - | - | - | - |
| 1897-98 | 5 | 4 | 1 | - | 2 | - | - | 1 | 1 | - | 1 | - | - | - | - | - | - | - | - | - | - | - |
| 1901-02 | 5 | 4 | 1 | - | 2 | - | - | 1 | 1 | - | 1 | - | - | - | - | - | - | - | - | - | - | - |
| 1903-04 | 5 | 2 | 3 | - | 1 | 1 | - | - | 2 | - | 1 | - | - | - | - | - | - | - | - | - | - | - |
| 1907-08 | 5 | 4 | 1 | - | 1 | 1 | - | 2 | - | - | 1 | - | - | - | - | - | - | - | - | - | - | - |
| 1911-12 | 5 | 1 | 4 | - | - | 2 | - | 1 | 1 | - | - | 1 | - | - | - | - | - | - | - | - | - | - |
| 1920-21 | 5 | 5 | - | - | 2 | - | - | 2 | - | - | 1 | - | - | - | - | - | - | - | - | - | - | - |
| 1924-25 | 5 | 4 | 1 | - | 1 | 1 | - | 2 | - | - | 1 | - | - | - | - | - | - | - | - | - | - | - |
| 1928-29 | 5 | 1 | 4 | - | 1 | 1 | - | - | 1 | - | - | 1 | - | - | 1 | - | - | - | - | - | - | - |
| 1932-33 | 5 | 1 | 4 | - | 1 | - | - | - | 2 | - | - | 1 | - | - | - | - | - | 1 | - | - | - | - |
| 1936-37 | 5 | 3 | 2 | - | 2 | - | - | - | 1 | - | 1 | - | - | - | - | - | - | 1 | - | - | - | - |
| 1946-47 | 5 | 3 | - | 2 | - | - | 1 | 2 | - | - | - | - | 1 | - | - | - | 1 | - | - | - | - | - |
| 1950-51 | 5 | 4 | 1 | - | 1 | 1 | - | 1 | - | - | 1 | - | - | - | - | - | 1 | - | - | - | - | - |
| 1954-55 | 5 | 1 | 3 | 1 | - | 1 | - | - | 1 | 1 | - | 1 | - | - | - | - | 1 | - | - | - | - | - |
| 1958-59 | 5 | 4 | - | 1 | 2 | - | - | - | - | 1 | 1 | - | - | - | - | - | 1 | - | - | - | - | - |
| 1962-63 | 5 | 1 | 1 | 3 | - | 1 | - | 1 | - | 1 | - | - | 1 | - | - | - | - | - | 1 | - | - | - |
| 1965-66 | 5 | 1 | 1 | 3 | - | - | 2 | - | 1 | - | 1 | - | - | - | - | - | - | - | 1 | - | - | - |
| 1970-71 | 6 | - | 2 | 4 | - | - | 1 | - | 2 | - | - | - | 1 | - | - | - | - | - | 1 | - | - | 1 |
| 1974-75 | 6 | 4 | 1 | 1 | - | 1 | 1 | 1 | - | - | 1 | - | - | - | - | - | 1 | - | - | 1 | - | - |
| 1976-77 | 1 | 1 | - | - | 1 | - | - | - | - | - | - | - | - | - | - | - | - | - | - | - | - | - |
| 1978-79 | 6 | 1 | 5 | - | 1 | - | - | - | 2 | - | - | 1 | - | - | - | - | - | 1 | - | - | 1 | - |
| 1979-80 | 3 | 3 | - | - | 1 | - | - | 1 | - | - | - | - | - | - | - | - | - | - | - | 1 | - | - |
| 1982-83 | 5 | 2 | 1 | 2 | - | 1 | - | - | - | 1 | 1 | - | - | - | - | - | 1 | - | - | - | - | 1 |
| 1986-87 | 5 | 1 | 2 | 2 | - | 1 | - | 1 | - | - | - | - | 1 | - | - | - | - | 1 | - | - | - | 1 |
| 1987-88 | 1 | - | - | 1 | - | - | - | - | - | 1 | - | - | - | - | - | - | - | - | - | - | - | - |
| 1990-91 | 5 | 3 | - | 2 | 1 | - | - | - | - | 1 | - | - | 1 | - | - | - | 1 | - | - | 1 | - | - |
| 1994-95 | 5 | 3 | 1 | - | 1 | - | - | - | - | 1 | - | 1 | - | - | - | - | 1 | - | - | 1 | - | - |
| | 150 | 73 | 52 | 25 | 25 | 18 | 7 | 23 | 20 | 7 | 13 | 8 | 5 | - | 1 | - | 8 | 4 | 3 | 4 | 1 | 3 |

**AUSTRALIA v ENGLAND-IN ENGLAND**

| | | Result | | | The Oval | | | Manch. | | | Lord's | | | Notting. | | | Leeds | | | Birming. | | | Sheffield | | |
|---|---|---|---|---|---|---|---|---|---|---|---|---|---|---|---|---|---|---|---|---|---|---|---|---|---|---|---|---|
| | Tests | A | E | D | A | E | D | A | E | D | A | E | D | A | E | D | A | E | D | A | E | D | A | E | D |
| 1880 | 1 | - | 1 | - | - | 1 | - | - | - | - | - | - | - | - | - | - | - | - | - | - | - | - | - | - | - |
| 1882 | 1 | 1 | - | - | 1 | - | - | - | - | - | - | - | - | - | - | - | - | - | - | - | - | - | - | - | - |
| 1884 | 3 | - | 1 | 2 | - | - | 1 | - | - | 1 | - | 1 | - | - | - | - | - | - | - | - | - | - | - | - | - |
| 1886 | 3 | - | 3 | - | - | 1 | - | - | 1 | - | - | 1 | - | - | - | - | - | - | - | - | - | - | - | - | - |
| 1888 | 3 | 1 | 2 | - | - | 1 | - | - | 1 | - | 1 | - | - | - | - | - | - | - | - | - | - | - | - | - | - |
| 1890 | 2 | - | 2 | - | - | 1 | - | - | - | - | - | 1 | - | - | - | - | - | - | - | - | - | - | - | - | - |
| 1893 | 3 | - | 1 | 2 | - | 1 | - | - | - | 1 | - | - | 1 | - | - | - | - | - | - | - | - | - | - | - | - |
| 1896 | 3 | 1 | 2 | - | - | 1 | - | 1 | - | - | - | 1 | - | - | - | - | - | - | - | - | - | - | - | - | - |
| 1899 | 5 | 1 | - | 4 | - | - | 1 | - | - | 1 | 1 | - | - | - | - | 1 | - | - | 1 | - | - | - | - | - | - |
| 1902 | 5 | 2 | 1 | 2 | - | 1 | - | 1 | - | - | - | - | 1 | - | - | - | - | - | - | - | - | 1 | 1 | - | - |
| 1905 | 5 | - | 2 | 3 | - | - | 1 | - | 1 | - | - | - | 1 | - | 1 | - | - | - | 1 | - | - | - | - | - | - |
| 1909 | 5 | 2 | 1 | 2 | - | - | 1 | - | - | 1 | 1 | - | - | - | - | - | 1 | - | - | - | 1 | - | - | - | - |
| 1912 | 3 | - | 1 | 2 | - | 1 | - | - | - | 1 | - | - | 1 | - | - | - | - | - | - | - | - | - | - | - | - |
| 1921 | 5 | 3 | - | 2 | - | - | 1 | - | - | 1 | 1 | - | - | 1 | - | - | 1 | - | - | - | - | - | - | - | - |
| 1926 | 5 | - | 1 | 4 | - | 1 | - | - | - | 1 | - | - | 1 | - | - | 1 | - | - | 1 | - | - | - | - | - | - |
| 1930 | 5 | 2 | 1 | 2 | 1 | - | - | - | - | 1 | 1 | - | - | - | 1 | - | - | - | 1 | - | - | - | - | - | - |
| 1934 | 5 | 2 | 1 | 2 | 1 | - | - | - | - | 1 | - | 1 | - | 1 | - | - | - | - | 1 | - | - | - | - | - | - |
| 1938 | 4 | 1 | 1 | 2 | - | 1 | - | - | - | - | - | - | 1 | - | - | 1 | 1 | - | - | - | - | - | - | - | - |
| 1948 | 5 | 4 | - | 1 | 1 | - | - | - | - | 1 | 1 | - | - | 1 | - | - | 1 | - | - | - | - | - | - | - | - |
| 1953 | 5 | - | 1 | 4 | - | 1 | - | - | - | 1 | - | - | 1 | - | - | 1 | - | - | 1 | - | - | - | - | - | - |
| 1956 | 5 | 1 | 2 | 2 | - | - | 1 | - | 1 | - | 1 | - | - | - | - | 1 | - | 1 | - | - | - | - | - | - | - |
| 1961 | 5 | 2 | 1 | 2 | - | - | 1 | 1 | - | - | 1 | - | - | - | - | - | - | 1 | - | - | - | 1 | - | - | - |
| 1964 | 5 | 1 | - | 4 | - | - | 1 | - | - | 1 | - | - | 1 | - | - | 1 | 1 | - | - | - | - | - | - | - | - |
| 1968 | 5 | 1 | 1 | 3 | - | 1 | - | 1 | - | - | - | - | 1 | - | - | - | - | - | 1 | - | - | 1 | - | - | - |
| 1972 | 5 | 2 | 2 | 1 | 1 | - | - | - | 1 | - | 1 | - | - | - | - | 1 | - | 1 | - | - | - | - | - | - | - |
| 1975 | 4 | 1 | - | 3 | - | - | 1 | - | - | - | - | - | 1 | - | - | - | - | - | 1 | 1 | - | - | - | - | - |
| 1977 | 5 | - | 3 | 2 | - | - | 1 | - | 1 | - | - | - | 1 | - | 1 | - | - | 1 | - | - | - | - | - | - | - |
| 1980 | 1 | - | - | 1 | - | - | - | - | - | - | - | - | 1 | - | - | - | - | - | - | - | - | - | - | - | - |
| 1981 | 6 | 1 | 3 | 2 | - | - | 1 | - | 1 | - | - | - | 1 | 1 | - | - | - | 1 | - | - | 1 | - | - | - | - |
| 1985 | 6 | 1 | 3 | 2 | - | 1 | - | - | - | 1 | 1 | - | - | - | - | 1 | - | 1 | - | - | 1 | - | - | - | - |
| 1989 | 6 | 4 | - | 2 | - | - | 1 | 1 | - | - | 1 | - | - | 1 | - | - | 1 | - | - | - | - | 1 | - | - | - |
| 1993 | 6 | 4 | 1 | 1 | - | 1 | - | 1 | - | - | 1 | - | - | - | - | 1 | 1 | - | - | 1 | - | - | - | - | - |
| 1997 | 6 | 3 | 2 | 1 | - | 1 | - | 1 | - | - | - | - | 1 | 1 | - | - | 1 | - | - | - | 1 | - | - | - | - |
| | 141 | 41 | 40 | 60 | 5 | 15 | 12 | 7 | 7 | 13 | 12 | 5 | 14 | 6 | 3 | 9 | 8 | 6 | 8 | 2 | 4 | 4 | 1 | - | - |
| Totals | 291 | 114 | 92 | 85 | | | | | | | | | | | | | | | | | | | | | |

*Key to ground abbreviations: Manch. - Manchester; Notting. - Nottingham; Birming. - Birmingham.*

*The matches abandoned without a ball being bowled at Manchester in 1890 and 1938 and at Melbourne in 1970-71 are excluded from these tables.*

**HIGHEST INNINGS TOTALS**

| | | | |
|---|---|---|---|
| Australia in England | 6d-729 | Lord's | 1930 |
| Australia in Australia | 8d-659 | Sydney | 1946-47 |
| England in England | 7d-903 | The Oval | 1938 |
| England in Australia | 636 | Sydney | 1928-29 |

**LOWEST INNINGS TOTALS**

| | | | |
|---|---|---|---|
| Australia in England | 36 | Birmingham | 1902 |
| Australia in Australia | 42 | Sydney | 1887-88 |
| England in England | 52 | The Oval | 1948 |
| England in Australia | 45 | Sydney | 1886-87 |

| | | | |
|---|---|---|---|
| **HIGHEST MATCH AGGREGATE** | 1753 for 40 wickets | Adelaide | 1920-21 |
| **LOWEST MATCH AGGREGATE** | 291 for 40 wickets | Lord's | 1888 |

**HIGHEST INDIVIDUAL INNINGS**

| | | | | |
|---|---|---|---|---|
| Australia in England | 334 | D.G.Bradman | Leeds | 1930 |
| Australia in Australia | 307 | R.M.Cowper | Melbourne | 1965-66 |
| England in England | 364 | L.Hutton | The Oval | 1938 |
| England in Australia | 287 | R.E.Foster | Sydney | 1903-04 |

**HIGHEST AGGREGATE OF RUNS IN A SERIES**

| | | | |
|---|---|---|---|
| Australia in England | 974 (av 139.14) | D.G.Bradman | 1930 |
| Australia in Australia | 810 (av 90.00) | D.G.Bradman | 1936-37 |
| England in England | 732 (av 81.33) | D.I.Gower | 1985 |
| England in Australia | 905 (av 113.12) | W.R.Hammond | 1928-29 |

**RECORD WICKET PARTNERSHIPS-AUSTRALIA**

| | | | | |
|---|---|---|---|---|
| 1st | 329 | G.R.Marsh (138), M.A.Taylor(219) | Nottingham | 1989 |
| 2nd | 451 | W.H.Ponsford (266), D.G.Bradman (244) | The Oval | 1934 |
| 3rd | 276 | D.G.Bradman (187), A.L.Hassett (128) | Brisbane[2] | 1946-47 |
| 4th | 388 | W H.Ponsford (181), D.G.Bradman (304) | Leeds | 1934 |
| 5th | 405 | S.G.Barnes (234), D.G.Bradman (234) | Sydney | 1946-47 |
| 6th | 346 | J.H.W Fingleton (136), D.G Bradman (270) | Melbourne | 1936-37 |
| 7th | 165 | C.Hill (188), H.Trumble (46) | Melbourne | 1897-98 |
| 8th | 243 | R.J.Hartigan (113), C.Hill (160) | Adelaide | 1907-08 |
| 9th | 154 | S.E.Gregory (201), J.M.Blackham (74) | Sydney | 1894-95 |
| 10th | 127 | J.M.Taylor (108), A.A.Mailey (46*) | Sydney | 1924-25 |

**RECORD WICKET PARTNERSHIPS-ENGLAND**

| | | | | |
|---|---|---|---|---|
| 1st | 323 | J.B.Hobbs (178), W.Rhodes (179) | Melbourne | 1911-12 |
| 2nd | 382 | L.Hutton (364), M.Leyland (187) | The Oval | 1938 |
| 3rd | 262 | W.R.Hammond (177), D.R.Jardine (98) | Adelaide | 1928-29 |
| 4th | 288 | N.Hussain (207), G.P.Thorpe (138) | Birmingham | 1997 |
| 5th | 206 | E.Paynter (216*), D.C.S.Compton (102) | Nottingham | 1938 |
| 6th | 215 | L.Hutton (364), J.Hardstaff, jr (169*) | The Oval | 1938 |
| | 215 | G.Boycott (107), A.P.E.Knott (135) | Nottingham | 1977 |
| 7th | 143 | F.E.Woolley (133*), J.Vine (36) | Sydney | 1911-12 |
| 8th | 124 | E.H.Hendren (169), H.Larwood (70) | Brisbane[1] | 1928-29 |
| 9th | 151 | W.H.Scotton (90), W.W.Read (117) | The Oval | 1884 |
| 10th | 130 | R.E.Foster (287), W.Rhodes (40*) | Sydney | 1903-04 |

**BEST INNINGS BOWLING ANALYSIS**

| | | | | |
|---|---|---|---|---|
| Australia in England | 8-31 | F.J.Laver | Manchester | 1909 |
| Australia in Australia | 9-121 | A.A.Mailey | Melbourne | 1920-21 |
| England in England | 10-53 | J.C.Laker | Manchester | 1956 |
| England in Australia | 8-35 | G.A.Lohmann | Sydney | 1886-87 |

**BEST MATCH BOWLING ANALYSIS**

| | | | | |
|---|---|---|---|---|
| Australia in England | 16-137 | R.A.L.Massie | Lord's | 1972 |
| Australia in Australia | 13-77 | M.A.Noble | Melbourne | 1901-02 |
| England in England | 19-90 | J.C.Laker | Manchester | 1956 |
| England in Australia | 15-124 | W.Rhodes | Melbourne | 1903-04 |

**HIGHEST AGGREGATE OF WICKETS IN A SERIES**

| | | | |
|---|---|---|---|
| Australia in England | 42 (av 21.26) | T.M.Alderman | 1981 |
| Australia in Australia | 41 (av 12.85) | R.M.Hogg | 1978-79 |
| England in England | 46 (av 9.60) | J.C.Laker | 1956 |
| England in Australia | 38 (av 23.18) | M.W.Tate | 1924-25 |

| AUSTRALIA v SOUTH AFRICA | Australia | | South Africa | | Captains | |
|---|---|---|---|---|---|---|
| Venue and Result | 1st | 2nd | 1st | 2nd | Australia | South Africa |
| **1902-03 in SOUTH AFRICA** | | | | | | |
| Johannesburg[1]-Drawn | 296 | 7d-372 | •454 | 4-101 | J.Darling | H.M.Taberer |
| Johannesburg[1]-Australia 159 runs | •175 | 309 | 240 | 85 | | J.H.Anderson |
| Cape Town-Australia 10 wkts | •252 | 0-59 | 85 | 225 | | E.A.Halliwell |
| **1910-11 in AUSTRALIA** | | | | | | |
| Sydney-Australia inns &114 runs | •528 | - | 174 | 240 | C.Hill | P.W.Sherwell |
| Melbourne-Australia 89 runs | •348 | 327 | 506 | 80 | | |
| Adelaide-South Africa 38 runs | 465 | 339 | •482 | 360 | | |
| Melbourne-Australia 530 runs | •328 | 578 | 205 | 171 | | |
| Sydney-Australia 7 wkts | •364 | 3-198 | 160 | 401 | | |
| **1912 in ENGLAND** | | | | | | |
| Manchester-Australia inns & 88 runs | •448 | - | 265 | 95 | S.E.Gregory | F.Mitchell |
| Lord's-Australia 10 wkts | 390 | 0-48 | •263 | 173 | | F.Mitchell |
| Nottingham-Drawn | 219 | - | •329 | - | | L.J.Tancred |
| **1921-22 in SOUTH AFRICA** | | | | | | |
| Durban[1]-Drawn | •299 | 7d-324 | 232 | 7-184 | H.L.Collins | H.W.Taylor |
| Johannesburg[1]-Drawn | •450 | 0-7 | 243 | 8d-472 | | |
| Cape Town-Australia 10 wkts | 396 | 0-1 | •180 | 216 | | |
| **1931-32 in AUSTRALIA** | | | | | | |
| Brisbane[2]-Australia inns & 163 runs | •450 | - | 170 | 117 | W.M.Woodfull | H.B.Cameron |
| Sydney-Australia inns & 155 runs | 469 | - | •153 | 161 | | |
| Melbourne-Australia 169 runs | •198 | 554 | 358 | 225 | | |
| Adelaide-Australia 10 wkts | 513 | 0-73 | •308 | 274 | | |
| Melbourne-Australia inns & 72 runs | 153 | - | •36 | 45 | | |
| **1935-36 in SOUTH AFRICA** | | | | | | |
| Durban[2]-Australia 9 wkts | 429 | 1-102 | •248 | 282 | V.Y.Richardson | H.F.Wade |
| Johannesburg[1]-Drawn | 250 | 2-274 | •157 | 491 | | |
| Cape Town-Australia inns & 78 runs | •8d-362 | - | 102 | 182 | | |
| Johannesburg[1]-Australia inns &184 runs | 439 | - | •157 | 98 | | |
| Durban[2]-Australia inns & 6 runs | 455 | - | •222 | 227 | | |
| **1949-50 in SOUTH AFRICA** | | | | | | |
| Johannesburg[2]-Australia inns & 85 runs | •413 | - | 137 | 191 | A.L.Hassett | A.D.Nourse |
| Cape Town-Australia 8 wkts | •7d-526 | 2-87 | 278 | 333 | | |
| Durban[2]-Australia 5 wkts | 75 | 5-336 | •311 | 99 | | |
| Johannesburg[2]-Drawn | •8d-465 | 2-259 | 352 | - | | |
| Port Elizabeth-Australia inns &259 runs | •7d-549 | - | 158 | 132 | | |
| **1952-53 in AUSTRALIA** | | | | | | |
| Brisbane[2]-Australia 96 runs | •280 | 277 | 221 | 240 | A.L.Hassett | J.E.Cheetham |
| Melbourne-South Africa 82 runs | 243 | 290 | •227 | 388 | | |
| Sydney-Australia inns & 38 runs | 443 | - | •173 | 232 | | |
| Adelaide-Drawn | •530 | 3d-233 | 387 | 6-177 | | |
| Melbourne-South Africa 6 wkts | •520 | 209 | 435 | 4-297 | | |
| **1957-58 in SOUTH AFRICA** | | | | | | |
| Johannesburg[3]-Drawn | 368 | 3-162 | •9d-470 | 201 | I.D.Craig | D.J.McGlew |
| Cape Town-Australia inns & 141 runs | •449 | - | 209 | 99 | | C.B.van Ryneveld |
| Durban[2]-Drawn | •163 | 7-292 | 384 | - | | C.B.van Ryneveld |
| Johannesburg[3]-Australia 10 wkts | •401 | 0-1 | 203 | 198 | | C.B.van Ryneveld |
| Port Elizabeth-Australia 8 wkts | 291 | 2-68 | •214 | 144 | | C.B.van Ryneveld |

| **AUSTRALIA v SOUTH AFRICA** (cont) | Australia | | South Africa | | Captains | |
|---|---|---|---|---|---|---|
| Venue and Result | 1st | 2nd | 1st | 2nd | Australia | South Africa |
| **1963-64 in AUSTRALIA** | | | | | | |
| Brisbane[2]-Drawn | •435 | 1d-144 | 346 | 1-13 | R.Benaud | T.L.Goddard |
| Melbourne-Australia 8 wkts | 447 | 2-136 | •274 | 306 | R.B.Simpson | |
| Sydney-Drawn | •260 | 9d-450 | 302 | 5-326 | R.B.Simpson | |
| Adelaide-South Africa 10 wkts | •345 | 331 | 595 | 0-82 | R.B.Simpson | |
| Sydney-Drawn | •311 | 270 | 411 | 0-76 | R.B.Simpson | |
| **1966-67 in SOUTH AFRICA** | | | | | | |
| Johannesburg[3]-South Africa 233 runs | 325 | 261 | •199 | 620 | R.B.Simpson | P.L.van der Merwe |
| Cape Town-Australia 6 wkts | •542 | 4-180 | 353 | 367 | | |
| Durban[2]-South Africa 8 wkts | 147 | 334 | •300 | 2-185 | | |
| Johannesburg[3]-Drawn | •143 | 8-148 | 9d-332 | - | | |
| Port Elizabeth-South Africa 7 wkts | •173 | 278 | 276 | 3-179 | | |
| **1969-70 in SOUTH AFRICA** | | | | | | |
| Cape Town-South Africa 170 runs | 164 | 280 | •382 | 232 | W.M.Lawry | A.Bacher |
| Durban[2]-South Africa inns &129 runs | 157 | 336 | •9d-622 | - | | |
| Johannesburg[3]-South Africa 307 runs | 202 | 178 | •279 | 408 | | |
| Port Elizabeth-South Africa 323 runs | 212 | 246 | •311 | 8d-470 | | |
| **1993-94 in AUSTRALIA** | | | | | | |
| Melbourne-Drawn | •7d-342 | - | 3-258 | - | A.R.Border | K.C.Wessels |
| Sydney-South Africa 5 runs | 292 | 111 | •169 | 239 | | K.C.Wessels |
| Adelaide-Australia 191 runs | •7d-469 | 6d-124 | 273 | 129 | | W.J.Cronje |
| **1993-94 in SOUTH AFRICA** | | | | | | |
| Johannesburg[3]-South Africa 197 runs | 248 | 256 | •251 | 9d-450 | A.R.Border | K.C.Wessels |
| Cape Town-Australia 9 wkts | 435 | 1-92 | •361 | 164 | | |
| Durban[2]-Drawn | •269 | 4-297 | 422 | - | | |
| **1996-97 in SOUTH AFRICA** | | | | | | |
| Johannesburg[3]-Australia inn & 196 runs | 8d-628 | - | •302 | 130 | M.A.Taylor | W.J.Cronje |
| Port Elizabeth-Australia 2 wkts | 108 | 8-271 | •209 | 168 | | |
| Centurion-South Africa 8 wkts | •227 | 185 | 384 | 2-32 | | |
| **1997-98 in AUSTRALIA** | | | | | | |
| Melbourne-Drawn | •309 | 257 | 186 | 7-273 | M.A.Taylor | W.J.Cronje |
| Sydney-Australia inn & 21 runs | 421 | - | •287 | 113 | | |
| Adelaide-Drawn | 350 | 7-227 | •517 | 6d-193 | | |

# Test Match Results Summary

### AUSTRALIA v SOUTH AFRICA-IN AUSTRALIA

| | | Result | | | Sydney | | | Melbourne | | | Adelaide | | | Brisbane[2] | | |
|---|---|---|---|---|---|---|---|---|---|---|---|---|---|---|---|---|
| | Tests | A | SA | D | A | SA | D | A | SA | D | A | SA | D | A | SA | D |
| 1910-11 | 5 | 4 | 1 | - | 2 | - | - | 2 | - | - | - | 1 | - | - | - | - |
| 1931-32 | 5 | 5 | - | - | 1 | - | - | 2 | - | - | 1 | - | - | 1 | - | - |
| 1952-53 | 5 | 2 | 2 | 1 | 1 | - | - | - | 2 | - | - | - | 1 | 1 | - | - |
| 1963-64 | 5 | 1 | 1 | 3 | - | - | 2 | 1 | - | - | - | 1 | - | - | - | 1 |
| 1993-94 | 3 | 1 | 1 | 1 | - | 1 | - | - | - | 1 | 1 | - | - | - | - | - |
| 1997-98 | 3 | 1 | - | 2 | 1 | - | - | - | - | 1 | - | - | 1 | - | - | - |
| | 26 | 14 | 5 | 7 | 5 | 1 | 2 | 5 | 2 | 2 | 2 | 2 | 2 | 2 | - | 1 |

### AUSTRALIA v SOUTH AFRICA-IN SOUTH AFRICA

| | | Result | | | Jo'burg[1] | | | C.Town | | | Durban[1] | | | Durban[2] | | | Jo'burg[2] | | | P.Elizabeth | | | Jo'burg[3] | | | Centurion | | |
|---|---|---|---|---|---|---|---|---|---|---|---|---|---|---|---|---|---|---|---|---|---|---|---|---|---|---|---|---|
| | Tests | A | S | D | A | S | D | A | S | D | A | S | D | A | S | D | A | S | D | A | S | D | A | S | D | A | S | D |
| 1902-03 | 3 | 2 | - | 1 | 1 | - | 1 | 1 | - | - | - | - | - | - | - | - | - | - | - | - | - | - | - | - | - | - | - | - |
| 1921-22 | 3 | 1 | - | 2 | - | - | 1 | 1 | - | - | - | - | 1 | - | - | - | - | - | - | - | - | - | - | - | - | - | - | - |
| 1935-36 | 5 | 4 | - | 1 | 1 | - | 1 | 1 | - | - | - | - | - | 2 | - | - | - | - | - | - | - | - | - | - | - | - | - | - |
| 1949-50 | 5 | 4 | - | 1 | - | - | - | 1 | - | - | - | - | - | 1 | - | - | 1 | - | 1 | 1 | - | - | - | - | - | - | - | - |
| 1957-58 | 5 | 3 | - | 2 | - | - | - | 1 | - | - | - | - | - | - | - | 1 | - | - | - | 1 | - | - | 1 | - | 1 | - | - | - |
| 1966-67 | 5 | 1 | 3 | 1 | - | - | - | 1 | - | - | - | - | - | - | 1 | - | - | - | - | - | 1 | - | - | 1 | 1 | - | - | - |
| 1969-70 | 4 | - | 4 | - | - | - | - | - | 1 | - | - | - | - | - | 1 | - | - | - | - | - | 1 | - | - | 1 | - | - | - | - |
| 1993-94 | 3 | 1 | 1 | 1 | - | - | - | 1 | - | - | - | - | - | - | - | 1 | - | - | - | - | - | - | - | 1 | - | - | - | - |
| 1996-97 | 3 | 2 | 1 | - | - | - | - | - | - | - | - | - | - | - | - | - | - | - | - | 1 | - | - | 1 | - | - | - | 1 | - |
| | 36 | 18 | 9 | 9 | 2 | - | 3 | 7 | 1 | - | - | - | 1 | 3 | 2 | 2 | 1 | - | 1 | 2 | 2 | - | 1 | 3 | 2 | - | 1 | - |

### AUSTRALIA v SOUTH AFRICA-IN ENGLAND

| | | Result | | | Manchester | | | Lord's | | | Nottingham | | |
|---|---|---|---|---|---|---|---|---|---|---|---|---|---|
| | Tests | A | SA | D | A | SA | D | A | SA | D | A | SA | D |
| 1912 | 3 | 2 | - | 1 | 1 | - | - | 1 | - | - | - | - | 1 |
| Totals | 65 | 34 | 14 | 17 | | | | | | | | | |

### HIGHEST INNINGS TOTALS

| | | | |
|---|---|---|---|
| Australia in Australia | 578 | Melbourne | 1910-11 |
| Australia in South Africa | 8d-628 | Johannesburg[3] | 1996-97 |
| South Africa in Australia | 595 | Adelaide | 1963-64 |
| South Africa in South Africa | 9d-622 | Durban[2] | 1969-70 |

### LOWEST INNINGS TOTALS

| | | | |
|---|---|---|---|
| Australia in Australia | 111 | Sydney | 1993-94 |
| Australia in South Africa | 75 | Durban[2] | 1949-50 |
| South Africa in Australia | 36 | Melbourne | 1931-32 |
| South Africa in South Africa | 85 | Johannesburg[1] | 1902-03 |
| | 85 | Cape Town | 1902-03 |

| | | | |
|---|---|---|---|
| **HIGHEST MATCH AGGREGATE** | 1646 for 40 wickets | Adelaide | 1910-11 |
| **LOWEST MATCH AGGREGATE** | 234 for 29 wickets | Melbourne | 1931-32 |

### HIGHEST INDIVIDUAL INNINGS

| | | | | |
|---|---|---|---|---|
| Australia in Australia | 299* | D.G.Bradman | Adelaide | 1931-32 |
| Australia in South Africa | 214 | G.S.Blewett | Johannesburg[3] | 1996-97 |
| South Africa in Australia | 204 | G.A.Faulkner | Melbourne | 1910-11 |
| South Africa in South Africa | 274 | R.G.Pollock | Durban[2] | 1969-70 |

**HIGHEST AGGREGATE OF RUNS IN A SERIES**

| | | | |
|---|---|---|---|
| Australia in Australia | 834 (av 92.66) | R.N.Harvey | 1952-53 |
| Australia in South Africa | 660 (av 132.00) | R.N.Harvey | 1949-50 |
| South Africa in Australia | 732 (av 73.20) | G.A.Faulkner | 1910-11 |
| South Africa in South Africa | 606 (av 86.57) | D.T.Lindsay | 1966-67 |

**RECORD WICKET PARTNERSHIPS-AUSTRALIA**

| | | | | |
|---|---|---|---|---|
| 1st | 233 | J.H.W.Fingleton (112), W.A.Brown (121) | Cape Town | 1935-36 |
| 2nd | 275 | C.C.McDonald (154), A.L.Hassett (163) | Adelaide | 1952-53 |
| 3rd | 242 | C.Kelleway (102), W.Bardsley (164) | Lord's | 1912 |
| 4th | 169 | M.A.Taylor (170), M.E.Waugh (84) | Melbourne | 1993-94 |
| 5th | 385 | S.R.Waugh (160), G.S.Blewett (214) | Johannesburg[3] | 1996-97 |
| 6th | 107 | C.Kelleway (59), V.S.Ransford (75) | Melbourne | 1910-11 |
| 7th | 160 | R.Benaud (90), G.D.McKenzie (76) | Sydney | 1963-64 |
| 8th | 83 | A.G.Chipperfield (109), C.V.Grimmett (15) | Durban[2] | 1935-36 |
| 9th | 78 | D.G.Bradman (299*), W.J.O'Reilly (23) | Adelaide | 1931-32 |
| | 78 | K.D.Mackay (83*), I.Meckiff (26) | Johannesburg[3] | 1957-58 |
| 10th | 82 | V.S.Ransford (95), W.J.Whitty (39*) | Melbourne | 1910-11 |

**RECORD WICKET PARTNERSHIPS-SOUTH AFRICA**

| | | | | |
|---|---|---|---|---|
| 1st | 176 | D.J.McGlew (108), T.L.Goddard (90) | Johannesburg[3] | 1957-58 |
| 2nd | 173 | L.J.Tancred (97), C.B.Llewellyn (90) | Johannesburg[1] | 1902-03 |
| 3rd | 341 | E.J.Barlow (201), R.G.Pollock (175) | Adelaide | 1963-64 |
| 4th | 206 | C.N.Frank (152), A.W.Nourse (111) | Johannesburg[1] | 1921-22 |
| 5th | 129 | J.H.B.Waite (59), W.R.Endean (77) | Johannesburg[3] | 1957-58 |
| 6th | 200 | R.G.Pollock (274), H.R.Lance (61) | Durban[2] | 1969-70 |
| 7th | 221 | D.T.Lindsay (182), P.L.van der Merwe (76) | Johannesburg[3] | 1966-67 |
| 8th | 124 | A.W.Nourse (72), E.A.Halliwell (57) | Johannesburg[1] | 1902-03 |
| 9th | 85 | R.G.Pollock (209), P.M.Pollock (41) | Cape Town | 1966-67 |
| 10th | 74 | B.M.McMillan (87*), P.L.Symcox (54) | Adelaide | 1997-98 |

**BEST INNINGS BOWLING ANALYSIS**

| | | | | |
|---|---|---|---|---|
| Australia in Australia | 7-56 | S.K.Warne | Sydney | 1993-94 |
| Australia in South Africa | 7-34 | J.V.Saunders | Johannesburg[1] | 1902-03 |
| South Africa in Australia | 7-81 | H.J.Tayfield | Melbourne | 1952-53 |
| South Africa in South Africa | 7-23 | H.J.Tayfield | Durban[2] | 1949-50 |

**BEST MATCH BOWLING ANALYSIS**

| | | | | |
|---|---|---|---|---|
| Australia in Australia | 14-199 | C.V.Grimmett | Adelaide | 1931-32 |
| Australia in South Africa | 13-173 | C.V.Grimmett | Durban[2] | 1935-36 |
| South Africa in Australia | 13-165 | H.J.Tayfield | Melbourne | 1952-53 |
| South Africa in South Africa | 10-116 | C.B.Llewellyn | Johannesburg[1] | 1902-03 |

**HIGHEST AGGREGATE OF WICKETS IN A SERIES**

| | | | |
|---|---|---|---|
| Australia in Australia | 37 (av 17.08) | W.J.Whitty | 1910-11 |
| Australia in South Africa | 44 (av 14.59) | C.V.Grimmett | 1935-36 |
| South Africa in Australia | 30 (av 28.10) | H.J.Tayfield | 1952-53 |
| South Africa in South Africa | 26 (av 16.23) | T.L.Goddard | 1966-67 |
| | 26 (av 13.57) | M.J.Procter | 1969-70 |

| AUSTRALIA v WEST INDIES | Australia | | West Indies | | Captains | |
|---|---|---|---|---|---|---|
| Venue and Result | 1st | 2nd | 1st | 2nd | Australia | West Indies |
| **1930-31 in AUSTRALIA** | | | | | | |
| Adelaide-Australia 10 wkts | 376 | 0-172 | •296 | 249 | W.M.Woodfull | G.C.Grant |
| Sydney-Australia inns & 172 runs | •369 | - | 107 | 90 | | |
| Brisbane[1]-Australia inns & 217 runs | •558 | - | 193 | 148 | | |
| Melbourne-Australia inns & 122 runs | 8d-328 | - | •99 | 107 | | |
| Sydney-West Indies 30 runs | 224 | 220 | •6d-350 | 5d-124 | | |
| **1951-52 in AUSTRALIA** | | | | | | |
| Brisbane[2]-Australia 3 wkts | 226 | 7-236 | •216 | 245 | A.L.Hassett | J.D.C.Goddard |
| Sydney-Australia 7 wkts | 517 | 3-137 | •362 | 290 | A.L.Hassett | J.D.C.Goddard |
| Adelaide-West Indies 6 wkts | •82 | 255 | 105 | 4-233 | A.R.Morris | J.D.C.Goddard |
| Melbourne-Australia 1 wkt | 216 | 9-260 | •272 | 203 | A.L.Hassett | J.D.C.Goddard |
| Sydney-Australia 202 runs | •116 | 377 | 78 | 213 | A.L.Hassett | J.B.Stollmeyer |
| **1954-55 in WEST INDIES** | | | | | | |
| Kingston-Australia 9 wkts | •9d-515 | 1-20 | 259 | 275 | I.W.Johnson | D.S.Atkinson |
| Port-of-Spain-Drawn | 9d-600 | - | •382 | 4-273 | | J.B.Stollmeyer |
| Georgetown-Australia 8 wkts | 257 | 2-133 | •182 | 207 | | J.B.Stollmeyer |
| Bridgetown-Drawn | •668 | 249 | 510 | 6-234 | | D.S.Atkinson |
| Kingston-Australia inns & 82 runs | 8d-758 | - | •357 | 319 | | D.S.Atkinson |
| **1960-61 in AUSTRALIA** | | | | | | |
| Brisbane[2]-Tied | 505 | 232 | •453 | 284 | R.Benaud | F.M.M.Worrell |
| Melbourne-Australia 7 wkts | •348 | 3-70 | 181 | 233 | | |
| Sydney-West Indies 222 runs | 202 | 241 | •339 | 326 | | |
| Adelaide-Drawn | 366 | 9-273 | •393 | 6d-432 | | |
| Melbourne-Australia 2 wkts | 356 | 8-258 | •292 | 321 | | |
| **1964-65 in WEST INDIES** | | | | | | |
| Kingston-West Indies 179 runs | 217 | 216 | •239 | 373 | R.B.Simpson | G.S.Sobers |
| Port-of-Spain-Drawn | 516 | - | •429 | 386 | | |
| Georgetown-West Indies 212 runs | 179 | 144 | •355 | 180 | | |
| Bridgetown-Drawn | •6d-650 | 4d-175 | 573 | 5-242 | | |
| Port-of-Spain-Australia 10 wkts | 294 | 0-63 | •224 | 131 | | |
| **1968-69 in AUSTRALIA** | | | | | | |
| Brisbane [2]-West Indies 125 runs | 284 | 240 | •296 | 353 | W.M.Lawry | G.S.Sobers |
| Melbourne-Australia inns & 30 runs | 510 | - | •200 | 280 | | |
| Sydney-Australia 10 wkts | 547 | 0-42 | •264 | 324 | | |
| Adelaide-Drawn | 533 | 9-339 | •276 | 616 | | |
| Sydney-Australia 382 runs | •619 | 8d-394 | 279 | 352 | | |
| **1972-73 in WEST INDIES** | | | | | | |
| Kingston-Drawn | •7d-428 | 2d-260 | 428 | 3-67 | I.M.Chappell | R.B.Kanhai |
| Bridgetown-Drawn | •324 | 2d-300 | 391 | 0-36 | | |
| Port-of-Spain-Australia 44 runs | •332 | 281 | 280 | 289 | | |
| Georgetown-Australia 10 wkts | 341 | 0-135 | •366 | 109 | | |
| Port-of-Spain-Drawn | •8d-419 | 7d-218 | 319 | 5-135 | | |
| **1975-76 in AUSTRALIA** | | | | | | |
| Brisbane[2]-Australia 8 wkts | 366 | 2-219 | •214 | 370 | G.S.Chappell | C.H.Lloyd |
| Perth-West Indies inns & 87 runs | •329 | 169 | 585 | - | | |
| Melbourne-Australia 8 wkts | 485 | 2-55 | •224 | 312 | | |
| Sydney-Australia 7 wkts | 405 | 3-82 | •355 | 128 | | |
| Adelaide-Australia 190 runs | •418 | 7d-345 | 274 | 299 | | |
| Melbourne-Australia 165 runs | •351 | 3d-300 | 160 | 326 | | |

| **AUSTRALIA v WEST INDIES** (cont.) | Australia | | West Indies | | Captains | |
|---|---|---|---|---|---|---|
| Venue and Result | 1st | 2nd | 1st | 2nd | Australia | West Indies |
| **1977-78 in WEST INDIES** | | | | | | |
| Port-of-Spain-West Indies inns & 106 runs | •90 | 209 | 405 | - | R.B.Simpson | C.H.Lloyd |
| Bridgetown-West Indies 9 wkts | •250 | 178 | 288 | 1-141 | | C.H.Lloyd |
| Georgetown-Australia 3 wkts | 286 | 7-362 | •205 | 439 | | A.I.Kallicharran |
| Port-of-Spain-West Indies 198 runs | 290 | 94 | •292 | 290 | | A.I.Kallicharran |
| Kingston-Drawn | •343 | 3d-305 | 280 | 9-258 | | A.I.Kallicharran |
| **1979-80 in AUSTRALIA** | | | | | | |
| Brisbane[2]-Drawn | •268 | 6d-448 | 441 | 3-40 | G.S.Chappell | D L.Murray |
| Melbourne-West Indies 10 wkts | •156 | 259 | 397 | 0-22 | | C.H.Lloyd |
| Adelaide-West Indies 408 runs | 203 | 165 | •328 | 448 | | C.H.Lloyd |
| **1981-82 in AUSTRALIA** | | | | | | |
| Melbourne-Australia 58 runs | •198 | 222 | 201 | 161 | G.S.Chappell | C H.Lloyd |
| Sydney-Drawn | 267 | 4-200 | •384 | 255 | | |
| Adelaide-West Indies 5 wkts | •238 | 386 | 389 | 5-239 | | |
| **1983-84 in WEST INDIES** | | | | | | |
| Georgetown-Drawn | •279 | 9d-273 | 230 | 0-250 | K.J.Hughes | C.H.Lloyd |
| Port-of-Spain-Drawn | •255 | 9d-299 | 8d-468 | - | | I.V.A.Richards |
| Bridgetown-West Indies 10 wkts | •429 | 97 | 509 | 0-21 | | C.H.Lloyd |
| St John's-West Indies inns & 36 runs | •262 | 200 | 498 | - | | C.H.Lloyd |
| Kingston-West Indies 10 wkts | •199 | 160 | 305 | 0-55 | | C.H.Lloyd |
| **1984-85 in AUSTRALIA** | | | | | | |
| Perth-West Indies inns & 112 runs | 76 | 228 | •416 | - | K.J.Hughes | C.H.Lloyd |
| Brisbane[2]-West Indies 8 wkts | •175 | 271 | 424 | 2-26 | K.J.Hughes | |
| Adelaide-West Indies 191 runs | 284 | 173 | •356 | 7d-292 | A.R.Border | |
| Melbourne-Drawn | 298 | 8-198 | •479 | 5d-186 | A.R.Border | |
| Sydney-Australia inns & 55 runs | •9d-471 | - | 163 | 253 | A.R.Border | |
| **1988-89 in AUSTRALIA** | | | | | | |
| Brisbane[2]-West Indies 8 wkts | •167 | 289 | 394 | 2-63 | A.R.Border | I.V.A.Richards |
| Perth-West Indies 169 runs | 8d-395 | 234 | •449 | 9d-349 | | |
| Melbourne-West Indies 285 runs | 242 | 114 | •280 | 9d-361 | | |
| Sydney-Australia 7 wkts | 401 | 3-82 | •224 | 256 | | |
| Adelaide-Drawn | •515 | 4d-224 | 369 | 4-233 | | |
| **1990-91 in WEST INDIES** | | | | | | |
| Kingston-Drawn | 371 | - | •264 | 3-334 | A.R.Border | I.V.A.Richards |
| Georgetown-West Indies 10 wkts | •348 | 248 | 569 | 0-31 | | |
| Port-of-Spain-Drawn | •294 | 3-123 | 227 | - | | |
| Bridgetown-West Indies 343 runs | 134 | 208 | •149 | 9d-536 | | |
| St John's-Australia 157 runs | •403 | 265 | 214 | 297 | | |
| **1992-93 in AUSTRALIA** | | | | | | |
| Brisbane[2]-Drawn | •293 | 308 | 371 | 8-133 | A.R.Border | R.B.Richardson |
| Melbourne-Australia 139 runs | •395 | 196 | 233 | 219 | | |
| Sydney-Drawn | •9d-503 | 0-117 | 616 | - | | |
| Adelaide-West Indies 1 run | 213 | 184 | •252 | 146 | | |
| Perth-West Indies inns & 25 runs | •119 | 178 | 322 | - | | |
| **1994-95 in WEST INDIES** | | | | | | |
| Bridgetown-Australia 10 wkts | 346 | 0-39 | •195 | 189 | M.A.Taylor | R.B.Richardson |
| St John's-Drawn | •216 | 7d-300 | 260 | 2-80 | | |
| Port-of-Spain-West Indies 9 wkts | •128 | 105 | 136 | 1-98 | | |
| Kingston-Australia inns & 53 runs | 531 | - | •265 | 213 | | |

| AUSTRALIA v WEST INDIES (cont.) | Australia | | West Indies | | Captains | |
|---|---|---|---|---|---|---|
| Venue and Result | 1st | 2nd | 1st | 2nd | Australia | West Indies |
| **1996-97 in AUSTRALIA** | | | | | | |
| Brisbane[2]-Australia 123 runs | •479 | 6d-217 | 277 | 296 | M.A.Taylor | C.A.Walsh |
| Sydney-Australia 124 runs | •331 | 4d-312 | 304 | 215 | | |
| Melbourne-West Indies 6 wkts | •219 | 122 | 255 | 4-87 | | |
| Adelaide-Australia inns & 183 runs | 517 | - | •130 | 204 | | |
| Perth-West Indies 10 wkts | •243 | 194 | 384 | 0-57 | | |

## Test Match Results Summary

### AUSTRALIA v WEST INDIES-IN AUSTRALIA

| | Tests | Result | Adelaide | Sydney | Brisbane[1] | Melbourne | Brisbane[2] | Perth |
|---|---|---|---|---|---|---|---|---|
| | | A W D T | A W D T | A W D T | A W D T | A W D T | A W D T | A W D T |
| 1930-31 | 5 | 4 1 - - | 1 - - - | 1 1 - - | 1 - - - | 1 - - - | - - - - | - - - - |
| 1951-52 | 5 | 4 1 - - | - 1 - - | 2 - - - | - - - - | 1 - - - | 1 - - - | - - - - |
| 1960-61 | 5 | 2 1 1 1 | - - 1 - | - 1 - - | - - - - | 2 - - - | - - - 1 | - - - - |
| 1968-69 | 5 | 3 1 1 - | - - 1 - | 2 - - - | - - - - | 1 - - - | - 1 - - | - - - - |
| 1975-76 | 6 | 5 1 - - | 1 - - - | 1 - - - | - - - - | 2 - - - | 1 - - - | - 1 - - |
| 1979-80 | 3 | - 2 1 - | - 1 - - | - - - - | - - - - | - 1 - - | - - 1 - | - - - - |
| 1981-82 | 3 | 1 1 1 - | - 1 - - | - - 1 - | - - - - | 1 - - - | - - - - | - - - - |
| 1984-85 | 5 | 1 3 1 - | - 1 - - | 1 - - - | - - - - | - - 1 - | - 1 - - | - 1 - - |
| 1988-89 | 5 | 1 3 1 - | - - 1 - | 1 - - - | - - - - | - 1 - - | - 1 - - | - 1 - - |
| 1992-93 | 5 | 1 2 2 - | - 1 - - | - - 1 - | - - - - | 1 - - - | - - 1 - | - 1 - - |
| 1996-97 | 5 | 3 2 - - | 1 - - - | 1 - - - | - - - - | - 1 - - | 1 - - - | - 1 - - |
| | 52 | 25 18 8 1 | 3 5 3 - | 9 2 2 - | 1 - - - | 9 3 1 - | 3 3 2 1 | - 5 - - |

### AUSTRALIA v WEST INDIES-IN WEST INDIES

| | Tests | Result | Kingston | Port-of-Spain | Georgetown | Bridgetown | St John's |
|---|---|---|---|---|---|---|---|
| | | A W D T | A W D T | A W D T | A W D T | A W D T | A W D T |
| 1954-55 | 5 | 3 - 2 - | 2 - - - | - - 1 - | 1 - - - | - - 1 - | - - - - |
| 1964-65 | 5 | 1 2 2 - | - 1 - - | 1 - 1 - | - 1 - - | - - 1 - | - - - - |
| 1972-73 | 5 | 2 - 3 - | - - 1 - | 1 - 1 - | 1 - - - | - - 1 - | - - - - |
| 1977-78 | 5 | 1 3 1 - | - - 1 - | - 2 - - | 1 - - - | - 1 - - | - - - - |
| 1983-84 | 5 | - 3 2 - | - 1 - - | - - 1 - | - - 1 - | - 1 - - | - 1 - - |
| 1990-91 | 5 | 1 2 2 - | - - 1 - | - - 1 - | - 1 - - | - 1 - - | 1 - - - |
| 1994-95 | 4 | 2 1 1 - | 1 - - - | - 1 - - | - - - - | 1 - - - | - - 1 - |
| | 34 | 10 11 13 - | 3 2 3 - | 2 3 5 - | 3 2 1 - | 1 3 3 - | 1 1 1 - |
| Totals | 86 | 35 29 21 1 | | | | | |

### HIGHEST INNINGS TOTALS

| | | | |
|---|---|---|---|
| Australia in Australia | 619 | Sydney | 1968-69 |
| Australia in West Indies | 8d-758 | Kingston | 1954-55 |
| West Indies in Australia | 616 | Adelaide | 1968-69 |
| West Indies in West Indies | 573 | Bridgetown | 1964-65 |

### LOWEST INNINGS TOTALS

| | | | |
|---|---|---|---|
| Australia in Australia | 76 | Perth | 1984-85 |
| Australia in West Indies | 90 | Port-of-Spain | 1977-78 |
| West Indies in Australia | 78 | Sydney | 1951-52 |
| West Indies in West Indies | 109 | Georgetown | 1972-73 |

| | | | |
|---|---|---|---|
| **HIGHEST MATCH AGGREGATE** | 1764 for 39 wickets | Adelaide | 1968-69 |
| **LOWEST MATCH AGGREGATE** | 467 for 31 wickets | Port-of-Spain | 1994-95 |

**HIGHEST INDIVIDUAL INNINGS**

| | | | | |
|---|---|---|---|---|
| Australia in Australia | 242 | K.D.Walters | Sydney | 1968-69 |
| Australia in West Indies | 210 | W.M.Lawry | Bridgetown | 1964-65 |
| West Indies in Australia | 277 | B.C.Lara | Sydney | 1992-93 |
| West Indies in West Indies | 226 | C.G.Greenidge | Bridgetown | 1990-91 |

**HIGHEST AGGREGATE OF RUNS IN A SERIES**

| | | | |
|---|---|---|---|
| Australia in Australia | 702 (av 117.00) | G.S.Chappell | 1975-76 |
| Australia in West Indies | 650 (av 108.33) | R.N.Harvey | 1954-55 |
| West Indies in Australia | 537 (av 59.66) | D.L.Haynes | 1988-89 |
| West Indies in West Indies | 827 (av 82.70) | C.L.Walcott | 1954-55 |

**RECORD WICKET PARTNERSHIPS-AUSTRALIA**

| | | | | |
|---|---|---|---|---|
| 1st | 382 | W.M.Lawry (210), R.B.Simpson (201) | Bridgetown | 1964-65 |
| 2nd | 298 | W.M.Lawry (205), I.M.Chappell (165) | Melbourne | 1968-69 |
| 3rd | 295 | C.C.McDonald (127), R.N.Harvey (204) | Kingston | 1954-55 |
| 4th | 336 | W.M.Lawry (151), K.D.Walters (242) | Sydney | 1968-69 |
| 5th | 220 | K.R.Miller (109), R.G.Archer (128) | Kingston | 1954-55 |
| 6th | 206 | K.R.Miller (137), R.G.Archer (98) | Bridgetown | 1954-55 |
| 7th | 134 | R.Benaud (52), A.K.Davidson (80) | Brisbane[2] | 1960-61 |
| 8th | 137 | R.Benaud (128), I.W.Johnson (27*) | Kingston | 1954-55 |
| 9th | 114 | D.M.Jones (216), M.G.Hughes (72*) | Adelaide | 1988-89 |
| 10th | 97 | T.G.Hogan (42*), R.M.Hogg (52) | Georgetown | 1983-84 |

**RECORD WICKET PARTNERSHIPS-WEST INDIES**

| | | | | |
|---|---|---|---|---|
| 1st | 250* | C.G.Greenidge (120*), D.L.Haynes (103*) | Georgetown | 1983-84 |
| 2nd | 297 | D.L.Haynes (111), R.B.Richardson (182) | Georgetown | 1990-91 |
| 3rd | 308 | R.B.Richardson (154), I.V.A.Richards (178) | St Jone's | 1983-84 |
| 4th | 198 | L.G.Rowe (107), A.I.Kallicharran (101) | Brisbane[2] | 1975-76 |
| 5th | 210 | R.B.Kanhai (84), M.L.C.Foster (125) | Kingston | 1972-73 |
| 6th | 165 | R.B.Kanhai (105), D.L.Murray (90) | Bridgetown | 1972-73 |
| 7th | 347 | D.S.Atkinson (219), C.C.Depeiza (122) | Bridgetown | 1954-55 |
| 8th | 87 | P.J.L.Dujon (70), C.E.L.Ambrose (53) | Port-of-Spain | 1990-91 |
| 9th | 122 | D.A.J.Holford (80), J.L.Hendriks (37*) | Adelaide | 1968-69 |
| 10th | 56 | J.Garner (60), C.E.H.Croft (2*) | Brisbane[2] | 1979-80 |

**BEST INNINGS BOWLING ANALYSIS**

| | | | | |
|---|---|---|---|---|
| Australia in Australia | 8-71 | G.D.McKenzie | Melbourne | 1968-69 |
| Australia in West Indies | 7-44 | I.W.Johnson | Georgetown | 1954-55 |
| West Indies in Australia | 7-25 | C.E.L.Ambrose | Perth | 1992-93 |
| West Indies in West Indies | 6-29 | L R.Gibbs | Georgetown | 1964-65 |

**BEST MATCH BOWLING ANALYSIS**

| | | | | |
|---|---|---|---|---|
| Australia in Australia | 13-217 | M.G.Hughes | Perth | 1988-89 |
| Australia in West Indies | 10-115 | N.J.N.Hawke | Georgetown | 1964-65 |
| West Indies in Australia | 11-107 | M.A.Holding | Melbourne | 1981-82 |
| West Indies in West Indies | 9-80 | L.R.Gibbs | Georgetown | 1964-65 |

**HIGHEST AGGREGATE OF WICKETS IN A SERIES**

| | | | |
|---|---|---|---|
| Australia in Australia | 33 (av 17 96) | C.V.Grimmett | 1930-31 |
| | 33 (av 18 54) | A.K.Davidson | 1960-61 |
| Australia in West Indies | 26 (av 20.73) | M.H.N.Walker | 1972-73 |
| West Indies in Australia | 33 (av 16.42) | C.E.L.Ambrose | 1992-93 |
| West Indies in West Indies | 31 (av 16.87) | J.Garner | 1983-84 |

| AUSTRALIA v NEW ZEALAND | Australia | | New Zealand | | Captains | |
|---|---|---|---|---|---|---|
| Venue and Result | 1st | 2nd | 1st | 2nd | Australia | New Zealand |
| **1945-46 in NEW ZEALAND** | | | | | | |
| Wellington-Australia inns & 103 runs | 8d-199 | - | •42 | 54 | W.A.Brown | W.A.Hadlee |
| **1973-74 in AUSTRALIA** | | | | | | |
| Melbourne-Australia inns & 25 runs | •8d-462 | - | 237 | 200 | I.M.Chappell | B.E.Congdon |
| Sydney-Drawn | 162 | 2-30 | •312 | 9d-305 | | |
| Adelaide-Australia inns & 57 runs | •477 | - | 218 | 202 | | |
| **1973-74 in NEW ZEALAND** | | | | | | |
| Wellington-Drawn | •6d-511 | 8-460 | 484 | - | I.M.Chappell | B.E.Congdon |
| Christchurch-New Zealand 5 wkts | •223 | 259 | 255 | 5-230 | | |
| Auckland-Australia 297 runs | •221 | 346 | 112 | 158 | | |
| **1976-77 in NEW ZEALAND** | | | | | | |
| Christchurch-Drawn | •552 | 4d-154 | 357 | 8-293 | G.S.Chappell | G.M.Turner |
| Auckland-Australia 10 wkts | 377 | 0-28 | •229 | 175 | | |
| **1980-81 in AUSTRALIA** | | | | | | |
| Brisbane[2]-Australia 10 wkts | 305 | 0-63 | •225 | 142 | G.S.Chappell | G.P.Howarth |
| Perth-Australia 8 wkts | 265 | 2-55 | •196 | 121 | | M.G.Burgess |
| Melbourne-Drawn | •321 | 188 | 317 | 6-128 | | G.P.Howarth |
| **1981-82 in NEW ZEALAND** | | | | | | |
| Wellington-Drawn | 1-85 | - | •7d-266 | - | G.S.Chappell | G.P.Howarth |
| Auckland-New Zealand 5 wkts | •210 | 280 | 387 | 5-109 | | |
| Christchurch-Australia 8 wkts | •353 | 2-69 | 149 | 272 | | |
| **1985-86 in AUSTRALIA** | | | | | | |
| Brisbane[2]-New Zealand inns & 41 runs | •179 | 333 | 7d-553 | - | A.R.Border | J.V.Coney |
| Sydney-Australia 4 wkts | 227 | 6-260 | •293 | 193 | | |
| Perth-New Zealand 6 wkts | •203 | 259 | 299 | 4-164 | | |
| **1985-86 in NEW ZEALAND** | | | | | | |
| Wellington-Drawn | •435 | - | 6-379 | - | A.R.Border | J.V.Coney |
| Auckland-Drawn | •364 | 7d-219 | 339 | 1-16 | | |
| Christchurch-New Zealand 8 wkts | •314 | 103 | 258 | 2-160 | | |
| **1987-88 in AUSTRALIA** | | | | | | |
| Brisbane[2]-Australia 9 wkts | 305 | 1-97 | •186 | 212 | A.R.Border | J.J.Crowe |
| Adelaide-Drawn | 496 | - | •9d-485 | 7-182 | | |
| Melbourne-Drawn | 357 | 9-230 | •317 | 286 | | |
| **1989-90 in AUSTRALIA** | | | | | | |
| Perth-Drawn | •9d-521 | - | 231 | 7-322 | A.R.Border | J.G.Wright |
| **1989-90 in NEW ZEALAND** | | | | | | |
| Wellington-New Zealand 9 wkts | •110 | 269 | 202 | 1-181 | A.R.Border | J.G.Wright |
| **1992-93 in NEW ZEALAND** | | | | | | |
| Canterbury-Australia inns & 60 runs | •485 | - | 182 | 243 | A.R.Border | M.D.Crowe |
| Wellington-Drawn | 298 | - | •329 | 7-210 | | |
| Auckland-New Zealand 5 wkts | •139 | 285 | 224 | 5-201 | | |
| **1993-94 in AUSTRALIA** | | | | | | |
| Perth-Drawn | •398 | 1d-323 | 9d-419 | 4-166 | A.R.Border | M.D.Crowe |
| Hobart-Australia inns & 222 runs | •6d-544 | - | 161 | 161 | | K.R.Rutherford |
| Brisbane[2]-Australia inns & 96 runs | 6d-607 | - | •233 | 278 | | K.R.Rutherford |

| **AUSTRALIA v NEW ZEALAND** (cont.) | Australia | | New Zealand | | Captains | |
|---|---|---|---|---|---|---|
| Venue and Result | 1st | 2nd | 1st | 2nd | Australia | New Zealand |
| **1997-98 in AUSTRALIA** | | | | | | |
| Brisbane[2]-Australia 186 runs | •373 | 6d-294 | 349 | 132 | M.A.Taylor | S.P.Fleming |
| Perth-Australia inns & 70 runs | 461 | - | •217 | 174 | | |
| Hobart-Drawn | •400 | 2d-138 | 6d-251 | 9-223 | | |

## Test Match Results Summary

**AUSTRALIA v NEW ZEALAND-IN AUSTRALIA**

| | | Result | | | Melbourne | | | Sydney | | | Adelaide | | | Brisbane[2] | | | Perth | | | Hobart | | |
|---|---|---|---|---|---|---|---|---|---|---|---|---|---|---|---|---|---|---|---|---|---|---|
| | Tests | A | NZ | D | A | NZ | D | A | NZ | D | A | NZ | D | A | NZ | D | A | NZ | D | A | NZ | D |
| 1973-74 | 3 | 2 | - | 1 | 1 | - | - | - | - | 1 | 1 | - | - | - | - | - | - | - | - | - | - | - |
| 1980-81 | 3 | 2 | - | 1 | - | - | 1 | - | - | - | - | - | - | 1 | - | - | 1 | - | - | - | - | - |
| 1985-86 | 3 | 1 | 2 | - | - | - | - | 1 | - | - | - | - | - | - | 1 | - | - | 1 | - | - | - | - |
| 1987-88 | 3 | 1 | - | 2 | - | - | 1 | - | - | - | - | - | 1 | 1 | - | - | - | - | - | - | - | - |
| 1989-90 | 1 | - | - | 1 | - | - | - | - | - | - | - | - | - | - | - | - | - | - | 1 | - | - | - |
| 1993-94 | 3 | 2 | - | 1 | - | - | - | - | - | - | - | - | - | 1 | - | - | - | - | 1 | 1 | - | - |
| 1997-98 | 3 | 2 | - | 1 | - | - | - | - | - | - | - | - | - | 1 | - | - | 1 | - | - | - | - | 1 |
| | 19 | 10 | 2 | 7 | 1 | - | 2 | 1 | - | 1 | 1 | - | 1 | 4 | 1 | - | 2 | 1 | 2 | 1 | - | 1 |

**AUSTRALIA v NEW ZEALAND-IN NEW ZEALAND**

| | | Result | | | Wellington | | | Christchurch | | | Auckland | | |
|---|---|---|---|---|---|---|---|---|---|---|---|---|---|
| | Tests | A | NZ | D | A | NZ | D | A | NZ | D | A | NZ | D |
| 1945-46 | 1 | 1 | - | - | 1 | - | - | - | - | - | - | - | - |
| 1973-74 | 3 | 1 | 1 | 1 | - | - | 1 | - | 1 | - | 1 | - | - |
| 1976-77 | 2 | 1 | - | 1 | - | - | - | - | - | 1 | 1 | - | - |
| 1981-82 | 3 | 1 | 1 | 1 | - | - | 1 | 1 | - | - | - | 1 | - |
| 1985-86 | 3 | - | 1 | 2 | - | - | 1 | - | - | 1 | - | 1 | - |
| 1989-90 | 1 | - | 1 | - | - | 1 | - | - | - | - | - | - | - |
| 1992-93 | 3 | 1 | 1 | 1 | - | - | 1 | 1 | - | - | - | 1 | - |
| | 16 | 5 | 5 | 6 | 1 | 1 | 4 | 2 | 1 | 2 | 2 | 3 | - |
| Totals | 35 | 15 | 7 | 13 | | | | | | | | | |

**HIGHEST INNINGS TOTALS**

| | | | |
|---|---|---|---|
| Australia in Australia | 6d-607 | Brisbane[2] | 1993-94 |
| Australia in New Zealand | 552 | Christchurch | 1976-77 |
| New Zealand in Australia | 7d-553 | Brisbane[2] | 1985-86 |
| New Zealand in New Zealand | 484 | Wellington | 1973-74 |

**LOWEST INNINGS TOTALS**

| | | | |
|---|---|---|---|
| Australia in Australia | 162 | Sydney | 1973-74 |
| Australia in New Zealand | 103 | Auckland | 1985-86 |
| New Zealand in Australia | 121 | Perth | 1980-81 |
| New Zealand in New Zealand | 42 | Wellington | 1945-46 |

| | | | |
|---|---|---|---|
| **HIGHEST MATCH AGGREGATE** | 1455 for 24 wickets | Wellington | 1973-74 |
| **LOWEST MATCH AGGREGATE** | 295 for 28 wickets | Wellington | 1945-46 |

**HIGHEST INDIVIDUAL INNINGS**

| | | | | |
|---|---|---|---|---|
| Australia in Australia | 205 | A.R.Border | Adelaide | 1987-88 |
| Australia in New Zealand | 250 | K.D.Walters | Christchurch | 1976-77 |
| New Zealand in Australia | 188 | M.D.Crowe | Sydney | 1985-86 |
| New Zealand in New Zealand | 161 | B.A.Edgar | Auckland | 1981-82 |

### HIGHEST AGGREGATE OF RUNS IN A SERIES

| | | | |
|---|---|---|---|
| Australia in Australia | 305 (av 76.25) | M.J.Slater | 1993-94 |
| Australia in New Zealand | 449 (av 89.80) | G.S.Chappell | 1973-74 |
| New Zealand in Australia | 396 (av 66.00) | M.D.Crowe | 1987-88 |
| New Zealand in New Zealand | 403 (av 100.75) | G.M.Turner | 1973-74 |

### RECORD WICKET PARTNERSHIPS-AUSTRALIA

| | | | | |
|---|---|---|---|---|
| 1st | 198 | M.J.Slater (99), M.A.Taylor (142*) | Perth | 1993-94 |
| 2nd | 235 | M.J.Slater (168), D.C.Boon (106) | Hobart | 1993-94 |
| 3rd | 264 | I.M.Chappell (145), G.S.Chappell (247*) | Wellington | 1973-74 |
| 4th | 153 | M.E.Waugh (86), S.R.Waugh (96) | Perth | 1997-98 |
| 5th | 213 | G.M.Ritchie (92), G.R.J.Matthews (130) | Wellington | 1985-86 |
| 6th | 197 | A.R.Border (152*), G.R.J.Matthews (115) | Brisbane[2] | 1985-86 |
| 7th | 217 | K.D.Walters (250), G.J.Gilmour (101) | Christchurch | 1976-77 |
| 8th | 93 | G.J.Gilmour (64), K.J.O'Keeffe (32) | Auckland | 1976-77 |
| 9th | 69 | I.A.Healy (113*), C.J.McDermott (35) | Perth | 1993-94 |
| 10th | 60 | K.D.Walters (107), J.D.Higgs (6*) | Melbourne | 1980-81 |

### RECORD WICKET PARTNERSHIPS-NEW ZEALAND

| | | | | |
|---|---|---|---|---|
| 1st | 112 | M.J.Greatbatch (61), J.G.Wright (72) | Wellington | 1992-93 |
| 2nd | 132 | M.J.Horne (133), A.C.Parore (44) | Hobart | 1997-98 |
| 3rd | 224 | J.F.Reid (108), M.D.Crowe (188) | Brisbane[2] | 1985-86 |
| 4th | 229 | B.E.Congdon (132), B.F.Hastings (101) | Wellington | 1973-74 |
| 5th | 88 | J.V.Coney (71), M.G.Burgess (43) | Perth | 1980-81 |
| 6th | 109 | K.R.Rutherford (65), J.V.Coney (101*) | Wellington | 1985-86 |
| 7th | 132* | J.V.Coney (101*), R.J.Hadlee (81*) | Wellington | 1985-86 |
| 8th | 88* | M.J.Greatbatch (146*), M.C.Snedden (33*) | Perth | 1989-90 |
| 9th | 73 | H.J.Howarth (60), D.R.Hadlee (37) | Christchurch | 1976-77 |
| 10th | 124 | J.G.Bracewell (83*), S.L.Boock (37) | Sydney | 1985-86 |

### BEST INNINGS BOWLING ANALYSIS

| | | | | |
|---|---|---|---|---|
| Australia in Australia | 6-31 | S.K.Warne | Hobart | 1993-94 |
| Australia in New Zealand | 6-72 | D.K.Lillee | Auckland | 1976-77 |
| New Zealand in Australia | 9-52 | R.J.Hadlee | Brisbane[2] | 1985-86 |
| New Zealand in New Zealand | 7-89 | D.K.Morrison | Wellington | 1992-93 |

### BEST MATCH BOWLING ANALYSIS

| | | | | |
|---|---|---|---|---|
| Australia in Australia | 10-174 | R.G.Holland | Sydney | 1985-86 |
| Australia in New Zealand | 11-123 | D.K.Lillee | Auckland | 1976-77 |
| New Zealand in Australia | 15-123 | R.J.Hadlee | Brisbane[2] | 1985-86 |
| New Zealand in New Zealand | 10-146 | J.G.Bracewell | Auckland | 1985-86 |

### HIGHEST AGGREGATE OF WICKETS IN A SERIES

| | | | |
|---|---|---|---|
| Australia in Australia | 19 (av 25.05) | S.K.Warne | 1997-98 |
| Australia in New Zealand | 17 (av 15.05) | S.K.Warne | 1992-93 |
| New Zealand in Australia | 33 (av 12.15) | R.J.Hadlee | 1985-86 |
| New Zealand in New Zealand | 17 (av 25.64) | R.O.Collinge | 1973-74 |
| | 17 (av 16.94) | D.K.Morrison | 1992-93 |

| **AUSTRALIA v INDIA** | Australia | | India | | Captains | |
|---|---|---|---|---|---|---|
| Venue and Result | 1st | 2nd | 1st | 2nd | Australia | India |
| **1947-48 in AUSTRALIA** | | | | | | |
| Brisbane²-Australia inns & 226 runs | •8d-382 | - | 58 | 98 | D.G.Bradman | N.B.Amarnath |
| Sydney-Drawn | 107 | - | •188 | 7-61 | | |
| Melbourne-Australia 233 runs | •394 | 4d-255 | 9d-291 | 125 | | |
| Adelaide-Australia inns & 16 runs | •674 | - | 381 | 277 | | |
| Melbourne-Australia inns & 177 runs | •8d-575 | - | 331 | 67 | | |
| **1956-57 in INDIA** | | | | | | |
| Madras²-Australia inns & 5 runs | 319 | - | •161 | 153 | I.W.Johnson | P.R.Umrigar |
| Bombay²-Drawn | 7d-523 | - | •251 | 5-250 | R.R.Lindwall | |
| Calcutta-Australia 94 runs | •177 | 9d-189 | 136 | 136 | I.W.Johnson | |
| **1959-60 in INDIA** | | | | | | |
| Delhi-Australia inns & 127 runs | 468 | - | •135 | 206 | R.Benaud | G.S.Ramchand |
| Kanpur-India 119 runs | 219 | 105 | •152 | 291 | | |
| Bombay²-Drawn | 8d-387 | 1-34 | •289 | 5d-226 | | |
| Madras²-Australia inns & 55 runs | •342 | - | 149 | 138 | | |
| Calcutta-Drawn | 331 | 2-121 | •194 | 339 | | |
| **1964-65 in INDIA** | | | | | | |
| Madras²-Australia 139 runs | •211 | 397 | 276 | 193 | R.B.Simpson | Nawab of Pataudi, jr |
| Bombay²-India 2 wkts | •320 | 274 | 341 | 8-256 | | |
| Calcutta-Drawn | •174 | 1-143 | 235 | - | | |
| **1967-68 in AUSTRALIA** | | | | | | |
| Adelaide-Australia 146 runs | •335 | 369 | 307 | 251 | R.B.Simpson | C.G Borde |
| Melbourne-Australia inns & 4 runs | 529 | - | •173 | 352 | R.B.Simpson | Nawab of Pataudi, jr |
| Brisbane²-Australia 39 runs | •379 | 294 | 279 | 355 | W M.Lawry | Nawab of Pataudi, jr |
| Sydney-Australia 144 runs | •317 | 292 | 268 | 197 | W.M.Lawry | Nawab of Pataudi, jr |
| **1969-70 in INDIA** | | | | | | |
| Bombay²-Australia 8 wkts | 345 | 2-67 | •271 | 137 | W.M.Lawry | Nawab of Pataudi, jr |
| Kanpur-Drawn | 348 | 0-95 | •320 | 7d-312 | | |
| Delhi-India 7 wkts | •296 | 107 | 223 | 3-181 | | |
| Calcutta-Australia 10 wkts | 335 | 0-42 | •212 | 161 | | |
| Madras¹-Australia 77 runs | •258 | 153 | 163 | 171 | | |
| **1977-78 in AUSTRALIA** | | | | | | |
| Brisbane²-Australia 16 runs | •166 | 327 | 153 | 324 | R.B.Simpson | B.S.Bedi |
| Perth-Australia 2 wkts | 394 | 8-342 | •402 | 9d-330 | | |
| Melbourne-India 222 runs | 213 | 164 | •256 | 343 | | |
| Sydney-India inns & 2 runs | •131 | 263 | 8d-396 | - | | |
| Adelaide-Australia 47 runs | •505 | 256 | 269 | 445 | | |
| **1979-80 in INDIA** | | | | | | |
| Madras¹-Drawn | •390 | 7-212 | 425 | - | K.J.Hughes | S.M.Gavaskar |
| Bangalore-Drawn | •333 | 3-77 | 5d-457 | - | | |
| Kanpur-India 153 runs | 304 | 125 | •271 | 311 | | |
| Delhi-Drawn | 298 | 413 | •7d-510 | - | | |
| Calcutta-Drawn | •442 | 6d-151 | 347 | 4-200 | | |
| Bombay³-India inns & 100 runs | 160 | 198 | •8d-458 | - | | |
| **1980-81 In AUSTRALIA** | | | | | | |
| Sydney-Australia inns & 4 runs | 406 | - | •201 | 201 | G.S.Chappell | S.M.Gavaskar |
| Adelaide-Drawn | •528 | 7d-221 | 419 | 8-135 | | |
| Melbourne-India 59 runs | 419 | 83 | •237 | 324 | | |

| **AUSTRALIA v INDIA** (cont.) | Australia | | India | | Captains | |
|---|---|---|---|---|---|---|
| Venue and Result | 1st | 2nd | 1st | 2nd | Australia | India |
| **1985-86 In AUSTRALIA** | | | | | | |
| Adelaide-Drawn | •381 | 0-17 | 520 | - | A.R.Border | Kapil Dev |
| Melbourne-Drawn | •262 | 308 | 445 | 2-59 | | |
| Sydney-Drawn | 396 | 6-119 | •4d-600 | - | | |
| **1986-87 in INDIA** | | | | | | |
| Madras[1]-Tied | •7d-574 | 5d-170 | 397 | 347 | A.R.Border | Kapil Dev |
| Delhi-Drawn | •3d-207 | - | 3-107 | - | | |
| Bombay[3]-Drawn | •345 | 2-216 | 5d-517 | - | | |
| **1991-92 in AUSTRALIA** | | | | | | |
| Brisbane[2]-Australia 10 wkts | 340 | 0-58 | •239 | 156 | A.R.Border | M.Azharuddin |
| Melbourne-Australia 8 wkts | 349 | 2-128 | •263 | 213 | | |
| Sydney-Drawn | •313 | 8-173 | 483 | - | | |
| Adelaide-Australia 38 runs | •145 | 451 | 225 | 333 | | |
| Perth-Australia 300 runs | •346 | 6d-367 | 272 | 141 | | |
| **1986-87 in INDIA** | | | | | | |
| Delhi-India 7 wkts | •182 | 234 | 361 | 3-58 | M.A.Taylor | S.R.Tendulkar |
| **1997-98 in INDIA** | | | | | | |
| Chennai[1]-India 179 runs | 328 | 168 | •257 | 4d-418 | M.A.Taylor | M.Azharuddin |
| Calcutta-India inns & 219 runs | •233 | 181 | 5d-633 | - | | |
| Bangalore-Australia 8 wkts | 400 | 2-195 | •424 | 169 | | |

## Test Match Results Summary

**AUSTRALIA v INDIA-IN AUSTRALIA**

| | | Result | | | | Brisbane[2] | | | | Sydney | | | | Melbourne | | | | Adelaide | | | | Perth | | | |
|---|---|---|---|---|---|---|---|---|---|---|---|---|---|---|---|---|---|---|---|---|---|---|---|---|---|
| | Tests | A | I | D | T | A | I | D | T | A | I | D | T | A | I | D | T | A | I | D | T | A | I | D | T |
| 1947-48 | 5 | 4 | - | 1 | - | 1 | - | - | - | - | - | 1 | - | 2 | - | - | - | 1 | - | - | - | - | - | - | - |
| 1967-68 | 4 | 4 | - | - | - | 1 | - | - | - | 1 | - | - | - | 1 | - | - | - | 1 | - | - | - | - | - | - | - |
| 1977-78 | 5 | 3 | 2 | - | - | 1 | - | - | - | - | 1 | - | - | - | 1 | - | - | 1 | - | - | - | 1 | - | - | - |
| 1980-81 | 3 | 1 | 1 | 1 | - | - | - | - | - | 1 | - | - | - | - | 1 | - | - | - | - | 1 | - | - | - | - | - |
| 1985-86 | 3 | - | - | 3 | - | - | - | - | - | - | - | 1 | - | - | - | 1 | - | - | - | 1 | - | - | - | - | - |
| 1991-92 | 5 | 4 | - | 1 | - | 1 | - | - | - | - | - | 1 | - | 1 | - | - | - | 1 | - | - | - | 1 | - | - | - |
| | 25 | 16 | 3 | 6 | - | 4 | - | - | - | 2 | 1 | 3 | - | 4 | 2 | 1 | - | 4 | - | 2 | - | 2 | - | - | - |

**AUSTRALIA v INDIA-IN INDIA**

| | | Result | | | | Madras[2] | | | | Bombay[2] | | | | Calcutta | | | | Delhi | | | | Kanpur | | | | Bangalore | | | | Chennai[1] | | | | Bombay[3] | | | |
|---|---|---|---|---|---|---|---|---|---|---|---|---|---|---|---|---|---|---|---|---|---|---|---|---|---|---|---|---|---|---|---|---|---|---|---|---|---|
| | Tests | A | I | D | T | A | I | D | T | A | I | D | T | A | I | D | T | A | I | D | T | A | I | D | T | A | I | D | T | A | I | D | T | A | I | D | T |
| 1956-57 | 3 | 2 | - | 1 | - | 1 | - | - | - | - | - | 1 | - | 1 | - | - | - | - | - | - | - | - | - | - | - | - | - | - | - | - | - | - | - | - | - | - | - |
| 1959-60 | 5 | 2 | 1 | 2 | - | 1 | - | - | - | - | - | 1 | - | - | - | 1 | - | 1 | - | - | - | - | 1 | - | - | - | - | - | - | - | - | - | - | - | - | - | - |
| 1964-65 | 3 | 1 | 1 | 1 | - | 1 | - | - | - | - | 1 | - | - | - | - | 1 | - | - | - | - | - | - | - | - | - | - | - | - | - | - | - | - | - | - | - | - | - |
| 1969-70 | 5 | 3 | 1 | 1 | - | - | - | - | - | 1 | - | - | - | 1 | - | - | - | - | 1 | - | - | - | - | 1 | - | - | - | - | - | 1 | - | - | - | - | - | - | - |
| 1979-80 | 6 | - | 2 | 4 | - | - | - | - | - | - | - | - | - | - | - | 1 | - | - | - | 1 | - | - | 1 | - | - | - | - | 1 | - | - | - | 1 | - | - | 1 | - | - |
| 1986-87 | 3 | - | - | 2 | 1 | - | - | - | - | - | - | - | - | - | - | - | - | - | - | 1 | - | - | - | - | - | - | - | - | - | - | - | - | 1 | - | - | 1 | - |
| 1996-97 | 1 | - | 1 | - | - | - | - | - | - | - | - | - | - | - | - | - | - | - | 1 | - | - | - | - | - | - | - | - | - | - | - | - | - | - | - | - | - | - |
| 1997-98 | 3 | 1 | 2 | - | - | - | 1 | - | - | - | - | - | - | - | 1 | - | - | - | - | - | - | - | - | - | - | 1 | - | - | - | - | - | - | - | - | - | - | - |
| | 29 | 9 | 8 | 11 | 1 | 3 | 1 | - | - | 1 | 1 | 2 | - | 2 | 1 | 3 | - | 1 | 2 | 2 | - | - | 2 | 1 | - | 1 | - | 1 | - | 1 | - | 1 | 1 | - | 1 | 1 | - |
| Totals | 54 | 25 | 11 | 17 | 1 | | | | | | | | | | | | | | | | | | | | | | | | | | | | | | | | |

**HIGHEST INNINGS TOTALS**

| | | | |
|---|---|---|---|
| Australia in Australia | 674 | Adelaide | 1947-48 |
| Australia in India | 7d-574 | Madras[1] | 1986-87 |
| India in Australia | 4d-600 | Sydney | 1985-86 |
| India in India | 5d-633 | Calcutta | 1997-98 |

**LOWEST INNINGS TOTALS**

| | | | |
|---|---|---|---|
| Australia in Australia | 83 | Melbourne | 1980-81 |
| Australia in India | 105 | Kanpur | 1959-60 |
| India in Australia | 58 | Brisbane[2] | 1947-48 |
| India in India | 135 | Delhi | 1959-60 |

| | | | |
|---|---|---|---|
| **HIGHEST MATCH AGGREGATE** | 1488 for 32 wickets | Madras[1] | 1986-87 |
| **LOWEST MATCH AGGREGATE** | 538 for 28 wickets | Brisbane[2] | 1947-48 |

**HIGHEST INDIVIDUAL INNINGS**

| | | | | |
|---|---|---|---|---|
| Australia in Australia | 213 | K.J.Hughes | Adelaide | 1980-81 |
| Australia in India | 210 | D.M.Jones | Madras[1] | 1986-87 |
| India in Australia | 206 | R.J.Shastri | Sydney | 1991-92 |
| India in India | 177 | S.R.Tendulkar | Bangalore | 1997-98 |

**HIGHEST AGGREGATE OR RUNS IN A SERIES**

| | | | |
|---|---|---|---|
| Australia in Australia | 715 (av 178.75) | D.G.Bradman | 1947-48 |
| Australia in India | 594 (av 59.40) | K.J.Hughes | 1979-80 |
| India in Australia | 473 (av 52.55) | G.R.Viswanath | 1977-78 |
| India in India | 518 (av 74.00) | G.R.Viswanath | 1979-80 |

**RECORD WICKET PARTNERSHIPS-AUSTRALIA**

| | | | | |
|---|---|---|---|---|
| 1st | 217 | D.C.Boon (172), G.R.Marsh (116) | Sydney | 1985-86 |
| 2nd | 236 | S.G.Barnes (112), D.G.Bradman (201) | Adelaide | 1947-48 |
| 3rd | 222 | A.R.Border (162), K.J.Hughes (100) | Madras[1] | 1979-80 |
| 4th | 178 | D.M.Jones (210), A.R.Border (106) | Madras[1] | 1986-87 |
| 5th | 223* | A.R.Morris (100*), D.G.Bradman (127*) | Melbourne | 1947-48 |
| 6th | 151 | T.R.Veivers (67), B.N.Jarman (78) | Bombay[2] | 1964-65 |
| 7th | 66 | G.R.J.Matthews (100), R.J.Bright (28) | Melbourne | 1985-86 |
| 8th | 73 | T.R.Veivers (74), G.D.McKenzie (27) | Madras[2] | 1964-65 |
| 9th | 96 | I.A.Healy (90), G.R.Robertson (57) | Madras[1] | 1997-98 |
| 10th | 77 | A.R.Border (163), D.R.Gilbert (10*) | Melbourne | 1985-86 |

**RECORD WICKET PARTNERSHIPS-INDIA**

| | | | | |
|---|---|---|---|---|
| 1st | 192 | S.M.Gavaskar (123), C.P.S.Chauhan (73) | Bombay[3] | 1979-80 |
| 2nd | 224 | S.M.Gavaskar (172), M.Amarnath (138) | Sydney | 1985-86 |
| 3rd | 159 | S.M.Gavaskar (115), G.R.Viswanath (131) | Delhi | 1979-80 |
| 4th | 159 | D.B.Vengsarkar (112), G.R.Viswanath (161*) | Bangalore | 1979-80 |
| 5th | 196 | R.J.Shastri (206), S.R.Tendulkar (148*) | Sydney | 1991-92 |
| 6th | 298* | D.B.Vengsarkar (164*), R.J.Shastri (121*) | Bombay[3] | 1986-87 |
| 7th | 132 | V.S.Hazare (145), H.R.Adhikari (51) | Adelaide | 1947-48 |
| 8th | 127 | S.M.H.Kirmani (101*), K.D.Ghavri (86) | Bombay[3] | 1979-80 |
| 9th | 81 | S.R.Tendulkar (114), K.S.More (67*) | Perth | 1991-92 |
| 10th | 94 | S.M.Gavaskar (166*), N.S.Yadav (41) | Adelaide | 1985-86 |

**BEST INNINGS BOWLING ANALYSIS**

| | | | | |
|---|---|---|---|---|
| Australia in Australia | 7-27 | M.R.Whitney | Perth | 1991-92 |
| Australia in India | 7-43 | R.R.Lindwall | Madras[2] | 1956-57 |
| India in Australia | 6-52 | B.S.Chandrasekhar | Melbourne | 1977-78 |
| India in India | 9-69 | J.M.Patel | Kanpur | 1959-60 |

**BEST MATCH BOWLING ANALYSIS**

| | | | | |
|---|---|---|---|---|
| Australia in Australia | 12-126 | B.A.Reid | Melbourne | 1991-92 |
| Australia in India | 12-124 | A.K.Davidson | Kanpur | 1959-60 |
| India in Australia | 12-104 | B.S.Chandrasekhar | Melbourne | 1977-78 |
| India in India | 14-124 | J.M.Patel | Kanpur | 1959-60 |

**HIGHEST AGGREGATE OF WICKETS IN A SERIES**

| | | | |
|---|---|---|---|
| Australia in Australia | 31 (av 21.61) | C.J.McDermott | 1991-92 |
| Australia in India | 29 (av 14 86) | A.K.Davidson | 1959-60 |
| | 29 (av 19.58) | R.Benaud | 1959-60 |
| India in Australia | 31 (av 23.87) | B.S.Bedi | 1977-78 |
| India in India | 28 (av 22.32) | Kapil Dev | 1979-80 |

| **AUSTRALIA v PAKISTAN** | Australia | | Pakistan | | Captains | |
|---|---|---|---|---|---|---|
| Venue and Result | 1st | 2nd | 1st | 2nd | Australia | Pakistan |
| **1956-57 In PAKISTAN** | | | | | | |
| Karachi[1]-Pakistan 9 wkts | •80 | 187 | 199 | 1-69 | I.W.Johnson | A.H.Kardar |
| **1959-60 In PAKISTAN** | | | | | | |
| Dacca-Australia 8 wkts | 225 | 2-112 | •200 | 134 | R.Benaud | Fazal Mahmood |
| Lahore[2]-Australia 7 wkts | 9d-391 | 3-123 | •146 | 366 | | Imtiaz Ahmed |
| Karachi[1]-Drawn | 257 | 2-83 | •287 | 8d-194 | | Fazal Mahmood |
| **1964-65 in PAKISTAN** | | | | | | |
| Karachi[1]-Drawn | 352 | 2-227 | •414 | 8d-279 | R.B.Simpson | Hanif Mohammad |
| **1964-65 in AUSTRALIA** | | | | | | |
| Melbourne-Drawn | 448 | 2-88 | •287 | 326 | R.B.Simpson | Hanif Mohammad |
| **1972-73 in AUSTRALIA** | | | | | | |
| Adelaide-Australia inns & 114 runs | 585 | - | •257 | 214 | I.M.Chappell | Intikhab Alam |
| Melbourne-Australia 92 runs | •5d-441 | 425 | 8d-574 | 200 | | |
| Sydney-Australia 52 runs | •334 | 184 | 360 | 106 | | |
| **1976-77 in AUSTRALIA** | | | | | | |
| Adelaide-Drawn | 454 | 6-261 | •272 | 466 | G.S.Chappell | Mushtaq Mohammad |
| Melbourne-Australia 348 runs | •8d-517 | 8d-315 | 333 | 151 | | |
| Sydney-Pakistan 8 wkts | •211 | 180 | 360 | 232 | | |
| **1978-79 in AUSTRALIA** | | | | | | |
| Melbourne-Pakistan 71 runs | 168 | 310 | •196 | 9d-353 | G.N.Yallop | Mushtaq Mohammad |
| Perth-Australia 7 wkts | 327 | 3-236 | •277 | 285 | K.J.Hughes | |
| **1979-80 in PAKISTAN** | | | | | | |
| Karachi[1]-Pakistan 7 wkts | •225 | 140 | 292 | 3-76 | G.S.Chappell | Javed Miandad |
| Faisalabad-Drawn | •617 | - | 2-382 | - | | |
| Lahore[2]-Drawn | •7d-407 | 8-391 | 9d-420 | - | | |
| **1981-82 in AUSTRALIA** | | | | | | |
| Perth-Australia 286 runs | •180 | 8d-424 | 62 | 256 | G.S.Chappell | Javed Miandad |
| Brisbane[2]-Australia 10 wkts | 9d-512 | 0-3 | •291 | 223 | | |
| Melbourne-Pakistan inns & 82 runs | 293 | 125 | •8d-500 | - | | |
| **1982-83 in PAKISTAN** | | | | | | |
| Karachi[1]-Pakistan 9 wkts | •284 | 179 | 9d-419 | 1-47 | K.J.Hughes | Javed Miandad |
| Faisalabad-Pakistan inns & 3 runs | 168 | 330 | •6d-501 | - | | |
| Lahore[2]-Pakistan 9 wkts | •316 | 214 | 7d-467 | 1-64 | | |
| **1983-84 in AUSTRALIA** | | | | | | |
| Perth-Australia inns & 9 runs | •9d-436 | - | 129 | 298 | K.J.Hughes | Zaheer Abbas |
| Brisbane[2]-Drawn | 7d-506 | - | •156 | 3-82 | | Zaheer Abbas |
| Adelaide-Drawn | •465 | 7-310 | 624 | - | | Zaheer Abbas |
| Melbourne-Drawn | 555 | - | •470 | 7-238 | | Imran Khan |
| Sydney-Australia 10 wkts | 6d-454 | 0-35 | •278 | 210 | | Imran Khan |
| **1988-89 in PAKISTAN** | | | | | | |
| Karachi[1]-Pakistan inns & 188 runs | 185 | 116 | •9d-469 | - | A.R.Border | Javed Miandad |
| Faisalabad-Drawn | 321 | 3-67 | •316 | 9d-378 | | |
| Lahore[2]-Drawn | •340 | 3d-161 | 233 | 8-153 | | |

| AUSTRALIA v PAKISTAN (cont.) | Australia | | Pakistan | | Captains | |
|---|---|---|---|---|---|---|
| Venue and Result | 1st | 2nd | 1st | 2nd | Australia | Pakistan |
| **1989-90 in AUSTRALIA** | | | | | | |
| Melbourne-Australia 92 runs | •223 | 8d-312 | 107 | 336 | A.R.Border | Imran Khan |
| Adelaide-Drawn | 341 | 6-233 | •257 | 9d-387 | | |
| Sydney-Drawn | 2-176 | - | •199 | - | | |
| **1994-95 in PAKISTAN** | | | | | | |
| Karachi[1]-Pakistan 1 wkt | •337 | 232 | 256 | 9-315 | M.A.Taylor | Saleem Malik |
| Rawalpindi[2]-Drawn | •9d-521 | 1-14 | 260 | 537 | | |
| Lahore[2]-Drawn | 455 | - | •373 | 404 | | |
| **1995-96 in AUSTRALIA** | | | | | | |
| Brisbane[2]-Australia inns & 126 runs | •463 | - | 97 | 240 | M.A.Taylor | Wasim Akram |
| Hobart-Australia 155 runs | •267 | 306 | 198 | 220 | | |
| Sydney-Pakistan 74 runs | 257 | 172 | •299 | 204 | | |

## Test Match Results Summary

### AUSTRALIA v PAKISTAN-IN AUSTRALIA

| | | Result | | | Melbourne | | | Adelaide | | | Sydney | | | Perth | | | Brisbane[2] | | | Hobart | | |
|---|---|---|---|---|---|---|---|---|---|---|---|---|---|---|---|---|---|---|---|---|---|---|
| | Tests | A | P | D | A | P | D | A | P | D | A | P | D | A | P | D | A | P | D | A | P | D |
| 1964-65 | 1 | - | - | 1 | - | - | 1 | - | - | - | - | - | - | - | - | - | - | - | - | - | - | - |
| 1972-73 | 3 | 3 | - | - | 1 | - | - | 1 | - | - | 1 | - | - | - | - | - | - | - | - | - | - | - |
| 1976-77 | 3 | 1 | 1 | 1 | 1 | - | - | - | - | 1 | - | 1 | - | - | - | - | - | - | - | - | - | - |
| 1978-79 | 2 | 1 | 1 | - | - | 1 | - | - | - | - | - | - | - | 1 | - | - | - | - | - | - | - | - |
| 1981-82 | 3 | 2 | 1 | - | - | 1 | - | - | - | - | - | - | - | 1 | - | - | 1 | - | - | - | - | - |
| 1983-84 | 5 | 2 | - | 3 | - | - | 1 | - | - | 1 | 1 | - | - | 1 | - | - | - | - | 1 | - | - | - |
| 1989-90 | 3 | 1 | - | 2 | 1 | - | - | - | - | 1 | - | - | 1 | - | - | - | - | - | - | - | - | - |
| 1995-96 | 3 | 2 | 1 | - | - | - | - | - | - | - | - | 1 | - | - | - | - | 1 | - | - | 1 | - | - |
| | 23 | 12 | 4 | 7 | 3 | 2 | 2 | 1 | - | 3 | 2 | 2 | 1 | 3 | - | - | 2 | - | 1 | 1 | - | - |

### AUSTRALIA v PAKISTAN-IN PAKISTAN

| | | Result | | | Karachi[1] | | | Dacca | | | Lahore[2] | | | Faisalabad | | | Rawalpindi[2] | | |
|---|---|---|---|---|---|---|---|---|---|---|---|---|---|---|---|---|---|---|---|
| | Tests | A | P | D | A | P | D | A | P | D | A | P | D | A | P | D | A | P | D |
| 1956-57 | 1 | - | 1 | - | - | 1 | - | - | - | - | - | - | - | - | - | - | - | - | - |
| 1959-60 | 3 | 2 | - | 1 | - | - | 1 | 1 | - | - | 1 | - | - | - | - | - | - | - | - |
| 1964-65 | 1 | - | - | 1 | - | - | 1 | - | - | - | - | - | - | - | - | - | - | - | - |
| 1979-80 | 3 | - | 1 | 2 | - | 1 | - | - | - | - | - | - | 1 | - | - | 1 | - | - | - |
| 1982-83 | 3 | - | 3 | - | - | 1 | - | - | - | - | - | 1 | - | - | 1 | - | - | - | - |
| 1988-89 | 3 | - | 1 | 2 | - | 1 | - | - | - | - | - | - | 1 | - | - | 1 | - | - | - |
| 1994-95 | 3 | - | 1 | 2 | - | 1 | - | - | - | - | - | - | 1 | - | - | - | - | - | 1 |
| | 17 | 2 | 7 | 8 | - | 5 | 2 | 1 | - | - | 1 | 1 | 3 | - | 1 | 2 | - | - | 1 |
| Totals | 40 | 14 | 11 | 15 | | | | | | | | | | | | | | | |

### HIGHEST INNINGS TOTALS

| | | | |
|---|---|---|---|
| Australia in Australia | 585 | Adelaide | 1972-73 |
| Australia in Pakistan | 617 | Faisalabad | 1979-80 |
| Pakistan in Australia | 624 | Adelaide | 1983-84 |
| Pakistan in Pakistan | 537 | Rawalpindi[2] | 1994-95 |

**LOWEST INNINGS TOTALS**

| | | | |
|---|---|---|---|
| Australia in Australia | 125 | Melbourne | 1981-82 |
| Australia in Pakistan | 80 | Karachi[1] | 1956-57 |
| Pakistan in Australia | 62 | Perth | 1981-82 |
| Pakistan in Pakistan | 134 | Dacca | 1959-60 |

| | | | |
|---|---|---|---|
| **HIGHEST MATCH AGGREGATE** | 1640 for 33 wickets | Melbourne | 1972-73 |
| **LOWEST MATCH AGGREGATE** | 535 for 31 wickets | Karachi[1] | 1956-57 |

**HIGHEST INDIVIDUAL INNINGS**

| | | | | |
|---|---|---|---|---|
| Australia in Australia | 268 | G.N.Yallop | Melbourne | 1983-84 |
| Australia in Pakistan | 235 | G.S.Chappell | Faisalabad | 1979-80 |
| Pakistan in Australia | 158 | Majid Khan | Melbourne | 1972-73 |
| Pakistan in Pakistan | 237 | Saleem Malik | Rawalpindi[2] | 1994-95 |

**HIGHEST AGGREGATE ON RUNS IN A SERIES**

| | | | |
|---|---|---|---|
| Australia in Australia | 554 (av 92.33) | G.N.Yallop | 1983-84 |
| Australia in Pakistan | 395 (av 131.66) | A.R.Border | 1979-80 |
| Pakistan in Australia | 390 (av 43.33) | Mohsin Khan | 1983-84 |
| Pakistan in Pakistan | 557 (av 92.83) | Saleem Malik | 1994-95 |

**RECORD WICKET PARTNERSHIPS-AUSTRALIA**

| | | | | |
|---|---|---|---|---|
| 1st | 176 | M.A.Taylor (69), M.J.Slater (110) | Rawalpindi[2] | 1994-95 |
| 2nd | 259 | W.B.Phillips (159), G.N.Yallop (141) | Perth | 1983-84 |
| 3rd | 203 | G.N.Yallop (268), K.J.Hughes (94) | Melbourne | 1983-84 |
| 4th | 217 | G.S.Chappell (235), G.N.Yallop (172) | Faisalabad | 1979-80 |
| 5th | 171 | G.S.Chappell (121), G.J.Cosier (168) | Melbourne | 1976-77 |
| 5th | 171 | A.R.Border (118), G.S.Chappell (150*) | Brisbane[2] | 1983-84 |
| 6th | 139 | R.M.Cowper (83), T.R.Veivers (88) | Melbourne | 1964-65 |
| 7th | 185 | G.N.Yallop (268), G.R.J.Matthews (75) | Melbourne | 1983-84 |
| 8th | 117 | G.J.Cosier (168), K.J.O'Keeffe (28*) | Melbourne | 1976-77 |
| 9th | 83 | J.R.Watkins (36), R.A.L.Massie (42) | Sydney | 1972-73 |
| 10th | 52 | D.K.Lillee (14), M.H.N.Walker (34*) | Sydney | 1976-77 |
| 10th | 52 | G.F.Lawson (57*), T.M.Alderman (7) | Lahore[2] | 1982-83 |

**RECORD WICKET PARTNERSHIPS-PAKISTAN**

| | | | | |
|---|---|---|---|---|
| 1st | 249 | Khalid Ibadulla (166), Abdul Kadir (95) | Karachi[1] | 1964-65 |
| 2nd | 233 | Mohsin Khan (149), Qasim Omar (113) | Adelaide | 1983-84 |
| 3rd | 223* | Taslim Arif (210*), Javed Miandad (106*) | Faisalabad | 1979-80 |
| 4th | 155 | Mansoor Akhtar (111), Zaheer Abbas (126) | Faisalabad | 1982-83 |
| 5th | 186 | Javed Miandad (131), Saleem Malik (77) | Adelaide | 1983-84 |
| 6th | 196 | Saleem Malik (143), Aamer Sohail (105) | Lahore[2] | 1994-95 |
| 7th | 104 | Intikhab Alam (64), Wasim Bari (72) | Adelaide | 1972-73 |
| 8th | 111 | Majid Khan (110*), Imran Khan (56) | Lahore[2] | 1979-80 |
| 9th | 56 | Intikhab Alam (61), Afaq Hussain (13*) | Melbourne | 1964-65 |
| 10th | 87 | Asif Iqbal (152*), Iqbal Qasim (4) | Adelaide | 1976-77 |

**BEST INNINGS BOWLING ANALYSIS**

| | | | | |
|---|---|---|---|---|
| Australia in Australia | 8-59 | A.A.Mallett | Adelaide | 1972-73 |
| Australia in Pakistan | 7-75 | L.F.Kline | Lahore[2] | 1959-60 |
| Pakistan in Australia | 9-86 | Sarfraz Nawaz | Melbourne | 1978-79 |
| Pakistan in Pakistan | 7-49 | Iqbal Qasim | Karachi[1] | 1979-80 |

**BEST MATCH BOWLING ANALYSIS**

| | | | | |
|---|---|---|---|---|
| Australia in Australia | 11-77 | S.K.Warne | Brisbane[2] | 1995-96 |
| Australia in Pakistan | 10-111 | R.J.Bright | Karachi[1] | 1979-80 |
| Pakistan in Australia | 12-165 | Imran Khan | Sydney | 1976-77 |
| Pakistan in Pakistan | 13-114 | Fazal Mahmood | Karachi[1] | 1956-57 |

**HIGHEST AGGREGATE OF WICKETS IN A SERIES**

| | | | |
|---|---|---|---|
| Australia in Australia | 24 (av 24.16) | G.F.Lawson | 1983-84 |
| Australia in Pakistan | 18 (av 21.05) | R.Benaud | 1959-60 |
| | 18 (av 28.00) | S.K.Warne | 1994-95 |
| Pakistan in Australia | 19 (av 38.52) | Azeem Hafeez | 1983-84 |
| Pakistan in Pakistan | 22 (av 25.54) | Abdul Qadir | 1982-83 |

| **AUSTRALIA v SRI LANKA** | Australia | | Sri Lanka | | Captains | |
|---|---|---|---|---|---|---|
| Venue and Result | 1st | 2nd | 1st | 2nd | Australia | Sri Lanka |
| **1982-83 in SRI LANKA** | | | | | | |
| Kandy-Australia inns & 38 runs | •4d-514 | - | 271 | 205 | G.S.Chappell | L.R.D.Mendis |
| **1987-88 in AUSTRALIA** | | | | | | |
| Perth-Australia inns & 108 runs | •455 | - | 194 | 153 | A.R.Border | R.S.Madugalle |
| **1989-90 in AUSTRALIA** | | | | | | |
| Brisbane²-Drawn | •367 | 6-375 | 418 | - | A.R.Border | A.Ranatunga |
| Hobart-Australia 173 runs | •224 | 5d-513 | 216 | 348 | | |
| **1992-93 in SRI LANKA** | | | | | | |
| Colombo (SSC)-Australia 16 runs | •256 | 471 | 8d-547 | 164 | A.R.Border | A.Ranatunga |
| Colombo (PIS)-Drawn | •247 | 6d-296 | 258 | 2-136 | | |
| Moratuwa-Drawn | •337 | 8-271 | 9d-274 | - | | |
| **1995-96 in AUSTRALIA** | | | | | | |
| Perth-Australia inns & 36 runs | 5d-617 | - | •251 | 330 | M.A.Taylor | A.Ranatunga |
| Melbourne-Australia 10 wkts | •6d-500 | 0-41 | 233 | 307 | | A.Ranatunga |
| Adelaide-Australia 148 runs | •9d-502 | 6d-215 | 317 | 252 | | P.A.de Silva |

## Test Match Results Summary

**AUSTRALIA v SRI LANKA-IN AUSTRALIA**

| | | Result | | | Perth | | | Brisbane² | | | Hobart | | | Melbourne | | | Adelaide | | |
|---|---|---|---|---|---|---|---|---|---|---|---|---|---|---|---|---|---|---|---|
| | Tests | A | SL | D | A | SL | D | A | SL | D | A | SL | D | A | SL | D | A | SL | D |
| 1987-88 | 1 | 1 | - | - | 1 | - | - | - | - | - | - | - | - | - | - | - | - | - | - |
| 1989-90 | 2 | 1 | - | 1 | - | - | - | - | - | 1 | 1 | - | - | - | - | - | - | - | - |
| 1995-96 | 3 | 3 | - | - | 1 | - | - | - | - | - | - | - | - | 1 | - | - | 1 | - | - |
| | 6 | 5 | - | 1 | 2 | - | - | - | - | 1 | 1 | - | - | 1 | - | - | 1 | - | - |

**AUSTRALIA v SRI LANKA-IN SRI LANKA**

| | | Result | | | Kandy | | | Colombo (SSC) | | | Colombo (PIS) | | | Moratuwa | | |
|---|---|---|---|---|---|---|---|---|---|---|---|---|---|---|---|---|
| | Tests | A | SL | D | A | SL | D | A | SL | D | A | SL | D | A | SL | D |
| 1982-83 | 1 | 1 | - | - | 1 | - | - | - | - | - | - | - | - | - | - | - |
| 1992-93 | 3 | 1 | - | 2 | - | - | - | 1 | - | - | - | - | 1 | - | - | 1 |
| | 4 | 2 | - | 2 | 1 | - | - | 1 | - | - | - | - | 1 | - | - | 1 |
| Totals | 10 | 7 | - | 3 | | | | | | | | | | | | |

**HIGHEST INNINGS TOTALS**

| | | | |
|---|---|---|---|
| Australia in Australia | 5d-617 | Perth | 1995-96 |
| Australia in Sri Lanka | 4d-514 | Kandy | 1982-83 |
| Sri Lanka in Australia | 418 | Brisbane² | 1989-90 |
| Sri Lanka in Sri Lanka | 8d-547 | Colombo (SSC) | 1992-93 |

**LOWEST INNINGS TOTALS**

| | | | |
|---|---|---|---|
| Australia in Australia | 224 | Hobart | 1989-90 |
| Australia in Sri Lanka | 247 | Colombo (PIS) | 1992-93 |
| Sri Lanka in Australia | 153 | Perth | 1987-88 |
| Sri Lanka in Sri Lanka | 164 | Colombo (SSC) | 1992-93 |

| | | | |
|---|---|---|---|
| **HIGHEST MATCH AGGREGATE** | 1438 for 39 wickets | Colombo (SSC) | 1992-93 |
| **LOWEST MATCH AGGREGATE** | 802 for 30 wickets | Perth | 1987-88 |

**HIGHEST INDIVIDUAL INNINGS**

| | | | | |
|---|---|---|---|---|
| Australia in Australia | 219 | M.J.Slater | Perth | 1995-96 |
| Australia in Sri Lanka | 143* | D.W.Hookes | Kandy | 1982-83 |
| Sri Lanka in Australia | 167 | P.A.de Silva | Brisbane[2] | 1989-90 |
| Sri Lanka in Sri Lanka | 137 | A.P.Gurusinha | Colombo (SSC) | 1992-93 |

**HIGHEST AGGREGATE ON RUNS IN A SERIES**

| | | | |
|---|---|---|---|
| Australia in Australia | 362 (av 362.00) | S.R.Waugh | 1995-96 |
| Australia in Sri Lanka | 329 (av 54.83) | G.R.J.Matthews | 1992-93 |
| Sri Lanka in Australia | 314 (av 104.66) | P.A.de Silva | 1989-90 |
| Sri Lanka in Sri Lanka | 250 (av 50.00) | R.S.Mahanama | 1992-93 |

**RECORD WICKET PARTNERSHIPS-AUSTRALIA**

| | | | | |
|---|---|---|---|---|
| 1st | 228 | M.J.Slater (219), M.A.Taylor (96) | Perth | 1995-96 |
| 2nd | 170 | K.C.Wessels (141), G.N.Yallop (98) | Kandy | 1982-83 |
| 3rd | 158 | T.M.Moody (106), A.R.Border (56) | Brisbane[2] | 1989-90 |
| 3rd | 158 | M.J.Slater (219), M.E.Waugh (111) | Perth | 1995-96 |
| 4th | 163 | M.A.Taylor (108), A.R.Border (85) | Hobart | 1989-90 |
| 5th | 155* | D.W.Hookes (143*), A.R.Border (47*) | Kandy | 1982-83 |
| 6th | 260* | D.M.Jones (118*), S.R.Waugh (134*) | Hobart | 1989-90 |
| 7th | 129 | G.R.J.Matthews (96), I.A.Healy (49) | Moratuwa | 1992-93 |
| 8th | 56 | G.R.J.Matthews (64), C.J.McDermott (40) | Colombo (SSC) | 1992-93 |
| 9th | 45 | I.A.Healy (66*), S.K.Warne (24) | Colombo (SSC) | 1992-93 |
| 10th | 49 | I.A.Healy (66*), M.R.Whitney (13) | Colombo (SSC) | 1992-93 |

**RECORD WICKET PARTNERSHIPS-SRI LANKA**

| | | | | |
|---|---|---|---|---|
| 1st | 110 | R.S.Mahanama (69), U.C.Hathurusingha (49) | Colombo (PIS) | 1992-93 |
| 2nd | 92 | R.S.Mahanama (78), A.P.Gurusinha (137) | Colombo (SSC) | 1992-93 |
| 3rd | 125 | S.T.Jayasuriya (125), S.Ranatunga (65) | Adelaide | 1995-96 |
| 4th | 230 | A.P.Gurusinha (137), A.Ranatunga (127) | Colombo (SSC) | 1992-93 |
| 5th | 116 | H.P.Tillakaratne (82), A.Ranatunga (48) | Moratuwa | 1992-93 |
| 6th | 96 | A.P.Gurusinha (137), R.S.Kaluwitharana (132*) | Colombo (SSC) | 1992-93 |
| 7th | 144 | P.A.de Silva (167), J.R.Ratnayeke (56) | Brisbane[2] | 1989-90 |
| 8th | 33 | A.Ranatunga (55), C.P.H.Ramanayake (9) | Perth | 1987-88 |
| 9th | 46 | H.D.P.K.Dharmasena (30), G.P.Wickramasinghe (28) | Perth | 1995-96 |
| 10th | 27 | P.A.de Silva (167), C.P.H.Ramanayake (10*) | Brisbane[2] | 1989-90 |

**BEST INNINGS BOWLING ANALYSIS**

| | | | | |
|---|---|---|---|---|
| Australia in Australia | 5-39 | P.R.Reiffel | Adelaide | 1995-96 |
| Australia in Sri Lanka | 5-66 | T.G.Hogan | Kandy | 1982-83 |
| Sri Lanka in Australia | 6-66 | R.J.Ratnayake | Hobart | 1989-90 |
| Sri Lanka in Sri Lanka | 5-82 | C.P.H.Ramanayake | Moratuwa | 1992-93 |

**BEST MATCH BOWLING ANALYSIS**

| | | | | |
|---|---|---|---|---|
| Australia in Australia | 8-156 | M.G.Hughes | Hobart | 1989-90 |
| Australia in Sri Lanka | 7-166 | B.Yardley | Kandy | 1982-83 |
| Sri Lanka in Australia | 8-189 | R.J.Ratnayake | Hobart | 1989-90 |
| Sri Lanka in Sri Lanka | 8-157 | C.P.H.Ramanayake | Moratuwa | 1992-93 |

**HIGHEST AGGREGATE OF WICKETS IN A SERIES**

| | | | |
|---|---|---|---|
| Australia in Australia | 21 (av 20.85) | G.D.McGrath | 1995-96 |
| Australia in Sri Lanka | 14 (av 24.42) | C.J.McDermott | 1992-93 |
| Sri Lanka in Australia | 9 (av 41.22) | W.P.U.J.C.Vaas | 1995-96 |
| Sri Lanka in Sri Lanka | 17 (av 25.52) | C.P.H.Ramanayake | 1992-93 |

| **ENGLAND v SOUTH AFRICA** | England | | South Africa | | Captains | |
|---|---|---|---|---|---|---|
| Venue and Result | 1st | 2nd | 1st | 2nd | England | South Africa |
| **1888-89 in SOUTH AFRICA** | | | | | | |
| Port Elizabeth-England 8 wkts | 148 | 2-67 | •84 | 129 | C.A.Smith | O.R.Dunell |
| Cape Town-England inns & 202 runs | •292 | - | 47 | 43 | M.P.Bowden | W.H.Milton |
| **1891-92 in SOUTH AFRICA** | | | | | | |
| Cape Town-England inns & 189 runs | 369 | - | •97 | 83 | W.W.Read | W.H.Milton |
| **1895-96 in SOUTH AFRICA** | | | | | | |
| Port Elizabeth-England 288 runs | •185 | 226 | 93 | 30 | Sir T.C.O'Brien | E.A.Halliwell |
| Johannesburg[1]-England inns & 197 runs | •482 | - | 151 | 134 | Lord Hawke | E.A.Halliwell |
| Cape Town-England inns & 33 runs | 265 | - | •115 | 117 | Lord Hawke | A.R.Richards |
| **1898-99 in SOUTH AFRICA** | | | | | | |
| Johannesburg[1]-England 32 runs | •145 | 237 | 251 | 99 | Lord Hawke | M.Bisset |
| Cape Town-England 210 runs | •92 | 330 | 177 | 35 | | |
| **1905-06 in SOUTH AFRICA** | | | | | | |
| Johannesburg[1]-South Africa 1 wkt | •184 | 190 | 91 | 9-287 | P.F.Warner | P.W.Sherwell |
| Johannesburg[1]-South Africa 9 wkts | •148 | 160 | 277 | 1-33 | | |
| Johannesburg[1]-South Africa 243 runs | 295 | 196 | •385 | 5d-349 | | |
| Cape Town-England 4 wkts | 198 | 6-160 | •218 | 138 | | |
| Cape Town-South Africa inns & 16 runs | •187 | 130 | 333 | - | | |
| **1907 in ENGLAND** | | | | | | |
| Lord's-Drawn | •428 | - | 140 | 3-185 | R.E.Foster | P.W.Sherwell |
| Leeds-England 53 runs | •76 | 162 | 110 | 75 | | |
| The Oval-Drawn | •295 | 138 | 178 | 5-159 | | |
| **1909-10 in SOUTH AFRICA** | | | | | | |
| Johannesburg[1]-South Africa 19 runs | 310 | 224 | •208 | 345 | H.D.G.Leveson Gower | S.J.Snooke |
| Durban[1]-South Africa 95 runs | 199 | 252 | •199 | 347 | H.D.G.Leveson Gower | |
| Johannesburg[1]-England 3 wkts | 322 | 7-221 | •305 | 237 | H.D.G.Leveson Gower | |
| Cape Town-South Africa 4 wkts | •203 | 178 | 207 | 6-175 | F.L.Fane | |
| Cape Town-England 9 wkts | •417 | 1-16 | 103 | 327 | F.L.Fane | |
| **1912 in ENGLAND** | | | | | | |
| Lord's-England inns & 62 runs | 337 | - | •58 | 217 | C.B.Fry | F.Mitchell |
| Leeds-England 174 runs | •242 | 238 | 147 | 159 | | L.J.Tancred |
| The Oval-England 10 wkts | 176 | 0-14 | •95 | 93 | | L.J.Tancred |
| **1913-14 in SOUTH AFRICA** | | | | | | |
| Durban[1]-England inns & 157 runs | 450 | - | •182 | 111 | J.W.H.T.Douglas | H.W.Taylor |
| Johannesburg[1]-England inns & 12 runs | 403 | - | •160 | 231 | | |
| Johannesburg[1]-England 91 runs | •238 | 308 | 151 | 304 | | |
| Durban[1]-Drawn | 163 | 5-154 | •170 | 9d-305 | | |
| Port Elizabeth-England 10 wkts | 411 | 0-11 | •193 | 228 | | |
| **1922-23 in SOUTH AFRICA** | | | | | | |
| Johannesburg[1]-South Africa 168 runs | 182 | 218 | •148 | 420 | F.T.Mann | H.W.Taylor |
| Cape Town-England 1 wkt | 183 | 9-173 | •113 | 242 | | |
| Durban[2]-Drawn | •428 | 1-11 | 368 | - | | |
| Johannesburg[1]-Drawn | •244 | 6d-376 | 295 | 4-247 | | |
| Durban[2]-England 109 runs | •281 | 241 | 179 | 234 | | |

| **ENGLAND v SOUTH AFRICA** (cont.) Venue and Result | England 1st | England 2nd | South Africa 1st | South Africa 2nd | Captains England | Captains South Africa |
|---|---|---|---|---|---|---|
| **1924 in ENGLAND** | | | | | | |
| Birmingham-England inns & 18 runs | •438 | - | 30 | 390 | A.E.R.Gilligan | H.W.Taylor |
| Lord's-England inns & 18 runs | 2d-531 | - | •273 | 240 | A.E.R.Gilligan | |
| Leeds-England 9 wkts | •396 | 1-60 | 132 | 323 | A.E.R.Gilligan | |
| Manchester-Drawn | - | - | •4-116 | - | J.W.H.T.Douglas | |
| The Oval-Drawn | 8-421 | - | •342 | - | A.E.R.Gilligan | |
| **1927-28 in SOUTH AFRICA** | | | | | | |
| Johannesburg[1]-England 10 wkts | 313 | 0-57 | •196 | 170 | R.T.Stanyforth | H.G.Deane |
| Cape Town-England 87 runs | •133 | 428 | 250 | 224 | R.T.Stanyforth | |
| Durban[2]-Drawn | 430 | 2-132 | •246 | 8d-464 | R.T.Stanyforth | |
| Johannesburg[1]-South Africa 4 wkts | •265 | 215 | 328 | 6-156 | R.T.Stanyforth | |
| Durban[2]-South Africa 8 wkts | •282 | 118 | 7d-332 | 2-69 | G.T.S.Stevens | |
| **1929 in ENGLAND** | | | | | | |
| Birmingham-Drawn | •245 | 4d-308 | 250 | 1-171 | J C.White | H.G.Deane |
| Lord's-Drawn | •302 | 8d-312 | 322 | 5-90 | J C.White | |
| Leeds-England 5 wkts | 328 | 5-186 | •236 | 275 | J C.White | |
| Manchester-England inns & 32 runs | •7d-427 | - | 130 | 265 | A.W.Carr | |
| The Oval-Drawn | •258 | 1-264 | 8d-492 | - | A.W.Carr | |
| **1930-31 in SOUTH AFRICA** | | | | | | |
| Johannesburg[1]-South Africa 28 runs | 193 | 211 | •126 | 306 | A.P.F.Chapman | E.P.Nupen |
| Cape Town-Drawn | 350 | 252 | •8d-513 | - | | H.G.Deane |
| Durban[2]-Drawn | 1d-223 | - | •177 | 8-145 | | H.G.Deane |
| Johannesburg[1]-Drawn | •442 | 9d-169 | 295 | 7-280 | | H.B.Cameron |
| Durban[2]-Drawn | 230 | 4-72 | •252 | 7d-219 | | H.B.Cameron |
| **1935 in ENGLAND** | | | | | | |
| Nottingham-Drawn | •7d-384 | - | 220 | 1-17 | R.E.S.Wyatt | H.F.Wade |
| Lord's-South Africa 157 runs | 198 | 151 | •228 | 7d-278 | | |
| Leeds-Drawn | •216 | 7d-294 | 171 | 5-194 | | |
| Manchester-Drawn | •357 | 6d-231 | 318 | 2-169 | | |
| The Oval-Drawn | 6d-534 | - | •476 | 6-287 | | |
| **1938-39 in SOUTH AFRICA** | | | | | | |
| Johannesburg[1]-Drawn | •422 | 4d-291 | 390 | 1-108 | W.R.Hammond | A.Melville |
| Cape Town-Drawn | •9d-559 | - | 286 | 2-201 | | |
| Durban[2]-England inns & 13 runs | •4d-469 | - | 103 | 353 | | |
| Johannesburg[1]-Drawn | •215 | 4-203 | 8d-349 | - | | |
| Durban[2]-Drawn | 316 | 6-654 | •530 | 481 | | |
| **1947 in ENGLAND** | | | | | | |
| Nottingham-Drawn | 208 | 551 | •533 | 1-166 | N.W.D.Yardley | A.Melville |
| Lord's-England 10 wkts | •8d-554 | 0-26 | 327 | 252 | | |
| Manchester-England 7 wkts | 478 | 3-130 | •339 | 267 | | |
| Leeds-England 10 wkts | 7d-317 | 0-47 | •175 | 184 | | |
| The Oval-Drawn | •427 | 6d-325 | 302 | 7-423 | | |
| **1948-49 in SOUTH AFRICA** | | | | | | |
| Durban[2]-England 2 wkts | 253 | 8-128 | •161 | 219 | F.G.Mann | A.D.Nourse |
| Johannesburg[2]-Drawn | •608 | - | 315 | 2-270 | | |
| Cape Town-Drawn | •308 | 3d-276 | 356 | 4-142 | | |
| Johannesburg[2]-Drawn | •379 | 7d-253 | 9d-257 | 4-194 | | |
| Port Elizabeth-England 3 wkts | 395 | 7-174 | •379 | 3d-187 | | |

| ENGLAND v SOUTH AFRICA (cont.) | England | | South Africa | | Captains | |
|---|---|---|---|---|---|---|
| Venue and Result | 1st | 2nd | 1st | 2nd | England | South Africa |
| **1951 in ENGLAND** | | | | | | |
| Nottingham-South Africa 71 runs | 9d-419 | 114 | •9d-483 | 121 | F.R.Brown | A.D.Nourse |
| Lord's-England 10 wkts | •311 | 0-16 | 115 | 211 | | |
| Manchester-England 9 wkts | 211 | 1-142 | •158 | 191 | | |
| Leeds-Drawn | 505 | - | •538 | 0-87 | | |
| The Oval-England 4 wkts | 194 | 6-164 | •202 | 154 | | |
| **1955 in ENGLAND** | | | | | | |
| Nottingham-England inns & 5 runs | •334 | - | 181 | 148 | P.B.H.May | J.E.Cheetham |
| Lord's-England 71 runs | •133 | 353 | 304 | 111 | | J.E.Cheetham |
| Manchester-South Africa 3 wkts | •284 | 381 | 8d-521 | 7-145 | | D.J.McGlew |
| Leeds-South Africa 224 runs | 191 | 256 | •171 | 500 | | D.J.McGlew |
| The Oval-England 92 runs | •151 | 204 | 112 | 151 | | J.E.Cheetham |
| **1956-57 in SOUTH AFRICA** | | | | | | |
| Johannesburg³-England 131 runs | •268 | 150 | 215 | 72 | P.B.H.May | C.B.van Ryneveld |
| Cape Town-England 312 runs | •369 | 6d-220 | 205 | 72 | | D.J.McGlew |
| Durban²-Drawn | •218 | 254 | 283 | 6-142 | | C.B.van Ryneveld |
| Johannesburg³-South Africa 17 runs | 251 | 214 | •340 | 142 | | C.B.van Ryneveld |
| Port Elizabeth-South Africa 58 runs | 110 | 130 | •164 | 134 | | C.B.van Ryneveld |
| **1960 in ENGLAND** | | | | | | |
| Birmingham-England 100 runs | •292 | 203 | 186 | 209 | M.C.Cowdrey | D.J.McGlew |
| Lord's-England inns & 73 runs | •8d-362 | - | 152 | 137 | | |
| Nottingham-England 8 wkts | •287 | 2-49 | 88 | 247 | | |
| Manchester-Drawn | •260 | 7d-153 | 229 | 0-46 | | |
| The Oval-Drawn | •155 | 9d-479 | 419 | 4-97 | | |
| **1964-65 in SOUTH AFRICA** | | | | | | |
| Durban²-England inns & 104 runs | •5d-485 | - | 155 | 226 | M J K.Smith | T L.Goddard |
| Johannesburg³-Drawn | •531 | - | 317 | 6-336 | | |
| Cape Town-Drawn | 442 | 0 15 | •7d-501 | 346 | | |
| Johannesburg³-Drawn | 384 | 6-153 | •6d-390 | 3d-307 | | |
| Port Elizabeth-Drawn | 435 | 1-29 | •502 | 4d-178 | | |
| **1965 in ENGLAND** | | | | | | |
| Lord's-Drawn | 338 | 7-145 | •280 | 248 | M.J.K.Smith | P L.van der Merwe |
| Nottingham-South Africa 94 runs | 240 | 224 | •269 | 289 | | |
| The Oval-Drawn | 202 | 4-308 | •208 | 392 | | |
| **1994 in ENGLAND** | | | | | | |
| Lord's-South Africa 356 runs | 180 | 99 | •357 | 8d-278 | M.A.Atherton | K.C.Wessels |
| Leeds-Drawn | •9d-477 | 5d-267 | 447 | 3-116 | | |
| The Oval-England 8 wickets | 304 | 2-205 | •332 | 175 | | |
| **1995-96 in SOUTH AFRICA** | | | | | | |
| Centurion-Drawn | •9d-381 | - | - | - | M.A.Atherton | W.J.Cronje |
| Johannesburg³-Drawn | 200 | 5-351 | •332 | 9d-346 | | |
| Durban²-Drawn | 5-152 | - | •225 | - | | |
| Port Elizabeth-Drawn | 263 | 3-189 | •428 | 9d-162 | | |
| Cape Town-South Africa 10 wkts | •153 | 157 | 244 | 0-70 | | |
| **1998 in ENGLAND** | | | | | | |
| Birmingham-Drawn | •462 | 8-170 | 343 | - | A.J.Stewart | W.J.Cronje |
| Lord's-South Africa 10 wkts | 110 | 264 | •360 | 0-15 | | |
| Manchester-Drawn | 183 | 9-369 | 5d-552 | | | |
| Nottingham-England 8 wkts | 336 | 2-247 | •374 | 208 | | |
| Leeds-England 23 | •230 | 240 | 252 | 195 | | |

## Test Match Results Summary

### ENGLAND v SOUTH AFRICA-IN ENGLAND

| | Tests | Result | | | Lord's | | | Leeds | | | The Oval | | | Birmingham | | | Manchester | | | Nottingham | | |
|---|---|---|---|---|---|---|---|---|---|---|---|---|---|---|---|---|---|---|---|---|---|---|
| | | E | SA | D | E | SA | D | E | SA | D | E | SA | D | E | SA | D | E | SA | D | E | SA | D |
| 1907 | 3 | 1 | - | 2 | - | - | 1 | 1 | - | - | - | - | 1 | - | - | - | - | - | - | - | - | - |
| 1912 | 3 | 3 | - | - | 1 | - | - | 1 | - | - | 1 | - | - | - | - | - | - | - | - | - | - | - |
| 1924 | 5 | 3 | - | 2 | 1 | - | - | 1 | - | - | - | - | 1 | 1 | - | - | - | - | 1 | - | - | - |
| 1929 | 5 | 2 | - | 3 | - | - | 1 | 1 | - | - | - | - | 1 | - | - | 1 | 1 | - | - | - | - | - |
| 1935 | 5 | - | 1 | 4 | - | 1 | - | - | - | 1 | - | - | 1 | - | - | - | - | - | 1 | - | - | 1 |
| 1947 | 5 | 3 | - | 2 | 1 | - | - | 1 | - | - | - | - | 1 | - | - | - | 1 | - | - | - | - | 1 |
| 1951 | 5 | 3 | 1 | 1 | 1 | - | - | - | - | 1 | 1 | - | - | - | - | - | 1 | - | - | - | 1 | - |
| 1955 | 5 | 3 | 2 | - | 1 | - | - | - | 1 | - | 1 | - | - | - | - | - | - | 1 | - | 1 | - | - |
| 1960 | 5 | 3 | - | 2 | 1 | - | - | - | - | - | - | - | 1 | 1 | - | - | - | - | 1 | 1 | - | - |
| 1965 | 3 | - | 1 | 2 | - | - | 1 | - | - | - | - | - | 1 | - | - | - | - | - | - | - | 1 | - |
| 1994 | 3 | 1 | 1 | 1 | - | 1 | - | - | - | 1 | 1 | - | - | - | - | - | - | - | - | - | - | - |
| 1998 | 5 | 2 | 1 | 2 | - | 1 | - | 1 | - | - | - | - | - | - | - | 1 | - | - | 1 | 1 | - | - |
| | 52 | 24 | 7 | 21 | 6 | 3 | 3 | 6 | 1 | 3 | 4 | - | 7 | 2 | - | 2 | 3 | 1 | 4 | 3 | 2 | 2 |

### ENGLAND v SOUTH AFRICA-IN SOUTH AFRICA

| | Tests | Result | | | P.Elizabeth | | | Cape Town | | | Johannesburg | | | Durban | | | Centurion | | |
|---|---|---|---|---|---|---|---|---|---|---|---|---|---|---|---|---|---|---|---|
| | | E | SA | D | E | SA | D | E | SA | D | E | SA | D | E | SA | D | E | SA | D |
| 1888-89 | 2 | 2 | - | - | 1 | - | - | 1 | - | - | - | - | - | - | - | - | - | - | - |
| 1891-92 | 1 | 1 | - | - | - | - | - | 1 | - | - | - | - | - | - | - | - | - | - | - |
| 1895-96 | 3 | 3 | - | - | 1 | - | - | 1 | - | - | 1 | - | - | - | - | - | - | - | - |
| 1898-99 | 2 | 2 | - | - | - | - | - | 1 | - | - | 1 | - | - | - | - | - | - | - | - |
| 1905-06 | 5 | 1 | 4 | - | - | - | - | 1 | 1 | - | - | 3 | - | - | - | - | - | - | - |
| 1909-10 | 5 | 2 | 3 | - | - | - | - | 1 | 1 | - | 1 | 1 | - | - | 1 | - | - | - | - |
| 1913-14 | 5 | 4 | - | 1 | 1 | - | - | - | - | - | 2 | - | - | 1 | - | 1 | - | - | - |
| 1922-23 | 5 | 2 | 1 | 2 | - | - | - | 1 | - | - | - | 1 | 1 | 1 | - | 1 | - | - | - |
| 1927-28 | 5 | 2 | 2 | 1 | - | - | - | 1 | - | - | 1 | 1 | - | - | 1 | 1 | - | - | - |
| 1930-31 | 5 | - | 1 | 4 | - | - | - | - | - | 1 | - | 1 | 1 | - | - | 2 | - | - | - |
| 1938-39 | 5 | 1 | - | 4 | - | - | - | - | - | 1 | - | - | 2 | 1 | - | 1 | - | - | - |
| 1948-49 | 5 | 2 | - | 3 | 1 | - | - | - | - | 1 | - | - | 2 | 1 | - | - | - | - | - |
| 1956-57 | 5 | 2 | 2 | 1 | - | 1 | - | 1 | - | - | 1 | 1 | - | - | - | 1 | - | - | - |
| 1964-65 | 5 | 1 | - | 4 | - | - | 1 | - | - | 1 | - | - | 2 | 1 | - | - | - | - | - |
| 1995-96 | 5 | - | 1 | 4 | - | - | 1 | - | 1 | - | - | - | 1 | - | - | 1 | - | - | 1 |
| | 63 | 25 | 14 | 24 | 4 | 1 | 2 | 9 | 3 | 4 | 7 | 8 | 9 | 5 | 2 | 8 | - | - | 1 |
| Totals | 115 | 49 | 21 | 45 | | | | | | | | | | | | | | | |

### HIGHEST INNINGS TOTALS

| | | | |
|---|---|---|---|
| England in England | 8d-554 | Lord's | 1947 |
| England in South Africa | 5-654 | Durban[2] | 1938-39 |
| South Africa in England | 5d-552 | Manchester | 1998 |
| South Africa in South Africa | 530 | Durban[2] | 1938-39 |

### LOWEST INNINGS TOTALS

| | | | |
|---|---|---|---|
| England in England | 76 | Leeds | 1907 |
| England in South Africa | 92 | Cape Town | 1898-99 |
| South Africa in England | 30 | Birmingham | 1924 |
| South Africa in South Africa | 30 | Port Elizabeth | 1895-96 |

| | | | |
|---|---|---|---|
| **HIGHEST MATCH AGGREGATE** | 1981 for 35 wickets | Durban[2] | 1938-39 |
| **LOWEST MATCH AGGREGATE** | 378 for 30 wickets | The Oval | 1912 |

## HIGHEST INDIVIDUAL INNINGS

| | | | | |
|---|---|---|---|---|
| England in England | 211 | J.B.Hobbs | Lord's | 1924 |
| England in South Africa | 243 | E.Paynter | Durban[2] | 1938-39 |
| South Africa in England | 236 | E.A.B.Rowan | Leeds | 1951 |
| South Africa in South Africa | 176 | H.W.Taylor | Johannesburg[1] | 1922-23 |

## HIGHEST AGGREGATE OF RUNS IN A SERIES

| | | | |
|---|---|---|---|
| England in England | 753 (av 94.12) | D.C.S.Compton | 1947 |
| England in South Africa | 653 (av 81.62) | E.Paynter | 1938-39 |
| South Africa in England | 621 (av 69.00) | A.D.Nourse | 1947 |
| South Africa in South Africa | 582 (av 64.66) | H.W.Taylor | 1922-23 |

## RECORD WICKET PARTNERSHIPS-ENGLAND

| | | | | |
|---|---|---|---|---|
| 1st | 359 | L.Hutton (158), C.Washbrook (195) | Johannesburg[2] | 1948-49 |
| 2nd | 280 | P.A.Gibb (120), W.J.Edrich (219) | Durban[2] | 1938-39 |
| 3rd | 370 | W.J.Edrich (189), D.C.S.Compton (208) | Lord's | 1947 |
| 4th | 197 | W.R.Hammond (181), L.E.G.Ames (115) | Cape Town | 1938-39 |
| 5th | 237 | D.C.S.Compton (163), N.W.D.Yardley (99) | Nottingham | 1947 |
| 6th | 206* | K.F.Barrington (148*), J.M.Parks (108*) | Durban[2] | 1964-65 |
| 7th | 115 | J.W.H.T.Douglas (119), M.C.Bird (61) | Durban[1] | 1913-14 |
| 8th | 154 | C.W.Wright (71), H.R Bromley-Davenport (84) | Johannesburg[1] | 1895-96 |
| 9th | 71 | H.Wood (134), J.T.Hearne (40) | Cape Town | 1891-92 |
| 10th | 92 | C.A.G.Russell (111), A.E.R.Gilligan (39*) | Durban[2] | 1922-23 |

## RECORD WICKET PARTNERSHIPS-SOUTH AFRICA

| | | | | |
|---|---|---|---|---|
| 1st | 260 | B.Mitchell (123), I.J.Siedle (141) | Cape Town | 1930-31 |
| 2nd | 238 | G.Kirsten (210). J.H.Kallis (132) | Manchester | 1998 |
| 3rd | 319 | A.Melville (189), A.D.Nourse (149) | Nottingham | 1947 |
| 4th | 214 | H.W.Taylor (121), H.G.Deane (93) | The Oval | 1929 |
| 5th | 157 | A.J.Pithey (95), J.H.B.Waite (64) | Johannesburg[3] | 1964-65 |
| 6th | 171 | J.H.B.Waite (113), P.L.Winslow (108) | Manchester | 1955 |
| 7th | 123 | H.G.Deane (73), E.P.Nupen (69) | Durban[2] | 1927-28 |
| 8th | 109* | B.Mitchell (189*), L.Tuckett (40*) | The Oval | 1947 |
| 9th | 137 | E.L.Dalton (117), A.B.C.Langton (73*) | The Oval | 1935 |
| 10th | 103 | H.G.Owen-Smith (129), A.J.Bell (26*) | Leeds | 1929 |

## BEST INNINGS BOWLING ANALYSIS

| | | | | |
|---|---|---|---|---|
| England in England | 9-57 | D.E.Malcolm | The Oval | 1994 |
| England in South Africa | 9-28 | G.A.Lohmann | Johannesburg[1] | 1895-96 |
| South Africa in England | 7-65 | S.J.Pegler | Lord's | 1912 |
| South Africa in South Africa | 9-113 | H.J.Tayfield | Johannesburg[3] | 1956-57 |

## BEST MATCH BOWLING ANALYSIS

| | | | | |
|---|---|---|---|---|
| England in England | 15-99 | C.Blythe | Leeds | 1907 |
| England in South Africa | 17-159 | S.F.Barnes | Johannesburg[1] | 1913-14 |
| South Africa in England | 10-87 | P.M.Pollock | Nottingham | 1965 |
| South Africa in South Africa | 13-192 | H.J.Tayfield | Johannesburg[3] | 1956-57 |

## HIGHEST AGGREGATE OF WICKETS IN A SERIES

| | | | |
|---|---|---|---|
| England in England | 34 (av 8.29) | S F Barnes | 1912 |
| England in South Africa | 49 (av 10.93) | S.F.Barnes | 1913-14 |
| South Africa in England | 33 (av 19.79) | A.A.Donald | 1998 |
| South Africa in South Africa | 37 (av 17.18) | H.J.Tayfield | 1956-57 |

| **ENGLAND v WEST INDIES** | England | | West Indies | | Captains | |
|---|---|---|---|---|---|---|
| Venue and Result | 1st | 2nd | 1st | 2nd | England | West Indies |
| **1928 in ENGLAND** | | | | | | |
| Lord's-England inns & 58 runs | •401 | - | 177 | 166 | A.P.F.Chapman | R.K.Nunes |
| Manchester-England inns & 30 runs | 351 | - | •206 | 115 | | |
| The Oval-England inns & 71 runs | 438 | - | •238 | 129 | | |
| **1929-30 in WEST INDIES** | | | | | | |
| Bridgetown-Drawn | 467 | 3-167 | •369 | 384 | Hon F.S.G.Calthorpe | E.L.G.Hoad |
| Port-of-Spain-England 167 runs | •208 | 8d-425 | 254 | 212 | | N.Betancourt |
| Georgetown-West Indies 289 runs | 145 | 327 | •471 | 290 | | M.P.Fernandes |
| Kingston-Drawn | •849 | 9d-272 | 286 | 5-408 | | R.K.Nunes |
| **1933 in ENGLAND** | | | | | | |
| Lord's-England inns & 27 runs | •296 | - | 97 | 172 | D.R.Jardine | G.C.Grant |
| Manchester-Drawn | 374 | - | •375 | 225 | D.R.Jardine | |
| The Oval-England inns & 17 runs | •312 | - | 100 | 195 | R.E.S.Wyatt | |
| **1934-35 in WEST INDIES** | | | | | | |
| Bridgetown-England 4 wkts | 7d-81 | 6-75 | •102 | 6d-51 | R.E.S.Wyatt | G.C.Grant |
| Port-of-Spain-West Indies 217 runs | 258 | 107 | •302 | 6d-280 | | |
| Georgetown-Drawn | •226 | 6d-160 | 184 | 5-104 | | |
| Kingston-West Indies inns & 161 runs | 271 | 103 | •7d-535 | - | | |
| **1939 in ENGLAND** | | | | | | |
| Lord's-England 8 wkts | 5d-404 | 2-100 | •277 | 225 | W.R.Hammond | R.S.Grant |
| Manchester-Drawn | •7d-164 | 6d-128 | 133 | 4-43 | | |
| The Oval-Drawn | •352 | 3d-366 | 498 | - | | |
| **1947-48 in WEST INDIES** | | | | | | |
| Bridgetown-Drawn | 253 | 4-86 | •296 | 9d-351 | K.Cranston | G.A.Headley |
| Port-of-Spain-Drawn | •362 | 275 | 497 | 3-72 | G.O.B.Allen | G.E.Gomez |
| Georgetown-West Indies 7 wkts | 111 | 263 | •8d-297 | 3-78 | G.O.B.Allen | J.D.C.Goddard |
| Kingston-West Indies 10 wkts | •227 | 336 | 490 | 0-76 | G.O.B.Allen | J.D.C.Goddard |
| **1950 in ENGLAND** | | | | | | |
| Manchester-England 202 runs | •312 | 288 | 215 | 183 | N.W.D.Yardley | J.D.C.Goddard |
| Lord's-West Indies 326 runs | 151 | 274 | •326 | 6d-425 | N.W.D Yardley | |
| Nottingham-West Indies 10 wkts | •223 | 436 | 558 | 0-103 | N.W.D.Yardley | |
| The Oval-West Indies inns & 56 runs | 344 | 103 | •503 | - | F.R.Brown | |
| **1953-54 in WEST INDIES** | | | | | | |
| Kingston-West Indies 140 runs | 170 | 316 | •417 | 6d-209 | L.Hutton | J.B.Stollmeyer |
| Bridgetown-West Indies 181 runs | 181 | 313 | •383 | 2d-292 | | |
| Georgetown-England 9 wkts | •435 | 1-75 | 251 | 256 | | |
| Port-of-Spain-Drawn | 537 | 3-98 | •8d-681 | 4d-212 | | |
| Kingston-England 9 wkts | 414 | 1-72 | •139 | 346 | | |
| **1957 in ENGLAND** | | | | | | |
| Birmingham-Drawn | •186 | 4d-583 | 474 | 7-72 | P.B.H.May | J.D.C.Goddard |
| Lord s-England inns & 36 runs | 424 | - | •127 | 261 | | |
| Nottingham-Drawn | •6d-619 | 1-64 | 372 | 367 | | |
| Leeds-England inns & 5 runs | 279 | - | •142 | 132 | | |
| The Oval-England inns & 237 runs | •412 | - | 89 | 86 | | |

| **ENGLAND v WEST INDIES** (cont.) Venue and Result | England 1st | England 2nd | West Indies 1st | West Indies 2nd | Captains England | Captains West Indies |
|---|---|---|---|---|---|---|
| **1959-60 in WEST INDIES** | | | | | | |
| Bridgetown-Drawn | •482 | 0-71 | 8d-563 | - | P.B.H.May | F.C.M.Alexander |
| Port-of-Spain-England 256 runs | •382 | 9d-230 | 112 | 244 | P.B.H.May | |
| Kingston-Drawn | •277 | 305 | 353 | 6-175 | P.B.H.May | |
| Georgetown-Drawn | •295 | 8-334 | 8d-402 | - | M.C.Cowdrey | |
| Port-of-Spain-Drawn | •393 | 7d-350 | 8d-338 | 5-209 | M.C.Cowdrey | |
| **1963 in ENGLAND** | | | | | | |
| Manchester-West Indies 10 wkts | 205 | 296 | •6d-501 | 0-1 | E.R.Dexter | F.M.M.Worrell |
| Lord's-Drawn | 297 | 9-228 | •301 | 229 | | |
| Birmingham-England 217 runs | •216 | 9d-278 | 186 | 91 | | |
| Leeds-West Indies 221 runs | 174 | 231 | •397 | 229 | | |
| The Oval-West Indies 8 wkts | •275 | 223 | 246 | 2-255 | | |
| **1966 in ENGLAND** | | | | | | |
| Manchester-West Indies inns & 40 runs | 167 | 277 | •484 | - | M.J.K.Smith | G.S.Sobers |
| Lord's-Drawn | 355 | 4-197 | •269 | 5d-369 | M.C.Cowdrey | |
| Nottingham-West Indies 139 runs | 325 | 253 | •235 | 5d-482 | M.C.Cowdrey | |
| Leeds-West Indies inns & 55 runs | 240 | 205 | •9d-500 | - | M.C.Cowdrey | |
| The Oval-England inns & 34 runs | 527 | - | •268 | 225 | D.B.Close | |
| **1967-68 in WEST INDIES** | | | | | | |
| Port-of-Spain-Drawn | •568 | - | 363 | 8-243 | M.C.Cowdrey | G.S.Sobers |
| Kingston-Drawn | •376 | 8-68 | 143 | 9d-391 | | |
| Bridgetown-Drawn | 449 | - | •349 | 6-284 | | |
| Port-of-Spain-England 7 wkts | 404 | 3-215 | •7d-526 | 2d-92 | | |
| Georgetown-Drawn | 371 | 9-206 | •414 | 264 | | |
| **1969 in ENGLAND** | | | | | | |
| Manchester-England 10 wkts | •413 | 0-12 | 147 | 275 | R.Illingworth | G.S.Sobers |
| Lord's-Drawn | 344 | 7-295 | •380 | 9d-295 | | |
| Leeds-England 30 runs | •223 | 240 | 161 | 272 | | |
| **1973 in ENGLAND** | | | | | | |
| The Oval-West Indies 158 runs | 257 | 255 | •415 | 255 | R.Illingworth | R.B.Kanhai |
| Birmingham-Drawn | 305 | 2-182 | •327 | 302 | | |
| Lord's-West Indies inns & 226 runs | 233 | 193 | •8d-652 | - | | |
| **1973-74 in WEST INDIES** | | | | | | |
| Port-of-Spain-West Indies 7 wkts | •131 | 392 | 392 | 3-132 | M.H.Denness | R.B.Kanhai |
| Kingston-Drawn | •353 | 9-432 | 9d-583 | - | | |
| Bridgetown-Drawn | •395 | 7-277 | 8d-596 | - | | |
| Georgetown-Drawn | •448 | - | 4-198 | - | | |
| Port-of-Spain-England 26 runs | •267 | 263 | 305 | 199 | | |
| **1976 in ENGLAND** | | | | | | |
| Nottingham-Drawn | 332 | 2-156 | •494 | 5d-176 | A.W.Greig | C.H.Lloyd |
| Lord's-Drawn | •250 | 254 | 182 | 6-241 | | |
| Manchester-West Indies 425 runs | 71 | 126 | •211 | 5d-411 | | |
| Leeds-West Indies 55 runs | 387 | 204 | •450 | 196 | | |
| The Oval-West Indies 231 runs | 435 | 203 | •8d-687 | 0d-182 | | |
| **1980 in ENGLAND** | | | | | | |
| Nottingham-West Indies 2 wkts | •263 | 252 | 308 | 8-209 | I.T.Botham | C.H.Lloyd |
| Lord's-Drawn | •269 | 2-133 | 518 | - | | C.H.Lloyd |
| Manchester-Drawn | •150 | 7-391 | 260 | - | | C.H.Lloyd |
| The Oval-Drawn | •370 | 9d-209 | 265 | - | | C.H.Lloyd |
| Leeds-Drawn | •143 | 6d-227 | 245 | - | | I.V.A.Richards |

| **ENGLAND v WEST INDIES** (cont.) | England | | West Indies | | Captains | |
|---|---|---|---|---|---|---|
| Venue and Result | 1st | 2nd | 1st | 2nd | England | West Indies |
| **1980-81 in WEST INDIES** | | | | | | |
| Port-of-Spain-West Indies inns & 79 runs | 178 | 169 | •9-426 | - | I.T.Botham | C.H.Lloyd |
| Georgetown-match cancelled | - | - | - | - | | |
| Bridgetown-West Indies 298 runs | 122 | 224 | •265 | 7d-379 | | |
| St John's-Drawn | •271 | 3-234 | 9d-468 | - | | |
| Kingston-Drawn | •285 | 6d-302 | 442 | - | | |
| **1984 in ENGLAND** | | | | | | |
| Birmingham-West Indies inns & 180 runs | •191 | 235 | 606 | - | D.I.Gower | C.H.Lloyd |
| Lord's-West Indies 9 wkts | •286 | 9d-300 | 245 | 1-344 | | |
| Manchester-West Indies 8 wkts | •270 | 159 | 302 | 2-131 | | |
| Leeds-West Indies inns & 64 runs | 280 | 156 | •500 | - | | |
| The Oval-West Indies 172 runs | 190 | 346 | 162 | 202 | | |
| **1985-86 in WEST INDIES** | | | | | | |
| Kingston-West Indies 10 wkts | •159 | 152 | 307 | 0-5 | D.I.Gower | I.V.A.Richards |
| Port-of-Spain-West Indies 7 wkts | •176 | 315 | 399 | 3-95 | | |
| Bridgetown-West Indies inns & 30 runs | 189 | 199 | •418 | - | | |
| Port-of-Spain-West Indies 10 wkts | •200 | 150 | 312 | 0-39 | | |
| St John's-West Indies 240 runs | 310 | 170 | •474 | 2d-246 | | |
| **1988 in ENGLAND** | | | | | | |
| Nottingham-Drawn | •245 | 3-301 | 9d-448 | - | M.W.Gatting | I.V.A.Richards |
| Lord's-West Indies 134 runs | 165 | 307 | •209 | 397 | J.E.Emburey | |
| Manchester-West Indies inns & 156 runs | •135 | 93 | 7d-384 | - | J.E.Emburey | |
| Leeds-West Indies 10 wkts | •201 | 138 | 275 | 0-67 | C.S.Cowdrey | |
| The Oval-West Indies 8 wkts | •205 | 202 | 183 | 2-226 | G.A.Gooch | |
| **1989-90 in WEST INDIES** | | | | | | |
| Kingston-England 9 wkts | 364 | 1-21 | •164 | 240 | G.A.Gooch | I.V.A.Richards |
| Georgetown-match abandoned | - | - | - | - | G.A.Gooch | I.V.A.Richards |
| Port-of-Spain-Drawn | 288 | 5-120 | •199 | 239 | G.A.Gooch | D.L.Haynes |
| Bridgetown-West Indies 164 runs | 358 | 191 | •446 | 8d-267 | A.J.Lamb | I.V.A.Richards |
| St John's-West Indies inns & 32 runs | •260 | 154 | 446 | - | A.J.Lamb | I.V.A.Richards |
| **1991 in ENGLAND** | | | | | | |
| Leeds-England 115 runs | •198 | 252 | 173 | 162 | G.A.Gooch | I.V.A.Richards |
| Lord's-Drawn | 354 | - | •419 | 2-12 | | |
| Nottingham-West Indies 9 wkts | •300 | 211 | 397 | 1-115 | | |
| Birmingham-West Indies 7 wkts | •188 | 255 | 292 | 3-157 | | |
| The Oval-England 5 wkts | •419 | 5-146 | 176 | 385 | | |
| **1993-94 in WEST INDIES** | | | | | | |
| Kingston- West Indies 8 wkts | •234 | 267 | 407 | 2-95 | M.A.Atherton | R.B.Richardson |
| Georgetown-West Indies inns & 44 runs | •322 | 190 | 556 | - | | R.B.Richardson |
| Port-of-Spain-West Indies 147 runs | 328 | 46 | •252 | 269 | | R.B.Richardson |
| Bridgetown-England 208 runs | •355 | 7d-394 | 304 | 237 | | R.B.Richardson |
| St John's-Drawn | 493 | - | •5d•593 | 0-43 | | C.A.Walsh |
| **1995 in ENGLAND** | | | | | | |
| Leeds-West Indies 9 wkts | •199 | 208 | 282 | 1-129 | M.A.Atherton | R.B.Richardson |
| Lord's-England 72 runs | •283 | 336 | 324 | 223 | | |
| Birmingham-West Indies inns & 64 runs | •147 | 89 | 300 | - | | |
| Manchester-England 6 wkts | 437 | 4-94 | •216 | 314 | | |
| Nottingham-Drawn | •440 | 9d-269 | 417 | 2-42 | | |
| The Oval-Drawn | •454 | 4-223 | 8d-692 | - | | |

| **ENGLAND v WEST INDIES** (cont.) | England | | West Indies | | Captains | |
|---|---|---|---|---|---|---|
| Venue and Result | 1st | 2nd | 1st | 2nd | England | West Indies |
| **1997-98 in WEST INDIES** | | | | | | |
| Kingston- Drawn | •3-17 | - | - | - | M.A.Atherton | B.C.Lara |
| Port-of-Spain-West Indies 3 wkts | •214 | 257 | 191 | 7-282 | | |
| Port-of-Spain-England 3 wkts | 145 | 7-225 | •159 | 210 | | |
| Georgetown-West Indies 242 runs | 170 | 137 | •352 | 197 | | |
| Bridgetown-Drawn | •403 | 3d-233 | 262 | 2-112 | | |
| St John's-West Indies inns & 52 runs | •127 | 321 | 7d-500 | - | | |

## Test Match Results Summary

### ENGLAND v WEST INDIES-IN ENGLAND

| | | Result | | | Lord's | | | Manchester | | | The Oval | | | Nottingham | | | Birmingham | | | Leeds | | |
|---|---|---|---|---|---|---|---|---|---|---|---|---|---|---|---|---|---|---|---|---|---|---|
| | Tests | E | WI | D | E | WI | D | E | WI | D | E | WI | D | E | WI | D | E | WI | D | E | WI | D |
| 1928 | 3 | 3 | - | - | 1 | - | - | 1 | - | - | 1 | - | - | - | - | - | - | - | - | - | - | - |
| 1933 | 3 | 2 | - | 1 | 1 | - | - | - | - | 1 | 1 | - | - | - | - | - | - | - | - | - | - | - |
| 1939 | 3 | 1 | - | 2 | 1 | - | - | - | - | 1 | - | - | 1 | - | - | - | - | - | - | - | - | - |
| 1950 | 4 | 1 | 3 | - | - | 1 | - | 1 | - | - | - | 1 | - | - | 1 | - | - | - | - | - | - | - |
| 1957 | 5 | 3 | - | 2 | 1 | - | - | - | - | - | 1 | - | - | - | - | 1 | - | - | 1 | 1 | - | - |
| 1963 | 5 | 1 | 3 | 1 | - | - | 1 | - | 1 | - | - | 1 | - | - | - | - | 1 | - | - | - | 1 | - |
| 1966 | 5 | 1 | 3 | 1 | - | - | 1 | - | 1 | - | - | 1 | - | - | - | - | 1 | - | - | - | 1 | - |
| 1969 | 3 | 2 | - | 1 | - | - | 1 | 1 | - | - | - | - | - | - | - | - | - | - | - | 1 | - | - |
| 1973 | 3 | - | 2 | 1 | - | 1 | - | - | - | - | - | 1 | - | - | - | - | - | - | 1 | - | - | - |
| 1976 | 5 | - | 3 | 2 | - | - | 1 | - | 1 | - | - | 1 | - | - | - | 1 | - | - | - | - | 1 | - |
| 1980 | 5 | - | 1 | 4 | - | - | 1 | - | - | 1 | - | - | 1 | - | 1 | - | - | - | - | - | 1 | - |
| 1984 | 5 | - | 5 | - | - | 1 | - | - | 1 | - | - | 1 | - | - | - | - | - | 1 | - | - | 1 | - |
| 1988 | 5 | - | 4 | 1 | - | 1 | - | - | 1 | - | - | 1 | - | - | - | - | - | 1 | - | - | - | 1 |
| 1991 | 5 | 2 | 2 | - | - | - | 1 | 1 | - | - | 1 | - | - | - | - | 1 | - | - | - | - | - | 1 |
| 1995 | 6 | 2 | 2 | 2 | 1 | - | - | 1 | - | - | - | - | 1 | - | - | 1 | - | 1 | - | - | 1 | - |
| | 65 | 18 | 28 | 19 | 5 | 4 | 6 | 5 | 5 | 3 | 5 | 6 | 3 | - | 3 | 5 | 1 | 2 | 2 | 2 | 6 | 2 |

### ENGLAND v WEST INDIES-IN WEST INDIES

| | | Result | | | Bridgetown | | | Port-of-Spain | | | Georgetown | | | Kingston | | | St John's | | |
|---|---|---|---|---|---|---|---|---|---|---|---|---|---|---|---|---|---|---|---|
| | Tests | E | WI | D | E | WI | D | E | WI | D | E | WI | D | E | WI | D | E | WI | D |
| 1929-30 | 4 | 1 | 1 | 2 | - | - | 1 | 1 | - | - | - | 1 | - | - | - | 1 | - | - | - |
| 1934-35 | 4 | 1 | 2 | 1 | 1 | - | - | - | 1 | - | - | - | 1 | - | 1 | - | - | - | - |
| 1947-48 | 4 | - | 2 | 2 | - | - | 1 | - | - | 1 | - | 1 | - | - | 1 | - | - | - | - |
| 1953-54 | 5 | 2 | 2 | 1 | - | 1 | - | - | - | 1 | 1 | - | - | 1 | 1 | - | - | - | - |
| 1959-60 | 5 | 1 | - | 4 | - | - | 1 | 1 | - | 1 | - | - | 1 | - | - | 1 | - | - | - |
| 1967-68 | 5 | 1 | - | 4 | - | - | 1 | 1 | - | 1 | - | - | 1 | - | - | 1 | - | - | - |
| 1973-74 | 5 | 1 | 1 | 3 | - | - | 1 | 1 | 1 | - | - | - | 1 | - | - | 1 | - | - | - |
| 1980-81 | 4 | - | 2 | 2 | - | 1 | - | - | 1 | - | - | - | - | - | - | 1 | - | - | 1 |
| 1985-86 | 5 | - | 5 | - | - | 1 | - | - | 2 | - | - | - | - | - | 1 | - | - | 1 | - |
| 1989-90 | 4 | 1 | 2 | 1 | - | 1 | - | - | - | 1 | - | - | - | 1 | - | - | - | 1 | - |
| 1993-94 | 5 | 1 | 3 | 1 | 1 | - | - | - | 1 | - | - | 1 | - | - | 1 | - | - | - | 1 |
| 1997-98 | 6 | 1 | 3 | 2 | - | - | 1 | 1 | 1 | - | - | 1 | - | - | - | 1 | - | 1 | - |
| | 56 | 10 | 23 | 23 | 2 | 4 | 6 | 5 | 7 | 5 | 1 | 4 | 4 | 2 | 5 | 6 | - | 3 | 2 |
| Totals | 121 | 28 | 51 | 42 | | | | | | | | | | | | | | | |

**HIGHEST INNINGS TOTALS**

| | | | |
|---|---|---|---|
| England in England | 6d-619 | Nottingham | 1957 |
| England in West Indies | 849 | Kingston | 1929-30 |
| West Indies in England | 8d-692 | The Oval | 1995 |
| West Indies in West Indies | 8d-681 | Port-of-Spain | 1953-54 |

**LOWEST INNINGS TOTALS**

| | | | |
|---|---|---|---|
| England in England | 71 | Manchester | 1976 |
| England in West Indies | 46 | Port-of-Spain | 1993-94 |
| West Indies in England | 86 | The Oval | 1957 |
| West Indies in West Indies | 102 | Bridgetown | 1934-35 |

| | | | |
|---|---|---|---|
| **HIGHEST MATCH AGGREGATE** | 1815 for 34 wickets | Kingston | 1929-30 |
| **LOWEST MATCH AGGREGATE** | 309 for 29 wickets | Bridgetown | 1934-35 |

**HIGHEST INDIVIDUAL INNINGS**

| | | | | |
|---|---|---|---|---|
| England in England | 285* | P.B.H.May | Birmingham | 1957 |
| England in West Indies | 325 | A.Sandham | Kingston | 1929-30 |
| West Indies in England | 291 | I.V.A.Richards | The Oval | 1976 |
| West Indies in West Indies | 375 | B.C.Lara | St John's | 1993-94 |

**HIGHEST AGGREGATE OF RUNS IN A SERIES**

| | | | |
|---|---|---|---|
| England in England | 489 (av 97.80) | P.B.H.May | 1957 |
| England in West Indies | 693 (av 115.50) | E.H.Hendren | 1929-30 |
| West Indies in England | 829 (av 118.42) | I.V.A.Richards | 1976 |
| West Indies in West Indies | 798 (av 99.75) | B.C.Lara | 1993-94 |

**RECORD WICKET PARTNERSHIPS-ENGLAND**

| | | | | |
|---|---|---|---|---|
| 1st | 212 | C.Washbrook (102), R.T.Simpson (94) | Nottingham | 1950 |
| 2nd | 266 | P.E.Richardson (126), T.W.Graveney (258) | Nottingham | 1957 |
| 3rd | 303 | M.A.Atherton (135), R.A.Smith (175) | St John's | 1993-94 |
| 4th | 411 | P.B.H.May (285*), M.C.Cowdrey (154) | Birmingham | 1957 |
| 5th | 150 | A.J.Stewart (143), G.P.Thorpe (84) | Brigetown | 1993-94 |
| 6th | 196 | G.A.Hick (96), R.C.Russell (91) | The Oval | 1995 |
| 7th | 197 | M.J.K.Smith (96), J.M.Parks (101*) | Port-of-Spain | 1959-60 |
| 8th | 217 | T.W.Graveney (165), J.T.Murray (112) | The Oval | 1966 |
| 9th | 109 | G.A.R.Lock (89), P.I.Pocock (13) | Georgetown | 1967-68 |
| 10th | 128 | K.Higgs (63), J.A.Snow (59*) | The Oval | 1966 |

**RECORD WICKET PARTNERSHIPS-WEST INDIES**

| | | | | |
|---|---|---|---|---|
| 1st | 298 | C.G.Greenidge (149), D.L.Haynes (167) | St John's | 1989-90 |
| 2nd | 287* | C.G.Greenidge (214*), H.A.Gomes (92*) | Lord's | 1984 |
| 3rd | 338 | E.D.Weekes (206), F.M.M.Worrell (167) | Port-of-Spain | 1953-54 |
| 4th | 399 | G.S.Sobers (226), F.M.M.Worrell (197*) | Bridgetown | 1959-60 |
| 5th | 265 | S.M.Nurse (137), G.S.Sobers (174) | Leeds | 1966 |
| 6th | 274* | G.S.Sobers (163*), D.A.J.Holford (105*) | Lord's | 1966 |
| 7th | 155*† | G.S.Sobers (150*), B.D.Julien (121) | Lord's | 1973 |
| 8th | 99 | C.A.McWatt (54), J.K.Holt (48*) | Georgetown | 1953-54 |
| 9th | 150 | E.A.E.Baptiste (87*), M.A.Holding (69) | Birmingham | 1984 |
| 10th | 70 | I.R.Bishop (44*), D.Ramnarine (19) | Georgetown | 1997-98 |

*† 231 runs were added for this wicket, G.S.Sobers retired ill and was replaced by K.D.Boyce after 155 had been scored.*

**BEST INNINGS BOWLING ANALYSIS**

| | | | | |
|---|---|---|---|---|
| England in England | 8-103 | I.T.Botham | Lord's | 1984 |
| England in West Indies | 8-53 | A.R.C.Fraser | Port-of-Spain | 1997-98 |
| West Indies in England | 8-92 | M.A.Holding | The Oval | 1976 |
| West Indies in West Indies | 8-45 | C.E.L.Ambrose | Bridgetown | 1989-90 |

**BEST MATCH BOWLING ANALYSIS**

| | | | | |
|---|---|---|---|---|
| England in England | 12-119 | F.S.Trueman | Birmingham | 1963 |
| England in West Indies | 13-156 | A.W.Greig | Port-of-Spain | 1973-74 |
| West Indies in England | 14-149 | M.A.Holding | The Oval | 1976 |
| West Indies in West Indies | 11-84 | C.E.L.Ambrose | Bridgetown | 1993-94 |

**HIGHEST AGGREGATE OF WICKETS IN A SERIES**

| | | | |
|---|---|---|---|
| England in England | 34 (av 17.47) | F.S.Trueman | 1963 |
| England in West Indies | 27 (av 18.66) | J.A.Snow | 1967-68 |
| | 27 (av 18.22) | A.R.C.Fraser | 1997-98 |
| West Indies in England | 35 (av 12.65) | M.D.Marshall | 1950 |
| West Indies in West Indies | 30 (av 14.26) | C.E.L.Ambrose | 1997-98 |

| ENGLAND v NEW ZEALAND | England | | New Zealand | | Captains | |
|---|---|---|---|---|---|---|
| Venue and Result | 1st | 2nd | 1st | 2nd | England | New Zealand |
| **1929-30 in NEW ZEALAND** | | | | | | |
| Christchurch-England 8 wkts | 181 | 2-66 | •112 | 131 | A.H.H.Gilligan | T.C.Lowry |
| Wellington-Drawn | 320 | 4-107 | •440 | 4d-164 | | |
| Auckland-Drawn | •4d-330 | - | 1-96 | - | | |
| Auckland-Drawn | •540 | 3-22 | 387 | - | | |
| **1931 in ENGLAND** | | | | | | |
| Lord's-Drawn | 454 | 5-146 | •224 | 9d-469 | D.R.Jardine | T.C.Lowry |
| The Oval-England inns & 26 runs | •4d-416 | - | 193 | 197 | | |
| Manchester-Drawn | •3-224 | - | - | - | | |
| **1932-33 in NEW ZEALAND** | | | | | | |
| Christchurch-Drawn | •8d-560 | - | 223 | 0-35 | D.R.Jardine | M.L.Page |
| Auckland-Drawn | 7d-548 | - | •158 | 0-16 | R.E.S.Wyatt | |
| **1937 in ENGLAND** | | | | | | |
| Lord's-Drawn | •424 | 4d-226 | 295 | 8-175 | R.W.V.Robins | M.L.Page |
| Manchester-England 130 runs | •9d-358 | 187 | 281 | 134 | | |
| The Oval-Drawn | 7d-254 | 1-31 | •249 | 187 | | |
| **1946-47 in NEW ZEALAND** | | | | | | |
| Christchurch-Drawn | 7d-265 | - | •9d-345 | - | W.R.Hammond | W.A.Hadlee |
| **1949 in ENGLAND** | | | | | | |
| Leeds-Drawn | •372 | 4d-267 | 341 | 2-195 | F.G.Mann | W.A.Hadlee |
| Lord's-Drawn | •9d-313 | 5-306 | 484 | - | F.G.Mann | |
| Manchester-Drawn | 9d-440 | - | •293 | 7-348 | F.R.Brown | |
| The Oval-Drawn | 482 | - | •345 | 9d-308 | F.R.Brown | |
| **1950-51 in NEW ZEALAND** | | | | | | |
| Christchurch-Drawn | 550 | - | •8d-417 | 3-46 | F.R.Brown | W.A.Hadlee |
| Wellington-England 6 wkts | 227 | 4-91 | •125 | 189 | | |
| **1954-55 in NEW ZEALAND** | | | | | | |
| Dunedin-England 8 wkts | 8d-209 | 2-49 | •125 | 132 | L.Hutton | G.O.Rabone |
| Auckland-England inns & 20 runs | 246 | - | •200 | 26 | | |
| **1958 in ENGLAND** | | | | | | |
| Birmingham-England 205 runs | •221 | 6d-215 | 94 | 137 | P.B.H.May | J.R.Reid |
| Lord's-England inns & 148 runs | •269 | - | 47 | 74 | | |
| Leeds-England inns & 71 runs | 2d-267 | - | •67 | 129 | | |
| Manchester-England inns & 13 runs | 9d-365 | - | •267 | 85 | | |
| The Oval-Drawn | 9d-219 | - | •161 | 3-91 | | |
| **1958-59 in NEW ZEALAND** | | | | | | |
| Christchurch-England inns & 99 runs | •374 | - | 142 | 133 | P.B.H.May | J.R.Reid |
| Auckland-Drawn | 7-311 | - | •181 | - | | |
| **1962-63 in NEW ZEALAND** | | | | | | |
| Auckland-England inns & 215 runs | •7d-562 | - | 258 | 89 | E.R.Dexter | J.R.Reid |
| Wellington-England inns & 47 runs | 8d-428 | - | •194 | 187 | | |
| Christchurch-England 7 wkts | 253 | 3-173 | •266 | 159 | | |
| **1965 in ENGLAND** | | | | | | |
| Birmingham-England 9 wkts | •435 | 1-96 | 116 | 413 | M.J.K.Smith | J.R.Reid |
| Lord's-England 7 wkts | 307 | 3-218 | •175 | 347 | | |
| Leeds-England inns & 187 runs | •4d-546 | - | 193 | 166 | | |

| **ENGLAND v NEW ZEALAND** (cont.) | England | | New Zealand | | Captains | |
|---|---|---|---|---|---|---|
| Venue and Result | 1st | 2nd | 1st | 2nd | England | New Zealand |
| **1965-66 in NEW ZEALAND** | | | | | | |
| Christchurch-Drawn | •342 | 5d-201 | 347 | 8-48 | M.J.K.Smith | M.E.Chapple |
| Dunedin-Drawn | 8d-254 | - | •192 | 9-147 | | B.W.Sinclair |
| Auckland-Drawn | 222 | 4-159 | •296 | 129 | | B.W.Sinclair |
| **1969 in ENGLAND** | | | | | | |
| Lord's-England 230 runs | •190 | 340 | 169 | 131 | R.Illingworth | G.T.Dowling |
| Nottingham-Drawn | 8d-451 | - | •294 | 1-66 | | |
| The Oval-England 8 wkts | 242 | 2-138 | •150 | 229 | | |
| **1970-71 in NEW ZEALAND** | | | | | | |
| Christchurch-England 8 wkts | 231 | 2-89 | •65 | 254 | R.Illingworth | G.T.Dowling |
| Auckland-Drawn | •321 | 237 | 7d-313 | 0-40 | | |
| **1973 in ENGLAND** | | | | | | |
| Nottingham-England 38 runs | •250 | 8d-325 | 97 | 440 | R.Illingworth | B.E.Congdon |
| Lord's-Drawn | •253 | 9-463 | 9d-551 | - | | |
| Leeds-England inns &1 run | 419 | - | •276 | 142 | | |
| **1974-75 in NEW ZEALAND** | | | | | | |
| Auckland-England inns & 83 runs | •6d-593 | - | 326 | 184 | M.H.Denness | B.E.Congdon |
| Christchurch-Drawn | 2-272 | - | •342 | - | | |
| **1977-78 in NEW ZEALAND** | | | | | | |
| Wellington-New Zealand 72 runs | 215 | 64 | •228 | 123 | G.Boycott | M.G.Burgess |
| Christchurch-England 174 runs | •418 | 4d-96 | 235 | 105 | | |
| Auckland-Drawn | 429 | - | •315 | 8-382 | | |
| **1978 in ENGLAND** | | | | | | |
| The Oval-England 7 wkts | 279 | 3-138 | •234 | 182 | J.M.Brearley | M.G.Burgess |
| Nottingham-England inns &119 runs | •429 | - | 120 | 190 | | |
| Lord's-England 7 wkts | 289 | 3-118 | •339 | 67 | | |
| **1983 in ENGLAND** | | | | | | |
| The Oval-England 189 runs | •209 | 6d-446 | 196 | 270 | R.G.D.Willis | G.P.Howarth |
| Leeds-New Zealand 5 wkts | •225 | 252 | 377 | 5-103 | | |
| Lord's-England 127 runs | •326 | 211 | 191 | 219 | | |
| Nottingham-England 165 runs | •420 | 297 | 207 | 345 | | |
| **1983-84 in NEW ZEALAND** | | | | | | |
| Wellington-Drawn | 463 | 0-69 | •219 | 537 | R.G.D.Willis | G.P.Howarth |
| Christchurch-New Zealand inns & 132 runs | 82 | 93 | •307 | - | | |
| Auckland-Drawn | 439 | - | •9d-496 | 0-16 | | |
| **1986 in ENGLAND** | | | | | | |
| Lord's-Drawn | •317 | 6d-295 | 342 | 2-41 | M.W.Gatting | J.V.Coney |
| Nottingham-New Zealand 8 wkts | •256 | 230 | 413 | 2-77 | | |
| The Oval-Drawn | 5d-388 | - | •287 | 0-7 | | |
| **1987-88 in NEW ZEALAND** | | | | | | |
| Christchurch-Drawn | •319 | 152 | 168 | 4-130 | M.W.Gatting | J.J.Crowe |
| Auckland-Drawn | 323 | - | •301 | 7-350 | | J.J.Crowe |
| Wellington-Drawn | 2-183 | - | •6d-512 | - | | J.G.Wright |
| **1990 in ENGLAND** | | | | | | |
| Nottingham-Drawn | 9d-345 | - | •208 | 2-36 | G.A.Gooch | J.G.Wright |
| Lord's-Drawn | •334 | 4d-272 | 9d-462 | - | | |
| Birmingham-England 114 runs | •435 | 158 | 249 | 230 | | |

| **ENGLAND v NEW ZEALAND** (cont.) | England | | New Zealand | | Captains | |
|---|---|---|---|---|---|---|
| Venue and Result | 1st | 2nd | 1st | 2nd | England | New Zealand |
| **1991-92 in NEW ZEALAND** | | | | | | |
| Christchurch-England inns & 4 runs | •9d-580 | - | 312 | 264 | G.A.Gooch | M.D.Crowe |
| Auckland-England 168 runs | •203 | 321 | 142 | 214 | | |
| Wellington-Drawn | •305 | 7d-359 | 9d-432 | 3-43 | | |
| **1994 in ENGLAND** | | | | | | |
| Nottingham-England inns & 90 runs | 9d-567 | - | •251 | 226 | M.A.Atherton | K.R.Rutherford |
| Lord's-Drawn | 281 | 8-254 | •476 | 5d-211 | | |
| Birmingham-Drawn | •382 | - | 151 | 7-308 | | |
| **1996-97 in NEW ZEALAND** | | | | | | |
| Auckland-Drawn | 521 | - | •390 | 9-248 | M.A.Atherton | L.K.Germon |
| Wellington-England inns & 68 runs | 383 | - | •124 | 191 | | L.K.Germon |
| Christchurch-England 4 wkts | 228 | 6-307 | •346 | 186 | | S.P.Fleming |

## Test Match Results Summary

### ENGLAND v NEW ZEALAND-IN ENGLAND

| | | Result | | | Lord's | | | The Oval | | | Manchester | | | Leeds | | | Birmingham | | | Nottingham | | |
|---|---|---|---|---|---|---|---|---|---|---|---|---|---|---|---|---|---|---|---|---|---|---|
| | Tests | E | NZ | D | E | NZ | D | E | NZ | D | E | NZ | D | E | NZ | D | E | NZ | D | E | NZ | D |
| 1931 | 3 | 1 | - | 2 | - | - | 1 | 1 | - | - | - | - | 1 | - | - | - | - | - | - | - | - | - |
| 1937 | 3 | 1 | - | 2 | - | - | - | - | - | 1 | 1 | - | - | - | - | - | - | - | - | - | - | - |
| 1949 | 4 | - | - | 4 | - | - | 1 | - | - | 1 | - | - | 1 | - | - | 1 | - | - | - | - | - | - |
| 1958 | 5 | 4 | - | 1 | 1 | - | - | - | - | 1 | 1 | - | - | 1 | - | - | 1 | - | - | - | - | - |
| 1965 | 3 | 3 | - | - | 1 | - | - | - | - | - | - | - | - | 1 | - | - | 1 | - | - | - | - | - |
| 1969 | 3 | 2 | - | 1 | 1 | - | - | 1 | - | - | - | - | - | - | - | - | - | - | - | - | - | 1 |
| 1973 | 3 | 2 | - | 1 | - | - | 1 | - | - | - | - | - | - | 1 | - | - | - | - | - | 1 | - | - |
| 1978 | 3 | 3 | - | - | 1 | - | - | 1 | - | - | - | - | - | - | - | - | - | - | - | 1 | - | - |
| 1983 | 4 | 3 | 1 | - | 1 | - | - | 1 | - | - | - | - | - | - | 1 | - | - | - | - | 1 | - | - |
| 1986 | 3 | - | 1 | 2 | - | - | 1 | - | - | 1 | - | - | - | - | - | - | - | - | - | - | - | 1 |
| 1990 | 3 | 1 | - | 2 | - | - | 1 | - | - | - | - | - | - | - | - | - | 1 | - | - | - | - | 1 |
| 1994 | 3 | 1 | - | 2 | - | - | 1 | - | - | - | - | - | 1 | - | - | - | - | - | - | 1 | - | - |
| | 40 | 21 | 2 | 17 | 5 | - | 7 | 4 | - | 4 | 2 | - | 3 | 3 | 1 | 1 | 3 | - | - | 4 | 1 | 2 |

### ENGLAND v NEW ZEALAND-IN NEW ZEALAND

| | | Result | | | Christchurch | | | Wellington | | | Auckland | | | Dunedin | | |
|---|---|---|---|---|---|---|---|---|---|---|---|---|---|---|---|---|
| | Tests | E | NZ | D | E | NZ | D | E | NZ | D | E | NZ | D | E | NZ | D |
| 1929-30 | 4 | 1 | - | 3 | 1 | - | - | - | - | 1 | - | - | 2 | - | - | - |
| 1932-33 | 2 | - | - | 2 | - | - | 1 | - | - | - | - | - | 1 | - | - | - |
| 1946-47 | 1 | - | - | 1 | - | - | 1 | - | - | - | - | - | - | - | - | - |
| 1950-51 | 2 | 1 | - | 1 | - | - | 1 | 1 | - | - | - | - | - | - | - | - |
| 1954-55 | 2 | 2 | - | - | - | - | - | - | - | - | 1 | - | - | 1 | - | - |
| 1958-59 | 2 | 1 | - | 1 | 1 | - | - | - | - | - | - | - | 1 | - | - | - |
| 1962-63 | 3 | 3 | - | - | 1 | - | - | 1 | - | - | 1 | - | - | - | - | - |
| 1965-66 | 3 | - | - | 3 | - | - | 1 | - | - | - | - | - | 1 | - | - | 1 |
| 1970-71 | 2 | 1 | - | 1 | 1 | - | - | - | - | - | - | - | 1 | - | - | - |
| 1974-75 | 2 | 1 | - | 1 | - | - | 1 | - | - | - | 1 | - | - | - | - | - |
| 1977-78 | 3 | 1 | 1 | 1 | 1 | - | - | - | 1 | - | - | - | 1 | - | - | - |
| 1983-84 | 3 | - | 1 | 2 | - | 1 | - | - | - | 1 | - | - | 1 | - | - | - |
| 1987-88 | 3 | - | - | 3 | - | - | 1 | - | - | 1 | - | - | 1 | - | - | - |
| 1991-92 | 3 | 2 | - | 1 | 1 | - | - | - | - | 1 | 1 | - | - | - | - | - |
| 1996-97 | 3 | 2 | - | 1 | 1 | - | - | 1 | - | - | - | - | 1 | - | - | - |
| | 38 | 15 | 2 | 21 | 6 | 1 | 6 | 2 | 1 | 4 | 4 | - | 9 | 1 | - | 1 |
| Totals | 78 | 36 | 4 | 38 | | | | | | | | | | | | |

**HIGHEST INNINGS TOTALS**

| | | | |
|---|---|---|---|
| England In England | 8d-567 | Nottingham | 1994 |
| England in New Zealand | 6d-593 | Auckland | 1974-75 |
| New Zealand in England | 9d-551 | Lord's | 1973 |
| New Zealand in New Zealand | 537 | Wellington | 1983-84 |

**LOWEST INNINGS TOTALS**

| | | | |
|---|---|---|---|
| England in England | 158 | Birmingham | 1990 |
| England in New Zealand | 64 | Wellington | 1977-78 |
| New Zealand in England | 47 | Lord's | 1958 |
| New Zealand in New Zealand | 26 | Auckland | 1954-55 |

| | | | |
|---|---|---|---|
| **HIGHEST MATCH AGGREGATE** | 1293 for 34 wickets | Lord's | 1931 |
| **LOWEST MATCH AGGREGATE** | 390 for 30 wickets | Lord's | 1958 |

**HIGHEST INDIVIDUAL INNINGS**

| | | | | |
|---|---|---|---|---|
| England in England | 310* | J.H.Edrich | Leeds | 1965 |
| England in New Zealand | 336* | W.R.Hammond | Auckland | 1932-33 |
| New Zealand in England | 206 | M.P.Donnelly | Lord's | 1949 |
| New Zealand in New Zealand | 174* | J.V.Coney | Wellington | 1983-84 |

**HIGHEST AGGREGATE OF RUNS IN A SERIES**

| | | | |
|---|---|---|---|
| England in England | 469 (av 78.16) | L.Hutton | 1949 |
| England in New Zealand | 563 (av 563.00) | W.R.Hammond | 1932-33 |
| New Zealand in England | 462 (av 77.00) | M.P.Donnelly | 1949 |
| New Zealand in New Zealand | 341 (av 85.25) | C.S.Dempster | 1929-30 |

**RECORD WICKET PARTNERSHIPS-ENGLAND**

| | | | | |
|---|---|---|---|---|
| 1st | 223 | G.Fowler (105), C.J.Tavare (109) | The Oval | 1983 |
| 2nd | 369 | J.H.Edrich (310*), K.F.Barrington (163) | Leeds | 1965 |
| 3rd | 245 | J.Hardstaff, jr (114), W.R.Hammond (140) | Lord's | 1937 |
| 4th | 266 | M H.Denness (188), K.W.R.Fletcher (216) | Auckland | 1974-75 |
| 5th | 242 | W.R.Hammond (227), L.E.G.Ames (103) | Christchurch | 1932-33 |
| 6th | 240 | P.H.Parfitt (131*), 8.R.Knight (125) | Auckland | 1962-63 |
| 7th | 149 | A.P.E.Knott (104), P.Lever (64) | Auckland | 1970-71 |
| 8th | 246 | L.E.G.Ames (137), G.O.B.Allen (122) | Lord's | 1931 |
| 9th | 163* | M.C.Cowdrey (128*), A.C.Smith (69*) | Wellington | 1962-63 |
| 10th | 59 | A.P.E.Knott (49), N.Gifford (25*) | Nottingham | 1973 |

**RECORD WICKET PARTNERSHIPS-NEW ZEALAND**

| | | | | |
|---|---|---|---|---|
| 1st | 276 | C.S.Dempster (136), J.E.Mills (117) | Wellington | 1929-30 |
| 2nd | 241 | J.G.Wright (116), A.H.Jones (143) | Wellington | 1991-92 |
| 3rd | 210 | B.A.Edgar (83), M.D.Crowe (106) | Lord's | 1986 |
| 4th | 155 | M.D.Crowe (143), M.J.Greatbatch (68) | Wellington | 1987-88 |
| 5th | 180 | M.D.Crowe (142), S.A.Thomson (69) | Lord's | 1994 |
| 6th | 141 | M.D.Crowe (115), A.C.Parore (71) | Manchester | 1994 |
| 7th | 117 | D.N.Patel (99), C.L.Cairns (61) | Christchurch | 1991-92 |
| 8th | 104 | D.A.R.Moloney (64), A.W.Roberts (66*) | Lord's | 1937 |
| 9th | 118 | J.V.Coney (174*), B.L.Cairns (64) | Wellington | 1983-84 |
| 10th | 106* | N.J.Astle (102*), D.K.Morrison (14*) | Auckland | 1996-97 |

**BEST INNINGS BOWLING ANALYSIS**

| | | | | |
|---|---|---|---|---|
| England in England | 7-32 | D.L.Underwood | Lord's | 1969 |
| England in New Zealand | 7-47 | P.C.R.Tufnell | Christchurch | 1991-92 |
| New Zealand in England | 7-74 | B.L.Cairns | Leeds | 1983 |
| New Zealand in New Zealand | 7-143 | B.L.Cairns | Wellington | 1983-84 |

**BEST MATCH BOWLING ANALYSIS**

| | | | | |
|---|---|---|---|---|
| England in England | 12-101 | D.L.Underwood | The Oval | 1969 |
| England in New Zealand | 12-97 | D.L.Underwood | Christchurch | 1970-71 |
| New Zealand in England | 11-169 | D.J.Nash | Lord's | 1994 |
| New Zealand in New Zealand | 10-100 | R.J.Hadlee | Wellington | 1977-78 |

**HIGHEST AGGREGATE OF WICKETS IN A SERIES**

| | | | |
|---|---|---|---|
| England in England | 34 (av 7.47) | G.A.R.Lock | 1958 |
| England in New Zealand | 19 (av 19.00) | D.Gough | 1996-97 |
| New Zealand in England | 21 (av 26.61) | R.J.Hadlee | 1983 |
| New Zealand in New Zealand | 15 (av 19.53) | R.O.Collinge | 1977-78 |
| | 15 (av 24.73) | R.J.Hadlee | 1977-78 |

| ENGLAND v INDIA | England | | India | | Captains | |
|---|---|---|---|---|---|---|
| Venue and Result | 1st | 2nd | 1st | 2nd | England | India |
| **1932 in ENGLAND** | | | | | | |
| Lord's-England 158 runs | •259 | 8d-275 | 189 | 187 | D.R.Jardine | C.K.Nayudu |
| **1933-34 in INDIA** | | | | | | |
| Bombay[1]-England 9 wkts | 438 | 1-40 | •219 | 258 | D.R.Jardine | C.K.Nayudu |
| Calcutta-Drawn | •403 | 2-7 | 247 | 237 | | |
| Madras[1]-England 202 runs | •335 | 7d-261 | 145 | 249 | | |
| **1936 in ENGLAND** | | | | | | |
| Lord's-England 9 wkts | 134 | 1-108 | •147 | 93 | G.O.B.Allen | Maharaj Vizianagram |
| Manchester-Drawn | 8d-571 | - | •203 | 5-390 | | |
| The Oval-England 9 wkts | •8d-471 | 1-64 | 222 | 312 | | |
| **1946 in ENGLAND** | | | | | | |
| Lord's-England 10 wkts | 428 | 0-48 | •200 | 275 | W.R.Hammond | Nawab of Pataudi, sr |
| Manchester-Drawn | •294 | 5d-153 | 170 | 9-152 | | |
| The Oval-Drawn | 3-95 | - | •331 | - | | |
| **1951-52 in INDIA** | | | | | | |
| Delhi-Drawn | •203 | 6-368 | 6d-418 | - | N.D.Howard | V.S.Hazare |
| Bombay[2]-Drawn | 456 | 2-55 | •9d-485 | 208 | N.D.Howard | |
| Calcutta-Drawn | •342 | 5d-252 | 344 | 0-103 | N.D.Howard | |
| Kanpur-England 8 wkts | 203 | 2-76 | •121 | 157 | N.D.Howard | |
| Madras[1]-India inns & 8 runs | •266 | 183 | 9d-457 | - | D.B.Carr | |
| **1952 in ENGLAND** | | | | | | |
| Leeds-England 7 wkts | 334 | 3-128 | •293 | 165 | L.Hutton | V.S.Hazare |
| Lord's-England 8 wkts | 537 | 2-79 | •235 | 378 | | |
| Manchester-England inns & 207 runs | •9d-347 | - | 58 | 82 | | |
| The Oval-Drawn | •6d-326 | - | 98 | - | | |
| **1959 in ENGLAND** | | | | | | |
| Nottingham-England inns & 59 runs | •422 | - | 206 | 157 | P.B.H.May | D.K.Gaekwad |
| Lord's-England 8 wkts | 226 | 2-108 | •168 | 165 | P.B.H.May | P.Roy |
| Leeds-England inns & 173 runs | 8d-483 | - | •161 | 149 | P.B.H.May | D.K.Gaekwad |
| Manchester-England 171 runs | •490 | 8d-265 | 208 | 376 | M C Cowdrey | D.K.Gaekwad |
| The Oval-England inns & 27 runs | 361 | - | •140 | 194 | M C Cowdrey | D.K.Gaekwad |
| **1961-62 in INDIA** | | | | | | |
| Bombay[2]-Drawn | •8d-500 | 5d-184 | 390 | 5-180 | E.R.Dexter | N.J.Contractor |
| Kanpur-Drawn | 244 | 5-497 | •8d-467 | - | | |
| Delhi-Drawn | 3-256 | - | •466 | - | | |
| Calcutta-India 187 runs | 212 | 233 | •380 | 252 | | |
| Madras[2]-India 128 runs | 281 | 209 | •428 | 190 | | |
| **1963-64 in INDIA** | | | | | | |
| Madras[2]-Drawn | 317 | 5-241 | •7d-457 | 9d-152 | M.J.K.Smith | Nawab of Pataudi, jr |
| Bombay[2]-Drawn | 233 | 3-206 | •300 | 8d-249 | | |
| Calcutta-Drawn | 267 | 2-145 | •241 | 7d-300 | | |
| Delhi-Drawn | 451 | - | •344 | 4 463 | | |
| Kanpur-Drawn | •8d-559 | - | 266 | 3-347 | | |
| **1967 in ENGLAND** | | | | | | |
| Leeds-England 6 wkts | •4d-550 | 4-126 | 164 | 510 | D.B.Close | Nawab of Pataudi, jr |
| Lord's-England inns & 124 runs | 386 | - | •152 | 110 | | |
| Birmingham-England 132 runs | •298 | 203 | 92 | 277 | | |

| **ENGLAND v INDIA** (cont.) | England | | India | | Captains | |
|---|---|---|---|---|---|---|
| Venue and Result | 1st | 2nd | 1st | 2nd | England | India |
| **1971 in ENGLAND** | | | | | | |
| Lord's-Drawn | •304 | 191 | 313 | 8-145 | R.Illingworth | A.L.Wadekar |
| Manchester-Drawn | •386 | 3d-245 | 212 | 3-65 | | |
| The Oval-India 4 wkts | •355 | 101 | 284 | 6-174 | | |
| **1972-73 In INDIA** | | | | | | |
| Delhi-England 6 wkts | 200 | 4-208 | •173 | 233 | A.R.Lewis | A.L.Wadekar |
| Calcutta-India 28 runs | 174 | 163 | •210 | 155 | | |
| Madras[1]-India 4 wkts | •242 | 159 | 316 | 6-86 | | |
| Kanpur-Drawn | 397 | - | •357 | 6-186 | | |
| Bombay[2]-Drawn | 480 | 2-67 | •448 | 5d-244 | | |
| **1974 in ENGLAND** | | | | | | |
| Manchester-England 113 runs | •9d-328 | 3d-213 | 246 | 182 | M.H.Denness | A.L.Wadekar |
| Lord's-England inns & 285 runs | •629 | - | 302 | 42 | | |
| Birmingham-England inns & 78 runs | 2d-459 | - | •165 | 216 | | |
| **1976-77 in INDIA** | | | | | | |
| Delhi-England inns & 25 runs | •381 | - | 122 | 234 | A.W.Greig | B.S.Bedi |
| Calcutta-England 10 wkts | 321 | 0-16 | •155 | 181 | | |
| Madras[1]-England 200 runs | •262 | 9d-185 | 164 | 83 | | |
| Bangalore-India 140 runs | 195 | 177 | •253 | 9d-259 | | |
| Bombay[3]-Drawn | 317 | 7-152 | •338 | 192 | | |
| **1979 in ENGLAND** | | | | | | |
| Birmingham-England inns & 83 runs | •5d-633 | - | 297 | 253 | J.M.Brearley | S.Venkataraghavan |
| Lord's-Drawn | 9d-419 | - | •96 | 4-318 | | |
| Leeds-Drawn | •270 | - | 6-223 | - | | |
| The Oval-Drawn | •305 | 8d-334 | 202 | 8-429 | | |
| **1979-80 in INDIA** | | | | | | |
| Bombay[3]-England 10 wkts | 296 | 0-98 | •242 | 149 | J.M.Brearley | G.R.Viswanath |
| **1981-82 in India** | | | | | | |
| Bombay[3]-India 138 runs | 166 | 102 | •179 | 227 | K.W.R.Fletcher | S.M.Gavaskar |
| Bangalore-Drawn | •400 | 3-174 | 428 | - | | |
| Delhi-Drawn | •9d-476 | 0-68 | 487 | - | | |
| Calcutta-Drawn | •248 | 5d-265 | 208 | 3-170 | | |
| Madras[1]-Drawn | 328 | - | •4d-481 | 3-160 | | |
| Kanpur-Drawn | •9d-378 | - | 7-377 | - | | |
| **1982 in ENGLAND** | | | | | | |
| Lord's-England 7 wkts | •433 | 3-67 | 128 | 369 | R.G.D.Willis | S.M.Gavaskar |
| Manchester-Drawn | •425 | - | 8-379 | - | | |
| The Oval-Drawn | •594 | 3d-191 | 410 | 3-111 | | |
| **1984-85 in India** | | | | | | |
| Bombay[3]-India 8 wkts | •195 | 317 | 8d-465 | 2-51 | D.I.Gower | S.M.Gavaskar |
| Delhi-England 8 wkts | 418 | 2-127 | •307 | 235 | | |
| Calcutta-Drawn | 276 | - | •7d-437 | 1-29 | | |
| Madras[1]-England 9 wkts | 7d-652 | 1-35 | •272 | 412 | | |
| Kanpur-Drawn | 417 | 0-91 | •8d-553 | 1d-97 | | |
| **1986 in ENGLAND** | | | | | | |
| Lord's-India 5 wkts | •294 | 180 | 341 | 5-136 | D.I.Gower | Kapil Dev |
| Manchester-India 279 runs | 102 | 128 | •272 | 237 | M.W.Gatting | |
| The Oval-Drawn | •390 | 235 | 390 | 5-174 | M.W.Gatting | |

| ENGLAND v INDIA (cont.) | England | | India | | Captains | |
|---|---|---|---|---|---|---|
| Venue and Result | 1st | 2nd | 1st | 2nd | England | India |
| **1990 in ENGLAND** | | | | | | |
| Lord's-England 247 runs | •4d-653 | 4d-272 | 454 | 224 | G.A.Gooch | M.Azharuddin |
| Manchester-Drawn | •519 | 4d-320 | 432 | 6-343 | | |
| The Oval-Drawn | 340 | 4d-477 | •9d-606 | - | | |
| **1992-93 in India** | | | | | | |
| Calcutta-India 8 wkts | 163 | 286 | •371 | 2-82 | G.A.Gooch | M.Azharuddin |
| Madras[1]-India inns & 22 runs | 286 | 252 | •6d-560 | - | A.J.Stewart | |
| Bombay[3]-India inns & 15 runs | •347 | 227 | 591 | | G.A.Gooch | |
| **1996 in ENGLAND** | | | | | | |
| Birmingham-England 8 wkts | 313 | 2-121 | •214 | 219 | M.A.Atherton | M.Azharuddin |
| Lord's-Drawn | •344 | 9d-278 | 429 | - | | |
| Nottingham-Drawn | 564 | - | •521 | 211 | | |

## Test Match Results Summary

### ENGLAND v INDIA-IN ENGLAND

| | | Result | | | Lord's | | | Manchester | | | The Oval | | | Leeds | | | Nottingham | | | Birmingham | | |
|---|---|---|---|---|---|---|---|---|---|---|---|---|---|---|---|---|---|---|---|---|---|---|
| | Tests | E | I | D | E | I | D | E | I | D | E | I | D | E | I | D | E | I | D | E | I | D |
| 1932 | 1 | 1 | - | - | 1 | - | - | - | - | - | - | - | - | - | - | - | - | - | - | - | - | - |
| 1936 | 3 | 2 | - | 1 | 1 | - | - | - | - | 1 | 1 | - | - | - | - | - | - | - | - | - | - | - |
| 1946 | 3 | 1 | - | 2 | 1 | - | - | - | - | 1 | - | - | 1 | - | - | - | - | - | - | - | - | - |
| 1952 | 4 | 3 | - | 1 | 1 | - | - | 1 | - | - | - | - | 1 | 1 | - | - | - | - | - | - | - | - |
| 1959 | 5 | 5 | - | - | 1 | - | - | 1 | - | - | 1 | - | - | 1 | - | - | - | - | - | - | - | - |
| 1967 | 3 | 3 | - | - | 1 | - | - | - | - | - | - | - | - | - | - | - | 1 | - | - | 1 | - | - |
| 1971 | 3 | - | 1 | 2 | - | - | 1 | - | - | 1 | - | 1 | - | - | - | - | - | - | - | - | - | - |
| 1974 | 3 | 3 | - | - | 1 | - | - | 1 | - | - | - | - | - | - | - | - | - | - | - | 1 | - | - |
| 1979 | 4 | 1 | - | 3 | - | - | 1 | - | - | - | - | - | 1 | - | - | 1 | - | - | - | 1 | - | - |
| 1982 | 3 | 1 | - | 2 | 1 | - | - | - | - | 1 | - | - | 1 | - | - | - | - | - | - | - | - | - |
| 1986 | 3 | - | 2 | 1 | - | 1 | - | - | - | - | - | - | - | - | 1 | - | - | - | - | - | - | 1 |
| 1990 | 3 | 1 | - | 2 | 1 | - | - | - | - | 1 | - | - | 1 | - | - | - | - | - | - | - | - | - |
| 1996 | 3 | 1 | - | - | 1 | - | - | - | - | - | - | - | - | - | - | - | - | - | 1 | - | - | 1 |
| | 41 | 22 | 3 | 16 | 10 | 1 | 2 | 3 | - | 5 | 2 | 1 | 5 | 3 | 1 | 1 | 1 | - | 1 | 3 | - | 2 |

### ENGLAND v INDIA-IN INDIA

| | | Result | | | Bombay | | | Calcutta | | | Madras | | | Delhi | | | Kanpur | | | Bangalore | | |
|---|---|---|---|---|---|---|---|---|---|---|---|---|---|---|---|---|---|---|---|---|---|---|
| | Tests | E | I | D | E | I | D | E | I | D | E | I | D | E | I | D | E | I | D | E | I | D |
| 1933-34 | 3 | 2 | - | 1 | 1 | - | - | - | - | 1 | 1 | - | - | - | - | - | - | - | - | - | - | - |
| 1951-52 | 5 | 1 | 1 | 3 | - | - | 1 | - | - | 1 | - | 1 | - | - | - | 1 | 1 | - | - | - | - | - |
| 1961-62 | 5 | - | 2 | 3 | - | - | 1 | - | 1 | - | - | 1 | - | - | - | 1 | - | - | 1 | - | - | - |
| 1963-64 | 5 | - | - | 5 | - | - | 1 | - | - | 1 | - | - | 1 | - | - | 1 | - | - | 1 | - | - | - |
| 1972-73 | 5 | 1 | 2 | 2 | - | - | 1 | - | 1 | - | - | 1 | - | 1 | - | - | - | - | 1 | - | - | - |
| 1976-77 | 5 | 3 | 1 | 1 | - | - | 1 | 1 | - | - | 1 | - | - | 1 | - | - | - | - | - | - | - | 1 |
| 1979-80 | 1 | 1 | - | - | 1 | - | - | - | - | - | - | - | - | - | - | - | - | - | - | - | - | - |
| 1981-82 | 6 | - | 1 | 5 | - | 1 | - | - | - | 1 | - | - | 1 | - | - | 1 | - | - | 1 | - | - | 1 |
| 1984-85 | 5 | 2 | 1 | 2 | - | 1 | - | - | - | 1 | 1 | - | - | 1 | - | - | - | - | 1 | - | - | - |
| 1992-93 | 3 | - | 3 | - | - | 1 | - | - | 1 | - | - | 1 | - | - | - | - | - | - | - | - | - | - |
| | 43 | 10 | 11 | 22 | 2 | 3 | 5 | 1 | 3 | 5 | 3 | 4 | 2 | 3 | - | 4 | 1 | - | 5 | - | 1 | 1 |
| Totals | 84 | 32 | 14 | 38 | | | | | | | | | | | | | | | | | | |

**HIGHEST INNINGS TOTALS**

| | | | |
|---|---|---|---|
| England in England | 4d-653 | Lord's | 1990 |
| England in India | 7d-652 | Madras[1] | 1984-85 |
| India in England | 9d-606 | The Oval | 1990 |
| India in India | 591 | Bombay[3] | 1992-93 |

**LOWEST INNINGS TOTALS**

| | | | |
|---|---|---|---|
| England in England | 101 | The Oval | 1971 |
| England in India | 102 | Bombay[3] | 1981-82 |
| India in England | 42 | Lord's | 1974 |
| India in India | 83 | Madras[1] | 1976-77 |

| | | | |
|---|---|---|---|
| **HIGHEST MATCH AGGREGATE** | 1614 for 30 wickets | Manchester | 1990 |
| **LOWEST MATCH AGGREGATE** | 482 for 31 wickets | Lord's | 1936 |

**HIGHEST INDIVIDUAL INNINGS**

| | | | | |
|---|---|---|---|---|
| England in England | 333 | G.A.Gooch | Lord's | 1990 |
| England in India | 207 | M.W.Gatting | Madras[1] | 1984-85 |
| India In England | 221 | S.M.Gavaskar | The Oval | 1979 |
| India in India | 224 | V.G.Kambli | Bombay[3] | 1992-93 |

**HIGHEST AGGREGATE OF RUNS IN A SERIES**

| | | | |
|---|---|---|---|
| England in England | 752 (av 125.33) | G.A.Gooch | 1990 |
| England in India | 594 (av 99.00) | K.F.Barrington | 1961-62 |
| India in England | 542 (av 77.42) | S.M.Gavaskar | 1979 |
| India in India | 586 (av 83.71) | V.L.Manjrekar | 1961-62 |

**RECORD WICKET PARTNERSHIPS-ENGLAND**

| | | | | |
|---|---|---|---|---|
| 1st | 225 | G.A.Gooch(116), M.A.Atherton(131) | Manchester | 1990 |
| 2nd | 241 | G.Fowler (201), M.W.Gatting (207) | Madras[1] | 1984-85 |
| 3rd | 308 | G.A.Gooch(333), A.J.Lamb(139) | Lord's | 1990 |
| 4th | 266 | W.R.Hammond (217), T.S.Worthington (128) | Oval | 1936 |
| 5th | 254 | K.W.R.Fletcher (113), A.W.Greig (148) | Bombay[2] | 1972-73 |
| 6th | 171 | I.T.Botham (114), R.W.Taylor (43) | Bombay[3] | 1979-80 |
| 7th | 125 | D.W.Randall (126), P.H.Edmonds (64) | Lord's | 1982 |
| 8th | 168 | R.Illingworth (107), P.Lever (88*) | Manchester | 1971 |
| 9th | 83 | K.W.R.Fletcher (97*), N.Gifford (19) | Madras[1] | 1972-73 |
| 10th | 70 | P.J.W.Allott (41*), R.G.D.Willis (28) | Lord's | 1982 |

**RECORD WICKET PARTNERSHIPS-INDIA**

| | | | | |
|---|---|---|---|---|
| 1st | 213 | S.M.Gavaskar (221), C.P.S.Chauhan (80) | The Oval | 1979 |
| 2nd | 192 | F.M.Engineer (121), A.L.Wadekar (87) | Bombay[2] | 1972-73 |
| 3rd | 316† | G.R.Viswanath (222), Yashpal Sharma (140) | Madras[1] | 1981-82 |
| 4th | 222 | V.S.Hazare (89), V.L.Manjrekar (133) | Leeds | 1952 |
| 5th | 214 | M.Azharuddin (110), R.J.Shastri (111) | Calcutta | 1984-85 |
| 6th | 130 | S.M.H.Kirmani (43), Kapil Dev (97) | The Oval | 1982 |
| 7th | 235 | R.J.Shastri (142), S.M.H.Kirmani (102) | Bombay[3] | 1984-85 |
| 8th | 128 | R.J.Shastri (93), S.M.H.Kirmani (67) | Delhi | 1981-82 |
| 9th | 104 | R.J.Shastri (93), S.Madan Lal (44) | Delhi | 1981-82 |
| 10th | 51 | R.G.Nadkarni (43'), B.S.Chandrasekhar (16) | Calcutta | 1963-64 |
| | 51 | S.M.H.Kirmani (75), C.Sharma (17*) | Madras[1] | 1984-85 |

*† 415 runs were added for this wicket. D.B.Vengsarkar retired hurt after he had added 99 with Viswanath.*

**BEST INNINGS BOWLING ANALYSIS**

| | | | | |
|---|---|---|---|---|
| England in England | 8-31 | F.S.Trueman | Manchester | 1952 |
| England in India | 7-46 | J.K.Lever | Delhi | 1976-77 |
| India in England | 6-35 | L.Amar Singh | Lord's | 1936 |
| India in India | 8-55 | M.H.Mankad | Madras[1] | 1951-52 |

**BEST MATCH BOWLING ANALYSIS**

| | | | | |
|---|---|---|---|---|
| England in England | 11-93 | A.V.Bedser | Manchester | 1946 |
| England in India | 13-106 | I.T.Botham | Bombay[3] | 1979-80 |
| India in England | 10-188 | C.Sharma | Birmingham | 1986 |
| India in India | 12-108 | M.H.Mankad | Madras[1] | 1951-52 |

**HIGHEST AGGREGATE OF WICKETS IN A SERIES**

| | | | |
|---|---|---|---|
| England in England | 29 (av 13.31) | F.S.Trueman | 1952 |
| England in India | 29 (av 17.55) | D.L.Underwood | 1976-77 |
| India in England | 17 (av 34.64) | S.P.Gupte | 1959 |
| India in India | 35 (av 18.91) | B.S.Chandrasekhar | 1972-73 |

| **ENGLAND v PAKISTAN** | England | | Pakistan | | Captains | |
|---|---|---|---|---|---|---|
| Venue and Result | 1st | 2nd | 1st | 2nd | England | Pakistan |
| **1954 in ENGLAND** | | | | | | |
| Lord's-Drawn | 9d-117 | - | •87 | 3-121 | L.Hutton | A.H.Kardar |
| Nottingham-England inns &129 runs | 6d-558 | - | •157 | 272 | D.S.Sheppard | |
| Manchester-Drawn | •8d-359 | - | 90 | 4-25 | D.S.Sheppard | |
| The Oval-Pakistan 24 runs | 130 | 143 | •133 | 164 | L.Hutton | |
| **1961-62 in PAKISTAN** | | | | | | |
| Lahore[2]-England 5 wkts | 380 | 5-209 | •9d-387 | 200 | E.R.Dexter | Imtiaz Ahmed |
| Dacca-Drawn | 439 | 0-38 | •7d-393 | 216 | | |
| Karachi[1]-Drawn | 507 | - | •253 | 8-404 | | |
| **1962 in ENGLAND** | | | | | | |
| Birmingham-England inns & 24 runs | •5d-544 | - | 246 | 274 | E.R.Dexter | Javed Burki |
| Lord's-England 9 wkts | 370 | 1-86 | •100 | 355 | E.R.Dexter | |
| Leeds-England inns & 117 runs | •428 | - | 131 | 180 | M.C.Cowdrey | |
| Nottingham-Drawn | •5d-428 | - | 219 | 6-216 | E.R.Dexter | |
| The Oval-England 10 wkts | •5d-480 | 0-27 | 183 | 323 | E.R.Dexter | |
| **1967 in ENGLAND** | | | | | | |
| Lord's-Drawn | •369 | 9d-241 | 354 | 3-88 | D.B.Close | Hanif Mohammad |
| Nottingham-England 10 wkts | 8d-252 | 0-3 | •140 | 114 | | |
| The Oval-England 8 wkts | 440 | 2-34 | •216 | 255 | | |
| **1968-69 In PAKISTAN** | | | | | | |
| Lahore[2]-Drawn | •306 | 9d-225 | 209 | 5-203 | M.C.Cowdrey | Saeed Ahmed |
| Dacca-Drawn | 274 | 0-33 | •246 | 6d-195 | | |
| Karachi[1]-Drawn | •7-502 | - | - | - | | |
| **1971 in ENGLAND** | | | | | | |
| Birmingham-Drawn | 353 | 5-229 | •7d-608 | - | R.Illingworth | Intikhab Alam |
| Lord's-Drawn | •2d-241 | 0-117 | 148 | - | | |
| Leeds-England 25 runs | •316 | 264 | 350 | 205 | | |
| **1972-73 in PAKISTAN** | | | | | | |
| Lahore[2]-Drawn | •355 | 7d-306 | 422 | 3-124 | A.R.Lewis | Majid Khan |
| Hyderabad-Drawn | •487 | 6-218 | 9d-569 | - | | |
| Karachi[1]-Drawn | 386 | 1-30 | •6d-445 | 199 | | |
| **1974 in ENGLAND** | | | | | | |
| Leeds-Drawn | 183 | 6-238 | •285 | 179 | M.H.Denness | Intikhab Alam |
| Lord's-Drawn | 270 | 0-27 | •9d-130 | 226 | | |
| The Oval-Drawn | 545 | - | •7d-600 | 4-94 | | |
| **1977-78 in PAKISTAN** | | | | | | |
| Lahore[2]-Drawn | 288 | - | •9d-407 | 3-106 | J.M.Brearley | Wasim Bari |
| Hyderabad-Drawn | 191 | 1-186 | •275 | 4d-259 | J.M.Brearley | |
| Karachi[1]-Drawn | •266 | 5-222 | 281 | - | G.Boycott | |
| **1978 in ENGLAND** | | | | | | |
| Birmingham-England inns & 57 runs | 8d-452 | - | •164 | 231 | J.M.Brearley | Wasim Bari |
| Lord's-England inns &120 runs | •364 | - | 105 | 139 | | |
| Leeds-Drawn | 7-119 | - | •201 | - | | |
| **1982 in ENGLAND** | | | | | | |
| Birmingham-England 113 runs | •272 | 291 | 251 | 199 | R.G.D.Willis | Imran Khan |
| Lord's-Pakistan 10 wkts | 227 | 276 | •8d-428 | 0-77 | D.I.Gower | |
| Leeds-England 3 wkts | 256 | 7-219 | •275 | 199 | R.G.D.Willis | |

| **ENGLAND v PAKISTAN** (cont.) | England | | Pakistan | | Captains | |
|---|---|---|---|---|---|---|
| Venue and Result | 1st | 2nd | 1st | 2nd | England | Pakistan |
| **1983-84 in PAKISTAN** | | | | | | |
| Karachi[1]-Pakistan 3 wkts | •182 | 159 | 277 | 7-66 | R.G.D.Willis | Zaheer Abbas |
| Faisalabad-Drawn | 8d-546 | - | •8d-449 | 4-137 | D.I.Gower | |
| Lahore[2]-Drawn | •241 | 9d-344 | 343 | 6-217 | D.I.Gower | |
| **1987 in ENGLAND** | | | | | | |
| Manchester-Drawn | •447 | - | 5-140 | - | M.W.Gatting | Imran Khan |
| Lord's-Drawn | •368 | - | - | - | | |
| Leeds-Pakistan inns & 18 runs | •136 | 199 | 353 | - | | |
| Birmingham-Drawn | 521 | 7-109 | •439 | 205 | | |
| The Oval-Drawn | 232 | 4-315 | •708 | - | | |
| **1987-88 in PAKISTAN** | | | | | | |
| Lahore[2]-Pakistan inns & 87 runs | •175 | 130 | 392 | - | M.W.Gatting | Javed Miandad |
| Faisalabad-Drawn | •292 | 6d-137 | 191 | 1-51 | | |
| Karachi[1]-Drawn | •294 | 9-258 | 353 | - | | |
| **1992 in ENGLAND** | | | | | | |
| Birmingham-Drawn | 7-459 | - | •4d-448 | - | G.A.Gooch | Javed Miandad |
| Lord's-Pakistan 2 wkts | •255 | 175 | 293 | 8-141 | | |
| Manchester-Drawn | 390 | - | •505 | 5d-239 | | |
| Leeds-England 6 wkts | 320 | 4-99 | •197 | 221 | | |
| The Oval-Pakistan 10 wkts | •207 | 174 | 380 | 0-5 | | |
| **1996 in ENGLAND** | | | | | | |
| Lord's-Pakistan 164 runs | 285 | 243 | •340 | 5d-352 | M.A.Atherton | Wasim Akram |
| Leeds-Drawn | 501 | - | •448 | 7d-242 | | |
| The Oval-Pakistan 9 wickets | •326 | 242 | 8d-521 | 1-48 | | |

## Test Match Results Summary

**ENGLAND v PAKISTAN-IN ENGLAND**

| | | Result | | | Lords | | | Nottingham | | | Manchester | | | The Oval | | | Birmingham | | | Leeds | | |
|---|---|---|---|---|---|---|---|---|---|---|---|---|---|---|---|---|---|---|---|---|---|---|
| | Tests | E | P | D | E | P | D | E | P | D | E | P | D | E | P | D | E | P | D | E | P | D |
| 1954 | 4 | 1 | 1 | 2 | - | - | 1 | 1 | - | - | - | - | 1 | - | 1 | - | - | - | - | - | - | - |
| 1962 | 5 | 4 | - | 1 | 1 | - | - | - | - | 1 | - | - | - | 1 | - | - | 1 | - | - | 1 | - | - |
| 1967 | 3 | 2 | - | 1 | - | - | 1 | 1 | - | - | - | - | - | 1 | - | - | - | - | - | - | - | - |
| 1971 | 3 | 1 | - | 2 | - | - | 1 | - | - | - | - | - | - | - | - | - | - | - | 1 | 1 | - | - |
| 1974 | 3 | - | - | 3 | - | - | 1 | - | - | - | - | - | - | - | - | 1 | - | - | - | - | - | 1 |
| 1978 | 3 | 2 | - | 1 | 1 | - | - | - | - | - | - | - | - | - | - | - | 1 | - | - | - | - | 1 |
| 1982 | 3 | 2 | 1 | - | - | 1 | - | - | - | - | - | - | - | - | - | - | 1 | - | - | 1 | - | - |
| 1987 | 5 | - | 1 | 4 | - | - | 1 | - | - | - | - | - | 1 | - | - | 1 | - | - | 1 | - | 1 | - |
| 1992 | 5 | 1 | 2 | 2 | - | 1 | - | - | - | - | - | - | 1 | - | 1 | - | - | - | 1 | 1 | - | - |
| 1996 | 3 | - | 2 | 1 | - | 1 | - | - | - | - | - | - | - | - | 1 | 2 | - | - | - | - | - | 1 |
| | 37 | 13 | 7 | 17 | 2 | 3 | 5 | 2 | - | 1 | - | - | 3 | 2 | 3 | 2 | 3 | - | 3 | 4 | 1 | 3 |

**ENGLAND v PAKISTAN-IN PAKISTAN**

| | Tests | Result | | | Lahore[2] | | | Dacca | | | Karachi[1] | | | Hyderabad | | | Faisalabad | | |
|---|---|---|---|---|---|---|---|---|---|---|---|---|---|---|---|---|---|---|---|
| | | E | P | D | E | P | D | E | P | D | E | P | D | E | P | D | E | P | D |
| 1961-62 | 3 | 1 | - | 2 | 1 | - | - | - | - | 1 | - | - | 1 | - | - | - | - | - | - |
| 1968-69 | 3 | - | - | 3 | - | - | 1 | - | - | - | - | - | 1 | - | - | 1 | - | - | - |
| 1972-73 | 3 | - | - | 3 | - | - | 1 | - | - | - | - | - | 1 | - | - | 1 | - | - | - |
| 1977-78 | 3 | - | - | 3 | - | - | 1 | - | - | 1 | - | - | 1 | - | - | - | - | - | - |
| 1983-84 | 3 | - | 1 | 2 | - | - | 1 | - | - | - | - | 1 | - | - | - | - | - | - | 1 |
| 1987-88 | 3 | - | 1 | 2 | - | 1 | - | - | - | - | - | - | 1 | - | - | - | - | - | 1 |
| | 18 | 1 | 2 | 15 | 1 | 1 | 4 | - | - | 2 | - | 1 | 5 | - | - | 2 | - | - | 2 |
| Totals | 55 | 14 | 9 | 32 | | | | | | | | | | | | | | | |

**HIGHEST INNINGS TOTALS**

| | | | |
|---|---|---|---|
| England in England | 6d-558 | Nottingham | 1954 |
| England in Pakistan | 8d-546 | Faisalabad | 1983-84 |
| Pakistan in England | 708 | The Oval | 1987 |
| Pakistan in Pakistan | 9d-569 | Hyderabad | 1972-73 |

**LOWEST INNINGS TOTALS**

| | | | |
|---|---|---|---|
| England in England | 130 | The Oval | 1954 |
| England in Pakistan | 130 | Lahore[2] | 1987-88 |
| Pakistan in England | 87 | Lord's | 1954 |
| Pakistan in Pakistan | 191 | Faisalabad | 1987-88 |

| | | | |
|---|---|---|---|
| **HIGHEST MATCH AGGREGATE** | 1274 for 25 wickets | Hyderabad | 1972-73 |
| **LOWEST MATCH AGGREGATE** | 509 for 28 wickets | Nottingham | 1967 |

**HIGHEST INDIVIDUAL INNINGS**

| | | | | |
|---|---|---|---|---|
| England in England | 278 | D.C.S.Compton | Nottingham | 1954 |
| England in Pakistan | 205 | E.R.Dexter | Karachi[1] | 1961-62 |
| Pakistan in England | 274 | Zaheer Abbas | Birmingham | 1971 |
| Pakistan in Pakistan | 157 | Mushtaq Mohammad | Hyderabad | 1972-73 |

**HIGHEST AGGREGATE OF RUNS IN A SERIES**

| | | | |
|---|---|---|---|
| England in England | 453 (av 90.60) | D.C.S.Compton | 1954 |
| England in Pakistan | 449 (av 112.25) | D.I.Gower | 1983-84 |
| Pakistan in England | 488 (av 81.33) | Saleem Malik | 1992 |
| Pakistan in Pakistan | 407 (av 67.83) | Hanif Mohammad | 1961-62 |

**RECORD WICKET PARTNERSHIPS-ENGLAND**

| | | | | |
|---|---|---|---|---|
| 1st | 198 | G.Pullar (165), R.W.Barber (86) | Dacca | 1961-62 |
| 2nd | 248 | M.C.Cowdrey (182), E.R.Dexter (172) | The Oval | 1962 |
| 3rd | 227 | A.J.Stewart (190), R.A.Smith (127) | Birmingham | 1992 |
| 4th | 188 | E.R.Dexter (205), P.H.Parfitt (111) | Karachi[1] | 1961-62 |
| 5th | 192 | D.C.S.Compton (278), T.E.Bailey (36*) | Nottingham | 1954 |
| 6th | 153* | P.H.Parfitt (101*), D.A.Allen (79*) | Birmingham | 1962 |
| 7th | 167 | D.I.Gower (152), V.J.Marks (83) | Faisalabad | 1983-84 |
| 8th | 99 | P.H.Parfitt (119), D.A.Allen (62) | Leeds | 1962 |
| 9th | 76 | T.W.Graveney (153), F.S.Trueman (29) | Lord's | 1962 |
| 10th | 79 | R.W.Taylor (54), R.G.D.Willis (28*) | Birmingham | 1982 |

### RECORD WICKET PARTNERSHIPS-PAKISTAN

| | | | | |
|---|---|---|---|---|
| 1st | 173 | Mohsin Khan (104), Shoaib Mohammad (80) | Lahore[2] | 1983-84 |
| 2nd | 291 | Zaheer Abbas (274), Mushtaq Mohammad (100) | Birmingham | 1971 |
| 3rd | 180 | Mudassar Nazar (114), Haroon Rashid (122) | Lahore[2] | 1977-78 |
| 4th | 332 | Javed Miandad (153*), Saleem Malik (165) | Birmingham | 1992 |
| 5th | 197 | Javed Burki (101), Nasim-ul-Ghani (101) | Lord's | 1962 |
| 6th | 145 | Mushtaq Mohammad (157), Intikhab Alam (138) | Hyderabad | 1972-73 |
| 7th | 112 | Asif Mujtaba (51), Moin Khan (105) | Leeds | 1996 |
| 8th | 130 | Hanif Mohammad (187*), Asif Iqbal (76) | Lord's | 1967 |
| 9th | 190 | Asif Iqbal (146), Intikhab Alam (51) | The Oval | 1967 |
| 10th | 62 | Sarfraz Nawaz (53), Asif Masood (4*) | Leeds | 1974 |

### BEST INNINGS BOWLING ANALYSIS

| | | | | |
|---|---|---|---|---|
| England in England | 8-34 | I.T.Botham | Lord's | 1978 |
| England in Pakistan | 7-66 | P.H.Edmonds | Karachi[1] | 1977-78 |
| Pakistan in England | 7-40 | Imran Khan | Leeds | 1987 |
| Pakistan in Pakistan | 9-56 | Abdul Qadir | Lahore[2] | 1987-88 |

### BEST MATCH BOWLING ANALYSIS

| | | | | |
|---|---|---|---|---|
| England in England | 13-71 | D.L.Underwood | Lord's | 1974 |
| England in Pakistan | 11-83 | N.G.B.Cook | Karachi[1] | 1983-84 |
| Pakistan in England | 12-99 | Fazal Mahmood | The Oval | 1954 |
| Pakistan in Pakistan | 13-101 | Abdul Qadir | Lahore[2] | 1987-88 |

### HIGHEST AGGREGATE OF WICKETS IN A SERIES

| | | | |
|---|---|---|---|
| England in England | 22 (av 19.95) | F.S.Trueman | 1962 |
| England in Pakistan | 14 (av 31.71) | N.G.B.Cook | 1983-84 |
| Pakistan in England | 22 (av 25.31) | Waqar Younis | 1992 |
| Pakistan in Pakistan | 30 (av 14.56) | Abdul Qadir | 1987-88 |

| **ENGLAND v SRI LANKA** Venue and Result | England 1st | England 2nd | Sri Lanka 1st | Sri Lanka 2nd | Captains England | Captains Sri Lanka |
|---|---|---|---|---|---|---|
| **1981-82 in SRI LANKA** | | | | | | |
| Colombo (PSS)-England 7 wkts | 223 | 3-171 | •218 | 175 | K.W.R.Fletcher | B.Warnapura |
| **1984 in ENGLAND** | | | | | | |
| Lord's-Drawn | 370 | - | •7d-491 | 7d-294 | D.I.Gower | L.R.D.Mendis |
| **1988 in ENGLAND** | | | | | | |
| Lord's-England 7 wkts | 429 | 3-100 | •194 | 331 | G.A.Gooch | R.S.Madugalle |
| **1991 in ENGLAND** | | | | | | |
| Lord's-England 137 runs | •282 | 3d-364 | 224 | 285 | G.A.Gooch | P.A.de Silva |
| **1992-93 in SRI LANKA** | | | | | | |
| Colombo (SSC)-Sri Lanka 5 wickets | •380 | 228 | 469 | 5-142 | A.J.Stewart | A.Ranatunga |

## Test Match Results Summary

**ENGLAND v SRI LANKA-IN ENGLAND**

| | | Result | | | Lord's | | |
|---|---|---|---|---|---|---|---|
| | Tests | E | SL | D | E | SL | D |
| 1984 | 1 | - | - | 1 | - | - | 1 |
| 1988 | 1 | 1 | - | - | 1 | - | - |
| 1991 | 1 | 1 | - | - | 1 | - | - |
| 1998 | 1 | | | | | | |
| | 3 | 2 | - | 1 | 2 | - | 1 |

**ENGLAND v SRI LANKA-IN SRI LANKA**

| | | Result | | | Colombo (PSS) | | | Colombo (SSC) | | |
|---|---|---|---|---|---|---|---|---|---|---|
| | Tests | E | SL | D | E | SL | D | E | SL | D |
| 1981-82 | 1 | 1 | - | - | 1 | - | - | - | - | - |
| 1992-93 | 1 | - | 1 | - | - | - | - | - | 1 | - |
| | 2 | 1 | 1 | - | 1 | - | - | - | 1 | - |
| Totals | 5 | 3 | 1 | 1 | | | | | | |

**HIGHEST INNINGS TOTALS**

| | | | |
|---|---|---|---|
| England in England | 429 | Lord's | 1988 |
| England in Sri Lanka | 380 | Colombo (SSC) | 1992-93 |
| Sri Lanka in England | 7d-491 | Lord's | 1984 |
| Sri Lanka in Sri Lanka | 469 | Colombo (SSC) | 1992-93 |

**LOWEST INNINGS TOTALS**

| | | | |
|---|---|---|---|
| England in England | 282 | Lord's | 1991 |
| England in Sri Lanka | 223 | Colombo (PSS) | 1981-82 |
| Sri Lanka in England | 194 | Lord's | 1988 |
| Sri Lanka in Sri Lanka | 195 | Colombo (PSS) | 1981-82 |

| | | | |
|---|---|---|---|
| **HIGHEST MATCH AGGREGATE** | 1219 for 37 wickets | Colombo (SSC) | 1992-93 |
| **LOWEST MATCH AGGREGATE** | 787 for 33 wickets | Colombo (PSS) | 1981-82 |

### HIGHEST INDIVIDUAL INNINGS

| | | | | |
|---|---|---|---|---|
| England in England | 174 | G.A.Gooch | Lord's | 1991 |
| England in Sri Lanka | 128 | R.A.Smith | Colombo (SSC) | 1992-93 |
| Sri Lanka in England | 190 | S.Wettimuny | Lord's | 1984 |
| Sri Lanka in Sri Lanka | 93* | H.P.Tillakaratne | Colombo (SSC) | 1992-93 |

### HIGHEST AGGREGATE OF RUNS IN A SERIES

| | | | |
|---|---|---|---|
| England in England | 212 (av 90.60) | G.A.Gooch | 1991 |
| England in Sri Lanka | 163 (av 81.50) | R.A.Smith | 1992-93 |
| Sri Lanka in England | 205 (av 44.55) | L.R.D.Mendis | 1984 |
| Sri Lanka in Sri Lanka | 129 (av —.—) | H.P.Tillakaratne | 1992-93 |

### RECORD WICKET PARTNERSHIPS-ENGLAND

| | | | | |
|---|---|---|---|---|
| 1st | 78 | G.A.Gooch (174), H.Morris (23) | Lord's | 1991 |
| 2nd | 139 | G.A.Gooch (174), A.J.Stewart (43) | Lord's | 1991 |
| 3rd | 112 | R.A.Smith (128), G.A.Hick (68) | Colombo (SSC) | 1992-93 |
| 4th | 122 | R.A.Smith (128), A.J.Stewart (63) | Colombo (SSC) | 1992-93 |
| 5th | 40 | A.J.Stewart (113*), I.T.Botham (22) | Lord's | 1991 |
| 6th | 87 | A.J.Lamb (107), R.M.Ellison (41) | Lord's | 1984 |
| 7th | 63 | A.J.Stewart (113*), R.C.Russell (17) | Lord's | 1991 |
| 8th | 20 | J.E.Emburey (59), P.W.Jarvis (3) | Colombo (SSC) | 1992-93 |
| 9th | 37 | P.J.Newport (26), N.A.Foster (14*) | Lord's | 1988 |
| 10th | 40 | J.E.Emburey (59), D.E.Malcolm (8*) | Colombo (SSC) | 1992-93 |

### RECORD WICKET PARTNERSHIPS-SRI LANKA

| | | | | |
|---|---|---|---|---|
| 1st | 99 | R.S.Mahanama (64), U.C.Hathurusingha (59) | Colombo (SSC) | 1992-93 |
| 2nd | 83 | B.Warnaweera (38), R.L.Dias (77) | Colombo (PSS) | 1981-82 |
| 3rd | 101 | S.Wettimuny (190), R.L.Dias (32) | Lord's | 1984 |
| 4th | 148 | S.Wettimuny (190), A.Ranatunga (84) | Lord's | 1984 |
| 5th | 150 | S.Wettimuny (190), L.R.D.Mendis(111) | Lord's | 1984 |
| 6th | 138 | S.A.R.Silva (102*), L.R.D.Mendis (94) | Lord's | 1984 |
| 7th | 74 | U.C.Hathurusingha (66), R.J.Ratnayake (52) | Lord's | 1991 |
| 8th | 28 | R.J.Ratnayake (17), C.P.H.Ramanayake (34*) | Lord's | 1991 |
| 9th | 83 | H.P.Tillakaratne (93*), M.Muralidaran (19) | Colombo (SSC) | 1992-93 |
| 10th | 64 | J.R.Ratnayeke (59*), G.F.Labrooy (42) | Lord's | 1988 |

### BEST INNINGS BOWLING ANALYSIS

| | | | | |
|---|---|---|---|---|
| England in England | 7-70 | P.A.J.DeFreitas | Lord's | 1991 |
| England in Sri Lanka | 6-33 | J.E.Emburey | Colombo (PSS) | 1981-82 |
| Sri Lanka in England | 5-69 | R.J.Ratnayake | Lord's | 1991 |
| Sri Lanka in Sri Lanka | 4-70 | A.L.F.de Mel | Colombo (PSS) | 1981-82 |

### BEST MATCH BOWLING ANALYSIS

| | | | | |
|---|---|---|---|---|
| England in England | 8-115 | P.A.J.DeFreitas | Lord's | 1991 |
| England in Sri Lanka | 8-95 | D.L.Underwood | Colombo (PSS) | 1981-82 |
| Sri Lanka in England | 5-160 | R.J.Ratnayake | Lord's | 1991 |
| Sri Lanka in Sri Lanka | 8-188 | K.P.J.Warnaweera | Colombo (SSC) | 1992-93 |

### HIGHEST AGGREGATE OF WICKETS IN A SERIES

| | | | |
|---|---|---|---|
| England in England | 8 (av 14.37) | P.A.J.DeFreitas | 1991 |
| England in Sri Lanka | 8 (av 11.87) | D.L.Underwood | 1981-82 |
| Sri Lanka in England | 5 (av 32.00) | R.J.Ratnayake | 1991 |
| | 5 (av 36.00) | S.D.Anurasiri | 1991 |
| Sri Lanka in Sri Lanka | 8 (av 23.50) | K.P.J.Warnaweera | 1992-93 |

| **ENGLAND v ZIMBABWE** | England | | Zimbabwe | | Captains | |
|---|---|---|---|---|---|---|
| Venue and Result | 1st | 2nd | 1st | 2nd | England | Zimbabwe |
| **1996-97 in ZIMBABWE** | | | | | | |
| Bulawayo[2]-Drawn | 406 | 6-204 | •376 | 234 | M.A.Atherton | A.D.R.Campbell |
| Harare-Drawn | •156 | 3-195 | 215 | - | | |

## Test Match Results Summary

### ENGLAND v ZIMBABWE-IN ZIMBABWE

| | Tests | Result | | | Bulawayo[2] | | | Harare | | |
|---|---|---|---|---|---|---|---|---|---|---|
| | | E | Z | D | E | SL | D | E | SL | D |
| 1996-97 | 2 | - | - | - | - | - | 1 | - | - | 1 |

**HIGHEST INNINGS TOTALS**

| | | | |
|---|---|---|---|
| England in Zimbabwe | 406 | Bulawayo[2] | 1996-97 |
| Zimbabwe in Zimbabwe | 376 | Bulawayo[2] | 1996-97 |

**LOWEST INNINGS TOTALS**

| | | | |
|---|---|---|---|
| England in Zimbabwe | 156 | Harare | 1996-97 |
| Zimbabwe in Zimbabwe | 215 | Harare | 1996-97 |

| | | | |
|---|---|---|---|
| **HIGHEST MATCH AGGREGATE** | 1220 for 36 wickets | Bulawayo[2] | 1996-97 |
| **LOWEST MATCH AGGREGATE** | 566 for 23 wickets | Harare | 1996-97 |

**HIGHEST INDIVIDUAL INNINGS**

| | | | | |
|---|---|---|---|---|
| England in Zimbabwe | 113 | N.Hussain | Bulawayo[2] | 1996-97 |
| Zimbabwe in Zimbabwe | 112 | A.Flower | Bulawayo[2] | 1996-97 |

**HIGHEST AGGREGATE OF RUNS IN A SERIES**

| | | | |
|---|---|---|---|
| England in Zimbabwe | 241 (av 80.33) | A.J.Stewart | 1996-97 |
| Zimbabwe in Zimbabwe | 135 (av 45.00) | A.D.R.Campbell | 1996-97 |

**RECORD WICKET PARTNERSHIPS-ENGLAND**

| | | | | |
|---|---|---|---|---|
| 1st | 48 | N.V.Knight (56), M.A.Atherton (16) | Bulawayo[2] | 1996-97 |
| 2nd | 137 | N.V.Knight (96), A.J.Stewart (73) | Bulawayo[2] | 1996-97 |
| 3rd | 68 | A.J.Stewart (48), N.Hussain (113) | Bulawayo[2] | 1996-97 |
| 4th | 106* | A.J.Stewart (101*), G.P.Thorpe (50*) | Harare | 1996-97 |
| 5th | 148 | N.Hussain (113), J.Crawley (112) | Bulawayo[2] | 1996-97 |
| 6th | 22 | N.V.Knight (96), D.Gough (3*) | Bulawayo[2] | 1996-97 |
| 7th | 34 | J.P.Crawley (47*), R.D.B.Croft (14) | Harare | 1996-97 |
| 8th | 9 | J.P.Crawley (112), C.E.W.Silverwood (0) | Bulawayo[2] | 1996-97 |
| 9th | 25 | J.P.Crawley (112), A.D.Mullally (4) | Bulawayo[2] | 1996-97 |
| 10th | 28 | J.P.Crawley (112), P.C.R.Tufnell (2*) | Bulawayo[2] | 1996-97 |

**RECORD WICKET PARTNERSHIPS-ZIMBABWE**

| | | | | |
|---|---|---|---|---|
| 1st | 6 | G.W.Flower (0), S.V.Carlisle (4) | Bulawayo[2] | 1996-97 |
| 2nd | 126 | G.W.Flower (43), A.D.R.Campbell (84) | Bulawayo[2] | 1996-97 |
| 3rd | 64 | G.W.Flower (73), D.L.Houghton (29) | Harare | 1996-97 |
| 4th | 70 | D.L.Houghton (34), A.Flower (112) | Bulawayo[2] | 1996-97 |
| 5th | 30 | A.Flower (112), A.C.Waller (15) | Bulawayo[2] | 1996-97 |
| 6th | 17 | A.Flower (112), G.J.Whittall (7) | Bulawayo[2] | 1996-97 |
| 7th | 67 | A.C.Waller (50), G.J.Whittall (56) | Bulawayo[2] | 1996-97 |
| 8th | 41 | A.Flower (112), H.H.Streak (19) | Bulawayo[2] | 1996-97 |
| 9th | 14 | G.J.Whittall (56), H.H.Streak (8*) | Bulawayo[2] | 1996-97 |
| | 14 | P.A.Strang (47*), E.A.Brandes (9) | Harare | |
| 10th | 4 | P.A.Strang (47*), H.K.Olonga (0) | Harare | 1996-97 |

**BEST INNINGS BOWLING ANALYSIS**

| | | | | |
|---|---|---|---|---|
| England in Zimbabwe | 4-40 | D.Gough | Bulawayo[2] | 1996-97 |
| Zimbabwe in Zimbabwe | 5-123 | P.A.Strang | Bulawayo[2] | 1996-97 |

**BEST MATCH BOWLING ANALYSIS**

| | | | | |
|---|---|---|---|---|
| England in Zimbabwe | 6-137 | P.C.R.Tufnell | Bulawayo[2] | 1996-97 |
| Zimbabwe in Zimbabwe | 7-186 | P.A.Strang | Bulawayo[2] | 1996-97 |

**HIGHEST AGGREGATE OF WICKETS IN A SERIES**

| | | | |
|---|---|---|---|
| England in Zimbabwe | 8 (av 22.25) | R.D.B.Croft | 1996-97 |
| Zimbabwe in Zimbabwe | 10 (av 25.90) | P.A.Strang | 1996-97 |

| **SOUTH AFRICA v NEW ZEALAND** | South Africa | | New Zealand | | Captains | |
|---|---|---|---|---|---|---|
| Venue and Result | 1st | 2nd | 1st | 2nd | South Africa | New Zealand |
| **1931-32 In NEW ZEALAND** | | | | | | |
| Christchurch-South Africa inns & 12 runs | 451 | - | •293 | 146 | H.B.Cameron | M.L.Page |
| Wellington-South Africa 8 wkts | 410 | 2-150 | •364 | 193 | | |
| **1952-53 In NEW ZEALAND** | | | | | | |
| Wellington-South Africa inns & 180 runs | •8d-524 | - | 172 | 172 | J.E.Cheetham | W.M.Wallace |
| Auckland-Drawn | •377 | 5d-200 | 245 | 2-31 | | |
| **1953-54 In SOUTH AFRICA** | | | | | | |
| Durban[2]-South Africa inns & 58 runs | •9d-437 | - | 230 | 149 | J.E.Cheetham | G.O.Rabone |
| Johannesburg[2]-South Africa 132 runs | •271 | 148 | 187 | 100 | | G.O.Rabone |
| Cape Town-Drawn | 326 | 3-159 | •505 | - | | G.O.Rabone |
| Johannesburg[2]-South Africa 9 wkts | •243 | 1-25 | 79 | 188 | | B.Sutcliffe |
| Port Elizabeth-South Africa 5 wkts | 237 | 5-215 | •226 | 222 | | B.Sutcliffe |
| **1961-62 In SOUTH AFRICA** | | | | | | |
| Durban[2]-South Africa 30 runs | •292 | 149 | 245 | 166 | D.J.McGlew | J.R.Reid |
| Johannesburg[3]-Drawn | •322 | 6d-178 | 223 | 4-165 | | |
| Cape Town-New Zealand 72 runs | 190 | 335 | •385 | 9d-212 | | |
| Johannesburg[3]-South Africa inns & 51 runs | 464 | - | •164 | 249 | | |
| Port Elizabeth-New Zealand 40 runs | 190 | 273 | •275 | 228 | | |
| **1963-64 in NEW ZEALAND** | | | | | | |
| Wellington-Drawn | •302 | 2d-218 | 253 | 6-138 | T.L.Goddard | J.R.Reid |
| Dunedin-Drawn | 223 | 3-42 | •149 | 138 | | |
| Auckland-Drawn | •371 | 5d-200 | 263 | 8-191 | | |
| **1994-95 In SOUTH AFRICA** | | | | | | |
| Johannesburg[3]-New Zealand 137 runs | 279 | 1189 | •411 | 194 | W.J.Cronje | K.R.Rutherford |
| Cape Town-South Africa 8 wkts | 226 | 2-153 | •185 | 192 | | |
| Durban[2]-South Africa 7 wkts | 440 | 3-89 | •288 | 239 | | |
| **1994-95 in NEW ZEALAND** | | | | | | |
| Auckland-South Africa 93 runs | •294 | 6d-308 | 328 | 181 | W.J.Cronje | K.R.Rutherford |

## Test Match Results Summary

### SOUTH AFRICA v NEW ZEALAND-IN SOUTH AFRICA

| | | Result | | | Durban[2] | | | Johannesburg | | | Cape Town | | | P.Elizabeth | | |
|---|---|---|---|---|---|---|---|---|---|---|---|---|---|---|---|---|
| | Tests | SA | NZ | D | SA | NZ | D | SA | NZ | D | SA | NZ | D | SA | NZ | D |
| 1953-54 | 5 | 4 | - | 1 | 1 | - | - | 2 | - | - | - | - | 1 | 1 | - | - |
| 1961-62 | 5 | 2 | 2 | 1 | 1 | - | - | 1 | - | 1 | - | 1 | - | - | 1 | - |
| 1994-95 | 3 | 2 | 1 | - | 1 | - | - | - | 1 | - | 1 | - | - | - | - | - |
| | 13 | 8 | 3 | 2 | 2 | - | - | 3 | - | 1 | - | 1 | 1 | 1 | 1 | - |

### SOUTH AFRICA v NEW ZEALAND-IN NEW ZEALAND

| | | Result | | | Christchurch | | | Wellington | | | Auckland | | | Dunedin | | |
|---|---|---|---|---|---|---|---|---|---|---|---|---|---|---|---|---|
| | Tests | SA | NZ | D | SA | NZ | D | SA | NZ | D | SA | NZ | D | SA | NZ | D |
| 1931-32 | 2 | 2 | - | - | 1 | - | - | 1 | - | - | - | - | - | - | - | - |
| 1952-53 | 2 | 1 | - | 1 | - | - | - | 1 | - | - | - | - | 1 | - | - | - |
| 1963-64 | 3 | - | - | 3 | - | - | - | - | - | 1 | - | - | 1 | - | - | 1 |
| 1994-95 | 1 | 1 | - | - | - | - | - | - | - | - | 1 | - | - | - | - | - |
| | 8 | 4 | - | 4 | 1 | - | - | 2 | - | 1 | - | - | 2 | - | - | 1 |
| Totals | 21 | 12 | 3 | 6 | | | | | | | | | | | | |

**HIGHEST INNINGS TOTALS**

| | | | |
|---|---|---|---|
| South Africa in South Africa | 464 | Johannesburg[3] | 1961-62 |
| South Africa in New Zealand | 8d-524 | Wellington | 1952-53 |
| New Zealand in South Africa | 505 | Cape Town | 1953-54 |
| New Zealand in New Zealand | 364 | Wellington | 1931-32 |

**LOWEST INNINGS TOTALS**

| | | | |
|---|---|---|---|
| South Africa in South Africa | 148 | Johannesburg[2] | 1953-54 |
| South Africa in New Zealand | 223 | Dunedin | 1963-64 |
| New Zealand in South Africa | 79 | Johannesburg[2] | 1953-54 |
| New Zealand in New Zealand | 138 | Dunedin | 1963-64 |

| | | | |
|---|---|---|---|
| **HIGHEST MATCH AGGREGATE** | 1122 for 39 wickets | Cape Town | 1961-62 |
| **LOWEST MATCH AGGREGATE** | 535 for 31 wickets | Johannesburg[2] | 1953-54 |

**HIGHEST INDIVIDUAL INNINGS**

| | | | | |
|---|---|---|---|---|
| South Africa in South Africa | 127* | D.J.McGlew | Durban[2] | 1961-62 |
| South Africa in New Zealand | 255* | D.J.McGlew | Wellington | 1952-53 |
| New Zealand in South Africa | 142 | J.R.Reid | Johannesburg[3] | 1961-62 |
| New Zealand in New Zealand | 138 | B.W.Sinclair | Auckland | 1963-64 |

**HIGHEST AGGREGATE OF RUNS IN A SERIES**

| | | | |
|---|---|---|---|
| South Africa in South Africa | 426 (av 60.85) | D.J.McGlew | 1961-62 |
| South Africa in New Zealand | 323 (av 161.50) | D.J.McGlew | 1952-53 |
| New Zealand in South Africa | 546 (av 60.66) | J.R.Reid | 1961-62 |
| New Zealand in New Zealand | 264 (av 44.00) | B.W.Sinclair | 1963-64 |

**RECORD WICKET PARTNERSHIPS-SOUTH AFRICA**

| | | | | |
|---|---|---|---|---|
| 1st | 196 | J.A.J.Christy (103), B.Mitchell (113) | Christchurch | 1931-32 |
| 2nd | 97 | G.Kirsten (66*), J.B.Commins (45) | Durban[2] | 1994-95 |
| 3rd | 112 | D.J.McGlew (120), R.A.McLean (78) | Johannesburg[3] | 1961-62 |
| 4th | 135 | K.J.Funston (39), R.A McLean (101) | Durban[2] | 1953-54 |
| 5th | 130 | W.R.Endean (116), J.E.Cheetham (54) | Auckland | 1952-53 |
| 6th | 83 | K.C.Bland (83), D.T.Lindsay (37) | Auckland | 1963-64 |
| 7th | 246 | D.J.McGlew (255*), A.R.A.Murray (109) | Wellington | 1952-53 |
| 8th | 95 | J.E.Cheetham (89), H.J.Tayfield (34) | Cape Town | 1953-54 |
| 9th | 60 | P.M.Pollock (54), N.A.T.Adcock (24) | Port Elizabeth | 1961-62 |
| 10th | 47 | D.J.McGlew (28*), H.D.Bromfield (21) | Port Elizabeth | 1961-62 |

**RECORD WICKET PARTNERSHIPS-NEW ZEALAND**

| | | | | |
|---|---|---|---|---|
| 1st | 126 | G.O.Rabone (56), M.E.Chapple (76) | Cape Town | 1953-54 |
| 2nd | 72 | D.J.Murray (25), S.P.Fleming (48) | Johannesburg[3] | 1994-95 |
| 3rd | 94 | M.B.Poore (44), B.Sutcliffe (66) | Cape Town | 1953-54 |
| 4th | 171 | B.W.Sinclair (138), S.N.McGregor (62) | Auckland | 1963-64 |
| 5th | 174 | J.R.Reid (135), J.E.F.Beck (99) | Cape Town | 1953-54 |
| 6th | 100 | H.G.Vivian (100), F.T Badcock (53) | Wellington | 1931-32 |
| 7th | 84 | J.R.Reid (142), G.A.Bartlett (33) | Johannesburg[3] | 1961-62 |
| 8th | 74 | S.A.Thomson (84), D.J.Nash (18) | Johannesburg[3] | 1994-95 |
| 9th | 69 | C.F.W.Allcott (26), I.B.Cromb (51*) | Wellington | 1931-32 |
| 10th | 57 | S.B.Doull (31*), R.P.de Groen (21) | Johannesburg[3] | 1994-95 |

**BEST INNINGS BOWLING ANALYSIS**

| | | | | |
|---|---|---|---|---|
| South Africa in South Africa | 8-53 | G.B.Lawrence | Johannesburg[3] | 1961-62 |
| South Africa in New Zealand | 6-47 | P.M.Pollock | Wellington | 1963-64 |
| New Zealand in South Africa | 6-68 | G.O.Rabone | Cape Town | 1953-54 |
| New Zealand in New Zealand | 6-60 | J.R.Reid | Dunedin | 1963-64 |

**BEST MATCH BOWLING ANALYSIS**

| | | | | |
|---|---|---|---|---|
| South Africa in South Africa | 11-196 | S.F.Burke | Cape Town | 1961-62 |
| South Africa in New Zealand | 9-127 | Q.McMillan | Christchurch | 1931-32 |
| New Zealand in South Africa | 8-134 | M.N.Hart | Johannesburg[3] | 1994-95 |
| New Zealand in New Zealand | 7-142 | R.W.Blair | Auckland | 1963-64 |

**HIGHEST AGGREGATE OF WICKETS IN A SERIES**

| | | | |
|---|---|---|---|
| South Africa in South Africa | 28 (av 18.28) | G.B.Lawrence | 1961-62 |
| South Africa in New Zealand | 16 (av 20.18) | Q.McMillan | 1931-32 |
| New Zealand in South Africa | 22 (av 20.63) | A.R.MacGibbon | 1953-54 |
| | 22 (av 28.04) | J.C.Alabaster | 1961-62 |
| New Zealand in New Zealand | 12 (av 23.16) | J.R.Reid | 1963-64 |
| | 12 (av 27.16) | R.W.Blair | 1963-64 |

| **SOUTH AFRICA v WEST INDIES** | South Africa | | West Indies | | Captains | |
|---|---|---|---|---|---|---|
| Venue and Result | 1st | 2nd | 1st | 2nd | South Africa | West Indies |
| **1991-92 In WEST INDIES** | | | | | | |
| Bridgetown-West Indies 52 runs | 345 | 148 | •262 | 283 | K.C.Wessels | R.B.Richardson |

## Test Match Results Summary

**SOUTH AFRICA v WEST INDIES-IN WEST INDIES**

| | | Result | | | Bridgetown | | |
|---|---|---|---|---|---|---|---|
| | Tests | SA | W | D | SA | W | D |
| 1991-92 | 1 | - | 1 | - | - | 1 | - |

**HIGHEST INNINGS TOTALS**

| | | | |
|---|---|---|---|
| South Africa in West Indies | 345 | Bridgetown | 1991-92 |
| West Indies in West Indies | 283 | Bridgetown | 1991-92 |

**LOWEST INNINGS TOTALS**

| | | | |
|---|---|---|---|
| South Africa in West Indies | 148 | Bridgetown | 1991-92 |
| West Indies in West Indies | 262 | Bridgetown | 1991-92 |

**HIGHEST MATCH AGGREGATE** 1038 for 40 wickets Bridgetown 1991-92

**HIGHEST INDIVIDUAL INNINGS**

| | | | | |
|---|---|---|---|---|
| South Africa in West Indies | 163 | A.C.Hudson | Bridgetown | 1991-92 |
| West Indies in West Indies | 79* | J.C.Adams | Bridgetown | 1991-92 |

**HIGHEST AGGREGATE OF RUNS IN A SERIES**

| | | | |
|---|---|---|---|
| South Africa in West Indies | 163 (av 81.50) | A.C.Hudson | 1991-92 |
| West Indies in West Indies | 90 (av 90.00) | J.C.Adams | 1991-92 |

**HIGHEST WICKET PARTNERSHIP-SOUTH AFRICA**

| | | | | |
|---|---|---|---|---|
| 1st | 14 | M.W.Rushmere (3), A.C.Hudson (163) | Bridgetown | 1991-92 |
| 2nd | 125 | A.C.Hudson (163), K.C.Wessels (59) | Bridgetown | 1991-92 |
| 3rd | 96 | K.C.Wessels (74), P.N.Kirsten (52) | Bridgetown | 1991-92 |
| 4th | 19 | A.C.Hudson (163), W.J.Cronje (5) | Bridgetown | 1991-92 |
| 5th | 92 | A.C.Hudson (163), A.P.kuiper (34) | Bridgetown | 1991-92 |
| 6th | 14 | A.C.Hudson (163), D.J.Richardson (8) | Bridgetown | 1991-92 |
| 7th | 19 | A.C.Hudson (163), R.P.Snell (16) | Bridgetown | 1991-92 |
| 8th | 5 | D.J.Richardson (2), M.W.Pringle (4) | Bridgetown | 1991-92 |
| 9th | 20 | M.W.Pringle (15), A.A.Donald (0) | Bridgetown | 1991-92 |
| 10th | 9 | M.W.Pringle (15), T.Bosch (5*) | Bridgetown | 1991-92 |

**HIGHEST WICKET PARTNERSHIP-WEST INDIES**

| | | | | |
|---|---|---|---|---|
| 1st | 99 | D.L.Haynes (58), P.V.Simmons (35) | Bridgetown | 1991-92 |
| 2nd | 56 | D.L.Haynes (23), B.C.Lara (64) | Bridgetown | 1991-92 |
| 3rd | 31 | B.C.Lara (17), R.B.Richardson (44) | Bridgetown | 1991-92 |
| 4th | 82 | R.B.Richardson (44), K.L.T.Arthurton (59) | Bridgetown | 1991-92 |
| 5th | 21 | K.L.T.Arthurton (59), J.C.Adams (11) | Bridgetown | 1991-92 |
| 6th | 25 | J.C.Adams (79*), D.Williams (5) | Bridgetown | 1991-92 |
| 7th | 10 | J.C.Adams (79*), C.E.L.Ambrose (6) | Bridgetown | 1991-92 |
| 8th | 22 | J.C.Adams (79*), K.C.G.Benajmin (7) | Bridgetown | 1991-92 |
| 9th | 27 | J.C.Adams (79*), C.A.Walsh (13) | Bridgetown | 1991-92 |
| 10th | 62 | J.C.Adams (79*), B.P.Patterson (11) | Bridgetown | 1991-92 |

**BEST INNINGS BOWLING ANALYSIS**

| | | | | |
|---|---|---|---|---|
| South Africa in South Africa | | | | |
| South Africa in West Indies | 4-74 | R.P.Snell | Bridgetown | 1991-92 |
| West Indies in South Africa | | | | |
| West Indies in West Indies | 6-34 | C.E.L.Ambrose | Bridgetown | 1991-92 |

**BEST MATCH BOWLING ANALYSIS**

| | | | | |
|---|---|---|---|---|
| South Africa in South Africa | | | | |
| South Africa in West Indies | 4-74 | R.P.Snell | Bridgetown | 1991-92 |
| West Indies in South Africa | | | | |
| West Indies in West Indies | 8-81 | C.E.L.Ambrose | Bridgetown | 1991-92 |

**HIGHEST AGGREGATE OF WICKETS IN A SERIES**

| | | | |
|---|---|---|---|
| South Africa in South Africa | | | |
| South Africa in West Indies | 8 (av 19.62) | R.P.Snell | 1991-92 |
| West Indies in South Africa | | | |
| West Indies in West Indies | 8 (av 10.12) | C.E.L.Ambrose | 1991-92 |

| **SOUTH AFRICA v INDIA** | South Africa | | India | | Captains | |
|---|---|---|---|---|---|---|
| Venue and Result | 1st | 2nd | 1st | 2nd | South Africa | West Indies |
| **1992-93 In SOUTH AFRICA** | | | | | | |
| Durban[2]-Drawn | •254 | 3-176 | 277 | - | K.C.Wessels | M.Azharuddin |
| Johannesburg[3]-Drawn | •292 | 252 | 227 | 4-141 | | |
| Port Elizabeth-South Africa 9 wkts | 275 | 1-155 | •212 | 215 | | |
| Cape Town-Drawn | •9d-360 | 6d-130 | 276 | 1-29 | | |
| **1996-97 In INDIA** | | | | | | |
| Ahmedabad-India 64 runs | 244 | 105 | •223 | 190 | W.J.Cronje | S.R.Tendulkar |
| Calcutta-South Africa 329 runs | •428 | 3d-367 | 329 | 137 | | |
| Kanpur-India 280 runs | 177 | 180 | •237 | 7d-400 | | |
| **1996-97 In SOUTH AFRICA** | | | | | | |
| Durban[2]-South Africa 328 runs | •235 | 259 | 100 | 66 | W.J.Cronje | S.R.Tendulkar |
| Cape Town-South Africa 282 runs | •7d-529 | 6d-256 | 359 | 144 | | |
| Johannesburg[3]-Drawn | 321 | 8-228 | •410 | 266 | | |

## Test Match Results Summary

**SOUTH AFRICA v INDIA-IN SOUTH AFRICA**

| | | Result | | | Durban[2] | | | Johannesburg[3] | | | P.Elizabeth | | | Cape Town | | |
|---|---|---|---|---|---|---|---|---|---|---|---|---|---|---|---|---|
| | Tests | SA | I | D | SA | I | D | SA | I | D | SA | I | D | SA | I | D |
| 1992-93 | 4 | 1 | - | 3 | - | - | 1 | - | - | 1 | 1 | - | - | - | - | 1 |
| 1996-97 | 3 | 2 | - | 1 | 1 | - | - | - | - | 1 | - | - | - | 1 | - | - |
| | 7 | 3 | - | 4 | 1 | - | 1 | - | - | 2 | 1 | - | - | 1 | - | 1 |

**SOUTH AFRICA v INDIA-IN INDIA**

| | | Result | | | Ahmedabad | | | Calcutta | | | Kanpur | | |
|---|---|---|---|---|---|---|---|---|---|---|---|---|---|
| | Tests | SA | I | D | SA | I | D | SA | I | D | SA | I | D |
| 1996-97 | 3 | 1 | 2 | - | - | 1 | - | 1 | - | - | - | 1 | - |
| | 3 | 1 | 2 | - | - | 1 | - | 1 | - | - | - | 1 | - |
| Totals | 10 | 4 | 2 | 4 | | | | | | | | | |

**HIGHEST INNINGS TOTALS**

| | | | |
|---|---|---|---|
| South Africa in South Africa | 7d-529 | Cape Town | 1996-97 |
| South Africa in India | 428 | Calcutta | 1996-97 |
| India in South Africa | 359 | Cape Town | 1996-97 |
| India in India | 7d-400 | Kanpur | 1996-97 |

**LOWEST INNINGS TOTALS**

| | | | |
|---|---|---|---|
| South Africa in South Africa | 235 | Durban[2] | 1996-97 |
| South Africa in India | 105 | Ahmedabad | 1996-97 |
| India in South Africa | 66 | Durban[2] | 1996-97 |
| India in India | 137 | Calcutta | 1996-97 |

| | | | |
|---|---|---|---|
| **HIGHEST MATCH AGGREGATE** | 1288 for 33 wickets | Cape Town | 1996-97 |
| **LOWEST MATCH AGGREGATE** | 670 for 40 wickets | Durban[2] | 1996-97 |

**HIGHEST INDIVIDUAL INNINGS**

| | | | | |
|---|---|---|---|---|
| South Africa in South Africa | 135 | W.J.Cronje | Port Elizabeth | 1992-93 |
| South Africa in India | 153* | D.J.Cullinan | Calcutta | 1996-97 |
| India in South Africa | 169 | S.R.Tendulkar | Port Elizabeth | 1996-97 |
| India in India | 163* | M.Azharuddin | Kanpur | 1996-97 |

**HIGHEST AGGREGATE OF RUNS IN A SERIES**

| | | | |
|---|---|---|---|
| South Africa in South Africa | 296 (av 98.66) | B.M.McMillan | 1996-97 |
| South Africa in India | 322 (av 53.66) | G.Kirsten | 1996-97 |
| India in South Africa | 277 (av 55.40) | R.S.Dravid | 1996-97 |
| India in India | 388 (av 77.60) | M.Azharuddin | 1996-97 |

**HIGHEST WICKET PARTNERSHIP-SOUTH AFRICA**

| | | | | |
|---|---|---|---|---|
| 1st | 236 | A.C.Hudson (146), G.Kirsten (102) | Calcutta | 1996-97 |
| 2nd | 212 | G.Kirsten (133), D.J.Cullinan (153*) | Calcutta | 1996-97 |
| 3rd | 114 | G.Kirsten (103), D.J.Cullinan (77) | Cape Town | 1996-97 |
| 4th | 94 | A.C.Hudson (55), D.J.Cullinan (55) | Cape Town | 1996-97 |
| 5th | 99 | D.J.Cullinan (46), J.N.Rhodes (86) | Cape Town | 1992-93 |
| 6th | 112 | B.M.McMillan (47), S.M.Pollock (79) | Johannesburg[3] | 1996-97 |
| 7th | 101* | B.M.McMillan (59*), S.M.Pollock (40*) | Cape Town | 1996-97 |
| 8th | 147* | B.M.McMillan (103*), L.Klusener (102*) | Cape Town | 1996-97 |
| 9th | 60 | P.S.de Villiers (67*), A.A.Donald (17) | Ahmedabad | 1996-97 |
| 10th | 74 | B.M.McMillan (51*), A.A.Donald (26) | Durban[2] | 1996-97 |

**HIGHEST WICKET PARTNERSHIP-INDIA**

| | | | | |
|---|---|---|---|---|
| 1st | 90 | V.Rathore (44), N.R.Mongia (50) | Johannesburg[3] | 1996-97 |
| 2nd | 85 | M.Prabhakar (62), S.V.Manjrekar (46) | Cape Town | 1992-93 |
| 3rd | 54 | R.S.Dravid (148), S.R.Tendulkar (35) | Johannesburg[3] | 1996-97 |
| 4th | 145 | R.S.Dravid (148), S.C.Ganguly (73) | Johannesburg[3] | 1996-97 |
| 5th | 87 | M.Azharuddin (36), P.K.Amre (103) | Durban[2] | 1992-93 |
| 6th | 222 | S.R.Tendulkar (169), M.Azharuddin (115) | Cape Town | 1996-97 |
| 7th | 128 | S.R.Tendulkar (111), Kapil Dev (25) | Johannesburg[3] | 1992-93 |
| 8th | 161 | M.Azharuddin (109), A.R.Kumble (88) | Calcutta | 1996-97 |
| 9th | 77 | Kapil Dev (129), A.R.Kumble (17) | Port Elizabeth | 1992-93 |
| 10th | 19 | S.R.Tendulkar (169), D.Ganesh (2*) | Cape Town | 1996-97 |

**BEST INNINGS BOWLING ANALYSIS**

| | | | | |
|---|---|---|---|---|
| South Africa in South Africa | 7-84 | A.A.Donald | Port Elizabeth | 1992-93 |
| South Africa in India | 8-64 | L.Klusener | Calcutta | 1996-97 |
| India in South Africa | 6-53 | A.R.Kumble | Johannesburg[3] | 1992-93 |
| India in India | 6-21 | J.Srinath | Ahmedabad | 1996-97 |

**BEST MATCH BOWLING ANALYSIS**

| | | | | |
|---|---|---|---|---|
| South Africa in South Africa | 12-139 | A.A.Donald | Port Elizabeth | 1992-93 |
| South Africa in India | 8-139 | L.Klusener | Calcutta | 1996-97 |
| | 8-139 | P.R.Adams | Kanpur | 1996-97 |
| India in South Africa | 8-113 | B.K.Venkatesh Prasad | Johannesburg[3] | 1996-97 |
| India in India | 8-68 | J.Srinath | Ahmedabad | 1996-97 |

**HIGHEST AGGREGATE OF WICKETS IN A SERIES**

| | | | |
|---|---|---|---|
| South Africa in South Africa | 20 (av 19.70) | A.A.Donald | 1992-93 |
| | 20 (av 15.95) | A.A.Donald | 1996-97 |
| South Africa in India | 14 (av 20.28) | P.R.Adams | 1996-97 |
| India in South Africa | 18 (av 25.94) | A.R.Kumble | 1992-93 |
| | 18 (av 28.72) | J.Srinath | 1996-97 |
| India in India | 17 (av 25.94) | J.Srinath | 1996-97 |

| SOUTH AFRICA v SRI LANKA | South Africa | | Sri Lanka | | Captains | |
|---|---|---|---|---|---|---|
| Venue and Result | 1st | 2nd | 1st | 2nd | South Africa | Sri Lanka |
| **1993-94 in SRI LANKA** | | | | | | |
| Moratuwa-Drawn | 267 | 7-251 | •331 | 6d-300 | K.C.Wessels | A.Ranatunga |
| Colombo(SSC)-Sth Africa inns & 208 runs | 495 | - | •168 | 119 | | |
| Colombo(PSS)-Drawn | •316 | 4-159 | 9d-296 | - | | |
| **1997-98 in SOUTH AFRICA** | | | | | | |
| Cape Town-Sth.Africa 70 runs | •418 | 264 | 306 | 306 | W.J.Cronje | A.Ranatunga |
| Centurion-Sth.Africa 6 wkts | 200 | 4-226 | •303 | 122 | | |

## Test Match Results Summary

**SOUTH AFRICA v SRI LANKA-IN SOUTH AFRICA**

| | | Result | | | Cape Town | | | Centurion | | |
|---|---|---|---|---|---|---|---|---|---|---|
| | Tests | SA | SL | D | SA | SL | D | SA | SL | D |
| 1997-98 | 2 | 2 | - | - | 1 | - | - | 1 | - | - |

**SOUTH AFRICA v SRI LANKA-IN SRI LANKA**

| | | Result | | | Moratuwa | | | Colombo(SSC) | | | Colombo(PSS) | | |
|---|---|---|---|---|---|---|---|---|---|---|---|---|---|
| | Tests | SA | SL | D | SA | SL | D | SA | SL | D | SA | SL | D |
| 1993-94 | 3 | 1 | - | 2 | - | - | 1 | 1 | - | - | - | - | 1 |
| Totals | 5 | 3 | - | 2 | | | | | | | | | |

**HIGHEST INNINGS TOTALS**

| | | | |
|---|---|---|---|
| South Africa in South Africa | 418 | Cape Town | 1997-98 |
| South Africa in Sri Lanka | 495 | Colombo (SSC) | 1993-94 |
| Sri Lanka in South Africa | 306 (twice) | Cape Town | 1997-98 |
| Sri Lanka in Sri Lanka | 331 | Moratuwa | 1993-94 |

**LOWEST INNINGS TOTALS**

| | | | |
|---|---|---|---|
| South Africa in South Africa | 200 | Centurion | 1997-98 |
| South Africa in Sri Lanka | 495 | Colombo (SSC) | 1993-94 |
| Sri Lanka in South Africa | 122 | Centurion | 1997-98 |
| Sri Lanka in Sri Lanka | 119 | Colombo (SSC) | 1993-94 |

| | | | |
|---|---|---|---|
| **HIGHEST MATCH AGGREGATE** | 1294 for 40 wickets | Cape Town | 1997-98 |
| **LOWEST MATCH AGGREGATE** | 771 for 23 wickets | Colombo (PSS) | 1993-94 |

**HIGHEST INDIVIDUAL INNINGS**

| | | | | |
|---|---|---|---|---|
| South Africa in South Africa | 113 | D.J.Cullinan | Cape Town | 1997-98 |
| South Africa in Sri Lanka | 122 | W.J.Cronje | Colombo (SSC) | 1993-94 |
| Sri Lanka in South Africa | 77 | P.A.de Silva | Cape Town | 1997-98 |
| Sri Lanka in Sri Lanka | 131 | A.Ranatunga | Moratuwa | 1993-94 |

**HIGHEST AGGREGATE OF RUNS IN A SERIES**

| | | | |
|---|---|---|---|
| South Africa in South Africa | 284 (av 71.00) | D.J.Cullinan | 1997-98 |
| South Africa in Sri Lanka | 237 (av 59.25) | W.J.Cronje | 1993-94 |
| | 237 (av 47.40) | D.J.Cullinan | 1993-94 |
| Sri Lanka in South Africa | 156 (av 39.00) | P.A.de Silva | 1997-98 |
| Sri Lanka in Sri Lanka | 250 (av 40.40) | A.Ranatunga | 1993-94 |

**HIGHEST WICKET PARTNERSHIP-SOUTH AFRICA**

| | | | | |
|---|---|---|---|---|
| 1st | 137 | K.C.Wessels (92), A.C.Hudson (58) | Colombo (SSC) | 1993-94 |
| 2nd | 48 | A.C.Hudson (90), W.J.Cronje (17) | Moratuwa | 1993-94 |
| 3rd | 116 | J.H.Kallis (49), D.J.Cullinan (69) | Cape Town | 1997-98 |
| 4th | 116 | G.Kirsten (75*), W.J.Cronje (82) | Centurion | 1997-98 |
| 5th | 35 | D.J.Cullinan (46), J.N.Rhodes (101*) | Moratuwa | 1993-94 |
| 6th | 122 | D.J.Cullinan (102), D.J.Richardson (63) | Colombo (PSS) | 1993-94 |
| 7th | 95 | S.M.Pollock (92), M.V.Boucher (33) | Cape Town | 1997-98 |
| 8th | 79 | P.L.Symcox (50), R.P.Snell (48) | Colombo (SSC) | 1993-94 |
| 9th | 7 | S.M.Pollock (92), P.R.Adams (2) | Cape Town | 1997-98 |
| 10th | 8 | P.R.Adams (12), M.Ntimi (2*) | Centurion | 1997-98 |

**HIGHEST WICKET PARTNERSHIP-SRI LANKA**

| | | | | |
|---|---|---|---|---|
| 1st | 53 | S.T.Jayasuriya (51), M.S.Atapattu (12) | Centurion | 1997-98 |
| 2nd | 72 | R.S.Mahanama (53), A.P.Gurusinha (26) | Moratuwa | 1993-94 |
| 3rd | 129 | M.S.Atapattu (60), P.A.de Silva (77) | Cape Town | 1997-98 |
| 4th | 118 | R.S.Mahanama (50), A.Ranatunga (73) | Centurion | 1997-98 |
| 5th | 121 | P.A.de Silva (68), A.Ranatunga (131) | Moratuwa | 1993-94 |
| 6th | 103 | A.Ranatunga (131), H.P.Tillakaratne (33*) | Moratuwa | 1993-94 |
| 7th | 43 | P.A.de Silva (41), G.P.Wickramasinghe (21) | Centurion | 1997-98 |
| 8th | 29 | W.P.U.J.C.Vaas (30), G.P.Wickramasinghe (11) | Cape Town | 1997-98 |
| 9th | 48 | G.P.Wickramasinghe (51), M.Muralidaran (10) | Cape Town | 1997-98 |
| 10th | 19 | G.P.Wickramasinghe (51), K.R.Pushpakumara (9*) | Cape Town | 1997-98 |

**BEST INNINGS BOWLING ANALYSIS**

| | | | | |
|---|---|---|---|---|
| South Africa in South Africa | 5-54 | A.A.Donald | Centurion | 1997-98 |
| South Africa in Sri Lanka | 5-48 | B.N.Schultz | Colombo (SSC) | 1993-94 |
| Sri Lanka in South Africa | 5-62 | M.Muralidaran | Centurion | 1997-98 |
| Sri Lanka in Sri Lanka | 5-101 | M.Muralidaran | Colombo (SSC) | 1993-94 |

**BEST MATCH BOWLING ANALYSIS**

| | | | | |
|---|---|---|---|---|
| South Africa in South Africa | 8-127 | A.A.Donald | Centurion | 1997-98 |
| South Africa in Sri Lanka | 9-106 | B.N.Schultz | Colombo (SSC) | 1993-94 |
| Sri Lanka in South Africa | 8-167 | M.Muralidaran | Centurion | 1997-98 |
| Sri Lanka in Sri Lanka | 6-152 | M.Muralidaran | Moratuwa | 1993-94 |

**HIGHEST AGGREGATE OF WICKETS IN A SERIES**

| | | | |
|---|---|---|---|
| South Africa in South Africa | 14 (av 18.35) | A.A.Donald | 1997-98 |
| South Africa in Sri Lanka | 20 (av 16.30) | B.N.Schultz | 1993-94 |
| Sri Lanka in South Africa | 16 (av 22.25) | M.Muralidaran | 1997-98 |
| Sri Lanka in Sri Lanka | 16 (av 25.00) | M.Muralidaran | 1993-94 |

| SOUTH AFRICA v PAKISTAN | South Africa | | Pakistan | | Captains | |
|---|---|---|---|---|---|---|
| Venue and Result | 1st | 2nd | 1st | 2nd | South Africa | Pakistan |
| **1994-95 In SOUTH AFRICA** | | | | | | |
| Johannesburg[3]-South Africa 324 runs | •460 | 7d-259 | 230 | 165 | W.J.Cronje | Saleem Malik |
| **1997-98 In PAKISTAN** | | | | | | |
| Rawalpindi[1]-Drawn | 403 | - | •456 | 6d-182 | W.J.Cronje | Saeed Anwar |
| Sheikhupura-Drawn | •402 | - | 1-53 | - | | |
| Faisalabad-South Africa 53 runs | •239 | 214 | 308 | 92 | | |
| **1997-98 In SOUTH AFRICA** | | | | | | |
| Johannesburg[3]-Drawn | •364 | 0-44 | 329 | - | W.J.Cronje | Aamer Sohail |
| Durban[2]-Pakistan 29 runs | 231 | 225 | •259 | 226 | | Aamer Sohail |
| Port Elizabeth-South Africa 259 runs | •293 | 7d-206 | 106 | 134 | | Rashid Latif |

## Test Match Results Summary

**SOUTH AFRICA v PAKISTAN-IN SOUTH AFRICA**

| | | Result | | | Johannesburg[3] | | | Durban[2] | | | Port Elizabeth | | |
|---|---|---|---|---|---|---|---|---|---|---|---|---|---|
| | Tests | SA | P | D | SA | P | D | SA | P | D | SA | P | D |
| 1994-95 | 1 | 1 | - | - | 1 | - | - | - | - | - | - | - | - |
| 1997-98 | 3 | 1 | 1 | 1 | - | - | 1 | - | 1 | - | 1 | - | - |
| | 4 | 2 | 1 | 1 | 1 | - | 1 | - | 1 | - | 1 | - | - |

**SOUTH AFRICA v PAKISTAN-IN PAKISTAN**

| | | Result | | | Rawalpindi[1] | | | Sheikhupura | | | Faisalabad | | |
|---|---|---|---|---|---|---|---|---|---|---|---|---|---|
| | Tests | SA | P | D | SA | P | D | SA | P | D | SA | P | D |
| 1997-98 | 3 | 1 | - | 2 | - | - | 1 | - | - | 1 | 1 | - | - |
| Totals | 7 | 3 | 1 | 3 | | | | | | | | | |

**HIGHEST INNINGS TOTALS**

| | | | |
|---|---|---|---|
| South Africa in South Africa | 460 | Johannesburg[3] | 1994-95 |
| South Africa in Pakistan | 403 | Rawalpindi[1] | 1997-98 |
| Pakistan in South Africa | 329 | Johannesburg[3] | 1997-98 |
| Pakistan in Pakistan | 456 | Rawalpindi[1] | 1997-98 |

**LOWEST INNINGS TOTALS**

| | | | |
|---|---|---|---|
| South Africa in South Africa | 225 | Durban[2] | 1997-98 |
| South Africa in Pakistan | 214 | Faisalabad | 1997-98 |
| Pakistan in South Africa | 106 | Port Elizabeth | 1997-98 |
| Pakistan in Pakistan | 92 | Faisalabad | 1997-98 |

| | | | |
|---|---|---|---|
| **HIGHEST MATCH AGGREGATE** | 1114 for 37 wickets | Johannesburg[3] | 1994-95 |
| **LOWEST MATCH AGGREGATE** | 455 for 11 wickets | Sheikhupara | 1997-98 |

**HIGHEST INDIVIDUAL INNINGS**

| | | | | |
|---|---|---|---|---|
| South Africa in South Africa | 113 | B.M.McMillan | Johannesburg[3] | 1994-95 |
| South Africa in Pakistan | 100* | G.Kirsten | Faisalabad | 1997-98 |
| Pakistan in South Africa | 99 | Saleem Malik | Johannesburg[3] | 1994-95 |
| Pakistan in Pakistan | 128* | Azhar Mahmood | Rawalpindi[1] | 1997-98 |

**HIGHEST AGGREGATE OF RUNS IN A SERIES**

| | | | |
|---|---|---|---|
| South Africa in South Africa | 188 (av 73.00) | M.V.Boucher | 1997-98 |
| South Africa in Pakistan | 258 (av 86.00) | G.Kirsten | 1997-98 |
| Pakistan in South Africa | 327 (av 65.40) | Azhar Mahmood | 1997-98 |
| Pakistan in Pakistan | 203 (av 101.50) | Azhar Mahmood | 1997-98 |

**HIGHEST WICKET PARTNERSHIP-SOUTH AFRICA**

| | | | | |
|---|---|---|---|---|
| 1st | 135 | G.Kirsten (56), A.M.Bacher (96) | Sheikhupura | 1997-98 |
| 2nd | 114 | G.Kirsten (98), J.H.Kallis (61) | Rawalpindi[1] | 1997-98 |
| 3rd | 83 | J.H.Kallis (22), H.D.Ackerman (57) | Durban[2] | 1997-98 |
| 4th | 79 | G.Kirsten (62), W.J.Cronje (41) | Johannesburg[3] | 1994-95 |
| 5th | 43 | P.L.Symcox (55), W.J.Cronje (21) | Faisalabad | 1997-98 |
| 6th | 157 | J.N.Rhodes (72), B.M.McMillan (113) | Johannesburg[3] | 1994-95 |
| 7th | 106 | S.M.Pollock (48), D.J.Richardson (45*) | Rawalpindi[1] | 1997-98 |
| 8th | 124 | G.Kirsten (100*), P.L.Symcox (81) | Faisalabad | 1997-98 |
| 9th | 195 | M.V.Boucher (78), P.L.Symcox (108) | Johannesburg[3] | 1997-98 |
| 10th | 71 | P.S.de Villiers (66*), A.A.Donald (15) | Durban[2] | 1994-95 |

**HIGHEST WICKET PARTNERSHIP-PAKISTAN**

| | | | | |
|---|---|---|---|---|
| 1st | 101 | Saeed Anwar (118), Aamer Sohail (36) | Durban[2] | 1997-98 |
| 2nd | 69 | Ali Naqvi (115), Mohammad Razdan (29) | Rawalpindi[1] | 1997-98 |
| 3rd | 72 | Ijaz Ahmed (34), Mohammad Wasim (44) | Johannesburg[3] | 1997-98 |
| 4th | 93 | Asif Mujtaba (26), Inzamamul Haq (95) | Johannesburg[3] | 1994-95 |
| 5th | 44 | Ali Naqvi (115), Mohammad Wasim (11) | Rawalpindi[1] | 1997-98 |
| 6th | 144 | Inzamamul Haq (96), Moin Khan (80) | Johannesburg[3] | 1997-98 |
| 7th | 35 | Saleem Malik (99), Wasim Akram (41) | Johannesburg[3] | 1994-95 |
| 8th | 40 | Inzamamul Haq (95), Kabir Khan (10) | Johannesburg[3] | 1994-95 |
| 9th | 80 | Azhar Mahmood (132), Shoaib Akhtar (6) | Johannesburg[3] | 1997-98 |
| 10th | 151 | Azhar Mahmood (128*), Mushtaq Ahmed (59) | Rawalpindi[1] | 1997-98 |

**BEST INNINGS BOWLING ANALYSIS**

| | | | | |
|---|---|---|---|---|
| South Africa in South Africa | 6-23 | P.S.de Villiers | Johannesburg[3] | 1997-98 |
| South Africa in Pakistan | 5-37 | S.M.Pollock | Faisalabad | 1997-98 |
| Pakistan in South Africa | 6-78 | Mushtaq Ahmed | Durban[2] | 1997-98 |
| | 6-78 | Waqar Younis | Port Elizabeth | 1997-98 |
| Pakistan in Pakistan | 5-129 | Saqlain Mushtaq | Rawalpindi[1] | 1997-98 |

**BEST MATCH BOWLING ANALYSIS**

| | | | | |
|---|---|---|---|---|
| South Africa in South Africa | 10-108 | P.S.de Villiers | Johannesburg[3] | 1994-95 |
| South Africa in Pakistan | 7-101 | S.M.Pollock | Faisalabad | 1997-98 |
| Pakistan in South Africa | 10-133 | Waqar Younis | Port Elizabeth | 1997-98 |
| Pakistan in Pakistan | 7-138 | Mushtaq Ahmed | Faisalabad | 1997-98 |

**HIGHEST AGGREGATE OF WICKETS IN A SERIES**

| | | | |
|---|---|---|---|
| South Africa in South Africa | 16 (av 16.37) | A.A.Donald | 1997-98 |
| South Africa in Pakistan | 10 (av 23.20) | S.M.Pollock | 1997-98 |
| Pakistan in South Africa | 16 (av 22.12) | Waqar Younis | 1997-98 |
| Pakistan in Pakistan | 14 (av 27.57) | Mushtaq Ahmed | 1997-98 |

| **SOUTH AFRICA v ZIMBABWE** | South Africa | | Zimbabwe | | Captains | |
|---|---|---|---|---|---|---|
| Venue and Result | 1st | 2nd | 1st | 2nd | South Africa | Zimbabwe |
| **1995-96 in ZIMBABWE** | | | | | | |
| Harare-South Africa 7 wkts | 346 | 3-108 | •170 | 283 | W.J.Cronje | A.Flower |

## Test Match Results Summary

**SOUTH AFRICA v ZIMBABWE-IN ZIMBABWE**

| | | Result | | | Harare | | |
|---|---|---|---|---|---|---|---|
| | Tests | SA | Z | D | SA | Z | D |
| 1995-96 | 1 | 1 | - | - | 1 | - | - |

**HIGHEST INNINGS TOTALS**

| | | | |
|---|---|---|---|
| South Africa in Zimbabwe | 346 | Harare | 1995-96 |
| Zimbabwe in Zimbabwe | 283 | Harare | 1995-96 |

**LOWEST INNINGS TOTALS**

| | | | |
|---|---|---|---|
| South Africa in Zimbabwe | 346 | Harare | 1995-96 |
| Zimbabwe in Zimbabwe | 170 | Harare | 1995-96 |

**HIGHEST MATCH AGGREGATE** 907 for 33 wickets Harare 1995-96

**HIGHEST INDIVIDUAL INNINGS**

| | | | | |
|---|---|---|---|---|
| South Africa in Zimbabwe | 135 | A.C.Hudson | Harare | 1995-96 |
| Zimbabwe in Zimbabwe | 63 | A.Flower | Harare | 1995-96 |

**HIGHEST AGGREGATE ON RUNS IN A SERIES**

| | | | |
|---|---|---|---|
| South Africa in Zimbabwe | 139 (av 69.50) | A.C.Hudson | 1995-96 |
| Zimbabwe in Zimbabwe | 70 (av 35.00) | A.Flower | 1995-96 |

**RECORD WICKET PARTNERSHIPS-SOUTH AFRICA**

| | | | | |
|---|---|---|---|---|
| 1st | 6 | G.Kirsten (13), A.C.Hudson (4) | Harare | 1995-96 |
| 2nd | 30 | G.Kirsten (13), W.J.Cronje (56*) | Harare | 1995-96 |
| 3rd | 35 | A.C.Hudson (135), D.J.Cullinan (11) | Harare | 1995-96 |
| 4th | 60* | W.J.Cronje (56*), B.M.McMillan (25*) | Harare | 1995-96 |
| 5th | 60 | A.C.Hudson (135), J.N.Rhodes (15) | Harare | 1995-96 |
| 6th | 101 | A.C.Hudson (135), B.M.McMillan (98*) | Harare | 1995-96 |
| 7th | 15 | B.M.McMillan (98*), D.J.Richardson (13) | Harare | 1995-96 |
| 8th | 4 | B.M.McMillan (98*), P.L.Symcox (4) | Harare | 1995-96 |
| 9th | 79 | B.M.McMillan (98*), A.A.Donald (33) | Harare | 1995-96 |
| 10th | 2 | B.M.McMillan (98*), B.N.Schultz (0) | Harare | 1995-96 |

**RECORD WICKET PARTNERSHIPS-ZIMBABWE**

| | | | | |
|---|---|---|---|---|
| 1st | 13 | M.H.Dekker (24), G.W.Flower (5) | Harare | 1995-96 |
| 2nd | 51 | M.H.Dekker (24), A.D.R.Campbell (28) | Harare | 1995-96 |
| 3rd | 10 | G.W.Flower (24), D.L.Houghton (5) | Harare | 1995-96 |
| 4th | 31 | D.L.Houghton (21), A.Flower (63) | Harare | 1995-96 |
| 5th | 97 | A.Flower (63), G.J.Whittall (38) | Harare | 1995-96 |
| 6th | 13 | G.J.Whittall (29), C.B.Wishart (24) | Harare | 1995-96 |
| 7th | 25 | C.B.Wishart (13), P.A.Strang (37) | Harare | 1995-96 |
| 8th | 43 | C.B.Wishart (24), H.H.Streak (53) | Harare | 1995-96 |
| 9th | 48 | P.A.Strang (37), B.C.Strang (25*) | Harare | 1995-96 |
| 10th | 42 | H.H.Streak (53), A.C.I.Lock (8*) | Harare | 1995-96 |

**BEST INNINGS BOWLING ANALYSIS**

| | | | | |
|---|---|---|---|---|
| South Africa in Zimbabwe | 8-71 | A.A.Donald | Harare | 1995-96 |
| Zimbabwe in Zimbabwe | 5-101 | B.C.Strang | Harare | 1995-96 |

**BEST MATCH BOWLING ANALYSIS**

| | | | | |
|---|---|---|---|---|
| South Africa in Zimbabwe | 11-113 | A.A.Donald | Harare | 1995-96 |
| Zimbabwe in Zimbabwe | 5-105 | A.C.I.Lock | Harare | 1995-96 |

**HIGHEST AGGREGATE OF WICKETS IN A SERIES**

| | | | |
|---|---|---|---|
| South Africa in Zimbabwe | 11 (av 10.27) | A.A.Donald | 1995-96 |
| Zimbabwe in Zimbabwe | 5 (av 21.00) | A.C.I.Lock | 1995-96 |
| | 5 (av 23.80) | B.C.Strang | 1995-96 |

| **WEST INDIES v NEW ZEALAND** | West Indies | | New Zealand | | Captains | |
|---|---|---|---|---|---|---|
| Venue and Result | 1st | 2nd | 1st | 2nd | West Indies | New Zealand |
| **1951-52 in NEW ZEALAND** | | | | | | |
| Christchurch-West Indies 5 wkts | 287 | 5-142 | •236 | 189 | J.D.C.Goddard | B.Sutcliffe |
| Auckland-Drawn | •6d-546 | - | 160 | 1-17 | | |
| **1955-56 in NEW ZEALAND** | | | | | | |
| Dunedin-West Indies inns & 71 runs | 353 | - | •74 | 208 | D.S.Atkinson | H.B.Cave |
| Christchurch-West Indies inns & 64 runs | •386 | - | 158 | 164 | | J.R.Reid |
| Wellington-West Indies 9 wkts | •404 | 1-13 | 208 | 208 | | J.R.Reid |
| Auckland-New Zealand 190 runs | 145 | 77 | •255 | 9d-157 | | J.R.Reid |
| **1968-69 in NEW ZEALAND** | | | | | | |
| Auckland-West Indies 5 wkts | 276 | 5-348 | •323 | 8d-297 | G.S.Sobers | G.T.Dowling |
| Wellington-New Zealand 6 wkts | •297 | 148 | 282 | 4-166 | | |
| Christchurch-Drawn | •417 | - | 217 | 6-367 | | |
| **1971-72 in WEST INDIES** | | | | | | |
| Kingston-Drawn | •4d-508 | 3d-218 | 386 | 6-236 | G.S.Sobers | G.T.Dowling |
| Port-of-Spain-Drawn | 341 | 5-121 | •348 | 3d-288 | | G.T.Dowling |
| Bridgetown-Drawn | •133 | 8-564 | 422 | - | | B.E.Congdon |
| Georgetown-Drawn | •7d-365 | 0-86 | 3d-543 | - | | B.E.Congdon |
| Port-of-Spain-Drawn | •368 | 194 | 162 | 7-253 | | B.E.Congdon |
| **1979-80 in NEW ZEALAND** | | | | | | |
| Dunedin-New Zealand 1 wkt | •140 | 212 | 249 | 9-104 | C.H.Lloyd | G.P.Howarth |
| Christchurch-Drawn | •228 | 5d-447 | 460 | - | | |
| Auckland-Drawn | •220 | 9d-264 | 305 | 4-73 | | |
| **1984-85 in WEST INDIES** | | | | | | |
| Port-of-Spain-Drawn | •307 | 8d-261 | 262 | 6-187 | I.V.A.Richards | G.P.Howarth |
| Georgetown-Drawn | •6d-511 | 6d-268 | 440 | - | | |
| Bridgetown-West Indies 10 wkts | 336 | 0-10 | •94 | 248 | | |
| Kingston-West Indies 10 wkts | •363 | 0-59 | 138 | 283 | | |
| **1986-87 in NEW ZEALAND** | | | | | | |
| Wellington-Drawn | 345 | 2-50 | •228 | 5d-386 | I.V.A.Richards | J.V.Coney |
| Auckland-West Indies 10 wkts | •9d-419 | 0-16 | 157 | 273 | | |
| Christchurch-New Zealand 5 wkts | •100 | 264 | 9d-332 | 5-33 | | |
| **1994-95 in NEW ZEALAND** | | | | | | |
| Christchurch-Drawn | 312 | - | •8d-341 | 2-61 | C.A.Walsh | K.R.Rutherford |
| Wellington-West Indies inns & 322 runs | •5d-660 | - | 216 | 122 | | |
| **1995-96 in WEST INDIES** | | | | | | |
| Bridgetown-West Indies 10 wkts | 472 | 0-29 | •195 | 305 | C.A.Walsh | L.K.Germon |
| St John's-Drawn | •7d-548 | 184 | 437 | 5-130 | | |

## Test Match Results Summary

**WEST INDIES v NEW ZEALAND-IN WEST INDIES**

| | | Result | | | Kingston | | | Port-of-Spain | | | Bridgetown | | | Georgetown | | | St John's | | |
|---|---|---|---|---|---|---|---|---|---|---|---|---|---|---|---|---|---|---|---|
| | Tests | WI | NZ | D | WI | NZ | D | WI | NZ | D | WI | NZ | D | WI | NZ | D | WI | NZ | D |
| 1971-72 | 5 | - | - | 5 | - | - | 1 | - | - | 2 | - | - | 1 | - | - | 1 | - | - | - |
| 1984-85 | 4 | 2 | - | 2 | 1 | - | - | - | - | 1 | 1 | - | - | - | - | 1 | - | - | - |
| 1995-96 | 2 | 1 | - | 1 | - | - | - | - | - | - | 1 | - | - | - | - | - | - | - | 1 |
| | 11 | 3 | - | 8 | 1 | - | 1 | - | - | 3 | 2 | - | 1 | - | - | 2 | - | - | 1 |

**WEST INDIES v NEW ZEALAND-IN NEW ZEALAND**

| | | Result | | | Christchurch | | | Auckland | | | Dunedin | | | Wellington | | |
|---|---|---|---|---|---|---|---|---|---|---|---|---|---|---|---|---|
| | Tests | WI | NZ | D | WI | NZ | D | WI | NZ | D | WI | NZ | D | WI | NZ | D |
| 1951-52 | 2 | 1 | - | 1 | 1 | - | - | - | - | 1 | - | - | - | - | - | - |
| 1955-56 | 4 | 3 | 1 | - | 1 | - | - | - | 1 | - | 1 | - | - | 1 | - | - |
| 1968-69 | 3 | 1 | 1 | 1 | - | - | 1 | 1 | - | - | - | - | - | - | 1 | - |
| 1979-80 | 3 | - | 1 | 2 | - | - | 1 | - | - | 1 | - | 1 | - | - | - | - |
| 1986-87 | 3 | 1 | 1 | 1 | - | 1 | - | 1 | - | - | - | - | - | - | - | 1 |
| 1994-95 | 2 | 1 | - | 1 | - | - | 1 | - | - | - | - | - | - | 1 | - | - |
| | 17 | 7 | 4 | 6 | 2 | 1 | 3 | 2 | 1 | 2 | 1 | 1 | - | 2 | 1 | 1 |
| Totals | 28 | 10 | 4 | 14 | | | | | | | | | | | | |

**HIGHEST INNINGS TOTALS**

| | | | |
|---|---|---|---|
| West Indies in West Indies | 8-564 | Bridgetown | 1971-72 |
| West Indies in New Zealand | 5d-660 | Wellington | 1994-95 |
| New Zealand in West Indies | 3d-543 | Georgetown | 1971-72 |
| New Zealand in New Zealand | 460 | Christchurch | 1979-80 |

**LOWEST INNINGS TOTALS**

| | | | |
|---|---|---|---|
| West Indies in West Indies | 133 | Bridgetown | 1971-72 |
| West Indies in New Zealand | 77 | Auckland | 1955-56 |
| New Zealand in West Indies | 94 | Bridgetown | 1984-85 |
| New Zealand in New Zealand | 74 | Dunedin | 1955-56 |

| | | | |
|---|---|---|---|
| **HIGHEST MATCH AGGREGATE** | 1348 for 23 wickets | Kingston | 1971-72 |
| **LOWEST MATCH AGGREGATE** | 634 for 39 wickets | Auckland | 1955-56 |

**HIGHEST INDIVIDUAL INNINGS**

| | | | | |
|---|---|---|---|---|
| West Indies in West Indies | 214 | L.G.Rowe | Kingston | 1971-72 |
| West Indies in New Zealand | 258 | S.M.Nurse | Christchurch | 1968-69 |
| New Zealand in West Indies | 259 | G.M.Turner | Georgetown | 1971-72 |
| New Zealand in New Zealand | 147 | G.P.Howarth | Christchurch | 1979-80 |

**HIGHEST AGGREGATE OF RUNS IN A SERIES**

| | | | |
|---|---|---|---|
| West Indies in West Indies | 487 (av 54.11) | R.C.Fredericks | 1971-72 |
| New Zealand in New Zealand | 558 (av 111.60) | S.M.Nurse | 1968-69 |
| New Zealand in West Indies | 672 (av 98.00) | G.M.Turner | 1971-72 |
| New Zealand in New Zealand | 328 (av 65.60) | M.D.Crowe | 1986-87 |

**RECORD WICKET PARTNERSHIPS-WEST INDIES**

| | | | | |
|---|---|---|---|---|
| 1st | 225 | C.G.Greenidge (97), D.L.Haynes (122) | Christchurch | 1979-80 |
| 2nd | 269 | R.C.Fredericks (163), L.G.Rowe (214) | Kingston | 1971-72 |
| 3rd | 221 | B.C.Lara (147), J.C.Adams (151) | Wellington | 1994-95 |
| 4th | 162 | E.D.Weekes (123), O.G.Smith (64) | Dunedin | 1955-56 |
| | 162 | C.G.Greenidge (91), A.I.Kallicharran (75) | Christchurch | 1979-80 |
| 5th | 189 | F.M.M.Worrell (100), C.L.Walcott (115) | Auckland | 1951-52 |
| 6th | 254 | C.A.Davis (183), G.S.Sobers (142) | Bridgetown | 1971-72 |
| 7th | 143 | D.S Atkinson (85), J.D.C.Goddard (83*) | Christchurch | 1955-56 |
| 8th | 83 | I.V.A.Richards (105), M.D.Marshall (63) | Bridgetown | 1984-85 |
| 9th | 70 | M.D.Marshall (63), J.Garner (37*) | Bridgetown | 1984-85 |
| 10th | 31 | T.M.Findlay (44*), G.C.Shillingford (15) | Bridgetown | 1971-72 |

### RECORD WICKET PARTNERSHIPS-NEW ZEALAND

| | | | | |
|---|---|---|---|---|
| 1st | 387 | G.M.Turner (259), T.W.Jarvis (182) | Georgetown | 1971-72 |
| 2nd | 210 | G.P.Howarth (84), J.J.Crowe (112) | Kingston | 1984-85 |
| 3rd | 241 | J.G.Wright (138), M.D.Crowe (119) | Wellington | 1986-87 |
| 4th | 175 | B.E.Congdon (126), B.F.Hastings (105) | Bridgetown | 1971-72 |
| 5th | 144 | N.J.Astle (125), J.T.C.Vaughan (24) | Bridgetown | 1995-96 |
| 6th | 220 | G.M.Turner (223*), K.J.Wadsworth (78) | Kingston | 1971-72 |
| 7th | 143 | M.D.Crowe (188), I.D.S.Smith (53) | Georgetown | 1984-85 |
| 8th | 136 | B.E.Congdon (166*), R.S.Cunis (51) | Port-of-Spain | 1971-72 |
| 9th | 62* | V.Pollard (51*), R.S.Cunis (20*) | Auckland | 1968-69 |
| 10th | 45 | D.K.Morrison (26*), R.J.Kennedy (22) | Bridgetown | 1995-96 |

### BEST INNINGS BOWLING ANALYSIS

| | | | | |
|---|---|---|---|---|
| West Indies in West Indies | 7-80 | M.D.Marshall | Bridgetown | 1984-85 |
| West Indies in New Zealand | 7-37 | C.A.Walsh | Wellington | 1994-95 |
| New Zealand in West Indies | 7-74 | B.R.Taylor | Bridgetown | 1971-72 |
| New Zealand in New Zealand | 6-50 | R.J.Hadlee | Christchurch | 1986-87 |

### BEST MATCH BOWLING ANALYSIS

| | | | | |
|---|---|---|---|---|
| West Indies in West Indies | 11-120 | M.D.Marshall | Bridgetown | 1984-85 |
| West Indies in New Zealand | 13-55 | C.A.Walsh | Wellington | 1994-95 |
| New Zealand in West Indies | 10-124 | E.J.Chatfield | Port-of-Spain | 1984-85 |
| New Zealand in New Zealand | 11-102 | R.J Hadlee | Dunedin | 1979-80 |

### HIGHEST AGGREGATE OF WICKETS IN A SERIES

| | | | |
|---|---|---|---|
| West Indies in West Indies | 27 (av 18.00) | M.D.Marshall | 1984-85 |
| West Indies In New Zealand | 20 (av 15.80) | S.Ramadhin | 1955-56 |
| New Zealand in West Indies | 27 (av 17.70) | B.R.Taylor | 1971-72 |
| New Zealand In New Zealand | 19 (av 19.00) | R.J Hadlee | 1979-80 |

| WEST INDIES v INDIA | West Indies | | India | | Captains | |
|---|---|---|---|---|---|---|
| Venue and Result | 1st | 2nd | 1st | 2nd | West Indies | India |
| **1948-49 in INDIA** | | | | | | |
| Delhi-Drawn | •631 | - | 454 | 6-220 | J.D.C.Goddard | N.B.Amarnath |
| Bombay[2]-Drawn | •6d-629 | - | 273 | 3-333 | | |
| Calcutta-Drawn | •366 | 9d-336 | 272 | 3-325 | | |
| Madras[1]-West Indies inns & 193 runs | •582 | - | 245 | 144 | | |
| Bombay[2]-Drawn | •286 | 267 | 193 | 8-355 | | |
| **1952-53 in WEST INDIES** | | | | | | |
| Port-of-Spain-Drawn | 438 | 0-142 | •417 | 294 | J.B.Stollmeyer | V.S.Hazare |
| Bridgetown-West Indies 142 runs | •296 | 228 | 253 | 129 | | |
| Port-of-Spain-Drawn | 315 | 2-192 | •279 | 7d-362 | | |
| Georgetown-Drawn | 364 | - | •262 | 5-190 | | |
| Kingston-Drawn | 576 | 4-92 | •312 | 444 | | |
| **1958-59 in INDIA** | | | | | | |
| Bombay[2]-Drawn | •227 | 4d-323 | 152 | 5-289 | F.C.M.Alexander | P.R.Umrigar |
| Kanpur-West Indies 203 runs | •222 | 7d-443 | 222 | 240 | | Ghulam Ahmed |
| Calcutta-West Indies inns & 336 runs | •5d-614 | - | 124 | 154 | | Ghulam Ahmed |
| Madras[2]-West Indies 295 runs | •500 | 5d-168 | 222 | 151 | | M.H.Mankad |
| Delhi-Drawn | 8d-644 | - | •415 | 275 | | H.R.Adhikari |
| **1961-62 in WEST INDIES** | | | | | | |
| Port-of-Spain-West Indies 10 wkts | 289 | 0-15 | •203 | 98 | F.M.M.Worrell | N.J.Contractor |
| Kingston-West Indies inns & 18 runs | 8d-631 | - | •395 | 218 | | N.J.Contractor |
| Bridgetown-West Indies inns & 30 runs | 475 | - | •258 | 187 | - | Nawab of Pataudi, jr |
| Port-of-Spain-West Indies 7 wkts | •9d-444 | 3-176 | 197 | 422 | | Nawab of Pataudi, jr |
| Kingston-West Indies 123 runs | •253 | 283 | 178 | 235 | | Nawab of Pataudi, jr |
| **1966-67 in INDIA** | | | | | | |
| Bombay[2]-West Indies 6 wkts | 421 | 4-192 | •296 | 316 | G.S.Sobers | Nawab of Pataudi, jr |
| Calcutta-West Indies inns & 45 runs | •390 | - | 167 | 178 | | |
| Madras[1]-Drawn | 406 | 7-270 | •404 | 323 | | |
| **1970-71 in WEST INDIES** | | | | | | |
| Kingston-Drawn | 217 | 5-385 | •387 | - | G.S.Sobers | A.L.Wadekar |
| Port-of-Spain-India 7 wkts | •214 | 261 | 352 | 3-125 | | |
| Georgetown-Drawn | •363 | 3d-307 | 376 | 0-123 | | |
| Bridgetown-Drawn | •5d-501 | 6d-180 | 347 | 5-221 | | |
| Port-of-Spain-Drawn | 526 | 8-165 | •360 | 427 | | |
| **1974-75 in INDIA** | | | | | | |
| Bangalore-West Indies 267 runs | •289 | 6d-356 | 260 | 118 | C.H.Lloyd | Nawab of Pataudi, jr |
| Delhi-West Indies inns & 17 runs | 493 | - | •220 | 256 | | S.Venkataraghavan |
| Calcutta-India 85 runs | 240 | 224 | •233 | 316 | | Nawab of Pataudi, jr |
| Madras[1]-India 100 runs | 192 | 154 | •190 | 256 | | Nawab of Pataudi, jr |
| Bombay[3]-West Indies 201 runs | •6d-604 | 3d-205 | 406 | 202 | | Nawab of Pataudi, jr |
| **1975-76 in WEST INDIES** | | | | | | |
| Bridgetown-West Indies inns & 97 runs | 9d-488 | - | •177 | 214 | C.H.Lloyd | B.S.Bedi |
| Port-of-Spain-Drawn | •241 | 8-215 | 5d-402 | - | | |
| Port-of-Spain-India 6 wkts | •359 | 6d-271 | 228 | 4-406 | | |
| Kingston-West Indies 10 wkts | 391 | 0-13 | •6d-306 | 97 | | |

| **WEST INDIES v INDIA** (cont.) | West Indies | | India | | Captains | |
|---|---|---|---|---|---|---|
| Venue and Result | 1st | 2nd | 1st | 2nd | West Indies | India |
| **1978-79 in INDIA** | | | | | | |
| Bombay[3]-Drawn | 493 | - | •424 | 2-224 | A.I.Kallicharran | S.M.Gavaskar |
| Bangalore-Drawn | •437 | 8-200 | 371 | - | | |
| Calcutta-Drawn | 327 | 9-197 | •300 | 1d-361 | | |
| Madras[1]-India 3 wkts | •228 | 151 | 255 | 7-125 | | |
| Delhi-Drawn | 172 | 3-179 | •8d-566 | - | | |
| Kanpur-Drawn | 8-452 | - | •7d-644 | - | | |
| **1982-83 in WEST INDIES** | | | | | | |
| Kingston-West Indies 4 wkts | 254 | 6-173 | •251 | 174 | C.H.Lloyd | Kapil Dev |
| Port-of-Spain-Drawn | 394 | - | •175 | 7-469 | | |
| Georgetown-Drawn | •470 | - | 3-284 | - | | |
| Bridgetown-West Indies 10 wkts | 486 | 0-1 | •209 | 277 | | |
| St John's-Drawn | 550 | - | •457 | 5d-247 | | |
| **1983-84 in INDIA** | | | | | | |
| Kanpur-West Indies inns & 83 runs | •454 | - | 207 | 164 | C.H.Lloyd | Kapil Dev |
| Delhi-Drawn | 384 | 2-120 | •464 | 233 | | |
| Ahmedabad-West Indies 138 runs | •281 | 201 | 241 | 103 | | |
| Bombay[3]-Drawn | 393 | 4-104 | •463 | 5d-173 | | |
| Calcutta-West Indies inns & 46 runs | 377 | - | •241 | 90 | | |
| Madras[1]-Drawn | •313 | 1-64 | 8d-451 | - | | |
| **1987-88 in INDIA** | | | | | | |
| Delhi-West Indies 5 wkts | 127 | 5-276 | •75 | 327 | I.V.A.Richards | D.B.Vengsarkar |
| Bombay[3]-Drawn | 337 | 1-4 | •281 | 173 | | D.B.Vengsarkar |
| Calcutta-Drawn | •5d-530 | 2-157 | 565 | - | | D.B.Vengsarkar |
| Madras[1]-India 255 runs | 184 | 160 | •382 | 8d-217 | | R.J.Shastri |
| **1988-89 in WEST INDIES** | | | | | | |
| Georgetown-Drawn | •437 | - | 1-86 | - | I.V.A.Richards | D.B.Vengsarkar |
| Bridgetown-West Indies 8 wkts | 377 | 2-196 | •321 | 251 | | |
| Port-of-Spain-West Indies 217 runs | •314 | 266 | 150 | 213 | | |
| Kingston-West Indies 7 wkts | 384 | 3-60 | •289 | 152 | | |
| **1994-95 in INDIA** | | | | | | |
| Bombay[3]-India 96 runs | 243 | 266 | •272 | 333 | C.A.Walsh | M.Azharuddin |
| Nagpur-Drawn | 428 | 5-132 | •9d-546 | 7d-208 | | |
| Mohali-West Indies 243 runs | •443 | 3d-301 | 387 | 114 | | |
| **1996-97 in WEST INDIES** | | | | | | |
| Kingston-Drawn | •427 | 4d-241 | 349 | 2-99 | C.A.Walsh | S.R.Tendulkar |
| Port-of-Spain-Drawn | 296 | 6-299 | 436 | - | C.A.Walsh | |
| Bridgetown-West Indies 8 wkts | •298 | 140 | 319 | 81 | B.C.Lara | |
| St John's-Drawn | •333 | - | 2-212 | - | C.A.Walsh | |
| Georgetown-Drawn | 3-145 | - | •355 | - | C.A.Walsh | |

## Test Match Results Summary

### WEST INDIES v INDIA-IN WEST INDIES

| | | Result | | | Port-of-Spain | | | Bridgetown | | | Georgetown | | | Kingston | | | St John's | | |
|---|---|---|---|---|---|---|---|---|---|---|---|---|---|---|---|---|---|---|---|
| | Tests | WI | I | D | WI | I | D | WI | I | D | WI | I | D | WI | I | D | WI | I | D |
| 1952-53 | 5 | 1 | - | 4 | - | - | 2 | 1 | - | - | - | - | 1 | - | - | 1 | - | - | - |
| 1961-62 | 5 | 5 | - | - | 2 | - | - | 1 | - | - | - | - | - | 2 | - | - | - | - | - |
| 1970-71 | 5 | - | 1 | 4 | - | 1 | 1 | - | - | 1 | - | - | 1 | - | - | 1 | - | - | - |
| 1975-76 | 4 | 2 | 1 | 1 | - | 1 | 1 | 1 | - | - | - | - | - | 1 | - | - | - | - | - |
| 1982-83 | 5 | 2 | - | 3 | - | - | 1 | 1 | - | - | - | - | 1 | 1 | - | - | - | - | 1 |
| 1988-89 | 4 | 3 | - | 1 | 1 | - | - | 1 | - | - | - | - | 1 | 1 | - | - | - | - | - |
| 1996-97 | 5 | 1 | - | 4 | - | - | 1 | 1 | - | - | - | - | 1 | - | - | 1 | - | - | 1 |
| | 33 | 14 | 2 | 17 | 3 | 2 | 6 | 6 | - | 1 | - | - | 5 | 5 | - | 3 | - | - | 2 |

### WEST INDIES v INDIA-IN INDIA

| | | Result | | | Delhi | | | Bombay | | | Calcutta | | | Madras | | |
|---|---|---|---|---|---|---|---|---|---|---|---|---|---|---|---|---|
| | Tests | WI | I | D | WI | I | D | WI | I | D | WI | I | D | WI | I | D |
| 1948-49 | 5 | 1 | - | 4 | - | - | 1 | - | - | 2 | - | - | 1 | 1 | - | - |
| 1958-59 | 5 | 3 | - | 2 | - | - | 1 | - | - | 1 | 1 | - | - | 1 | - | - |
| 1966-67 | 3 | 2 | - | 1 | - | - | - | 1 | - | - | 1 | - | - | - | - | 1 |
| 1974-75 | 5 | 3 | 2 | - | 1 | - | - | 1 | - | - | - | 1 | - | - | 1 | - |
| 1978-79 | 6 | - | 1 | 5 | - | - | 1 | - | - | 1 | - | - | 1 | - | 1 | - |
| 1983-84 | 6 | 3 | - | 3 | - | - | 1 | - | - | 1 | 1 | - | - | - | - | 1 |
| 1987-88 | 4 | 1 | 1 | 2 | 1 | - | - | - | - | 1 | - | - | 1 | - | 1 | - |
| 1994-95 | 3 | 1 | 1 | 1 | - | - | - | - | 1 | - | - | - | - | - | - | - |
| | 37 | 14 | 5 | 18 | 2 | - | 4 | 2 | - | 6 | 3 | 1 | 3 | 2 | 3 | 2 |
| Totals | 70 | 28 | 7 | 35 | | | | | | | | | | | | |

| | Kanpur | | | Bang. | | | Ahmed. | | | Nagpur | | | Mohali | | |
|---|---|---|---|---|---|---|---|---|---|---|---|---|---|---|---|
| | WI | I | D | WI | I | D | WI | I | D | WI | I | D | WI | I | D |
| 1948-49 | - | - | - | - | - | - | - | - | - | - | - | - | - | - | - |
| 1958-59 | 1 | - | - | - | - | - | - | - | - | - | - | - | - | - | - |
| 1966-67 | - | - | - | - | - | - | - | - | - | - | - | - | - | - | - |
| 1974-75 | - | - | - | 1 | - | - | - | - | - | - | - | - | - | - | - |
| 1978-79 | - | - | 1 | - | - | 1 | - | - | - | - | - | - | - | - | - |
| 1983-84 | 1 | - | - | - | - | - | 1 | - | - | - | - | - | - | - | - |
| 1987-88 | - | - | - | - | - | - | - | - | - | - | - | - | - | - | - |
| 1994-95 | - | - | - | - | - | - | - | - | - | - | - | 1 | 1 | - | - |
| | 2 | - | 1 | 1 | - | 1 | 1 | - | - | - | - | 1 | 1 | - | - |

*Key to ground abbreviation: Bang. - Bangalore; Ahmed. - Ahmedabad.*

### HIGHEST INNINGS TOTALS

| | | | |
|---|---|---|---|
| West Indies in West Indies | 8d-631 | Kingston | 1961-62 |
| West Indies in India | 8d-644 | Delhi | 1958-59 |
| India in West Indies | 7-469 | Port-of-Spain | 1982-83 |
| India in India | 7d-644 | Kanpur | 1978-79 |

### LOWEST INNINGS TOTALS

| | | | |
|---|---|---|---|
| West Indies in West Indies | 140 | Bridgetown | 1996-97 |
| West Indies in India | 127 | Delhi | 1987-88 |
| India in West Indies | 81 | Bridgetown | 1996-97 |
| India in India | 75 | Delhi | 1987-88 |

| | | | |
|---|---|---|---|
| **HIGHEST MATCH AGGREGATE** | 1478 for 38 wickets | Port-of-Spain | 1970-71 |
| **LOWEST MATCH AGGREGATE** | 605 for 30 wickets | Port-of-Spain | 1961-62 |

### HIGHEST INDIVIDUAL INNINGS

| | | | | |
|---|---|---|---|---|
| West Indies in West Indies | 237 | F.M.M.Worrell | Kingston | 1952-53 |
| West Indies in India | 256 | R.B.Kanhai | Calcutta | 1958-59 |
| India in West Indies | 220 | S.M.Gavaskar | Port-of-Spain | 1970-71 |
| India in India | 236* | S.M.Gavaskar | Madras[1] | 1983-84 |

### HIGHEST AGGREGATE OF RUNS IN A SERIES

| | | | |
|---|---|---|---|
| West Indies in West Indies | 716 (av 102.28) | E.D.Weekes | 1952-53 |
| West Indies in India | 779 (av 111.28) | E.D.Weekes | 1948-49 |
| India in West Indies | 774 (av 154.80) | S.M.Gavaskar | 1970-71 |
| India in India | 732 (av 91.50) | S.M.Gavaskar | 1978-79 |

**RECORD WICKET PARTNERSHIPS-WEST INDIES**

| | | | | |
|---|---|---|---|---|
| 1st | 296 | C.G.Greenidge (154*), D.L.Haynes (136) | St John's | 1982-83 |
| 2nd | 255 | E.D A.S.McMorris (125), R.B.Kanhai (158) | Kingston | 1961-62 |
| 3rd | 220 | I V.A Richards (142), A.I.Kallicharran (93) | Bridgetown | 1975-76 |
| 4th | 267 | C.L.Walcott (152), G.E.Gomez (101) | Delhi | 1948-49 |
| 5th | 219 | E.D.Weekes (207), B.H.Pairaudeau (115) | Port-of-Spain | 1952-53 |
| 6th | 250 | C.H.Lloyd (242), D.L.Murray (91) | Bombay[3] | 1974-75 |
| 7th | 130 | C.G.Greenidge (194), M.D.Marshall (92) | Kanpur | 1983-84 |
| 8th | 124 | I.V.A Richards (192), K.D.Boyce (68) | Delhi | 1974-75 |
| 9th | 161 | C.H.Lloyd (161*), A.M.E.Roberts (68) | Calcutta | 1983-84 |
| 10th | 98* | F.M.M.Worrell (73*), W.W.Hall (50*) | Port-of-Spain | 1961-62 |

**RECORD WICKET PARTNERSHIPS-INDIA**

| | | | | |
|---|---|---|---|---|
| 1st | 153 | S.M.Gavaskar (73), C.P.S.Chauhan (84) | Bombay[3] | 1978-79 |
| 2nd | 344* | S.M.Gavaskar (182), D.B.Vengsarkar (157) | Calcutta | 1978-79 |
| 3rd | 177 | N.S.Sidhu (107), S.R.Tendulkar (179) | Nagpur | 1994-95 |
| 4th | 172 | G.R.Viswanath (179), A.D.Gaekwad (102) | Kanpur | 1978-79 |
| 5th | 204 | S.M.Gavaskar (156), B.P.Patel (115) | Port-of-Spain | 1975-76 |
| 6th | 170 | S.M.Gavaskar (236*), R.J.Shastri (72) | Madras[1] | 1983-84 |
| 7th | 186 | D.N.Sardesai (150), E.D.Solkar (65) | Bridgetown | 1970-71 |
| 8th | 107 | Yashpal Sharma (63), B.S.Sandhu (68) | Kingston | 1982-83 |
| 9th | 143* | S.M.Gavaskar (236*), S.M.H.Kirmani (63*) | Madras[1] | 1983-84 |
| 10th | 62 | D.N.Sardesai (150), B.S.Bedi (20*) | Bridgetown | 1970-71 |

**BEST INNINGS BOWLING ANALYSIS**

| | | | | |
|---|---|---|---|---|
| West Indies in West Indies | 9-95 | J.M.Noreiga | Port-of-Spain | 1970-71 |
| West Indies in India | 7-64 | A.M.E.Roberts | Madras[1] | 1974-75 |
| India in West Indies | 7-162 | S.P.Gupte | Port-of-Spain | 1952-53 |
| India in India | 9-83 | Kapil Dev | Ahmedabad | 1983-84 |

**BEST MATCH BOWLING ANALYSIS**

| | | | | |
|---|---|---|---|---|
| West Indies in West Indies | 11-89 | M.D.Marshall | Port-of-Spain | 1988-89 |
| West Indies in India | 12-121 | A.M.E.Roberts | Madras[1] | 1974-75 |
| India in West Indies | 8-118 | Kapil Dev | Kingston | 1982-83 |
| India in India | 16-136 | N.D.Hirwani | Madras[1] | 1987-88 |

**HIGHEST AGGREGATE OF WICKETS IN A SERIES**

| | | | |
|---|---|---|---|
| West Indies in West Indies | 28 (av 29.57) | A.L.Valentine | 1952-53 |
| West Indies in India | 33 (av 18.81) | M.D.Marshall | 1983-84 |
| India in West Indies | 27 (av 29.22) | S.P.Gupte | 1952-53 |
| India in India | 29 (av 18.51) | Kapil Dev | 1983-84 |

| WEST INDIES v PAKISTAN | West Indies | | Pakistan | | Captains | |
|---|---|---|---|---|---|---|
| Venue and Result | 1st | 2nd | 1st | 2nd | West Indies | Pakistan |
| **1957-58 In WEST INDIES** | | | | | | |
| Bridgetown-Drawn | •9d-579 | 0-28 | 106 | 8d-657 | F.C.M.Alexander | A.H.Kardar |
| Port-of-Spain-West Indies 120 runs | •325 | 312 | 282 | 235 | | |
| Kingston-West Indies inns & 174 runs | 3d-790 | - | •328 | 288 | | |
| Georgetown-West Indies 8 wkts | 410 | 2-317 | •408 | 318 | | |
| Port-of-Spain-Pakistan inns & 1 run | •268 | 227 | 496 | - | | |
| **1958-59 In PAKISTAN** | | | | | | |
| Karachi[1]-Pakistan 10 wkts | •146 | 245 | 304 | 0-88 | F.C.M.Alexander | Fazal Mahmood |
| Dacca-Pakistan 41 runs | 76 | 172 | •145 | 144 | | |
| Lahore[1]-West Indies & 156 runs | •469 | - | 209 | 104 | | |
| **1974-75 In PAKISTAN** | | | | | | |
| Lahore[2]-Drawn | 214 | 4-258 | •199 | 7d-373 | C.H.Lloyd | Intikhab Alam |
| Karachi[1]-Drawn | 493 | 0-1 | •8d-406 | 256 | | |
| **1976-77 In WEST INDIES** | | | | | | |
| Bridgetown-Drawn | 421 | 9-251 | •435 | 291 | C.H.Lloyd | Mushtaq Mohammad |
| Port-of-Spain-West Indies 6 wkts | 316 | 4-206 | •180 | 340 | | |
| Georgetown-Drawn | 448 | 1-154 | •194 | 540 | | |
| Port-of-Spain-Pakistan 266 runs | 154 | 222 | •341 | 9d-301 | | |
| Kingston-West Indies 140 runs | •280 | 359 | 198 | 301 | | |
| **1980-81 In PAKISTAN** | | | | | | |
| Lahore[2]-Drawn | 297 | - | •369 | 7-156 | C.H.Lloyd | Javed Miandad |
| Faisalabad-West Indies 156 runs | •235 | 242 | 176 | 145 | | |
| Karachi[1]-Drawn | 169 | - | •128 | 9-204 | | |
| Multan-Drawn | •249 | 5-116 | 166 | - | | |
| **1986-87 In PAKISTAN** | | | | | | |
| Faisalabad-Pakistan 186 runs | 248 | 53 | •159 | 328 | I.V.A.Richards | Imran Khan |
| Lahore[2]-West Indies inns & 10 runs | 218 | - | •131 | 77 | | |
| Karachi[1]-Drawn | •240 | 211 | 239 | 7-125 | | |
| **1987-88 In WEST INDIES** | | | | | | |
| Georgetown-Pakistan 9 wkts | •292 | 172 | 435 | 1-32 | C.G.Greenidge | Imran Khan |
| Port-of-Spain-Drawn | •174 | 391 | 194 | 9-341 | I.V.A.Richards | |
| Bridgetown-West Indies 2 wkts | 306 | 8-268 | •309 | 262 | I.V.A.Richards | |
| **1990-91 In PAKISTAN** | | | | | | |
| Karachi[1]-Pakistan 8 wkts | •216 | 181 | 345 | 2-98 | D.L.Haynes | Imran Khan |
| Faisalabad-West Indies 7 wkts | 195 | 3-130 | •170 | 154 | | |
| Lahore[2]-Drawn | •294 | 173 | 122 | 6-242 | | |
| **1992-93 In WEST INDIES** | | | | | | |
| Port-of-Spain-West Indies 204 runs | •127 | 382 | 140 | 165 | R.B.Richardson | Wasim Akram |
| Bridgetown-West Indies 10 wkts | •455 | 0-29 | 221 | 262 | | |
| St John's-Drawn | •438 | 4-153 | 326 | | | |
| **1997-98 In PAKISTAN** | | | | | | |
| Peshawar[2]-Pakistan inns & 19 runs | 381 | - | •151 | 211 | C.A.Walsh | Wasim Akram |
| Rawalpindi[2]-Pakistan inns & 29 runs | 471 | - | •303 | 139 | | |
| Karachi[1]-Pakistan 10 wkts | 417 | 0-15 | •216 | 212 | | |

## Test Match Results Summary

**WEST INDIES v PAKISTAN-IN WEST INDIES**

| | Tests | Result | | | Bridgetown | | | Port-of-Spain | | | Kingston | | | Georgetown | | | St John's | | |
|---|---|---|---|---|---|---|---|---|---|---|---|---|---|---|---|---|---|---|---|
| | | WI | P | D | WI | P | D | WI | P | D | WI | P | D | WI | P | D | WI | P | D |
| 1957-58 | 5 | 3 | 1 | 1 | - | - | 1 | 1 | 1 | - | 1 | - | - | 1 | - | - | - | - | - |
| 1976-77 | 5 | 2 | 1 | 2 | - | - | 1 | 1 | 1 | - | 1 | - | - | - | - | 1 | - | - | - |
| 1987-88 | 3 | 1 | 1 | 1 | 1 | - | - | - | - | 1 | - | - | - | - | 1 | - | - | - | - |
| 1992-93 | 3 | 2 | - | 1 | 1 | - | - | 1 | - | - | - | - | - | - | - | - | - | - | 1 |
| | 16 | 8 | 3 | 5 | 2 | - | 2 | 3 | 2 | 1 | 2 | - | - | 1 | 1 | 1 | - | - | 1 |

**WEST INDIES v PAKISTAN-IN PAKISTAN**

| | Tests | Result | | | Karachi[1] | | | Dacca | | | Lahore | | | Faisalabad | | | Multan | | | Peshawar[2] | | | Rawalpindi[2] | | |
|---|---|---|---|---|---|---|---|---|---|---|---|---|---|---|---|---|---|---|---|---|---|---|---|---|---|
| | | W | P | D | W | P | D | W | P | D | W | P | D | W | P | D | W | P | D | W | P | D | W | P | D |
| 1955-56 | 3 | - | 2 | 1 | - | 1 | - | - | 1 | - | - | - | 1 | - | - | - | - | - | - | - | - | - | - | - | - |
| 1958-59 | 3 | 1 | 2 | - | - | 1 | - | - | 1 | - | 1 | - | - | - | - | - | - | - | - | - | - | - | - | - | - |
| 1974-75 | 2 | - | - | 2 | - | - | 1 | - | - | - | - | - | 1 | - | - | - | - | - | - | - | - | - | - | - | - |
| 1980-81 | 4 | 1 | - | 3 | - | - | 1 | - | - | - | - | - | 1 | 1 | - | - | - | - | 1 | - | - | - | - | - | - |
| 1986-87 | 3 | 1 | 1 | 1 | - | - | 1 | - | - | - | 1 | - | - | - | 1 | - | - | - | - | - | - | - | - | - | - |
| 1990-91 | 3 | 1 | 1 | 1 | - | 1 | - | - | - | - | - | - | 1 | 1 | - | - | - | - | - | - | - | - | - | - | - |
| 1997-98 | 3 | - | 3 | - | - | 1 | - | - | - | - | - | - | - | - | - | - | - | - | - | - | 1 | - | - | 1 | - |
| | 18 | 4 | 7 | 7 | - | 3 | 3 | - | 1 | - | 2 | - | 3 | 2 | 1 | - | - | - | 1 | - | 1 | - | - | 1 | - |
| Totals | 34 | 12 | 10 | 12 | | | | | | | | | | | | | | | | | | | | | |

**HIGHEST INNINGS TOTALS**

| | | | |
|---|---|---|---|
| West Indies in West Indies | 3d-790 | Kingston | 1957-58 |
| West Indies in Pakistan | 493 | Karachi[1] | 1974-75 |
| Pakistan in West Indies | 8d-657 | Bridgetown | 1957-58 |
| Pakistan in Pakistan | 471 | Rawalpindi[2] | 1997-98 |

**LOWEST INNINGS TOTALS**

| | | | |
|---|---|---|---|
| West Indies in West Indies | 127 | Port-of-Spain | 1992-93 |
| West Indies in Pakistan | 53 | Faisalabad | 1986-87 |
| Pakistan in West Indies | 106 | Bridgetown | 1957-58 |
| Pakistan in Pakistan | 77 | Lahore[2] | 1986-87 |

| | | | |
|---|---|---|---|
| **HIGHEST MATCH AGGREGATE** | 1453 for 32 wickets | Georgetown | 1957-58 |
| **LOWEST MATCH AGGREGATE** | 426 for 30 wickets | Lahore[2] | 1986-87 |

**HIGHEST INDIVIDUAL INNINGS**

| | | | | |
|---|---|---|---|---|
| West Indies in West Indies | 365 | G.S.Sobers | Kingston | 1957-58 |
| West Indies in Pakistan | 217 | R.B.Kanhai | Lahore[1] | 1958-59 |
| Pakistan in West Indies | 337 | Hanif Mohammad | Bridgetown | 1957-58 |
| Pakistan in Pakistan | 177 | Inzamamul Haq | Rawalpindi[2] | 1997-98 |

**HIGHEST AGGREGATE OF RUNS IN A SERIES**

| | | | |
|---|---|---|---|
| West Indies in West Indies | 824 (av 137.33) | G.S.Sobers | 1957-58 |
| West Indies in Pakistan | 364 (av 72.80) | I.V.A.Richards | 1980-81 |
| Pakistan in West Indies | 628 (av 69.77) | Hanif Mohammad | 1957-58 |
| Pakistan in Pakistan | 285 (av 57.00) | Aamer Sohail | 1997-98 |

**RECORD WICKET PARTNERSHIPS-WEST INDIES**

| | | | | |
|---|---|---|---|---|
| 1st | 182 | R.C.Fredericks (83), C.G.Greenidge (82) | Kingston | 1976-77 |
| 2nd | 446 | C.C.Hunte (260), G.S.Sobers (365*) | Kingston | 1957-58 |
| 3rd | 169 | D.L.Haynes (143*), B.C.Lara (96) | Port-of-Spain | 1992-93 |
| 4th | 188* | G.S Sobers (365*), C.L.Walcott (88*) | Kingston | 1957-58 |
| 5th | 185 | E.D.Weekes (197), O.G Smith (78) | Bridgetown | 1957-58 |
| 6th | 151 | C.H.Lloyd (157), D.L.Murray (52) | Bridgetown | 1976-77 |
| 7th | 70 | C.H.Lloyd (157), J.Garner (43) | Bridgetown | 1976-77 |
| 8th | 60 | C.L.Hooper (178*) A.C.Cummins (14) | St John's | 1992-93 |
| 9th | 61* | P.J.L.Dujon (29*), W.K.M.Benjamin (40*) | Bridgetown | 1987-88 |
| 10th | 106 | C.L.Hooper (178*), C.A.Walsh (30) | St John's | 1992-93 |

**RECORD WICKET PARTNERSHIPS-PAKISTAN**

| | | | | |
|---|---|---|---|---|
| 1st | 298 | Aamer Sohail (160), Ijaz Ahmed (151) | Karachi[1] | 1997-98 |
| 2nd | 178 | Hanif Mohammad (103), Saeed Ahmed (78) | Karachi[1] | 1958-59 |
| 3rd | 323 | Aamer Sohail (160), Inzamamul Haq (177) | Rawalpindi[2] | 1997-98 |
| 4th | 174 | Shoaib Mohammad (86), Saleem Malik (102) | Karachi[1] | 1990-91 |
| 5th | 88 | Basit Ali (56), Inzamamul Haq (123) | St John's | 1992-93 |
| 6th | 166 | Wazir Mohammad (106), A.H.Kardar (57) | Kingston | 1957-58 |
| 7th | 128 | Wasim Raja (107*), Wasim Bari (58) | Karachi[1] | 1974-75 |
| 8th | 94 | Saleem Malik (66), Saleem Yousuf (39) | Port-of-Spain | 1987-88 |
| 9th | 96 | Inzamamul Haq (123), Nadeem Khan (25) | St John's | 1992-93 |
| 10th | 133 | Wasim Raja (71), Wasim Bari (60*) | Bridgetown | 1976-77 |

**BEST INNINGS BOWLING ANALYSIS**

| | | | | |
|---|---|---|---|---|
| West Indies in West Indies | 8-29 | C.E.H.Croft | Port-of-Spain | 1976-77 |
| West Indies in Pakistan | 5-33 | M.D.Marshall | Lahore[2] | 1986-87 |
| Pakistan in West Indies | 7-80 | Imran Khan | Georgetown | 1987-88 |
| Pakistan in Pakistan | 6-16 | Abdul Qadir | Faisalabad | 1986-87 |

**BEST MATCH BOWLING ANALYSIS**

| | | | | |
|---|---|---|---|---|
| West Indies in West Indies | 9-95 | C.E.H.Croft | Port-of-Spain | 1976-77 |
| West Indies in Pakistan | 9-187 | A.M.E.Roberts | Lahore[2] | 1974-75 |
| Pakistan in West Indies | 11-121 | Imran Khan | Georgetown | 1987-88 |
| Pakistan in Pakistan | 12-100 | Fazal Mahmood | Dacca | 1959-60 |

**HIGHEST AGGREGATE OF WICKETS IN A SERIES**

| | | | |
|---|---|---|---|
| West Indies in West Indies | 33 (av 20.48) | C E.H.Croft | 1976-77 |
| West Indies in Pakistan | 17 (av 17.76) | C.E.H.Croft | 1980-81 |
| Pakistan in West Indies | 25 (av 31.60) | Imran Khan | 1976-77 |
| Pakistan in Pakistan | 21 (av 15.85) | Fazal Mahmood | 1958-59 |
| | 21 (av 14.19) | Wasim Akram | 1990-91 |

| **WEST INDIES v SRI LANKA** | West Indies | | Sri Lanka | | Captains | |
|---|---|---|---|---|---|---|
| Venue and Result | 1st | 2nd | 1st | 2nd | West Indies | Sri Lanka |
| **1993-94 in SRI LANKA** | | | | | | |
| Moratuwa-Drawn | •190 | 2-43 | 204 | - | R.B.Richardson | A.Ranatunga |
| **1997-98 in WEST INDIES** | | | | | | |
| St John's-West Indies 6 wkts | 189 | 4-189 | •223 | 152 | C.A.Walsh | A.Ranatunga |
| Kingstown-Drawn | •147 | 343 | 222 | 8-233 | | |

## Test Match Results Summary

**WEST INDIES v SRI LANKA-IN SRI LANKA**

| | | Result | | | Moratuwa | | |
|---|---|---|---|---|---|---|---|
| | Tests | WI | SL | D | WI | SL | D |
| 1993-94 | 1 | - | - | 1 | - | - | 1 |

**WEST INDIES v SRI LANKA-IN WEST INDIES**

| | | Result | | | St John's | | | Kingstown | | |
|---|---|---|---|---|---|---|---|---|---|---|
| | Tests | W | SL | D | W | SL | D | W | SL | D |
| 1997-98 | 2 | 1 | - | 1 | 1 | - | - | - | - | 1 |
| Totals | 3 | 1 | - | 2 | | | | | | |

**HIGHEST INNINGS TOTALS**

| | | | |
|---|---|---|---|
| West Indies in West Indies | 343 | Kingstown | 1997-98 |
| West Indies in Sri Lanka | 204 | Moratuwa | 1993-94 |
| Sri Lanka in West Indies | 8-233 | Kingstown | 1997-98 |
| Sri Lanka in Sri Lanka | 190 | Moratuwa | 1993-94 |

**LOWEST INNINGS TOTALS**

| | | | |
|---|---|---|---|
| West Indies in West Indies | 147 | Kingstown | 1997-98 |
| West Indies in Sri Lanka | 204 | Moratuwa | 1993-94 |
| Sri Lanka in West Indies | 152 | St John's | 1997-98 |
| Sri Lanka in Sri Lanka | 190 | Moratuwa | 1993-94 |

| | | | |
|---|---|---|---|
| **HIGHEST MATCH AGGREGATE** | 949 for 38 wickets | Kingstown | 1997-98 |
| **LOWEST MATCH AGGREGATE** | 437 for 22 wickets | Moratuwa | 1993-94 |

**HIGHEST INDIVIDUAL INNINGS**

| | | | | |
|---|---|---|---|---|
| West Indies in West Indies | 115 | B.C.Lara | Kingstown | 1997-98 |
| West Indies in Sri Lanka | 62 | C.L.Hooper | Moratuwa | 1993-94 |
| Sri Lanka in West Indies | 90 | S.T.Jayasuriya | Kingstown | 1997-98 |
| Sri Lanka in Sri Lanka | 53 | P.A.de Silva | Moratuwa | 1993-94 |

**HIGHEST AGGREGATE OF RUNS IN A SERIES**

| | | | |
|---|---|---|---|
| West Indies in West Indies | 182 (av 45.50) | S.L.Campbell | 1997-98 |
| West Indies in Sri Lanka | 62 (av 62.00) | C.L.Hooper | 1993-94 |
| Sri Lanka in West Indies | 192 (av 48.00) | S.T.Jayasuriya | 1997-98 |
| Sri Lanka in Sri Lanka | 68 (av 68.00) | P.A.de Silva | 1993-94 |

**HIGHEST WICKET PARTNERSHIP-WEST INDIES**

| | | | | |
|---|---|---|---|---|
| 1st | 160 | S.L.Campbell (79), S.C.Williams (83) | St John's | 1997-98 |
| 2nd | 54 | S.L.Campbell (50), F.L.Reiffer (29) | St John's | 1997-98 |
| 3rd | 51 | B.C.Lara (115), F.L.Reiffer (18) | Kingstown | 1997-98 |
| 4th | 97 | B.C.Lara (115), C.L.Hooper (34) | Kingstown | 1997-98 |
| 5th | 84 | R.B.Richardson (51), C.L.Hooper (62) | Moratuwa | 1993-94 |
| 6th | 24 | C.L.Hooper (81), I.R.Bishop (11) | Kingstown | 1997-98 |
| 7th | 14 | R.I.C..Holder (34), C.O.Browne (0) | Kingstown | 1997-98 |
| 8th | 51 | R.I.C..Holder (34), C.E.L.Ambrose (31) | Kingstown | 1997-98 |
| 9th | 13 | W.K.M.Benjamin (2), C.E.L.Ambrose (7*) | Moratuwa | 1993-94 |
| 10th | 2 | F.A.Rose (1), C.A.Walsh (1*) | Kingstown | 1997-98 |

**HIGHEST WICKET PARTNERSHIP-SRI LANKA**

| | | | | |
|---|---|---|---|---|
| 1st | 62 | S.T.Jayasuriya (90), R.S.Mahanama (28) | Kingstown | 1997-98 |
| 2nd | 29 | R.S.Mahanama (29), M.S.Atapattu (10) | Kingstown | 1997-98 |
| 3rd | 76 | S.T.Jayasuriya (90), P.A.de Silva (35) | Kingstown | 1997-98 |
| 4th | 110 | S.T.Jayasuriya (85), A.Ranatunga (42) | St John's | 1997-98 |
| 5th | 32 | S.T.Jayasuriya (85), R.S.Kaluwitharana (23) | St John's | 1997-98 |
| 6th | 35 | R.S.Kaluwitharana (23), H.D.P.K.Dharmasena (29) | St John's | 1997-98 |
| 7th | 51 | R.S.Kalpage (39), P.B.Dasanayake (18) | Moratuwa | 1993-94 |
| 8th | 11 | H.D.P.K.Dharmasena (31), K.S.C.de Silva (2*) | St John's | 1997-98 |
| 9th | 7 | K.S.C.de Silva (6), M.Muralidaran (6*) | St John's | 1997-98 |
| 10th | 7 | K.S.C.de Silva (4*), M.Muralidaran (4) | Kingstown | 1997-98 |

**BEST INNINGS BOWLING ANALYSIS**

| | | | | |
|---|---|---|---|---|
| West Indies in West Indies | 5-26 | C.L.Hooper | Kingstown | 1997-98 |
| West Indies in Sri Lanka | 4-46 | W.K.M.Benjamin | Moratuwa | 1993-94 |
| Sri Lanka in West Indies | 5-34 | M.Muralidaran | St John's | 1997-98 |
| Sri Lanka in Sri Lanka | 4-47 | M.Muralidaran | Moratuwa | 1993-94 |

**BEST MATCH BOWLING ANALYSIS**

| | | | | |
|---|---|---|---|---|
| West Indies in West Indies | 8-78 | C.E.L.Ambrose | St John's | 1997-98 |
| West Indies in Sri Lanka | 5-51 | W.K.M.Benjamin | Moratuwa | 1993-94 |
| Sri Lanka in West Indies | 8-106 | M.Muralidaran | St John's | 1997-98 |
| Sri Lanka in Sri Lanka | 4-47 | M.Muralidaran | Moratuwa | 1993-94 |

**HIGHEST AGGREGATE OF WICKETS IN A SERIES**

| | | | |
|---|---|---|---|
| West Indies in West Indies | 11 (av 14.81) | C.E.L.Ambrose | 1997-98 |
| West Indies in Sri Lanka | 5 (av 10.20) | W.K.M.Benjamin | 1993-94 |
| Sri Lanka in West Indies | 16 (av 15.43) | M.Muralidaran | 1997-98 |
| Sri Lanka in Sri Lanka | 4 (av 11.75) | M.Muralidaran | 1993-94 |

| **NEW ZEALAND v INDIA** | New Zealand | | India | | Captains | |
|---|---|---|---|---|---|---|
| Venue and Result | 1st | 2nd | 1st | 2nd | New Zealand | India |
| **1955-56 in INDIA** | | | | | | |
| Hyderabad-Drawn | 326 | 2-212 | •4d-498 | - | H.B.Cave | Ghulam Ahmed |
| Bombay[2]-India inns & 27 runs | 258 | 136 | •8d-421 | - | | P.R.Umrigar |
| Delhi-Drawn | •2d-450 | 1-112 | 7d-531 | - | | P.R.Umrigar |
| Calcutta-Drawn | 336 | 6-75 | •132 | 7d-438 | | P.R.Umrigar |
| Madras[2]-India inns & 109 runs | 209 | 219 | •3d-537 | - | | P.R.Umrigar |
| **1964-65 in INDIA** | | | | | | |
| Madras[2]-Drawn | 315 | 0-62 | •397 | 2d-199 | J.R.Reid | Nawab of Pataudi, jr |
| Calcutta-Drawn | •9d-462 | 9d-191 | 380 | 3-92 | | |
| Bombay[2]-Drawn | •297 | 8-80 | 88 | 5d-463 | | |
| Delhi-India 7 wkts | •262 | 272 | 8d-465 | 3-73 | | |
| **1967-68 in NEW ZEALAND** | | | | | | |
| Dunedin-India 5 wkts | •350 | 208 | 359 | 5-200 | B.W.Sinclair | Nawab of Pataudi, jr |
| Christchurch-New Zealand 6 wkts | •502 | 4-88 | 288 | 301 | G.T.Dowling | |
| Wellington-India 8 wkts | •186 | 199 | 327 | 2-59 | G.T.Dowling | |
| Auckland-India 272 runs | 140 | 101 | •252 | 5d-261 | G.T.Dowling | |
| **1969-70 in INDIA** | | | | | | |
| Bombay[2]-India 60 runs | 229 | 127 | •156 | 260 | G.T.Dowling | Nawab of Pataudi, jr |
| Nagpur-New Zealand 167 runs | •319 | 214 | 257 | 109 | | |
| Hyderabad-Drawn | •181 | 8d-175 | 89 | 7-67 | | |
| **1975-76 in NEW ZEALAND** | | | | | | |
| Auckland-India 8 wkts | •266 | 215 | 414 | 2-71 | G.M.Turner | S.M.Gavaskar |
| Christchurch-Drawn | 403 | - | •270 | 6-255 | | B.S.Bedi |
| Wellington-New Zealand inns & 33 runs | 334 | - | •220 | 81 | | B.S.Bedi |
| **1976-77 in INDIA** | | | | | | |
| Bombay[3]-India 162 runs | 298 | 141 | •399 | 4d-202 | G.M.Turner | B.S.Bedi |
| Kanpur-Drawn | 350 | 7-193 | •9d-524 | 2d-208 | | |
| Madras[1]-India 216 runs | 140 | 143 | •298 | 5d-201 | | |
| **1980-81 in NEW ZEALAND** | | | | | | |
| Wellington-New Zealand 62 runs | •375 | 100 | 223 | 190 | G.P.Howarth | S.M.Gavaskar |
| Christchurch-Drawn | 5-286 | - | •255 | - | | |
| Auckland-Drawn | 366 | 5-95 | •238 | 284 | | |
| **1988-89 in INDIA** | | | | | | |
| Bangalore-India 172 runs | 189 | 164 | •9d-384 | 1d-141 | J.G.Wright | D.B.Vengsarkar |
| Bombay[3]-New Zealand 136 runs | •236 | 279 | 234 | 145 | | |
| Hyderabad-India 10 wkts | •254 | 124 | 358 | 0-22 | | |
| **1989-90 in NEW ZEALAND** | | | | | | |
| Christchurch-New Zealand 10 wkts | •459 | 0-2 | 164 | 296 | J.G.Wright | M.Azharuddin |
| Napier-Drawn | 1-178 | - | •358 | - | | |
| Auckland-Drawn | •391 | 5d-483 | 482 | 0-149 | | |
| **1993-94 in NEW ZEALAND** | | | | | | |
| Hamilton-Drawn | •187 | 7d-368 | 246 | 3-177 | K.R.Rutherford | M.Azharuddin |
| **1995-96 in INDIA** | | | | | | |
| Bangalore-India 8 wkts | 228 | 2-151 | •145 | 233 | L.K.Germon | M.Azharuddin |
| Madras[1]-Drawn | - | - | •2-144 | - | | |
| Cuttack-Drawn | 8-175 | - | •8d-296 | - | | |

# Test Match Results Summary

### NEW ZEALAND v INDIA-IN NEW ZEALAND

| | | Result | | | Dunedin | | | Christchurch | | | Wellington | | | Auckland | | | Napier | | | Hamilton | | |
|---|---|---|---|---|---|---|---|---|---|---|---|---|---|---|---|---|---|---|---|---|---|---|
| | Tests | NZ | I | D | NZ | I | D | NZ | I | D | NZ | I | D | NZ | I | D | NZ | I | D | NZ | I | D |
| 1967-68 | 4 | 1 | 3 | - | - | 1 | - | 1 | - | - | - | 1 | - | - | 1 | - | - | - | - | - | - | - |
| 1975-76 | 3 | 1 | 1 | 1 | - | - | - | - | - | 1 | 1 | - | - | - | 1 | - | - | - | - | - | - | - |
| 1980-81 | 3 | 1 | - | 2 | - | - | - | - | - | 1 | 1 | - | - | - | - | 1 | - | - | - | - | - | - |
| 1989-90 | 3 | 1 | - | 2 | - | - | - | 1 | - | - | - | - | - | - | - | 1 | - | - | 1 | - | - | - |
| 1993-94 | 1 | - | - | 1 | - | - | - | - | - | - | - | - | - | - | - | - | - | - | - | - | - | 1 |
| | 14 | 4 | 4 | 6 | - | 1 | - | 2 | - | 2 | 2 | 1 | - | - | 2 | 2 | - | - | 1 | - | - | 1 |

### NEW ZEALAND v INDIA-IN INDIA

| | | Result | | | Hyder. | | | Bombay | | | Delhi | | | Calcutta | | | Madras | | | Nagpur | | | Kanpur | | | Bangalore | | | Cuttack | | |
|---|---|---|---|---|---|---|---|---|---|---|---|---|---|---|---|---|---|---|---|---|---|---|---|---|---|---|---|---|---|---|---|
| | Tests | NZ | I | D | NZ | I | D | NZ | I | D | NZ | I | D | NZ | I | D | NZ | I | D | NZ | I | D | NZ | I | D | NZ | I | D | NZ | I | D |
| 1955-56 | 5 | - | 2 | 3 | - | - | 1 | - | 1 | - | - | - | 1 | - | - | 1 | - | 1 | - | - | - | - | - | - | - | - | - | - | - | - | - |
| 1964-65 | 4 | - | 1 | 3 | - | - | - | - | - | 1 | - | 1 | - | - | - | 1 | - | - | 1 | - | - | - | - | - | - | - | - | - | - | - | - |
| 1969-70 | 3 | 1 | 1 | 1 | - | - | 1 | - | 1 | - | - | - | - | - | - | - | - | - | - | 1 | - | - | - | - | - | - | - | - | - | - | - |
| 1976-77 | 3 | - | 2 | 1 | - | - | - | - | 1 | - | - | - | - | - | - | - | - | 1 | - | - | - | - | - | - | 1 | - | - | - | - | - | - |
| 1988-89 | 3 | 1 | 2 | - | - | 1 | - | 1 | - | - | - | - | - | - | - | - | - | - | - | - | - | - | - | - | - | - | 1 | - | - | - | - |
| 1995-96 | 3 | - | 1 | 2 | - | - | - | - | - | - | - | - | - | - | - | - | - | - | 1 | - | - | - | - | - | - | 1 | - | - | - | - | 1 |
| | 21 | 2 | 9 | 10 | - | 1 | 2 | 1 | 3 | 1 | - | 1 | 1 | - | - | 2 | - | 2 | 2 | 1 | - | - | - | - | 1 | 1 | 1 | - | - | - | 1 |
| Totals | 35 | 6 | 13 | 16 | | | | | | | | | | | | | | | | | | | | | | | | | | | |

*Key to ground abbreviation: Hyder. - Hyderabad.*

**HIGHEST INNINGS TOTALS**

| | | | |
|---|---|---|---|
| New Zealand in New Zealand | 502 | Christchurch | 1967-68 |
| New Zealand in India | 9d-462 | Calcutta | 1964-65 |
| India in New Zealand | 482 | Auckland | 1989-90 |
| India in India | 3d-537 | Madras[2] | 1955-56 |

**LOWEST INNINGS TOTALS**

| | | | |
|---|---|---|---|
| New Zealand in New Zealand | 100 | Wellington | 1980-81 |
| New Zealand in India | 124 | Hyderabad | 1988-89 |
| India in New Zealand | 81 | Wellington | 1975-76 |
| India in India | 88 | Bombay[2] | 1964-65 |

| | | | |
|---|---|---|---|
| **HIGHEST MATCH AGGREGATE** | 1505 for 25 wickets | Auckland | 1989-90 |
| **LOWEST MATCH AGGREGATE** | 635 for 29 wickets | Wellington | 1975-76 |

**HIGHEST INDIVIDUAL INNINGS**

| | | | | |
|---|---|---|---|---|
| New Zealand in New Zealand | 239 | G.T.Dowling | Christchurch | 1967-68 |
| New Zealand in India | 230* | B.Sutcliffe | Delhi | 1955-56 |
| India in New Zealand | 192 | M.Azharuddin | Auckland | 1989-90 |
| India in India | 231 | M.H.Mankad | Madras[2] | 1955-56 |

**HIGHEST AGGREGATE OF RUNS IN A SERIES**

| | | | |
|---|---|---|---|
| New Zealand in New Zealand | 471 (av 58.87) | G.T.Dowling | 1967-68 |
| New Zealand in India | 611 (av 87.28) | B.Sutcliffe | 1955-56 |
| India in New Zealand | 330 (av 47.14) | A.L.Wadekar | 1967-68 |
| India in India | 526 (av 105.20) | M.H.Mankad | 1955-56 |

**RECORD WICKET PARTNERSHIPS-NEW ZEALAND**

| | | | | |
|---|---|---|---|---|
| 1st | 149 | T.J.Franklin (50), J.G.Wright (113*) | Napier | 1989-90 |
| 2nd | 155 | G.T.Dowling (143), B.E.Congdon (58) | Dunedin | 1967-68 |
| 3rd | 222* | B.Sutcliffe (230*), J.R Reid (119*) | Delhi | 1955-56 |
| 4th | 125 | J.G.Wright (185), M.J.Greatbatch (46) | Christchurch | 1989-90 |
| 5th | 119 | G.T.Dowling (239), K Thomson (69) | Christchurch | 1967-68 |
| 6th | 87 | J.W.Guy (102), A.R MacGibbon (59) | Hyderabad | 1955-56 |
| 7th | 163 | B.Sutcliffe (151*), B.R Taylor (105) | Calcutta | 1964-65 |
| 8th | 103 | R.J.Hadlee (87), I.D.S.Smith (173) | Auckland | 1989-90 |
| 9th | 136 | I.D.S.Smith (173), M.C.Snedden (22) | Auckland | 1989-90 |
| 10th | 61 | J.T.Ward (35*), R.O.Collinge (34) | Madras[2] | 1964-65 |

**RECORD WICKET PARTNERSHIPS-INDIA**

| | | | | |
|---|---|---|---|---|
| 1st | 413 | M.H.Mankad (231), P.Roy (173) | Madras[2] | 1955-56 |
| 2nd | 204 | S.M Gavaskar (116), S Amarnath (124) | Auckland | 1975-76 |
| 3rd | 238 | P.R Umrigar (223), V.L.Manjrekar (118) | Hyderabad | 1955-56 |
| 4th | 171 | P R Umrigar (223), A.G Kripal Singh (100*) | Hyderabad | 1955-56 |
| 5th | 127 | V.L.Manjrekar (177), G.S Ramchand (72) | Delhi | 1955-56 |
| 6th | 193* | D.N Sardesai (200), Hanumant Singh (75*) | Bombay[2] | 1964-65 |
| 7th | 128 | S.R.Tendulkar (88), K.S.More (73) | Napier | 1989-90 |
| 8th | 143 | R.G.Nadkarni (75), F.M.Engineer (90) | Madras[2] | 1964-65 |
| 9th | 105 | S.M.H.Kirmani (88), B.S.Bedi (36) | Bombay[3] | 1976-77 |
| | 105 | S.M.H.Kirmani (78), N.S.Yadav (43) | Auckland | 1980-81 |
| 10th | 57 | R.B.Desai (32*), B.S.Bedi (22) | Dunedin | 1967-68 |

**BEST INNINGS BOWLING ANALYSIS**

| | | | | |
|---|---|---|---|---|
| New Zealand in New Zealand | 7-23 | R.J.Hadlee | Wellington | 1975-76 |
| New Zealand in India | 6-49 | R.J.Hadlee | Bombay[2] | 1964-65 |
| India in New Zealand | 8-76 | E.A.S.Prasanna | Auckland | 1975-76 |
| India in India | 8-72 | S.Venkataraghavan | Delhi | 1964-65 |

**BEST MATCH BOWLING ANALYSIS**

| | | | | |
|---|---|---|---|---|
| New Zealand in New Zealand | 11-58 | R.J.Hadlee | Wellington | 1975-76 |
| New Zealand in India | 10-88 | R.J.Hadlee | Bombay[2] | 1969-70 |
| India in New Zealand | 11-140 | E.A.S.Prasanna | Auckland | 1975-76 |
| India in India | 12-152 | S.Venkataraghavan | Delhi | 1964-65 |

**HIGHEST AGGREGATE OF WICKETS IN A SERIES**

| | | | |
|---|---|---|---|
| New Zealand in New Zealand | 16 (av 27.87) | D.K.Morrison | 1989-90 |
| New Zealand in India | 18 (av 14.00) | R.J.Hadlee | 1988-89 |
| India in New Zealand | 24 (av 18.79) | E.A.S.Prasanna | 1967-68 |
| India in India | 34 (av 19.17) | S.P.Gupte | 1955-55 |

| NEW ZEALAND v PAKISTAN | New Zealand | | Pakistan | | Captains | |
|---|---|---|---|---|---|---|
| Venue and Result | 1st | 2nd | 1st | 2nd | New Zealand | Pakistan |
| **1955-56 in PAKISTAN** | | | | | | |
| Karachi[1]-Pakistan inns & 1 run | •164 | 124 | 289 | - | H.B.Cave | A.H.Kardar |
| Lahore[1]-Pakistan 4 wkts | •348 | 328 | 561 | 6-117 | | |
| Dacca-Drawn | •70 | 6-69 | 6d-195 | - | | |
| **1964-65 in NEW ZEALAND** | | | | | | |
| Wellington-Drawn | •266 | 7d-179 | 187 | 7-140 | J.R.Reid | Hanif Mohammad |
| Auckland-Drawn | 214 | 7-166 | •226 | 207 | | |
| Christchurch-Drawn | 202 | 5-223 | •206 | 8d-309 | | |
| **1964-65 in PAKISTAN** | | | | | | |
| Rawalpindi[1]-Pakistan inns & 64 runs | •175 | 79 | 318 | - | J.R.Reid | Hanif Mohammad |
| Lahore[2]-Drawn | 6d-482 | - | •7d-385 | 8d-194 | | |
| Karachi[1]-Pakistan 8 wkts | •285 | 223 | 8d-307 | 2-202 | | |
| **1969-70 in PAKISTAN** | | | | | | |
| Karachi[1]-Drawn | 274 | 5-112 | •220 | 8d-283 | G.T.Dowling | Intikhab Alam |
| Lahore[2]-New Zealand 5 wkts | 241 | 5-82 | •114 | 208 | | |
| Dacca-Drawn | •273 | 200 | 7d-290 | 4-51 | | |
| **1972-73 in NEW ZEALAND** | | | | | | |
| Wellington-Drawn | 325 | 3-78 | •357 | 6d-290 | B.E.Congdon | Intikhab Alam |
| Dunedin-Pakistan inns & 166 runs | 156 | 185 | •6d-507 | - | | |
| Auckland-Drawn | 402 | 3-92 | •402 | 271 | | |
| **1976-77 in PAKISTAN** | | | | | | |
| Lahore[2]-Pakistan 6 wkts | 157 | 360 | •417 | 4-105 | G.M.Turner | Mushtaq Mohammad |
| Hyderabad-Pakistan 10 wkts | 219 | 254 | •8d-473 | 0-4 | G.M.Turner | |
| Karachi[1]-Drawn | 468 | 7-262 | •9d-565 | 5d-290 | J.M.Parker | |
| **1978-79 in NEW ZEALAND** | | | | | | |
| Christchurch-Pakistan 128 runs | 290 | 176 | •271 | 6d-323 | M.G.Burgess | Mushtaq Mohammad |
| Napier-Drawn | 402 | - | •360 | 3d-234 | | |
| Auckland-Drawn | •254 | 8d-281 | 359 | 0-8 | | |
| **1984-85 in PAKISTAN** | | | | | | |
| Lahore[2]-Pakistan 6 wkts | •157 | 241 | 221 | 4-181 | J.V.Coney | Zaheer Abbas |
| Hyderabad-Pakistan 7 wkts | •267 | 189 | 230 | 3-230 | | |
| Karachi[1]-Drawn | 426 | - | •328 | 5-308 | | |
| **1984-85 in NEW ZEALAND** | | | | | | |
| Wellington-Drawn | •492 | 4-103 | 322 | - | G.P.Howarth | Javed Miandad |
| Christchurch-New Zealand inns & 99 runs | 9d-451 | - | •169 | 183 | | |
| Dunedin-New Zealand 2 wkts | 220 | 8-278 | •274 | 223 | | |
| **1988-89 in NEW ZEALAND** | | | | | | |
| Dunedin-Abandoned | - | - | - | - | J.G.Wright | Imran Khan |
| Wellington-Drawn | •447 | 8-186 | 7d-438 | - | | |
| Auckland-Drawn | 403 | 3-99 | •5d-616 | - | | |
| **1990-91 in PAKISTAN** | | | | | | |
| Karachi[1]-Pakistan inns & 43 runs | •196 | 194 | 6d-433 | - | M.D.Crowe | Javed Miandad |
| Lahore[2]-Pakistan 9 wkts | •160 | 287 | 9d-373 | 1-77 | | |
| Faisalabad-Pakistan 65 runs | 217 | 177 | •102 | 357 | | |
| **1992-93 in NEW ZEALAND** | | | | | | |
| Auckland-Pakistan 33 runs | 264 | 93 | •216 | 174 | K.R.Rutherford | Javed Miandad |

| **NEW ZEALAND v PAKISTAN** (cont.) | New Zealand | | Pakistan | | Captains | |
|---|---|---|---|---|---|---|
| Venue and Result | 1st | 2nd | 1st | 2nd | New Zealand | Pakistan |
| **1993-94 in NEW ZEALAND** | | | | | | |
| Auckland-Pakistan 5 wkts | •242 | 110 | 215 | 5-141 | K.R.Rutherford | Saleem Malik |
| Wellington-Pakistan inns & 12 runs | •175 | 361 | 5d-548 | - | | |
| Christchurch-New Zealand 5 wkts | 200 | 5-324 | •344 | 179 | | |
| **1995-96 in NEW ZEALAND** | | | | | | |
| Christchurch-Pakistan 161 runs | 286 | 195 | •208 | 434 | L.K.Germon | Wasim Akram |
| **1996-97 in PAKISTAN** | | | | | | |
| Lahore[2]-New Zealand 44 runs | •155 | 311 | 191 | 231 | L.K.Germon | Saeed Anwar |
| Rawalpindi[2]-Pakistan inns & 13 runs | •249 | 168 | 430 | - | | |

## Test Match Results Summary

### NEW ZEALAND v PAKISTAN-IN NEW ZEALAND

| | | Result | | | Wellington | | | Auckland | | | Christchurch | | | Dunedin | | | Napier | | | Hamilton | | |
|---|---|---|---|---|---|---|---|---|---|---|---|---|---|---|---|---|---|---|---|---|---|---|
| | Tests | NZ | P | D | NZ | P | D | NZ | P | D | NZ | P | D | NZ | P | D | NZ | P | D | NZ | P | D |
| 1964-65 | 3 | - | - | 3 | - | - | 1 | - | - | 1 | - | - | 1 | - | - | - | - | - | - | - | - | - |
| 1972-73 | 3 | - | 1 | 2 | - | - | 1 | - | - | 1 | - | - | - | - | 1 | - | - | - | - | - | - | - |
| 1978-79 | 3 | - | 1 | 2 | - | - | - | - | - | 1 | - | 1 | - | - | - | - | - | - | 1 | - | - | - |
| 1984-85 | 3 | 2 | - | 1 | - | - | 1 | 1 | - | - | - | - | - | 1 | - | - | - | - | - | - | - | - |
| 1988-89 | 2 | - | - | 2 | - | - | 1 | - | - | 1 | - | - | - | - | - | - | - | - | - | - | - | - |
| 1992-93 | 1 | - | 1 | - | - | - | - | - | - | - | - | - | - | - | - | - | - | - | - | - | 1 | - |
| 1993-94 | 3 | 1 | 2 | - | - | - | 1 | - | - | 1 | 1 | - | - | - | - | - | - | - | - | - | - | - |
| 1995-96 | 1 | - | 1 | - | - | - | - | - | - | - | - | 1 | - | - | - | - | - | - | - | - | - | - |
| | 19 | 3 | 6 | 10 | - | - | 5 | 1 | - | 5 | 1 | 2 | 1 | 1 | 1 | - | - | - | 1 | - | 1 | - |

### NEW ZEALAND v PAKISTAN-IN PAKISTAN

| | | Result | | | Karachi[1] | | | Lahore | | | Dacca | | | Rawalpindi[1] | | | Hyderabad | | | Faisalabad | | | Rawalpindi[2] | | |
|---|---|---|---|---|---|---|---|---|---|---|---|---|---|---|---|---|---|---|---|---|---|---|---|---|---|
| | Tests | NZ | P | D | NZ | P | D | NZ | P | D | NZ | P | D | NZ | P | D | NZ | P | D | NZ | P | D | NZ | P | D |
| 1955-56 | 3 | - | 2 | 1 | - | 1 | - | - | 1 | - | - | - | 1 | - | - | - | - | - | - | - | - | - | - | - | - |
| 1964-65 | 3 | - | 2 | 1 | - | 1 | - | - | - | 1 | - | - | - | - | 1 | - | - | - | - | - | - | - | - | - | - |
| 1969-70 | 3 | 1 | - | 2 | - | - | 1 | 1 | - | - | - | - | 1 | - | - | - | - | - | - | - | - | - | - | - | - |
| 1976-77 | 3 | - | 2 | 1 | - | - | 1 | - | 1 | - | - | - | - | - | - | - | - | 1 | - | - | - | - | - | - | - |
| 1984-85 | 3 | - | 2 | 1 | - | - | 1 | - | 1 | - | - | - | - | - | - | - | - | 1 | - | - | - | - | - | - | - |
| 1990-91 | 3 | - | 3 | - | - | 1 | - | - | 1 | - | - | - | - | - | - | - | - | - | - | - | 1 | - | - | - | - |
| 1996-97 | 2 | 1 | 1 | - | - | - | - | 1 | - | - | - | - | - | - | - | - | - | - | - | - | - | - | - | 1 | - |
| | 20 | 2 | 12 | 6 | - | 3 | 3 | 2 | 4 | 1 | - | - | 2 | - | 1 | - | - | 2 | - | - | 1 | - | - | 1 | - |
| Totals | 39 | 5 | 18 | 16 | | | | | | | | | | | | | | | | | | | | | |

**HIGHEST INNINGS TOTALS**

| | | | |
|---|---|---|---|
| New Zealand in New Zealand | 492 | Wellington | 1984-85 |
| New Zealand in Pakistan | 6d-482 | Lahore[2] | 1964-65 |
| Pakistan in New Zealand | 5d-616 | Auckland | 1988-89 |
| Pakistan in Pakistan | 9d-565 | Karachi[1] | 1976-77 |

**LOWEST INNINGS TOTALS**

| | | | |
|---|---|---|---|
| New Zealand in New Zealand | 93 | Hamilton | 1992-93 |
| New Zealand in Pakistan | 70 | Dacca | 1955-56 |
| Pakistan in New Zealand | 169 | Auckland | 1984-85 |
| Pakistan in Pakistan | 102 | Faisalabad | 1990-91 |

| | | | |
|---|---|---|---|
| **HIGHEST MATCH AGGREGATE** | 1585 for 31 wickets | Karachi[1] | 1976-77 |
| **LOWEST MATCH AGGREGATE** | 572 for 30 wickets | Rawalpindi[1] | 1964-65 |

**HIGHEST INDIVIDUAL INNINGS**

| | | | | |
|---|---|---|---|---|
| New Zealand in New Zealand | 174 | M.D.Crowe | Wellington | 1988-89 |
| New Zealand in Pakistan | 152 | W.K.Lees | Karachi[1] | 1976-77 |
| Pakistan in New Zealand | 201 | Javed Miandad | Auckland | 1988-89 |
| Pakistan in Pakistan | 209 | Imtiaz Ahmed | Lahore[1] | 1955-56 |

**HIGHEST AGGREGATE OF RUNS IN A SERIES**

| | | | |
|---|---|---|---|
| New Zealand in New Zealand | 333 (av 83.25) | J.F.Reid | 1984-85 |
| New Zealand in Pakistan | 296 (av 59.20) | J.R.Reid | 1964-65 |
| Pakistan in New Zealand | 389 (av 194.50) | Javed Miandad | 1988-89 |
| Pakistan in Pakistan | 507 (av 169.00) | Shoaib Mohammad | 1990-91 |

**RECORD WICKET PARTNERSHIPS-NEW ZEALAND**

| | | | | |
|---|---|---|---|---|
| 1st | 159 | R.E.Redmond (107), G.M.Turner (58) | Auckland | 1972-73 |
| 2nd | 195 | J.G.Wright (88), G.P.Howarth (114) | Napier | 1978-79 |
| 3rd | 178 | B.W.Sinclair (130), J.R.Reid (88) | Lahore[2] | 1964-65 |
| 4th | 128 | B.F.Hastings (72), M.G.Burgess (79) | Wellington | 1972-73 |
| 5th | 183 | M.G.Burgess (111), R.W.Anderson (92) | Lahore[2] | 1976-77 |
| 6th | 145 | J.F.Reid (148), R.J.Hadlee (87) | Wellington | 1984-85 |
| 7th | 186 | W.K.Lees (152), R.J.Hadlee (87) | Karachi[1] | 1976-77 |
| 8th | 100 | B.W.Yuile (47*), D.R.Hadlee (56) | Karachi[1] | 1969-70 |
| 9th | 96 | M.G.Burgess (119*), R.S.Cunis (23) | Dacca | 1969-70 |
| 10th | 151 | B.F.Hastings (110), R.O.Collinge (68*) | Auckland | 1972-73 |

**RECORD WICKET PARTNERSHIPS-PAKISTAN**

| | | | | |
|---|---|---|---|---|
| 1st | 172 | Rameez Raja (78), Shoaib Mohammad (203*) | Karachi[1] | 1990-91 |
| 2nd | 262 | Saeed Anwar (149), Ijaz Ahmed (125) | Rawalpindi[2] | 1996-97 |
| 3rd | 248 | Shoaib Mohammad (112), Javed Miandad (271) | Auckland | 1988-89 |
| 4th | 350 | Mushtaq Mohammad (201), Asif Iqbal (175) | Dunedin | 1972-73 |
| 5th | 281 | Javed Miandad (163), Asif Iqbal (166) | Lahore[2] | 1976-77 |
| 6th | 217 | Hanif Mohammad (203*), Majid Khan (80) | Lahore[2] | 1964-65 |
| 7th | 308 | Waqar Hassan (189), Imtiaz Ahmed (209) | Lahore[1] | 1955-56 |
| 8th | 89 | Anil Dalpat (52), Iqbal Qasim (45*) | Karachi[1] | 1984-85 |
| 9th | 52 | Intikhab Alam (45), Arif Butt (20) | Auckland | 1964-65 |
| 10th | 65 | Salahuddin (34*), Mohammad Farooq (47) | Rawalpindi[1] | 1964-65 |

**BEST INNINGS BOWLING ANALYSIS**

| | | | | |
|---|---|---|---|---|
| New Zealand in New Zealand | 6-51 | R.J.Hadlee | Dunedin | 1984-85 |
| New Zealand in Pakistan | 7-52 | C.Pringle | Faisalabad | 1990-91 |
| Pakistan in New Zealand | 7-52 | Intikhab Alam | Dunedin | 1972-73 |
| Pakistan in Pakistan | 7-52 | Waqar Younis | Faisalabad | 1990-91 |

**BEST MATCH BOWLING ANALYSIS**

| | | | | |
|---|---|---|---|---|
| New Zealand in New Zealand | 9-70 | F.J.Cameron | Auckland | 1964-65 |
| New Zealand in Pakistan | 11-152 | C.Pringle | Faisalabad | 1990-91 |
| Pakistan in New Zealand | 11-130 | Intikhab Alam | Dunedin | 1972-73 |
| Pakistan in Pakistan | 12-130 | Waqar Younis | Faisalabad | 1990-91 |

**HIGHEST AGGREGATE OF WICKETS IN A SERIES**

| | | | |
|---|---|---|---|
| New Zealand in New Zealand | 18 (av 23.00) | R.J.Hadlee | 1978-79 |
| New Zealand in Pakistan | 16 (av 20.18) | H.J.Howarth | 1969-70 |
| Pakistan in New Zealand | 25 (av 17.24) | Wasim Akram | 1993-94 |
| Pakistan in Pakistan | 29 (av 10.86) | Waqar Younis | 1990-91 |

| **NEW ZEALAND v SRI LANKA** | New Zealand | | Sri Lanka | | Captains | |
|---|---|---|---|---|---|---|
| Venue and Result | 1st | 2nd | 1st | 2nd | New Zealand | Sri Lanka |
| **1982-83 in NEW ZEALAND** | | | | | | |
| Christchurch-New Zealand inns & 25 runs | •344 | - | 144 | 175 | G.P.Howarth | D.S.de Silva |
| Wellington-New Zealand 6 wkts | 201 | 4-134 | •240 | 93 | | |
| **1983-84 in SRI LANKA** | | | | | | |
| Kandy-New Zealand 165 runs | •276 | 8d-201 | 215 | 97 | G.P.Howarth | L.R.D.Mendis |
| Colombo (SSC)-Drawn | 198 | 4-123 | •174 | 9d-289 | | |
| Colombo (CCC)-New Zealand inns & 61 runs | 459 | - | •256 | 142 | | |
| **1986-87 in SRI LANKA** | | | | | | |
| Colombo (CCC)-Drawn | 5-406 | - | •9d-397 | - | J.J.Crowe | L.R.D.Mendis |
| **1990-91 in NEW ZEALAND** | | | | | | |
| Wellington-Drawn | •174 | 4-671 | 497 | - | M.D.Crowe | A.Ranatunga |
| Hamilton-Drawn | •296 | 6d-374 | 253 | 6-344 | M.D.Crowe | |
| Auckland-Drawn | 317 | 5-261 | •380 | 319 | I.D.S.Smith | |
| **1992-93 in SRI LANKA** | | | | | | |
| Moratuwa-Drawn | •288 | 5-195 | 6d-327 | - | M.D.Crowe | A.Ranatunga |
| Colombo (SSC)-Sri Lanka 9 wkts | 102 | 361 | •394 | 1-70 | | |
| **1994-95 in NEW ZEALAND** | | | | | | |
| Napier-Sri Lanka 241 runs | 109 | 185 | •183 | 352 | K.R.Rutherford | A.Ranatunga |
| Dunedin-Drawn | 307 | 0-0 | •233 | 411 | | |
| **1996-97 in NEW ZEALAND** | | | | | | |
| Dunedin-New Zealand inns & 36 runs | •7d-586 | - | 222 | 328 | S.P.Fleming | A.Ranatunga |
| Hamilton-New Zealand 120 runs | •222 | 273 | 170 | 205 | | |
| **1997-98 in SRI LANKA** | | | | | | |
| Colombo (PIS)-New Zealand 167 runs | •305 | 6d-444 | 285 | 297 | S.P.Fleming | A.Ranatunga |
| Galle-Sri Lanka inns & 16 runs | •193 | 114 | 323 | - | | |
| Colombo (SSC)-Sri Lanka 164 runs | 193 | 131 | •206 | 282 | | |

## Test Match Results Summary

**NEW ZEALAND v SRI LANKA-IN NEW ZEALAND**

| | | Result | | | Christchurch | | | Wellington | | | Hamilton | | | Auckland | | | Napier | | | Dunedin | | |
|---|---|---|---|---|---|---|---|---|---|---|---|---|---|---|---|---|---|---|---|---|---|---|
| | Tests | NZ | SL | D | NZ | SL | D | NZ | SL | D | NZ | SL | D | NZ | SL | D | NZ | SL | D | NZ | SL | D |
| 1982-83 | 2 | 2 | - | - | 1 | - | - | 1 | - | - | - | - | - | - | - | - | - | - | - | - | - | - |
| 1990-91 | 3 | - | - | 3 | - | - | - | - | - | 1 | - | - | 1 | - | - | 1 | - | - | - | - | - | - |
| 1994-95 | 2 | - | 1 | 1 | - | - | - | - | - | - | - | - | - | - | - | - | - | 1 | - | - | - | 1 |
| 1996-97 | 2 | 2 | - | - | - | - | - | - | - | - | 1 | - | - | - | - | - | - | - | - | 1 | - | - |
| | 9 | 4 | 1 | 4 | 1 | - | - | 1 | - | 1 | 1 | - | 1 | - | - | 1 | - | 1 | - | 1 | - | 1 |

**NEW ZEALAND v SRI LANKA-IN SRI LANKA**

| | | Result | | | Kandy | | | Colombo(SSC) | | | Colombo(CCC) | | | Moratuwa | | | Colombo(PIS) | | | Galle | | |
|---|---|---|---|---|---|---|---|---|---|---|---|---|---|---|---|---|---|---|---|---|---|---|
| | Tests | NZ | SL | D | NZ | SL | D | NZ | SL | D | NZ | SL | D | NZ | SL | D | NZ | SL | D | NZ | SL | D |
| 1983-84 | 3 | 2 | - | 1 | 1 | - | - | - | - | 1 | 1 | - | - | - | - | - | - | - | - | - | - | - |
| 1986-87 | 1 | - | - | 1 | - | - | - | - | - | - | - | - | 1 | - | - | - | - | - | - | - | - | - |
| 1992-93 | 2 | - | 1 | 1 | - | - | - | - | 1 | - | - | - | - | - | - | 1 | - | - | - | - | - | - |
| 1997-98 | 3 | 1 | 2 | - | - | - | - | - | 1 | - | - | - | - | - | - | - | 1 | - | - | - | 1 | - |
| | 9 | 3 | 3 | 3 | 1 | - | - | - | 2 | 1 | 1 | - | 1 | - | - | 1 | 1 | - | - | - | 1 | - |
| Totals | 18 | 7 | 4 | 7 | | | | | | | | | | | | | | | | | | |

**HIGHEST INNINGS TOTALS**

| | | | |
|---|---|---|---|
| New Zealand in New Zealand | 4-671 | Wellington | 1990-91 |
| New Zealand in Sri Lanka | 459 | Colombo (CCC) | 1983-84 |
| Sri Lanka in New Zealand | 497 | Wellington | 1990-91 |
| Sri Lanka in Sri Lanka | 9d-397 | Colombo (CCC) | 1986-87 |

**LOWEST INNINGS TOTALS**

| | | | |
|---|---|---|---|
| New Zealand in New Zealand | 109 | Napier | 1994-95 |
| New Zealand in Sri Lanka | 102 | Colombo (SSC) | 1992-93 |
| Sri Lanka in New Zealand | 93 | Wellington | 1987-88 |
| Sri Lanka in Sri Lanka | 97 | Kandy | 1983-84 |

| | | | |
|---|---|---|---|
| **HIGHEST MATCH AGGREGATE** | 1342 for 23 wickets | Wellington | 1990-91 |
| **LOWEST MATCH AGGREGATE** | 663 for 30 wickets | Christchurch | 1982-83 |

**HIGHEST INDIVIDUAL INNINGS**

| | | | | |
|---|---|---|---|---|
| New Zealand in New Zealand | 299 | M.D.Crowe | Wellington | 1990-91 |
| New Zealand in Sri Lanka | 180 | J.F.Reid | Colombo (CCC) | 1983-84 |
| Sri Lanka in New Zealand | 267 | P.A.de Silva | Wellington | 1990-91 |
| Sri Lanka in Sri Lanka | 201* | D.S.B.P.Kuruppu | Colombo (CCC) | 1986-87 |

**HIGHEST AGGREGATE ON RUNS IN A SERIES**

| | | | |
|---|---|---|---|
| New Zealand in New Zealand | 513 (av 102.60) | A.H.Jones | 1990-91 |
| New Zealand in Sri Lanka | 359 (av 71.80) | S.P.Fleming | 1983-84 |
| Sri Lanka in New Zealand | 493 (av 98.60) | P.A.de Silva | 1990-91 |
| Sri Lanka in Sri Lanka | 300 (av 60.00) | D.P.M.Jayawardene | 1997-98 |

**RECORD WICKET PARTNERSHIPS-NEW ZEALAND**

| | | | | |
|---|---|---|---|---|
| 1st | 161 | T.J.Franklin (69), J.G.Wright (101) | Hamilton | 1990-91 |
| 2nd | 141 | B.A.Young (267*), M.J.Horne (66) | Dunedin | 1996-97 |
| 3rd | 467 | A.H.Jones (188), M.D.Crowe (299) | Wellington | 1990-91 |
| 4th | 240 | S.P.Fleming (176*), C.D.McMillan (142) | Colombo (PIS) | 1997-98 |
| 5th | 151 | K.R.Rutherford (105), C.Z.Harris (56) | Moratuwa | 1992-93 |
| 6th | 246* | J.J.Crowe (120*), R.J.Hadlee (151*) | Colombo (CCC) | 1986-87 |
| 7th | 47 | D.N.Patel (52), M.L.Su'a (20*) | Dunedin | 1994-95 |
| 8th | 79 | J.V.Coney (84), W.K.Lees (89) | Christchurch | 1982-83 |
| 9th | 43 | A.C.Parore (30), P.J.Wiseman (23) | Galle | 1997-98 |
| 10th | 52 | W.K.Lees (89), E.J.Chatfield (10*) | Christchurch | 1982-83 |

**RECORD WICKET PARTNERSHIPS-SRI LANKA**

| | | | | |
|---|---|---|---|---|
| 1st | 102 | R.S.Mahanama (109), U.C.Hathurusingha (27) | Colombo (SSC) | 1992-93 |
| 2nd | 137 | R.S.Mahanama (153), A.P.Gurusinha (43) | Moratuwa | 1992-93 |
| 3rd | 159*† | S.Wettimuny (65), R.L.Dias (108) | Colombo (SSC) | 1983-84 |
| 4th | 192 | A.P.Gurusinha (127), H.P.Tillakaratne (108) | Dunedin | 1994-95 |
| 5th | 130 | R.S.Madugalle (79), D.S.de Silva (61) | Wellington | 1982-83 |
| 6th | 109§ | R.S.Madugalle (89*), A.Ranatunga (37) | Colombo (CCC) | 1983-84 |
| | 109 | D.S.B.P.Kuruppu (201*), R.S.Madugalle (60) | Colombo (CCC) | 1986-87 |
| 7th | 138 | R.S.Kaluwitharana (103), W.P.U.J.C.Vaas (57) | Dunedin | 1996-97 |
| 8th | 73 | H.P.Tillakaratne (55), G.P.Wickramasinghe (43) | Dunedin | 1996-97 |
| 9th | 31 | G.F.Labrooy (70*), R.J.Ratnayake (18) | Auckland | 1990-91 |
| | 31 | S.T.Jayasuriya (12*), R.J.Ratnayake (20) | Auckland | 1990-91 |
| 10th | 71 | R.S.Kaluwitharana (88), M.Muralidaran (26*) | Colombo (SSC) | 1997-98 |

*† 163 runs were added for this wicket, S.Wettimuny retired hurt and was replaced by L.R.D.Mendis after 159 had been scored.*

*§ 119 runs were added for this wicket, R.S.Madugalle retired hurt and was replaced by D.S.de Silva after 109 had been scored.*

**BEST INNINGS BOWLING ANALYSIS**

| | | | | |
|---|---|---|---|---|
| New Zealand in New Zealand | 5-58 | S.B.Doull | Dunedin | 1996-97 |
| New Zealand in Sri Lanka | 5-28 | D.L.Vettori | Colombo (SSC) | 1997-98 |
| Sri Lanka in New Zealand | 6-87 | W.P.J.U.C.Vaas | Dunedin | 1994-95 |
| Sri Lanka in Sri Lanka | 6-72 | H.D.P.K.Dharmasena | Galle | 1997-98 |

**BEST MATCH BOWLING ANALYSIS**

| | | | | |
|---|---|---|---|---|
| New Zealand in New Zealand | 9-130 | D.L.Vettori | Hamilton | 1996-97 |
| New Zealand in Sri Lanka | 10-102 | R.J.Hadlee | Colombo (CCC) | 1983-84 |
| Sri Lanka in New Zealand | 10-90 | W.P.J.U.C.Vaas | Napier | 1994-95 |
| Sri Lanka in Sri Lanka | 9-83 | M.L.C.N.Bandaratilleke | Galle | 1997-98 |

**HIGHEST AGGREGATE OF WICKETS IN A SERIES**

| | | | |
|---|---|---|---|
| New Zealand in New Zealand | 13 (av 36.61) | D.K.Morrison | 1990-91 |
| New Zealand in Sri Lanka | 23 (av 10.00) | R.J.Hadlee | 1983-84 |
| Sri Lanka in New Zealand | 16 (av 11.06) | W.P.J.U.C.Vaas | 1994-95 |
| Sri Lanka in Sri Lanka | 19 (av 19.78) | M.Muralidaran | 1997-98 |

| **NEW ZEALAND v ZIMBABWE** | New Zealand | | Zimbabwe | | Captains | |
|---|---|---|---|---|---|---|
| Venue and Result | 1st | 2nd | 1st | 2nd | New Zealand | Zimbabwe |
| **1992-93 in ZIMBABWE** | | | | | | |
| Bulawayo[1]-Drawn | •3d-325 | 5d-222 | 219 | 1-197 | M.D.Crowe | D.L.Houghton |
| Harare-New Zealand won by 177 runs | •335 | 5d-262 | 9d-283 | 137 | | |
| **1995-96 in NEW ZEALAND** | | | | | | |
| Hamilton-Drawn | •8d230 | 5d222 | 196 | 6-208 | L.K.Germon | A.Flower |
| Auckland-Drawn | •251 | 5d-441 | 9d-326 | 4-246 | | |
| **1997-98 in ZIMBABWE** | | | | | | |
| Harare-Drawn | 207 | 8-304 | •298 | 9d-311 | S.P.Fleming | A.D.R.Campbell |
| Bulawayo[2]-Drawn | 403 | 8-275 | •461 | 8d-227 | | |
| **1997-98 in NEW ZEALAND** | | | | | | |
| Wellington-New Zealand 10 wkts | 411 | 0-20 | •180 | 250 | S.P.Fleming | A.D.R.Campbell |
| Auckland-New Zealand inns & 13 runs | 460 | - | •170 | 277 | | |

## Test Match Results Summary

**\NEW ZEALAND v ZIMBABWE-IN NEW ZEALAND**

| | | Result | | | Auckland | | | Hamilton | | | Wellington | | |
|---|---|---|---|---|---|---|---|---|---|---|---|---|---|
| | Tests | NZ | Z | D | NZ | Z | D | NZ | Z | D | NZ | Z | D |
| 1995-96 | 2 | - | - | 2 | - | - | 1 | - | - | 1 | - | - | - |
| 1997-98 | 2 | 2 | - | - | 1 | - | - | - | - | - | 1 | - | - |
| | 4 | 2 | - | 2 | 1 | - | 1 | - | - | 1 | 1 | - | - |

**NEW ZEALAND v ZIMBABWE-IN ZIMBABWE**

| | | Result | | | Harare | | | Bulawayo[1] | | | Bulawayo[2] | | |
|---|---|---|---|---|---|---|---|---|---|---|---|---|---|
| | Tests | NZ | Z | D | NZ | Z | D | NZ | Z | D | NZ | Z | D |
| 1992-93 | 2 | 1 | - | 1 | 1 | - | - | - | - | 1 | - | - | - |
| 1997-98 | 2 | - | - | 2 | - | - | 1 | - | - | - | - | - | 1 |
| | 4 | 1 | - | 3 | 1 | - | 1 | - | - | 1 | - | - | 1 |
| Totals | 8 | 3 | - | 5 | | | | | | | | | |

**HIGHEST INNINGS TOTALS**

| | | | |
|---|---|---|---|
| New Zealand in New Zealand | 460 | Auckland | 1997-98 |
| New Zealand in Zimbabwe | 403 | Bulawayo[2] | 1997-98 |
| Zimbabwe in New Zealand | 9-326 | Auckland | 1995-96 |
| Zimbabwe in Zimbabwe | 461 | Bulawayo[2] | 1997-98 |

**LOWEST INNINGS TOTALS**

| | | | |
|---|---|---|---|
| New Zealand in New Zealand | 251 | Auckland | 1995-96 |
| New Zealand in Zimbabwe | 335 | Harare | 1992-93 |
| Zimbabwe in New Zealand | 170 | Auckland | 1997-98 |
| Zimbabwe in Zimbabwe | 137 | Harare | 1992-93 |

| | | | |
|---|---|---|---|
| **HIGHEST MATCH AGGREGATE** | 1417 for 34 wickets | Harare | 1992-93 |
| **LOWEST MATCH AGGREGATE** | 852 for 29 wickets | Hamilton | 1995-96 |

**HIGHEST INDIVIDUAL INNINGS**

| | | | | |
|---|---|---|---|---|
| New Zealand in New Zealand | 157 | M.J.Horne | Auckland | 1997-98 |
| New Zealand in Zimbabwe | 140 | M.D.Crowe | Harare | 1992-93 |
| Zimbabwe in New Zealand | 104+ | D.L.Houghton | Auckland | 1995-96 |
| Zimbabwe in Zimbabwe | 203* | G.J.Whittall | Bulawayo[2] | 1997-98 |

**HIGHEST AGGREGATE ON RUNS IN A SERIES**

| | | | |
|---|---|---|---|
| New Zealand in New Zealand | 227 (av 113.50) | C.D.McMillan | 1997-98 |
| New Zealand in Zimbabwe | 249 (av 62.25) | M.D.Crowe | 1992-93 |
| Zimbabwe in New Zealand | 166 (av 83.00) | D.L.Houghton | 1995-96 |
| Zimbabwe in Zimbabwe | 387 (av 96.75) | G.J.Whittall | 1997-98 |

**RECORD WICKET PARTNERSHIPS-NEW ZEALAND**

| | | | | |
|---|---|---|---|---|
| 1st | 214 | C.M.Spearman (112), R.G.Twose (94) | Auckland | 1995-96 |
| 2nd | 127 | R.T.Latham (119), A.H.Jones (67*) | Bulawayo[1] | 1992-93 |
| 3rd | 71 | A.H.Jones (67*), M.D.Crowe (42) | Bulawayo[1] | 1992-93 |
| 4th | 243 | M.J.Horne (157), N.J.Astle (114) | Auckland | 1997-98 |
| 5th | 166 | A.C.Parore (76*), C.L.Cairns (120) | Auckland | 1995-96 |
| 6th | 82* | A.C.Parore (84*), L.K.Germon (22*) | Hamilton | 1995-96 |
| 7th | 108 | C.D.McMillan (139), D.J.Nash (41) | Wellington | 1997-98 |
| 8th | 112 | C.Z.Harris (71), D.L.Vettori (90) | Bulawayo[2] | 1997-98 |
| 9th | 18 | D.L.Vettori (90), S.B.O'Connor (7) | Bulawayo[2] | 1997-98 |
| 10th | 27 | C.D.McMillan (88), S.B.Doull (6*) | Auckland | 1997-98 |

**RECORD WICKET PARTNERSHIPS-ZIMBABWE**

| | | | | |
|---|---|---|---|---|
| 1st | 156 | G.J.Rennie (57), G.W.Flower (151) | Harare | 1997-98 |
| 2nd | 107 | K.J.Arnott (68), A.D.R.Campbell (52) | Harare | 1992-93 |
| 3rd | 70 | A.Flower (39), G.J.Whittall (203*) | Bulawayo[2] | 1997-98 |
| 4th | 88 | D.L.Houghton (104+), A.Flower (35) | Auckland | 1995-96 |
| 5th | 78 | G.J.Whittall (203*), D.L.Houghton (32) | Bulawayo[2] | 1997-98 |
| 6th | 70 | D.L.Houghton (36), A.Flower (81) | Bulawayo[1] | 1992-93 |
| 7th | 91 | G.J.Whittall (54), P.A.Strang (49) | Hamilton | 1995-96 |
| 8th | 94 | A.D.R.Campbell (56), H.H.Streak (43*) | Wellington | 1997-98 |
| 9th | 46 | G.J.Crocker (33), M.G.Burmester (17*) | Harare | 1992-93 |
| 10th | 40 | G.J.Whittall (203*), E.Matambanadzo (4) | Bulawayo[2] | 1997-98 |

**BEST INNINGS BOWLING ANALYSIS**

| | | | | |
|---|---|---|---|---|
| New Zealand in New Zealand | 4-35 | S.B.Doull | Auckland | 1997-98 |
| New Zealand in Zimbabwe | 6-50 | D.N.Patel | Harare | 1992-93 |
| Zimbabwe in New Zealand | 4-52 | H.H.Streak | Hamilton | 1995-96 |
| Zimbabwe in Zimbabwe | 6-109 | A.G.Huckle | Bulawayo[2] | 1997-98 |

**BEST MATCH BOWLING ANALYSIS**

| | | | | |
|---|---|---|---|---|
| New Zealand in New Zealand | 8-85 | S.B.Doull | Auckland | 1997-98 |
| New Zealand in Zimbabwe | 8-131 | D.N.Patel | Harare | 1992-93 |
| Zimbabwe in New Zealand | 7-160 | H.H.Streak | Auckland | 1995-96 |
| Zimbabwe in Zimbabwe | 11-255 | A.G.Huckle | Bulawayo[2] | 1997-98 |

**HIGHEST AGGREGATE OF WICKETS IN A SERIES**

| | | | |
|---|---|---|---|
| New Zealand in New Zealand | 11 (av 13.63) | S.B.Doull | 1997-98 |
| | 11 (av 22.09) | C.L.Cairns | 1997-98 |
| New Zealand in Zimbabwe | 15 (av 20.26) | D.N.Patel | 1992-93 |
| Zimbabwe in New Zealand | 12 (av 22.33) | H.H.Streak | 1995-96 |
| Zimbabwe in Zimbabwe | 16 (av 23.18) | A.G.Huckle | 1997-98 |

| INDIA v PAKISTAN | India | | Pakistan | | Captains | |
|---|---|---|---|---|---|---|
| Venue and Result | 1st | 2nd | 1st | 2nd | India | Pakistan |
| **1952-53 In INDIA** | | | | | | |
| Delhi-India inns & 70 runs | •372 | - | 150 | 152 | N.B.Amarnath | A.H.Kardar |
| Lucknow[1]-Pakistan inns & 43 runs | •106 | 182 | 331 | - | | |
| Bombay[2]-India 10 wkts | 4d-387 | 0-45 | •186 | 242 | | |
| Madras[1]-Drawn | 6-175 | - | •344 | - | | |
| Calcutta-Drawn | 397 | 0-28 | •257 | 7d-236 | | |
| **1954-55 In PAKISTAN** | | | | | | |
| Dacca-Drawn | 148 | 2-147 | •257 | 158 | M.H.Mankad | A.H.Kardar |
| Bahawalpur-Drawn | •235 | 5-209 | 9d-312 | - | | |
| Lahore[1]-Drawn | 251 | 2-74 | •328 | 5d-136 | | |
| Peshawar[1]-Drawn | 245 | 1-23 | •188 | 182 | | |
| Karachi[1]-Drawn | 145 | 2-69 | •162 | 5d-241 | | |
| **1960-61 In INDIA** | | | | | | |
| Bombay[2]-Drawn | 9d-449 | - | •350 | 4-166 | N.J.Contractor | Fazal Mahmood |
| Kanpur-Drawn | 404 | - | •335 | 3-140 | | |
| Calcutta-Drawn | 180 | 4-127 | •301 | 3d-146 | | |
| Madras[2]-Drawn | 9d-539 | - | •8d-448 | 0-59 | | |
| Delhi-Drawn | •463 | 0-16 | 286 | 250 | | |
| **1978-79 In PAKISTAN** | | | | | | |
| Faisalabad-Drawn | 9d-462 | 0-43 | •8d-503 | 4d-264 | B.S.Bedi | Mushtaq Mohammad |
| Lahore[2]-Pakistan 8 wkts | •199 | 465 | 6d-539 | 2-182 | | |
| Karachi[1]-Pakistan 8 wkts | •344 | 300 | 9d-481 | 2-164 | | |
| **1979-80 IN INDIA** | | | | | | |
| Bangalore-Drawn | 416 | - | •9d-431 | 2-108 | S.M.Gavaskar | Asif Iqbal |
| Delhi-Drawn | 126 | 6-364 | •273 | 242 | S.M.Gavaskar | |
| Bombay[3]-India 131 runs | •334 | 160 | 173 | 190 | S.M.Gavaskar | |
| Kanpur-Drawn | •162 | 2-193 | 249 | - | S.M.Gavaskar | |
| Madras[1]-India 10 wkts | 430 | 0-78 | •272 | 233 | S.M.Gavaskar | |
| Calcutta-Drawn | •331 | 205 | 4d-272 | 6-179 | G.R.Viswanath | |
| **1982-83 In PAKISTAN** | | | | | | |
| Lahore[2]-Drawn | 379 | - | •485 | 1-135 | S.M.Gavaskar | Imran Khan |
| Karachi[1]-Pakistan inns & 86 runs | •169 | 197 | 452 | - | | |
| Faisalabad-Pakistan 10 wkts | •372 | 286 | 652 | 0-10 | | |
| Hyderabad-Pakistan inns & 119 runs | 189 | 273 | •3d-581 | - | | |
| Lahore[2]-Drawn | 3-235 | - | •323 | - | | |
| Karachi[1]-Drawn | •8d-393 | 2-224 | 6d-420 | - | | |
| **1983-84 IN INDIA** | | | | | | |
| Bangalore-Drawn | •275 | 0-176 | 288 | - | Kapil Dev | Zaheer Abbas |
| Jullundur-Drawn | 374 | - | •337 | 0-16 | | |
| Nagpur-Drawn | •245 | 8d-262 | 322 | 1-42 | | |
| **1984-85 In PAKISTAN** | | | | | | |
| Lahore[2]-Drawn | 156 | 6-371 | •9d-428 | - | S.M.Gavaskar | Zaheer Abbas |
| Faisalabad-Drawn | •500 | - | 6-674 | - | | |
| **1986-87 IN INDIA** | | | | | | |
| Madras[1]-Drawn | 9d-527 | - | •9d-487 | 3-182 | Kapil Dev | Imran Khan |
| Calcutta-Drawn | •403 | 3d-181 | 229 | 5-179 | | |
| Jaipur-Drawn | •8d-465 | 2-114 | 341 | - | | |
| Ahmedabad-Drawn | 323 | - | •395 | 2-135 | | |
| Bangalore-Pakistan 16 runs | 145 | 204 | •116 | 249 | | |

| INDIA v PAKISTAN (cont.) Venue and Result | India 1st | India 2nd | Pakistan 1st | Pakistan 2nd | Captains India | Captains Pakistan |
|---|---|---|---|---|---|---|
| **1989-90 In PAKISTAN** | | | | | | |
| Karachi[1]-Drawn | 262 | 3-303 | •409 | 5d-305 | K.Srikkanth | Imran Khan |
| Faisalabad-Drawn | •288 | 7-398 | 9d-423 | - | | |
| Lahore[2]-Drawn | •509 | - | 5-699 | - | | |
| Sialkot-Drawn | •324 | 7-234 | 250 | - | | |

## Test Match Results Summary

**INDIA v PAKISTAN-IN INDIA**

| | T | Result I P D | Delhi I P D | Luck. I P D | Bomb. I P D | Madras I P D | Calc. I P D | Kanpur I P D | Bang. I P D | Jull. I P D | Nagpur I P D | Jaipur I P D | Ahmed. I P D |
|---|---|---|---|---|---|---|---|---|---|---|---|---|---|
| 1952-53 | 5 | 2 1 2 | 1 - - | - 1 - | 1 - - | - - 1 | - - 1 | - - - | - - - | - - - | - - - | - - - | - - - |
| 1960-61 | 5 | - - 5 | - - 1 | - - - | - - 1 | - - 1 | - - 1 | - - 1 | - - - | - - - | - - - | - - - | - - - |
| 1979-80 | 6 | 2 - 4 | - - 1 | - - - | 1 - - | 1 - - | - - 1 | - - 1 | - - 1 | - - - | - - - | - - - | - - - |
| 1983-84 | 3 | - - 3 | - - - | - - - | - - - | - - - | - - - | - - - | - - 1 | - - 1 | - - 1 | - - - | - - - |
| 1986-87 | 5 | - 1 4 | - - - | - - - | - - - | - - 1 | - - 1 | - - - | - 1 - | - - - | - - - | - - 1 | - - 1 |
| | 24 | 4 2 18 | 1 - 2 | - 1 - | 2 - 1 | 1 - 3 | - - 4 | - - 2 | - 1 2 | - - 1 | - - 1 | - - 1 | - - 1 |

**INDIA v PAKISTAN-IN PAKISTAN**

| | Tests | Result I | Result P | Result D | Dacca I P D | Bah. I P D | Lahore I P D | Pesh. I P D | Karachi[1] I P D | Fais. I P D | Hyd. I P D | Sialkot I P D |
|---|---|---|---|---|---|---|---|---|---|---|---|---|
| 1954-55 | 5 | - | - | 5 | - - 1 | - - 1 | - - 1 | - - 1 | - - 1 | - - - | - - - | - - - |
| 1978-79 | 3 | - | 2 | 1 | - - - | - - - | - 1 - | - - - | - 1 - | - - 1 | - - - | - - - |
| 1982-83 | 6 | - | 3 | 3 | - - - | - - - | - - 2 | - - - | - 1 1 | - 1 - | - 1 - | - - - |
| 1984-85 | 2 | - | - | 2 | - - - | - - - | - - 1 | - - - | - - - | - - 1 | - - - | - - - |
| 1989-90 | 4 | - | - | 4 | - - - | - - - | - - 1 | - - - | - - 1 | - - 1 | - - - | - - 1 |
| | 20 | - | 5 | 15 | - - 1 | - - 1 | - 1 5 | - - 1 | - 2 3 | - 1 3 | - 1 - | - - 1 |
| Totals | 44 | 4 | 7 | 33 | | | | | | | | |

*Key to ground abbreviations: Luck. - Lucknow[1]; Bomb. - Mumbai; Calc. - Calcutta; Bang. - Bangalore; Jull. - Jullundur; Ahmed. - Ahmedabad; Bah. - Bahawalpur; Pesh. - Peshawar[1]; Fais. - Faisalabad; Hyd. - Hyderabad.*

**HIGHEST INNINGS TOTALS**

| | | | |
|---|---|---|---|
| India in India | 9d-539 | Madras[2] | 1960-61 |
| India in Pakistan | 509 | Lahore[2] | 1989-90 |
| Pakistan in India | 9d-487 | Madras[2] | 1960-61 |
| Pakistan in Pakistan | 5-699 | Lahore[2] | 1989-90 |

**LOWEST INNINGS TOTALS**

| | | | |
|---|---|---|---|
| India in India | 106 | Lucknow[1] | 1952-53 |
| India in Pakistan | 145 | Karachi[1] | 1954-55 |
| Pakistan in India | 116 | Delhi | 1986-87 |
| Pakistan in Pakistan | 158 | Dacca | 1954-55 |

| | | | |
|---|---|---|---|
| **HIGHEST MATCH AGGREGATE** | 1331 for 28 wickets | Lahore[2] | 1978-79 |
| **LOWEST MATCH AGGREGATE** | 619 for 30 wickets | Lucknow[1] | 1952-53 |

**HIGHEST INDIVIDUAL INNINGS**

| | | | | |
|---|---|---|---|---|
| India in India | 201 | A.D.Gaekwad | Jullundur | 1983-84 |
| India in Pakistan | 218 | S.V.Manjrekar | Lahore[2] | 1989-90 |
| Pakistan in India | 160 | Hanif Mohammad | Bombay[2] | 1960-61 |
| Pakistan in Pakistan | 280* | Javed Miandad | Hyderabad | 1982-83 |

**HIGHEST AGGREGATE OF RUNS IN A SERIES**

| | | | |
|---|---|---|---|
| India in India | 529 (av 52.90) | S.M.Gavaskar | 1979-80 |
| India in Pakistan | 584 (av 73.00) | M.Amarnath | 1982-83 |
| Pakistan in India | 460 (av 51.11) | Saeed Ahmed | 1960-61 |
| Pakistan in Pakistan | 761 (av 126.83) | Mudassar Nazar | 1982-83 |

**RECORD WICKET PARTNERSHIPS-INDIA**

| | | | | |
|---|---|---|---|---|
| 1st | 200 | S.M.Gavaskar (91), K.Srikkanth (123) | Madras[1] | 1986-87 |
| 2nd | 135 | N.S.Sidhu (85), S.V.Manjrekar (113) | Karachi[1] | 1989-90 |
| 3rd | 190 | M.Amarnath (120), Yasdhpal Sharma (63*) | Lahore[2] | 1982-83 |
| 4th | 186 | S.V.Manjrekar (218), R.J.Shastri (61) | Lahore[2] | 1989-90 |
| 5th | 200 | S.M.Patil (127), R.J.Shastri (139) | Faisalabad | 1984-85 |
| 6th | 143 | M.Azharuddin (141), Kapil Dev (66) | Calcutta | 1986-87 |
| 7th | 155 | R.M.H.Binny (83*), S.Madan Lal (74) | Bangalore | 1983-84 |
| 8th | 122 | S.M.H.Kirmani (66), S.Madan Lal (54) | Faisalabad | 1982-83 |
| 9th | 149 | P.G.Joshi (52*), R.B.Desai (85) | Bombay[2] | 1960-61 |
| 10th | 109 | H.R.Adhikari (81*), Ghulam Ahmed (50) | Delhi | 1952-53 |

**RECORD WICKET PARTNERSHIPS-PAKISTAN**

| | | | | |
|---|---|---|---|---|
| 1st | 162 | Hanif Mohammad (62), Imtiaz Ahmed (135) | Madras[2] | 1960-61 |
| 2nd | 250 | Mudassar Nazar (199), Qasim Omar (210) | Faisalabad | 1984-85 |
| 3rd | 451 | Mudassar Nazar (230), Javed Miandad (280*) | Hyderabad | 1982-83 |
| 4th | 287 | Javed Miandad (126), Zaheer Abbas (168) | Faisalabad | 1982-83 |
| 5th | 213 | Zaheer Abbas (186), Mudassar Nazar (119) | Karachi[1] | 1982-83 |
| 6th | 207 | Saleem Malik (107), Imran Khan (117) | Faisalabad | 1982-83 |
| 7th | 154 | Imran Khan (72), Ijaz Faqih (105) | Ahmedabad | 1986-87 |
| 8th | 112 | Imran Khan (135*), Wasim Akram (62) | Madras[1] | 1986-87 |
| 9th | 60 | Wasim Bari (49*), Iqbal Qasim (20) | Bangalore | 1979-80 |
| 10th | 104 | Zulfiqar Ahmed (63*), Amir Elahi (47) | Madras[1] | 1952-53 |

**BEST INNINGS BOWLING ANALYSIS**

| | | | | |
|---|---|---|---|---|
| India in India | 8-52 | M.H.Mankad | Delhi | 1952-53 |
| India in Pakistan | 8-85 | Kapil Dev | Lahore[2] | 1982-83 |
| Pakistan In India | 8-69 | Sikander Bakht | Delhi | 1979-80 |
| Pakistan in Pakistan | 8-60 | Imran Khan | Karachi[1] | 1982-83 |

**BEST MATCH BOWLING ANALYSIS**

| | | | | |
|---|---|---|---|---|
| India in India | 13-131 | M.H.Mankad | Delhi | 1952-53 |
| India in Pakistan | 8-85 | Kapil Dev | Lahore[2] | 1982-83 |
| Pakistan in India | 12-94 | Fazal Mahmood | Lucknow[1] | 1952-53 |
| Pakistan in Pakistan | 11-79 | Imran Khan | Karachi[1] | 1982-83 |

**HIGHEST AGGREGATE OF WICKETS IN A SERIES**

| | | | |
|---|---|---|---|
| India in India | 32 (av 17.68) | Kapil Dev | 1979-80 |
| India in Pakistan | 21 (av 22.61) | Kapil Dev | 1982-83 |
| Pakistan in India | 24 (av 26.70) | Sikander Bakht | 1979-80 |
| Pakistan in Pakistan | 22 (av 15.86) | Imran Khan | 1982-83 |

| **INDIA v SRI LANKA** | India | | Sri Lanka | | Captains | |
|---|---|---|---|---|---|---|
| Venue and Result | 1st | 2nd | 1st | 2nd | India | Sri Lanka |
| **1982-83 in INDIA** | | | | | | |
| Madras[1]-Drawn | 6d-566 | 7-135 | •346 | 394 | S.M.Gavaskar | B.Warnaweera |
| **1985-86 in SRI LANKA** | | | | | | |
| Colombo (SSC)-Drawn | •218 | 251 | 347 | 4-61 | Kapil Dev | L.R.D.Mendis |
| Colombo (PSS)-Sri Lanka 149 runs | 244 | 198 | •385 | 3d-206 | | |
| Kandy-Drawn | •249 | 5d-325 | 198 | 7-307 | | |
| **1986-87 in INDIA** | | | | | | |
| Kanpur-Drawn | 7-676 | - | •420 | - | Kapil Dev | L.R.D.Mendis |
| Nagpur-India inns & 106 runs | 6d-451 | - | •204 | 141 | | |
| Cuttack-India inns & 67 runs | •400 | - | 191 | 142 | | |
| **1990-91 in INDIA** | | | | | | |
| Chandigarh-India inns & 8 runs | •288 | - | 82 | 198 | M.Azharuddin | A.Ranatunga |
| **1993-94 in SRI LANKA** | | | | | | |
| Kandy-Drawn | - | - | •3-24 | - | M.Azharuddin | A.Ranatunga |
| Colombo (SSC)-India 235 runs | •366 | 4d-359 | 254 | 236 | | |
| Colombo (PSS)-Drawn | 446 | - | •351 | 6-352 | | |
| **1993-94 in INDIA** | | | | | | |
| Lucknow[2]-India inns & 119 runs | •511 | - | 218 | 174 | M.Azharuddin | A.Ranatunga |
| Bangalore-India inns & 95 runs | •6d-541 | - | 231 | 215 | | |
| Ahmedabad-India inns & 17 runs | 358 | - | •119 | 222 | | |
| **1997-98 in SRI LANKA** | | | | | | |
| Colombo (PIS)-Drawn | •8d-537 | - | 6d-952 | - | S.R.Tendulkar | A.Ranatunga |
| Colombo (SSC)-Drawn | 375 | 5-281 | •332 | 7d-415 | | |
| **1997-98 in INDIA** | | | | | | |
| Mohali-Drawn | 9d-515 | - | •369 | 6-251 | S.R.Tendulkar | A.Ranatunga |
| Nagpur-Drawn | •485 | - | - | - | | |
| Mumbai-Drawn | •512 | 9d-181 | 361 | 7-166 | | |

## Test Match Results Summary

**INDIA v SRI LANKA-IN INDIA**

| | T | Result | Madras | Kanpur | Nagpur | Cuttack | Chand. | Luck. | Banga. | Ahmed. | Mohali | Mumbai |
|---|---|---|---|---|---|---|---|---|---|---|---|---|
| | T | I S D | I S D | I S D | I S D | I S D | I S D | I S D | I S D | I S D | I S D | I S D |
| 1982-83 | 1 | - - 1 | - - 1 | - - - | - - - | - - - | - - - | - - - | - - - | - - - | - - - | - - - |
| 1986-87 | 3 | 2 - 1 | - - - | 1 - - | - - 1 | 1 - - | - - - | - - - | - - - | - - - | - - - | - - - |
| 1990-91 | 1 | 1 - - | - - - | - - - | - - - | - - - | - - 1 | - - - | - - - | - - - | - - - | - - - |
| 1993-94 | 3 | 3 - - | - - - | - - - | - - - | - - - | - - - | 1 - - | 1 - - | 1 - - | - - - | - - - |
| 1997-98 | 3 | - - 3 | - - - | - - - | - - 1 | - - - | - - - | - - - | - - - | - - - | - - 1 | - - 1 |
| | 11 | 6 - 5 | - - 1 | 1 - - | - - 2 | 1 - - | - - 1 | 1 - - | 1 - - | 1 - - | - - 1 | - - 1 |

**INDIA v SRI LANKA-IN SRI LANKA**

| | Tests | Result I | Result SL | Result D | Colombo (SSC) I | Colombo (SSC) SL | Colombo (SSC) D | Colombo (PSS) I | Colombo (PSS) SL | Colombo (PSS) D | Kandy I | Kandy SL | Kandy D | Colombo (PIS) I | Colombo (PIS) SL | Colombo (PIS) D |
|---|---|---|---|---|---|---|---|---|---|---|---|---|---|---|---|---|
| 1985-86 | 3 | - | 1 | 2 | - | - | 1 | - | 1 | - | - | - | 1 | - | - | - |
| 1993-94 | 3 | 1 | - | 2 | 1 | - | - | - | - | 1 | - | - | 1 | - | - | - |
| 1997-98 | 2 | - | - | 2 | - | - | 1 | - | - | - | - | - | - | - | - | 1 |
| | 8 | 1 | 1 | 6 | 1 | - | 2 | - | 1 | 1 | - | - | 2 | - | - | 1 |
| Totals | 19 | 7 | 1 | 11 | | | | | | | | | | | | |

*Key to ground abbreviations: Chand. - Chandigarh; Luck. - Lucknow; Bang. - Bangalore; Ahmed. - Ahmedabad.*

**HIGHEST INNINGS TOTALS**

| | | | |
|---|---|---|---|
| India in India | 7-676 | Kanpur | 1986-87 |
| India in Sri Lanka | 446 | Colombo (PSS) | 1993-94 |
| Sri Lanka in India | 8d-537 | Mohali | 1997-98 |
| Sri Lanka in Sri Lanka | 6d-952 | Colombo (PIS) | 1997-98 |

**LOWEST INNINGS TOTALS**

| | | | |
|---|---|---|---|
| India in India | 288 | Chandigarh | 1990-91 |
| India in Sri Lanka | 198 | Colombo (PSS) | 1985-86 |
| Sri Lanka in India | 82 | Chandigarh | 1990-91 |
| Sri Lanka in Sri Lanka | 198 | Kandy | 1985-86 |

| | | | |
|---|---|---|---|
| **HIGHEST MATCH AGGREGATE** | 1489 for 14 wickets | Colombo (PIS) | 1997-98 |
| **LOWEST MATCH AGGREGATE** | 568 for 30 wickets | Chandigarh | 1990-91 |

**HIGHEST INDIVIDUAL INNINGS**

| | | | | |
|---|---|---|---|---|
| India in India | 199 | M.Azharuddin | Kanpur | 1986-87 |
| India in Sri Lanka | 147 | S.C.Ganguly | Colombo (SSC) | 1997-98 |
| Sri Lanka in India | 110* | P.A.de Silva | Mohali | 1997-98 |
| Sri Lanka in Sri Lanka | 340 | S.T.Jayasuriya | Colombo (PIS) | 1997-98 |

**HIGHEST AGGREGATE ON RUNS IN A SERIES**

| | | | |
|---|---|---|---|
| India in India | 392 (av 98.00) | S.C.Ganguly | 1997-98 |
| India in Sri Lanka | 290 (av 96.66) | S.R.Tendulkar | 1997-98 |
| Sri Lanka in India | 282 (av 47.00) | R.S.Mahanama | 1993-94 |
| Sri Lanka in Sri Lanka | 571 (av 190.33) | S.T.Jayasuriya | 1997-98 |

**RECORD WICKET PARTNERSHIPS-INDIA**

| | | | | |
|---|---|---|---|---|
| 1st | 171 | M.Prabhakar (94), N.S.Sidhu (104) | Colombo (SSC) | 1993-94 |
| 2nd | 173 | S.M.Gavaskar (155), D.B.Vengsarkar (90) | Madras[1] | 1982-83 |
| 3rd | 173 | M.Amarnath (131), D.B.Vengsarkar (153) | Nagpur | 1986-87 |
| 4th | 255 | S.C.Ganguly (173), S.R.Tendulkar (148) | Mumbai[3] | 1997-98 |
| 5th | 150 | S.R.Tendulkar (139), S.C.Ganguly (147) | Colombo (SSC) | 1997-98 |
| 6th | 272 | M.Azharuddin (199), Kapil Dev (163) | Kanpur | 1986-87 |
| 7th | 78* | S.M.Patil (114*), S.Madan Lal (37*) | Madras[1] | 1982-83 |
| 8th | 70 | Kapil Dev (78), L.Sivaramakrishnan (21) | Colombo (PSS) | 1985-86 |
| 9th | 89 | S.C.Ganguly (109), A.Kuruvilla (35*) | Mohali | 1997-98 |
| 10th | 29 | Kapil Dev (78), C.Sharma (0*) | Colombo (PSS) | 1985-86 |

**RECORD WICKET PARTNERSHIPS-SRI LANKA**

| | | | | |
|---|---|---|---|---|
| 1st | 159 | S.Wettimuny (79), J.R.Ratnayeke (93) | Kanpur | 1986-87 |
| 2nd | 576 | S.T.Jayasuriya (340), R.S.Mahanama (225) | Colombo (PIS) | 1997-98 |
| 3rd | 218 | S.T.Jayasuriya (199), P.A.de Silva (120) | Colombo (SSC) | 1997-98 |
| 4th | 216 | R.L.Dias (106), L.R.D.Mendis (124) | Kandy | 1985-86 |
| 5th | 144 | R.S.Madugalle (103), A.Ranatunga (111) | Colombo (SSC) | 1985-86 |
| 6th | 103 | P.A.de Silva (110*), H.D.P.K.Dharmasena (25) | Mohali | 1997-98 |
| 7th | 77 | R.S.Madugalle (46), D.S.de Silva (49) | Madras[1] | 1982-83 |
| 8th | 48 | P.A.de Silva (146), M.Muralidaran (39) | Colombo (PIS) | 1997-98 |
| 9th | 60 | H.P.Tillakaratne (55), M.A.W.R.Madurasinghe (11) | Madras[1] | 1982-83 |
| 10th | 44 | R.J.Ratnayake (32*), E.A.R.de Silva (16) | Nagpur | 1986-87 |

**BEST INNINGS BOWLING ANALYSIS**

| | | | | |
|---|---|---|---|---|
| India in India | 7-51 | Maninder Singh | Nagpur | 1986-87 |
| India in Sri Lanka | 5-87 | A.R.Kumble | Colombo (SSC) | 1993-94 |
| Sri Lanka in India | 5-57 | H.D.P.K.Dharmasena | Mumbai[3] | 1997-98 |
| Sri Lanka in Sri Lanka | 6-85 | R.J.Ratnayake | Colombo (SSC) | 1985-86 |

**BEST MATCH BOWLING ANALYSIS**

| | | | | |
|---|---|---|---|---|
| India in India | 11-128 | A.R.Kumble | Lucknow[2] | 1993-94 |
| India in Sri Lanka | 8-172 | A.R.Kumble | Colombo (SSC) | 1993-94 |
| Sri Lanka in India | 8-201 | H.D.P.K.Dharmasena | Mumbai[3] | 1997-98 |
| Sri Lanka in Sri Lanka | 9-125 | R.J.Ratnayake | Colombo (PSS) | 1985-86 |

**HIGHEST AGGREGATE OF WICKETS IN A SERIES**

| | | | |
|---|---|---|---|
| India in India | 18 (av 15.50) | Maninder Singh | 1986-87 |
| India in Sri Lanka | 14 (av 27.35) | C.Sharma | 1985-86 |
| Sri Lanka in India | 12 (av 35.00) | M.Muralidaran | 1993-94 |
| Sri Lanka in Sri Lanka | 20 (av 22.95) | R.J.Ratnayake | 1985-86 |

| **INDIA v ZIMBABWE** | India | | Zimbabwe | | Captains | |
|---|---|---|---|---|---|---|
| Venue and Result | 1st | 2nd | 1st | 2nd | India | Zimbabwe |
| **1992-93 in ZIMBABWE** | | | | | | |
| Harare-Drawn | 307 | - | •456 | 4-146 | M.Azharuddin | D.L.Houghton |
| **1992-93 in India** | | | | | | |
| Delhi-India inns & 13 runs | •7d-536 | - | 322 | 201 | M.Azharuddin | D.L.Houghton |

## Test Match Results Summary

**INDIA v ZIMBABWE-IN ZIMBABWE**

| | | Result | | | Harare | | |
|---|---|---|---|---|---|---|---|
| | Tests | I | Z | D | I | Z | D |
| 1992-93 | 1 | - | - | 1 | - | - | 1 |

**INDIA v ZIMBABWE-IN INDIA**

| | | Result | | | Delhi | | |
|---|---|---|---|---|---|---|---|
| | Tests | I | Z | D | I | Z | D |
| 1992-93 | 1 | 1 | - | - | 1 | - | - |
| Totals | 2 | 1 | - | 1 | | | |

**HIGHEST INNINGS TOTALS**

| | | | |
|---|---|---|---|
| India in Zimbabwe | 307 | Harare | 1992-93 |
| India in India | 7d-536 | Delhi | 1992-93 |
| Zimbabwe in Zimbabwe | 456 | Harare | 1992-93 |
| Zimbabwe in India | 322 | Delhi | 1992-93 |

**LOWEST INNINGS TOTALS**

| | | | |
|---|---|---|---|
| India in Zimbabwe | 307 | Harare | 1992-93 |
| India in India | no instance | Delhi | 1992-93 |
| Zimbabwe in Zimbabwe | 456 | Harare | 1992-93 |
| Zimbabwe in India | 201 | Delhi | 1992-93 |

| | | | |
|---|---|---|---|
| **HIGHEST MATCH AGGREGATE** | 1059 for 27 wickets | Delhi | 1992-93 |
| **LOWEST MATCH AGGREGATE** | 909 for 24 wickets | Harare | 1992-93 |

**HIGHEST INDIVIDUAL INNINGS**

| | | | | |
|---|---|---|---|---|
| India in Zimbabwe | 104 | S.V.Manjrekar | Harare | 1992-93 |
| India in India | 227 | V.G.Kambli | Delhi | 1992-93 |
| Zimbabwe in Zimbabwe | 121 | D.L.Houghton | Harare | 1992-93 |
| Zimbabwe in India | 115 | A.Flower | Delhi | 1992-93 |

**HIGHEST AGGREGATE ON RUNS IN A SERIES**

| | | | |
|---|---|---|---|
| India in Zimbabwe | 104 (av 104.00) | S.V.Manjrekar | 1992-93 |
| India in India | 227 (av 227.00) | V.G.Kambli | 1992-93 |
| Zimbabwe in Zimbabwe | 162 (av 162.00) | D.L.Houghton | 1992-93 |
| Zimbabwe in India | 177 (av 177.00) | A.Flower | 1992-93 |

**HIGHEST WICKET PARTNERSHIP-INDIA**

| | | | | |
|---|---|---|---|---|
| 1st | 29 | R.J.Shastri (11), W.V.Raman (43) | Harare | 1992-93 |
| 2nd | 107 | N.S.Sidhu (61), V.G.Kambli (227) | Delhi | 1992-93 |
| 3rd | 137 | V.G.Kambli (227), S.R.Tendulkar (62) | Delhi | 1992-93 |
| 4th | 107 | V.G.Kambli (227), M.Azharuddin (42) | Delhi | 1992-93 |
| 5th | 64 | V.G.Kambli (227), P.K.Amre (52*) | Delhi | 1992-93 |
| 6th | 96 | S.V.Manjrekar (104), Kapil Dev (60) | Harare | 1992-93 |
| 7th | 43 | P.K.Amre (52*), V.Yadav (14) | Delhi | 1992-93 |
| 8th | 68 | S.V.Manjrekar (104), K.S.More (41) | Harare | 1992-93 |
| 9th | 7 | K.S.More (41), A.R.Kumble (0) | Harare | 1992-93 |
| 10th | 13 | K.S.More (41), J.Srinath (6*) | Harare | 1992-93 |

**HIGHEST WICKET PARTNERSHIP-ZIMBABWE**

| | | | | |
|---|---|---|---|---|
| 1st | 100 | K.J.Arnott (40), G.W.Flower (82) | Harare | 1992-93 |
| 2nd | 75 | G.W.Flower (82), A.D.R.Campbell (45) | Harare | 1992-93 |
| 3rd | 77 | K.J.Arnott(32), A.J.Pycroft (46) | Harare | 1992-93 |
| 4th | 192 | G.W.Flower (96), A.Flower (115) | Delhi | 1992-93 |
| 5th | 51 | A.J.Pycroft (39), D.L.Houghton (121) | Harare | 1992-93 |
| 6th | 165 | D.L.Houghton (121), A.Flower (59) | Harare | 1992-93 |
| 7th | 28 | D.L.Houghton (121), G.J.Crocker (23*) | Harare | 1992-93 |
| 8th | 1 | A.H.Shah (25), D.H.Brain (0) | Delhi | 1992-93 |
| 8th | 1 | A.Flower (62*), D.H.Brain (0) | Delhi | 1992-93 |
| 9th | 31 | A.H.Shah(25), U.Ranchod (7) | Delhi | 1992-93 |
| 10th | 13 | A.Flower (62*), A.J.Traicos (1) | Delhi | 1992-93 |

**BEST INNINGS BOWLING ANALYSIS**

| | | | | |
|---|---|---|---|---|
| India in Zimbabwe | 3-66 | M.Prabhakar | Harare | 1992-93 |
| India in India | 5-70 | A.R.Kumble | Delhi | 1992-93 |
| Zimbabwe in Zimbabwe | 5-86 | A.J.Traicos | Harare | 1992-93 |
| Zimbabwe in India | 3-186 | A.J.Traicos | Delhi | 1992-93 |

**BEST MATCH BOWLING ANALYSIS**

| | | | | |
|---|---|---|---|---|
| India in Zimbabwe | 4-88 | M.Prabhakar | Harare | 1992-93 |
| India in India | 8-160 | A.R.Kumble | Delhi | 1992-93 |
| Zimbabwe in Zimbabwe | 5-86 | A.J.Traicos | Harare | 1992-93 |
| Zimbabwe in India | 3-186 | A.J.Traicos | Delhi | 1992-93 |

**HIGHEST AGGREGATE OF WICKETS IN A SERIES**

| | | | |
|---|---|---|---|
| India in Zimbabwe | 4 (av 22.00) | M.Prabhakar | 1992-93 |
| India in India | 4 (av 22.00) | A.R.Kumble | 1992-93 |
| Zimbabwe in Zimbabwe | 5 (av 17.20) | A.J.Traicos | 1992-93 |
| Zimbabwe in India | 3 (av 62.00) | A.J.Traicos | 1992-93 |

| PAKISTAN v SRI LANKA | Pakistan | | Sri Lanka | | Captains | |
|---|---|---|---|---|---|---|
| Venue and Result | 1st | 2nd | 1st | 2nd | Pakistan | Sri Lanka |
| **1981-82 in PAKISTAN** | | | | | | |
| Karachi[1]-Pakistan 204 runs | •396 | 4d-301 | 344 | 149 | Javed Miandad | B Warnapura |
| Faisalabad-Drawn | 270 | 7-186 | •454 | 8d-154 | | L. R. D. Mendis |
| Lahore[2]-Pakistan inns & 102 runs | 7d-500 | - | •240 | 158 | | B. Warnapura |
| **1985-86 in PAKISTAN** | | | | | | |
| Faisalabad-Drawn | 3-555 | - | •479 | - | Javed Miandad | L. R. D. Mendis |
| Sialkot-Pakistan 8 wkts | 259 | 2-100 | •157 | 200 | | |
| Karachi[1]-Pakistan 10 wkts | 295 | 0-98 | •162 | 230 | | |
| **1985-86 in SRI LANKA** | | | | | | |
| Kandy-Pakistan inns & 20 runs | 230 | - | •109 | 101 | Imran Khan | L. R. D. Mendis |
| Colombo (CCC)-Sri Lanka 149 runs | •132 | 172 | 273 | 2-32 | | |
| Colombo (PSS)-Drawn | 318 | - | •281 | 3-323 | | |
| **1991-92 in PAKISTAN** | | | | | | |
| Sialkot-Drawn | 5d-423 | - | •270 | 5-137 | Imran Khan | P.A.de Silva |
| Gujranwala-Drawn | •2-109 | - | - | - | | |
| Faisalabad-Pakistan 3 wkts | 221 | 7-188 | •240 | 165 | | |
| **1994-95 in SRI LANKA** | | | | | | |
| Colombo (PSS)-Pakistan 301 runs | •390 | 4d-318 | 226 | 181 | Saleem Malik | A.Ranatunga |
| Colombo (SSC)-Match cancelled | | | | | | |
| Kandy-Pakistan inns & 52 runs | 9d-357 | - | 71 | 234 | | |
| **1995-96 in PAKISTAN** | | | | | | |
| Peshawar[2]-Pakistan inns & 40 runs | •9d-459 | - | 186 | 233 | Rameez Raja | A.Ranatunga |
| Faisalabad-Sri Lanka 42 runs | 333 | 209 | •223 | 361 | | |
| Sialkot-Sri Lanka 144 runs | 214 | 212 | •232 | 9d-338 | | |
| **1996-97 in SRI LANKA** | | | | | | |
| Colombo (PIS)-Drawn | 378 | - | •330 | 8-423 | Rameez Raja | A.Ranatunga |
| Colombo (SSC)-Drawn | 292 | 5-285 | •331 | 4d-386 | | |

## Test Match Results Summary

**PAKISTAN v SRI LANKA-IN PAKISTAN**

| | | Results | | | Karachi[1] | | | Faisalabad | | | Lahore[2] | | | Sialkot | | | Gujranwala | | | Peshawar[2] | | |
|---|---|---|---|---|---|---|---|---|---|---|---|---|---|---|---|---|---|---|---|---|---|---|
| | Tests | P | SL | D | P | SL | D | P | SL | D | P | SL | D | P | SL | D | P | SL | D | P | SL | D |
| 1981-82 | 3 | 2 | - | 1 | 1 | - | - | - | - | 1 | 1 | - | - | - | - | - | - | - | - | - | - | - |
| 1985-86 | 3 | 2 | - | 1 | 1 | - | - | - | - | 1 | - | - | - | 1 | - | - | - | - | - | - | - | - |
| 1991-92 | 3 | 1 | - | 2 | - | - | 1 | 1 | - | - | - | - | - | - | - | 1 | - | - | 1 | - | - | - |
| 1995-96 | 3 | 1 | 2 | - | - | - | - | - | 1 | - | - | - | - | - | 1 | - | - | - | - | 1 | - | - |
| | 12 | 6 | 2 | 4 | 2 | - | 1 | 1 | 1 | 2 | 1 | - | - | 1 | 1 | 1 | - | - | 1 | 1 | - | - |

**PAKISTAN v SRI LANKA-IN SRI LANKA**

| | Tests | Result | | | Kandy | | | Col. CCC) | | | Col. PSS) | | | Col. (SSC) | | | Col. (PIS) | | |
|---|---|---|---|---|---|---|---|---|---|---|---|---|---|---|---|---|---|---|---|
| | | P | SL | D | P | SL | D | P | SL | D | P | SL | D | P | SL | D | P | SL | D |
| 1985-86 | 3 | 1 | 1 | 1 | 1 | - | - | - | 1 | - | - | - | 1 | - | - | - | - | - | - |
| 1994-95 | 2 | 2 | - | - | 1 | - | - | - | - | - | 1 | - | - | - | - | - | - | - | - |
| 1996-97 | 2 | - | - | 2 | - | - | - | - | - | - | - | - | - | - | - | 1 | - | - | 1 |
| | 7 | 3 | 1 | 3 | 2 | - | - | - | 1 | - | 1 | - | 1 | - | - | 1 | - | - | 1 |
| Totals | 19 | 9 | 3 | 7 | | | | | | | | | | | | | | | |

**HIGHEST INNINGS TOTALS**

| | | | |
|---|---|---|---|
| Pakistan in Pakistan | 3-555 | Faisalabad | 1985-86 |
| Pakistan in Sri Lanka | 390 | Colombo (PSS) | 1994-95 |
| Sri Lanka in Pakistan | 479 | Faisalabad | 1985-86 |
| Sri Lanka in Sri Lanka | 8-423 | Colombo (PIS) | 1996-97 |

**LOWEST INNINGS TOTALS**

| | | | |
|---|---|---|---|
| Pakistan in Pakistan | 209 | Faisalabad | 1995-96 |
| Pakistan in Sri Lanka | 132 | Colombo (CCC) | 1985-86 |
| Sri Lanka in Pakistan | 149 | Karachi[1] | 1981-82 |
| Sri Lanka in Sri Lanka | 71 | Kandy | 1994-95 |

| | | | |
|---|---|---|---|
| **HIGHEST MATCH AGGREGATE** | 1294 for 29 wickets | Colombo (SSC) | 1996-97 |
| **LOWEST MATCH AGGREGATE** | 440 for 30 wickets | Kandy | 1985-86 |

**HIGHEST INDIVIDUAL INNINGS**

| | | | | |
|---|---|---|---|---|
| Pakistan in Pakistan | 206 | Qasim Omar | Faisalabad | 1985-86 |
| Pakistan in Sri Lanka | 155 | Saleem Malik | Colombo (SSC) | 1996-97 |
| Sri Lanka in Pakistan | 157 | S.Wettimuny | Faisalabad | 1981-82 |
| Sri Lanka in Sri Lanka | 168 | P.A.de Silva | Colombo (PIS) | 1996-97 |

**HIGHEST AGGREGATE OF RUNS IN A SERIES**

| | | | |
|---|---|---|---|
| Pakistan in Pakistan | 306 (av 153.00) | Javed Miandad | 1985-86 |
| Pakistan in Sri Lanka | 261 (av 87.00) | Saaed Anwar | 1994-95 |
| Sri Lanka in Pakistan | 316 (av 52.66) | S.Wettimuny | 1985-86 |
| Sri Lanka in Sri Lanka | 432 (av 216.00) | P.A.de Silva | 1996-97 |

**RECORD WICKET PARTNERSHIPS-PAKISTAN**

| | | | | |
|---|---|---|---|---|
| 1st | 128 | Rameez Raja (98), Shoaib Mohammad (43) | Sialkot | 1991-92 |
| | 128 | Saeed Anwar (136), Aamer Sohail (65) | Colombo (PSS) | 1994-95 |
| 2nd | 151 | Mohsin Khan (129), Majid Khan (63) | Lahore[2] | 1981-82 |
| 3rd | 397 | Qasim Omar (206), Javed Miandad (203*) | Faisalabad | 1985-86 |
| 4th | 162 | Saleem Malik (100*), Javed Miandad (92) | Karachi[1] | 1981-82 |
| 5th | 132 | Saleem Malik (101), Imran Khan (93*) | Sialkot | 1991-92 |
| 6th | 100 | Zaheer Abbas (134), Imran Khan (39) | Lahore[2] | 1981-82 |
| 7th | 104 | Haroon Rashid (153), Tahir Naqqash (57) | Karachi[1] | 1981-82 |
| 8th | 38 | Saqlain Mushtaq (58), Mushtaq Ahmed (26) | Colombo (PIS) | 1996-97 |
| 9th | 127 | Haroon Rashid (153), Rashid Khan (59) | Karachi[1] | 1981-82 |
| 10th | 65 | Moin Khan (117*), Aamer Nazir (11) | Sialkot | 1995-96 |

**RECORD WICKET PARTNERSHIPS-SRI LANKA**

| | | | | |
|---|---|---|---|---|
| 1st | 157 | S.T.Jayasuriya (113), R.P.Arnold (50) | Colombo (SSC) | 1996-97 |
| 2nd | 217 | S.Wettimuny (157), R.L.Dias (98) | Faisalabad | 1981-82 |
| 3rd | 176 | U.C.Hathurusingha (83), P.A.de Silva (105) | Faisalabad | 1995-96 |
| 4th | 240* | A.P.Gurusinha (116*), A.Ranatunga (135*) | Colombo (PSS) | 1985-86 |
| 5th | 125 | A.Ranatunga (76), H.P.Tillakaratne (48) | Peshawar[2] | 1995-96 |
| 6th | 121 | A.Ranatunga (79), P.A.de Silva (122) | Faisalabad | 1985-86 |
| 7th | 76 | P.A.de Silva (138*), W.P.U.J.C.Vaas (17) | Colombo (SSC) | 1996-97 |
| 8th | 65 | H.D.P.K.Dharmasena (49), W.P.J.U.C.Vaas (40) | Faisalabad | 1995-96 |
| 9th | 52 | P.A.de Silva (122), R.J.Ratnayake (56) | Faisalabad | 1985-86 |
| 10th | 36 | R.J.Ratnayake (356), R.G.C.E.Wijesuriya (7*) | Faisalabad | 1985-86 |

**BEST INNINGS BOWLING ANALYSIS**

| | | | | |
|---|---|---|---|---|
| Pakistan in Pakistan | 8-58 | Imran Khan | Lahore[2] | 1981-82 |
| Pakistan in Sri Lanka | 6-34 | Waqar Younis | Kandy | 1994-95 |
| Sri Lanka in Pakistan | 8-83 | J.R.Ratnayeke | Faisalabad | 1985-86 |
| Sri Lanka in Sri Lanka | 6-98 | M.Muralidaran | Colombo (PIS) | 1996-97 |

**BEST MATCH BOWLING ANALYSIS**

| | | | | |
|---|---|---|---|---|
| Pakistan in Pakistan | 14-116 | Imran Khan | Lahore[2] | 1981-82 |
| Pakistan in Sri Lanka | 11-119 | Waqar Younis | Kandy | 1994-95 |
| Sri Lanka in Pakistan | 9-162 | D.S.de Silva | Faisalabad | 1981-82 |
| Sri Lanka in Sri Lanka | 8-183 | H.D.P.K.Dharmasena | Colombo (PSS) | 1994-95 |

**HIGHEST AGGREGATE OF WICKETS IN SERIES**

| | | | |
|---|---|---|---|
| Pakistan in Pakistan | 17 (av 15.94) | Imran Khan | 1985-86 |
| Pakistan in Sri Lanka | 15 (av 18.00) | Imran Khan | 1985-86 |
| Sri Lanka in Pakistan | 17 (av 28.94) | D.S.de Silva | 1981-82 |
| Sri Lanka in Sri Lanka | 12 (av 21.50) | H.D.P.K.Dharmasena | 1994-95 |

| **PAKISTAN v ZIMBABWE** | Pakistan | | Zimbabwe | | Captains | |
|---|---|---|---|---|---|---|
| Venue and Result | 1st | 2nd | 1st | 2nd | Pakistan | Zimbabwe |
| **1993-94 in PAKISTAN** | | | | | | |
| Karachi[2]-Pakistan 131 runs | •8d-423 | 3d-131 | 289 | 134 | Waqar Younis | A.Flower |
| Rawalpindi[2]-Pakistan 52 runs | •245 | 248 | 254 | 187 | Wasim Akram | |
| Lahore[2]-Drawn | •147 | 1-174 | 230 | - | Wasim Akram | |
| **1994-95 in ZIMBABWE** | | | | | | |
| Harare-Zimbabwe inns & 64 runs | 322 | 158 | •4d-544 | - | Saleem Malik | A.Flower |
| Bulawayo[2]-Pakistan 8 wkts | 260 | 2-61 | •174 | 146 | | |
| Harare-Pakistan 99 runs | •231 | 250 | 243 | 139 | | |
| **1996-97 in PAKISTAN** | | | | | | |
| Sheikhupura-Drawn | 553 | - | •375 | 7-241 | Wasim Akram | A.D.R.Campbell |
| Faisalabad-Pakistan 10 wkts | 267 | 0-69 | •133 | 200 | | |
| **1994-95 in ZIMBABWE** | | | | | | |
| Bulawayo[2]-Drawn | 256 | 6-258 | •321 | 4d-302 | Rashid Latif | A.D.R.Campbell |
| Harare-Pakistan 3 wkts | 354 | 7-192 | •277 | 268 | | |

## Test Match Results Summary

**PAKISTAN v ZIMBABWE-IN PAKISTAN**

| | | Result | | | Karachi[1] | | | Rawalpindi[2] | | | Lahore[2] | | | Sheikhupura | | | Faisalabad | | |
|---|---|---|---|---|---|---|---|---|---|---|---|---|---|---|---|---|---|---|---|
| | Tests | P | Z | D | P | Z | D | P | Z | D | P | Z | D | P | Z | D | P | Z | D |
| 1993-94 | 3 | 2 | - | 1 | 1 | - | - | 1 | - | - | - | - | 1 | - | - | - | - | - | - |
| 1996-97 | 2 | 1 | - | 1 | - | - | - | - | - | - | - | - | - | - | - | 1 | 1 | - | - |
| | 5 | 3 | - | 2 | 1 | - | - | 1 | - | - | - | - | 1 | - | - | 1 | 1 | - | - |

## PAKISTAN v ZIMBABWE-IN ZIMBABWE

| | Tests | Result | | | Harare | | | Bulawayo[2] | | |
|---|---|---|---|---|---|---|---|---|---|---|
| | | P | Z | D | P | Z | D | P | Z | D |
| 1994-95 | 3 | 2 | 1 | - | 1 | 1 | - | 1 | - | - |
| 1997-98 | 2 | 1 | - | 1 | 1 | - | - | - | - | 1 |
| | 5 | 3 | 1 | 1 | 2 | 1 | - | 1 | - | 1 |
| Totals | 10 | 6 | 1 | 3 | | | | | | |

### HIGHEST INNINGS TOTALS

| | | | |
|---|---|---|---|
| Pakistan in Pakistan | 553 | Sheikhupura | 1996-97 |
| Pakistan in Zimbabwe | 354 | Harare | 1997-98 |
| Zimbabwe in Pakistan | 375 | Sheikhupura | 1996-97 |
| Zimbabwe in Zimbabwe | 4d-544 | Harare | 1994-95 |

### LOWEST INNINGS TOTALS

| | | | |
|---|---|---|---|
| Pakistan in Pakistan | 147 | Lahore[2] | 1993-94 |
| Pakistan in Zimbabwe | 158 | Harare | 1994-95 |
| Zimbabwe in Pakistan | 133 | Faisalabad | 1996-97 |
| Zimbabwe in Zimbabwe | 139 | Harare | 1994-95 |

| | | | |
|---|---|---|---|
| **HIGHEST MATCH AGGREGATE** | 1137 for 30 wickets | Harare | 1997-98 |
| **LOWEST MATCH AGGREGATE** | 551 for 21 wickets | Lahore[2] | 1993-94 |

### HIGHEST INDIVIDUAL INNINGS

| | | | | |
|---|---|---|---|---|
| Pakistan in Pakistan | 257* | Wasim Akram | Sheikhupura | 1996-97 |
| Pakistan in Zimbabwe | 192 | Mohammad Wasim | Harare | 1997-98 |
| Zimbabwe in Pakistan | 110 | G.W.Flower | Sheikhupura | 1996-97 |
| Zimbabwe in Zimbabwe | 201* | G.W.Flower | Harare | 1994-95 |

### HIGHEST AGGREGATE OF RUNS IN A SERIES

| | | | |
|---|---|---|---|
| Pakistan in Pakistan | 292 (av 292.00) | Wasim Akram | 1996-97 |
| Pakistan in Zimbabwe | 367 (av 73.40) | Inzamamul Haq | 1994-95 |
| Zimbabwe in Pakistan | 205 (av 41.00) | A.D.R.Campbell | 1996-97 |
| Zimbabwe in Zimbabwe | 300 (av 100.00) | M.W.Goodwin | 1997-98 |

### RECORD WICKET PARTNERSHIPS-PAKISTAN

| | | | | |
|---|---|---|---|---|
| 1st | 95 | Aamer Sohail (63), Shoaib Mohammad (81) | Karachi[2] | 1993-94 |
| 2nd | 118* | Shoaib Mohammad (53*), Asif Mujtaba (65*) | Lahore[2] | 1993-94 |
| 3rd | 83 | Shoaib Mohammad (81), Javed Miandad (70) | Karachi[2] | 1993-94 |
| 4th | 116 | Inzamamul Haq (83), Ijaz Ahmed (55) | Harare | 1994-95 |
| 5th | 110 | Yousuf Youhana (64), Moin Khan (97) | Bulawayo[2] | 1997-98 |
| 6th | 96 | Ijaz Ahmed (65), Inzamamul Haq (71) | Harare | 1994-95 |
| 7th | 120 | Inzamamul Haq (71), Wasim Akram (27) | Harare | 1994-95 |
| 8th | 313 | Wasim Akram(257*), Saqlain Mushtaq (79) | Sheikhupura | 1996-97 |
| 9th | 147 | Mohammad Wasim (192), Mushtaq Ahmed (57) | Harare | 1997-98 |
| 10th | 27 | Waqar Younis (17), Ashfaq Ahmed (1*) | Harare | 1994-95 |

### RECORD WICKET PARTNERSHIPS-ZIMBABWE

| | | | | |
|---|---|---|---|---|
| 1st | 47 | G.W.Flower (39), G.J.Rennie (13) | Harare | 1997-98 |
| 2nd | 135 | M.H.Dekker (68*), A.D.R.Campbell (75) | Rawalpindi[2] | 1993-94 |
| 3rd | 269 | G.W.Flower (30), D.L.Houghton (50) | Harare | 1994-95 |
| 4th | 233* | D.L.Houghton (50), A.Flower (62*) | Harare | 1994-95 |
| 5th | 277* | M.W.Goodwin (166*), A.Flower (100*) | Bulawayo[2] | 1997-98 |
| 6th | 72 | M.H.Dekker (68), H.H.Streak (29) | Rawalpindi[2] | 1993-94 |
| 7th | 131 | G.W.Flower (110), P.A.Strang (106*) | Sheikhupura | 1996-97 |
| 8th | 110 | G.J.Whittall (62), B.C.Strang (53) | Harare | 1997-98 |
| 9th | 87 | P.A.Strang 106*), B.C..Strang (42) | Sheikhupura | 1996-97 |
| 10th | 19 | M.H.Dekker (68*), S.G.Peall (10) | Rawalpindi[2] | 1993-94 |

**BEST INNINGS BOWLING ANALYSIS**

| | | | | |
|---|---|---|---|---|
| Pakistan in Pakistan | 7-91 | Waqar Younis | Karachi[2] | 1993-94 |
| Pakistan in Zimbabwe | 5-43 | Wasim Akram | Bulawayo[2] | 1994-95 |
| Zimbabwe in Pakistan | 5-42 | D.H.Brain | Lahore[2] | 1993-94 |
| Zimbabwe in Zimbabwe | 6-90 | H.H.Streak | Harare | 1994-95 |

**BEST MATCH BOWLING ANALYSIS**

| | | | | |
|---|---|---|---|---|
| Pakistan in Pakistan | 13-135 | Waqar Younis | Karachi[2] | 1993-94 |
| Pakistan in Zimbabwe | 8-83 | Wasim Akram | Bulawayo[2] | 1994-95 |
| Zimbabwe in Pakistan | 8-114 | H.H.Streak | Rawalpindi[2] | 1993-94 |
| Zimbabwe in Zimbabwe | 9-105 | H.H.Streak | Harare | 1994-95 |

**HIGHEST AGGREGATE OF WICKETS IN SERIES**

| | | | |
|---|---|---|---|
| Pakistan in Pakistan | 27 (av 13.81) | Waqar Younis | 1993-94 |
| Pakistan in Zimbabwe | 13 (av 24.07) | Wasim Akram | 1994-95 |
| | 13 (av 17.76) | Waqar Younis | 1997-98 |
| Zimbabwe in Pakistan | 13 (av 30.30) | E.A.Brandes | 1993-94 |
| Zimbabwe in Zimbabwe | 22 (av 13.54) | H.H.Streak | 1994-95 |

| **SRI LANKA v ZIMBABWE** Venue and Result | Sri Lanka 1st | Sri Lanka 2nd | Zimbabwe 1st | Zimbabwe 2nd | Captains Sri Lanka | Captains Zimbabwe |
|---|---|---|---|---|---|---|
| **1994-95 in ZIMBABWE** | | | | | | |
| Harare-Drawn | •383 | - | 8-319 | - | A.Ranatunga | A.Flower |
| Bulawayo[2]-Drawn | 218 | 4-193 | •9d-462 | - | | |
| Harare-Drawn | •402 | 3-89 | 375 | - | | |
| **1996-97 in SRI LANKA** | | | | | | |
| Colombo (PIS)-Sri Lanka inns & 77 runs | •349 | - | 145 | 127 | A.Ranatunga | A.D.R.Campbell |
| Colombo (SSC)-Sri Lanka 10 wkts | 8d-350 | 0-30 | •141 | 235 | | |
| **1996-97 in SRI LANKA** | | | | | | |
| Kandy-Sri Lanka 8 wkts | •9d-469 | 2-10 | 140 | 338 | A.Ranatunga | A.D.R.Campbell |
| Colombo (SSC)-Sri Lanka 5 wkts | 225 | 5-326 | •251 | 299 | | |

**Test Match Results Summary**

**SRI LANKA v ZIMBABWE-IN SRI LANKA**

| | Tests | Result SL | Result Z | Result D | Colombo (PIS) SL | Colombo (PIS) Z | Colombo (PIS) D | Colombo (SSC) SL | Colombo (SSC) Z | Colombo (SSC) D | Kandy SL | Kandy Z | Kandy D |
|---|---|---|---|---|---|---|---|---|---|---|---|---|---|
| 1996-97 | 2 | 2 | - | - | 1 | - | - | 1 | - | - | - | - | - |
| 1997-98 | 2 | 2 | - | - | - | - | - | 1 | - | - | 1 | - | - |
| | 4 | 4 | - | - | 1 | - | - | 2 | - | - | 1 | - | - |

**SRI LANKA v ZIMBABWE-IN ZIMBABWE**

| | Tests | Result SL | Result Z | Result D | Harare SL | Harare Z | Harare D | Bulawayo[2] SL | Bulawayo[2] Z | Bulawayo[2] D |
|---|---|---|---|---|---|---|---|---|---|---|
| 1994-95 | 3 | - | - | 3 | - | - | 2 | - | - | 1 |
| Totals | 7 | 4 | - | 3 | | | | | | |

**HIGHEST INNINGS TOTALS**

| | | | |
|---|---|---|---|
| Sri Lanka in Sri Lanka | 9d-469 | Kandy | 1997-98 |
| Sri Lanka in Zimbabwe | 402 | Harare | 1994-95 |
| Zimbabwe in Sri Lanka | 338 | Kandy | 1997-98 |
| Zimbabwe in Zimbabwe | 9-462 | Bulawayo[2] | 1994-95 |

**LOWEST INNINGS TOTALS**

| | | | |
|---|---|---|---|
| Sri Lanka in Sri Lanka | 225 | Colombo (PIS) | 1997-98 |
| Sri Lanka in Zimbabwe | 218 | Bulawayo[2] | 1994-95 |
| Zimbabwe in Sri Lanka | 127 | Colombo (PIS) | 1996-97 |
| Zimbabwe in Zimbabwe | 8-319 | Harare | 1994-95 |

| | | | |
|---|---|---|---|
| **HIGHEST MATCH AGGREGATE** | 1101 for 34 wickets | Colombo (SSC) | 1997-98 |
| **LOWEST MATCH AGGREGATE** | 621 for 30 wickets | Colombo (PIS) | 1996-97 |

**HIGHEST INDIVIDUAL INNINGS**

| | | | | |
|---|---|---|---|---|
| Sri Lanka in Sri Lanka | 223 | M.S.Atapattu | Kandy | 1997-98 |
| Sri Lanka in Zimbabwe | 128 | A.P.Gurusinha | Harare | 1994-95 |
| Zimbabwe in Sri Lanka | 105* | A.Flower | Colombo (SSC) | 1997-98 |
| Zimbabwe in Zimbabwe | 266 | D.L.Houghton | Bulawayo[2] | 1994-95 |

**HIGHEST AGGREGATE OF RUNS IN A SERIES**

| | | | |
|---|---|---|---|
| Sri Lanka in Sri Lanka | 277 (av 92.33) | M.S.Atapattu | 1997-98 |
| Sri Lanka in Zimbabwe | 273 (av 68.25) | S.Ranatunga | 1994-95 |
| Zimbabwe in Sri Lanka | 188 (av 62.66) | A.Flower | 1997-98 |
| Zimbabwe in Zimbabwe | 466 (av 155.33) | D.L.Houghton | 1994-95 |

**RECORD WICKET PARTNERSHIPS-SRI LANKA**

| | | | | |
|---|---|---|---|---|
| 1st | 64 | R.S.Mahanama (24), A.P.Gurusinha (54) | Harare | 1994-95 |
| 2nd | 217 | A.P.Gurusinha (128), S.Ranatunga (118) | Harare | 1994-95 |
| 3rd | 140 | M.S.Atapattu (223), P.A.de Silva (75) | Kandy | 1997-98 |
| 4th | 84 | S.Ranatunga (100*), P.A.de Silva (27) | Bulawayo[2] | 1994-95 |
| 5th | 114 | A.P.Gurusinha (88), H.P.Tillakaratne (116) | Colombo (SSC) | 1996-97 |
| 6th | 189* | P.A.de Silva (143*), A.Ranatunga (87*) | Colombo (SSC) | 1997-98 |
| 7th | 57 | M.S.Atapattu (223), W.P.U.J.C.Vaas (26) | Kandy | 1997-98 |
| 8th | 74 | H.P.D.K.Dharmasena (42*), W.P.U.J.C.Vaas (34) | Colombo (PIS) | 1996-97 |
| 9th | 22 | H.P.D.K.Dharmasena (54), G.P.Wickramasinghe (7) | Bulawayo[2] | 1994-95 |
| 10th | 25 | H.P.D.K.Dharmasena (54), M.Muralidaran (15*) | Bulawayo[2] | 1994-95 |

**RECORD WICKET PARTNERSHIPS-ZIMBABWE**

| | | | | |
|---|---|---|---|---|
| 1st | 113 | G.W.Flower (41), M.H.Dekker (40) | Harare | 1994-95 |
| 2nd | 40 | G.J.Rennie (50), M.W.Goodwin (73) | Colombo (SSC) | 1997-98 |
| 3rd | 194 | A.D.R.Campbell (99), D.L.Houghton (142) | Harare | 1994-95 |
| 4th | 121 | D.L.Houghton (266), A.Flower (50) | Bulawayo[2] | 1994-95 |
| 5th | 76 | A.D.R.Campbell (40), A.Flower (67) | Kandy | 1997-98 |
| 6th | 100 | D.L.Houghton (266), W.R.James (33) | Bulawayo[2] | 1994-95 |
| 7th | 63 | A.Flower (105*), C.B.Wishart (18) | Colombo (SSC) | 1997-98 |
| 8th | 84 | D.L.Houghton (266), J.A.Rennie (19*) | Bulawayo[2] | 1994-95 |
| 9th | 43 | J.A.Rennie (19*), S.G.Peall (30) | Bulawayo[2] | 1994-95 |
| 10th | 34 | P.A.Strang (50), H.K.Olonga (3*) | Colombo (SSC) | 1996-97 |

**BEST INNINGS BOWLING ANALYSIS**

| | | | | |
|---|---|---|---|---|
| Sri Lanka in Sri Lanka | 7-94 | M.Muralidaran | Kandy | 1997-98 |
| Sri Lanka in Zimbabwe | 7-116 | K.R.Pushpakumara | Harare | 1994-95 |
| Zimbabwe in Sri Lanka | 5-106 | P.A.Strang | Colombo (PIS) | 1996-97 |
| Zimbabwe in Zimbabwe | 5-129 | H.H.Streak | Harare | 1994-95 |

**BEST MATCH BOWLING ANALYSIS**

| | | | | |
|---|---|---|---|---|
| Sri Lanka in Sri Lanka | 12-117 | M.Muralidaran | Kandy | 1997-98 |
| Sri Lanka in Zimbabwe | 7-116 | K.R.Pushpakumara | Harare | 1994-95 |
| Zimbabwe in Sri Lanka | 6-112 | H.H.Streak | Colombo (SSC) | 1997-98 |
| Zimbabwe in Zimbabwe | 4-70 | G.J.Whittall | Harare | 1994-95 |

**HIGHEST AGGREGATE OF WICKETS IN SERIES**

| | | | |
|---|---|---|---|
| Sri Lanka in Sri Lanka | 14 (av 13.92) | M.Muralidaran | 1997-98 |
| Sri Lanka in Zimbabwe | 10 (av 23.50) | W.P.U.J.C.Vaas | 1994-95 |
| Zimbabwe in Sri Lanka | 10 (av 21.20) | H.H.Streak | 1997-98 |
| Zimbabwe in Zimbabwe | 13 (av 23.38) | H.H.Streak | 1994-95 |

## The Teams

### HIGHEST INNINGS TOTALS

| | | | | | |
|---|---|---|---|---|---|
| 952-6d | Sri Lanka | v | India | Colombo (PIS) | 1997-98 |
| 903-7d | England | v | Australia | The Oval | 1938 |
| 849 | England | v | West Indies | Kingston | 1929-30 |
| 790-3d | West Indies | v | Pakistan | Kingston | 1957-58 |
| 758-8d | Australia | v | West Indies | Kingston | 1954-55 |
| 729-6d | Australia | v | England | Lord's | 1930 |
| 708 | Pakistan | v | England | The Oval | 1987 |
| 701 | Australia | v | England | The Oval | 1934 |
| 699-5 | Pakistan | v | India | Lahore[2] | 1989-90 |
| 695 | Australia | v | England | The Oval | 1930 |
| 692-8d | West Indies | v | England | The Oval | 1995 |
| 687-8d | West Indies | v | England | The Oval | 1976 |
| 681-8d | West Indies | v | England | Port-of-Spain | 1953-54 |
| 676-7 | India | v | Sri Lanka | Kanpur | 1986-87 |
| 674-6 | Pakistan | v | India | Faisalabad | 1984-85 |
| 674 | Australia | v | India | Adelaide | 1947-48 |
| 671-4 | New Zealand | v | Sri Lanka | Wellington | 1990-91 |
| 668 | Australia | v | West Indies | Bridgetown | 1954-55 |
| 660-5d | West Indies | v | New Zealand | Wellington | 1994-95 |
| 659-8d | Australia | v | England | Sydney | 1946-47 |
| 658-8d | England | v | Australia | Nottingham | 1938 |
| 657-8d | Pakistan | v | West Indies | Bridgetown | 1957-58 |
| 656-8d | Australia | v | England | Manchester | 1964 |
| 654-5 | England | v | South Africa | Durban[2] | 1938-39 |
| 653-4d | England | v | India | Lord's | 1990 |
| 653-4d | Australia | v | England | Leeds | 1993 |
| 652-7d | England | v | India | Madras[1] | 1984-85 |
| 652-8d | West Indies | v | England | Lord's | 1973 |
| 652 | Pakistan | v | India | Faisalabad | 1982-83 |
| 650-6d | Australia | v | West Indies | Bridgetown | 1964-65 |
| 645 | Australia | v | England | Brisbane[2] | 1946-47 |
| 644-7d | India | v | West Indies | Kanpur | 1978-79 |
| 644-8d | West Indies | v | India | Delhi | 1958-59 |
| 636 | England | v | Australia | Sydney | 1928-29 |
| 633-5d | England | v | India | Birmingham | 1979 |
| 633-5d | India | v | Australia | Calcutta | 1997-98 |
| 632-4d | Australia | v | England | Lord's | 1993 |
| 631-8d | West Indies | v | India | Kingston | 1961-62 |
| 631 | West Indies | v | India | Delhi | 1948-49 |
| 629-6d | West Indies | v | India | Bombay[2] | 1948-49 |
| 629 | England | v | India | Lord's | 1974 |
| 628-8d | Australia | v | South Africa | Johannesburg[3] | 1996-97 |
| 627-9d | England | v | Australia | Manchester | 1934 |
| 624 | Pakistan | v | Australia | Adelaide | 1983-84 |
| 622-9d | South Africa | v | Australia | Durban[2] | 1969-70 |
| 620 | South Africa | v | Australia | Johannesburg[3] | 1966-67 |
| 619-6d | England | v | West Indies | Nottingham | 1957 |
| 619 | Australia | v | West Indies | Sydney | 1968-69 |
| 617-5d | Australia | v | Sri Lanka | Perth | 1995-96 |
| 617 | Australia | v | Pakistan | Faisalabad | 1979-80 |
| 616-5d | Pakistan | v | New Zealand | Auckland | 1988-89 |
| 616 | West Indies | v | Australia | Adelaide | 1968-69 |
| 614-5d | West Indies | v | India | Calcutta | 1958-59 |
| 611 | England | v | Australia | Manchester | 1964 |
| 608-7d | Pakistan | v | England | Birmingham | 1971 |
| 608 | England | v | South Africa | Johannesburg[2] | 1948-49 |
| 606 | West Indies | v | England | Birmingham | 1984 |

| | | | | | |
|---|---|---|---|---|---|
| 606-9d | India | v | England | The Oval | 1990 |
| 606 | West Indies | v | Australia | Sydney | 1992-93 |
| 604-6d | West Indies | v | India | Bombay[3] | 1974-75 |
| 604 | Australia | v | England | Melbourne | 1936-37 |
| 602-6d | Australia | v | England | Nottingham | 1989 |
| 601-7d | Australia | v | England | Leeds | 1989 |
| 601-8d | Australia | v | England | Brisbane[2] | 1954-55 |
| 600-4d | India | v | Australia | Sydney | 1985-86 |
| 600-7d | Pakistan | v | England | The Oval | 1974 |
| 600-9d | Australia | v | West Indies | Port-of-Spain | 1954-55 |
| 600 | Australia | v | England | Melbourne | 1924-25 |

*The highest total for the other countries are:*

| | | | | | |
|---|---|---|---|---|---|
| 544-5d | Zimbabwe | v | Pakistan | Harare | 1994-95 |

## BOTH TEAMS SCORING 600

| | | | | |
|---|---|---|---|---|
| Australia (8d-656) | v | England (611) | Manchester | 1964 |

## HIGHEST SECOND INNINGS TOTALS *First innings in brackets (§ After following on.)*

| | | | | | | |
|---|---|---|---|---|---|---|
| 671-4 | (174) | New Zealand | v | Sri Lanka | Wellington | 1990-91 |
| 657-8d § | (106) | Pakistan | v | West Indies | Bridgetown | 1957-58 |
| 654-5 | (316) | England | v | South Africa | Durban[2] | 1938-39 |
| 620 | (199) | South Africa | v | Australia | Johannesburg[3] | 1966-67 |
| 616 | (276) | West Indies | v | Australia | Adelaide | 1968-69 |
| 583-4d | (186) | England | v | West Indies | Birmingham | 1957 |
| 582 | (354) | Australia | v | England | Adelaide | 1920-21 |
| 581 | (267) | Australia | v | England | Sydney | 1920-21 |
| 578 | (328) | Australia | v | South Africa | Melbourne | 1910-11 |
| 564-8 | (133) | West Indies | v | New Zealand | Bridgetown | 1971-72 |
| 564 | (200-9d) | Australia | v | England | Melbourne | 1936-37 |
| 554 | (198) | Australia | v | South Africa | Melbourne | 1931-32 |
| 551 § | (208) | England | v | South Africa | Nottingham | 1947 |

## HIGHEST FOURTH INNINGS TOTALS

| | | | | | | Runs set in 4th innings |
|---|---|---|---|---|---|---|
| *TO WIN* | | | | | | |
| 406-4 | India | v | West Indies | Port-of-Spain | 1975-76 | 403 |
| 404-3 | Australia | v | England | Leeds | 1948 | 404 |
| 362-7 | Australia | v | West Indies | Georgetown | 1977-78 | 359 |
| 348-5 | West Indies | v | New Zealand | Auckland | 1968-69 | 345 |
| 344-1 | West Indies | v | England | Lord's | 1984 | 342 |
| 342-8 | Australia | v | India | Perth | 1977-78 | 339 |
| 336-5 | Australia | v | South Africa | Durban[2] | 1949-50 | 336 |
| 332-7 | England | v | Australia | Melbourne | 1928-29 | 332 |
| 326-5 | Sri Lanka | v | Zimbabwe | Colombo (SSC) | 1997-98 | 326 |
| 324-5 | New Zealand | v | Pakistan | Christchurch | 1993-94 | 323 |
| 317-2 | West Indies | v | Pakistan | Georgetown | 1957-58 | 317 |
| 315-6 | Australia | v | England | Adelaide | 1901-02 | 315 |
| 315-9 | Pakistan | v | Australia | Karachi[1] | 1994-95 | 314 |
| 307-6 | England | v | New Zealand | Christchurch | 1996-97 | 305 |
| *TO TIE* | | | | | | |
| 347 | India | v | Australia | Madras[1] | | 1986-87 |
| *TO LOSE* | | | | | | Losing Margin |
| 445 | India | v | Australia | Adelaide | 1977-78 | 47 |
| 440 | New Zealand | v | England | Nottingham | 1973 | 38 |
| 417 | England | v | Australia | Melbourne | 1976-77 | 45 |
| 411 | England | v | Australia | Sydney | 1924-25 | 193 |
| 402 | Australia | v | England | Manchester | 1981 | 103 |
| 376 | India | v | England | Manchester | 1959 | 171 |
| 370 | England | v | Australia | Adelaide | 1920-21 | 119 |
| 363 | England | v | Australia | Adelaide | 1924-25 | 11 |

Aravinda de Silva on his way to a score of 167 at the Gabba in Brisbane in 1989 — the highest innings score by a Sri Lankan against Australia.

Indian captain Bishen Bedi leads his side to a 16-run victory over Australia at the Gabba in Brisbane in 1977.

The West Indies' Clive Lloyd looks ferocious, cutting square of the wicket, Adelaide, 1979/80.

David Gower, a fine batsman and former English captain, made 114 against Australia in Adelaide in December 1982.

England's Dennis Compton made 147 against Australia in Adelaide in February 1947. Don Tallon kept wicket with Ian Johnson fielding at slip.

The Australian team celebrates Shane Warne's historic hat-trick against England at the MCG in 1994. Warne dismissed Philip de Freitas, Darren Gough and Devon Malcolm with successive balls.

Frank Tyson bowled a devastating spell against Australia at the MCG in January 1955, taking 7 for 27 and spearheading England to victory.

Fred Trueman captured 8 for 31 against India at Old Trafford, Manchester, in 1952.

South Africa's Graeme Pollock made 122 against Australia at the SCG in 1964. The wicketkeeper is the legendary Wally Grout.

Pakistan's Hanif Mohammed scored 104 in Pakistan's first Test in Australia at the MCG in 1964.

Herbert Sutcliffe scored a massive 194 runs for England against Australia at the SCG in 1932.

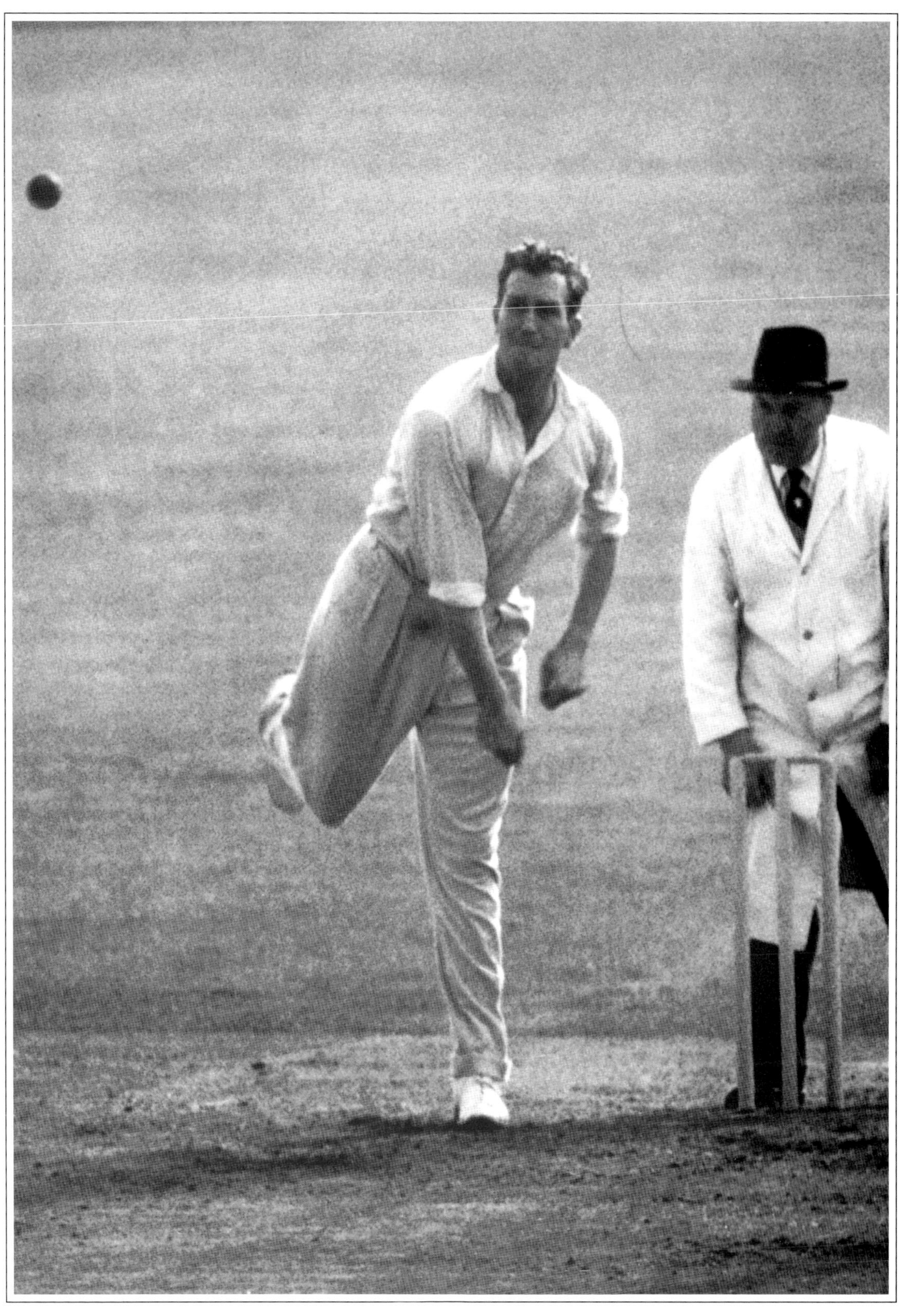

Jim Laker bowled a record-breaking spell against Australia at Old Trafford, Manchester, in 1956. He took 10 for 153 — the only player to take all ten wickets in an innings in the history of Test cricket.

West Indian fast bowler Joel Garner, known as 'Big Bird', took 3 for 49 against Australia at the MCG in 1984, with umpire Steve Randall looking on.

Keith Miller, Australia's greatest all-rounder, batting in characteristically aggressive style at the peak of his career.

Peter Pollock bowls for South Africa against Australia at the MCG in December 1963.

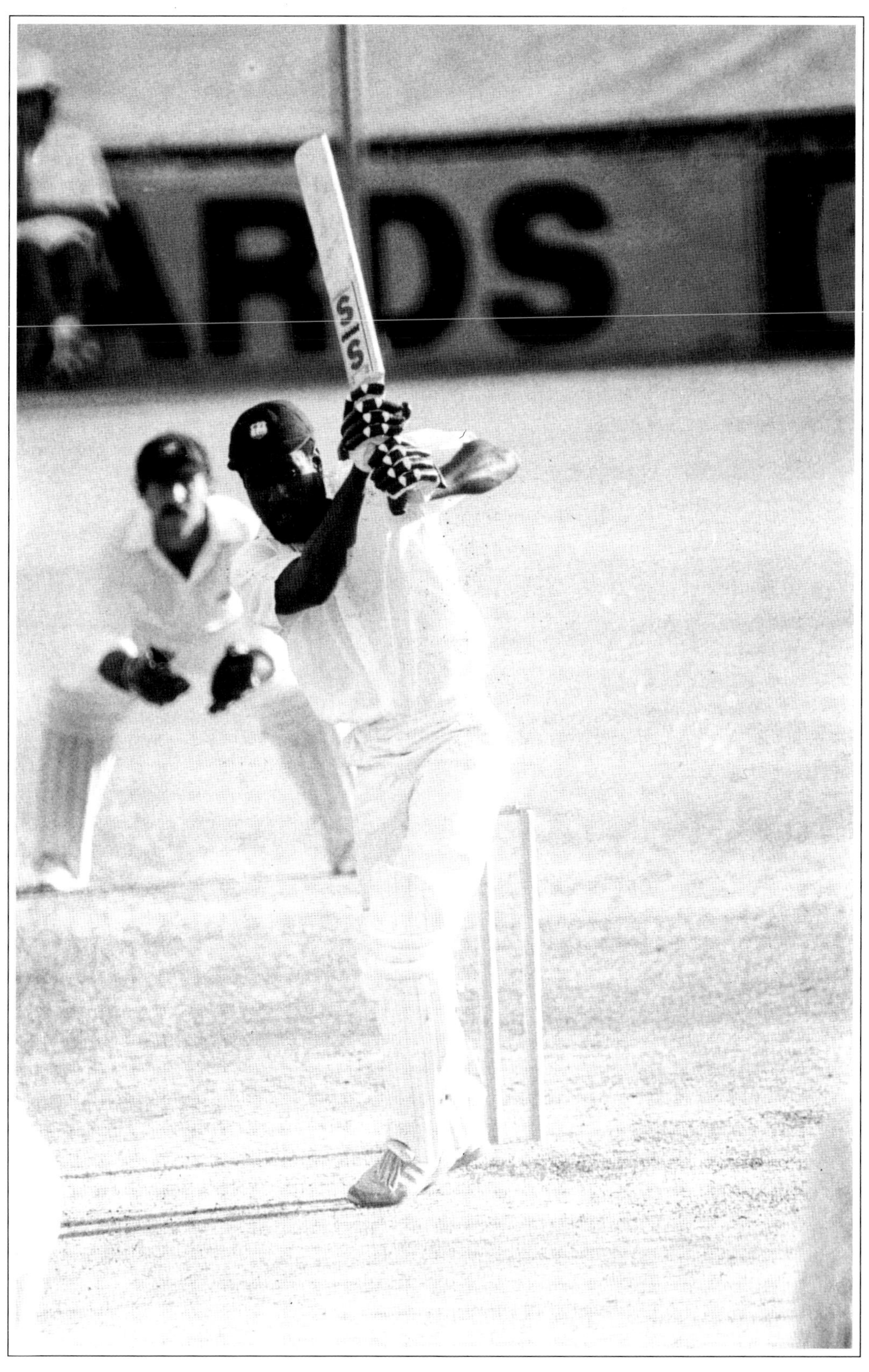

The great Viv Richards, West Indies v Australia, Port of Spain, 1984. Richards' record for the fastest century came in just 56 balls, against England at St John's in 1985–6.

The great New Zealand bowler Sir Richard Hadlee claims one of his ten wickets in the third Test against Australia in Melbourne, December 1987.

| | | | | | | |
|---|---|---|---|---|---|---|
| 355 | India | v | Australia | Brisbane[2] | 1967-68 | 39 |
| 352 | West Indies | v | Australia | Sydney | 1968-69 | 382 |
| 348 | Sri Lanka | v | Australia | Hobart | 1989-90 | 173 |
| 345 | New Zealand | v | England | Nottingham | 1983 | 165 |
| 339 | Australia | v | South Africa | Adelaide | 1910-11 | 38 |
| 336 | Australia | v | England | Adelaide | 1928-29 | 12 |
| 336 | Pakistan | v | Australia | Melbourne | 1989-90 | 92 |
| 335 | Australia | v | England | Nottingham | 1930 | 93 |
| 335 | South Africa | v | New Zealand | Cape Town | 1961-62 | 72 |
| 333 | Australia | v | England | Melbourne | 1894-95 | 94 |
| 333 | India | v | Australia | Adelaide | 1991-92 | 38 |
| 332 | England | v | Australia | Manchester | 1993 | 179 |
| 327 | England | v | West Indies | Georgetown | 1929-30 | 289 |
| 326 | West Indies | v | Australia | Melbourne | 1975-76 | 165 |
| 324 | India | v | Australia | Brisbane[2] | 1977-78 | 16 |
| 323 | England | v | Australia | Melbourne | 1936-37 | 365 |
| 323 | England | v | Australia | Brisbane[2] | 1994-95 | 184 |
| 316 | England | v | West Indies | Kingston | 1953-54 | 140 |
| 313 | England | v | West Indies | Bridgetown | 1953-54 | 181 |
| 310 | Australia | v | Pakistan | Melbourne | 1978-79 | 71 |
| 307 | England | v | West Indies | Lord's | 1988 | 134 |
| 306 | Sri Lanka | v | South Africa | Cape Town | 1997-98 | 377 |
| 304 | South Africa | v | England | Johannesburg[1] | 1913-14 | 91 |
| 301 | Pakistan | v | West Indies | Kingston | 1976-77 | 140 |

| *TO DRAW* | | | | | | Runs set in 4th innings |
|---|---|---|---|---|---|---|
| 654-5 | England | v | South Africa | Durban[2] | 1938-39 | 696 |
| 429-8 | India | v | England | The Oval | 1979 | 438 |
| 423-7 | South Africa | v | England | The Oval | 1947 | 451 |
| 408-5 | West Indies | v | England | Kingston | 1929-30 | 836 |
| 364-6 | India | v | Pakistan | Delhi | 1979-80 | 390 |
| 355-8 | India | v | West Indies | Bombay[2] | 1948-49 | 361 |
| 351-5 | England | v | South Africa | Johannesburg[3] | 1995-96 | 479 |
| 344-6 | Sri Lanka | v | New Zealand | Hamilton | 1990-91 | 418 |
| 344-7 | Australia | v | England | Sydney | 1994-95 | 449 |
| 343-6 | India | v | England | Manchester | 1990 | 408 |
| 341-9 | Pakistan | v | West Indies | Port-of-Spain | 1987-88 | 372 |
| 339-9 | Australia | v | West Indies | Adelaide | 1968-69 | 360 |
| 335-5 | England | v | Australia | Adelaide | 1990-91 | 472 |
| 329-3 | Australia | v | England | Lord's | 1975 | 484 |
| 328-3 | Australia | v | England | Adelaide | 1970-71 | 469 |
| 326-5 | South Africa | v | Australia | Sydney | 1963-64 | 409 |
| 325-3 | India | v | West Indies | Calcutta | 1948-49 | 431 |
| 314-7 | England | v | Australia | Sydney | 1982-83 | 460 |
| 310-7 | England | v | Australia | Melbourne | 1946-47 | 551 |
| 308-4 | England | v | South Africa | The Oval | 1965 | 399 |
| 307-7 | Sri Lanka | v | India | Kandy | 1985-86 | 377 |
| 307-6 | England | v | New Zealand | Christchurch | 1996-97 | 305 |
| 304-8 | New Zealand | v | Zimbabwe | Harare | 1997-98 | 403 |
| 303-3 | India | v | Pakistan | Karachi[1] | 1989-90 | 453 |

## HIGHEST MATCH AGGREGATES - BOTH SIDES

| Runs | Played | | | | | | Days Played |
|---|---|---|---|---|---|---|---|
| 1981 | 35 | South Africa | v | England | Durban[2] | 1938-39 | §10 |
| 1815 | 34 | West Indies | v | England | Kingston | 1929-30 | †9 |
| 1764 | 39 | Australia | v | West Indies | Adelaide | 1968-69 | 5 |
| 1753 | 40 | Australia | v | England | Adelaide | 1920-21 | 6 |
| 1723 | 31 | England | v | Australia | Leeds | 1948 | 5 |
| 1661 | 36 | West Indies | v | Australia | Bridgetown | 1954-55 | 6 |

| | | | | | | | |
|---|---|---|---|---|---|---|---|
| 1646 | 40 | Australia | v | South Africa | Adelaide | 1910-11 | 6 |
| 1644 | 38 | Australia | v | West Indies | Sydney | 1968-69 | 6 |
| 1640 | 24 | West Indies | v | Australia | Bridgetown | 1964-65 | 6 |
| 1640 | 33 | Australia | v | Pakistan | Melbourne | 1972-73 | 5 |
| 1619 | 20 | Australia | v | England | Melbourne | 1924-25 | 7 |
| 1614 | 30 | England | v | India | Manchester | 1990 | 5 |
| 1611 | 40 | Australia | v | England | Sydney | 1924-25 | 7 |
| 1603 | 28 | England | v | India | Lord's | 1990 | 5 |
| 1601 | 29 | England | v | Australia | Lord's | 1930 | 4 |
| 1585 | 31 | Pakistan | v | New Zealand | Karachi[1] | 1976-77 | 5 |
| 1562 | 37 | Australia | v | England | Melbourne | 1946-47 | 6 |
| 1554 | 35 | Australia | v | England | Melbourne | 1928-29 | 8 |
| 1541 | 35 | Australia | v | England | Sydney | 1903-04 | 6 |
| 1528 | 24 | West Indies | v | England | Port-of-Spain | 1953-54 | 6 |
| 1514 | 40 | Australia | v | England | Sydney | 1894-95 | 6 |
| 1507 | 28 | England | v | West Indies | The Oval | 1976 | 5 |
| 1505 | 25 | New Zealand | v | India | Auckland | 1989-90 | 5 |
| 1502 | 29 | Australia | v | England | Adelaide | 1946-47 | 6 |

*§ No play on one day. † No play on two days.*

## HIGHEST MATCH AGGREGATES - ONE SIDE

| Runs | Wkts | | | | | |
|---|---|---|---|---|---|---|
| 1121 | 19 | England | v | West Indies | Kingston | 1929-30 |
| 1028 | 20 | Australia | v | England | The Oval | 1934 |
| 1013 | 18 | Australia | v | West Indies | Sydney | 1968-69 |
| 1011 | 20 | South Africa | v | England | Durban[2] | 1938-39 |

## LOWEST MATCH AGGREGATES *(Completed match)*

| Runs | Wkts | | | | | | Days Played |
|---|---|---|---|---|---|---|---|
| 234 | 29 | Australia | v | South Africa | Melbourne | 1931-32 | §3 |
| 291 | 40 | England | v | Australia | Lord's | 1888 | 2 |
| 295 | 28 | New Zealand | v | Australia | Wellington | 1945-46 | 2 |
| 309 | 29 | West Indies | v | England | Bridgetown | 1934-35 | 3 |
| 323 | 30 | England | v | Australia | Manchester | 1888 | 2 |
| 363 | 40 | England | v | Australia | The Oval | 1882 | 2 |
| 374 | 40 | Australia | v | England | Sydney | 1887-88 | †5 |
| 378 | 30 | England | v | South Africa | The Oval | 1912 | 2 |
| 382 | 30 | South Africa | v | England | Cape Town | 1888-89 | 2 |
| 389 | 38 | England | v | Australia | The Oval | 1890 | 2 |
| 390 | 30 | England | v | New Zealand | Lord's | 1958 | 3 |
| 392 | 40 | England | v | Australia | The Oval | 1896 | 3 |

*§ No play on one day. † No play on two days.*

## LOWEST COMPLETED INNINGS TOTALS

| | | | | | |
|---|---|---|---|---|---|
| 26 | New Zealand | v | England | Auckland | 1954-55 |
| 30 | South Africa | v | England | Port Elizabeth | 1895-96 |
| 30 | South Africa | v | England | Birmingham | 1924 |
| 35 | South Africa | v | England | Cape Town | 1898-99 |
| 36 | Australia | v | England | Birmingham | 1902 |
| 36 | South Africa | v | Australia | Melbourne | 1931-32 |
| 42 | Australia | v | England | Sydney | 1887-88 |
| 42 | New Zealand | v | Australia | Wellington | 1945-46 |
| 42 § | India | v | England | Lord's | 1974 |
| 43 | South Africa | v | England | Cape Town | 1888-89 |
| 44 | Australia | v | England | The Oval | 1896 |
| 45 | England | v | Australia | Sydney | 1886-87 |
| 45 | South Africa | v | Australia | Melbourne | 1931-32 |
| 46 | England | v | West Indies | Port-of-Spain | 1993-94 |
| 47 | South Africa | v | England | Cape Town | 1888-89 |
| 47 | New Zealand | v | England | Lord's | 1958 |

| | | | | | |
|---|---|---|---|---|---|
| 52 | England | v | Australia | The Oval | 1948 |
| 53 | England | v | Australia | Lord's | 1888 |
| 53 | Australia | v | England | Lord's | 1896 |
| 53 | West Indies | v | Pakistan | Faisalabad | 1986-87 |
| 54 | New Zealand | v | Australia | Wellington | 1945-46 |
| 58 | South Africa | v | England | Lord's | 1912 |
| 58 § | Australia | v | England | Brisbane[2] | 1936-37 |
| 58 | India | v | Australia | Brisbane[2] | 1947-48 |
| 58 | India | v | England | Manchester | 1952 |
| 60 | Australia | v | England | Lord's | 1888 |
| 61 | Australia | v | England | Melbourne | 1901-02 |
| 61 | England | v | Australia | Melbourne | 1903-04 |
| 62 | England | v | Australia | Lord's | 1888 |
| 62 | Pakistan | v | Australia | Perth | 1981-82 |
| 63 | Australia | v | England | The Oval | 1882 |
| 64 | England | v | New Zealand | Wellington | 1977-78 |
| 65 | England | v | Australia | Sydney | 1894-95 |
| 65 | Australia | v | England | The Oval | 1912 |
| 65 | New Zealand | v | England | Christchurch | 1970-71 |

*§ One batsman absent hurt/ill.*

*The lowest completed innings total for the other countries are:*

| | | | | | |
|---|---|---|---|---|---|
| 71 | Sri Lanka | v | Pakistan | Kandy | 1994-95 |
| 127 | Zimbabwe | v | Sri Lanka | Colombo (PIS) | 1996-97 |

*The following innings were closed at a low total:*

| | | | | | |
|---|---|---|---|---|---|
| 32-7d | Australia | v | England | Brisbane[2] | 1950-51 |
| 35-8 | Australia | v | England | Manchester | 1953 |
| 48-8 | New Zealand | v | England | Christchurch | 1965-66 |
| 51-6d | West Indies | v | England | Bridgetown | 1934-35 |

## DISMISSED FOR UNDER 100 IN BOTH INNINGS

| | | | | | | |
|---|---|---|---|---|---|---|
| 42 | 82 | Australia | v | England | Sydney | 1887-88 |
| 53 | 62 | England | v | Australia | Lord's | 1888 |
| 81 | 70 | Australia | v | England | Manchester | 1888 |
| 47 | 43 | South Africa | v | England | Cape Town | 1888-89 |
| 97 | 83 | South Africa | v | England | Cape Town | 1891-92 |
| 65 | 72 | England | v | Australia | Sydney | 1894-95 |
| 93 | 30 | South Africa | v | England | Port Elizabeth | 1895-96 |
| 95 | 93 | South Africa | v | England | The Oval | 1912 |
| 36 | 45 | South Africa | v | Australia | Melbourne | 1931-32 |
| 42 | 54 | New Zealand | v | Australia | Wellington | 1945-46 |
| 58 | 98 | India | v | Australia | Brisbane[2] | 1947-48 |
| 58 | 82 | India | v | England | Manchester | 1952 |
| 89 | 86 | West Indies | v | England | The Oval | 1957 |
| 47 | 74 | New Zealand | v | England | Lord's | 1958 |
| 82 | 93 | England | v | New Zealand | Christchurch | 1983-84 |

## RESULTS BY NARROW MARGINS - TIE

| | | | | |
|---|---|---|---|---|
| Australia (505 + 232) | v | West Indies (453 + 284) | Brisbane[2] | 1960-61 |
| India (397 + 347) | v | Australia (7d-574 + 5d-170) | Madras[1] | 1986-87 |

## RESULTS BY NARROW MARGINS - WON BY ONE WICKET

| | | | | 10th Wicket Partnership | |
|---|---|---|---|---|---|
| England (183 + 9-263) | v | Australia (324 + 121) | The Oval | 15* | 1902 |
| South Africa (91 + 9-287) | v | England (184 + 190) | Johannesburg[1] | 48* | 1905-06 |
| England (382 + 9-282) | v | Australia (266 + 397) | Melbourne | 39* | 1907-08 |
| England (183 + 9-173) | v | South Africa (113 + 242) | Cape Town | 5* | 1922-23 |
| Australia (216 + 9-260) | v | West Indies (272 + 203 | Melbourne | 38* | 1951-52 |
| New Zealand (249 + 9-104) | v | West Indies (140 + 212) | Dunedin | 4* | 1979-80 |
| Pakistan (256 + 9-315) | v | Australia (337 + 232) | Karachi[1] | 57* | 1994-95 |

* *(unbroken)*

## RESULTS BY NARROW MARGINS - WON BY TWO WICKETS

| | | | | |
|---|---|---|---|---|
| England (100 + 8-95) | v | Australia (92 + 102) | The Oval | 1890 |
| Australia (300 + 8-275) | v | England (273 + 100) | Sydney | 1907-08 |
| § England (253 + 8-128) | v | South Africa (161 + 219) | Durban[2] | 1948-49 |
| Australia (356 + 8-258) | v | West Indies (292 + 321) | Melbourne | 1960-61 |
| India (341 + 8-256) | v | Australia (320 + 274) | Bombay[2] | 1964-65 |
| Australia (394 + 8-342) | v | India (402 + 9d-330) | Perth | 1977-78 |
| West Indies (308+ 8-209) | v | England (263 + 252) | Nottingham | 1980 |
| New Zealand (220 + 8-278) | v | Pakistan (274 + 223) | Dunedin | 1984-85 |
| West Indies (306 + 8-268) | v | Pakistan (309 + 262) | Bridgetown | 1987-88 |
| Pakistan (293 + 8-141) | v | England (255 + 175) | Lord's | 1992 |
| Australia (108 + 8-271) | v | South Africa (209 + 168) | Port Elizabeth | 1996-97 |

*§ England won by a leg bye off the last possible ball*

## RESULTS BY NARROW MARGINS - LESS THAN TWENTY RUNS

| | | | | | |
|---|---|---|---|---|---|
| 1 | West Indies (252 + 146) | v | Australia (213 + 184) | Adelaide | 1992-93 |
| 3 | Australia (299 + 86) | v | England (262 + 120) | Manchester | 1902 |
| 3 | England (284 + 294) | v | Australia (287 + 288) | Melbourne | 1982-83 |
| 5 | South Africa (169 + 239) | v | Australia (292 + 111) | Sydney | 1993-94 |
| 6 | Australia (182 + 165) | v | England (133 + 207) | Sydney | 1884-85 |
| 7 | Australia (63 + 122) | v | England (101 + 77) | The Oval | 1882 |
| 10 | England (325 + 437) | v | Australia (586 + 166) | Sydney | 1894-95 |
| 11 | Australia (489 + 250) | v | England (365 + 363) | Adelaide | 1924-25 |
| 12 | England (334 + 383) | v | Australia (369 + 336) | Adelaide | 1928-29 |
| 13 | England (115 + 184) | v | Australia (119 + 97) | Sydney | 1886-87 |
| 16 | Australia (166 + 327) | v | India (153 + 324) | Brisbane[2] | 1977-78 |
| 16 | Pakistan (116 + 249) | v | India (145 + 204) | Bangalore | 1986-87 |
| 16 | Australia (256 + 471) | v | Sri Lanka (8d-547 + 164) | Colombo (SSC) | 1992-93 |
| 17 | South Africa (340 + 142) | v | England (251 + 214) | Johannesburg[3] | 1956-57 |
| 18 | England (174 + 356) | v | Australia (9d-401 + 111) | Leeds | 1981 |
| 19 | South Africa (208 + 345) | v | England (310 + 224) | Johannesburg[1] | 1909-10 |
| 19 | England (180 + 163) | v | Australia (220 + 104) | The Oval | 1997 |

*At Port-of-Spain in 1934-35, West Indies took England's last second innings wicket with the fifth ball of the last possible over to win by 217 runs.*

| DRAWS | Target | Total | Opponents | | |
|---|---|---|---|---|---|
| India | 361 | 355-8 | West Indies | Bombay[2] | 1948-49 |
| England | 234 | 228-9 | West Indies | Lord's | 1963 |
| Australia | 360 | 339-9 | West Indies | Adelaide | 1968-69 |
| Australia | 246 | 238-8 | England | Melbourne | 1974-75 |
| India | 438 | 429-8 | England | The Oval | 1979 |
| Australia | 247 | 230-9 | New Zealand | Melbourne | 1987-88 |
| Pakistan | 372 | 341-9 | West Indies | Port-of-Spain | 1987-88 |
| England | 205 | 204-6 | Zimbabwe | Bulawayo[2] | 1996-97 |
| New Zealand | 288 | 9-223 | Australia | Hobart | 1997-98 |

## GREATEST TEST VICTORIES BY AN INNINGS

| | | | | | |
|---|---|---|---|---|---|
| Inns and 579 runs | England | v | Australia | The Oval | 1938 |
| Inns and 336 runs | West Indies | v | India | Calcutta | 1958-59 |
| Inns and 332 runs | Australia | v | England | Brisbane[2] | 1946-47 |
| Inns and 322 runs | West Indies | v | New Zealand | Wellington | 1994-95 |
| Inns and 285 runs | England | v | India | Lord's | 1974 |
| Inns and 259 runs | Australia | v | South Africa | Port Elizabeth | 1949-50 |
| Inns and 237 runs | England | v | West Indies | The Oval | 1957 |
| Inns and 230 runs | England | v | Australia | Adelaide | 1891-92 |
| Inns and 226 runs | Australia | v | India | Brisbane[2] | 1947-48 |
| Inns and 226 runs | West Indies | v | England | Lord's | 1973 |
| Inns and 225 runs | England | v | Australia | Melbourne | 1911-12 |
| Inns and 222 runs | Australia | v | New Zealand | Hobart | 1993-94 |

| | | | | | |
|---|---|---|---|---|---|
| Inns and 219 runs | India | v | Australia | Calcutta | 1997-98 |
| Inns and 217 runs | England | v | Australia | The Oval | 1886 |
| Inns and 217 runs | Australia | v | West Indies | Brisbane[1] | 1930-31 |
| Inns and 215 runs | England | v | New Zealand | Auckland | 1962-63 |
| Inns and 208 runs | South Africa | v | Sri Lanka | Colombo (SSC) | 1993-94 |
| Inns and 207 runs | England | v | India | Manchester | 1952 |
| Inns and 202 runs | England | v | South Africa | Cape Town | 1888-89 |
| Inns and 200 runs | Australia | v | England | Melbourne | 1936-37 |

## GREATEST TEST VICTORIES BY A RUN MARGIN

| | | | | | |
|---|---|---|---|---|---|
| 675 runs | England | v | Australia | Brisbane[1] | 1928-29 |
| 562 runs | Australia | v | England | The Oval | 1934 |
| 530 runs | Australia | v | South Africa | Melbourne | 1910-11 |
| 425 runs | West Indies | v | England | Manchester | 1976 |
| 409 runs | Australia | v | England | Lord's | 1948 |
| 408 runs | West Indies | v | Australia | Adelaide | 1979-80 |
| 382 runs | Australia | v | England | Adelaide | 1894-95 |
| 382 runs | Australia | v | West Indies | Sydney | 1968-69 |
| 377 runs | Australia | v | England | Sydney | 1920-21 |
| 365 runs | Australia | v | England | Melbourne | 1936-37 |
| 356 runs | South Africa | v | England | Lord's | 1994 |
| 348 runs | Australia | v | Pakistan | Melbourne | 1976-77 |
| 343 runs | West Indies | v | Australia | Bridgetown | 1990-91 |
| 338 runs | England | v | Australia | Adelaide | 1932-33 |
| 329 runs | Australia | v | England | Perth | 1994-95 |
| 329 runs | South Africa | v | India | Calcutta | 1996-97 |
| 328 runs | South Africa | v | India | Durban[2] | 1996-97 |
| 326 runs | West Indies | v | England | Lord's | 1950 |
| 324 runs | South Africa | v | Pakistan | Johannesburg[3] | 1994-95 |
| 323 runs | South Africa | v | Australia | Port Elizabeth | 1969-70 |
| 322 runs | England | v | Australia | Brisbane[2] | 1936-37 |
| 312 runs | England | v | South Africa | Cape Town | 1956-57 |
| 308 runs | Australia | v | England | Melbourne | 1907-08 |
| 307 runs | Australia | v | England | Sydney | 1924-25 |
| 307 runs | South Africa | v | Australia | Johannesburg[3] | 1969-70 |
| 301 runs | Pakistan | v | Sri Lanka | Colombo (PSS) | 1994-95 |
| 300 runs | Australia | v | India | Perth | 1991-92 |

## VICTORY LOSING FEWEST WICKETS

*TWO WICKETS*

| | | | | |
|---|---|---|---|---|
| England (2d-531) | v | South Africa (273 + 240) | Lord's | 1924 |
| England (2d-267) | v | New Zealand (67 + 129) | Leeds | 1958 |
| England (2d-459) | v | India (165 + 216) | Birmingham | 1974 |

## VICTORY AFTER FOLLOWING-ON

| | | | | |
|---|---|---|---|---|
| England (325 + 437) | beat | Australia (586 +166) by 10 runs | Sydney | 1894-95 |
| England (174 + 356) | beat | Australia (9d-401 + 111) by 12 runs | Leeds | 1981 |

## BATSMEN'S PARADISE (Over 60 runs per wicket)

| Runs per Wkt | Runs-Wkts | | | | | |
|---|---|---|---|---|---|---|
| 109.30 | (1093-10) | India | v | New Zealand | Delhi | 1955-56 |
| 106.35 | (1489-14) | Sri Lanka | v | India | Colombo (PIS) | 1997-98 |
| 99.40 | (994-10) | West Indies | v | New Zealand | Georgetown | 1971-72 |
| 86.87 | (695-8) | New Zealand | v | England | Wellington | 1987-88 |
| 83.25 | (999-12) | Pakistan | v | Australia | Faisalabad | 1979-80 |
| 82.27 | (905-11) | England | v | Pakistan | Birmingham | 1992 |
| 81.93 | (1229-15) | West Indies | v | England | St John's | 1993-94 |
| 80.53 | (1208-15) | Pakistan | v | India | Lahore[2] | 1989-90 |
| 79.53 | (1034-13) | Pakistan | v | Sri Lanka | Faisalabad | 1985-86 |

| | | | | | | |
|---|---|---|---|---|---|---|
| 78.25 | (1252-16) | India | v | West Indies | Calcutta | 1987-88 |
| 73.37 | (1174-16) | Pakistan | v | India | Faisalabad | 1984-85 |
| 73.06 | (1096-15) | India | v | West Indies | Kanpur | 1978-79 |
| 70.61 | (1271-18) | England | v | Australia | Manchester | 1964 |
| 68.33 | (1640-24) | West Indies | v | Australia | Bridgetown | 1964-65 |
| 66.95 | (1406-21) | West Indies | v | Pakistan | Kingston | 1957-58 |
| 65.35 | (1307-20) | England | v | Australia | Manchester | 1934 |
| 65.00 | (1235-19) | India | v | West Indies | Bombay[2] | 1948-49 |
| 64.75 | (1036-16) | India | v | New Zealand | Hyderabad | 1955-56 |
| 64.52 | (1226-19) | Australia | v | West Indies | Sydney | 1992-93 |
| 64.47 | (1096-17) | India | v | Sri Lanka | Kanpur | 1986-87 |
| 63.66 | (1528-24) | West Indies | v | England | Port-of-Spain | 1953-54 |
| 63.41 | (1078-17) | India | v | Australia | Bombay[3] | 1986-87 |
| 62.33 | (1496-24) | England | v | Australia | Nottingham | 1938 |
| 62.22 | (1369-22) | England | v | West Indies | The Oval | 1995 |
| 62.11 | (1118-18) | New Zealand | v | Pakistan | Auckland | 1988-89 |
| 62.00 | (1116-18) | West Indies | v | England | Bridgetown | 1959-60 |
| 61.86 | (1423-23) | England | v | India | The Oval | 1990 |
| 61.52 | (1042-17) | India | v | Pakistan | Madras[2] | 1960-61 |
| 60.94 | (1158-12) | India | v | England | Kanpur | 1984-85 |
| 60.62 | (1455-24) | New Zealand | v | Australia | Wellington | 1973-74 |
| 60.57 | (1272-21) | Pakistan | v | India | Faisalabad | 1978-79 |
| 60.45 | (1209-20) | Australia | v | England | Adelaide | 1986-87 |
| 60.20 | (1505-25) | New Zealand | v | India | Auckland | 1989-90 |

## MOST CENTURIES IN AN INNINGS

| | | | | | |
|---|---|---|---|---|---|
| 5 | Australia (8d-758) | v | West Indies | Kingston | 1954-55 |
| 4 | England (8d-658) | v | Australia | Nottingham | 1938 |
| 4 | West Indies (631) | v | India | Delhi | 1948-49 |
| 4 | Pakistan (652) | v | India | Faisalabad | 1982-83 |
| 4 | West Indies (550) | v | India | St John's | 1982-83 |

*The most fifties in a Test innings is seven by England (9d-627) v Australia at Manchester in 1934.*

## MOST CENTURIES IN A MATCH (BOTH TEAMS)

| | | | | | |
|---|---|---|---|---|---|
| 7 | England (4) | v | Australia (3) | Nottingham | 1938 |
| 7 | West Indies (2) | v | Australia (5) | Kingston | 1954-55 |

*The most fifties in a Test match is 17 by Australia (10) and West Indies (7) at Adelaide in 1968-69.*

## MOST CENTURIES IN A SERIES (ONE TEAM)

| | | | | Venue | | Tests |
|---|---|---|---|---|---|---|
| 12 | Australia | v | West Indies | West Indies | 1954-55 | 5 |
| 12 | Pakistan | v | India | Pakistan | 1982-83 | 6 |
| 11 | England | v | South Africa | South Africa | 1938-39 | 5 |
| 11 | West Indies | v | India | India | 1948-49 | 5 |
| 11 | Australia | v | South Africa | South Africa | 1949-50 | 5 |
| 11 | India | v | West Indies | India | 1978-79 | 6 |

## MOST CENTURIES IN A SERIES (BOTH TEAMS)

| | | | | Venue | | Tests |
|---|---|---|---|---|---|---|
| 21 | West Indies (9) | v | Australia (12) | West Indies | 1954-55 | 5 |
| 17 | Australia (9) | v | England (8) | Australia | 1928-29 | 5 |
| 17 | South Africa (6) | v | England (11) | South Africa | 1938-39 | 5 |
| 17 | Pakistan (12) | v | India (5) | Pakistan | 1982-83 | 6 |
| 16 | India (5) | v | West Indies (11) | India | 1948-49 | 5 |
| 16 | Australia (10) | v | West Indies (6) | Australia | 1968-69 | 5 |
| 16 | Australia (10) | v | West Indies (6) | Australia | 1975-76 | 6 |
| 15 | Australia (10) | v | England (5) | Australia | 1946-47 | 5 |
| 15 | England (9) | v | India (6) | England | 1990 | 3 |

## WINNING EVERY TEST IN A SERIES (Minimum: 4 matches)

| | | | Venue | | Tests |
|---|---|---|---|---|---|
| Australia | v | England | Australia | 1920-21 | 5 |
| Australia | v | South Africa | Australia | 1931-32 | 5 |
| England | v | India | England | 1959 | 5 |
| West Indies | v | India | West Indies | 1961-62 | 5 |
| Australia | v | India | Australia | 1967-68 | 4 |
| South Africa | v | Australia | South Africa | 1969-70 | 4 |
| West Indies | v | England | England | 1984 | 5 |
| West Indies | v | England | West Indies | 1985-86 | 5 |

*The following countries won 6-match series in Australia by 5 Tests to one: Australia (v West Indies 1975-76) England (v Australia 1978-79).*

## DRAWING EVERY TEST IN A FIVE-MATCH SERIES

| | | | |
|---|---|---|---|
| Pakistan | v | India | 1954-55 |
| India | v | Pakistan | 1960-61 |
| India | v | England | 1963-64 |
| West Indies | v | New Zealand | 1971-72 |

## MOST CONSECUTIVE WINS

| | | | | | | |
|---|---|---|---|---|---|---|
| 11 | West Indies | Bridgetown | 1983-84 | to | Adelaide | 1984-85 |
| 8 | Australia | Sydney | 1920-21 | to | Leeds | 1921 |
| 7 | England | Melbourne | 1884-85 | to | Sydney | 1887-88 |
| 7 | England | Lord's | 1928 | to | Adelaide | 1928-29 |
| 7 | West Indies | Bridgetown | 1984-85 | to | St John's | 1985-86 |
| 7 | West Indies | Lord's | 1988 | to | Melbourne | 1988-89 |
| 6 | England | The Oval | 1888 | to | The Oval | 1890 |
| 6 | England | Leeds | 1957 | to | Manchester | 1958 |
| 6 | West Indies | Port-of-Spain | 1961-62 | to | Manchester | 1963 |

## MOST CONSECUTIVE MATCHES WITHOUT DEFEAT

| | | | | | | |
|---|---|---|---|---|---|---|
| 27 | West Indies | Sydney | 1981-82 | to | Melbourne | 1984-85 |
| 26 | England | Lord's | 1968 | to | Manchester | 1971 |
| 25 | Australia | Wellington | 1945-46 | to | Adelaide | 1950-51 |
| 18 | England | Christchurch | 1958-59 | to | Birmingham | 1961 |
| 17 | Australia | Madras[2] | 1956-57 | to | Delhi | 1959-60 |
| 17 | India | Kandy | 1985-86 | to | Ahmedabad | 1986-87 |
| 16 | Australia | Sydney | 1920-21 | to | Adelaide | 1924-25 |
| 16 | Pakistan | Karachi[1] | 1986-87 | to | Port-of-Spain | 1987-88 |
| 15 | England | Melbourne | 1911-12 | to | Port Elizabeth | 1913-14 |
| 15 | Pakistan | Wellington | 1972-73 | to | Adelaide | 1976-77 |
| 15 | India | Lord's | 1979 | to | Calcutta | 1979-80 |
| 15 | West Indies | Christchurch | 1979-80 | to | Kingston | 1980-81 |
| 14 | Australia | Sydney | 1988-89 | to | Sydney | 1989-90 |
| 13 | India | Port-of-Spain | 1952-53 | to | Madras[2] | 1955-56 |
| 13 | Australia | The Oval | 1972 | to | Wellington | 1973-74 |
| 12 | England | The Oval | 1938 | to | The Oval | 1946 |
| 12 | Pakistan | Manchester | 1954 | to | Bridgetown | 1957-58 |
| 12 | England | The Oval | 1966 | to | Georgetown | 1967-68 |
| 12 | Pakistan | Karachi[1] | 1982-83 | to | Nagpur | 1983-84 |

## MOST CONSECUTIVE DEFEATS

| | | | | | | |
|---|---|---|---|---|---|---|
| 8 † | South Africa | Port Elizabeth | 1888-89 | to | Cape Town | 1898-99 |
| 8 | England | Sydney | 1920-21 | to | Leeds | 1921 |
| 7 | Australia | Melbourne | 1884-85 | to | Sydney | 1887-88 |
| 7 | England | Lord's | 1950 | to | Adelaide | 1950-51 |
| 7 | India | Leeds | 1967 | to | Sydney | 1967-68 |
| 7 | England | Kingston | 1985-86 | to | Leeds | 1986 |
| 7 | England | The Oval | 1992 | to | Lord's | 1993 |
| 6 | South Africa | Melbourne | 1910-11 | to | Lord's | 1912 |

| | | | | | | |
|---|---|---|---|---|---|---|
| 6 | New Zealand | Johannesburg[2] | 1953-54 | to | Lahore[1] | 1955-56 |
| 6 | India | Nottingham | 1959 | to | Delhi | 1959-60 |
| 6 | Australia | Bridgetown | 1983-84 | to | Adelaide | 1984-85 |

*† South Africa's first 8 Tests*

## MOST CONSECUTIVE MATCHES WITHOUT VICTORY

| | | | | | | |
|---|---|---|---|---|---|---|
| 44 † | New Zealand | Christchurch | 1929-30 | to | Wellington | 1955-56 |
| 31 | India | Bangalore | 1981-82 | to | Faisalabad | 1984-85 |
| 28 | South Africa | Leeds | 1935 | to | Port Elizabeth | 1949-50 |
| 24 | India | Lord's | 1932 | to | Kanpur | 1951-52 |
| 23 | New Zealand | Auckland | 1962-63 | to | Dunedin | 1967-68 |
| 22 | Pakistan | Lahore[1] | 1958-59 | to | Christchurch | 1964-65 |
| 21 | Sri Lanka | Colombo (PSS) | 1985-86 | to | Moratuwa | 1992-93 |
| 20 | West Indies | Wellington | 1968-69 | to | Port-of-Spain | 1972-73 |
| 18 | New Zealand | Dacca | 1969-70 | to | Wellington | 1973-74 |
| 18 | England | Sydney | 1986-87 | to | The Oval | 1988 |
| 16 | South Africa | Melbourne | 1910-11 | to | Cape Town | 1921-22 |
| 16 | Pakistan | Lord's | 1967 | to | Wellington | 1972-73 |
| 14 | India | Madras[2] | 1956-57 | to | Delhi | 1959-60 |
| 14 | Australia | Perth | 1985-86 | to | Melbourne | 1986-87 |
| 14 | India | Georgetown | 1988-89 | to | The Oval | 1990 |
| 14 | New Zealand | Durban[2] | 1994-95 | to | St John's | 1995-96 |
| 13 | India | Madras[1] | 1952-53 | to | Hyderabad | 1955-56 |
| 13 | England | Wellington | 1983-84 | to | Bombay[3] | 1984-85 |
| 13 | Sri Lanka | Colombo (PSS) | 1981-82 | to | Colombo (SSC) | 1985-86 |
| 13 | New Zealand | Nottingham | 1990 | to | Bulawayo[1] | 1992-93 |
| 13 | Sri Lanka | Kandy | 1993-94 | to | Harare | 1994-95 |
| 12 | South Africa | Cape Town | 1922-23 | to | Durban[2] | 1927-28 |
| 12 | England | Leeds | 1963 | to | The Oval | 1964 |
| 12 | England | Nottingham | 1980 | to | Lord's | 1981 |

*† New Zealand's first 44 Tests.*

## MOST CONSECUTIVE DRAWS

| | | | | | | |
|---|---|---|---|---|---|---|
| 10 | West Indies | Georgetown | 1970-71 | to | Bridgetown | 1972-73 |
| 9 | India | Port-of-Spain | 1952-53 | to | Hyderabad | 1955-56 |
| 9 | India | Calcutta | 1959-60 | to | Delhi | 1961-62 |

## MOST RUNS IN ONE DAY - BY ONE TEAM

| | | | | | | Day |
|---|---|---|---|---|---|---|
| 503-2 | England (0-28 to 2d-531) | v | South Africa | Lord's | 1924 | 2nd |
| 494-6 | Australia (6-496) | v | South Africa | Sydney | 1910-11 | 1st |
| 475-2 | Australia (2-475) | v | England | The Oval | 1934 | 1st |
| 471-8 | England (8d-471) | v | India | The Oval | 1936 | 1st |
| 458-3 | Australia (3-458) | v | England | Leeds | 1930 | 1st |
| 455-1 | Australia (3-93 to 4-494) | v | England | Leeds | 1934 | 2nd |
| 451-10 | South Africa (451) | v | New Zealand | Christchurch | 1931-32 | 2nd |
| 450-10 | Australia (450) | v | South Africa | Johannesburg[1] | 1921-22 | 1st |

## MOST RUNS IN ONE DAY - BY BOTH TEAMS

| | | | | | | Day |
|---|---|---|---|---|---|---|
| 588-6 | England (2-173 to 8d-571) | v | India (0-190) | Manchester | 1936 | 2nd |
| 522-2 | England (0-28 to 2d-531) | v | South Africa (0-19) | Lord's | 1924 | 2nd |
| 508-8 | England (4-313- to 6d-534) | v | South Africa (6-287) | The Oval | 1935 | 3rd |
| 496-4 | England (2-121 to 6d-558) | v | Pakistan (0-59) | Nottingham | 1952 | 2nd |
| 492-8 | South Africa (6-297 to 476) | v | England (4-313) | The Oval | 1935 | 2nd |
| 491-7 | New Zealand (9-312 to 341 + 2-195) | v | England (4d-267) | Leeds | 1949 | 3rd |
| 473-4 | South Africa (5-283 to 8d-492) | v | England (1-264) | The Oval | 1929 | 3rd |
| 471-9 | Australia (3-162 to 389) | v | England (2-244) | The Oval | 1921 | 3rd |
| 469-7 | West Indies (6-395 to 498) | v | England (3d-366) | The Oval | 1939 | 3rd |
| 464-11 | Australia (448) | v | South Africa (1-16) | Manchester | 1912 | 1st |
| 458-12 | Australia (3-239 to 8d-394) | v | West Indies (7-303) | Sydney | 1968-69 | 5th |

## FEWEST RUNS IN A FULL DAY'S PLAY

| | | | | | | Day |
|---|---|---|---|---|---|---|
| 95-12 | Australia (80 all out) | v | Pakistan (2-15) | Karachi[1] | 1956-57 | 1st |
| 104-5 | Pakistan (5-104) | v | Australia | Karachi[1] | 1959-60 | 4th |
| 106-8 | England (2-92 to 198 all out) | v | Australia | Brisbane[2] | 1958-59 | 4th |
| 112-5 | Australia (6-138 to 187 all out) | v | Pakistan (1-63) | Karachi[1] | 1956-57 | 4th |
| 115-18 | Australia (7-116 to 165 all out + 5-66) | v | Pakistan | Karachi[1] | 1988-89 | 4th |
| 117-5 | India (5-117) | v | Australia | Madras[2] | 1956-57 | 1st |
| 117-4 | New Zealand (0-6 to 1-123) | v | Sri Lanka | Colombo (SSC) | 1983-84 | 5th |
| 122-8 | England (9-110 to 110) | v | South Africa (7-122) | Port Elizabeth | 1956-57 | 3rd |
| 122-6 | Australia (6-156 to 186) | v | England (2-92) | Brisbane[1] | 1958-59 | 3rd |
| 122-15 | Australia (6-282 to 306 + 1-9) | v | England (87) | Melbourne | 1958-59 | 4th |
| 122-14 | Australia (4-243 to 258) | v | England (8-107) | Melbourne | 1978-79 | 2nd |
| 123-9 | England (2-123 to 191) | v | Pakistan (1-55) | Hyderabad | 1977-78 | 3rd |
| 124-7 | Pakistan (4-74 to 134) | v | Australia (1-64) | Dacca | 1959-60 | 4th |
| 124-6 | India (6-226 to 291) | v | Australia (2-59) | Kanpur | 1959-60 | 4th |
| 127-8 | India (3-162 to 245) | v | Pakistan (1-44) | Peshawar[1] | 1954-55 | 3rd |
| 127-8 | West Indies (2-291 to 353) | v | England (0-65) | Kingston | 1959-60 | 4th |
| 128-7 | England (2-53 to 9-181) | v | West Indies | Bridgetown | 1953-54 | 3rd |
| 129-6 | Pakistan (6-129) | v | India | Peshawar[1] | 1954-55 | 1st |
| 129-11 | India (1-46 to 149 + 2-26) | v | Australia | Madras[2] | 1959-60 | 3rd |
| 130-14 | South Africa (7-200 to 243) | v | New Zealand (78 + 1-8) | Johannesburg[2] | 1953-54 | 2nd |
| 130-6 | India (5-115 to 148) | v | Pakistan (1-97) | Dacca | 1954-55 | 3rd |
| 130-8 | West Indies (7-349 to 386) | v | New Zealand (5-93) | Christchurch | 1955-56 | 2nd |
| 130-4 | Pakistan (4-130) | v | India | Ahmedabad | 1986-87 | 1st |
| 134-9 | England (1-333 to 439) | v | Pakistan (0-28) | Dacca | 1961-62 | 4th |
| 136-14 | South Africa (5-138 to 164) | v | England (9-110) | Port Elizabeth | 1956-57 | 2nd |
| 136-6 | New Zealand (0-9 to 6-145) | v | India | Bangalore | 1988-89 | 3rd |
| 138-6 | Australia (6-138) | v | Pakistan | Karachi[1] | 1956-57 | 3rd |
| 138-5 | South Africa (5-138) | v | England | Port Elizabeth | 1956-57 | 1st |
| 140-5 | New Zealand (1-8 to 6-148) | v | South Africa | Johannesburg[2] | 1953-54 | 3rd |

## E XTRAS TOP SCORING IN A COMPLETED INNINGS

| | Total | HS | Extras | Opponents | | |
|---|---|---|---|---|---|---|
| South Africa | 58 | 13 | 17 | England | Lord's | 1912 |
| South Africa | 30 | 7 | 11 | England | Birmingham | 1924 |
| New Zealand | 97 | 19 | 20 | England | Nottingham | 1973 |
| England | 126 | 24 | 25 | West Indies | Manchester | 1976 |
| England | 227 | 33 | 46 | Pakistan | Lord's | 1982 |
| Australia | 200 | 29 | 36 | West Indies | St John's | 1983-84 |
| England | 315 | 47 | 59 | West Indies | Port-of-Spain | 1985-86 |
| New Zealand | 160 | 33 | 38 | Pakistan | Lahore[2] | 1990-91 |
| Australia | 248 | 47 | 53 | West Indies | Georgetown | 1990-91 |
| New Zealand | 93 | 22 | 19 | Pakistan | Hamilton | 1992-93 |
| (Zimbabwe | 8-319 | 58 | 65 | Sri Lanka | Harare | 1994-95) |

## COMPLETED INNINGS WITHOUT EXTRAS

| Total | Wicketkeeper | | | | | |
|---|---|---|---|---|---|---|
| 328 | N.S.Tamhane | India | v | Pakistan | Lahore[1] | 1954-55 |
| 252 | W.Farrimond | England | v | South Africa | Durban[2] | 1930-31 |
| 247 | J.M.Parks | England | v | South Africa | Nottingham | 1960 |
| 236 | G.MacGregor | England | v | Australia | Melbourne | 1891-92 |
| 200 | R.W.Marsh | Australia | v | Pakistan | Melbourne | 1972-73 |
| 174 | J.J.Kelly | Australia | v | England | Melbourne | 1897-98 |
| 134 | M.V.Boucher | South Africa | v | Pakistan | Port Elizabeth | 1997-98 |
| 128 | R.W.Marsh | Australia | v | West Indies | Sydney | 1975-76 |
| 126 | J.Hunter | England | v | Australia | Melbourne | 1884-85 |
| 111 | A.F.A.Lilley | England | v | Australia | Melbourne | 1903-04 |
| 96 | R.W.Taylor | England | v | India | Lord's | 1979 |
| 94 | T.G.Evans | England | v | New Zealand | Birmingham | 1958 |
| 92 | G.MacGregor | England | v | Australia | The Oval | 1890 |

| | | | | | | |
|---|---|---|---|---|---|---|
| 84 | T.G.Evans | England | v | Australia | Manchester | 1956 |
| 77 | S.C.Guillen | New Zealand | v | West Indies | Auckland | 1955-56 |
| 74 | T.G.Evans | England | v | New Zealand | Lord's | 1958 |
| 62 | J.M.Blackham | Australia | v | England | Lord's | 1888 |
| 42 | A.P.E.Knott | England | v | India | Lord's | 1974 |
| 30 | H.R.Butt | England | v | South Africa | Port Elizabeth | 1895-96 |
| 26 | T.G.Evans | England | v | New Zealand | Auckland | 1954-55 |

## 50 OR MORE EXTRAS IN AN INNINGS

| | | | | | |
|---|---|---|---|---|---|
| 71 (B 21, LB 8, NB 38, W 4) | Pakistan (435) | v | West Indies | Georgetown | 1987-88 |
| 68 (B 29, LB 11, NB 28) | Pakistan (291) | v | West Indies | Bridgetown | 1976-77 |
| 65 (B 10, LB 18, NB 36, W 1) | Zimbabwe (8-319) | v | Sri Lanka | Harare | 1994-95 |
| 64 (B 12, LB 25, NB 27) | India (565) | v | West Indies | Calcutta | 1987-88 |
| 64 (B 4, LB 18, NB 36, W 6) | South Africa (460) | v | Pakistan | Johannesburg[3] | 1994-95 |
| 64 (B 18, LB 11, NB 34, W 1) | England (437) | v | West Indies | Manchester | 1995 |
| 61 (B 17, LB 17, NB 25, W 2) | Pakistan (9-341) | v | West Indies | Port-of-Spain | 1987-88 |
| 61 (B 6, LB 23, NB 29, W 3) | Australia (6d-602) | v | England | Nottingham | 1989 |
| 60 (B 4, LB 27, NB 18, W 11) | England (5d-633) | v | India | Birmingham | 1979 |
| 59 (B 20, LB 11, NB 27, W 1) | England (315) | v | West Indies | Port-of-Spain | 1985-86 |
| 58 (LB 18, NB 40) | Australia (515) | v | West Indies | Adelaide | 1988-89 |
| 58 (LB 23, NB 34, W 1) | Australia (471) | v | Sri Lanka | Colombo (SSC) | 1992-93 |
| 57 (B 31, LB 16, NB 10) | New Zealand (387) | v | England | Auckland | 1929-30 |
| 57 (B 7, LB 21, NB 19, W 10) | England (370) | v | West Indies | The Oval | 1980 |
| 57 (B 16, LB 14, NB 26, W 1) | India (463) | v | West Indies | Bombay[3] | 1983-84 |
| 55 (B 6, LB 11, NB 32, W 6) | Australia (345) | v | England | Lord's | 1981 |
| 55 (B 2, LB 16, NB 22, W 15) | India (288) | v | Pakistan | Faisalabad | 1989-90 |
| 55 (B 16, LB 22, NB 12, W 5) | England (4-477) | v | India | The Oval | 1990 |
| 55 (B 11, LB25,, NB 9, W 10) | India (429) | v | England | Lord's | 1996 |
| 54 (B 7, LB 13, NB 34) | India (8d-566) | v | West Indies | Delhi | 1978-79 |
| 54 (B 8, LB 10, NB 35, W 1) | England (419) | v | West Indies | The Oval | 1991 |
| 54 (B 9, LB 10, NB35) | Australia (9d-501) | v | England | Leeds | 1997 |
| 54 (B 18, LB 26, NB 2, W 2) | England (462) | v | South Africa | Birmingham | 1998 |
| 53 (B 20, LB 8, NB 21, W 4) | India (487) | v | England | Delhi | 1981-82 |
| 53 (B 6, LB 17, NB 28, W 2) | West Indies (606) | v | England | Birmingham | 1984 |
| 53 (B 17, LB 6, NB 28, W 2) | Australia (248) | v | West Indies | Georgetown | 1990-91 |
| 53 (B 8, LB 8, NB 35, W 2) | England (390) | v | Pakistan | Manchester | 1992 |
| 53 (B 13, LB 9, NB 25, W 6) | Pakistan (471) | v | West indies | Rawalpindi[2] | 1997-98 |
| 52 (B 12, LB 7, NB 33) | New Zealand (468) | v | Pakistan | Karachi[1] | 1976-77 |
| 52 (B 19, LB 13, NB 10, W 10) | England (252) | v | West Indies | Nottingham | 1980 |
| 52 (B 8, LB 8, NB 35, W 1) | England (309) | v | Australia | Brsbane[2] | 1982-83 |
| 52 (B 1, LB 24, NB 16, W 11) | England (521) | v | Pakistan | Birmingham | 1987 |
| 52 (B 4, LB 23, NB 21, W 4) | Australia (371) | v | West Indies | Kingston | 1990-91 |
| 52 (B 9, LB 20, NB 23) | England (593) | v | West Indies | Port-of-Spain | 1993-94 |
| 51 (B 10, LB 20, NB 21) | India (7-469) | v | West Indies | Port-of-Spain | 1982-83 |
| 51 (B 5, LB 6, NB 40) | England (310) | v | West Indies | St John's | 1985-86 |
| 51 (B 14, LB 9, NB 25, W 3) | England (358) | v | West Indies | Bridgetown | 1989-90 |
| 50 (B 37, LB 8, NB 4, W 1) | Australia (327) | v | England | The Oval | 1934 |
| 50 (B 22, LB 19, NB 8, W 1) | England (7d-903) | v | Australia | The Oval | 1938 |
| 50 (B 11, LB 8, NB 29, W 2) | India (6d-566) | v | Sri Lanka | Madras[1] | 1982-83 |
| 50 (B 13, LB 9, NB 28) | India (8d-393) | v | Pakistan | Karachi[1] | 1982-83 |
| 50 (B 13, LB 11, NB 26) | England (464) | v | Australia | The Oval | 1985 |
| 50 (B 8, LB 6, NB 36) | England (7d-394) | v | West Indies | Bridgetown | 1993-94 |
| 50 (B 18, LB 18, NB 14) | England (564) | v | India | Nottingham | 1996 |

## 25 OR MORE BYES IN AN INNINGS

| | | | | | |
|---|---|---|---|---|---|
| 37 | Australia (327) | v | England | The Oval | 1934 |
| 33 | India (390) | v | England | Bombay[2] | 1961-62 |
| 33 | West Indies (9d-391) | v | England | Kingston | 1967-68 |
| 31 | New Zealand (387) | v | England | Auckland | 1929-30 |
| 31 | Pakistan (366) | v | Australia | Lahore[2] | 1959-60 |
| 30 | England (417) | v | South Africa | Cape Town | 1909-10 |
| 30 | South Africa (329) | v | Australia | Nottingham | 1912 |
| 30 | England (327) | v | West Indies | Georgetown | 1929-30 |
| 30 | New Zealand (189) | v | England | Wellington | 1950-51 |
| 29 | India (378) | v | England | Lord's | 1952 |
| 29 | England (559) | v | India | Kanpur | 1952 |
| 29 | Pakistan (291) | v | West Indies | Bridgetown | 1976-77 |
| 28 | India (372) | v | Pakistan | Delhi | 1952-53 |

## 25 OR MORE LEG BYES IN AN INNINGS

| | | | | | |
|---|---|---|---|---|---|
| 30 | West Indies (5d-411) | v | England | Manchester | 1976 |
| 28 | New Zealand (307) | v | Sri Lanka | Dunedin | 1994-95 |
| 27 | England (5d-633) | v | India | Birmingham | 1979 |
| 27 | England (336) | v | West Indies | Lord's | 1995 |
| 26 | England (8d-452) | v | Pakistan | Birmingham | 1978 |
| 26 | England (462) | v | South Africa | Birmingham | 1998 |
| 25 | West Indies (509) | v | Australia | Bridgetown | 1983-84 |
| 25 | India (565) | v | West Indies | Calcutta | 1987-88 |
| 25 | India (429) | v | England | Lord's | 1996 |

## 35 OR MORE NO BALLS IN AN INNINGS *(from which no runs were scored by batsmen)*

| | | | | | |
|---|---|---|---|---|---|
| 40 | England (310) | v | West Indies | St John's | 1985-86 |
| 40 | Australia (515) | v | West Indies | Adelaide | 1988-89 |
| 38 | Pakistan (435) | v | West Indies | Georgetown | 1987-88 |
| 37 | Australia (234) (2nd innings) | v | West Indies | Perth | 1988-89 |
| 36 | England (7d-394) | v | West Indies | Bridgetown | 1993-94 |
| 36 | Zimbabwe (8-319) | v | Sri Lanka | Harare | 1994-95 |
| 36 | South Africa (460) | v | Pakistan | Johannesburg[3] | 1994-95 |
| 35 | West Indies (8d-596) | v | England | Bridgetown | 1973-74 |
| 35 | England (309) | v | Australia | Brisbane[2] | 1982-83 |
| 35 | Australia (8d-395) (1st innings) | v | West Indies | Perth | 1988-89 |
| 35 | New Zealand (4-671) | v | Sri Lanka | Wellington | 1990-91 |
| 35 | England (419) | v | West Indies | The Oval | 1991 |
| 35 | England (390) | v | Pakistan | Manchester | 1992 |
| 35 | Australia (9d-501) | v | England | Leeds | 1997 |

## 10 OR MORE WIDES IN AN INNINGS

| | | | | | |
|---|---|---|---|---|---|
| 15 | India (288) | v | Pakistan | Faisalabad | 1989-90 |
| 15 | England (260) | v | West Indies | St John's | 1989-90 |
| 15 | South Africa (7d-259) | v | Pakistan | Johannesburg[3] | 1994-95 |
| 13 | England (227) | v | Pakistan | Lord's | 1982 |
| 12 | India (6d-306) | v | West Indies | Kingston | 1975-76 |
| 11 | England (288) | v | Australia | Leeds | 1975 |
| 11 | England (5d-633) | v | India | Birmingham | 1979 |
| 11 | England (521) | v | Pakistan | Birmingham | 1987 |
| 10 | England (252) | v | West Indies | Nottingham | 1980 |
| 10 | England (370) | v | West Indies | The Oval | 1980 |
| 10 | India (371) | v | England | Calcutta | 1992-93 |
| 10 | India (366) | v | Sri Lanka | Colombo (SSC) | 1993-94 |
| 10 | India (429) | v | England | Lord's | 1996 |

## 100 EXTRAS IN A MATCH

| | | | | |
|---|---|---|---|---|
| 173 (B 37, LB 31, NB 103, W 2) West Indies | v | Pakistan | Bridgetown | 1976-77 |
| 149 (B 25, LB 34, NB 90) Australia | v | West Indies | Perth | 1988-89 |
| 140 (B 20, LB 48, NB 71, W 1) Australia | v | West Indies | Adelaide | 1988-89 |
| 136 (B 28, LB 29, NB 75, W 4) West Indies | v | Australia | Georgetown | 1990-91 |
| 129 (B 18, LB 35, NB 54, W 22) South Africa | v | Pakistan | Johannesburg[3] | 1994-95 |
| 127 (B 22, LB 38, NB 62, W 5) West Indies | v | England | Bridgetown | 1989-90 |
| 124 (B 21, LB 36, NB 63, W 4) West Indies | v | England | St John's | 1985-86 |
| 122 (B 19, LB 33, NB 58, W 12) England | v | West Indies | Leeds | 1976 |
| 122 (B 31, LB 39, NB 37, W 15) England | v | India | The Oval | 1990 |
| 120 (B 4, LB 43, NB 68, W 5) Sri Lanka | v | Australia | Colombo (SSC) | 1992-93 |
| 119 (B 25, LB 27, NB 66, W 1) West Indies | v | South Africa | Bridgetown | 1991-92 |
| 117 (B 41, LB 43, NB 33) India | v | West Indies | Bombay[3] | 1994-95 |
| 117 (B 40, LB 36, NB 41) Pakistan | v | Sri Lanka | Sialkot | 1995-96 |
| 117 (B33, LB 38, NB45, W 1) West Indies | v | England | Port-of-Spain | 1997-98 |
| 114 (B 53, LB 30, NB 25, W 6) West Indies | v | Australia | Bridgetown | 1964-65 |
| 114 (B 5, LB 36, NB 72, W 1) New Zealand | v | Sri Lanka | Auckland | 1990-91 |
| 114 (B 25, LB 62, NB 26, W 1) England | v | Sri Lanka | Lord's | 1991 |
| 114 (B 7, LB 30, NB 67, W 10) Australia | v | West Indies | Perth | 1996-97 |
| 113 (B 26, LB 32, NB 54, W1) Pakistan | v | West Indies | Lahore[2] | 1990-91 |
| 112 (B 7, LB 39, NB 54, W 12) England | v | West Indies | The Oval | 1980 |
| 112 (B 11, LB32, NB39, W30) Pakistan | v | India | Faisalabad | 1989-90 |
| 112 (B 9, LB 22, NB81) West Indies | v | England | Bridgetown | 1993-94 |
| 111 (B 10, LB 23, NB 68, W 10) Australia | v | West Indies | Brisbane[2] | 1988-89 |
| 110 (B 27, LB 41, NB 27, W 15) England | v | West Indies | Nottingham | 1980 |
| 110 (B 23, LB 36, NB 50, W 1) Pakistan | v | West Indies | Karachi[1] | 1990-91 |
| 109 (B 16, LB 33, NB 59, W 1) New Zealand | v | India | Christchurch | 1967-68 |
| 109 (B 25, LB 49, NB 16, W 19) England | v | Pakistan | Lord's | 1982 |
| 108 (B 23, LB 25, NB 59, W 1) India | v | Australia | Delhi | 1979-80 |
| 108 (B 19, LB 24, NB 61, W 4) Ebgland | v | West Indies | The Oval | 1991 |
| 107 (B 36, LB 42, NB 29) Australia | v | England | Melbourne | 1970-71 |
| 107 (B 51, LB 38, NB 17, W 1) West Indies | v | Australia | Port-of-Spain | 1972-73 |
| 107 (B 10, LB 18, NB 79) West Indies | v | England | Bridgetown | 1973-74 |
| 106 (B 26, LB 39, NB 38, W 3) Australia | v | England | Perth | 1986-87 |
| 106 (B 36, LB 32, NB 32, W 6) India | v | Sri Lanka | Mohali | 1997-98 |
| 105 (B 26, LB 36, NB 42, W 1) West Indies | v | England | Kingston | 1973-74 |
| 105 (B 27, LB 39, NB 36, W 3) Pakistan | v | India | Karachi[1] | 1978-79 |
| 105 (B 47, LB 42, NB 12, W 4) Pakistan | v | West Indies | Karachi[1] | 1986-87 |
| 105 (B 27, LB 37, NB 39, W 2) West Indies | v | Pakistan | Port-of-Spain | 1987-88 |
| 105 (B 16, LB 34, NB 52, W 3) South Africa | v | England | Johannesburg[3] | 1995-96 |
| 104 (B 28, LB 32, NB 35, W 9) England | v | West Indies | The Oval | 1976 |
| 104 (B 30, LB 36, NB 38) West Indies | v | New Zealand | Port-of-Spain | 1984-85 |
| 104 (B 26, LB 25, NB 47, W 6) Pakistan | v | New Zealand | Lahore[2] | 1990-91 |
| 104 (B 25, LB 41, NB 28, W 10) England | v | India | Lord's | 1996 |
| 103 (B 20, LB 43, NB 32, W 8) West Indies | v | New Zealand | Georgetown | 1984-85 |
| 103 (B 22, LB 33, NB 42, W 6) India | v | West Indies | Mohali | 1994-95 |
| 103 (B 23, LB 23, NB 50, W 7) England | v | West Indies | Manchester | 1995 |
| 102 (B 24, LB 29, NB 48, W 1) West Indies | v | England | Georgetown | 1997-98 |
| 101 (B 12, LB 43, NB 32, W 14) England | v | India | Birmingham | 1979 |
| 101 (B 18, LB 39, NB 44) India | v | West Indies | Calcutta | 1987-88 |
| 100 (B 65, LB 22, NB 12, W 1) West Indies | v | England | Kingston | 1967-68 |
| 100 (B 15, LB 30, NB 42, W 13) England | v | Australia | Leeds | 1981 |
| 100 (B 27, LB 19, NB 50, W 4) West Indies | v | Pakistan | Georgetown | 1987-88 |
| 100 (B 19, LB 35, NB 40, W 6) West Indies | v | Australia | Kingston | 1990-91 |
| 100 (B 25, LB 31, NB 36, W 8) England | v | India | Nottingham | 1996 |

# Batting

## 6000 RUNS IN TESTS

| Player (Country) | M | I | Runs | A | E | SA | WI | NZ | I | P | SL | Z |
|---|---|---|---|---|---|---|---|---|---|---|---|---|
| | | | | *Opponent* | | | | | | | | |
| A.R.Border (A) | 156 | 265 | **11174** | - | 3548 | 298 | 2052 | 1500 | 1567 | 1666 | 543 | - |
| S.M.Gavaskar (I) | 125 | 214 | **10122** | 1550 | 2483 | - | 2749 | 651 | - | 2089 | 600 | - |
| G.A.Gooch (E) | 118 | 215 | **8900** | 2632 | - | 139 | 2197 | 1148 | 1725 | 683 | 376 | - |
| Javed Miandad (P) | 124 | 189 | **8832** | 1797 | 1329 | - | 834 | 1919 | 2228 | - | 582 | 143 |
| I.V.A.Richards (W) | 121 | 182 | **8540** | 2266 | 2869 | - | - | 387 | 1927 | 1091 | - | - |
| D.I.Gower (E) | 117 | 204 | **8231** | 3269 | - | - | 1149 | 1051 | 1391 | 1185 | 186 | - |
| G.Boycott (E) | 108 | 193 | **8114** | 2945 | - | 373 | 2205 | 916 | 1084 | 591 | - | - |
| G.S.Sobers (W) | 93 | 160 | **8032** | 1510 | 3214 | - | - | 404 | 1920 | 984 | - | - |
| M.C.Cowdrey (E) | 114 | 188 | **7624** | 2433 | - | 1021 | 1751 | 1133 | 653 | 633 | - | - |
| C.G.Greenidge (W) | 108 | 185 | **7558** | 1819 | 2318 | - | - | 882 | 1678 | 861 | - | - |
| C.H.Lloyd (W) | 110 | 175 | **7515** | 2211 | 2120 | - | - | 234 | 2344 | 606 | - | - |
| D.L.Haynes (W) | 116 | 202 | **7487** | 2233 | 2392 | 81 | - | 843 | 990 | 928 | 20 | - |
| D.C.Boon (A) | 107 | 190 | **7422** | - | 2237 | 433 | 1437 | 1187 | 1204 | 431 | 493 | - |
| W.R.Hammond (E) | 85 | 140 | **7249** | 2852 | - | 2188 | 639 | 1015 | 555 | - | - | - |
| G.S.Chappell (A) | 87 | 151 | **7110** | - | 2619 | - | 1400 | 1076 | 368 | 1581 | 66 | - |
| D.G.Bradman (A) | 52 | 80 | **6996** | - | 5028 | 806 | 447 | - | 715 | - | - | - |
| L.Hutton (E) | 79 | 138 | **6971** | 2428 | - | 1564 | 1661 | 777 | 522 | 19 | - | - |
| D.B.Vengsarkar (I) | 116 | 185 | **6868** | 1304 | 1589 | - | 1596 | 440 | - | 1284 | 655 | - |
| K.F.Barrington (E) | 82 | 131 | **6806** | 2111 | - | 989 | 1042 | 594 | 1355 | 715 | - | - |
| M.A.Taylor (A) | 96 | 171 | **6784** | - | 2268 | 746 | 984 | 666 | 675 | 834 | 611 | - |
| S.R.Waugh (A) | 103 | 162 | **6480** | - | 2076 | 911 | 1208 | 825 | 304 | 507 | 649 | - |
| R.B.Kanhai (W) | 79 | 137 | **6227** | 1694 | 2267 | - | - | - | 1693 | 573 | - | - |
| R.N.Harvey (A) | 79 | 137 | **6149** | - | 2416 | 1625 | 1054 | - | 775 | 279 | - | - |
| G.R.Viswanath (I) | 91 | 155 | **6080** | 1538 | 1880 | - | 1455 | 585 | - | 611 | 11 | - |

## 2000 RUNS IN TESTS

| **AUSTRALIA** | Tests | I | NO | Runs | HS | Avge | 100 | 50 |
|---|---|---|---|---|---|---|---|---|
| A.R.Border | 156 | 265 | 44 | 11174 | 205 | 50.56 | 27 | 63 |
| D.C.Boon | 107 | 190 | 20 | 7422 | 200 | 43.65 | 21 | 32 |
| G.S.Chappell | 87 | 151 | 19 | 7110 | 247* | 53.86 | 24 | 31 |
| D.G.Bradman | 52 | 80 | 10 | 6996 | 334 | 99.94 | 29 | 13 |
| M.A.Taylor | 96 | 171 | 12 | 6784 | 219 | 42.66 | 18 | 36 |
| S.R.Waugh | 103 | 162 | 29 | 6480 | 200 | 48.72 | 14 | 38 |
| R.N.Harvey | 79 | 137 | 10 | 6149 | 205 | 48.41 | 21 | 24 |
| K.D.Walters | 74 | 125 | 14 | 5357 | 250 | 48.26 | 15 | 33 |
| I.M.Chappell | 75 | 136 | 10 | 5345 | 196 | 42.42 | 14 | 26 |
| W.M.Lawry | 67 | 123 | 12 | 5234 | 210 | 47.15 | 13 | 27 |
| M.E.Waugh | 78 | 128 | 7 | 5219 | 153* | 43.13 | 14 | 32 |
| R.B.Simpson | 62 | 111 | 7 | 4869 | 311 | 46.81 | 10 | 27 |
| I.R.Redpath | 66 | 120 | 11 | 4737 | 171 | 43.45 | 8 | 31 |
| K.J.Hughes | 70 | 124 | 6 | 4415 | 213 | 37.41 | 9 | 22 |
| I.A.Healy | 103 | 157 | 21 | 3906 | 161* | 28.72 | 3 | 21 |
| R.W.Marsh | 96 | 150 | 13 | 3633 | 132 | 26.51 | 3 | 16 |
| D.M.Jones | 52 | 89 | 11 | 3631 | 216 | 46.55 | 11 | 14 |
| A.R.Morris | 46 | 79 | 3 | 3533 | 206 | 46.48 | 12 | 12 |
| C.Hill | 49 | 89 | 2 | 3412 | 191 | 39.21 | 7 | 19 |
| G.M.Wood | 59 | 112 | 6 | 3374 | 172 | 31.83 | 9 | 12 |
| V.T.Trumper | 48 | 89 | 8 | 3163 | 214* | 39.04 | 8 | 13 |
| C.C.McDonald | 47 | 83 | 4 | 3107 | 170 | 39.32 | 5 | 17 |
| A.L.Hassett | 43 | 69 | 3 | 3073 | 198* | 46.56 | 10 | 11 |
| K.R.Miller | 55 | 87 | 7 | 2958 | 147 | 36.97 | 7 | 13 |
| W.W.Armstrong | 50 | 84 | 10 | 2863 | 159* | 38.68 | 6 | 8 |
| G.R.Marsh | 50 | 93 | 7 | 2854 | 138 | 33.18 | 4 | 15 |
| M.J.Slater | 37 | 65 | 3 | 2817 | 219 | 45.43 | 7 | 11 |
| K.R.Stackpole | 43 | 80 | 5 | 2807 | 207 | 37.42 | 7 | 14 |

| | | | | | | | | |
|---|---|---|---|---|---|---|---|---|
| N.C.O'Neill | 42 | 69 | 8 | 2779 | 181 | 45.55 | 6 | 15 |
| G.N.Yallop | 39 | 70 | 3 | 2756 | 268 | 41.13 | 8 | 9 |
| S.J.McCabe | 39 | 62 | 5 | 2748 | 232 | 48.21 | 6 | 13 |
| W.Bardsley | 41 | 66 | 5 | 2469 | 193* | 40.47 | 6 | 14 |
| W.M.Woodfull | 35 | 54 | 4 | 2300 | 161 | 46.00 | 7 | 13 |
| P.J.P.Burge | 42 | 68 | 8 | 2290 | 181 | 38.16 | 4 | 12 |
| S.E.Gregory | 58 | 100 | 7 | 2282 | 201 | 24.53 | 4 | 8 |
| R.Benaud | 63 | 97 | 7 | 2201 | 122 | 24.45 | 3 | 9 |
| C.G.Macartney | 35 | 55 | 4 | 2131 | 170 | 41.78 | 7 | 9 |
| W.H.Ponsford | 29 | 48 | 4 | 2122 | 266 | 48.22 | 7 | 6 |
| R.M.Cowper | 27 | 46 | 2 | 2061 | 307 | 46.84 | 5 | 10 |
| **ENGLAND** | Tests | I | NO | Runs | HS | Avge | 100 | 50 |
| G.A.Gooch | 118 | 215 | 6 | 8900 | 333 | 42.58 | 20 | 46 |
| D.I.Gower | 117 | 204 | 18 | 8231 | 215 | 44.25 | 18 | 39 |
| G.Boycott | 108 | 193 | 23 | 8114 | 246* | 47.72 | 22 | 42 |
| M.C.Cowdrey | 114 | 188 | 15 | 7624 | 182 | 44.06 | 22 | 38 |
| W.R.Hammond | 85 | 140 | 16 | 7249 | 336* | 58.45 | 22 | 24 |
| L.Hutton | 79 | 138 | 15 | 6971 | 364 | 56.67 | 19 | 33 |
| K.F.Barrington | 82 | 131 | 15 | 6806 | 256 | 58.67 | 20 | 35 |
| M.A.Atherton | 84 | 155 | 6 | 5935 | 185 | 39.83 | 12 | 37 |
| D.C.S.Compton | 78 | 131 | 15 | 5807 | 278 | 50.06 | 17 | 28 |
| A.J.Stewart | 80 | 144 | 10 | 5618 | 190 | 41.92 | 11 | 28 |
| J.B.Hobbs | 61 | 102 | 7 | 5410 | 211 | 56.94 | 15 | 28 |
| I.T.Botham | 102 | 161 | 6 | 5200 | 208 | 33.54 | 14 | 22 |
| J.H.Edrich | 77 | 127 | 9 | 5138 | 310* | 43.54 | 12 | 24 |
| T.W.Graveney | 79 | 123 | 13 | 4882 | 258 | 44.38 | 11 | 20 |
| A.J.Lamb | 79 | 139 | 10 | 4656 | 142 | 36.09 | 14 | 18 |
| H.Sutcliffe | 54 | 84 | 9 | 4555 | 194 | 60.73 | 16 | 23 |
| P.B.H.May | 66 | 106 | 9 | 4537 | 285* | 46.77 | 13 | 22 |
| E.R.Dexter | 62 | 102 | 8 | 4502 | 205 | 47.89 | 9 | 27 |
| M.W.Gatting | 79 | 138 | 14 | 4409 | 207 | 35.55 | 10 | 21 |
| A.P.E.Knott | 95 | 149 | 15 | 4389 | 135 | 32.75 | 5 | 30 |
| R.A.Smith | 62 | 112 | 15 | 4236 | 175 | 43.67 | 9 | 28 |
| D.L.Amiss | 50 | 88 | 10 | 3612 | 262* | 46.30 | 11 | 11 |
| A.W.Greig | 58 | 93 | 4 | 3599 | 148 | 40.43 | 8 | 20 |
| E.H.Hendren | 51 | 83 | 9 | 3525 | 205* | 47.63 | 7 | 21 |
| G.P.Thorpe | 49 | 89 | 11 | 3303 | 138 | 42.34 | 6 | 23 |
| F.E.Woolley | 64 | 98 | 7 | 3283 | 154 | 36.07 | 5 | 23 |
| K.W.R.Fletcher | 59 | 96 | 14 | 3272 | 216 | 39.90 | 7 | 19 |
| M.Leyland | 41 | 65 | 5 | 2764 | 187 | 46.06 | 9 | 10 |
| G.A.Hick | 48 | 83 | 6 | 2681 | 178 | 34.81 | 4 | 15 |
| C.Washbrook | 37 | 66 | 6 | 2569 | 195 | 42.81 | 6 | 12 |
| B.L.D'Oliveira | 44 | 70 | 8 | 2484 | 158 | 40.06 | 5 | 15 |
| D.W.Randall | 47 | 79 | 5 | 2470 | 174 | 33.37 | 7 | 12 |
| W.J.Edrich | 39 | 63 | 2 | 2440 | 219 | 40.00 | 6 | 13 |
| T.G.Evans | 91 | 133 | 14 | 2439 | 104 | 20.49 | 2 | 8 |
| L.E.G.Ames | 47 | 72 | 12 | 2434 | 149 | 40.56 | 8 | 7 |
| W.Rhodes | 58 | 98 | 21 | 2325 | 179 | 30.19 | 2 | 11 |
| T.E.Bailey | 61 | 91 | 14 | 2290 | 134* | 29.74 | 1 | 10 |
| M.J.K.Smith | 50 | 78 | 6 | 2278 | 121 | 31.63 | 3 | 11 |
| P.E.Richardson | 34 | 56 | 1 | 2061 | 126 | 37.47 | 5 | 9 |
| N. Hussain | 34 | 61 | 5 | 2033 | 207 | 36.30 | 7 | 6 |
| **SOUTH AFRICA** | Tests | I | NO | Runs | HS | Avge | 100 | 50 |
| B.Mitchell | 42 | 80 | 9 | 3471 | 189* | 48.88 | 8 | 21 |
| W.J.Cronje | 51 | 88 | 9 | 3079 | 135 | 38.97 | 6 | 18 |
| A.D.Nourse | 34 | 62 | 7 | 2960 | 231 | 53.81 | 9 | 14 |
| H.W.Taylor | 42 | 76 | 4 | 2936 | 176 | 40.77 | 7 | 17 |
| G.Kirsten | 45 | 81 | 7 | 2895 | 210 | 39.12 | 7 | 15 |

| | | | | | | | | |
|---|---|---|---|---|---|---|---|---|
| T.L.Goddard | 41 | 78 | 5 | 2516 | 112 | 34.46 | 1 | 18 |
| D.J.McGlew | 34 | 64 | 6 | 2440 | 255* | 42.06 | 7 | 10 |
| J.H.B.Waite | 50 | 86 | 7 | 2405 | 134 | 30.44 | 4 | 16 |
| D.J.Cullinan | 40 | 68 | 6 | 2403 | 153* | 38.75 | 5 | 15 |
| R.G.Pollock | 23 | 41 | 4 | 2256 | 274 | 60.97 | 7 | 11 |
| A.W.Nourse | 45 | 83 | 8 | 2234 | 111 | 29.78 | 1 | 15 |
| R.A.McLean | 40 | 73 | 3 | 2120 | 142 | 30.28 | 5 | 10 |
| D.J.Cullinan | 35 | 59 | 5 | 2116 | 153* | 38.47 | 5 | 12 |
| A.C.Hudson | 35 | 63 | 3 | 2007 | 163 | 33.45 | 4 | 13 |

| **WEST INDIES** | Tests | I | NO | Runs | HS | Avge | 100 | 50 |
|---|---|---|---|---|---|---|---|---|
| I.V.A.Richards | 121 | 182 | 12 | 8540 | 291 | 50.23 | 24 | 45 |
| G.S.Sobers | 93 | 160 | 21 | 8032 | 365* | 57.78 | 26 | 30 |
| C.G.Greenidge | 108 | 185 | 16 | 7558 | 226 | 44.72 | 19 | 34 |
| C.H.Lloyd | 110 | 175 | 14 | 7515 | 242* | 46.67 | 19 | 39 |
| D.L.Haynes | 116 | 202 | 25 | 7487 | 184 | 42.29 | 18 | 39 |
| R.B.Kanhai | 79 | 137 | 6 | 6227 | 256 | 47.53 | 15 | 28 |
| R.B.Richardson | 86 | 146 | 12 | 5949 | 194 | 44.39 | 16 | 27 |
| B.C.Lara | 54 | 91 | 3 | 4550 | 375 | 51.70 | 10 | 23 |
| E.D.Weekes | 48 | 81 | 5 | 4455 | 207 | 58.61 | 15 | 19 |
| A.I.Kallicharran | 66 | 109 | 10 | 4399 | 187 | 44.43 | 12 | 21 |
| R.C.Fredericks | 59 | 109 | 7 | 4334 | 169 | 42.49 | 8 | 26 |
| F.M.M.Worrell | 51 | 87 | 9 | 3860 | 261 | 49.48 | 9 | 22 |
| C.L.Hooper | 73 | 122 | 13 | 3826 | 178* | 35.10 | 9 | 17 |
| C.L.Walcott | 44 | 74 | 7 | 3798 | 220 | 56.68 | 15 | 14 |
| P.J.L.Dujon | 81 | 115 | 11 | 3322 | 139 | 31.94 | 5 | 16 |
| C.C.Hunte | 44 | 78 | 6 | 3245 | 260 | 45.06 | 8 | 13 |
| H.A.Gomes | 60 | 91 | 11 | 3171 | 143 | 39.63 | 9 | 13 |
| B.F.Butcher | 44 | 78 | 6 | 3104 | 209* | 43.11 | 7 | 16 |
| S.M.Nurse | 29 | 54 | 1 | 2523 | 258 | 47.60 | 6 | 10 |
| A.L.Logie | 52 | 78 | 9 | 2470 | 130 | 35.79 | 2 | 16 |
| G.A.Headley | 22 | 40 | 4 | 2190 | 270* | 60.83 | 10 | 5 |
| J.B.Stollmeyer | 32 | 56 | 5 | 2159 | 160 | 42.33 | 4 | 12 |
| J.C.Adams | 33 | 52 | 11 | 2104 | 208* | 51.31 | 5 | 10 |
| L.G.Rowe | 30 | 49 | 2 | 2047 | 302 | 43.55 | 7 | 7 |

| **NEW ZEALAND** | Tests | I | NO | Runs | HS | Avge | 100 | 50 |
|---|---|---|---|---|---|---|---|---|
| M.D.Crowe | 77 | 131 | 11 | 5444 | 299 | 45.36 | 17 | 18 |
| J.G.Wright | 82 | 148 | 7 | 5334 | 185 | 37.82 | 12 | 23 |
| B.E.Congdon | 61 | 114 | 7 | 3448 | 176 | 32.22 | 7 | 19 |
| J..R.Reid | 58 | 108 | 5 | 3428 | 142 | 33.28 | 6 | 22 |
| R.J.Hadlee | 86 | 134 | 19 | 3124 | 151* | 27.16 | 2 | 15 |
| G.M.Turner | 41 | 73 | 6 | 2991 | 259 | 44.64 | 7 | 14 |
| A.H.Jones | 39 | 74 | 8 | 2922 | 186 | 44.27 | 7 | 11 |
| B.Sutcliffe | 42 | 76 | 8 | 2727 | 230* | 40.10 | 5 | 15 |
| M.G.Burgess | 50 | 92 | 6 | 2684 | 119* | 31.20 | 5 | 14 |
| J.V.Coney | 52 | 85 | 14 | 2668 | 174* | 37.57 | 3 | 16 |
| G.P.Howarth | 47 | 83 | 5 | 2531 | 147 | 32.44 | 6 | 11 |
| K.R.Rutherford | 56 | 99 | 8 | 2463 | 107* | 27.06 | 3 | 15 |
| S.P.Fleming | 37 | 65 | 3 | 2349 | 176* | 37.88 | 2 | 18 |
| G.T.Dowling | 39 | 77 | 3 | 2306 | 239 | 31.16 | 3 | 11 |
| M.J.Greatbatch | 41 | 71 | 5 | 2021 | 146* | 30.62 | 3 | 10 |

| **INDIA** | Tests | I | NO | Runs | HS | Avge | 100 | 50 |
|---|---|---|---|---|---|---|---|---|
| S.M.Gavaskar | 125 | 214 | 16 | 10122 | 236* | 51.12 | 34 | 45 |
| D.B.Vengsarkar | 116 | 185 | 22 | 6868 | 166 | 42.13 | 17 | 35 |
| G.R.Viswanath | 91 | 155 | 10 | 6080 | 222 | 41.93 | 14 | 35 |
| M.Azharuddin | 91 | 132 | 8 | 5697 | 199 | 45.94 | 20 | 19 |
| Kapil Dev | 131 | 184 | 15 | 5248 | 163 | 31.05 | 8 | 27 |
| S.R.Tendulkar | 61 | 92 | 9 | 4552 | 179 | 54.84 | 16 | 19 |
| M.Amarnath | 69 | 113 | 10 | 4378 | 138 | 42.50 | 11 | 24 |

| | | | | | | | | |
|---|---|---|---|---|---|---|---|---|
| R.J.Shastri | 80 | 121 | 14 | 3830 | 206 | 35.79 | 11 | 12 |
| P.R.Umrigar | 59 | 94 | 8 | 3631 | 223 | 42.22 | 12 | 14 |
| V.L.Manjrekar | 55 | 92 | 10 | 3208 | 189* | 39.12 | 7 | 15 |
| N.S.Sidhu | 48 | 72 | 2 | 3148 | 201 | 44.97 | 9 | 15 |
| C.G.Borde | 55 | 97 | 11 | 3061 | 177* | 35.59 | 5 | 18 |
| Nawab of Pataudi, jr | 46 | 83 | 3 | 2793 | 203* | 34.91 | 6 | 16 |
| S.M.H.Kirmani | 88 | 124 | 22 | 2759 | 102 | 27.04 | 2 | 12 |
| F.M.Engineer | 46 | 87 | 3 | 2611 | 121 | 31.08 | 2 | 16 |
| Pankaj Roy | 43 | 79 | 4 | 2442 | 173 | 32.56 | 5 | 9 |
| V.S.Hazare | 30 | 52 | 6 | 2192 | 164* | 47.65 | 7 | 9 |
| A.L.Wadekar | 37 | 71 | 3 | 2113 | 143 | 31.07 | 1 | 14 |
| M.H.Mankad | 44 | 72 | 5 | 2109 | 231 | 31.47 | 5 | 6 |
| C.P.S.Chauhan | 40 | 68 | 2 | 2084 | 97 | 31.57 | - | 16 |
| K.Srikkanth | 43 | 72 | 3 | 2062 | 123 | 29.88 | 2 | 12 |
| M.L.Jaisimha | 39 | 71 | 4 | 2056 | 129 | 30.68 | 3 | 12 |
| S.V.Manjrekar | 37 | 61 | 6 | 2043 | 218 | 37.14 | 4 | 9 |
| D.N.Sardesai | 30 | 55 | 4 | 2001 | 212 | 39.23 | 5 | 9 |

| **PAKISTAN** | Tests | I | NO | Runs | HS | Avge | 100 | 50 |
|---|---|---|---|---|---|---|---|---|
| Javed Miandad | 124 | 189 | 21 | 8832 | 280* | 52.57 | 23 | 43 |
| Saleem Malik | 96 | 142 | 21 | 5528 | 237 | 45.68 | 15 | 28 |
| Zaheer Abbas | 78 | 124 | 11 | 5062 | 274 | 44.79 | 12 | 20 |
| Mudassar Nazar | 76 | 116 | 8 | 4114 | 231 | 38.09 | 10 | 17 |
| Majid Khan | 63 | 106 | 5 | 3930 | 167 | 38.91 | 8 | 19 |
| Hanif Mohammad | 55 | 97 | 8 | 3915 | 337 | 43.98 | 12 | 15 |
| Imran Khan | 88 | 126 | 25 | 3807 | 136 | 37.69 | 6 | 18 |
| Mushtaq Mohammad | 57 | 100 | 7 | 3643 | 201 | 39.17 | 10 | 19 |
| Asif Iqbal | 58 | 99 | 7 | 3575 | 175 | 38.85 | 11 | 12 |
| Inzamamul Haq | 46 | 77 | 9 | 2998 | 177 | 44.08 | 5 | 17 |
| Saeed Ahmed | 41 | 78 | 4 | 2991 | 172 | 40.41 | 5 | 16 |
| Rameez Raja | 57 | 94 | 5 | 2833 | 122 | 31.83 | 2 | 22 |
| Wasim Raja | 57 | 92 | 14 | 2821 | 125 | 36.16 | 4 | 18 |
| Mohsin Khan | 48 | 79 | 6 | 2709 | 200 | 37.10 | 7 | 9 |
| Shoaib Mohammad | 45 | 68 | 7 | 2705 | 203* | 44.34 | 7 | 13 |
| Sadiq Mohammad | 41 | 74 | 2 | 2579 | 166 | 35.81 | 5 | 10 |
| Aamer Sohail | 41 | 72 | 3 | 2554 | 205 | 37.01 | 4 | 13 |
| Ijaz Ahmed | 46 | 68 | 3 | 2416 | 151 | 37.16 | 8 | 10 |
| Saeed Anwar | 32 | 54 | 1 | 2261 | 176 | 42.66 | 5 | 16 |
| Imtiaz Ahmed | 41 | 72 | 1 | 2079 | 209 | 29.28 | 3 | 11 |
| Wasim Akram | 79 | 109 | 15 | 2019 | 257* | 21.47 | 2 | 4 |

| **SRI LANKA** | Tests | I | NO | Runs | HS | Avge | 100 | 50 |
|---|---|---|---|---|---|---|---|---|
| P.A.de Silva | 73 | 127 | 9 | 4977 | 267 | 42.17 | 16 | 18 |
| A.Ranatunga | 81 | 137 | 8 | 4544 | 135* | 35.22 | 4 | 32 |
| H.P.Tillakaratne | 81 | 137 | 8 | 4544 | 135* | 35.22 | 4 | 32 |
| R.S.Mahanama | 52 | 89 | 1 | 2576 | 225 | 29.27 | 4 | 11 |
| A.P.Gurusinha | 41 | 70 | 7 | 2452 | 143 | 38.92 | 7 | 8 |
| S.T.Jayasuriya | 37 | 62 | 6 | 2375 | 340 | 42.41 | 4 | 14 |

500 runs for Zimbabwe:

| **ZIMBABWE** | Tests | I | NO | Runs | HS | Avge | 100 | 50 |
|---|---|---|---|---|---|---|---|---|
| G.W.Flower | 30 | 54 | 2 | 1991 | 201* | 38.28 | 5 | 8 |
| A.Flower | 30 | 53 | 7 | 1942 | 156 | 42.21 | 5 | 12 |
| A.D.R.Campbell | 30 | 54 | 2 | 1531 | 99 | 29.44 | 0 | 11 |
| D.L.Houghton | 22 | 36 | 2 | 1466 | 266 | 43.11 | 4 | 4 |
| G.J.Whittall | 25 | 43 | 3 | 1045 | 203* | 26.12 | 2 | 4 |
| P.A.Strang | 20 | 34 | 7 | 747 | 106* | 27.66 | 1 | 2 |

## MOST CENTURIES

| Player | Country | 100 | Inns | A | E | SA | WI | NZ | I | P | SL | Z |
|---|---|---|---|---|---|---|---|---|---|---|---|---|
| S.M.Gavaskar | India | **34** | 214 | 8 | 4 | - | 13 | 2 | - | 5 | 2 | - |
| D.G.Bradman | Australia | **29** | 80 | - | 19 | 4 | 2 | - | 4 | - | - | - |
| A.R.Border | Australia | **27** | 265 | - | 8 | 0 | 3 | 5 | 4 | 6 | 1 | - |
| G.S.Sobers | West Indies | **26** | 160 | 4 | 10 | - | - | 1 | 8 | 3 | - | - |
| G.S.Chappell | Australia | **24** | 151 | - | 9 | - | 5 | 3 | 1 | 6 | - | - |
| I.V.A.Richards | West Indies | **24** | 161 | 5 | 8 | - | - | 1 | 8 | 2 | - | - |
| Javed Miandad | Pakistan | **23** | 189 | 6 | 2 | - | 2 | 7 | 5 | - | 1 | - |
| G.Boycott | England | **22** | 193 | 7 | - | 1 | 5 | 2 | 4 | 3 | - | - |
| M.C.Cowdrey | England | **22** | 188 | 5 | - | 3 | 6 | 2 | 3 | 3 | - | - |
| W.R.Hammond | England | **22** | 140 | 9 | - | 6 | 1 | 4 | 2 | - | - | - |
| D.C.Boon | Australia | **21** | 190 | - | 7 | 0 | 3 | 3 | 6 | 1 | 1 | - |
| R.N.Harvey | Australia | **21** | 137 | - | 6 | 8 | 3 | - | 4 | 0 | - | - |
| M.Azharuddin | India | **20** | 132 | 2 | 6 | 3 | 0 | 1 | - | 3 | 5 | 0 |
| K.F.Barrington | England | **20** | 131 | 5 | - | 2 | 3 | 3 | 3 | 4 | - | - |
| G.A.Gooch | England | **20** | 215 | 4 | - | 0 | 5 | 4 | 5 | 1 | 1 | - |
| C.G.Greenidge | West Indies | **19** | 185 | 4 | 7 | - | - | 2 | 5 | 1 | - | - |
| L.Hutton | England | **19** | 138 | 5 | - | 4 | 5 | 3 | 2 | - | - | - |
| C.H.Lloyd | West Indies | **19** | 175 | 6 | 5 | - | - | 0 | 7 | 1 | - | - |
| D.I.Gower | England | **18** | 204 | 9 | - | - | 1 | 4 | 2 | 2 | 0 | - |
| D.L.Haynes | West Indies | **18** | 202 | 5 | 5 | - | - | 3 | 2 | 3 | 0 | - |
| M.A.Taylor | Australia | **18** | 171 | - | 6 | 2 | 1 | 2 | 2 | 3 | 2 | - |
| D.C.S.Compton | England | **17** | 131 | 5 | - | 7 | 2 | 2 | - | 1 | - | - |
| M.D.Crowe | New Zealand | **17** | 131 | 3 | 5 | 0 | 3 | - | 1 | 2 | 2 | 1 |
| D.B.Vengsarkar | India | **17** | 185 | 2 | 5 | - | 6 | - | - | 2 | 2 | - |
| P.A.de Silva | Sri Lanka | **16** | 127 | 1 | 0 | 0 | 0 | 2 | 5 | 7 | - | 1 |
| R.B.Richardson | West Indies | **16** | 146 | 9 | 4 | 0 | - | 1 | 2 | 0 | 0 | - |
| H.Sutcliffe | England | **16** | 84 | 8 | - | 6 | 0 | 2 | 0 | - | - | - |
| S.R.Tendulkar | India | **16** | 92 | 4 | 4 | 2 | 1 | 0 | - | 0 | 5 | 0 |
| J.B.Hobbs | England | **15** | 102 | 12 | - | 2 | 1 | - | - | - | - | - |
| R.B.Kanhai | West Indies | **15** | 137 | 5 | 5 | - | - | - | 4 | 1 | - | - |
| Saleem Malik | Pakistan | **15** | 142 | 2 | 4 | 0 | 1 | 2 | 3 | - | 3 | 0 |
| C.L.Walcott | West Indies | **15** | 74 | 5 | 4 | - | - | 1 | 4 | 1 | - | - |
| K.D.Walters | Australia | **15** | 125 | - | 4 | - | 6 | 3 | 1 | 1 | - | - |
| E.D.Weekes | West Indies | **15** | 81 | 1 | 3 | - | - | 3 | 7 | 1 | - | - |
| I.T.Botham | England | **14** | 161 | 4 | - | - | - | 3 | 5 | 2 | - | - |
| I.M.Chappell | Australia | **14** | 136 | - | 4 | - | 5 | 2 | 2 | 1 | - | - |
| A.J.Lamb | England | **14** | 139 | 1 | - | - | 6 | 3 | 3 | - | 1 | - |
| G.R.Viswanath | India | **14** | 155 | 4 | 4 | - | 4 | 1 | - | 1 | - | - |
| M.E.Waugh | Australia | **14** | 128 | - | 3 | 3 | 3 | 2 | 1 | 1 | 1 | - |
| S.R.Waugh | Australia | **14** | 162 | - | 5 | 2 | 2 | 1 | - | 1 | 3 | - |
| W.M.Lawry | Australia | **13** | 123 | - | 7 | 1 | 4 | - | 1 | - | - | - |
| P.B.H.May | England | **13** | 106 | 3 | - | 3 | 3 | 3 | 1 | - | - | - |
| M.A.Atherton | England | **12** | 155 | 1 | - | 2 | 3 | 3 | 2 | 0 | 0 | 1 |
| J.H.Edrich | England | **12** | 127 | 7 | - | - | 1 | 3 | 1 | - | - | - |
| Hanif Mohammad | Pakistan | **12** | 97 | 2 | 3 | - | 2 | 3 | 2 | - | - | - |
| A.I.Kallicharran | West Indies | **12** | 109 | 4 | 2 | - | - | 2 | 3 | 1 | - | - |
| A.R.Morris | Australia | **12** | 79 | - | 8 | 2 | 1 | - | 1 | - | - | - |
| P.R.Umrigar | India | **12** | 94 | - | 3 | - | 3 | 1 | - | 5 | - | - |
| J.G.Wright | New Zealand | **12** | 148 | 2 | 4 | - | 1 | - | 3 | 1 | 1 | - |
| Zaheer Abbas | Pakistan | **12** | 124 | 2 | 2 | - | - | 1 | 6 | - | 1 | - |
| M.Amarnath | India | **11** | 113 | 2 | - | - | 3 | - | - | 4 | 2 | - |
| D.L.Amiss | England | **11** | 88 | - | - | - | 4 | 2 | 2 | 3 | - | - |
| Asif Iqbal | Pakistan | **11** | 99 | 3 | 3 | - | 1 | 3 | 1 | - | - | - |
| T.W.Graveney | England | **11** | 123 | 1 | - | - | 5 | - | 2 | 3 | - | - |
| D.M.Jones | Australia | **11** | 89 | - | 3 | - | 1 | - | 2 | 2 | 3 | - |
| R.J.Shastri | India | **11** | 121 | 2 | 4 | - | 2 | - | - | 3 | - | - |
| A.J.Stewart | England | **11** | 144 | 0 | - | 1 | 2 | 4 | 0 | 2 | 1 | 1 |
| M.W.Gatting | England | **10** | 138 | 4 | - | - | - | 1 | 3 | 2 | - | - |

| | | | | | | | | | | | | |
|---|---|---|---|---|---|---|---|---|---|---|---|---|
| A.L.Hassett | Australia | **10** | 69 | - | 4 | 3 | 2 | - | 1 | - | - | - |
| G.A.Headley | West Indies | **10** | 40 | 2 | 8 | - | - | - | - | - | - | - |
| B.C.Lara | West Indies | **10** | 91 | 2 | 5 | 0 | - | 1 | 1 | 0 | 1 | - |
| Mudassar Nazar | Pakistan | **10** | 116 | - | 3 | - | - | 1 | 6 | - | - | - |
| Mushtaq Mohammad | Pakistan | **10** | 100 | 1 | 3 | - | 2 | 3 | 1 | - | - | - |
| R.B.Simpson | Australia | **10** | 111 | - | 2 | 1 | 1 | - | 4 | 2 | - | - |

*The leading century-maker for South Africa is A.D.Nourse (9 in 62 innings) and for Zimbabwe A.Flower (5 in 53 innings) and G.W.Flower (5 in 54 innings).*

## HIGHEST BATTING AVERAGES *(Qualification: 15 innings)*

| Player | Country | Tests | I | NO | Runs | HS | Avge | 100 | 50 |
|---|---|---|---|---|---|---|---|---|---|
| D.G.Bradman | Australia | 52 | 80 | 10 | 6996 | 334 | **99.94** | 29 | 13 |
| C.S.Dempster | New Zealand | 10 | 15 | 4 | 723 | 136 | **65.72** | 2 | 5 |
| S.G.Barnes | Australia | 13 | 19 | 2 | 1072 | 234 | **63.05** | 3 | 5 |
| R.G.Pollock | South Africa | 23 | 41 | 4 | 2256 | 274 | **60.97** | 7 | 11 |
| G.A.Headley | West Indies | 22 | 40 | 4 | 2190 | 270* | **60.83** | 10 | 5 |
| H.Sutcliffe | England | 54 | 84 | 9 | 4555 | 194 | **60.73** | 16 | 23 |
| E.Paynter | England | 20 | 31 | 5 | 1540 | 243 | **59.23** | 4 | 7 |
| K.F.Barrington | England | 82 | 131 | 15 | 6806 | 256 | **58.67** | 20 | 35 |
| E.D.Weekes | West Indies | 48 | 81 | 5 | 4455 | 207 | **58.61** | 15 | 19 |
| K.S.Duleepsinhji | England | 12 | 19 | 2 | 995 | 173 | **58.52** | 3 | 5 |
| W.R.Hammond | England | 85 | 140 | 16 | 7249 | 336* | **58.46** | 22 | 24 |
| G.S.Sobers | West Indies | 93 | 160 | 21 | 8032 | 365* | **57.78** | 26 | 30 |
| J.B.Hobbs | England | 61 | 102 | 7 | 5410 | 211 | **56.94** | 15 | 28 |
| C.A.G.Russell | England | 10 | 18 | 2 | 990 | 140 | **56.87** | 5 | 2 |
| C.L.Walcott | West Indies | 44 | 74 | 7 | 3798 | 220 | **56.68** | 15 | 14 |
| L.Hutton | England | 79 | 138 | 15 | 6971 | 364 | **56.67** | 19 | 33 |
| G.E.Tyldesley | England | 14 | 20 | 2 | 990 | 122 | **55.00** | 3 | 6 |
| S.R.Tendulkar | India | 61 | 92 | 9 | 4552 | 179 | **54.84** | 16 | 19 |
| C.A.Davis | West Indies | 15 | 29 | 5 | 1301 | 183 | **54.20** | 4 | 4 |
| V.G.Kambli | India | 17 | 21 | 1 | 1084 | 227 | **54.20** | 4 | 3 |
| G.S.Chappell | Australia | 87 | 151 | 19 | 7110 | 247* | **53.86** | 24 | 31 |
| S.Chanderpaul | West Indies | 21 | 33 | 6 | 1454 | 137* | **53.85** | 1 | 14 |
| A.D.Nourse | South Africa | 34 | 62 | 7 | 2960 | 231 | **53.81** | 9 | 14 |
| A.Melville | South Africa | 11 | 19 | 2 | 894 | 189* | **52.58** | 4 | 3 |
| Javed Miandad | Pakistan | 124 | 189 | 21 | 8832 | 280* | **52.57** | 23 | 43 |
| C.F.Walters | England | 11 | 18 | 3 | 784 | 102 | **52.26** | 1 | 7 |
| S.L.Campbell | West Indies | 11 | 18 | 1 | 885 | 208 | **52.05** | 1 | 6 |
| B.C.Lara | West Indies | 54 | 91 | 3 | 4550 | 375 | **51.70** | 10 | 23 |
| J.Ryder | Australia | 20 | 32 | 5 | 1394 | 201* | **51.62** | 3 | 9 |
| R.S.Dravid | India | 22 | 35 | 3 | 1643 | 148 | **51.34** | 1 | 15 |
| J.C.Adams | West Indies | 33 | 52 | 11 | 2104 | 208* | **51.31** | 5 | 10 |
| S.C.Ganguly | India | 20 | 31 | 2 | 1483 | 173 | **51.13** | 5 | 5 |
| S.M.Gavaskar | India | 125 | 214 | 12 | 10122 | 236* | **51.12** | 34 | 45 |
| A.R.Border | Australia | 156 | 265 | 44 | 11174 | 205 | **50.56** | 27 | 63 |
| I.V.A.Richards | West Indies | 121 | 182 | 12 | 8540 | 291 | **50.23** | 24 | 45 |
| D.C.S.Compton | England | 78 | 131 | 15 | 5807 | 278 | **50.06** | 17 | 28 |

## HIGHEST INDIVIDUAL INNINGS

| | | | | | | |
|---|---|---|---|---|---|---|
| 375 | B.C.Lara | West Indies | v | England | St John's | 1993-94 |
| 365* | G.S.Sobers | West Indies | v | Pakistan | Kingston | 1957-58 |
| 364 | L.Hutton | England | v | Australia | The Oval | 1938 |
| 340 | S.T.Jayasuriya | Sri Lanka | v | India | Colombo (PIS) | 1997-98 |
| 337 | Hanif Mohammad | Pakistan | v | West Indies | Bridgetown | 1957-58 |
| 336* | W.R.Hammond | England | v | New Zealand | Auckland | 1932-33 |
| 334 | D.G.Bradman | Australia | v | England | Leeds | 1930 |
| 333 | G.A.Gooch | England | v | India | Lord's | 1990 |
| 325 | A.Sandham | England | v | West Indies | Kingston | 1929-30 |
| 311 | R.B.Simpson | Australia | v | England | Manchester | 1964 |
| 310* | J.H.Edrich | England | v | New Zealand | Leeds | 1965 |

| | | | | | | |
|---|---|---|---|---|---|---|
| 307 | R.M.Cowper | Australia | v | England | Melbourne | 1965-66 |
| 304 | D.G.Bradman | Australia | v | England | Leeds | 1934 |
| 302 | L.G.Rowe | West Indies | v | England | Bridgetown | 1973-74 |
| 299* | D.G.Bradman | Australia | v | South Africa | Adelaide | 1931-32 |
| 299 | M.D.Crowe | New Zealand | v | Sri Lanka | Wellington | 1990-91 |
| 291I | .V.A.Richards | West Indies | v | England | The Oval | 1976 |
| 287 | R.E.Foster | England | v | Australia | Sydney | 1903-04 |
| 285* | P.B.H.May | England | v | West Indies | Birmingham | 1957 |
| 280* | Javed Miandad | Pakistan | v | India | Hyderabad | 1982-83 |
| 278 | D.C.S.Compton | England | v | Pakistan | Nottingham | 1954 |
| 277 | B.C.Lara | West Indies | v | Australia | Sydney | 1992-93 |
| 274 | R.G.Pollock | South Africa | v | Australia | Durban[2] | 1969-70 |
| 274 | Zaheer Abbas | Pakistan | v | England | Birmingham | 1971 |
| 271 | Javed Miandad | Pakistan | v | New Zealand | Auckland | 1988-89 |
| 270* | G.A.Headley | West Indies | v | England | Kingston | 1934-35 |
| 270 | D.G.Bradman | Australia | v | England | Melbourne | 1936-37 |
| 268 | G.N.Yallop | Australia | v | Pakistan | Melbourne | 1983-84 |
| 267* | B.A.Young | New Zealand | v | Sri Lanka | Dunedin | 1996-97 |
| 267 | P.A.de Silva | Sri Lanka | v | New Zealand | Wellington | 1990-91 |
| 266 | W.H.Ponsford | Australia | v | England | The Oval | 1934 |
| 266 | D.L.Houghton | Zimbabwe | v | Sri Lanka | Bulawayo[2] | 1994-95 |
| 262* | D.L.Amiss | England | v | West Indies | Kingston | 1973-74 |
| 261 | F.M.M.Worrell | West Indies | v | England | Nottingham | 1950 |
| 260 | C.C.Hunte | West Indies | v | Pakistan | Kingston | 1957-58 |
| 260 | Javed Miandad | Pakistan | v | England | The Oval | 1987 |
| 259 | G.M.Turner | New Zealand | v | West Indies | Georgetown | 1971-72 |
| 258 | T.W.Graveney | England | v | West Indies | Nottingham | 1957 |
| 258 | S.M.Nurse | West Indies | v | New Zealand | Christchurch | 1968-69 |
| 257* | Wasim Akram | Pakistan | v | Zimbabwe | Sheikhupura | 1996-97 |
| 256 | R.B.Kanhai | West Indies | v | India | Calcutta | 1958-59 |
| 256 | K.F.Barrington | England | v | Australia | Manchester | 1964 |
| 255* | D.J.McGlew | South Africa | v | New Zealand | Wellington | 1952-53 |
| 254 | D.G.Bradman | Australia | v | England | Lord's | 1930 |
| 251 | W.R.Hammond | England | v | Australia | Sydney | 1928-29 |
| 250 | K.D.Walters | Australia | v | New Zealand | Christchurch | 1976-77 |
| 250 | S.F.A.F.Bacchus | West Indies | v | India | Kanpur | 1978-79 |
| 247* | G.S.Chappell | Australia | v | New Zealand | Wellington | 1973-74 |
| 246* | G.Boycott | England | v | India | Leeds | 1967 |
| 244 | D.G.Bradman | Australia | v | England | The Oval | 1934 |
| 243 | E.Paynter | England | v | South Africa | Durban[2] | 1938-39 |
| 242* | C.H.Lloyd | West Indies | v | India | Bombay[3] | 1974-75 |
| 242 | K.D.Walters | Australia | v | West Indies | Sydney | 1968-69 |
| 240 | W.R.Hammond | England | v | Australia | Lord's | 1938 |
| 240 | Zaheer Abbas | Pakistan | v | England | The Oval | 1974 |
| 239 | G.T.Dowling | New Zealand | v | India | Christchurch | 1967-68 |
| 237 | F.M.M.Worrell | West Indies | v | India | Kingston | 1952-53 |
| 237 | Saleem Malik | Pakistan | v | Australia | Rawalpindi[2] | 1994-95 |
| 236* | S.M.Gavaskar | India | v | West Indies | Madras[1] | 1983-84 |
| 236 | E.A.B.Rowan | South Africa | v | England | Leeds | 1951 |
| 235* | Zaheer Abbas | Pakistan | v | India | Lahore[2] | 1978-79 |
| 235 | G.S.Chappell | Australia | v | Pakistan | Faisalabad | 1979-80 |
| 234 | D.G.Bradman | Australia | v | England | Sydney | 1946-47 |
| 234 | S.G.Barnes | Australia | v | England | Sydney | 1946-47 |
| 232 | D.G.Bradman | Australia | v | England | The Oval | 1930 |
| 232 | S.J.McCabe | Australia | v | England | Nottingham | 1938 |
| 232 | I.V.A.Richards | West Indies | v | England | Nottingham | 1976 |
| 231* | W.R.Hammond | England | v | Australia | Sydney | 1936-37 |
| 231 | A.D.Nourse | South Africa | v | Australia | Johannesburg[1] | 1935-36 |
| 231 | M.H.Mankad | India | v | New Zealand | Madras[2] | 1955-56 |
| 231 | Mudassar Nazar | Pakistan | v | India | Hyderabad | 1982-83 |

| | | | | | | |
|---|---|---|---|---|---|---|
| 230* | B.Sutcliffe | New Zealand | v | India | Delhi | 1955-56 |
| 227 | W.R.Hammond | England | v | New Zealand | Christchurch | 1932-33 |
| 227 | V.G.Kambli | India | v | Zimbabwe | Delhi | 1992-93 |
| 226 | D.G.Bradman | Australia | v | South Africa | Brisbane[2] | 1931-32 |
| 226 | G.S.Sobers | West Indies | v | England | Bridgetown | 1959-60 |
| 226 | C.G.Greenidge | West Indies | v | Australia | Bridgetown | 1990-91 |
| 225 | R.B.Simpson | Australia | v | England | Adelaide | 1965-66 |
| 225 | R.S.Mahanama | Sri Lanka | v | India | Colombo (PIS) | 1997-98 |
| 224 | V.G.Kambli | India | v | England | Bombay[3] | 1992-93 |
| 223* | G.M.Turner | New Zealand | v | West Indies | Kingston | 1971-72 |
| 223 | G.A.Headley | West Indies | v | England | Kingston | 1929-30 |
| 223 | D.G.Bradman | Australia | v | West Indies | Brisbane[1] | 1930-31 |
| 223 | P.R.Umrigar | India | v | New Zealand | Hyderabad | 1955-56 |
| 223 | M.H.Mankad | India | v | New Zealand | Bombay[2] | 1955-56 |
| 223 | C.G.Greenidge | West Indies | v | England | Manchester | 1984 |
| 223 | M.S.Atapattu | Sri Lanka | v | Zimbabwe | Kandy | 1997-98 |
| 222 | G.R.Viswanath | India | v | England | Madras[1] | 1981-82 |
| 221 | S.M.Gavaskar | India | v | England | The Oval | 1979 |
| 220 | C.L.Walcott | West Indies | v | England | Bridgetown | 1953-54 |
| 220 | S.M.Gavaskar | India | v | West Indies | Port-of-Spain | 1970-71 |
| 219 | W.J.Edrich | England | v | South Africa | Durban[2] | 1938-39 |
| 219 | D.S.Atkinson | West Indies | v | Australia | Bridgetown | 1954-55 |
| 219 | M.A.Taylor | Australia | v | England | Nottingham | 1989 |
| 219 | M.J.Slater | Australia | v | Sri Lanka | Perth | 1995-96 |
| 218 | S.V.Manjrekar | India | v | Pakistan | Lahore[2] | 1989-90 |
| 217 | W.R.Hammond | England | v | India | The Oval | 1936 |
| 217 | R.B.Kanhai | West Indies | v | Pakistan | Lahore[1] | 1958-59 |
| 216* | E.Paynter | England | v | Australia | Nottingham | 1938 |
| 216 | K.W.R.Fletcher | England | v | New Zealand | Auckland | 1974-75 |
| 216 | D.M.Jones | Australia | v | West Indies | Adelaide | 1988-89 |
| 215 | Zaheer Abbas | Pakistan | v | India | Lahore[2] | 1982-83 |
| 215 | D.I.Gower | England | v | West Indies | Birmingham | 1985 |
| 214* | V.T.Trumper | Australia | v | South Africa | Adelaide | 1910-11 |
| 214* | D.Lloyd | England | v | India | Birmingham | 1974 |
| 214* | C.G.Greenidge | West Indies | v | England | Lord's | 1984 |
| 214 | L.G.Rowe | West Indies | v | New Zealand | Kingston | 1971-72 |
| 214 | G.S.Blewett | Australia | v | South Africa | Johannesburg[3] | 1996-97 |
| 213 | K.J.Hughes | Australia | v | India | Adelaide | 1980-81 |
| 213 | C.G.Greenidge | West Indies | v | New Zealand | Auckland | 1986-87 |
| 212 | D.G.Bradman | Australia | v | England | Adelaide | 1936-37 |
| 212 | D.N.Sardesai | India | v | West Indies | Kingston | 1970-71 |
| 211 | W.L.Murdoch | Australia | v | England | The Oval | 1884 |
| 211 | J.B.Hobbs | England | v | South Africa | Lord's | 1924 |
| 211 | Javed Miandad | Pakistan | v | Australia | Karachi[1] | 1988-89 |
| 210* | Taslim Arif | Pakistan | v | Australia | Faisalabad | 1979-80 |
| 210 | W.M.Lawry | Australia | v | West Indies | Bridgetown | 1964-65 |
| 210 | Qasim Omar | Pakistan | v | India | Faisalabad | 1984-85 |
| 210 | D.M.Jones | Australia | v | India | Madras[1] | 1986-87 |
| 210 | G.A.Gooch | England | v | New Zealand | Nottingham | 1994 |
| 210 | G.Kirsten | South Africa | v | England | Manchester | 1998 |
| 209* | B.F.Butcher | West Indies | v | England | Nottingham | 1966 |
| 209 | C.A.Roach | West Indies | v | England | Georgetown | 1929-30 |
| 209 | Imtiaz Ahmed | Pakistan | v | New Zealand | Lahore[1] | 1955-56 |
| 209 | R.G.Pollock | South Africa | v | Australia | Cape Town | 1966-67 |
| 208* | J.C.Adams | West Indies | v | New Zealand | St John's | 1995-96 |
| 208 | D.C.S.Compton | England | v | South Africa | Lord's | 1947 |
| 208 | A.D.Nourse | South Africa | v | England | Nottingham | 1951 |
| 208 | I.T.Botham | England | v | India | The Oval | 1982 |
| 208 | I.V.A.Richards | West Indies | v | Australia | Melbourne | 1984-85 |
| 208 | S.L.Campbell | West Indies | v | New Zealand | Bridgetown | 1995-96 |

| | | | | | | |
|---|---|---|---|---|---|---|
| 207 | E.D.Weekes | West Indies | v | India | Port-of-Spain | 1952-53 |
| 207 | K.R.Stackpole | Australia | v | England | Brisbane[2] | 1970-71 |
| 207 | M.W.Gatting | England | v | India | Madras[1] | 1984-85 |
| 207 | N.Hussain | England | v | Australia | Birmingham | 1997 |
| 206* | W.A.Brown | Australia | v | England | Lord's | 1938 |
| 206 | M.P.Donnelly | New Zealand | v | England | Lord's | 1949 |
| 206 | L.Hutton | England | v | New Zealand | The Oval | 1949 |
| 206 | A.R.Morris | Australia | v | England | Adelaide | 1950-51 |
| 206 | E.D.Weekes | West Indies | v | England | Port-of-Spain | 1953-54 |
| 206 | Javed Miandad | Pakistan | v | New Zealand | Karachi[1] | 1976-77 |
| 206 | Qasim Omar | Pakistan | v | Sri Lanka | Faisalabad | 1985-86 |
| 206 | R.J.Shastri | India | v | Australia | Sydney | 1991-92 |
| 205* | E.H.Hendren | England | v | West Indies | Port-of-Spain | 1929-30 |
| 205* | J.Hardstaff, jr | England | v | India | Lord's | 1946 |
| 205 | R.N.Harvey | Australia | v | South Africa | Melbourne | 1952-53 |
| 205 | L.Hutton | England | v | West Indies | Kingston | 1953-54 |
| 205 | E.R.Dexter | England | v | Pakistan | Karachi[1] | 1961-62 |
| 205 | W.M.Lawry | Australia | v | West Indies | Melbourne | 1968-69 |
| 205 | S.M.Gavaskar | India | v | West Indies | Bombay[3] | 1978-79 |
| 205 | A.R.Border | Australia | v | New Zealand | Adelaide | 1987-88 |
| 205 | Aamer Sohail | Pakistan | v | England | Manchester | 1992 |
| 204 | G.A.Faulkner | South Africa | v | Australia | Melbourne | 1910-11 |
| 204 | R.N.Harvey | Australia | v | West Indies | Kingston | 1954-55 |
| 204 | G.S.Chappell | Australia | v | India | Sydney | 1980-81 |
| 203* | Nawab of Pataudi, jr | India | v | England | Delhi | 1963-64 |
| 203* | Hanif Mohammad | Pakistan | v | New Zealand | Lahore[2] | 1964-65 |
| 203* | Javed Miandad | Pakistan | v | Sri Lanka | Faisalabad | 1985-86 |
| 203* | Shoaib Mohammad | Pakistan | v | India | Lahore[2] | 1989-90 |
| 203* | Shoaib Mohammad | Pakistan | v | New Zealand | Karachi[1] | 1990-91 |
| 203* | G.J.Whittall | Zimbabwe | v | New Zealand | Bulawayo[2] | 1997-98 |
| 203 | H.L.Collins | Australia | v | South Africa | Johannesburg[1] | 1921-22 |
| 203 | D.L.Amiss | England | v | West Indies | The Oval | 1976 |
| 202* | L.Hutton | England | v | West Indies | The Oval | 1950 |
| 201* | J.Ryder | Australia | v | England | Adelaide | 1924-25 |
| 201* | D.S.B.P.Kuruppu | Sri Lanka | v | New Zealand | Colombo (CCC) | 1986-87 |
| 201* | G.W.Flower | Zimbabwe | v | Pakistan | Harare | 1994-95 |
| 201 | S.E.Gregory | Australia | v | England | Sydney | 1894-95 |
| 201 | D.G.Bradman | Australia | v | India | Adelaide | 1947-48 |
| 201 | E.J.Barlow | South Africa | v | Australia | Adelaide | 1963-64 |
| 201 | R.B.Simpson | Australia | v | West Indies | Bridgetown | 1964-65 |
| 201 | S.M.Nurse | West Indies | v | Australia | Bridgetown | 1964-65 |
| 201 | Mushtaq Mohammad | Pakistan | v | New Zealand | Dunedin | 1972-73 |
| 201 | G.S.Chappell | Australia | v | Pakistan | Brisbane[2] | 1981-82 |
| 201 | A.D.Gaekwad | India | v | Pakistan | Jullundur | 1983-84 |
| 201 | G.Fowler | England | v | India | Madras[1] | 1984-85 |
| 201 | N.S.Sidhu | India | v | West Indies | Port-of-Spain | 1996-97 |
| 200* | D.N.Sardesai | India | v | New Zealand | Bombay[2] | 1964-65 |
| 200* | D.I.Gower | England | v | India | Birmingham | 1979 |
| 200* | A.R.Border | Australia | v | England | Leeds | 1993 |
| 200 | W.R.Hammond | England | v | Australia | Melbourne | 1928-29 |
| 200 | Mohsin Khan | Pakistan | v | England | Lord's | 1982 |
| 200 | D.C.Boon | Australia | v | New Zealand | Perth | 1989-90 |
| 200 | S.R.Waugh | Australia | v | West Indies | Kingston | 1994-95 |

## 500 RUNS IN A TEST SERIES *(§ first Test series. # last Test series. † only Test Series)*

| AUSTRALIA | Opp | Season | Tests | I | NO | Runs | HS | Avge | 100 | 50 |
|---|---|---|---|---|---|---|---|---|---|---|
| D.G.Bradman | ENG | 1930 | 5 | 7 | 0 | 974 | 334 | 139.14 | 4 | - |
| M.A.Taylor | ENG | 1989 | 6 | 11 | 1 | 839 | 219 | 83.90 | 2 | 5 |
| R.N.Harvey | SA | 1952-53 | 5 | 9 | 0 | 834 | 205 | 92.66 | 4 | 3 |
| D.G.Bradman | ENG | 1936-37 | 5 | 9 | 0 | 810 | 270 | 90.00 | 3 | 1 |

| | | | | | | | | | | |
|---|---|---|---|---|---|---|---|---|---|---|
| D.G.Bradman | SA | 1931-32 | 5 | 5 | 1 | 806 | 299* | 201.50 | 4 | - |
| D.G.Bradman | ENG | 1934 | 5 | 8 | 0 | 758 | 304 | 94.75 | 2 | 1 |
| D.G.Bradman | IND | 1947-48 | 5 | 6 | 2 | 715 | 201 | 178.75 | 4 | 1 |
| G.S.Chappell | WI | 1975-76 | 6 | 11 | 5 | 702 | 182* | 117.00 | 3 | 3 |
| K.D.Walters | WI | 1968-69 | 4 | 6 | 0 | 699 | 242 | 116.50 | 4 | 2 |
| A.R.Morris | ENG | 1948 | 5 | 9 | 1 | 696 | 196 | 87.00 | 3 | 3 |
| D.G.Bradman | ENG | 1946-47 | 5 | 8 | 1 | 680 | 234 | 97.14 | 2 | 3 |
| W.M.Lawry | WI | 1968-69 | 5 | 8 | 0 | 667 | 205 | 83.38 | 3 | 2 |
| V.T.Trumper | SA | 1910-11 | 5 | 9 | 2 | 661 | 214* | 94.42 | 2 | 2 |
| R.N.Harvey | SA | 1949-50 | 5 | 8 | 3 | 660 | 178 | 132.00 | 4 | 1 |
| R.N.Harvey | WI | 1954-55 | 5 | 7 | 1 | 650 | 204 | 108.33 | 3 | 1 |
| K.R.Stackpole | ENG | 1970-71 | 6 | 12 | 0 | 627 | 207 | 52.25 | 2 | 2 |
| M.J.Slater | ENG | 1994-95 | 5 | 10 | 0 | 623 | 176 | 62.30 | 3 | 1 |
| G.S.Chappell | ENG | 1974-75 | 6 | 11 | 0 | 608 | 144 | 55.27 | 2 | 5 |
| A.R.Border | ENG | 1985 | 6 | 11 | 2 | 597 | 196 | 66.33 | 2 | 1 |
| K.J.Hughes | IND | 1979-80 | 6 | 12 | 2 | 594 | 100 | 59.40 | 1 | 5 |
| W.M.Lawry | ENG | 1965-66 | 5 | 7 | 0 | 592 | 166 | 84.57 | 3 | 2 |
| I.R.Redpath | WI | 1975-76 | 6 | 11 | 0 | 575 | 103 | 52.27 | 3 | 2 |
| V.T.Trumper | ENG | 1903-04 | 5 | 10 | 1 | 574 | 185* | 63.77 | 2 | 3 |
| W.Bardsley | SA | 1910-11 | 5 | 9 | 0 | 573 | 132 | 63.66 | 1 | 5 |
| W.H.Ponsford # | ENG | 1934 | 4 | 7 | 1 | 569 | 266 | 94.83 | 2 | 1 |
| D.M.Jones | ENG | 1989 | 6 | 9 | 1 | 566 | 157 | 70.75 | 2 | 3 |
| H.L.Collins § | ENG | 1920-21 | 5 | 9 | 0 | 557 | 162 | 61.88 | 2 | 3 |
| D.C.Boon | IND | 1991-92 | 5 | 9 | 2 | 556 | 135 | 79.42 | 3 | 1 |
| M.T.G.Elliott | ENG | 1997 | 6 | 10 | 0 | 556 | 199 | 55.60 | 2 | 2 |
| D.C.Boon | ENG | 1993 | 6 | 10 | 2 | 555 | 164* | 69.37 | 3 | 1 |
| G.N.Yallop | PAK | 1983-84 | 5 | 6 | 0 | 554 | 268 | 92.33 | 2 | 1 |
| M.E.Waugh | ENG | 1993 | 6 | 10 | 1 | 550 | 137 | 61.11 | 1 | 5 |
| I.M.Chappell | WI | 1968-69 | 5 | 8 | 0 | 548 | 165 | 68.50 | 2 | 3 |
| I.M.Chappell | WI | 1972-73 | 5 | 9 | 2 | 542 | 109 | 77.42 | 2 | 3 |
| J.M.Taylor | ENG | 1924-25 | 5 | 10 | 0 | 541 | 108 | 54.10 | 1 | 4 |
| R.B.Simpson | IND | 1977-78 | 5 | 10 | 0 | 539 | 176 | 53.90 | 2 | 2 |
| J.Darling | ENG | 1897-98 | 5 | 8 | 0 | 537 | 178 | 67.12 | 3 | - |
| A.R.Border | ENG | 1981 | 6 | 12 | 3 | 533 | 123* | 59.22 | 2 | 3 |
| B.C.Booth | SA | 1963-64 | 4 | 7 | 1 | 531 | 169 | 88.50 | 2 | 3 |
| D.C.Boon | ENG | 1990-91 | 5 | 9 | 2 | 530 | 121 | 75.71 | 1 | 3 |
| N.C.O'Neill | WI | 1960-61 | 5 | 10 | 0 | 522 | 181 | 52.20 | 1 | 3 |
| C.Hill | ENG | 1901-02 | 5 | 10 | 0 | 521 | 99 | 52.10 | - | 4 |
| A.R.Border | IND | 1979-80 | 6 | 12 | 0 | 521 | 162 | 49.63 | 1 | 3 |
| A.R.Border | WI | 1983-84 | 5 | 10 | 3 | 521 | 100* | 74.42 | 1 | 4 |
| C.C.McDonald | ENG | 1958-59 | 5 | 9 | 1 | 519 | 170 | 64.87 | 2 | 1 |
| W.A.Brown | ENG | 1938 | 4 | 8 | 1 | 512 | 206* | 73.14 | 2 | 1 |
| D.M.Jones | ENG | 1986-87 | 5 | 10 | 1 | 511 | 184* | 56.77 | 1 | 3 |
| D.G.Bradman # | ENG | 1948 | 5 | 9 | 2 | 508 | 173* | 72.57 | 2 | 1 |
| S.R.Waugh | ENG | 1989 | 6 | 8 | 4 | 506 | 177* | 126.50 | 2 | 1 |
| K.C.Wessels | WI | 1984-85 | 5 | 9 | 0 | 505 | 173 | 56.11 | 1 | 4 |
| A.R.Morris § | ENG | 1946-47 | 5 | 8 | 1 | 503 | 155 | 71.85 | 3 | 1 |

| **ENGLAND** | Opp | Season | Tests | I | NO | Runs | HS | Avge | 100 | 50 |
|---|---|---|---|---|---|---|---|---|---|---|
| W.R.Hammond | AUST | 1928-29 | 5 | 9 | 1 | 905 | 251 | 113.12 | 4 | - |
| D.C.S.Compton | SA | 1947 | 5 | 8 | 0 | 753 | 208 | 94.12 | 4 | 2 |
| G.A.Gooch | IND | 1990 | 3 | 6 | 0 | 752 | 333 | 125.33 | 3 | 2 |
| H.Sutcliffe | AUST | 1924-25 | 5 | 9 | 0 | 734 | 176 | 81.56 | 4 | 2 |
| D.I.Gower | AUST | 1985 | 6 | 9 | 0 | 732 | 215 | 81.33 | 3 | 1 |
| E.H.Hendren | WI | 1929-30 | 4 | 8 | 2 | 693 | 205* | 115.50 | 2 | 5 |
| L.Hutton | WI | 1953-54 | 5 | 8 | 1 | 677 | 205 | 96.71 | 2 | 3 |
| G.A.Gooch | AUST | 1993 | 6 | 12 | 0 | 673 | 133 | 56.08 | 2 | 4 |
| D.L.Amiss | WI | 1973-74 | 5 | 9 | 1 | 663 | 262* | 82.87 | 3 | - |
| J.B.Hobbs | AUST | 1911-12 | 5 | 9 | 1 | 662 | 187 | 82.75 | 3 | 1 |
| G.Boycott | AUST | 1970-71 | 5 | 10 | 3 | 657 | 142* | 93.85 | 2 | 5 |

| | | | | | | | | | | |
|---|---|---|---|---|---|---|---|---|---|---|
| E.Paynter # | SA | 1938-39 | 5 | 8 | 0 | 653 | 243 | 81.62 | 3 | 2 |
| J.H.Edrich | AUST | 1970-71 | 6 | 11 | 2 | 648 | 130 | 72.00 | 2 | 4 |
| W.R.Hammond | SA | 1938-39 | 5 | 8 | 1 | 609 | 181 | 87.00 | 3 | 2 |
| K.F.Barrington | IND | 1961-62 | 5 | 9 | 3 | 594 | 172 | 99.00 | 3 | 1 |
| A.Sandham # | WI | 1929-30 | 4 | 8 | 0 | 592 | 325 | 74.00 | 2 | 2 |
| K.F.Barrington | AUST | 1962-63 | 5 | 10 | 2 | 582 | 132 | 72.75 | 2 | 3 |
| P.B.H.May | SA | 1955 | 5 | 9 | 1 | 582 | 117 | 72.75 | 2 | 3 |
| L.Hutton | SA | 1948-49 | 5 | 9 | 0 | 577 | 158 | 64.11 | 2 | 2 |
| M.W.Gatting | IND | 1984-85 | 5 | 9 | 3 | 575 | 207 | 95.83 | 2 | 1 |
| J.B.Hobbs | AUST | 1924-25 | 5 | 9 | 0 | 573 | 154 | 63.66 | 3 | 2 |
| W.R.Hammond | NZ | 1932-33 | 2 | 2 | 1 | 563 | 336* | 64.49 | 2 | - |
| D.C.S.Compton | AUST | 1948 | 5 | 10 | 1 | 562 | 184 | 62.44 | 2 | 2 |
| J.H.Edrich | AUST | 1968 | 5 | 9 | 0 | 554 | 164 | 61.55 | 1 | 4 |
| R.A.Smith | AUST | 1989 | 5 | 10 | 1 | 553 | 143 | 61.44 | 2 | 3 |
| M.A.Atherton | AUST | 1993 | 6 | 12 | 0 | 553 | 99 | 46.08 | 0 | 6 |
| W.J.Edrich | SA | 1947 | 4 | 6 | 1 | 552 | 191 | 110.40 | 2 | 2 |
| C.Washbrook | SA | 1948-49 | 5 | 9 | 0 | 542 | 195 | 60.22 | 1 | 2 |
| J.B.Hobbs | SA | 1909-10 | 5 | 9 | 1 | 539 | 187 | 67.37 | 1 | 4 |
| M.C.Cowdrey | WI | 1967-68 | 5 | 8 | 0 | 534 | 148 | 66.75 | 2 | 4 |
| L.Hutton | AUST | 1950-51 | 5 | 10 | 4 | 533 | 156* | 88.83 | 1 | 4 |
| K.F.Barrington | AUST | 1964 | 5 | 8 | 1 | 531 | 256 | 75.85 | 1 | 2 |
| M.W.Gatting | AUST | 1985 | 6 | 9 | 3 | 527 | 160 | 87.83 | 2 | 3 |
| E.R.Dexter | WI | 1959-60 | 5 | 9 | 1 | 526 | 136* | 65.75 | 2 | 2 |
| G.E.Tyldesley | SA | 1927-28 | 5 | 9 | 1 | 520 | 122 | 65.00 | 2 | 3 |
| W.R.Hammond | SA | 1930-31 | 5 | 9 | 1 | 517 | 136* | 64.62 | 1 | 4 |
| H.Sutcliffe | AUST | 1929 | 5 | 9 | 1 | 513 | 114 | 64.12 | 4 | - |
| M.A.Atherton | WI | 1993-94 | 5 | 9 | 0 | 510 | 144 | 56.66 | 2 | 2 |
| K.F.Barrington | SA | 1964-65 | 5 | 7 | 2 | 508 | 148* | 101.60 | 2 | 2 |
| G.P.Thorpe | WI | 1995 | 6 | 12 | 0 | 506 | 94 | 42.16 | 0 | 5 |
| J.B.Hobbs | AUST | 1920-21 | 5 | 10 | 0 | 505 | 123 | 50.50 | 2 | 1 |

| **SOUTH AFRICA** | Opp | Season | Tests | I | NO | Runs | HS | Avge | 100 | 50 |
|---|---|---|---|---|---|---|---|---|---|---|
| G.A.Faulkner | AUST | 1910-11 | 5 | 10 | 0 | 732 | 204 | 73.20 | 2 | 5 |
| A.D.Nourse | ENG | 1947 | 5 | 9 | 0 | 621 | 149 | 69.00 | 2 | 5 |
| D.T.Lindsay | AUST | 1966-67 | 5 | 7 | 0 | 606 | 182 | 86.57 | 3 | 1 |
| E.J.Barlow | AUST | 1963-64 | 5 | 10 | 2 | 603 | 201 | 75.37 | 3 | 1 |
| B.Mitchell | ENG | 1947 | 5 | 10 | 1 | 597 | 189* | 66.33 | 2 | 3 |
| H.W.Taylor | ENG | 1922-23 | 5 | 9 | 0 | 582 | 176 | 64.66 | 3 | 2 |
| K.C.Bland | ENG | 1964-65 | 5 | 10 | 2 | 572 | 144* | 71.50 | 1 | 4 |
| A.Melville | ENG | 1947 | 5 | 10 | 1 | 569 | 189 | 63.22 | 3 | 1 |
| E.J.Barlow | ENG | 1964-65 | 5 | 10 | 0 | 558 | 138 | 55.80 | 1 | 4 |
| G.A.Faulkner | ENG | 1909-10 | 5 | 10 | 1 | 545 | 123 | 60.55 | 1 | 3 |
| R.G.Pollock | AUST | 1966-67 | 5 | 9 | 2 | 537 | 209 | 76.71 | 2 | 2 |
| A.D.Nourse | ENG | 1948-49 | 5 | 10 | 3 | 536 | 129* | 76.57 | 2 | 2 |
| A.D.Nourse | AUST | 1935-36 | 5 | 10 | 1 | 518 | 231 | 57.55 | 1 | 2 |
| R.G.Pollock # | AUST | 1969-70 | 4 | 7 | 0 | 517 | 274 | 73.85 | 1 | 3 |
| E.A.B.Rowan # | ENG | 1951 | 5 | 10 | 1 | 515 | 236 | 57.22 | 1 | 3 |
| B.A.Richards † | AUST | 1969-70 | 4 | 7 | 0 | 508 | 140 | 72.57 | 2 | 2 |
| H.W.Taylor | ENG | 1913-14 | 5 | 10 | 0 | 508 | 109 | 35.10 | 1 | 3 |

| **WEST INDIES** | Opp | Season | Tests | I | NO | Runs | HS | Avge | 100 | 50 |
|---|---|---|---|---|---|---|---|---|---|---|
| I.V.A.Richards | ENG | 1976 | 4 | 7 | 0 | 829 | 291 | 118.42 | 3 | 2 |
| C.L.Walcott | AUST | 1954-55 | 5 | 10 | 0 | 827 | 155 | 82.70 | 5 | 2 |
| G.S.Sobers | PAK | 1957-58 | 5 | 8 | 2 | 824 | 365* | 137.33 | 3 | 3 |
| B.C.Lara | ENG | 1993-94 | 5 | 8 | 0 | 798 | 375 | 99.75 | 2 | 2 |
| E.D.Weekes | IND | 1948-49 | 5 | 7 | 0 | 779 | 194 | 111.28 | 4 | 2 |
| B.C.Lara | ENG | 1995 | 6 | 10 | 1 | 765 | 179 | 85.00 | 3 | 3 |
| G.S.Sobers | ENG | 1966 | 5 | 8 | 1 | 722 | 174 | 103.14 | 3 | 2 |
| E.D.Weekes | IND | 1952-53 | 5 | 8 | 1 | 716 | 207 | 102.28 | 3 | 2 |
| G.S.Sobers | ENG | 1959-60 | 5 | 8 | 1 | 709 | 226 | 101.28 | 3 | 1 |

| | | | | | | | | | | |
|---|---|---|---|---|---|---|---|---|---|---|
| G.A.Headley § | ENG | 1929-30 | 4 | 8 | 0 | 703 | 223 | 87.87 | 4 | - |
| C.L.Walcott | ENG | 1953-54 | 5 | 10 | 2 | 698 | 220 | 87.25 | 3 | 3 |
| C.H.Lloyd | IND | 1974-75 | 5 | 9 | 1 | 636 | 242* | 79.50 | 2 | 1 |
| C.C.Hunte § | PAK | 1957-58 | 5 | 9 | 1 | 622 | 260 | 79.75 | 3 | - |
| R.B.Richardson | IND | 1988-89 | 4 | 7 | 0 | 619 | 194 | 88.42 | 2 | 3 |
| L.G.Rowe | ENG | 1973-74 | 5 | 7 | 0 | 616 | 302 | 88.00 | 3 | - |
| G.S.Sobers | IND | 1970-71 | 5 | 10 | 2 | 597 | 178* | 74.62 | 3 | 1 |
| C.G.Greenidge | ENG | 1976 | 5 | 10 | 1 | 592 | 134 | 65.66 | 3 | 2 |
| C.G.Greenidge | ENG | 1984 | 5 | 8 | 1 | 572 | 223 | 81.71 | 2 | - |
| S.M.Nurse † | NZ | 1968-69 | 3 | 5 | 0 | 558 | 258 | 111.60 | 2 | 1 |
| G.S.Sobers | IND | 1958-59 | 5 | 8 | 2 | 557 | 198 | 92.83 | 3 | - |
| I.V.A.Richards | IND | 1975-76 | 4 | 7 | 0 | 556 | 177 | 92.66 | 3 | 1 |
| C.C.Hunte | AUST | 1964-65 | 5 | 10 | 1 | 550 | 89 | 61.11 | - | 6 |
| G.S.Sobers | ENG | 1967-68 | 5 | 9 | 3 | 545 | 152 | 90.83 | 2 | 2 |
| F.M.M.Worrell | ENG | 1950 | 4 | 6 | 0 | 539 | 261 | 89.33 | 2 | 1 |
| A.I.Kallicharran | IND | 1978-79 | 6 | 10 | 1 | 538 | 187 | 59.77 | 1 | 3 |
| R.B.Kanhai | IND | 1958-59 | 5 | 8 | 0 | 538 | 256 | 67.25 | 1 | 2 |
| C.G.Greenidge | PAK | 1976-77 | 5 | 10 | 0 | 536 | 100 | 53.60 | 1 | 4 |
| R.B.Kanhai | ENG | 1967-68 | 5 | 10 | 1 | 535 | 153 | 59.44 | 2 | 1 |
| C.A.Davis | IND | 1970-71 | 4 | 8 | 4 | 529 | 125* | 132.25 | 2 | 3 |
| J.C.Adams | IND | 1994-95 | 3 | 6 | 3 | 520 | 174* | 173.33 | 2 | 2 |
| R.C.Fredericks | ENG | 1976 | 5 | 10 | 1 | 517 | 138 | 57.44 | 2 | 3 |
| R.B.Kanhai | AUST | 1960-61 | 5 | 10 | 0 | 503 | 117 | 50.30 | 2 | 2 |
| S.M.Nurse | ENG | 1966 | 5 | 8 | 0 | 501 | 137 | 62.65 | 1 | 4 |

| **NEW ZEALAND** | Opp | Season | Tests | I | NO | Runs | HS | Avge | 100 | 50 |
|---|---|---|---|---|---|---|---|---|---|---|
| G.M.Turner | WI | 1971-72 | 5 | 8 | 1 | 672 | 259 | 96.00 | 2 | 2 |
| B.Sutcliffe | IND | 1955-56 | 5 | 9 | 2 | 611 | 230* | 87.28 | 2 | 1 |
| J.R.Reid | SA | 1961-62 | 5 | 10 | 1 | 546 | 142 | 60.66 | 1 | 4 |
| B.E.Congdon | WI | 1971-72 | 5 | 8 | 2 | 531 | 166* | 88.50 | 2 | 3 |
| A.H.Jones | SL | 1990-91 | 3 | 6 | 1 | 513 | 186 | 102.60 | 3 | 1 |

| **INDIA** | Opp | Season | Tests | I | NO | Runs | HS | Avge | 100 | 50 |
|---|---|---|---|---|---|---|---|---|---|---|
| S.M.Gavaskar § | WI | 1970-71 | 4 | 8 | 3 | 774 | 220 | 154.80 | 4 | 3 |
| S.M.Gavaskar | WI | 1978-79 | 6 | 9 | 1 | 732 | 205* | 91.50 | 4 | 1 |
| D.N.Sardesai | WI | 1970-71 | 5 | 8 | 0 | 642 | 212 | 80.25 | 3 | 1 |
| M.Amarnath | WI | 1982-83 | 5 | 9 | 0 | 598 | 117 | 66.44 | 2 | 4 |
| V.L.Manjrekar | ENG | 1961-62 | 5 | 8 | 1 | 586 | 189* | 83.71 | 1 | 4 |
| M.Amarnath | PAK | 1982-83 | 6 | 10 | 2 | 584 | 120 | 73.00 | 3 | 3 |
| S.V.Manjrekar | PAK | 1989-90 | 4 | 7 | 1 | 569 | 218 | 94.83 | 2 | 3 |
| G.R.Viswanath | WI | 1974-75 | 5 | 10 | 1 | 568 | 139 | 63.11 | 1 | 3 |
| R.S.Modi | WI | 1948-49 | 5 | 10 | 0 | 560 | 112 | 56.00 | 1 | 5 |
| P.R.Umrigar | WI | 1952-53 | 5 | 10 | 1 | 560 | 130 | 62.22 | 2 | 4 |
| V.S.Hazare | WI | 1948-49 | 5 | 10 | 2 | 543 | 134* | 67.87 | 2 | 3 |
| S.M.Gavaskar | ENG | 1979 | 4 | 7 | 0 | 542 | 221 | 77.42 | 1 | 4 |
| S.M.Gavaskar | PAK | 1979-80 | 6 | 11 | 1 | 529 | 166 | 52.90 | 1 | 2 |
| M.H.Mankad | NZ | 1955-56 | 4 | 5 | 0 | 526 | 231 | 105.20 | 2 | - |
| B.K.Kunderan | ENG | 1963-64 | 5 | 10 | 0 | 525 | 192 | 52.50 | 2 | 1 |
| G.R.Viswanath | A | 1979-80 | 6 | 8 | 1 | 518 | 161* | 74.00 | 2 | 2 |
| S.M.Gavaskar | WI | 1983-84 | 6 | 11 | 1 | 505 | 236* | 50.50 | 2 | 1 |
| S.M.Gavaskar | ENG | 1981-82 | 6 | 9 | 1 | 500 | 172 | 62.50 | 1 | 3 |

| **PAKISTAN** | Opp | Season | Tests | I | NO | Runs | HS | Avge | 100 | 50 |
|---|---|---|---|---|---|---|---|---|---|---|
| Mudassar Nazar | IND | 1982-83 | 6 | 8 | 2 | 761 | 231 | 126.83 | 4 | 1 |
| Zaheer Abbas | IND | 1982-83 | 6 | 6 | 1 | 650 | 215 | 130.00 | 3 | - |
| Hanif Mohammad | WI | 1957-58 | 5 | 9 | 0 | 628 | 337 | 39.10 | 1 | 3 |
| Javed Miandad | IND | 1982-83 | 6 | 6 | 1 | 594 | 280* | 118.88 | 2 | 1 |
| Zaheer Abbas | IND | 1978-79 | 3 | 5 | 2 | 583 | 235 | 174.33 | 2 | 1 |
| Saleem Malik | AUS | 1994-95 | 3 | 6 | 0 | 557 | 237 | 92.83 | 2 | 1 |
| Majid.J.Khan | WI | 1976-77 | 5 | 10 | 0 | 530 | 167 | 53.00 | 1 | 3 |

| | | | | | | | | | | |
|---|---|---|---|---|---|---|---|---|---|---|
| Wasim Raja | WI | 1976-77 | 5 | 10 | 1 | 517 | 117* | 57.44 | 1 | 5 |
| Saeed Ahmed § | WI | 1957-58 | 5 | 9 | 0 | 508 | 150 | 56.44 | 1 | 4 |
| Shoaib Mohammad | NZ | 1990-91 | 3 | 5 | 2 | 507 | 203* | 169.00 | 3 | - |
| Javed Miandad § | NZ | 1976-77 | 3 | 5 | 1 | 504 | 206 | 126.00 | 2 | 1 |

Most runs in a Test series for the other countries:

| **SRI LANKA** | Opp | Season | Tests | I | NO | Runs | HS | Avge | 100 | 50 |
|---|---|---|---|---|---|---|---|---|---|---|
| S.T.Jayassuriya | IND | 1997-98 | 2 | 3 | 0 | 571 | 340 | 190.33 | 2 | 0 |
| P.A.de Silva | NZ | 1990-91 | 3 | 5 | 0 | 493 | 267 | 98.60 | 2 | 1 |

| **ZIMBABWE** | Opp | Season | Tests | I | NO | Runs | HS | Avge | 100 | 50 |
|---|---|---|---|---|---|---|---|---|---|---|
| D.L.Houghton | SL | 1994-95 | 3 | 3 | 0 | 466 | 266 | 155.33 | 2 | 1 |

## MOST CENTURIES IN A SERIES

| | | | | |
|---|---|---|---|---|
| **FIVE** | | | | |
| C.L Walcott | West Indies | v | Australia | 1954-55 |
| **FOUR** | | | | |
| D.G Bradman | Australia | v | England | 1930 |
| | Australia | v | South Africa | 1931-32 |
| | Australia | v | India | 1947-48 |
| D.C.S.Compton | England | v | South Africa | 1947 |
| S.M.Gavaskar | India | v | West Indies | 1970-71 |
| | India | v | West Indies | 1978-79 |
| W.R.Hammond | England | v | Australia | 1928-29 |
| R.N.Harvey | Australia | v | South Africa | 1949-50 |
| | Australia | v | South Africa | 1952-53 |
| G.A.Headley | West Indies | v | England | 1929-30 |
| Mudassar Nazar | Pakistan | v | India | 1982-83 |
| H.Sutcliffe | England | v | Australia | 1924-25 |
| | England | v | South Africa | 1929 |
| K.D.Walters | Australia | v | West Indies | 1968-69 |
| E.D.Weekes | West Indies | v | India | 1948-49 |

## MOST DOUBLE CENTURIES IN A SERIES

| | | | | |
|---|---|---|---|---|
| **THREE** | | | | |
| D.G.Bradman | Australia | v | England | 1930 |
| **TWO** | | | | |
| D.G.Bradman | Australia | v | South Africa | 1931-32 |
| | Australia | v | England | 1934 |
| | Australia | v | England | 1936-37 |
| C.G.Greenidge | West Indies | v | England | 1984 |
| W.R.Hammond | England | v | Australia | 1928-29 |
| | England | v | New Zealand | 1932-33 |
| M.H.Mankad | India | v | New Zealand | 1955-56 |
| I.V.A.Richards | West Indies | v | England | 1976 |
| G.M.Turner | New Zealand | v | West Indies | 1971-72 |

## CENTURIES IN MOST CONSECUTIVE INNINGS

| | | | | | |
|---|---|---|---|---|---|
| **FIVE** | | | Opponents | | |
| E.D.Weekes | West Indies | 141 | England | Kingston | 1947-48 |
| | | 128 | India | Delhi | 1948-49 |
| | | 194 | India | Bombay[2] | 1948-49 |
| | | 162) | India | Calcutta | 1948-49 |
| | | 101) | | | |

*Weekes was run out for 90 in his next innings (Madras[1] 1948-49).*

| | | | | | |
|---|---|---|---|---|---|
| **FOUR** | | | Opponents | | |
| J.H.W.Fingleton | Australia | 112 | South Africa | Cape Town | 1935-36 |
| | | 108 | South Africa | Johannesburg[1] | 1935-36 |
| | | 118 | South Africa | Durban[2] | 1935-36 |
| | | 100 | England | Brisbane[2] | 1936-37 |

| | | | | | |
|---|---|---|---|---|---|
| A.Melville | South Africa | 103 | England | Durban[2] | 1938-39 |
| | | 189 ) | England | Nottingham | 1947 |
| | | 104*) | | | |
| | | 117 | England | Lord's | 1947 |
| **THREE** | | | Opponents | | |
| W.Bardsley | Australia | 136) | England | The Oval | 1909 |
| | | 130) | | | |
| | | 132 | South Africa | Sydney | 1910-11 |
| G.Boycott | England | 119* | Australia | Adelaide | 1970-71 |
| | | 121* | Pakistan | Lord's | 1971 |
| | | 112 | Pakistan | Leeds | 1971 |
| D G Bradman | Australia | 132 ) | India | Melbourne | 1947-48 |
| | | 127*) | | | |
| | | 201 | India | Adelaide | 1947-48 |
| D.C.S.Compton | England | 163 | South Africa | Nottingham | 1947 |
| | | 208 | South Africa | Lord's | 1947 |
| | | 115 | South Africa | Manchester | 1947 |
| P.A.de Silva | Sri Lanka | 168 | Pakistan | Colombo (PIS) | 1996-97 |
| | | 138*) | Pakistan | Colombo (SSC) | 1996-97 |
| | | 103*) | | | |
| P.A.de Silva | Sri Lanka | 125 | India | Colombo (PIS) | 1997-98 |
| | | 146) | India | Colombo (SSC) | 1997-98 |
| | | 120) | | | |
| S.M.Gavaskar | India | 117* | West Indies | Bridgetown | 1970-71 |
| | | 124) | West Indies | Port-of-Spain | 1970-71 |
| | | 220) | | | |
| S.M.Gavaskar | | 111) | Pakistan | Karachi[1] | 1978-79 |
| | | 137) | | | |
| | | 205 | West Indies | Bombay[3] | 1978-79 |
| G.A.Gooch | England | 333) | India | Lord's | 1990 |
| | | 123) | | | |
| | | 116 | India | Manchester | 1990 |
| C G Greenidge | West Indies | 134) | England | Manchester | 1976 |
| | | 101) | | | |
| | | 115 | England | Leeds | 1976 |
| V.S.Hazare | India | 122 | West Indies | Bombay[2] | 1948-49 |
| | | 164* | England | Delhi | 1951-52 |
| | | 155 | England | Bombay[2] | 1951-52 |
| G.A.Headley | West Indies | 270* | England | Kingston | 1934-35 |
| | | 106) | England | Lord's | 1939 |
| | | 107) | | | |
| A.H.Jones | New Zealand | 186 | Sri Lanka | Wellington | 1990-91 |
| | | 122 ) | Sri Lanka | Hamilton | 1990-91 |
| | | 100*) | | | |
| V.G.Kambli | India | 224 | England | Bombay[3] | 1992-93 |
| | | 227 | Zimbabwe | Delhi | 1992-93 |
| | | 125 | Sri Lanka | Colombo (SSC) | 1993-94 |
| C.G.Macartney | Australia | 133* | England | Lord's | 1926 |
| | | 151 | England | Leeds | 1926 |
| | | 109 | England | Manchester | 1926 |
| A.R.Morris | Australia | 155 | England | Melbourne | 1946-47 |
| | | 122 ) | England | Adelaide | 1946-47 |
| | | 124*) | | | |
| Mudassar Nazar | Pakistan | 231 | India | Hyderabad | 1982-83 |
| | | 152* | India | Lahore[2] | 1982-83 |
| | | 152 | India | Karachi[1] | 1982-83 |
| G.S.Sobers | West Indies | 365* | Pakistan | Kingston | 1957-58 |
| | | 125 ) | Pakistan | Georgetown | 1957-58 |
| | | 109*) | | | |

| | | | | | |
|---|---|---|---|---|---|
| H.Sutcliffe | England | 115 | Australia | Sydney | 1924-25 |
| | | 176) | Australia | Melbourne | 1924-25 |
| | | 127) | | | |
| P.R.Umrigar | India | 117 | Pakistan | Madras[2] | 1960-61 |
| | | 112 | Pakistan | Delhi | 1960-61 |
| | | 147* | England | Kanpur | 1961-62 |
| E.D.Weekes | West Indies | 123 | New Zealand | Dunedin | 1955-56 |
| | | 103 | New Zealand | Christchurch | 1955-56 |
| | | 156 | New Zealand | Wellington | 1955-56 |
| Zaheer Abbas | Pakistan | 215 | India | Lahore[2] | 1982-83 |
| | | 186 | India | Karachi[1] | 1982-83 |
| | | 168 | India | Faisalabad | 1982-83 |

## CENTURIES IN MOST CONSECUTIVE MATCHES

*SIX*

| | | | |
|---|---|---|---|
| D.G.Bradman | Australia | 270, 212, 169, 144*, 102*, 103 | 1936-37 to 1938 |

*Because of injury Bradman was unable to bat in his next Test but scored 187 and 234 in his following two matches in 1946-47.*

## CARRYING BAT THROUGH A COMPLETED INNINGS

*(§ on Test debut. # one or more batsmen absent or retired hurt)*

| **AUSTRALIA** | Score | Total | Opponents | | |
|---|---|---|---|---|---|
| J.E.Barrett | 67* | 176 § | England | Lord's | 1890 |
| W.W.Armstrong | 159* | 309 | South Africa | Johannesburg[1] | 1902-03 |
| W.Bardsley | 193* | 383 | England | Lord's | 1926 |
| W.M.Woodfull | 30* | 66# | England | Brisbane[1] | 1928-29 |
| W.M.Woodfull | 73* | 193# | England | Adelaide | 1932-33 |
| W.A.Brown | 206* | 422 | England | Lord's | 1938 |
| W.M.Lawry | 49* | 107 | India | Delhi | 1969-70 |
| W.M.Lawry | 60* | 116# | England | Sydney | 1970-71 |
| I.R.Redpath | 159* | 346 | New Zealand | Auckland | 1973-74 |
| D.C.Boon | 58* | 103 | New Zealand | Auckland | 1985-86 |
| M.A.Taylor | 169* | 350 | South Africa | Adelaide | 1997-98 |

| **ENGLAND** | Score | Total | Opponents | | |
|---|---|---|---|---|---|
| R.Abel | 132* | 307 | Australia | Sydney | 1891-92 |
| P.F.Warner | 132* | 237 § | South Africa | Johannesburg[1] | 1898-99 |
| L.Hutton | 202* | 344 | West Indies | The Oval | 1950 |
| L.Hutton | 156* | 272 | Australia | Adelaide | 1950-51 |
| G.Boycott | 99* | 215 | Australia | Perth | 1979-80 |
| G.A.Gooch | 154* | 252 | West Indies | Leeds | 1991 |
| A.J.Stewart | 69* | 175 | Pakistan | Lord's | 1992 |
| M.A.Atherton | 94* | 228 | New Zealand | Christchurch | 1996-97 |

| **SOUTH AFRICA** | Score | Total | Opponents | | |
|---|---|---|---|---|---|
| A.B.Tancred | 26* | 47 | England | Cape Town | 1888-89 |
| J.W.Zulch | 43* | 103 | England | Cape Town | 1909-10 |
| T.L.Goddard | 56* | 99 | Australia | Cape Town | 1957-58 |
| D.J.McGlew | 127* | 292 | New Zealand | Durban[2] | 1961-62 |
| G.Kirsten | 100* | 239 | Pakistan | Faisalabad | 1997-98 |

| **WEST INDIES** | Score | Total | Opponents | | |
|---|---|---|---|---|---|
| F.M.M.Worrell | 191* | 372 | England | Nottingham | 1957 |
| C.C.Hunte | 60* | 131 | Australia | Port-of-Spain | 1964-65 |
| D.L.Haynes | 88* | 211 | Pakistan | Karachi[1] | 1986-87 |
| D.L.Haynes | 75* | 176 | England | The Oval | 1991 |
| D.L.Haynes | 143* | 382 | Pakistan | Port-of-Spain | 1992-93 |

| NEW ZEALAND | Score | Total | Opponents | | |
|---|---|---|---|---|---|
| G.M.Turner | 43* | 131 | England | Lord's | 1969 |
| G.M.Turner | 223* | 386 | West Indies | Kingston | 1971-72 |

| INDIA | Score | Total | Opponents | | |
|---|---|---|---|---|---|
| S.M.Gavaskar | 127* | 286 | Pakistan | Faisalabad | 1982-83 |

| PAKISTAN | Score | Total | Opponents | | |
|---|---|---|---|---|---|
| Nazar Mohammad | 124* | 331 | India | Lucknow[1] | 1952-53 |
| Mudassar Nazar | 152* | 323 | India | Lahore[2] | 1982-83 |

| SRI LANKA | Score | Total | Opponents | | |
|---|---|---|---|---|---|
| S.Wettimuny | 63* | 144 | New Zealand | Christchurch | 1982-83 |

| ZIMBABWE | Score | Total | Opponents | | |
|---|---|---|---|---|---|
| M.H.Dekker | 68* | 187 | Pakistan | Rawalpindi[2] | 1993-94 |
| G.W.Flower | 156* | 321 | Pakistan | Bulawayo[2] | 1997-98 |

## CENTURY IN EACH INNINGS OF A MATCH

| AUSTRALIA | | | Opponents | | |
|---|---|---|---|---|---|
| W.Bardsley | 136 | 130 | England | The Oval | 1909 |
| A.R.Morris | 122 | 124* | England | Adelaide | 1946-47 |
| D.G.Bradman | 132 | 127* | India | Melbourne | 1947-48 |
| J.Moroney | 118 | 101* | South Africa | Johannesburg[2] | 1949-50 |
| R.B.Simpson | 153 | 115 | Pakistan | Karachi[1] | 1964-65 |
| K.D.Walters | 242 | 103 | West Indies | Sydney | 1968-69 |
| I.M.Chappell | 145 | 121 | New Zealand | Wellington | 1973-74 |
| G.S.Chappell | 247* | 133 | New Zealand | Wellington | 1973-74 |
| G.S.Chappell | 123 | 109* | West Indies | Brisbane[2] | 1975-76 |
| A.R.Border | 150* | 153 | Pakistan | Lahore[2] | 1979-80 |
| A.R.Border | 140 | 114* | New Zealand | Christchurch | 1985-86 |
| D.M.Jones | 116 | 121* | Pakistan | Adelaide | 1989-90 |
| S.R.Waugh | 108 | 116 | England | Manchester | 1997 |

| ENGLAND | | | Opponents | | |
|---|---|---|---|---|---|
| C.A.G.Russell | 140 | 111 | South Africa | Durban[2] | 1922-23 |
| H.Sutcliffe | 176 | 127 | Australia | Melbourne | 1924-25 |
| W.R.Hammond | 119* | 177 | Australia | Adelaide | 1928-29 |
| H.Sutcliffe | 104 | 109* | South Africa | The Oval | 1929 |
| E.Paynter | 117 | 100 | South Africa | Johannesburg[1] | 1938-39 |
| D.C.S.Compton | 147 | 103* | Australia | Adelaide | 1946-47 |
| G.A.Gooch | 333 | 123 | India | Lord's | 1990 |
| A.J.Stewart | 118 | 143 | West Indies | Bridgetown | 1993-94 |

| SOUTH AFRICA | | | Opponents | | |
|---|---|---|---|---|---|
| A.Melville | 189 | 104* | England | Nottingham | 1947 |
| B.Mitchell | 120 | 189* | England | The Oval | 1947 |
| G.Kirsten | 102 | 133 | India | Calcutta | 1996-97 |

| WEST INDIES | | | Opponents | | |
|---|---|---|---|---|---|
| G.A.Headley | 114 | 112 | England | Georgetown | 1929-30 |
| G.A.Headley | 106 | 107 | England | Lord's | 1939 |
| E.D.Weekes | 162 | 101 | India | Calcutta | 1948-49 |
| C.L.Walcott | 126 | 110 | Australia | Port-of-Spain | 1954-55 |
| C.L.Walcott | 155 | 110 | Australia | Kingston | 1954-55 |
| G.S.Sobers | 125 | 109* | Pakistan | Georgetown | 1957-58 |
| R.B.Kanhai | 117 | 115 | Australia | Adelaide | 1960-61 |
| L.G.Rowe | 214 | 100* | New Zealand | Kingston | 1971-72 |
| C.G.Greenidge | 134 | 101 | England | Manchester | 1976 |

| NEW ZEALAND | | | Opponents | | |
|---|---|---|---|---|---|
| G.M.Turner | 101 | 110* | Australia | Christchurch | 1973-74 |
| G.P.Howarth | 122 | 102 | England | Auckland | 1977-78 |
| A.H.Jones | 122 | 100* | Sri Lanka | Hamilton | 1990-91 |

| INDIA | | | Opponents | | |
|---|---|---|---|---|---|
| V.S.Hazare | 116 | 145 | Australia | Adelaide | 1947-48 |
| S.M.Gavaskar | 124 | 220 | West Indies | Port-of-Spain | 1970-71 |
| S.M.Gavaskar | 111 | 137 | Pakistan | Karachi[1] | 1978-79 |
| S.M.Gavaskar | 107 | 182* | West Indies | Calcutta | 1978-79 |

| PAKISTAN | | | Opponents | | |
|---|---|---|---|---|---|
| Hanif Mohammad | 111 | 104 | England | Dacca | 1961-62 |
| Javed Miandad | 104 | 103* | New Zealand | Hyderabad | 1984-85 |

| SRI LANKA | | | Opponents | | |
|---|---|---|---|---|---|
| L.R.D.Mendis | 105 | 105 | India | Madras[1] | 1982-83 |
| A.P.Gurusinha | 119 | 102 | New Zealand | Hamilton | 1990-91 |
| P.A.de Silva | 138* | 103* | Pakistan | Colombo (SSC) | 1996-97 |
| P.A.de Silva | 146 | 120 | India | Colombo (SSC) | 1997-98 |

| ZIMBABWE | | | Opponents | | |
|---|---|---|---|---|---|
| G.W.Flower | 104 | 151 | New Zealand | Harare | 1997-98 |

## CENTURY AND A NINETY IN A MATCH *(§ In first Test. † in last Test)*

| AUSTRALIA | | | Opponents | | |
|---|---|---|---|---|---|
| R.M.Cowper | 92 | 108 | India | Adelaide | 1967-68 |
| P.M.Toohey | 122 | 97 | West Indies | Kingston | 1977-78 |
| A.R.Border | 98* | 100* | West Indies | Port-of-Spain | 1983-84 |

| ENGLAND | | | Opponents | | |
|---|---|---|---|---|---|
| P.A.Gibb § | 93 | 106 | South Africa | Johannesburg[1] | 1938-39 |
| M.C.Cowdrey | 114 | 97 | West Indies | Kingston | 1959-60 |
| K.F.Barrington | 101 | 94 | Australia | Sydney | 1962-63 |
| A.P.E.Knott | 101 | 96 | New Zealand | Auckland | 1970-71 |
| G.Boycott | 99 | 112 | West Indies | Port-of-Spain | 1973-74 |
| M.A.Atherton | 94* | 118 | New Zealand | Christchurch | 1996-97 |

| SOUTH AFRICA | | | Opponents | | |
|---|---|---|---|---|---|
| P.G.V.van der Bijl † | 125 | 97 | England | Durban[2] | 1938-39 |

| WEST INDIES | | | Opponents | | |
|---|---|---|---|---|---|
| G.S.Sobers | 152 | 92* | England | Georgetown | 1967-68 |
| S.M.Nurse | 95 | 168 | New Zealand | Auckland | 1968-69 |
| C.G.Greenidge § | 93 | 107 | India | Bangalore | 1974-75 |

| INDIA | | | Opponents | | |
|---|---|---|---|---|---|
| C.G.Borde | 109 | 96 | West Indies | Delhi | 1958-59 |
| M.Amarnath | 90 | 100 | Australia | Perth | 1977-78 |

| PAKISTAN | | | Opponents | | |
|---|---|---|---|---|---|
| Hanif Mohammad | 104 | 93 | Australia | Melbourne | 1964-65 |
| Zaheer Abbas | 176 | 96 | India | Faisalabad | 1978-79 |
| Mohsin Khan | 94 | 101* | India | Lahore[2] | 1982-83 |
| Saeed Anwar | 94 | 136 | Sri Lanka | Colombo (PSS) | 1993-94 |

| SRI LANKA | | | Opponents | | |
|---|---|---|---|---|---|
| L.R.D.Mendis | 111 | 94 | England | Lord's | 1984 |
| P.A.de Silva | 96 | 123 | New Zealand | Auckland | 1990-91 |

## NINETY IN EACH INNINGS OF A MATCH

| AUSTRALIA | | | Opponents | | |
|---|---|---|---|---|---|
| C.Hill | 98 | 97 | England | Adelaide | 1901-02 |

| ENGLAND | | | Opponents | | |
|---|---|---|---|---|---|
| F.E.Woolley | 95 | 93 | Australia | Lord's | 1921 |

| WEST INDIES | | | Opponents | | |
|---|---|---|---|---|---|
| C.G.Greenidge | 91 | 96 | Pakistan | Georgetown | 1976-77 |
| C.G.Greenidge | 91 | 97 | New Zealand | Christchurch | 1979-80 |

## CENTURY ON DEBUT

| | | | | | | |
|---|---|---|---|---|---|---|
| *IN BOTH INNINGS* | | | | | | |
| L.G.Rowe | 214 )<br>100*) | West Indies | v | New Zealand | Kingston | 1971-72 |
| *IN FIRST INNINGS* | | | | | | |
| C.Bannerman | 165* | Australia | v | England | Melbourne | 1876-77 |
| W.G.Grace | 152 | England | v | Australia | The Oval | 1880 |
| H.Graham | 107 | Australia | v | England | Lord's | 1893 |
| R.E.Foster | 287 | England | v | Australia | Sydney | 1903-04 |
| G.Gunn | 119 | England | v | Australia | Sydney | 1907-08 |
| W.H.Ponsford †Ω | 110 | Australia | v | England | Sydney | 1924-25 |
| A.Jackson | 164 | Australia | v | England | Adelaide | 1928-29 |
| J.E.Mills | 117 | New Zealand | v | England | Wellington | 1929-30 |
| Nawab of Pataudi, sr | 102 | England | v | Australia | Sydney | 1932-33 |
| B.H.Valentine | 136 | England | v | India | Bombay[1] | 1933-34 |
| S.C.Griffith | 140 | England | v | West Indies | Port-of-Spain | 1947-48 |
| A.G.Ganteaume # | 112 | West Indies | v | England | Port-of-Spain | 1947-48 |
| P.B.H.May | 138 | England | v | South Africa | Leeds | 1951 |
| R.H.Shodhan | 110 | India | v | Pakistan | Calcutta | 1952-53 |
| B.H.Pairaudeau | 115 | West Indies | v | India | Port-of-Spain | 1952-53 |
| A.G.Kripal Singh | 100* | India | v | New Zealand | Hyderabad | 1955-56 |
| C.C.Hunte | 142 | West Indies | v | Pakistan | Bridgetown | 1957-58 |
| C.A.Milton | 104* | England | v | New Zealand | Leeds | 1958 |
| Hanumant Singh | 105 | India | v | England | Delhi | 1963-64 |
| Khalid Ibadulla | 166 | Pakistan | v | Australia | Karachi[1] | 1964-65 |
| B.R.Taylor | 105 | New Zealand | v | India | Calcutta | 1964-65 |
| K.D.Walters Ω | 155 | Australia | v | England | Brisbane[2] | 1965-66 |
| J.H.Hampshire | 107 | England | v | West Indies | Lord's | 1969 |
| G.S.Chappell † | 108 | Australia | v | England | Perth | 1970-71 |
| A.I.Kallicharran Ω | 100* | West Indies | v | New Zealand | Georgetown | 1971-72 |
| R.E.Redmond # | 107 | New Zealand | v | Pakistan | Auckland | 1972-73 |
| G.J.Cosier | 109 | Australia | v | West Indies | Melbourne | 1975-76 |
| S.Amarnath ∇ | 124 | India | v | New Zealand | Auckland | 1975-76 |
| Javed Miandad | 163 | Pakistan | v | New Zealand | Lahore[2] | 1976-77 |
| K.C.Wessels | 162 | Australia | v | England | Brisbane[2] | 1982-83 |
| W.B.Phillips | 159 | Australia | v | Pakistan | Perth | 1983-84 |
| M.Azharuddin ¶ | 110 | India | v | England | Calcutta | 1984-85 |
| D.S.B.P.Kuruppu | 201* | Sri Lanka | v | New Zealand | Colombo (CCC) | 1986-87 |
| M.E.Waugh | 138 | Australia | v | England | Adelaide | 1990-91 |
| A.C.Hudson | 163 | South Africa | v | West Indies | Bridgetown | 1991-92 |
| R.S.Kaluwitharana | 132* | Sri Lanka | v | Australia | Colombo (SSC) | 1992-93 |
| D.L.Houghton | 121 | Zimbabwe | v | India | Harare | 1992-93 |
| P.K.Amre | 103 | India | v | South Africa | Durban[2] | 1992-93 |
| G.S.Blewett Ω | 102* | Australia | v | England | Adelaide | 1994-95 |
| S.C.Ganguly Ω | 131 | India | v | England | Lord's | 1996 |
| Ali Naqvi Σ | 115 | Pakistan | v | South Africa | Rawalpindi[2] | 1997-98 |
| Azhar Mahmood Σ | 128* | Pakistan | v | South Africa | Rawalpindi[2] | 1997-98 |
| *IN SECOND INNINGS* | | | | | | |
| K.S.Ranjitsinhji | 154* | England | v | Australia | Manchester | 1896 |

| | | | | | | |
|---|---|---|---|---|---|---|
| P.F.Warner | 132* | England | v | South Africa | Johannesburg[1] | 1898-99 |
| R.A.Duff † | 104 | Australia | v | England | Melbourne | 1901-02 |
| R.J.Hartigan | 116 | Australia | v | England | Adelaide | 1907-08 |
| H.L.Collins | 104 | Australia | v | England | Sydney | 1920-21 |
| G.A.Headley | 176 | West Indies | v | England | Bridgetown | 1929-30 |
| N.B.Amarnath ∇ | 118 | India | v | England | Bombay[1] | 1933-34 |
| P.A.Gibb § | 106 | England | v | South Africa | Johannesburg[1] | 1938-39 |
| J.W.Burke | 101* | Australia | v | England | Adelaide | 1950-51 |
| O.G.Smith | 104 | West Indies | v | Australia | Kingston | 1954-55 |
| A.A.Baig | 112 | India | v | England | Manchester | 1959 |
| G.R.Viswanath | 137 | India | v | Australia | Kanpur | 1969-70 |
| F.C.Hayes | 106* | England | v | West Indies | The Oval | 1973 |
| C.G.Greenidge § | 107 | West Indies | v | India | Bangalore | 1974-75 |
| L.Baichan | 105* | West Indies | v | Pakistan | Lahore[2] | 1974-75 |
| A.B.Williams | 100 | West Indies | v | Australia | Georgetown | 1977-78 |
| D.M.Wellham | 103 | Australia | v | England | The Oval | 1981 |
| Saleem Malik | 100* | Pakistan | v | Sri Lanka | Karachi[1] | 1981-82 |
| M.J.Greatbatch | 107* | New Zealand | v | England | Auckland | 1987-88 |
| G.P.Thorpe | 114* | England | v | Australia | Nottingham | 1993 |
| Mohammad Wasim | 109* | Pakistan | v | New Zealand | Lahore[2] | 1996-97 |

*# Only Test. § Gibb and Greenidge both scored 93 in the first innings. † Duff, Ponsford and Chappell also scored a century in their last Test (Chappell also scored a century in each innings of his first Test as captain). Ω Ponsford, Walters, Kallicharran, Blewett and Ganguly also scored a century in their second Test. ¶ Azharuddin scored a century in each of his first three Tests. ∇ N.B. and S.Amarnath provide the only instance of a father and son scoring a century on debut. Σ Ali Naqvi and Azhar Mahmood achieved the feat in the same innings.*

## MOST RUNS IN FIRST TEST MATCH

| | | | | | | | |
|---|---|---|---|---|---|---|---|
| 314 | L.G.Rowe | (214 + 100*) | West Indies | v | New Zealand | Kingston | 1971-72 |
| 306 | R.E.Foster | (287 + 19) | England | v | Australia | Sydney | 1903-04 |

*B.M.Laird (92 and 75) scored 167 runs for Australia v West Indies at Brisbane[2] in 1979-80 the highest aggregate without a century by a player in his first Test.*

## MAIDEN FIRST-CLASS CENTURY IN A TEST MATCH

| | | | | | | |
|---|---|---|---|---|---|---|
| C.Bannerman § † | 165* | Australia | v | England | Melbourne | 1876-77 |
| W.L.Murdoch | 153* | Australia | v | England | The Oval | 1880 |
| P.S.McDonnell | 147 | Australia | v | England | Sydney | 1881-82 |
| H.Wood † | 134* | England | v | South Africa | Cape Town | 1891-92 |
| H.Graham § | 107 | Australia | v | England | Lord's | 1893 |
| A.J.L.Hill | 124 | England | v | South Africa | Cape Town | 1895-96 |
| J.H.Sinclair | 106 | South Africa | v | England | Cape Town | 1898-99 |
| P.W.Sherwell | 115 | South Africa | v | England | Lord's | 1907 |
| H.G.Owen-Smith | 129 | South Africa | v | England | Leeds | 1929 |
| C.A.Roach | 122 | West Indies | v | England | Bridgetown | 1929-30 |
| S.C.Griffith § | 140 | England | v | West Indies | Port-of-Spain | 1947-48 |
| V.L.Manjrekar | 133 | India | v | England | Leeds | 1952 |
| C.C.Depeiza † | 122 | West Indies | v | Australia | Bridgetown | 1954-55 |
| P.L.Winslow | 108 | South Africa | v | England | Manchester | 1955 |
| S.N.McGregor | 111 | New Zealand | v | Pakistan | Lahore[1] | 1955-56 |
| F.C.M.Alexander † | 108 | West Indies | v | Australia | Sydney | 1960-61 |
| Nasim-ul-Ghani | 101 | Pakistan | v | England | Lord's | 1962 |
| B.R.Taylor § | 105 | New Zealand | v | India | Calcutta | 1964-65 |
| B.D.Julien | 121 | West Indies | v | England | Lord's | 1973 |
| W.K.Lees | 152 | New Zealand | v | Pakistan | Karachi[1] | 1976-77 |
| Kapil Dev | 126* | India | v | West Indies | Delhi | 1978-79 |
| S.Wettimuny | 157 | Sri Lanka | v | Pakistan | Faisalabad | 1981-82 |
| S.A.R.Silva | 102* | Sri Lanka | v | England | Lord's | 1984 |
| D.S.B.P.Kuruppu § | 201* | Sri Lanka | v | New Zealand | Colombo (CCC) | 1986-87 |
| R.C.Russell | 128* | England | v | Australia | Manchester | 1989 |
| I.A.Healy | 102* | Australia | v | England | Manchester | 1993 |

| | | | | | | |
|---|---|---|---|---|---|---|
| Azhar Mahmood § | 128* | Pakistan | v | South Africa | Rawalpindi[2] | 1997-98 |

*§ On Test debut. † Only century in first-class cricket. H.Graham (105 v England at Sydney in 1894-95), C.A.Roach (209 v England at Georgetown in 1929-30) and B.R.Taylor (124 v West Indies at Auckland in 1968-69) also scored their second first-class century in a Test match, whilst I.A.Healy (113* v New Zealand at Perth in 1993-94 and 161* v West Indies at Brisbane[2] in 1996-97) scored his first three first-class centuries in a Test match.*

## YOUNGEST PLAYERS TO SCORE A CENTURY

| Years | Days | | | | | | | |
|---|---|---|---|---|---|---|---|---|
| 17 | 82 | Mushtaq Mohammad | 101 | Pakistan | v | India | Delhi | 1960-61 |
| 17 | 112 | S.R.Tendulkar | 119* | India | v | England | Manchester | 1990 |
| 18 | 251 | Mushtaq Mohammad | 100* | Pakistan | v | England | Nottingham | 1962 |
| 18 | 256 | S.R.Tendulkar | 148* | India | v | Australia | Sydney | 1991-92 |
| 18 | 285 | S.R.Tendulkar | 114 | India | v | Australia | Perth | 1991-92 |
| 18 | 328 | Saleem Malik | 100* | Pakistan | v | Sri Lanka | Karachi[1] | 1981-82 |
| 19 | 26 | Mohammad Ilyas | 126 | Pakistan | v | New Zealand | Karachi[1] | 1964-65 |
| 19 | 108 | Mohammad Wasim | 109* | Pakistan | v | New Zealand | Lahore[2] | 1996-97 |
| 19 | 119 | Javed Miandad | 163 | Pakistan | v | New Zealand | Lahore[2] | 1976-77 |
| 19 | 121 | H.G.Vivian | 100 | New Zealand | v | South Africa | Wellington | 1931-32 |
| 19 | 121 | R.N.Harvey | 153 | Australia | v | India | Melbourne | 1947-48 |
| 19 | 140 | Javed Miandad | 206 | Pakistan | v | New Zealand | Karachi[1] | 1976-77 |
| 19 | 152 | A.Jackson | 164 | Australia | v | England | Adelaide | 1928-29 |
| 19 | 192 | A.P.Gurusinha | 116* | Sri Lanka | v | Pakistan | Colombo (PSS) | 1985-86 |
| 19 | 218 | S.R.Tendulkar | 111 | India | v | South Africa | Johannesburg[3] | 1992-93 |
| 19 | 264 | Saleem Malik | 107 | Pakistan | v | India | Faisalabad | 1982-83 |
| 19 | 290 | R.N.Harvey | 112 | Australia | v | England | Leeds | 1948 |
| 19 | 294 | S.R.Tendulkar | 165 | India | v | England | Madras[1] | 1992-93 |
| 19 | 318 | R.G.Pollock | 122 | South Africa | v | Australia | Sydney | 1963-64 |
| 19 | 332 | R.G.Pollock | 175 | South Africa | v | Australia | Adelaide | 1963-64 |
| 19 | 357 | K.D.Walters | 155 | Australia | v | England | Brisbane[2] | 1965-66 |
| 20 | 1 | P.A.de Silva | 122 | Sri Lanka | v | Pakistan | Faisalabad | 1985-86 |
| 20 | 3 | Ijaz Ahmed | 122 | Pakistan | v | Australia | Faisalabad | 1988-89 |
| 20 | 14 | K.D.Walters | 115 | Australia | v | England | Melbourne | 1965-66 |
| 20 | 19 | D.C.S.Compton | 102 | England | v | Australia | Nottingham | 1938 |
| 20 | 21 | Kapil Dev | 126* | India | v | West Indies | Delhi | 1978-79 |
| 20 | 23 | P.A.de Silva | 105 | Sri Lanka | v | Pakistan | Karachi[1] | 1985-86 |
| 20 | 58 | Hanif Mohammad | 142 | Pakistan | v | India | Bahawalpur | 1954-55 |
| 20 | 96 | S.R.Tendulkar | 104* | India | v | Sri Lanka | Colombo (SSC) | 1993-94 |
| 20 | 129 | D.G.Bradman | 112 | Australia | v | England | Melbourne | 1928-29 |
| 20 | 131 | A.A.Baig | 112 | India | v | England | Manchester | 1959 |
| 20 | 148 | H.G.Owen-Smith | 129 | South Africa | v | England | Leeds | 1929 |
| 20 | 154 | Saeed Ahmed | 150 | Pakistan | v | West Indies | Georgetown | 1957-58 |
| 20 | 197 | D.G.Bradman | 123 | Australia | v | England | Melbourne | 1928-29 |
| 20 | 201 | Ali Naqvi | 115 | Pakistan | v | South Africa | Rawalpindi[2] | 1997-98 |
| 20 | 230 | G.A.Headley | 176 | West Indies | v | England | Bridgetown | 1929-30 |
| 20 | 240 | J.W.Burke | 101* | Australia | v | England | Adelaide | 1950-51 |
| 20 | 249 | R.J.Shastri | 128 | India | v | Pakistan | Karachi[1] | 1982-83 |
| 20 | 253 | V.L.Manjrekar | 133 | India | v | England | Leeds | 1952 |
| 20 | 268 | G.A.Headley | 114 | West Indies | v | England | Georgetown | 1929-30 |
| 20 | 271 | G.A.Headley | 112 | West Indies | v | England | Georgetown | 1929-30 |
| 20 | 271 | S.R.Tendulkar | 142 | India | v | Sri Lanka | Lucknow[2] | 1993-94 |
| 20 | 281 | G.R.Viswanath | 137 | India | v | Australia | Kanpur | 1969-70 |
| 20 | 314 | G.A.Headley | 223 | West Indies | v | England | Kingston | 1929-30 |
| 20 | 317 | C.Hill | 188 | Australia | v | England | Melbourne | 1897-98 |
| 20 | 324 | J.W.Hearne | 114 | England | v | Australia | Melbourne | 1911-12 |
| 20 | 330 | O.G.Smith | 104 | West Indies | v | Australia | Kingston | 1954-55 |
| 20 | 332 | Saleem Malik | 116 | Pakistan | v | England | Faislabad | 1984-85 |
| 20 | 337 | R.J.Shastri | 102 | India | v | West Indies | St John's | 1982-83 |
| 20 | 351 | R.G.Pollock | 137 | South Africa | v | England | Port Elizabeth | 1964-65 |

## YOUNGEST PLAYERS TO SCORE A DOUBLE CENTURY

| Years | Days | | | | | | | |
|---|---|---|---|---|---|---|---|---|
| 19 | 141 | Javed Miandad | 206 | Pakistan | v | New Zealand | Karachi[1] | 1976-77 |
| 20 | 315 | G.A.Headley | 223 | West Indies | v | England | Kingston | 1929-30 |

## YOUNGEST PLAYERS TO SCORE A TRIPLE CENTURY

| Years | Days | | | | | | | |
|---|---|---|---|---|---|---|---|---|
| 21 | 216 | G.S.Sobers | 365* | West Indies | v | Pakistan | Kingston | 1957-58 |
| 21 | 318 | D.G.Bradman | 334 | Australia | v | England | Leeds | 1930 |

## OLDEST PLAYERS TO SCORE A CENTURY

| Years | Days | | | | | | | |
|---|---|---|---|---|---|---|---|---|
| 46 | 82 | J.B.Hobbs | 142 | England | v | Australia | Melbourne | 1928-29 |
| 45 | 241 | J.B.Hobbs | 159 | England | v | West Indies | The Oval | 1928 |
| 45 | 151 | E.H.Hendren | 132 | England | v | Australia | Manchester | 1934 |
| 43 | 294 | A.W.Nourse | 111 | South Africa | v | Australia | Johannesburg[1] | 1921-22 |
| 43 | 244 | J.B.Hobbs | 100 | England | v | Australia | The Oval | 1926 |
| 43 | 194 | J.B.Hobbs | 119 | England | v | Australia | Lord's | 1926 |
| 43 | 201 | W.Bardsley | 193* | Australia | v | England | Lord's | 1926 |
| 42 | 61 | F.E.Woolley | 154 | England | v | South Africa | Manchester | 1929 |
| 42 | 35 | J.B.Hobbs | 119 | England | v | Australia | Adelaide | 1924-25 |
| 42 | 18 | J.B.Hobbs | 154 | England | v | Australia | Melbourne | 1924-25 |
| 42 | 6 | J.B.Hobbs | 115 | England | v | Australia | Sydney | 1924-25 |
| 42 | 6 | E.A.B.Rowan | 236 | South Africa | v | England | Leeds | 1951 |
| 41 | 360 | R.B.Simpson | 100 | Australia | v | India | Adelaide | 1977-78 |
| 41 | 318 | R.B.Simpson | 176 | Australia | v | India | Perth | 1977-78 |
| 41 | 266 | W.W.Armstrong | 123* | Australia | v | England | Melbourne | 1920-21 |
| 41 | 264 | T.W.Graveney | 105 | England | v | Pakistan | Karachi[1] | 1968-69 |
| 41 | 242 | H.W.Taylor | 117 | South Africa | v | England | Cape Town | 1930-31 |
| 41 | 241 | W.W.Armstrong | 121 | Australia | v | England | Adelaide | 1920-21 |
| 41 | 213 | W.W.Armstrong | 158 | Australia | v | England | Sydney | 1920-21 |
| 41 | 197 | J.B.Hobbs | 211 | England | v | South Africa | Lord's | 1924 |
| 41 | 109 | B.Sutcliffe | 151* | New Zealand | v | India | Calcutta | 1964-65 |
| 41 | 64 | G.Boycott | 105 | England | v | India | Delhi | 1981-82 |
| 41 | 21 | E.H.Hendren | 123 | England | v | West Indies | Georgetown | 1929-30 |
| 40 | 364 | E.H.Hendren | 205* | England | v | West Indies | Port-of-Spain | 1929-30 |
| 40 | 315 | G.A.Gooch | 210 | England | v | New Zealand | Nottingham | 1994 |
| 40 | 312 | G.Boycott | 137 | England | v | Australia | The Oval | 1981 |
| 40 | 218 | T.W.Graveney | 118 | England | v | West Indies | Port-of-Spain | 1967-68 |
| 40 | 208 | A.D.Nourse | 208 | South Africa | v | England | Nottingham | 1951 |
| 40 | 184 | E.A.B.Rowan | 143 | South Africa | v | Australia | Durban[2] | 1949-50 |
| 40 | 162 | G.Boycott | 104* | England | v | West Indies | St John's | 1980-81 |
| 40 | 105 | H.W.Taylor | 121 | South Africa | v | England | The Oval | 1929 |
| 40 | 85 | C.H.Lloyd | 114 | West Indies | v | Australia | Brisbane[2] | 1984-85 |
| 40 | 76 | A.L.Hassett | 115 | Australia | v | England | Nottingham | 1953 |
| 40 | 29 | C.G.Macartney | 109 | Australia | v | England | Manchester | 1926 |
| 40 | 22 | V.J.Merchant | 154 | India | v | England | Delhi | 1951-52 |
| 40 | 13 | C.G.Macartney | 151 | Australia | v | England | Leeds | 1926 |
| 40 | 8 | T.W.Graveney | 151 | England | v | India | Lord's | 1967 |
| 40 | 2 | C.G.Macartney | 133* | Australia | v | England | Lord's | 1926 |

## OLDEST PLAYERS TO SCORE A DOUBLE CENTURY

| Years | Days | | | | | | | |
|---|---|---|---|---|---|---|---|---|
| 42 | 7 | E.A.B.Rowan | 236 | South Africa | v | England | Leeds | 1951 |
| 41 | 197 | J.B.Hobbs | 211 | England | v | South Africa | Lord's | 1924 |
| 41 | 0 | E.H.Hendren | 205* | England | v | West Indies | Port-of-Spain | 1929-30 |
| 40 | 316 | G.A.Gooch | 210 | England | v | New Zealand | Nottingham | 1994 |
| 40 | 208 | A.D.Nourse | 208 | South Africa | v | England | Nottingham | 1951 |
| 39 | 355 | C.G.Greenidge | 226 | West Indies | v | Australia | Bridgetown | 1990-91 |

| | | | | | | | | |
|---|---|---|---|---|---|---|---|---|
| 39 | 349 | A.Sandham | 325 | England | v | West Indies | Kingston | 1929-30 |
| 39 | 149 | D.G.Bradman | 201 | Australia | v | India | Adelaide | 1947-48 |
| 38 | 270 | M.H.Mankad | 231 | India | v | New Zealand | Madras[2] | 1955-56 |
| 38 | 112 | D.G.Bradman | 234 | Australia | v | England | Sydney | 1946-47 |

## OLDEST PLAYERS TO SCORE A MAIDEN CENTURY

| Years | Days | | | | | | | |
|---|---|---|---|---|---|---|---|---|
| 43 | 294 | A.W.Nourse | 111 | South Africa | v | Australia | Johannesburg[1] | 1921-22 |
| 39 | 256 | E.H.Bowley | 109 | England | v | New Zealand | Auckland | 1929-30 |
| 39 | 191 | A.Sandham | 152 | England | v | West Indies | Bridgetown | 1929-30 |
| 39 | 173 | J.W.H.Makepeace | 117 | England | v | Australia | Melbourne | 1920-21 |
| 39 | 163 | E.A.B.Rowan | 156* | South Africa | v | England | Johannesburg[2] | 1948-49 |
| 39 | 84 | P.N.Kirsten | 104 | South Africa | v | England | Leeds | 1994 |
| 38 | 324 | G.E.Tyldesley | 122 | England | v | South Africa | Johannesburg[1] | 1927-28 |
| 38 | 98 | H.Wood | 134* | England | v | South Africa | Cape Town | 1891-92 |
| 37 | 353 | A.J.Richardson | 100 | Australia | v | England | Leeds | 1926 |
| 37 | 308 | P.L.Symmcox | 108 | South Africa | v | Pakistan | Johannesburg[3] | 1997-98 |
| 37 | 253 | G.M.Carew | 107 | West Indies | v | England | Port-of-Spain | 1947-48 |
| 37 | 138 | F.R.Martin | 123* | West Indies | v | Australia | Sydney | 1930-31 |
| 37 | 22 | R.Illingworth | 113 | England | v | West Indies | Lord's | 1969 |
| 36 | 218 | E.Paynter | 216* | England | v | Australia | Nottingham | 1938 |
| 35 | 262 | G.Giffen | 161 | Australia | v | England | Sydney | 1894-95 |
| 35 | 248 | B.L.D'Oliveira | 109 | England | v | India | Leeds | 1967 |
| 35 | 239 | D.Denton | 104 | England | v | South Africa | Johannesburg[1] | 1909-10 |
| 35 | 157 | E.H.Hendren | 132 | England | v | South Africa | Leeds | 1924 |
| 35 | 118 | D.L.Houghton | 121 | Zimbabwe | v | India | Harare | 1992-93 |

## DISTRIBUTION OF TEST MATCH CENTURIES

| Conceded By | Scored For | | | | | | | | | Total Conceded |
|---|---|---|---|---|---|---|---|---|---|---|
| | A | E | SA | WI | NZ | I | P | SL | Z | |
| Australia | 0 | 204 | 40 | 81 | 20 | 39 | 36 | 7 | - | 427 |
| England | 239 | 0 | 65 | 110 | 40 | 64 | 38 | 3 | 1 | 561 |
| South Africa | 65 | 93 | 0 | 0 | 7 | 8 | 5 | 1 | 0 | 180 |
| West Indies | 78 | 98 | 1 | 0 | 20 | 57 | 22 | 0 | - | 276 |
| New Zealand | 32 | 83 | 14 | 31 | 0 | 22 | 41 | 11 | 5 | 239 |
| India | 53 | 76 | 10 | 82 | 21 | 0 | 41 | 17 | 2 | 302 |
| Pakistan | 42 | 47 | 3 | 25 | 21 | 31 | 0 | 14 | 8 | 191 |
| Sri Lanka | 15 | 4 | 5 | 1 | 13 | 27 | 13 | 0 | 3 | 81 |
| Zimbabwe | - | 3 | 1 | - | 7 | 2 | 3 | 7 | 0 | 23 |
| Total Scored | 524 | 609 | 140 | 330 | 149 | 250 | 199 | 60 | 19 | 2280 |

## CENTURIES IN TEST CRICKET

*§ Denotes century on first appearance against that country. Where known I have shown the batting time, balls faced and boundary details of the complete innings. The following abbreviations are used: m - minutes; h - minutes where time has been converted from hours e.g. $4^3/_4$ hours converts to 285h; a - about; n - nearly; > more than; † just over; < less than; # just under; ∇ indicates that the ball was hit over the boundary but the match was played in Australia at a time when such hits were awarded only five runs, the ball having to be hit clear out of the ground for a six. Such sixes are indicated thus: !. The majority of this information was supplied by Dr Colin Clowes.*

| **AUSTRALIA** (524) | | | Time | Balls | 6/4 | Opponents | | |
|---|---|---|---|---|---|---|---|---|
| Archer,RG | | 128 | 213m | | 2/19 | West Indies | Kingston | 1954-55 |
| Armstrong,WW | (6) | 159* | | | -/16 | South Africa | Johannesburg[1] | 1902-03 |
| | | 133* | 289m | | 2!/14 | England | Melbourne | 1907-08 |
| | | 132 | 208m | | -/13 | South Africa | Melbourne | 1910-11 |
| | | 158 | 205m | 209 | -/17 | England | Sydney | 1920-21 |
| | | 121 | 206m | | -/11 | England | Adelaide | 1920-21 |
| | | 123* | 214m | | -/9 | England | Melbourne | 1920-21 |
| Badcock,CL | | 118 | 205m | | -/15 | England | Melbourne | 1936-37 |

| | | | | | | | | |
|---|---|---|---|---|---|---|---|---|
| Bannerman,C | | 165* § | 285h | | -/18 | England | Melbourne | 1876-77 |
| | | (The first century in Test cricket) | | | | | | |
| Bardsley,W | (6) | 136) | 228m | 230 | 1/12 | England | The Oval | 1909 |
| | | 130) | 200m | 250 | -/10 | | | |
| | | 132 § | 150m | | -/16 | South Africa | Sydney | 1910-11 |
| | | 121 | 150m | 157 | 2/11 | South Africa | Manchester | 1912 |
| | | 164 | 216m | 283 | 1/16 | South Africa | Lord's | 1912 |
| | | 193* | 398m | | -/14 | England | Lord's | 1926 |
| Barnes,SG | (3) | 234 | 642m | 661 | -/17 | England | Sydney | 1946-47 |
| | | 112 | 227m | | 1/6 | India | Adelaide | 1947-48 |
| | | 141 | 227m | 286 | 2/14 | England | Lord's | 1948 |
| Benaud,J | | 142 | 211m | 207 | 2/18 | Pakistan | Melbourne | 1972-73 |
| Benaud,R | (3) | 121 | 96m | | 2/18 | West Indies | Kingston | 1954-55 |
| | | 122 | 220m | | -/20 | South Africa | Johannesburg[3] | 1957-58 |
| | | 100 | 186m | | 1/9 | South Africa | Johannesburg[3] | 1957-58 |
| Blewett,GS | (4) | 102* § | 261m | 180 | -/12 | England | Adelaide | 1994-95 |
| | | 115 | 202m | 158 | -/19 | England | Perth | 1994-95 |
| | | 214 § | 519m | 420 | -/33 | South Africa | Johannesburg[3] | 1996-97 |
| | | 125 | 300m | 228 | 1/19 | England | Birmingham | 1997 |
| Bonnor,GJ | | 128 | 115m | | 3∇/14 | England | Sydney | 1884-85 |
| Boon,DC | (21) | 123 § | 336m | 255 | -/14 | India | Adelaide | 1985-86 |
| | | 131 | 345m | 311 | -/16 | India | Sydney | 1985-86 |
| | | 122 | 332m | 258 | -/21 | India | Madras[1] | 1986-87 |
| | | 103 | 305m | 274 | -/14 | England | Adelaide | 1986-87 |
| | | 143 | 342m | 255 | -/15 | New Zealand | Brisbane[2] | 1987-88 |
| | | 184* | 492m | 431 | -/14 | England | Sydney | 1987-88 |
| | | 149 | 479m | 425 | -/10 | West Indies | Sydney | 1988-89 |
| | | 200 | 451m | 326 | -/28 | New Zealand | Perth | 1989-90 |
| | | 121 | 368m | 276 | -/9 | England | Adelaide | 1990-91 |
| | | 109* | 388m | 253 | -/9 | West Indies | Kingston | 1990-91 |
| | | 129* | 444m | 361 | -/13 | India | Sydney | 1991-92 |
| | | 135 | 465m | 352 | -/16 | India | Adelaide | 1991-92 |
| | | 107 | 377m | 304 | -/14 | India | Perth | 1991-92 |
| | | 111 | 325m | 259 | -/13 | West Indies | Brisbane[2] | 1992-93 |
| | | 164* | 471m | 378 | -/15 | England | Lord's | 1993 |
| | | 101 | 257m | 177 | -/17 | England | Nottingham | 1993 |
| | | 107 | 310m | 225 | -/17 | England | Leeds | 1993 |
| | | 106 | 317m | 242 | -/9 | New Zealand | Hobart | 1993-94 |
| | | 114 | 336m | 220 | -/10 | Pakistan | Karachi[1] | 1994-95 |
| | | 131 | 378m | 277 | -/14 | England | Melbourne | 1994-95 |
| | | 110 | 408m | 312 | -/11 | Sri Lanka | Melbourne | 1995-96 |
| Booth,BC | (5) | 112 | 217m | | -/14 | England | Brisbane[2] | 1962-63 |
| | | 103 | 348m | | -/19 | England | Melbourne | 1962-63 |
| | | 169 § | 330m | | -/19 | South Africa | Brisbane[2] | 1963-64 |
| | | 102* | 306m | 235 | -/5 | South Africa | Sydney | 1963-64 |
| | | 117 | 315m | | -/13 | West Indies | Port-of-Spain | 1964-65 |
| Border,AR | (27) | 105 § | 373m | 275 | -/7 | Pakistan | Melbourne | 1978-79 |
| | | 162 § | 416m | | 1/24 | India | Madras[1] | 1979-80 |
| | | 115 | 384m | 296 | -/13 | England | Perth | 1979-80 |
| | | 150*) | 397m | | 2/16 | Pakistan | Lahore[2] | 1979-80 |
| | | 153 ) | 214m | | 5/16 | | | |
| | | 124 | 303m | 265 | -/12 | India | Melbourne | 1980-81 |
| | | 123* | 415m | 356 | -/17 | England | Manchester | 1981 |
| | | 106* | 290m | 230 | -/13 | England | The Oval | 1981 |
| | | 126 | 336m | 278 | -/9 | West Indies | Adelaide | 1981-82 |
| | | 118 | 347m | 254 | -/10 | Pakistan | Brisbane[2] | 1983-84 |
| | | 117* | 310m | 208 | -/11 | Pakistan | Adelaide | 1983-84 |
| | | 100* | 279m | 269 | -/12 | West Indies | Port-of-Spain | 1983-84 |
| | | 196 | 450m | 317 | -/22 | England | Lord's | 1985 |
| | | 146* | 346m | 333 | -/13 | England | Manchester | 1985 |

| | | | | | | | | |
|---|---|---|---|---|---|---|---|---|
| | | 152* | 458m | 301 | 2/20 | New Zealand | Brisbane[2] | 1985-86 |
| | | 163 | 410m | 358 | -/16 | India | Melbourne | 1985-86 |
| | | 140 ) | 386m | 338 | 1/15 | New Zealand | Christchurch | 1985-86 |
| | | 114*) | 280m | 201 | -/10 | | | |
| | | 106 | 252m | 172 | 1/14 | India | Madras[1] | 1986-87 |
| | | 125 | 372m | 282 | -/17 | England | Perth | 1986-87 |
| | | 100* | 303m | 253 | -/11 | England | Adelaide | 1986-87 |
| | | 205 | 599m | 485 | -/20 | New Zealand | Adelaide | 1987-88 |
| | | 113* | 354m | 237 | -/13 | Pakistan | Faisalabad | 1988-89 |
| | | 106 | 217m | 164 | -/16 | Sri Lanka | Moratuwa | 1992-93 |
| | | 110 | 350m | 274 | 1/5 | West Indies | Melbourne | 1992-93 |
| | | 200* | 565m | 399 | -/26 | England | Leeds | 1993 |
| | | 105 | 275m | 193 | -/15 | New Zealand | Brisbane[2] | 1993-94 |
| Bradman,DG | (29) | 112 | 247m | 281 | -/7 | England | Melbourne | 1928-29 |
| | | 123 | 217m | 247 | -/8 | England | Melbourne | 1928-29 |
| | | 131 | 258m | 287 | -/10 | England | Nottingham | 1930 |
| | | 254 | 339m | 376 | -/25 | England | Lord's | 1930 |
| | | 334 | 378m | 446 | -/46 | England | Leeds | 1930 |
| | | 232 | 408m | 410 | -/16 | England | The Oval | 1930 |
| | | 223 | 297m | | -/24 | West Indies | Brisbane[1] | 1930-31 |
| | | 152 | 154m | | -/13 | West Indies | Melbourne | 1930-31 |
| | | 226 § | 277m | | -/22 | South Africa | Brisbane[2] | 1931-32 |
| | | 112 | 155m | | -/10 | South Africa | Sydney | 1931-32 |
| | | 167 | 183m | | -/18 | South Africa | Melbourne | 1931-32 |
| | | 299* | 396m | | -/23 | South Africa | Adelaide | 1931-32 |
| | | 103* | 185m | 146 | -/7 | England | Melbourne | 1932-33 |
| | | 304 | 430m | 466 | 2/44 | England | Leeds | 1934 |
| | | 244 | 316m | 277 | 1/32 | England | The Oval | 1934 |
| | | 270 | 458m | 375 | -/22 | England | Melbourne | 1936-37 |
| | | 212 | 441m | 393 | -/14 | England | Adelaide | 1936-37 |
| | | 169 | 223m | | -/15 | England | Melbourne | 1936-37 |
| | | 144* | 363m | 377 | -/5 | England | Nottingham | 1938 |
| | | 102* | 147m | 132 | -/15 | England | Lord's | 1938 |
| | | 103 | 176m | 181 | -/9 | England | Leeds | 1938 |
| | | 187 | 318m | 313 | -/19 | England | Brisbane[2] | 1946-47 |
| | | 234 | 393m | 396 | -/24 | England | Sydney | 1946-47 |
| | | 185 § | 288m | | -/20 | India | Brisbane[2] | 1947-48 |
| | | 132 ) | 197m | | -/8 | India | Melbourne | 1947-48 |
| | | 127*) | 178m | | -/12 | | | |
| | | 201 | 272m | | 1/21 | India | Adelaide | 1947-48 |
| | | 138 | 288m | 315 | -/10 | England | Nottingham | 1948 |
| | | 173* | 255m | 294 | -/29 | England | Leeds | 1948 |
| Brown,WA | (4) | 105 | 199m | 199 | -/14 | England | Lord's | 1934 |
| | | 121 | 207m | 225 | 1/5 | South Africa | Cape Town | 1935-36 |
| | | 133 | 320m | 377 | -/13 | England | Nottingham | 1938 |
| | | 206* | 370m | 386 | -/22 | England | Lord's | 1938 |
| Burge,PJP | (4) | 181 | 411m | | -/22 | England | The Oval | 1961 |
| | | 103 | 331m | 293 | -/9 | England | Sydney | 1962-63 |
| | | 160 | 314m | 307 | -/24 | England | Leeds | 1964 |
| | | 120 | 255m | | -/12 | England | Melbourne | 1965-66 |
| Burke,JW | (3) | 101* § | 245m | | -/9 | England | Adelaide | 1950-51 |
| | | 161 | 504m | | -/15 | India | Bombay[2] | 1956-57 |
| | | 189 | 578m | | -/15 | South Africa | Cape Town | 1957-58 |
| Chappell,GS | (24) | 108 § | 272m | | -/10 | England | Perth | 1970-71 |
| | | 131 | 372m | | -/14 | England | Lord's | 1972 |
| | | 113 | 272m | | -/17 | England | The Oval | 1972 |
| | | 116* | 230m | | -/12 | Pakistan | Melbourne | 1972-73 |
| | | 106 | 255m | | -/10 | West Indies | Bridgetown | 1972-73 |
| | | 247*) | 410m | 356 | 1/30 | New Zealand | Wellington | 1973-74 |
| | | 133 ) | 186m | 175 | -/8 | | | |

| | | | | | | | | |
|---|---|---|---|---|---|---|---|---|
| | | 144 | 252m | 209 | -/16 | England | Sydney | 1974-75 |
| | | 102 | 249m | 177 | -/11 | England | Melbourne | 1974-75 |
| | | 123 ) | 231m | 232 | 2/15 | West Indies | Brisbane[2] | 1975-76 |
| | | 109*) | 161m | 172 | 1/14 | | | |
| | | 182* | 366m | 274 | -/22 | West Indies | Sydney | 1975-76 |
| | | 121 | 246m | | -/9 | Pakistan | Melbourne | 1976-77 |
| | | 112 | 282m | 230 | 1/15 | England | Manchester | 1977 |
| | | 124 | 376m | 299 | -/12 | West Indies | Brisbane[2] | 1979-80 |
| | | 114 | 288m | 213 | -/14 | England | Melbourne | 1979-80 |
| | | 235 | 441m | | -/24 | Pakistan | Faisalabad | 1979-80 |
| | | 204 § | 408m | 296 | -/27 | India | Sydney | 1980-81 |
| | | 201 | 417m | 296 | -/22 | Pakistan | Brisbane[2] | 1981-82 |
| | | 176 | 257m | 218 | 2/23 | New Zealand | Christchurch | 1981-82 |
| | | 117 | 259m | 174 | 2/11 | England | Perth | 1982-83 |
| | | 115 | 239m | 201 | -/19 | England | Adelaide | 1982-83 |
| | | 150* | 334m | 250 | -/17 | Pakistan | Brisbane[2] | 1983-84 |
| | | 182 | 526m | 400 | -/17 | Pakistan | Sydney | 1983-84 |
| Chappell,IM | (14) | 151 | 252m | | -/21 | India | Melbourne | 1967-68 |
| | | 117 § | 247m | | -/17 | West Indies | Brisbane[2] | 1968-69 |
| | | 165 | 319m | | -/16 | West Indies | Melbourne | 1968-69 |
| | | 138 | 276m | | -/21 | India | Delhi | 1969-70 |
| | | 111 | 243m | | -/12 | England | Melbourne | 1970-71 |
| | | 104 | 326m | | -/9 | England | Adelaide | 1970-71 |
| | | 118 | 330m | | -/20 | England | The Oval | 1972 |
| | | 196 | 295m | 243 | 4/21 | Pakistan | Adelaide | 1972-73 |
| | | 106* | 247m | | -/15 | West Indies | Bridgetown | 1972-73 |
| | | 109 | 302m | | -/10 | West Indies | Georgetown | 1972-73 |
| | | 145) | 283m | 268 | 1/17 | New Zealand | Wellington | 1973-74 |
| | | 121) | 199m | 218 | 1/13 | | | |
| | | 192 | 442m | 367 | -/17 | England | The Oval | 1975 |
| | | 156 | 377m | 261 | -/19 | West Indies | Perth | 1975-76 |
| Chipperfield,AG | | 109 § | 171m | 193 | -/8 | South Africa | Durban[2] | 1935-36 |
| Collins,HL | (4) | 104 § | 219m | 278 | -/11 | England | Sydney | 1920-21 |
| | | 162 | 258m | | -/20 | England | Adelaide | 1920-21 |
| | | 203 | 277m | | -/26 | South Africa | Johannesburg[1] | 1921-22 |
| | | 114 | 236m | | -/9 | England | Sydney | 1924-25 |
| Cosier,GJ | (2) | 109 § | 254m | 186 | -/13 | West Indies | Melbourne | 1975-76 |
| | | 168 | 228m | | -/20 | Pakistan | Melbourne | 1976-77 |
| Cowper,RM | (5) | 143 | 339m | | -/18 | West Indies | Port-of-Spain | 1964-65 |
| | | 102 | 183m | | -/13 | West Indies | Bridgetown | 1964-65 |
| | | 307 | 727m | 589 | -/20 | England | Melbourne | 1965-66 |
| | | 108 | 212m | | -/13 | India | Adelaide | 1967-68 |
| | | 165 | 321m | 346 | -/13 | India | Sydney | 1967-68 |
| Darling,J | (3) | 101 | 195m | | -/19 | England | Sydney | 1897-98 |
| | | 178 | 285m | | 1!/26 | England | Adelaide | 1897-98 |
| | | 160 | 175m | | -/30 | England | Sydney | 1897-98 |
| Davis,IC | | 105 § | 229m | | 1/14 | Pakistan | Adelaide | 1976-77 |
| Duff,RA | (2) | 104 § | 206m | | -/11 | England | Melbourne | 1901-02 |
| | | 146 | 197m | | -/20 | England | The Oval | 1905 |
| Dyson,J | (2) | 102 | 292m | 233 | -/14 | England | Leeds | 1981 |
| | | 127* § | 377m | 321 | -/11 | West Indies | Sydney | 1981-82 |
| Edwards,R | (2) | 170* | 344m | | -/13 | England | Nottingham | 1972 |
| | | 115 | 322m | 252 | -/6 | England | Perth | 1974-75 |
| Elliott,MTG | (3) | 112 | 240m | 180 | -/20 | England | Lord's | 1997 |
| | | 199 | 450m | 351 | 3/23 | England | Leeds | 1997 |
| | | 114 | 338m | 265 | -/18 | New Zealand | Hobart | 1997-98 |
| Favell,LE | | 101 | | | | India | Madras[2] | 1959-60 |
| Fingleton,JHW | (5) | 112 | 191m | 212 | -/7 | South Africa | Cape Town | 1935-36 |
| | | 108 | 132m | 169 | -/7 | South Africa | Johannesburg[1] | 1935-36 |
| | | 118 | 224m | 212 | -/9 | South Africa | Durban[2] | 1935-36 |

| | | | | | | | | |
|---|---|---|---|---|---|---|---|---|
| | | 100 | 301m | | -/6 | England | Brisbane[2] | 1936-37 |
| | | 136 | 386m | | -/6 | England | Melbourne | 1936-37 |
| Giffen,G | | 161 | 254m | | 1_/22 | England | Sydney | 1894-95 |
| Gilmour,GJ | | 101 | 187m | 146 | 1/20 | New Zealand | Christchurch | 1976-77 |
| Graham,H | (2) | 107 § | 140m | | -/12 | England | Lord's | 1893 |
| | | 105 | 135m | | -/14 | England | Sydney | 1894-95 |
| Gregory,JM | (2) | 100 | 137m | | -/12 | England | Melbourne | 1920-21 |
| | | 119 | 85m | | 2/19 | South Africa | Johannesburg[1] | 1921-22 |
| | | (Including the fastest Test century in 70 minutes) | | | | | | |
| Gregory,SE | (4) | 201 | 243m | | -/28 | England | Sydney | 1894-95 |
| | | 103 | 160m | | -/17 | England | Lord's | 1896 |
| | | 117 | 195m | | -/15 | England | The Oval | 1899 |
| | | 112 | 122m | | -/15 | England | Adelaide | 1903-04 |
| Hartigan,RJ | | 116 § | 319m | | -/18 | England | Adelaide | 1907-08 |
| Harvey,RN | (21) | 153 | 249m | | -/11 | India | Melbourne | 1947-48 |
| | | 112 § | 188m | 186 | -/17 | England | Leeds | 1948 |
| | | 178 | 237m | 253 | -/16 | South Africa | Cape Town | 1949-50 |
| | | 151* | 325m | 361 | -/14 | South Africa | Durban[2] | 1949-50 |
| | | 100 | 133m | 132 | -/13 | South Africa | Johannesburg[2] | 1949-50 |
| | | 116 | 130m | 128 | -/14 | South Africa | Port Elizabeth | 1949-50 |
| | | 109 | 155m | | -/16 | South Africa | Brisbane[2] | 1952-53 |
| | | 190 | 361m | | -/21 | South Africa | Sydney | 1952-53 |
| | | 116 | 125m | | -/14 | South Africa | Adelaide | 1952-53 |
| | | 205 | 295m | | -/19 | South Africa | Melbourne | 1952-53 |
| | | 122 | 240m | 248 | -/11 | England | Manchester | 1953 |
| | | 162 | 380m | | -/17 | England | Brisbane[2] | 1954-55 |
| | | 133 | 306m | | -/20 | West Indies | Kingston | 1954-55 |
| | | 133 | 242m | | -/18 | West Indies | Port-of-Spain | 1954-55 |
| | | 204 | 426m | | 1/24 | West Indies | Kingston | 1954-55 |
| | | 140 | 244m | | -/18 | India | 5 9 7 5 16 2 | 1956-57 |
| | | 167 | 370m | 325 | -/16 | England | Melbourne | 1958-59 |
| | | 114 | 240h | | -/14 | India | Delhi | 1959-60 |
| | | 102 | 287m | | -/9 | India | 5 9 7 5 16 2 | 1959-60 |
| | | 114 | 212m | | -/18 | England | Birmingham | 1961 |
| | | 154 | 326m | | -/18 | England | Adelaide | 1962-63 |
| Hassett,AL | (10) | 128 | 394m | 395 | -/10 | England | Brisbane[2] | 1946-47 |
| | | 198* | 342m | | -/16 | India | Adelaide | 1947-48 |
| | | 137 | 352m | 385 | 1/20 | England | Nottingham | 1948 |
| | | 112 § | 261m | 283 | -/7 | South Africa | Johannesburg[1] | 1949-50 |
| | | 167 | 314m | 314 | 1/14 | South Africa | Port Elizabeth | 1949-50 |
| | | 132 | 381m | | -/10 | West Indies | Sydney | 1951-52 |
| | | 102 | 323m | | -/10 | West Indies | Melbourne | 1951-52 |
| | | 163 | 359m | | -/15 | South Africa | Adelaide | 1952-53 |
| | | 115 | 394m | 315 | -/9 | England | Nottingham | 1953 |
| | | 104 | 296m | 251 | -/11 | England | Lord's | 1953 |
| Hayden,ML | | 125 | 354m | 226 | 1/15 | West Indies | Adelaide | 1996-97 |
| Healy,IA | (3) | 102* | 164m | 133 | -/12 | England | Manchester | 1993 |
| | | 113* | 262m | 181 | -/11 | New Zealand | Perth | 1993-94 |
| | | 161* | 356m | 250 | -/20 | West Indies | Brisbane[2] | 1996-97 |
| Hendry,HSTL | | 112 | 233m | 305 | -/7 | England | Sydney | 1928-29 |
| Hilditch,AMJ | (2) | 113 § | 339m | 273 | -/7 | West Indies | Melbourne | 1984-85 |
| | | 119 | 245m | 182 | 2/17 | England | Leeds | 1985 |
| Hill,C | (7) | 188 | 294m | | -/21 | England | Melbourne | 1897-98 |
| | | 135 | 240m | | -/17 | England | Lord's | 1899 |
| | | 119 | 145m | | -/19 | England | Sheffield | 1902 |
| | | 142 § | 135m | | 1!/16 | South Africa | Johannesburg[1] | 1902-03 |
| | | 160 | 254m | | -/12 | England | Adelaide | 1907-08 |
| | | 191 | 202m | | -/18 | South Africa | Sydney | 1910-11 |
| | | 100 | <100m | | -/13 | South Africa | Melbourne | 1910-11 |
| Hookes,DW | | 143* § | 201m | 152 | 2/17 | Sri Lanka | Kandy | 1982-83 |

| | | | | | | | | |
|---|---|---|---|---|---|---|---|---|
| Horan,TP | | 124 | 250m | | -/7 | England | Melbourne | 1881-82 |
| Hughes,KJ | (9) | 129 | 481m | 411 | 2/8 | England | Brisbane[2] | 1978-79 |
| | | 100 | 278m | | 1/10 | India | Madras[1] | 1979-80 |
| | | 130* § | 376m | 244 | 1/17 | West Indies | Brisbane[2] | 1979-80 |
| | | 117 | 205m | 213 | 3/14 | England | Lord's | 1980 |
| | | 213 | 383m | 301 | -/21 | India | Adelaide | 1980-81 |
| | | 106 | 271m | 198 | -/17 | Pakistan | Perth | 1981-82 |
| | | 100* | 266m | 200 | -/11 | West Indies | Melbourne | 1981-82 |
| | | 137 | 379m | 316 | 3/12 | England | Sydney | 1982-83 |
| | | 106 | 269m | 245 | 1/11 | Pakistan | Adelaide | 1983-84 |
| Iredale,FA | (2) | 140 | 245m | | -/17 | England | Adelaide | 1894-95 |
| | | 108 | 220m | | -/16 | England | Manchester | 1896 |
| Jackson,AA | | 164 § | 318m | 331 | -/15 | England | Adelaide | 1928-29 |
| Jones,DM | (11) | 210 § | 502m | 330 | 2/27 | India | Madras[1] | 1986-87 |
| | | 184* | 540m | 421 | 1/12 | England | Sydney | 1986-87 |
| | | 102 § | 251m | 174 | -/13 | Sri Lanka | Perth | 1987-88 |
| | | 216 | 538m | 347 | -/16 | West Indies | Adelaide | 1988-89 |
| | | 157 | 391m | 295 | -/17 | England | Birmingham | 1989 |
| | | 122 | 214m | 180 | -/17 | England | The Oval | 1989 |
| | | 118* | 252m | 178 | -/6 | Sri Lanka | Hobart | 1989-90 |
| | | 116 ) | 331m | 239 | -/7 | Pakistan | Adelaide | 1989-90 |
| | | 121*) | 260m | 205 | 1/11 | | | |
| | | 150* | 395m | 265 | 1/14 | India | Perth | 1991-92 |
| | | 100* | 281m | 213 | 2/7 | Sri Lanka | Colombo (PIS) | 1992-93 |
| Kelleway,C | (3) | 114 | 201m | 244 | -/5 | South Africa | Manchester | 1912 |
| | | 102 | 196m | 279 | -/7 | South Africa | Lord's | 1912 |
| | | 147 | 422m | | -/13 | England | Adelaide | 1920-21 |
| Kippax,AF | (2) | 100 | 217m | 255 | -/9 | England | Melbourne | 1928-29 |
| | | 146 § | 229m | | -/18 | West Indies | Adelaide | 1930-31 |
| Lawry,WM | (13) | 130 | 369m | | -/18 | England | Lord's | 1961 |
| | | 102 | 270m | | -/13 | England | Manchester | 1961 |
| | | 157 | 329m | | -/19 | South Africa | Melbourne | 1963-64 |
| | | 106 | 281m | 311 | 3/5 | England | Manchester | 1964 |
| | | 210 | 544m | | 3/25 | West Indies | Bridgetown | 1964-65 |
| | | 166 | 419m | | 1/23 | England | Brisbane[2] | 1965-66 |
| | | 119 | 255m | | 1/9 | England | Adelaide | 1965-66 |
| | | 108 | 369m | | -/7 | England | Melbourne | 1965-66 |
| | | 100 | 179m | 186 | -/8 | India | Melbourne | 1967-68 |
| | | 135 | 447m | | -/22 | England | The Oval | 1968 |
| | | 105 | 286m | | -/12 | West Indies | Brisbane[2] | 1968-69 |
| | | 205 | 461m | | 1/12 | West Indies | Melbourne | 1968-69 |
| | | 151 | 500m | 367 | -/12 | West Indies | Sydney | 1968-69 |
| Lindwall,RR | (2) | 100 | 113m | 90 | 1/13 | England | Melbourne | 1946-47 |
| | | 118 | 159m | | 2/15 | West Indies | Bridgetown | 1954-55 |
| Loxton,SJE | | 101 § | 144m | 193 | -/14 | South Africa | Johannesburg[2] | 1949-50 |
| Lyons,JJ | | 134 | 165h | | -/16 | England | Sydney | 1891-92 |
| Macartney,CG | (7) | 137 | 193m | | -/16 | South Africa | Sydney | 1910-11 |
| | | 170 | 244m | 227 | -/20 | England | Sydney | 1920-21 |
| | | 115 | 186m | 176 | -/13 | England | Leeds | 1921 |
| | | 116 | 114m | | 1/17 | South Africa | Durban[1] | 1921-22 |
| | | 133* | 205m | | -/13 | England | Lord's | 1926 |
| | | 151 | 170m | | -/21 | England | Leeds | 1926 |
| | | 109 | 178m | | -/14 | England | Manchester | 1926 |
| McCabe,SJ | (6) | 187* | 242m | 233 | -/25 | England | Sydney | 1932-33 |
| | | 137 | 214m | 205 | -/22 | England | Manchester | 1934 |
| | | 149 | 268m | 266 | -/6 | South Africa | Durban[2] | 1935-36 |
| | | 189* | 197m | 232 | -/29 | South Africa | Johannesburg[1] | 1935-36 |
| | | 112 | 163m | | -/16 | England | Melbourne | 1936-37 |
| | | 232 | 235m | 276 | 1/34 | England | Nottingham | 1938 |
| McCool,CL | | 104* | 183m | 194 | -/8 | England | Melbourne | 1946-47 |

| | | | | | | | | |
|---|---|---|---|---|---|---|---|---|
| McCosker,RB | (4) | 127 | 372m | 294 | -/21 | England | The Oval | 1975 |
| | | 109* | 249m | 267 | -/7 | West Indies | Melbourne | 1975-76 |
| | | 105 | 222m | | -/10 | Pakistan | Melbourne | 1976-77 |
| | | 107 | 371m | 307 | 1/10 | England | Nottingham | 1977 |
| McDonald,CC | (5) | 154 | 316m | | 1/16 | South Africa | Adelaide | 1952-53 |
| | | 110 | 257m | | -/12 | West Indies | Port-of-Spain | 1954-55 |
| | | 127 | 323m | | -/11 | West Indies | Kingston | 1954-55 |
| | | 170 | 487m | 315 | -/12 | England | Adelaide | 1958-59 |
| | | 133 | 339m | 249 | -/7 | England | Melbourne | 1958-59 |
| McDonnell,PS | (3) | 147 | 250m | | 1▽/16 | England | Sydney | 1881-82 |
| | | 103 | 136m | 168 | -/14 | England | The Oval | 1884 |
| | | 124 | 195m | | -/9 | England | Adelaide | 1884-85 |
| McLeod,CE | | 112 | 244m | | -/4 | England | Melbourne | 1897-98 |
| Mann,AL | | 105 | 184m | | -/11 | India | Perth | 1977-78 |
| Marsh,GR | (4) | 118 | 346m | 287 | -/14 | New Zealand | Auckland | 1985-86 |
| | | 101 | 370m | 300 | -/11 | India | Bombay[3] | 1986-87 |
| | | 110 § | 392m | 311 | -/12 | England | Brisbane[2] | 1986-87 |
| | | 138 | 432m | 382 | -/15 | England | Nottingham | 1989 |
| Marsh,RW | (3) | 118 § | 164m | | 4/10 | Pakistan | Adelaide | 1972-73 |
| | | 132 | 305m | 266 | -/9 | New Zealand | Adelaide | 1973-74 |
| | | 110* | 297m | 173 | -/10 | England | Melbourne | 1976-77 |
| Matthews,GRJ | (4) | 115 § | 229m | 205 | 1/10 | New Zealand | Brisbane[2] | 1985-86 |
| | | 100* | 195m | 152 | 2/9 | India | Melbourne | 1985-86 |
| | | 130 | 306m | 235 | -/12 | New Zealand | Wellington | 1985-86 |
| | | 128 | 242m | 175 | -/17 | England | Sydney | 1990-91 |
| Miller,KR | (7) | 141* | 270m | 198 | 1/9 | England | Adelaide | 1946-47 |
| | | 145* | 354m | | 1/6 | England | Sydney | 1950-51 |
| | | 129 | 246m | | -/15 | West Indies | Sydney | 1951-52 |
| | | 109 | 292m | 269 | 1/14 | England | Lord's | 1953 |
| | | 147 | 346m | | -/15 | West Indies | Kingston | 1954-55 |
| | | 137 | 237m | | -/22 | West Indies | Bridgetown | 1954-55 |
| | | 109 | 328m | | 1/15 | West Indies | Kingston | 1954-55 |
| Moody,TM | (2) | 106 § | 218m | 179 | -/12 | Sri Lanka | Brisbane[2] | 1989-90 |
| | | 101 § | 186m | 149 | -/9 | India | Perth | 1991-92 |
| Moroney,J | (2) | 118 ) | 321m | 334 | -/13 | South Africa | Johannesburg[2] | 1949-50 |
| | | 101*) | 225m | 197 | -/17 | | | |
| Morris,AR | (12) | 155 | 364m | 317 | -/8 | England | Melbourne | 1946-47 |
| | | 122 ) | 268m | 255 | 2/12 | England | Adelaide | 1946-47 |
| | | 124*) | 198m | 171 | -/12 | | | |
| | | 100* | 196m | | -/7 | India | Melbourne | 1947-48 |
| | | 105 | 209m | 214 | 1/14 | England | Lord's | 1948 |
| | | 182 | 291m | 294 | -/33 | England | Leeds | 1948 |
| | | 196 | 406m | 493 | -/16 | England | The Oval | 1948 |
| | | 111 | 267m | 242 | 1/9 | South Africa | Johannesburg[2] | 1949-50 |
| | | 157 | 301m | 226 | 1/14 | South Africa | Port Elizabeth | 1949-50 |
| | | 206 | 462m | | -/23 | England | Adelaide | 1950-51 |
| | | 153 | 419m | | 2/18 | England | Brisbane[2] | 1954-55 |
| | | 111 | 322m | | -/18 | West Indies | Port-of-Spain | 1954-55 |
| Murdoch,WL | (2) | 153* | 330m | | -/18 | England | The Oval | 1880 |
| | | 211 | 484m | 525 | -/24 | England | The Oval | 1884 |
| Noble,MA | | 133 | 287m | | -/17 | England | Sydney | 1903-04 |
| O'Neill,NC | (6) | 134 | | | -/17 | Pakistan | Lahore[2] | 1959-60 |
| | | 163 | 360h | | -/14 | India | Bombay[2] | 1959-60 |
| | | 113 | | | -/15 | India | Calcutta | 1959-60 |
| | | 181 § | 401m | | -/22 | West Indies | Brisbane[2] | 1960-61 |
| | | 117 | 200m | | -/14 | England | The Oval | 1961 |
| | | 100 | 171m | | -/13 | England | Adelaide | 1962-63 |
| Pellew,CE | (2) | 116 | 203m | | -/8 | England | Melbourne | 1920-21 |
| | | 104 | 123m | | -/14 | England | Adelaide | 1920-21 |
| Phillips,WB | (2) | 159 § | 307m | 240 | -/20 | Pakistan | Perth | 1983-84 |

| | | | | | | | | |
|---|---|---|---|---|---|---|---|---|
| | | 120 | 227m | 197 | 4/14 | West Indies | Bridgetown | 1983-84 |
| Ponsford,WH | (7) | 110 § | 228m | | -/8 | England | Sydney | 1924-25 |
| | | 128 | 222m | | -/6 | England | Melbourne | 1924-25 |
| | | 110 | 159m | 206 | -/11 | England | The Oval | 1930 |
| | | 183 | 348m | | -/11 | West Indies | Sydney | 1930-31 |
| | | 109 | 165m | | -/12 | West Indies | Brisbane[1] | 1930-31 |
| | | 181 | 387m | 425 | -/19 | England | Leeds | 1934 |
| | | 266 | 460m | 418 | -/27 | England | The Oval | 1934 |
| Ponting,RT | (2) | 127 § | 261m | 202 | 1/19 | England | Leeds | 1997 |
| | | 105 § | 269m | 208 | -/14 | South Africa | Melbourne | 1997-98 |
| Ransford,VS | | 143* | 252m | 260 | -/21 | England | Lord's | 1909 |
| Redpath,IR | (8) | 132 | 267m | 277 | -/11 | West Indies | Sydney | 1968-69 |
| | | 171 | 484m | | -/14 | England | Perth | 1970-71 |
| | | 135 | 277m | | -/14 | Pakistan | Melbourne | 1972-73 |
| | | 159* | 348m | 310 | -/20 | New Zealand | Auckland | 1973-74 |
| | | 105 | 344m | 239 | -/9 | England | Sydney | 1974-75 |
| | | 102 | 320m | 258 | -/10 | West Indies | Melbourne | 1975-76 |
| | | 103 | 220m | 175 | 2/6 | West Indies | Adelaide | 1975-76 |
| | | 101 | 325m | 230 | -/11 | West Indies | Melbourne | 1975-76 |
| Richardson,AJ | | 100 | 186m | | -/10 | England | Leeds | 1926 |
| Richardson,VY | | 138 | 198m | | -/13 | England | Melbourne | 1924-25 |
| Rigg,KE | | 127 § | 240m | | -/12 | South Africa | Sydney | 1931-32 |
| Ritchie,GM | (3) | 106* | 293m | 216 | 3/9 | Pakistan | Faisalabad | 1982-83 |
| | | 146 | 361m | 308 | -/16 | England | Nottingham | 1985 |
| | | 128 § | 389m | 321 | -/11 | India | Adelaide | 1985-86 |
| Ryder,J | (3) | 142 | 181m | | -/12 | South Africa | Cape Town | 1921-22 |
| | | 201* | 385m | | 1/12 | England | Adelaide | 1924-25 |
| | | 112 | 224m | 219 | 1/6 | England | Melbourne | 1928-29 |
| Scott,HJH | | 102 | 203m | 216 | -/15 | England | The Oval | 1884 |
| Serjeant,CS | | 124 | 268m | | 1/18 | West Indies | Georgetown | 1977-78 |
| Sheahan,AP | (2) | 114 | 257m | | -/20 | India | Kanpur | 1969-70 |
| | | 127 | 275m | 207 | -/12 | Pakistan | Melbourne | 1972-73 |
| Simpson, RB | (10) | 311 | 762m | 740 | 1/23 | England | Manchester | 1964 |
| | | 153 §) | 408m | 361 | -/12 | Pakistan | Karachi[1] | 1964-65 |
| | | 115 §) | 200m | 192 | -/15 | | | |
| | | 201 | 414m | | -/22 | West Indies | Bridgetown | 1964-65 |
| | | 225 | 545m | | 1/18 | England | Adelaide | 1965-66 |
| | | 153 | 386m | | -/12 | South Africa | Cape Town | 1966-67 |
| | | 103 | 232m | | -/12 | India | Adelaide | 1967-68 |
| | | 109 | 220m | 170 | -/8 | India | Melbourne | 1967-68 |
| | | 176 | 391m | 343 | -/17 | India | Perth | 1977-78 |
| | | 100 | 264m | | -/6 | India | Adelaide | 1977-78 |
| Slater,MJ | (7) | 152 | 293m | 263 | -/18 | England | Lord's | 1993 |
| | | 168 | 328m | 235 | -/17 | New Zealand | Hobart | 1993-94 |
| | | 110 | 250m | 155 | -/14 | Pakistan | Rawalpindi[2] | 1994-95 |
| | | 176 | 324m | 244 | -/25 | England | Brisbane[2] | 1994-95 |
| | | 103 | 283m | 236 | -/10 | England | Sydney | 1994-95 |
| | | 124 | 296m | 231 | -/13 | England | Perth | 1994-95 |
| | | 219 § | 460m | 321 | 5/15 | Sri Lanka | Perth | 1995-96 |
| Stackpole,KR | (7) | 134 | 196m | | 2/18 | South Africa | Cape Town | 1966-67 |
| | | 103 § | 290m | | -/14 | India | Bombay[2] | 1969-70 |
| | | 207 | 454m | | 1/25 | England | Brisbane[2] | 1970-71 |
| | | 136 | 410m | | -/16 | England | Adelaide | 1970-71 |
| | | 114 | 335m | | -/10 | England | Nottingham | 1972 |
| | | 142 | 265m | | -/22 | West Indies | Kingston | 1972-73 |
| | | 122 § | 222m | 191 | -/13 | New Zealand | Melbourne | 1973-74 |
| Taylor,JM | | 108 | 164m | | -/8 | England | Sydney | 1924-25 |
| Taylor,MA | (18) | 136 § | 394m | 315 | -/16 | England | Leeds | 1989 |
| | | 219 | 551m | 461 | -/23 | England | Nottingham | 1989 |
| | | 164 § | 425m | 334 | 2/17 | Sri Lanka | Brisbane[2] | 1989-90 |

| | | | | | | | | |
|---|---|---|---|---|---|---|---|---|
| | | 108 | 291m | 291 | -/12 | Sri Lanka | Hobart | 1989-90 |
| | | 101 § | 322m | 240 | -/11 | Pakistan | Melbourne | 1989-90 |
| | | 101* | 258m | 227 | -/8 | Pakistan | Sydney | 1989-90 |
| | | 144 | 361m | 277 | -/12 | West Indies | St John's | 1990-91 |
| | | 100 | 395m | 303 | -/9 | India | Adelaide | 1991-92 |
| | | 124 | 325m | 234 | 2/12 | England | Manchester | 1993 |
| | | 111 | 323m | 245 | 1/10 | England | Lord's | 1993 |
| | | 142* | 360m | 255 | -/8 | New Zealand | Perth | 1993-94 |
| | | 170 § | 495m | 349 | -/12 | South Africa | Melbourne | 1993-94 |
| | | 113 | 364m | 248 | -/9 | England | Sydney | 1994-95 |
| | | 123 | 356m | 243 | -/13 | Pakistan | Hobart | 1995-96 |
| | | 129 | 396m | 298 | 1/13 | England | Birmingham | 1997 |
| | | 112 | 313m | 258 | -/10 | New Zealand | Brisbane[2] | 1997-98 |
| | | 169* | 524m | 376 | -/21 | South Africa | Adelaide | 1997-98 |
| | | 102* | 209m | 193 | -/17 | India | Bangalore | 1997-98 |
| Toohey,PM | | 122 | 313m | 293 | -/10 | West Indies | Kingston | 1977-78 |
| Trott,G HS | | 143 | 210m | | -/24 | England | Lord's | 1896 |
| Trumper,VT | (8) | 135* | 195m | | -/20 | England | Lord's | 1899 |
| | | 104 | 115m | | -/14 | England | Manchester | 1902 |
| | | 185* | 230m | | -/25? | England | Sydney | 1903-04 |
| | | 113 | 189m | | -/12 | England | Adelaide | 1903-04 |
| | | 166 | 241m | | -/18 | England | Sydney | 1907-08 |
| | | 159 | 178m | | 1/15 | South Africa | Melbourne | 1910-11 |
| | | 214* | 242m | | -/26 | South Africa | Adelaide | 1910-11 |
| | | 113 | 226m | 206 | -/12 | England | Sydney | 1911-12 |
| Turner,A | | 136 | 279m | 222 | -/15 | West Indies | Adelaide | 1975-76 |
| Walters,KD | (15) | 155 § | 322m | | 2/11 | England | Brisbane[2] | 1965-66 |
| | | 115 | 263m | | -/5 | England | Melbourne | 1965-66 |
| | | 118 | 214m | 185 | -/12 | West Indies | Sydney | 1968-69 |
| | | 110 | 194m | | -/13 | West Indies | Adelaide | 1968-68 |
| | | 242) | 480m | 412 | -/24 | West Indies | Sydney | 1968-69 |
| | | 103) | 196m | 181 | -/7 | | | |
| | | 102 | 208m | | 2/14 | India | Madras[1] | 1969-70 |
| | | 112 | 328m | | -/9 | England | Brisbane[2] | 1970-71 |
| | | 102* | 200m | | -/15 | West Indies | Bridgetown | 1972-73 |
| | | 112 | 148m | | 1/19 | West Indies | Port-of-Spain | 1972-73 |
| | | 104* | 165m | 138 | -/15 | New Zealand | Auckland | 1973-74 |
| | | 103 | 140m | 119 | 1/11 | England | Perth | 1974-75 |
| | | 107 | 247m | | -/9 | Pakistan | Adelaide | 1976-77 |
| | | 250 | 394m | 342 | 2/30 | New Zealand | Christchurch | 1976-77 |
| | | 107 | 276m | 206 | -/6 | New Zealand | Melbourne | 1980-81 |
| Waugh,ME | (14) | 138 § | 237m | 186 | -/18 | England | Adelaide | 1990-91 |
| | | 139* | 307m | 188 | 3/11 | West Indies | St John's | 1990-91 |
| | | 112 | 327m | 234 | -/9 | West Indies | Melbourne | 1992-93 |
| | | 137 | 239m | 219 | -/18 | England | Birmingham | 1993 |
| | | 111 | 187m | 139 | -/15 | New Zealand | Hobart | 1993-94 |
| | | 113* | 283m | 222 | -/13 | South Africa | Durban[2] | 1993-94 |
| | | 140 | 323m | 215 | 1/14 | England | Brisbane[2] | 1994-95 |
| | | 126 | 276m | 192 | -/12 | West Indies | Kingston | 1994-95 |
| | | 116 | 262m | 106 | 1/8 | Pakistan | Sydney | 1995-96 |
| | | 111 | 261m | 223 | 1/7 | Sri Lanka | Perth | 1995-96 |
| | | 116 | 323m | 229 | 1/17 | South Africa | Port Elizabeth | 1996-97 |
| | | 100 | 211m | 186 | 1/12 | South Africa | Sydney | 1997-98 |
| | | 115* | 404m | 305 | -/16 | South Africa | Adelaide | 1997-98 |
| | | 153* | 334m | 266 | 4/13 | India | Bangalore | 1997-98 |
| Waugh,SR | (14) | 177* | 308m | 242 | -/24 | England | Leeds | 1989 |
| | | 152* | 329m | 249 | -/17 | England | Lord's | 1989 |
| | | 134* | 234m | 234 | -/14 | Sri Lanka | Hobart | 1989-90 |
| | | 100 | 269m | 207 | -/5 | West Indies | Sydney | 1992-93 |
| | | 157* | 405m | 305 | -/19 | England | Leeds | 1993 |

| | | | | | | | | |
|---|---|---|---|---|---|---|---|---|
| | | 147* | 380m | 281 | -/15 | New Zealand | Brisbane[2] | 1993-94 |
| | | 164 § | 380m | 276 | -/19 | South Africa | Adelaide | 1993-94 |
| | | 200 | 555m | 425 | 1/17 | West Indies | Kingston | 1994-95 |
| | | 112* | 366m | 275 | -/7 | Pakistan | Brisbane[2] | 1995-96 |
| | | 131* | 329m | 252 | -/12 | Sri Lanka | Melbourne | 1995-96 |
| | | 170 | 421m | 316 | -/13 | Sri Lanka | Adelaide | 1995-96 |
| | | 160 | 501m | 366 | -/22 | South Africa | Johannesburg[3] | 1996-97 |
| | | 108) | 241m | 173 | -/13 | England | Manchester | 1997 |
| | | 116) | 383m | 270 | -/10 | | | |
| Wellham,DM | | 103 § | 266m | 222 | -/12 | England | The Oval | 1981 |
| Wessels,KC | (4) | 162 § | 464m | 343 | -/17 | England | Brisbane[2] | 1982-83 |
| | | 141 § | 252m | 188 | -/21 | Sri Lanka | Kandy | 1982-83 |
| | | 179 | 330m | 233 | 1/24 | Pakistan | Adelaide | 1983-84 |
| | | 173 | 482m | 351 | -/14 | West Indies | Sydney | 1984-85 |
| Wood,GM | (9) | 126 | 337m | | 1/8 | West Indies | Georgetown | 1977-78 |
| | | 100 | 392m | 283 | -/6 | England | Melbourne | 1978-79 |
| | | 112 | 363m | 295 | -/10 | England | Lord's | 1980 |
| | | 111 § | 318m | 229 | -/12 | New Zealand | Brisbane[2] | 1980-81 |
| | | 125 | 286m | 217 | 1/10 | India | Adelaide | 1980-81 |
| | | 100 | 375m | 305 | -/3 | Pakistan | Melbourne | 1981-82 |
| | | 100 | 261m | 249 | -/10 | New Zealand | Auckland | 1981-82 |
| | | 172 | 601m | 449 | -/21 | England | Nottingham | 1985 |
| | | 111 | 391m | 287 | -/14 | West Indies | Perth | 1988-89 |
| Woodfull,WM | (7) | 141 | 295m | | -/12 | England | Leeds | 1926 |
| | | 117 | 259m | | -/6 | England | Manchester | 1926 |
| | | 111 | 258m | 286 | -/6 | England | Sydney | 1928-29 |
| | | 107 | 271m | 309 | -/7 | England | Melbourne | 1928-29 |
| | | 102 | 325m | 381 | -/3 | England | Melbourne | 1928-29 |
| | | 155 | 325m | 391 | -/9 | England | Lord's | 1930 |
| | | 161 | 300m | | -/5 | South Africa | Melbourne | 1931-32 |
| Yallop,GN | (8) | 121 § | 228m | | -/13 | India | Adelaide | 1977-78 |
| | | 102 § | 347m | 307 | -/8 | England | Brisbane[2] | 1978-79 |
| | | 121 | 266m | 212 | -/13 | England | Sydney | 1978-79 |
| | | 167 | 520m | 392 | -/14 | India | Calcutta | 1979-80 |
| | | 172 | 504m | | -/19 | Pakistan | Faisalabad | 1979-80 |
| | | 114 | 177m | 125 | -/17 | England | Manchester | 1981 |
| | | 141 | 402m | 274 | -/13 | Pakistan | Perth | 1983-84 |
| | | 268 | 716m | 517 | -/29 | Pakistan | Melbourne | 1983-84 |

| **ENGLAND** (609) | | | Time | Balls | 6/4 | Opponents | | |
|---|---|---|---|---|---|---|---|---|
| Abel,R | (2) | 120 | n240h | | -/11 | South Africa | Cape Town | 1888-89 |
| | | 132* | 325m | | -/11 | Australia | Sydney | 1891-92 |
| Allen,GOB | | 122 § | 170m | | 1/14 | New Zealand | Lord's | 1931 |
| Ames,LEG | (8) | 105 | 220m | | -/17 | West Indies | Port-of-Spain | 1929-30 |
| | | 149 | 160m | | -/17 | West Indies | Kingston | 1929-30 |
| | | 137 § | 205m | | 2/18 | New Zealand | Lord's | 1931 |
| | | 103 | 144m | | -/11 | New Zealand | Christchurch | 1932-33 |
| | | 120 | 262m | 333 | -/14 | Australia | Lord's | 1934 |
| | | 126 | 251m | | -/16 | West Indies | Kingston | 1934-35 |
| | | 148* | 210m | | 1/14 | South Africa | The Oval | 1935 |
| | | 115 | 145m | 168 | -/13 | South Africa | Cape Town | 1938-39 |
| Amiss,DL | (11) | 112 | 304m | | -/15 | Pakistan | Lahore[2] | 1972-73 |
| | | 158 | 326m | | -/27 | Pakistan | Hyderabad | 1972-73 |
| | | 138* § | 365m | | -/12 | New Zealand | Nottingham | 1973 |
| | | 174 | 396m | 429 | -/19 | West Indies | Port-of-Spain | 1973-74 |
| | | 262* | 570m | 563 | 1/40 | West Indies | Kingston | 1973-74 |
| | | 118 | 340m | 246 | -/15 | West Indies | Georgetown | 1973-74 |
| | | 188 | >360h | | -/29 | India | Lord's | 1974 |
| | | 183 | 421m | 370 | -/19 | Pakistan | The Oval | 1974 |
| | | 164* | 406m | 351 | -/25 | New Zealand | Christchurch | 1974-75 |

| | | | | | | | | |
|---|---|---|---|---|---|---|---|---|
| | | 203 | 443m | 320 | -/28 | West Indies | The Oval | 1976 |
| | | 179 | 496m | 393 | 1/22 | India | Delhi | 1976-77 |
| Atherton,MA | (12) | 151 | 497m | 382 | -/16 | New Zealand | Nottingham | 1990 |
| | | 131 | 338m | 276 | -/12 | India | Manchester | 1990 |
| | | 105 | 451m | 349 | -/8 | Australia | Sydney | 1990-91 |
| | | 144 | 412m | 296 | -/17 | West Indies | Georgetown | 1993-94 |
| | | 135 | 539m | 383 | -/13 | West Indies | St John's | 1993-94 |
| | | 101 | 325m | 264 | -/13 | New Zealand | Nottingham | 1994 |
| | | 111 | 408m | 307 | -/14 | New Zealand | Manchester | 1994 |
| | | 113 | 336m | 247 | -/17 | West Indies | Nottingham | 1995 |
| | | 185* | 645m | 492 | -/29 | South Africa | Johannesburg[3] | 1995-96 |
| | | 160 | 467m | 376 | -/20 | India | Nottingham | 1996 |
| | | 118 | 398m | 311 | -/11 | New Zealand | Christchurch | 1996-97 |
| | | 103 | 365m | 279 | -/12 | South Africa | Birmingham | 1998 |
| Athey,CWJ | | 123 | 315m | 203 | -/14 | Pakistan | Lord's | 1987 |
| Bailey,TE | | 134* | 390m | | -/13 | New Zealand | Christchurch | 1950-51 |
| Bakewell,AH | | 107 § | 230m | | -/10 | West Indies | The Oval | 1933 |
| Barber,RW | | 185 | 296m | 272 | -/19 | Australia | Sydney | 1965-66 |
| Barnes,W | | 134 | 285h | | -/7 | Australia | Adelaide | 1884-85 |
| Barnett,CJ | (2) | 129 | 341m | | 1/13 | Australia | Adelaide | 1936-37 |
| | | 126 | 172m | 183 | -/18 | Australia | Nottingham | 1938 |
| Barrington,KF | (20) | 128 § | 330h | | -/20 | West Indies | Bridgetown | 1959-60 |
| | | 121 | 350m | | -/10 | West Indies | Port-of-Spain | 1959-60 |
| | | 139 § | 430m | | -/19 | Pakistan | Lahore[2] | 1961-62 |
| | | 151* | 420m | | -/15 | India | Bombay[2] | 1961-62 |
| | | 172 | 406m | | -/26 | India | Kanpur | 1961-62 |
| | | 113* | 360h | | -/13 | India | Delhi | 1961-62 |
| | | 132* | 227m | | 2/16 | Australia | Adelaide | 1962-63 |
| | | 101 | 320m | 344 | -/4 | Australia | Sydney | 1962-63 |
| | | 126 § | 254m | | 1/15 | New Zealand | Auckland | 1962-63 |
| | | 256 | 685m | 621 | -/26 | Australia | Manchester | 1964 |
| | | 148* | 432m | | -/9 | South Africa | Durban[2] | 1964-65 |
| | | 121 | 329m | | 1/16 | South Africa | Johannesburg[3] | 1964-65 |
| | | 137 | 437m | | 1/11 | New Zealand | Birmingham | 1965 |
| | | 163 | 339m | 291 | -/26 | New Zealand | Leeds | 1965 |
| | | 102 | 329m | | -/4 | Australia | Adelaide | 1965-66 |
| | | 115 | 178m | | 2/8 | Australia | Melbourne | 1965-66 |
| | | 148 | 310m | | -/17 | Pakistan | Lord's | 1967 |
| | | 109* | 410m | | -/5 | Pakistan | Nottingham | 1967 |
| | | 142 | 347m | | -/14 | Pakistan | The Oval | 1967 |
| | | 143 | 390m | | 2/14 | West Indies | Port-of-Spain | 1967-68 |
| Botham,IT | (14) | 103 | 313m | | 1/12 | New Zealand | Christchurch | 1977-78 |
| | | 100 § | 190m | | -/11 | Pakistan | Birmingham | 1978 |
| | | 108 | a180h | | | Pakistan | Lord's | 1978 |
| | | 137 | 201m | 152 | 5/16 | India | Leeds | 1979 |
| | | 119* | 224m | 212 | -/15 | Australia | Melbourne | 1979-80 |
| | | 114 | 206m | 144 | -/17 | India | Bombay[3] | 1979-80 |
| | | 149* | 219m | 148 | 1/27 | Australia | Leeds | 1981 |
| | | 118 | 123m | 102 | 6/13 | Australia | Manchester | 1981 |
| | | 142 | 347m | | 2/12 | India | Kanpur | 1981-82 |
| | | 128 | 199m | 169 | 2/19 | India | Manchester | 1982 |
| | | 208 | 276m | 226 | 4/19 | India | The Oval | 1982 |
| | | 103 | 156m | 103 | 3/14 | New Zealand | Nottingham | 1983 |
| | | 138 | 236m | 167 | 2/22 | New Zealand | Wellington | 1983-84 |
| | | 138 | 249m | 174 | 4/13 | Australia | Brisbane[2] | 1986-87 |
| Bowley,EH | | 109 | 128m | | 1/11 | New Zealand | Auckland | 1929-30 |
| Boycott,G | (22) | 113 | 297m | 314 | -/10 | Australia | The Oval | 1964 |
| | | 117 | 423m | 396 | -/12 | South Africa | Port Elizabeth | 1964-65 |
| | | 246* § | 573m | 555 | 1/29 | India | Leeds | 1967 |
| | | 116 | 293m | 254 | -/20 | West Indies | Georgetown | 1967-68 |

| | | | | | | | | |
|---|---|---|---|---|---|---|---|---|
| | | 128 | 335m | | -/18 | West Indies | Manchester | 1969 |
| | | 106 | 269m | 273 | -/16 | West Indies | Lord's | 1969 |
| | | 142* | 412m | | -/12 | Australia | Sydney | 1970-71 |
| | | 119* | 250m | | -/12 | Australia | Adelaide | 1970-71 |
| | | 121* | 309m | | -/12 | Pakistan | Lord's | 1971 |
| | | 112 | 265m | 206 | 1/14 | Pakistan | Leeds | 1971 |
| | | 115 | 221m | | -/20 | New Zealand | Leeds | 1973 |
| | | 112 | 415m | 385 | -/12 | West Indies | Port-of-Spain | 1973-74 |
| | | 107 | 419m | 314 | -/11 | Australia | Nottingham | 1977 |
| | | 191 | 620m | 469 | -/23 | Australia | Leeds | 1977 |
| | | (His 100th first-class century) | | | | | | |
| | | 100* | 325m | | -/8 | Pakistan | Hyderabad | 1977-78 |
| | | 131 | 417m | | -/10 | New Zealand | Nottingham | 1978 |
| | | 155 | 458m | 341 | -/12 | India | Birmingham | 1979 |
| | | 125 | 418m | 293 | -/6 | India | The Oval | 1979 |
| | | 128* | 316m | 252 | -/12 | Australia | Lord's | 1980 |
| | | 104* | 345m | | -/8 | West Indies | St John's | 1980-81 |
| | | 137 | 441m | 321 | -/7 | Australia | The Oval | 1981 |
| | | 105 | 441m | 278 | -/7 | India | Delhi | 1981-82 |
| Braund,LC | (3) | 103* | 222m | | 1_/12 | Australia | Adelaide | 1901-02 |
| | | 102 | 171m | | -/15 | Australia | Sydney | 1903-04 |
| | | 104 § | 240h | | -/12 | South Africa | Lord's | 1907 |
| Briggs,J | | 121 | 150h | | -/15 | Australia | Melbourne | 1884-85 |
| Broad,BC | (6) | 162 | 435m | 314 | -/25 | Australia | Perth | 1986-87 |
| | | 116 | 307m | 263 | 1/12 | Australia | Adelaide | 1986-87 |
| | | 112 | 329m | 225 | -/9 | Australia | Melbourne | 1986-87 |
| | | 116 | 421m | 339 | -/13 | Pakistan | Faisalabad | 1987-88 |
| | | 139 | 434m | 361 | -/13 | Australia | Sydney | 1987-88 |
| | | 114 § | 341m | 244 | -/11 | New Zealand | Christchurch | 1987-88 |
| Brown,JT | | 140 | 148m | | -/16 | Australia | Melbourne | 1894-95 |
| Butcher,MA | | 116 | 322m | 252 | -/18 | South Africa | Leeds | 1998 |
| Chapman,APF | | 121 | 152m | 166 | 4/12 | Australia | Lord's | 1930 |
| Compton,DCS | (17) | 102 § | 138m | 172 | -/15 | Australia | Nottingham | 1938 |
| | | 120 § | 140m | | -/16 | West Indies | Lord's | 1939 |
| | | 147 ) | 286m | 350 | -/14 | Australia | Adelaide | 1946-47 |
| | | 103*) | 284m | 353 | -/10 | | | |
| | | 163 § | 270m | | -/19 | South Africa | Nottingham | 1947 |
| | | 208 | 355m | | -/20 | South Africa | Lord's | 1947 |
| | | 115 | 190m | | -/17 | South Africa | Manchester | 1947 |
| | | 113 | 110m | | -/15 | South Africa | The Oval | 1947 |
| | | 184 | 410m | 482 | -/19 | Australia | Nottingham | 1948 |
| | | 145* | 327m | 322 | -/16 | Australia | Manchester | 1948 |
| | | 114 | 156m | 201 | -/14 | South Africa | Johannesburg[2] | 1948-49 |
| | | 114 | 240h | | -/13 | New Zealand | Leeds | 1949 |
| | | 116 | 220m | | -/11 | New Zealand | Lord's | 1949 |
| | | 112 | 320m | | -/11 | South Africa | Nottingham | 1951 |
| | | 133 | 349m | | -/17 | West Indies | Port-of-Spain | 1953-54 |
| | | 278 | 290m | | 1/34 | Pakistan | Nottingham | 1954 |
| | | 158 | 339m | | -/22 | South Africa | Manchester | 1955 |
| Cowdrey,MC | (22) | 102 | 239m | | -/15 | Australia | Melbourne | 1954-55 |
| | | 101 | 369m | | 1/9 | South Africa | Cape Town | 1956-57 |
| | | 154 § | 500m | | -/16 | West Indies | Birmingham | 1957 |
| | | 152 | 321m | | -/14 | West Indies | Lord's | 1957 |
| | | 100* | 365m | 302 | -/7 | Australia | Sydney | 1958-59 |
| | | 160 | 278m | 279 | 4/14 | India | Leeds | 1959 |
| | | 114 | 406m | | -/11 | West Indies | Kingston | 1959-60 |
| | | 119 | 270h | | -/15 | West Indies | Port-of-Spain | 1959-60 |
| | | 155 | 260m | | -/22 | South Africa | The Oval | 1960 |
| | | 159 § | 263m | | -/21 | Pakistan | Birmingham | 1962 |
| | | 182 | 323m | | 1/23 | Pakistan | The Oval | 1962 |
| | | 113 | 270m | | -/7 | Australia | Melbourne | 1962-63 |

| | | | | | | | | |
|---|---|---|---|---|---|---|---|---|
| | | 128* | 235m | | -/10 | New Zealand | Wellington | 1962-63 |
| | | 107 | 380m | | -/17 | India | Calcutta | 1963-64 |
| | | 151 | 374m | | 1/23 | India | Delhi | 1963-64 |
| | | 119 | 298m | | -/13 | New Zealand | Lord's | 1965 |
| | | 105 | 188m | 170 | -/11 | South Africa | Nottingham | 1965 |
| | | 104 | 197m | | | Australia | Melbourne | 1965-66 |
| | | 101 | 345m | | -/12 | West Indies | Kingston | 1967-68 |
| | | 148 | 271m | | -/21 | West Indies | Port-of-Spain | 1967-68 |
| | | 104 | 244m | | -/15 | Australia | Birmingham | 1968 |
| | | (In his 100th Test match) | | | | | | |
| | | 100 | 227m | | -/12 | Pakistan | Lahore[2] | 1968-69 |
| Crawley,JP | (2) | 106 | 257 | 217 | -/12 | Pakistan | The Oval | 1996 |
| | | 112 § | 358m | 198 | 1/9 | Zimbabwe | Bulawayo[2] | 1996-97 |
| Denness,MH | (4) | 118 | 244m | 228 | -/12 | India | Lord's | 1974 |
| | | 100 | 214m | 193 | -/10 | India | Birmingham | 1974 |
| | | 188 | 492m | 448 | -/17 | Australia | Melbourne | 1974-75 |
| | | 181 | 414m | 392 | -/25 | New Zealand | Auckland | 1974-75 |
| Denton, D | | 104 | 100m | | -/18 | South Africa | Johannesburg[1] | 1909-10 |
| Dexter,ER | (9) | 141 | 257m | | -/24 | New Zealand | Christchurch | 1958-59 |
| | | 136* § | 285h | | 1/19 | West Indies | Bridgetown | 1959-60 |
| | | 110 | 255h | | | West Indies | Georgetown | 1959-60 |
| | | 180 | 344m | | -/31 | Australia | Birmingham | 1961 |
| | | 126* | 256m | | -/15 | India | Kanpur | 1961-62 |
| | | 205 | 495m | | -/22 | Pakistan | Karachi[1] | 1961-62 |
| | | 172 | 228m | | 5/18 | Pakistan | The Oval | 1962 |
| | | 174 | 481m | 382 | -/22 | Australia | Manchester | 1964 |
| | | 172 | 339m | | -/27 | South Africa | Johannesburg[3] | 1964-65 |
| D'Oliveira,BL | (5) | 109 § | 185m | | -/13 | India | Leeds | 1967 |
| | | 158 | 315m | | -/21 | Australia | The Oval | 1968 |
| | | 114* | 285m | | -/9 | Pakistan | Dacca | 1968-69 |
| | | 117 | 346m | | -/11 | Australia | Melbourne | 1970-71 |
| | | 100 | 216m | | 2/13 | New Zealand | Christchurch | 1970-71 |
| Douglas,JWHT | | 119 § | 225m | | -/14 | South Africa | Durban[1] | 1913-14 |
| Duleepsinhji,KS | (3) | 117 | 131m | | 1/10 | New Zealand | Auckland | 1929-30 |
| | | 173 § | 292m | 321 | -/21 | Australia | Lord's | 1930 |
| | | 109 | 135h | | -/13 | New Zealand | The Oval | 1931 |
| Edrich,JH | (12) | 120 § | 318m | 287 | 2/9 | Australia | Lord's | 1964 |
| | | 310* § | 532m | 450 | 5/52 | New Zealand | Leeds | 1965 |
| | | 109 | 310m | | -/11 | Australia | Melbourne | 1965-66 |
| | | 103 | 253m | | -/12 | Australia | Sydney | 1965-66 |
| | | 146 | 469m | | 1/10 | West Indies | Bridgetown | 1967-68 |
| | | 164 | 462m | | -/20 | Australia | The Oval | 1968 |
| | | 115 | 296m | 306 | -/20 | New Zealand | Lord's | 1969 |
| | | 155 | 347m | | -/19 | New Zealand | Nottingham | 1969 |
| | | 115* | 346m | | -/16 | Australia | Perth | 1970-71 |
| | | 130 | 354m | | -/14 | Australia | Adelaide | 1970-71 |
| | | 100* | 198m | | 1/9 | India | Manchester | 1974 |
| | | 175 | 542m | 420 | -/21 | Australia | Lord's | 1975 |
| Edrich,WJ | (6) | 219 | 436m | | -/25 | South Africa | Durban[2] | 1938-39 |
| | | 119 | 314m | 379 | -/7 | Australia | Sydney | 1946-47 |
| | | 189 | 362m | | 1/24 | South Africa | Lord's | 1947 |
| | | 191 | 320m | | 3/22 | South Africa | Manchester | 1947 |
| | | 111 | 314m | 312 | 1/13 | Australia | Leeds | 1948 |
| | | 100 | 185m | | -/14 | New Zealand | The Oval | 1949 |
| Evans,TG | (2) | 104 | 140m | | -/17 | West Indies | Manchester | 1950 |
| | | 104 | 130m | | -/16 | India | Lord's | 1952 |
| Fane,FL | | 143 | n240h | | -/17 | South Africa | Johannesburg[1] | 1905-06 |
| Fletcher,KWR | (7) | 113 | 295m | 259 | -/13 | India | Bombay[2] | 1972-73 |
| | | 178 | 379m | | 2/21 | New Zealand | Lord's | 1973 |
| | | 129* | 365m | 357 | -/19 | West Indies | Bridgetown | 1973-74 |

| | | | | | | | | |
|---|---|---|---|---|---|---|---|---|
| | | 123* | 334m | | -/8 | India | Manchester | 1974 |
| | | 122 | 513m | 377 | -/10 | Pakistan | The Oval | 1974 |
| | | 146 | 446m | 424 | -/11 | Australia | Melbourne | 1974-75 |
| | | 216 | 443m | 413 | -/30 | New Zealand | Auckland | 1974-75 |
| Foster,RE | | 287 § | 419m | | -/37 | Australia | Sydney | 1903-04 |
| Fowler,G | (3) | 105 § | 324m | 303 | -/8 | New Zealand | The Oval | 1983 |
| | | 106 | 366m | 259 | -/13 | West Indies | Lord's | 1984 |
| | | 201 | 565m | 411 | 3/21 | India | Madras[1] | 1984-85 |
| Fry,CB | (2) | 144 | 213m | | -/23 | Australia | The Oval | 1905 |
| | | 129 | 285h | | -/7 | South Africa | The Oval | 1907 |
| Gatting,MW | (10) | 136 | 310m | 255 | -/21 | India | Bombay[3] | 1984-85 |
| | | 207 | 504m | 308 | 3/20 | India | Madras[1] | 1984-85 |
| | | 160 | 356m | 266 | -/21 | Australia | Manchester | 1985 |
| | | 100* | 216m | 127 | -/13 | Australia | Birmingham | 1985 |
| | | 183* | 383m | 294 | 2/20 | India | Birmingham | 1986 |
| | | 121 | 259m | 198 | -/13 | New Zealand | The Oval | 1986 |
| | | 100 | 180m | 141 | -/15 | Australia | Adelaide | 1986-87 |
| | | 124 | 401m | 281 | -/16 | Pakistan | Birmingham | 1987 |
| | | 150* | 346m | 302 | -/21 | Pakistan | The Oval | 1987 |
| | | 117 | 410m | 286 | -/14 | Australia | Adelaide | 1994-95 |
| Gibb,PA | (2) | 106 § | 192m | 192 | -/7 | South Africa | Johannesburg[1] | 1938-39 |
| | | 120 | 451m | | -/2 | South Africa | Durban[2] | 1938-39 |
| Gooch,GA | (20) | 123 | 211m | 162 | 1/17 | West Indies | Lord's | 1980 |
| | | 116 | 310m | | -/13 | West Indies | Bridgetown | 1980-81 |
| | | 153 | 315m | | 2/21 | West Indies | Kingston | 1980-81 |
| | | 127 | 227m | | -/20 | India | Madras[1] | 1981-82 |
| | | 196 | 423m | 310 | -/27 | Australia | The Oval | 1985 |
| | | 114 | 355m | 280 | 1/12 | India | Lord's | 1986 |
| | | 183 | 441m | 368 | -/22 | New Zealand | Lord's | 1986 |
| | | 146 | 410m | 303 | -/15 | West Indies | Nottingham | 1988 |
| | | 154 | 393m | 281 | 1/19 | New Zealand | Birmingham | 1990 |
| | | 333) | 627m | 485 | 3/43 | India | Lord's | 1990 |
| | | 123) | 147m | 113 | 4/13 | | | |
| | | 116 | 237m | 163 | -/16 | India | Manchester | 1990 |
| | | 117 | 214m | 188 | -/12 | Australia | Adelaide | 1990-91 |
| | | 154* | 452m | 331 | -/18 | West Indies | Leeds | 1991 |
| | | 174 | 329m | 252 | -/19 | Sri Lanka | Lord's | 1991 |
| | | 114 | 294m | 220 | 2/15 | New Zealand | Auckland | 1991-92 |
| | | 135 | 415m | 301 | 1/19 | Pakistan | Leeds | 1992 |
| | | 133 | 309m | 247 | 2/21 | Australia | Manchester | 1993 |
| | | 120 | 324m | 265 | 1/18 | Australia | Nottingham | 1993 |
| | | 210 | 418m | 317 | -/29 | New Zealand | Nottingham | 1994 |
| Gower,DI | (18) | 111 § | 251m | 253 | -/14 | New Zealand | The Oval | 1978 |
| | | 102 | 254m | 221 | -/9 | Australia | Perth | 1978-79 |
| | | 200* § | 365m | 279 | 1/24 | India | Birmingham | 1979 |
| | | 154* | 461m | | 1/16 | West Indies | Kingston | 1980-81 |
| | | 114 | 370m | 259 | -/16 | Australia | Adelaide | 1982-83 |
| | | 112* | 281m | 196 | -/14 | New Zealand | Leeds | 1983 |
| | | 108 | 228m | 198 | -/16 | New Zealand | Lord's | 1983 |
| | | 152 | 426m | 318 | -/16 | Pakistan | Faisalabad | 1983-84 |
| | | 173* | 423m | 284 | -/16 | Pakistan | Lahore[2] | 1983-84 |
| | | 166 | 379m | 283 | -/17 | Australia | Nottingham | 1985 |
| | | 215 | 449m | 314 | 1/25 | Australia | Birmingham | 1985 |
| | | 157 | 337m | 215 | -/20 | Australia | The Oval | 1985 |
| | | 131 | 281m | 202 | -/14 | New Zealand | The Oval | 1986 |
| | | 136 | 277m | 175 | -/19 | Australia | Perth | 1986-87 |
| | | 106 | 273m | 198 | -/16 | Australia | Lord's | 1989 |
| | | 157* | 365m | 271 | -/21 | India | The Oval | 1990 |
| | | 100 | 254m | 170 | -/8 | Australia | Melbourne | 1990-91 |
| | | 123 | 312m | 236 | -/15 | Australia | Sydney | 1990-91 |

| | | | | | | | | |
|---|---|---|---|---|---|---|---|---|
| Grace,WG | (2) | 152 § | 235m | | -/12 | Australia | The Oval | 1880 |
| | | 170 | 270m | | -/22 | Australia | The Oval | 1886 |
| Graveney,TW | (11) | 175 § | 503m | | -/17 | India | Bombay[2] | 1951-52 |
| | | 111 | 166m | 168 | -/14 | Australia | Sydney | 1954-55 |
| | | 258 | 471m | | -/30 | West Indies | Nottingham | 1957 |
| | | 164 | 324m | | -/17 | West Indies | The Oval | 1957 |
| | | 153 | 247m | | -/22 | Pakistan | Lord's | 1962 |
| | | 114 | 200m | 214 | -/15 | Pakistan | Nottingham | 1962 |
| | | 109 | 230m | | 1/11 | West Indies | Nottingham | 1966 |
| | | 165 | 361m | | -/19 | West Indies | The Oval | 1966 |
| | | 151 | 300h | | 2/12 | India | Lord's | 1967 |
| | | 118 | 250m | | -/20 | West Indies | Port-of-Spain | 1967-68 |
| | | 105 | 275m | | -/9 | Pakistan | Karachi[1] | 1968-69 |
| Greig,AW | (8) | 148 | 360m | 291 | -/24 | India | Bombay[2] | 1972-73 |
| | | 139 § | 197m | | -/16 | New Zealand | Nottingham | 1973 |
| | | 148 | 404m | 320 | 2/15 | West Indies | Bridgetown | 1973-74 |
| | | 121 | 311m | 254 | 1/14 | West Indies | Georgetown | 1973-74 |
| | | 106 | 188m | 180 | 1/8 | India | Lord's | 1974 |
| | | 110 | 296m | 229 | -/17 | Australia | Brisbane[2] | 1974-75 |
| | | 116 | 340m | 264 | -/15 | West Indies | Leeds | 1976 |
| | | 103 | 426m | 343 | 1/7 | India | Calcutta | 1976-77 |
| Griffith,SC | | 140 § | 354m | | -/15 | West Indies | Port-of-Spain | 1947-48 |
| Gunn,G | (2) | 119 § | 150m | | -/20 | Australia | Sydney | 1907-08 |
| | | 122* | 287m | | 1!/7 | Australia | Sydney | 1907-08 |
| Gunn,W | | 102* | 250m | | -/8 | Australia | Manchester | 1893 |
| Hammond,WR | (22) | 251 | 461m | 605 | -/30 | Australia | Sydney | 1928-29 |
| | | 200 | 398m | 472 | -/17 | Australia | Melbourne | 1928-29 |
| | | 119*) | 263m | 374 | -/19 | Australia | Adelaide | 1928-29 |
| | | 177 ) | 440m | 603 | -/17 | | | |
| | | 138* | 200m | | -/13 | South Africa | Birmingham | 1929 |
| | | 101* | >120h | | 1/5 | South Africa | The Oval | 1929 |
| | | 113 | 325m | 356 | -/14 | Australia | Leeds | 1930 |
| | | 136* | 220m | | -/6 | South Africa | Durban[2] | 1930-31 |
| | | 100* | 100m | | -/13 | New Zealand | The Oval | 1931 |
| | | 112 | 192m | 242 | -/16 | Australia | Sydney | 1932-33 |
| | | 101 | 208m | 205 | -/12 | Australia | Sydney | 1932-33 |
| | | 227 | 396m | | -/22 | New Zealand | Christchurch | 1932-33 |
| | | 336* | 325m | 398 | 10/34 | New Zealand | Auckland | 1932-33 |
| | | 167 | 190m | | -/21 | India | Manchester | 1936 |
| | | 217 | 290m | | -/30 | India | The Oval | 1936 |
| | | 231* | 458m | | -/27 | Australia | Sydney | 1936-37 |
| | | 140 | 219m | | 1/14 | New Zealand | Lord's | 1937 |
| | | 240 | 369m | 385 | -/32 | Australia | Lord's | 1938 |
| | | 181 | 337m | 371 | -/16 | South Africa | Cape Town | 1938-39 |
| | | 120 | 178m | 177 | -/16 | South Africa | Durban[2] | 1938-39 |
| | | 140 | 349m | | -/7 | South Africa | Durban[2] | 1938-39 |
| | | 138 | 180h | | -/21 | West Indies | The Oval | 1939 |
| Hampshire,JH | | 107 § | 288m | 258 | -/15 | West Indies | Lord's | 1969 |
| Hardstaff,J,jr | (4) | 114 § | 250m | | -/9 | New Zealand | Lord's | 1937 |
| | | 103 | n180h | | -/16 | New Zealand | The Oval | 1937 |
| | | 169* | 326m | 395 | -/20 | Australia | The Oval | 1938 |
| | | 205* | 315m | | -/16 | India | Lord's | 1946 |
| Hayes,FC | | 106* § | 240m | | -/12 | West Indies | The Oval | 1973 |
| Hayward,TW | (3) | 122 | >180h | | 1!/15 | South Africa | Johannesburg[1] | 1895-96 |
| | | 130 | 255h | | -/18 | Australia | Manchester | 1899 |
| | | 137 | 270h | | -/20 | Australia | The Oval | 1899 |
| Hearne,JW | | 114 | 225m | 243 | -/11 | Australia | Melbourne | 1911-12 |
| Hendren,EH | (7) | 132 | 140m | | -/20 | South Africa | Leeds | 1924 |
| | | 142 | 190m | | 2/14 | South Africa | The Oval | 1924 |
| | | 127* | 208m | | -/18 | Australia | Lord's | 1926 |

| | | | | | | | | |
|---|---|---|---|---|---|---|---|---|
| | | 169 | 308m | 314 | -/16 | Australia | Brisbane[1] | 1928-29 |
| | | 205* | 398m | | -/29 | West Indies | Port-of-Spain | 1929-30 |
| | | 123 | | | -/21 | West Indies | Georgetown | 1929-30 |
| | | 132 | 243m | 245 | -/22 | Australia | Manchester | 1934 |
| Hick,GA | (4) | 178 | 390m | 319 | 1/20 | India | Bombay[3] | 1992-93 |
| | | 110 | 272m | 182 | 3/6 | South Africa | Leeds | 1994 |
| | | 118* | 302m | 213 | -/17 | West Indies | Nottingham | 1995 |
| | | 141 | 393m | 252 | -/25 | South Africa | Centurion | 1995-96 |
| Hill,AJL | | 124 | | | | South Africa | Cape Town | 1895-96 |
| Hobbs,JB | (15) | 187 | 225m | | -/23 | South Africa | Cape Town | 1909-10 |
| | | 126* | 227m | 206 | -/8 | Australia | Melbourne | 1911-12 |
| | | 187 | 334m | 351 | -/16 | Australia | Adelaide | 1911-12 |
| | | 178 | 268m | | -/22 | Australia | Melbourne | 1911-12 |
| | | 107 | 167m | 203 | -/15 | Australia | Lord's | 1912 |
| | | 122 | 210m | | -/10 | Australia | Melbourne | 1920-21 |
| | | 123 | 151m | | -/13 | Australia | Adelaide | 1920-21 |
| | | 211 | 280m | | -/16 | South Africa | Lord's | 1924 |
| | | 115 | 219m | | -/7 | Australia | Sydney | 1924-25 |
| | | 154 | 288m | | -/11 | Australia | Melbourne | 1924-25 |
| | | 119 | 294m | | -/7 | Australia | Adelaide | 1924-25 |
| | | 119 | 247m | | -/10 | Australia | Lord's | 1926 |
| | | 100 | 227m | | -/10 | Australia | The Oval | 1926 |
| | | 159 | 240h | | -/20 | West Indies | The Oval | 1928 |
| | | 142 | 278m | 301 | -/11 | Australia | Melbourne | 1928-29 |
| Hussain,N | (7) | 128 § | 327m | 227 | 1/18 | India | Birmingham | 1996 |
| | | 107® | 239m | 180 | -/12 | India | Nottingham | 1996 |
| | | 113 § | 357m | 276 | -/14 | Zimbabwe | Bulawayo[2] | 1996-97 |
| | | 207 | 437m | 336 | -/38 | Australia | Birmingham | 1997 |
| | | 105 | 250m | 181 | -/15 | Australia | Leeds | 1997 |
| | | 106 | 378m | 318 | -/14 | West Indies | St John's | 1997-98 |
| | | 105 | 391m | 294 | -/17 | South Africa | Lord's | 1998 |
| Hutchings,KL | | 126 | 163m | | 1!/21 | Australia | Melbourne | 1907-08 |
| Hutton,L | (19) | 100 | 202m | | -/8 | New Zealand | Manchester | 1937 |
| | | 100 § | 199m | 227 | -/14 | Australia | Nottingham | 1938 |
| | | 364 | 797m | 844 | -/35 | Australia | The Oval | 1938 |
| | | 196 § | 310m | | -/21 | West Indies | Lord's | 1939 |
| | | 165* | 310m | | -/17 | West Indies | The Oval | 1939 |
| | | 122* | 300m | 356 | -/5 | Australia | Sydney | 1946-47 |
| | | 100 | 277m | | -/8 | South Africa | Leeds | 1947 |
| | | 158 | 290m | 362 | -/16 | South Africa | Johannesburg[2] | 1948-49 |
| | | 123 | 249m | | -/13 | South Africa | Johannesburg[2] | 1948-49 |
| | | 101 | >240h | | -/14 | New Zealand | Leeds | 1949 |
| | | 206 | 300h | | -/25 | New Zealand | The Oval | 1949 |
| | | 202* | 470m | | -/22 | West Indies | The Oval | 1950 |
| | | 156* | 370m | | -/11 | Australia | Adelaide | 1950-51 |
| | | 100 | 300h | | | South Africa | Leeds | 1951 |
| | | 150 | 317m | | -/20 | India | Lord's | 1952 |
| | | 104 | 315m | | -/10 | India | Manchester | 1952 |
| | | 145 | 325m | 308 | -/16 | Australia | Lord's | 1953 |
| | | 169 | 457m | | 1/24 | West Indies | Georgetown | 1953-54 |
| | | 205 | 534m | | 1/23 | West Indies | Kingston | 1953-54 |
| Illingworth,R | (2) | 113 | 195h | | -/12 | West Indies | Lord's | 1969 |
| | | 107 | 270m | | 1/8 | India | Manchester | 1971 |
| Insole,DJ | | 110* | 373m | | -/7 | South Africa | Durban[2] | 1956-57 |
| Jackson,Hon.FS | (5) | 103 | 135h | | -/13 | Australia | The Oval | 1893 |
| | | 118 | 173m | | -/18 | Australia | The Oval | 1899 |
| | | 128 | 255m | | -/16 | Australia | Manchester | 1902 |
| | | 144* | 268m | | -/18 | Australia | Leeds | 1905 |
| | | 113 | 223m | | -/12 | Australia | Manchester | 1905 |
| Jardine,DR | | 127 | 300h | | -/5 | West Indies | Manchester | 1933 |

| | | | | | | | | |
|---|---|---|---|---|---|---|---|---|
| Jessop,GL | | 104 | 77m | | -/17 | Australia | The Oval | 1902 |
| Knight,B R | (2) | 125 § | 218m | | -/14 | New Zealand | Auckland | 1962-63 |
| | | 127 | 224m | | -/16 | India | Kanpur | 1963-64 |
| Knight,NV | | 113 | 258m | 176 | -/16 | Pakistan | Leeds | 1996 |
| Knott,APE | (5) | 101 | 181m | | 1/11 | New Zealand | Auckland | 1970-71 |
| | | 116 | 188m | 173 | -/22 | Pakistan | Birmingham | 1971 |
| | | 106* | 227m | 205 | -/9 | Australia | Adelaide | 1974-75 |
| | | 116 | 305m | 212 | -/14 | West Indies | Leeds | 1976 |
| | | 135 | 292m | 214 | -/18 | Australia | Nottingham | 1977 |
| Lamb,AJ | (14) | 107 | 260m | 202 | 1/8 | India | The Oval | 1982 |
| | | 102* § | 297m | 293 | -/10 | New Zealand | The Oval | 1983 |
| | | 137* | 262m | 219 | -/22 | New Zealand | Nottingham | 1983 |
| | | 110 | 360m | 259 | -/13 | West Indies | Lord's | 1984 |
| | | 100 | 228m | 186 | -/15 | West Indies | Leeds | 1984 |
| | | 100* | 251m | 185 | -/15 | West Indies | Manchester | 1984 |
| | | 107 § | 267m | 195 | 1/10 | Sri Lanka | Lord's | 1984 |
| | | 113 | 338m | 212 | -/15 | West Indies | Lord's | 1988 |
| | | 125 | 281m | 205 | -/24 | Australia | Leeds | 1989 |
| | | 132 | 364m | 209 | -/16 | West Indies | Kingston | 1989-90 |
| | | 119 | 338m | 225 | -/14 | West Indies | Bridgetown | 1989-90 |
| | | 139 | 276m | 187 | -/22 | India | Lord's | 1990 |
| | | 109 | 205m | 231 | 2/8 | India | Manchester | 1990 |
| | | 142 | 303m | 141 | -/15 | New Zealand | Wellington | 1991-92 |
| Legge,GB | | 196 | 281m | | -/23 | New Zealand | Auckland | 1929-30 |
| Lewis,AR | | 125 | 267m | 228 | 1/16 | India | Kanpur | 1972-73 |
| Lewis,CC | | 117 | 170m | 140 | 2/15 | India | Madras[1] | 1992-93 |
| Leyland,M | (9) | 137 § | 301m | 330 | -/18 | Australia | Melbourne | 1928-29 |
| | | 102 | | | -/10 | South Africa | Lord's | 1929 |
| | | 109 | 211m | 258 | 1/14 | Australia | Lord's | 1934 |
| | | 153 | 314m | 314 | -/19 | Australia | Manchester | 1934 |
| | | 110 | 165m | 174 | 1/15 | Australia | The Oval | 1934 |
| | | 161 | 235m | | 1/17 | South Africa | The Oval | 1935 |
| | | 126 | 251m | | -/11 | Australia | Brisbane[2] | 1936-37 |
| | | 111* | 194m | | -/11 | Australia | Melbourne | 1936-37 |
| | | 187 | 381m | 431 | -/17 | Australia | The Oval | 1938 |
| Lloyd,D | | 214* | 448m | 396 | -/17 | India | Birmingham | 1974 |
| Luckhurst,BW | (4) | 131 | 340m | | -/13 | Australia | Perth | 1970-71 |
| | | 109 | 328m | | -/11 | Australia | Melbourne | 1970-71 |
| | | 108* § | 327m | 279 | -/14 | Pakistan | Birmingham | 1971 |
| | | 101 | 231m | 170 | 1/10 | India | Manchester | 1971 |
| MacLaren,AC | (5) | 120 | 220m | | -/12 | Australia | Melbourne | 1894-95 |
| | | 109 | 189m | | -/15 | Australia | Sydney | 1897-98 |
| | | 124 | 317m | | -/10 | Australia | Adelaide | 1897-98 |
| | | 116 | 206m | | -/20 | Australia | Sydney | 1901-02 |
| | | 140 | 217m | | -/22 | Australia | Nottingham | 1905 |
| Makepeace,JWH | | 117 | 260m | | -/4 | Australia | Melbourne | 1920-21 |
| Mann,FG | | 136* | 237m | | 1/12 | South Africa | Port Elizabeth | 1948-49 |
| May,PBH | (13) | 138 § | 380m | | -/19 | South Africa | Leeds | 1951 |
| | | 135 | 249m | | -/24 | West Indies | Port-of-Spain | 1953-54 |
| | | 104 | 298m | 281 | -/10 | Australia | Sydney | 1954-55 |
| | | 112 | 270m | | -/18 | South Africa | Lord's | 1955 |
| | | 117 | 270h | | -/16 | South Africa | Manchester | 1955 |
| | | 101 | 317m | | -/12 | Australia | Leeds | 1956 |
| | | 285* | 595m | | 2/25 | West Indies | Birmingham | 1957 |
| | | 104 | 183m | | -/14 | West Indies | Nottingham | 1957 |
| | | 113* | 174m | | 2/12 | New Zealand | Leeds | 1958 |
| | | 101 | 156m | | 4/7 | New Zealand | Manchester | 1958 |
| | | 113 | 315m | 298 | -/11 | Australia | Melbourne | 1958-59 |
| | | 124* | 251m | | -/14 | New Zealand | Auckland | 1958-59 |
| | | 106 | 218m | | -/18 | India | Nottingham | 1959 |

| | | | | | | | | |
|---|---|---|---|---|---|---|---|---|
| Mead,CP | (4) | 102 | >210h | | -/12 | South Africa | Johannesburg[1] | 1913-14 |
| | | 117 | 225h | | -/8 | South Africa | Port Elizabeth | 1913-14 |
| | | 182* | 309m | | -/21 | Australia | The Oval | 1921 |
| | | 181 | 454m | | -/13 | South Africa | Durban[2] | 1922-23 |
| Milburn,C | (2) | 126* | 179m | | 3/17 | West Indies | Lord's | 1966 |
| | | 139 | 301m | | 1/17 | Pakistan | Karachi[1] | 1968-69 |
| Milton,CA | | 104* § | 297m | | -/12 | New Zealand | Leeds | 1958 |
| Murray,JT | | 112 § | 267m | | -/13 | West Indies | The Oval | 1966 |
| Parfitt,PH | (7) | 111 | 312m | | -/11 | Pakistan | Karachi[1] | 1961-62 |
| | | 101* | 197m | | 2/9 | Pakistan | Birmingham | 1962 |
| | | 119 | 265m | | -/18 | Pakistan | Leeds | 1962 |
| | | 101* | 225m | 187 | -/9 | Pakistan | Nottingham | 1962 |
| | | 131* § | 289m | | -/14 | New Zealand | Auckland | 1962-63 |
| | | 121 | 328m | | -/18 | India | Kanpur | 1963-64 |
| | | 122* | 333m | 289 | -/18 | South Africa | Johannesburg[3] | 1964-65 |
| Parks,JM | (2) | 101* § | 210m | | | West Indies | Port-of-Spain | 1959-60 |
| | | 108* | 247m | | -/10 | South Africa | Durban[2] | 1964-65 |
| Pataudi,Nawab of,sr | | 102 § | 317m | 380 | -/6 | Australia | Sydney | 1932-33 |
| Paynter,E | (4) | 216* | 319m | 331 | 1/26 | Australia | Nottingham | 1938 |
| | | 117 §) | 176m | 179 | 1/8 | South Africa | Johannesburg[1] | 1938-39 |
| | | 100 §) | 192m | 162 | -/10 | | | |
| | | 243 | 334m | 419 | -/24 | South Africa | Durban[2] | 1938-39 |
| Place,W | | 107 | 367m | | -/6 | West Indies | Kingston | 1947-48 |
| Pullar,G | (4) | 131 | 320m | | -/14 | India | Manchester | 1959 |
| | | 175 | 360m | 354 | 1/15 | South Africa | The Oval | 1960 |
| | | 119 | 313m | | -/14 | India | Kanpur | 1961-62 |
| | | 165 | 414m | | -/16 | Pakistan | Dacca | 1961-62 |
| Radley,CT | (2) | 158 | 648m | 500 | -/15 | New Zealand | Auckland | 1977-78 |
| | | 106 § | 310m | | -/11 | Pakistan | Birmingham | 1978 |
| Ramprakash,MR | | 154 | 529m | 388 | -/20 | West Indies | Bridgetown | 1997-98 |
| Randall,DW | (7) | 174 § | 448m | 353 | -/21 | Australia | Melbourne | 1976-77 |
| | | 150 | 582m | 498 | -/13 | Australia | Sydney | 1978-79 |
| | | 126 | 353m | 290 | 1/11 | India | Lord's | 1982 |
| | | 105 | 249m | 156 | -/11 | Pakistan | Birmingham | 1982 |
| | | 115 | 266m | 215 | -/13 | Australia | Perth | 1982-83 |
| | | 164 | 365m | 269 | 2/20 | New Zealand | Wellington | 1983-84 |
| | | 104 | 347m | 338 | -/12 | New Zealand | Auckland | 1983-84 |
| Ranjitsinhji,KS | (2) | 154* § | 185m | | -/23 | Australia | Manchester | 1896 |
| | | 175 | 223m | | -/24 | Australia | Sydney | 1897-98 |
| Read,WW | | 117 | 137m | 155 | -/20 | Australia | The Oval | 1884 |
| Rhodes,W | (2) | 179 | 397m | | -/14 | Australia | Melbourne | 1911-12 |
| | | 152 | 310m | | -/21 | South Africa | Johannesburg[1] | 1913-14 |
| Richards,CJ | | 133 | 240m | 207 | -/16 | Australia | Perth | 1986-87 |
| Richardson,PE | (5) | 104 | 222m | | -/11 | Australia | Manchester | 1956 |
| | | 117 § | 528m | | -/6 | South Africa | Johannesburg[3] | 1956-57 |
| | | 126 | 278m | | -/10 | West Indies | Nottingham | 1957 |
| | | 107 | 295m | | -/10 | West Indies | The Oval | 1957 |
| | | 100 § | 286m | | -/7 | New Zealand | Birmingham | 1958 |
| Robertson,JDB | (2) | 133 | 345m | | -/14 | West Indies | Port-of-Spain | 1947-48 |
| | | 121 § | 225h | | 1/11 | New Zealand | Lord's | 1949 |
| Robins,RWV | | 108 | 130m | | -/12 | South Africa | Manchester | 1935 |
| Robinson,RT | (4) | 160 | 508m | 391 | -/17 | India | Delhi | 1984-85 |
| | | 175 § | 408m | 271 | -/27 | Australia | Leeds | 1985 |
| | | 148 | 392m | 293 | -/18 | Australia | Birmingham | 1985 |
| | | 166 § | 528m | 366 | -/16 | Pakistan | Manchester | 1987 |
| Russell,CAG | (5) | 135* | 250m | | 1/10 | Australia | Adelaide | 1920-21 |
| | | 101 | 244m | | -/9 | Australia | Manchester | 1921 |
| | | 102* | 163m | | -/11 | Australia | The Oval | 1921 |
| | | 140) | 320m | | -/11 | South Africa | Durban[2] | 1922-23 |
| | | 111) | 265m | | -/10 | | | |

| | | | | | | | | |
|---|---|---|---|---|---|---|---|---|
| Russell,RC | (2) | 128* | 350m | 294 | -/14 | Australia | Manchester | 1989 |
| | | 124 | 383m | 261 | -/13 | India | Lord's | 1996 |
| Sandham,A | (2) | 152 § | 360m | | -/16 | West Indies | Bridgetown | 1929-30 |
| | | 325 | 600m | | -/28 | West Indies | Kingston | 1929-30 |
| Sharp,J | | 105 | 176m | 174 | -/11 | Australia | The Oval | 1909 |
| Sharpe,PJ | | 111 | 269m | | -/14 | New Zealand | Nottingham | 1969 |
| Sheppard,Rev.DS | (3) | 119 | 350m | | -/9 | India | The Oval | 1952 |
| | | 113 | 296m | | 1/15 | Australia | Manchester | 1956 |
| | | 113 | 301m | | -/5 | Australia | Melbourne | 1962-63 |
| Shrewsbury,A | (3) | 105* | 320m | | -/10 | Australia | Melbourne | 1884-85 |
| | | 164 | 411m | | -/16 | Australia | Lord's | 1886 |
| | | 106 | 250m | | -/9 | Australia | Lord's | 1893 |
| Simpson,RT | (4) | 103 § | a145m | | 3/11 | New Zealand | Manchester | 1949 |
| | | 156* | 338m | | -/12 | Australia | Melbourne | 1950-51 |
| | | 137 | 250m | | -/21 | South Africa | Nottingham | 1951 |
| | | 101 | 203m | | -/9 | Pakistan | Nottingham | 1954 |
| Smith,MJK | (3) | 100 § | 214m | | -/12 | India | Manchester | 1959 |
| | | 108 | a300h | | 2/? | West Indies | Port-of-Spain | 1959-60 |
| | | 121 | 320m | | 1/12 | South Africa | Cape Town | 1964-65 |
| Smith,RA | (9) | 143 | 355m | 285 | -/15 | Australia | Manchester | 1989 |
| | | 101 | 206m | 150 | -/16 | Australia | Nottingham | 1989 |
| | | 100* § | 196m | 155 | -/14 | India | Lord's | 1990 |
| | | 121* | 243m | 197 | -/11 | India | Manchester | 1990 |
| | | 148* | 413m | 271 | -/20 | West Indies | Lord's | 1991 |
| | | 109 | 353m | 256 | -/13 | West Indies | The Oval | 1991 |
| | | 127 § | 326m | 231 | -/18 | Pakistan | Birmingham | 1992 |
| | | 128 | 448m | 338 | -/20 | Sri Lanka | Colombo (SSC) | 1992-93 |
| | | 175 | 418m | 315 | 3/25 | West Indies | St John's | 1993-94 |
| Spooner,RH | | 119 § | <180h | | 1/13 | South Africa | Lord's | 1912 |
| Steel,AG | (2) | 135* | 238m | | -/16 | Australia | Sydney | 1882-83 |
| | | 148 | 230m | | -/13 | Australia | Lord's | 1884 |
| Steele,DS | | 106 § | 368m | 296 | -/9 | West Indies | Nottingham | 1976 |
| Stewart,AJ | (11) | 113* § | 308m | 240 | -/14 | Sri Lanka | Lord's | 1991 |
| | | 148 | 355m | 265 | -/17 | New Zealand | Christchurch | 1991-92 |
| | | 107 | 320m | 243 | -/13 | New Zealand | Wellington | 1991-92 |
| | | 190 § | 351m | 261 | -/31 | Pakistan | Birmingham | 1992 |
| | | 118) | 347m | 221 | -/18 | West Indies | Bridgetown | 1993-94 |
| | | 143) | 475m | 319 | -/20 | | | |
| | | 119 | 289m | 229 | -/20 | New Zealand | Lord's | 1994 |
| | | 170 | 438m | 315 | -/24 | Pakistan | Leeds | 1996 |
| | | 101* | 408m | 267 | -/8 | Zimbabwe | Harare | 1996-97 |
| | | 173 | 364m | 277 | 1/23 | New Zealand | Aucklamd | 1996-97 |
| | | 164 | 422m | 317 | -/24 | South Africa | Manchester | 1998 |
| Stoddart,AE | (2) | 134 | 230m | | -/15 | Australia | Adelaide | 1891-92 |
| | | 173 | 320m | | 1∇/14 | Australia | Melbourne | 1894-95 |
| Subba Row,R | (3) | 100 | 270m | | | West Indies | Georgetown | 1959-60 |
| | | 112 | 244m | | -/13 | Australia | Birmingham | 1961 |
| | | 137 | 400m | | 1/15 | Australia | The Oval | 1961 |
| Sutcliffe,H | (16) | 122 | 200m | | -/11 | South Africa | Lord's | 1924 |
| | | 115 § | 247m | | -/11 | Australia | Sydney | 1924-25 |
| | | 176) | 431m | | -/17 | Australia | Melbourne | 1924-25 |
| | | 127) | 379m | | -/12 | | | |
| | | 143 | 295m | | -/14 | Australia | Melbourne | 1924-25 |
| | | 161 | 439m | | -/16 | Australia | The Oval | 1926 |
| | | 102 | | | | South Africa | Johannesburg[1] | 1927-28 |
| | | 135 | 385m | 462 | -/9 | Australia | Melbourne | 1928-29 |
| | | 114 | 225m | | -/7 | South Africa | Birmingham | 1929 |
| | | 100 | 176m | | -/10 | South Africa | Lord's | 1929 |
| | | 104 ) | 210m | | -/9 | South Africa | The Oval | 1929 |
| | | 109*) | 200m | | -/11 | | | |

| | | | | | | | | |
|---|---|---|---|---|---|---|---|---|
| | | 161 | 404m | 387 | -/10 | Australia | The Oval | 1930 |
| | | 117 § | 220m | | -/10 | New Zealand | The Oval | 1931 |
| | | 109* | 195m | | 1/9 | New Zealand | Manchester | 1931 |
| | | 194 | 436m | 496 | -/13 | Australia | Sydney | 1932-33 |
| Tate,MW | | 100* | <120h | | -/12 | South Africa | Lord's | 1929 |
| Tavare,CJ | (2) | 149 | 455m | 303 | -/18 | India | Delhi | 1981-82 |
| | | 109 § | 312m | 255 | -/11 | New Zealand | The Oval | 1983 |
| Thorpe,GP | (6) | 114* § | 334m | 280 | -/11 | Australia | Nottingham | 1993 |
| | | 123 | 301m | 218 | -/19 | Australia | Perth | 1994-95 |
| | | 119 | 338m | 245 | -/17 | New Zealand | Aucklamd | 1996-97 |
| | | 108 | 330m | 249 | -/12 | New Zealand | Wellington | 1996-97 |
| | | 138 | 290m | 245 | -/19 | Australia | Birmingham | 1997 |
| | | 103 | 392m | 268 | -/8 | West Indies | Bridgetown | 1997-98 |
| Tyldesley,GE | (3) | 122 | 253m | | -/16 | South Africa | Johannesburg[1] | 1927-28 |
| | | 100 | 165m | | -/5 | South Africa | Durban[2] | 1927-28 |
| | | 122 § | 210h | | 1/13 | West Indies | Birmingham | 1928 |
| Tyldesley,JT | (4) | 112 | | | | South Africa | Cape Town | 1898-99 |
| | | 138 | 262m | | -/20 | Australia | Birmingham | 1902 |
| | | 100 | 168m | | -/12 | Australia | Leeds | 1905 |
| | | 112* | 212m | | -/15 | Australia | The Oval | 1905 |
| Ulyett,G | | 149 | 240m | | -/13 | Australia | Melbourne | 1881-82 |
| Valentine,BH | (2) | 136 § | 177m | | 1/13 | India | Bombay[1] | 1933-34 |
| | | 112 | 160m | 147 | 1/12 | South Africa | Cape Town | 1938-39 |
| Walters,CF | | 102 | 151m | | -/14 | India | Madras[1] | 1933-34 |
| Ward,Albert | | 117 | 224m | | -/11 | Australia | Sydney | 1894-95 |
| Warner,PF | | 132* § | | | -/19 | South Africa | Johannesburg[1] | 1898-99 |
| Washbrook,C | (6) | 112 | 247m | 299 | 1/8 | Australia | Melbourne | 1946-47 |
| | | 143 | 317m | 312 | -/22 | Australia | Leeds | 1948 |
| | | 195 | 297m | 308 | -/18 | South Africa | Johannesburg[2] | 1948-49 |
| | | 103* | 180h | | -/12 | New Zealand | Leeds | 1949 |
| | | 114 § | 320m | | 1/14 | West Indies | Lord's | 1950 |
| | | 102 | 320m | | -/9 | West Indies | Nottingham | 1950 |
| Watkins,AJ | (2) | 111 | 220m | | -/15 | South Africa | Johannesburg[2] | 1948-49 |
| | | 137 § | 540h | | -/15 | India | Delhi | 1951-52 |
| Watson,W | (2) | 109 § | 346m | 356 | -/16 | Australia | Lord's | 1953 |
| | | 116 § | 259m | | -/16 | West Indies | Kingston | 1953-54 |
| Willey,P | (2) | 100* | 236m | 203 | -/16 | West Indies | The Oval | 1980 |
| | | 102* | 223m | 203 | 1/15 | West Indies | St John's | 1980-81 |
| Wood,H | | 134* | | | | South Africa | Cape Town | 1891-92 |
| Woolley,FE | (5) | 133* | 215m | | -/12 | Australia | Sydney | 1911-12 |
| | | 115* | 206m | | 1/11 | South Africa | Johannesburg[1] | 1922-23 |
| | | 134* | 145m | | -/20 | South Africa | Lord's | 1924 |
| | | 123 | 146m | | 1/15 | Australia | Sydney | 1924-25 |
| | | 154 | 165m | | -/20 | South Africa | Manchester | 1929 |
| Woolmer,RA | (3) | 149 | 499m | 390 | -/20 | Australia | The Oval | 1975 |
| | | 120 | 306m | 247 | -/13 | Australia | Lord's | 1977 |
| | | 137 | 386m | 338 | -/22 | Australia | Manchester | 1977 |
| Worthington,TS | | 128 | >210h | | -/19 | India | The Oval | 1936 |
| Wyatt,RES | (2) | 113 | 245m | | -/14 | South Africa | Manchester | 1929 |
| | | 149 | 305m | | -/17 | South Africa | Nottingham | 1935 |
| **SOUTH AFRICA** (140) | | | Time | Balls | 6/4 | Opponents | | |
| Balaskas,XC | | 122* | 198m | | -/15 | New Zealand | Wellington | 1931-32 |
| Barlow,EJ | (6) | 114 § | 354m | | -/13 | Australia | Brisbane[2] | 1963-64 |
| | | 109 | 273m | | -/11 | Australia | Melbourne | 1963-64 |
| | | 201 | 392m | | -/27 | Australia | Adelaide | 1963-64 |
| | | 138 | 344m | | -/16 | England | Cape Town | 1964-65 |
| | | 127 | 362m | | 1/11 | Australia | Cape Town | 1969-70 |
| | | 110 | 323m | 247 | 1/13 | Australia | Johannesburg[3] | 1969-70 |
| Bland,KC | (3) | 126 | 324m | 333 | 1/13 | Australia | Sydney | 1963-64 |

| | | | | | | | | |
|---|---|---|---|---|---|---|---|---|
| | | 144* | 248m | | 2/17 | England | Johannesburg[3] | 1964-65 |
| | | 127 | #270h | | -/16 | England | The Oval | 1965 |
| Catterall,RH | (3) | 120 | 195m | | 2/15 | England | Birmingham | 1924 |
| | | 120 | 200m | | -/16 | England | Lord's | 1924 |
| | | 119 | 135m | | 2/14 | England | Durban[2] | 1927-28 |
| Christy,JAJ | | 103 § | 126m | | -/10 | New Zealand | Christchurch | 1931-32 |
| Cronje,WJ | (5) | 135 | 527m | 411 | -/12 | India | Port Elizabeth | 1992-93 |
| | | 122 | 412m | 297 | -/11 | Sri Lanka | Colombo (SSC) | 1993-94 |
| | | 122 | 250m | 122 | 1/16 | Australia | Johannesburg[3] | 1993-94 |
| | | 112 | 288m | 235 | 1/10 | New Zealand | Cape Town | 1994-95 |
| | | 101 | 227m | 155 | 3/7 | New Zealand | Auckland | 1994-95 |
| Cullinan,DJ | (5) | 102 | 358m | 232 | -/17 | Sri Lanka | Colombo (PSS) | 1993-94 |
| | | 153* | 354m | 261 | 1/15 | India | Calcutta | 1996-97 |
| | | 122* | 262m | 194 | 1/15 | India | Johannesburg[3] | 1996-97 |
| | | 113 | 222m | 159 | 1/13 | Sri Lanka | Cape Town | 1997-98 |
| | | 103 | 307m | 185 | -/13 | Sri Lanka | Centurion | 1997-98 |
| Dalton,EL | (2) | 117 | 140m | | -/18 | England | The Oval | 1935 |
| | | 102 | 209m | 237 | -/9 | England | Johannesburg[1] | 1938-39 |
| Endean,WR | (3) | 162* | 452m | | -/9 | Australia | Melbourne | 1952-53 |
| | | 116 | 275m | | -/9 | New Zealand | Auckland | 1952-53 |
| | | 116* | †240h | | -/16 | England | Leeds | 1955 |
| Faulkner,GA | (4) | 123 | 170m | | -/17 | England | Johannesburg[1] | 1909-10 |
| | | 204 | 313m | | -/26 | Australia | Melbourne | 1910-11 |
| | | 115 | 239m | | -/10 | Australia | Adelaide | 1910-11 |
| | | 122* | 257m | 270 | -/13 | Australia | Manchester | 1912 |
| Frank,CN | | 152 | 512m | | -/17 | Australia | Johannesburg[1] | 1921-22 |
| Goddard,TL | | 112 | 251m | | 3/10 | England | Johannesburg[3] | 1964-65 |
| Hathorn,CMH | | 102 | 135h | | -/15 | England | Johannesburg[1] | 1905-06 |
| Hudson,AC | (4) | 163 § | 521m | 384 | -/24 | West Indies | Bridgetown | 1991-92 |
| | | 102 | 249m | 175 | -/13 | Australia | Cape Town | 1993-94 |
| | | 135 § | 311m | 236 | 2/18 | Zimbabwe | Harare | 1994-95 |
| | | 146 | 302m | 244 | -/24 | India | Calcutta | 1996-97 |
| Irvine,BL | | 102 | 178m | 146 | 2/9 | Australia | Port Elizabeth | 1969-70 |
| Kallis,JH | (2) | 101 | 357m | 279 | -/6 | Australia | Melbourne | 1997-98 |
| | | 132 | 357m | 266 | -/16 | England | Manchester | 1998 |
| Kirsten,G | (7) | 110 | 353m | 241 | -/16 | England | Johannesburg[3] | 1995-96 |
| | | 102 ) | 241m | 171 | -/15 | India | Calcutta | 1996-97 |
| | | 133 ) | 315m | 197 | -/18 | | | |
| | | 103 | 290m | 204 | -/15 | India | Cape Town | 1996-97 |
| | | 100* | 299m | 208 | -/15 | Pakistan | Faisalabad | 1997-98 |
| | | 108* | 235m | 159 | 1/17 | Australia | Adelaide | 1997-98 |
| | | 210 | 652m | 525 | 1/24 | England | Manchester | 1998 |
| Kirsten,PN | | 104 | 295m | 226 | -/13 | England | Leeds | 1994 |
| Klusener,L | | 102* | 143m | 100 | -/13 | India | Cape Town | 1996-97 |
| Lindsay,DT | (3) | 182 | 274m | | 5/25 | Australia | Johannesburg[3] | 1966-67 |
| | | 137 | 253m | | -/14 | Australia | Durban[2] | 1966-67 |
| | | 131 | 160m | | 4/14 | Australia | Johannesburg[3] | 1966-67 |
| McGlew,DJ | (7) | 255* § | 534m | | -/19 | New Zealand | Wellington | 1952-53 |
| | | 104* | 280m | | -/19 | England | Manchester | 1955 |
| | | 133 | 398m | | -/13 | England | Leeds | 1955 |
| | | 108 | 315m | | 1/12 | Australia | Johannesburg[3] | 1957-58 |
| | | 105 | 572m | | -/4 | Australia | Durban[2] | 1957-58 |
| | | 127* | 312m | | -/10 | New Zealand | Durban[2] | 1961-62 |
| | | 120 | 302m | | 1/10 | New Zealand | Johannesburg[3] | 1961-62 |
| McLean,RA | (5) | 101 | 144m | | -/11 | New Zealand | Durban[2] | 1953-54 |
| | | 142 | 205m | | 1/21 | England | Lord's | 1955 |
| | | 100 | 260m | | -/14 | England | Durban[2] | 1956-57 |
| | | 109 | 157m | 153 | -/14 | England | Manchester | 1960 |
| | | 113 | 174m | | 1/16 | New Zealand | Cape Town | 1961-62 |
| McMillan,BM | (3) | 113 § | 226m | 180 | -/15 | Pakistan | Johannesburg[3] | 1994-95 |

| | | | | | | | | |
|---|---|---|---|---|---|---|---|---|
| | | 100* | 299m | 168 | 3/9 | England | Johannesburg[3] | 1995-96 |
| | | 103* | 348m | 235 | -/9 | India | Cape Town | 1996-97 |
| Melville,A | (4) | 103 | 210m | | -/10 | England | Durban[2] | 1938-39 |
| | | 189 ) | 360h | | 1/16 | England | Nottingham | 1947 |
| | | 104*) | 138m | | -/15 | | | |
| | | 117 | 253m | | -/13 | England | Lord's | 1947 |
| Mitchell,B | (8) | 123 | 340m | | -/9 | England | Cape Town | 1930-31 |
| | | 113 § | 181m | | -/6 | New Zealand | Christchurch | 1931-32 |
| | | 164* | 333m | | -/17 | England | Lord's | 1935 |
| | | 128 | 280m | | -/11 | England | The Oval | 1935 |
| | | 109 | 190m | 234 | -/14 | England | Durban[2] | 1938-39 |
| | | 120 ) | 391m | | -/14 | England | The Oval | 1947 |
| | | 189*) | 410m | | | | | |
| | | 120 | 344m | | -/11 | England | Cape Town | 1948-49 |
| Murray,ARA | | 109 § | 219m | | | New Zealand | Wellington | 1952-53 |
| Nourse,AD | (9) | 231 | 298m | 346 | -/36 | Australia | Johannesburg[1] | 1935-36 |
| | | 120 | 268m | 295 | 1/12 | England | Cape Town | 1938-39 |
| | | 103 | 364m | 345 | -/6 | England | Durban[2] | 1938-39 |
| | | 149 | 240m | | 1/15 | England | Nottingham | 1947 |
| | | 115 | 145m | | 2/13 | England | Manchester | 1947 |
| | | 112 | 209m | | -/11 | England | Cape Town | 1948-49 |
| | | 129* | 319m | | -/11 | England | Johannesburg[2] | 1948-49 |
| | | 114 | 274m | 279 | -/9 | Australia | Cape Town | 1949-50 |
| | | 208 | 555m | | -/25 | England | Nottingham | 1951 |
| Nourse,AW | | 111 | 228m | | -/13 | Australia | Johannesburg[1] | 1921-22 |
| Owen-Smith,HG | | 129 | 160m | | 2/15 | England | Leeds | 1929 |
| Pithey,AJ | | 154 | 440m | | 1/13 | England | Cape Town | 1964-65 |
| Pollock,RG | (7) | 122 | 221m | 234 | 1/19 | Australia | Sydney | 1963-64 |
| | | 175 | 283m | | 3/18 | Australia | Adelaide | 1963-64 |
| | | 137 | 272m | 236 | -/18 | England | Port Elizabeth | 1964-65 |
| | | 125 | 140m | 145 | -/21 | England | Nottingham | 1965 |
| | | 209 | 361m | | -/30 | Australia | Cape Town | 1966-67 |
| | | 105 | 179m | | 1/13 | Australia | Port Elizabeth | 1966-67 |
| | | 274 | 417m | 401 | -/43 | Australia | Durban[2] | 1969-70 |
| Rhodes,JN | | 101* § | 255m | 202 | 1/14 | Sri Lanka | Moratuwa | 1993-94 |
| | | 117 | 298m | 200 | -/14 | England | Lord's | 1998 |
| Richards,BA | (2) | 140 | 181m | 164 | 1/20 | Australia | Durban[2] | 1969-70 |
| | | 126 | 236m | 212 | 3/16 | Australia | Port Elizabeth | 1969-70 |
| Richardson,DJ | | 109 | 302m | 206 | -/7 | New Zealand | Cape Town | 1994-95 |
| Rowan,EAB | (3) | 156* | 368m | | -/18 | England | Johannesburg[2] | 1948-49 |
| | | 143 | 388m | 369 | -/14 | Australia | Durban[2] | 1949-50 |
| | | 236 | 550m | | -/28 | England | Leeds | 1951 |
| Sherwell,PW | | 115 | 105m | | -/18 | England | Lord's | 1907 |
| Siedle,IJ | | 141 | 297m | | -/13 | England | Cape Town | 1930-31 |
| Sinclair,JH | (3) | 106 | 142m | | 1!/9 | England | Cape Town | 1898-99 |
| | | 101 | 125m | | 2!/14 | Australia | Johannesburg[1] | 1902-03 |
| | | 104 | 83m | | 6!/18 | Australia | Cape Town | 1902-03 |
| Snooke,SJ | | 103 | 215m | | | Australia | Adelaide | 1910-11 |
| Symcox,PL | | 108 | 226m | 157 | -/17 | Pakistan | Johannesburg[3] | 1997-98 |
| Taylor,HW | (7) | 109 | 198m | | 1/11 | England | Durban[1] | 1913-14 |
| | | 176 | 308m | | -/25 | England | Johannesburg[1] | 1922-23 |
| | | 101 | 225h | | 1/11 | England | Johannesburg[1] | 1922-23 |
| | | 102 | 270m | | 1/6 | England | Durban[2] | 1922-23 |
| | | 101 | 145m | | -/9 | England | Johannesburg[1] | 1927-28 |
| | | 121 | 220m | | -/12 | England | The Oval | 1929 |
| | | 117 | 167m | | -/15 | England | Cape Town | 1930-31 |
| Van der Bijl,PGV | | 125 | 438m | 458 | 1/11 | England | Durban[2] | 1938-39 |
| Viljoen,KG | (2) | 111 | 210m | | 1/9 | Australia | Melbourne | 1931-32 |
| | | 124 | 280m | | -/10 | England | Manchester | 1935 |
| Wade,WW | | 125 | 290m | | -/12 | England | Port Elizabeth | 1948-49 |

| | | | | | | | | |
|---|---|---|---|---|---|---|---|---|
| Waite,JHB | (4) | 113 | 340m | | -/12 | England | Manchester | 1955 |
| | | 115 | 305m | | -/11 | Australia | Johannesburg[3] | 1957-58 |
| | | 134 | 513m | | -/6 | Australia | Durban[2] | 1957-58 |
| | | 101 | 206m | | -/13 | New Zealand | Johannesburg[3] | 1961-62 |
| Wessels,KC | (2) | 118 § | 372m | 264 | -/18 | India | Durban[2] | 1992-93 |
| | | 105 § | 298m | 217 | -/15 | England | Lord' | 1994 |
| White,GC | (2) | 147 | >240h | | 2/19 | England | Johannesburg[1] | 1905-06 |
| | | 118 | 240h | | 1/10 | England | Durban[1] | 1909-10 |
| Winslow,PL | | 108 | 190m | | 3/13 | England | Manchester | 1955 |
| Zulch,JW | (2) | 105 | 184m | | -/9 | Australia | Adelaide | 1910-11 |
| | | 150 | 298m | | -/15 | Australia | Sydney | 1910-11 |
| **WEST INDIES** (330) | | | Time | Balls | 6/4 | Opponents | | |
| Adams,JC | (5) | 137 | 414m | 262 | -/21 | England | Georgetown | 1993-94 |
| | | 125* | 406m | 312 | -/14 | India | Nagpur | 1994-95 |
| | | 174* | 451m | 371 | -/19 | India | Mohali | 1994-95 |
| | | 151 | 308m | 226 | -/24 | New Zealand | Wellington | 1994-95 |
| | | 208* | 433m | 333 | 1/31 | New Zealand | St John's | 1995-96 |
| Alexander,FCM | | 108 | 212m | 186 | 1/9 | Australia | Sydney | 1960-61 |
| Arthurton,KLT | (2) | 157* § | 447m | 343 | 1/16 | Australia | Brisbane[2] | 1992-93 |
| | | 126 | 323m | 232 | 2/11 | England | Kingston | 1993-94 |
| Atkinson,DS | | 219 | 411m | | 1/29 | Australia | Bridgetown | 1954-55 |
| Bacchus,SFAF | | 250 | 512m | 375 | -/33 | India | Kanpur | 1978-79 |
| Baichan,L | | 105* § | 373m | | -/5 | Pakistan | Lahore[2] | 1974-75 |
| Barrow,I | | 105 | 235m | | -/9 | England | Manchester | 1933 |
| Best,CA | | 164 | 423m | 245 | -/19 | England | Bridgetown | 1989-90 |
| Butcher,BF | (7) | 103 | †180h | | -/15 | India | Calcutta | 1958-59 |
| | | 142 | 335m | | -/10 | India | Madras[2] | 1958-59 |
| | | 133 | 244m | 261 | 2/17 | England | Lord's | 1963 |
| | | 117 | 210m | | 1/10 | Australia | Port-of-Spain | 1964-65 |
| | | 209* | 461m | | -/22 | England | Nottingham | 1966 |
| | | 101 | 249m | 134 | -/14 | Australia | Sydney | 1968-69 |
| | | 118 | 191m | | -/18 | Australia | Adelaide | 1968-69 |
| Campbell,SL | (2) | 208 | 675m | 496 | -/29 | New Zealand | Bridgetown | 1995-96 |
| | | 113 | 407m | 327 | -/9 | Australia | Brisbane[2] | 1996-97 |
| Carew,GM | | 107 | 162m | | -/16 | England | Port-of-Spain | 1947-48 |
| Carew,MC | | 109 § | 318m | | -/12 | New Zealand | Auckland | 1968-69 |
| Chanderpaul,S | (2) | 137* | 442m | 272 | -/13 | India | Bridgetown | 1996-97 |
| | | 118 | 385m | 263 | 1/15 | England | Georgetown | 1997-98 |
| Christiani,RJ | | 107 § | 194m | | -/9 | India | Delhi | 1948-49 |
| Davis,CA | (4) | 103 | 372m | | -/6 | England | Lord's | 1969 |
| | | 125* | n300h | | -/15 | India | Georgetown | 1970-71 |
| | | 105 | 330h | | | India | Port-of-Spain | 1970-71 |
| | | 183 | 602m | | -/21 | New Zealand | Bridgetown | 1971-72 |
| Depeiza,CC | | 122 | 330m | | -/16 | Australia | Bridgetown | 1954-55 |
| Dujon,PJL | (5) | 110 | 239m | | -/14 | India | St John's | 1982-83 |
| | | 130 | 262m | 187 | 2/15 | Australia | Port-of-Spain | 1983-84 |
| | | 101 | 247m | 228 | -/12 | England | Manchester | 1984 |
| | | 139 | 240m | 158 | -/21 | Australia | Perth | 1984-85 |
| | | 106* | 316m | 175 | -/13 | Pakistan | Port-of-Spain | 1987-88 |
| Foster,MLC | | 125 § | 232m | | -/16 | Australia | Kingston | 1972-73 |
| Fredericks,RC | (8) | 163 | 408m | | -/20 | New Zealand | Kingston | 1971-72 |
| | | 150 | 510m | | -/17 | England | Birmingham | 1973 |
| | | 100 | 212m | | -/13 | India | Calcutta | 1974-75 |
| | | 104 | 215m | | -/17 | India | Bombay[3] | 1974-75 |
| | | 169 | 212m | 145 | 1/27 | Australia | Perth | 1975-76 |
| | | 138 | 282m | 253 | 1/14 | England | Lord's | 1976 |
| | | 109 | 156m | 124 | -/18 | England | Leeds | 1976 |
| | | 120 | 380m | | -/12 | Pakistan | Port-of-Spain | 1976-77 |
| Ganteaume,AG | | 112 § | 300m | | -/13 | England | Port-of-Spain | 1947-48 |

| | | | | | | | | |
|---|---|---|---|---|---|---|---|---|
| Gomes,HA | (9) | 101 § | 205m | | -/11 | Australia | Georgetown | 1977-78 |
| | | 115 | 343m | 269 | -/11 | Australia | Kingston | 1977-78 |
| | | 126* | 344m | 252 | -/11 | Australia | Sydney | 1981-82 |
| | | 124* | 402m | 273 | -/9 | Australia | Adelaide | 1981-82 |
| | | 123 | 446m | 333 | -/12 | India | Port-of-Spain | 1982-83 |
| | | 143 | 380m | 279 | -/16 | England | Birmingham | 1984 |
| | | 104* | 314m | 197 | -/14 | England | Leeds | 1984 |
| | | 127 | 472m | 297 | -/9 | Australia | Perth | 1984-85 |
| | | 120* | 304m | 217 | -/10 | Australia | Adelaide | 1984-85 |
| Gomez,GE | | 101 § | 255m | | -/7 | India | Delhi | 1948-49 |
| Greenidge,CG | (19) | 107 § | 260m | 208 | 2/14 | India | Bangalore | 1974-75 |
| | | 134) | 250m | 198 | -/18 | England | Manchester | 1976 |
| | | 101) | 245m | 155 | -/13 | | | |
| | | 115 | 214m | 147 | 2/14 | England | Leeds | 1976 |
| | | 100 | †210h | | 3/15 | Pakistan | Kingston | 1976-77 |
| | | 154* | 248m | | 1/14 | India | St John's | 1982-83 |
| | | 194 | 552m | 368 | -/23 | India | Kanpur | 1983-84 |
| | | 120* | 270m | 189 | 3/10 | Australia | Georgetown | 1983-84 |
| | | 127 | 286m | 193 | -/17 | Australia | Kingston | 1983-84 |
| | | 214* | 300m | 241 | -/29 | England | Lord's | 1984 |
| | | 223 | 598m | 425 | -/30 | England | Manchester | 1984 |
| | | 100 | 316m | 235 | -/12 | New Zealand | Port-of-Spain | 1984-85 |
| | | 213 | 534m | 381 | 7/20 | New Zealand | Auckland | 1986-87 |
| | | 141 | 362m | 265 | 4/14 | India | Calcutta | 1987-88 |
| | | 103 | 246m | 192 | -/14 | England | Lord's | 1988 |
| | | 104 | 294m | 249 | -/8 | Australia | Adelaide | 1988-89 |
| | | 117 | 236m | 182 | 1/11 | India | Bridgetown | 1988-89 |
| | | 149 | 380m | 207 | 3/18 | England | St John's | 1989-90 |
| | | (In his 100th Test match) | | | | | | |
| | | 226 | 677m | 480 | 3/11 | Australia | Bridgetown | 1990-91 |
| Haynes,DL | (18) | 105 § | 435m | 323 | -/16 | New Zealand | Dunedin | 1979-80 |
| | | 122 | 263m | 199 | 3/17 | New Zealand | Christchurch | 1979-80 |
| | | 184 | 490m | 395 | 1/27 | England | Lord's | 1980 |
| | | 136 | 372m | | 1/10 | India | St John's | 1982-83 |
| | | 103* | 270m | 184 | -/9 | Australia | Georgetown | 1983-84 |
| | | 145 | 383m | 222 | 1/19 | Australia | Bridgetown | 1983-84 |
| | | 125 | 436m | 269 | -/17 | England | The Oval | 1984 |
| | | 131 | 472m | 283 | -/14 | England | St John's | 1985-86 |
| | | 121 | 311m | 269 | -/20 | New Zealand | Wellington | 1986-87 |
| | | 100 | 243m | 176 | -/12 | Australia | Perth | 1988-89 |
| | | 143 | 316m | 272 | -/16 | Australia | Sydney | 1988-89 |
| | | 112* | 177m | 128 | 3/11 | India | Bridgetown | 1988-89 |
| | | 109 | 303m | 176 | -/10 | England | Bridgetown | 1989-90 |
| | | 167 | 533m | 317 | 1/24 | England | St John's | 1989-90 |
| | | 117 | 351m | 204 | -/8 | Pakistan | Karachi[1] | 1990-91 |
| | | 111 | 318m | 223 | -/17 | Australia | Georgetown | 1990-91 |
| | | 143* | 406m | 289 | -/20 | Pakistan | Port-of-Spain | 1992-93 |
| | | 125 | 351m | 206 | 1/14 | Pakistan | Bridgetown | 1992-93 |
| Headley,GA | (10) | 176 § | 390h | | -/16 | England | Bridgetown | 1929-30 |
| | | 114) | 200m | | -/10 | England | Georgetown | 1929-30 |
| | | 112) | 257m | | 1/12 | | | |
| | | 223 | 390h | | -/28 | England | Kingston | 1929-30 |
| | | 102* | 247m | | -/10 | Australia | Brisbane[1] | 1930-31 |
| | | 105 | 146m | | -/13 | Australia | Sydney | 1930-31 |
| | | 169* | 375h | | -/18 | England | Manchester | 1933 |
| | | 270* | 493m | | -/30 | England | Kingston | 1934-35 |
| | | 106) | 250m | | -/13 | England | Lord's | 1939 |
| | | 107) | 230m | | -/8 | | | |
| Holford,DAJ | | 105* | 320m | | -/6 | England | Lord's | 1966 |
| Holt,JK | (2) | 166 | 284m | | 1/26 | England | Bridgetown | 1953-54 |

| | | | | | | | | |
|---|---|---|---|---|---|---|---|---|
| | | 123 | 255m | | -/17 | India | Delhi | 1958-59 |
| Hooper,CL | (9) | 100* | 277m | 171 | 3/7 | India | Calcutta | 1987-88 |
| | | 134 | 315m | 226 | 2/11 | Pakistan | Lahore[2] | 1990-91 |
| | | 111 | 282m | 202 | 1/14 | England | Lord's | 1991 |
| | | 178* | 297m | 248 | 4/19 | Pakistan | St John's | 1992-93 |
| | | 127 | 285m | 180 | 2/14 | England | The Oval | 1995 |
| | | 102 | 306m | 228 | 1/10 | Australia | Brisbane[2] | 1996-97 |
| | | 129 | 275m | 212 | -/17 | India | Kingston | 1996-97 |
| | | 106 | 135m | 90 | 4/14 | Pakistan | Karachi[1] | 1997-98 |
| | | 108* | 216m | 150 | -/17 | England | St John's | 1997-98 |
| Hunte,CC | (8) | 142 § | 300h | | -/17 | Pakistan | Bridgetown | 1957-58 |
| | | 260 | 506m | | 1/28 | Pakistan | Kingston | 1957-58 |
| | | 114 | 253m | | -/9 | Pakistan | Georgetown | 1957-58 |
| | | 110 | 270m | | -/9 | Australia | Melbourne | 1960-61 |
| | | 182 | 500m | | -/27 | England | Manchester | 1963 |
| | | 108* | 300h | | | England | The Oval | 1963 |
| | | 135 | 300h | | -/19 | England | Manchester | 1966 |
| | | 101 | 285m | | -/16 | India | Bombay[2] | 1966-67 |
| Julien,BD | (2) | 121 | 171m | | 2/18 | England | Lord's | 1973 |
| | | 101 | 192m | | -/12 | Pakistan | Karachi[1] | 1974-75 |
| Kallicharran,AI | (12) | 100* § | 258m | | 1/7 | New Zealand | Georgetown | 1971-72 |
| | | 101 | 179m | | 1/13 | New Zealand | Port-of-Spain | 1971-72 |
| | | 158 | 369m | 334 | -/18 | England | Port-of-Spain | 1973-74 |
| | | 119 | 251m | 191 | -/18 | England | Bridgetown | 1973-74 |
| | | 124 § | 281m | 226 | 2/15 | India | Bangalore | 1974-75 |
| | | 115 | | | 1/18 | Pakistan | Karachi[1] | 1974-75 |
| | | 101 | 267m | 207 | -/13 | Australia | Brisbane[2] | 1975-76 |
| | | 103* | 257m | | -/8 | India | Port-of-Spain | 1975-76 |
| | | 127 | 256m | | -/17 | Australia | Port-of-Spain | 1977-78 |
| | | 126 | 263m | 260 | 1/18 | Australia | Kingston | 1977-78 |
| | | 187 | 396m | | -/26 | India | Bombay[3] | 1978-79 |
| | | 106 | 221m | 176 | -/14 | Australia | Adelaide | 1979-80 |
| Kanhai,RB | (15) | 256 | 400m | | -/42 | India | Calcutta | 1958-59 |
| | | 217 | 420h | | -/32 | Pakistan | Lahore[1] | 1958-59 |
| | | 110 | 378m | | 1/19 | England | Port-of-Spain | 1959-60 |
| | | 117) | 149m | | 2/14 | Australia | Adelaide | 1960-61 |
| | | 115) | 222m | | -/12 | | | |
| | | 138 | 298m | | -/19 | India | Kingston | 1961-62 |
| | | 139 | | | 2/11 | India | Port-of-Spain | 1961-62 |
| | | 129 | 372m | | -/17 | Australia | Bridgetown | 1964-65 |
| | | 121 | 182m | | 2/12 | Australia | Port-of-Spain | 1964-65 |
| | | 104 | 215m | | -/14 | England | The Oval | 1966 |
| | | 153 | 300m | | 1/19 | England | Port-of-Spain | 1967-68 |
| | | 150 | 412m | 301 | -/21 | England | Georgetown | 1967-68 |
| | | 158* | 390h | | -/17 | India | Kingston | 1970-71 |
| | | 105 | 305m | | -/11 | Australia | Bridgetown | 1972-73 |
| | | 157 | 340m | | -/21 | England | Lord's | 1973 |
| King,CL | | 100* | 129m | 109 | 4/10 | New Zealand | Christchurch | 1979-80 |
| Lambert,CB | | 104 | 364m | 232 | 1/10 | England | St John's | 1997-98 |
| Lara,BC | (10) | 277 | 474m | 372 | -/38 | Australia | Sydney | 1992-93 |
| | | 167 | 256m | 210 | 2/25 | England | Georgetown | 1993-94 |
| | | 375 | 766m | 538 | -/45 | England | St John's | 1993-94 |
| | | 147 | 247m | 181 | -/23 | New Zealand | Wellington | 1994-95 |
| | | 145 | 281m | 216 | -/16 | England | Manchester | 1995 |
| | | 152 | 253m | 182 | -/28 | England | Nottingham | 1995 |
| | | 179 | 267m | 206 | 1/26 | England | The Oval | 1995 |
| | | 132 | 223m | 185 | 1/22 | Australia | Perth | 1996-97 |
| | | 103 | 215m | 175 | 1/11 | India | St John's | 1996-97 |
| | | 115 | 266m | 207 | 1/11 | Sri Lanka | Kingstown | 1996-97 |
| Lloyd,CH | (19) | 118 § | 273m | | 1/17 | England | Port-of-Spain | 1967-68 |

| | | | | | | | | |
|---|---|---|---|---|---|---|---|---|
| | | 113* | 178m | | 2/14 | England | Bridgetown | 1967-68 |
| | | 129 § | 208m | | 1/18 | Australia | Brisbane[2] | 1968-69 |
| | | 178 | 358m | | 1/24 | Australia | Georgetown | 1972-73 |
| | | 132 | a240h | | 2/15 | England | The Oval | 1973 |
| | | 163 | 205m | 149 | 2/22 | India | Bangalore | 1974-75 |
| | | 242* | 429m | | 4/19 | India | Bombay[3] | 1974-75 |
| | | 149 | 218m | 186 | 1/22 | Australia | Perth | 1975-76 |
| | | 102 | 206m | 121 | -/14 | Australia | Melbourne | 1975-76 |
| | | 102 | 175m | | 2/12 | India | Bridgetown | 1975-76 |
| | | 157 | 290m | | 3/21 | Pakistan | Bridgetown | 1976-77 |
| | | 121 | 187m | 156 | -/17 | Australia | Adelaide | 1979-80 |
| | | 101 | 205m | 159 | -/11 | England | Manchester | 1980 |
| | | 100 | 238m | | -/17 | England | Bridgetown | 1980-81 |
| | | 143 | 310mm | | 2/13 | India | Port-of-Spain | 1982-83 |
| | | 106 | 218m | | 1/11 | India | St John's | 1982-83 |
| | | 103 | 320m | | -/7 | India | Delhi | 1983-84 |
| | | 161* | 496m | | -/12 | India | Calcutta | 1983-84 |
| | | 114 | 208m | 154 | 3/14 | Australia | Brisbane[2] | 1984-85 |
| Logie,AL | (2) | 130 | 273m | | 2/12 | India | Bridgetown | 1982-83 |
| | | 101 | 188m | 136 | -/15 | India | Calcutta | 1987-88 |
| McMorris,EDAS | | 125 § | 342m | | -/11 | India | Kingston | 1961-62 |
| Martin,FR | | 123* | 347m | | -/11 | Australia | Sydney | 1930-31 |
| Murray,JR | | 101* | 114m | 88 | 2/11 | New Zealand | Wellington | 1994-95 |
| Nurse,SM | (6) | 201 | 382m | | -/30 | Australia | Bridgetown | 1964-65 |
| | | 137 | 345m | | 2/14 | England | Leeds | 1966 |
| | | 136 | 331m | | -/12 | England | Port-of-Spain | 1967-68 |
| | | 137 | 200m | | 1/18 | Australia | Sydney | 1968-69 |
| | | 168 § | 215m | | 2/22 | New Zealand | Auckland | 1968-69 |
| | | 258 | 476m | | 1/35 | New Zealand | Christchurch | 1968-69 |
| Pairaudeau,BH | | 115 § | 272m | | -/16 | India | Port-of-Spain | 1952-53 |
| Rae,AF | (4) | 104 | 255m | | -/11 | India | Bombay[2] | 1948-49 |
| | | 109 | 230m | | 3/5 | India | Madras[1] | 1948-49 |
| | | 106 | 280m | | -/15 | England | Lord's | 1950 |
| | | 109 | 300h | | | England | The Oval | 1950 |
| Richards,IVA | (24) | 192* | 319m | 297 | 6/20 | India | Delhi | 1974-75 |
| | | 101 | 182m | 136 | -/17 | Australia | Adelaide | 1975-76 |
| | | 142 | 242m | | 1/10 | India | Bridgetown | 1975-76 |
| | | 130 | 290m | 203 | -/21 | India | Port-of-Spain | 1975-76 |
| | | 177 | 343m | 296 | 2/23 | India | Port-of-Spain | 1975-76 |
| | | 232 § | 438m | 313 | 4/31 | England | Nottingham | 1976 |
| | | 135 | 288m | 261 | -/18 | England | Manchester | 1976 |
| | | 291 | 472m | 386 | -/38 | England | The Oval | 1976 |
| | | 140 | 329m | 259 | -/20 | Australia | Brisbane[2] | 1979-80 |
| | | 145 | 196m | 159 | 1/25 | England | Lord's | 1980 |
| | | 120 | 417m | 263 | -/15 | Pakistan | Multan | 1980-81 |
| | | 182* | 383m | | 2/23 | England | Bridgetown | 1980-81 |
| | | 114 | 305m | | 1/21 | England | St John's | 1980-81 |
| | | 109 | 258m | | 2/9 | India | Georgetown | 1982-83 |
| | | 120 | 267m | | 1/13 | India | Bombay[3] | 1983-84 |
| | | 178 | 377m | 229 | -/30 | Australia | St John's | 1983-84 |
| | | 117 | 204m | 154 | 1/17 | England | Birmingham | 1984 |
| | | 208 | 376m | 245 | 3/22 | Australia | Melbourne | 1984-85 |
| | | 105 | 192m | 147 | 3/13 | New Zealand | Bridgetown | 1984-85 |
| | | 110* | 87m | 58 | 7/7 | England | St John's | 1985-86 |
| | | 109* | 179m | 114 | -/13 | India | Delhi | 1987-88 |
| | | 123 | 302m | 169 | -/13 | Pakistan | Port-of-Spain | 1987-88 |
| | | 146 | 195m | 150 | 3/21 | Australia | Perth | 1988-89 |
| | | 110 | 304m | 178 | 1/13 | India | Kingston | 1988-89 |
| Richardson,RB | (16) | 131* | 481m | 313 | -/17 | Australia | Bridgetown | 1983-84 |
| | | 154 | 468m | 326 | 1/21 | Australia | St John's | 1983-84 |

| | | | | | | | | |
|---|---|---|---|---|---|---|---|---|
| | | 138 | 331m | 232 | -/24 | Australia | Brisbane[2] | 1984-85 |
| | | 185 | 455m | 346 | -/26 | New Zealand | Georgetown | 1984-85 |
| | | 102 | 176m | 140 | 1/19 | England | Port-of-Spain | 1985-86 |
| | | 160 | 348m | 278 | -/18 | England | Bridgetown | 1985-86 |
| | | 122 | 286m | 194 | -/12 | Australia | Melbourne | 1988-89 |
| | | 106 | 194m | 160 | -/16 | Australia | Adelaide | 1988-89 |
| | | 194 | 459m | 367 | -/20 | India | Georgetown | 1988-89 |
| | | 156 | 482m | 314 | -/20 | India | Kingston | 1988-89 |
| | | 104* | 315m | 240 | -/15 | Australia | Kingston | 1990-91 |
| | | 182 | 344m | 259 | 2/26 | Australia | Georgetown | 1990-91 |
| | | 104 | 273m | 229 | -/13 | England | Birmingham | 1991 |
| | | 121 | 458m | 312 | 1/11 | England | The Oval | 1991 |
| | | 109 | 330m | 253 | -/11 | Australia | Sydney | 1992-93 |
| | | 100 | 344m | 223 | 1/12 | Australia | Kingston | 1994-95 |
| Roach,CA | (2) | 122 | 165m | | -/20 | England | Bridgetown | 1929-30 |
| | | 209 | 303m | | 3/22 | England | Georgetown | 1929-30 |
| Rowe,LG | (7) | 214 § ) | 427m | | 1/19 | New Zealand | Kingston | 1971-72 |
| | | 100* §) | 153m | | -/13 | | | |
| | | 120 | 303m | 258 | 1/17 | England | Kingston | 1973-74 |
| | | 302 | 612m | 430 | 1/36 | England | Bridgetown | 1973-74 |
| | | 123 | 437m | 340 | 1/10 | England | Port-of-Spain | 1973-74 |
| | | 107 | 267m | 235 | -/14 | Australia | Brisbane[2] | 1975-76 |
| | | 100 | 186m | 165 | 1/10 | New Zealand | Christchurch | 1979-80 |
| Samuels,RG | | 125 | 329m | 219 | 3/15 | New Zealand | St John's | 1995-96 |
| Shillingford,IT | | 120 | 345m | | 1/15 | Pakistan | Georgetown | 1976-77 |
| Simmons,PV | | 110 | 253m | 178 | 2/8 | Australia | Melbourne | 1992-93 |
| Smith,OG | (4) | 104 § | 218m | | -/14 | Australia | Kingston | 1954-55 |
| | | 161 § | 412m | | 1/18 | England | Birmingham | 1957 |
| | | 168 | 416m | | 3/10 | England | Nottingham | 1957 |
| | | 100 | <180h | | 2/10 | India | Delhi | 1958-59 |
| Sobers,GS | (26) | 365* | 614m | | -/38 | Pakistan | Kingston | 1957-58 |
| | | 125 ) | 260m | | -/15 | Pakistan | Georgetown | 1957-58 |
| | | 109*) | | | -/9 | | | |
| | | 142* § | 365m | | 1/8 | India | Bombay[2] | 1958-59 |
| | | 198 | 340m | | -/28 | India | Kanpur | 1958-59 |
| | | 106* | a195h | | -/11 | India | Calcutta | 1958-59 |
| | | 226 | 647m | | -/24 | England | Bridgetown | 1959-60 |
| | | 147 | 371m | | -/17 | England | Kingston | 1959-60 |
| | | 145 | 420h | | 1/18 | England | Georgetown | 1959-60 |
| | | 132 | 174m | | -/21 | Australia | Brisbane[2] | 1960-61 |
| | | 168 | 270m | 224 | 1/25 | Australia | Sydney | 1960-61 |
| | | 153 | 280m | | 4/11 | India | Kingston | 1961-62 |
| | | 104 | | | 2/13 | India | Kingston | 1961-62 |
| | | 102 | 251m | | -/14 | England | Leeds | 1963 |
| | | 161 | 248m | | 1/26 | England | Manchester | 1966 |
| | | 163* | 330m | | -/13 | England | Lord's | 1966 |
| | | 174 | 243m | | -/24 | England | Leeds | 1966 |
| | | 113* | 357m | | 1/14 | England | Kingston | 1967-68 |
| | | 152 | 440m | 362 | -/18 | England | Georgetown | 1967-68 |
| | | 110 | 134m | | 2/15 | Australia | Adelaide | 1968-69 |
| | | 113 | 144m | 126 | -/20 | Australia | Sydney | 1968-69 |
| | | 108* | 150m | | 2/14 | India | Georgetown | 1970-71 |
| | | 178 | 329m | | 1/19 | India | Bridgetown | 1970-71 |
| | | 132 | | | | India | Port-of-Spain | 1970-71 |
| | | 142 | 363m | | -/18 | New Zealand | Bridgetown | 1971-72 |
| | | 150* | 288m | 227 | -/19 | England | Lord's | 1973 |
| Solomon,JS | | 100* | 281m | | -/9 | India | Delhi | 1958-59 |
| Stollmeyer,JB | (4) | 160 | 308m | | -/12 | India | Madras[1] | 1948-49 |
| | | 104 | 242m | | -/6 | Australia | Sydney | 1951-52 |
| | | 152 | 326m | | -/14 | New Zealand | Auckland | 1951-52 |

| | | | | | | | | |
|---|---|---|---|---|---|---|---|---|
| | | 104* | 163m | | | India | Port-of-Spain | 1952-53 |
| Walcott,CL | (15) | 152 § | 259m | | -/12 | India | Delhi | 1948-49 |
| | | 108 | 164m | | 2/11 | India | Calcutta | 1948-49 |
| | | 168* | 285m | | -/24 | England | Lord's | 1950 |
| | | 115 | 168m | | -/13 | New Zealand | Auckland | 1951-52 |
| | | 125 | 255m | | 1/15 | India | Georgetown | 1952-53 |
| | | 118 | 241m | | -/11 | India | Kingston | 1952-53 |
| | | 220 | 428m | | 1/28 | England | Bridgetown | 1953-54 |
| | | 124 | 211m | | 1/18 | England | Port-of-Spain | 1953-54 |
| | | 116 | 262m | | -/20 | England | Kingston | 1953-54 |
| | | 108 | 208m | | -/14 | Australia | Kingston | 1954-55 |
| | | 126) | 267m | | -/14 | Australia | Port-of-Spain | 1954-55 |
| | | 110) | 147m | | -/17 | | | |
| | | 155) | 294m | | -/23 | Australia | Kingston | 1954-55 |
| | | 110) | 196m | | -/14 | | | |
| | | 145 | 273m | | -/19 | Pakistan | Georgetown | 1957-58 |
| Weekes,ED | (15) | 141 | 232m | | -/15 | England | Kingston | 1947-48 |
| | | 128 § | 194m | | -/16 | India | Delhi | 1948-49 |
| | | 194 | 368m | | -/18 | India | Bombay[2] | 1948-49 |
| | | 162) | 199m | | -/24 | India | Calcutta | 1948-49 |
| | | 101) | 187m | | -/5 | | | |
| | | 129 | 220m | | -/17 | England | Nottingham | 1950 |
| | | 207 | 431m | | -/20 | India | Port-of-Spain | 1952-53 |
| | | 161 | 338m | | -/22 | India | Port-of-Spain | 1952-53 |
| | | 109 | 173m | | -/13 | India | Kingston | 1952-53 |
| | | 206 | 354m | | -/25 | England | Port-of-Spain | 1953-54 |
| | | 139 | 210m | | 1/24 | Australia | Port-of-Spain | 1954-55 |
| | | 123 | 148m | | -/17 | New Zealand | Dunedin | 1955-56 |
| | | 103 | 142m | | -/16 | New Zealand | Christchurch | 1955-56 |
| | | 156 | 211m | | -/19 | New Zealand | Wellington | 1955-56 |
| | | 197 § | 330m | | -/18 | Pakistan | Bridgetown | 1957-58 |
| Weekes,KH | | 137 | 135m | | 1/18 | England | The Oval | 1939 |
| Williams,AB | (2) | 100 § | 169m | 118 | -/19 | Australia | Georgetown | 1977-78 |
| | | 111 | 214m | | -/11 | India | Calcutta | 1978-79 |
| Williams,SC | | 128 | 452m | 299 | 1/11 | India | Port-of-Spain | 1996-97 |
| Worrell,FMM | (9) | 131* | 215m | | -/14 | England | Georgetown | 1947-48 |
| | | 261 | 335m | | 2/35 | England | Nottingham | 1950 |
| | | 138 | 305m | | -/17 | England | The Oval | 1950 |
| | | 108 | 247m | | -/7 | Australia | Melbourne | 1951-52 |
| | | 100 | 151m | | -/13 | New Zealand | Auckland | 1951-52 |
| | | 237 | 569m | | -/35 | India | Kingston | 1952-53 |
| | | 167 | 438m | | -/23 | England | Port-of-Spain | 1953-54 |
| | | 191* | 575m | | -/26 | England | Nottingham | 1957 |
| | | 197* | 682m | | 2/17 | England | Bridgetown | 1959-60 |

| **NEW ZEALAND** (149) | | | Time | Balls | 6/4 | Opponents | | |
|---|---|---|---|---|---|---|---|---|
| Astle,NJ | (4) | 125 | 214m | 154 | 2/22 | West Indies | Bridgetown | 1995-96 |
| | | 103 | 217m | 165 | 1/12 | West Indies | St John's | 1995-96 |
| | | 102* § | 278m | 214 | -/13 | England | Aucklamd | 1996-97 |
| | | 114 | | 192 | -/16 | Zimbabwe | Auckland | 1997-98 |
| Barton,PT | | 109 | 276m | | -/20 | South Africa | Port Elizabeth | 1961-62 |
| Bracewell,JG | | 110 | 270m | 200 | -/10 | England | Nottingham | 1986 |
| Burgess,MG | (5) | 119* | 255m | | -/12 | Pakistan | Dacca | 1969-70 |
| | | 104 | 237m | 176 | 1/12 | England | Auckland | 1970-71 |
| | | 101 | 185m | | 1/15 | West Indies | Kingston | 1971-72 |
| | | 105 | 228m | | -/12 | England | Lord's | 1973 |
| | | 111 | 254m | | -/9 | Pakistan | Lahore[2] | 1976-77 |
| Cairns,CL | | 120 | 122m | 96 | 9/10 | Zimbabwe | Auckland | 1995-96 |
| Coney,JV | (3) | 174* | 488m | 374 | 1/26 | England | Wellington | 1983-84 |
| | | 111* | 385m | 243 | -/12 | Pakistan | Dunedin | 1984-85 |

| | | | | | | | | |
|---|---|---|---|---|---|---|---|---|
| | | 101* | 282m | 192 | -/14 | Australia | Wellington | 1985-86 |
| Congdon,BE | (7) | 104 | 320m | | -/7 | England | Christchurch | 1965-66 |
| | | 166* | 527m | | 1/14 | West Indies | Port-of-Spain | 1971-72 |
| | | 126 | 258m | | -/11 | West Indies | Bridgetown | 1971-72 |
| | | 176 | 409m | | -/19 | England | Nottingham | 1973 |
| | | 175 | 515m | | -/12 | England | Lord's | 1973 |
| | | 132 | 390m | 360 | -/14 | Australia | Wellington | 1973-74 |
| | | 107* | 297m | 251 | -/11 | Australia | Christchurch | 1976-77 |
| Crowe,JJ | (3) | 128 | 384m | 285 | -/20 | England | Auckland | 1983-84 |
| | | 112 | 286m | 207 | 1/10 | West Indies | Kingston | 1984-85 |
| | | 120* | 609m | 397 | -/13 | Sri Lanka | Colombo (CCC) | 1986-87 |
| Crowe,MD | (17) | 100 | 276m | 247 | -/19 | England | Wellington | 1983-84 |
| | | 188 | 571m | 462 | 1/26 | West Indies | Georgetown | 1984-85 |
| | | 188 | 472m | 328 | -/26 | Australia | Brisbane[2] | 1985-86 |
| | | 137 | 283m | 226 | -/21 | Australia | Christchurch | 1985-86 |
| | | 106 | 339m | 247 | -/11 | England | Lord's | 1986 |
| | | 119 | 381m | 308 | -/15 | West Indies | Wellington | 1986-87 |
| | | 104 | 382m | 264 | 1/8 | West Indies | Auckland | 1986-87 |
| | | 137 | 234m | 184 | 1/17 | Australia | Adelaide | 1987-88 |
| | | 143 | 402m | 333 | -/14 | England | Wellington | 1987-88 |
| | | 174 | 592m | 410 | -/16 | Pakistan | Wellington | 1988-89 |
| | | 113 | 227m | 174 | -/17 | India | Auckland | 1989-90 |
| | | 108* | 552m | 306 | 1/14 | Pakistan | Lahore[2] | 1990-91 |
| | | 299 | 610m | 523 | 3/29 | Sri Lanka | Wellington | 1990-91 |
| | | 140 | 182m | 163 | 3/17 | Zimbabwe | Harare | 1992-93 |
| | | 107 | 159m | 121 | 4/10 | Sri Lanka | Colombo (SSC) | 1992-93 |
| | | 142 | 366m | 255 | 3/20 | England | Lord's | 1994 |
| | | 115 | 333m | 237 | -/15 | England | Manchester | 1994 |
| Dempster,CS | (2) | 136 | 274m | | -/8 | England | Wellington | 1929-30 |
| | | 120 | 235m | | -/10 | England | Lord's | 1931 |
| Donnelly,MP | | 206 | 355m | | -/26 | England | Lord's | 1949 |
| Dowling,GT | (3) | 129 | 378m | | -/17 | India | Bombay[2] | 1964-65 |
| | | 143 | 343m | | 2/16 | India | Dunedin | 1967-68 |
| | | 239 | 556m | 519 | 5/28 | India | Christchurch | 1967-68 |
| Edgar,BA | (3) | 129 § | 414m | | -/14 | Pakistan | Christchurch | 1978-79 |
| | | 127 | 432m | 317 | -/7 | West Indies | Auckland | 1979-80 |
| | | 161 | 516m | 418 | -/22 | Australia | Auckland | 1981-82 |
| Fleming,SP | (2) | 127 | 367m | 253 | 1/18 | England | Auckland | 1996-97 |
| | | 176* | | 332 | 1/15 | Sri Lanka | Colombo (PIS) | 1997-98 |
| Franklin,TJ | | 101 | 432m | 310 | -/8 | England | Lord's | 1990 |
| Greatbatch,MJ | (3) | 107* § | 407m | 325 | -/12 | England | Auckland | 1987-88 |
| | | 146* § | 656m | 485 | -/17 | Australia | Perth | 1989-90 |
| | | 133 | 427m | 317 | -/16 | Pakistan | Hamilton | 1992-93 |
| Guy,J W | | 102 § | 473m | | -/13 | India | Hyderabad | 1955-56 |
| Hadlee,RJ | (2) | 103 | 114m | 92 | 2/11 | West Indies | Christchurch | 1979-80 |
| | | 151* | 407m | 243 | 2/14 | Sri Lanka | Colombo (CCC) | 1986-87 |
| Hadlee,WA | | 116 | 147m | | -/11 | England | Christchurch | 1946-47 |
| Harris,PGZ | | 101 | 266m | | 2/10 | South Africa | Cape Town | 1961-62 |
| Hastings,BF | (4) | 117* | 278m | | 2/12 | West Indies | Christchurch | 1968-69 |
| | | 105 | 273m | | -/15 | West Indies | Bridgetown | 1971-72 |
| | | 110 | 275m | | -/10 | Pakistan | Auckland | 1972-73 |
| | | 101 | 281m | 274 | -/8 | Australia | Wellington | 1973-74 |
| Horne,MJ | (2) | 133 § | 326m | 259 | 2/9 | Australia | Hobart | 1997-98 |
| | | 157 | | 260 | 4/19 | Zimbabwe | Auckland | 1997-98 |
| Howarth,GP | (6) | 122) | 515m | | -/12 | England | Auckland | 1977-78 |
| | | 102) | 320m | | -/13 | | | |
| | | 123 | 340m | | -/14 | England | Lord's | 1978 |
| | | 114 | 286m | | 1/11 | Pakistan | Napier | 1978-79 |
| | | 147 | 358m | 261 | -/13 | West Indies | Christchurch | 1979-80 |
| | | 137 § | 353m | | -/15 | India | Wellington | 1980-81 |

| | | | | | | | | |
|---|---|---|---|---|---|---|---|---|
| Jarvis,TW | | 182 | 540m | 555 | -/19 | West Indies | Georgetown | 1971-72 |
| Jones,AH | (7) | 150 | 444m | 383 | -/11 | Australia | Adelaide | 1987-88 |
| | | 170 | 634m | 448 | 2/15 | India | Auckland | 1989-90 |
| | | 186 | 562m | 454 | -/15 | Sri Lanka | Wellington | 1990-91 |
| | | 122 ) | 288m | 217 | -/8 | Sri Lanka | Hamilton | 1990-91 |
| | | 100*) | 255m | 175 | -/8 | | | |
| | | 143 | 462m | 398 | -/15 | England | Wellington | 1991-92 |
| | | 143 | 351m | 283 | -/11 | Australia | Perth | 1993-94 |
| Latham,RT | | 119 § | 282m | 214 | 1/14 | Zimbabwe | Bulawayo[1] | 1992-93 |
| Lees,WK | | 152 | 338m | | 2/21 | Pakistan | Karachi[1] | 1976-77 |
| McGregor,SN | | 111 | 340m | | -/12 | Pakistan | Lahore[1] | 1955-56 |
| McMillan,CD | (2) | 139 § | | 209 | -/18 | Zimbabwe | Wellington | 1997-98 |
| | | 142 § | | 179 | 6/13 | Sri Lanka | Colombo (PIS) | 1997-98 |
| Mills,JE | | 117 § | 258m | | -/13 | England | Wellington | 1929-30 |
| Morrison,JFM | | 117 | 261m | 246 | -/11 | Australia | Sydney | 1973-74 |
| Page,ML | | 104 | 215m | | -/15 | England | Lord's | 1931 |
| Parore,AC | | 100* § | 298m | 249 | -/9 | New Zealand | Christchurch | 1994-95 |
| Parker,JM | (3) | 108 | 258m | 233 | -/10 | Australia | Sydney | 1973-74 |
| | | 121 | 408m | 297 | -/18 | England | Auckland | 1974-75 |
| | | 104 | 289m | | -/11 | India | Bombay[3] | 1976-77 |
| Pollard,V | (2) | 116 | 437m | | -/10 | England | Nottingham | 1973 |
| | | 105* | 235m | | -/14 | England | Lord's | 1973 |
| Rabone,GO | | 107 | n360h | | -/9 | South Africa | Durban[2] | 1953-54 |
| Redmond,RE | | 107 § | 145m | | -/20 | Pakistan | Auckland | 1972-73 |
| Reid,JF | (6) | 123* | 446m | | -/11 | India | Christchurch | 1980-81 |
| | | 180 | 685m | 445 | -/16 | Sri Lanka | Colombo (CCC) | 1983-84 |
| | | 106 | 291m | 325 | -/8 | Pakistan | Hyderabad | 1984-85 |
| | | 148 | 572m | 427 | -/15 | Pakistan | Wellington | 1984-85 |
| | | 158* | 486m | 318 | -/17 | Pakistan | Auckland | 1984-85 |
| | | 108 § | 365m | 256 | -/16 | Australia | Brisbane[2] | 1985-86 |
| Reid,JR | (6) | 135 | 196m | | 2/18 | South Africa | Cape Town | 1953-54 |
| | | 119* | 210h | | 1/10 | India | Delhi | 1955-56 |
| | | 120 | 273m | | -/15 | India | Calcutta | 1955-56 |
| | | 142 | 259m | | 2/21 | South Africa | Johannesburg[3] | 1961-62 |
| | | 100 | 252m | | -/13 | England | Christchurch | 1962-63 |
| | | 128 | 268m | | 3/15 | Pakistan | Karachi[1] | 1964-65 |
| Rutherford,KR | (3) | 107* | 263m | 181 | -/12 | England | Wellington | 1987-88 |
| | | 105 | 277m | 227 | 2/13 | Sri Lanka | Moratuwa | 1992-93 |
| | | 102 | 260m | 215 | 1/9 | Australia | Christchurch | 1992-93 |
| Sinclair,BW | (3) | 138 | 346m | | -/22 | South Africa | Auckland | 1963-64 |
| | | 130 | 373m | | -/12 | Pakistan | Lahore[2] | 1964-65 |
| | | 114 | 229m | | -/11 | England | Auckland | 1965-66 |
| Smith,IDS | (2) | 113* | 239m | 182 | 2/9 | England | Auckland | 1983-84 |
| | | 173 | 237m | 136 | 3/23 | India | Auckland | 1989-90 |
| Spearman,CM | | 112 | 334m | 219 | 1/9 | Zimbabwe | Auckland | 1995-96 |
| Sutcliffe,B | (5) | 101 | 170m | | -/12 | England | Manchester | 1949 |
| | | 116 | 267m | | -/12 | England | Christchurch | 1950-51 |
| | | 137* § | 300h | | -/15 | India | Hyderabad | 1955-56 |
| | | 230* | >480h | | -/30 | India | Delhi | 1955-56 |
| | | 151* | 357m | | -/24 | India | Calcutta | 1964-65 |
| Taylor,BR | (2) | 105 § | 158m | | 3/14 | India | Calcutta | 1964-65 |
| | | 124 § | 111m | 102 | 5/14 | West Indies | Auckland | 1968-69 |
| Thomson,SA | | 120* | 233m | 167 | 2/12 | Pakistan | Christchurch | 1993-94 |
| Turner,GM | (7) | 110 § | 445m | | -/7 | Pakistan | Dacca | 1969-70 |
| | | 223* | 572m | | -/26 | West Indies | Kingston | 1971-72 |
| | | 259 | 704m | 759 | -/22 | West Indies | Georgetown | 1971-72 |
| | | 101 ) | 282m | 260 | -/9 | Australia | Christchurch | 1973-74 |
| | | 110*) | 370m | 355 | -/11 | | | |
| | | 117 | 411m | | -/9 | India | Christchurch | 1975-76 |
| | | 113 | 246m | 236 | -/14 | India | Kanpur | 1976-77 |

| | | | | | | | | |
|---|---|---|---|---|---|---|---|---|
| Vivian,HG | | 100 § | 139m | | -/14 | South Africa | Wellington | 1931-32 |
| Wright,JG | (12) | 110 | 460m | 434 | 1/10 | India | Auckland | 1980-81 |
| | | 141 | 352m | 262 | -/26 | Australia | Christchurch | 1981-82 |
| | | 130 | 387m | 297 | -/24 | England | Auckland | 1983-84 |
| | | 107 | 235m | 200 | 1/17 | Pakistan | Karachi[1] | 1984-85 |
| | | 119 | 427m | 344 | -/8 | England | The Oval | 1986 |
| | | 138 | 575m | 466 | -/14 | West Indies | Wellington | 1986-87 |
| | | 103 | 352m | 276 | -/16 | England | Auckland | 1987-88 |
| | | 185 | 553m | 443 | -/23 | India | Christchurch | 1989-90 |
| | | 113* | 278m | 208 | 1/12 | India | Napier | 1989-90 |
| | | 117* | 248m | 197 | 1/17 | Australia | Wellington | 1989-90 |
| | | 101 | 185m | 140 | -/14 | Sri Lanka | Hamilton | 1990-91 |
| | | 116 | 406m | 334 | -/15 | England | Wellington | 1991-92 |
| Young,BA | (2) | 120 | 416m | 314 | -/7 | Pakistan | Christchurch | 1993-94 |
| | | 267* | 605m | 421 | -/37 | Sri Lanka | Dunedin | 1996-97 |

| | | | Time | Balls | 6/4 | Opponents | | |
|---|---|---|---|---|---|---|---|---|
| **INDIA** (250) | | | | | | | | |
| Adhikari,HR | | 114* § | 245m | | -/10 | West Indies | Delhi | 1948-49 |
| Amarnath,M | (11) | 100 | 264m | | -/4 | Australia | Perth | 1977-78 |
| | | 101* | 288m | 223 | -/5 | West Indies | Kanpur | 1978-79 |
| | | 109* | 391m | 284 | -/15 | Pakistan | Lahore[2] | 1982-83 |
| | | 120 | 282m | 200 | 1/15 | Pakistan | Lahore[2] | 1982-83 |
| | | 103* | 236m | 188 | -/12 | Pakistan | Karachi[1] | 1982-83 |
| | | 117 | 375m | | -/14 | West Indies | Port-of-Spain | 1982-83 |
| | | 116 | 282m | | -/10 | West Indies | St John's | 1982-83 |
| | | 101* | 408m | | -/8 | Pakistan | Lahore[2] | 1984-85 |
| | | 116* | 395m | 201 | -/9 | Sri Lanka | Kandy | 1985-86 |
| | | 138 | 382m | 312 | -/10 | Australia | Sydney | 1985-86 |
| | | 131 | 454m | 301 | -/14 | Sri Lanka | Nagpur | 1986-87 |
| Amarnath,NB | | 118 § | 203m | | -/21 | England | Bombay[1] | 1933-34 |
| Amarnath,S | | 124 § | 259m | | 1/16 | New Zealand | Auckland | 1975-76 |
| Amre,PK | | 103 § | 374m | 298 | -/11 | South Africa | Durban[2] | 1992-93 |
| Apte,ML | | 163* | 584m | | | West Indies | Port-of-Spain | 1952-53 |
| Azharuddin,M | (20) | 110 § | 442m | 324 | -/10 | England | Calcutta | 1984-85 |
| | | 105 | 279m | 218 | -/18 | England | Madras[1] | 1984-85 |
| | | 122 | 374m | 270 | -/16 | England | Kanpur | 1984-85 |
| | | 199 | 500m | | 1/16 | Sri Lanka | Kanpur | 1986-87 |
| | | 141 | 400m | | -/11 | Pakistan | Calcutta | 1986-87 |
| | | 110 | 308m | 211 | -/14 | Pakistan | Jaipur | 1986-87 |
| | | 109 | 249m | 175 | -/10 | Pakistan | Faisalabad | 1989-90 |
| | | 192 | 421m | 259 | -/26 | New Zealand | Auckland | 1989-90 |
| | | 121 | 174m | 112 | -/22 | England | Lord's | 1990 |
| | | 179 | 279m | 243 | 1/21 | England | Manchester | 1990 |
| | | 106 | 185m | 162 | -/17 | Australia | Adelaide | 1991-92 |
| | | 182 | 326m | 197 | 1/26 | England | Calcutta | 1992-93 |
| | | 108 | 290m | 217 | 1/11 | Sri Lanka | Bangalore | 1993-94 |
| | | 152 | 361m | 260 | 1/16 | Sri Lanka | Ahmedabad | 1993-94 |
| | | 109 | 126m | 78 | 1/18 | South Africa | Calcutta | 1996-97 |
| | | 163* | 312m | 222 | 1/25 | South Africa | Kanpur | 1996-97 |
| | | 115 | 175m | 109 | 1/19 | South Africa | Cape Town | 1996-97 |
| | | 126 | 289m | 199 | -/11 | Sri Lanka | Colombo (PIS) | 1997-98 |
| | | 108* | 227m | 174 | -/14 | Sri Lanka | Colombo (SSC) | 1997-98 |
| | | 163* | 311m | 246 | 3/18 | Australia | Calcutta | 1997-98 |
| Baig,AA | | 112 § | 261m | | -/12 | England | Manchester | 1959 |
| Borde,CG | (5) | 109 | 255m | | -/16 | West Indies | Delhi | 1958-59 |
| | | 177* | 533 | | -/13 | Pakistan | Madras[2] | 1960-61 |
| | | 109 | 152m | | -/17 | New Zealand | Bombay[2] | 1964-65 |
| | | 121 | | | -/15 | West Indies | Bombay[2] | 1966-67 |
| | | 125 | 340m | | -/14 | West Indies | Madras[1] | 1966-67 |
| Contractor,NJ | | 108 | 397m | | -/10 | Australia | Bombay[2] | 1959-60 |

| | | | | | | | | |
|---|---|---|---|---|---|---|---|---|
| Dravid,RS | | 148 | 540m | 362 | -/21 | South Africa | Johannesburg[3] | 1996-97 |
| Durani,SA | | 104 | 194m | | -/14 | West Indies | Port-of-Spain | 1961-62 |
| Engineer,FM | (2) | 109 | 159m | | -/18 | West Indies | Madras[1] | 1966-67 |
| | | 121 | 283m | 182 | -/14 | England | Bombay[2] | 1972-73 |
| Gaekwad,AD | (2) | 102 | 357m | | -/10 | West Indies | Kanpur | 1978-79 |
| | | 201 | 671m | 436 | -/17 | Pakistan | Jullundur | 1983-84 |
| Ganguly,S | (5) | 131 § | 434m | 301 | -/20 | England | Lord's | 1996 |
| | | 136 | 361m | 268 | 2/17 | England | Nottingham | 1996 |
| | | 147 | 426m | 390 | 2/19 | Sri Lanka | Colombo (SSC) | 1997-98 |
| | | 109 | 324m | 240 | 2/10 | Sri Lanka | Mohali | 1997-98 |
| | | 173 | 516m | 361 | 2/25 | Sri Lanka | Mumbai[3] | 1997-98 |
| Gavaskar,SM | (34) | 116 | 265m | | -/11 | West Indies | Georgetown | 1970-71 |
| | | 117* | 340m | | -/10 | West Indies | Bridgetown | 1970-71 |
| | | 124) | 392m | | -/11 | West Indies | Port-of-Spain | 1970-71 |
| | | 220) | 505m | | -/22 | | | |
| | | 101 | 290m | | -/8 | England | Manchester | 1974 |
| | | 116 § | 368m | | 1/15 | New Zealand | Auckland | 1975-76 |
| | | 156 | 488m | 352 | -/13 | West Indies | Port-of-Spain | 1975-76 |
| | | 102 | 245m | | -/13 | West Indies | Port-of-Spain | 1975-76 |
| | | 119 | 265m | | -/20 | New Zealand | Bombay[3] | 1976-77 |
| | | 108 | 341m | 220 | -/13 | England | Bombay[3] | 1976-77 |
| | | 113 § | 320m | 264 | -/12 | Australia | Brisbane[2] | 1977-78 |
| | | 127 | 270m | | -/20 | Australia | Perth | 1977-78 |
| | | 118 | 354m | | -12 | Australia | Melbourne | 1977-78 |
| | | 111) | 357m | | -/15 | Pakistan | Karachi[1] | 1978-79 |
| | | 137) | 315m | 240 | -/20 | | | |
| | | 205 | 398m | | 2/29 | West Indies | Bombay[3] | 1978-79 |
| | | 107 ) | 315h | | -/18 | West Indies | Calcutta | 1978-79 |
| | | 182*) | 399m | 264 | -/19 | | | |
| | | 120 | 344m | 218 | -/18 | West Indies | Delhi | 1978-79 |
| | | 221 | 489m | 443 | -/21 | England | The Oval | 1979 |
| | | 115 | 329m | 238 | 1/17 | Australia | Delhi | 1979-80 |
| | | 123 | 303m | 239 | -/17 | Australia | Bombay[3] | 1979-80 |
| | | 166 | 593m | 393 | 1/15 | Pakistan | Madras[1] | 1979-80 |
| | | 172 | 708m | 476 | -/21 | England | Bangalore | 1981-82 |
| | | 155 § | 399m | 293 | 1/24 | Sri Lanka | Madras[1] | 1982-83 |
| | | 127* | 433m | 262 | -/19 | Pakistan | Faisalabad | 1982-83 |
| | | 147* | 330m | | 1/17 | West Indies | Georgetown | 1982-83 |
| | | 103* | 236m | 190 | -/10 | Pakistan | Bangalore | 1983-84 |
| | | 121 | 224m | 128 | 2/15 | West Indies | Delhi | 1983-84 |
| | | 236* | 644m | 425 | -/23 | West Indies | Madras[1] | 1983-84 |
| | | 166* | 551m | 416 | -/16 | Australia | Adelaide | 1985-86 |
| | | 172 | 413m | 400 | -/19 | Australia | Sydney | 1985-86 |
| | | 103 | 302m | 203 | -/11 | Australia | Bombay[3] | 1986-87 |
| | | 176 | 506m | 302 | -/22 | Sri Lanka | Kanpur | 1986-87 |
| Hanumant Singh | | 105 § | 149m | | -/16 | England | Delhi | 1963-64 |
| Hazare,VS | (7) | 116) | 275m | | -/14 | Australia | Adelaide | 1947-48 |
| | | 145) | 313m | | -/17 | | | |
| | | 134* | 371m | | -/18 | West Indies | Bombay[2] | 1948-49 |
| | | 122 | 241m | | -/14 | West Indies | Bombay[2] | 1948-49 |
| | | 164* | 515m | | -/15 | England | Delhi | 1951-52 |
| | | 155 | 321m | | -/19 | England | Bombay[2] | 1951-52 |
| | | 146* | 285m | | -/18 | Pakistan | Bombay[2] | 1952-53 |
| Jaisimha,ML | (3) | 127 | 249m | | 2/14 | England | Delhi | 1961-62 |
| | | 129 | 299m | | 1/18 | England | Calcutta | 1963-64 |
| | | 101 | 291m | | -/9 | Australia | Brisbane[2] | 1967-68 |
| Kambli,VG | (4) | 224 | 608m | 411 | -/23 | England | Bombay[3] | 1992-93 |
| | | 227 | 413m | 301 | -/28 | Zimbabwe | Delhi | 1992-93 |
| | | 125 | 358m | 220 | 1/16 | Sri Lanka | Colombo (SSC) | 1993-94 |
| | | 120 | 315m | 240 | 2/15 | Sri Lanka | Colombo (PSS) | 1993-94 |

| | | | | | | | | |
|---|---|---|---|---|---|---|---|---|
| Kapil Dev | (8) | 126* | 224m | 124 | 1/11 | West Indies | Delhi | 1978-79 |
| | | 116 | 173m | 98 | 2/16 | England | Kanpur | 1981-82 |
| | | 100* | 142m | 95 | 3/13 | West Indies | Port-of-Spain | 1982-83 |
| | | 119 | 214m | 138 | -/21 | Australia | Madras[1] | 1986-87 |
| | | 163 | 240m | 165 | 1/19 | Sri Lanka | Kanpur | 1986-87 |
| | | 109 | 164m | 124 | -/18 | West Indies | Madras[1] | 1987-88 |
| | | 110 | 197m | 142 | -/19 | England | The Oval | 1990 |
| | | 129 | 256m | 180 | 1/14 | South Africa | Port Elizabeth | 1992-93 |
| Kirmani,SMH | (2) | 101* | 306m | 206 | -/16 | Australia | Bombay[3] | 1979-80 |
| | | 102 | 319m | 230 | -/10 | England | Bombay[3] | 1984-85 |
| Kripal Singh,AG | | 100* § | 246m | | -/12 | New Zealand | Hyderabad | 1955-56 |
| Kunderan,BK | (2) | 192 | 410m | | -/31 | England | Madras[2] | 1963-64 |
| | | 100 | 241m | | -/15 | England | Delhi | 1963-64 |
| Manjrekar,SV | (4) | 108 | 343m | 221 | -/15 | West Indies | Bridgetown | 1988-89 |
| | | 113* | 351m | 243 | -/13 | Pakistan | Karachi[1] | 1989-90 |
| | | 218 | 511m | 401 | -/28 | Pakistan | Lahore[2] | 1989-90 |
| | | 100* § | 529m | 422 | -/7 | Zimbabwe | Harare | 1992-93 |
| Manjrekar,VL | (7) | 133 | 266m | | -/19 | England | Leeds | 1952 |
| | | 118 | 249m | | -/15 | West Indies | Kingston | 1952-53 |
| | | 118 § | 235m | | -/20 | New Zealand | Hyderabad | 1955-56 |
| | | 177 | 555h | | -/20 | New Zealand | Delhi | 1955-56 |
| | | 189* | 444m | | -/28 | England | Delhi | 1961-62 |
| | | 108 | 294m | | -/14 | England | Madras[2] | 1963-64 |
| | | 102* | 200m | | -/14 | New Zealand | Madras[2] | 1964-65 |
| Mankad,MH | (5) | 116 | 180h | | 1/13 | Australia | Melbourne | 1947-48 |
| | | 111 | 300m | | -/6 | Australia | Melbourne | 1947-48 |
| | | 184 | 270m | | 1/19 | England | Lord's | 1952 |
| | | 223 | 472m | | -/22 | New Zealand | Bombay[2] | 1955-56 |
| | | 231 | 525m | | -/21 | New Zealand | Madras[2] | 1955-56 |
| Merchant,VM | (3) | 114 | 255m | | -/13 | England | Manchester | 1936 |
| | | 128 | 315h | | -/15 | England | The Oval | 1946 |
| | | 154 | 440m | | -/20 | England | Delhi | 1951-52 |
| Modi,RS | | 112 | 284m | | -/12 | West Indies | Bombay[2] | 1948-49 |
| Mongia,NR | | 152 § | 497m | 365 | 1/18 | Australia | Delhi | 1996-97 |
| Mushtaq Ali | (2) | 112 | 160m | | -/17 | England | Manchester | 1936 |
| | | 106 § | 203m | | -/9 | West Indies | Calcutta | 1948-49 |
| Nadkarni,RG | | 122* | 418m | | -/15 | England | Kanpur | 1963-64 |
| Pataudi,Nawab of,jr | (6) | 103 | 168m | | 2/16 | England | Madras[2] | 1961-62 |
| | | 203* | 430m | | 2/23 | England | Delhi | 1963-64 |
| | | 128* § | 343m | 311 | -/17 | Australia | Madras[2] | 1964-65 |
| | | 153 | 285m | | -/29 | New Zealand | Calcutta | 1964-65 |
| | | 113 | 233m | | 2/16 | New Zealand | Delhi | 1964-65 |
| | | 148 | 350m | | 1/15 | England | Leeds | 1967 |
| Patel,BP | | 115* | 420m | | -/10 | West Indies | Port-of-Spain | 1975-76 |
| Patil,SM | (4) | 174 | 301m | 240 | 1/22 | Australia | Adelaide | 1980-81 |
| | | 129* | 212m | 196 | 2/18 | England | Manchester | 1982 |
| | | 114* § | 216m | | 1/13 | Sri Lanka | Madras[1] | 1982-83 |
| | | 127 | 330h | 231 | -/18 | Pakistan | Faisalabad | 1984-85 |
| Phadkar,DG | (2) | 123 | 254m | | -/15 | Australia | Adelaide | 1947-48 |
| | | 115 | 389m | | 1/10 | England | Calcutta | 1951-52 |
| Prabhakar,M | | 120 | 405m | 274 | -/16 | West Indies | Mohali | 1994-95 |
| Ramchand,GS | (2) | 106* | 220m | | -/14 | New Zealand | Calcutta | 1955-56 |
| | | 109 | 248m | | -/19 | Australia | Bombay[2] | 1956-57 |
| Roy,Pankaj | (5) | 140 | 329m | | -/20 | England | Bombay[2] | 1951-52 |
| | | 111 | 232m | | -/15 | England | Madras[1] | 1951-52 |
| | | 150 | 376m | | -/20 | West Indies | Kingston | 1952-53 |
| | | 100 | 308m | | -/15 | New Zealand | Calcutta | 1955-56 |
| | | 173 | 472m | | -/12 | New Zealand | Madras[2] | 1955-56 |
| Sardesai,DN | (5) | 200* | 550m | | -/25 | New Zealand | Bombay[2] | 1964-65 |
| | | 106 | 140m | | -/18 | New Zealand | Delhi | 1964-65 |

| | | | | | | | | |
|---|---|---|---|---|---|---|---|---|
| | | 212 | 487m | | 1/17 | West Indies | Kingston | 1970-71 |
| | | 112 | 278m | | -/11 | West Indies | Port-of-Spain | 1970-71 |
| | | 150 | 288m | | -/20 | West Indies | Bridgetown | 1970-71 |
| Shastri,RJ | (11) | 128 | 488m | 327 | -/15 | Pakistan | Karachi[1] | 1982-83 |
| | | 102 | 370m | | -/5 | West Indies | St John's | 1982-83 |
| | | 139 | 405m | 270 | 2/16 | Pakistan | Faisalabad | 1984-85 |
| | | 142 | 389m | 322 | 1/17 | England | Bombay[3] | 1984-85 |
| | | 111 | 455m | 357 | -/13 | England | Calcutta | 1984-85 |
| | | 121* | 388m | 287 | 6/9 | Australia | Bombay[3] | 1986-87 |
| | | 125 | >450h | | 1/8 | Pakistan | Jaipur | 1986-87 |
| | | 107 | 441m | 282 | -/12 | West Indies | Bridgetown | 1988-89 |
| | | 100 | 245m | 185 | 1/12 | England | Lord's | 1990 |
| | | 187 | 559m | 435 | -/23 | England | The Oval | 1990 |
| | | 206 | 572m | 472 | 2/17 | Australia | Sydney | 1991-92 |
| Shodhan,RH | | 110 § | 215m | | -/15 | Pakistan | Calcutta | 1952-53 |
| Sidhu,NS | (9) | 116 § | 295m | 195 | 4/12 | New Zealand | Bangalore | 1988-89 |
| | | 116 | 358m | 237 | -/13 | West Indies | Kingston | 1988-89 |
| | | 106 | 403m | 273 | -/9 | England | Madras[1] | 1992-93 |
| | | 104 | 384m | 273 | -/7 | Sri Lanka | Colombo (SSC) | 1993-94 |
| | | 124 | 280m | 223 | 8/9 | Sri Lanka | Lucknow[2] | 1993-94 |
| | | 107 | 296m | 240 | -/17 | West Indies | Nagpur | 1994-95 |
| | | 201 | 673m | 491 | 1/19 | West Indies | Port-of-Spain | 1996-97 |
| | | 111 | 260m | 200 | 2/13 | Sri Lanka | Colombo (PIS) | 1997-98 |
| | | 131 | 476m | 372 | 2/14 | Sri Lanka | Mohali | 1997-98 |
| Solkar,ED | | 102 | 363m | | -/8 | West Indies | Bombay[3] | 1974-75 |
| Srikkanth,K | (2) | 116 | 190m | 119 | 1/19 | Australia | Sydney | 1985-86 |
| | | 123 | | 149 | 2/18 | Pakistan | Madras[1] | 1986-87 |
| Tendulkar,SR | (16) | 119* | 225m | 189 | -/17 | England | Manchester | 1990 |
| | | 148* | 298m | 215 | -/14 | Australia | Sydney | 1991-92 |
| | | 114 | 228m | 161 | -/16 | Australia | Perth | 1991-92 |
| | | 111 | 370m | 270 | -/19 | South Africa | Johannesburg[3] | 1992-93 |
| | | 165 | 361m | 296 | 1/24 | England | Madras[1] | 1992-93 |
| | | 104* | 217m | 163 | 1/11 | Sri Lanka | Colombo (SSC) | 1993-94 |
| | | 142 | 260m | 224 | -/22 | Sri Lanka | Lucknow[2] | 1993-94 |
| | | 179 | 412m | 319 | 1/24 | West Indies | Nagpur | 1994-95 |
| | | 122 | 262m | 176 | 1/19 | England | Birmingham | 1996 |
| | | 177 | 462m | 360 | -/26 | England | Nottingham | 1996 |
| | | 169 | 333m | 253 | -/26 | South Africa | Cape Town | 1996-97 |
| | | 143 | 294m | 247 | -/20 | Sri Lanka | Colombo (PIS) | 1997-98 |
| | | 139 | 403m | 266 | -/16 | Sri Lanka | Colombo (SSC) | 1997-98 |
| | | 148 | 320m | 244 | 3/21 | Sri Lanka | Mumbai[3] | 1997-98 |
| | | 155* | 286m | 191 | 4/14 | Australia | Chennai[1] | 1997-98 |
| | | 177 | 298m | 207 | 3/29 | Australia | Bangalore | 1997-98 |
| Umrigar,PR | (12) | 130* | 262m | | -/11 | England | Madras[1] | 1951-52 |
| | | 102 | 168m | | 1/15 | Pakistan | Bombay[2] | 1952-53 |
| | | 130 | 327m | | 2/12 | West Indies | Port-of-Spain | 1952-53 |
| | | 117 | 232m | | -/16 | West Indies | Kingston | 1952-53 |
| | | 108 | 280m | | -/13 | Pakistan | Peshawar[1] | 1954-55 |
| | | 223 § | 503m | | -/26 | New Zealand | Hyderabad | 1955-56 |
| | | 118 | 260m | | -/13 | England | Manchester | 1959 |
| | | 115 | 339m | | -/11 | Pakistan | Kanpur | 1960-61 |
| | | 117 | | | -/14 | Pakistan | Madras[2] | 1960-61 |
| | | 112 | | | | Pakistan | Delhi | 1960-61 |
| | | 147* | 400m | | -/16 | England | Kanpur | 1961-62 |
| | | 172* | 248m | | | West Indies | Port-of-Spain | 1961-62 |
| Vengsarkar,DB | (17) | 157* | 379m | 299 | 1/18 | West Indies | Calcutta | 1978-79 |
| | | 109 | 336m | 223 | -/11 | West Indies | Delhi | 1978-79 |
| | | 103 | 353m | 295 | -/13 | England | Lord's | 1979 |
| | | 112 | 366m | 283 | 2/12 | Australia | Bangalore | 1979-80 |
| | | 146* | 522m | 370 | 1/11 | Pakistan | Delhi | 1979-80 |

| | | | | | | | | |
|---|---|---|---|---|---|---|---|---|
| | | 157 | 334m | 264 | -/21 | England | Lord's | 1982 |
| | | 159 | 370m | 238 | 1/20 | West Indies | Delhi | 1983-84 |
| | | 100 | | 142 | -/13 | West Indies | Bombay[3] | 1983-84 |
| | | 137 | 360m | 255 | 1/17 | England | Kanpur | 1984-85 |
| | | 126* | 327m | 213 | -/16 | England | Lord's | 1986 |
| | | 102* | 282m | 216 | -/10 | England | Leeds | 1986 |
| | | 164* | 432m | 303 | 1/21 | Australia | Bombay[3] | 1986-87 |
| | | 153 | | | | Sri Lanka | Nagpur | 1986-87 |
| | | 166 | 429m | 266 | -/14 | Sri Lanka | Cuttack | 1986-87 |
| | | 109 | | 295 | -/10 | Pakistan | Ahmedabad | 1986-87 |
| | | 102 | 405m | 257 | -/8 | West Indies | Delhi | 1987-88 |
| | | 102* | 346m | 266 | -/11 | West Indies | Calcutta | 1987-88 |
| Viswanath,GR | (14) | 137 § | 354m | | -/25 | Australia | Kanpur | 1969-70 |
| | | 113 | 267m | 214 | 1/18 | England | Bombay[2] | 1972-73 |
| | | 139 | 376m | 263 | -/23 | West Indies | Calcutta | 1974-75 |
| | | 112 | 220m | | -/15 | West Indies | Port-of-Spain | 1975-76 |
| | | 103* | 147m | | -/8 | New Zealand | Kanpur | 1976-77 |
| | | 145 § | 360m | | -/16 | Pakistan | Faisalabad | 1978-79 |
| | | 124 | 346m | | -/17 | West Indies | Madras[1] | 1978-79 |
| | | 179 | 419m | 261 | -/21 | West Indies | Kanpur | 1978-79 |
| | | 113 | 351m | 337 | -/14 | England | Lord's | 1979 |
| | | 161* | 405m | 297 | 1/11 | Australia | Bangalore | 1979-80 |
| | | 131 | 277m | 207 | -/18 | Australia | Delhi | 1979-80 |
| | | 114 | 274m | 222 | -/11 | Australia | Melbourne | 1980-81 |
| | | 107 | 268m | 200 | -/14 | England | Delhi | 1981-82 |
| | | 222 | 638m | 373 | -/31 | England | Madras[1] | 1981-82 |
| Wadekar,AL | | 143 | 371m | | -/12 | New Zealand | Wellington | 1967-68 |
| Yashpal Sharma | (2) | 100* | 280m | 239 | 3/10 | Australia | Delhi | 1979-80 |
| | | 140 | 492m | 301 | 2/18 | England | Madras[1] | 1981-82 |
| **PAKISTAN** (199) | | | Time | Balls | 6/4 | Opponents | | |
| Aamer Malik | (2) | 117 | 409m | 300 | -/15 | India | Faisalabad | 1989-90 |
| | | 113 | 344m | 276 | -/11 | India | Lahore[2] | 1989-90 |
| Aamer Sohail | (4) | 205 | 343m | 284 | -/32 | England | Manchester | 1992 |
| | | 105 | 280m | 200 | -/17 | Australia | Lahore[2] | 1994-95 |
| | | 160 | 441m | 297 | 1/17 | West Indies | Rawalpindi[2] | 1997-98 |
| | | 160 | 354m | 255 | -/21 | West Indies | Karachi[1] | 1997-98 |
| Ali Naqvi | | 115 § | 356m | 270 | -/14 | South Africa | Rawalpindi[2] | 1997-98 |
| Alimuddin | (2) | 103* | 325m | | -/15 | India | Karachi[1] | 1954-55 |
| | | 109 | 232m | | -/17 | England | Karachi[1] | 1961-62 |
| Asif Iqbal | (11) | 146 | 190m | 244 | 2/21 | England | The Oval | 1967 |
| | | 104* | 192m | 170 | -/16 | England | Birmingham | 1971 |
| | | 175 | 274m | | 1/18 | New Zealand | Dunedin | 1972-73 |
| | | 102 | 195m | | -/16 | England | Lahore[2] | 1972-73 |
| | | 166 | 334m | | -/15 | New Zealand | Lahore[2] | 1976-77 |
| | | 152* | 268m | | -/14 | Australia | Adelaide | 1976-77 |
| | | 120 | 245m | | -/15 | Australia | Sydney | 1976-77 |
| | | 135 | 245m | | 1/20 | West Indies | Kingston | 1976-77 |
| | | 104 § | 178m | | -/15 | India | Faisalabad | 1978-79 |
| | | 104 | 237m | | -/10 | New Zealand | Napier | 1978-79 |
| | | 134* | 306m | | 1/18 | Australia | Perth | 1978-79 |
| Azhar Mahmood | (3) | 128* § | 351m | 267 | 1/11 | South Africa | Rawalpindi[2] | 1997-98 |
| | | 136 | 304m | 215 | 2/16 | South Africa | Johannesburg[3] | 1997-98 |
| | | 132 | 198m | 163 | -/24 | South Africa | Durban[2] | 1997-98 |
| Basit Ali | | 103 | 197m | 139 | 3/9 | New Zealand | Christchurch | 1993-94 |
| Hanif Mohammad | (12) | 142 | 518m | | 1/17 | India | Bahawalpur | 1954-55 |
| | | 103 | 270h | | -/8 | New Zealand | Dacca | 1955-56 |
| | | 337 § | 973m | | -/24 | West Indies | Bridgetown | 1957-58 |
| | | 103 | 390h | | -/7 | West Indies | Karachi[1] | 1958-59 |
| | | 101* | 365m | | -/10 | Australia | Karachi[1] | 1959-60 |

| | | | | | | | | |
|---|---|---|---|---|---|---|---|---|
| | | 160 | 380m | | -/17 | India | Bombay[2] | 1960-61 |
| | | 111) | 497m | | -/14 | England | Dacca | 1961-62 |
| | | 104) | 396m | | -/8 | | | |
| | | 104 | 193m | | -/8 | Australia | Melbourne | 1964-65 |
| | | 100* | 203m | | -/18 | New Zealand | Christchurch | 1964-65 |
| | | 203* | 445m | | -/33 | New Zealand | Lahore[2] | 1964-65 |
| | | 187* | 540h | | -/21 | England | Lord's | 1967 |
| Haroon Rashid | (3) | 122 § | 298m | | 1/18 | England | Lahore[2] | 1977-78 |
| | | 108 | 214m | | 6/10 | England | Hyderabad | 1977-78 |
| | | 153 § | 323m | 242 | 3/16 | Sri Lanka | Karachi[1] | 1981-82 |
| Ijaz Ahmed | (8) | 122 | 297m | 221 | 2/17 | Australia | Faisalabad | 1988-89 |
| | | 121 | 450m | 331 | -/11 | Australia | Melbourne | 1989-90 |
| | | 137 | 442m | 332 | 2/17 | Australia | Sydney | 1995-96 |
| | | 103 | 312m | 213 | 2/13 | New Zealand | Christchurch | 1995-96 |
| | | 141 | 279m | 201 | 2/20 | England | Leeds | 1996 |
| | | 125 | 269m | 201 | 1/19 | New Zealand | Rawalpindi[2] | 1996-97 |
| | | 113 | 324m | 245 | -/11 | Sri Lanka | Colombo (PIS) | 1996-97 |
| | | 151 | 485m | 337 | 1/15 | West Indies | Karachi[1] | 1997-98 |
| Ijaz Faqih | | 105 § | | 241 | 4/7 | India | Ahmedabad | 1986-87 |
| Imran Khan | (6) | 123 | 302m | 199 | -/13 | West Indies | Lahore[2] | 1980-81 |
| | | 117 | 192m | 121 | 5/10 | India | Faisalabad | 1982-83 |
| | | 135* | | 230 | 5/14 | India | Madras[1] | 1986-87 |
| | | 118 | 256m | 201 | 1/11 | England | The Oval | 1987 |
| | | 109* | 201m | 145 | 1/17 | India | Karachi[1] | 1989-90 |
| | | 136 | 485m | 361 | -/10 | Australia | Adelaide | 1989-90 |
| Imtiaz Ahmed | (3) | 209 | 380m | | -/28 | New Zealand | Lahore[2] | 1955-56 |
| | | 122 | 250m | | -/14 | West Indies | Kingston | 1957-58 |
| | | 135 | 320m | | -/11 | India | Madras[2] | 1960-61 |
| Intikhab Alam | | 138 | 270m | | 4/15 | England | Hyderabad | 1972-73 |
| Inzamamul Haq | (6) | 123 | 314m | 225 | 1/11 | West Indies | St John's | 1992-93 |
| | | 135* | 251m | 195 | 1/19 | New Zealand | Wellington | 1993-94 |
| | | 100* | 197m | 125 | -/13 | Sri Lanka | Kandy | 1994-95 |
| | | 101 | 205m | 168 | 2/12 | Zimbabwe | Harare | 1994-95 |
| | | 148 | 299m | 218 | 1/19 | England | Lord's | 1996 |
| | | 177 | 443m | 320 | 2/19 | West Indies | Rawalpindi[2] | 1997-98 |
| Javed Burki | (3) | 138 § | 375h | | 1/17 | England | Lahore[2] | 1961-62 |
| | | 140 | 356m | | -/18 | England | Dacca | 1961-62 |
| | | 101 | 225m | | -/15 | England | Lord's | 1962 |
| Javed Miandad | (23) | 163 § | 259m | | -/22 | New Zealand | Lahore[2] | 1976-77 |
| | | 206 | 410m | | 2/29 | New Zealand | Karachi[1] | 1976-77 |
| | | 154* § | 430m | | 3/13 | India | Faisalabad | 1978-79 |
| | | 100 | 311m | | 1/8 | India | Karachi[1] | 1978-79 |
| | | 160* | 420m | | 1/17 | New Zealand | Christchurch | 1978-79 |
| | | 129* | 388m | 284 | -/15 | Australia | Perth | 1978-79 |
| | | 106* | 217m | | 1/11 | Australia | Faisalabad | 1979-80 |
| | | 138 | 416m | 264 | 2/13 | Australia | Lahore[2] | 1982-83 |
| | | 126 | 276m | 200 | 3/10 | India | Faisalabad | 1982-83 |
| | | 280* | 606m | 460 | 1/19 | India | Hyderabad | 1982-83 |
| | | 131 | 361m | 271 | -/13 | Australia | Adelaide | 1983-84 |
| | | 104 ) | 269m | 217 | -/12 | New Zealand | Hyderabad | 1984-85 |
| | | 103*) | 245m | 198 | 1/13 | | | |
| | | 203* | 465m | | 1/22 | Sri Lanka | Faisalabad | 1985-86 |
| | | 260 | 617m | 521 | 1/28 | England | The Oval | 1987 |
| | | 114 | 405m | 235 | -/12 | West Indies | Georgetown | 1987-88 |
| | | 102 | 436m | 265 | -/18 | West Indies | Port-of-Spain | 1987-88 |
| | | 211 | 636m | 441 | 1/29 | Australia | Karachi[1] | 1988-89 |
| | | 107 | 254m | 186 | -/17 | Australia | Faisalabad | 1988-89 |
| | | 118 | 360m | 277 | -/8 | New Zealand | Wellington | 1988-89 |
| | | 271 | 558m | 465 | 5/28 | New Zealand | Auckland | 1988-89 |
| | | 145 | 369m | 291 | -/10 | India | Lahore[2] | 1989-90 |

| | | | | | | | | |
|---|---|---|---|---|---|---|---|---|
| | | (In his 100th Test match) | | | | | | |
| | | 153* | 415m | 337 | -/19 | England | Birmingham | 1992 |
| Khalid Ibadulla | | 166 § | 330m | 319 | -/20 | Australia | Karachi[1] | 1964-65 |
| Majid Khan | (8) | 158 | 303m | | -/18 | Australia | Melbourne | 1972-73 |
| | | 110 | 269m | | -/15 | New Zealand | Auckland | 1972-73 |
| | | 100 | 247m | | -/9 | West Indies | Karachi[1] | 1974-75 |
| | | 112 | 128m | | 2/18 | New Zealand | Karachi[1] | 1976-77 |
| | | 167 | 360h | | -/25 | West Indies | Georgetown | 1976-77 |
| | | 119* | 411m | | -/13 | New Zealand | Napier | 1978-79 |
| | | 108 | 219m | | -/16 | Australia | Melbourne | 1978-79 |
| | | 110* | 282m | | -/14 | Australia | Lahore[2] | 1979-80 |
| Mansoor Akhtar | | 111 | 289m | 191 | -/18 | Australia | Faisalabad | 1982-83 |
| Mohammad Ilyas | | 126 | 205m | | 1/15 | New Zealand | Karachi[1] | 1964-65 |
| Mohammad Wasim | | 109* § | 217m | 165 | -/17 | New Zealand | Lahore[2] | 1996-97 |
| | | 192 § | 560m | 407 | -/23 | Zimbabwe | Harare | 1997-98 |
| Mohsin Khan | (7) | 129 | 296m | 173 | -/17 | Sri Lanka | Lahore[2] | 1981-82 |
| | | 200 | 496m | 386 | -/23 | England | Lord's | 1982 |
| | | 135 | 349m | 218 | -/17 | Australia | Lahore[2] | 1982-83 |
| | | 101* § | 168m | 161 | 1/10 | India | Lahore[2] | 1982-83 |
| | | 149 | 393m | 296 | -/16 | Australia | Adelaide | 1983-84 |
| | | 152 | 354m | 239 | 1/19 | Australia | Melbourne | 1983-84 |
| | | 104 | 258m | 136 | -/3 | England | Lahore[2] | 1983-84 |
| Moin Khan | (3) | 115* | 233m | 185 | 1/13 | Australia | Lahore[2] | 1994-95 |
| | | 117* | 283m | 208 | 2/13 | Sri Lanka | Sialkot | 1994-95 |
| | | 105 | 282m | 191 | 1/10 | England | Leeds | 1996 |
| Mudassar Nazar | (10) | 114 § | 591m | | -/12 | England | Lahore[2] | 1977-78 |
| | | 126 | 447m | 337 | -/13 | India | Bangalore | 1979-80 |
| | | 119 | 294m | 199 | -/10 | India | Karachi[1] | 1982-83 |
| | | 231 | 627m | 444 | 1/21 | India | Hyderabad | 1982-83 |
| | | 152* | 495m | 296 | -/15 | India | Lahore[2] | 1982-83 |
| | | 152 | 458m | 308 | -/14 | India | Karachi[1] | 1982-83 |
| | | 199 | 552m | 408 | -/24 | India | Faisalabad | 1984-85 |
| | | 106 | 255m | 187 | -/11 | New Zealand | Hyderabad | 1984-85 |
| | | 124 | 416m | 362 | -/16 | England | Birmingham | 1987 |
| | | 120 | 323m | 257 | -/18 | England | Lahore[2] | 1987-88 |
| Mushtaq Mohammad | (10) | 101 | 210m | | -/19 | India | Delhi | 1960-61 |
| | | 100* | 324m | | -/9 | England | Nottingham | 1962 |
| | | 100 | 351m | 283 | -/13 | England | Birmingham | 1971 |
| | | 121 | 292m | 271 | -/14 | Australia | Sydney | 1972-73 |
| | | 201 | 383m | | -/20 | New Zealand | Dunedin | 1972-73 |
| | | 157 | 469m | | -/17 | England | Hyderabad | 1972-73 |
| | | 123 | 466m | | -/12 | West Indies | Lahore[2] | 1974-75 |
| | | 101 | | | -/9 | New Zealand | Hyderabad | 1976-77 |
| | | 107 | 298m | | -/11 | New Zealand | Karachi[1] | 1976-77 |
| | | 121 | 371m | | -/14 | West Indies | Port-of-Spain | 1976-77 |
| Nasim-ul-Ghani | | 101 | 180m | | 1/16 | England | Lord's | 1962 |
| Nazir Mohammad | | 124* | 517m | | | India | Lucknow[1] | 1952-53 |
| Qasim Omar | (3) | 113 | 283m | 224 | -/12 | Australia | Adelaide | 1983-84 |
| | | 210 | 685m | 442 | -/27 | India | Faisalabad | 1984-85 |
| | | 206 § | | | | Sri Lanka | Faisalabad | 1985-86 |
| Rameez Raja | (2) | 122 | 388m | 242 | -/17 | Sri Lanka | Colombo (PSS) | 1985-86 |
| | | 114 | 302m | 279 | 1/12 | India | Jaipur | 1986-87 |
| Sadiq Mohammad | (5) | 137 | 313m | | -/15 | Australia | Melbourne | 1972-73 |
| | | 166 | 362m | | -/19 | New Zealand | Wellington | 1972-73 |
| | | 119 | 375m | | -/12 | England | Lahore[2] | 1972-73 |
| | | 103* | | | -/14 | New Zealand | Hyderabad | 1976-77 |
| | | 105 | 296m | | -/10 | Australia | Melbourne | 1976-77 |
| Saeed Ahmed | (5) | 150 | 349m | | -/16 | West Indies | Georgetown | 1957-58 |
| | | 166 | 461m | | -/19 | Australia | Lahore[2] | 1959-60 |
| | | 121 § | 345m | | -/11 | India | Bombay[2] | 1960-61 |

| | | | Time | Balls | 6/4 | Opponents | | |
|---|---|---|---|---|---|---|---|---|
| | | 103 | 245m | | -/10 | India | Madras[2] | 1960-61 |
| | | 172 | 341m | | 1/17 | New Zealand | Karachi[1] | 1964-65 |
| Saeed Anwar | (5) | 169 | 307m | 248 | -/26 | New Zealand | Wellington | 1993-94 |
| | | 136 | 319m | 218 | -/12 | Sri Lanka | Colombo (PPS) | 1994-95 |
| | | 176 | 378m | 264 | -/26 | England | The Oval | 1996 |
| | | 149 | 305m | 214 | -/20 | New Zealand | Rawalpindi[2] | 1996-97 |
| | | 118 | 312m | 209 | -/18 | South Africa | Durban[2] | 1997-98 |
| Saleem Malik | (15) | 100* § | 272m | 191 | -/10 | Sri Lanka | Karachi[1] | 1981-82 |
| | | 107 | 251m | 168 | -/14 | India | Faisalabad | 1982-83 |
| | | 116 | 393m | 270 | -/17 | England | Faisalabad | 1983-84 |
| | | 102* | 205m | 157 | -/15 | India | Faisalabad | 1984-85 |
| | | 119* | 267m | 169 | 1/21 | New Zealand | Karachi[1] | 1984-85 |
| | | 102 | 267m | 237 | -/6 | England | The Oval | 1987 |
| | | 102* | 216m | 144 | -/13 | India | Karachi[1] | 1989-90 |
| | | 102 | 268m | 208 | -/7 | West Indies | Karachi[1] | 1990-91 |
| | | 101 | 287m | 201 | -/10 | Sri Lanka | Sialkot | 1991-92 |
| | | 165 | 370m | 297 | 1/19 | England | Birmingham | 1992 |
| | | 140 | 285m | 200 | -/20 | New Zealand | Christchurch | 1993-94 |
| | | 237 | 443m | 328 | -/34 | Australia | Rawalpindi[2] | 1994-95 |
| | | 143 | 313m | 242 | -/19 | Australia | Lahore[2] | 1994-95 |
| | | 100* | 289m | 223 | -/10 | England | The Oval | 1996 |
| | | 155 | 338m | 240 | -/26 | Sri Lanka | Colombo (SSC) | 1996-97 |
| Shoaib Mohammad | (7) | 101 | | | -/10 | India | Madras[1] | 1986-87 |
| | | 163 | 720m | 516 | 1/17 | New Zealand | Wellington | 1988-89 |
| | | 112 | 350m | 254 | -/17 | New Zealand | Auckland | 1988-89 |
| | | 203* | 486m | 335 | -/19 | India | Lahore[2] | 1989-90 |
| | | 203* | 656m | 411 | -/23 | New Zealand | Karachi[1] | 1990-91 |
| | | 105 | 351m | 223 | 1/15 | New Zealand | Lahore[2] | 1990-91 |
| | | 142 | 527m | 368 | -/20 | New Zealand | Faisalabad | 1990-91 |
| Taslim Arif | | 210* | 435m | | -/20 | Australia | Faisalabad | 1979-80 |
| Waqar Hassan | | 189 | 430m | | -/30 | New Zealand | Lahore[1] | 1955-56 |
| Wasim Akram | (2) | 123 | 244m | 195 | 1/18 | Australia | Adelaide | 1989-90 |
| | | 257* | 489m | 370 | 12/22 | Zimbabwe | Sheikhapura | 1996-97 |
| Wasim Raja | (4) | 107* | 340m | | 1/10 | West Indies | Karachi[1] | 1974-75 |
| | | 117* | 260m | | 1/12 | West Indies | Bridgetown | 1976-77 |
| | | 125 | 258m | 207 | 2/17 | India | Jullundur | 1983-84 |
| | | 112 | 300m | 210 | 2/14 | England | Faisalabad | 1983-84 |
| Wazir Mohammad | (2) | 106 | a180h | | -/17 | West Indies | Kingston | 1957-58 |
| | | 189 | 403m | | -/22 | West Indies | Port-of-Spain | 1957-58 |
| Zaheer Abbas | (12) | 274 § | 550m | | -/38 | England | Birmingham | 1971 |
| | | 240 | 550m | 410 | -/22 | England | The Oval | 1974 |
| | | 101 | 224m | | 1/13 | Australia | Adelaide | 1976-77 |
| | | 176 § | 315m | | 2/24 | India | Faisalabad | 1978-79 |
| | | 235* | 391m | | 2/29 | India | Lahore[2] | 1978-79 |
| | | 135 | 388m | 282 | 1/15 | New Zealand | Auckland | 1978-79 |
| | | 134 § | 269m | 148 | 2/12 | Sri Lanka | Lahore[2] | 1981-82 |
| | | 126 | 279m | 205 | 3/12 | Australia | Faisalabad | 1982-83 |
| | | 215 | 334m | 254 | 2/23 | India | Lahore[2] | 1982-83 |
| | | (His 100th first-class century) | | | | | | |
| | | 186 | 328m | 246 | -/23 | India | Karachi[1] | 1982-83 |
| | | 168 | 264m | 176 | 1/23 | India | Faisalabad | 1982-83 |
| | | 168* | 500m | 341 | 1/6 | India | Lahore[2] | 1984-85 |
| **SRI LANKA** (60) | | | Time | Balls | 6/4 | Opponents | | |
| Atapattu,MS | (2) | 108 | 341m | 244 | -/14 | India | Mohali | 1997-98 |
| | | 223 § | | 446 | 1/29 | Zimbabwe | Kandy | 1997-98 |
| de Silva,PA | (16) | 122 § | 510m | | 3/17 | Pakistan | Faisalabad | 1985-86 |
| | | 105 | 265m | | -/16 | Pakistan | Karachi[1] | 1985-86 |
| | | 167 | 491m | 361 | 1/17 | Australia | Brisbane[2] | 1989-90 |
| | | 267 | 509m | 380 | -/40 | New Zealand | Wellington | 1990-91 |

| | | | | | | | | |
|---|---|---|---|---|---|---|---|---|
| | | 123 | 261m | 193 | 5/6 | New Zealand | Auckland | 1990-91 |
| | | 148 | 388m | 297 | 1/17 | India | Colombo (PSS) | 1993-94 |
| | | 127 | 211m | 156 | 1/19 | Pakistan | Colombo (PSS) | 1994-95 |
| | | 105 | 402m | 316 | -/11 | Pakistan | Faisalabad | 1994-95 |
| | | 168 | 508m | 383 | 1/14 | Pakistan | Colombo (PIS) | 1996-97 |
| | | 138*) | 273m | 208 | -/19 | Pakistan | Colombo (SSC) | 1996-97 |
| | | 103*) | 169m | 99 | 1/11 | | | |
| | | 126 | 293m | 211 | -/16 | India | Colombo (PIS) | 1997-98 |
| | | 146) | 365m | 228 | -/20 | India | Colombo (SSC) | 1997-98 |
| | | 120) | 267m | 198 | -/13 | | | |
| | | 110* | 378m | 263 | 1/15 | India | Mohali | 1997-98 |
| | | 143* | 459m | 312 | 2/16 | Zimbabwe | Colombo (SSC) | 1997-98 |
| Dias,RL | (3) | 109 | 260m | 179 | 1/14 | Pakistan | Lahore[2] | 1981-82 |
| | | 108 § | 272m | 215 | -/18 | New Zealand | Colombo (SSC) | 1983-84 |
| | | 106 | 312m | 216 | -/17 | India | Kandy | 1985-86 |
| Gurusinha,AP | (7) | 116* | 495m | 307 | -/14 | Pakistan | Colombo (PSS) | 1985-86 |
| | | 119) | 362m | 261 | 1/17 | New Zealand | Hamilton | 1990-91 |
| | | 102) | 331m | 239 | 1/9 | | | |
| | | 137 | 525m | 399 | -/18 | Australia | Colombo (SSC) | 1992-93 |
| | | 128 § | 607m | 461 | 1/14 | Zimbabwe | Harare | 1994-95 |
| | | 127 | 516m | 429 | 1/11 | New Zealand | Dunedin | 1994-95 |
| | | 143 | 353m | 274 | 1/15 | Australia | Melbourne | 1995-96 |
| Jayasuriya,ST | (4) | 112 | 272m | 188 | 2/14 | Australia | Adelaide | 1995-96 |
| | | 113 | 290m | 212 | 1/9 | Pakistan | Colombo (SSC) | 1996-97 |
| | | 340 | 799m | 578 | 2/36 | India | Colombo (PIS) | 1997-98 |
| | | 199 | 419m | 226 | -/16 | India | Colombo (SSC) | 1997-98 |
| Jayawardene,DPM | | 167 | | 273 | -/18 | New Zealand | Colombo (PIS) | 1997-98 |
| Kaluwitharana,RS | (2) | 132* § | 203m | 158 | -/26 | Australia | Colombo (SSC) | 1992-93 |
| | | 103 § | 134m | 104 | 2/13 | New Zealand | Dunedin | 1996-97 |
| Kuruppu,DSBP | | 201* § | 778m | 562 | -/24 | New Zealand | Colombo (CCC) | 1986-87 |
| Madugalle,RS | | 103 | 403m | 280 | -/10 | India | Colombo (SSC) | 1985-86 |
| Mahanama,RS | (4) | 153 | 361m | 297 | -/18 | New Zealand | Moratuwa | 1992-93 |
| | | 109 | 217m | 154 | -/14 | New Zealand | Colombo (SSC) | 1992-93 |
| | | 151 | 520m | 362 | -/19 | India | Colombo (PSS) | 1993-94 |
| | | 225 | 753m | 561 | -/27 | India | Colombo (PIS) | 1997-98 |
| Mendis,LRD | (4) | 105 §) | 179m | 123 | 1/17 | India | Madras[1] | 1982-83 |
| | | 105 §) | 236m | | -/12 | | | |
| | | 111 | 197m | 143 | 3/11 | England | Lord's | 1984 |
| | | 124 | 318m | 228 | 2/12 | India | Kandy | 1985-86 |
| Ranatunga,A | (4) | 111 | 400m | 290 | 1/4 | India | Colombo (SSC) | 1985-86 |
| | | 135* | 341m | 208 | 4/14 | Pakistan | Colombo (PSS) | 1985-86 |
| | | 127 | 266m | 192 | 3/15 | Australia | Colombo (SSC) | 1992-93 |
| | | 131 § | 204m | 140 | 1/18 | South Africa | Moratuwa | 1992-93 |
| Ranatunga,S | (2) | 118 | 467m | 342 | -/17 | Zimbabwe | Harare | 1994-95 |
| | | 100* | 421m | 352 | -/15 | Zimbabwe | Bulawayo[2] | 1994-95 |
| Silva,SAR | (2) | 102* § | 316m | 255 | -/12 | England | Lord's | 1984 |
| | | 111 | 492m | 347 | -/11 | India | Colombo (PSS) | 1985-86 |
| Tillakaratne,HP | (6) | 116 | 451m | 287 | -/14 | Zimbabwe | Harare | 1994-95 |
| | | 108 | 332m | 258 | -/14 | New Zealand | Dunedin | 1994-95 |
| | | 115 | 226m | 176 | -/20 | Pakistan | Faisalabad | 1994-95 |
| | | 119 | 267m | 206 | -/12 | Australia | Perth | 1995-96 |
| | | 126* | 409m | 326 | -/13 | Zimbabwe | Colombo (SSC) | 1996-97 |
| | | 103 | 349m | 228 | -/10 | Pakistan | Colombo (PIS) | 1996-97 |
| Wettimuny,S | (2) | 157 | 372m | 330 | -/21 | Pakistan | Faisalabad | 1981-82 |
| | | 190 | 636m | 471 | -/21 | England | Lord's | 1984 |

| **ZIMBABWE** (19) | | | Time | Balls | 6/4 | Opponents | | |
|---|---|---|---|---|---|---|---|---|
| Arnott,KJ | | 101* § | 248m | 200 | -/12 | New Zealand | Bulawayo[1] | 1992-93 |
| Flower,A | (5) | 115 | 289m | 236 | -/15 | India | Delhi | 1992-93 |
| | | 156 | 336m | 245 | 1/18 | Pakistan | Harare | 1994-95 |

| | | | | | | | | |
|---|---|---|---|---|---|---|---|---|
| | | 112 § | 364m | 331 | -/12 | England | Bulawayo[2] | 1996-97 |
| | | 105* | | 240 | -/10 | Sri Lanka | Colombo (SSC) | 1997-98 |
| | | 100* | | 217 | -/6 | Pakistan | Bulawayo[2] | 1997-98 |
| Flower,GW | (5) | 201* | 654m | 523 | 1/10 | Pakistan | Harare | 1994-95 |
| | | 110 | 392m | 287 | 1/14 | Pakistan | Sheikhapura | 1996-97 |
| | | 104) | | 286 | -/10 | New Zealand | Harare | 1997-98 |
| | | 151) | | 239 | 3/12 | | | |
| | | 156* | | 329 | 2/13 | Pakistan | Bulawayo[2] | 1997-98 |
| Goodwin,MW | | 166* § | | 204 | -/17 | Pakistan | Bulawayo[2] | 1997-98 |
| Houghton,DL | (4) | 121 § | 414m | 322 | -/15 | India | Harare | 1992-93 |
| | | 266 | 675m | 541 | 3/30 | Sri Lanka | Bulawayo[2] | 1994-95 |
| | | 142 | 394m | 268 | 2/17 | Sri Lanka | Harare | 1994-95 |
| | | 104+ | 306m | 204 | -/12 | New Zealand | Auckland | 1995-96 |
| Strang,PA | | 106* | 325m | 207 | -/10 | Pakistan | Sheikhapura | 1996-97 |
| Whittall,GJ | (2) | 113* | 243m | 192 | -/9 | Pakistan | Harare | 1994-95 |
| | | 203* | | 360 | 2/22 | New Zealand | Bulawayo[2] | 1997-98 |

## NINETY-NINES IN TEST MATCHES

*Over the years many batsmen have scored ninety-nine runs in a Test innings. M.J.K.Smith, G.Boycott (* Boycott and S.R.Waugh are the only players to register a not out 99), R.B.Richardson, J.G.Wright, M.A.Atherton, Saleem Malik and G.S.Blewett are the only batsmen to score 99 twice in their careers. In the Third Test between England and Pakistan at Karachi[1] in 1972-73 three batsmen, Majid Khan, Mushtaq Mohammad and D.L.Amiss were dismissed for 99.*

| **AUSTRALIA** *(§ on debut)* | How out | Opponent | | |
|---|---|---|---|---|
| C.Hill | caught | England | Melbourne | 1901-02 |
| C.G.Macartney | caught | England | Lord's | 1912 |
| A.G.Chipperfield § | caught | England | Nottingham | 1934 |
| W.A.Brown | run out | India | Melbourne | 1947-48 |
| K.R.Miller | bowled | England | Adelaide | 1950-51 |
| A.R.Morris | run out | South Africa | Melbourne | 1952-53 |
| C.C.McDonald | caught | South Africa | Cape Town | 1957-58 |
| R.M.Cowper | caught | England | Melbourne | 1965-66 |
| I.M.Chappell | caught | India | Calcutta | 1969-70 |
| R.Edwards | lbw | England | Lord's | 1975 |
| K.J.Hughes | caught | England | Perth | 1979-80 |
| D.M.Jones | lbw | New Zealand | Perth | 1989-90 |
| M.E.Waugh | bowled | England | Lord's | 1993 |
| M.J.Slater | caught | New Zealand | Perth | 1993-94 |
| S.R.Waugh | not out | England | Perth | 1994-95 |
| G.S.Blewett | bowled | West Indies | Adelaide | 1996-97 |
| G.S.Blewett | bowled | New Zealand | Hobart | 1997-98 |

| **ENGLAND** | How out | Opponent | | |
|---|---|---|---|---|
| H.Sutcliffe | bowled | South Africa | Cape Town | 1927-28 |
| E.Paynter | lbw | Australia | Lord's | 1938 |
| N.W.D.Yardley | caught | South Africa | Nottingham | 1947 |
| M.J.K.Smith | caught | South Africa | Lord's | 1960 |
| M.J.K.Smith | run out | Pakistan | Lahore[2] | 1961-62 |
| E.R.Dexter | bowled | Australia | Brisbane[2] | 1962-63 |
| D.L.Amiss | caught | Pakistan | Karachi[1] | 1972-73 |
| G.Boycott | caught | West Indies | Port-of-Spain | 1973-74 |
| G.Boycott* | not out | Australia | Perth | 1979-80 |
| G.A.Gooch | run out | Australia | Melbourne | 1979-80 |
| M.D.Moxon | caught | New Zealand | Auckland | 1987-88 |
| M.A.Atherton | run out | Australia | Lord's | 1993 |
| M.A.Atherton | c and b | South Africa | Leeds | 1994 |

| **SOUTH AFRICA** | How out | Opponent | | |
|---|---|---|---|---|
| G.A.Faulkner | caught | England | Cape Town | 1909-10 |
| B.Mitchell | caught | England | Port Elizabeth | 1948-49 |
| T.L.Goddard | caught | England | The Oval | 1960 |

| **WEST INDIES** (*§ on debut*) | How out | Opponent | | |
|---|---|---|---|---|
| R.J.Christiani § | lbw | England | Bridgetown | 1947-48 |
| A.F.Rae | bowled | New Zealand | Auckland | 1951-52 |
| R.B.Kanhai | run out | India | Madras[2] | 1958-59 |
| M.L.C.Foster | bowled | India | Port-of-Spain | 1970-71 |
| R.B.Richardson | bowled | India | Port-of-Spain | 1988-89 |
| R.B.Richardson | lbw | Australia | Bridgetown | 1990-91 |

| **NEW ZEALAND** | How out | Opponent | | |
|---|---|---|---|---|
| J.E.F.Beck | run out | South Africa | Cape Town | 1953-54 |
| R.J.Hadlee | caught | England | Christchurch | 1983-84 |
| J.G.Wright | caught | Australia | Melbourne | 1987-88 |
| D.N.Patel | run out | England | Christchurch | 1991-92 |
| J.G.Wright | stumped | England | Christchurch | 1991-92 |

| **INDIA** | How out | Opponent | | |
|---|---|---|---|---|
| Pankaj Roy | caught | Australia | Delhi | 1959-60 |
| M.L.Jaisimha | run out | Pakistan | Kanpur | 1960-61 |
| A.L.Wadekar | caught | Australia | Melbourne | 1967-68 |
| R.F.Surti | caught | New Zealand | Auckland | 1967-68 |
| N.S.Sidhu | lbw | Sri Lanka | Bangalore | 1993-94 |
| S.C.Ganguly | caught | Sri Lanka | Nagpur | 1997-98 |

| **PAKISTAN** | How out | Opponent | | |
|---|---|---|---|---|
| Maqsood Ahmed | stumped | India | Lahore[1] | 1954-55 |
| Majid Khan | caught | England | Karachi[1] | 1972-73 |
| Mushtaq Mohammad | run out | England | Karachi[1] | 1972-73 |
| Javed Miandad | caught | India | Bangalore | 1983-84 |
| Saleem Malik | caught | England | Leeds | 1987 |
| Saleem Malik | caught | South Africa | Johannesburg[3] | 1994-95 |
| Aamer Sohail | bowled | Australia | Brisbane[2] | 1995-96 |

| **ZIMBABWE** | How out | Opponent | | |
|---|---|---|---|---|
| A.D.R.Campbell | caught | Sri Lanka | Harare | 1994-95 |

## THE NERVOUS NINETIES IN TEST MATCHES

*There have been 543 scores in the nineties recorded in Test cricket (114 for Australia; 131 for England; 46 for South Africa; 87 for West Indies; 35 for New Zealand; 59 for India; 53 for Pakistan; 16 for Sri Lanka; and 2 for Zimbabwe). The following players scored these nineties:*

8 A.I.Kallicharran(W), S.R.Waugh(A)

6 G.Boycott(E), C.G.Greenidge(W), C.Hill(A), R.B.Kanhai(W)

5 M.A.Atherton(E), K.F.Barrington(E), D.C.Boon(A), S.M.Gavaskar(I), G.S.Sobers(W)

4 I.M.Chappell(A), M.C.Cowdrey(E), R.S.Dravid(I), T.W.Graveney(E), Inzamamul Haq(P), Javed Miandad(P), A.P.E.Knott(E), A.L.Logie(W), Majid Khan(P), R.W.Marsh(A), P.B.H.May(E), R.B.Richardson(W), N.S.Sidhu(I), R.B.Simpson(A), M.J.Slater(A), M.J.K.Smith(E), D.B.Vengsarkar(I), A.L.Wadekar(I), E.D.Weekes(W), K.C.Wessels(A2/SA2), J.G.Wright(N), Zaheer Abbas(P)

3 M.Amarnath(I),(E), G.S.Blewett(A), A.R.Border(A), D.C.S.Compton(E), J.V.Coney(N), D.J.Cullinan(SA), R.L.Dias(SL), J.H.Edrich(E), S.P.Fleming(N), R.C.Fredericks(W), T.L.Goddard(SA), H.A.Gomes(W), G.A.Gooch(E), J.Hardstaff jr(E), D.L.Haynes(W), E.H.Hendren(E), G.A.Hick(E), J.B.Hobbs(E), K.J.Hughes(A), L.Hutton(E), B.C.Lara(W), W.M.Lawry(A), C.H.Lloyd(W), B.M.McMillan(SA), I.R.Redpath(A), J.R.Reid(N), I.V.A.Richards(W), Sadiq Mohammad(P), R.A.Smith(E), H.W.Taylor(SA), H.P.Tillakaratne(SL), G.R.Viswanath, K.D.Walters(A), F.E.Woolley(E)

2 D.L.Amiss(E), T.J.E.Andrews(A), A.M.Bacher(SA), T.E.Bailey(E), A.C.Bannerman(A), E.J.Barlow(SA), R.Benaud(A), C.G.Borde(I), M.C.Carew(W), R.H.Catterall(SA), C.P.S.Chauhan(I), N.J.Contractor(I), R.M.Cowper(A), P.A.de Silva(SL), E.R.Dexter(E), G.A.Faulkner(SA), D.I.Gower(E), A.W.Greig(E), R.J.Hadlee(N), Hanif Mohammad(P), R.N.Harvey(A), T.W.Hayward(E), A.C.Hudson(SA), Imtiaz Ahmed(P), D.M.Jones(A), Kapil Dev(I), A.J.Lamb(E), S.J.McCabe(A), C.C.McDonald(A), V.L.Manjrekar(I), G.R.Marsh(A), G.Miller(E), B.Mitchell(SA), Mohsin Khan(P), Moin Khan(P), D.L.Murray(W), A.D.Nourse(SA), A.W.Nourse(SA), S.M.Nurse(W), A.F.Rae(W), A.Ranatunga(SL), G.M.Ritchie(A), Pankaj Roy(I), M.Prabhakar(I), J.N.Rhodes(SA),

R.C.Russell(E), Saeed Ahmed(P), Saleem Malik(P), J.E.D.Sealy(W), Shoaib Mohammad(P), R.Subba Row(E), H.Sutcliffe(E), M.A.Taylor(A), G.H.S.Trott(A), G.M.Turner(N), C.L.Walcott(W), C.Washbrook(E), Wasim Raja(P), F.M.M.Worrell(W)

1 Aamer Malik(P), Abdul Kadir(P), R.Abel(E), J.C.Adams(W), R.W.Anderson(N), R.G.Archer(A), W.W.Armstrong(A), Arun Lal(I), Asif Iqbal(P), N.J.Astle(N), M.S.Atapattu(SL), C.W.J.Athey(E), M.Azahruddin(I), S.F.A.F.Bacchus(A), R.W.Barber(E), W.Bardsley(A), Basit Ali(P), J.E.F.Beck(N), M.G.Bevan(A), R.C.Blunt(N), B.C.Booth(A), K.D.Boyce(W), J.M.Brearley(E), W.A.Brown(A), P.J.P.Burge(A), M.G.Burgess(N), B.F.Butcher(W), C.L.Cairns(N), H.B.Cameron(SA), A.D.R.Campbell(Z), S.L.Campbell(W), D.J.Capel(E), S.Chanderpaul(W), G.S.Chappell(A), A.G.Chipperfield(A), R.J.Christiani(W), L.N.Constantine(W), W.M.Darling(A), C.A.Davis(W), H.G.Deane(SA), P.J.L.Dujon(W), C.I.Dunusinghe(SL), S.A.Durani(I), R.Edwards(A), W.R.Endean(SA), F.M.Engineer(I), K.W.R.Fletcher(E), G.W.Flower(Z), M.L.C.Foster(W), K.J.Funston(SA), S.C.Ganguly(I), M.W.Gatting(E), P.A.Gibb(E), G.J.Gilmour(A), M.J.Greatbatch(N), J.M.Gregory(A), J.W.Guy(N), W.A.Hadlee(N), W.R.Hammond(E), Hanumant Singh(I), N.S.Harford(N), A.L.Hassett(A), G.A.Headley(W), I.A.Healy(A), E.E.Hemmings(E), R.I.C.Holder(W), J.K.Holt(W), C.L.Hooper(W), G.P.Howarth(N), C.C.Hunte(W), N.Hussain(E), Imran Khan(P), F.S.Jackson(E), A.D.Jadeja(I), M.L.Jaisimha(I), D.R.Jardine(E), S.T.Jayasuriya(SL), G.L.Jessop(E), A.H.Kardar(P), G.Kirsten(SA), N.V.Knight(E), B.M.Laird(A), H.Larwood(E), V.V.S.Laxman(I), M.Leyland(E), C.B.Llewellyn(SA), S.J.E.Loxton(A), B.W.Luckhurst(E), C.G.Macartney(A), C.L.McCool(A), R.B.McCosker(A), A.C.MacLaren(E), R.A.McLean(SA), R.S.Madugalle(SL), S.V.Manjrekar(I), A.V.Mankad(I), M.H.Mankad(I), P.N.F.Mansell(SA), Maqsood Ahmed(P), M.D.Marshall(W), G.R.J.Matthews(A), L.R.D.Mendis(SL), C.Milburn(E), K.R.Miller(A), R.B.Minnett(A), R.W.Morgan(N), A.R.Morris(A), M.D.Moxon(E), Mudassar Nazar(P), B.A.G.Murray(N), Mushtaq Mohammad(P), R.K.Nunes(W), S.O'Linn(SA), J.M.Parks(E), Nawab of Pataudi, jr(I), D.N.Patel(N), E.Paynter(E), W.B.Phillips(A), A.J.Pithey(SA), R.G.Pollock(SA), W.H.Ponsford(A), Qasim Omar(P), W.V.Raman(I), Rameez Raja(P), D.W.Randall(E), K.S.Ranjitsinhji(E), V.S.Ransford(A), J.R.Ratnayeke(SL), W.W.Read(E), J.F.Reid(N), W.Rhodes(E), A.J.Richardson(A), D.J.Richardson(SA), R.T.Robinson(E), C.A.G.Russell(E), Saeed Anwar(P), Saleem Yousuf(P), Sarfraz Nawaz(P), W.H.Scotton(E), Shafqat Rana(P), R.J.Shastri(I), B.K.Shepherd(A), R.T.Simpson(E), P.R.Sleep(A), C.L.Smith(E), F.B.Smith(N), J.S.Solomon(W), R.T.Spooner(E), K.Srikkanth(I), D.S.Steele(E), A.J.Stewart(E), V.H.Stollmeyer(W), R.F.Surti(I), D.Tallon(A), L.J.Tancred(SA), Taslim Arif(P), J.M.Taylor(A), R.W.Taylor(E), S.R.Tendulkar(I), G.P.Thorpe(E), P.M.Toohey(A), J.T.Tyldesley(E), B.H.Valentine(E), P.G.V.van der Bijl(SA), D.L.Vettori(N), K.G.Viljoen(SA), P.A.Wallace(W), Waqar Hassan(P), A.Ward(E), J.C.Watkins(SA), M.E.Waugh(A), Wazir Mohammad(P), S.Wettimuny(SL), J.M.Wiener(A), B.Wood(E), G.M.Wood(A), R.E.S.Wyatt(E), G.N.Yallop(A), N.W.D.Yardley(E), B.A.Young(N)

## MOST FIFTIES *(All scores of 50 and over)*

| Player | Country | 50's | Inns | A | E | SA | WI | NZ | I | P | SL | Z |
|---|---|---|---|---|---|---|---|---|---|---|---|---|
| A.R.Border | Australia | **90** | 265 | 0 | 29 | 1 | 17 | 11 | 13 | 14 | 5 | 0 |
| S.M.Gavaskar | India | **79** | 214 | 12 | 20 | 0 | 20 | 5 | 0 | 17 | 5 | 0 |
| I.V.A.Richards | West Indies | **69** | 182 | 19 | 23 | 0 | 0 | 3 | 16 | 8 | 0 | 0 |
| Javed Miandad | Pakistan | **66** | 189 | 13 | 11 | 0 | 6 | 13 | 19 | 0 | 3 | 1 |
| G.A.Gooch | England | **66** | 215 | 20 | 0 | 0 | 18 | 7 | 13 | 6 | 2 | 0 |
| G.Boycott | England | **64** | 193 | 21 | 0 | 3 | 20 | 8 | 6 | 6 | 0 | 0 |
| M.C.Cowdrey | England | **60** | 188 | 16 | 0 | 10 | 16 | 10 | 5 | 3 | 0 | 0 |
| C.H.Lloyd | West Indies | **58** | 175 | 18 | 18 | 0 | 0 | 0 | 19 | 3 | 0 | 0 |
| D.L.Haynes | West Indies | **57** | 202 | 19 | 18 | 1 | 0 | 8 | 6 | 5 | 0 | 0 |
| D.I.Gower | England | **57** | 204 | 21 | 0 | 0 | 7 | 8 | 8 | 11 | 2 | 0 |
| G.S.Sobers | West Indies | **56** | 160 | 10 | 23 | 0 | 0 | 1 | 15 | 7 | 0 | 0 |
| K.F.Barrington | England | **55** | 131 | 18 | 0 | 8 | 7 | 4 | 12 | 6 | 0 | 0 |
| G.S.Chappell | Australia | **55** | 151 | 0 | 21 | 0 | 12 | 6 | 3 | 12 | 0 | 0 |
| M.A.Taylor | Australia | **54** | 171 | 0 | 19 | 5 | 6 | 7 | 5 | 9 | 3 | 0 |
| C.G.Greenidge | West Indies | **53** | 185 | 12 | 15 | 1 | 0 | 7 | 13 | 6 | 0 | 0 |
| D.C.Boon | Australia | **53** | 190 | 0 | 15 | 3 | 11 | 11 | 8 | 2 | 3 | 0 |
| L.Hutton | England | **52** | 138 | 19 | 0 | 11 | 11 | 7 | 4 | 0 | 0 | 0 |
| S.R.Waugh | Australia | **52** | 162 | 0 | 15 | 8 | 10 | 7 | 2 | 4 | 6 | 0 |
| D.B.Vengsarkar | India | **52** | 185 | 9 | 11 | 0 | 13 | 3 | 0 | 10 | 6 | 0 |
| M.A.Atherton | England | **49** | 149 | 14 | 0 | 9 | 8 | 9 | 6 | 3 | 0 | 0 |
| G.R.Viswanath | India | **49** | 155 | 13 | 16 | 0 | 11 | 5 | 0 | 4 | 0 | 0 |
| K.D.Walters | Australia | **48** | 123 | 0 | 17 | 3 | 11 | 7 | 8 | 2 | 0 | 0 |
| W.R.Hammond | England | **46** | 140 | 16 | 0 | 20 | 2 | 5 | 3 | 0 | 0 | 0 |
| M.E.Waugh | Australia | **45** | 128 | 0 | 12 | 6 | 12 | 4 | 2 | 6 | 4 | 0 |

| | | | | | | | | | | | | | |
|---|---|---|---|---|---|---|---|---|---|---|---|---|---|
| D.C.S.Compton | England | **45** | 131 | 14 | 0 | 18 | 4 | 4 | 2 | 3 | 0 | 0 |
| R.N.Harvey | Australia | **45** | 137 | 0 | 18 | 13 | 6 | 0 | 6 | 2 | 0 | 0 |
| J.B.Hobbs | England | **43** | 102 | 27 | 0 | 14 | 2 | 0 | 0 | 0 | 0 | 0 |
| R.B.Kanhai | West Indies | **43** | 137 | 15 | 14 | 0 | 0 | 0 | 11 | 3 | 0 | 0 |
| Saleem Malik | Pakistan | **43** | 142 | 6 | 13 | 1 | 4 | 7 | 5 | 0 | 6 | 1 |
| R.B.Richardson | West Indies | **43** | 146 | 16 | 10 | 0 | 0 | 3 | 7 | 6 | 1 | 0 |
| D.G.Bradman | Australia | **42** | 80 | 0 | 31 | 4 | 2 | 0 | 5 | 0 | 0 | 0 |
| W.M.Lawry | Australia | **40** | 123 | 0 | 20 | 5 | 7 | 0 | 8 | 0 | 0 | 0 |
| I.M.Chappell | Australia | **40** | 136 | 0 | 20 | 0 | 12 | 3 | 3 | 2 | 0 | 0 |

Most for the other countries:

| | | | | | | | | | | | | |
|---|---|---|---|---|---|---|---|---|---|---|---|---|
| B.Mitchell | South Africa | **29** | 80 | 4 | 23 | 0 | 0 | 2 | 0 | 0 | 0 | 0 |
| M.D.Crowe | New Zealand | **35** | 131 | 9 | 8 | 1 | 4 | 0 | 1 | 8 | 2 | 2 |
| J.G.Wright | New Zealand | **35** | 148 | 6 | 11 | 0 | 4 | 0 | 6 | 4 | 4 | 0 |
| A.Ranatunga | Sri Lanka | **36** | 137 | 4 | 4 | 3 | 1 | 7 | 5 | 8 | 0 | 4 |
| A.Flower | Zimbabwe | **17** | 53 | 0 | 1 | 1 | 0 | 4 | 3 | 5 | 3 | 0 |

## MOST CONSECUTIVE FIFTIES

**SEVEN**

| | | | | | | | | | |
|---|---|---|---|---|---|---|---|---|---|
| E.D.Weekes | West Indies | 141 | 128 | 194 | 162 | 101 | 90 | 56 | 1947-48 to 1948-49 |

**SIX**

| | | | | | | | | |
|---|---|---|---|---|---|---|---|---|
| J.Ryder | Australia | 78* | 58 | 56 | 142 | 201* | 88 | 1921-22 to 1924-25 |
| E.H.Hendren | England | 77 | 205* | 56 | 123 | 61 | 55 | 1929-30 |
| G.A.Headley | West Indies | 93 | 53 | 270* | 106 | 107 | 51 | 1934-35 to 1939 |
| A.Melville | South Africa | 67 | 78 | 103 | 189 | 104* | 117 | 1938-39 to 1947 |
| G.S.Sobers | West Indies | 52 | 52 | 80 | 365* | 125 | 109* | 1957-58 |
| E.R.Dexter | England | 85 | 172 | 70 | 99 | 93 | 52 | 1962 to 1962-63 |
| K.F.Barrington | England | 63 | 132* | 101 | 94 | 126 | 76 | 1962-63 |
| K.D.Walters | Australia | 76 | 118 | 110 | 50 | 242 | 103 | 1968-69 |
| G.S.Chappell | Australia | 68 | 54* | 52 | 70 | 121 | 67 | 1975-76 to 1976-77 |
| G.R.Viswanath | India | 59 | 54 | 79 | 89 | 73 | 145 | 1977-78 to 1978-79 |
| Zaheer Abbas | Pakistan | 91 | 126 | 52 | 215 | 186 | 168 | 1982-83 |
| A.R.Border | Australia | 80 | 65* | 76 | 51* | 50 | 56 | 1989 to 1989-90 |
| M.A.Taylor | Australia | 108 | 52 | 101 | 77 | 59 | 101* | 1989-90 |
| R.S.Dravid | India | 92 | 93 | 85 | 52 | 56 | 86 | 1997-98 |

*G.Boycott (England) scored nine fifties in ten innings in 1970-71 and 1971: 70, 50, 77, 142*,12, 76*, 58, 119*, 121*, 112.*

*M.A.Noble (Australia) is the only player to score two separate fifties on the same day: 60* and 59* v England at Manchester in 1899 on the second day.*

## CENTURY BEFORE LUNCH

| FIRST DAY | Lunch score | | | | | |
|---|---|---|---|---|---|---|
| V.T.Trumper (104) | 103* | Australia | v | England | Manchester | 1902 |
| C.G.Macartney (151) | 112* | Australia | v | England | Leeds | 1926 |
| D.G.Bradman (334) | 105* | Australia | v | England | Leeds | 1930 |
| Majid Khan (112) | 108* | Pakistan | v | New Zealand | Karachi[1] | 1976-77 |

| OTHER DAYS | Overnight score | Lunch score | | | | | | Day |
|---|---|---|---|---|---|---|---|---|
| K.S.Ranjitsinhji (154*) | 41* | 154* | England | v | Australia | Manchester | 1896 | 3 |
| C.Hill (142) | 22* | 138* | Australia | v | South Africa | Johannesburg[1] | 1902-03 | 3 |
| W.Bardsley (164) | 32* | 150* | Australia | v | South Africa | Lord's | 1912 | 2 |
| C.P.Mead (182* | 19* | 128* | England | v | Australia | The Oval | 1921 | 2 |
| J.B.Hobbs (211) | 12* | 114* | England | v | South Africa | Lord's | 1924 | 2 |
| H.G.Owen-Smith (129) | 27* | 129 | South Africa | v | England | Leeds | 1929 | 3 |
| W.R.Hammond (336*) | 41* | 152* | England | v | New Zealand | Auckland | 1932-33 | 2 |
| L.E.G.Ames (148*) | 25* | 148* | England | v | South Africa | The Oval | 1935 | 3 |
| S.J.McCabe (189*) | 59* | 159* | Australia | v | South Africa | Johannesburg[1] | 1935-36 | 4 |
| G.S.Chappell (176) | 76* | 176 | Australia | v | New Zealand | Christchurch | 1981-82 | 2 |

## 100 RUNS BETWEEN LUNCH AND TEA

| | | | | | | |
|---|---|---|---|---|---|---|
| 112 | J.M.Gregory (119) | Australia | v | South Africa | Johannesburg[1] | 1921-22 |
| 115 | D.G.Bradman (334) | Australia | v | England | Leeds | 1930 |
| 145+ | W.R.Hammond (336*) | England | v | New Zealand | Christchurch | 1932-33 |
| 107 | D.G.Bradman (244) | Australia | v | England | The Oval | 1934 |
| 127 | S.J.McCabe (232) | Australia | v | England | Nottingham | 1938 |
| 114 | F.M.M.Worrell (261) | West Indies | v | England | Nottingham | 1950 |
| 173 | D.C.S.Compton (278) | England | v | Pakistan | Nottingham | 1954 |
| 121 | R.Benaud (121) | Australia | v | West Indies | Kingston[1] | 1954-55 |
| 103 | G.S.Sobers (174) | West Indies | v | England | Leeds | 1966 |
| 100 | K.R.Stackpole (138) | Australia | v | South Africa | Cape Town | 1966-67 |
| 100 | K.D.Walters (112) | Australia | v | West Indies | Port-of-Spain | 1972-73 |
| 106 | D.W.Hookes (143*) | Australia | v | Sri Lanka | Kandy | 1982-83 |
| 103 | M.Azharuddin (179) | India | v | England | Manchester | 1990 |

## 100 RUNS BETWEEN TEA AND STUMPS

| | | | | | | |
|---|---|---|---|---|---|---|
| 113 | G.J.Bonnor (128) | Australia | v | England | Sydney | 1884-85 |
| 112 | V.T.Trumper (185*) | Australia | v | England | Sydney | 1903-04 |
| 133 | V.T.Trumper (159) | Australia | v | South Africa | Melbourne | 1910-11 |
| 101 | D.G.Bradman (254) | Australia | v | England | Lord's | 1930 |
| 102 | D.G.Bradman (304) | Australia | v | England | Leeds | 1934 |
| 104 | A.Melville (104*) | South Africa | v | England | Nottingham | 1947 |
| 107 | D.G.Bradman (201) | Australia | v | INDIA | Adelaide | 1947-48 |
| 105 | D.T.Lindsay (131) | South Africa | v | Australia | Johannesburg[3] | 1966-67 |
| 103 | K.D.Walters (103) | Australia | v | England | Perth | 1974-75 |
| 106 | I.T.Botham (149*) | England | v | Australia | Leeds | 1981 |
| 106 | R.B.Richardson (182) | West Indies | v | Australia | Georgetown | 1990-91 |
| 110 | M.E.Waugh (139*) | Australia | v | West Indies | St John's | 1990-91 |

## FASTEST FIFTIES

| Min | | | | | | |
|---|---|---|---|---|---|---|
| 22 | V.T.Trumper (63) | Australia | v | South Africa | Johannesburg[1] | 1902-03 |
| 28 | J.T Brown (140) | England | v | Australia | Melbourne | 1894-95 |
| 29 | S.A.Durani (61*) | India | v | England | Kanpur | 1963-64 |
| 30 | E.A.V.Williams (72) | West Indies | v | England | Bridgetown | 1947-48 |
| 30 | B.R.Taylor (124) | New Zealand | v | West Indies | Auckland | 1968-69 |
| 31 | W.J.O'Reilly (56*) | Australia | v | South Africa | Johannesburg[1] | 1935-36 |
| 32 | W.J.Cronje (82) | South Africa | v | Sri Lanka | Centurion | 1997-98 |
| 33 | C.A.Roach (56) | West Indies | v | England | The Oval | 1933 |
| 34 | C.R.Browne (70*) | West Indies | v | England | Georgetown | 1929-30 |
| 35 | J.H.Sinclair (104) | South Africa | v | Australia | Cape Town | 1902-03 |
| 35 | C.G.Macartney (56) | Australia | v | South Africa | Sydney | 1910-11 |
| 35 | J.W.Hitch (51*) | England | v | Australia | The Oval | 1921 |
| 38 | R.Benaud (121) | Australia | v | West Indies | Kingston | 1954-55 |
| 40 | J.Darling (160) | Australia | v | England | Sydney | 1897-98 |
| 40 | S.J.McCabe (189*) | Australia | v | South Africa | Johannesburg[1] | 1935-36 |
| 41 | J.M.Gregory (119) | Australia | v | South Africa | Johannesburg[1] | 1921-22 |
| 42 | T.G.Evans (73) | England | v | India | Nottingham | 1959 |
| 43 | G.L.Jessop (104) | England | v | Australia | The Oval | 1902 |
| 45 | J.J.Lyons (55) | Australia | v | England | Lord's | 1890 |
| 45 | G.L.Jessop (93) | England | v | South Africa | Lord's | 1907 |
| 45 | P.W.Sherwell (115) | South Africa | v | England | Lord's | 1907 |
| 45 | F.B.Smith (54*) | New Zealand | v | England | Leeds | 1949 |
| 45 | R.R.Lindwall (50) | Australia | v | England | Lord's | 1953 |
| 45 | L.K.Germon (55) | New Zealand | v | Pakistan | Lahore[2] | 1996-97 |

## FASTEST FIFTIES (by balls)

| Balls | | | | | | |
|---|---|---|---|---|---|---|
| 30 | Kapil Dev (73) | India | v | Pakistan | Karachi[1] | 1982-83 |
| 31 | W.J.Cronje (82) | South Africa | v | Sri Lanka | Centurion | 1997-98 |
| 32 | I.V.A.Richards (61) | West Indies | v | India | Kingston | 1982-83 |
| 32 | I.T.Botham (59) | England | v | New Zealand | The Oval | 1986 |
| 33 | R.C.Fredericks (169) | West Indies | v | Australia | Perth | 1975-76 |
| 33 | Kapil Dev (59) | India | v | Pakistan | Karachi | 1978-79 |
| 33 | Kapil Dev (65) | India | v | England | Manchester | 1982 |
| 33 | A.J.Lamb (60) | England | v | New Zealand | Auckland | 1991-92 |
| 34 | I.D.S.Smith (61) | New Zealand | v | Pakistan | Faisalabad | 1990-91 |
| 35 | I.V.A.Richards (110*) | West Indies | v | England | St John's | 1985-86 |
| 35 | R.B.Richardson (106) | West Indies | v | Australia | Adelaide | 1988-89 |
| 35 | M.Azahruddin (109) | India | v | South Africa | Calcutta | 1996-97 |
| 36 | B.R.Taylor (124) | New Zealand | v | West Indies | Auckland | 1968-69 |
| 37 | S.M.Gavaskar (121) | India | v | West Indies | Delhi | 1983-84 |
| 38 | S.Chanderpaul (71) | West Indies | v | Australia | Sydney | 1996-97 |
| 39 | M.J.Greatbatch (87) | New Zealand | v | Zimbabwe | Bulawayo[1] | 1992-93 |
| 39 | A.D.R.Campbell (63) | Zimbabwe | v | Pakistan | Rawalpindi[2] | 1993-94 |
| 39 | G.P.Wickramasinghe (51) | Sri Lanka | v | South Africa | Cape Town | 1997-98 |
| 40 | B.C.Lara (53) | West Indies | v | England | Leeds | 1995 |
| 40 | G.P.Thorpe (82*) | England | v | Australia | Nottingham | 1997 |
| 40 | S.T.Jayasuriya (50) | Sri Lanka | v | India | Mumbai[3] | 1997-98 |
| 40 | P.L.Symcox (54) | South Africa | v | Australia | Adelaide | 1997-98 |
| 42 | D.I.Gower (73) | England | v | Pakistan | Manchester | 1992 |
| 43 | J.M.Gregory (119) | Australia | v | South Africa | Johannesburg[1] | 1921-22 |
| 43 | A.Ranatunga (131) | Sri Lanka | v | South Africa | Moratuwa | 1993-94 |
| 43 | B.C.Lara (152) | West Indies | v | England | Nottingham | 1995 |
| 45 | W.J.O'Reilly (56*) | Australia | v | South Africa | Johannesburg[1] | 1935-36 |
| 45 | C.L.Hooper (73*) | West Indies | v | England | Leeds | 1995 |
| 46 | R.S.Kaluwitharana (103) | Sri Lanka | v | New Zealand | Dunedin | 1996-97 |
| 46 | L.Klusener (58) | South Africa | v | Pakistan | Sheikhupura | 1997-98 |
| 46 | R.S.Kaluwitharana (51) | Sri Lanka | v | Zimbabwe | Kandy | 1997-98 |
| 47 | P.V.Simmons (87) | West Indies | v | Pakistan | Bridgetown | 1992-93 |
| 47 | C.L.Cairns (120) | New Zealand | v | Zimbabwe | Auckland | 1995-96 |
| 47 | S.T.Jayasuriya (72) | Sri Lanka | v | Pakistan | Colombo (SSC) | 1996-97 |
| 47 | P.A.de Silva (78) | Sri Lanka | v | West Indies | Kingstown | 1997-98 |
| 47 | S.T.Jayasuriya (59) | Sri Lanka | v | New Zealand | Cilombo (PIS) | 1997-98 |
| 48 | B.C.Lara (88) | West Indies | v | Australia | St John's | 1994-95 |
| 48 | A.J.Stewart (73) | England | v | Zimbabwe | Bulwayo[2] | 1996-97 |
| 48 | I.A.Healy (63) | Australia | v | England | Nottingham | 1997 |
| 48 | C.L.Hooper (106) | West Indies | v | Pakistan | Karachi[1] | 1997-98 |
| 50 | R.S.Mahanama (109) | Sri Lanka | v | New Zealand | Colombo (SSC) | 1992-93 |
| 50 | M.E.Waugh (70) | Australia | v | England | Nottingham | 1993 |
| 50 | M.E.Waugh (126) | Australia | v | West Indies | Kingston | 1994-95 |

## FASTEST CENTURIES

| Min | | | | | | |
|---|---|---|---|---|---|---|
| 70 | J.M.Gregory (119) | Australia | v | South Africa | Johannesburg[1] | 1921-22 |
| 75 | G.L.Jessop (104) | England | v | Australia | The Oval | 1902 |
| 78 | R.Benaud (121) | Australia | v | West Indies | Kingston | 1954-55 |
| 80 | J.H.Sinclair (104) | South Africa | v | Australia | Cape Town | 1902-03 |
| 81 | I.V.A.Richards (110*) | West Indies | v | England | St John's | 1985-86 |
| 86 | B.R.Taylor (124) | New Zealand | v | West Indies | Auckland | 1968-69 |
| 91 | J.Darling (160) | Australia | v | England | Sydney | 1897-98 |
| 91 | S.J.McCabe (189*) | Australia | v | South Africa | Johannesburg[1] | 1935-36 |
| 94 | V.T.Trumper (185*) | Australia | v | England | Sydney | 1903-04 |
| 95 | J.T.Brown (140) | England | v | Australia | Melbourne | 1894-95 |
| 95 | P.W.Sherwell (115) | South Africa | v | England | Lord's | 1907 |
| 98 | D.Denton (104) | England | v | South Africa | Johannesburg[1] | 1909-10 |

| | | | | | | |
|---|---|---|---|---|---|---|
| 98 | C.Hill (191) | Australia | v | South Africa | Sydney | 1910-11 |
| 98 | D.G.Bradman (167) | Australia | v | South Africa | Melbourne | 1931-32 |
| 99 | C.G.Macartney (116) | Australia | v | South Africa | Durban[1] | 1921-22 |
| 99 | D.G.Bradman (334) | Australia | v | England | Leeds | 1948 |
| 100 | G.J.Bonnor (128) | Australia | v | England | Sydney | 1884-85 |
| 100 | C.Hill (100) | Australia | v | South Africa | Mebourne | 1910-11 |
| 100 | L.E.G.Ames (149) | England | v | West Indies | Kingston | 1929-30 |
| 100 | W.R.Hammond (100*) | England | v | New Zealand | The Oval | 1931 |
| 100 | W.R.Hammond (167) | England | v | India | Manchester | 1936 |

## FASTEST CENTURIES *(by balls)*

| Balls | | | | | | |
|---|---|---|---|---|---|---|
| 56 | I.V.A.Richards (110*) | West Indies | v | England | St John's | 1985-86 |
| 67 | J.M.Gregory (119) | Australia | v | South Africa | Johannesburg[1] | 1921-22 |
| 71 | R.C.Fredericks (169) | West Indies | v | Australia | Perth | 1975-76 |
| 74 | Majid Khan (112) | Pakistan | v | New Zealand | Karachi[1] | 1976-77 |
| 74 | Kapil Dev (163) | India | v | Sri Lanka | Kanpur | 1986-87 |
| 74 | M.Azahruddin (109) | India | v | South Africa | Calcutta | 1996-97 |
| 76 | G.L.Jessop (104) | England | v | Australia | The Oval | 1902 |
| 80 | C.L.Hooper (106) | West Indies | v | Pakistan | Karachi[1] | 1997-98 |
| 83 | B.R.Taylor (124) | New Zealand | v | West Indies | Auckland | 1968-69 |
| 85 | C.H.Lloyd (163) | West Indies | v | India | Bangalore | 1974-75 |
| 86 | I.T.Botham (118) | England | v | Australia | Manchester | 1981 |
| 86 | Kapil Dev (116) | India | v | England | Kanpur | 1981-82 |
| 86 | C.L.Cairns (120) | New Zealand | v | Zimbabwe | Auckland | 1995-96 |
| 87 | I.T.Botham (147*) | England | v | Australia | Leeds | 1981 |
| 87 | M.Azharuddin (121) | India | v | England | Lord's | 1990 |
| 88 | R.R.Lindwall (100) | Australia | v | England | Melbourne | 1946-47 |
| 88 | R.J.Hadlee (103) | New Zealand | v | West Indies | Christchurch | 1979-80 |
| 94 | Zaheer Abbas (168) | Pakistan | v | India | Faisalabad | 1982-83 |
| 94 | S.M.Gavaskar (121) | India | v | West Indies | Delhi | 1983-84 |
| 95 | D.T.Lindsay (131) | South Africa | v | Australia | Johannesburg[3] | 1966-67 |
| 95 | Kapil Dev (100*) | India | v | West Indies | Port-of-Spain | 1982-83 |
| 95 | I.D.S.Smith (173) | New Zealand | v | India | Auckland | 1989-90 |
| 95 | G.A.Gooch (123) | England | v | India | Lord's | 1990 |
| 96 | M.Azahruddin (115) | India | v | South Africa | Cape Town | 1996-97 |
| 97 | K.Srikkanth (116) | India | v | Australia | Sydney | 1985-86 |
| 98 | G.S.Sobers (113) | West Indies | v | Australia | Sydney | 1968-69 |
| 98 | R.S.Kaluwitharana (103) | Sri Lanka | v | New Zealand | Dunedin | 1996-97 |
| 99 | I.T.Botham (103) | England | v | New Zealand | Nottingham | 1983 |
| 99 | P.A.de Silva (103*) | Sri Lanka | v | Pakistan | Colombo (SSC) | 1996-97 |
| 100 | L.Klusener (102*) | South Africa | v | India | Cape Town | 1996-97 |
| 101 | Kapil Dev (126*) | India | v | West Indies | Delhi | 1978-79 |
| 102 | I.V.A.Richards (109*) | West Indies | v | India | Delhi | 1987-88 |
| 104 | I.T.Botham (108) | England | v | Pakistan | Lord's | 1978 |
| 105 | I.V.A.Richards (145) | West Indies | v | England | Lord's | 1980 |
| 105 | Kapil Dev (109) | India | v | West Indies | Madras[1] | 1987-88 |
| 107 | C.H.Lloyd (242*) | West Indies | v | India | Bombay[3] | 1974-75 |
| 108 | M.D.Crowe (107) | New Zealand | v | Sri Lanka | Colombo (SSC) | 1992-93 |
| 109 | D.C.S.Compton (113) | England | v | South Africa | The Oval | 1947 |
| 109 | C.L.King (100*) | West Indies | v | New Zealand | Christchurch | 1979-80 |
| 109 | Kapil Dev (119) | India | v | Australia | Madras[1] | 1986-87 |
| 110 | R.E.Redmond (107) | New Zealand | v | Pakistan | Auckland | 1972-73 |
| 110 | R.C.Fredericks (109) | West Indies | v | England | Leeds | 1976 |
| 110 | L.R.D.Mendis (105) | Sri Lanka | v | India | Madras[1] | 1982-83 |
| 110 | S.R.Waugh (134*) | Australia | v | Sri Lanka | Hobart | 1989-90 |
| 114 | A.Rantunga (131) | Sri Lanka | v | South Africa | Moratuwa | 1993-94 |

## FASTEST DOUBLE CENTURIES

| Min | | | | | | |
|---|---|---|---|---|---|---|
| 214 | D.G.Bradman (334) | Australia | v | England | Leeds | 1930 |
| 223 | S.J.McCabe (232) | Australia | v | England | Nottingham | 1938 |
| 226 | V.T.Trumper (214*) | Australia | v | South Africa | Adelaide | 1910-11 |
| 234 | D.G.Bradman (254) | Australia | v | England | Lord's | 1930 |
| 240 | W.R.Hammond (336*) | England | v | New Zealand | Auckland | 1932-33 |
| 241 | S.E.Gregory (201) | Australia | v | England | Sydney | 1894-95 |
| 245 | D.C S.Compton (278) | England | v | Pakistan | Nottingham | 1954 |
| 251 | D.G Bradman (223) | Australia | v | West Indies | Brisbane[1] | 1930-31 |
| 253 | D.G.Bradman (226) | Australia | v | South Africa | Brisbane[2] | 1931-32 |

## FASTEST TRIPLE CENTURIES

| Min | | | | | | |
|---|---|---|---|---|---|---|
| 288 | W.R.Hammond (336*) | England | v | New Zealand | Auckland | 1932-33 |
| 336 | D.G.Bradman (334) | Australia | v | England | Leeds | 1930 |

*W.R.Hammond's third hundred was scored in 48 minutes.*
*D.G.Bradman scored his three hundreds in 99, 115 and 122 minutes respectively and reached 309* at the end of the first day.*

## MOST RUNS IN A DAY

| | | | | | | |
|---|---|---|---|---|---|---|
| 309(0-309*) | D.G.Bradman (334) | Australia | v | England | Leeds | 1930 |
| 295(41*-336*) | W.R.Hammond (336*) | England | v | New Zealand | Auckland | 1932-33 |
| 273(5*-278) | D.C.S.Compton (278) | England | v | Pakistan | Nottingham | 1954 |
| 271(0-271*) | D.G.Bradman (304) | Australia | v | England | Leeds | 1934 |
| 244(0-244) | D.G.Bradman (244) | Australia | v | England | The Oval | 1934 |
| 239(0-239*) | F.M.M.Worrell (261) | West Indies | v | England | Nottingham | 1950 |
| 223(0-223*) | W.R.Hammond (227) | England | v | New Zealand | Christchurch | 1932-33 |
| 223(0-223*) | D.G.Bradman (223) | Australia | v | West Indies | Brisbane[1] | 1930-31 |
| 217(0-217) | W.R.Hammond (217) | England | v | India | The Oval | 1936 |
| 214(73*-287) | R.E.Foster (287) | England | v | Australia | Sydney | 1903-04 |
| 213(19*-232) | S.J.McCabe (232) | Australia | v | England | Nottingham | 1938 |
| 210(0-210*) | W.R.Hammond (240) | England | v | Australia | Lord's | 1938 |
| 209(0-209) | C.A.Roach (209) | West Indies | v | England | Georgetown | 1929-30 |
| 208(20*-228*) | G.S.Sobers (365*) | West Indies | v | Pakistan | Kingston | 1957-58 |
| 208(0-208*) | V.T.Trumper (214*) | Australia | v | South Africa | Adelaide | 1910-11 |
| 206(0-206) | L.Hutton (206) | England | v | New Zealand | The Oval | 1949 |
| 205(0-205*) | W.H.Ponsford (266) | Australia | v | England | The Oval | 1934 |
| 205(0-205) | Aamer Sohail (205) | Pakistan | v | England | Manchester | 1992 |
| 203(0-203) | H.L.Collins (203) | Australia | v | South Africa | Johannesburg[1] | 1921-22 |
| 203(0-203*) | R B Kanhai (256) | West Indies | v | India | Calcutta | 1958-59 |
| 203(0*-203*) | P.A.de Silva (267) | Sri Lanka | v | New Zealand | Wellington | 1990-91 |
| 201(0-201) | D.G.Bradman (201) | Australia | v | India | Adelaide | 1947-48 |
| 200(0-200*) | D.G.Bradman (226) | Australia | v | South Africa | Brisbane[2] | 1931-32 |
| 200(0-200*) | I.V.A.Richards (291) | West Indies | v | England | The Oval | 1976 |

## SLOWEST FIFTIES

| Min | | | | | | |
|---|---|---|---|---|---|---|
| 357 | T.E.Bailey (68) | England | v | Australia | Brisbane[2] | 1958-59 |
| 350 | C.J.Tavare (82) | England | v | Pakistan | Lord's | 1982 |
| 333 | B.A.Young (51) | New Zealand | v | South Africa | Durban[2] | 1994-95 |
| 326 | S.M.Gavaskar (51) | India | v | Sri Lanka | Colombo (SSC) | 1985-86 |
| 318 | Rameez Raja (62) | Pakistan | v | West Indies | Karachi[1] | 1986-87 |
| 316 | C.P.S.Chauhan (61) | India | v | Pakistan | Kanpur | 1979-80 |
| 315 | Shoaib Mohammad (53*) | Pakistan | v | Zimbabwe | Lahore[2] | 1993-94 |
| 313 | D.J.McGlew (70) | South Africa | v | Australia | Johannesburg[3] | 1957-58 |
| 312 | J.J.Crowe (120*) | New Zealand | v | Sri Lanka | Colombo (CCC) | 1986-87 |
| 310 | B.A.Edgar (55) | New Zealand | v | Australia | Wellington | 1981-82 |
| 310 | A.R.Border (75) | Australia | v | West Indies | Sydney | 1988-89 |

| | | | | | | |
|---|---|---|---|---|---|---|
| 306 | C.J.Tavare (78) | England | v | Australia | Manchester | 1981 |
| 304 | P.L.Taylor (54*) | Australia | v | Pakistan | Karachi[1] | 1988-89 |
| 302 | D.N.Sardesai (60) | India | v | West Indies | Bridgetown | 1961-62 |
| 300 | G.S.Camacho (57) | West Indies | v | England | Bridgetown | 1967-68 |
| 296 | C.Z.Harris (56) | New Zealand | v | Sri Lanka | Moratuwa | 1992-93 |
| 296 | B.A.Young (56) | New Zealand | v | England | Wellington | 1996-97 |
| 294 | C.L.Smith (91) | England | v | New Zealand | Auckland | 1983-84 |
| 290 | G.Boycott (63) | England | v | Pakistan | Lahore[2] | 1977-78 |
| 290 | K.R.Rutherford (50*) | New Zealand | v | Australia | Auckland | 1985-86 |
| 290 | E.J.Gray (50) | New Zealand | v | England | Nottingham | 1986 |
| 290 | H.D.P.K.Dharmasena (54) | Sri Lanka | v | Zimbabwe | Bulawayo[2] | 1994-95 |
| 289 | C.J.Tavare (56) | England | v | India | Bombay[3] | 1981-82 |
| 289 | B.A.Edgar (74) | New Zealand | v | Australia | Perth | 1985-86 |
| 288 | R.J.Shastri (109) | India | v | West Indies | Bridgetown | 1988-89 |
| 285 | P.R.Umrigar (78) | India | v | Australia | Bombay[2] | 1956-57 |
| 285 | G.A.Gooch (84) | England | v | West Indies | The Oval | 1988 |
| 284 | K.S.More (55) | India | v | South Africa | Durban[2] | 1992-93 |
| 284 | J.G.Wright (72) | New Zealand | v | Australia | Wellington | 1992-93 |
| 282 | E.D.A.S.McMorris (73) | West Indies | v | England | Kingston | 1959-60 |
| 280 | P.E.Richardson (117) | England | v | South Africa | Johannesburg[3] | 1956-57 |
| 279 | Asif Mujtaba (54*) | Pakistan | v | Zimbabwe | Rawalpindi[2] | 1993-94 |
| 278 | G.Boycott (77) | England | v | Australia | Perth | 1978-79 |
| 277 | P.A.de Silva (110*) | Sri Lanka | v | India | Mohali | 1997-98 |
| 275 | W.M.Lawry (57) | Australia | v | England | Melbourne | 1962-63 |
| 275 | S.Ranatunga (118) | Sri Lanka | v | Zimbabwe | Harare | 1994-95 |
| 272 | A.P.Gurusinha (128) | Sri Lanka | v | Zimbabwe | Harare | 1994-95 |
| 271 | B.A.Young (51) | New Zealand | v | South Africa | Cape Town | 1994-95 |
| 270 | Mudassar Nazar (111) | Pakistan | v | England | Lahore[2] | 1977-78 |
| 270 | M.D.Crowe (108*) | New Zealand | v | Pakistan | Lahore[2] | 1990-91 |
| 270 | Saqlain Mushtaq (78) | Pakistan | v | Zimbabwe | Sheikhupura | 1996-97 |

## SLOWEST CENTURIES

| Min | | | | | | |
|---|---|---|---|---|---|---|
| 557 | Mudassar Nazar (111) | Pakistan | v | England | Lahore[2] | 1977-78 |
| 545 | D.J.McGlew (105) | South Africa | v | Australia | Durban[2] | 1957-58 |
| 535 | A.P.Gurusinha (128) | Sri Lanka | v | Zimbabwe | Harare | 1994-95 |
| 516 | J.J.Crowe (120*) | New Zealand | v | Sri Lanka | Colombo (CCC) | 1986-87 |
| 500 | S.V.Manjrekar (104) | India | v | Zimbabwe | Harare | 1992-93 |
| 488 | P.E.Richardson (117) | England | v | South Africa | Johannesburg[3] | 1956-57 |
| 487 | C.T.Radley (158) | England | v | New Zealand | Auckland | 1977-78 |
| 468 | Hanif Mohammad (142) | Pakistan | v | India | Bahawalpur | 1954-55 |
| 462 | M.J.Greatbatch (146*) | New Zealand | v | Australia | Perth | 1989-90 |
| 461 | M.D.Crowe (108*) | New Zealand | v | Pakistan | Lahore[2] | 1990-91 |
| 460 | Hanif Mohammad (111) | Pakistan | v | England | Dacca | 1961-62 |
| 458 | K.W.R.Fletcher (122) | England | v | Pakistan | The Oval | 1974 |
| 457 | S.A.R.Silva (111) | Sri Lanka | v | India | Colombo (SSC) | 1985-86 |
| 455 | G.P.Howarth (122) | New Zealand | v | England | Auckland | 1977-78 |
| 440 | A.J.Watkins (137*) | England | v | India | Delhi | 1951-52 |
| 438 | G.Boycott (105) | England | v | India | Delhi | 1981-82 |
| 437 | D.B.Vengsarkar (146*) | India | v | Pakistan | Delhi | 1979-80 |
| 437 | A.P.Gurusinha (116*) | Sri Lanka | v | Pakistan | Colombo (PSS) | 1985-86 |
| 435 | J.W.Guy (102) | New Zealand | v | India | Hyderabad | 1955-56 |
| 434 | M.C.Cowdrey (154) | England | v | West Indies | Birmingham | 1957 |
| 434 | T.J.Franklin (101) | New Zealand | v | England | Lord's | 1990 |
| 430 | S.Ranatunga (118) | Sri Lanka | v | Zimbabwe | Harare | 1994-95 |
| 428 | S.M.Gavaskar (172) | India | v | England | Bangalore | 1981-82 |
| 427 | R.J.Shastri (109) | India | v | West Indies | Bridgetown | 1988-89 |
| 425 | H.A.Gomes (127) | West Indies | v | Australia | Perth | 1984-85 |
| 424 | R.J.Shastri (125) | India | v | Pakistan | Jaipur | 1986-87 |
| 424 | M.A.Atherton (105) | England | v | Australia | Sydney | 1990-91 |

| | | | | | | |
|---|---|---|---|---|---|---|
| 422 | R.J.Shastri (111) | India | v | England | Calcutta | 1984-85 |
| 421 | S.Ranatunga (100*) | Sri Lanka | v | Zimbabwe | Bulawayo[2] | 1994-95 |
| 420 | M.D.Crowe (188) | New Zealand | v | West Indies | Georgetown | 1984-85 |
| 416 | W.J.Cronje (135) | South Africa | v | India | Port Elizabeth | 1992-93 |
| 416 | A.J.Stewart (143) | England | v | West Indies | Bridgetown | 1993-94 |
| 416 | N.S.Sidhu (131) | India | v | Sri Lanka | Mohali | 1996-97 |
| 414 | J.H.B.Waite (134) | South Africa | v | Australia | Durban[2] | 1957-58 |
| 414 | A.W.Greig (103) | England | v | India | Calcutta | 1976-77 |
| 414 | J.G.Wright (110) | New Zealand | v | India | Auckland | 1980-81 |
| 412 | J.G.Wright (138) | New Zealand | v | West Indies | Wellington | 1986-87 |
| 411 | D.W.Randall (150) | England | v | Australia | Sydney | 1978-79 |
| 410 | M.A.Atherton (151) | England | v | New Zealand | Nottingham | 1990 |
| 409 | M.L.Apte (163*) | India | v | West Indies | Port-of-Spain | 1952-53 |
| 408 | M.Amarnath (101) | India | v | Pakistan | Lahore[2] | 1984-85 |
| 404 | J.F.Reid (148) | New Zealand | v | Pakistan | Wellington | 1984-85 |
| 396 | R.A.Woolmer (149) | England | v | Australia | The Oval | 1975 |
| 395 | A.P.Gurusinha (127) | Sri Lanka | v | New Zealand | Dunedin | 1994-95 |
| 392 | J.F.Reid (180) | New Zealand | v | Sri Lanka | Colombo (CCC) | 1983-84 |
| 392 | M.J.Greatbatch (107*) | New Zealand | v | England | Auckland | 1987-88 |
| 390 | R.A.Smith (128) | England | v | Sri Lanka | Colombo (SSC) | 1992-93 |
| 390 | K.F.Barrington (109*) | England | v | Pakistan | Nottingham | 1967 |
| 388 | H.A.Gomes (127*) | West Indies | v | Australia | Adelaide | 1981-82 |
| 387 | M.A.Atherton (111) | England | v | New Zealand | Manchester | 1994 |
| 386 | C.A.Davis (183) | West Indies | v | New Zealand | Bridgetown | 1971-72 |
| 385 | D.M.Jones (210) | Australia | v | India | Madras[1] | 1986-87 |
| 385 | Imran Khan (136) | Pakistan | v | Australia | Adelaide | 1989-90 |
| 385 | R.S.Dravid (148) | India | v | South Africa | Johannesburg[3] | 1996-97 |
| 384 | M.A.Taylor (100) | Australia | v | India | Adelaide | 1991-92 |
| 382 | D.L.Haynes (105) | West Indies | v | New Zealand | Dunedin | 1979-80 |
| 379 | G.Boycott (107) | England | v | Australia | Nottingham | 1977 |
| 377 | M.R.Ramprakash (154) | England | v | West Indies | Bridgetown | 1997-98 |
| 376 | B.A.Edgar (127) | New Zealand | v | West Indies | Auckland | 1979-80 |
| 375 | G.P.Thorpe (103) | England | v | West Indies | Bridgetown | 1997-98 |
| 370 | H.P.Tillakaratne (116) | Sri Lanka | v | Zimbabwe | Harare | 1994-95 |

## SLOWEST DOUBLE CENTURIES

| Min | | | | | | |
|---|---|---|---|---|---|---|
| 776 | D.S.B.P.Kuruppu (201*) | Sri Lanka | v | New Zealand | Colombo (CCC) | 1986-87 |
| 685 | V.G.Kambli (224) | India | v | England | Madras[1] | 1992-93 |
| 671 | N.S.Sidhu (201) | India | v | West Indies | Port-of-Spain | 1996-97 |
| 666 | G.W.Flower (201*) | Zimbabwe | v | Pakistan | Harare | 1994-95 |
| 656 | Shoaib Mohammad (203*) | Pakistan | v | New Zealand | Karachi[1] | 1990-91 |
| 652 | A.D.Gaekwad (201) | India | v | Pakistan | Jullundur | 1983-84 |
| 652 | R.S.Mahanama (225) | Sri Lanka | v | India | Colombo (PIS) | 1997-98 |
| 608 | R.B.Simpson (311) | Australia | v | England | Manchester | 1964 |
| 596 | A.R.Border (205) | Australia | v | New Zealand | Adelaide | 1987-88 |
| 595 | G.S.Sobers (226) | West Indies | v | England | Bridgetown | 1959-60 |
| 591 | Javed Miandad (211) | Pakistan | v | Australia | Karachi[1] | 1988-89 |
| 584 | Hanif Mohammad (337) | Pakistan | v | West Indies | Bridgetown | 1957-58 |
| 570 | S.G.Barnes (234) | Australia | v | England | Sydney | 1946-47 |
| 568 | G.R.Viswanath (222) | India | v | England | Madras[1] | 1981-82 |
| 566 | A.R.Border (200*) | Australia | v | England | Leeds | 1993 |
| 562 | C.G.Greenidge (226) | West Indies | v | Australia | Bridgetown | 1990-91 |
| 556 | R.J.Shastri (206) | India | v | Australia | Sydney | 1991-92 |
| 555 | G.N.Yallop (268) | Australia | v | Pakistan | Melbourne | 1983-84 |
| 550 | S.R.Waugh (200) | Australia | v | West Indies | Kingston | 1994-95 |
| 550 | M.S.Atapattu (223) | Sri Lanka | v | Zimbabwe | Kandy | 1997-98 |
| 535 | R.M.Cowper (307) | Australia | v | England | Melbourne | 1965-66 |
| 531 | W.M.Lawry (210) | Australia | v | West Indies | Bridgetown | 1964-65 |
| 524 | D.L.Houghton (266) | Zimbabwe | v | Sri Lanka | Bulawayo[2] | 1994-95 |

| | | | | | | |
|---|---|---|---|---|---|---|
| 519 | B.A.Young (267*) | New Zealand | v | Sri Lanka | Dunedin | 1996-97 |
| 518 | K.F.Barrington (256) | England | v | Australia | Manchester | 1964 |
| 515 | D.M.Jones (216) | Australia | v | West Indies | Adelaide | 1988-89 |
| 513 | V.G.Kambli (224) | India | v | England | Bombay[3] | 1992-93 |
| 512 | M.A.Taylor (219) | Australia | v | England | Nottingham | 1989 |
| 511 | B.A.Young (267*) | New Zealand | v | Sri Lanka | Dunedin | 1996-97 |

## SLOWEST TRIPLE CENTURIES

| Min | | | | | | |
|---|---|---|---|---|---|---|
| 858 | Hanif Mohammad (337) | Pakistan | v | West Indies | Bridgetown | 1957-58 |
| 753 | R.B.Simpson (311) | Australia | v | England | Manchester | 1964 |
| 723 | S.T.Jayasuriya (340) | Sri Lanka | v | India | Colombo (PIS) | 1997-98 |
| 693 | R.M.Cowper (307) | Australia | v | England | Melbourne | 1965-66 |
| 662 | L.Hutton (364) | England | v | Australia | The Oval | 1938 |
| 610 | B.C.Lara (375) | West Indies | v | England | St John's | 1993-94 |
| 605 | L.G.Rowe (302) | West Indies | v | England | Bridgetown | 1973-74 |

## AN HOUR BEFORE SCORING FIRST RUN

| Min | | | | | | |
|---|---|---|---|---|---|---|
| 97 | T.G.Evans (10*) | England | v | Australia | Adelaide | 1946-47 |
| 84 | R.K.Chauhan (9) | India | v | Sri Lanka | Ahmedabad | 1993-94 |
| 82 | P.I.Pocock (13) | England | v | West Indies | Georgetown | 1967-68 |
| 74 | J.T.Murray (3*) | England | v | Australia | Sydney | 1962-63 |
| 72 | C.G.Rackemann (9) | Australia | v | England | Sydney | 1990-91 |
| 72 | H.H.Streak (19*) | Zimbabwe | v | Pakistan | Karachi[2] | 1993-94 |
| 70 | W.L.Murdoch (17) | Australia | v | England | Sydney | 1882-83 |
| 69 | R.M.Hogg (7*) | Australia | v | West Indies | Adelaide | 1984-85 |
| 67 | C.J.Tavare (82) | England | v | Pakistan | Lord's | 1982 |
| 66 | J.G.Wright (38) | New Zealand | v | Australia | Wellington | 1981-82 |
| 65 | Shujauddin (45) | Pakistan | v | Australia | Lahore[2] | 1959-60 |
| 64 | C.E.Eksteen (21) | South Africa | v | New Zealand | Auckland | 1994-95 |
| 63 | C.J.Tavare (9) | England | v | Australia | Perth | 1982-83 |
| 63 | P.C.R.Tufnell (2*) | England | v | India | Bombay[3] | 1992-93 |
| 62 | M.A.Taylor (49) | Australia | v | England | Sydney | 1994-95 |

## AN HOUR WITHOUT ADDING TO SCORE

| Min | | | | | | |
|---|---|---|---|---|---|---|
| 94 | M.C.Snedden (23) | New Zealand | v | Australia | Wellington | 1989-90 |
| 91 | J.J.Crowe (21) | New Zealand | v | West Indies | Bridgetown | 1984-85 |
| 90 | B.Mitchell (58) | South Africa | v | Australia | Brisbane[2] | 1931-32 |
| 90 | C.J.Tavare (89) | England | v | Australia | Perth | 1982-83 |
| 89 | R.J.Shastri (23) | India | v | South Africa | Johannesburg[3] | 1992-93 |
| 79 | T.E.Bailey (8) | England | v | South Africa | Leeds | 1955 |
| 77 | D.B.Close (20) | England | v | West Indies | Manchester | 1976 |
| 75 | A.Ranatunga (37) | Sri Lanka | v | New Zealand | Colombo (CCC) | 1983-84 |
| 70 | D.L.Haynes (9) | West Indies | v | New Zealand | Auckland | 1979-80 |
| 70 | R.C.Russell (29*) | England | v | South Africa | Johannesburg[3] | 1995-96 |
| 69 | G.A.Gooch (84) | England | v | West Indies | The Oval | 1988 |
| 67 | W.H.Scotton (34) | England | v | Australia | The Oval | 1886 |
| 66 | S.M.Gavaskar (52) | India | v | Sri Lanka | Colombo (PSS) | 1985-86 |
| 65 | Nawab of Pataudi, jr (5) | India | v | England | Bombay[2] | 1972-73 |
| 64 | Anil Dalpat (15) | Pakistan | v | New Zealand | Wellington | 1984-85 |
| 64 | M.A.Taylor (11) | Australia | v | England | Sydney | 1990-91 |
| 64 | S.Chanderpaul (80) | West Indies | v | England | The Oval | 1995 |
| 63 | D.R.Jardine (24) | England | v | Australia | Brisbane[2] | 1932-33 |
| 63 | W.R.Endean (18) | South Africa | v | England | Johannesburg[3] | 1956-57 |
| 63 | W.R.Playle (18) | New Zealand | v | England | Leeds | 1958 |
| 63 | J.M.Brearley (48) | England | v | Australia | Birmingham | 1981 |
| 63 | S.R.Waugh (47*) | Australia | v | England | Nottingham | 1993 |
| 62 | K.F.Barrington (137) | England | v | New Zealand | Birmingham | 1965 |

| | | | | | | |
|---|---|---|---|---|---|---|
| 61 | J.F.Reid (148) | New Zealand | v | Pakistan | Wellington | 1984-85 |
| 61 | M.D.Marshall (6*) | West Indies | v | England | Birmingham | 1991 |
| 60 | B.Mitchell (73) | South Africa | v | England | Johannesburg[1] | 1938-39 |
| 60 | T.E.Bailey (80) | England | v | South Africa | Durban[2] | 1956-57 |
| 60 | C.J.Tavare (82) | England | v | Pakistan | Lord's | 1982 |
| 60 | A.R.Border (9) | Australia | v | Pakistan | Faisalabad | 1982-83 |
| 60 | S.M.Gavaskar (51) | India | v | Sri Lanka | Colombo (SSC) | 1985-86 |
| 60 | J.J.Crowe (120*) | New Zealand | v | Sri Lanka | Colombo (CCC) | 1986-87 |

## BATSMEN DISMISSED FOR A 'PAIR'

**FOUR TIMES**

B.S.Chandrasekhar (India): v NZ 1975-76; v E 1976-77; v A 1977-78 (twice).

**THREE TIMES**

R.Peel (England):v A 1894-95 (twice), 1896.
R.W.Blair (New Zealand): v WI 1955-56; v E 1962-63; v SA 1963-64.
D.L.Underwood (England):v WI 1966; v A 1974-75; v WI 1976.
B.S.Bedi (India):v E 1974; v WI 1974-75; v E 1976-77.
A.G.Hurst (Australia):v E 1978-79 (twice); v P 1978-79.
C.E.L.Ambrose (West Indies):v E 1988; v P 1990-91; v E 1991.
D.K.Morrison (New Zealand) v A 1987-88; v SL 1990-91; v A 1993-94.
D.E.Malcolm v NZ 1990; v P 1992; v A 1997.

**TWICE**

*AUSTRALIA*: K.D.Mackay v E 1956; v I 1959-60. G.D.McKenzie v SA 1963-64; v E 1968. J.W.Gleeson v SA 1969-70; v E 1970-71. W.M.Clark v WI 1977-78 (twice). R.M.Hogg v I 1979-80; v WI 1984-85. R.G.Holland v E 1985; v NZ 1985-86. M.E.Waugh v SL 1992-93 (twice).
*ENGLAND*: A.V.Bedser v A 1948; v WI 1950. D.L.Amiss v A 1968, 1974-75. P.I.Pocock v WI 1984 (twice). N.A.Foster v WI 1985-86; v P 1987-88. A.R.Caddick v A 1997; v W 1997-98.
*SOUTH AFRICA*: L.J.Tancred v E 1907, 1912. Q.McMillan v A 1931-32 (twice). R.J.Crisp v A 1935-36 (twice).
*WEST INDIES*: C.A.Roach v E 1929-30, 1933. A.L.Valentine v E 1950, 1953-54. A.I.Kallicharran v E 1973-74; v NZ 1979-80.
*NEW ZEALAND*: S.B.Doull v W 1994-95; v E 1996-97.
*INDIA*: M.Amarnath v WI 1983-84 (twice). Maninder Singh v P 1982-83; v WI 1987-88.
*PAKISTAN*: Aaqib Javed v A 1989-90; v E 1992.
*SRI LANKA*: M.S.Ataputta v I 1990-91; v I 1993-94.
*ZIMBABWE*: A.G.Huckle v SL 1997-98; v P 1997-98.

**ONCE**

*AUSTRALIA*: P.S.McDonnell v E 1882-83. T.W.Garrett v E 1882-83. E.Evans v E 1886. P.G.McShane v E 1887-88. A.C.Bannerman v E 1888. M.A.Noble v E 1899. S.E.Gregory v E 1899. C.E.McLeod v E 1901-02. J.Darling v E 1902. J.J.Kelly v E 1902. H.Trumble v E 1903-04. V.T.Trumper v E 1907-08. J.V.Saunders v E 1907-08. C.V.Grimmett v E 1930. W.A.S.Oldfield v SA 1931-32. J.H.W.Fingleton v E 1932-33. V.Y.Richardson v E 1932-33. C.L.Badcock v E 1938. I.W.Johnson v E 1946-47. J.Moroney v E 1950-51. J.B.Iverson v E 1950-51. L.V.Maddocks v E 1956. R.N.Harvey v E 1956. A.T.W.Grout v WI 1960-61. R.Benaud v E 1961. A.N.Connolly v WI 1968-69. R.Edwards v E 1972. K.R.Stackpole v NZ 1973-74. G.Dymock v E 1974-75. R.W.Marsh v E 1977. J.R.Thomson v E 1977. C.S.Serjeant v I 1977-78. A.L.Mann v I 1977-78. D.W.Hookes v P 1979-80. G.M.Wood v NZ 1980-81. M.R.Whitney v E 1981. B.Yardley v P 1982-83. R.J.Bright v P 1982-83. C.G.Rackemann v WI 1984-85. K.J.Hughes v WI 1984-85. M.G.Hughes v E 1986-87. D.M.Jones v P 1988-89. B.A.Reid v WI 1990-91. I.A.Healy v WI 1992-93. A.R.Border v WI 1992-93. J.L.Langer v NZ 1992-93. M.A.Taylor v P 1994-95. P.E.McIntyre v A 1994-95. B.P.Julian v W 1994-95. C.J.McDermott v P 1995-96. G.D.McGrath v P 1995-96.
*ENGLAND*: G.F.Grace v A 1880. W.Attewell v A 1891-92. G.A.Lohmann v SA 1895-96. E.G.Arnold v A 1903-04. A.E.Knight v A 1903-04. E.G.Hayes v SA 1905-06. M.C.Bird v SA 1909-10. H.Strudwick v A 1921. P.Holmes v SA 1927-28. C.I.J.Smith v WI 1934-35. J.T.Ikin v A 1946-47. J.J.Warr v A 1950-51. F.Ridgway v I 1951-52. R.T.Spooner v SA 1955. J.H.Wardle v A 1956. F.S.Trueman v A 1958-59. T.E.Bailey v A 1958-59. G.Pullar v P 1961-62. M.J.K.Smith v I 1961-62. J.T.Murray v P 1967. B.W.Luckhurst v P 1971. A.P.E.Knott v NZ 1973. G.G.Arnold v A 1974-75. G.A.Gooch v A 1975. A.Ward v WI 1976. J.C.Balderstone v WI 1976. M.Hendrick v NZ 1977-78. R.A.Woolmer v A 1981. I.T.Botham v A 1981. E.E.Hemmings v A 1982-83. N.G.Cowans v I 1984-85. D.J.Capel v P 1987-88. W.Larkins v WI 1989-90. R.J.Bailey v WI 1989-90. C.C.Lewis v A 1993. P.C.R.Tufnell v A 1994-95. J.P.Crawley v A 1994-95. P.A.J.DeFreitas v A 1994-95. M.R.Ramprakash v W 1995. D.Gough v A 1997. M.A.Butcher v W 1997-98. G.P.Thorpe v SA 1998. A.Flintoff v SA 1998.
*SOUTH AFRICA*: C.S.Wimble v E 1891-92. J.T.Willoughby v E 1895-96. J.J.Kotze v A 1902-03. P.S.Twentyman-Jones v A 1902-03. A.E.E.Vogler v A 1910-11. T.A.Ward v A 1912. C.B.Llewellyn v E 1912. P.T.Lewis v E 1913-14. J.L.Cox v E

1913-14. C.D.Dixon v E 1913-14. G.A.L.Hearne v E 1922-23. A.E.Hall v E 1922-23. F.Nicholson v A 1935-36. X.C.Balaskas v A 1935-36. C.N.McCarthy v E 1948-49. D.J.McGlew v E 1955. W.R.Endean v E 1955. P.S.Heine v E 1956-57. C.Wesley v E 1960. M.A.Seymour v A 1969-70. A.A.Donald v WI 1991-92. C.R.Matthews v E 1994. D.J.Richardson v P 1994-95.

*WEST INDIES*: C.R.Browne v E 1929-30. H.C.Griffith v E 1933. E.E.Achong v E 1934-35. J.Trim v A 1951-52. A.P.Binns v A 1954-55. O.G.Smith v A 1954-55. S.Ramadhin v E 1957. E.D.Weekes v E 1957. F.C.M.Alexander v E 1957. L.R.Gibbs v P 1958-59. F.M.M.Worrell v A 1960-61. J.S.Solomon v I 1961-62. J.L.Hendriks v E 1966. W.W.Hall v E 1967-68. D.L.Murray v I 1974-75. C.G.Greenidge v A 1975-76. J.Garner v P 1976-77. D.A.Murray v P 1980-81. A.L.Logie v I 1983-84. M.A.Holding v A 1984-85. P.J.L.Dujon v P 1986-87. A.H.Gray v P 1986-87. D.Williams v A 1992-93. K.L.T.Arthurton v A 1992-93. J.R.Murray v P 1992-93. C.A.Walsh v P 1997-98.

*NEW ZEALAND*: K.C.James v E 1929-30. F.T.Badcock v E 1929-30. J.Cowie v E 1937. C.G.Rowe v A 1945-46. L.A.Butterfield v A 1945-46. L.S.M.Miller v SA 1953-54. M.B.Poore v E 1954-55. I.A.Colquhoun v E 1954-55. J.A.Hayes v E 1954-55. A.R.MacGibbon v I 1955-56. H.B.Cave v WI 1955-56. N.S.Harford v E 1958. R.C.Motz v SA 1961-62. M.J.F.Shrimpton v SA 1963-64. A.E.Dick v P 1964-65. G.A.Bartlett v E 1965-66. T.W.Jarvis v P 1972-73. W.K.Lees v E 1977-78. B.P.Bracewell v E 1978. B.L.Cairns v A 1980-81. B.A.Edgar v A 1980-81. G.B.Troup v I 1980-81. J.V.Coney v A 1981-82. I.D.S.Smith v A 1981-82. J.G.Bracewell v P 1984-85. K.R.Rutherford v WI 1984-85. J.G.Wright v E 1986. C.M.Kuggeleijn v I 1988-89. M.C.Snedden v I 1988-89. B.R.Hartland v E 1991-92. M.L.Su'a v P 1992-93. D.J.Nash v SL 1994-95. C.Z.Harris N v W 1995-96. D.N.Patel v E 1996-97. S.P.Fleming v A 1997-98. D.L.Vettori v SL 1997-98.

*INDIA*: V.S.Hazare v E 1951-52. G.S.Ramchand v E 1952. Pankaj Roy v E 1952. P.G.Joshi v WI 1952-53. C.V.Gadkari v WI 1952-53. N.S.Tamhane v WI 1958-59. Surendranath v E 1959. R.B.Desai v A 1959-60. D.N.Sardesai v WI 1961-62. M.L.Jaisimha v NZ 1969-70. E.A.S.Prasanna v WI 1974-75. F.M.Engineer v WI 1974-75. D.B.Vengsarkar v WI 1978-79. Yashpal Sharma v A 1979-80. R.M.H.Binny v P 1979-80. D.R.Doshi v P 1982-83. S.Venkataraghavan v WI 1982-83. R.G.Patel v NZ 1988-89. B.K.Venkatesh Prasad v W 1996-97. Harvinder Singh 1997-98.

*PAKISTAN*: M.E.Z.Ghazali v E 1954. Nasim-ul-Ghani v WI 1957-58. Wazir Mohammad v WI 1957-58. Imtiaz Ahmed v E 1961-62. Javed Burki v NZ 1964-65. Salim Altaf v A 1976-77. Iqbal Qasim v E 1978. Majid Khan v A 1978-79. Wasim Bari v A 1978-79. Sikander Bakht v A 1978-79. Mudassar Nazar v E 1982. Wasim Akram v SL 1985-86. Waqar Younis v NZ 1990-91. Saeed Anwar v WI 1990-91. Aamer Sohail v NZ 1992-93. Mushtaq Ahmed v A 1994-95. Manzoor Elahi v Z 1994-95. Rashid Latif v SA 1997-98.

*SRI LANKA*: B.R.Jurangpathy v I 1986-87. R.G.de Alwis v I 1986-87. R.J.Ratnayake v I 1990-91. G.F.Labrooy v I 1990-91. A.Ranatunga v P 1991-92. S.D.Anurasiri v P 1991-92. C.I.Dunusinghe v N 1994-95.

*ZIMBABWE*: D.H.Brain v I 1992-93. S.G.Peall v P 1993-94. G.W.Flower v P 1993-94. H.K.Olonga v E 1996-97. H.H.Streak v N 1997-98. G.J.Rennie v N 1997-98. M.Mbangwa v N 1997-98. D.P.Viljoen v P 1997-98.

## BATSMEN DISMISSED FOR A 'KING PAIR'

| | | | | | |
|---|---|---|---|---|---|
| A.E.E.Vogler | South Africa | v | Australia | Sydney | 1910-11 |
| T.A.Ward | South Africa | v | Australia | Manchester | 1912 |
| R.J.Crisp | South Africa | v | Australia | Durban[2] | 1935-36 |
| C.Wesley | South Africa | v | England | Nottingham | 1960 |
| G.B.Troup | New Zealand | v | India | Wellington | 1980-81 |
| D.J.Richardson | South Africa | v | Pakistan | Johannesburg[3] | 1994-95 |
| A.G.Huckle | Zimbabwe | v | Pakistan | Harare | 1997-98 |

## FASTEST 'PAIRS' *Timed from the start of first innings to dismissal in the second innings*

| | | | | | | |
|---|---|---|---|---|---|---|
| 120 mins | M.E.Z.Ghazali | Pakistan | v | England | Manchester | 1954 |
| 124 mins | R.N.Harvey | Australia | v | England | Manchester | 1956 |
| 164 mins | Pankaj Roy | India | v | England | Manchester | 1952 |

## DISMISSED FOR A 'PAIR' BY THE SAME FIELDING COMBINATION

| | | | | | | |
|---|---|---|---|---|---|---|
| R.Peel | st Jarvis b Turner | England | v | Australia | Sydney | 1894-95 |
| J.Darling | c Braund b Barnes | Australia | v | England | Sheffield | 1902 |
| P.T.Lewis | c Woolley b Barnes | South Africa | v | England | Durban[1] | 1913-14 |
| P.G.Joshi | c Worrell b Valentine | India | v | West Indies | Bridgetown | 1952-53 |
| K.D.Mackay | c Oakman b Laker | Australia | v | England | Manchester | 1956 |
| Maninder Singh | c Richardson b Walsh | India | v | West Indies | Bombay[3] | 1987-88 |

## THREE 'PAIRS' IN A MATCH BY THE SAME TEAM

| | | | | | |
|---|---|---|---|---|---|
| M.B.Poore, I.A.Colquhoun, J A.Hayes | New Zealand | v | England | Auckland | 1954-55 |
| D L.Amiss, D L.Underwood, G G.Arnold | England | v | Australia | Adelaide | 1974-75 |
| Majid Khan, Wasim Bari, Sikander Bakht | Pakistan | v | Australia | Perth | 1978-79 |
| M.S.Ataputta, R.J.Ratnayake, G.F.Labrooy | Sri Lanka | v | India | Chandigarh | 1990-91 |

## MOST 'DUCKS' IN A SERIES

| | | | | | Innings | |
|---|---|---|---|---|---|---|
| *SIX* | A.G.Hurst | Australia | v | England | 12 | 1978-79 |
| *FIVE* | Pankaj Roy | India | v | England | 7 | 1952 |
| | R.C.Motz | New Zealand | v | South Africa | 9 | 1961-62 |
| | W.M.Clark | Australia | v | West Indies | 7 | 1977-78 |
| | M.Amarnath | India | v | West Indies | 6 | 1983-84 |

## MOST CONSECUTIVE 'DUCKS'

| | | | | | |
|---|---|---|---|---|---|
| *FIVE* | | | | | |
| R.G.Holland | (including two pairs | Australia | v | England | 1985 |
| | in consecutive Tests) | Australia | v | New Zealand | 1985-86 |
| *FOUR* | | | | | |
| R.Peel | (2 pairs in consecutive Tests) | England | v | Australia | 1894-95 |
| R.J.Crisp | (2 pairs in consecutive Tests) | South Africa | v | Australia | 1935-36 |
| Pankaj Roy | (including one pair) | India | v | England | 1952 |
| L.S.M.Miller | (including one pair) | New Zealand | v | South Africa | 1953-54 |
| R.B.Desai | | India | v | England | 1959 |
| | (including one pair) | India | v | Australia | 1959-60 |
| W.M.Clark | (2 pairs in consecutive Tests) | Australia | v | West Indies | 1977-78 |
| P.I.Pocock | (2 pairs in consecutive Tests) | England | v | West Indies | 1984 |
| N.A.Foster | (including one pair) | England | v | Australia | 1985 |
| | | England | v | West Indies | 1985-86 |
| R.G.de Alwis | (including one pair) | Sri Lanka | v | India | 1986-87 |
| | | Sri Lanka | v | Australia | 1987-88 |
| M.E.Waugh | (2 pairs in consecutive Tests) | Australia | v | Sri Lanka | 1992-93 |
| M.L.Su'a | (including one pair) | New Zealand | v | Sri Lanka | 1992-93 |
| | | New Zealand | v | Pakistan | 1992-93 |
| | | New Zealand | v | Australia | 1992-93 |
| D.K.Morrison | (including one pair) | New Zealand | v | Australia | 1993-94 |
| M.Mbangwa | (including one pair) | Zimbabwe | v | New Zealand | 1997-98 |
| | | Zimbabwe | v | Pakistan | 1997-98 |

*R.J.Crisp was dismissed four times in five balls.*

## MOST 'DUCKS'

| Player | Country | 0's | Tests | A | E | SA | WI | NZ | I | P | SL | Z |
|---|---|---|---|---|---|---|---|---|---|---|---|---|
| C.A.Walsh | West Indies | **29** | 103 | 8 | 7 | - | - | - | 3 | 8 | 3 | - |
| D.K.Morrison | New Zealand | **24** | 48 | 7 | 4 | 1 | 1 | - | 2 | 6 | 3 | - |
| B.S.Chandrasekhar | India | **23** | 58 | 6 | 8 | - | 4 | 3 | - | 2 | - | - |
| B.S.Bedi | India | **20** | 67 | 11 | 1 | - | 7 | 1 | - | - | - | - |
| Wasim Bari | Pakistan | **19** | 81 | 11 | 4 | - | 2 | - | 2 | - | - | - |
| D.L.Underwood | England | **19** | 86 | 8 | - | - | 7 | - | 2 | 1 | 1 | - |
| J.Garner | West Indies | **18** | 59 | 5 | 5 | - | - | 4 | - | 4 | - | - |
| C.E.L.Ambrose | West Indies | **18** | 80 | 6 | 8 | - | - | - | - | 4 | - | - |
| K.R.Rutherford | New Zealand | **17** | 56 | 3 | 3 | 2 | 3 | - | 1 | 2 | 3 | - |
| T.G.Evans | England | **17** | 91 | 5 | - | 6 | 1 | 3 | 1 | 1 | - | - |
| D.E.Malcolm | England | **16** | 40 | 6 | - | - | 3 | 2 | 2 | 3 | - | - |
| J.A.Snow | England | **16** | 49 | 6 | - | 1 | 7 | - | 1 | 1 | - | - |
| J.E.Emburey | England | **16** | 65 | 5 | - | - | 6 | - | 2 | 1 | 2 | - |
| S.K.Warne | Australia | **16** | 67 | - | 6 | 3 | 4 | - | 1 | 2 | - | - |
| M.W.Gatting | England | **16** | 79 | 6 | - | - | 2 | 2 | 3 | 3 | - | - |
| D.C.Boon | Australia | **16** | 107 | - | 5 | - | 3 | 3 | - | 2 | 3 | - |
| Kapil Dev | India | **16** | 131 | 3 | 4 | - | 4 | 2 | - | 2 | 1 | - |
| E.A.S.Prasanna | India | **15** | 49 | 7 | 4 | - | 2 | 2 | - | - | - | - |

| Player | Country | 0's | Tests | A | E | SA | WI | NZ | I | P | SL | Z |
|---|---|---|---|---|---|---|---|---|---|---|---|---|
| M.A.Holding | West Indies | **15** | 60 | 5 | 4 | - | - | 2 | 4 | - | - | - |
| G.D.McKenzie | Australia | **15** | 60 | - | 7 | 3 | 1 | - | 4 | - | - | - |
| I.T.Botham | England | **15** | 102 | 11 | - | - | 1 | 1 | 1 | 1 | - | - |
| I.A.Healy | Australia | **15** | 103 | - | 2 | 1 | 8 | 2 | - | 1 | 1 | - |
| S.R.Waugh | Australia | **15** | 103 | - | 6 | 1 | 2 | 2 | 2 | 2 | - | - |
| D.B.Vengsarkar | India | **15** | 116 | 1 | 3 | - | 5 | 3 | - | 2 | 1 | - |
| D.R.Doshi | India | **14** | 33 | 4 | 4 | - | - | 1 | - | 5 | - | - |
| G.D.McGrath | Australia | **14** | 37 | - | 2 | 2 | 5 | 1 | 1 | 3 | - | - |
| R.M.Hogg | Australia | **14** | 38 | - | 7 | - | 2 | 1 | 3 | 1 | - | - |
| S.Ramadhin | West Indies | **14** | 43 | 7 | 6 | - | - | 1 | - | - | - | - |
| Pankaj Roy | India | **14** | 43 | 8 | 1 | - | 2 | 1 | - | 2 | - | - |
| J.R.Thomson | Australia | **14** | 43 | - | 5 | - | 6 | - | 2 | 1 | - | - |
| D.W.Randall | England | **14** | 47 | 6 | - | - | 1 | 2 | 3 | 2 | - | - |
| L.R.Gibbs | West Indies | **14** | 79 | 5 | 5 | - | - | - | 1 | 3 | - | - |
| Wasim Akram | Pakistan | **14** | 79 | - | 1 | - | 6 | 1 | 2 | - | 2 | 2 |
| M.D.Marshall | West Indies | **14** | 81 | 3 | 6 | - | - | 1 | 1 | 3 | - | - |
| P.C.R.Tufnell | England | **13** | 34 | 7 | - | - | 4 | - | - | 1 | 1 | - |
| T.M.Alderman | Australia | **13** | 41 | - | 4 | - | 6 | - | - | 2 | 1 | - |
| C.G.Borde | India | **13** | 55 | 4 | 4 | - | 4 | - | - | 1 | - | - |
| S.Venkataraghavan | India | **13** | 57 | 5 | 2 | - | 5 | 1 | - | - | - | - |
| F.E.Woolley | England | **13** | 64 | 7 | - | 6 | - | - | - | - | - | - |
| J.B.Statham | England | **13** | 70 | 5 | - | 5 | 2 | - | - | 1 | - | - |
| C.J.McDermott | Australia | **13** | 71 | - | 4 | - | 3 | - | 3 | 3 | - | - |
| C.L.Hooper | West Indies | **13** | 73 | 5 | 3 | - | - | - | - | 5 | - | - |
| M.A.Atherton | England | **14** | 84 | 3 | - | 3 | 5 | 1 | 1 | 1 | - | - |
| G.S.Chappell | Australia | **13** | 87 | - | 5 | - | 3 | 3 | 1 | 1 | - | - |
| R.W.Marsh | Australia | **13** | 96 | - | 6 | - | 1 | 2 | 1 | 3 | - | - |
| G.A.Gooch | England | **13** | 118 | 5 | - | - | 3 | 4 | 1 | - | - | - |
| R.W.Blair | New Zealand | **12** | 19 | - | 6 | 4 | 2 | - | - | - | - | - |
| R.C.Motz | New Zealand | **12** | 32 | - | 2 | 6 | - | - | 1 | 3 | - | - |
| A.L.Valentine | West Indies | **12** | 36 | 5 | 4 | - | - | 1 | 2 | - | - | - |
| R.A.McLean | South Africa | **12** | 40 | 3 | 6 | - | - | 3 | - | - | - | - |
| J.G.Bracewell | New Zealand | **12** | 41 | 3 | 3 | - | - | - | 1 | 4 | 1 | - |
| S.E.Gregory | Australia | **12** | 58 | - | 11 | 1 | - | - | - | - | - | - |
| M.Amarnath | India | **12** | 69 | 3 | 3 | - | 5 | - | - | 1 | - | - |
| A.Ranatunga | Sri Lanka | **12** | 81 | 1 | 1 | 1 | - | 1 | 2 | 6 | - | - |
| R.J.Hadlee | New Zealand | **12** | 86 | 3 | 5 | - | 1 | - | 3 | 2 | - | - |
| R.G.D.Willis | England | **12** | 90 | 5 | - | - | 3 | 1 | 2 | - | 1 | - |
| G.S.Sobers | West Indies | **12** | 93 | 6 | 1 | - | - | 2 | 2 | 1 | - | - |
| S.M.Gavaskar | India | **12** | 125 | 3 | 2 | - | 5 | - | - | 1 | 1 | - |
| J.W.Gleeson | Australia | **11** | 29 | - | 5 | 3 | 2 | - | 1 | - | - | - |
| Maninder Singh | India | **11** | 35 | - | 1 | - | 4 | - | - | 5 | 1 | - |
| M.Muralidaran | Sri Lanka | **11** | 41 | 1 | - | 1 | 1 | 2 | 1 | 2 | - | 2 |
| E.J.Chatfield | New Zealand | **11** | 43 | 5 | - | - | 1 | - | 3 | 2 | - | - |
| M.J.K.Smith | England | **11** | 50 | 2 | - | 2 | 2 | 2 | 3 | - | - | - |
| A.V.Bedser | England | **11** | 51 | 5 | - | 2 | 3 | 1 | - | - | - | - |
| A.T.W.Grout | Australia | **11** | 51 | - | 4 | 2 | 3 | - | 1 | 1 | - | - |
| F.M.M.Worrell | West Indies | **11** | 51 | 8 | 2 | - | - | - | 1 | - | - | - |
| D.M.Jones | Australia | **11** | 52 | - | 3 | - | 1 | 2 | 2 | 3 | - | - |
| Waqar Younis | Pakistan | **11** | 53 | 1 | - | 2 | 1 | 2 | 1 | - | 1 | 3 |
| V.L.Manjrekar | India | **11** | 55 | 4 | - | - | 5 | 1 | - | 1 | - | - |
| F.S.Trueman | England | **11** | 67 | 6 | - | 2 | 1 | 1 | 1 | - | - | - |
| Saleem Malik | Pakistan | **11** | 96 | 3 | 1 | - | 1 | 4 | 2 | - | - | - |
| A.R.Border | Australia | **11** | 156 | - | 3 | - | 4 | 2 | 2 | - | - | - |
| A.G.Hurst | Australia | **10** | 12 | - | 6 | - | - | - | 2 | 2 | - | - |
| P.I.Pocock | England | **10** | 25 | - | - | - | 7 | - | 3 | - | - | - |
| S.L.Boock | New Zealand | **10** | 28 | 2 | - | - | 3 | - | - | 5 | - | - |
| G.P.Wickramasinghe | Sri Lanka | **10** | 30 | 1 | - | - | 1 | 3 | 2 | 3 | - | - |
| J.Briggs | England | **10** | 33 | 9 | - | 1 | - | - | - | - | - | - |

| Player | Country | 0's | Tests | A | E | SA | WI | NZ | I | P | SL | Z |
|---|---|---|---|---|---|---|---|---|---|---|---|---|
| Fazal Mahmood | Pakistan | **10** | 34 | 3 | - | - | 5 | - | 2 | - | - | - |
| A.F.A.Lilley | England | **10** | 35 | 9 | - | 1 | - | - | - | - | - | - |
| D.N.Patel | New Zealand | **10** | 37 | 2 | 3 | - | 1 | - | - | 4 | - | - |
| A.A.Mallett | Australia | **10** | 38 | - | 4 | - | 3 | 1 | 1 | 1 | - | - |
| G.R.Dilley | England | **10** | 39 | 2 | - | - | 5 | 1 | 1 | 1 | - | - |
| I.R.Bishop | West Indies | **10** | 43 | 5 | 1 | - | - | - | 1 | 2 | 1 | - |
| P.A.J.DeFreitas | England | **10** | 44 | 4 | - | - | 4 | 1 | - | 1 | - | - |
| I.W.Johnson | Australia | **10** | 45 | - | 6 | 1 | 1 | - | 1 | 1 | - | - |
| A.A.Donald | South Africa | **10** | 47 | 2 | 3 | - | 2 | - | 1 | 2 | - | - |
| Intikhab Alam | Pakistan | **10** | 47 | 4 | 1 | - | 1 | 3 | 1 | - | - | - |
| Iqbal Qasim | Pakistan | **10** | 47 | 5 | - | - | 2 | - | 3 | - | - | - |
| W.W.Hall | West Indies | **10** | 48 | 2 | 4 | - | - | - | 2 | 2 | - | - |
| D.L.Amiss | England | **10** | 50 | 7 | - | - | - | - | 2 | 1 | - | - |
| M.G.Hughes | Australia | **10** | 53 | - | 3 | 1 | 5 | - | 1 | - | - | - |
| R.W.Taylor | England | **10** | 57 | 3 | - | - | - | 3 | 2 | 2 | - | - |
| A.I.Kallicharran | West Indies | **10** | 66 | 4 | 1 | - | - | 3 | 2 | - | - | - |
| K.J.Hughes | Australia | **10** | 70 | - | 3 | - | 4 | 1 | 1 | 1 | - | - |
| I.M.Chappell | Australia | **10** | 75 | - | 4 | 4 | - | - | 2 | - | - | - |
| M.E.Waugh | Australia | **10** | 78 | - | - | 1 | 3 | - | 2 | - | 4 | - |
| Zaheer Abbas | Pakistan | **10** | 78 | 2 | 3 | - | 2 | 2 | 1 | - | - | - |
| G.R.Viswanath | India | **10** | 91 | 3 | 1 | - | 1 | 2 | - | 3 | - | - |
| C.G.Greenidge | West Indies | **10** | 96 | 3 | 5 | - | - | - | 2 | - | - | - |
| G.Boycott | England | **10** | 108 | 3 | - | 1 | 4 | 2 | - | - | - | - |
| D.L.Haynes | West Indies | **10** | 116 | 1 | 2 | - | - | 3 | 1 | 3 | - | - |
| Most 'ducks' for Zimbabwe: | | | | | | | | | | | | |
| H.H.Streak | Zimbabwe | **8** | 23 | - | - | 1 | - | 2 | - | 4 | 1 | - |

## MOST INNINGS BEFORE FIRST 'DUCK'

| | | | | | |
|---|---|---|---|---|---|
| 75 | P.A.de Silva | Sri Lanka | 1984 | to | 1994-95 |
| 58 | C.H.Lloyd | West Indies | 1966-67 | to | 1973-74 |
| 51 | A.K.Davidson | Australia | 1953 | to | 1961 |
| 46 | B.F.Butcher | West Indies | 1958-59 | to | 1966-67 |
| 44 | M.J.Slater | Australia | 1993 | to | 1994-95 |
| 41 | R.N.Harvey | Australia | 1947-48 | to | 1953 |
| 41 | G.S.Sobers | West Indies | 1953-54 | to | 1958-59 |
| 41 | K.D.Ghavri | India | 1974-75 | to | 1979-80 |
| 40 | W.H.Ponsford | Australia | 1924-25 | to | 1932-33 |
| 40 | Sadiq Mohammad | Pakistan | 1969-70 | to | 1976-77 |

## MOST CONSECUTIVE INNINGS WITHOUT A 'DUCK'

| | | | | | |
|---|---|---|---|---|---|
| 119 | D.I.Gower | England | 1982 | to | 1990-91 |
| 96 | R.B.Richardson | West Indies | 1984-85 | to | 1991 |
| 89 | A.R.Border | Australia | 1982-83 | to | 1988-89 |
| 78 | K.F.Barrington | England | 1962 | to | 1967-68 |
| 75 | P.A.de Silva | Sri Lanka | 1984 | to | 1994-95 |
| 74 | C.H.Lloyd | West Indies | 1976 | to | 1984 |
| 72 | H.W.Taylor | South Africa | 1912 | to | 1931-32 |
| 72 | G.M.Turner | New Zealand | 1968-69 | to | 1982-83 |
| 68 | K.D.Walters | Australia | 1969-70 | to | 1976-77 |
| 67 | W.R.Hammond | England | 1929 | to | 1936 |
| 67 | G.Boycott | England | 1969 | to | 1978-79 |
| 66 | H.A.Gomes | West Indies | 1977-78 | to | 1984-85 |
| 62 | A.P.E.Knott | England | 1974 | to | 1981 |
| 62 | G.R.Marsh | Australia | 1986-87 | to | 1990-91 |

## FEWEST 'DUCKS' IN A CAREER

| Ducks | Innings | | | | | |
|---|---|---|---|---|---|---|
| 0 | 44 | J.W.Burke | Australia | 1950-51 | to | 1958-59 |
| 0 | 40 | R.A.Duff | Australia | 1901-02 | to | 1907-08 |

| | | | | | | |
|---|---|---|---|---|---|---|
| 0 | 37 | R.J.Christiani | West Indies | 1947-48 | to | 1953-54 |
| 0 | 36 | D.L.Houghton | Zimbabwe | 1992-93 | to | 1997-98 |
| 0 | 35 | Waqar Hassan | Pakistan | 1952-53 | to | 1959-60 |
| 0 | 35 | R.S.Dravid | India | 1996 | to | 1997-98 |
| 0 | 34 | B.D.Julien | West Indies | 1973 | to | 1976-77 |
| 0 | 33 | S.Chanderpaul | West Indies | 1993-94 | to | 1996-97 |
| 1 | 74 | C.L.Walcott | West Indies | 1947-48 | to | 1959-60 |
| 1 | 73 | G.M.Turner | New Zealand | 1968-69 | to | 1982-83 |
| 1 | 69 | A.L.Hassett | Australia | 1938 | to | 1953 |
| 1 | 61 | A.K.Davidson | Australia | 1953 | to | 1962-63 |
| 1 | 56 | P.E.Richardson | England | 1956 | to | 1963 |
| 1 | 55 | C.G.Macartney | Australia | 1907-08 | to | 1926 |
| 1 | 53 | G.M.Ritchie | Australia | 1982-83 | to | 1986-87 |
| 1 | 48 | W.M.Ponsford | Australia | 1924-25 | to | 1934 |
| 1 | 48 | E.D.Solkar | India | 1969-70 | to | 1976-77 |
| 1 | 48 | W.B.Phillips | Australia | 1983-84 | to | 1985-86 |
| 1 | 46 | S.J.Snooke | South Africa | 1905-06 | to | 1922-23 |
| 1 | 45 | R.W.Barber | England | 1960 | to | 1968 |
| 1 | 43 | J.E.Cheetham | South Africa | 1948-49 | to | 1955 |
| 1 | 42 | U.C.Hathurusingha | Sri Lanka | 1990-91 | to | 1995-96 |
| 1 | 41 | R.G.Pollock | South Africa | 1963-64 | to | 1969-70 |
| 1 | 40 | A.Shrewsbury | England | 1881-82 | to | 1893 |
| 2 | 84 | H.Sutcliffe | England | 1924 | to | 1935 |
| 2 | 83 | C.C.McDonald | Australia | 1951-52 | to | 1961 |
| 2 | 78 | Saeed Ahmed | Pakistan | 1957-58 | to | 1972-73 |
| 2 | 76 | H.W.Taylor | South Africa | 1912 | to | 1931-32 |
| 2 | 74 | A.H.Jones | New Zealand | 1986-87 | to | 1994-95 |
| 2 | 66 | C.Washbrook | England | 1937 | to | 1956 |
| 2 | 62 | B.M.McMillan | South Africa | 1992-93 | to | 1996-97 |
| 2 | 59 | A.C.Parore | New Zealand | 1990 | to | 1996-97 |
| 2 | 57 | K.D.Ghavri | India | 1974-75 | to | 1980-81 |
| 2 | 56 | J.B.Stollmeyer | West Indies | 1939 | to | 1954-55 |
| 2 | 54 | Ijaz Ahmed | Pakistan | 1988-89 | to | 1996-97 |
| 2 | 53 | G.R.J.Matthews | Australia | 1983-84 | to | 1992-93 |
| 2 | 52 | N.J.Contractor | India | 1955-56 | to | 1961-62 |
| 2 | 50 | P.Willey | England | 1976 | to | 1986 |
| 3 | 93 | G.R.Marsh | Australia | 1985-86 | to | 1991-92 |
| 3 | 85 | J.V.Coney | New Zealand | 1973-74 | to | 1986-87 |
| 3 | 83 | A.W.Nourse | South Africa | 1902-03 | to | 1924 |
| 3 | 83 | G.A.Hick | England | 1991 | to | 1998 |
| 3 | 80 | B.Mitchell | South Africa | 1930-31 | to | 1948-49 |
| 3 | 79 | Mohsin Khan | Pakistan | 1977-78 | to | 1986-87 |
| 3 | 78 | B.F.Butcher | West Indies | 1958-59 | to | 1969 |
| 3 | 70 | G.N.Yallop | Australia | 1975-76 | to | 1984-85 |
| 3 | 70 | R.C.Russell | England | 1988 | to | 1995-96 |
| 3 | 70 | A.P.Gurusinha | Sri Lanka | 1985-86 | to | 1996-97 |
| 4 | 175 | C.H.Lloyd | West Indies | 1966-67 | to | 1984-85 |
| 4 | 171 | M.A.Taylor | Australia | 1988-89 | to | 1996-97 |
| 4 | 144 | A.J.Stewart | England | 1989-90 | to | 1998 |
| 4 | 140 | W.R.Hammond | England | 1927-28 | to | 1946-47 |
| 4 | 125 | K.D.Walters | Australia | 1965-66 | to | 1980-81 |
| 4 | 123 | M.Azharuddin | India | 1984-85 | to | 1997-98 |
| 4 | 102 | J.B.Hobbs | England | 1907-08 | to | 1930 |
| 4 | 100 | Mushtaq Mohammad | Pakistan | 1958-59 | to | 1978-79 |
| 5 | 138 | L.Hutton | England | 1937 | to | 1954-55 |
| 5 | 131 | K.F.Barrington | England | 1955 | to | 1968 |
| 6 | 189 | Javed Miandad | Pakistan | 1976-77 | to | 1993-94 |
| 7 | 202 | D.I.Gower | England | 1978 | to | 1990-91 |

## Partnerships

### HIGHEST PARTNERSHIP FOR EACH WICKET

| | | | | | | | |
|---|---|---|---|---|---|---|---|
| 1st | 413 | M.H.Mankad (231), Pankaj Roy (173) | IND | v | NZ | Madras[2] | 1955-56 |
| 2nd | 576 | S.T.Jayasuriya (340), R.S.Mahanama (225) | SL | v | IND | Colombo (PIS) | 1997-98 |
| 3rd | 467 | A.H.Jones (186), M.D.Crowe (299) | NZ | v | SL | Wellington | 1990-91 |
| 4th | 411 | P.B.H.May (285*), M.C.Cowdrey (154) | ENG | v | WI | Birmingham | 1957 |
| 5th | 405 | S.G.Barnes (234), D.G.Bradman (234) | AUST | v | ENG | Sydney | 1946-47 |
| 6th | 346 | J.H.W.Fingleton (136), D.G.Bradman (270) | AUST | v | ENG | Melbourne | 1936-37 |
| 7th | 347 | D.S.Atkinson (219), C.C.Depeiza (122) | WI | v | AUST | Bridgetown | 1954-55 |
| 8th | 313 | Wasim Akram (257*), Saqlain Mushtaq (78) | PAK | v | ZIM | Sheikhupura | 1996-97 |
| 9th | 195 | M.V.Boucher (78), P.L.Symcox (108) | SAF | v | PAK | Johannesburg[3] | 1997-98 |
| 10th | 151 | B.F.Hastings (110), R.O.Collinge (68*) | NZ | v | PAK | Auckland | 1972-73 |
| | 151 | Azhar Mahmood (128*), Mushtaq Ahmed (59) | PAK | v | SAF | Rawalpindi[2] | 1997-98 |

### PARTNERSHIPS OF 300 AND OVER

| Runs | Wkt | | | | |
|---|---|---|---|---|---|
| 576 | 2nd | S.T.Jayasuriya (340), R.S.Mahanama (225) | SL v IND | Colombo (PIS) | 1997-98 |
| 467 | 3rd | A.H.Jones (186), M.D.Crowe (299) | NZ v SL | Wellington | 1990-91 |
| 451 | 2nd | W.H.Ponsford (266), D.G.Bradman (244) | AUST v ENG | The Oval | 1938 |
| 451 | 3rd | Mudassar Nazar (231), Javed Miandad (280*) | PAK v IND | Hyderabad | 1982-83 |
| 446 | 2nd | C.C.Hunte (260), G.S.Sobers (365*) | WI v PAK | Kingston | 1957-58 |
| 413 | 1st | M.H.Mankad (231), Pankaj Roy (173) | IND v NZ | Madras[2] | 1955-56 |
| 411 | 4th | P.B.H.May (285*), M.C.Cowdrey (154) | ENG v WI | Birmingham | 1957 |
| 405 | 5th | S.G.Barnes (234), D.G.Bradman (234) | AUST v ENG | Sydney | 1946-47 |
| 399 | 4th | G.S.Sobers (226), F.M.M.Worrell (197*) | WI v E | Bridgetown | 1959-60 |
| 397 | 3rd | Qasim Omar (206), Javed Miandad (203*) | PAK v SL | Faisalabad | 1985-86 |
| 388 | 4th | W.H.Ponsford (181), D.G.Bradman (304) | AUST v ENG | Leeds | 1934 |
| 387 | 1st | G.M.Turner (259), T.W.Jarvis (182) | NZ v WI | Georgetown | 1971-72 |
| 385 | 5th | S.R.Waugh (160), G.S.Blewett (214*) | AUST v SA | Johannesburg[3] | 1996-97 |
| 382 | 2nd | L.Hutton (364), M.Leyland (187) | ENG v AUST | The Oval | 1938 |
| 382 | 1st | W.M.Lawry (210), R.B.Simpson (201) | AUST v WI | Bridgetown | 1964-65 |
| 370 | 3rd | W.J.Edrich (189), D.C.S.Compton (208) | ENG v SA | Lord's | 1947 |
| 369 | 2nd | J.H.Edrich (310*), K.F.Barrington (163) | ENG v NZ | Leeds | 1965 |
| 359 | 1st | L.Hutton (158), C.Washbrook (195) | ENG v SA | Johannesburg[2] | 1948-49 |
| 351 | 2nd | G.A.Gooch (196), D.I.Gower (157) | ENG v AUST | The Oval | 1985 |
| 350 | 4th | Mushtaq Mohammad (201), Asif Iqbal (175) | PAK v NZ | Dunedin | 1972-73 |
| 347 | 7th | D.S.Atkinson (219), C.C.Depeiza (122) | WI v AUST | Bridgetown | 1954-55 |
| 346 | 6th | J.H.W.Fingleton (136), D.G.Bradman (270) | AUST v ENG | Melbourne | 1936-37 |
| 344* | 2nd | S.M.Gavaskar (182*), D.B.Vengsarkar (157*) | IND v WI | Calcutta | 1978-79 |
| 341 | 3rd | E.J.Barlow (201), R.G.Pollock (175) | SA v AUST | Adelaide | 1963-64 |
| 338 | 3rd | E.D.Weekes (206), F.M.M.Worrell (167) | WI v ENG | Port-of-Spain | 1953-54 |
| 336 | 4th | W.M.Lawry (151), K.D.Walters (242) | AUST v WI | Sydney | 1968-69 |
| 332* | 5th | A.R.Border (200*), S.R.Waugh (157*) | AUST v ENG | Leeds | 1993 |
| 331 | 2nd | R.T.Robinson (148), D.I.Gower (215) | ENG v AUST | Birmingham | 1985 |
| 329 | 1st | G.R.Marsh (138), M.A.Taylor (219) | AUST v ENG | Nottingham | 1989 |
| 323 | 1st | J.B.Hobbs (178), W.Rhodes (179) | ENG v AUST | Melbourne | 1911-12 |
| 323 | 3rd | Aamer Sohail (160), Inzamamul Haq (177) | PAK v WI | Rawalpindi[2] | 1997-98 |
| 322 | 4th | Javed Miandad (153*), Saleem Malik (165) | PAK v ENG | Birmingham | 1992 |
| 319 | 3rd | A.Melville (189), A.D.Nourse (149) | SA v ENG | Nottingham | 1947 |
| 316† | 3rd | G.R.Viswanath (222), Yashpal Sharma (140) | IND v ENG | Madras[1] | 1981-82 |
| 313 | 8th | Wasim Akram (257*), Saqlain Mushtaq (78) | PAK v ZIM | Sheikhupura | 1996-97 |
| 308 | 7th | Waqar Hassan (189), Imtiaz Ahmed (209) | PAK v IND | Lahore[1] | 1955-56 |
| 308 | 3rd | R.B.Richardson (154), I.V.A.Richards (178) | WI v AUST | St John's | 1983-84 |
| 308 | 3rd | G.A.Gooch (333), A.J.Lamb (139) | ENG v IND | Lord's | 1990 |
| 303 | 3rd | I.V.A.Richards (232), A.I.Kallicharran (97) | WI v ENG | Nottingham | 1976 |
| 303 | 3rd | M.A.Atherton (135), R.A.Smith (175) | ENG v WI | St John's | 1993-94 |
| 301 | 2nd | A.R.Morris (182), D.G.Bradman (173*) | AUST v ENG | Leeds | 1948 |

*† 415 runs were scored for this wicket in two separate partnerships, D.B.Vengsarkar retiring hurt and being succeeded by Yashpal Sharma after 99 runs had been added.*

## MOST CENTURY PARTNERSHIPS IN AN INNINGS

| *FOUR* | | Opponents | | |
|---|---|---|---|---|
| England | 382 (2nd), 135 (3rd), 215 (6th), 106 (7th) | Australia | The Oval | 1938 |
| West Indies | 267 (4th), 101 (6th), 118 (7th), 106 (9th) | India | Delhi | 1948-49 |
| Pakistan | 152 (1st), 112 (2nd), 154 (3rd), 121 (4th) | West Indies | Bridgetown | 1957-58 |
| India | 144 (3rd), 172 (4th), 109 (5th), 102 (6th) | West Indies | Kanpur | 1978-79 |

## SUMMARY OF CENTURY PARTNERSHIPS

| Country | 1st | 2nd | 3rd | 4th | 5th | 6th | 7th | 8th | 9th | 10th | Total |
|---|---|---|---|---|---|---|---|---|---|---|---|
| Australia | 75 | 112 | 109 | 106 | 78 | 46 | 25 | 12 | 7 | 2 | 572 |
| England | 140 | 139 | 116 | 112 | 74 | 72 | 36 | 12 | 7 | 3 | 707 |
| South Africa | 37 | 27 | 35 | 27 | 12 | 16 | 15 | 9 | 2 | 1 | 181 |
| West Indies | 46 | 63 | 68 | 68 | 49 | 48 | 15 | 1 | 4 | 1 | 363 |
| New Zealand | 26 | 26 | 29 | 23 | 29 | 16 | 11 | 6 | 2 | 3 | 171 |
| India | 40 | 52 | 59 | 50 | 34 | 27 | 15 | 8 | 7 | 1 | 293 |
| Pakistan | 28 | 34 | 46 | 35 | 25 | 21 | 8 | 5 | 4 | 3 | 209 |
| Sri Lanka | 5 | 7 | 19 | 12 | 13 | 9 | 3 | - | - | - | 68 |
| Zimbabwe | 5 | 5 | 2 | 3 | 1 | 2 | 2 | 1 | - | - | 21 |
| Total | 402 | 461 | 483 | 436 | 315 | 257 | 130 | 54 | 33 | 14 | 2585 |

## BATSMEN SHARING IN MOST CENTURY PARTNERSHIPS

| Player | Country | Total | 1st | 2nd | 3rd | 4th | 5th | 6th | 7th | 8th | 9th | 10th |
|---|---|---|---|---|---|---|---|---|---|---|---|---|
| A.R.Border | Australia | **62** | - | 2 | 14 | 20 | 16 | 8 | 1 | 1 | - | - |
| S.M.Gavaskar | India | **58** | 22 | 18 | 8 | 6 | 2 | 1 | - | - | 1 | - |
| Javed Miandad | Pakistan | **50** | - | 2 | 22 | 15 | 8 | 3 | - | - | - | - |
| G.Boycott | England | **47** | 20 | 8 | 9 | 8 | - | 2 | - | - | - | - |
| C.G.Greenidge | West Indies | **46** | 22 | 9 | 5 | 4 | 2 | 3 | 1 | - | - | - |
| G.S.Chappell | Australia | **44** | - | 2 | 15 | 13 | 11 | 2 | 1 | - | - | - |
| I.V.A.Richards | West Indies | **44** | - | 11 | 12 | 12 | 5 | 2 | 1 | 1 | - | - |
| G.S.Sobers | West Indies | **43** | - | 3 | 4 | 12 | 12 | 10 | 2 | - | - | - |
| D.C.Boon | Australia | **42** | 6 | 13 | 16 | 5 | 1 | 1 | - | - | - | - |
| M.C.Cowdrey | England | **42** | 5 | 9 | 6 | 13 | 4 | 3 | 1 | - | 1 | - |
| G.A.Gooch | England | **41** | 18 | 11 | 7 | 2 | 2 | 1 | - | - | - | - |
| L.Hutton | England | **41** | 17 | 13 | 7 | 1 | - | 2 | 1 | - | - | - |
| C.H.Lloyd | West Indies | **41** | - | - | 6 | 14 | 9 | 10 | 1 | - | 1 | - |
| D.L.Haynes | West Indies | **39** | 18 | 14 | 5 | 1 | - | 1 | - | - | - | - |
| D.I.Gower | England | **38** | - | 7 | 10 | 11 | 5 | 3 | 2 | - | - | - |
| K.F.Barrington | England | **35** | - | 6 | 10 | 14 | 4 | 1 | - | - | - | - |
| D.G.Bradman | Australia | **35** | - | 14 | 11 | 3 | 6 | 1 | - | - | - | - |
| M.A.Atherton | England | **34** | 16 | 9 | 5 | 3 | - | 1 | - | - | - | - |
| R.B.Kanhai | West Indies | **34** | 2 | 9 | 11 | 7 | 3 | 2 | - | - | - | - |
| M.A.Taylor | Australia | **34** | 17 | 10 | 3 | 3 | - | 1 | - | - | - | - |
| W.R.Hammond | England | **33** | 1 | 6 | 12 | 11 | 2 | 1 | - | - | - | - |
| H.Sutcliffe | England | **33** | 21 | 10 | 1 | - | - | 1 | - | - | - | - |
| S.R.Waugh | Australia | **33** | - | 1 | - | 5 | 14 | 9 | 3 | - | 1 | - |
| J.H.Edrich | England | **32** | 9 | 11 | 6 | 5 | 1 | - | - | - | - | - |
| R.N.Harvey | Australia | **32** | - | 6 | 13 | 9 | 3 | 1 | - | - | - | - |
| J.B.Hobbs | England | **32** | 24 | 6 | 1 | - | - | - | 1 | - | - | - |
| M.Azharuddin | India | **31** | - | 1 | 4 | 15 | 4 | 4 | 2 | 1 | - | - |
| I.M.Chappell | Australia | **30** | - | 18 | 8 | 1 | 1 | 2 | - | - | - | - |
| D.C.S.Compton | England | **30** | - | - | 14 | 7 | 7 | 1 | - | 1 | - | - |
| D.B.Vengsarkar | India | **30** | - | 9 | 9 | 9 | 1 | 2 | - | - | - | - |
| M.E.Waugh | Australia | **30** | - | - | 15 | 8 | 5 | 1 | 1 | - | - | - |
| The most for the other countries is: | | | | | | | | | | | | |
| B.Mitchell | South Africa | **24** | 9 | 3 | 8 | 2 | - | - | 1 | 1 | - | - |
| M.D.Crowe | New Zealand | **26** | - | 1 | 12 | 3 | 7 | 2 | 1 | - | - | - |
| P.A.de Silva | Sri Lanka | **26** | - | - | 14 | 5 | 3 | 3 | 1 | - | - | - |
| G.W.Flower | Zimbabwe | **11** | 5 | 1 | 1 | 2 | - | - | 2 | - | - | - |

# HIGHEST WICKET PARTNERSHIPS FOR EACH COUNTRY

## AUSTRALIA

| | | | | | | |
|---|---|---|---|---|---|---|
| 1st | 382 | W.M.Lawry (210), R.B.Simpson (201) | v | West Indies | Bridgetown | 1964-65 |
| 2nd | 451 | W.H.Ponsford (266), D.G.Bradman (244) | v | England | The Oval | 1934 |
| 3rd | 295 | C.C.McDonald (127), R.N.Harvey (204) | v | West Indies | Kingston | 1954-55 |
| 4th | 388 | W.H.Ponsford (181), D.G.Bradman (304) | v | England | Leeds | 1934 |
| 5th | 405 | S.G.Barnes (234), D.G.Bradman (234) | v | England | Sydney | 1946-47 |
| 6th | 346 | J.H.W.Fingleton (136), D.G.Bradman (270) | v | England | Melbourne | 1936-37 |
| 7th | 217 | K.D.Walters (250), G.J.Gilmour (101) | v | New Zealand | Christchurch | 1976-77 |
| 8th | 243 | R.J.Hartigan (116), C.Hill (160) | v | England | Adelaide | 1907-08 |
| 9th | 154 | S.E.Gregory (201), J.M.Blackham (74) | v | England | Sydney | 1894-95 |
| 10th | 127 | J.M.Taylor (108), A.A.Mailey (46*) | v | England | Sydney | 1924-25 |

## ENGLAND

| | | | | | | |
|---|---|---|---|---|---|---|
| 1st | 359 | L.Hutton (158), C.Washbrook (195) | v | South Africa | Johannesburg[2] | 1948-49 |
| 2nd | 382 | L.Hutton (364), M.Leyland (187) | v | Australia | The Oval | 1938 |
| 3rd | 370 | W.J.Edrich (189), D.C.S.Compton (208) | v | South Africa | Lord's | 1947 |
| 4th | 411 | P.B.H.May (285*), M.C.Cowdrey (154) | v | West Indies | Birmingham | 1957 |
| 5th | 254 | K.W.R.Fletcher (113), A.W.Greig (148) | v | India | Bombay[2] | 1972-73 |
| 6th | 240 | P.H.Parfitt (131*), B.R.Knight (125) | v | New Zealand | Auckland | 1962-62 |
| 7th | 197 | M.K.J.Smith (96), J.M.Parks (101*) | v | West Indies | Port-of-Spain | 1959-60 |
| 8th | 246 | L.E.G.Ames (137), G.O.B.Allen (122) | v | New Zealand | Lord's | 1931 |
| 9th | 163* | M.C.Cowdrey (128*), A.C.Smith (69*) | v | New Zealand | Wellington | 1962-62 |
| 10th | 130 | R.E.Foster (287), W.Rhodes (40*) | v | Australia | Sydney | 1903-04 |

## SOUTH AFRICA

| | | | | | | |
|---|---|---|---|---|---|---|
| 1st | 260 | B.Mitchell (123), I.J.Siedle (141) | v | England | Cape Town | 1930-31 |
| 2nd | 238 | G.Kirsten (210), J.H.Kallis (132) | v | England | Manchester | 1998 |
| 3rd | 341 | E.J.Barlow (201), R.G.Pollock (175) | v | Australia | Adelaide | 1963-64 |
| 4th | 214 | H.W.Taylor (121), H.G.Deane (93) | v | England | The Oval | 1929 |
| 5th | 157 | A.J.Pithey (95), J.H.B.Waite (64) | v | England | Johannesburg[2] | 1964-65 |
| 6th | 200 | R.G.Pollock (274), H.R.Lance (61) | v | Australia | Durban[2] | 1969-70 |
| 7th | 246 | D.J.McGlew (255*), A.R.A.Murray (109) | v | New Zealand | Wellington | 1952-53 |
| 8th | 147* | B.M.McMillan (103*), L.Klusener (102*) | v | India | Cape Town | 1996-97 |
| 9th | 195 | M.V.Boucher (78), P.L.Symcox (108) | v | Pakistan | Johannesburg[3] | 1997-98 |
| 10th | 103 | H.G.Owen-Smith (129), A.J.Bell (26*) | v | England | Leeds | 1929 |

## WEST INDIES

| | | | | | | |
|---|---|---|---|---|---|---|
| 1st | 298 | C.G.Greenidge (149), D.L.Haynes (167) | v | England | St John's | 1989-90 |
| 2nd | 446 | C.C.Hunte (260), G.S.Sobers (365*) | v | Pakistan | Kingston | 1957-58 |
| 3rd | 338 | E.D.Weekes (206), F.M.M.Worrell (167) | v | England | Port-of-Spain | 1953-54 |
| 4th | 399 | G.S.Sobers (226), F.M.M.Worrell (197*) | v | England | Bridgetown | 1959-60 |
| 5th | 265 | S.M.Nurse (137), G.S.Sobers (174) | v | England | Leeds | 1966 |
| 6th | 274* | G.S.Sobers (163*), D.A.J.Holford (105*) | v | England | Lord's | 1966 |
| 7th | 347 | D.S.Atkinson (219), C.C.Depeiza (122) | v | Australia | Bridgetown | 1954-55 |
| 8th | 124 | I.V.A.Richards (192*), K.D.Boyce (68) | v | India | Delhi | 1974-75 |
| 9th | 161 | C.H.Lloyd (161*), A.M.E.Roberts (68) | v | India | Calcutta | 1983-84 |
| 10th | 106 | C.L.Hooper (178*), C.A.Walsh (30) | v | Pakistan | St John's | 1992-93 |

## NEW ZEALAND

| | | | | | | |
|---|---|---|---|---|---|---|
| 1st | 387 | G.M.Turner (259), T.W.Jarvis (182) | v | West Indies | Georgetown | 1971-72 |
| 2nd | 241 | J.G.Wright (116), A.H.Jones (143) | v | England | Wellington | 1991-92 |
| 3rd | 467 | A.H.Jones (186), M.D.Crowe (299) | v | Sri Lanka | Wellington | 1990-91 |
| 4th | 243 | M.J.Horne (157), N.J.Astle (114) | v | Zimbabwe | Auckland | 1997-98 |
| 5th | 183 | M.G.Burgess (111), R.W.Anderson (92) | v | Pakistan | Lahore[2] | 1976-77 |
| 6th | 246* | J.J.Crowe (120*), R.J.Hadlee (151*) | v | Sri Lanka | Colombo (CCC) | 1986-87 |
| 7th | 186 | W.K.Lees (152), R.J.Hadlee (87) | v | Pakistan | Karachi[1] | 1976-77 |
| 8th | 136 | B.E.Congdon (166*), R.S.Cunis (51) | v | West Indies | Port-of-Spain | 1971-72 |
| 9th | 136 | I.D.S.Smith (173), M.C.Snedden (22) | v | India | Auckland | 1989-90 |
| 10th | 151 | B.F.Hastings (110), R.O.Collinge (68*) | v | Pakistan | Auckland | 1972-73 |

**INDIA**

| | | | | | | |
|---|---|---|---|---|---|---|
| 1st | 413 | M.H.Mankad (231), Pankaj Roy (173) | v | New Zealand | Madras[2] | 1955-56 |
| 2nd | 344* | S.M.Gavaskar (182*), D.B.Vengsarkar (157*) | v | West Indies | Calcutta | 1978-79 |
| 3rd | 316 | G.R.Viswanath (222), Yashpal Sharma (140) | v | England | Madras[1] | 1981-82 |
| 4th | 255 | S.C.Ganguly (173), M.Azharuddin (148) | v | Sri Lanka | Mumbai[3] | 1997-98 |
| 5th | 214 | M.Azharuddin (110), R.J.Shastri (111) | v | England | Calcutta | 1984-85 |
| 6th | 298* | D.B.Vengsarkar (164*), R.J.Shastri (121*) | v | Australia | Bombay[3] | 1986-87 |
| 7th | 235 | R.J.Shastri (142), S.M.H.Kirmani (102) | v | England | Bombay[3] | 1984-85 |
| 8th | 161 | M.Azharuddin (109), A.R.Kumble (88) | v | South Africa | Calcutta | 1996-97 |
| 9th | 149 | P.G.Joshi (52*), R.B.Desai (85) | v | Pakistan | Bombay[2] | 1960-61 |
| 10th | 109 | H.R.Adhikari (81*), Ghulam Ahmed (50) | v | Pakistan | Delhi | 1952-53 |

**PAKISTAN**

| | | | | | | |
|---|---|---|---|---|---|---|
| 1st | 298 | Aamer Soahil (160), Ijaz Ahmed (151) | v | West Indies | Karachi[1] | 1997-98 |
| 2nd | 291 | Zaheer Abbas (274), Mushtaq Mohammad (100) | v | England | Birmingham | 1971 |
| 3rd | 451 | Mudassar Nazar (231), Javed Miandad (280*) | v | India | Hyderabad | 1982-83 |
| 4th | 350 | Mushtaq Mohammad (201), Asif Iqbal (175) | v | New Zealand | Dunedin | 1972-73 |
| 5th | 281 | Javed Miandad (163), Asif Iqbal (166) | v | New Zealand | Lahore[2] | 1976-77 |
| 6th | 217 | Hanif Mohammad (203*), Majid Khan (80) | v | New Zealand | Lahore[2] | 1964-65 |
| 7th | 308 | Waqar Hassan (189), Imtiaz Ahmed (209) | v | New Zealand | Lahore[1] | 1955-56 |
| 8th | 313 | Wasim Akram (257*), Saqlain Mushtaq (78) | v | Zimbabwe | Sheikhupura | 1996-97 |
| 9th | 190 | Asif Iqbal (146), Intikhab Alam (51) | v | England | The Oval | 1967 |
| 10th | 151 | Azhar Mahmood (128*), Mushtaq Ahmed (59) | v | South Africa | Rawalpindi[2] | 1997-98 |

**SRI LANKA**

| | | | | | | |
|---|---|---|---|---|---|---|
| 1st | 159 | S.Wettimuny (79), J.R.Ratnayeke (93) | v | India | Kanpur | 1986-87 |
| 2nd | 576 | S.T.Jayasuriya (340), R.S.Mahanama (225) | v | India | Colombo (PIS) | 1997-98 |
| 3rd | 218 | S.T.Jayasuriya (199), P.A.de Silva (120) | v | India | Colombo (SSC) | 1997-98 |
| 4th | 240* | A.P.Gurusinha (116*), A.Ranatunga (135*) | v | Pakistan | Colombo (PSS) | 1985-86 |
| 5th | 150 | S.Wettimuny (190), L.R.D.Mendis (111) | v | England | Lord's | 1984 |
| 6th | 189* | P.A.de Silva (143*), A.Ranatunga (87*) | v | Zimbabwe | Colombo (SSC) | 1997-98 |
| 7th | 144 | P A de Silva (167), J R Ratnayeke (56) | v | Australia | Brisbane[2] | 1989-90 |
| 8th | 83 | H.P.Tillakaratne (93*), M.Muralidaran (19) | v | England | Colombo (SSC) | 1992-93 |
| 9th | 52 | P.A.de Silva (122), R.J.Ratnayake (56) | v | Pakistan | Faisalabad | 1985-86 |
| 10th | 71 | R.S.Kaluwitharana (88), M.Muralidaran (26*) | v | New Zealand | Colombo (SSC) | 1997-98 |

**ZIMBABWE**

| | | | | | | |
|---|---|---|---|---|---|---|
| 1st | 156 | G.J.Rennie(57), G.W.Flower (151) | v | New Zealand | Bulawayo[2] | 1997-98 |
| 2nd | 135 | M.H.Dekker (68*), A.D.R.Campbell (75) | v | Pakistan | Rawalpindi[2] | 1993-94 |
| 3rd | 269 | G.W.Flower (201*), A.Flower (156) | v | Pakistan | Harare | 1994-95 |
| 4th | 233* | G.W.Flower (201*), G.J.Whittall (113*) | v | Pakistan | Harare | 1994-95 |
| 5th | 277* | M.W.Goodwin (166*), A.Flower (100*) | v | Pakistan | Bulawayo[2] | 1997-98 |
| 6th | 165 | D.L.Houghton (121), A.Flower (59) | v | India | Harare | 1992-93 |
| 7th | 131 | G.W.Flower (110), P.A.Strang (106*) | v | Pakistan | Sheikhupura | 1996-97 |
| 8th | 110 | G.J.Whittall (62), J.A.Rennie (19*) | v | Pakistan | Harare | 1997-98 |
| 9th | 87 | P.A.Strang (106*), B.C.Strang (42) | v | Pakistan | Sheikhupura | 1996-97 |
| 10th | 42 | H.H.Streak (53), A.C.I.Lock (8*) | v | South Africa | Harare | 1995-96 |

## Bowling

### 200 TEST WICKETS

| Player (Country) | Tests | Wkts | Avge | A | E | SA | WI | NZ | I | P | SL | Z |
|---|---|---|---|---|---|---|---|---|---|---|---|---|
| | | | | *Opponents* | | | | | | | | |
| Kapil Dev (I) | 131 | **434** | 29.64 | 79 | 85 | 8 | 89 | 25 | - | 99 | 45 | 4 |
| R.J.Hadlee (N) | 86 | **431** | 22.29 | 130 | 97 | - | 51 | - | 65 | 51 | 37 | - |
| I.T.Botham (E) | 102 | **383** | 28.40 | 148 | - | - | 61 | 64 | 59 | 40 | 11 | - |
| M.D.Marshall (W) | 81 | **376** | 20.94 | 87 | 127 | - | - | 36 | 76 | 50 | - | - |
| C.A.Walsh (W) | 102 | **375** | 25.78 | 98 | 111 | 4 | - | 40 | 65 | 49 | 8 | - |
| Imran Khan (P) | 88 | **362** | 22.81 | 64 | 47 | - | 80 | 31 | 94 | - | 46 | - |
| D.K.Lillee (A) | 70 | **355** | 23.92 | - | 167 | - | 55 | 38 | 21 | 71 | 3 | - |
| Wasim Akram (P) | 79 | **341** | 22.59 | 40 | 50 | 13 | 64 | 60 | 31 | - | 44 | 39 |
| C.E.L.Ambrose (W) | 80 | **337** | 21.16 | 109 | 147 | 8 | - | 13 | 15 | 31 | 14 | - |
| R.G.D.Willis (E) | 90 | **325** | 25.20 | 128 | - | - | 38 | 60 | 62 | 34 | 3 | - |
| S.K.Warne (A) | 67 | **313** | 24.77 | - | 85 | 64 | 47 | 54 | 11 | 37 | 15 | - |
| L.R.Gibbs (W) | 79 | **309** | 29.09 | 103 | 100 | - | - | 11 | 63 | 32 | - | - |
| F.S.Trueman (E) | 67 | **307** | 21.57 | 79 | - | 27 | 86 | 40 | 53 | 22 | - | - |
| D.L.Underwood (E) | 86 | **297** | 25.83 | 105 | - | - | 38 | 48 | 62 | 36 | 8 | - |
| C.J.McDermott (A) | 71 | **291** | 28.63 | - | 84 | 21 | 59 | 48 | 34 | 18 | 27 | - |
| Waqar Younis (P) | 53 | **267** | 21.52 | 22 | 38 | 20 | 42 | 62 | 6 | - | 31 | 46 |
| B.S.Bedi (I) | 67 | **266** | 28.71 | 56 | 85 | - | 62 | 57 | - | 6 | - | - |
| J.Garner (W) | 58 | **259** | 20.97 | 89 | 92 | - | - | 36 | 7 | 35 | - | - |
| J.B.Statham (E) | 70 | **252** | 24.84 | 69 | - | 69 | 42 | 20 | 25 | 27 | - | - |
| M.A.Holding (W) | 60 | **249** | 23.68 | 76 | 96 | - | - | 16 | 61 | - | - | - |
| R.Benaud (A) | 63 | **248** | 27.03 | - | 83 | 52 | 42 | - | 47 | 15 | - | - |
| G.D.McKenzie (A) | 60 | **246** | 29.78 | - | 96 | 41 | 47 | - | 47 | 15 | - | - |
| B.S.Chandrasekhar (I) | 58 | **242** | 29.74 | 38 | 95 | - | 65 | 36 | - | 8 | - | - |
| A.A.Donald (SA) | 47 | 237 | 22.07 | 48 | 64 | - | 6 | 5 | 50 | 27 | 26 | 11 |
| A.V.Bedser (E) | 51 | **236** | 24.89 | 104 | - | 54 | 11 | 13 | 44 | 10 | - | - |
| Abdul Qadir (P) | 67 | **236** | 32.80 | 45 | 82 | - | 42 | 26 | 27 | - | 14 | - |
| G.S.Sobers (W) | 93 | **235** | 34.03 | 51 | 102 | - | - | 19 | 59 | 4 | - | - |
| R.R.Lindwall (A) | 61 | **228** | 23.03 | - | 114 | 31 | 41 | 2 | 36 | 4 | - | - |
| C.V.Grimmett (A) | 37 | **216** | 24.21 | - | 106 | 77 | 33 | - | - | - | - | - |
| M.G.Hughes (A) | 53 | **212** | 28.38 | - | 75 | 4 | 53 | 25 | 23 | 16 | 16 | - |
| A.A.Donald (SA) | 43 | **210** | 22.47 | 48 | 37 | - | 6 | 5 | 50 | 27 | 26 | 11 |
| A.M.E.Roberts (W) | 47 | **202** | 25.61 | 51 | 50 | - | - | 3 | 67 | 31 | - | - |
| J.A.Snow (E) | 49 | **202** | 26.66 | 83 | - | 4 | 72 | 20 | 16 | 7 | - | - |
| J.R.Thomson (A) | 51 | **200** | 28.00 | - | 100 | - | 62 | 6 | 22 | 10 | - | - |

### 100 OR MORE TEST WICKETS

| **AUSTRALIA** | Tests | Balls | Runs | Wkts | Avge | 5wi | 10wm | Best |
|---|---|---|---|---|---|---|---|---|
| D.K.Lillee | 70 | 18467 | 8493 | 355 | 23.92 | 23 | 7 | 7/83 |
| S.K.Warne | 67 | 19791 | 7756 | 313 | 24.77 | 14 | 4 | 8/71 |
| C.J.McDermott | 71 | 16586 | 8332 | 291 | 28.63 | 14 | 2 | 8/97 |
| R.Benaud | 63 | 19108 | 6704 | 248 | 27.03 | 16 | 1 | 7/72 |
| G.D.McKenzie | 60 | 17681 | 7328 | 246 | 29.78 | 16 | 3 | 8/71 |
| R.R.Lindwall | 61 | 13650 | 5251 | 228 | 23.03 | 12 | 0 | 7/38 |
| C.V.Grimmett | 37 | 14513 | 5231 | 216 | 24.21 | 21 | 7 | 7/40 |
| M.G.Hughes | 53 | 12285 | 6017 | 212 | 28.38 | 7 | 1 | 8/87 |
| J.R.Thomson | 51 | 10535 | 5601 | 200 | 28.00 | 8 | 0 | 6/46 |
| A.K.Davidson | 44 | 11587 | 3819 | 186 | 20.53 | 14 | 2 | 7/93 |
| G.F.Lawson | 46 | 11118 | 5501 | 180 | 30.56 | 11 | 2 | 8/112 |
| K.R.Miller | 55 | 10461 | 3906 | 170 | 22.97 | 7 | 1 | 7/60 |
| T.M.Alderman | 41 | 10181 | 4616 | 170 | 27.15 | 14 | 1 | 6/47 |
| G.D.McGrath | 37 | 8849 | 3900 | 166 | 23.49 | 9 | 0 | 8/38 |
| W.A.Johnston | 40 | 11048 | 3826 | 160 | 23.91 | 7 | 0 | 6/44 |
| W.J.O'Reilly | 27 | 10024 | 3254 | 144 | 22.59 | 11 | 3 | 7/54 |
| H.Trumble | 32 | 8099 | 3072 | 141 | 21.78 | 9 | 3 | 8/65 |
| M.H.N.Walker | 34 | 10094 | 3792 | 138 | 27.47 | 6 | 0 | 8/143 |
| A.A.Mallett | 38 | 9990 | 3940 | 132 | 29.84 | 6 | 1 | 8/59 |

| | | | | | | | | |
|---|---|---|---|---|---|---|---|---|
| B.Yardley | 33 | 8909 | 3986 | 126 | 31.63 | 6 | 1 | 7/98 |
| R.M.Hogg | 38 | 7633 | 3503 | 123 | 28.47 | 6 | 2 | 6/74 |
| M.A.Noble | 42 | 7159 | 3025 | 121 | 25.00 | 9 | 2 | 7/17 |
| B.A.Reid | 27 | 6244 | 2784 | 113 | 24.63 | 5 | 2 | 7/51 |
| I.W.Johnson | 45 | 8780 | 3182 | 109 | 29.19 | 3 | 0 | 7/44 |
| P.R.Reiffel | 35 | 6403 | 2804 | 104 | 26.96 | 5 | 0 | 6/71 |
| G.Giffen | 31 | 6391 | 2791 | 103 | 27.09 | 7 | 1 | 7/117 |
| A.N.Connolly | 29 | 7818 | 2981 | 102 | 29.22 | 4 | 0 | 6/47 |
| C.T.B.Turner | 17 | 5179 | 1670 | 101 | 16.53 | 11 | 2 | 7/43 |

| **ENGLAND** | Tests | Balls | Runs | Wkts | Avge | 5wi | 10wm | Best |
|---|---|---|---|---|---|---|---|---|
| I.T.Botham | 102 | 21815 | 10878 | 383 | 28.40 | 27 | 4 | 8/34 |
| R.G.D.Willis | 90 | 17357 | 8190 | 325 | 25.20 | 16 | 0 | 8/43 |
| F.S.Trueman | 67 | 15178 | 6625 | 307 | 21.57 | 17 | 3 | 8/31 |
| D.L.Underwood | 86 | 21862 | 7674 | 297 | 25.83 | 17 | 6 | 8/51 |
| J.B.Statham | 70 | 16056 | 6261 | 252 | 24.84 | 9 | 1 | 7/39 |
| A.V.Bedser | 51 | 15918 | 5876 | 236 | 24.89 | 15 | 5 | 7/44 |
| J.A.Snow | 49 | 12021 | 5387 | 202 | 26.66 | 8 | 1 | 7/40 |
| J.C.Laker | 46 | 12027 | 4101 | 193 | 21.24 | 9 | 3 | 10/53 |
| S.F.Barnes | 27 | 7873 | 3106 | 189 | 16.43 | 24 | 7 | 9/103 |
| G.A.R.Lock | 49 | 13147 | 4451 | 174 | 25.58 | 9 | 3 | 7/35 |
| A.R.C.Fraser | 43 | 10312 | 4493 | 170 | 26.42 | 13 | 2 | 8/53 |
| M.W.Tate | 39 | 12523 | 4055 | 155 | 26.16 | 7 | 1 | 6/42 |
| F.J.Titmus | 53 | 15118 | 4931 | 153 | 32.22 | 7 | 0 | 7/79 |
| J.E.Emburey | 65 | 15571 | 5728 | 147 | 38.96 | 6 | 0 | 7/78 |
| H.Verity | 40 | 11173 | 3510 | 144 | 24.37 | 5 | 2 | 8/43 |
| C.M.Old | 46 | 8858 | 4020 | 143 | 28.11 | 4 | 0 | 7/50 |
| A.W.Greig | 58 | 9802 | 4541 | 141 | 32.20 | 6 | 2 | 8/86 |
| P.A.J.DeFreitas | 44 | 9838 | 4700 | 140 | 33.57 | 4 | 0 | 7/70 |
| G.R.Dilley | 41 | 8192 | 4107 | 138 | 29.76 | 6 | 0 | 6/38 |
| T.E.Bailey | 61 | 9712 | 3856 | 132 | 29.21 | 5 | 1 | 7/34 |
| D.E.Malcolm | 40 | 8468 | 4748 | 128 | 37.09 | 5 | 2 | 9/57 |
| W.Rhodes | 58 | 8231 | 3425 | 127 | 26.96 | 6 | 1 | 8/68 |
| P.H.Edmonds | 51 | 12028 | 4273 | 125 | 34.18 | 2 | 0 | 7/66 |
| D.A.Allen | 39 | 11297 | 3779 | 122 | 30.97 | 4 | 0 | 5/30 |
| R.Illingworth | 61 | 11934 | 3807 | 122 | 31.20 | 3 | 0 | 6/29 |
| J.Briggs | 33 | 5332 | 2094 | 118 | 17.74 | 9 | 4 | 8/11 |
| G.G.Arnold | 34 | 7650 | 3254 | 115 | 28.29 | 6 | 0 | 6/45 |
| G.A.Lohmann | 18 | 3821 | 1205 | 112 | 10.75 | 9 | 5 | 9/28 |
| D.V.P.Wright | 34 | 8135 | 4224 | 108 | 39.11 | 6 | 1 | 7/105 |
| R.Peel | 20 | 5216 | 1715 | 101 | 16.98 | 5 | 1 | 7/31 |
| J.H.Wardle | 28 | 6597 | 2080 | 102 | 20.39 | 5 | 1 | 7/36 |
| D.Gough | 25 | 5307 | 2789 | 102 | 27.34 | 4 | 0 | 6/42 |
| C.Blythe | 19 | 4546 | 1863 | 100 | 18.63 | 9 | 4 | 8/59 |
| P.C.R.Tufnell | 34 | 9230 | 3637 | 100 | 36.37 | 5 | 2 | 7/47 |

| **SOUTH AFRICA** | Tests | Balls | Runs | Wkts | Avge | 5wi | 10wm | Best |
|---|---|---|---|---|---|---|---|---|
| A.A.Donald | 47 | 11005 | 5232 | 237 | 22.07 | 15 | 2 | 8/71 |
| H.J.Tayfield | 37 | 13568 | 4405 | 170 | 25.91 | 14 | 2 | 9/113 |
| T.L.Goddard | 41 | 11736 | 3226 | 123 | 26.22 | 5 | 0 | 6/53 |
| P.M.Pollock | 28 | 6522 | 2806 | 116 | 24.18 | 9 | 1 | 6/38 |
| N.A.T.Adcock | 26 | 6391 | 2195 | 104 | 21.10 | 5 | 0 | 6/43 |

| **WEST INDIES** | Tests | Balls | Runs | Wkts | Avge | 5wi | 10wm | Best |
|---|---|---|---|---|---|---|---|---|
| M.D.Marshall | 81 | 17585 | 7876 | 376 | 20.94 | 22 | 4 | 7/22 |
| C.A.Walsh | 102 | 22026 | 9669 | 375 | 25.78 | 15 | 2 | 7/37 |
| C.E.L.Ambrose | 80 | 17953 | 7132 | 337 | 21.16 | 20 | 3 | 8/45 |
| L.R.Gibbs | 79 | 27115 | 8989 | 309 | 29.09 | 18 | 2 | 8/38 |
| J.Garner | 58 | 13175 | 5433 | 259 | 20.97 | 7 | 0 | 6/56 |
| M.A.Holding | 60 | 12680 | 5898 | 249 | 23.68 | 13 | 2 | 8/92 |
| G.S.Sobers | 93 | 21599 | 7999 | 235 | 34.03 | 6 | 0 | 6/73 |

| | | | | | | | | |
|---|---|---|---|---|---|---|---|---|
| A.M.E.Roberts | 47 | 11136 | 5174 | 202 | 25.61 | 11 | 2 | 7/54 |
| W.W.Hall | 48 | 10421 | 5066 | 192 | 26.38 | 9 | 1 | 7/69 |
| I.R.Bishop | 43 | 8407 | 3910 | 161 | 24.28 | 6 | 0 | 6/40 |
| S.Ramadhin | 43 | 13939 | 4579 | 158 | 28.98 | 10 | 1 | 7/49 |
| A.L.Valentine | 36 | 12953 | 4215 | 139 | 30.32 | 8 | 2 | 8/104 |
| C.E.H.Croft | 27 | 6165 | 2913 | 125 | 23.30 | 3 | 0 | 8/29 |
| V.A.Holder | 40 | 9095 | 3627 | 109 | 33.27 | 3 | 0 | 6/28 |

| **NEW ZEALAND** | Tests | Balls | Runs | Wkts | Avge | 5wi | 10wm | Best |
|---|---|---|---|---|---|---|---|---|
| R.J.Hadlee | 86 | 21918 | 9611 | 431 | 22.29 | 36 | 9 | 9/52 |
| D.K.Morrison | 48 | 10064 | 5549 | 160 | 34.68 | 10 | 0 | 7/89 |
| B.L.Cairns | 43 | 10628 | 4279 | 130 | 32.91 | 6 | 1 | 7/74 |
| E.J.Chatfield | 43 | 10360 | 3958 | 123 | 32.17 | 3 | 1 | 6/73 |
| R.O.Collinge | 35 | 7689 | 3393 | 116 | 29.25 | 3 | 0 | 6/63 |
| B.R.Taylor | 30 | 6334 | 2953 | 111 | 26.60 | 4 | 0 | 7/74 |
| J.G.Bracewell | 41 | 8403 | 3653 | 102 | 35.81 | 4 | 1 | 6/32 |
| R.C.Motz | 32 | 7034 | 3148 | 100 | 31.48 | 5 | 0 | 6/63 |

| **INDIA** | Tests | Balls | Runs | Wkts | Avge | 5wi | 10wm | Best |
|---|---|---|---|---|---|---|---|---|
| Kapil Dev | 131 | 28741 | 12867 | 434 | 29.64 | 23 | 2 | 9/83 |
| B.S.Bedi | 67 | 21367 | 7637 | 266 | 28.71 | 14 | 1 | 7/98 |
| B.S.Chandrasekhar | 58 | 15963 | 7199 | 242 | 29.74 | 16 | 2 | 8/79 |
| A.R.Kumble | 46 | 13984 | 5603 | 197 | 28.44 | 11 | 1 | 7/59 |
| E.A.S.Prasanna | 49 | 14353 | 5742 | 189 | 30.38 | 10 | 2 | 8/76 |
| M.H.Mankad | 44 | 14686 | 5236 | 162 | 32.32 | 8 | 2 | 8/52 |
| S.Venkataraghavan | 57 | 14877 | 5634 | 156 | 36.11 | 3 | 1 | 8/72 |
| R.J.Shastri | 80 | 15751 | 6187 | 151 | 40.97 | 2 | 0 | 5/75 |
| S.P.Gupte | 36 | 11284 | 4403 | 149 | 29.55 | 12 | 1 | 9/102 |
| D.R.Doshi | 33 | 9322 | 3502 | 114 | 30.71 | 6 | 0 | 6/102 |
| J.Srinath | 32 | 7224 | 3414 | 109 | 31.32 | 2 | 0 | 6/21 |
| K.D.Ghavri | 39 | 7042 | 3656 | 109 | 33.54 | 4 | 0 | 5/33 |
| N.S.Yadav | 35 | 8349 | 3580 | 102 | 35.09 | 3 | 0 | 5/76 |

| **PAKISTAN** | Tests | Balls | Runs | Wkts | Avge | 5wi | 10wm | Best |
|---|---|---|---|---|---|---|---|---|
| Imran Khan | 88 | 19458 | 8258 | 362 | 22.81 | 23 | 6 | 8/58 |
| Wasim Akram | 79 | 17904 | 7705 | 341 | 22.59 | 21 | 4 | 7/119 |
| Waqar Younis | 53 | 10798 | 5748 | 267 | 21.52 | 21 | 5 | 7/76 |
| Abdul Qadir | 67 | 17126 | 7742 | 236 | 32.80 | 15 | 5 | 9/56 |
| Sarfraz Nawaz | 55 | 13931 | 5798 | 177 | 32.75 | 4 | 1 | 9/86 |
| Iqbal Qasim | 50 | 13019 | 4807 | 171 | 28.11 | 8 | 2 | 7/49 |
| Mushtaq Ahmed | 38 | 9544 | 4427 | 160 | 27.66 | 10 | 3 | 7/56 |
| Fazal Mahmood | 34 | 9834 | 3434 | 139 | 24.70 | 13 | 4 | 7/42 |
| Intikhab Alam | 47 | 10474 | 4494 | 125 | 35.92 | 5 | 2 | 7/52 |

Most Test wickets for the other countries:

| **SRI LANKA** | Tests | Balls | Runs | Wkts | Avge | 5wi | 10wm | Best |
|---|---|---|---|---|---|---|---|---|
| M.Muralidaran | 41 | 12356 | 5244 | 187 | 28.04 | 14 | 1 | 7/94 |
| W.P.U.J.C.Vaas | 26 | 5555 | 2409 | 83 | 29.02 | 4 | 1 | 6/87 |
| R.J.Ratnayake | 23 | 4955 | 2563 | 73 | 35.11 | 5 | 0 | 6/66 |

| **ZIMBABWE** | Tests | Balls | Runs | Wkts | Avge | 5wi | 10wm | Best |
|---|---|---|---|---|---|---|---|---|
| H.H.Streak | 23 | 5285 | 2335 | 94 | 24.84 | 3 | 0 | 6/90 |
| P.A.Strang | 20 | 4852 | 2153 | 57 | 37.77 | 3 | 0 | 5/106 |
| G.J.Whittall | 25 | 3040 | 1314 | 36 | 36.50 | 0 | 0 | 4/18 |
| B.C.Strang | 13 | 2633 | 980 | 32 | 30.62 | 1 | 0 | 5/101 |
| D.H.Brain | 9 | 1810 | 915 | 30 | 30.50 | 1 | 0 | 5/42 |

## BEST BOWLING AVERAGES *(Qualification: 25 wicket)*

| Player | Country | Tests | Balls | Runs | Wkts | Avge | 5wi | 10wm |
|---|---|---|---|---|---|---|---|---|
| G.A.Lohmann | England | 18 | 3821 | 1205 | 112 | **10.75** | 9 | 5 |
| J.J.Ferris | Australia/England | 9 | 2302 | 775 | 61 | **12.70** | 6 | 1 |
| A.E.Trott | Australia/England | 5 | 948 | 390 | 26 | **15.00** | 2 | 0 |
| M.J.Proctor | South Africa | 7 | 1514 | 616 | 41 | **15.02** | 1 | 0 |
| W.Barnes | England | 21 | 2289 | 793 | 51 | **14.54** | 3 | 0 |
| W.Bates | England | 15 | 2364 | 821 | 50 | **16.42** | 4 | 1 |
| S.F.Barnes | England | 27 | 7873 | 3106 | 189 | **16.43** | 24 | 7 |
| C.T.B.Turner | Australia | 17 | 5179 | 1670 | 101 | **16.53** | 11 | 2 |
| R.Peel | England | 20 | 5216 | 1715 | 101 | **16.98** | 5 | 1 |
| J.Briggs | England | 33 | 5332 | 2094 | 118 | **17.74** | 9 | 4 |
| R.Appleyard | England | 9 | 1596 | 534 | 31 | **17.87** | 1 | 0 |
| W.S.Lees | England | 5 | 1256 | 467 | 26 | **17.96** | 2 | 0 |
| H.Ironmonger | Australia | 14 | 4695 | 1330 | 74 | **17.97** | 4 | 2 |
| G.B.Lawrence | South Africa | 5 | 1334 | 512 | 28 | **18.28** | 2 | 0 |
| F.R.Spofforth | Australia | 18 | 4185 | 1731 | 94 | **18.41** | 7 | 4 |
| F.H.Tyson | England | 17 | 3452 | 1413 | 76 | **18.56** | 4 | 1 |
| C.Blythe | England | 19 | 4446 | 1863 | 100 | **18.63** | 9 | 4 |
| G.F.Bissett | South Africa | 4 | 989 | 469 | 25 | **18.76** | 2 | 0 |
| A.S.Kennedy | England | 5 | 1683 | 599 | 31 | **19.32** | 2 | 0 |

## 25 OR MORE WICKETS IN A TEST SERIES *(§ in first series. # in last series. † in only series.)*

| AUSTRALIA | Opp | Season | Tests | Balls | Mdns | Runs | Wkts | Avge | 5wi | 10wm | Best |
|---|---|---|---|---|---|---|---|---|---|---|---|
| C.V.Grimmett # | SA | 1935-36 | 5 | 2077 | 140 | 642 | 44 | 14.59 | 5 | 3 | 7/40 |
| T.M.Alderman § | ENG | 1981 | 6 | 1950 | 76 | 893 | 42 | 21.26 | 4 | 0 | 6/135 |
| R.M.Hogg § | ENG | 1978-79 | 6 | 1740 | 60 | 527 | 41 | 12.85 | 5 | 2 | 6/74 |
| T.M.Alderman | ENG | 1989 | 6 | 1622 | 68 | 712 | 41 | 17.36 | 6 | 1 | 6/128 |
| D.K.Lillee | ENG | 1981 | 6 | 1870 | 81 | 870 | 39 | 22.30 | 2 | 1 | 7/89 |
| W.J.Whitty | SA | 1910-11 | 5 | 1395 | 55 | 632 | 37 | 17.08 | 2 | 0 | 6/17 |
| A.A.Mailey § | ENG | 1920-21 | 5 | 1465 | 27 | 946 | 36 | 26.27 | 4 | 2 | 9/121 |
| G.D.McGrath | ENG | 1997 | 6 | 1499 | 67 | 701 | 36 | 19.47 | 2 | 0 | 8/38 |
| G.Giffen | ENG | 1894-95 | 5 | 2060 | 111 | 820 | 34 | 24.11 | 3 | 0 | 6/155 |
| G.F.Lawson | ENG | 1982-83 | 5 | 1384 | 51 | 687 | 34 | 20.20 | 4 | 1 | 6/47 |
| S.K.Warne | ENG | 1993 | 6 | 2639 | 178 | 877 | 34 | 25.79 | 1 | 0 | 5/82 |
| C.V.Grimmett | WI | 1930-31 | 5 | 1433 | 60 | 593 | 33 | 17.96 | 2 | 1 | 7/87 |
| C.V.Grimmett | SA | 1931-32 | 5 | 1836 | 108 | 557 | 33 | 16.87 | 3 | 1 | 7/83 |
| A.K.Davidson | WI | 1960-61 | 4 | 1391 | 25 | 612 | 33 | 18.54 | 5 | 1 | 6/53 |
| J.R.Thomson | ENG | 1974-75 | 5 | 1401 | 34 | 592 | 33 | 17.93 | 2 | 0 | 6/46 |
| M.A.Noble | ENG | 1901-02 | 5 | 1380 | 68 | 608 | 32 | 19.00 | 4 | 1 | 7/17 |
| H.V.Hordern # | ENG | 1911-12 | 5 | 1665 | 43 | 780 | 32 | 24.37 | 4 | 2 | 7/90 |
| C.J.McDermott | ENG | 1994-95 | 5 | 1397 | 56 | 675 | 32 | 21.09 | 4 | 0 | 6/38 |
| J.V.Saunders # | ENG | 1907-08 | 5 | 1603 | 52 | 716 | 31 | 23.09 | 3 | 0 | 5/28 |
| H.Ironmonger | SA | 1931-32 | 4 | 1331 | 112 | 296 | 31 | 9.54 | 3 | 1 | 6/18 |
| R.Benaud | ENG | 1958-59 | 5 | 1866 | 65 | 584 | 31 | 18.83 | 2 | 0 | 5/83 |
| D.K.Lillee | ENG | 1972 | 5 | 1499 | 83 | 548 | 31 | 17.67 | 3 | 1 | 6/66 |
| C.J.McDermott | IND | 1991-92 | 5 | 1586 | 75 | 670 | 31 | 21.61 | 3 | 1 | 5/54 |
| M.G.Hughes | ENG | 1993 | 6 | 1778 | 79 | 845 | 31 | 27.25 | 1 | 0 | 5/92 |
| R.Benaud | SA | 1957-58 | 5 | 1937 | 56 | 658 | 30 | 21.93 | 4 | 0 | 5/49 |
| G.D.McKenzie | WI | 1968-69 | 5 | 1649 | 27 | 758 | 30 | 25.26 | 1 | 1 | 8/71 |
| C.J.McDermott | ENG | 1985 | 6 | 1406 | 21 | 901 | 30 | 30.03 | 2 | 0 | 8/141 |
| C.V.Grimmett | ENG | 1930 | 5 | 2098 | 78 | 925 | 29 | 31.89 | 4 | 1 | 6/167 |
| A.K.Davidson | IND | 1959-60 | 5 | 1469 | 85 | 431 | 29 | 14.86 | 2 | 1 | 7/93 |
| R.Benaud | IND | 1959-60 | 5 | 1934 | 146 | 568 | 29 | 19.58 | 2 | 0 | 5/43 |
| G.D.McKenzie | ENG | 1964 | 5 | 1536 | 61 | 654 | 29 | 22.55 | 2 | 0 | 7/153 |
| J.R.Thomson | WI | 1975-76 | 6 | 1205 | 15 | 831 | 29 | 28.65 | 2 | 0 | 6/50 |
| G.F.Lawson | ENG | 1989 | 6 | 1663 | 68 | 791 | 29 | 27.27 | 1 | 0 | 6/72 |
| H.Trumble | ENG | 1901-02 | 5 | 1604 | 93 | 561 | 28 | 20.03 | 2 | 0 | 6/74 |
| W.J.O'Reilly | ENG | 1934 | 5 | 2002 | 128 | 698 | 28 | 24.92 | 2 | 1 | 7/54 |
| A.A.Mallett | IND | 1969-70 | 5 | 1792 | 129 | 535 | 28 | 19.10 | 3 | 1 | 6/64 |

| | | | | | | | | | | | |
|---|---|---|---|---|---|---|---|---|---|---|---|
| W.M.Clark § | IND | 1977-78 | 5 | 1585 | 27 | 701 | 28 | 25.03 | 0 | 0 | 4/46 |
| E.A.McDonald | ENG | 1921 | 5 | 1235 | 32 | 668 | 27 | 24.74 | 2 | 0 | 5/32 |
| W.J.O'Reilly | ENG | 1932-33 | 5 | 2302 | 144 | 724 | 27 | 26.81 | 2 | 1 | 5/63 |
| W.J.O'Reilly | SA | 1935-36 | 5 | 1502 | 112 | 460 | 27 | 17.03 | 2 | 0 | 5/20 |
| R.R.Lindwall | ENG | 1948 | 5 | 1337 | 57 | 530 | 27 | 19.62 | 2 | 0 | 6/20 |
| W.A.Johnston | ENG | 1948 | 5 | 1856 | 91 | 630 | 27 | 23.33 | 1 | 0 | 5/36 |
| D.K.Lillee | WI | 1975-76 | 5 | 1035 | 7 | 712 | 27 | 26.37 | 1 | 0 | 5/63 |
| B.A.Reid | ENG | 1990-91 | 4 | 1039 | 47 | 432 | 27 | 16.00 | 2 | 1 | 7/51 |
| S.K.Warne | ENG | 1994-95 | 5 | 1537 | 84 | 549 | 27 | 20.33 | 2 | 1 | 8/71 |
| E.Jones | ENG | 1899 | 5 | 1276 | 73 | 657 | 26 | 25.26 | 2 | 1 | 7/88 |
| H.Trumble | ENG | 1902 | 3 | 1036 | 55 | 371 | 26 | 14.26 | 2 | 2 | 8/65 |
| R.R.Lindwall | ENG | 1953 | 5 | 1444 | 62 | 490 | 26 | 18.84 | 3 | 0 | 5/54 |
| J.W.Gleeson | WI | 1968-69 | 5 | 2006 | 57 | 844 | 26 | 32.46 | 2 | 0 | 5/61 |
| M.H.N.Walker | WI | 1972-73 | 5 | 1627 | 83 | 539 | 26 | 20.73 | 3 | 0 | 6/114 |
| G.D.McGrath | WI | 1996-97 | 5 | 1205 | 61 | 453 | 26 | 17.42 | 1 | 0 | 5/50 |
| C.V.Grimmett | ENG | 1934 | 5 | 2379 | 148 | 668 | 25 | 26.72 | 2 | 0 | 7/83 |
| W.J.O'Reilly | ENG | 1936-37 | 5 | 1982 | 89 | 555 | 25 | 22.20 | 2 | 0 | 5/51 |
| A.K.Davidson | SA | 1957-58 | 5 | 1613 | 47 | 425 | 25 | 17.00 | 2 | 0 | 6/34 |
| D.K.Lillee | ENG | 1974-75 | 6 | 1462 | 36 | 596 | 25 | 23.84 | 0 | - | 4/49 |
| A.G.Hurst | ENG | 1978-79 | 6 | 1634 | 44 | 577 | 25 | 23.08 | 1 | 0 | 5/28 |

| **ENGLAND** | Opp | Season | Tests | Balls | Mdns | Runs | Wkts | Avge | 5wi | 10wm | Best |
|---|---|---|---|---|---|---|---|---|---|---|---|
| S.F.Barnes # | SA | 1913-14 | 4 | 1356 | 56 | 536 | 49 | 10.93 | 7 | 3 | 9/103 |
| J.C.Laker | AUST | 1956 | 5 | 1703 | 127 | 442 | 46 | 9.60 | 4 | 2 | 10/53 |
| A.V.Bedser | AUST | 1953 | 5 | 1591 | 58 | 682 | 39 | 17.48 | 5 | 1 | 7/44 |
| M.W.Tate | AUST | 1924-25 | 5 | 2528 | 62 | 881 | 38 | 23.18 | 5 | 1 | 6/99 |
| G.A.Lohmann | SA | 1895-96 | 3 | 520 | 38 | 203 | 35 | 5.80 | 4 | 2 | 9/28 |
| S.F.Barnes | AUST | 1911-12 | 5 | 1782 | 64 | 778 | 34 | 22.88 | 3 | 0 | 5/44 |
| S.F.Barnes | SA | 1912 | 3 | 768 | 38 | 282 | 34 | 8.29 | 5 | 3 | 8/29 |
| G.A.R.Lock | NZ | 1958 | 5 | 1056 | 93 | 254 | 34 | 7.47 | 3 | 1 | 7/35 |
| F.S.Trueman | WI | 1963 | 5 | 1420 | 53 | 594 | 34 | 17.47 | 4 | 2 | 7/44 |
| I.T.Botham | AUST | 1981 | 6 | 1635 | 81 | 700 | 34 | 20.58 | 3 | 1 | 6/95 |
| H.Larwood # | AUST | 1932-33 | 5 | 1322 | 42 | 644 | 33 | 19.51 | 2 | 1 | 5/28 |
| T.Richardson | AUST | 1894-95 | 5 | 1747 | 63 | 849 | 32 | 26.53 | 4 | 0 | 6/104 |
| F.R.Foster § | AUST | 1911-12 | 5 | 1660 | 58 | 692 | 32 | 21.62 | 3 | 0 | 6/91 |
| W.Rhodes | AUST | 1903-04 | 5 | 1032 | 36 | 488 | 31 | 15.74 | 3 | 1 | 8/68 |
| A.S.Kennedy † | SA | 1922-23 | 5 | 1683 | 91 | 599 | 31 | 19.32 | 2 | 0 | 5/76 |
| J.A.Snow | AUST | 1970-71 | 6 | 1805 | 47 | 708 | 31 | 22.83 | 2 | 0 | 7/40 |
| I.T.Botham | AUST | 1985 | 6 | 1510 | 36 | 855 | 31 | 27.58 | 1 | 0 | 5/109 |
| J.N.Crawford # | AUST | 1907-08 | 5 | 1426 | 36 | 742 | 30 | 24.73 | 3 | 0 | 5/48 |
| A.V.Bedser | AUST | 1950-51 | 5 | 1560 | 34 | 482 | 30 | 16.06 | 2 | 1 | 5/46 |
| A.V.Bedser | SA | 1951 | 5 | 1655 | 84 | 517 | 30 | 17.23 | 3 | 1 | 7/58 |
| F.S.Trueman § | IND | 1952 | 4 | 718 | 25 | 386 | 29 | 13.31 | 2 | 0 | 8/31 |
| D.L.Underwood | IND | 1976-77 | 5 | 1517 | 95 | 509 | 29 | 17.55 | 1 | 0 | 5/84 |
| R.G.D.Willis | AUST | 1981 | 6 | 1516 | 56 | 666 | 29 | 22.96 | 1 | 0 | 8/43 |
| F.H.Tyson | AUST | 1954-55 | 5 | 1208 | 16 | 583 | 28 | 20.82 | 2 | 1 | 7/27 |
| R.Peel | AUST | 1894-95 | 5 | 1831 | 77 | 721 | 27 | 26.70 | 1 | 0 | 6/67 |
| M.W.Tate § | SA | 1924 | 5 | 1304 | 68 | 424 | 27 | 15.70 | 1 | 0 | 6/42 |
| J.B.Statham | SA | 1960 | 5 | 1218 | 54 | 491 | 27 | 18.18 | 2 | 1 | 6/63 |
| F.J.Titmus | IND | 1963-64 | 5 | 2393 | 156 | 747 | 27 | 27.66 | 2 | 0 | 6/73 |
| J.A.Snow | WI | 1967-68 | 4 | 990 | 29 | 504 | 27 | 18.66 | 3 | 1 | 7/49 |
| R.G.D.Willis | AUST | 1977 | 5 | 1000 | 36 | 534 | 27 | 19.77 | 3 | 0 | 7/78 |
| A.R.C.Fraser | WI | 1997-98 | 6 | 1124 | 50 | 492 | 27 | 18.22 | 2 | 1 | 8/53 |
| W.S.Lees † | SA | 1905-06 | 5 | 1256 | 69 | 467 | 26 | 17.96 | 2 | 0 | 6/78 |
| C.Blythe | SA | 1907 | 3 | 603 | 26 | 270 | 26 | 10.38 | 3 | 1 | 8/59 |
| W.Voce | AUST | 1936-37 | 5 | 1297 | 20 | 560 | 26 | 21.53 | 1 | 1 | 6/41 |
| J.H.Wardle | SA | 1956-57 | 4 | 1118 | 37 | 359 | 26 | 13.80 | 3 | 1 | 7/36 |
| J.K.Lever § | IND | 1976-77 | 5 | 898 | 29 | 380 | 26 | 14.61 | 2 | 1 | 7/46 |
| D.G.Cork § | WI | 1995 | 5 | 1106 | 30 | 661 | 26 | 25.42 | 1 | 0 | 7/43 |
| A.Fielder # | AUST | 1907-08 | 4 | 1299 | 31 | 627 | 25 | 25.08 | 1 | 0 | 6/82 |
| J.C.White | AUST | 1928-29 | 5 | 2440 | 134 | 760 | 25 | 30.40 | 3 | 1 | 8/126 |
| F.S.Trueman | SA | 1960 | 5 | 1083 | 31 | 508 | 25 | 20.32 | 1 | 0 | 5/27 |

| SOUTH AFRICA | Opp | Season | Tests | Balls | Mdns | Runs | Wkts | Avge | 5wi | 10wm | Best |
|---|---|---|---|---|---|---|---|---|---|---|---|
| H.J.Tayfield | ENG | 1956-57 | 5 | 2280 | 105 | 636 | 37 | 17.18 | 4 | 1 | 9/113 |
| A.E.E.Vogler | ENG | 1909-10 | 5 | 1349 | 33 | 783 | 36 | 21.75 | 4 | 1 | 7/94 |
| A.A.Donald | ENG | 1998 | 5 | 1460 | 69 | 653 | 33 | 19.78 | 4 | 0 | 6/88 |
| H.J.Tayfield | AUST | 1952-53 | 5 | 2228 | 58 | 843 | 30 | 28.10 | 2 | 1 | 7/81 |
| G.A.Faulkner | ENG | 1909-10 | 5 | 1255 | 45 | 635 | 29 | 21.89 | 2 | 0 | 6/87 |
| G.B.Lawrence † | NZ | 1961-62 | 5 | 1334 | 62 | 512 | 28 | 18.28 | 2 | 0 | 8/53 |
| A.E.Hall § | ENG | 1922-23 | 4 | 1505 | 82 | 501 | 27 | 18.55 | 2 | 1 | 7/63 |
| H.J.Tayfield | ENG | 1955 | 5 | 1881 | 124 | 568 | 26 | 21.84 | 3 | 0 | 5/60 |
| N.A.T.Adcock | ENG | 1960 | 5 | 1578 | 69 | 587 | 26 | 22.57 | 2 | 0 | 6/65 |
| T.L.Goddard | AUST | 1966-67 | 5 | 1533 | 101 | 422 | 26 | 16.23 | 1 | 0 | 6/53 |
| M.J.Procter # | AUST | 1969-70 | 4 | 858 | 50 | 353 | 26 | 13.57 | 1 | 0 | 6/73 |
| C.B.Llewellyn | AUST | 1902-03 | 3 | 796 | 23 | 448 | 25 | 17.92 | 4 | 1 | 6/92 |
| R.O.Schwarz | AUST | 1910-11 | 5 | 1006 | 19 | 651 | 25 | 26.04 | 2 | 0 | 6/47 |
| J.M.Blanckenberg | ENG | 1922-23 | 5 | 1510 | 60 | 613 | 25 | 24.52 | 2 | 0 | 6/76 |
| G.F.Bissett † | ENG | 1927-28 | 4 | 989 | 28 | 469 | 25 | 18.76 | 2 | 0 | 7/29 |
| T.L.Goddard § | ENG | 1955 | 5 | 1894 | 148 | 528 | 25 | 21.12 | 2 | 0 | 5/31 |
| J.T.Partridge § | AUST | 1963-64 | 5 | 1980 | 33 | 833 | 25 | 33.32 | 2 | 0 | 7/91 |
| P.M.Pollock | AUST | 1963-64 | 5 | 1275 | 11 | 710 | 25 | 28.40 | 2 | 0 | 6/95 |

| WEST INDIES | Opp | Season | Tests | Balls | Mdns | Runs | Wkts | Avge | 5wi | 10wm | Best |
|---|---|---|---|---|---|---|---|---|---|---|---|
| M.D.Marshall | ENG | 1988 | 5 | 1219 | 49 | 443 | 35 | 12.66 | 3 | 1 | 7/22 |
| A.L.Valentine § | ENG | 1950 | 4 | 2535 | 197 | 674 | 33 | 20.42 | 2 | 2 | 8/104 |
| C.E.H.Croft § | PAK | 1976-77 | 5 | 1307 | 45 | 676 | 33 | 20.48 | 1 | 0 | 8/29 |
| M.D.Marshall | IND | 1983-84 | 6 | 1326 | 59 | 621 | 33 | 18.81 | 2 | 0 | 6/37 |
| C.E.L.Ambrose | AUST | 1992-93 | 5 | 1563 | 77 | 542 | 33 | 16.42 | 3 | 1 | 7/25 |
| C.C.Griffith | ENG | 1963 | 5 | 1343 | 54 | 519 | 32 | 16.21 | 3 | 0 | 6/36 |
| A.M.E.Roberts | IND | 1974-75 | 5 | 1251 | 51 | 585 | 32 | 18.28 | 3 | 1 | 7/64 |
| J.Garner | AUST | 1983-84 | 5 | 1253 | 55 | 523 | 31 | 16.87 | 3 | 0 | 6/60 |
| W.W.Hall | IND | 1958-59 | 5 | 1330 | 65 | 530 | 30 | 17.66 | 2 | 1 | 6/50 |
| M.A.Holding | IND | 1983-84 | 6 | 1342 | 43 | 663 | 30 | 22.10 | 1 | 0 | 5/102 |
| C.E.L.Ambrose | WI | 1997-98 | + | 1235 | 61 | 428 | 30 | 14.25 | 2 | 0 | 5/25 |
| J.Garner | ENG | 1984 | 5 | 1307 | 60 | 540 | 29 | 18.62 | 1 | 0 | 5/55 |
| A.L.Valentine | IND | 1952-53 | 5 | 2580 | 178 | 828 | 28 | 29.57 | 2 | 0 | 5/64 |
| M.A.Holding | ENG | 1976 | 4 | 957 | 54 | 356 | 28 | 12.71 | 3 | 1 | 8/92 |
| A.M.E.Roberts | ENG | 1976 | 5 | 1330 | 69 | 537 | 28 | 19.17 | 3 | 1 | 6/37 |
| .M.D.Marshall | AUST | 1984-85 | 5 | 1277 | 47 | 554 | 28 | 19.78 | 4 | 1 | 5/38 |
| C.E.L.Ambrose | ENG | 1991 | 5 | 1494 | 63 | 560 | 28 | 20.00 | 2 | 0 | 6/52 |
| W.W.Hall | IND | 1961-62 | 5 | 1006 | 37 | 475 | 27 | 15.74 | 2 | 0 | 6/49 |
| M.D.Marshall | NZ | 1984-85 | 4 | 1021 | 30 | 486 | 27 | 18.00 | 1 | 1 | 7/80 |
| J.Garner | ENG | 1985-86 | 5 | 937 | 30 | 436 | 27 | 16.14 | 0 | 0 | 4/43 |
| M.D.Marshall | ENG | 1985-86 | 5 | 1017 | 36 | 482 | 27 | 17.85 | 0 | 0 | 4/38 |
| I.R.Bishop | ENG | 1995 | 6 | 1455 | 49 | 649 | 27 | 24.03 | 1 | 0 | 5/32 |
| S.Ramadhin § | ENG | 1950 | 4 | 2267 | 170 | 604 | 26 | 23.23 | 3 | 1 | 6/86 |
| R.Gilchrist # | IND | 1958-59 | 4 | 1189 | 73 | 419 | 26 | 16.11 | 1 | 0 | 6/55 |
| L.R.Gibbs | ENG | 1963 | 5 | 1497 | 74 | 554 | 26 | 21.30 | 2 | 1 | 5/98 |
| L.R.Gibbs | AUST | 1972-73 | 5 | 1950 | 108 | 696 | 26 | 26.76 | 1 | 0 | 5/102 |
| J.Garner | ENG | 1980 | 5 | 1276 | 73 | 371 | 26 | 14.26 | 0 | 0 | 4/30 |
| C.A.Walsh | IND | 1987-88 | 4 | 823 | 24 | 437 | 26 | 16.80 | 2 | 0 | 5/54 |
| C.E.L.Ambrose | AUST | 1988-89 | 5 | 1227 | 38 | 558 | 26 | 21.46 | 1 | 0 | 5/72 |
| C.E.L.Ambrose | ENG | 1993-94 | 5 | 1346 | 62 | 519 | 26 | 19.96 | 2 | 1 | 6/24 |
| C.A.Walsh | ENG | 1995 | 6 | 1740 | 57 | 786 | 26 | 30.23 | 1 | 0 | 5/45 |
| J.Garner § | PAK | 1976-77 | 5 | 1317 | 41 | 688 | 25 | 27.52 | 0 | 0 | 4/48 |

| NEW ZEALAND | Opp | Season | Tests | Balls | Mdns | Runs | Wkts | Avge | 5wi | 10wm | Best |
|---|---|---|---|---|---|---|---|---|---|---|---|
| R.J.Hadlee | AUST | 1985-86 | 3 | 1017 | 42 | 401 | 33 | 12.15 | 5 | 2 | 9/52 |
| B.R.Taylor | WI | 1971-72 | 4 | 1034 | 39 | 478 | 27 | 17.70 | 2 | 0 | 7/74 |

| **INDIA** | Opp | Season | Tests | Balls | Mdns | Runs | Wkts | Avge | 5wi | 10wm | Best |
|---|---|---|---|---|---|---|---|---|---|---|---|
| B.S.Chandrasekhar | ENG | 1972-73 | 5 | 1747 | 83 | 662 | 35 | 18.91 | 4 | 0 | 8/79 |
| M.H.Mankad | ENG | 1951-52 | 5 | 2224 | 151 | 571 | 34 | 16.79 | 1 | 1 | 8/55 |
| S.P.Gupte | NZ | 1955-56 | 5 | 2140 | 152 | 669 | 34 | 19.67 | 4 | 0 | 7/128 |
| Kapil Dev | PAK | 1979-80 | 6 | 1271 | 53 | 566 | 32 | 17.68 | 3 | 1 | 7/56 |
| B.S.Bedi | AUST | 1977-78 | 5 | 1759 | 39 | 740 | 31 | 23.87 | 3 | 1 | 5/55 |
| Kapil Dev | WI | 1983-84 | 6 | 1223 | 39 | 537 | 29 | 18.51 | 2 | 1 | 9/83 |
| B.S.Chandrasekhar | AUST | 1977-78 | 5 | 1579 | 24 | 704 | 28 | 25.14 | 3 | 1 | 6/52 |
| Kapil Dev | AUST | 1979-80 | 6 | 1339 | 53 | 625 | 28 | 22.32 | 2 | 0 | 5/74 |
| S.P.Gupte | WI | 1952-53 | 5 | 1977 | 87 | 789 | 27 | 29.22 | 3 | 0 | 7/162 |
| K.D.Ghavri | WI | 1978-79 | 6 | 1230 | 42 | 634 | 27 | 23.48 | 1 | 0 | 5/51 |
| D.R.Doshi § | AUST | 1979-80 | 6 | 1838 | 87 | 630 | 27 | 23.33 | 2 | 0 | 6/103 |
| E.A.S.Prasanna | AUST | 1969-70 | 5 | 1770 | 107 | 672 | 26 | 25.84 | 3 | 1 | 6/74 |
| M.H.Mankad | PAK | 1952-53 | 4 | 1592 | 100 | 514 | 25 | 20.56 | 3 | 1 | 8/52 |
| E.A.S.Prasanna | AUST | 1967-68 | 4 | 1581 | 34 | 686 | 25 | 27.44 | 2 | 0 | 6/104 |
| B.S.Bedi | ENG | 1972-73 | 5 | 2237 | 134 | 632 | 25 | 25.28 | 1 | 0 | 5/63 |
| B.S.Bedi | ENG | 1976-77 | 5 | 1788 | 106 | 574 | 25 | 22.96 | 2 | 0 | 6/71 |
| Kapil Dev | AUST | 1991-92 | 5 | 1704 | 76 | 645 | 25 | 25.80 | 2 | 0 | 5/97 |

| **PAKISTAN** | Opp | Season | Tests | Balls | Mdns | Runs | Wkts | Avge | 5wi | 10wm | Best |
|---|---|---|---|---|---|---|---|---|---|---|---|
| Imran Khan | IND | 1982-83 | 6 | 1339 | 69 | 558 | 40 | 13.95 | 4 | 2 | 8/60 |
| Abdul Qadir | ENG | 1987-88 | 3 | 1408 | 69 | 437 | 30 | 14.56 | 3 | 2 | 9/56 |
| Waqar Younis | NZ | 1990-91 | 3 | 869 | 50 | 315 | 29 | 10.86 | 3 | 2 | 7/76 |
| Waqar Younis | ZIM | 1993-94 | 3 | 784 | 31 | 373 | 27 | 13.81 | 4 | 1 | 7/91 |
| Imran Khan | WI | 1976-77 | 5 | 1417 | 54 | 790 | 25 | 31.60 | 1 | 0 | 6/90 |
| Wasim Akram | NZ | 1993-94 | 3 | 958 | 41 | 431 | 25 | 17.24 | 2 | 0 | 7/119 |

Most wickets in a series for the other countries:

| **SRI LANKA** | Opp | Season | Tests | Balls | Mdns | Runs | Wkts | Avge | 5wi | 10wm | Best |
|---|---|---|---|---|---|---|---|---|---|---|---|
| R.J.Ratnayake | IND | 1985-86 | 3 | 977 | 35 | 459 | 20 | 22.95 | 2 | 0 | 6/85 |

| **ZIMBABWE** | Opp | Season | Tests | Balls | Mdns | Runs | Wkts | Avge | 5wi | 10wm | Best |
|---|---|---|---|---|---|---|---|---|---|---|---|
| H.H.Streak | P | 1995 | 3 | 708 | 31 | 298 | 22 | 13.54 | 2 | 0 | 6/90 |

## TEN WICKETS IN A MATCH *(§ In first Test. # In last Test. † In only Test)*

| **AUSTRALIA** (75) | | Opponents | | |
|---|---|---|---|---|
| R.A.L.Massie § | 16-137 | England | Lord's | 1972 |
| F.R.Spofforth | 14-90 | England | The Oval | 1882 |
| C.V.Grimmett | 14-199 | South Africa | Adelaide | 1931-32 |
| M.A.Noble | 13-77 | England | Melbourne | 1901-02 |
| F.R.Spofforth | 13-110 | England | Melbourne | 1878-79 |
| B.A.Reid | 13-148 | England | Melbourne | 1990-91 |
| C.V.Grimmett # | 13-173 | South Africa | Durban[2] | 1935-36 |
| M.G.Hughes | 13-217 | West Indies | Perth | 1988-89 |
| A.A.Mailey | 13-236 | England | Melbourne | 1920-21 |
| C.T.B.Turner | 12-87 | England | Sydney | 1887-88 |
| H.Trumble | 12-89 | England | The Oval | 1896 |
| A.K.Davidson | 12-124 | India | Kanpur | 1959-60 |
| B.A.Reid | 12-126 | India | Melbourne | 1991-92 |
| S.K.Warne | 12-128 | South Africa | Sydney | 1993-94 |
| G.Dymock | 12-166 | India | Kanpur | 1979-80 |
| H.Trumble | 12-173 | England | The Oval | 1902 |
| H.V.Hordern | 12-175 | England | Sydney | 1911-12 |
| H.Ironmonger | 11-24 | South Africa | Melbourne | 1931-32 |
| E.R.H.Toshack | 11-31 | India | Brisbane[2] | 1947-48 |
| S.K.Warne | 11-77 | Pakistan | Brisbane[2] | 1995-96 |
| H.Ironmonger | 11-79 | West Indies | Melbourne | 1930-31 |
| C.V.Grimmett § | 11-82 | England | Sydney | 1924-25 |
| C.G.Macartney | 11-85 | England | Leeds | 1909 |
| M.R.Whitney | 11-95 | India | Perth | 1991-92 |

| | | | | |
|---|---|---|---|---|
| A.R.Border | 11-96 | West Indies | Sydney | 1988-89 |
| M.A.Noble | 11-103 | England | Sheffield | 1902 |
| R.Benaud | 11-105 | India | Calcutta | 1956-57 |
| S.K.Warne | 11-109 | South Africa | Sydney | 1997-98 |
| S.K.Warne | 11-110 | England | Brisbane[2] | 1994-95 |
| F.R.Spofforth | 11-117 | England | Sydney | 1882-83 |
| C.G.Rackemann | 11-118 | Pakistan | Perth | 1983-84 |
| D.K.Lillee | 11-123 | New Zealand | Auckland | 1976-77 |
| W.J.O'Reilly | 11-129 | England | Nottingham | 1934 |
| G.F.Lawson | 11-134 | England | Brisbane[2] | 1982-83 |
| D.K.Lillee | 11-138 | England | Melbourne | 1979-80 |
| C.J.McDermott | 11-157 | England | Perth | 1990-91 |
| D.K.Lillee | 11-159 | England | The Oval | 1981 |
| G.E.Palmer | 11-165 | England | Sydney | 1881-82 |
| D.K.Lillee | 11-165 | England | Melbourne | 1976-77 |
| G.F.Lawson | 11-181 | West Indies | Adelaide | 1984-85 |
| C.V.Grimmett | 11-183 | West Indies | Adelaide | 1930-31 |
| A.K.Davidson | 11-222 | West Indies | Brisbane[2] | 1960-61 |
| C.T.B.Turner | 10-63 | England | Lord's | 1888 |
| R.M.Hogg | 10-66 | England | Melbourne | 1978-79 |
| C.V.Grimmett | 10-88 | South Africa | Cape Town | 1935-36 |
| G.D.McKenzie | 10-91 | India | Madras[2] | 1964-65 |
| C.V.Grimmett | 10-110 | South Africa | Johannesburg[1] | 1935-36 |
| R.J.Bright | 10-111 | Pakistan | Karachi[1] | 1979-80 |
| M.G.Bevan | 10-113 | West indies | Adelaide | 1996-97 |
| N.J.N.Hawke | 10-115 | West Indies | Georgetown | 1964-65 |
| W.J.O'Reilly | 10-122 | England | Leeds | 1938 |
| R.M.Hogg | 10-122 | England | Perth | 1978-79 |
| G.E.Palmer | 10-126 | England | Melbourne | 1882-83 |
| D.K.Lillee | 10-127 | West Indies | Melbourne | 1981-82 |
| H.Trumble | 10-128 | England | Manchester | 1902 |
| W.J.O'Reilly | 10-129 | England | Melbourne | 1932-33 |
| D.K.Lillee | 10-135 | Pakistan | Melbourne | 1976-77 |
| F R.Spofforth | 10-144 | England | Sydney | 1884-85 |
| A.A.Mallett | 10-144 | India | Madras[1] | 1969-70 |
| R.G.Holland | 10-144 | West Indies | Sydney | 1984-85 |
| G.D.McKenzie | 10-151 | India | Melbourne | 1967-68 |
| T.M.Alderman | 10-151 | England | Leeds | 1989 |
| K.R.Miller | 10-152 | England | Lord's | 1956 |
| G.D.McKenzie | 10-159 | West Indies | Melbourne | 1968-69 |
| G.Giffen | 10-160 | England | Sydney | 1891-92 |
| H.V.Hordern # | 10-161 | England | Sydney | 1911-12 |
| E.Jones | 10-164 | England | Lord's | 1899 |
| C.J.McDermott | 10-168 | India | Adelaide | 1991-92 |
| R.G.Holland | 10-174 | New Zealand | Sydney | 1985-86 |
| D.K.Lillee | 10-181 | England | The Oval | 1972 |
| B.Yardley | 10-185 | West Indies | Sydney | 1981-82 |
| C.V.Grimmett | 10-201 | England | Nottingham | 1930 |
| L.O.Fleetwood-Smith | 10-239 | England | Adelaide | 1936-37 |
| G.R.J.Matthews | 10-249 | India | Madras[1] | 1986-87 |
| A.A.Mailey | 10-302 | England | Adelaide | 1920-21 |

| **ENGLAND** (91) | | Opponents | | |
|---|---|---|---|---|
| J.C.Laker | 19-90 | Australia | Manchester | 1956 |
| S.F.Barnes | 17-159 | South Africa | Johannesburg[1] | 1913-14 |
| J.Briggs | 15-28 | South Africa | Cape Town | 1888-89 |
| G.A Lohmann | 15-45 | South Africa | Port Elizabeth | 1895-96 |
| C.Blythe | 15-99 | South Africa | Leeds | 1907 |
| H.Verity | 15-104 | Australia | Lord's | 1934 |
| W.Rhodes | 15-124 | Australia | Melbourne | 1903-04 |

| | | | | |
|---|---|---|---|---|
| A.V.Bedser | 14-99 | Australia | Nottingham | 1953 |
| W.Bates | 14-102 | Australia | Melbourne | 1882-83 |
| S.F.Barnes # | 14-144 | South Africa | Durban[1] | 1913-14 |
| S.F.Barnes | 13-57 | South Africa | The Oval | 1912 |
| D.L.Underwood | 13-71 | Pakistan | Lord's | 1974 |
| J.J.Ferris ¶ | 13-91 | South Africa | Cape Town | 1891-92 |
| I.T.Botham | 13-106 | India | Bombay[3] | 1979-80 |
| A.W.Greig | 13-156 | West Indies | Port-of-Spain | 1973-74 |
| S.F.Barnes | 13-163 | Australia | Melbourne | 1901-02 |
| T.Richardson | 13-244 | Australia | Manchester | 1896 |
| J.C.White | 13-256 | Australia | Adelaide | 1928-29 |
| G.A.Lohmann | 12-71 | South Africa | Johannesburg[1] | 1895-96 |
| J.H.Wardle | 12-89 | South Africa | Cape Town | 1956-57 |
| D.L.Underwood | 12-97 | New Zealand | Christchurch | 1970-71 |
| R.Tattersall | 12-101 | South Africa | Lord's | 1951 |
| D.L.Underwood | 12-101 | New Zealand | The Oval | 1969 |
| F.Martin § | 12-102 | Australia | The Oval | 1890 |
| G.A.Lohmann | 12-104 | Australia | The Oval | 1886 |
| A.V.Bedser | 12-112 | South Africa | Manchester | 1951 |
| F.S.Trueman | 12-119 | West Indies | Birmingham | 1963 |
| G.Geary | 12-130 | South Africa | Johannesburg[1] | 1927-28 |
| J.Briggs | 12-136 | Australia | Adelaide | 1891-92 |
| A.P.Freeman | 12-171 | South Africa | Manchester | 1929 |
| G.A.R.Lock | 11-48 | West Indies | The Oval | 1957 |
| G.A.R.Lock | 11-65 | New Zealand | Leeds | 1958 |
| R.Peel | 11-68 | Australia | Manchester | 1888 |
| D.L.Underwood | 11-70 | New Zealand | Lord's | 1969 |
| J.Briggs | 11-74 | Australia | Lord's | 1886 |
| W.H.Lockwood | 11-76 | Australia | Manchester | 1902 |
| N.G.B.Cook | 11-83 | Pakistan | Karachi[1] | 1983-84 |
| G.A.R.Lock | 11-84 | New Zealand | Christchurch | 1958-59 |
| F.S.Trueman | 11-88 | Australia | Leeds | 1961 |
| A.E.R.Gilligan | 11-90 | South Africa | Birmingham | 1924 |
| A.V.Bedser | 11-93 | India | Manchester | 1946 |
| P.C.R.Tufnell | 11-93 | Australia | The Oval | 1997 |
| C.S.Marriott † | 11-96 | West Indies | The Oval | 1933 |
| J.B.Statham | 11-97 | South Africa | Lord's | 1960 |
| T.E.Bailey | 11-98 | West Indies | Lord's | 1957 |
| C.Blythe | 11-102 | Australia | Birmingham | 1909 |
| S.F.Barnes | 11-110 | South Africa | Lord's | 1912 |
| A.R.C.Fraser | 11-110 | West Indies | Port-of-Spain | 1997-98 |
| J.C.Laker | 11-113 | Australia | Leeds | 1956 |
| C.Blythe | 11-118 | South Africa | Cape Town | 1905-06 |
| I.T.Botham | 11-140 | New Zealand | Lord's | 1978 |
| A.V.Bedser § | 11-145 | India | Lord's | 1946 |
| P.C.R.Tufnell | 11-147 | New Zealand | Christchurch | 1991-92 |
| W.Voce | 11-149 | West Indies | Port-of-Spain | 1929-30 |
| F.S.Trueman | 11-152 | West Indies | Lord's | 1963 |
| H.Verity | 11-153 | India | Madras[1] | 1933-34 |
| N.A.Foster | 11-163 | India | Madras[1] | 1984-85 |
| T.Richardson | 11-173 | Australia | Lord's | 1896 |
| I.T.Botham | 11-176 | Australia | Perth | 1979-80 |
| D.L.Underwood | 11-215 | Australia | Adelaide | 1974-75 |
| M.W.Tate | 11-228 | Australia | Sydney | 1924-25 |
| F.E.Woolley | 10-49 | Australia | The Oval | 1912 |
| W.Voce | 10-57 | Australia | Brisbane[2] | 1936-37 |
| J.T.Hearne | 10-60 | Australia | The Oval | 1896 |
| J.K.Lever § | 10-70 | India | Delhi | 1976-77 |
| G.O.B.Allen | 10-78 | India | Lord's | 1936 |
| D.L.Underwood | 10-82 | Australia | Leeds | 1972 |

| | | | | |
|---|---|---|---|---|
| G.A.Lohmann | 10-87 | Australia | Sydney | 1886-87 |
| A.P.Freeman | 10-93 | West Indies | Manchester | 1928 |
| C.Blythe # | 10-104 | South Africa | Cape Town | 1909-10 |
| R.M.Ellison | 10-104 | Australia | Birmingham | 1985 |
| A.V.Bedser | 10-105 | Australia | Melbourne | 1950-51 |
| S.F.Barnes | 10-105 | South Africa | Durban[1] | 1913-14 |
| S.F.Barnes | 10-115 | South Africa | Leeds | 1912 |
| J.C.Laker | 10-119 | South Africa | The Oval | 1951 |
| A.R.C.Fraser | 10-122 | South Aftica | Nottingham | 1998 |
| H.Larwood | 10-124 | Australia | Sydney | 1932-33 |
| F.H.Tyson | 10-130 | Australia | Sydney | 1954-55 |
| D.E.Malcolm | 10-137 | West Indies | Port-of-Spain | 1989-90 |
| D.E.Malcolm | 10-138 | South Africa | The Oval | 1994 |
| G.A Lohmann | 10-142 | Australia | Sydney | 1891-92 |
| J.A.Snow | 10-142 | West Indies | Georgetown | 1967-68 |
| J.Briggs | 10-148 | Australia | The Oval | 1893 |
| A.W.Greig | 10-149 | New Zealand | Auckland | 1977 |
| T.Richardson § | 10-156 | Australia | Manchester | 1893 |
| D.V.P.Wright | 10-175 | South Africa | Lord's | 1947 |
| K.Farnes § | 10-179 | Australia | Nottingham | 1934 |
| G.T.S.Stevens | 10-195 | West Indies | Bridgetown | 1929-30 |
| T.Richardson # | 10-204 | Australia | Sydney | 1897-98 |
| A.P.Freeman | 10-207 | South Africa | Leeds | 1929 |
| I.T.Botham | 10-253 | Australia | The Oval | 1981 |

*¶ Ferris's only Test for England.*

| **SOUTH AFRICA** (13) | | Opponents | | |
|---|---|---|---|---|
| H.J.Tayfield | 13-165 | Australia | Melbourne | 1952-53 |
| H.J.Tayfield | 13-192 | England | Johannesburg[3] | 1956-57 |
| S.J.Snooke | 12-127 | England | Johannesburg[1] | 1905-06 |
| A.A.Donald | 12-139 | India | Port Elizabeth | 1992-93 |
| A.E.E.Vogler | 12-181 | England | Johannesburg[1] | 1909-10 |
| A.E.Hall § | 11-112 | England | Cape Town | 1922-23 |
| A.A.Donald | 11-113 | Zimbabwe | Harare | 1995-96 |
| E.P.Nupen | 11-150 | England | Johannesburg[1] | 1930-31 |
| S.F.Burke § | 11-196 | New Zealand | Cape Town | 1961-62 |
| P.M.Pollock | 10-87 | England | Nottingham | 1965 |
| P.S.de Villiers | 10-108 | Pakistan | Johannesburg[3] | 1994-95 |
| C.B.Llewellyn | 10-116 | Australia | Johannesburg[1] | 1902-03 |
| P.S.de Villiers | 10-123 | Australia | Sydney | 1993-94 |

| **WEST INDIES** (24) | | Opponents | | |
|---|---|---|---|---|
| M.A.Holding | 14-149 | England | The Oval | 1976 |
| C.A.Walsh | 13-55 | New Zealand | Wellington | 1994-95 |
| A.M.E.Roberts | 12-121 | India | Madras[1] | 1974-75 |
| C.E.L.Ambrose | 11-84 | England | Port-of-Spain | 1993-94 |
| M.D.Marshall | 11-89 | India | Port-of-Spain | 1988-89 |
| M.A.Holding | 11-107 | Australia | Melbourne | 1981-82 |
| M.D.Marshall | 11-120 | New Zealand | Bridgetown | 1984-85 |
| W.W.Hall | 11-126 | India | Kanpur | 1958-59 |
| K.D.Boyce | 11-147 | England | The Oval | 1973 |
| S.Ramadhin | 11-152 | England | Lord's | 1950 |
| L.R.Gibbs | 11-157 | England | Manchester | 1963 |
| A.L.Valentine § | 11-204 | England | Manchester | 1950 |
| W.Ferguson | 11-229 | England | Port-of-Spain | 1947-48 |
| M.D.Marshall | 10-92 | England | Lord's | 1988 |
| H.H.H.Johnson § | 10-96 | England | Kingston | 1947-48 |
| C A Walsh | 10-101 | India | Kingston | 1988-89 |
| L R Gibbs | 10-106 | England | Manchester | 1966 |
| M.D.Marshall | 10-107 | Australia | Adelaide | 1984-85 |
| G.E.Gomez | 10-113 | Australia | Sydney | 1951-52 |
| C.E.L.Ambrose | 10-120 | Australia | Adelaide | 1992-93 |

| | | | | |
|---|---|---|---|---|
| A.M.E.Roberts | 10-123 | England | Lord's | 1976 |
| C.E.L.Ambrose | 10-127 | England | Bridgetown | 1989-90 |
| A.L.Valentine | 10-160 | England | The Oval | 1950 |
| K.C.G.Benjamin | 10-174 | England | Nottingham | 1995 |

| **NEW ZEALAND** (16) | | Opponents | | |
|---|---|---|---|---|
| R.J.Hadlee | 15-123 | Australia | Brisbane[2] | 1985-86 |
| R.J.Hadlee | 11-58 | India | Wellington | 1975-76 |
| R.J.Hadlee | 11-102 | West Indies | Dunedin | 1979-80 |
| C.Pringle | 11-152 | Pakistan | Faisalabad | 1990-91 |
| R.J.Hadlee | 11-155 | Australia | Perth | 1985-86 |
| D.J.Nash | 11-169 | England | Lord's | 1994 |
| R.J.Hadlee | 10-88 | India | Bombay[3] | 1988-89 |
| R.J.Hadlee | 10-100 | England | Wellington | 1977-78 |
| R.J.Hadlee | 10-102 | Sri Lanka | Colombo (CCC) | 1983-84 |
| J.G.Bracewell | 10-106 | Australia | Auckland | 1985-86 |
| E.J.Chatfield | 10-124 | West Indies | Port-of-Spain | 1984-85 |
| J.Cowie | 10-140 | England | Manchester | 1937 |
| R.J.Hadlee | 10-140 | England | Nottingham | 1986 |
| B.L.Cairns | 10-144 | England | Leeds | 1983 |
| G.B.Troup | 10-166 | West Indies | Auckland | 1979-80 |
| R.J.Hadlee | 10-176 | Australia | Melbourne | 1987-88 |

| **INDIA** (23) | | Opponents | | |
|---|---|---|---|---|
| N.D.Hirwani § | 16-136 | West Indies | Madras[1] | 1987-88 |
| J.M.Patel | 14-124 | Australia | Kanpur | 1959-60 |
| M.H.Mankad | 13-131 | Pakistan | Delhi | 1952-53 |
| B.S.Chandrasekhar | 12-104 | Australia | Melbourne | 1977-78 |
| M.H.Mankad | 12-108 | England | Madras[1] | 1951-52 |
| S.Venkataraghavan | 12-152 | New Zealand | Delhi | 1964-65 |
| L.Sivaramakrishnan | 12-181 | England | Bombay[3] | 1984-85 |
| R.G.Nadkarni | 11-122 | Australia | Madras[2] | 1964-65 |
| S.L.Venkatapathy Raju | 11-125 | Sri Lanka | Ahmedabad | 1993-94 |
| A.R.Kumble | 11-128 | Sri Lanka | Lucknow[2] | 1993-94 |
| E.A.S.Prasanna | 11-140 | New Zealand | Auckland | 1975-76 |
| Kapil Dev | 11-146 | Pakistan | Madras[1] | 1979-80 |
| B.S.Chandrasekhar | 11-235 | West Indies | Bombay[2] | 1966-67 |
| Maninder Singh | 10-107 | Sri Lanka | Nagpur | 1986-87 |
| Maninder Singh | 10-126 | Pakistan | Bangalore | 1986-87 |
| Ghulam Ahmed | 10-130 | Australia | Calcutta | 1956-57 |
| Kapil Dev | 10-135 | West Indies | Ahmedabad | 1983-84 |
| B.K.Venkatesh Prasad | 10-153 | South Africa | Durban[2] | 1996-97 |
| E.A.S.Prasanna | 10-174 | Australia | Madras[1] | 1969-70 |
| S.A.Durani | 10-177 | England | Madras[2] | 1961-62 |
| C.Sharma | 10-188 | England | Birmingham | 1986 |
| B.S.Bedi | 10-194 | Australia | Perth | 1977-78 |
| S.P.Gupte | 10-223 | West Indies | Kanpur | 1958-59 |

| **PAKISTAN** (35) | | Opponents | | |
|---|---|---|---|---|
| Imran Khan | 14-116 | Sri Lanka | Lahore[2] | 1981-82 |
| Abdul Qadir | 13-101 | England | Lahore[2] | 1987-88 |
| Fazal Mahmood | 13-114 | Australia | Karachi[1] | 1956-57 |
| Waqar Younis | 13-135 | Zimbabwe | Karachi[2] | 1993-94 |
| Fazal Mahmood | 12-94 | India | Lucknow[1] | 1952-53 |
| Fazal Mahmood | 12-99 | England | The Oval | 1954 |
| Fazal Mahmood | 12-100 | West Indies | Dacca | 1958-59 |
| Waqar Younis | 12-130 | New Zealand | Faisalabad | 1990-91 |
| Imran Khan | 12-165 | Australia | Sydney | 1976-77 |
| Zulfiqar Ahmed | 11-79 | New Zealand | Karachi[1] | 1955-56 |
| Imran Khan | 11-79 | India | Karachi[1] | 1982-83 |
| Iqbal Qasim | 11-118 | Australia | Karachi[1] | 1979-80 |

| | | | | |
|---|---|---|---|---|
| Waqar Younis | 11-119 | Sri Lanka | Kandy | 1994-95 |
| Imran Khan | 11-121 | West Indies | Georgetown | 1987-88 |
| Sarfraz Nawaz | 11-125 | Australia | Melbourne | 1978-79 |
| Intikhab Alam | 11-130 | New Zealand | Dunedin | 1972-73 |
| Mohammad Zahid | 11-130 | New Zealand | Rawalpindi[2] | 1996-97 |
| Wasim Akram | 11-160 | Australia | Melbourne | 1989-90 |
| Wasim Akram | 11-179 | New Zealand | Wellington | 1993-94 |
| Imran Khan | 11-180 | India | Faisalabad | 1982-83 |
| Sikander Bakht | 11-190 | India | Delhi | 1979-80 |
| Abdul Qadir | 11-218 | Australia | Faisalabad | 1982-83 |
| Imran Khan | 10-77 | England | Leeds | 1987 |
| Wasim Akram | 10-106 | Zimbabwe | Faisalabad | 1996-97 |
| Waqar Younis | 10-106 | New Zealand | Lahore[1] | 1990-91 |
| Mushtaq Ahmed | 10-106 | West Indies | Peshawar[2] | 1997-98 |
| Wasim Akram | 10-128 | New Zealand | Dunedin | 1984-85 |
| Waqar Younis | 10-133 | South Africa | Port Elizabeth | 1997-98 |
| Mushtaq Ahmed | 10-143 | New Zealand | Lahore[2] | 1996-97 |
| Mushtaq Ahmed | 10-171 | New Zealand | Christchurch | 1995-96 |
| Iqbal Qasim | 10-175 | India | Bombay[3] | 1979-80 |
| Intikhab Alam | 10-182 | New Zealand | Dacca | 1969-70 |
| Abdul Qadir | 10-186 | England | Karachi[1] | 1987-88 |
| Abdul Qadir | 10-194 | England | Lahore[2] | 1983-84 |
| Abdul Qadir | 10-211 | England | The Oval | 1987 |

| **SRI LANKA** (2) | | Opponents | | |
|---|---|---|---|---|
| M.Muralidaran | 12-117 | Zimbabwe | Kandy | 1997-98 |
| W.P.U.J.C.Vaas | 10-90 | New Zealand | Napier | 1994-95 |

| **ZIMBABWE** (1) | | Opponents | | |
|---|---|---|---|---|
| A.G.Huckle | 11-257 | New Zealand | Bulawayo[2] | 1997-98 |

## SIX WICKETS IN AN INNINGS ON DEBUT

### IN BOTH INNINGS

| | | | | | | |
|---|---|---|---|---|---|---|
| F.Martin | 6/50)<br>6/52) | England | v | Australia | The Oval | 1890 |
| R.A.L.Massie | 8/84)<br>8/52) | Australia | v | England | Lord's | 1972 |
| N.D.Hirwani | 8/61)<br>8/75) | India | v | West Indies | Madras[1] | 1987-88 |

### IN FIRST INNINGS

| | | | | | | |
|---|---|---|---|---|---|---|
| W.H.Ashley | 7/95 | South Africa | v | England | Port Elizabeth | 1888-89 |
| W.H.Lockwood | 6/101 | England | v | Australia | Lord's | 1893 |
| G.H.T.Simpson-Hayward | 6/43 | England | v | South Africa | Johannesburg[1] | 1909-10 |
| G.M.Parker | 6/152 | South Africa | v | England | Birmingham | 1924 |
| A.J.Bell | 6/99 | South Africa | v | England | Lord's | 1929 |
| A.V.Bedser | 7/49 | England | v | India | Lord's | 1946 |
| J.C.Laker | 7/103 | England | v | West Indies | Bridgetown | 1947-48 |
| T.E.Bailey | 6/118 | England | v | New Zealand | Leeds | 1949 |
| G.F.Cresswell | 6/168 | New Zealand | v | England | The Oval | 1949 |
| A.L.Valentine | 8/104 | West Indies | v | England | Manchester | 1950 |
| A.M.Moir | 6/155 | New Zealand | v | England | Christchurch | 1950-51 |
| S.F.Burke | 6/128 | South Africa | v | New Zealand | Cape Town | 1961-62 |
| Arif Butt | 6/89 | Pakistan | v | Australia | Melbourne | 1964-65 |
| S.Abid Ali | 6/55 | India | v | Australia | Adelaide | 1967-68 |
| Mohammad Nazir | 7/99 | Pakistan | v | New Zealand | Karachi[1] | 1969-70 |
| J.K.Lever | 7/46 | England | v | India | Delhi | 1976-77 |
| R.M.Hogg | 6/74 | Australia | v | England | Brisbane[2] | 1978-79 |
| D.R.Doshi | 6/103 | India | v | Australia | Madras[1] | 1979-80 |
| P.L.Taylor | 6/78 | Australia | v | England | Sydney | 1986-87 |
| P.M.Such | 6/67 | England | v | Australia | Manchester | 1993 |
| F.A.Rose | 6/100 | West Indies | v | India | Kingston | 1996-97 |

**IN SECOND INNINGS**

| | | | | | | |
|---|---|---|---|---|---|---|
| T.K.Kendall | 7/55 | Australia | v | England | Melbourne | 1876-77 |
| W.H.Cooper | 6/120 | Australia | v | England | Melbourne | 1881-82 |
| A.E.Trott | 8/43 | Australia | v | England | Adelaide | 1894-95 |
| M.A.Noble | 6/49 | Australia | v | England | Melbourne | 1897-98 |
| A.E.Hall | 7/63 | South Africa | v | England | Cape Town | 1922-23 |
| C.V.Grimmett | 6/37 | Australia | v | England | Sydney | 1924-25 |
| J.Langridge | 7/56 | England | v | West Indies | Manchester | 1933 |
| C.S.Marriott | 6/59 | England | v | West Indies | The Oval | 1933 |
| F.A.Ward | 6/102 | Australia | v | England | Brisbane[2] | 1936-37 |
| C.N.McCarthy | 6/43 | South Africa | v | England | Durban[2] | 1948-49 |
| P.S.Pollock | 6/38 | South Africa | v | New Zealand | Durban[2] | 1961-62 |
| L.J.Coldwell | 6/85 | England | v | Pakistan | Lord's | 1962 |
| A.I.C.Dodemaide | 6/58 | Australia | v | New Zealand | Melbourne | 1987-88 |
| D.G.Cork | 7/43 | England | v | West Indies | Lord's | 1995 |
| Mohammad Zahid | 7/66 | Pakistan | v | New Zealand | Rawalpindi[2] | 1996-97 |
| L.Klusener | 8/64 | South Africa | v | India | Calcutta | 1996-97 |

## TEN WICKETS IN A MATCH ON DEBUT

| | | | | | | |
|---|---|---|---|---|---|---|
| F.Martin | 10/104 | England | v | Australia | The Oval | 1890 |
| T.Richardson | 10/156 | England | v | Australia | Manchester | 1893 |
| A.E.Hall | 11/112 | South Africa | v | England | Cape Town | 1922-23 |
| C.V.Grimmett | 11/82 | Australia | v | England | Sydney | 1924-25 |
| C.S.Marriott | 11/96 | England | v | West Indies | The Oval | 1933 |
| K.Farnes | 10/179 | England | v | Australia | Nottingham | 1934 |
| A.V.Bedser | 11/145 | England | v | India | Lord's | 1946 |
| H.H.H.Johnson | 10/96 | West Indies | v | England | Kingston | 1947-48 |
| A.L.Valentine | 11/204 | West Indies | v | England | Manchester | 1950 |
| S.F.Burke | 11/196 | South Africa | v | New Zealand | Cape Town | 1961-62 |
| R.A.L.Massie | 16/137 | Australia | v | England | Lord's | 1972 |
| J.K.Lever | 10/70 | England | v | India | Delhi | 1976-77 |
| N.D.Hirwani | 16/136 | India | v | West Indies | Madras[1] | 1987-88 |
| Mohammad Zahid | 11/130 | Pakistan | v | New Zealand | Rawalpindi[2] | 1996-97 |

## EIGHT WICKETS IN AN INNINGS *(§ In first Test. # In last Test)*

| **AUSTRALIA** (15) | | Opponents | | |
|---|---|---|---|---|
| A.A.Mailey | 9-121 | England | Melbourne | 1920-21 |
| F.Laver | 8-31 | England | Manchester | 1909 |
| G.D.McGrath | 8-38 | England | Lord's | 1997 |
| A.E.Trott § | 8-43 | England | Adelaide | 1894-95 |
| R.A.L.Massie § | 8-53 | England | Lord's | 1972 |
| A.A.Mallett | 8-59 | Pakistan | Adelaide | 1972-73 |
| H.Trumble | 8-65 | England | The Oval | 1902 |
| G.D.McKenzie | 8-71 | West Indies | Melbourne | 1968-69 |
| S.K.Warne | 8-71 | England | Brisbane[2] | 1994-95 |
| R.A.L.Massie § | 8-84 | England | Lord's | 1972 |
| M.G.Hughes | 8-87 | West Indies | Perth | 1988-89 |
| C.J.McDermott | 8-97 | England | Perth | 1990-91 |
| G.F.Lawson | 8-112 | West Indies | Adelaide | 1984-85 |
| C.J.McDermott | 8-141 | England | Manchester | 1985 |
| M.H.N.Walker | 8-143 | England | Melbourne | 1974-75 |

| **ENGLAND** (26) | | Opponents | | |
|---|---|---|---|---|
| J.C.Laker | 10-53 | Australia | Manchester | 1956 |
| G.A.Lohmann | 9-28 | South Africa | Johannesburg[1] | 1895-96 |
| J.C.Laker | 9-37 | Australia | Manchester | 1956 |
| D.E.Malcolm | 9-57 | South Africa | The Oval | 1994 |
| S.F.Barnes | 9-103 | South Africa | Johannesburg[1] | 1913-14 |
| G.A.Lohmann | 8-7 | South Africa | Port Elizabeth | 1895-96 |
| J.Briggs | 8-11 | South Africa | Cape Town | 1888-89 |

| | | | | |
|---|---|---|---|---|
| S.F.Barnes | 8-29 | South Africa | The Oval | 1912 |
| F.S.Trueman | 8-31 | India | Manchester | 1952 |
| I.T.Botham | 8-34 | Pakistan | Lord's | 1978 |
| G.A.Lohmann | 8-35 | Australia | Sydney | 1886-87 |
| H.Verity | 8-43 | Australia | Lord's | 1934 |
| R.G.D.Willis | 8-43 | Australia | Leeds | 1981 |
| D.L.Underwood | 8-51 | Pakistan | Lord's | 1974 |
| A.R.C.Fraser | 8-75 | West Indies | Bridgetown | 1993-94 |
| S.F.Barnes | 8-56 | South Africa | Johannesburg[1] | 1913-14 |
| G.A.Lohmann | 8-58 | Australia | Sydney | 1891-92 |
| C.Blythe | 8-59 | South Africa | Leeds | 1907 |
| W.Rhodes | 8-68 | Australia | Melbourne | 1903-04 |
| A.R.C.Fraser | 8-53 | West Indies | Port-of-Spain | 1997-98 |
| L.C.Braund | 8-81 | Australia | Melbourne | 1903-04 |
| A.W.Greig | 8-86 | West Indies | Port-of-Spain | 1973-74 |
| T.Richardson # | 8-94 | Australia | Sydney | 1897-98 |
| I.T.Botham | 8-103 | West Indies | Lord's | 1984 |
| B.J.T.Bosanquet | 8-107 | Australia | Nottingham | 1905 |
| N.A.Foster | 8-107 | Pakistan | Leeds | 1987 |
| J.C.White | 8-126 | Australia | Adelaide | 1928-29 |
| **SOUTH AFRICA** (6) | | Opponents | | |
| H.J.Tayfield | 9-113 | England | Johannesburg[3] | 1956-57 |
| G.B.Lawrence | 8-53 | New Zealand | Johannesburg[3] | 1961-62 |
| L.Klusener | 8-64 | India | Calcutta | 1996-97 |
| H.J.Tayfield | 8-69 | England | Durban[2] | 1956-57 |
| S.J.Snooke | 8-70 | England | Johannesburg[1] | 1905-06 |
| A.A.Donald | 8-71 | Zimbabwe | Harare | 1995-96 |
| **WEST INDIES** (6) | | Opponents | | |
| J.M.Noreiga | 9-95 | India | Port-of-Spain | 1970-71 |
| C.E.H.Croft | 8-29 | Pakistan | Port-of-Spain | 1976-77 |
| L.R.Gibbs | 8-38 | India | Bridgetown | 1961-62 |
| C.E.L.Ambrose | 8-45 | England | Bridgetown | 1989-90 |
| M.A.Holding | 8-92 | England | The Oval | 1976 |
| A.L.Valentine § | 8-104 | England | Manchester | 1950 |
| **NEW ZEALAND** (1) | | Opponents | | |
| R.J.Hadlee | 9-52 | Australia | Brisbane[2] | 1985-86 |
| **INDIA** (12) | | Opponents | | |
| J.M.Patel | 9-69 | Australia | Kanpur | 1959-60 |
| Kapil Dev | 9-83 | West Indies | Ahmedabad | 1983-84 |
| S.P.Gupte | 9-102 | West Indies | Kanpur | 1958-59 |
| M.H.Mankad | 8-52 | Pakistan | Delhi | 1952-53 |
| M.H.Mankad | 8-55 | England | Madras[1] | 1951-52 |
| N.D.Hirwani § | 8-61 | West Indies | Madras[1] | 1987-88 |
| S.Venkataraghavan | 8-72 | New Zealand | Delhi | 1964-65 |
| N.D.Hirwani § | 8-75 | West Indies | Madras[1] | 1987-88 |
| E.A.S.Prasanna | 8-76 | New Zealand | Auckland | 1975-76 |
| B.S.Chandrasekhar | 8-79 | England | Delhi | 1972-73 |
| Kapil Dev | 8-85 | Pakistan | Lahore[2] | 1982-83 |
| Kapil Dev | 8-106 | Australia | Adelaide | 1985-86 |
| **PAKISTAN** (5) | | Opponents | | |
| Abdul Qadir | 9-56 | England | Lahore[2] | 1887-88 |
| Sarfraz Nawaz | 9-86 | Australia | Melbourne | 1978-79 |
| Imran Khan | 8-58 | Sri Lanka | Lahore[2] | 1981-82 |
| Imran Khan | 8-60 | India | Karachi[1] | 1982-83 |
| Sikander Bakht | 8-69 | India | Delhi | 1979-80 |

| **SRI LANKA** (1) | | Opponents | | |
|---|---|---|---|---|
| J.R.Ratnayeke | 8-83 | Pakistan | Sialkot | 1985-86 |

Best for Zimbabwe:

| **ZIMBABWE** | | | | |
|---|---|---|---|---|
| H.H.Streak | 6-90 | Pakistan | Harare | 1994-95 |

## YOUNGEST PLAYERS TO TAKE 10 OR MORE WICKETS IN A MATCH

| Years | Days | | | | | | | |
|---|---|---|---|---|---|---|---|---|
| 18 | 256 | Wasim Akram | 10-128 | Pakistan | v | New Zealand | Dunedin | 1984-85 |
| 18 | 335 | S.Venkataraghavan | 12-152 | India | v | New Zealand | Delhi | 1964-65 |
| 18 | 338 | L.Shivaramakrishnan | 12-181 | India | v | England | Bombay[3] | 1984-85 |
| 18 | 341 | Waqar Younis | 10-106 | Pakistan | v | New Zealand | Lahore[1] | 1990-91 |
| 18 | 349 | Waqar Younis | 12-130 | Pakistan | v | New Zealand | Faisalabad | 1990-91 |
| 19 | 89 | N.D.Hirwani | 16-136 | India | v | West Indies | Madras[1] | 1987-88 |
| 20 | 41 | A.L.Valentine | 11-204 | West Indies | v | England | Manchester | 1950 |
| 20 | 47 | W.P.U.J.C.Vaas | 10-90 | Sri Lanka | v | New Zealand | Napier | 1994-95 |
| 20 | 109 | A.L.Valentine | 10-160 | West Indies | v | England | The Oval | 1950 |
| 20 | 182 | W.Voce | 11-149 | England | v | West Indies | Port-of-Spain | 1929-30 |
| 20 | 186 | C.Sharma | 10-188 | India | v | England | Birmingham | 1986 |

Youngest for the other countries:

| | | | | | | | | |
|---|---|---|---|---|---|---|---|---|
| 22 | 277 | C.Pringle | 11-152 | New Zealand | v | Pakistan | Faisalabad | 1990-91 |
| 23 | 212 | D.J.Nash | 11-169 | New Zealand | v | England | Lord's | 1994 |
| 24 | 40 | P.M.Pollock | 10-87 | South Africa | v | England | Nottingham | 1965 |
| 26 | 8 | A.G.Huckle | 11-257 | Zimbabwe | v | New Zealand | Bulawayo[2] | 1997-98 |

## YOUNGEST PLAYERS TO TAKE 5 OR MORE WICKETS IN AN INNINGS

| Years | Days | | | | | | | |
|---|---|---|---|---|---|---|---|---|
| 16 | 307 | Nasim-ul-Ghani | 5/116 | Pakistan | v | West Indies | Georgetown | 1957-58 |
| 16 | 321 | Nasim-ul-Ghani | 6/67 | Pakistan | v | West Indies | Port-of-Spain | 1957-58 |
| 18 | 49 | D.L.Vettori | 5/84 | New Zealand | v | Sri Lanka | Hamilton | 1996-97 |
| 18 | 253 | Wasim Akram | 5/56 | Pakistan | v | New Zealand | Dunedin | 1984-85 |
| 18 | 256 | Wasim Akram | 5/72 | Pakistan | v | New Zealand | Dunedin | 1984-85 |
| 18 | 294 | R.J.Shastri | 5/125 | India | v | New Zealand | Auckland | 1980-81 |
| 18 | 318 | Shahid Nazir | 5/53 | Pakistan | v | Zimbabwe | Sheikhupura | 1996-97 |
| 18 | 333 | S.Venkataraghavan | 8/72 | India | v | New Zealand | Delhi | 1964-65 |
| 18 | 334 | L.Shivaramakrishnan | 6/64 | India | v | England | Bombay[3] | 1984-85 |
| 18 | 338 | L.Shivaramakrishnan | 6/117 | India | v | England | Bombay[3] | 1984-85 |
| 18 | 341 | Waqar Younis | 7/86 | Pakistan | v | New Zealand | Lahore[2] | 1990-91 |
| 18 | 346 | Waqar Younis | 7/76 | Pakistan | v | New Zealand | Faisalabad | 1990-91 |
| 18 | 349 | Waqar Younis | 5/54 | Pakistan | v | New Zealand | Faisalabad | 1990-91 |
| 18 | 351 | L.Shivaramakrishnan | 6/99 | India | v | England | Delhi | 1984-85 |
| 18 | 364 | Waqar Younis | 5/76 | Pakistan | v | West Indies | Karachi[1] | 1990-91 |
| 19 | 8 | Waqar Younis | 5/46 | Pakistan | v | West Indies | Faisalabad | 1990-91 |
| 19 | 88 | N.D.Hirwani | 8/61 | India | v | West Indies | Madras[1] | 1987-88 |
| 19 | 89 | N.D.Hirwani | 8/75 | India | v | West Indies | Madras[1] | 1987-88 |
| 19 | 95 | A.Cotter | 6/40 | Australia | v | England | Melbourne | 1903-04 |
| 19 | 101 | K.R.Pushpakumara | 7/116 | Sri Lanka | v | Zimbabwe | Harare | 1994-95 |
| 19 | 136 | D.L.Vettori | 5/84 | New Zealand | v | Sri Lanka | Hamilton | 1996-97 |
| 19 | 232 | P.R.Adams | 6/55 | South Africa | v | India | Kanpur | 1996-97 |
| 19 | 247 | C.Sharma | 5/118 | India | v | Sri Lanka | Colombo (PSS) | 1985-86 |
| 19 | 253 | M.G.Melle | 5/113 | South Africa | v | Australia | Johannesburg[2] | 1949-50 |
| 19 | 254 | J.J.Ferris | 5/76 | Australia | v | England | Sydney | 1886-87 |
| 19 | 271 | C.N.McCarthy | 6/43 | South Africa | v | England | Durban[2] | 1948-49 |
| 19 | 272 | J.J.Ferris | 5/71 | Australia | v | England | Sydney | 1886-87 |
| 19 | 273 | H.H.Streak | 5/56 | Zimbabwe | v | Pakistan | Rawalpindi[2] | 1993-94 |
| 19 | 327 | C.N.McCarthy | 5/114 | South Africa | v | England | Johannesburg[2] | 1948-49 |
| 19 | 363 | J.M.Blanckenberg | 5/83 | South Africa | v | England | Johannesburg[1] | 1913-14 |
| 19 | 364 | R.B.Desai | 5/89 | India | v | England | Lord's | 1959 |

| | | | | | | | | |
|---|---|---|---|---|---|---|---|---|
| 20 | 2 | G.D.McKenzie | 5/37 | Australia | v | England | Lord's | 1961 |
| 20 | 27 | Waqar Younis | 5/84 | Pakistan | v | Sri Lanka | Sialkot | 1991-92 |
| 20 | 30 | N.D.Hirwani | 6/59 | India | v | New Zealand | Bangalore | 1988-89 |
| 20 | 40 | A.L.Valentine | 8/104 | West Indies | v | England | Manchester | 1950 |
| 20 | 44 | W.P.U.J.C.Vaas | 5/47 | Sri Lanka | v | New Zealand | Napier | 1994-95 |
| 20 | 47 | W.P.U.J.C.Vaas | 5/43 | Sri Lanka | v | New Zealand | Napier | 1994-95 |
| 20 | 51 | Waqar Younis | 5/65 | Pakistan | v | Sri Lanka | Faisalabad | 1991-92 |
| 20 | 52 | W.P.U.J.C.Vaas | 6/87 | Sri Lanka | v | New Zealand | Dunedin | 1994-95 |
| 20 | 75 | C.J.McDermott | 6/70 | Australia | v | England | Lord's | 1985 |
| 20 | 106 | Azeem Hafeez | 5/100 | Pakistan | v | Australia | Perth | 1983-84 |
| 20 | 109 | A.L.Valentine | 6/39 | West Indies | v | England | The Oval | 1950 |
| 20 | 110 | V.Razdan | 5/79 | India | v | Pakistan | Sialkot | 1989-90 |
| 20 | 111 | C.J.McDermott | 8/141 | Australia | v | England | Manchester | 1985 |
| 20 | 121 | Mohammad Zahid | 7/66 | Pakistan | v | New Zealand | Rawalpindi[2] | 1996-97 |
| 20 | 134 | Azeem Hafeez | 5/167 | Pakistan | v | Australia | Adelaide | 1983-84 |
| 20 | 143 | G.P.Wickramasinghe | 5/73 | Sri Lanka | v | Pakistan | Faisalabad | 1991-92 |
| 20 | 144 | Saqlain Mushtaq | 5/89 | Pakistan | v | Sri Lanka | Colombo (PIS) | 1996-97 |
| 20 | 154 | C.Sharma | 5/64 | India | v | England | Lord's | 1986 |
| 20 | 165 | P.M.Pollock | 6/38 | South Africa | v | New Zealand | Durban[2] | 1961-62 |
| 20 | 182 | W.Voce | 7/70 | England | v | West Indies | Port-of-Spain | 1929-30 |
| 20 | 185 | C.Sharma | 6/58 | India | v | England | Birmingham | 1986 |
| 20 | 188 | Kapil Dev | 5/146 | India | v | England | Birmingham | 1979 |
| 20 | 204 | Arif Butt | 6/89 | Pakistan | v | Australia | Melbourne | 1964-65 |
| 20 | 215 | Waqar Younis | 5/91 | Pakistan | v | England | Lord's | 1992 |
| 20 | 253 | Waqar Younis | 5/113 | Pakistan | v | England | Leeds | 1992 |
| 20 | 255 | A.Cotter | 7/148 | Australia | v | England | The Oval | 1905 |
| 20 | 265 | C.L.Cairns | 5/75 | New Zealand | v | Sri Lanka | Auckland | 1990-91 |
| 20 | 267 | Waqar Younis | 5/52 | Pakistan | v | England | The Oval | 1992 |
| 20 | 283 | Kapil Dev | 5/82 | India | v | Australia | Delhi | 1979-80 |
| 20 | 285 | H.H.Streak | 6/90 | Zimbabwe | v | Pakistan | Harare | 1994-95 |
| 20 | 289 | H.H.Streak | 5/70 | Zimbabwe | v | Pakistan | Bulawayo[2] | 1994-95 |
| 20 | 294 | Kapil Dev | 5/74 | India | v | Australia | Calcutta | 1979-80 |
| 20 | 317 | Saqlain Mushtaq | 5/129 | Pakistan | v | Pakistan | Faisalabad | 1997-98 |
| 20 | 333 | Kapil Dev | 5/58 | India | v | Pakistan | Delhi | 1979-80 |
| 20 | 355 | Kapil Dev | 6/63 | India | v | Pakistan | Kanpur | 1979-80 |
| 20 | 356 | H.J.Tayfield | 7/23 | South Africa | v | Australia | Durban[2] | 1949-50 |
| 20 | 361 | E.P.Nupen | 5/53 | South Africa | v | England | Johannesburg[1] | 1922-23 |

## OLDEST PLAYERS TO TAKE 10 OR MORE WICKETS IN A MATCH

| Years | Days | | | | | | | |
|---|---|---|---|---|---|---|---|---|
| 49 | 313 | H.Ironmonger | 11-79 | Australia | v | West Indies | Melbourne | 1930-31 |
| 44 | 69 | C.V.Grimmett | 13-173 | Australia | v | South Africa | Durban[2] | 1935-36 |
| 44 | 54 | C.V.Grimmett | 10-110 | Australia | v | South Africa | Johannesburg[1] | 1935-36 |
| 44 | 10 | C.V.Grimmett | 10-88 | Australia | v | South Africa | Cape Town | 1935-36 |
| 41 | 74 | A.P.Freeman | 10-207 | England | v | South Africa | Leeds | 1929 |
| 41 | 60 | A.P.Freeman | 12-171 | England | v | South Africa | Manchester | 1929 |
| 41 | 52 | H.Ironmonger | 11-24 | Australia | v | South Africa | Melbourne | 1931-32 |
| 41 | 39 | C.V.Grimmett | 14-199 | Australia | v | South Africa | Adelaide | 1931-32 |
| 40 | 304 | S.F.Barnes | 14-144 | England | v | South Africa | Durban[1] | 1913-14 |
| 40 | 254 | S.F.Barnes | 17-159 | England | v | South Africa | Johannesburg[1] | 1913-14 |
| 40 | 242 | S.F.Barnes | 10-105 | England | v | South Africa | Durban[1] | 1913-14 |
| 40 | 68 | A.P.Freeman | 10-93 | England | v | West Indies | Manchester | 1928 |
| 39 | 116 | S.F.Barnes | 13-57 | England | v | South Africa | The Oval | 1912 |
| 39 | 82 | S.F.Barnes | 10-115 | England | v | South Africa | Leeds | 1912 |
| 39 | 54 | S.F.Barnes | 11-110 | England | v | South Africa | Lord's | 1912 |
| 39 | 37 | R.G.Holland | 10-174 | Australia | v | New Zealand | Sydney | 1985-86 |
| 38 | 355 | C.V.Grimmett | 11-183 | Australia | v | West Indies | Adelaide | 1930-31 |
| 38 | 173 | C.V.Grimmett | 10-201 | Australia | v | England | Nottingham | 1930 |
| 38 | 75 | R.G.Holland | 10-144 | Australia | v | West Indies | Sydney | 1984-85 |
| 37 | 354 | J.C.White | 13-256 | England | v | Australia | Adelaide | 1928-29 |

| | | | | | | | | |
|---|---|---|---|---|---|---|---|---|
| 37 | 335 | C.S.Marriott | 11-96 | England | v | West Indies | The Oval | 1933 |
| 37 | 259 | H.H.H.Johnson | 10-96 | West Indies | v | England | Kingston | 1947-48 |
| 37 | 149 | R.J.Hadlee | 10-88 | New Zealand | v | India | Bombay[3] | 1988-89 |
| 36 | 211 | K.R.Miller | 10-152 | Australia | v | England | Lord's | 1956 |
| 36 | 180 | R.J.Hadlee | 10-176 | New Zealand | v | Australia | Melbourne | 1987-88 |
| 35 | 251 | E.A.S.Prasanna | 11-140 | India | v | New Zealand | Auckland | 1975-76 |
| 35 | 133 | Imran Khan | 11-121 | Pakistan | v | West Indies | Georgetown | 1987-88 |
| 35 | 103 | H.Trumble | 10-128 | Australia | v | England | Manchester | 1902 |
| 35 | 75 | H.Trumble | 12-173 | Australia | v | England | The Oval | 1902 |
| 35 | 40 | R.J.Hadlee | 10-140 | New Zealand | v | England | Nottingham | 1986 |
| 35 | 27 | J.M.Patel | 14-124 | India | v | Australia | Kanpur | 1959-60 |
| Oldest for the other countries: | | | | | | | | |
| 33 | 38 | A.E.E.Vogler | 12-181 | South Africa | v | England | Johannesburg[1] | 1909-10 |
| 26 | 8 | A.G.Huckle | 11-257 | Zimbabwe | v | New Zealand | Bulawayo[2] | 1997-98 |
| 25 | 269 | M.Muralidaran | 12-117 | Sri Lanka | v | Zimbabwe | Kandy | 1997-98 |

## OLDEST PLAYERS TO TAKE 5 OR MORE WICKETS IN AN INNINGS

| | | | | | | | | |
|---|---|---|---|---|---|---|---|---|
| 49 | 314 | H.Ironmonger | 6/18 | Australia | v | South Africa | Melbourne | 1931-32 |
| 49 | 311 | H.Ironmonger | 5/6 | Australia | v | South Africa | Melbourne | 1931-32 |
| 49 | 239 | H.Ironmonger | 5/42 | Australia | v | South Africa | Brisbane[2] | 1931-32 |
| 48 | 312 | H.Ironmonger | 7/23 | Australia | v | West Indies | Melbourne | 1930-31 |
| 46 | 272 | D.D.Blackie | 6/94 | Australia | v | England | Melbourne | 1928-29 |
| 45 | 157 | A.J.Traicos | 5/85 | Zimbabwe | v | India | Harare | 1992-93 |
| 44 | 69 | C.V.Grimmett | 6/73 | Australia | v | South Africa | Durban2 | 1935-36 |
| 44 | 65 | C.V.Grimmett | 7/100 | Australia | v | South Africa | Durban2 | 1935-36 |
| 44 | 54 | C.V.Grimmett | 7/40 | Australia | v | South Africa | Johannesburg[1] | 1935-36 |
| 44 | 10 | C.V.Grimmett | 5/56 | Australia | v | South Africa | Cape Town | 1935-36 |
| 44 | 9 | C.V.Grimmett | 5/32 | Australia | v | South Africa | Cape Town | 1935-36 |
| 42 | 243 | F.E.Woolley | 7/76 | England | v | New Zealand | Wellington | 1929-30 |
| 42 | 240 | C.V.Grimmett | 5/64 | Australia | v | England | The Oval | 1934 |
| 42 | 168 | C.V.Grimmett | 5/81 | Australia | v | England | Nottingham | 1934 |
| 42 | 91 | L.R.Gibbs | 5/102 | West Indies | v | Australia | Brisbane[2] | 1975-76 |
| 41 | 137 | E.E.Hemmings | 6/58 | England | v | New Zealand | Birmingham | 1990 |
| 41 | 73 | A.P.Freeman | 5/100 | England | v | South Africa | Manchester | 1929 |
| 41 | 72 | A.P.Freeman | 7/71 | England | v | South Africa | Manchester | 1929 |
| 41 | 56 | A.P.Freeman | 7/115 | England | v | South Africa | Leeds | 1929 |
| 40 | 307 | S.F.Barnes | 7/88 | England | v | South Africa | Durban[1] | 1913-14 |
| 40 | 302 | S.F.Barnes | 7/56 | England | v | South Africa | Durban[1] | 1913-14 |
| 40 | 262 | S.F.Barnes | 5/102 | England | v | South Africa | Johannesburg[1] | 1913-14 |
| 40 | 256 | S.F.Barnes | 9/103 | England | v | South Africa | Johannesburg[1] | 1913-14 |
| 40 | 252 | S.F.Barnes | 8/56 | England | v | South Africa | Johannesburg[1] | 1913-14 |
| 40 | 243 | S.F.Barnes | 5/48 | England | v | South Africa | Durban[1] | 1913-14 |
| 40 | 239 | S.F.Barnes | 5/57 | England | v | South Africa | Durban[1] | 1913-14 |
| 40 | 223 | A.A.Mailey | 6/138 | Australia | v | England | The Oval | 1926 |
| 40 | 196 | C.P.Carter | 6/91 | South Africa | v | Australia | Johannesburg[1] | 1921-22 |
| 40 | 121 | L.R.Gibbs | 7/98 | West Indies | v | India | Bombay[3] | 1974-75 |
| 40 | 87 | G.W.A.Chubb | 6/51 | South Africa | v | England | Manchester | 1951 |
| 40 | 77 | L.R.Gibbs | 6/76 | West Indies | v | India | Delhi | 1974-75 |
| 40 | 72 | F.R.Brown | 5/49 | England | v | Australia | Melbourne | 1950-51 |
| 40 | 70 | G.W.A.Chubb | 5/77 | South Africa | v | England | Lord's | 1951 |
| 40 | 68 | A.P.Freeman | 5/39 | England | v | West Indies | Manchester | 1928 |
| 40 | 68 | W.J.O'Reilly | 5/14 | Australia | v | New Zealand | Wellington | 1945-46 |
| 40 | 65 | A.P.Freeman | 5/54 | England | v | West Indies | Manchester | 1928 |
| 40 | 39 | C.V.Grimmett | 7/83 | Australia | v | South Africa | Adelaide | 1931-32 |
| 40 | 35 | C.V.Grimmett | 7/116 | Australia | v | South Africa | Adelaide | 1931-32 |
| 40 | 12 | C.V.Grimmett | 6/92 | Australia | v | South Africa | Melbourne | 1931-32 |
| 39 | 281 | D.S.de Silva | 5/59 | Sri Lanka | v | Pakistan | Faisalabad | 1981-82 |
| 39 | 231 | F.J.Laver | 8/31 | Australia | v | England | Manchester | 1909 |
| 39 | 181 | R.Peel | 6/23 | England | v | Australia | The Oval | 1896 |
| 39 | 130 | L.R.Gibbs | 6/108 | West Indies | v | England | Port-of-Spain | 1973-74 |

| | | | | | | | | |
|---|---|---|---|---|---|---|---|---|
| 39 | 124 | S.F.Barnes | 5/30 | England | v | Australia | The Oval | 1912 |
| 39 | 116 | S.F.Barnes | 8/29 | England | v | South Africa | The Oval | 1912 |
| 39 | 115 | S.F.Barnes | 5/28 | England | v | South Africa | The Oval | 1912 |
| 39 | 80 | S.F.Barnes | 6/52 | England | v | South Africa | Leeds | 1912 |
| 39 | 75 | R.Illingworth | 5/70 | England | v | India | The Oval | 1971 |
| 39 | 54 | S.F.Barnes | 6/85 | England | v | South Africa | Lord's | 1912 |
| 39 | 52 | S.F.Barnes | 5/25 | England | v | South Africa | Lord's | 1912 |
| 39 | 34 | R.G.Holland | 6/106 | Australia | v | New Zealand | Sydney | 1985-86 |
| 39 | 26 | C.V.Grimmett | 5/49 | Australia | v | West Indies | Brisbane[1] | 1930-31 |
| 39 | 6 | R.J.Hadlee | 5/53 | New Zealand | v | England | Birmingham | 1990 |
| 39 | 5 | A.A.Mailey | 5/92 | Australia | v | England | Melbourne | 1924-25 |

## DISTRIBUTION OF FIVE WICKETS IN AN INNINGS

| Taken Against | Taken For A | E | SA | WI | NZ | I | P | SL | Z | Total Against |
|---|---|---|---|---|---|---|---|---|---|---|
| Australia | 0 | 218 | 37 | 53 | 23 | 38 | 22 | 3 | 0 | 394 |
| England | 253 | 0 | 81 | 82 | 29 | 50 | 30 | 1 | 1 | 527 |
| South Africa | 57 | 92 | 0 | 1 | 6 | 6 | 4 | 3 | 1 | 170 |
| West Indies | 61 | 73 | 0 | 0 | 15 | 33 | 24 | 3 | 0 | 209 |
| New Zealand | 16 | 55 | 19 | 17 | 0 | 23 | 36 | 12 | 2 | 180 |
| India | 33 | 47 | 5 | 46 | 19 | 0 | 29 | 10 | 1 | 190 |
| Pakistan | 28 | 31 | 5 | 15 | 15 | 27 | 0 | 11 | 5 | 137 |
| Sri Lanka | 6 | 5 | 4 | 2 | 12 | 10 | 13 | 0 | 1 | 53 |
| Zimbabwe | 0 | 0 | 1 | 0 | 4 | 1 | 10 | 4 | 0 | 20 |
| Total For | 454 | 521 | 152 | 216 | 123 | 188 | 168 | 47 | 11 | 1880 |

## FIVE WICKETS IN AN INNINGS

*(§ In first Test appearances against that country; † on Test debut; # Ferris & Trott had previously played for Australia and Traicos for South Africa.)*

**AUSTRALIA *(454)***

| | | | Opponents | | |
|---|---|---|---|---|---|
| Alderman,TM | (14) | † 5/62 | England | Nottingham | 1981 |
| | | 6/135 | England | Leeds | 1981 |
| | | 5/42 | England | Birmingham | 1981 |
| | | 5/109 | England | Manchester | 1981 |
| | | 6/128 | West Indies | Perth | 1984-85 |
| | | 5/107) | England | Leeds | 1989 |
| | | 5/44 ) | | | |
| | | 6/128 | England | Lord's | 1989 |
| | | 5/66 | England | Manchester | 1989 |
| | | 5/69 | England | Nottingham | 1989 |
| | | 5/66 | England | The Oval | 1989 |
| | | 5/105 | Pakistan | Melbourne | 1989-90 |
| | | 5/65 | Pakistan | Sydney | 1989-90 |
| | | 6/47 | England | Brisbane[2] | 1990-91 |
| Archer,RG | | 5/53 | England | The Oval | 1956 |
| Armstrong,WW | (3) | 5/122 | England | Leeds | 1905 |
| | | 5/27 | England | Birmingham | 1909 |
| | | 6/34 | England | Lord's | 1909 |
| Benaud,R | (16) | § 7/72 | India | Madras[2] | 1956-57 |
| | | 6/52) | India | Calcutta | 1956-57 |
| | | 5/53) | | | |
| | | 5/49 | South Africa | Cape Town | 1957-58 |
| | | 5/114 | South Africa | Durban[2] | 1957-58 |
| | | 5/84 | South Africa | Johannesburg[3] | 1957-58 |
| | | 5/82 | South Africa | Port Elizabeth | 1957-58 |
| | | 5/83 | England | Sydney | 1958-59 |
| | | 5/91 | England | Adelaide | 1958-59 |
| | | 5/93 | Pakistan | Karachi[1] | 1959-60 |

| | | | | | |
|---|---|---|---|---|---|
| | | 5/76 | India | Delhi | 1959-60 |
| | | 5/43 | India | Madras[2] | 1959-60 |
| | | 5/96 | West Indies | Adelaide | 1960-61 |
| | | 6/70 | England | Manchester | 1961 |
| | | 6/115 | England | Brisbane[2] | 1962-63 |
| | | 5/68 | South Africa | Brisbane[2] | 1963-64 |
| Bevan,MG | | 6/82 | West Indies | Adelaide | 1996-97 |
| Blackie,DD | | 6/94 | England | Melbourne | 1928-29 |
| Border,AR | (2) | 7/46 | West Indies | Sydney | 1988-89 |
| | | 5/68 | West Indies | Georgetown | 1990-91 |
| Boyle,HF | | 6/42 | England | Manchester | 1884 |
| Bright,RJ | (4) | § 7/87 | Pakistan | Karachi[1] | 1979-80 |
| | | 5/172 | Pakistan | Lahore[2] | 1979-80 |
| | | 5/68 | England | Birmingham | 1981 |
| | | 5/94 | India | Madras[1] | 1986-87 |
| Callaway,ST | | 5/37 | England | Adelaide | 1894-95 |
| Chappell,GS | | 5/61 | Pakistan | Sydney | 1972-73 |
| Connolly,AN | (4) | 5/72 | England | Leeds | 1968 |
| | | 5/122 | West Indies | Adelaide | 1968-69 |
| | | 5/47 | South Africa | Cape Town | 1969-70 |
| | | 6/47 | South Africa | Port Elizabeth | 1969-70 |
| Cook,SH | | †§ 5/39 | New Zealand | Perth | 1997-98 |
| Cooper,WH | | †§ 6/120 | England | Melbourne | 1881-82 |
| Cotter,A | (7) | 6/40 | England | Melbourne | 1903-04 |
| | | 7/148 | England | The Oval | 1905 |
| | | 6/101 | England | Sydney | 1907-08 |
| | | 5/142 | England | Melbourne | 1907-08 |
| | | 5/38 | England | Leeds | 1909 |
| | | 6/95 | England | The Oval | 1909 |
| | | § 6/69 | South Africa | Sydney | 1910-11 |
| Davidson,AK | (14) | § 6/34 | South Africa | Johannesburg[3] | 1957-58 |
| | | 5/38 | South Africa | Port Elizabeth | 1957-58 |
| | | 6/64 | England | Melbourne | 1958-59 |
| | | 5/31) | India | Kanpur | 1959-60 |
| | | 7/93) | | | |
| | | § 5/135) | West Indies | Brisbane[2] | 1960-61 |
| | | 6/87 ) | | | |
| | | 6/83 | West Indies | Melbourne | 1960-61 |
| | | 5/80 | West Indies | Sydney | 1960-61 |
| | | 5/84 | West Indies | Melbourne | 1960-61 |
| | | 5/42 | England | Lord's | 1961 |
| | | 5/63 | England | Leeds | 1961 |
| | | 6/75 | England | Melbourne | 1962-63 |
| | | 5/25 | England | Sydney | 1962-63 |
| Dodemaide,AIC | | †§ 6/58 | New Zealand | Melbourne | 1987-88 |
| Dymock,G | (5) | †§ 5/58 | New Zealand | Adelaide | 1973-74 |
| | | 5/99) | India | Kanpur | 1979-80 |
| | | 7/67) | | | |
| | | 6/34 | England | Perth | 1979-80 |
| | | 5/104 | West Indies | Adelaide | 1979-80 |
| Ferris,JJ | (4) | †§ 5/76 | England | Sydney | 1886-87 |
| | | 5/71 | England | Sydney | 1886-87 |
| | | 5/26 | England | Lord's | 1888 |
| | | 5/49 | England | The Oval | 1890 |
| Fleetwood-Smith,LO | (2) | § 5/124 | England | Melbourne | 1936-37 |
| | | 6/110 | England | Adelaide | 1936-37 |
| Garrett,TW | (2) | 6/78 | England | Sydney | 1881-82 |
| | | 5/80 | England | Melbourne | 1881-82 |
| Giffen,G | (7) | 7/117 | England | Sydney | 1884-85 |
| | | 6/72 | England | Sydney | 1891-92 |

| | | | | | |
|---|---|---|---|---|---|
| | | 5/43 | England | Lord's | 1893 |
| | | 7/128 | England | The Oval | 1893 |
| | | 6/155 | England | Melbourne | 1894-95 |
| | | 5/76 | England | Adelaide | 1894-95 |
| | | 5/26 | England | Sydney | 1894-95 |
| Gillespie,JN | (1) | 5/54 | South Africa | Port Elizabeth | 1996-97 |
| | | 7/37 | Australia | Leeds | 1997 |
| Gilmour,GJ | (3) | 5/64 | New Zealand | Auckland | 1973-74 |
| | | § 6/85 | England | Leeds | 1975 |
| | | 5/34 | West Indies | Melbourne | 1975-76 |
| Gleeson,JW | (3) | § 5/122 | West Indies | Brisbane[2] | 1968-69 |
| | | 5/61 | West Indies | Melbourne | 1968-69 |
| | | 5/125 | South Africa | Johannesburg[3] | 1969-70 |
| Gregory,JM | (4) | 7/69 | England | Melbourne | 1920-21 |
| | | 6/58 | England | Nottingham | 1921 |
| | | § 6/77 | South Africa | Durban[1] | 1921-22 |
| | | 5/111 | England | Sydney | 1924-25 |
| Grimmett,CV | (21) | †§ 5/45) | England | Sydney | 1924-25 |
| | | 6/37) | | | |
| | | 5/88 | England | Leeds | 1926 |
| | | 6/131 | England | Brisbane[1] | 1928-29 |
| | | 5/102 | England | Adelaide | 1928-29 |
| | | 5/107) | England | Nottingham | 1930 |
| | | 5/94 ) | | | |
| | | 6/167 | England | Lord's | 1930 |
| | | 5/135 | England | Leeds | 1930 |
| | | § 7/87 | West Indies | Adelaide | 1930-31 |
| | | 5/49 | West Indies | Brisbane[1] | 1930-31 |
| | | 6/92 | South Africa | Melbourne | 1931-32 |
| | | 7/116) | South Africa | Adelaide | 1931-32 |
| | | 7/83 ) | | | |
| | | 5/81 | England | Nottingham | 1934 |
| | | 5/64 | England | The Oval | 1934 |
| | | 5/32) | South Africa | Cape Town | 1935-36 |
| | | 5/56) | | | |
| | | 7/40 | South Africa | Johannesburg[1] | 1935-36 |
| | | 7/100) | South Africa | Durban[2] | 1935-36 |
| | | 6/73 ) | | | |
| Hawke,NJN | (6) | 6/139 | South Africa | Adelaide | 1963-64 |
| | | 5/75 | England | Leeds | 1964 |
| | | 6/47 | England | The Oval | 1964 |
| | | 6/72 | West Indies | Georgetown | 1964-65 |
| | | 7/105 | England | Sydney | 1965-66 |
| | | 5/54 | England | Adelaide | 1965-66 |
| Hazlitt,GR | | 7/25 | England | The Oval | 1912 |
| Higgs,JD | (2) | 5/148 | England | Sydney | 1979-80 |
| | | § 7/143 | India | Madras[1] | 1979-80 |
| Hogan,TG | | †§ 5/66 | Sri Lanka | Kandy | 1982-83 |
| Hogg,RM | (6) | †§ 6/74 | England | Brisbane[2] | 1978-79 |
| | | 5/65) | England | Perth | 1978-79 |
| | | 5/57) | | | |
| | | 5/30) | England | Melbourne | 1978-79 |
| | | 5/36) | | | |
| | | 6/77 | West Indies | Bridgetown | 1983-84 |
| Holland,RG | (3) | 6/54 | West Indies | Sydney | 1984-85 |
| | | § 5/68 | England | Lord's | 1985 |
| | | 6/106 | New Zealand | Sydney | 1985-86 |
| Horan,TP | | 6/40 | England | Sydney | 1884-85 |
| Hordern,HV | (5) | †§ 5/66 | South Africa | Melbourne | 1910-11 |
| | | § 5/85) | England | Sydney | 1911-12 |

| | | | | | |
|---|---|---|---|---|---|
| | | 7/90) | | | |
| | | 5/95) | England | Sydney | 1911-12 |
| | | 5/66) | | | |
| Hornibrook,PM | | 7/92 | England | The Oval | 1930 |
| Howell,WP | | 5/81 | South Africa | Cape Town | 1902-03 |
| Hughes,MG | (7) | § 5/67 | Sri Lanka | Perth | 1987-88 |
| | | § 5/130) | West Indies | Perth | 1988-89 |
| | | 8/87 ) | | | |
| | | 5/88 | Sri Lanka | Hobart | 1989-90 |
| | | 5/111 | Pakistan | Adelaide | 1989-90 |
| | | 5/64 | West Indies | Adelaide | 1992-93 |
| | | 5/92 | England | Nottingham | 1993 |
| Hurst,AG | (2) | 5/28 | England | Sydney | 1978-79 |
| | | 5/94 | Pakistan | Perth | 1978-79 |
| Ironmonger,H | (4) | 7/23 | West Indies | Melbourne | 1930-31 |
| | | § 5/42 | South Africa | Brisbane[2] | 1931-32 |
| | | 5/6 ) | South Africa | Melbourne | 1931-32 |
| | | 6/18) | | | |
| Iverson,JB | | 6/27 | England | Sydney | 1950-51 |
| Jenner,TJ | | 5/90 | West Indies | Port-of-Spain | 1972-73 |
| Johnson,IW | (3) | § 6/42 | England | Sydney | 1946-47 |
| | | 5/34 | South Africa | Durban[2] | 1949-50 |
| | | 7/44 | West Indies | Georgetown | 1954-55 |
| Johnston,WA | (7) | § 5/36 | England | Nottingham | 1948 |
| | | § 6/44 | South Africa | Johannesburg[2] | 1949-50 |
| | | 5/35 | England | Brisbane[2] | 1950-51 |
| | | 6/62 | West Indies | Adelaide | 1951-52 |
| | | 5/110 | South Africa | Adelaide | 1952-53 |
| | | 6/152 | South Africa | Melbourne | 1952-53 |
| | | 5/85 | England | Melbourne | 1954-55 |
| Jones,E | (3) | 6/82 | England | Sydney | 1897-98 |
| | | 5/88 | England | Nottingham | 1899 |
| | | 7/88 | England | Lord's | 1899 |
| Kelleway,C | | 5/33 | South Africa | Manchester | 1912 |
| Kasprowicz,MS | (2) | 7/36 | England | The Oval | 1997 |
| | | 5/28 | India | Bangalore | 1997-98 |
| Kendall,TK | | †§ 7/55 | England | Melbourne | 1876-77 |
| Kline,LF | | § 7/75 | Pakistan | Lahore[2] | 1959-60 |
| Laughlin,TJ | | 5/101 | West Indies | Kingston | 1977-78 |
| Laver,FJ | (2) | 7/64 | England | Nottingham | 1905 |
| | | 8/31 | England | Manchester | 1909 |
| Lawson,GF | (11) | 7/81 | England | Lord's | 1981 |
| | | 5/108 | England | Perth | 1982-83 |
| | | 6/47) | England | Brisbane[2] | 1982-83 |
| | | 5/87) | | | |
| | | 5/66 | England | Adelaide | 1982-83 |
| | | 5/49 | Pakistan | Brisbane[2] | 1983-84 |
| | | 5/59 | Pakistan | Sydney | 1983-84 |
| | | 5/116 | West Indies | Brisbane[2] | 1984-85 |
| | | 8/112 | West Indies | Adelaide | 1984-85 |
| | | 5/103 | England | Nottingham | 1985 |
| | | 6/72 | England | Manchester | 1989 |
| Lillee,DK | (23) | †§ 5/84 | England | Adelaide | 1970-71 |
| | | 6/66 | England | Manchester | 1972 |
| | | 5/58 ) | England | The Oval | 1972 |
| | | 5/123) | | | |
| | | 5/15 | England | Birmingham | 1975 |
| | | 5/63 | West Indies | Melbourne | 1975-76 |
| | | 5/163 | Pakistan | Adelaide | 1976-77 |
| | | 6/82 | Pakistan | Melbourne | 1976-77 |

| | | | | | |
|---|---|---|---|---|---|
| | | 5/51) | New Zealand | Auckland | 1976-77 |
| | | 6/72) | | | |
| | | 6/26 ) | England | Melbourne | 1976-77 |
| | | 5/139) | | | |
| | | 5/78 | West Indies | Adelaide | 1979-80 |
| | | 6/60) | England | Melbourne | 1979-80 |
| | | 5/78) | | | |
| | | 6/53 | New Zealand | Brisbane[2] | 1980-81 |
| | | 5/65 | New Zealand | Perth | 1980-81 |
| | | 5/46 | England | Nottingham | 1981 |
| | | 7/89 | England | The Oval | 1981 |
| | | 5/18 | Pakistan | Perth | 1981-82 |
| | | 5/81 | Pakistan | Brisbane[2] | 1981-82 |
| | | 7/83 | West Indies | Melbourne | 1981-82 |
| | | 6/171 | Pakistan | Adelaide | 1983-84 |
| Lindwall,RR | (12) | 7/63 | England | Sydney | 1946-47 |
| | | 7/38 | India | Adelaide | 1947-48 |
| | | 5/70 | England | Lord's | 1948 |
| | | 6/20 | England | The Oval | 1948 |
| | | 5/32 | South Africa | Cape Town | 1949-50 |
| | | 5/52 | West Indies | Sydney | 1951-52 |
| | | 5/60 | South Africa | Brisbane[2] | 1952-53 |
| | | 5/57 | England | Nottingham | 1953 |
| | | 5/66 | England | Lord's | 1953 |
| | | 5/54 | England | Leeds | 1953 |
| | | 6/95 | West Indies | Georgetown | 1954-55 |
| | | 7/43 | India | Madras[2] | 1956-57 |
| Lyons,JJ | | 5/30 | England | Lord's | 1890 |
| Macartney,CG | (2) | 7/58 | England | Leeds | 1909 |
| | | 5/44 | South Africa | Cape Town | 1921-22 |
| McCool,CL | (3) | 5/109 | England | Sydney | 1946-47 |
| | | 5/44 | England | Sydney | 1946-47 |
| | | 5/41 | South Africa | Cape Town | 1949-50 |
| McDermott,CJ | (14) | 6/70 | England | Lord's | 1985 |
| | | 8/141 | England | Manchester | 1985 |
| | | 5/97 | New Zealand | Melbourne | 1987-88 |
| | | 5/97 | England | Adelaide | 1990-91 |
| | | 8/97 | England | Perth | 1990-91 |
| | | 5/80 | West Indies | Kingston | 1990-91 |
| | | 5/54 | India | Brisbane[2] | 1991-92 |
| | | 5/76) | India | Adelaide | 1991-92 |
| | | 5/62) | | | |
| | | 6/53 | England | Brisbane[2] | 1994-95 |
| | | 5/42 | England | Melbourne | 1994-95 |
| | | 5/101 | England | Sydney | 1994-95 |
| | | 6/38 | England | Perth | 1994-95 |
| | | 5/49 | Pakistan | Sydney | 1995-96 |
| McDonald,EA | (2) | 5/32 | England | Nottingham | 1921 |
| | | 5/143 | England | The Oval | 1921 |
| McGrath,GD | (9) | § 5/68 | West Indies | Bridgetown | 1994-95 |
| | | 6/47 | West Indies | Port-of-Spain | 1994-95 |
| | | 5/61 | Pakistan | Hobart | 1995-96 |
| | | 5/40 | Sri Lanka | Melbourne | 1995-96 |
| | | 5/50 | West Indies | Melbourne | 1996-97 |
| | | 6/86 | South Africa | Centurion | 1996-97 |
| | | 8/38 | England | Lord's | 1997 |
| | | 7/76 | England | The Oval | 1997 |
| | | 5/32 | New Zealand | Brisbane[2] | 1997-98 |
| Mackay,KD | (2) | § 6/42 | Pakistan | Dacca | 1959-60 |
| | | 5/121 | England | The Oval | 1961 |

| Player | No. | Figures | Opponent | Venue | Season |
|---|---|---|---|---|---|
| McKenzie,GD | (16) | †§ 5/37 | England | Lord's | 1961 |
| | | 5/89 | England | Adelaide | 1962-63 |
| | | 5/53 | England | Nottingham | 1964 |
| | | 7/153 | England | Manchester | 1964 |
| | | § 6/58 | India | Madras[2] | 1964-65 |
| | | § 6/69 | Pakistan | Karachi[1] | 1964-65 |
| | | 5/33 | West Indies | Port-of-Spain | 1964-65 |
| | | 5/134 | England | Melbourne | 1965-66 |
| | | 6/48 | England | Adelaide | 1965-66 |
| | | 5/46 | South Africa | Johannesburg[3] | 1966-67 |
| | | 5/65 | South Africa | Cape Town | 1966-67 |
| | | 5/65 | South Africa | Port Elizabeth | 1966-67 |
| | | 7/66 | India | Melbourne | 1967-68 |
| | | 8/71 | West Indies | Melbourne | 1968-69 |
| | | 5/69 | India | Bombay[2] | 1969-70 |
| | | 6/67 | India | Calcutta | 1969-70 |
| McLeod,CE | (2) | 5/65 | England | Adelaide | 1897-98 |
| | | 5/125 | England | Manchester | 1905 |
| McLeod,RW | | †§ 5/55 | England | Melbourne | 1891-92 |
| Mailey,AA | (6) | 5/160) | England | Adelaide | 1920-21 |
| | | 5/142) | | | |
| | | 9/121 | England | Melbourne | 1920-21 |
| | | 5/119 | England | Sydney | 1920-21 |
| | | 5/92 | England | Melbourne | 1924-25 |
| | | 6/138 | England | The Oval | 1926 |
| Mallett,AA | (6) | 6/64 | India | Delhi | 1969-70 |
| | | 5/91) | India | Madras[1] | 1969-70 |
| | | 5/53) | | | |
| | | § 5/126 | South Africa | Cape Town | 1969-70 |
| | | 5/114 | England | Leeds | 1972 |
| | | § 8/59 | Pakistan | Adelaide | 1972-73 |
| Malone,MF | | †§ 5/63 | England | The Oval | 1977 |
| Massie,RAL | (2) | †§ 8/84) | England | Lord's | 1972 |
| | | 8/53) | | | |
| Matthews,GRJ | (2) | 5/103) | India | Madras[1] | 1986-87 |
| | | 5/146) | | | |
| May,TBA | (3) | 5/9 | West Indies | Adelaide | 1992-93 |
| | | 5/89 | England | Birmingham | 1993 |
| | | 5/65 | New Zealand | Hobart | 1993-94 |
| Meckiff,I | (2) | †§ 5/125 | South Africa | Johannesburg[3] | 1957-58 |
| | | 6/38 | England | Melbourne | 1958-59 |
| Midwinter,WE | | †§ 5/78 | England | Melbourne | 1876-77 |
| Miller,KR | (7) | § 7/60 | England | Brisbane[2] | 1946-47 |
| | | § 5/40 | South Africa | Johannesburg[2] | 1949-50 |
| | | 5/60 | West Indies | Melbourne | 1951-52 |
| | | 5/26 | West Indies | Sydney | 1951-52 |
| | | 6/107 | West Indies | Kingston | 1954-55 |
| | | 5/72) | England | Lord's | 1956 |
| | | 5/80) | | | |
| Noble,MA | (9) | †§ 6/49 | England | Melbourne | 1897-98 |
| | | 5/84 | England | Melbourne | 1897-98 |
| | | 7/17) | England | Melbourne | 1901-02 |
| | | 6/60) | | | |
| | | 5/54 | England | Sydney | 1901-02 |
| | | 6/98 | England | Melbourne | 1901-02 |
| | | 5/51) | England | Sheffield | 1902 |
| | | 6/52) | | | |
| | | 7/11 | England | Sydney | 1903-04 |
| O'Connor,JDA | | †§ 5/40 | England | Adelaide | 1907-08 |
| O'Keeffe,KJ | | 5/101 | New Zealand | Christchurch | 1976-77 |

| | | | | | |
|---|---|---|---|---|---|
| O'Reilly,WJ | (11) | 5/63) | England | Melbourne | 1932-33 |
| | | 5/66) | | | |
| | | 7/54 | England | Nottingham | 1934 |
| | | 7/189 | England | Manchester | 1934 |
| | | 5/20 | South Africa | Johannesburg[1] | 1935-36 |
| | | 5/49 | South Africa | Durban[2] | 1935-36 |
| | | 5/102 | England | Brisbane[2] | 1936-37 |
| | | 5/51 | England | Melbourne | 1936-37 |
| | | 5/66) | England | Leeds | 1938 |
| | | 5/56) | | | |
| | | § 5/14 | New Zealand | Wellington | 1945-46 |
| Palmer,GE | (6) | 7/68 | England | Sydney | 1881-82 |
| | | 5/46 | England | Sydney | 1881-82 |
| | | 7/65 | England | Melbourne | 1882-83 |
| | | 5/103 | England | Melbourne | 1882-83 |
| | | 6/111 | England | Lord's | 1884 |
| | | 5/81 | England | Adelaide | 1884-85 |
| Pascoe,LS | | 5/59 | England | Lord's | 1980 |
| Philpott,PI | | § 5/90 | England | Brisbane[2] | 1965-66 |
| Rackemann,CG | (3) | § 5/32) | Pakistan | Perth | 1983-84 |
| | | 6/86) | | | |
| | | § 5/161 | West Indies | St John's | 1983-84 |
| Reid,BA | (5) | 6/97) | England | Melbourne | 1990-91 |
| | | 7/51) | | | |
| | | 6/66) | India | Melbourne | 1991-92 |
| | | 6/60) | | | |
| | | 5/112 | West Indies | Brisbane[2] | 1992-93 |
| Reiffel,PR | (5) | § 5/65 | England | Leeds | 1993 |
| | | 6/71 | England | Birmingham | 1993 |
| | | 5/39 | Sri Lanka | Adelaide | 1995-96 |
| | | 5/73 | West Indies | Perth | 1996-97 |
| | | 5/49 | England | Leeds | 1997 |
| Renneberg,DA | (2) | 5/97 | South Africa | Johannesburg[3] | 1966-67 |
| | | § 5/39 | India | Adelaide | 1967-68 |
| Ring,DT | (2) | § 6/80 | West Indies | Brisbane[2] | 1951-52 |
| | | § 6/72 | South Africa | Brisbane[2] | 1952-53 |
| Saunders,JV | (6) | †§ 5/43 | England | Sydney | 1901-02 |
| | | 5/50 | England | Sheffield | 1902 |
| | | § 7/34 | South Africa | Johannesburg[1] | 1902-03 |
| | | 5/65 | England | Adelaide | 1907-08 |
| | | 5/28 | England | Melbourne | 1907-08 |
| | | 5/82 | England | Sydney | 1907-08 |
| Sievers,MW | | 5/21 | England | Melbourne | 1936-37 |
| Simpson,RB | (2) | 5/57 | England | Sydney | 1962-63 |
| | | 5/59 | India | Sydney | 1967-68 |
| Sleep,PR | | 5/72 | England | Sydney | 1986-87 |
| Spofforth,FR | (7) | 6/48) | England | Melbourne | 1878-79 |
| | | 7/62) | | | |
| | | 7/46) | England | The Oval | 1882 |
| | | 7/44) | | | |
| | | 7/44 | England | Sydney | 1882-83 |
| | | 6/90 | England | Sydney | 1884-85 |
| | | 5/30 | England | Sydney | 1884-85 |
| Taylor,PL | | †§ 6/78 | England | Sydney | 1986-87 |
| Thomson,JR | (8) | § 6/46 | England | Brisbane[2] | 1974-75 |
| | | 5/93 | England | Perth | 1974-75 |
| | | 5/38 | England | Birmingham | 1975 |
| | | 5/62 | West Indies | Melbourne | 1975-76 |
| | | 6/50 | West Indies | Sydney | 1975-76 |
| | | 6/77 | West Indies | Bridgetown | 1977-78 |

| | | | | | |
|---|---|---|---|---|---|
| | | 5/73 | England | Brisbane[2] | 1982-83 |
| | | 5/50 | England | Sydney | 1982-83 |
| Toshack,ERH | (4) | § 6/82 | England | Brisbane[2] | 1946-47 |
| | | § 5/2 ) | India | Brisbane[2] | 1947-48 |
| | | 6/29) | | | |
| | | 5/40 | England | Lord's | 1948 |
| Trott,AE | | †§ 8/43 | England | Adelaide | 1894-95 |
| Trumble,H | (9) | 6/59) | England | The Oval | 1896 |
| | | 6/30) | | | |
| | | 5/60 | England | Leeds | 1899 |
| | | 6/74 | England | Adelaide | 1901-02 |
| | | 5/62 | England | Melbourne | 1901-02 |
| | | 6/53 | England | Manchester | 1902 |
| | | 8/65 | England | The Oval | 1902 |
| | | 5/34 | England | Melbourne | 1903-04 |
| | | 7/28 | England | Melbourne | 1903-04 |
| Turner,CTB | (11) | †§ 6/15 | England | Sydney | 1886-87 |
| | | 5/41 | England | Sydney | 1886-87 |
| | | 5/44) | England | Sydney | 1887-88 |
| | | 7/43) | | | |
| | | 5/27) | England | Lord's | 1888 |
| | | 5/36) | | | |
| | | 6/112 | England | The Oval | 1888 |
| | | 5/86 | England | Manchester | 1888 |
| | | 5/51 | England | Melbourne | 1891-92 |
| | | 6/67 | England | Lord's | 1893 |
| | | 5/32 | England | Melbourne | 1894-95 |
| Walker,MHN | (6) | 6/15 | Pakistan | Sydney | 1972-73 |
| | | § 6/114 | West Indies | Kingston | 1972-73 |
| | | 5/97 | West Indies | Bridgetown | 1972-73 |
| | | 5/75 | West Indies | Port-of-Spain | 1972-73 |
| | | 8/143 | England | Melbourne | 1974-75 |
| | | 5/48 | England | Birmingham | 1975 |
| Wall,TW | (3) | †§ 5/66 | England | Melbourne | 1928-29 |
| | | § 5/14 | South Africa | Brisbane[2] | 1931-32 |
| | | 5/72 | England | Adelaide | 1932-33 |
| Walters,KD | | 5/66 | West Indies | Georgetown | 1972-73 |
| Ward,FA | | †§ 6/102 | England | Brisbane[2] | 1936-37 |
| Warne,SK | (14) | § 7/52 | West Indies | Melbourne | 1992-93 |
| | | 5/82 | England | Birmingham | 1993 |
| | | 6/31 | New Zealand | Hobart | 1993-94 |
| | | 7/56) | South Africa | Sydney | 1993-94 |
| | | 5/72) | | | |
| | | § 5/89 | Pakistan | Karachi[1] | 1994-95 |
| | | § 6/136 | Pakistan | Lahore[2] | 1994-95 |
| | | 8/71 | England | Brsibane[2] | 1994-95 |
| | | 6/64 | England | Melbourne | 1994-95 |
| | | 7/23 | Pakistan | Brsibane[2] | 1995-96 |
| | | 6/48 | England | Manchester | 1997 |
| | | 5/88 | New Zealand | Hobart | 1997-98 |
| | | 5/75) | South Africa | Sydney | 1997-98 |
| | | 6/34) | | | |
| Waugh,ME | | 5/40 | England | Adelaide | 1994-95 |
| Waugh,SR | (3) | 5/69 | England | Perth | 1986-87 |
| | | 5/92 | West Indies | Melbourne | 1988-89 |
| | | 5/28 | South Africa | Cape Town | 1993-94 |
| Whitney,MR | (2) | § 7/89 | West Indies | Adelaide | 1988-89 |
| | | 7/27 | India | Perth | 1991-92 |
| Whitty,WJ | (3) | 6/17 | South Africa | Melbourne | 1910-11 |
| | | 6/104 | South Africa | Adelaide | 1910-11 |

| | | | | | |
|---|---|---|---|---|---|
| | | 5/55 | South Africa | Manchester | 1912 |
| Yardley,B | (6) | 6/84 | Pakistan | Perth | 1981-82 |
| | | 7/187 | Pakistan | Melbourne | 1981-82 |
| | | 7/98 | West Indies | Sydney | 1981-82 |
| | | 5/132 | West Indies | Adelaide | 1981-82 |
| | | 5/107 | England | Perth | 1982-83 |
| | | § 5/88 | Sri Lanka | Kandy | 1982-83 |

**ENGLAND *(523)***Opponents

| | | | | | |
|---|---|---|---|---|---|
| Allen,DA | (4) | 5/67 | India | Calcutta | 1961-62 |
| | | 5/30 | Pakistan | Dacca | 1961-62 |
| | | 5/41 | South Africa | Durban[2] | 1964-65 |
| | | 5/123 | New Zealand | Auckland | 1965-66 |
| Allen,GOB | (5) | 5/14 | New Zealand | The Oval | 1931 |
| | | § 5/35) | India | Lord's | 1936 |
| | | 5/43) | | | |
| | | 7/80 | India | The Oval | 1936 |
| | | 5/36 | Australia | Brisbane[2] | 1936-37 |
| Allom,MJC | | †§ 5/38 | New Zealand | Christchurch | 1929-30 |
| Allott,PJW | | § 6/61 | West Indies | Leeds | 1984 |
| Appleyard,R | | †§ 5/51 | Pakistan | Nottingham | 1954 |
| Arnold,EG | | § 5/37 | South Africa | Lord's | 1907 |
| Arnold,GG | (6) | 5/58 | Pakistan | The Oval | 1967 |
| | | § 6/45 | India | Delhi | 1972-73 |
| | | 5/131 | New Zealand | Nottingham | 1973 |
| | | 5/27 | New Zealand | Leeds | 1973 |
| | | § 5/113 | West Indies | The Oval | 1973 |
| | | 5/86 | Australia | Sydney | 1974-75 |
| Bailey,TE | (5) | †§ 6/118 | New Zealand | Leeds | 1949 |
| | | 6/84 | New Zealand | Manchester | 1949 |
| | | 7/34 | West Indies | Kingston | 1953-54 |
| | | 5/20 | South Africa | Johannesburg[3] | 1956-57 |
| | | 7/44 | West Indies | Lord's | 1957 |
| Barlow,RG | (3) | 5/19 | Australia | The Oval | 1882 |
| | | 7/40 | Australia | Sydney | 1882-83 |
| | | 7/44 | Australia | Manchester | 1886 |
| Barnes,SF | (24) | †§ 5/65 | Australia | Sydney | 1901-02 |
| | | 6/42 ) | Australia | Melbourne | 1901-02 |
| | | 7/121) | | | |
| | | 6/49 | Australia | Sheffield | 1902 |
| | | 5/72 | Australia | Melbourne | 1907-08 |
| | | 7/60 | Australia | Sydney | 1907-08 |
| | | 6/63 | Australia | Leeds | 1909 |
| | | 5/56 | Australia | Manchester | 1909 |
| | | 5/44 | Australia | Melbourne | 1911-12 |
| | | 5/105 | Australia | Adelaide | 1911-12 |
| | | 5/74 | Australia | Melbourne | 1911-12 |
| | | § 5/25) | South Africa | Lord's | 1912 |
| | | 6/85) | | | |
| | | 6/52 | South Africa | Leeds | 1912 |
| | | 5/28) | South Africa | The Oval | 1912 |
| | | 8/29) | | | |
| | | 5/30 | Australia | The Oval | 1912 |
| | | 5/57) | South Africa | Durban[1] | 1913-14 |
| | | 5/48) | | | |
| | | 8/56 ) | South Africa | Johannesburg[1] | 1913-14 |
| | | 9/103) | | | |
| | | 5/102 | South Africa | Johannesburg[1] | 1913-14 |
| | | 7/56) | South Africa | Durban[1] | 1913-14 |
| | | 7/88) | | | |

| | | | | | |
|---|---|---|---|---|---|
| Barnes,W | (3) | 6/31 | Australia | Melbourne | 1884-85 |
| | | 6/28 | Australia | Sydney | 1886-87 |
| | | 5/32 | Australia | The Oval | 1888 |
| Bates,W | (4) | 7/28) | Australia | Melbourne | 1882-83 |
| | | 7/74) | | | |
| | | 5/31 | Australia | Adelaide | 1884-85 |
| | | 5/24 | Australia | Sydney | 1884-85 |
| Bedser,AV | (15) | †§ 7/49 | India | Lord's | 1946 |
| | | 7/52 | India | Manchester | 1946 |
| | | 5/127 | West Indies | Nottingham | 1950 |
| | | 5/46) | Australia | Melbourne | 1950-51 |
| | | 5/59) | | | |
| | | 6/37 | South Africa | Nottingham | 1951 |
| | | 7/58) | South Africa | Manchester | 1951 |
| | | 5/54) | | | |
| | | 5/27 | India | Manchester | 1952 |
| | | 5/41 | India | The Oval | 1952 |
| | | 7/55) | Australia | Nottingham | 1953 |
| | | 7/44) | | | |
| | | 5/105 | Australia | Lord's | 1953 |
| | | 5/115 | Australia | Manchester | 1953 |
| | | 6/95 | Australia | Leeds | 1953 |
| Berry,R | | †§ 5/63 | West Indies | Manchester | 1950 |
| Birkenshaw,J | | § 5/57 | Pakistan | Karachi[1] | 1972-73 |
| Blythe,C | (9) | 6/68) | South Africa | Cape Town | 1905-06 |
| | | 5/50) | | | |
| | | 8/59) | South Africa | Leeds | 1907 |
| | | 7/40) | | | |
| | | 5/61 | South Africa | The Oval | 1907 |
| | | 6/44) | Australia | Birmingham | 1909 |
| | | 5/58) | | | |
| | | 5/63 | Australia | Manchester | 1909 |
| | | 7/46 | South Africa | Cape Town | 1909-10 |
| Bosanquet,BJT | (2) | 6/51 | Australia | Sydney | 1903-04 |
| | | 8/107 | Australia | Nottingham | 1905 |
| Botham,IT | (27) | †§ 5/74 | Australia | Nottingham | 1977 |
| | | 5/21 | Australia | Leeds | 1977 |
| | | 5/73 | New Zealand | Christchurch | 1977-78 |
| | | 5/109 | New Zealand | Auckland | 1977-78 |
| | | 8/34 | Pakistan | Lord's | 1978 |
| | | 6/34 | New Zealand | Nottingham | 1978 |
| | | 6/101) | New Zealand | Lord's | 1978 |
| | | 5/39 ) | | | |
| | | § 5/70 | India | Birmingham | 1979 |
| | | 5/35 | India | Lord's | 1979 |
| | | 6/78) | Australia | Perth | 1979-80 |
| | | 5/98) | | | |
| | | 6/58) | India | Bombay[3] | 1979-80 |
| | | 7/48) | | | |
| | | 6/95 | Australia | Leeds | 1981 |
| | | 5/11 | Australia | Birmingham | 1981 |
| | | 6/125 | Australia | The Oval | 1981 |
| | | 5/61 | India | Bombay[3] | 1981-82 |
| | | 5/46 | India | Lord's | 1982 |
| | | 5/74 | Pakistan | Leeds | 1982 |
| | | 5/59 | New Zealand | Wellington | 1983-84 |
| | | 8/103 | West Indies | Lord's | 1984 |
| | | 5/72 | West Indies | The Oval | 1984 |
| | | 6/90 | Sri Lanka | Lord's | 1984 |
| | | 5/109 | Australia | Lord's | 1985 |

| Player | | Figures | Opponent | Venue | Season |
|---|---|---|---|---|---|
| | | 5/71 | West Indies | Port-of-Spain | 1985-86 |
| | | 5/41 | Australia | Melbourne | 1986-87 |
| Bowes,WE | (6) | § 6/34 | New Zealand | Auckland | 1932-33 |
| | | 6/142 | Australia | Leeds | 1934 |
| | | 5/55 | Australia | The Oval | 1934 |
| | | 5/100 | South Africa | Manchester | 1935 |
| | | 5/49 | Australia | The Oval | 1938 |
| | | 6/33 | West Indies | Manchester | 1939 |
| Bradley,WM | | †§ 5/67 | Australia | Manchester | 1899 |
| Braund,LC | (3) | †§ 5/61 | Australia | Sydney | 1901-02 |
| | | 5/95 | Australia | Melbourne | 1901-02 |
| | | 8/81 | Australia | Melbourne | 1903-04 |
| Brearley,W | | 5/110 | Australia | The Oval | 1905 |
| Briggs,J | (9) | 5/29) | Australia | Lord's | 1886 |
| | | 6/45) | | | |
| | | 5/25 | Australia | The Oval | 1888 |
| | | 7/17) | South Africa | Cape Town | 1888-89 |
| | | 8/11) | | | |
| | | 6/49) | Australia | Adelaide | 1891-92 |
| | | 6/87) | | | |
| | | 5/34 ) | Australia | The Oval | 1893 |
| | | 5/114) | | | |
| Brown,DJ | (2) | 5/63 | Australia | Sydney | 1965-66 |
| | | 5/42 | Australia | Lord's | 1968 |
| Brown,FR | | 5/49 | Australia | Melbourne | 1950-51 |
| Buckenham,CP | | 5/115 | South Africa | Johannesburg[1] | 1909-10 |
| Caddick,AR | (5) | 6/65 | West Indies | Port-of-Spain | 1993-94 |
| | | 5/63 | West Indies | Bridgetown | 1993-94 |
| | | 5/50 | Australia | Birmingham | 1997 |
| | | 5/42 | Australia | The Oval | 1997 |
| | | 5/67 | West Indies | Port-of-Spain | 1997-98 |
| Carr,DW | | †§ 5/146 | Australia | The Oval | 1909 |
| Cartwright,TW | | 6/94 | South Africa | Nottingham | 1965 |
| Clark,EW | | 5/98 | Australia | The Oval | 1934 |
| Coldwell,LJ | | †§ 6/85 | Pakistan | Lord's | 1962 |
| Compton,DCS | | 5/70 | South Africa | Cape Town | 1948-49 |
| Cook,NGB | (4) | †§ 5/35 | New Zealand | Lord's | 1983 |
| | | 5/63 | New Zealand | Nottingham | 1983 |
| | | § 6/65) | Pakistan | Karachi[1] | 1983-84 |
| | | 5/18) | | | |
| Copson,WH | | †§ 5/85 | West Indies | Lord's | 1939 |
| Cork,DG | (5) | †§ 7/43 | West Indies | Lord's | 1995 |
| | | 5/84 | South Africa | Johannesburg[3] | 1995-96 |
| | | 5/113 | Pakistan | Leeds | 1996 |
| | | 5/93 | South Africa | Birmingham | 1998 |
| | | 6/119 | South Africa | Lord's | 1998 |
| Cowans,NG | (2) | 6/77 | Australia | Melbourne | 1982-83 |
| | | 5/42 | Pakistan | Lahore[2] | 1983-84 |
| Crawford,JN | (3) | 5/79 | Australia | Melbourne | 1907-08 |
| | | 5/48 | Australia | Melbourne | 1907-08 |
| | | 5/141 | Australia | Sydney | 1907-08 |
| Croft,RDB | | 5/95 | New Zealand | Christchurch | 1996-97 |
| DeFreitas,PAJ | (4) | 5/86 | Pakistan | Karachi[1] | 1987-88 |
| | | 5/53 | New Zealand | Nottingham | 1990 |
| | | § 7/70 | Sri Lanka | Lord's | 1991 |
| | | 5/71 | New Zealand | Nottingham | 1994 |
| Dilley,GR | (6) | 5/68 | Australia | Brisbane[2] | 1986-87 |
| | | 5/92 | Pakistan | Birmingham | 1987 |
| | | 6/154 | Pakistan | The Oval | 1987 |
| | | 6/38 | New Zealand | Christchurch | 1987-88 |

| | | | | | |
|---|---|---|---|---|---|
| | | 5/60 | New Zealand | Auckland | 1987-88 |
| | | 5/55 | West Indies | Lord's | 1988 |
| Douglas,JWHT | | 5/46 | Australia | Melbourne | 1911-12 |
| Edmonds,PH | (2) | †§ 5/28 | Australia | Leeds | 1975 |
| | | 7/66 | Pakistan | Karachi[1] | 1977-78 |
| Ellison,RM | (3) | § 6/77 | Australia | Birmingham | 1985 |
| | | 5/46 | Australia | The Oval | 1985 |
| | | 5/78 | West Indies | Kingston | 1985-86 |
| Emburey,JE | (6) | 5/124 | West Indies | Port-of-Spain | 1980-81 |
| | | § 6/33 | Sri Lanka | Colombo (PSS) | 1981-82 |
| | | 5/82 | Australia | Leeds | 1985 |
| | | 5/78 | West Indies | Port-of-Spain | 1985-86 |
| | | 5/80 | Australia | Brisbane[2] | 1986-87 |
| | | 7/78 | Australia | Sydney | 1986-87 |
| Emmett,T | | 7/68 | Australia | Melbourne | 1876-77 |
| Farnes,K | (3) | †§ 5/102) | Australia | Nottingham | 1934 |
| | | 5/77 ) | | | |
| | | 6/96 | Australia | Melbourne | 1936-37 |
| Fender,PGH | (2) | 5/122 | Australia | Melbourne | 1920-21 |
| | | 5/90 | Australia | Sydney | 1920-21 |
| Ferris,JJ # | (2) | †§ 6/54) | South Africa | Cape Town | 1891-92 |
| | | 7/37) | | | |
| Fielder,A | | 6/82 | Australia | Sydney | 1907-08 |
| Flowers,W | | 5/46 | Australia | Sydney | 1884-85 |
| Foster,FR | (4) | †§ 5/92 | Australia | Sydney | 1911-12 |
| | | 6/91 | Australia | Melbourne | 1911-12 |
| | | 5/36 | Australia | Adelaide | 1911-12 |
| | | § 5/16 | South Africa | Lord's | 1912 |
| Foster,NA | (5) | 5/67 | Pakistan | Lahore[2] | 1983-84 |
| | | 6/104) | India | Madras[1] | 1984-85 |
| | | 5/59 ) | | | |
| | | 8/107 | Pakistan | Leeds | 1987 |
| | | 5/64 | West Indies | The Oval | 1988 |
| Fraser,ARC | (13) | 5/28 | West Indies | Kingston | 1989-90 |
| | | 5/104 | India | Lord's | 1990 |
| | | 5/124 | India | Manchester | 1990 |
| | | 6/82 | Australia | Melbourne | 1990-91 |
| | | 5/87 | Australia | The Oval | 1993 |
| | | 8/75 | West Indies | Bridgetown | 1993-94 |
| | | 5/73 | Australia | Sydney | 1994-95 |
| | | 5/66 | West Indies | Lord's | 1995 |
| | | 8/53 | West Indies | Port-of-Spain | 1997-98 |
| | | 5/40 | West Indies | Port-of-Spain | 1997-98 |
| | | 5/60) | West Indies | Nottingham | 1998 |
| | | 5/62) | | | |
| | | 5/42 | South Africa | Leeds | 1998 |
| Freeman,AP | (5) | 5/54) | West Indies | Manchester | 1928 |
| | | 5/39) | | | |
| | | 7/115 | South Africa | Leeds | 1929 |
| | | 7/71 ) | South Africa | Manchester | 1929 |
| | | 5/100) | | | |
| Geary,G | (4) | 7/70) | South Africa | Johannesburg[1] | 1927-28 |
| | | 5/60) | | | |
| | | 5/35 | Australia | Sydney | 1928-29 |
| | | 5/105 | Australia | Melbourne | 1928-29 |
| Gifford,N | | 5/55 | Pakistan | Karachi[1] | 1972-73 |
| Gilligan,AER | (2) | 6/7 ) | South Africa | Birmingham | 1924 |
| | | 5/83) | | | |
| Goddard,TWJ | | § 6/29 | New Zealand | Manchester | 1937 |
| Gough,D | (4) | 6/49 | Australia | Sydney | 1994-95 |
| | | 5/40 | New Zealand | Wellington | 1996-97 |
| | | 5/149 | Australia | Leeds | 1997 |
| | | 6/42 | South Africa | Leeds | 1998 |

| | | | | | |
|---|---|---|---|---|---|
| Greenhough,T | | 5/35 | India | Lord's | 1959 |
| Greig,AW | (6) | 5/24 | India | Calcutta | 1972-73 |
| | | 6/164 | West Indies | Bridgetown | 1973-74 |
| | | 8/86) | West Indies | Port-of-Spain | 1973-74 |
| | | 5/70) | | | |
| | | 5/98) | New Zealand | Auckland | 1974-75 |
| | | 5/51) | | | |
| Gunn,J | | 5/76 | Australia | Adelaide | 1901-02 |
| Haigh,S | | 6/11 | South Africa | Cape Town | 1898-99 |
| Hammond,WR | (2) | †§ 5/36 | South Africa | Johannesburg[1] | 1927-28 |
| | | 5/57 | Australia | Adelaide | 1936-37 |
| Hearne,JT | (4) | § 5/76 | Australia | Lord's | 1896 |
| | | 6/41 | Australia | The Oval | 1896 |
| | | 5/42 | Australia | Sydney | 1897-98 |
| | | 6/98 | Australia | Melbourne | 1897-98 |
| Hearne,JW | | 5/49 | South Africa | Johannesburg[1] | 1913-14 |
| Hemmings,EE | | 6/58 | New Zealand | Birmingham | 1990 |
| Heseltine,C | | †§ 5/38 | South Africa | Johannesburg[1] | 1895-96 |
| Higgs,K | (2) | 6/91 | West Indies | Lord's | 1966 |
| | | 5/58 | Pakistan | The Oval | 1967 |
| Hilton,MJ | | § 5/61 | India | Kanpur | 1951-52 |
| Hirst,GH | (3) | 5/77 | Australia | The Oval | 1902 |
| | | 5/48 | Australia | Melbourne | 1903-04 |
| | | 5/58 | Australia | Birmingham | 1909 |
| Hollies,WE | (5) | 7/50 | West Indies | Georgetown | 1934-35 |
| | | § 5/123 | South Africa | Nottingham | 1947 |
| | | § 5/131 | Australia | The Oval | 1948 |
| | | 5/133 | New Zealand | Lord's | 1949 |
| | | 5/63 | West Indies | Manchester | 1950 |
| Howorth,R | | § 6/124 | West Indies | Bridgetown | 1947-48 |
| Illingworth,R | (3) | 6/29 | India | Lord's | 1967 |
| | | 6/87 | Australia | Leeds | 1968 |
| | | 5/70 | India | The Oval | 1971 |
| Jackson,Hon.FS | | 5/52 | Australia | Nottingham | 1905 |
| Jenkins,RO | | § 5/116 | West Indies | Lord's | 1950 |
| Jones,IJ | | 6/118 | Australia | Adelaide | 1965-66 |
| Kennedy,AS | (2) | 5/88 | South Africa | Durban[2] | 1922-23 |
| | | 5/76 | South Africa | Durban[2] | 1922-23 |
| Laker,JC | (9) | †§ 7/103 | West Indies | Bridgetown | 1947-48 |
| | | 6/55 | South Africa | The Oval | 1951 |
| | | 5/56 | South Africa | The Oval | 1955 |
| | | 5/58) | Australia | Leeds | 1956 |
| | | 6/55) | | | |
| | | 9/37) | Australia | Manchester | 1956 |
| | | 10/53) | | | |
| | | 5/17 | New Zealand | Leeds | 1958 |
| | | 5/107 | Australia | Sydney | 1958-59 |
| Langridge,J | (2) | †§ 7/56 | West Indies | Manchester | 1933 |
| | | 5/63 | India | Madras[1] | 1933-34 |
| Larter,JDF | (2) | †§ 5/57 | Pakistan | The Oval | 1962 |
| | | 5/68 | South Africa | Nottingham | 1965 |
| Larwood,H | (4) | 6/32 | Australia | Brisbane[1] | 1928-29 |
| | | § 5/57 | South Africa | Birmingham | 1929 |
| | | 5/96) | Australia | Sydney | 1932-33 |
| | | 5/28) | | | |
| Lawrence,DV | | 5/106 | West Indies | The Oval | 1991 |
| Lees,WS | (2) | †§ 5/34 | South Africa | Johannesburg[1] | 1905-06 |
| | | 6/78 | South Africa | Johannesburg[1] | 1905-06 |
| Lever,JK | (3) | †§ 7/46 | India | Delhi | 1976-77 |
| | | 5/59 | India | Madras[1] | 1976-77 |
| | | 5/100 | India | Bangalore | 1981-82 |

| | | | | | |
|---|---|---|---|---|---|
| Lever,P | (2) | § 5/70 | India | Manchester | 1971 |
| | | 6/38 | Australia | Melbourne | 1974-75 |
| Lewis,CC | (3) | 6/111 | West Indies | Birmingham | 1991 |
| | | 5/31 | New Zealand | Auckland | 1991-92 |
| | | 5/72 | India | Birmingham | 1996 |
| Loader,PJ | | § 6/36 | West Indies | Leeds | 1957 |
| Lock,GAR | (9) | 5/45 | Australia | The Oval | 1953 |
| | | 5/28) | West Indies | The Oval | 1957 |
| | | 6/20) | | | |
| | | 5/17 | New Zealand | Lord's | 1958 |
| | | 7/51 | New Zealand | Leeds | 1958 |
| | | 7/35 | New Zealand | Manchester | 1958 |
| | | 5/31) | New Zealand | Christchurch | 1958-59 |
| | | 6/53) | | | |
| | | 6/65 | India | Madras[2] | 1961-62 |
| Lockwood,WH | (5) | †§ 6/101 | Australia | Lord's | 1893 |
| | | 7/71 | Australia | The Oval | 1899 |
| | | 6/48) | Australia | Manchester | 1902 |
| | | 5/28) | | | |
| | | 5/45 | Australia | The Oval | 1902 |
| Lohmann,GA | (9) | 7/36) | Australia | The Oval | 1886 |
| | | 5/68) | | | |
| | | 8/35 | Australia | Sydney | 1886-87 |
| | | 5/17 | Australia | Sydney | 1887-88 |
| | | 8/58 | Australia | Sydney | 1891-92 |
| | | § 7/38) | South Africa | Port Elizabeth | 1895-96 |
| | | 8/7 ) | | | |
| | | 9/28 | South Africa | Johannesburg[1] | 1895-96 |
| | | 7/42 | South Africa | Cape Town | 1895-96 |
| Macaulay,GG | | †§ 5/64 | South Africa | Cape Town | 1922-23 |
| Malcolm,DE | (5) | 6/77 | West Indies | Port-of-Spain | 1989-90 |
| | | 5/94 | New Zealand | Lord's | 1990 |
| | | 5/46 | New Zealand | Birmingham | 1990 |
| | | 5/94 | Pakistan | The Oval | 1992 |
| | | § 9/57 | South Africa | The Oval | 1994 |
| Mallender,NA | | †§ 5/50 | Pakistan | Leeds | 1992 |
| Marriott,CS | (2) | †§ 5/37) | West Indies | The Oval | 1933 |
| | | 6/59) | | | |
| Martin,F | (2) | †§ 6/50) | Australia | The Oval | 1890 |
| | | 6/52) | | | |
| Miller,G | | 5/44 | Australia | Sydney | 1978-79 |
| Morley,F | | †§ 5/56 | Australia | The Oval | 1880 |
| Nichols,MS | (2) | § 5/55 | India | Bombay[1] | 1933-34 |
| | | § 6/35 | South Africa | Nottingham | 1935 |
| Old,CM | (4) | § 5/113 | New Zealand | Lord's | 1973 |
| | | 5/21 | India | Lord's | 1974 |
| | | 6/54 | New Zealand | Wellington | 1977-78 |
| | | 7/50 | Pakistan | Birmingham | 1978 |
| Paine,GAE | | 5/168 | West Indies | Kingston | 1934-35 |
| Parkin,CH | (2) | 5/60 | Australia | Adelaide | 1920-21 |
| | | 5/38 | Australia | Manchester | 1921 |
| Peate,E | (2) | 5/43 | Australia | Sydney | 1881-82 |
| | | 6/85 | Australia | Lord's | 1884 |
| Peebles,IAR | (3) | 6/204 | Australia | The Oval | 1930 |
| | | 6/63 | South Africa | Johannesburg[1] | 1930-31 |
| | | § 5/77 | New Zealand | Lord's | 1931 |
| Peel,R | (5) | †§ 5/51 | Australia | Adelaide | 1884-85 |
| | | 5/18 | Australia | Sydney | 1887-88 |
| | | 7/31 | Australia | Manchester | 1888 |
| | | 6/67 | Australia | Sydney | 1894-95 |

| | | | | | |
|---|---|---|---|---|---|
| | | 6/23 | Australia | The Oval | 1896 |
| Perks,RTD | (2) | § 5/100 | South Africa | Durban[2] | 1938-39 |
| | | § 5/156 | West Indies | The Oval | 1939 |
| Pocock,PI | (3) | § 6/79 | Australia | Manchester | 1968 |
| | | 5/169 | Pakistan | Hyderabad | 1972-73 |
| | | 5/110 | West Indies | Port-of-Spain | 1973-74 |
| Pollard,R | | †§ 5/24 | India | Manchester | 1946 |
| Price,JSE | | 5/73 | India | Calcutta | 1963-64 |
| Pringle,DR | (3) | § 5/108 | West Indies | Birmingham | 1984 |
| | | 5/95 | West Indies | Leeds | 1988 |
| | | 5/100 | West Indies | Lord's | 1991 |
| Relf,AE | | 5/85 | Australia | Lord's | 1909 |
| Rhodes,W | (6) | 7/17 | Australia | Birmingham | 1902 |
| | | 5/63 | Australia | Sheffield | 1902 |
| | | 5/94 | Australia | Sydney | 1903-04 |
| | | 7/56) | Australia | Melbourne | 1903-04 |
| | | 8/68) | | | |
| | | 5/83 | Australia | Manchester | 1909 |
| Richardson,T | (11) | †§ 5/49 ) | Australia | Manchester | 1893 |
| | | 5/107) | | | |
| | | 5/181 | Australia | Sydney | 1894-95 |
| | | 5/57 | Australia | Melbourne | 1894-95 |
| | | 5/75 | Australia | Adelaide | 1894-95 |
| | | 6/104 | Australia | Melbourne | 1894-95 |
| | | 6/39 ) | Australia | Lord's | 1896 |
| | | 5/134) | | | |
| | | 7/168) | Australia | Manchester | 1896 |
| | | 6/76 ) | | | |
| | | 8/94 | Australia | Sydney | 1897-98 |
| Robins,RWV | | § 6/32 | West Indies | Lord's | 1933 |
| Sharpe,JW | | 6/84 | Australia | Melbourne | 1891-92 |
| Shaw,A | | †§ 5/38 | Australia | Melbourne | 1876-77 |
| Shuttleworth,K | | †§ 5/47 | Australia | Brisbane[2] | 1970-71 |
| Simpson-Hayward,GHT | (2) | †§ 6/43 | South Africa | Johannesburg[1] | 1909-10 |
| | | 5/69 | South Africa | Johannesburg[1] | 1909-10 |
| Sims,JM | | § 5/73 | India | The Oval | 1936 |
| Small,GC | (2) | § 5/48 | Australia | Melbourne | 1986-87 |
| | | 5/75 | Australia | Sydney | 1986-87 |
| Smith,CA | | †§ 5/19 | South Africa | Port Elizabeth | 1888-89 |
| Smith,CIJ | | †§ 5/16 | West Indies | Bridgetown | 1934-35 |
| Snow,JA | (8) | 7/49 | West Indies | Kingston | 1967-68 |
| | | 5/86 | West Indies | Bridgetown | 1967-68 |
| | | 6/60 | West Indies | Georgetown | 1967-68 |
| | | 5/114 | West Indies | Lord's | 1969 |
| | | 6/114 | Australia | Brisbane[2] | 1970-71 |
| | | 7/40 | Australia | Sydney | 1970-71 |
| | | 5/57 | Australia | Lord's | 1972 |
| | | 5/92 | Australia | Nottingham | 1972 |
| Statham,JB | (9) | 5/60 | Australia | Melbourne | 1954-55 |
| | | 7/39 | South Africa | Lord's | 1955 |
| | | 5/118 | West Indies | Nottingham | 1957 |
| | | 7/57 | Australia | Melbourne | 1958-59 |
| | | 5/31 | India | Nottingham | 1959 |
| | | 6/63) | South Africa | Lord's | 1960 |
| | | 5/34) | | | |
| | | 5/53 | Australia | Manchester | 1961 |
| | | 5/40 | South Africa | The Oval | 1965 |
| Stevens,GTS | (2) | § 5/105) | West Indies | Bridgetown | 1929-30 |
| | | 5/90 ) | | | |
| Such,PM | | § 6/67 | Australia | Manchester | 1993 |

| | | | | | |
|---|---|---|---|---|---|
| Tate,MW | (7) | 6/42 | South Africa | Leeds | 1924 |
| | | § 6/130) | Australia | Sydney | 1924-25 |
| | | 5/98 ) | | | |
| | | 6/99 | Australia | Melbourne | 1924-25 |
| | | 5/75 | Australia | Melbourne | 1924-25 |
| | | 5/115 | Australia | Sydney | 1924-25 |
| | | 5/124 | Australia | Leeds | 1930 |
| Tattersall,R | (4) | 6/44 | New Zealand | Wellington | 1950-51 |
| | | 7/52) | South Africa | Lord's | 1951 |
| | | 5/49) | | | |
| | | 6/48 | India | Kanpur | 1951-52 |
| Titmus,FJ | (7) | 7/79 | Australia | Sydney | 1962-63 |
| | | 5/103 | Australia | Sydney | 1962-63 |
| | | § 5/116 | India | Madras[2] | 1963-64 |
| | | 6/73 | India | Kanpur | 1963-64 |
| | | 5/66 | South Africa | Durban[2] | 1964-65 |
| | | 5/19 | New Zealand | Leeds | 1965 |
| | | 5/83 | West Indies | Manchester | 1966 |
| Trott,AE # | | †§ 5/51 | South Africa | Johannesburg[1] | 1898-99 |
| Trueman,FS | (17) | 8/31 | India | Manchester | 1952 |
| | | 5/48 | India | The Oval | 1952 |
| | | 5/90 | Australia | Lord's | 1956 |
| | | 5/63 | West Indies | Nottingham | 1957 |
| | | § 5/31 | New Zealand | Birmingham | 1958 |
| | | 5/35 | West Indies | Port-of-Spain | 1959-60 |
| | | 5/27 | South Africa | Nottingham | 1960 |
| | | 5/58) | Australia | Leeds | 1961 |
| | | 6/30) | | | |
| | | 6/31 | Pakistan | Lord's | 1962 |
| | | 5/62 | Australia | Melbourne | 1962-63 |
| | | 7/75 | New Zealand | Christchurch | 1962-63 |
| | | 6/100) | West Indies | Lord's | 1963 |
| | | 5/52 ) | | | |
| | | 5/75) | West Indies | Birmingham | 1963 |
| | | 7/44) | | | |
| | | 5/48 | Australia | Lord's | 1964 |
| Tufnell,PCR | (5) | 5/61 | Australia | Sydney | 1990-91 |
| | | § 6/25 | West Indies | The Oval | 1991 |
| | | § 5/94 | Sri Lanka | Lord's | 1991 |
| | | § 7/47 | New Zealand | Christchurch | 1991-92 |
| | | 7/66 | Australia | The Oval | 1997 |
| Tyson,FH | (4) | 6/85 | Australia | Sydney | 1954-55 |
| | | 7/27 | Australia | Melbourne | 1954-55 |
| | | § 6/28 | South Africa | Nottingham | 1955 |
| | | 6/40 | South Africa | Port Elizabeth | 1956-57 |
| Ulyett,G | | 7/36 | Australia | Lord's | 1884 |
| Underwood,DL | (17) | § 5/52 | Pakistan | Nottingham | 1967 |
| | | 7/50 | Australia | The Oval | 1968 |
| | | 5/94 | Pakistan | Dacca | 1968-69 |
| | | § 7/32 | New Zealand | Lord's | 1969 |
| | | 6/41) | New Zealand | The Oval | 1969 |
| | | 6/60) | | | |
| | | 6/12) | New Zealand | Christchurch | 1970-71 |
| | | 6/85) | | | |
| | | 5/108 | New Zealand | Auckland | 1970-71 |
| | | 6/45 | Australia | Leeds | 1972 |
| | | 5/20) | Pakistan | Lord's | 1974 |
| | | 8/51) | | | |
| | | 7/113 | Australia | Adelaide | 1974-75 |
| | | 5/39 | West Indies | Lord's | 1976 |

| | | | | | |
|---|---|---|---|---|---|
| | | 5/84 | India | Bombay[3] | 1976-77 |
| | | 6/66 | Australia | Manchester | 1977 |
| | | § 5/28 | Sri Lanka | Colombo (PSS) | 1981-82 |
| Verity,H | (5) | 5/33 | Australia | Sydney | 1932-33 |
| | | 7/49 | India | Madras[1] | 1933-34 |
| | | 7/61) | Australia | Lord's | 1934 |
| | | 8/43) | | | |
| | | 5/70 | South Africa | Cape Town | 1938-39 |
| Voce,W | (3) | 7/70 | West Indies | Port-of-Spain | 1929-30 |
| | | 5/58 | South Africa | Durban[2] | 1930-31 |
| | | 6/41 | Australia | Brisbane[2] | 1936-37 |
| Wardle,JH | (5) | 7/56 | Pakistan | The Oval | 1954 |
| | | 5/79 | Australia | Sydney | 1954-55 |
| | | 5/53) | South Africa | Cape Town | 1956-57 |
| | | 7/36) | | | |
| | | 5/61 | South Africa | Durban[2] | 1956-57 |
| Warren,AR | | †§ 5/57 | Australia | Leeds | 1905 |
| White,JC | (3) | 5/107 | Australia | Melbourne | 1928-29 |
| | | 5/130) | Australia | Adelaide | 1928-29 |
| | | 8/126) | | | |
| Willis,RGD | (16) | 5/61 | Australia | Melbourne | 1974-75 |
| | | 5/42 | West Indies | Leeds | 1976 |
| | | 5/27 | India | Calcutta | 1976-77 |
| | | 6/53 | India | Bangalore | 1976-77 |
| | | 7/78 | Australia | Lord's | 1977 |
| | | 5/88 | Australia | Nottingham | 1977 |
| | | 5/102 | Australia | The Oval | 1977 |
| | | 5/32 | New Zealand | Wellington | 1977-78 |
| | | 5/47 | Pakistan | Lord's | 1978 |
| | | 5/42 | New Zealand | The Oval | 1978 |
| | | 5/44 | Australia | Perth | 1978-79 |
| | | 5/65 | West Indies | Nottingham | 1980 |
| | | 8/43 | Australia | Leeds | 1981 |
| | | 6/101 | India | Lord's | 1982 |
| | | 5/66 | Australia | Brisbane[2] | 1982-83 |
| | | 5/35 | New Zealand | Lord's | 1983 |
| Woolley,FE | (4) | 5/41 | South Africa | The Oval | 1912 |
| | | 5/29) | Australia | The Oval | 1912 |
| | | 5/20) | | | |
| | | 7/76 | New Zealand | Wellington | 1929-30 |
| Wright,DVP | (6) | 5/167 | Australia | Brisbane[2] | 1946-47 |
| | | 7/105 | Australia | Sydney | 1946-47 |
| | | 5/95) | South Africa | Lord's | 1947 |
| | | 5/80) | | | |
| | | 5/141 | West Indies | The Oval | 1950 |
| | | 5/48 | New Zealand | Wellington | 1950-51 |
| **SOUTH AFRICA *(152)*** | | | Opponents | | |
| Adams,PR | | 6/55 | India | Kanpur | 1996-97 |
| Adcock,NAT | (5) | 5/43 | New Zealand | Johannesburg[2] | 1953-54 |
| | | 5/45 | New Zealand | Johannesburg[2] | 1953-54 |
| | | 6/43 | Australia | Durban[2] | 1957-58 |
| | | 5/62 | England | Birmingham | 1960 |
| | | 6/65 | England | The Oval | 1960 |
| Ashley,WH | | †§ 7/95 | England | Cape Town | 1888-89 |
| Balaskas,XC | | 5/49 | England | Lord's | 1935 |
| Barlow,EJ | | 5/85 | Australia | Cape Town | 1966-67 |
| Bell,AJ | (4) | †§ 6/99 | England | Lord's | 1929 |
| | | 5/140 | Australia | Sydney | 1931-32 |
| | | 5/69 | Australia | Melbourne | 1931-32 |

| | | | | | |
|---|---|---|---|---|---|
| | | 5/142 | Australia | Adelaide | 1931-32 |
| Bissett,GF | (2) | †§ 5/37 | England | Cape Town | 1927-28 |
| | | 7/29 | England | Durban[2] | 1927-28 |
| Blanckenberg,JM | (4) | 5/83 | England | Johannesburg[1] | 1913-14 |
| | | § 5/78 | Australia | Durban[1] | 1921-22 |
| | | 6/76 | England | Johannesburg[1] | 1922-23 |
| | | 5/61 | England | Cape Town | 1922-23 |
| Bromfield,HD | | § 5/88 | England | Cape Town | 1964-65 |
| Burke,SF | (2) | †§ 6/128) | New Zealand | Cape Town | 1961-62 |
| | | 5/68 ) | | | |
| Carter,CP | (2) | 6/50 | England | Durban[1] | 1913-14 |
| | | 6/91 | Australia | Johannesburg[1] | 1921-22 |
| Chubb,GWA | (2) | 5/77 | England | Lord's | 1951 |
| | | 6/51 | England | Manchester | 1951 |
| Crisp,RJ | | 5/99 | England | Manchester | 1935 |
| de Villiers,PS | (5) | 6/43 | Australia | Sydney | 1993-94 |
| | | 5/64 | New Zealand | Dunedin[2] | 1994-95 |
| | | 5/61 | New Zealand | Cape Town | 1994-95 |
| | | § 6/81 | Pakistan | Johannesburg[3] | 1994-95 |
| | | 5/23 | Pakistan | Durban[2] | 1997-98 |
| Donald,AA | (15) | 5/55) | India | Port Elizabeth | 1992-93 |
| | | 7/84) | | | |
| | | § 5/69 | Sri Lanka | Moratuwa | 1993-94 |
| | | § 5/74 | England | Lord's | 1994 |
| | | § 8/71 | Zimbabwe | Harare | 1995-96 |
| | | 5/46 | England | Cape Town | 1995-96 |
| | | 5/40 | India | Durban[2] | 1996-97 |
| | | 5/36 | Australia | Centurion | 1996-97 |
| | | 5/79 | Pakistan | Durban[2] | 1997-98 |
| | | 6/59 | Australia | Melbourne | 1997-98 |
| | | 5/54 | Sri Lanka | Centurion | 1997-98 |
| | | 5/32 | England | Lord's | 1998 |
| | | 6/88 | England | Manchester | 1998 |
| | | 5/109 | England | Nottingham | 1998 |
| | | 5/71 | England | Leeds | 1998 |
| Faulkner,GA | (4) | 6/17 | England | Leeds | 1907 |
| | | 5/120 | England | Durban[1] | 1909-10 |
| | | 6/87 | England | Durban[1] | 1909-10 |
| | | 7/84 | England | The Oval | 1912 |
| Fuller,ERH | | 5/66 | Australia | Melbourne | 1952-53 |
| Goddard,TL | (5) | 5/69 | England | Leeds | 1955 |
| | | 5/31 | England | The Oval | 1955 |
| | | 5/80 | England | Nottingham | 1960 |
| | | 5/60 | Australia | Adelaide | 1963-64 |
| | | 6/53 | Australia | Johannesburg[3] | 1966-67 |
| Gordon,N | (2) | †§ 5/103 | England | Johannesburg[1] | 1938-39 |
| | | 5/157 | England | Cape Town | 1938-39 |
| Hall,AE | (3) | †§ 7/63 | England | Cape Town | 1922-23 |
| | | 6/82 | England | Johannesburg[1] | 1922-23 |
| | | 6/100 | England | Johannesburg[1] | 1927-28 |
| Heine,PS | (4) | †§ 5/60 | England | Lord's | 1955 |
| | | 5/86 | England | Manchester | 1955 |
| | | § 6/58 | Australia | Johannesburg[3] | 1957-58 |
| | | 6/96 | Australia | Johannesburg[3] | 1957-58 |
| Ironside,DEJ | | †§ 5/51 | New Zealand | Johannesburg[2] | 1953-54 |
| Klusener,L | | § 8/64 | India | Calcutta | 1996-97 |
| Langton,ABC | | 5/58 | England | Johannesburg[1] | 1938-39 |
| Lawrence,GB | (2) | 8/53 | New Zealand | Johannesburg[3] | 1961-62 |
| | | 5/52 | New Zealand | Johannesburg[3] | 1961-62 |
| Llewellyn,CB | (4) | § 6/92 | Australia | Johannesburg[1] | 1902-03 |
| | | 5/43) | Australia | Johannesburg[1] | 1902-03 |
| | | 5/73) | | | |

| Bowler | | Figures | Opponents | Venue | Season |
|---|---|---|---|---|---|
| | | 6/97 | Australia | Cape Town | 1902-03 |
| McCarthy,CN | (2) | †§ 6/43 | England | Durban[2] | 1948-49 |
| | | 5/114 | England | Johannesburg[2] | 1948-49 |
| McMillan,Q | (2) | § 5/66 | New Zealand | Christchurch | 1931-32 |
| | | 5/125 | New Zealand | Wellington | 1931-32 |
| Mann,NBF | | 6/59 | England | Durban[2] | 1948-49 |
| Matthews,CR | (2) | 5/80 | Australia | Cape Town | 1993-94 |
| | | § 5/42 | New Zealand | Johannesburg[3] | 1994-95 |
| Melle,MG | (2) | †§ 5/113 | Australia | Johannesburg[2] | 1949-50 |
| | | 6/71 | Australia | Brisbane[2] | 1952-53 |
| Middleton,J | (2) | †§ 5/64 | England | Port Elizabeth | 1895-96 |
| | | 5/51 | England | Johannesburg[1] | 1898-99 |
| Mitchell,B | | 5/87 | Australia | Durban[2] | 1935-36 |
| Nupen,EP | (5) | § 5/53 | England | Johannesburg[1] | 1922-23 |
| | | 5/83 | England | Durban[2] | 1927-28 |
| | | 5/63) | England | Johannesburg[1] | 1930-31 |
| | | 6/87) | | | |
| | | 6/46 | England | Johannesburg[1] | 1930-31 |
| Parker,GM | | †§ 6/152 | England | Birmingham | 1924 |
| Partridge,JT | (3) | 5/123 | Australia | Sydney | 1963-64 |
| | | 7/91 | Australia | Sydney | 1963-64 |
| | | 6/86 | New Zealand | Auckland | 1963-64 |
| Pegler,SJ | (2) | 6/105 | Australia | Manchester | 1912 |
| | | 7/65 | England | Lord's | 1912 |
| Pithey,DB | | 6/58 | New Zealand | Dunedin | 1963-64 |
| Pollock,PM | (9) | †§ 6/38 | New Zealand | Durban[2] | 1961-62 |
| | | § 6/95 | Australia | Brisbane[2] | 1963-64 |
| | | 5/83 | Australia | Sydney | 1963-64 |
| | | 6/47 | New Zealand | Wellington | 1963-64 |
| | | 5/129 | England | Johannesburg[3] | 1964-65 |
| | | 5/53) | England | Nottingham | 1965 |
| | | 5/34) | | | |
| | | 5/43 | England | The Oval | 1965 |
| | | 5/39 | Australia | Johannesburg[3] | 1969-70 |
| Pollock,SM | (5) | 5/32 | England | Cape Town | 1995-96 |
| | | 5/37 | Pakistan | Faisalabad | 1997-98 |
| | | 7/87 | Australia | Adelaide | 1997-98 |
| | | 6/50 | Pakistan | Durban[2] | 1997-98 |
| | | 5/33 | England | Leeds | 1998 |
| Procter,MJ | | 6/73 | Australia | Port Elizabeth | 1969-70 |
| Promnitz,HLE | | †§ 5/58 | England | Johannesburg[1] | 1927-28 |
| Quinn,NA | | 6/92 | England | Leeds | 1929 |
| Rose-Innes,A | | †§ 5/43 | England | Port Elizabeth | 1888-89 |
| Rowan,AMB | (4) | 5/80 | England | Cape Town | 1948-49 |
| | | 5/167 | England | Port Elizabeth | 1948-49 |
| | | 5/68 | England | Nottingham | 1951 |
| | | 5/174 | England | Leeds | 1951 |
| Rowe,GA | | § 5/115 | England | Johannesburg[1] | 1895-96 |
| Schultz,BN | (2) | 5/48 | Sri Lanka | Colombo (SSC) | 1993-94 |
| | | 5/63 | Sri Lanka | Colombo (PSS) | 1993-94 |
| Schwarz,RO | (2) | § 5/102 | Australia | Sydney | 1910-11 |
| | | 6/47 | Australia | Sydney | 1910-11 |
| Sinclair,JH | | 6/26 | England | Cape Town | 1898-99 |
| Snooke,SJ | | 8/70 | England | Johannesburg[1] | 1905-06 |
| Tayfield,HJ | (14) | 7/23 | Australia | Durban[2] | 1949-50 |
| | | 6/84) | Australia | Melbourne | 1952-53 |
| | | 7/81) | | | |
| | | 5/62 | New Zealand | Auckland | 1952-53 |
| | | 6/62 | New Zealand | Durban[2] | 1953-54 |
| | | 6/13 | New Zealand | Johannesburg[2] | 1953-54 |
| | | 5/80 | England | Lord's | 1955 |

| | | | | | |
|---|---|---|---|---|---|
| | | 5/94 | England | Leeds | 1955 |
| | | 5/60 | England | The Oval | 1955 |
| | | 5/130 | England | Cape Town | 1956-57 |
| | | 8/69 | England | Durban[2] | 1956-57 |
| | | 9/113 | England | Johannesburg[3] | 1956-57 |
| | | 6/78 | England | Port Elizabeth | 1956-57 |
| | | 5/120 | Australia | Cape Town | 1957-58 |
| Tuckett,L | (2) | †§ 5/68 | England | Nottingham | 1947 |
| | | 5/115 | England | Lord's | 1947 |
| Vincent,CL | (3) | 6/131 | England | Durban[2] | 1927-28 |
| | | 5/105 | England | The Oval | 1929 |
| | | 6/51 | England | Durban[2] | 1930-31 |
| Vogler,AEE | (5) | 7/128 | England | Lord's | 1907 |
| | | 5/87) | England | Johannesburg[1] | 1909-10 |
| | | 7/94) | | | |
| | | 5/83 | England | Johannesburg[1] | 1909-10 |
| | | 5/72 | England | Cape Town | 1909-10 |
| **WEST INDIES *(216)*** | | | Opponents | | |
| Adams,JC | | 5/17 | New Zealand | Bridgetown | 1995-96 |
| Ali,Inshan | | 5/59 | New Zealand | Port-of-Spain | 1971-72 |
| Ambrose,CEL | (20) | 5/72 | Australia | Perth | 1988-89 |
| | | 8/45 | England | Bridgetown | 1989-90 |
| | | 5/35 | Pakistan | Lahore[2] | 1990-91 |
| | | 6/52 | England | Leeds | 1991 |
| | | 5/74 | England | Nottingham | 1991 |
| | | § 6/34 | South Africa | Bridgetown | 1991-92 |
| | | 5/66 | Australia | Brisbane[2] | 1992-93 |
| | | 6/74 | Australia | Adelaide | 1992-93 |
| | | 7/25 | Australia | Perth | 1992-93 |
| | | 5/60) | England | Port-of-Spain | 1993-94 |
| | | 6/24) | | | |
| | | 5/45 | Australia | Port-of-Spain | 1994-95 |
| | | 5/96 | England | The Oval | 1995 |
| | | 5/68 | New Zealand | St John's | 1995-96 |
| | | 5/55 | Australia | Melbourne | 1996-97 |
| | | 5/43 | Australia | Perth | 1996-97 |
| | | 5/87 | India | Port-of-Spain | 1996-97 |
| | | 5/37 | Sri Lanka | St John's | 1996-97 |
| | | 5/52 | England | Port-of-Spain | 1997-98 |
| | | 5/25 | England | Port-of-Spain | 1997-98 |
| Atkinson,DS | (3) | 5/56 | Australia | Bridgetown | 1954-55 |
| | | 5/66 | New Zealand | Wellington | 1955-56 |
| | | 7/53 | New Zealand | Auckland | 1955-56 |
| Atkinson,ES | | 5/42 | Pakistan | Kingston | 1957-58 |
| Benjamin,KCG | (4) | 6/66 | England | Kingston | 1993-94 |
| | | 5/65 | India | Mohali | 1994-95 |
| | | 5/109) | England | Nottingham | 1995 |
| | | 5/69 ) | | | |
| Bishop,IR | (6) | 6/87 | India | Bridgetown | 1988-89 |
| | | 5/84 | England | St John's | 1989-90 |
| | | 5/41 | Pakistan | Lahore[2] | 1990-91 |
| | | 6/40 | Australia | Perth | 1992-93 |
| | | 5/43 | Pakistan | Port-of-Spain | 1992-93 |
| | | 5/32 | England | Leeds | 1995 |
| Boyce,KD | (2) | § 5/70) | England | The Oval | 1973 |
| | | 6/77) | | | |
| Butcher,BF | | 5/34 | England | Port-of-Spain | 1967-68 |
| Clarke,ST | | 5/126 | India | Bangalore | 1978-79 |
| Constantine,LN | (2) | 5/87 | England | Georgetown | 1929-30 |

| | | | | | |
|---|---|---|---|---|---|
| | | 5/73 | England | The Oval | 1939 |
| Croft,CEH | (3) | 8/29 | Pakistan | Port-of-Spain | 1976-77 |
| | | 5/40 | England | Port-of-Spain | 1980-81 |
| | | 6/74 | England | St John's | 1980-81 |
| Daniel,WW | | 5/39 | India | Ahmedabad | 1983-84 |
| Dewdney,DT | | 5/21 | New Zealand | Auckland | 1955-56 |
| Dillon,M | | § 5/111 | Pakistan | Karachi[1] | 1997-98 |
| Edwards,RM | | 5/84 | New Zealand | Wellington | 1968-69 |
| Ferguson,W | (3) | 5/137) | England | Port-of-Spain | 1947-48 |
| | | 6/92 ) | | | |
| | | 5/116 | England | Georgetown | 1947-48 |
| Garner,J | (7) | 6/56 | New Zealand | Auckland | 1979-80 |
| | | 5/56 | Australia | Adelaide | 1981-82 |
| | | 6/75 | Australia | Georgetown | 1983-84 |
| | | 6/60 | Australia | Port-of-Spain | 1983-84 |
| | | 5/63 | Australia | St John's | 1983-84 |
| | | 5/55 | England | Birmingham | 1984 |
| | | 5/51 | New Zealand | Wellington | 1986-87 |
| Gibbs,LR | (18) | 5/80 | Pakistan | Georgetown | 1957-58 |
| | | § 5/66 | Australia | Sydney | 1960-61 |
| | | 5/97 | Australia | Adelaide | 1960-61 |
| | | 8/38 | India | Bridgetown | 1961-62 |
| | | § 5/59) | England | Manchester | 1963 |
| | | 6/98) | | | |
| | | 6/29 | Australia | Georgetown | 1964-65 |
| | | 5/37) | England | Manchester | 1966 |
| | | 5/69) | | | |
| | | 6/39 | England | Leeds | 1966 |
| | | 5/51 | India | Calcutta | 1966-67 |
| | | 6/60 | England | Georgetown | 1967-68 |
| | | 5/88 | Australia | Brisbane[2] | 1968-69 |
| | | 5/102 | Australia | Port-of-Spain | 1972-73 |
| | | 6/108 | England | Port-of-Spain | 1973-74 |
| | | 6/76 | India | Delhi | 1974-75 |
| | | 7/98 | India | Bombay[3] | 1974-75 |
| | | 5/102 | Australia | Brisbane[2] | 1975-76 |
| Gilchrist,R | | 6/55 | India | Calcutta | 1958-59 |
| Goddard,JDC | | 5/31 | England | Georgetown | 1947-48 |
| Gomez,GE | | 7/55 | Australia | Sydney | 1951-52 |
| Griffith,CC | (5) | 5/91 | England | Lord's | 1963 |
| | | 6/36 | England | Leeds | 1963 |
| | | 6/71 | England | The Oval | 1963 |
| | | 6/46 | Australia | Port-of-Spain | 1964-65 |
| | | 5/69 | England | Port-of-Spain | 1967-68 |
| Griffith,HC | (2) | 6/103 | England | The Oval | 1928 |
| | | 5/63 | England | Port-of-Spain | 1929-30 |
| Hall,WW | (9) | 6/50) | India | Kanpur | 1958-59 |
| | | 5/76) | | | |
| | | 5/87 | Pakistan | Lahore[1] | 1958-59 |
| | | 7/69 | England | Kingston | 1959-60 |
| | | 6/90 | England | Georgetown | 1959-60 |
| | | § 5/63 | Australia | Brisbane[2] | 1960-61 |
| | | 6/49 | India | Kingston | 1961-62 |
| | | 5/20 | India | Port-of-Spain | 1961-62 |
| | | 5/60 | Australia | Kingston | 1964-65 |
| Harper,RA | | 6/57 | England | Manchester | 1984 |
| Holder,VA | (3) | 6/39 | India | Bombay[3] | 1974-75 |
| | | 5/108 | Australia | Adelaide | 1975-76 |
| | | 6/28 | Australia | Port-of-Spain | 1977-78 |
| Holding,MA | (13) | 6/65 | India | Port-of-Spain | 1975-76 |

| | | | | | |
|---|---|---|---|---|---|
| | | 5/17 | England | Manchester | 1976 |
| | | 8/92) | England | The Oval | 1976 |
| | | 6/57) | | | |
| | | 6/67 | England | Lord's | 1980 |
| | | 5/56 | England | Kingston | 1980-81 |
| | | 5/45) | Australia | Melbourne | 1981-82 |
| | | 6/62) | | | |
| | | 5/64 | Australia | Sydney | 1981-82 |
| | | 5/72 | Australia | Adelaide | 1981-82 |
| | | 5/102 | India | Bombay[3] | 1983-84 |
| | | 5/43 | England | The Oval | 1984 |
| | | 6/21 | Australia | Perth | 1984-85 |
| Holford,DAJ | | 5/23 | India | Bridgetown | 1975-76 |
| Hooper,CL | (4) | 5/40 | Pakistan | Bridgetown | 1992-93 |
| | | 5/116 | India | Nagpur | 1994-95 |
| | | 5/26 | Sri Lanka | Kingstown | 1996-97 |
| | | 5/80 | England | Bridgetown | 1997-98 |
| Johnson,HHH | (2) | †§ 5/41) | England | Kingston | 1947-48 |
| | | 5/55) | | | |
| Jones,PE | | 5/85 | India | Bombay[2] | 1948-49 |
| Julien,BD | | 5/57 | England | Bridgetown | 1973-74 |
| Kentish,ESM | | 5/49 | England | Kingston | 1953-54 |
| King,FM | | 5/74 | India | Port-of-Spain | 1952-53 |
| King,LA | | †§ 5/46 | India | Kingston | 1961-62 |
| Marshall,MD | (22) | 5/37 | India | Port-of-Spain | 1982-83 |
| | | 6/37 | India | Calcutta | 1983-84 |
| | | 5/72 | India | Madras[1] | 1983-84 |
| | | 5/42 | Australia | Bridgetown | 1983-84 |
| | | 5/51 | Australia | Kingston | 1983-84 |
| | | 6/85 | England | Lord's | 1984 |
| | | 7/53 | England | Leeds | 1984 |
| | | 5/35 | England | The Oval | 1984 |
| | | 5/82 | Australia | Brisbane[2] | 1984-85 |
| | | 5/69) | Australia | Adelaide | 1984-85 |
| | | 5/38) | | | |
| | | 5/86 | Australia | Melbourne | 1984-85 |
| | | 7/80 | New Zealand | Bridgetown | 1984-85 |
| | | 5/33 | Pakistan | Lahore[2] | 1986-87 |
| | | 5/65 | Pakistan | Bridgetown | 1987-88 |
| | | 6/69 | England | Nottingham | 1988 |
| | | 6/32 | England | Lord's | 1988 |
| | | 7/22 | England | Manchester | 1988 |
| | | 5/29 | Australia | Sydney | 1988-89 |
| | | 5/60 | India | Bridgetown | 1988-89 |
| | | 5/34) | India | Port-of-Spain | 1988-89 |
| | | 6/55) | | | |
| Martindale,EA | (3) | 5/73 | England | Manchester | 1933 |
| | | 5/93 | England | The Oval | 1933 |
| | | 5/22 | England | Bridgetown | 1934-35 |
| Noreiga,JM | (2) | 9/95 | India | Port-of-Spain | 1970-71 |
| | | 5/129 | India | Port-of-Spain | 1970-71 |
| Parry,DR | | 5/15 | Australia | Port-of-Spain | 1977-78 |
| Patterson,BP | (5) | § 5/24 | India | Delhi | 1987-88 |
| | | 5/68 | India | Bombay[3] | 1987-88 |
| | | 5/39 | Australia | Melbourne | 1988-89 |
| | | 5/83 | Australia | Kingston | 1990-91 |
| | | 5/81 | England | Birmingham | 1991 |
| Ramadhin,S | (10) | 5/66) | England | Lord's | 1950 |
| | | 6/86) | | | |
| | | 5/135 | England | Nottingham | 1950 |

| | | | | | |
|---|---|---|---|---|---|
| | | § 5/90 | Australia | Brisbane[2] | 1951-52 |
| | | § 5/86 | New Zealand | Christchurch | 1951-52 |
| | | 5/26 | India | Bridgetown | 1952-53 |
| | | 6/113 | England | Georgetown | 1953-54 |
| | | 6/23 | New Zealand | Dunedin | 1955-56 |
| | | 5/46 | New Zealand | Christchurch | 1955-56 |
| | | 7/49 | England | Birmingham | 1957 |
| Roberts,AME | (11) | 5/50 | India | Calcutta | 1974-75 |
| | | 7/64) | India | Madras[1] | 1974-75 |
| | | 5/57) | | | |
| | | § 5/66 | Pakistan | Lahore[2] | 1974-75 |
| | | 7/54 | Australia | Perth | 1975-76 |
| | | 5/60) | England | Lord's | 1976 |
| | | 5/63) | | | |
| | | 6/37 | England | Manchester | 1976 |
| | | 5/56 | Australia | Port-of-Spain | 1977-78 |
| | | 5/72 | England | Nottingham | 1980 |
| | | 5/39 | India | Kingston | 1982-83 |
| Rose,FA | | †§ 6/100 | India | Kingston | 1996-97 |
| Scott,OC | | 5/266 | England | Kingston | 1929-30 |
| Shepherd,JN | | †§ 5/104 | England | Manchester | 1969 |
| Smith,OG | | 5/90 | India | Delhi | 1958-59 |
| Sobers,GS | (6) | 5/120 | Australia | Melbourne | 1960-61 |
| | | 5/63 | India | Kingston | 1961-62 |
| | | 5/60 | England | Birmingham | 1963 |
| | | 5/41 | England | Leeds | 1966 |
| | | 6/73 | Australia | Brisbane[2] | 1968-69 |
| | | 5/42 | England | Leeds | 1969 |
| Taylor,J | | †§ 5/109 | Pakistan | Port-of-Spain | 1957-58 |
| Trim,J | | § 5/34 | Australia | Melbourne | 1951-52 |
| Valentine,AL | (8) | †§ 8/104 | England | Manchester | 1950 |
| | | 6/39 | England | The Oval | 1950 |
| | | § 5/99 | Australia | Brisbane[2] | 1951-52 |
| | | 6/102 | Australia | Adelaide | 1951-52 |
| | | 5/88 | Australia | Melbourne | 1951-52 |
| | | 5/127 | India | Georgetown | 1952-53 |
| | | 5/64 | India | Kingston | 1952-53 |
| | | 5/32 | New Zealand | Christchurch | 1955-56 |
| Walsh,CA | (15) | 5/73 | New Zealand | Auckland | 1986-87 |
| | | § 5/54 | India | Delhi | 1987-88 |
| | | 5/54 | India | Bombay[3] | 1987-88 |
| | | 6/62 | India | Kingston | 1988-89 |
| | | 5/68 | England | Kingston | 1989-90 |
| | | 5/94 | England | Bridgetown | 1993-94 |
| | | 6/79 | India | Bombay[3] | 1994-95 |
| | | 7/37) | New Zealand | Wellington | 1994-95 |
| | | 6/18) | | | |
| | | 6/54 | Australia | St John's | 1994-95 |
| | | 5/45 | England | Birmingham | 1995 |
| | | 5/98 | Australia | Sydney | 1996-97 |
| | | 5/74 | Australia | Perth | 1996-97 |
| | | 5/79 | Pakistan | Peshawar[2] | 1997-98 |
| | | 5/143 | Pakistan | Rawalpindi[2] | 1997-98 |
| Worrell,FMM | (2) | 6/38 | Australia | Adelaide | 1951-52 |
| | | 7/70 | England | Leeds | 1957 |
| | | | | | |
| **NEW ZEALAND *(123)*** | | | Opponents | | |
| Bartlett,GA | | § 6/38 | India | Christchurch | 1967-68 |
| Boock,SL | (4) | 5/67 | England | Auckland | 1977-78 |
| | | § 5/28 | Sri Lanka | Kandy | 1983-84 |

| | | | | | |
|---|---|---|---|---|---|
| | | 7/87 | Pakistan | Hyderabad | 1984-85 |
| | | 5/117 | Pakistan | Wellington | 1984-85 |
| Bracewell,JG | (4) | § 5/75 | India | Auckland | 1980-81 |
| | | 6/32 | Australia | Auckland | 1985-86 |
| | | 6/51 | India | Bombay[3] | 1988-89 |
| | | 6/85 | Australia | Wellington | 1989-90 |
| Burtt,TB | (3) | 5/97 | England | Leeds | 1949 |
| | | 6/162 | England | Manchester | 1949 |
| | | § 5/69 | West Indies | Christchurch | 1951-52 |
| Cairns,BL | (6) | 5/55 | India | Madras[1] | 1976-77 |
| | | 6/85 | West Indies | Christchurch | 1979-80 |
| | | 5/87 | Australia | Brisbane[2] | 1980-81 |
| | | 5/33 | India | Wellington | 1980-81 |
| | | 7/74 | England | Leeds | 1983 |
| | | 7/143 | England | Wellington | 1983-84 |
| Cairns,CL | (4) | 5/75 | Sri Lanka | Auckland | 1990-91 |
| | | 6/52 | England | Auckland | 1991-92 |
| | | 5/137 | Pakistan | Rawalpindi[2] | 1996-97 |
| | | 5/50 | Zimbabwe | Harare | 1997-98 |
| | | 5/62 | Sri Lanka | Colombo (SSC) | 1997-98 |
| Cameron,FJ | (3) | 5/83 | South Africa | Johannesburg[3] | 1961-62 |
| | | 5/48 | South Africa | Cape Town | 1961-62 |
| | | 5/34 | Pakistan | Auckland | 1964-65 |
| Chatfield,EJ | (3) | 5/95 | England | Leeds | 1983 |
| | | 5/63 | Sri Lanka | Colombo (CCC) | 1983-84 |
| | | 6/73 | West Indies | Port-of-Spain | 1984-85 |
| Collinge,RO | (3) | 5/74 | England | Leeds | 1973 |
| | | 5/82 | Australia | Auckland | 1973-74 |
| | | 6/63 | India | Christchurch | 1975-76 |
| Congdon,BE | | 5/65 | India | Auckland | 1975-76 |
| Cowie,J | (4) | 6/67 | England | Manchester | 1937 |
| | | § 6/40 | Australia | Wellington | 1945-46 |
| | | 6/83 | England | Christchurch | 1946-47 |
| | | 5/127 | England | Leeds | 1949 |
| Cresswell,GF | | †§ 6/168 | England | The Oval | 1949 |
| Cunis,RS | | 6/76 | England | Auckland | 1970-71 |
| Davis,HT | | 5/63 | Sri Lanka | Hamilton | 1996-97 |
| Doull,SB | (5) | 5/66 | Pakistan | Auckland | 1993-94 |
| | | 5/73 | South Africa | Dunedin[2] | 1994-95 |
| | | 5/46 | Pakistan | Lahore[2] | 1996-97 |
| | | 5/75 | England | Wellington | 1996-97 |
| | | § 5/58 | Sri Lanka | Dunedin | 1996-97 |
| Hadlee,RJ | (36) | 7/23 | India | Wellington | 1975-76 |
| | | 5/121 | Pakistan | Lahore[2] | 1976-77 |
| | | 6/26 | England | Wellington | 1977-78 |
| | | 5/84 | England | Lord's | 1978 |
| | | 5/62 | Pakistan | Christchurch | 1978-79 |
| | | 5/104 | Pakistan | Auckland | 1978-79 |
| | | § 5/34) | West Indies | Dunedin | 1979-80 |
| | | 6/68) | | | |
| | | 5/87 | Australia | Perth | 1980-81 |
| | | 6/57 | Australia | Melbourne | 1980-81 |
| | | 5/47 | India | Christchurch | 1980-81 |
| | | 5/63 | Australia | Auckland | 1981-82 |
| | | 6/100 | Australia | Christchurch | 1981-82 |
| | | 6/53 | England | The Oval | 1983 |
| | | 5/93 | England | Lord's | 1983 |
| | | 5/28 | England | Christchurch | 1983-84 |
| | | 5/73) | Sri Lanka | Colombo (CCC) | 1983-84 |
| | | 5/29) | | | |

| | | | | | |
|---|---|---|---|---|---|
| | | 6/51 | Pakistan | Dunedin | 1984-85 |
| | | 9/52) | Australia | Brisbane[2] | 1985-86 |
| | | 6/71) | | | |
| | | 5/65 | Australia | Sydney | 1985-86 |
| | | 5/65) | Australia | Perth | 1985-86 |
| | | 6/90) | | | |
| | | 7/116 | Australia | Christchurch | 1985-86 |
| | | 6/80 | England | Lord's | 1986 |
| | | 6/80 | England | Nottingham | 1986 |
| | | 6/105 | West Indies | Auckland | 1986-87 |
| | | 6/50 | West Indies | Christchurch | 1986-87 |
| | | 5/68 | Australia | Adelaide | 1987-88 |
| | | 5/109) | Australia | Melbourne | 1987-88 |
| | | 5/67 ) | | | |
| | | 5/65 | India | Bangalore | 1988-89 |
| | | 6/49 | India | Bombay[3] | 1988-89 |
| | | 5/39 | Australia | Wellington | 1989-90 |
| | | 5/53 | England | Birmingham | 1990 |
| Hart,MN | | § 5/77 | South Africa | Johannesburg[3] | 1994-95 |
| Howarth,HJ | (2) | 5/34 | India | Nagpur | 1969-70 |
| | | § 5/80 | Pakistan | Karachi[1] | 1969-70 |
| MacGibbon,AR | | 5/64 | England | Birmingham | 1958 |
| Moir,AM | (2) | †§ 6/155 | England | Christchurch | 1950-51 |
| | | 5/62 | England | Auckland | 1954-55 |
| Morrison,DK | (10) | § 5/69 | England | Christchurch | 1987-88 |
| | | 5/75 | India | Christchurch | 1989-90 |
| | | 5/98 | India | Napier | 1989-90 |
| | | 5/145 | India | Auckland | 1989-90 |
| | | 5/153 | Sri Lanka | Wellington | 1990-91 |
| | | 5/51 | Pakistan | Hamilton | 1992-93 |
| | | 7/89 | Australia | Wellington | 1992-93 |
| | | 6/37 | Australia | Christchurch | 1992-93 |
| | | § 6/69 | West Indies | Christchurch | 1994-95 |
| | | 5/61 | West Indies | St John's | 1995-96 |
| Motz,RC | (5) | 5/108 | England | Birmingham | 1965 |
| | | 5/86 | India | Dunedin | 1967-68 |
| | | 6/63 | India | Christchurch | 1967-68 |
| | | 6/69 | West Indies | Wellington | 1968-69 |
| | | 5/113 | West Indies | Christchurch | 1968-69 |
| Nash,DJ | (2) | 6/76) | England | Lord's | 1994 |
| | | 5/93) | | | |
| O'Sullivan,DR | | 5/148 | Australia | Adelaide | 1973-74 |
| Patel,DN | (3) | § 6/113 | Zimbabwe | Bulawayo[1] | 1992-93 |
| | | 6/50 | Zimbabwe | Harare | 1992-93 |
| | | 5/93 | Australia | Canterbruy | 1992-93 |
| Pringle,C | | 7/52 | Pakistan | Faisalabad | 1990-91 |
| Rabone,GO | | 6/68 | South Africa | Cape Town | 1953-54 |
| Reid,JR | | 6/60 | South Africa | Dunedin | 1963-64 |
| Snedden,MC | | 5/68 | West Indies | Christchurch | 1986-87 |
| Su'a.ML | (2) | 5/85 | Zimbabwe | Harare | 1992-93 |
| | | § 5/73 | Pakistan | Hamilton | 1992-93 |
| Taylor,BR | (4) | †§ 5/86 | India | Calcutta | 1964-65 |
| | | 5/26 | India | Bombay[2] | 1964-65 |
| | | 7/74 | West Indies | Bridgetown | 1971-72 |
| | | 5/41 | West Indies | Port-of-Spain | 1971-72 |
| Troup,GB | | 6/95 | West Indies | Auckland | 1979-80 |
| Vettori,DL | (2) | 5/84 | Sri Lanka | Hamilton | 1996-97 |
| | | 6/64 | Sri Lanka | Colombo (SSC) | 1997-98 |
| Watson,W | | 6/78 | Pakistan | Lahore[2] | 1990-91 |
| Wiseman,PJ | | †§ 5/82 | Sri Lanka | Colombo (PIS) | 1997-98 |

| **INDIA *(188)*** | | | Opponents | | |
|---|---|---|---|---|---|
| Abid Ali,S | | †§ 6/55 | Australia | Adelaide | 1967-68 |
| Amar Singh,L | (2) | 7/86 | England | Madras[1] | 1933-34 |
| | | 6/35 | England | Lord's | 1936 |
| Amarnath,NB | (2) | 5/118 | England | Lord's | 1946 |
| | | 5/96 | England | Manchester | 1946 |
| Arshad Ayub | (3) | 5/50 | New Zealand | Bombay[3] | 1988-89 |
| | | 5/104 | West Indies | Georgetown | 1988-89 |
| | | 5/117 | West Indies | Port-of-Spain | 1988-89 |
| Bedi,BS | (14) | 6/127 | New Zealand | Christchurch | 1967-68 |
| | | 6/42 | New Zealand | Bombay[2] | 1969-70 |
| | | 5/37 | Australia | Delhi | 1969-70 |
| | | 7/98 | Australia | Calcutta | 1969-70 |
| | | 5/63 | England | Calcutta | 1972-73 |
| | | 6/226 | England | Lord's | 1974 |
| | | 5/82 | West Indies | Port-of-Spain | 1975-76 |
| | | 5/27 | New Zealand | Bombay[3] | 1976-77 |
| | | 5/48 | New Zealand | Madras[1] | 1976-77 |
| | | 5/110 | England | Calcutta | 1976-77 |
| | | 6/71 | England | Bangalore | 1976-77 |
| | | 5/55 | Australia | Brisbane[2] | 1977-78 |
| | | 5/89 ) | Australia | Perth | 1977-78 |
| | | 5/105) | | | |
| Binny,RMH | (2) | 5/40 | England | Lords | 1986 |
| | | 6/56 | Pakistan | Calcutta | 1986-87 |
| Borde,CG | | 5/88 | England | Madras[2] | 1963-64 |
| Chandrasekhar,BS | (16) | § 7/157 | West Indies | Bombay[2] | 1966-67 |
| | | 5/127 | England | Lord's | 1967 |
| | | 6/38 | England | The Oval | 1971 |
| | | 8/79 | England | Delhi | 1972-73 |
| | | 5/65 | England | Calcutta | 1972-73 |
| | | 6/90 | England | Madras[1] | 1972-73 |
| | | 5/135 | England | Bombay[2] | 1972-73 |
| | | 6/94 | New Zealand | Auckland | 1975-76 |
| | | 6/120 | West Indies | Port-of-Spain | 1975-76 |
| | | 5/153 | West Indies | Kingston | 1975-76 |
| | | 5/50 | England | Madras[1] | 1976-77 |
| | | 6/76 | England | Bangalore | 1976-77 |
| | | 6/52) | Australia | Melbourne | 1977-78 |
| | | 6/52) | | | |
| | | 5/136 | Australia | Adelaide | 1977-78 |
| | | 5/115 | West Indies | Bombay[3] | 1978-79 |
| Desai,RB | (2) | 5/89 | England | Lord's | 1959 |
| | | 6/56 | New Zealand | Bombay[2] | 1964-65 |
| Doshi,DR | (6) | †§ 6/103 | Australia | Madras[1] | 1979-80 |
| | | 5/43 | Australia | Bombay[3] | 1979-80 |
| | | § 5/39 | England | Bombay[3] | 1981-82 |
| | | 6/102 | England | Manchester | 1982 |
| | | § 5/85 | Sri Lanka | Madras[1] | 1982-83 |
| | | 5/90 | Pakistan | Lahore[2] | 1982-83 |
| Durani,SA | (3) | 5/47 | England | Calcutta | 1961-62 |
| | | 6/105 | England | Madras[2] | 1961-62 |
| | | 6/73 | Australia | Calcutta | 1964-65 |
| Ghavri,KD | (4) | 5/33 | England | Bombay[3] | 1976-77 |
| | | 5/51 | West Indies | Bangalore | 1978-79 |
| | | 5/52 | England | Bombay[3] | 1979-80 |
| | | 5/107 | Australia | Sydney | 1980-81 |
| Ghulam Ahmed | (4) | § 5/70 | England | Kanpur | 1951-52 |
| | | 5/100 | England | Leeds | 1952 |

| | | | | | |
|---|---|---|---|---|---|
| | | 5/109 | Pakistan | Dacca | 1954-55 |
| | | 7/49 | Australia | Calcutta | 1956-57 |
| Gupte,SP | (12) | § 7/162 | West Indies | Port-of-Spain | 1952-53 |
| | | 5/107 | West Indies | Port-of-Spain | 1952-53 |
| | | 5/180 | West Indies | Kingston | 1952-53 |
| | | 5/18 | Pakistan | Dacca | 1954-55 |
| | | 5/133 | Pakistan | Lahore[1] | 1954-55 |
| | | 5/63 | Pakistan | Peshawar[1] | 1954-55 |
| | | § 7/128 | New Zealand | Hyderabad | 1955-56 |
| | | 5/45 | New Zealand | Bombay[2] | 1955-56 |
| | | 6/90 | New Zealand | Calcutta | 1955-56 |
| | | 5/72 | New Zealand | Madras[2] | 1955-56 |
| | | 9/102 | West Indies | Kanpur | 1958-59 |
| | | 5/90 | England | Kanpur | 1961-62 |
| Hirwani,ND | (4) | †§ 8/61) | West Indies | Madras[1] | 1987-88 |
| | | 8/75) | | | |
| | | § 6/59 | New Zealand | Bangalore | 1988-89 |
| | | 6/59 | New Zealand | Cuttack | 1994-95 |
| Kapil Dev | (23) | § 5/146 | England | Birmingham | 1979 |
| | | 5/82 | Australia | Delhi | 1979-80 |
| | | 5/74 | Australia | Calcutta | 1979-80 |
| | | 5/58 | Pakistan | Delhi | 1979-80 |
| | | 6/63 | Pakistan | Kanpur | 1979-80 |
| | | 7/56 | Pakistan | Madras[1] | 1979-80 |
| | | 5/97 | Australia | Sydney | 1980-81 |
| | | 5/28 | Australia | Melbourne | 1980-81 |
| | | 5/70 | England | Bombay[3] | 1981-82 |
| | | 6/91 | England | Calcutta | 1981-82 |
| | | 5/125 | England | Lord's | 1982 |
| | | § 5/110 | Sri Lanka | Madras[1] | 1982-83 |
| | | 5/102 | Pakistan | Karachi[1] | 1982-83 |
| | | 7/220 | Pakistan | Faisalabad | 1982-83 |
| | | 8/85 | Pakistan | Lahore[2] | 1982-83 |
| | | 5/68 | Pakistan | Bangalore | 1983-84 |
| | | 6/77 | West Indies | Delhi | 1983-84 |
| | | 9/83 | West Indies | Ahmedabad | 1983-84 |
| | | 8/106 | Australia | Adelaide | 1985-86 |
| | | 5/58 | West Indies | Port-of-Spain | 1988-89 |
| | | 6/84 | West Indies | Kingston | 1988-89 |
| | | 5/97 | Australia | Melbourne | 1991-92 |
| | | 5/130 | Australia | Adelaide | 1991-92 |
| Kumar,VV | | †§ 5/64 | Pakistan | Delhi | 1960-61 |
| Kumble,AR | (11) | 6/53 | South Africa | Johannesburg[3] | 1992-93 |
| | | 6/64 | England | Madras[1] | 1992-93 |
| | | § 5/70 | Zimbabwe | Delhi | 1992-93 |
| | | 5/87 | Sri Lanka | Colombo (SSC) | 1993-94 |
| | | 7/59 | Sri Lanka | Lucknow[2] | 1993-94 |
| | | 5/81 | New Zealand | Bangalore | 1994-95 |
| | | § 5/67 | Australia | Delhi | 1996-97 |
| | | 5/120 | West Indies | Kingston | 1996-97 |
| | | 5/104 | West Indies | Port-of-Spain | 1996-97 |
| | | 5/62 | Australia | Calcuttta | 1997-98 |
| | | 6/98 | Australia | Bangalore | 1997-98 |
| Kuruvilla,A | | 5/68 | West Indies | Bridgetown | 1996-97 |
| Madan Lal,S | (4) | 5/134 | New Zealand | Christchurch | 1975-76 |
| | | § 5/72 | Australia | Brisbane[2] | 1977-78 |
| | | 5/23 | England | Bombay[3] | 1981-82 |
| | | 5/85 | England | Delhi | 1981-82 |
| Maninder Singh | (3) | 7/51 | Sri Lanka | Nagpur | 1986-87 |
| | | 5/135 | Pakistan | Madras[1] | 1986-87 |

| | | | | | |
|---|---|---|---|---|---|
| | | 7/27 | Pakistan | Bangalore | 1986-87 |
| Mankad,MH | (8) | 5/101 | England | Manchester | 1946 |
| | | 8/55 | England | Madras[1] | 1951-52 |
| | | 5/196 | England | Lord's | 1952 |
| | | § 8/52) | Pakistan | Delhi | 1952-53 |
| | | 5/79) | | | |
| | | 5/72 | Pakistan | Bombay[2] | 1952-53 |
| | | 5/228 | West Indies | Kingston | 1952-53 |
| | | 5/64 | Pakistan | Peshawar[1] | 1954-55 |
| Nadkarni,RG | (4) | 6/105 | Australia | Bombay[2] | 1959-60 |
| | | 5/31) | Australia | Madras[2] | 1964-65 |
| | | 6/91) | | | |
| | | 6/43 | New Zealand | Wellington | 1967-68 |
| Nissar, Mahomed | (3) | †§ 5/93 | England | Lord's | 1932 |
| | | 5/90 | England | Bombay[1] | 1933-34 |
| | | 5/120 | England | The Oval | 1936 |
| Patel,JM | (2) | 9/69) | Australia | Kanpur | 1959-60 |
| | | 5/55) | | | |
| Phadkar,DG | (3) | 7/159 | West Indies | Madras[1] | 1948-49 |
| | | 5/72 | Pakistan | Calcutta | 1952-53 |
| | | 5/64 | West Indies | Bridgetown | 1952-53 |
| Prabhakar,M | (3) | 5/104 | Pakistan | Karachi[1] | 1989-90 |
| | | 6/132 | Pakistan | Faisalabad | 1989-90 |
| | | 5/101 | Australia | Perth | 1991-92 |
| Prasanna,EAS | (10) | 6/141 | Australia | Melbourne | 1967-68 |
| | | 6/104 | Australia | Brisbane[2] | 1967-68 |
| | | § 6/94 | New Zealand | Dunedin | 1967-68 |
| | | 5/32 | New Zealand | Wellington | 1967-68 |
| | | 5/51 | New Zealand | Nagpur | 1969-70 |
| | | 5/121 | Australia | Bombay[2] | 1969-70 |
| | | 5/42 | Australia | Delhi | 1969-70 |
| | | 6/74 | Australia | Madras[1] | 1969-70 |
| | | 5/70 | West Indies | Madras[1] | 1974-75 |
| | | 8/76 | New Zealand | Auckland | 1975-76 |
| Ramchand,GS | | 6/49 | Pakistan | Karachi[1] | 1954-55 |
| Rangachari,CR | | § 5/107 | West Indies | Delhi | 1948-49 |
| Razdan,V | | 5/79 | Pakistan | Sialkot | 1989-90 |
| Sharma,C | (4) | 5/118 | Sri Lanka | Colombo (PSS) | 1985-86 |
| | | 5/64 | England | Lord's | 1986 |
| | | 6/58 | England | Birmingham | 1986 |
| | | § 5/55 | West Indies | Delhi | 1987-88 |
| Shastri,RJ | (2) | 5/125 | New Zealand | Auckland | 1980-81 |
| | | 5/75 | Pakistan | Nagpur | 1983-84 |
| Shinde,SG | | 6/91 | England | Delhi | 1951-52 |
| Shivaramakrishnan,L | (3) | § 6/64 ) | England | Bombay[3] | 1984-85 |
| | | 6/117) | | | |
| | | 6/99 | England | Delhi | 1984-85 |
| Srinath,J | (2) | 6/21 | South Africa | Ahmedabad | 1996-97 |
| | | 5/104 | South Africa | Johannesburg[3] | 1996-97 |
| Surendranath,R | (2) | 5/115 | England | Manchester | 1959 |
| | | 5/89 | England | The Oval | 1959 |
| Surti,RF | | § 5/74 | Australia | Adelaide | 1967-68 |
| Umrigar,PR | (2) | 6/78 | Pakistan | Bahawalpur | 1954-55 |
| | | 5/107 | West Indies | Port-of-Spain | 1961-62 |
| Venkatapathy Raju,SL | (5) | § 6/12 | Sri Lanka | Chandigarh | 1990-91 |
| | | 5/38) | Sri Lanka | Ahmedabad | 1993-94 |
| | | 6/87) | | | |
| | | § 5/60 | West Indies | Bombay[3] | 1994-95 |
| | | 5/127 | West Indies | Nagpur | 1994-95 |
| Venkatesh Prasad,BK | (5) | 5/76 | England | Lord's | 1996 |

| | | | | | |
|---|---|---|---|---|---|
| | | 6/104 | South Africa | Calcutta | 1996-97 |
| | | 5/60) | South Africa | Durban[2] | 1996-97 |
| | | 5/93) | | | |
| | | 5/82 | West Indies | Bridgetown | 1996-97 |
| Venkataraghavan,S | (3) | 8/72 | New Zealand | Delhi | 1964-65 |
| | | 6/74 | New Zealand | Hyderabad | 1969-70 |
| | | 5/95 | West Indies | Port-of-Spain | 1970-71 |
| Yadav,NS | (3) | § 5/131 | West Indies | Bombay[3] | 1983-84 |
| | | 5/99 | Australia | Sydney | 1985-86 |
| | | § 5/76 | Sri Lanka | Nagpur | 1986-87 |
| | | | | | |
| **PAKISTAN *(168)*** | | | Opponents | | |
| Aamer Nazir | | 5/46 | Zimbabwe | Harare | 1994-95 |
| Aaqib Javed | | 5/84 | Sri Lanka | Faisalabad | 1995-96 |
| Abdul Qadir | (15) | 6/44 | England | Hyderabad | 1977-78 |
| | | § 5/76 | Australia | Karachi[1] | 1982-83 |
| | | 7/142 | Australia | Lahore[2] | 1982-83 |
| | | 5/166 | Australia | Melbourne | 1983-84 |
| | | 5/74 | England | Karachi[1] | 1983-84 |
| | | 5/84 ) | England | Lahore[2] | 1983-84 |
| | | 5/110) | | | |
| | | 5/108 | New Zealand | Hyderabad | 1984-85 |
| | | 5/44 | Sri Lanka | Karachi[1] | 1985-86 |
| | | 6/16 | West Indies | Faisalabad | 1986-87 |
| | | 7/96 | England | The Oval | 1987 |
| | | 9/56 | England | Lahore[2] | 1987-88 |
| | | 5/88) | England | Karachi[1] | 1987-88 |
| | | 5/98) | | | |
| | | 6/160 | New Zealand | Auckland | 1988-89 |
| Arif Butt | | †§ 6/89 | Australia | Melbourne | 1964-65 |
| Asif Iqbal | (2) | § 5/48 | New Zealand | Wellington | 1964-65 |
| | | 5/52 | New Zealand | Auckland | 1964-65 |
| Asif Masood | | 5/111 | England | Birmingham | 1971 |
| Azeem Hafeez | (4) | § 5/100 | Australia | Perth | 1983-84 |
| | | 5/167 | Australia | Adelaide | 1983-84 |
| | | 6/46 | India | Lahore[2] | 1984-85 |
| | | 5/127 | New Zealand | Wellington | 1984-85 |
| D'Souza,A | | 5/112 | England | Karachi[1] | 1961-62 |
| Ehteshamuddin | | 5/47 | India | Kanpur | 1979-80 |
| Fazal Mahmood | (13) | 5/52) | India | Lucknow[1] | 1952-53 |
| | | 7/42) | | | |
| | | 6/53) | England | The Oval | 1954 |
| | | 6/46) | | | |
| | | 5/48 | India | Karachi[1] | 1954-55 |
| | | § 6/34) | Australia | Karachi[1] | 1956-57 |
| | | 7/80) | | | |
| | | 6/83 | West Indies | Port-of-Spain | 1957-58 |
| | | 6/34) | West Indies | Dacca | 1958-59 |
| | | 6/66) | | | |
| | | 5/71 | Australia | Dacca | 1959-60 |
| | | 5/74 | Australia | Karachi[1] | 1959-60 |
| | | 5/26 | India | Calcutta | 1960-61 |
| Haseeb Ahsan | (2) | 5/121 | India | Kanpur | 1960-61 |
| | | 6/202 | India | Madras[2] | 1960-61 |
| Imran Khan | (23) | 5/122 | Australia | Melbourne | 1976-77 |
| | | 6/102) | Australia | Sydney | 1976-77 |
| | | 6/63 ) | | | |
| | | 6/90 | West Indies | Kingston | 1976-77 |
| | | 5/106 | New Zealand | Napier | 1978-79 |
| | | 5/114 | India | Madras[1] | 1979-80 |

| | | | | | |
|---|---|---|---|---|---|
| | | 5/63 | India | Calcutta | 1979-80 |
| | | 5/62 | West Indies | Multan | 1980-81 |
| | | § 8/58) | Sri Lanka | Lahore[2] | 1981-82 |
| | | 6/58) | | | |
| | | 7/52 | England | Birmingham | 1982 |
| | | 5/49 | England | Leeds | 1982 |
| | | 8/60 | India | Karachi[1] | 1982-83 |
| | | 6/98) | India | Faisalabad | 1982-83 |
| | | 5/82) | | | |
| | | 6/35 | India | Hyderabad | 1982-83 |
| | | 5/40 | Sri Lanka | Sialkot | 1985-86 |
| | | 5/59 | West Indies | Lahore[2] | 1986-87 |
| | | 6/46 | West Indies | Karachi[1] | 1986-87 |
| | | 7/40 | England | Leeds | 1987 |
| | | 6/129 | England | Birmingham | 1987 |
| | | 7/80 | West Indies | Georgetown | 1987-88 |
| | | 5/115 | West Indies | Port-of-Spain | 1987-88 |
| Intikhab Alam | (5) | 5/91) | New Zealand | Dacca | 1969-70 |
| | | 5/91) | | | |
| | | 7/52 | New Zealand | Dunedin | 1972-73 |
| | | 6/127 | New Zealand | Auckland | 1972-73 |
| | | 5/116 | England | The Oval | 1974 |
| Iqbal Qasim | (8) | 6/40 | India | Bombay[3] | 1979-80 |
| | | 7/49 | Australia | Karachi[1] | 1979-80 |
| | | 6/89 | West Indies | Faisalabad | 1980-81 |
| | | 6/141 | Sri Lanka | Faisalabad | 1981-82 |
| | | 5/78 | New Zealand | Hyderabad | 1984-85 |
| | | 5/48 | India | Bangalore | 1986-87 |
| | | 5/83 | England | Faisalabad | 1987-88 |
| | | 5/35 | Australia | Karachi[1] | 1988-89 |
| Khan Mohammad | (4) | § 5/61 | England | Lord's | 1954 |
| | | 5/74 | India | Bahawalpur | 1954-55 |
| | | 5/73 | India | Karachi[1] | 1954-55 |
| | | 6/21 | New Zealand | Dacca | 1955-56 |
| Mahmood Hussain | (2) | 6/67 | India | Dacca | 1954-55 |
| | | 5/129 | India | Bombay[2] | 1960-61 |
| Mohammad Nazir | (3) | †§ 7/99 | New Zealand | Karachi[1] | 1969-70 |
| | | 5/44 | West Indies | Faisalabad | 1980-81 |
| | | 5/72 | India | Nagpur | 1983-84 |
| Mohammad Zahid | | †§ 7/66 | New Zealand | Rawalpindi[2] | 1996-97 |
| Mudassar Nazar | | 6/32 | England | Lord's | 1982 |
| Munir Malik | | § 5/128 | England | Leeds | 1962 |
| Mushtaq Ahmed | (10) | 5/115 | Australia | Hobart | 1995-96 |
| | | 5/95 | Australia | Sydney | 1995-96 |
| | | § 7/56 | New Zealand | Christchurch | 1995-96 |
| | | 5/57 | England | Lord's | 1996-97 |
| | | 6/78 | England | The Oval | 1996-97 |
| | | 6/84 | New Zealand | Lahore[2] | 1996-97 |
| | | 6/87 | New Zealand | Rawalpindi[2] | 1996-97 |
| | | 5/35) | West Indies | Peshawar[2] | 1997-98 |
| | | 5/71) | | | |
| | | 6/78 | South Africa | Durban[2] | 1997-98 |
| Mushtaq Mohammad | (3) | 5/49 | New Zealand | Dunedin | 1972-73 |
| | | 5/28 | West Indies | Port-of-Spain | 1976-77 |
| | | 5/59 | New Zealand | Christchurch | 1978-79 |
| Nasim-ul-Ghani | (2) | 5/116 | West Indies | Georgetown | 1957-58 |
| | | 6/67 | West Indies | Port-of-Spain | 1957-58 |
| Pervez Sajjad | (3) | 5/42 | New Zealand | Auckland | 1964-65 |
| | | 5/33 | New Zealand | Karachi[1] | 1969-70 |
| | | 7/74 | New Zealand | Lahore[2] | 1969-70 |

| | | | | | |
|---|---|---|---|---|---|
| Saleem Jaffer | | § 5/40 | New Zealand | Wellington | 1988-89 |
| Saqlain Mushtaq | (3) | 5/89 | Sri Lanka | Colombo (PIS) | 1996-97 |
| | | § 5/129 | South Africa | Rawalpindi[2] | 1997-98 |
| | | § 5/54 | West Indies | Karachi[1] | 1997-98 |
| Sarfraz Nawaz | (4) | § 6/89 | West Indies | Lahore[2] | 1974-75 |
| | | 5/39 | England | Leeds | 1978 |
| | | 5/70 | India | Karachi[1] | 1978-79 |
| | | 9/86 | Australia | Melbourne | 1978-79 |
| Shahid Nazir | | § 5/53 | Zimbabwe | Sheikhupura | 1996-97 |
| Shoaib Akhtar | | 5/43 | South Africa | Durban[2] | 1997-98 |
| Sikander Bakht | (3) | 8/69 | India | Delhi | 1979-80 |
| | | 5/55 | India | Bombay[3] | 1979-80 |
| | | 5/56 | India | Kanpur | 1979-80 |
| Tahir Naqqash | (2) | § 5/40 | England | Birmingham | 1982 |
| | | 5/76 | India | Bangalore | 1983-84 |
| Tauseef Ahmed | (3) | 5/54 | Sri Lanka | Karachi[1] | 1985-86 |
| | | 6/45 | Sri Lanka | Kandy | 1985-86 |
| | | 5/54 | India | Bangalore | 1986-87 |
| Waqar Younis | (21) | 7/86 | New Zealand | Lahore[2] | 1990-91 |
| | | 7/76) | New Zealand | Faisalabad | 1990-91 |
| | | 5/54) | | | |
| | | 5/76 | West Indies | Karachi[1] | 1990-91 |
| | | 5/46 | West Indies | Faisalabad | 1990-91 |
| | | 5/84 | Sri Lanka | Sialkot | 1991-92 |
| | | 5/65 | Sri Lanka | Faisalabad | 1991-92 |
| | | 5/91 | England | Lord's | 1992 |
| | | 5/113 | England | Leeds | 1992 |
| | | 5/52 | England | The Oval | 1992 |
| | | 5/22 | New Zealand | Hamilton | 1992-93 |
| | | 5/104 | West indies | Bridgetown | 1992-93 |
| | | § 7/91) | Zimbabwe | Karachi[2] | 1993-94 |
| | | 6/44) | | | |
| | | 5/88 | Zimbabwe | Rawalpindi[2] | 1993-94 |
| | | 5/100 | Zimbabwe | Lahore[2] | 1993-94 |
| | | 6/78 | New Zealand | Christchurch | 1993-94 |
| | | 6/34) | Sri Lanka | Kandy | 1994-95 |
| | | 5/85) | | | |
| | | 6/78 | South Africa | Port Elizabeth | 1997-98 |
| | | 5/106 | Zimbabwe | Bulawayo[2] | 1997-98 |
| Wasim Akram | (21) | 5/56) | New Zealand | Dunedin | 1984-85 |
| | | 5/72) | | | |
| | | § 6/91 | West Indies | Faisalabad | 1986-87 |
| | | 5/96 | India | Calcutta | 1986-87 |
| | | 5/101 | India | Sialkot | 1989-90 |
| | | § 6/62) | Australia | Melbourne | 1989-90 |
| | | 5/98) | | | |
| | | 5/100 | Australia | Adelaide | 1989-90 |
| | | 5/28 | West Indies | Lahore[2] | 1990-91 |
| | | 5/128 | England | Manchester | 1992 |
| | | 6/67 | England | The Oval | 1992 |
| | | 5/45 | New Zealand | Hamilton | 1992-93 |
| | | § 5/65 | Zimbabwe | Rawalpindi[2] | 1993-94 |
| | | 6/43 | New Zealand | Auckland | 1993-94 |
| | | 7/119 | New Zealand | Wellington | 1993-94 |
| | | 5/43 | Sri Lanka | Colombo (PSS) | 1994-95 |
| | | 5/64 | Australia | Karachi[1] | 1994-95 |
| | | 5/43 | Zimbabwe | Bulawayo[2] | 1994-95 |
| | | 5/55 | Sri Lanka | Peshawar[2] | 1995-96 |
| | | 5/53 | New Zealand | Christchurch | 1995-96 |
| | | 6/48 | Zimbabwe | Faisalabad | 1996-97 |

| | | | | | |
|---|---|---|---|---|---|
| Zulfiqar Ahmed | (2) | § 5/37) | New Zealand | Karachi[1] | 1955-56 |
| | | 6/42) | | | |
| **SRI LANKA *(47)*** | | | Opponents | | |
| Ahangama,FS | | 5/52 | India | Kandy | 1985-86 |
| Bandaratilake,MLCN | | 5/36 | New Zealand | Galle | 1997-98 |
| de Mel,ALF | (4) | § 5/68 | India | Madras[1] | 1982-83 |
| | | 5/64 | India | Colombo (SSC) | 1985-86 |
| | | 6/109 | Pakistan | Karachi[1] | 1985-86 |
| | | 5/64 | India | Colombo (SSC) | 1985-86 |
| de Silva,DS | | 5/59 | Pakistan | Faisalabad | 1981-82 |
| de Silva,KSC | | § 5/85 | Pakistan | Colombo (SSC) | 1996-97 |
| Dharmasena,HDPK | (3) | § 6/99 | Pakistan | Colombo (PSS) | 1994-95 |
| | | 5/57 | India | Mumbai[3] | 1997-98 |
| | | 6/72 | New Zealand | Galle | 1997-98 |
| John,VB | (2) | 5/60 | New Zealand | Wellington | 1982-83 |
| | | 5/86 | New Zealand | Kandy | 1983-84 |
| Kuruppuarachchi,AK | | †§ 5/44 | Pakistan | Colombo (CCC) | 1985-86 |
| Labrooy,GF | | 5/133 | Australia | Brisbane[2] | 1989-90 |
| Muralidaran,M | (14) | § 5/104 | South Africa | Moratuwa | 1993-94 |
| | | 5/101 | South Africa | Colombo (SSC) | 1993-94 |
| | | 5/162 | India | Lucknow[2] | 1993-94 |
| | | 5/64 | New Zealand | Napier | 1994-95 |
| | | 5/68 | Pakistan | Faisalabad | 1995-96 |
| | | 5/33 | Zimbabwe | Faisalabad | 1996-97 |
| | | 6/98 | Pakistan | Colombo (PIS) | 1996-97 |
| | | 5/34 | West Indies | St John's | 1996-97 |
| | | 5/113 | West Indies | Kingstown | 1996-97 |
| | | 5/23) | Zimbabwe | Kandy | 1997-98 |
| | | 7/94) | | | |
| | | 5/63 | South Africa | Centurion | 1997-98 |
| | | 5/90 | New Zealand | Colombo (PIS) | 1997-98 |
| | | 5/30 | New Zealand | Colombo (SSC) | 1997-98 |
| Pushpakumara,KR | (3) | 7/116 | Zimbabwe | Harare | 1994-95 |
| | | 5/41 | West Indies | Kingstown | 1996-97 |
| | | 5/122 | India | Nagpur | 1997-98 |
| Ramanayake,CPH | | 5/82 | Australia | Moratuwa | 1992-93 |
| Ratnayake,RJ | (5) | § 6/85 | India | Colombo (SSC) | 1985-86 |
| | | 5/49 | India | Colombo (PSS) | 1985-86 |
| | | 6/66 | Australia | Hobart | 1989-90 |
| | | 5/77 | New Zealand | Hamilton | 1990-91 |
| | | § 5/69 | England | Lord's | 1991 |
| Ratnayeke,JR | (4) | 5/42 | New Zealand | Colombo (SSC) | 1983-84 |
| | | 8/83 | Pakistan | Sialkot | 1985-86 |
| | | 5/37 | Pakistan | Colombo (CCC) | 1985-86 |
| | | 5/85 | India | Cuttack | 1986-87 |
| Vaas,WPUJC | (4) | 5/47) | New Zealand | Napier | 1994-95 |
| | | 5/43) | | | |
| | | 6/87 | New Zealand | Dunedin | 1994-95 |
| | | 5/99 | Pakistan | Peshawar[2] | 1995-96 |
| Wickramasinghe,GP | | 5/73 | Pakistan | Faisalabad | 1991-92 |
| **ZIMBABWE *(11)*** | | | Opponents | | |
| Brain,DH | | 5/42 | Pakistan | Lahore[2] | 1993-94 |
| Huckle,AG | (2) | 6/111) | New Zealand | Bulawayo[2] | 1997-98 |
| | | 5/146) | | | |
| Strang,BC | | § 5/101 | South Africa | Harare | 1995-96 |
| Strang,PA | (3) | 5/106 | Sri Lanka | Colombo (SSC) | 1996-97 |
| | | 5/212 | Pakistan | Sheikhupura | 1996-97 |
| | | 5/123 | England | Bulawayo[2] | 1996-97 |

| | | | | | |
|---|---|---|---|---|---|
| Streak,HH | (3) | 5/56 | Pakistan | Rawalpindi[2] | 1993-94 |
| | | 6/90 | Pakistan | Harare | 1994-95 |
| | | 5/70 | Pakistan | Bulawayo[2] | 1994-95 |
| Traicos,AJ # | | †§ 5/85 | India | Harare | 1992-93 |

## FOUR WICKETS IN FIVE BALLS

| | | | | | |
|---|---|---|---|---|---|
| M.J.C.Allom | England | v | New Zealand | Christchurch | 1929-30 |

*In his first Test - in his eighth over (WOWWW).*

| | | | | | |
|---|---|---|---|---|---|
| C.M.Old | England | v | Pakistan | Birmingham | 1978 |

*In the same over (WWOWW) his third ball was a no ball.*

| | | | | | |
|---|---|---|---|---|---|
| Wasim Akram | Pakistan | v | West Indies | Lahore[2] | 1990-91 |

*In the same over (WW1WW) - a catch was dropped from the third ball.*

## HAT-TRICKS IN TEST MATCHES *(§ In first Test. # On final Test appearance. ¶ Over both innings.)*

| | | | | | |
|---|---|---|---|---|---|
| F.R.Spofforth | Australia | v | England | Melbourne | 1878-79 |
| W.Bates | England | v | Australia | Melbourne | 1882-83 |
| J.Briggs | England | v | Australia | Sydney | 1891-92 |
| G.A.Lohmann | England | v | South Africa | Port Elizabeth | 1895-96 |
| J.T.Hearne | England | v | Australia | Leeds | 1899 |
| H.Trumble | Australia | v | England | Melbourne | 1901-02 |
| H.Trumble # | Australia | v | England | Melbourne | 1903-04 |
| T.J.Matthews (2) | Australia | v | South Africa | Manchester | 1912 |
| M.J.C.Allom § | England | v | New Zealand | Christchurch | 1929-30 |
| T.W.J.Goddard | England | v | South Africa | Johannesburg[1] | 1938-39 |
| P.J.Loader | England | v | West Indies | Leeds | 1957 |
| L.F.Kline | Australia | v | South Africa | Cape Town | 1957-58 |
| W.W.Hall | West Indies | v | Pakistan | Lahore[1] | 1958-59 |
| G.M.Griffin # | South Africa | v | England | Lord's | 1960 |
| L.R.Gibbs | West Indies | v | Australia | Adelaide | 1960-61 |
| P.J.Petherick § | New Zealand | v | Pakistan | Lahore[2] | 1976-77 |
| C.A.Walsh ¶ | West Indies | v | Australia | Brisbane[2] | 1988-89 |
| M.G.Hughes ¶ | Australia | v | West Indies | Perth | 1988-89 |
| D.W.Fleming § | Australia | v | Pakistan | Rawalpindi[2] | 1994-95 |
| S.K.Warne | Australia | v | England | Melbourne | 1994-95 |
| D.G.Cork | England | v | West Indies | Lord's | 1995 |

*Matthews did the hat-trick in each innings on the second afternoon of the match.*

## THREE WICKETS IN FOUR BALLS

| | | | | | |
|---|---|---|---|---|---|
| F.R.Spofforth | Australia | v | England | The Oval | 1882 |
| F.R.Spofforth | Australia | v | England | Sydney | 1884-85 |
| J.Briggs | England | v | South Africa | Cape Town | 1888-89 |
| W.P.Howell | Australia | v | South Africa | Cape Town | 1902-03 |
| E.P.Nupen | South Africa | v | England | Johannesburg[1] | 1930-31 |
| W J.O'Reilly | Australia | v | England | Manchester | 1934 |
| W.Voce | England | v | Australia | Sydney | 1936-37 |
| R.R.Lindwall | Australia | v | England | Adelaide | 1946-47 |
| K.Cranston | England | v | South Africa | Leeds | 1947 |
| C.N.McCarthy | South Africa | v | England | Durban[2] | 1948-49 |
| R.Appleyard | England | v | New Zealand | Auckland | 1954-55 |
| R.Benaud | Australia | v | West Indies | Georgetown | 1954-55 |
| Fazal Mahmood | Pakistan | v | Australia | Karachi[1] | 1956-57 |
| J.W.Martin | Australia | v | West Indies | Melbourne | 1960-61 |
| L.R.Gibbs | West Indies | v | Australia | Sydney | 1960-61 |
| K.D.Mackay | Australia | v | England | Birmingham | 1961 |
| W.W.Hall | West Indies | v | India | Port-of-Spain | 1961-62 |
| D.Shackleton | England | v | West Indies | Lord's | 1963 |
| G.D.McKenzie | Australia | v | West Indies | Port-of-Spain | 1964-65 |
| F.J.Titmus | England | v | New Zealand | Leeds | 1965 |
| P.Lever | England | v | Pakistan | Leeds | 1971 |
| D.K.Lillee | Australia | v | England | Manchester | 1972 |

| | | | | | |
|---|---|---|---|---|---|
| D.K.Lillee | Australia | v | England | The Oval | 1972 |
| C.M.Old | England | v | Pakistan | Birmingham | 1978 |
| S.T.Clarke | West Indies | v | Pakistan | Karachi[1] | 1980-81 |
| R..Hadlee | New Zealand | v | Australia | Melbourne | 1980-81 |
| R..Shastri | India | v | New Zealand | Wellington | 1980-81 |
| I.T.Botham | England | v | Australia | Leeds | 1985 |
| Kapil Dev | India | v | Australia | Adelaide | 1985-86 |
| C.G.Rackemann | Australia | v | Pakistan | Adelaide | 1989-90 |
| D.E.Malcolm | England | v | West Indies | Port-of-Spain | 1989-90 |
| Wasim Akram | Pakistan | v | West Indies | Lahore[2] | 1990-91 |
| A.R.Border | Australia | v | West Indies | Georgetown | 1990-91 |
| Wasim Akram | Pakistan | v | England | Lord's | 1992 |
| S.K.Warne | Australia | v | England | Brisbane[2] | 1994-95 |
| P.A.Strang | Zimbabwe | v | Sri Lanka | Colombo (PIS) | 1996-97 |

*K.Cranston, F.J.Titmus, C.M.Old and Wasim Akram each took four wickets in an over.*

## BOWLERS UNCHANGED IN A COMPLETED INNINGS

| AUSTRALIA | | Opponents | | |
|---|---|---|---|---|
| G.E.Palmer (7-68) | E.Evans (3-64) | England (133) | Sydney | 1881-82 |
| F.R.Spofforth (5-30) | G.E.Palmer (4-32) | England (77) | Sydney | 1884-85 |
| C.T.B.Turner (6-15) | J.J.Ferris (4-27) | England (45) | Sydney | 1886-87 |
| C.T.B.Turner (5-36) | J.J.Ferris (5-26) | England (62) | Lord's | 1888 |
| G.Giffen (5-26) | C.T.B.Turner (4-33) | England (72) | Sydney | 1894-95 |
| H.Trumble (3-38) | M.A.Noble (7-17) | England (61) | Melbourne | 1901-02 |
| M.A.Noble (5-54) | J.V.Saunders (5-43) | England (99) | Sydney | 1901-02 |

| ENGLAND | | Opponents | | |
|---|---|---|---|---|
| F.Morley (2-34) | R.G.Barlow (7-40) | Australia (83) | Sydney | 1882-83 |
| G.A.Lohmann (7-36) | J.Briggs(3-28) | Australia (68) | The Oval | 1886 |
| G.A.Lohmann (5-17) | R.Peel (5-18) | Australia (42) | Sydney | 1887-88 |
| J.Briggs (8-11) | A.J.Fothergill (1-30) | South Africa (43) | Cape Town | 1888-89 |
| J.J.Ferris (7-37) | F.Martin (2-39) | South Africa (83) | Cape Town | 1891-92 |
| J.Briggs (6-49) | G.A.Lohmann (3-46) | Australia (100) | Adelaide | 1891-92 |
| T.Richardson (6-39) | G.A.Lohmann (3-13) | Australia (53) | Lord's | 1896 |
| S.Haigh (6-11) | A.E.Trott (4-19) | South Africa (35) | Cape Town | 1898-99 |
| S.F.Barnes (6-42) | C.Blythe (4-64) | Australia (112) | Melbourne | 1901-02 |
| G.H.Hirst (4-28) | C.Blythe (6-44) | Australia (74) | Birmingham | 1909 |
| F.R.Foster (5-16) | S.F.Barnes (5-25) | South Africa (58) | Lord's | 1912 |
| A.E.R.Gilligan (6-7) | M.W.Tate (4-12) | South Africa (30) | Birmingham | 1924 |
| G.O.B.Allen (5-36) | W.Voce (4-16) | Australia (58) | Brisbane[2] | 1936-37 |

| PAKISTAN | | Opponents | | |
|---|---|---|---|---|
| Fazal Mahmood (6-34) | Khan Mohammad (4-43) | Australia (80) | Karachi[1] | 1956-57 |
| Wasim Akram (4-32) | Waqar Younis (6-34) | Sri Lanka (71) | Kandy | 1994-95 |

| WEST INDIES | | Opponents | | |
|---|---|---|---|---|
| C.E.L.Ambrose (6-24) | C.A.Walsh (3-16) | England (46) | Port-of-Spain | 1993-94 |

## MOST LBWS IN AN INNINGS BY ONE BOWLER

| | | | | | |
|---|---|---|---|---|---|
| *FIVE* | | | | | |
| T.M.Alderman | Australia | v | Pakistan | Melbourne | 1989-90 |
| C.E.L.Ambrose | West Indies | v | England | Bridgetown | 1989-90 |
| Mohammad Zahid | Pakistan | v | New Zealand | Rawalpindi[2] | 1996-97 |
| *FOUR* | | | | | |
| P.S.Heine | South Africa | v | England | Leeds | 1955 |
| G.A.R.Lock | England | v | New Zealand | Leeds | 1958 |
| Abdul Qadir | Pakistan | v | England | Karachi[1] | 1977-78 |
| Kapil Dev | India | v | Australia | Kanpur | 1979-80 |
| R.J.Hadlee | New Zealand | v | West Indies | Dunedin | 1979-80 |
| L.S.Pascoe | Australia | v | England | Lord's | 1980 |

| | | | | | |
|---|---|---|---|---|---|
| R.M.Ellison | England | v | West Indies | Kingston | 1985-86 |
| Abdul Qadir | Pakistan | v | England | Faisalabad | 1987-88 |
| N.D.Hirwani | India | v | New Zealand | Bangalore | 1988-89 |
| T.M.Alderman | Australia | v | England | Leeds | 1989 |
| T.M.Alderman | Australia | v | England | Lord's | 1989 |
| G.P.Wickramasinghe | Sri Lanka | v | Pakistan | Faisalabad | 1991-92 |
| Waqar Younis | Pakistan | v | Zimbabwe | Karachi[2] | 1993-94 |
| Shahid Nazir | Pakistan | v | Zimbabwe | Sheikhupura | 1996-97 |
| Wasim Akram | Pakistan | v | West Indies | Peshawar[2] | 1997-98 |
| D.Gough | England | v | South Africa | Leeds | 1998 |

## MOST LBWS IN A MATCH BY ONE BOWLER

| | | | | | |
|---|---|---|---|---|---|
| *EIGHT* | | | | | |
| Mohammad Zahid | Pakistan | v | New Zealand | Rawalpindi[2] | 1996-97 |
| *SEVEN* | | | | | |
| R.J.Hadlee | New Zealand | v | West Indies | Dunedin | 1979-80 |
| Abdul Qadir | Pakistan | v | England | Faisalabad | 1987-88 |
| Waqar Younis | Pakistan | v | Zimbabwe | Karachi[2] | 1993-94 |
| *SIX* | | | | | |
| Imran Khan | Pakistan | v | India | Faisalabad | 1982-83 |
| T.M.Alderman | Australia | v | Pakistan | Melbourne | 1989-90 |
| C.E.L.Ambrose | West Indies | v | England | Bridgetown | 1989-90 |
| Waqar Younis | Pakistan | v | West Indies | St John's | 1992-93 |
| *FIVE* | | | | | |
| Fazal Mahmood | Pakistan | v | India | Lucknow[1] | 1952-53 |
| Kapil Dev | India | v | Australia | Kanpur | 1979-80 |
| N.D.Hirwani | India | v | New Zealand | Bangalore | 1988-89 |
| T.M.Alderman | Australia | v | England | Leeds | 1989 |
| T.M.Alderman | Australia | v | England | Lord's | 1989 |
| Wasim Akram | Pakistan | v | West Indies | Lahore[2] | 1990-91 |
| G.P.Wickramasinghe | Sri Lanka | v | Pakistan | Faisalabad | 1991-92 |
| C.C.Lewis | England | v | New Zealand | Auckland | 1991-92 |
| Mushtaq Ahmed | Pakistan | v | New Zealand | Lahore[2] | 1996-97 |

## BOWLERS WITH 100 OR MORE WICKETS AGAINST A COUNTRY

| Player | Country | Opponent | M | Balls | Mdns | Runs | Wkts | Avge | 5w | 10w | Best |
|---|---|---|---|---|---|---|---|---|---|---|---|
| Lillee,DK | Aust | England | 29 | 8516 | 361 | 3507 | 167 | 21.00 | 11 | 4 | 7/89 |
| Botham,IT | Eng | Australia | 36 | 8479 | 297 | 4093 | 148 | 27.65 | 9 | 2 | 6/78 |
| Ambrose,CEL | WI | England | 29 | 7197 | 317 | 2765 | 147 | 18.80 | 8 | 2 | 8/45 |
| Trumble,H | Aust | England | 31 | 7895 | 448 | 2945 | 141 | 20.88 | 9 | 3 | 8/65 |
| Hadlee,RJ | NZ | Australia | 23 | 6099 | 213 | 2674 | 130 | 20.56 | 14 | 3 | 9/52 |
| Willis,RDG | Eng | Australia | 35 | 7294 | 199 | 3346 | 128 | 26.14 | 7 | 0 | 8/43 |
| Malcolm,MD | WI | England | 26 | 5790 | 136 | 2436 | 127 | 19.18 | 6 | 1 | 7/22 |
| Noble,MA | Aust | England | 39 | 6845 | 353 | 2860 | 115 | 24.86 | 9 | 2 | 7/17 |
| Lindwall,RR | Aust | England | 29 | 6728 | 216 | 2559 | 114 | 22.44 | 6 | 0 | 7/63 |
| Walsh,CA | WI | England | 31 | 7496 | 268 | 3247 | 111 | 29.25 | 3 | 0 | 5/45 |
| Rhodes,W | Eng | Australia | 41 | 5796 | 334 | 2616 | 109 | 24.00 | 6 | 1 | 8/68 |
| Ambrose,CEL | WI | Australia | 23 | 5590 | 218 | 2294 | 109 | 21.04 | 7 | 1 | 7/25 |
| Grimmett,CV | Aust | England | 22 | 9164 | 427 | 3439 | 106 | 32.44 | 11 | 2 | 6/37 |
| Barnes,SF | Eng | Australia | 20 | 5749 | 262 | 2288 | 106 | 21.58 | 12 | 1 | 7/60 |
| Underwood,DL | Eng | Australia | 29 | 8000 | 407 | 2770 | 105 | 26.38 | 4 | 2 | 7/50 |
| Bedser,AV | Eng | Australia | 21 | 7065 | 209 | 2859 | 104 | 27.49 | 7 | 2 | 7/44 |
| Giffen,G | Aust | England | 31 | 6325 | 434 | 2791 | 103 | 27.09 | 7 | 1 | 7/117 |
| Gibbs,LR | WI | Australia | 24 | 9358 | 361 | 3222 | 103 | 31.28 | 6 | 0 | 6/29 |
| O'Reilly,WJ | Aust | England | 19 | 7864 | 441 | 2587 | 102 | 25.36 | 8 | 3 | 7/54 |
| Sobers,GS | WI | England | 36 | 8771 | 444 | 3323 | 102 | 32.57 | 3 | 0 | 5/41 |
| Peel,R | Eng | Australia | 20 | 5216 | 411 | 1715 | 101 | 16.98 | 6 | 2 | 7/31 |
| Turner,CTB | Aust | England | 17 | 5179 | 447 | 1670 | 101 | 16.53 | 11 | 2 | 7/43 |
| Alderman,TM | Aust | England | 17 | 4717 | 189 | 2117 | 100 | 21.17 | 11 | 1 | 6/47 |
| Thomson,JR | Aust | England | 21 | 4951 | 166 | 2418 | 100 | 24.18 | 5 | 0 | 6/46 |
| Gibbs,LR | WI | England | 26 | 8841 | 496 | 2889 | 100 | 28.89 | 7 | 2 | 6/39 |

## FOUR OR MORE BOWLERS CONCEDING 100 RUNS IN AN INNINGS

*FIVE BOWLERS*

Australia (8d-758) v West Indies Kingston 1954-55
(D.T.Dewdney 1/115; F.M.King 2/126; D.S.Atkinson 1/132; O.G.Smith 2/145; F.M.M.Worrell 1/116 - nb G.S.Sobers 1/99 in the same innings)

West Indies (8d-652) v England Lord's 1973
(G.G.Arnold 0/111; R.G.D.Willis 4/118; A.W.Greig 3/180; D.L.Underwood 0/105; R.Illingworth 1/114)

Australia (6d-607) v New Zealand Brisbane[2] 1993-94
(D.K.Morrison 0/104; C.L.Cairns 1/128; S.B.Doull 2/105; R.P.de Groen 1/120; D.N.Patel 1/125)

*FOUR BOWLERS*

England (849) v West Indies Kingston 1929-30
(H.C.Griffith 2/555; G.Gladstone 1/139; O.C.Scott 5/266; F.R.Martin 1/128)

Australia (6d-729) v England Lord's 1930
(G.O.B.Allen 0/115; M.W.Tate 1/148; J.C.White 1/172; R.W.V.Robins 1/172)

Australia (554) v South Africa Melbourne 1931-32
(A.J.Bell 1/101; N.A.Quinn 1/113; C.L.Vincent 4/154; Q.McMillan 4/150)

England (524) v Australia Sydney 1932-33
(T.W.Wall 3/104; L.E.Nagel 2/110; W.J.O'Reilly 3/117; C.V.Grimmett 1/118)

Australia (701) v England The Oval 1934
(W.E.Bowes 4/164; G.O.B.Allen 4/170; E.W.Clark 2/110; H.Verity 0/123)

England (8d-658) v Australia Nottingham 1938
(E.L.McCormick 1/108; W.J.O'Reilly 3/164; L.O.Flrrtwood-Smith 4/153; F.A.Ward 0/142)

England (5-654) v South Africa Durban[2] 1938-39
(A.B.C.Langton 1/132; N.Gordon 1/174; B.Mitchell 1/133; E.L.Dalton 2/100)

Australia (674) v India Adelaide 1947-48
(C.R.Rangachari 4/141; M.H.Mankad 2/170; C.T.Sarwate 0/121; V.S.Hazare 0/110)

Australia (7d-549) v South Africa Port Elizabeth 1949-50
(C.N.McCarthy 0/121; M.G.Melle 2/132; H.J.Tayfield 2/103; N.B.F.Mann 2/154)

Australia (530) v South Africa Adelaide 1952-53
(M.G.Melle 1/105; E.R.H.Fuller 2/119; H.J.Tayfield 4/142; P.N.F.Mansell 2/113)

West Indies (8d-681) v England Port-of-Spain 1953-54
(F.S.Trueman 1/131; T.E.Bailey 0/104; J.C.Laker 2/154; G.A.R.Lock 2/178)

England (6d-558) v Pakistan Nottingham 1954
(Fazal Mahmood 0/148; Khan Mohammad 3/155; A.H.Kardar 1/110; Khalid Wazir 2/116)

Australia (8d-601) v England Brisbane[2] 1954-55
(A.V.Bedser 1/131; J.B.Statham 2/123; F.H.Tyson 1/160; T.E.Bailey 3/140)

England (5d-544) v Pakistan Birmingham 1962
(Mahmood Hussain 2/130; A.D'Souza 1/161; Intikhab Alam 2/117; Nasim-ul-Ghani 0/109)

South Africa (595) v Australia Adelaide 1963-64
(R.A.Gaunt 2/115; G.D.McKenzie 1/135; N.J.N.Hawke 3/139; R.Benaud 0/101)

Australia (8d-656) v England Manchester 1964
(J.S.E.Price 3/183; T.W.Cartwright 2/118; F.J.Titmus 0/100; J.B.Mortimore 0/122)

Australia (6d-650) v West Indies Bridgetown 1964-65
(W.W.Hall 2/117; C.C.Griffith 0/131; G.S.Sobers 1/143; L.R.Gibbs 2/168)

Australia (516) v England Adelaide 1965-66
(I.J.Jones 6/118; D.J.Brown 1/109; F.J.Titmus 3/116; D.A.Allen 0/103)

Australia (547) v West Indies Sydney 1968-69
(W.W.Hall 3/113; R.M.Edwards 2/139; G.S.Sobers 0/109; L.R.Gibbs 2/124)

New Zealand (9d-551) v England Lord's 1973
(J.A.Snow 3/109; G.G.Arnold 1/108; C.M.Old 5/113; N.Gifford 0/107)

Australia (6d-511) v New Zealand Wellington 1973-74
(M.G.Webb 2/114; R.O.Collinge 1/103; D.R.Hadlee 2/107; H.J.Howarth 0/113)

Pakistan (7d-600) v England The Oval 1974
(G.G.Arnold 1/106; R.G.D.Willis 2/102; C.M.Old 0/143; D.L.Underwood 2/106)

West Indies (585) v Australia Perth 1975-76
(D.K.Lillee 2/123; J.R.Thomson 3/128; G.J.Gilmour 2/103; A.A.Mallett 0/103)

Pakistan (9d-565) v New Zealand Karachi[1] 1976-77
(R.O.Collinge 2/141; R.J.Hadlee 4/138; B.L.Cairns 1/142; D.R.O'Sullivan 2/131)

India (7d-644) v West Indies Kanpur 1978-79
(M.D.Marshall 1/123; V.A.Holder 0/118; R.R.Jumadeen 3/137; D.R.Parry 2/127)

England (5d-633) v India Birmingham 1979
(Kapil Dev 5/146; K.D.Ghavri 0/129; B.S.Chandrasekhar 0/113; S.Venkataraghavan 0/107)

Australia (528) v India Adelaide 1980-81
(Kapil Dev 2/112; K.D.Ghavri 0/106; D.R.Doshi 3/146; N.S.Yadav 4/143)

Pakistan (7d-500) v Sri Lanka Lahore[2] 1981-82
(A.L.F.de Mel 3/120; J.R.Ratnayeke 3/121; D.S.de Silva 1/129; R.G.C.E.Wijesuriya 0/105)

Pakistan (652) v India Faisalabad 1982-83
(Kapil Dev 7/220; S.Madan Lal 2/109; D.R.Doshi 0/130; Maninder Singh 1/103)

Pakistan (3d-581) v India Hyderabad 1982-83
(Kapil Dev 0/111; B.S.Sandhu 2/107; Maninder Singh 0/135; D.R.Doshi 1/143)

Pakistan (624) v Australia Adelaide 1983-84
(G.F.Lawson 2/127; R.M.Hogg 1/123; D.K.Lillee 6/171; T.G.Hogan 1/107)

West Indies (606) v England Birmingham 1984
(R.G.D.Willis 2/108; I.T.Botham 1/127; D.R.Pringle 5/108; N.G.B.Cook 1/127)

India (8d-553) v England Kanpur 1984-85
(N.G.Cowans 2/115; N.A.Foster 3/123; P.H.Edmonds 1/112; C.S.Cowdrey 1/103)

New Zealand (7d-533) v Australia Brisbane[2] 1985-86
(C.J.McDermott 1/119; D.R.Gilbert 2/102; G.R.J.Matthews 3/110; R.G.Holland 0/106)

England (8d-592) v Australia Perth 1986-87
(G.F.Lawson 0/126; C.D.Matthews 3/112; B.A.Reid 4/115; G.R.J.Matthews 1/124)

Australia (5d-514) v England Adelaide 1986-87
(G.R.Dilley 1/111; P.A.J.DeFreitas 1/128; J.E.Emburey 1/117; P.H.Edmonds 2/134)

India (7d-676) v Sri Lanka Kanpur 1986-87
(A.L.F.de Mel 1/119; G.F.Labrooy 1/164; J.R.Ratnayeke 4/132; E.A.R.de Silva 0/133)

Australia (7d-601) v England Leeds 1989
(P.A.J.DeFreitas 2/140; N.A.Foster 3/109; P.J.Newport 2/153; D.R.Pringle 0/123)

Pakistan (5-699) v India Lahore[2] 1989-90
(M.Prabhakar 1/107; Maninder Singh 2/191; Arshad Ayub 0/182; R.J.Shastri 105)

England (4d-653) v India Lord's 1990
(Kapil Dev 1/120; M.Prabhakar 1/187; S.K.Sharma 1/122; N.D.Hirwani 1/102)

India (454) v England Lord's 1990
D.E.Malcolm 1/106; A.R.C.Fraser 5/104; C.C.Lewis 1/108; E.E.Hemmings 2/109)

India (9d-606) v England The Oval 1990
(D.E.Malcolm 2/110; A.R.C.Fraser 2/112; N.F.Williams 2/148; E.E.Hemmings 2/117)

England (9d-580) v New Zealand Christchurch 1991-92
(D.K.Morrison 2/133; C.L.Cairns 1/118; C.Pringle 3/127; D.N.Patel 2/132)

Australia (4d-653) v England Leeds 1993
(M.J.McCague 0/110; M.C.Ilott 3/161; A.R.Caddick 0/138; M.P.Bicknell 1/155)

Pakistan (5d-548) v New Zealand Wellington 1993-94
(D.K.Morrison 2/139; R.P.de Groen 0/104; S.B.Doull 0/112; M.N.Hart 1/102)

West Indies (5d-593) v England St John's 1993-94
(A.R.C.Fraser 2/121; A.R.Caddick 3/158; P.C.R.Tufnell 0/110; C.C.Lewis 0/140)

West Indies (8d-592) v England The Oval 1995
(D.E.Malcolm 3/160; A.R.C.Fraser 1/155; M.Watkinson 0/113; D.G.Cork 3/145)

South Africa (5d-552) v England Manchester 1998
(D.Gough 3/116; D.G.Cork 0/109; R.D.B.Croft 0/103; A.F.Giles 1/106)

## Wicketkeeping

### MOST DISMISSALS IN TEST CAREER

| Player | Country | Tests | Dis | C | S | Opponents A | E | SA | WI | NZ | I | P | SL | Z |
|---|---|---|---|---|---|---|---|---|---|---|---|---|---|---|
| R.W.Marsh | A | 96 | **355** | 343 | 12 | - | 148 | - | 65 | 58 | 16 | 68 | - | - |
| I.A.Healy | A | 103 | **353** | 328 | 25 | - | 116 | 33 | 70 | 42 | 26 | 36 | 30 | - |
| P.J.L.Dujon | WI | 81 | **272** | 267 ¶ | 5 | 86 | 84 | - | - | 20 | 60 | 22 | - | - |
| A.P.E.Knott | E | 95 | **269** | 250 | 19 | 105 | - | - | 43 | 26 | 54 | 41 | - | - |
| Wasim Bari | P | 81 | **228** | 201 | 27 | 66 | 54 | - | 21 | 32 | 55 | - | - | - |
| T.G.Evans | E | 91 | **219** | 173 | 46 | 76 | - | 59 | 37 | 28 | 12 | 7 | - | - |
| S.M.H.Kirmani | I | 88 | **198** | 160 | 38 | 41 | 42 | - | 36 | 28 | - | 50 | 1 | - |
| D.L.Murray | WI | 62 | **189** | 181 | 8 | 40 | 94 | - | - | 7 | 27 | 21 | - | - |
| A.T.W.Grout | A | 51 | **187** | 163 | 24 | - | 76 | 33 | 41 | - | 20 | 17 | - | - |
| I.D.S.Smith | NZ | 63 | **176** | 168 | 8 | 39 | 42 | - | 16 | - | 29 | 23 | 27 | - |
| R.W.Taylor | E | 57 | **174** | 167 | 7 | 57 | - | - | - | 45 | 40 | 29 | 3 | - |
| R.C.Russell | E | 54 | **165** | 153 | 12 | 28 | - | 27 | 52 | 16 | 20 | 16 | 6 | - |
| D.J.Richardson | SA | 42 | **152** | 150 | 2 | 40 | 15 | - | 6 | 23 | 32 | 13 | 17 | 6 |
| A.J.Stewart | E | 80 | 146 | 139¡ | 7 | 48 | - | 25 | 23 | 27 | 4 | 8 | 6 | 5 |
| J.H.B.Waite | SA | 50 | **141** | 124 | 17 | 28 | 56 | - | - | 57 | - | - | - | - |
| W.A.S.Oldfield | A | 54 | **130** | 78 | 52 | - | 90 | 27 | 13 | - | - | - | - | - |
| K.S.More | I | 49 | **130** | 110 | 20 | 13 | 37 | 11 | 21 | 13 | - | 21 | 11 | 3 |
| J.M.Parks | E | 46 | **114** | 103 § | 11 | 21 | - | 30 | 31 | 22 | 9 | 1 | - | - |
| Saleem Yousuf | P | 32 | **104** | 91 | 13 | 15 | 15 | - | 22 | 22 | 11 | - | 19 | - |

Best for the other countries are:

| Player | Country | Tests | Dis | C | S | A | E | SA | WI | NZ | I | P | SL | Z |
|---|---|---|---|---|---|---|---|---|---|---|---|---|---|---|
| R.S.Kaluwitharana | SL | 23 | **54** | 44 | 10 | 10 | - | 7 | 6 | 8 | 7 | 4 | - | 12 |
| A.Flower | Z | 30 | **75** | 70 † | 5 | - | 3 | 2 | - | 23 | 3 | 30 | 14 | - |

*§ Including 2 catches in 3 Tests when not keeping wicket. ¶ Including 2 catches in 2 Tests when not keeping wicket. † includes 5 catches in 4 Tests when not keeping wicket. ¡ including 31 catches in 46 Tests when not keeping wickets.*

### MOST DISMISSALS IN A MATCH *(§ In first Test)*

**AUSTRALIA**

| | | | | |
|---|---|---|---|---|
| 9 (8c, 1s) | G.R.A.Langley | England | Lord's | 1956 |
| 9 (9c) | R.W.Marsh | England | Brisbane[2] | 1982-83 |
| 9 (9c) | I.A.Healy | England | Brisbane[2] | 1994-95 |
| 8 (8c) | J.J.Kelly | England | Sydney | 1901-02 |
| 8 (8c) | G.R.A.Langley | West Indies | Kingston | 1954-55 |
| 8 (6c, 2s) | A.T.W.Grout | Pakistan | Lahore[2] | 1959-60 |
| 8 (8c) | A.T.W.Grout | England | Lord's | 1961 |
| 8 (7c, 1s) § | H.B.Taber | South Africa | Johannesburg[3] | 1966-67 |
| 8 (8c) | R.W.Marsh | West Indies | Melbourne | 1975-76 |
| 8 (8c) | R.W.Marsh | New Zealand | Christchurch | 1976-77 |
| 8 (7c, 1s) | R.W.Marsh | India | Sydney | 1980-81 |
| 8 (8c) | R.W.Marsh | England | Adelaide | 1982-83 |
| 8 (8c) | I.A.Healy | West Indies | Adelaide | 1992-93 |
| 8 (8c) | I.A.Healy | England | Melbourne | 1994-95 |
| 8 (8c) | I.A.Healy | Sri Lanka | Adelaide | 1995-96 |

**ENGLAND**

| | | | | |
|---|---|---|---|---|
| 11 (11c) | R.C.Russell | South Africa | Johannesburg[3] | 1995-96 |
| 10 (10c) | R.W.Taylor | India | Bombay[3] | 1979-80 |
| 9 (7c, 2s) | R.C.Russell | South Africa | Port Elizabeth | 1995-96 |
| 8 (6c, 2s) | L.E.G.Ames | West Indies | The Oval | 1933 |
| 8 (8c) | J.M.Parks | New Zealand | Christchurch | 1965-66 |
| 8 (8c) | A.J.Stewart | Australia | Manchester | 1997 |
| 8 (8c) | A.J.Stewart | South Africa | Nottingham | 1998 |

**SOUTH AFRICA**

| | | | | |
|---|---|---|---|---|
| 9 (9c) | D.J.Richardson | India | Port Elizabeth | 1992-93 |

| | | | | |
|---|---|---|---|---|
| 9 (8c, s1) | M.V.Boucher | Pakistan | Port Elizabeth | 1997-98 |
| 8 (8c) | D.T.Lindsay | Australia | Johannesburg[3] | 1966-67 |
| 8 (8c) | D.J.Richardson | Sri Lanka | Colombo (SSC) | 1993-94 |

**WEST INDIES**

| | | | | |
|---|---|---|---|---|
| 9 (9c) | D.A.Murray | Australia | Melbourne | 1981-82 |
| 9 (9c) | C.O.Browne | England | Lord's | 1995 |
| 8 (8c) | J.R.Murray | Australia | Perth | 1992-93 |

**NEW ZEALAND**

| | | | | |
|---|---|---|---|---|
| 8 (8c) | W.K.Lees | Sri Lanka | Wellington | 1982-83 |
| 8 (8c) | I.D.S.Smith | Sri Lanka | Hamilton | 1990-91 |

**INDIA**

| | | | | |
|---|---|---|---|---|
| 8 (8c) | N.R.Mongia | South Africa | Durban[2] | 1996-97 |
| 7 (1c, 6s) | K.S.More | West Indies | Madras[1] | 1987-88 |
| 7 (5c, 2s) | K.S.More | England | Bombay[3] | 1992-93 |

**PAKISTAN**

| | | | | |
|---|---|---|---|---|
| 9 (9c) | Rashid Latif | New Zealand | Auckland | 1993-94 |
| 8 (8c) | Wasim Bari | England | Leeds | 1971 |
| 8 (7c, 1s) | Rashid Latif | Australia | Sydney | 1995-96 |

**SRI LANKA**

| | | | | |
|---|---|---|---|---|
| 9 (9c) | S.A.R.Silva | India | Colombo (SSC) | 1985-86 |
| 9 (8c, 1s) | S.A.R.Silva | India | Colombo (PSS) | 1985-86 |

**ZIMBABWE**

| | | | | |
|---|---|---|---|---|
| 7 (7c) | W.R.James | Sri Lanka | Bulawayo[2] | 1994-95 |

## MOST DISMISSALS IN A SERIES *(§ In first series. # In last series)*

**AUSTRALIA**

| Total | C | S | Tests | Player | Opponents | Season |
|---|---|---|---|---|---|---|
| 28 | 28 | - | 5 | R.W.Marsh | England | 1982-83 |
| 27 | 25 | 2 | 6 | I.A.Healy | England | 1997 |
| 26 | 26 | - | 6 | R.W.Marsh | West Indies | 1975-76 |
| 26 | 21 | 5 | 6 | I.A.Healy | England | 1993 |
| 25 | 23 | 2 | 5 | I.A.Healy | England | 1994-95 |
| 24 | 24 | - | 5 | I.A.Healy | England | 1990-91 |
| 23 | 20 | 3 | 5 | A.T.W.Grout | West Indies | 1960-61 |
| 23 | 21 | 2 | 5 | R.W.Marsh | England | 1972 |
| 23 | 23 | - | 6 | R.W.Marsh | England | 1981 |
| 23 | 19 | 4 | 5 | I.A.Healy | West Indies | 1992-93 |
| 22 § | 22 | - | 5 | S.J.Rixon | India | 1977-78 |
| 21 # | 13 | 8 | 5 | R.A.Saggers | South Africa | 1949-50 |
| 21 § | 16 | 5 | 5 | G.R.A.Langley | West Indies | 1951-52 |
| 21 | 20 | 1 | 5 | A.T.W.Grout | England | 1961 |
| 21 # | 21 | - | 5 | R.W.Marsh | Pakistan | 1983-84 |
| 20 | 16 | 4 | 5 | D.Tallon | England | 1946-47 |
| 20 | 16 | 4 | 4 | G.R.A.Langley | West Indies | 1954-55 |
| 20 | 17 | 3 | 5 | A.T.W.Grout | England | 1958-59 |
| 20 § | 19 | 1 | 5 | H.B.Taber | South Africa | 1966-67 |

**ENGLAND**

| Total | C | S | Tests | Player | Opponents | Season |
|---|---|---|---|---|---|---|
| 27 | 25 | 2 | 5 | R.C.Russell | South Africa | 1995-96 |
| 24 | 21 | 3 | 6 | A.P.E.Knott | Australia | 1970-71 |
| 23 | 22 | 1 | 6 | A.P.E.Knott | Australia | 1974-75 |
| 23 | 23 | 0 | 6 | A.J.Stewart | Australia | 1997 |
| 23 | 23 | 0 | 5 | A.J.Stewart | South Africa | 1998 |
| 21 | 21 | - | 5 | H.Strudwick | South Africa | 1913-14 |

| | | | | | | |
|---|---|---|---|---|---|---|
| 21 | 20 | 1 | 5 | S.J.Rhodes | Australia | 1994-95 |
| 20 | 20 | - | - | T.G.Evans | South Africa | 1956-57 |
| 20 | 18 | 2 | 6 | R.W.Taylor | Australia | 1978-79 |
| 20 | 19 | 1 | 6 | P.R.Downton | Australia | 1985 |

**SOUTH AFRICA**

| Total | C | S | Tests | Player | Opponents | Season |
|---|---|---|---|---|---|---|
| 26 | 23 | 3 | 5 | J.H.B.Waite | New Zealand | 1961-62 |
| 26 | 25 | 1 | 5 | M.V.Boucher | England | 1998 |
| 24 | 24 | - | 5 | D.T.Lindsay | Australia | 1966-67 |
| 23 | 16 | 7 | 5 | J.H.B.Waite | New Zealand | 1953-54 |

**WEST INDIES**

| Total | C | S | Tests | Player | Opponents | Season |
|---|---|---|---|---|---|---|
| 24 § | 22 | 2 | 5 | D.L.Murray | England | 1963 |
| 23 | 22 | 1 | 5 | F.C.M.Alexander | England | 1959-60 |
| 23 | 23 | - | 5 | P.J.L.Dujon | Australia | 1990-91 |
| 20 | 19 | 1 | 5 | P.J.L.Dujon | Australia | 1983-84 |
| 20 | 20 | - | 5 | P.J.L.Dujon | England | 1988 |

**NEW ZEALAND**

| Total | C | S | Tests | Player | Opponents | Season |
|---|---|---|---|---|---|---|
| 23 § | 21 | 2 | 5 | A.E.Dick | South Africa | 1961-62 |

**INDIA**

| Total | C | S | Tests | Player | Opponents | Season |
|---|---|---|---|---|---|---|
| 19 § | 12 | 7 | 5 | N.S.Tamhane | Pakistan | 1954-55 |
| 19 | 17 | 2 | 6 | S.M.H.Kirmani | Pakistan | 1979-80 |

**PAKISTAN**

| Total | C | S | Tests | Player | Opponents | Season |
|---|---|---|---|---|---|---|
| 17 | 15 | 2 | 6 | Wasim Bari | India | 1982-83 |

**SRI LANKA**

| Total | C | S | Tests | Player | Opponents | Season |
|---|---|---|---|---|---|---|
| 22 | 21 | 1 | 3 | S.A.R.Silva | India | 1985-86 |

**ZIMBABWE**

| Total | C | S | Tests | Player | Opponents | Season |
|---|---|---|---|---|---|---|
| 13 | 13 | 0 | 2 | W.R.James | Sri Lanka | 1994-95 |

## MOST DISMISSALS IN AN INNINGS *(§ In first Test. # in last Test)*

**AUSTRALIA**

| | | | | |
|---|---|---|---|---|
| 6 (6c) § | A.T.W.Grout | South Africa | Johannesburg[3] | 1957-58 |
| 6 (6c) | R.W.Marsh | England | Brisbane[2] | 1982-83 |
| 6 (6c) | I.A.Healy | England | Birmingham | 1997 |
| 5 (1c, 4s) | W.A.S.Oldfield | England | Melbourne | 1924-25 |
| 5 (2c, 3s) | G.R.A.Langley | West Indies | Georgetown | 1954-55 |
| 5 (5c) | G.R.A.Langley | West Indies | Kingston | 1954-55 |
| 5 (5c) | G.R.A.Langley | England | Lord's | 1956 |
| 5 (4c, 1s) | A.T.W.Grout | South Africa | Durban[2] | 1957-58 |
| 5 (5c) | A.T.W.Grout | Pakistan | Lahore[2] | 1959-60 |
| 5 (4c, 1s) | A.T.W.Grout | West Indies | Brisbane[2] | 1960-61 |
| 5 (5c) | A.T.W.Grout | England | Lord's | 1961 |
| 5 (5c) | A.T.W.Grout | England | Sydney | 1965-66 |
| 5 (5c) § | H.B.Taber | South Africa | Johannesburg[3] | 1966-67 |
| 5 (5c) | H.B.Taber | West Indies | Sydney | 1968-69 |
| 5 (5c) # | H.B.Taber | South Africa | Port Elizabeth | 1969-70 |
| 5 (5c) | R.W.Marsh | England | Manchester | 1972 |
| 5 (5c) | R.W.Marsh | England | Nottingham | 1972 |
| 5 (5c) | R.W.Marsh | New Zealand | Sydney | 1973-74 |

| | | | | |
|---|---|---|---|---|
| 5 (5c) | R.W.Marsh | New Zealand | Christchurch | 1973-74 |
| 5 (5c) | R.W.Marsh | West Indies | Melbourne | 1975-76 |
| 5 (5c) | R.W.Marsh | New Zealand | Christchurch | 1976-77 |
| 5 (5c) § | J.A.Maclean | England | Brisbane[2] | 1978-79 |
| 5 (5c) | K.J.Wright | Pakistan | Melbourne | 1978-79 |
| 5 (5c) | R.W.Marsh | West Indies | Brisbane[2] | 1979-80 |
| 5 (5c) | R.W.Marsh | India | Sydney | 1980-81 |
| 5 (5c) | R.W.Marsh | Pakistan | Perth | 1981-82 |
| 5 (5c) | R.W.Marsh | Pakistan | Perth | 1983-84 |
| 5 (5c) # | R.W.Marsh | Pakistan | Sydney | 1983-84 |
| 5 (5c) | W.B.Phillips | West Indies | Kingston | 1983-84 |
| 5 (5c) | I.A.Healy | Pakistan | Adelaide | 1989-90 |
| 5 (5c) | I.A.Healy | England | Melbourne | 1990-91 |
| 5 (5c) | I.A.Healy | England | Adelaide | 1990-91 |
| 5 (5c) | I.A.Healy | New Zealand | Brisbane[2] | 1993-94 |
| 5 (5c) | I.A.Healy | Pakistan | Rawalpindi[2] | 1994-95 |
| 5 (4c, 1s) § | P.A.Emery | Pakistan | Lahore[2] | 1994-95 |
| 5 (5c) | I.A.Healy | England | Brisbane[2] | 1994-95 |
| 5 (5c) | I.A.Healy | England | Melbourne | 1994-95 |
| 5 (5c) | I.A.Healy | Sri Lanka | Adelaide | 1995-96 |
| 5 (5c) | I.A.Healy | South Africa | Johannesburg[3] | 1996-97 |
| **ENGLAND** | | | | |
| 7 (7c) | R.W.Taylor | India | Bombay[3] | 1979-80 |
| 6 (6c) | J.T.Murray | India | Lord's | 1967 |
| 6 (6c) | R.C.Russell | Australia | Melbourne | 1990-91 |
| 6 (6c) | R.C.Russell | South Africa (1st Innings) | Johannesburg[3] | 1995-96 |
| 6 (6c) | A.J.Stewart | Australia | Manchester | 1997 |
| 5 (5c) | J.G.Binks | India | Calcutta | 1963-64 |
| 5 (3c, 2s) | J.M.Parks | Australia | Sydney | 1965-66 |
| 5 (5c) | J.M.Parks | New Zealand | Christchurch | 1965-66 |
| 5 (4c, 1s) | A.P.E.Knott | India | Manchester | 1974 |
| 5 (5c) | R.W.Taylor | New Zealand | Nottingham | 1978 |
| 5 (5c) | R.W.Taylor | Australia | Brisbane[2] | 1978-79 |
| 5 (5c) | C.J.Richards | Australia | Melbourne | 1986-87 |
| 5 (5c) | R.C.Russell | West Indies | Bridgetown | 1989-90 |
| 5 (5c) | R.C.Russell | South Africa (2nd Innings) | Johannesburg[3] | 1995-96 |
| 5 (4c, 1s) | R.C.Russell | South Africa | Port Elizabeth | 1995-96 |
| 5 (5c) | A.J.Stewart | South Africa | Lord's | 1998 |
| 5 (5c) | A.J.Stewart | South Africa | Nottingham | 1998 |
| **SOUTH AFRICA** | | | | |
| 6 (6c) | D.T.Lindsay | Australia | Johannesburg[3] | 1966-67 |
| 6 (6c) | M.V.Boucher | Pakistan | Port Elizabeth | 1997-98 |
| 6 (6c) | M.V.Boucher | Sri Lanka | Cape Town | 1997-98 |
| 5 (5c) | D.J.Richardson | India | Port Elizabeth | 1992-93 |
| 5 (5c) | M.V.Boucher | England | Lord's | 1998 |
| **WEST INDIES** | | | | |
| 5 (5c) | F.C.M.Alexander | England | Bridgetown | 1959-60 |
| 5 (5c) | D.L.Murray | England | Leeds | 1976 |
| 5 (5c) | D.L.Murray | Pakistan | Georgetown | 1976-77 |
| 5 (5c) | D.A.Murray | India | Delhi | 1978-79 |
| 5 (5c) | D.A.Murray | Australia | Melbourne | 1981-82 |
| 5 (5c) | P.J.L.Dujon | India | Kingston | 1982-83 |
| 5 (5c) | P.J.L.Dujon | England | Bridgetown | 1985-86 |
| 5 (5c) | P.J.L.Dujon | Australia | St John's | 1990-91 |
| 5 (5c) | D.Williams | Australia | Brisbane[2] | 1992-93 |
| 5 (5c) | J.R.Murray | Australia | Perth | 1992-93 |
| 5 (5c) | C.O.Browne | England | Nottingham | 1995 |
| 5 (5c) | C.O.Browne | New Zealand | St John's | 1995-96 |

**NEW ZEALAND**

| | | | | |
|---|---|---|---|---|
| 7 (7c) | I.D.S.Smith | Sri Lanka | Hamilton | 1990-91 |
| 5 (5c) | R.I.Harford | India | Wellington | 1967-68 |
| 5 (5c) | K.J.Wadsworth | Pakistan | Auckland | 1972-73 |
| 5 (5c) | W.K.Lees | Sri Lanka | Wellington | 1982-83 |
| 5 (4c, 1s) | I.D.S.Smith | England | Auckland | 1983-84 |
| 5 (5c) | I.D.S.Smith | Sri Lanka | Auckland | 1990-91 |
| 5 (5c) | A.C.Parore | England | Auckland | 1991-92 |
| 5 (4c, 1s) | A.C.Parore | Sri Lanka | Colombo (SSC) | 1992-93 |

**INDIA**

| | | | | |
|---|---|---|---|---|
| 6 (5c, 1s) | S.M.H.Kirmani | New Zealand | Christchurch | 1975-76 |
| 5 (3c, 2s) | B.K.Kunderan | England | Bombay[2] | 1961-62 |
| 5 (5c) | S.M.H.Kirmani | Pakistan | Faisalabad | 1982-83 |
| 5 (0c, 5s) | K.S.More | West Indies | Madras[1] | 1987-88 |
| 5 (5c) | N.R.Mongia | South Africa | Durban[2] | 1996-97 |

**PAKISTAN**

| | | | | |
|---|---|---|---|---|
| 7 (7c) | Wasim Bari | New Zealand | Auckland | 1978-79 |
| 6 (6c) | Rashid Latif | Zimbabwe | Bulawayo[2] | 1997-98 |
| 5 (4c, 1s) | Imtiaz Ahmed | Australia | Lahore[2] | 1959-60 |
| 5 (5c) | Wasim Bari | England | Leeds | 1971 |
| 5 (5c) | Saleem Yousuf | Sri Lanka | Karachi[1] | 1985-86 |
| 5 (5c) | Saleem Yousuf | New Zealand | Faisalabad | 1990-91 |
| 5 (4c, 1s) | Moin Khan | West Indies | Bridgetown | 1992-93 |
| 5 (5c) | Rashid Latif | Zimbabwe | Lahore[2] | 1993-94 |
| 5 (5c) | Rashid Latif | New Zealand | Auckland | 1993-94 |
| 5 (4c, s1) | Rashid Latif | Australia | Sydney | 1995-96 |
| 5 (5c) | Rashid Latif | New Zealand | Christchurch | 1995-96 |

**SRI LANKA**

| | | | | |
|---|---|---|---|---|
| 6 (6c) | S.A.R.Silva | India | Colombo (SSC) | 1985-86 |
| 5 (5c) | S.A.R.Silva | India | Colombo (PSS) | 1985-86 |
| 5 (5c) | H.P.Tillakaratne | New Zealand | Hamilton | 1990-91 |
| 5 (5c) | P.B.Dasanayake | Zimbabwe | Harare | 1994-95 |

**ZIMBABWE**

| | | | | |
|---|---|---|---|---|
| 5 (5c) | W.R.James | Sri Lanka | Bulawayo[2] | 1994-95 |
| 4 (4c) | A.Flower | New Zealand | Harare | 1992-93 |
| 4 (4c) | A.Flower | Pakistan | Karachi[2] | 1993-94 |
| 4 (4c) | W.R.James | Sri Lanka | Harare | 1994-95 |
| 4 (4c) | A.Flower | Pakistan | Harare | 1994-95 |

## NO BYES CONCEDED IN TOTAL OF 500 RUNS

| | | | | | | |
|---|---|---|---|---|---|---|
| 4-671 | H.P.Tillakaratne | Sri Lanka | v | New Zealand | Wellington | 1990-91 |
| 5d-660 | A.C.Parore | New Zealand | v | West Indies | Wellington | 1994-95 |
| 8d-659 | T.G.Evans | England | v | Australia | Sydney | 1946-47 |
| 652 | S.M.H.Kirmani | India | v | Pakistan | Faisalabad | 1982-83 |
| 4d-632 | A.J.Stewart | England | v | Australia | Lord's | 1993 |
| 619 | J.L.Hendriks | West Indies | v | Australia | Sydney | 1968-69 |
| 5d-616 | I.D.S.Smith | New Zealand | v | Pakistan | Auckland | 1988-89 |
| 7d-601 | R C Russell | England | v | Australia | Leeds | 1989 |
| 5d-593 | R.C.Russell | England | v | West Indies | St John's | 1993-94 |
| 7d-586 | R.S.Kaluwitharana | Sri Lanka | v | New Zealand | Dunedin | 1996-97 |
| 8d-567 | A.C.Parore | New Zealand | v | England | Nottingham | 1994 |
| 9d-559 | W.W.Wade | South Africa | v | England | Cape Town | 1938-39 |
| 551 | J.J.Kelly | Australia | v | England | Sydney | 1897-98 |
| 9d-551 | A.P.E.Knott | England | v | New Zealand | Lord's | 1973 |
| 7d-548 | L.K.Germon | New Zealand | v | West Indies | St John's | 1995-96 |
| 5d-544 | Imtiaz Ahmed | Pakistan | v | England | Birmingham | 1962 |
| 3d-543 | T.M.Findlay | West Indies | v | New Zealand | Georgetown | 1971-72 |
| 9d-536 | I.A.Healy | Australia | v | West Indies | Bridgetown | 1990-91 |
| 9d-532 | A.P.E.Knott | England | v | Australia | The Oval | 1975 |
| 531 | D.T.Lindsay | South Africa | v | England | Johannesburg[3] | 1964-65 |
| 528 | S.M.H.Kirmani | India | v | Australia | Adelaide | 1980-81 |
| 528 | R.C.Russell | England | v | Australia | Lord's | 1989 |
| 7d-526 | A.P.E.Knott | England | v | West Indies | Port-of-Spain | 1967-68 |
| 521 | W.A.S.Oldfield | Australia | v | England | Brisbane[1] | 1928-29 |
| 520 | J.H.B.Waite | South Africa | v | Australia | Melbourne | 1952-53 |
| 517 | I.A.Healy | Australia | v | South Africa | Adelaide | 1997-98 |
| 515 | P.J.L.Dujon | West Indies | v | Australia | Adelaide | 1988-89 |
| 4d-514 | R.G.de Alwis | Sri Lanka | v | Australia | Kandy | 1982-83 |
| 5d-514 | C.J.Richards | England | v | Australia | Adelaide | 1986-87 |
| 6d-512 | B.N.French | England | v | New Zealand | Wellington | 1987-88 |
| 510 | J.L.Hendriks | West Indies | v | Australia | Melbourne | 1968-69 |
| 509 | W.B.Phillips | Australia | v | West Indies | Bridgetown | 1983-84 |
| 6d-507 | K.J.Wadsworth | New Zealand | v | Pakistan | Dunedin | 1972-73 |
| 8d-503 | S.M.H.Kirmani | India | v | Pakistan | Faisalabad | 1978-79 |
| 6d-500 | R.S.Kaluwitharana | Sri Lanka | v | Australia | Melbourne | 1995-96 |
| 7d-500 | R.C.Russell | England | v | West Indies | St John's | 1997-98 |

## Fielding

### MOST CATCHES IN TESTS

| Player | Country | Tests | C | A | E | SA | WI | NZ | I | P | SL | Z |
|---|---|---|---|---|---|---|---|---|---|---|---|---|
| A.R.Border | A | 156 | **156** | - | 57 | 5 | 19 | 31 | 14 | 22 | 8 | - |
| M.A.Taylor | A | 96 | **144** | - | 37 | 17 | 28 | 25 | 10 | 16 | 11 | - |
| G.S.Chappell | A | 87 | **122** | - | 61 | - | 16 | 18 | 5 | 22 | 0 | - |
| I.V.A.Richards | WI | 121 | **122** | 24 | 29 | - | - | 7 | 39 | 23 | - | - |
| I.T.Botham | E | 102 | **120** | 61 | - | - | 15 | 14 | 14 | 14 | 2 | - |
| M.C.Cowdrey | E | 114 | **120** | 40 | - | 22 | 21 | 15 | 11 | 11 | - | - |
| R.B.Simpson | A | 62 | **110** | - | 30 | 27 | 29 | - | 21 | 3 | - | - |
| W.R.Hammond | E | 85 | **110** | 43 | - | 30 | 22 | 9 | 6 | - | - | - |
| G.S.Sobers | WI | 93 | **109** | 27 | 40 | - | - | 11 | 27 | 4 | - | - |
| S.M.Gavaskar | I | 125 | **108** | 19 | 35 | - | 17 | 11 | - | 19 | 7 | - |
| I.M.Chappell | A | 75 | **105** | - | 31 | 11 | 24 | 16 | 17 | 6 | - | - |
| G.A.Gooch | E | 118 | **103** | 29 | - | 1 | 28 | 13 | 21 | 7 | 4 | - |
| M.Azharuddin | I | 91 | **101** | 14 | 9 | 13 | 20 | 4 | - | 12 | 27 | 2 |

The most successful catchers for the other countries are:

| Player | Country | Tests | C | A | E | SA | WI | NZ | I | P | SL | Z |
|---|---|---|---|---|---|---|---|---|---|---|---|---|
| B.Mitchell | SA | 42 | **56** | 10 | 43 | - | - | 3 | - | - | - | - |
| M.D.Crowe | NZ | 77 | **70** | 10 | 19 | 7 | 12 | - | 2 | 15 | 4 | 1 |
| Javed Miandad | P | 124 | **93** | 10 | 22 | - | 12 | 20 | 18 | - | 11 | - |
| R.S.Mahanama | SL | 52 | **56** | 5 | 4 | 5 | 2 | 10 | 9 | 8 | - | 13 |
| † H.P.Tillakaratne | SL | 41 | **51** | 1 | 4 | 6 | 0 | 24 | 6 | 7 | - | 3 |
| A.D.R.Campbell | Z | 30 | **29** | - | 7 | 0 | - | 8 | 0 | 11 | 3 | - |

*Note: † H.P.Tillakaratne (SL) took 83 catches in 52 Tests including 32 catches in 11 Tests as a wicket-keeper.*

### MOST CATCHES IN A SERIES *(§ In first Test series)*

**AUSTRALIA**

| C | Tests | Player | Against | Season |
|---|---|---|---|---|
| 15 § | 5 | J.M.Gregory | England | 1920-21 |
| 14 | 6 | G.S.Chappell | England | 1974-75 |
| 13 § | 5 | R.B.Simpson | South Africa | 1957-58 |
| 13 | 5 | R.B.Simpson | West Indies | 1960-61 |
| 12 | 5 | D.F.Whatmore | India | 1979-80 |
| 12 | 6 | A.R.Border | England | 1981 |

**ENGLAND**

| C | Tests | Player | Against | Season |
|---|---|---|---|---|
| 12 § | 5 | L.C.Braund | Australia | 1901-02 |
| 12 | 5 | W.R.Hammond | Australia | 1934 |
| 12 | 3 | J.T.Ikin | South Africa | 1951 |
| 12 | 6 | A.W.Greig | Australia | 1974-75 |
| 12 | 6 | I.T.Botham | Australia | 1981 |

**SOUTH AFRICA**

| C | Tests | Player | Against | Season |
|---|---|---|---|---|
| 12 | 5 | A.E.E.Vogler | England | 1909-10 |
| 12 | 5 | B.Mitchell | England | 1930-31 |
| 12 | 5 | T.L.Goddard | England | 1956-57 |

**WEST INDIES**

| C | Tests | Player | Against | Season |
|---|---|---|---|---|
| 13 | 6 | B.C.Lara | England | 1997-98 |
| 12 | 5 | G.S.Sobers | Australia | 1960-61 |

**NEW ZEALAND**

| C | Tests | Player | Against | Season |
|---|---|---|---|---|
| 10 | 2 | S.P.Fleming | Zimbabwe | 1997-98 |
| 9 | 3 | B.A.Young | Pakistan | 1993-94 |
| 9 | 3 | S.P.Fleming | Australia | 1997-98 |
| 8 | 5 | B.Sutcliffe | South Africa | 1953-54 |
| 8 | 4 | B.A.G.Murray | India | 1967-68 |
| 8 | 4 | J.J.Crowe | West Indies | 1984-85 |

**INDIA**

| | | | | |
|---|---|---|---|---|
| 12 | 5 | E.D.Solkar | England | 1972-73 |
| 11 | 3 | M.Azharuddin | Sri Lanka | 1993-94 |
| 10 | 4 | A.L.Wadekar | New Zealand | 1967-68 |
| 10 | 4 | E.D.Solkar | Australia | 1969-70 |

**PAKISTAN**

| | | | | |
|---|---|---|---|---|
| 9 | 5 | W.Mathias | West Indies | 1957-58 |

**SRI LANKA**

| | | | | |
|---|---|---|---|---|
| 8 | 2 | H.P.Tillakaratne | New Zealand | 1992-93 |
| 8 | 2 | R.S.Mahanama | Zimbabwe | 1996-97 |
| 8 | 2 | R.S.Mahanama | New Zealand | 1996-97 |

**ZIMBABWE**

| | | | | |
|---|---|---|---|---|
| 7 | 3 | M.H.Dekker | Sri Lanka | 1994-95 |
| 7 | 2 | A.D.R.Campbell | England | 1996-97 |

## MOST CATCHES IN A MATCH *(§ In first Test. # In last Test)*

**AUSTRALIA**

| | | | | | |
|---|---|---|---|---|---|
| 7 | G.S.Chappell | v | England | Perth | 1974-75 |
| 6 | J.M.Gregory | v | England | Sydney | 1920-21 |
| 6 # | V.Y.Richardson | v | South Africa | Durban2 | 1935-36 |
| 6 # | R.N.Harvey | v | England | Sydney | 1962-63 |
| 6 | I.M.Chappell | v | New Zealand | Adelaide | 1973-74 |
| 6 | D.F.Whatmore | v | India | Kanpur | 1979-80 |

**ENGLAND**

| | | | | | |
|---|---|---|---|---|---|
| 6 | A.Shrewsbury | v | Australia | Sydney | 1887-88 |
| 6 | F.E.Woolley | v | Australia | Sydney | 1911-12 |
| 6 | M.C.Cowdrey | v | West Indies | Lord's | 1963 |
| 6 | A.W.Greig | v | Pakistan | Leeds | 1974 |
| 6 | A.J.Lamb | v | New Zealand | Lord's | 1983 |
| 6 | G.A.Hick | v | Pakistan | Leeds | 1992 |

**SOUTH AFRICA**

| | | | | | |
|---|---|---|---|---|---|
| 6 | A.E.E.Vogler | v | England | Durban[1] | 1909-10 |
| 6 | B.Mitchell | v | Australia | Melbourne | 1931-32 |

**WEST INDIES**

| | | | | | |
|---|---|---|---|---|---|
| 6 | G.S.Sobers | v | England | Lord's | 1973 |
| 6 | J.C.Adams | v | England | Bridgetown | 1993-94 |

**NEW ZEALAND**

| | | | | | |
|---|---|---|---|---|---|
| 7 | S.P.Fleming | v | Zimbabwe | Harare | 1997-98 |
| 6 | B.A.Young | v | Pakistan | Auckland | 1993-94 |
| 6 | S.P.Fleming | v | Australia | Brisbane[2] | 1997-98 |

**INDIA**

| | | | | | |
|---|---|---|---|---|---|
| 7 § | Yajurvindra Singh | v | England | Bangalore | 1976-77 |
| 6 | E.D.Solkar | v | West Indies | Port-of-Spain | 1970-71 |

**PAKISTAN**

| | | | | | |
|---|---|---|---|---|---|
| 5 | Majid Khan | v | Australia | Karachi[1] | 1979-80 |
| 5 | Inzamamul Haq | v | Zimbabwe | Rawalpindi[2] | 1993-94 |

**SRI LANKA**

| | | | | | |
|---|---|---|---|---|---|
| 7 | H.P.Tillakaratne | v | New Zealand | Colombo (SSC) | 1992-93 |

**ZIMBABWE**

| | | | | | |
|---|---|---|---|---|---|
| 4 | M.H.Dekker | v | Sri Lanka | Harare | 1994-95 |
| 4 | A.D.R.Campbell | v | England | Harare | 1996-97 |

## MOST CATCHES IN AN INNINGS *(§ In first Test. # In last Test)*

### AUSTRALIA

| | | | | | |
|---|---|---|---|---|---|
| 5 | V.Y.Richardson # | v | South Africa | Durban[2] | 1935-36 |
| 4 | H.Trumble | v | England | Lord's | 1899 |
| 4 | S.J.E.Loxton | v | England | Brisbane[2] | 1950-51 |
| 4 | G.B.Hole | v | South Africa | Sydney | 1952-53 |
| 4 | R.G.Archer | v | West Indies | Georgetown | 1954-55 |
| 4 | A.K.Davidson | v | India | Delhi | 1959-60 |
| 4 | R.B.Simpson | v | West Indies | Sydney | 1960-61 |
| 4 | R.N.Harvey # | v | England | Sydney | 1962-63 |
| 4 | R.B.Simpson | v | West Indies | Bridgetown | 1964-65 |
| 4 | I.M.Chappell | v | New Zealand | Adelaide | 1973-74 |
| 4 | G.S.Chappell | v | England | Perth | 1974-75 |
| 4 | A.Turner | v | Pakistan | Sydney | 1976-77 |
| 4 | D.F.Whatmore | v | India | Kanpur | 1979-80 |
| 4 | A.R.Border | v | Pakistan | Karachi[1] | 1979-80 |
| 4 | K.J.Hughes | v | New Zealand | Perth | 1980-81 |
| 4 | D.C.Boon | v | Pakistan | Karachi[1] | 1988-89 |
| 4 | M.A.Taylor | v | West Indies | Bridgetown | 1994-95 |

### ENGLAND

| | | | | | |
|---|---|---|---|---|---|
| 4 | L.C.Braund | v | Australia | Sheffield | 1902 |
| 4 | W.Rhodes | v | Australia | Manchester | 1905 |
| 4 | L.C.Braund | v | Australia | Sydney | 1907-08 |
| 4 | F.E.Woolley | v | Australia | Sydney | 1911-12 |
| 4 | H.Larwood | v | Australia | Brisbane[1] | 1928-29 |
| 4 | J.E.McConnon | v | Pakistan | Manchester | 1954 |
| 4 | P.B.H.May | v | Australia | Adelaide | 1954-55 |
| 4 | P.H.Parfitt | v | Australia | Nottingham | 1972 |
| 4 | A.W.Greig | v | Pakistan | Leeds | 1974 |
| 4 | P.H.Edmonds | v | New Zealand | Christchurch | 1977-78 |
| 4 | A.J.Lamb | v | New Zealand | Lord's | 1983 |
| 4 | G.A.Hick | v | Pakistan | Leeds | 1992 |
| 4 | G.A.Hick | v | India | Calcutta | 1992-93 |
| 4 | G.A.Hick | v | New Zealand | Nottingham | 1994 |
| 4 | N.V.Knight | v | New Zealand | Christchurch | 1996-97 |

### SOUTH AFRICA

| | | | | | |
|---|---|---|---|---|---|
| 4 | A.E.E.Vogler | v | England | Durban[1] | 1909-10 |
| 4 | A.W.Nourse | v | England | Durban[2] | 1922-23 |
| 4 | B.Mitchell | v | Australia | Melbourne | 1931-32 |
| 4 | T.L.Goddard | v | Australia | Sydney | 1963-64 |
| 4 | A.J.Traicos § | v | Australia | Durban[2] | 1969-70 |
| 4 | A.C.Hudson | v | India | Cape Town | 1992-93 |

### WEST INDIES

| | | | | | |
|---|---|---|---|---|---|
| 4 | E.D.Weekes | v | India | Kingston | 1952-53 |
| 4 | G.S.Sobers | v | England | Port-of-Spain | 1959-60 |
| 4 | G.S.Sobers | v | England | Nottingham | 1966 |
| 4 | R.C.Fredericks | v | Australia | Port-of-Spain | 1972-73 |
| 4 | G.S.Sobers | v | England | Lord's | 1973 |
| 4 | I.V.A.Richards | v | India | Kingston | 1988-89 |
| 4 | A.L.Logie | v | Pakistan | Lahore[2] | 1990-91 |
| 4 | J.C.Adams | v | England | Bridgetown | 1993-94 |
| 4 | B.C.Lara | v | Australia | Kingston | 1994-95 |

| | | | | | |
|---|---|---|---|---|---|
| **NEW ZEALAND** | | | | | |
| 5 | S.P.Fleming | v | Zimbabwe | Harare | 1997-98 |
| 4 | J.J.Crowe | v | West Indies | Bridgetown | 1984-85 |
| 4 | M.D.Crowe | v | West Indies | Kingston | 1984-85 |
| 4 | S.P.Fleming | v | Australia | Brisbane[2] | 1997-98 |
| **INDIA** | | | | | |
| 5 | Yajurvindra Singh § | v | England | Bangalore | 197-77 |
| 5 | M Azharuddin | v | Pakistan | Karachi[1] | 1989-90 |
| 5 | K.Srikkanth | v | Australia | Perth | 1991-92 |
| 4 | A.L.Wadekar | v | England | Birmingham | 1967 |
| 4 | A.L.Wadekar | v | New Zealand | Christchurch | 1967-68 |
| **PAKISTAN** | | | | | |
| 4 | W.Mathias | v | West Indies | Bridgetown | 1957-58 |
| 4 | Hanif Mohammad | v | England | Dacca | 1968-69 |
| 4 | Aamer Malik § | v | England | Faisalabad | 1987-88 |
| 4 | Inzamamul Haq | v | Zimbabwe | Rawalpindi[2] | 1993-94 |
| 4 | Saleem Elahi | v | Sri Lanka | Colombo (SSC) | 1996-97 |
| **SRI LANKA** | | | | | |
| 4 | Y.Goonasekera | v | New Zealand | Wellington | 1982-83 |
| 4 | H.P.Tillakaratne | v | New Zealand | Colombo (SSC) | 1992-93 |
| 4 | R.S.Mahanama | v | New Zealand | Dunedin | 1996-97 |
| 4 | R.S.Mahanama | v | Zimbabwe | Colombo (PIS) | 1996-97 |
| 4 | P.A.de Silva | v | India | Mumbai[3] | 1997-98 |
| **ZIMBABWE** | | | | | |
| 4 | M.H.Dekker | v | Sri Lanka | Harare | 1994-95 |

# All Round

## 1000 RUNS AND 100 WICKETS

| AUSTRALIA | Tests | Runs | Wkts | Tests for Double |
|---|---|---|---|---|
| R.Benaud | 63 | 2201 | 248 | 32 |
| A K.Davidson | 44 | 1328 | 186 | 34 |
| G Giffen | 31 | 1238 | 103 | 30 |
| M.G.Hughes | 53 | 1032 | 212 | 52 |
| I.W.Johnson | 45 | 1000 | 109 | 45 |
| R.R.Lindwall | 61 | 1502 | 228 | 38 |
| K.R.Miller | 55 | 2958 | 170 | 33 |
| M.A.Noble | 42 | 1997 | 121 | 27 |
| S.K.Warne | 67 | 1230 | 313 | 58 |
| **ENGLAND** | | | | |
| T.E.Bailey | 61 | 2290 | 132 | 47 |
| I.T.Botham | 102 | 5200 | 383 | 21 |
| J.E.Emburey | 64 | 1721 | 147 | 46 |
| A.W.Greig | 58 | 3599 | 141 | 37 |
| R.Illingworth | 61 | 1836 | 122 | 47 |
| W.Rhodes | 58 | 2325 | 127 | 44 |
| M W.Tate | 39 | 1198 | 155 | 33 |
| F.J.Titmus | 53 | 1449 | 153 | 40 |
| **SOUTH AFRICA** | | | | |
| T.L.Goddard | 41 | 2516 | 123 | 36 |
| **WEST INDIES** | | | | |
| C.E.L.Ambrose | 80 | 1188 | 337 | 69 |
| M.D.Marshall | 81 | 1810 | 376 | 49 |
| G.S.Sobers | 93 | 8032 | 235 | 48 |
| **NEW ZEALAND** | | | | |
| J.G.Bracewell | 41 | 1001 | 102 | 41 |
| R.J.Hadlee | 86 | 3124 | 431 | 28 |
| C.L.Cairns | 33 | 1442 | 103 | 33 |
| **INDIA** | | | | |
| Kapil Dev | 131 | 5248 | 434 | 25 |
| M.H.Mankad | 44 | 2109 | 162 | 23 |
| R.J.Shastri | 80 | 3830 | 151 | 44 |
| **PAKISTAN** | | | | |
| Abdul Qadir | 67 | 1029 | 236 | 62 |
| Imran Khan | 88 | 3807 | 362 | 30 |
| Intikhab Alam | 47 | 1493 | 125 | 41 |
| Sarfraz Nawaz | 55 | 1045 | 177 | 55 |
| Wasim Akram | 79 | 2020 | 341 | 45 |

## 1000 RUNS, 50 WICKETS AND 50 CATCHES

| AUSTRALIA | Tests | Runs | Wkts | Catches |
|---|---|---|---|---|
| R.Benaud | 63 | 2201 | 248 | 65 |
| R.B.Simpson | 62 | 4869 | 71 | 110 |
| S.R.Waugh | 103 | 6480 | 86 | 77 |
| **ENGLAND** | | | | |
| I.T.Botham | 102 | 5200 | 383 | 120 |
| A.W.Greig | 58 | 3599 | 141 | 87 |
| W.R.Hammond | 85 | 7249 | 83 | 110 |
| W.Rhodes | 58 | 2325 | 127 | 60 |
| F.E.Woolley | 64 | 3283 | 83 | 64 |

| | | | | |
|---|---|---|---|---|
| **WEST INDIES** | | | | |
| C.L.Hooper | 73 | 3826 | 80 | 79 |
| G.S.Sobers | 93 | 8032 | 235 | 109 |
| **INDIA** | | | | |
| Kapil Dev | 131 | 5248 | 434 | 64 |

## 1000 RUNS AND 100 WICKETKEEPING DISMISSALS

| **AUSTRALIA** | Tests | Runs | Dismissals | Tests for Double |
|---|---|---|---|---|
| I.A.Healy | 103 | 3906 | 353 | 36 |
| R.W.Marsh | 96 | 3633 | 355 | 25 |
| W.A.S.Oldfield | 54 | 1427 | 130 | 41 |
| **ENGLAND** | | | | |
| T.G.Evans | 91 | 2439 | 219 | 42 |
| A.P.E.Knott | 95 | 4389 | 269 | 30 |
| J.M.Parks | 46 | 1962 | 114 | 41 |
| R.C.Russell | 54 | 1897 | 152 | 37 |
| A.J.Stewart | 80 | 5618 | 146 | 65 |
| R.W.Taylor | 57 | 1156 | 174 | 47 |
| **SOUTH AFRICA** | | | | |
| J.H.B.Waite | 50 | 2405 | 141 | 36 |
| D.J.Richardson | 42 | 1359 | 152 | 28 |
| **WEST INDIES** | | | | |
| P.J.L.Dujon | 81 | 3322 | 272 | 30 |
| D.L.Murray | 62 | 1993 | 189 | 33 |
| **NEW ZEALAND** | | | | |
| I.D.S.Smith | 63 | 1815 | 177 | 42 |
| **INDIA** | | | | |
| S.M.H.Kirmani | 88 | 2759 | 198 | 42 |
| K.S.More | 46 | 1277 | 125 | 39 |
| **PAKISTAN** | | | | |
| Saleem Yousuf | 32 | 1055 | 104 | 32 |
| Wasim Bari | 81 | 1366 | 228 | 53 |

## 250 RUNS AND 20 WICKETS IN A SERIES *(§ In first Test series)*

| | Tests | Runs | Wkts | | | | |
|---|---|---|---|---|---|---|---|
| G.Giffen | 5 | 475 | 34 | Australia | v | England | 1894-95 |
| L.C.Braund § | 5 | 256 | 21 | England | v | Australia | 1901-02 |
| G.A.Faulkner | 5 | 545 | 29 | South Africa | v | England | 1909-10 |
| G.J.Thompson | 5 | 267 | 23 | England | v | South Africa | 1909-10 |
| J.M.Gregory § | 5 | 442 | 23 | Australia | v | England | 1920-21 |
| K.R.Miller | 5 | 362 | 20 | Australia | v | West Indies | 1951-52 |
| K.R.Miller | 5 | 439 | 20 | Australia | v | West Indies | 1954-55 |
| R.Benaud | 5 | 329 | 30 | Australia | v | South Africa | 1957-58 |
| G.S.Sobers | 5 | 424 | 23 | West Indies | v | India | 1961-62 |
| G.S.Sobers | 5 | 322 | 20 | West Indies | v | England | 1963 |
| G.S.Sobers | 5 | 722 | 20 | West Indies | v | England | 1966 |
| T.L.Goddard | 5 | 294 | 26 | South Africa | v | Australia | 1966-67 |
| A.W.Greig | 5 | 430 | 24 | England | v | West Indies | 1973-74 |
| I.T.Botham | 6 | 291 | 23 | England | v | Australia | 1978-79 |
| Kapil Dev | 6 | 278 | 32 | India | v | Pakistan | 1979-80 |
| I T.Botham | 6 | 399 | 34 | England | v | Australia | 1981 |
| Kapil Dev | 6 | 318 | 22 | India | v | England | 1981-82 |
| R.J.Hadlee | 4 | 301 | 21 | New Zealand | v | England | 1983 |
| I.T.Botham | 6 | 250 | 31 | England | v | Australia | 1985 |

## 250 RUNS AND 20 WICKETKEEPING DISMISSALS IN A SERIES

| | Tests | Runs | Dismissals | | | | |
|---|---|---|---|---|---|---|---|
| J H.B Waite | 5 | 263 | 26 | South Africa | v | New Zealand | 1961-62 |
| D T.Lindsay | 5 | 606 | 24 | South Africa | v | Australia | 1966-67 |
| A P.E.Knott | 6 | 364 | 23 | England | v | Australia | 1974-75 |
| P.J.L.Dujon | 5 | 305 | 20 | West Indies | v | England | 1988 |
| I.A.Healy | 6 | 296 | 26 | Australia | v | England | 1993 |
| A.J.Stewart | 6 | 268 | 23 | England | v | Australia | 1997 |
| A.J.Stewart | 5 | 465 | 23 | England | v | Australia | 1998 |

## 500 RUNS IN A SERIES BY A WICKETKEEPER

| | Tests | Runs | Avge | | | | |
|---|---|---|---|---|---|---|---|
| B.K.Kunderan | 5 | 525 | 52.50 | India | v | England | 1963-64 |
| D.T.Lindsay | 5 | 606 | 86.57 | South Africa | v | Australia | 1966-67 |

## MATCH DOUBLE - 100 RUNS AND 10 WICKETS

| | | | | | | | |
|---|---|---|---|---|---|---|---|
| A.K.Davidson | 44<br>80 | 5-135)<br>6-87 ) | Australia | v | West Indies | Brisbane[2] | 1960-61 |
| I.T.Botham | 114 | 6-58)<br>7-48) | England | v | India | Bombay[3] | 1979-80 |
| Imran Khan | 117 | 6-98)<br>5-82) | Pakistan | v | India | Faisalabad | 1982-83 |

## A CENTURY AND 5 WICKETS IN AN INNINGS OF THE SAME MATCH *(§ In first Test)*

| | | | Opponents | | |
|---|---|---|---|---|---|
| **AUSTRALIA** | | | | | |
| C.Kelleway | 114 | 5-33 | South Africa | Manchester | 1912 |
| J.M.Gregory | 100 | 7-69 | England | Melbourne | 1920-21 |
| K.R.Miller | 109 | 6-107 | West Indies | Kingston | 1954-55 |
| R.Benaud | 100 | 5-84 | South Africa | Johannesburg[3] | 1957-58 |
| **ENGLAND** | | | | | |
| A.W.Greig | 148 | 6-164 | West Indies | Bridgetown | 1973-74 |
| I.T.Botham | 103 | 5-73 | New Zealand | Christchurch | 1977-78 |
| I.T.Botham | 108 | 8-34 | Pakistan | Lord's | 1978 |
| I.T.Botham | 114 | 6-58 + 7-48 | India | Bombay[3] | 1979-80 |
| I.T.Botham | 149* | 6-95 | Australia | Leeds | 1981 |
| I.T.Botham | 138 | 5-59 | New Zealand | Wellington | 1983-84 |
| **SOUTH AFRICA** | | | | | |
| J.H.Sinclair | 106 | 6-26 | England | Cape Town | 1898-99 |
| G.A.Faulkner | 123 | 5-120 | England | Johannesburg[1] | 1909-10 |
| **WEST INDIES** | | | | | |
| D.S.Atkinson | 219 | 5-56 | Australia | Bridgetown | 1954-55 |
| O.G.Smith | 100 | 5-90 | India | Delhi | 1958-59 |
| G.S.Sobers | 104 | 5-63 | India | Kingston | 1961-62 |
| G.S.Sobers | 174 | 5-41 | England | Leeds | 1966 |
| **NEW ZEALAND** | | | | | |
| B.R.Taylor § | 105 | 5-86 | India | Calcutta | 1964-65 |
| **INDIA** | | | | | |
| M.H.Mankad | 184 | 5-196 | England | Lord's | 1952 |
| P.R.Umrigar | 172* | 5-107 | West Indies | Port-of-Spain | 1961-62 |
| **PAKISTAN** | | | | | |
| Mushtaq Mohammad | 201 | 5-49 | New Zealand | Dunedin | 1972-73 |
| Mushtaq Mohammad | 121 | 5-28 | West Indies | Port-of-Spain | 1976-77 |
| Imran Khan | 117 | 6-88 + 5-82 | India | Faisalabad | 1982-83 |
| Wasim Akram | 123 | 5-100 | Australia | Adelaide | 1989-90 |

| **ZIMBABWE** | | | | | |
|---|---|---|---|---|---|
| P.A.Strang | 106* | 5-212 | Pakistan | Sheikhupura | 1996-97 |

## A FIFTY AND TEN WICKETS IN THE SAME MATCH *(§ In first Test)*

| **AUSTRALIA** | | | Opponents | | |
|---|---|---|---|---|---|
| H.Trumble | 64* + 7* | 8-65 + 4-108 | England | The Oval | 1902 |
| A.K.Davidson | 44 + 80 | 5-132 + 6-87 | West Indies | Brisbane[2] | 1960-61 |
| A.R.Border | 75 + 16* | 7-46 + 4-50 | West Indies | Sydney | 1988-89 |
| M.G.Bevan | 85* | 4-31 + 6-82 | West Indies | Adelaide | 1996-97 |
| **ENGLAND** | | | Opponents | | |
| W.Bates | 55 | 7-28 + 7-74 | Australia | Melbourne | 1882-83 |
| F.E.Woolley | 62 + 4 | 5-29 + 5-20 | Australia | The Oval | 1912 |
| A.W.Greig | 51 | 5-98 + 5-51 | New Zealand | Auckland | 1974-75 |
| J.K.Lever § | 53 | 7-46 + 3-24 | India | Delhi | 1976-77 |
| I.T.Botham | 114 | 6-58 + 7-48 | India | Bombay[3] | 1979-80 |
| **SOUTH AFRICA** | | | Opponents | | |
| P.S.de Villiers | 66* | 6-81 + 4-27 | Pakistan | Johannesburg[3] | 1994-95 |
| **WEST INDIES** | | | Opponents | | |
| K.D.Boyce | 72 + 9 | 5-70 + 6-77 | England | The Oval | 1973 |
| M.D.Marshall | 63 | 4-40 + 7-80 | New Zealand | Bridgetown | 1984-85 |
| **NEW ZEALAND** | | | Opponents | | |
| R.J.Hadlee | 51 + 17 | 5-34 + 6-68 | West Indies | Dunedin | 1979-80 |
| R.J.Hadlee | 54 | 9-52 + 6-71 | Australia | Brisbane[2] | 1985-86 |
| R.J.Hadlee | 68 | 6-80 + 4-60 | England | Nottingham | 1986 |
| D.J.Nash | 56 | 6-76 + 5-93 | England | Lord's | 1994 |
| **INDIA** | | | Opponents | | |
| Kapil Dev | 84 | 4-90 + 7-56 | Pakistan | Madras[1] | 1979-80 |
| **PAKISTAN** | | | Opponents | | |
| Imran Khan | 117 | 6-98 + 5-82 | India | Faisalabad | 1982-83 |
| Abdul Qadir | 61 | 5-88 + 5-98 | England | Karachi[1] | 1987-88 |

## A CENTURY AND FIVE DISMISSALS IN AN INNINGS BY A WICKETKEEPER

| | | | | | | | |
|---|---|---|---|---|---|---|---|
| D.T.Lindsay | 182 | 6c | South Africa | v | Australia | Johannesburg[3] | 1966-67 |
| I.D.S.Smith | 113* | 4c, 1s | New Zealand | v | England | Auckland | 1983-84 |
| S.A.R.Silva | 111 | 5c | Sri Lanka | v | India | Colombo (PSS) | 1985-86 |

## The Captains

| **RESULT SUMMARY** | Tests as | | | Opponents | | | | | | Results | | | | Toss |
|---|---|---|---|---|---|---|---|---|---|---|---|---|---|---|
| **AUSTRALIA** (39) | Captain | E | SA | WI | NZ | I | P | SL | Z | W | L | D | Tie | Won |
| D.W.Gregory | **3** | 3 | - | - | - | - | - | - | - | 2 | 1 | - | - | 2 |
| W.L.Murdoch | **16** | 16 | - | - | - | - | - | - | - | 5 | 7 | 4 | - | 7 |
| T.P.Horan | **2** | 2 | - | - | - | - | - | - | - | - | 2 | - | - | 1 |
| H.H.Massie | **1** | 1 | - | - | - | - | - | - | - | 1 | - | - | - | 1 |
| J.M.Blackham | **8** | 8 | - | - | - | - | - | - | - | 3 | 3 | 2 | - | 4 |
| H.J.H.Scott | **3** | 3 | - | - | - | - | - | - | - | - | 3 | - | - | 1 |
| P.S.McDonnell | **6** | 6 | - | - | - | - | - | - | - | 1 | 5 | - | - | 4 |
| G.Giffen | **4** | 4 | - | - | - | - | - | - | - | 2 | 2 | - | - | 3 |
| G.H.S.Trott | **8** | 8 | - | - | - | - | - | - | - | 5 | 3 | - | - | 5 |
| J.Darling | **21** | 18 | 3 | - | - | - | - | - | - | 7 | 4 | 10 | - | 7 |
| H.Trumble | **2** | 2 | - | - | - | - | - | - | - | 2 | - | - | - | 1 |
| M.A.Noble | **15** | 15 | - | - | - | - | - | - | - | 8 | 5 | 2 | - | 11 |
| C.Hill | **10** | 5 | 5 | - | - | - | - | - | - | 5 | 5 | - | - | 5 |
| S.E.Gregory | **6** | 3 | 3 | - | - | - | - | - | - | 2 | 1 | 3 | - | 1 |
| W.W.Armstrong | **10** | 10 | - | - | - | - | - | - | - | 8 | - | 2 | - | 4 |
| H.L.Collins | **11** | 8 | 3 | - | - | - | - | - | - | 5 | 2 | 4 | - | 7 |
| W.Bardsley | **2** | 2 | - | - | - | - | - | - | - | - | - | 2 | - | 1 |
| J.Ryder | **5** | 5 | - | - | - | - | - | - | - | 1 | 4 | - | - | 2 |
| W.M.Woodfull | **25** | 15 | 5 | 5 | - | - | - | - | - | 14 | 7 | 4 | - | 12 |
| V.Y.Richardson | **5** | - | 5 | - | - | - | - | - | - | 4 | - | 1 | - | 1 |
| D.G.Bradman | **24** | 19 | - | - | - | 5 | - | - | - | 15 | 3 | 6 | - | 10 |
| W.A.Brown | **1** | - | - | - | 1 | - | - | - | - | 1 | - | - | - | 0 |
| A.L.Hassett | **24** | 10 | 10 | 4 | - | - | - | - | - | 14 | 4 | 6 | - | 18 |
| A.R.Morris | **2** | 1 | - | - | - | - | - | - | - | - | 2 | - | - | 2 |
| I.W.Johnson | **17** | 9 | - | 5 | - | 2 | 1 | - | - | 7 | 5 | 5 | - | 6 |
| R.R.Lindwall | **1** | - | - | - | - | 1 | - | - | - | - | - | 1 | - | 0 |
| I.D.Craig | **5** | - | 5 | - | - | - | - | - | - | 3 | - | 2 | - | 3 |
| R.Benaud | **28** | 14 | 1 | 5 | - | 5 | 3 | - | - | 12 | 4 | 11 | 1 | 11 |
| R.N.Harvey | **1** | 1 | - | - | - | - | - | - | - | 1 | - | - | - | 0 |
| R.B.Simpson | **39** | 8 | 9 | 10 | - | 10 | 2 | - | - | 12 | 12 | 15 | - | 19 |
| B.C.Booth | **2** | 2 | - | - | - | - | - | - | - | - | 1 | 1 | - | 1 |
| W.M.Lawry | **25** | 9 | 4 | 5 | - | 7 | - | - | - | 9 | 8 | 8 | - | 8 |
| B.N.Jarman | **1** | 1 | - | - | - | - | - | - | - | - | - | 1 | - | 1 |
| I.M.Chappell | **30** | 16 | - | 5 | 6 | - | 3 | - | - | 15 | 5 | 10 | - | 17 |
| G.S.Chappell | **48** | 15 | - | 12 | 8 | 3 | 9 | 1 | - | 21 | 13 | 14 | - | 29 |
| G.N.Yallop | **7** | 6 | - | - | - | - | 1 | - | - | 1 | 6 | - | - | 6 |
| K.J.Hughes | **28** | 6 | - | 7 | - | 6 | 9 | - | - | 4 | 13 | 11 | - | 13 |
| A.R.Border | **93** | 29 | 6 | 18 | 17 | 11 | 6 | 6 | - | 32 | 22 | 38 | 1 | 46 |
| M.A.Taylor | **42** | 11 | 6 | 9 | 3 | 4 | 6 | 3 | - | 22 | 12 | 8 | - | 19 |
| | **581** | 291 | 65 | 86 | 35 | 54 | 40 | 10 | - | 244 | 164 | 171 | 2 | 289 |

| | Tests as | | | Opponents | | | | | | Results | | | | Toss |
|---|---|---|---|---|---|---|---|---|---|---|---|---|---|---|
| **ENGLAND** (71) | Captain | A | SA | WI | NZ | I | P | SL | Z | W | L | D | Tie | Won |
| James Lillywhite | **2** | 2 | - | - | - | - | - | - | - | 1 | 1 | - | - | 0 |
| Lord Harris | **4** | 4 | - | - | - | - | - | - | - | 2 | 1 | 1 | - | 2 |
| A.Shaw | **4** | 4 | - | - | - | - | - | - | - | - | 2 | 2 | - | 4 |
| A.N.Hornby | **2** | 2 | - | - | - | - | - | - | - | - | 1 | 1 | - | 1 |
| Hon.I.F.W.Bligh | **4** | 4 | - | - | - | - | - | - | - | 2 | 2 | - | - | 3 |
| A.Shrewsbury | **7** | 7 | - | - | - | - | - | - | - | 5 | 2 | - | - | 3 |
| A.G.Steel | **4** | 4 | - | - | - | - | - | - | - | 3 | 1 | - | - | 2 |
| W.W.Read | **2** | 1 | 1 | - | - | - | - | - | - | 2 | - | - | - | 0 |
| W.G.Grace | **13** | 13 | - | - | - | - | - | - | - | 8 | 3 | 2 | - | 4 |
| C.A.Smith | **1** | - | 1 | - | - | - | - | - | - | 1 | - | - | - | 0 |
| M.P.Bowden | **1** | - | 1 | - | - | - | - | - | - | 1 | - | - | - | 1 |
| A.E.Stoddart | **8** | 8 | - | - | - | - | - | - | - | 3 | 4 | 1 | - | 2 |
| T.C.O'Brien | **1** | - | 1 | - | - | - | - | - | - | 1 | - | - | - | 0 |

| | | | | | | | | | | | | | | |
|---|---|---|---|---|---|---|---|---|---|---|---|---|---|---|
| Lord Hawke | **4** | - | 4 | - | - | - | - | - | - | 4 | - | - | - | 4 |
| A.C.MacLaren | **22** | 22 | - | - | - | - | - | - | - | 4 | 11 | 7 | - | 11 |
| P.F.Warner | **10** | 5 | 5 | - | - | - | - | - | - | 4 | 6 | - | - | 5 |
| Hon F.S.Jackson | **5** | 5 | - | - | - | - | - | - | - | 2 | - | 3 | - | 5 |
| R.E.Foster | **3** | - | 3 | - | - | - | - | - | - | 1 | - | 2 | - | 3 |
| F.L.Fane | **5** | 3 | 2 | - | - | - | - | - | - | 2 | 3 | - | - | 3 |
| A.O.Jones | **2** | 2 | - | - | - | - | - | - | - | - | 2 | - | - | 1 |
| H.D.G.Leveson Gower | **3** | - | 3 | - | - | - | - | - | - | 1 | 2 | - | - | 0 |
| J.W.H.T.Douglas | **18** | 12 | 6 | - | - | - | - | - | - | 8 | 8 | 2 | - | 7 |
| C.B Fry | **6** | 3 | 3 | - | - | - | - | - | - | 4 | - | 2 | - | 4 |
| Hon.L.H.Tennyson | **3** | 3 | - | - | - | - | - | - | - | - | 1 | 2 | - | 2 |
| F.T.Mann | **5** | - | 5 | - | - | - | - | - | - | 2 | 1 | 2 | - | 3 |
| A.E.R.Gilligan | **9** | 5 | 4 | - | - | - | - | - | - | 4 | 4 | 1 | - | 2 |
| A.W Carr | **6** | 4 | 2 | - | - | - | - | - | - | 1 | - | 5 | - | 3 |
| A.P.F.Chapman | **17** | 9 | 5 | 3 | - | - | - | - | - | 9 | 2 | 6 | - | 9 |
| R.T.Stanyforth | **4** | - | 4 | - | - | - | - | - | - | 2 | 1 | 1 | - | 0 |
| G.T.S.Stevens | **1** | - | 1 | - | - | - | - | - | - | - | 1 | - | - | 0 |
| J.C.White | **4** | 1 | 3 | - | - | - | - | - | - | 1 | 1 | 2 | - | 3 |
| A.H.H.Gilligan | **4** | - | - | - | 4 | - | - | - | - | 1 | - | 3 | - | 1 |
| Hon.F.S.G.Calthorpe | **4** | - | - | 4 | - | - | - | - | - | 1 | 1 | 2 | - | 2 |
| R.E.S.Wyatt | **16** | 5 | 5 | 5 | 1 | - | - | - | - | 3 | 5 | 8 | - | 12 |
| D.R.Jardine | **15** | 5 | - | 2 | 4 | 4 | - | - | - | 9 | 1 | 5 | - | 7 |
| C.F.Walters | **1** | 1 | - | - | - | - | - | - | - | - | 1 | - | - | 0 |
| G.O.B.Allen | **11** | 5 | - | 3 | - | 3 | - | - | - | 4 | 5 | 2 | - | 6 |
| R.W.V.Robins | **3** | - | - | - | 3 | - | - | - | - | 1 | - | 2 | - | 2 |
| W.R.Hammond | **20** | 8 | 5 | 3 | 1 | 3 | - | - | - | 4 | 3 | 13 | - | 12 |
| N.W.D.Yardley | **14** | 6 | 5 | 3 | - | - | - | - | - | 4 | 7 | 3 | - | 9 |
| K.Cranston | **1** | - | - | - | 1 | - | - | - | - | - | - | 1 | - | 0 |
| F.G.Mann | **7** | - | 5 | - | 2 | - | - | - | - | 2 | - | 5 | - | 5 |
| F.R.Brown | **15** | 5 | 5 | 1 | 4 | - | - | - | - | 5 | 6 | 4 | - | 3 |
| N.D.Howard | **4** | - | - | - | - | 4 | - | - | - | 1 | - | 3 | - | 2 |
| D.B.Carr | **1** | - | - | - | - | 1 | - | - | - | - | 1 | - | - | 1 |
| L.Hutton | **23** | 10 | - | 5 | 2 | 4 | 2 | - | - | 11 | 4 | 8 | - | 7 |
| Rev.D.S.Sheppard | **2** | - | - | - | - | - | 2 | - | - | 1 | - | 1 | - | 1 |
| P.B.H.May | **41** | 13 | 10 | 8 | 7 | 3 | - | - | - | 20 | 10 | 11 | - | 26 |
| M.C.Cowdrey | **27** | 6 | 5 | 10 | - | 2 | 4 | - | - | 8 | 4 | 15 | - | 17 |
| E.R.Dexter | **30** | 10 | - | 5 | 3 | 5 | 7 | - | - | 9 | 7 | 14 | - | 13 |
| M.J.K.Smith | **25** | 5 | 8 | 1 | 6 | 5 | - | - | - | 5 | 3 | 17 | - | 10 |
| D.B.Close | **7** | - | - | 1 | - | 3 | 3 | - | - | 6 | - | 1 | - | 4 |
| T.W.Graveney | **1** | 1 | - | - | - | - | - | - | - | - | - | 1 | - | 0 |
| R.Illingworth | **31** | 11 | - | 6 | 8 | 3 | 3 | - | - | 12 | 5 | 14 | - | 15 |
| A R.Lewis | **8** | - | - | - | - | 5 | 3 | - | - | 1 | 2 | 5 | - | 3 |
| M.H.Denness | **19** | 6 | - | 5 | 2 | 3 | 3 | - | - | 6 | 5 | 8 | - | 9 |
| J.H.Edrich | **1** | 1 | - | - | - | - | - | - | - | - | 1 | - | - | 0 |
| A.W.Greig | **14** | 4 | - | 5 | - | 5 | - | - | - | 3 | 5 | 6 | - | 6 |
| J.M.Brearley | **31** | 18 | - | - | 3 | 5 | 5 | - | - | 18 | 4 | 9 | - | 13 |
| G.Boycott | **4** | - | - | - | 3 | - | 1 | - | - | 1 | 1 | 2 | - | 3 |
| I.T.Botham | **12** | 3 | - | 9 | - | - | - | - | - | - | 4 | 8 | - | 6 |
| K.W.R.Fletcher | **7** | - | - | - | - | 6 | - | 1 | - | 1 | 1 | 5 | - | 5 |
| R.G.D.Willis | **18** | 5 | - | - | 7 | 3 | 3 | - | - | 7 | 5 | 6 | - | 8 |
| D.I.Gower | **32** | 12 | - | 10 | - | 6 | 3 | 1 | - | 5 | 18 | 9 | - | 14 |
| M.W.Gatting | **23** | 6 | - | 1 | 6 | 2 | 8 | - | - | 2 | 5 | 16 | - | 14 |
| J.E.Emburey | **2** | - | - | 2 | - | - | - | - | - | - | 2 | - | - | 1 |
| C.S.Cowdrey | **1** | - | - | 1 | - | - | - | - | - | - | 1 | - | - | 0 |
| G.A.Gooch | **34** | 8 | - | 8 | 6 | 5 | 5 | 2 | - | 10 | 12 | 12 | - | 16 |
| A.J.Lamb | **3** | 1 | - | 2 | - | - | - | - | - | - | 3 | - | - | 2 |
| A.J.Stewart | **7** | - | 5 | - | - | 1 | - | 1 | - | 2 | 3 | 2 | - | 4 |
| M.A.Atherton | **52** | 13 | 8 | 17 | 6 | 3 | 3 | - | 2 | 13 | 19 | 20 | - | 23 |
| | **751** | 291 | 115 | 122 | 78 | 84 | 55 | 5 | 2 | 254 | 214 | 283 | - | 368 |

| **SOUTH AFRICA** (27) | Tests as Captain | Opponents | | | | | | | | Results | | | | Toss |
|---|---|---|---|---|---|---|---|---|---|---|---|---|---|---|
| | | A | E | WI | NZ | I | P | SL | Z | W | L | D | Tie | Won |
| O.R.Dunell | **1** | - | 1 | - | - | - | - | - | - | - | - | - | - | 1 |
| W.H.Milton | **2** | - | 2 | - | - | - | - | - | - | - | 2 | - | - | 1 |
| E.A.Halliwell | **3** | 1 | 2 | - | - | - | - | - | - | - | 3 | - | - | 1 |
| A.R.Richards | **1** | - | 1 | - | - | - | - | - | - | - | 1 | - | - | 0 |
| M.Bisset | **2** | - | 2 | - | - | - | - | - | - | - | 2 | - | - | 0 |
| H.M.Taberer | **1** | 1 | - | - | - | - | - | - | - | - | - | 1 | - | 1 |
| J.H.Anderson | **1** | 1 | - | - | - | - | - | - | - | - | 1 | - | - | 0 |
| P.W.Sherwell | **13** | 5 | 8 | - | - | - | - | - | - | 5 | 6 | 2 | - | 5 |
| S.J.Snooke | **5** | - | 5 | - | - | - | - | - | - | 3 | 2 | - | - | 3 |
| F.Mitchell | **3** | 2 | 1 | - | - | - | - | - | - | - | 3 | - | - | 2 |
| L.J.Tancred | **3** | 1 | 2 | - | - | - | - | - | - | - | 2 | 1 | - | 2 |
| H.W.Taylor | **18** | 3 | 15 | - | - | - | - | - | - | 1 | 10 | 7 | - | 11 |
| H.G.Deane | **12** | - | 12 | - | - | - | - | - | - | 2 | 4 | 6 | - | 9 |
| E.P.Nupen | **1** | - | 1 | - | - | - | - | - | - | 1 | - | - | - | 0 |
| H.B.Cameron | **9** | 5 | 2 | - | 2 | - | - | - | - | 2 | 5 | 2 | - | 3 |
| H.F.Wade | **10** | 5 | 5 | - | - | - | - | - | - | 1 | 4 | 5 | - | 5 |
| A.Melville | **10** | - | 10 | - | - | - | - | - | - | - | 4 | 6 | - | 4 |
| A.D.Nourse | **15** | 5 | 10 | - | - | - | - | - | - | 1 | 9 | 5 | - | 7 |
| J.E.Cheetham | **15** | 5 | 3 | - | 7 | - | - | - | - | 7 | 5 | 3 | - | 6 |
| D.J.McGlew | **14** | 1 | 8 | - | 5 | - | - | - | - | 4 | 6 | 4 | - | 4 |
| C.B.van Ryneveld | **8** | 4 | 4 | - | - | - | - | - | - | 2 | 4 | 2 | - | 3 |
| T.L.Goddard | **13** | 5 | 5 | - | 3 | - | - | - | - | 1 | 2 | 10 | - | 4 |
| P.L.van der Merwe | **8** | 5 | 3 | - | - | - | - | - | - | 4 | 1 | 3 | - | 4 |
| A Bacher | **4** | 4 | - | - | - | - | - | - | - | 4 | - | - | - | 4 |
| K.C.Wessels | **16** | 5 | 3 | 1 | - | 4 | - | 3 | - | 5 | 3 | 8 | - | 11 |
| W.J.Cronje | **36** | 7 | 10 | - | 4 | 6 | 6 | 2 | 1 | 15 | 11 | 10 | - | 19 |
| G.Kirsten | **1** | - | - | - | - | - | 1 | - | - | - | - | 1 | - | - |
| | **225** | 65 | 115 | 1 | 21 | 10 | 7 | 5 | 1 | 58 | 89 | 76 | - | 109 |

| **WEST INDIES** (23) | Tests as Captain | Opponents | | | | | | | | Results | | | | Toss |
|---|---|---|---|---|---|---|---|---|---|---|---|---|---|---|
| | | A | E | SA | NZ | I | P | SL | Z | W | L | D | Tie | Won |
| R.K.Nunes | **4** | - | 4 | - | - | - | - | - | - | - | 3 | 1 | - | 2 |
| E.L.G.Hoad | **1** | - | 1 | - | - | - | - | - | - | - | - | 1 | - | 1 |
| N.Betancourt | **1** | - | 1 | - | - | - | - | - | - | - | - | 1 | - | 0 |
| M.P.Fernandes | **1** | - | 1 | - | - | - | - | - | - | 1 | - | - | - | 1 |
| G.C.Grant | **12** | 5 | 7 | - | - | - | - | - | - | 3 | 7 | 2 | - | 5 |
| R.C.Grant | **3** | - | 3 | - | - | - | - | - | - | - | 1 | 2 | - | 2 |
| G.A.Headley | **1** | - | 1 | - | - | - | - | - | - | - | - | 1 | - | 1 |
| J.D.C.Goddard | **22** | 4 | 11 | - | 2 | 5 | - | - | - | 8 | 7 | 7 | - | 12 |
| J.B.Stollmeyer | **13** | 3 | 5 | - | - | 5 | - | - | - | 3 | 4 | 6 | - | 7 |
| D.S.Atkinson | **7** | 3 | - | - | 4 | - | - | - | - | 3 | 3 | 1 | - | 3 |
| F.C.M.Alexander | **18** | - | 5 | - | - | 5 | 8 | - | - | 7 | 4 | 7 | - | 9 |
| F.M.M.Worrell | **15** | 5 | 5 | - | - | 5 | - | - | - | 9 | 3 | 2 | 1 | 9 |
| G.S.Sobers | **39** | 10 | 13 | - | 8 | 8 | - | - | - | 9 | 10 | 20 | - | 27 |
| R.B.Kanhai | **13** | 5 | 8 | - | - | - | - | - | - | 3 | 3 | 7 | - | 6 |
| C.H.Lloyd | **74** | 22 | 18 | - | 3 | 20 | 1 | - | - | 36 | 12 | 26 | - | 35 |
| A.I.Kallicharran | **9** | 3 | - | - | - | 6 | - | - | - | 1 | 2 | 6 | - | 4 |
| D.L.Murray | **1** | 1 | - | - | - | - | - | - | - | - | - | 1 | - | 1 |
| I.V.A.Richards | **50** | 11 | 19 | - | 7 | 8 | 5 | - | - | 27 | 8 | 15 | - | 24 |
| C.G.Greenidge | **1** | - | - | - | - | - | 1 | - | - | - | 1 | - | - | 1 |
| D.L.Haynes | **4** | - | 1 | - | - | - | 3 | - | - | 1 | 1 | 2 | - | 2 |
| R.B.Richardson | **24** | 9 | 10 | 1 | - | - | 3 | 1 | - | 11 | 6 | 7 | - | 12 |
| C.A.Walsh | **22** | 5 | 1 | - | 4 | 7 | 3 | 2 | - | 6 | 7 | 9 | - | 13 |
| B.C.Lara | **7** | - | 6 | - | - | 1 | - | - | - | 4 | 1 | 2 | - | 3 |
| | **343** | 86 | 121 | 1 | 28 | 70 | 34 | 3 | - | 132 | 84 | 126 | 1 | 180 |

| | Tests as | Opponents | | | | | | | | Results | | | | Toss |
|---|---|---|---|---|---|---|---|---|---|---|---|---|---|---|
| **NEW ZEALAND** (24) | Captain | A | E | SA | WI | I | P | SL | Z | W | L | D | Tie | Won |
| T.C.Lowry | **7** | 7 | 1 | - | - | - | - | - | - | - | 2 | 5 | - | 5 |
| M.L.Page | **7** | - | 5 | 2 | - | - | - | - | - | - | 3 | 4 | - | 4 |
| W.A.Hadlee | **8** | 1 | 7 | - | - | - | - | - | - | - | 2 | 6 | - | 4 |
| B.Sutcliffe | **4** | - | - | 2 | 2 | - | - | - | - | - | 3 | 1 | - | 4 |
| W.M.Wallace | **2** | - | - | 2 | - | - | - | - | - | - | 1 | 1 | - | 0 |
| G.O.Rabone | **5** | - | 2 | 3 | - | - | - | - | - | - | 4 | 1 | - | 2 |
| H.B.Cave | **9** | - | - | - | 1 | 5 | 3 | - | - | - | 5 | 4 | - | 5 |
| J.R.Reid | **34** | - | 13 | 8 | 3 | 4 | 6 | - | - | 3 | 18 | 13 | - | 17 |
| M.E.Chapple | **1** | - | 1 | - | - | - | - | - | - | - | - | 1 | - | 0 |
| B.W.Sinclair | **3** | - | 2 | - | - | 1 | - | - | - | - | 1 | 2 | - | 3 |
| G.T.Dowling | **19** | - | 5 | - | 5 | 6 | 3 | - | - | 4 | 7 | 8 | - | 10 |
| B.E.Congdon | **17** | 6 | 5 | - | 3 | - | 3 | - | - | 1 | 7 | 9 | - | 4 |
| G.M.Turner | **10** | 2 | - | - | - | 6 | 2 | - | - | 1 | 6 | 3 | - | 2 |
| J.M.Parker | **1** | - | - | - | - | - | 1 | - | - | - | - | 1 | - | 0 |
| M.G.Burgess | **10** | 1 | 6 | - | - | - | 3 | - | - | 1 | 6 | 3 | - | 4 |
| G.P.Howarth | **30** | 5 | 7 | - | 7 | 3 | 3 | 5 | - | 11 | 7 | 12 | - | 17 |
| J.V.Coney | **15** | 6 | 3 | - | 3 | - | 3 | - | - | 5 | 4 | 6 | - | 8 |
| J.J.Crowe | **6** | 3 | 2 | - | - | - | - | 1 | - | - | 1 | 5 | - | 3 |
| J.G.Wright | **14** | 2 | 4 | - | - | 6 | 2 | - | - | 3 | 3 | 8 | - | 8 |
| M.D.Crowe | **16** | 4 | 3 | - | - | - | 3 | 4 | 2 | 2 | 7 | 7 | - | 8 |
| I.D.S.Smith | **1** | - | - | - | - | - | - | 1 | - | - | - | 1 | - | 1 |
| K.R.Rutherford | **18** | 2 | 3 | 4 | 2 | 1 | 4 | 2 | - | 2 | 11 | 5 | - | 12 |
| L.K.Germon | **12** | - | 2 | - | 2 | 3 | 3 | - | 2 | 1 | 5 | 6 | - | 6 |
| S.P.Fleming | **13** | 3 | 1 | - | - | - | - | 5 | 4 | 5 | 5 | 3 | - | 6 |
| | **262** | 35 | 78 | 21 | 28 | 35 | 39 | 18 | 8 | 39 | 108 | 115 | - | 133 |

| | Tests as | Opponents | | | | | | | | Results | | | | Toss |
|---|---|---|---|---|---|---|---|---|---|---|---|---|---|---|
| **INDIA** (26) | Captain | A | E | SA | WI | NZ | P | SL | Z | W | L | D | Tie | Won |
| C.K.Nayudu | **4** | - | 4 | - | - | - | - | - | - | - | 3 | 1 | - | 1 |
| Maharajkumar of Vizianagram | **3** | - | 3 | - | - | - | - | - | - | - | 2 | 1 | - | 1 |
| Nawab of Pataudi, sr | **3** | - | 3 | - | - | - | - | - | - | - | 1 | 2 | - | 3 |
| N.B.Amarnath | **15** | 5 | - | - | 5 | - | 5 | - | - | 2 | 6 | 7 | - | 4 |
| V.S.Hazare | **14** | - | 9 | - | 5 | - | - | - | - | 1 | 5 | 8 | - | 8 |
| M.H.Mankad | **6** | - | - | - | 1 | - | 5 | - | - | - | 1 | 5 | - | 1 |
| Ghulam Ahmed | **3** | - | - | - | 2 | 1 | - | - | - | - | 2 | 1 | - | 1 |
| P.R.Umrigar | **8** | 3 | - | - | 1 | 4 | - | - | - | 2 | 2 | 4 | - | 6 |
| H.R.Adhikari | **1** | - | - | - | 1 | - | - | - | - | - | - | 1 | - | 1 |
| D.K.Gaekwad | **4** | - | 4 | - | - | - | - | - | - | - | 4 | - | - | 2 |
| Pankaj Roy | **1** | - | 1 | - | - | - | - | - | - | - | 1 | - | - | 1 |
| G.S.Ramchand | **5** | 5 | - | - | - | - | - | - | - | 1 | 2 | 2 | - | 4 |
| N.J.Contractor | **12** | - | 5 | - | 2 | - | 5 | - | - | 2 | 2 | 8 | - | 7 |
| Nawab of Pataudi, jr | **40** | 11 | 8 | - | 10 | 1 | - | - | - | 9 | 19 | 12 | - | 20 |
| C.G.Borde | **1** | 1 | - | - | - | - | - | - | - | - | 1 | - | - | 0 |
| A.L.Wadekar | **16** | - | 11 | - | 5 | - | - | - | - | 4 | 4 | 8 | - | 7 |
| S.Venkataraghavan | **5** | - | 4 | - | 1 | - | - | - | - | - | 2 | 3 | - | 2 |
| S.M.Gavaskar | **47** | 9 | 14 | - | 6 | 4 | 13 | 1 | - | 9 | 8 | 30 | - | 22 |
| B.S.Bedi | **22** | 5 | 5 | - | 4 | 5 | 3 | - | - | 6 | 11 | 5 | - | 13 |
| G.R.Viswanath | **2** | - | 1 | - | - | - | 1 | - | - | - | 1 | 1 | - | 2 |
| Kapil Dev | **34** | 6 | 3 | - | 11 | - | 8 | 6 | - | 4 | 7 | 22 | 1 | 15 |
| D.B.Vengsarkar | **10** | - | - | - | 7 | 3 | - | - | - | 2 | 5 | 3 | - | 4 |
| R.J.Shastri | **1** | - | - | - | 1 | - | - | - | - | 1 | - | - | - | 1 |
| K.Srikkanth | **4** | - | - | - | - | - | 4 | - | - | - | - | 4 | - | 2 |
| M.Azharuddin | **40** | 8 | 9 | 4 | 3 | 7 | - | 7 | 2 | 13 | 10 | 17 | - | 24 |
| S.R.Tendulkar | **17** | 1 | - | 6 | 5 | - | - | 5 | - | 3 | 4 | 10 | - | 10 |
| | **318** | 54 | 84 | 10 | 70 | 35 | 44 | 19 | 2 | 59 | 103 | 155 | 1 | 162 |

| PAKISTAN (21) | Tests as Captain | A | E | SA | WI | NZ | I | SL | Z | W | L | D | Tie | Toss Won |
|---|---|---|---|---|---|---|---|---|---|---|---|---|---|---|
| A.H.Kardar | **23** | 1 | 4 | - | 5 | 3 | 10 | - | - | 6 | 6 | 11 | - | 10 |
| Fazal Mahmood | **10** | 2 | - | - | 3 | - | 5 | - | - | 2 | 2 | 6 | - | 6 |
| Imtiaz Ahmed | **4** | 1 | 3 | - | - | - | - | - | - | - | 2 | 2 | - | 4 |
| Javed Burki | **5** | - | 5 | - | - | - | - | - | - | - | 4 | 1 | - | 3 |
| Hanif Mohammad | **11** | 2 | 3 | - | - | 6 | - | - | - | 2 | 2 | 7 | - | 6 |
| Saeed Ahmed | **3** | - | 3 | - | - | - | - | - | - | - | - | 3 | - | 1 |
| Intikhab Alam | **17** | 3 | 6 | - | 2 | 6 | - | - | - | 1 | 5 | 11 | - | 12 |
| Majid Khan | **3** | - | 3 | - | - | - | - | - | - | - | - | 3 | - | 1 |
| Mushtaq Mohammad | **19** | 5 | - | - | 5 | 6 | 3 | - | - | 8 | 4 | 7 | - | 10 |
| Wasim Bari | **6** | - | 6 | - | - | - | - | - | - | - | 2 | 4 | - | 4 |
| Asif Iqbal | **6** | - | - | - | - | - | 6 | - | - | - | 2 | 4 | - | 3 |
| Javed Miandad | **34** | 9 | 8 | - | 4 | 7 | - | 6 | - | 14 | 6 | 14 | - | 12 |
| Imran Khan | **48** | 8 | 8 | - | 9 | 2 | 15 | 6 | - | 14 | 8 | 26 | - | 25 |
| Zaheer Abbas | **14** | 3 | 3 | - | - | 3 | 5 | - | - | 3 | 1 | 10 | - | 6 |
| Wasim Akram | **17** | 3 | 3 | - | 6 | 1 | - | - | 4 | 9 | 4 | 4 | - | 4 |
| Waqar Younis | **1** | - | - | - | - | - | - | - | 1 | 1 | - | - | - | 1 |
| Saleem Malik | **12** | 3 | - | 1 | - | 3 | - | 2 | 3 | 7 | 3 | 2 | - | 6 |
| Rameez Raja | **5** | - | - | - | - | - | - | 5 | - | 1 | 2 | 2 | - | 2 |
| Saeed Anwar | **5** | - | - | 3 | - | 2 | - | - | - | 1 | 2 | 2 | - | 2 |
| Aamer Sohail | **2** | - | - | 2 | - | - | - | - | - | 1 | - | 1 | - | 1 |
| Rashid Latif | **3** | - | - | 1 | - | - | - | - | 2 | 1 | 1 | 1 | - | 1 |
| | **248** | 40 | 55 | 7 | 34 | 39 | 44 | 19 | 10 | 71 | 56 | 121 | - | 120 |

| SRI LANKA (6) | Tests as Captain | A | E | SA | WI | NZ | I | P | Z | W | L | D | Tie | Toss Won |
|---|---|---|---|---|---|---|---|---|---|---|---|---|---|---|
| B.Warnapura | **4** | 1 | 1 | - | - | - | 1 | 2 | - | - | 3 | 1 | - | 2 |
| L.R.D.Mendis | **19** | 1 | 1 | - | - | 4 | 6 | 7 | - | 2 | 8 | 9 | - | 10 |
| D.S.De Silva | **2** | - | - | - | - | 2 | - | - | - | - | 2 | - | - | 1 |
| R.S.Madugalle | **2** | 1 | 1 | - | - | - | - | - | - | - | 2 | - | - | - |
| A.Ranatunga | **54** | 7 | 1 | 5 | 3 | 12 | 12 | 7 | 7 | 11 | 19 | 24 | - | 29 |
| P.A.de Silva | **5** | 1 | 1 | - | - | - | - | 3 | - | - | 3 | 2 | - | 2 |
| | **87** | 10 | 5 | 5 | 3 | 18 | 19 | 19 | 7 | 13 | 37 | 36 | - | 44 |

| ZIMBABWE (3) | Tests as Captain | A | E | SA | WI | NZ | I | P | SL | W | L | D | Tie | Toss Won |
|---|---|---|---|---|---|---|---|---|---|---|---|---|---|---|
| D.L.Houghton | **4** | - | - | - | - | 2 | 2 | - | - | - | 2 | 2 | - | 1 |
| A.Flower | **12** | - | - | 1 | - | 2 | - | 6 | 3 | 1 | 5 | 6 | - | 7 |
| A.D.R.Campbell | **14** | - | 2 | - | - | 4 | - | 4 | 4 | - | 6 | 8 | - | 10 |
| | **30** | - | 2 | 1 | - | 8 | 2 | 10 | 7 | 1 | 13 | 16 | - | 18 |

(Columns A–Z/SL: Opponents; W, L, D, Tie: Results)

## MOST CONSECUTIVE MATCHES AS CAPTAIN# *to date.*

| | | | From | To |
|---|---|---|---|---|
| Australia | 93 | A.R.Border | 1984-85 | 1993-94 |
| England | 52 | M.A.Atherton | 1993 | 1997-98 |
| South Africa | 26 | W.J.Cronje | 1994-95 | 1997-98 |
| West Indies | 39 | G.S.Sobers | 1964-65 | 1971-72 |
| New Zealand | 34 | J.R.Reid | 1955-56 | 1965 |
| India | 37 | M.Azharuddin | 1989-90 | 1996 |
| Pakistan | 23 | A.H.Kardar | 1952-53 | 1957-58 |
| Sri Lanka | 30 | A.Ranatunga | 1992-93 | 1995-96 |
| Zimbabwe | 14 | A.D.R.Campbell | 1996-97 | # 1997-98 |

In addition to those listed above, the following had unbroken captaincy runs of 20 or more matches

42 M.A.Taylor (A)
35 P.B.H.May (E)

| | |
|---|---|
| 30 | I.M.Chappell (A) |
| 29 | C.H.Lloyd (WI) |
| 25 | W.M.Woodfull (A), R.Illingworth (E), D.I.Gower (E) |
| 23 | C.H.Lloyd (WI), M.W.Gatting (E) |
| 22 | B.S.Bedi(I), S.M.Gavaskar(I) |
| 21 | Nawab of Pataudi, jr (I) |
| 20 | M.J.K.Smith (E), W.M.Lawry (A), J.M.Brearley (E), Kapil Dev (I) |

## WINNING ALL FIVE TOSSES IN A SERIES

| Captains | | | | Venue | |
|---|---|---|---|---|---|
| Hon F.S.Jackson | England | v | Australia | England | 1905 |
| M.A.Noble | Australia | v | England | England | 1909 |
| H.G.Deane | South Africa | v | England | South Africa | 1927-28 |
| J.D.C.Goddard | West Indies | v | India | India | 1948-49 |
| A.L.Hassett | Australia | v | England | England | 1953 |
| P.B.H.May (3) ) | England | v | West Indies | West Indies | 1959-60 |
| M.C.Cowdrey (2) ) | | | | | |
| M.C.Cowdrey | England | v | South Africa | England | 1960 |
| Nawab of Pataudi, jr | India | v | England | India | 1963-64 |
| G.S.Sobers | West Indies | v | England | England | 1966 |
| G.S.Sobers | West Indies | v | New Zealand | West Indies | 1971-72 |
| C.H.Lloyd | West Indies | v | India | West Indies | 1982-83 |

*The following Australian captains won five tosses during six-match series in Australia: I.M.Chappell v England 1974-75; G.S.Chappell v West Indies 1975-76; G.N.Yallop v England 1978-79. K.W.R.Fletcher (England) won five successive tosses during the six-match series in India in 1981-82. M.A.Taylor (Australia) won five successive tosses during the six-match series in England in 1997. M.C.Cowdrey won the toss for England in nine consecutive Tests from 1959-60 to 1961. R.B.Richardson (West Indies) won the toss in all 4 Tests in the series against Australia in the West Indies in 1994-95 and 8 consecutive tosses from 1993-94 to 1995.*

## CAPTAINS WHO SENT THE OPPOSITION IN

*(§ In first match as captain. # In last Test as captain. ¶ In only Test as captain.)*

| **AUSTRALIA** | Opponents | Result | | |
|---|---|---|---|---|
| P.S.McDonnell § | England | Lost by 13 runs | Sydney | 1886-87 |
| P.S.McDonnell | England | Lost by 126 runs | Sydney | 1887-88 |
| G.Giffen § | England | Lost by 94 runs | Melbourne | 1894-95 |
| M.A.Noble | England | Won by 9 wkts | Lord's | 1909 |
| A.L.Hassett | West Indies | Won by 7 wkts | Sydney | 1951-52 |
| A.L.Hassett | England | Drawn | Leeds | 1953 |
| A.R.Morris # | England | Lost by 38 runs | Sydney | 1954-55 |
| I.W.Johnson | England | Drawn | Sydney | 1954-55 |
| R.Benaud | England | Won by 9 wkts | Melbourne | 1958-59 |
| R.Benaud | Pakistan | Won by 8 wkts | Dacca | 1959-60 |
| R.Benaud | West Indies | Won by 2 wkts | Melbourne | 1960-61 |
| R.B.Simpson § | South Africa | Won by 8 wkts | Melbourne | 1963-64 |
| R.B.Simpson | Pakistan | Drawn | Melbourne | 1964-65 |
| R.B.Simpson | West Indies | Drawn | Port-of-Spain | 1964-65 |
| R.B.Simpson | South Africa | Lost by 8 wkts | Durban[2] | 1966-67 |
| W.M.Lawry | West Indies | Won by Innings + 30 runs | Melbourne | 1968-69 |
| W.M.Lawry | India | Won by 10 wkts | Calcutta | 1969-70 |
| W.M.Lawry | England | Drawn | Perth | 1970-71 |
| I.M.Chappell § | England | Lost by 62 runs | Sydney | 1970-71 |
| I.M.Chappell | New Zealand | Drawn | Sydney | 1973-74 |
| I.M.Chappell | England | Won by 9 wkts | Perth | 1974-75 |
| I.M.Chappell | England | Drawn | Melbourne | 1974-75 |
| G.S.Chappell | West Indies | Won by 8 wkts | Melbourne | 1975-76 |
| G.S.Chappell | West Indies | Won by 7 wkts | Sydney | 1975-76 |
| G.S.Chappell | New Zealand | Won by 10 wkts | Auckland | 1976-77 |
| G.S.Chappell | England | Drawn | The Oval | 1977 |

| | | | | |
|---|---|---|---|---|
| R.B.Simpson | West Indies | Lost by 198 runs | Port-of-Spain | 1977-78 |
| G.N.Yallop | England | Lost by 166 runs | Perth | 1978-79 |
| G.N.Yallop | England | Lost by 205 runs | Adelaide | 1978-79 |
| G.N.Yallop # | Pakistan | Lost by 71 runs | Melbourne | 1978-79 |
| K.J.Hughes § | Pakistan | Won by 7 wkts | Perth | 1978-79 |
| G.S.Chappell | England | Won by 6 wkts | Sydney | 1979-80 |
| G.S.Chappell | West Indies | Lost by 408 runs | Adelaide | 1979-80 |
| G.S.Chappell | New Zealand | Won by 10 wkts | Brisbane[2] | 1980-81 |
| G.S.Chappell | New Zealand | Won by 8 wkts | Perth | 1980-81 |
| G.S.Chappell | India | Lost by 59 runs | Melbourne | 1980-81 |
| K.J.Hughes | England | Won by 4 wkts | Nottingham | 1981 |
| K.J.Hughes | England | Drawn | Lord's | 1981 |
| G.S.Chappell | Pakistan | Won by 10 wkts | Brisbane[2] | 1981-82 |
| G.S.Chappell | New Zealand | Drawn | Wellington | 1981-82 |
| G.S.Chappell | England | Drawn | Perth | 1982-83 |
| G.S.Chappell | England | Won by 7 wkts | Brisbane[2] | 1982-83 |
| G.S.Chappell | England | Lost by 3 runs | Melbourne | 1982-83 |
| K.J.Hughes | Pakistan | Won by 10 wkts | Sydney | 1983-84 |
| K.J.Hughes | West Indies | Lost by Innings + 112 runs | Perth | 1984-85 |
| A.R.Border | West Indies | Drawn | Melbourne | 1984-85 |
| A.R.Border | England | Won by 4 wkts | Lord's | 1985 |
| A.R.Border | New Zealand | Won by 4 wkts | Sydney | 1985-86 |
| A.R.Border | England | Lost by 7 wkts | Brisbane[2] | 1986-87 |
| A.R.Border | New Zealand | Won by 9 wkts | Brisbane[2] | 1987-88 |
| A.R.Border | New Zealand | Drawn | Melbourne | 1987-88 |
| A.R.Border | West Indies | Lost by 169 runs | Perth | 1988-89 |
| A.R.Border | West Indies | Lost by 285 runs | Melbourne | 1988-89 |
| A.R.Border | Pakistan | Drawn | Sydney | 1989-90 |
| A.R.Border | England | Won by 10 wkts | Brisbane[2] | 1990-91 |
| A.R.Border | West Indies | Lost by 343 runs | Bridgetown | 1990-91 |
| A.R.Border | India | Won by 10 wkts | Brisbane[2] | 1991-92 |
| A.R.Border | New Zealand | Drawn | Wellington | 1992-93 |
| M.A.Taylor | South Africa | Won by 2 wkts | Port Elizabeth | 1996-97 |
| M.A.Taylor | England | Drawn | Lord's | 1997 |
| M.A.Taylor | England | Won by Innings + 61 runs | Leeds | 1997 |

| **ENGLAND** | Opponents | Result | | |
|---|---|---|---|---|
| A.E.Stoddart | Australia | Lost by Innings + 147 runs | Sydney | 1894-95 |
| Lord Hawke | South Africa | Won by Innings + 33 runs | Cape Town | 1895-96 |
| A.C.MacLaren | Australia | Lost by 229 runs | Melbourne | 1901-02 |
| A.O.Jones # | Australia | Lost by 49 runs | Sydney | 1907-08 |
| J.W.H.T.Douglas | Australia | Won by Innings + 225 runs | Melbourne | 1911-12 |
| A.W.Carr | Australia | Drawn | Leeds | 1926 |
| A.P.F.Chapman | South Africa | Lost by 28 runs | Johannesburg[1] | 1930-31 |
| A.P.F.Chapman # | South Africa | Drawn | Durban[2] | 1930-31 |
| R.E.S.Wyatt | West Indies | Won by 4 wkts | Bridgetown | 1934-35 |
| R.E.S.Wyatt | West Indies | Lost by 217 runs | Port-of-Spain | 1934-35 |
| R.E.S.Wyatt # | South Africa | Drawn | The Oval | 1935 |
| G.O.B.Allen § | India | Won by 9 wkts | Lord's | 1936 |
| W.R.Hammond # | New Zealand | Drawn | Christchurch | 1946-47 |
| F.R.Brown § | New Zealand | Drawn | Manchester | 1949 |
| L.Hutton | Pakistan | Drawn | Lord's | 1954 |
| L.Hutton | Australia | Lost by Innings + 154 runs | Brisbane[2] | 1954-55 |
| L.Hutton # | New Zealand | Won by 8 wkts | Dunedin | 1954-55 |
| P.B.H.May | Australia | Lost by 10 wkts | Adelaide | 1958-59 |
| E.R.Dexter | New Zealand | Won by Innings + 47 runs | Wellington | 1962-63 |
| E.R.Dexter | Australia | Drawn | Lord's | 1964 |
| M.J.K.Smith | South Africa | Drawn | Johannesburg[3] | 1964-65 |
| M.J.K.Smith | South Africa | Drawn | The Oval | 1965 |
| D.B.Close # | Pakistan | Won by 8 wkts | The Oval | 1967 |

| | | | | |
|---|---|---|---|---|
| R.Illingworth | Australia | Drawn | Nottingham | 1972 |
| M.H.Denness | Australia | Lost by 163 runs | Adelaide | 1974-75 |
| M.H.Denness | New Zealand | Drawn | Christchurch | 1974-75 |
| M.H.Denness # | Australia | Lost by Innings + 85 runs | Birmingham | 1975 |
| A.W.Greig # | Australia | Lost by 45 runs | Melbourne | 1976-77 |
| G.Boycott | New Zealand | Lost by 72 runs | Wellington | 1977-78 |
| J.M.Brearley | Australia | Lost by 138 runs | Perth | 1979-80 |
| I.T.Botham | West Indies | Lost by Innings + 79 runs | Port-of-Spain | 1980-81 |
| I.T.Botham | West Indies | Lost by 298 runs | Bridgetown | 1980-81 |
| J.M.Brearley # | Australia | Drawn | The Oval | 1981 |
| K.W.R.Fletcher | India | Drawn | Madras[1] | 1981-82 |
| R.G.D.Willis | Australia | Lost by 8 wkts | Adelaide | 1982-83 |
| D.I.Gower | Sri Lanka | Drawn | Lord's | 1984 |
| D.I.Gower | Australia | Drawn | Manchester | 1985 |
| D.I.Gower | Australia | Won by Innings + 118 runs | Birmingham | 1985 |
| D.I.Gower | West Indies | Lost by Innings + 30 runs | Bridgetown | 1985-86 |
| D.I.Gower | West Indies | Lost by 240 runs | St John's | 1985-86 |
| M.W.Gatting | New Zealand | Drawn | The Oval | 1986 |
| M.W.Gatting | Australia | Won by Innings + 14 runs | Melbourne | 1986-87 |
| M.W.Gatting | Pakistan | Drawn | Birmingham | 1987 |
| M.W.Gatting | New Zealand | Drawn | Auckland | 1987-88 |
| G.A.Gooch | Sri Lanka | Won by 7 wkts | Lord's | 1988 |
| D.I.Gower | Australia | Lost by 210 runs | Leeds | 1989 |
| G.A.Gooch | West Indies | Drawn | Port-of-Spain | 1989-90 |
| A.J.Lamb § | West Indies | Lost by 164 runs | Bridgetown | 1989-90 |
| G.A.Gooch | Pakistan | Drawn | Birmingham | 1992 |
| G.A.Gooch | Australia | Lost by 179 runs | Manchester | 1993 |
| M.A.Atherton | Australia | Lost by 295 runs | Melbourne | 1994-95 |
| M.A.Atherton | South Africa | Drawn | Johannesburg[3] | 1995-96 |
| M.A.Atherton | Pakistan | Drawn | Leeds | 1996 |
| M.A.Atherton | New Zealand | Won by 4 wkts | Christchurch | 1996-97 |
| A.J.Stewart | South Africa | Lost by 10 wkts | Lord's | 1998 |
| A.J.Stewart | South Africa | Won by 8 wkts | Nottingham | 1998 |

| **SOUTH AFRICA** | Opponents | Result | | |
|---|---|---|---|---|
| E.A.Halliwell § | England | Lost by 288 runs | Port Elizabeth | 1895-96 |
| P.W.Sherwell | Australia | Lost by 530 runs | Melbourne | 1910-11 |
| P.W.Sherwell # | Australia | Lost by 7 wkts | Sydney | 1910-11 |
| H.W.Taylor | England | Lost by Innings + 18 runs | Birmingham | 1924 |
| H.G.Deane | England | Lost by 87 runs | Cape Town | 1927-28 |
| H.G.Deane | England | Won by 4 wkts | 1927-28 | |
| H.G.Deane | England | Won by 8 wkts | Durban[2] | 1927-28 |
| H.G Deane | England | Drawn | The Oval | 1929 |
| T.L.Goddard | Australia | Drawn | Sydney | 1963-64 |
| P.L.van der Merwe # | Australia | Won by 7 wkts | Port Elizabeth | 1966-67 |
| K.C.Wessels § | West Indies | Lost by 52 runs | Bridgetown | 1991-92 |
| K.C.Wessels | India | Won by 9 wickets | Port Elizabeth | 1992-93 |
| K.C.Wessels | Australia | Drawn | Durban[2] | 1993-94 |
| W.J.Cronje | England | Drawn | Centurion | 1995-96 |
| W.J.Cronje | Australia | Won by 8 wkts | Centurion | 1996-97 |
| W.J.Cronje | Pakistan | Lost by 29 runs | Durban[2] | 1997-98 |
| W.J.Cronje | England | Drawn | Birmingham | 1998 |

| **WEST INDIES** | Opponents | Result | | |
|---|---|---|---|---|
| R.S.Grant | England | Drawn | Manchester | 1939 |
| F.C.M.Alexander | Pakistan | Lost by 41 runs | Dacca | 1958-59 |
| F.M.M.Worrell | India | Won by Innings + 30 runs | Bridgetown | 1961-62 |
| G.S.Sobers | Australia | Lost by 382 runs | Sydney | 1968-69 |
| G.S.Sobers | New Zealand | Won by 5 wkts | Auckland | 1968-69 |
| G.S.Sobers | India | Drawn | Kingston | 1970-71 |
| G.S.Sobers | New Zealand | Drawn | Port-of-Spain | 1971-72 |

| | | | | |
|---|---|---|---|---|
| R.B.Kanhai | England | Won by 7 wkts | Port-of-Spain | 1973-74 |
| R.B.Kanhai | England | Drawn | Bridgetown | 1973-74 |
| C.H.Lloyd | Pakistan | Drawn | Lahore[2] | 1974-75 |
| C.H.Lloyd | India | Won by 10 wkts | Kingston | 1975-76 |
| C.H.Lloyd | Pakistan | Drawn | Georgetown | 1976-77 |
| C.H.Lloyd | Pakistan | Lost by 266 runs | Port-of-Spain | 1976-77 |
| C H Lloyd | Australia | Won by Innings + 106 runs | Port-of-Spain | 1977-78 |
| C H Lloyd | Australia | Won by 9 wkts | Bridgetown | 1977-78 |
| A.I.Kallicharran | India | Drawn | Bombay[3] | 1978-79 |
| D.L.Murray ¶ | Australia | Drawn | Brisbane[2] | 1979-80 |
| C.H.Lloyd | England | Drawn | Manchester | 1980 |
| I V A.Richards § | England | Drawn | Kingston | 1980 |
| C H Lloyd | Australia | Won by 5 wkts | Adelaide | 1981-82 |
| C.H.Lloyd | India | Won by 4 wkts | Kingston | 1982-83 |
| C.H.Lloyd | India | Drawn | Port-of-Spain | 1982-83 |
| C H Lloyd | India | Won by 10 wkts | Bridgetown | 1982-83 |
| C H Lloyd | India | Drawn | St John's | 1982-83 |
| I.V.A.Richards | Australia | Drawn | Port-of-Spain | 1983-84 |
| C.H.Lloyd | Australia | Won by 10 wkts | Bridgetown | 1983-84 |
| C.H.Lloyd | Australia | Won by 10 wkts | Kingston | 1983-84 |
| C.H.Lloyd | England | Won by 9 wkts | Lord's | 1984 |
| C.H.Lloyd | Australia | Won by 8 wkts | Brisbane[2] | 1984-85 |
| I.V.A.Richards | New Zealand | Won by 10 wkts | Bridgetown | 1984-85 |
| I.V.A.Richards | England | Won by 7 wkts | Port-of-Spain | 1985-86 |
| I.V.A.Richards | England | Won by 10 wkts | Port-of-Spain | 1985-86 |
| I.V.A.Richards | New Zealand | Drawn | Wellington | 1986-87 |
| I.V.A.Richards | India | Drawn | Bombay[3] | 1987-88 |
| I.V.A.Richards | Pakistan | Won by 2 wkts | Bridgetown | 1987-88 |
| I.V.A.Richards | England | Won by 10 wkts | Leeds | 1988 |
| I.V.A.Richards | India | Won by 8 wkts | Bridgetown | 1988-89 |
| I.V.A.Richards | India | Won by 7 wkts | Kingston | 1988-89 |
| I.V.A.Richards | Australia | Drawn | Port-of-Spain | 1990-91 |
| I.V.A.Richards | England | Lost by 115 runs | Leeds | 1991 |
| I.V.A.Richards | England | Won by 7 wkts | Birmingham | 1991 |
| R.B.Richardson | England | Lost by 208 runs | Bridgetown | 1993-94 |
| C.A.Walsh | New Zealand | Drawn | Christchurch | 1994-95 |
| R.B.Richardson | Australia | Drawn | St John's | 1994-95 |
| R.B.Richardson | Australia | Won by 9 wickets | Port-of-Spain | 1994-95 |
| R.B.Richardson | England | Won by 9 wickets | Leeds | 1995 |
| C.A.Walsh | New Zealand | Won by 10 wickets | Bridgetown | 1995-96 |
| C.A.Walsh | Australia | Lost by 123 runs | Brisbane[2] | 1996-97 |
| C.A.Walsh | Sri Lanka | Won by 6 wickets | St John's | 1996-97 |
| B.C.Lara | England | Srawn | Bridgetown | 1997-98 |
| B.C.Lara | England | Won by Innings + 52 runs | St John's | 1997-98 |

| **NEW ZEALAND** | Opponents | Result | | |
|---|---|---|---|---|
| T.C.Lowry | England | Drawn | Auckland | 1929-30 |
| T.C.Lowry # | England | Drawn | Manchester | 1931 |
| B.Sutcliffe | West Indies | Drawn | Auckland | 1951-52 |
| B.Sutcliffe | South Africa | Lost by 9 wkts | Johannesburg[2] | 1953-54 |
| J.R.Reid | South Africa | Drawn | Auckland | 1963-64 |
| J.R.Reid | Pakistan | Drawn | Lahore[2] | 1964-65 |
| G.T.Dowling | India | Lost by 272 runs | Auckland | 1967-68 |
| G.T.Dowling | West Indies | Won by 6 wkts | Wellington | 1968-69 |
| G.T.Dowling | England | Drawn | Auckland | 1970-71 |
| B.E.Congdon | England | Drawn | Lord's | 1973 |
| B.E.Congdon | Australia | Won by 5 wkts | Christchurch | 1973-74 |
| B.E.Congdon | Australia | Lost by 297 runs | Auckland | 1973-74 |
| G.M.Turner | Australia | Drawn | Christchurch | 1976-77 |
| M.G.Burgess | Pakistan | Lost by 128 runs | Christchurch | 1978-79 |

| | | | | |
|---|---|---|---|---|
| G.P.Howarth | West Indies | Drawn | Christchurch | 1979-80 |
| G.P.Howarth | West Indies | Drawn | Auckland | 1979-80 |
| G.P.Howarth | Australia | Drawn | Melbourne | 1980-81 |
| G.P.Howarth | Australia | Won by 5 wkts | Auckland | 1981-82 |
| G.P.Howarth | Australia | Lost by 8 wkts | Christchurch | 1981-82 |
| G.P.Howarth | Sri Lanka | Won by 6 wkts | Wellington | 1982-83 |
| G.P.Howarth | England | Won by 5 wkts | Leeds | 1983 |
| G.P Howarth | England | Lost by 127 runs | Lord s | 1983 |
| G.P.Howarth | Sri Lanka | Drawn | Colombo (SSC) | 1983-84 |
| G.P.Howarth | Pakistan | Won by Innings + 99 runs | Auckland | 1984-85 |
| G.P.Howarth | Pakistan | Won by 2 wkts | Dunedin | 1984-85 |
| G.P.Howarth # | West Indies | Lost by 10 wkts | Kingston | 1984-85 |
| J.V.Coney | Australia | Won by Innings + 41 runs | Brisbane[2] | 1985-86 |
| J.V.Coney | Australia | Won by 6 wkts | Perth | 1985-86 |
| J.V.Coney | Australia | Drawn | Wellington | 1985-86 |
| J.V.Coney | Australia | Drawn | Christchurch | 1985-86 |
| J.V.Coney | England | Won by 8 wkts | Nottingham | 1986 |
| J.V.Coney # | West Indies | Won by 5 wkts | Christchurch | 1986-87 |
| J.J.Crowe § | Sri Lanka | Drawn | Colombo (CCC) | 1986-87 |
| J.J.Crowe | England | Drawn | Christchurch | 1987-88 |
| J.G.Wright | Australia | Drawn | Perth | 1989-90 |
| J.G.Wright | England | Drawn | Lord's | 1990 |
| J.G.Wright # | England | Lost by 114 runs | Birmingham | 1990 |
| M.D.Crowe | Pakistan | Lost by 65 runs | Faisalabad | 1990-91 |
| I.D.S.Smith ¶ | Sri Lanka | Drawn | Auckland | 1990-91 |
| M.D.Crowe | England | Lost by Innings + 4 runs | Christchurch | 1991-92 |
| M.D.Crowe | England | Lost by 168 runs | Auckland | 1991-92 |
| K.R.Rutherford § | Pakistan | Lost by 33 runs | Hamilton | 1992-93 |
| M.D.Crowe | Australia | Lost by Innings + 60 runs | Christchurch | 1992-93 |
| M.D.Crowe | Australia | Drawn | Perth | 1993-94 |
| K.R.Rutherford | Pakistan | Won 5 wkts | Christchurch | 1993-94 |
| K.R.Rutherford | Sri Lanka | Lost by 241 runs | Napier | 1994-95 |
| K.R.Rutherford | Sri Lanka | Drawn | Dunedin | 1994-95 |
| L.K.Germon | Pakistan | Lost by 161 runs | Christchurch | 1995-96 |
| L.K.Germon | West indies | Drawn | St John's | 1995-96 |
| S.P.Fleming | Zimbabwe | Drawn | Harare | 1997-98 |
| S.P.Fleming | Australia | Lost by 186 runs | Brisbane[2] | 1997-98 |

| **INDIA** | Opponents | Result | | |
|---|---|---|---|---|
| Nawab of Pataudi, sr | England | Drawn | Manchester | 1946 |
| N.B.Amarnath | Pakistan | Drawn | Calcutta | 1952-53 |
| P.R.Umrigar | Australia | Lost by 94 runs | Calcutta | 1956-57 |
| Nawab of Pataudi, jr | England | Drawn | Kanpur | 1963-64 |
| Nawab of Pataudi, jr | Australia | Drawn | Calcutta | 1964-65 |
| Nawab of Pataudi, jr | Australia | Lost by 39 runs | Brisbane[2] | 1967-68 |
| Nawab of Pataudi, jr | Australia | Lost by 144 runs | Sydney | 1967-68 |
| Nawab of Pataudi, jr | New Zealand | Lost by 6 wkts | Christchurch | 1967-68 |
| A.L.Wadekar | West Indies | Drawn | Bridgetown | 1970-71 |
| Nawab of Pataudi, jr | West Indies | Lost by 267 runs | Bangalore | 1974-75 |
| B.S.Bedi | West Indies | Drawn | Port-of-Spain | 1975-76 |
| S.M.Gavaskar | Australia | Drawn | Adelaide | 1980-81 |
| S.M.Gavaskar | New Zealand | Lost by 62 runs | Wellington | 1980-81 |
| S.M.Gavaskar | Pakistan | Drawn | Lahore[2] (1st) | 1982-83 |
| S.M Gavaskar | Pakistan | Drawn | Lahore[2] (5th) | 1982-83 |
| Kapil Dev | Pakistan | Drawn | Jullundur | 1983-84 |
| Kapil Dev | West Indies | Lost by 138 runs | Ahmedabad | 1983-84 |
| Kapil Dev | Australia | Drawn | Melbourne | 1985-86 |
| Kapil Dev | England | Won by 5 wkts | Lord's | 1986 |
| D.B.Vengsarkar | West Indies | Drawn | Georgetown | 1988-89 |
| D.B.Vengsarkar | West Indies | Lost by 217 runs | Port-of-Spain | 1988-89 |

| | | | | |
|---|---|---|---|---|
| K.Srikkanth § | Pakistan | Drawn | Karachi[1] | 1989-90 |
| M.Azharuddin | New Zealand | Drawn | Auckland | 1990-91 |
| M.Azharuddin | England | Lost by 247 runs | Lord's | 1990 |
| M.Azharuddin | Australia | Drawn | Sydney | 1991-92 |
| M.Azharuddin | Australia | Lost by 38 runs | Adelaide | 1991-92 |
| M.Azharuddin | South Africa | Drawn | Durban[2] | 1992-93 |
| M.Azharuddin | Sri Lanka | Drawn | Kandy | 1993-94 |
| M.Azharuddin | England | Drawn | Lord's | 1996 |
| S.R.Tendulkar | India | Lost by 328 runs | Durban[2] | 1996-97 |
| S.R.Tendulkar | West Indies | Lost by 38 runs | Bridgetown | 1996-97 |
| S.R.Tendulkar | Sri Lanka | Drawn | Colombo (SSC) | 1997-98 |
| S.R.Tendulkar | Sri Lanka | Drawn | Mohali | 1997-98 |

| **PAKISTAN** | Opponents | Result | | |
|---|---|---|---|---|
| Fazal Mahmood § | West Indies | Won by 10 wkts | Karachi[1] | 1958-59 |
| Javed Burki | England | Lost by Innings + 117 runs | Leeds | 1962 |
| Javed Burki | England | Drawn | Nottingham | 1962 |
| Hanif Mohammad | New Zealand | Drawn | Wellington | 1964-65 |
| Hanif Mohammad | New Zealand | Won by Innings + 64 runs | Rawalpindi[1] | 1964-65 |
| Intikhab Alam | Australia | Lost by 52 runs | Sydney | 1972-73 |
| Mushtaq Mohammad | India | Won by 8 wkts | Lahore[2] | 1978-79 |
| Mushtaq Mohammad | New Zealand | Drawn | Auckland | 1978-79 |
| Javed Miandad | Australia | Lost by 286 runs | Perth | 1981-82 |
| Javed Miandad | Sri Lanka | Won by Innings + 102 runs | Lahore[2] | 1981-82 |
| Imran Khan | Australia | Won by 9 wkts | Lahore[2] | 1982-83 |
| Imran Khan | India | Won by Innings + 86 runs | Karachi[1] | 1982-83 |
| Imran Khan | India | Won by 10 wkts | Faisalabad | 1982-83 |
| Zaheer Abbas | Australia | Lost by Innings + 9 runs | Perth | 1983-84 |
| Zaheer Abbas | England | Drawn | Lahore[2] | 1983-84 |
| Javed Miandad | Sri Lanka | Won by 8 wkts | Sialkot | 1985-86 |
| Imran Khan | India | Drawn | Calcutta | 1986-87 |
| Imran Khan | England | Drawn | Manchester | 1987 |
| Imran Khan | West Indies | Drawn | Port-of-Spain | 1987-88 |
| Imran Khan | New Zealand | Drawn | Wellington | 1988-89 |
| Imran Khan | India | Drawn | Faisalabad | 1989-90 |
| Imran Khan | India | Drawn | Lahore[2] | 1989-90 |
| Imran Khan | India | Drawn | Sialkot | 1989-90 |
| Imran Khan | Australia | Lost by 92 runs | Melbourne | 1989-90 |
| Javed Miandad | New Zealand | Won by Innings + 43 runs | Faisalabad | 1990-91 |
| Imran Khan | Sri Lanka | Won by 3 wkts | Faisalabad | 1991-92 |
| Wasim Akram | West Indies | Lost by 10 wickets | Bridgetown | 1992-93 |
| Saleem Malik § | New Zealand | Won 5 wkts | Auckland | 1993-94 |
| Saleem Malik | Sri Lanka | Won by Innings + 52 runs | Kandy | 1994-95 |
| Saleem Malik | Australia | Drawn | Rawalpindi[2] | 1994-95 |
| Rameez Raja | Sri Lanka | Lost by 42 runs | Faisalabad | 1995-96 |
| Wasim Akram | West Indies | Won by Innings + 29 runs | Rawalpindi[2] | 1997-98 |
| Aamer Sohail | South Africa | Drawn | Johannesburg[3] | 1997-98 |
| Rashid Latif | South Africa | Lost by 259 runs | Port Elizabeth | 1997-98 |

| **SRI LANKA** | Opponents | Result | | |
|---|---|---|---|---|
| D.S.de Silva § | New Zealand | Lost by Innings + 25 runs | Christchurch | 1982-83 |
| L.R.D.Mendis | Pakistan | Won by 8 wkts | Colombo (CCC) | 1985-86 |
| A.Ranatunga § | Australia | Drawn | Brisbane[2] | 1989-90 |
| A.Ranatunga | Australia | Lost by 173 runs | Hobart | 1989-90 |
| A.Ranatunga | New Zealand | Drawn | Wellington | 1990-91 |
| A.Ranatunga | New Zealand | Drawn | Hamilton | 1990-91 |
| P.A.de Silva | Pakistan | Drawn | Gujranwala | 1991-92 |
| A.Ranatunga | Australia | Lost by 16 runs | Colombo (SSC) | 1992-93 |
| A.Ranatunga | Australia | Drawn | Colombo (PIS) | 1992-93 |
| A.Ranatunga | New Zealand | Drawn | Moratuwa | 1992-93 |

| | | | | |
|---|---|---|---|---|
| A.Ranatunga | Australia | Lost by 10 wickets | Melbourne | 1995-96 |
| A.Ranatunga | Zimbabwe | Won by 10 wkts | Colombo (SSC) | 1996-97 |
| A.Ranatunga | New Zealand | Lost by Innings + 36 runs | Dunedin | 1996-97 |
| A.Ranatunga | West Indies | Drawn | Kingstown | 1996-97 |
| A.Ranatunga | India | Drawn | Mumbai[3] | 1997-98 |

| **ZIMBABWE** | Opponents | Result | | |
|---|---|---|---|---|
| A.Flower | Pakistan | Lost by 52 runs | Rawalpindi[2] | 1993-94 |
| A.Flower | Pakistan | Drawn | Lahore[2] | 1993-94 |
| A.D.R.Campbell | England | Drawn | Harare | 1996-97 |

| **SUMMARY** | Captains | Instances | W | L | D |
|---|---|---|---|---|---|
| Australia | 15 | 61 | 27 | 18 | 16 |
| England | 29 | 55 | 12 | 21 | 22 |
| South Africa | 8 | 17 | 5 | 7 | 5 |
| West Indies | 12 | 52 | 26 | 6 | 20 |
| New Zealand | 14 | 50 | 12 | 16 | 22 |
| India | 12 | 33 | 1 | 13 | 19 |
| Pakistan | 13 | 35 | 13 | 8 | 14 |
| Sri Lanka | 4 | 15 | 2 | 5 | 8 |
| Zimbabwe | 2 | 3 | 0 | 1 | 2 |
| TOTAL | 109 | 321 | 98 | 95 | 128 |

## CENTURY ON DEBUT AS CAPTAIN

| | | | | | | | |
|---|---|---|---|---|---|---|---|
| 0 | 143 | G.H.S.Trott | Australia | v | England | Lord's | 1896 |
| 109 | 50* | A.C.MacLaren | England | v | Australia | Sydney | 1897-98 |
| 133 | 22 | M.A.Noble | Australia | v | England | Sydney | 1903-04 |
| 191 | | C.Hill | Australia | v | South Africa | Sydney | 1910-11 |
| 109 | 8 | H.W.Taylor | South Africa | v | England | Durban[1] | 1913-14 |
| 12 | 158 | W.W.Armstrong | Australia | v | England | Sydney | 1920-21 |
| 112 | | A.L.Hassett | Australia | v | South Africa | Johannesburg[2] | 1949-50 |
| 164* | | V.J.Hazare | India | v | England | Delhi | 1951-52 |
| 10 | 104 | J.B.Stollmeyer | West Indies | v | Australia | Sydney | 1951-52 |
| 107 | 68 | G.O.Rabone | New Zealand | v | South Africa | Durban[2] | 1953-54 |
| 104* | 48 | D.J.McGlew | South Africa | v | England | Manchester | 1955 |
| 239 | 5 | G.T.Dowling | New Zealand | v | India | Christchurch | 1967-68 |
| 126 | | B.E.Congdon | New Zealand | v | West Indies | Bridgetown | 1971-72 |
| 30 | 163 | C.H.Lloyd | West Indies | v | India | Bangalore | 1974-75 |
| 123 | 109* | G.S.Chappell | Australia | v | West Indies | Brisbane[2] | 1975-76 |
| 116 | 35* | S.M.Gavaskar | India | v | New Zealand | Auckland | 1975-76 |
| 7 | 102 | G.N.Yallop | Australia | v | England | Brisbane[2] | 1978-79 |
| 120* | | J.J.Crowe | New Zealand | v | Sri Lanka | Colombo (CCC) | 1986-87 |
| 10 | 102 | D.B.Vengsarkar | India | v | West Indies | Delhi | 1987-88 |
| 119 | 10 | A.J.Lamb | England | v | West Indies | Bridgetown | 1989-90 |
| 121 | | D.L.Houghton | Zimbabwe | v | India | Harare | 1992-93 |

## HIGHEST INDIVIDUAL INNINGS BY CAPTAINS

| | | | | | | |
|---|---|---|---|---|---|---|
| 333 | G.A.Gooch | England | v | India | Lord's | 1990 |
| 311 | R.B.Simpson | Australia | v | England | Manchester | 1964 |
| 299 | M.D.Crowe | New Zealand | v | Sri Lanka | Wellington | 1990-91 |
| 285* | P.B.H.May | England | v | West Indies | Birmingham | 1957 |
| 270 | D.G.Bradman | Australia | v | England | Melbourne | 1936-37 |
| 257* | Wasim Akram | Pakistan | v | Zimbabwe | Sheikhupura | 1996-97 |
| 242* | C.H.Lloyd | West Indies | v | India | Bombay[3] | 1974-75 |
| 240 | W.R.Hammond | England | v | Australia | Lord's | 1938 |
| 239 | G.T.Dowling | New Zealand | v | India | Christchurch | 1967-68 |
| 237 | Saleem Malik | Pakistan | v | Australia | Rawalpindi[2] | 1994-95 |
| 235 | G.S.Chappell | Australia | v | Pakistan | Faisalabad | 1979-80 |
| 234 | D.G.Bradman | Australia | v | England | Sydney | 1946-47 |
| 225 | R.B.Simpson | Australia | v | England | Adelaide | 1965-66 |

| | | | | | | |
|---|---|---|---|---|---|---|
| 219 | D.S.Atkinson | West Indies | v | Australia | Bridgetown | 1954-55 |
| 215 | D.I.Gower | England | v | Australia | Birmingham | 1985 |
| 212 | D.G.Bradman | Australia | v | England | Adelaide | 1936-37 |
| 211 | W.L.Murdoch | Australia | v | England | The Oval | 1884 |
| 211 | Javed Miandad | Pakistan | v | Australia | Karachi[1] | 1988-89 |
| 208 | A.D.Nourse | South Africa | v | England | Nottingham | 1951 |
| 205 | E.R.Dexter | England | v | Pakistan | Karachi[1] | 1961-62 |
| 205 | L.Hutton | England | v | West Indies | Kingston | 1953-54 |
| 205 | W.M.Lawry | Australia | v | West Indies | Melbourne | 1968-69 |
| 205 | S.M.Gavaskar | India | v | West Indies | Bombay[3] | 1978-79 |
| 205 | A.R.Border | Australia | v | New Zealand | Adelaide | 1987-88 |
| 204 | G.S.Chappell | Australia | v | India | Sydney | 1980-81 |
| 203* | Nawab of Pataudi jr | India | v | England | Delhi | 1963-64 |
| 203* | Hanif Mohammad | Pakistan | v | New Zealand | Lahore[2] | 1964-65 |
| 203* | Javed Miandad | Pakistan | v | Sri Lanka | Faisalabad | 1985-86 |
| 203 | H.L.Collins | Australia | v | South Africa | Johannesburg[1] | 1921-22 |
| 201* | J.Ryder | Australia | v | England | Adelaide | 1924-25 |
| 201 | D.G.Bradman | Australia | v | India | Adelaide | 1947-48 |
| 201 | R.B.Simpson | Australia | v | West Indies | Bridgetown | 1964-65 |
| 201 | G.S.Chappell | Australia | v | Pakistan | Brisbane[2] | 1981-82 |
| 200* | A.R.Border | Australia | v | England | Leeds | 1993 |

## CENTURY IN EACH INNINGS BY A CAPTAIN

| | | | | | | | |
|---|---|---|---|---|---|---|---|
| 189 | 104* | A.Melville | South Africa | v | England | Nottingham | 1947 |
| 132 | 127* | D.G.Bradman | Australia | v | India | Melbourne | 1947-48 |
| 153 | 115 | R.B.Simpson | Australia | v | Pakistan | Karachi[1] | 1964-65 |
| 145 | 121 | I.M.Chappell | Australia | v | New Zealand | Wellington | 1973-74 |
| 123 | 109* | G.S.Chappell | Australia | v | West Indies | Brisbane[2] | 1975-76 |
| 107 | 182* | S.M.Gavaskar | India | v | West Indies | Calcutta | 1978-79 |
| 140 | 114* | A.R.Border | Australia | v | New Zealand | Christchurch | 1985-86 |
| 333 | 123 | G.A.Gooch | England | v | India | Lord's | 1990 |

## CENTURY AND A NINETY IN SAME MATCH BY A CAPTAIN

| | | | | | | | |
|---|---|---|---|---|---|---|---|
| 104 | 93 | Hanif Mohammad | Pakistan | v | Australia | Melbourne | 1964-65 |
| 152 | 95* | G.S.Sobers | West Indies | v | England | Georgetown | 1967-68 |
| 119 | 94 | L.R.D.Mendis | Sri Lanka | v | England | Lord's | 1984 |
| 94* | 118 | M.A.Atherton | England | v | New Zealand | Christchurch | 1996-97 |

## CENTURIES BY RIVAL CAPTAINS IN THE SAME TEST

| | | | | | | | |
|---|---|---|---|---|---|---|---|
| H.W.Taylor | South Africa | 109 | J.W.H.T.Douglas | England | 119 | Durban[2] | 1913-14 |
| A.P.F.Chapman | England | 121 | W.M.Woodfull | Australia | 155 | Lord's | 1930 |
| W.R.Hammond | England | 240 | D.G.Bradman | Australia | 102* | Lord's | 1938 |
| A.Melville | South Africa | 103 | W.R.Hammond | England | 140 | Durban[2] | 1938-39 |
| L.Hutton | England | 145 | A.L.Hassett | Australia | 104 | Lord's | 1953 |
| P.B.H.May | England | 117 | D.J.McGlew | South Africa | 104* | Manchester | 1955 |
| D.J.McGlew | South Africa | 120 | J.R.Reid | New Zealand | 142 | Johannesburg[1] | 1961-62 |
| E.R.Dexter | England | 174 | R.B.Simpson | Australia | 311 | Manchester | 1964 |
| G.S.Sobers | West Indies | 113* | M.C.Cowdrey | England | 101 | Kingston | 1967-68 |
| W.M.Lawry | Australia | 151 | G.S.Sobers | West Indies | 113 | Sydney | 1968-69 |
| G.S.Sobers | West Indies | 142 | B.E.Congdon | New Zealand | 126 | Bridgetown | 1971-72 |
| R.B.Kanhai | West Indies | 105 | I.M.Chappell | Australia | 106* | Bridgetown | 1972-73 |
| B.E.Congdon | New Zealand | 132 | I.M.Chappell | Australia | 145 + 121 | Wellington | 1973-74 |
| S.M.Gavaskar | India | 205 | A.I.Kallicharran | West Indies | 187 | Bombay[3] | 1978-79 |
| Javed Miandad | Pakistan | 106* | G.S.Chappell | Australia | 235 | Faisalabad | 1979-80 |
| Imran Khan | Pakistan | 117 | S.M.Gavaskar | India | 127* | Faisalabad | 1982-83 |
| C.H.Lloyd | West Indies | 143 | Kapil Dev | India | 100* | Port-of-Spain | 1982-83 |
| Kapil Dev | India | 119 | A.R.Border | Australia | 106 | Madras[1] | 1986-87 |
| M.W.Gatting | England | 150* | Imran Khan | Pakistan | 118 | The Oval | 1987 |
| D.B.Vengsarkar | India | 102 | I.V.A.Richards | West Indies | 146 | Delhi | 1987-88 |
| Javed Miandad | Pakistan | 107 | A.R.Border | Australia | 113* | Faisalabad | 1988-89 |

| | | | | | | | |
|---|---|---|---|---|---|---|---|
| G.A.Gooch | England | 333 + 123 | M.Azharuddin | India | 121 | Lord's | 1990 |
| G.A.Gooch | England | 116 | M.Azharuddin | India | 179 | Manchester | 1990 |

## SEVEN WICKETS IN AN INNINGS BY A CAPTAIN

| | | | | | | |
|---|---|---|---|---|---|---|
| 9-83 | Kapil Dev | India | v | West Indies | Ahmedabad | 1983-84 |
| 8-60 | Imran Khan | Pakistan | v | India | Karachi[1] | 1982-83 |
| 8-106 | Kapil Dev | India | v | Australia | Adelaide | 1985-86 |
| 7-37 | C.A.Walsh | West Indies | v | New Zealand | Wellington | 1994-95 |
| 7-40 | Imran Khan | Pakistan | v | England | Leeds | 1987 |
| 7-44 | I.W.Johnson | Australia | v | West Indies | Georgetown | 1954-55 |
| 7-46 | A.R.Border | Australia | v | West Indies | Sydney | 1988-89 |
| 7-52 | Intikhab Alam | Pakistan | v | New Zealand | Dunedin | 1972-73 |
| 7-52 | Imran Khan | Pakistan | v | England | Birmingham | 1982 |
| 7-53 | D.S.Atkinson | West Indies | v | New Zealand | Auckland | 1955-56 |
| 7-80 | G.O.B.Allen | England | v | India | The Oval | 1936 |
| 7-80 | Imran Khan | Pakistan | v | West Indies | Georgetown | 1987-88 |
| 7-91 | Waqar Younis | Pakistan | v | Zimbabwe | Karachi[2] | 1993-94 |
| 7-100 | M.A.Noble | Australia | v | England | Sydney | 1903-04 |

## TEN WICKETS IN A MATCH BY A CAPTAIN

| | | | | | | |
|---|---|---|---|---|---|---|
| 13-55 | C.A.Walsh | West Indies | v | New Zealand | Wellington | 1994-95 |
| 13-135 | Waqar Younis | Pakistan | v | Zimbabwe | Karachi[2] | 1993-94 |
| 12-100 | Fazal Mahmood | Pakistan | v | West Indies | Dacca | 1958-59 |
| 11-79 | Imran Khan | Pakistan | v | India | Karachi[1] | 1982-83 |
| 11-90 | A.E.R.Gilligan | England | v | South Africa | Birmingham | 1924 |
| 11-96 | A.R.Border | Australia | v | West Indies | Sydney | 1988-89 |
| 11-121 | Imran Khan | Pakistan | v | West Indies | Georgetown | 1987-88 |
| 11-130 | Intikhab Alam | Pakistan | v | New Zealand | Dunedin | 1972-73 |
| 11-150 | E.P.Nupen | South Africa | v | England | Johannesburg[1] | 1930-31 |
| 11-180 | Imran Khan | Pakistan | v | India | Faisalabad | 1982-83 |
| 10-77 | Imran Khan | Pakistan | v | England | Leeds | 1987 |
| 10-78 | G.O.B.Allen | England | v | India | Lord's | 1936 |
| 10-106 | Wasim Akram | Pakistan | v | Zimbabwe | Faisalabad | 1996-97 |
| 10-135 | Kapil Dev | India | v | West Indies | Ahmedabad | 1983-84 |
| 10-182 | Intikhab Alam | Pakistan | v | New Zealand | Dacca | 1969-70 |
| 10-194 | B.S.Bedi | India | v | Australia | Perth | 1977-78 |

## A CENTURY AND FIVE WICKETS IN AN INNINGS BY A CAPTAIN

| | | | | | | | |
|---|---|---|---|---|---|---|---|
| 219 | 5-56 | D.S.Atkinson | West Indies | v | Australia | Bridgetown | 1954-55 |
| 174 | 5-41 | G.S.Sobers | West Indies | v | England | Leeds | 1966 |
| 121 | 5-28 | Mushtaq Mohammad | Pakistan | v | West Indies | Port-of-Spain | 1976-77 |
| 117 | 6-98)<br>5-82) | Imran Khan | Pakistan | v | India | Faisalabad | 1982-83 |

## HUNDRED RUNS AND EIGHT WICKETS IN A MATCH BY A CAPTAIN.

| | | | | | | | | | |
|---|---|---|---|---|---|---|---|---|---|
| 121 | 56 | 5-28 | 3-69 | Mushtaq Mohammad | Pakistan | v | West Indies | Port-of-Spain | 1976-77 |
| 174 | | 5-41 | 3-39 | G.S.Sobers | West Indies | v | England | Leeds | 1966 |
| 117 | | 6-98 | 5-82 | Imran Khan | Pakistan | v | India | Faisalabad | 1982-83 |
| 67* | 46 | 5-49 | 3-66 | Imran Khan | Pakistan | v | England | Leeds | 1982 |
| 35 | 68 | 3-71 | 5-36 | G.O.B.Allen | England | v | Australia | Brisbane[2] | 1936-37 |

## YOUNGEST CAPTAINS

| Years | Days | | | | | | |
|---|---|---|---|---|---|---|---|
| 21 | 77 | Nawab of Pataudi, jr | India | v | West Indies | Bridgetown | 1961-62 |
| 22 | 15 | Waqar Younis | Pakistan | v | Zimbabwe | Karachi[2] | 1993-94 |
| 22 | 194 | I.D.Craig | Australia | v | South Africa | Johannesburg[3] | 1957-58 |
| 22 | 260 | Javed Miandad | Pakistan | v | Australia | Karachi[1] | 1979-80 |
| 22 | 306 | M.Bisset | South Africa | v | England | Johannesburg[1] | 1898-99 |
| 23 | 144 | M.P.Bowden | England | v | South Africa | Cape Town | 1888-89 |

| | | | | | | | |
|---|---|---|---|---|---|---|---|
| 23 | 169 | S.R.Tendulkar | India | v | Australia | Delhi | 1996-97 |
| 23 | 217 | G.C.Grant | West Indies | v | Australia | Adelaide | 1930-31 |
| 23 | 230 | S.P.Fleming | New Zealand | v | England | Christchurch | 1996-97 |
| 23 | 292 | Hon I.F.W.Bligh | England | v | Australia | Melbourne | 1882-83 |
| 23 | 353 | A.D.R.Campbell | Zimbabwe | v | Sri Lanka | Colombo (PIS) | 1996-97 |
| 24 | 23 | Javed Burki | Pakistan | v | England | Birmingham | 1962 |
| 24 | 48 | Kapil Dev | India | v | West Indies | Kingston | 1982-83 |
| 24 | 125 | W.J.Cronje | South Africa | v | Australia | Adelaide | 1993-94 |
| 24 | 194 | I.T.Botham | England | v | West Indies | Nottingham | 1980 |
| 24 | 222 | H.W.Taylor | South Africa | v | England | Durban[1] | 1913-14 |
| 25 | 40 | D.B.Carr | England | v | India | Madras[1] | 1951-52 |
| 25 | 57 | K.J.Hughes | Australia | v | Pakistan | Perth | 1978-79 |
| 25 | 117 | D.S.Sheppard | England | v | Pakistan | Nottingham | 1954 |
| 25 | 133 | D.I.Gower | England | v | Pakistan | Lord's | 1982 |
| 25 | 135 | M.A.Atherton | England | v | Australia | Birmingham | 1993 |
| 25 | 217 | A.Flower | Zimbabwe | v | Pakistan | Karachi[2] | 1993-94 |

## OLDEST CAPTAINS

| Years | Days | | | | | | |
|---|---|---|---|---|---|---|---|
| 50 | 320 | W.G.Grace | England | v | Australia | Nottingham | 1899 |
| 45 | 245 | G.O.B.Allen | England | v | West Indies | Kingston | 1947-48 |
| 43 | 276 | W.R.Hammond | England | v | New Zealand | Christchurch | 1946-47 |
| 43 | 232 | W.Bardsley | Australia | v | England | Manchester | 1926 |
| 42 | 247 | N.Betancourt | West Indies | v | England | Port-of-Spain | 1929-30 |
| 42 | 130 | S.E.Gregory | Australia | v | England | The Oval | 1912 |
| 42 | 86 | W.W.Armstrong | Australia | v | England | The Oval | 1921 |
| 41 | 330 | J.W.H.T.Douglas | England | v | South Africa | Manchester | 1924 |
| 41 | 178 | V.Y.Richardson | Australia | v | South Africa | Durban[2] | 1935-36 |
| 41 | 95 | N.B.Amarnath | India | v | Pakistan | Calcutta | 1952-53 |
| 41 | 80 | R.Illingworth | England | v | West Indies | Lord's | 1973 |
| 41 | 44 | T.W.Graveney | England | v | Australia | Leeds | 1968 |
| 40 | 279 | A.D.Nourse | South Africa | v | England | The Oval | 1951 |
| 40 | 277 | D.S.de Silva | Sri Lanka | v | New Zealand | Wellington | 1982-83 |
| 40 | 245 | F.R.Brown | England | v | South Africa | The Oval | 1951 |
| 40 | 223 | J.M.Blackham | Australia | v | England | Sydney | 1894-95 |
| 40 | 125 | C.H.Lloyd | West Indies | v | Australia | Sydney | 1984-85 |
| 40 | 109 | C.B.Fry | England | v | Australia | The Oval | 1912 |
| 40 | 3 | G.A.Gooch | England | v | Australia | Leeds | 1993 |

## General

### MOST TEST MATCH APPEARANCES

| For | Total | | Opponents A | E | SA | WI | NZ | I | P | SL | Z |
|---|---|---|---|---|---|---|---|---|---|---|---|
| Australia | **156** | A.R.Border | - | 47 | 6 | 31 | 23 | 20 | 22 | 7 | - |
| England | **118** | G.A.Gooch | 42 | - | 3 | 26 | 15 | 19 | 10 | 3 | - |
| South Africa | **51** | W.J.Cronje | 12 | 13 | - | 1 | 4 | 9 | 6 | 5 | 1 |
| West Indies | **121** | I.V.A.Richards | 34 | 36 | - | - | 7 | 28 | 16 | - | - |
| New Zealand | **86** | R.J.Hadlee | 23 | 21 | - | 10 | - | 14 | 12 | 6 | - |
| India | **131** | Kapil Dev | 20 | 27 | 4 | 25 | 10 | - | 29 | 14 | 2 |
| Pakistan | **124** | Javed Miandad | 24 | 22 | - | 17 | 18 | 28 | - | 12 | 3 |
| Sri Lanka | **81** | A.Ranatunga | 9 | 4 | 5 | 3 | 16 | 19 | 18 | - | 7 |
| Zimbabwe | **30** | A.D.R.Campbell | - | 2 | - | - | 8 | 2 | 10 | 7 | - |
| | | A.Flower | - | 2 | - | - | 8 | 2 | 10 | 7 | - |
| | | G.W.Flower | - | 2 | - | - | 8 | 2 | 10 | 7 | - |

### MOST CONSECUTIVE APPEARANCES

| | | From | | To | |
|---|---|---|---|---|---|
| 153 | A.R.Border (Australia) | Melbourne | 1978-79 | Durban[2] | 1993-94 |
| 106 | S.M.Gavaskar (India) | Bombay[3] | 1974-75 | Madras[1] | 1986-87 |
| 87 | G.R.Viswanath (India) | Georgetown | 1970-71 | Karachi[1] | 1982-83 |
| 85 | G.S.Sobers (West Indies) | Port-of-Spain | 1954-55 | Port-of-Spain | 1971-72 |
| 72 | D.L.Haynes (West Indies) | Brisbane[2] | 1979-80 | Lord's | 1988 |
| 71 | I.M.Chappell (Australia) | Adelaide | 1965-66 | Melbourne | 1975-76 |
| 69 | M.Azharuddin (India) | Bombay[3] | 1987-88 | Bangalore | # 1997-98 |
| 66 | Kapil Dev (India) | Faisalabad | 1978-79 | Delhi | 1984-85 |
| 65 | A.P.E.Knott (England) | Auckland | 1970-71 | The Oval | 1977 |
| 65 | I.T.Botham (England) | Wellington | 1977-78 | Karachi[1] | 1983-84 |
| 65 | Kapil Dev (India) | Madras[1] | 1984-85 | Hamilton | 1993-94 |
| 64 | I.A.Healy (Australia) | Karachi[1] | 1988-89 | Rawalpindi[2] | 1994-95 |
| 64 | M.A.Atherton (England) | Bombay[3] | 1992-93 | Leeds | # 1998 |
| 61 | R.B.Kanhai (West Indies) | Birmingham | 1957 | Sydney | 1968-69 |
| 61 | I.V.A.Richards (West Indies) | Nottingham | 1980 | Madras[1] | 1987-88 |
| 58 § | J R.Reid (New Zealand) | Manchester | 1949 | Leeds | 1965 |
| 58 § | A.W.Greig (England) | Manchester | 1972 | The Oval | 1977 |
| 56 | S.M.H.Kirmani (India) | Madras[1] | 1979-80 | Kanpur | 1984-85 |
| 53 | K.J.Hughes (Australia) | Brisbane[2] | 1978-79 | Sydney | 1982-83 |
| 53 | Javed Miandad (Pakistan) | Lahore[2] | 1977-78 | Sydney | 1983-84 |
| 52 | F.E.Woolley (England) | The Oval | 1909 | The Oval | 1926 |
| 52 | P.B.H.May (England) | The Oval | 1953 | Leeds | 1959 |
| 52 | R.W.Marsh (Australia) | Brisbane[2] | 1970-71 | The Oval | 1977 |
| 51 | G.S.Chappell (Australia) | Perth | 1970-71 | The Oval | 1977 |
| 51 | D.I.Gower (England) | Bombay[3] | 1981-82 | Lord's | 1986 |

*The most for South Africa is 45 § by A.W.Nourse; for Sri Lanka 35 by P.A.de Silva; and for Zimbabwe 30 by the 3 players named above.*

*§ Entire Test career. # To date. Note: Kapil Dev played 66 consecutive Tests before being dropped for one Test because of disciplinary reasons. He then played a further 65 consecutive Tests.*

### LONGEST CAREERS *(From debut to final day of last match)*

| Years | Days | | Team (s) | From | | To | |
|---|---|---|---|---|---|---|---|
| 30 | 315 | W.Rhodes | England | Nottingham | 1899 | Kingston | 1929-30 |
| 26 | 355 | D.B.Close | England | Manchester | 1949 | Manchester | 1976 |
| 25 | 13 | F.E.Woolley | England | The Oval | 1909 | The Oval | 1934 |
| 24 | 10 | G.A.Headley | West Indies | Bridgetown | 1929-30 | Kingston | 1953-54 |
| 23 | 41 | A.J.Traicos | South Africa/Zimbabwe | Durban[2] | 1969-70 | Delhi | 1992-93 |
| 22 | 233 | J.B.Hobbs | England | Melbourne | 1907-08 | The Oval | 1930 |
| 22 | 120 | G.Gunn | England | Sydney | 1907-08 | Kingston | 1929-30 |
| 22 | 18 | S.E.Gregory | Australia | Lord's | 1890 | The Oval | 1912 |
| 21 | 336 | F.R.Brown | England | The Oval | 1931 | Lord's | 1953 |
| 21 | 313 | A.W.Nourse | South Africa | Johannesburg[1] | 1902-03 | The Oval | 1924 |

| | | | | | | | |
|---|---|---|---|---|---|---|---|
| 20 | 218 | Imran Khan | Pakistan | Birmingham | 1971 | Faisalabad | 1991-92 |
| 20 | 132 | R.B.Simpson | Australia | Johannesburg[1] | 1957-58 | Kingston | 1977-78 |
| 20 | 79 | M.C.Cowdrey | England | Brisbane[2] | 1954-55 | Melbourne | 1974-75 |
| 20 | 6 | G.S.Sobers | West Indies | Kingston | 1953-54 | Port-of-Spain | 1973-74 |
| 20 | 3 | Mushtaq Mohammed | Pakistan | Lahore[1] | 1958-59 | Perth | 1978-79 |

*Longest for the other countries:*

| | | | | | | | |
|---|---|---|---|---|---|---|---|
| 19 | 0 | N.B.Amarnath | India | Bombay[1] | 1933-34 | Calcutta | 1952-53 |
| 18 | 72 | B.Sutcliffe | New Zealand | Christchurch | 1946-47 | Birmingham | 1965 |
| 16 | 116 | A.Ranatunga | Sri Lanka | Colombo (PSS) | 1981-82 | Colombo (SSC) # | 1997-98 |

*# To date.*

## LONGEST INTERVALS BETWEEN APPEARANCES

| Years | Days | | Team (s) | From | | To | |
|---|---|---|---|---|---|---|---|
| 22 | 222 | A.J.Traicos | Sth Africa/Zimbabwe | Pt.Elizabeth | 1969-70 | Harare | 1992-93 |
| 17 | 316 | G.Gunn | England | Sydney | 1911-12 | Bridgetown | 1929-30 |
| 17 | 111 | Younis Ahmed | Pakistan | Lahore[2] | 1969-70 | Jaipur | 1986-87 |
| 14 | 92 | J.M.M.Commaille | South Africa | Cape Town | 1909-10 | Birmingham | 1924 |
| 14 | 28 | D.C.Cleverley | New Zealand | Christchurch | 1931-32 | Wellington | 1945-46 |
| 13 | 53 | F.Mitchell | England/South Africa | Cape Town | 1898-99 | Manchester | 1912 |
| 13 | 32 | G.M.Carew | West Indies | Bridgetown | 1934-35 | Port-of-Spain | 1947-48 |
| 12 | 160 | N.B.Amarnath | India | Madras[1] | 1933-34 | Lord's | 1946 |
| 12 | 81 | W.E.Hollies | England | Kingston | 1934-35 | Nottingham | 1947 |
| 12 | 10 | Nawab of Pataudi, sr | England/India | Nottingham | 1934 | Lord's | 1946 |
| 11 | 361 | F.R.Brown | England | Manchester | 1937 | The Oval | 1949 |
| 11 | 345 | H.L.Jackson | England | Manchester | 1949 | Leeds | 1961 |
| 11 | 320 | G.A.Faulkner | South Africa | The Oval | 1912 | Lord's | 1924 |
| 11 | 306 | S.J.Pegler | South Africa | The Oval | 1912 | Birmingham | 1924 |
| 11 | 298 | M.P.Donnelly | New Zealand | The Oval | 1937 | The Oval | 1949 |
| 11 | 225 | D.Shackleton | England | Delhi | 1951-52 | Lord's | 1963 |
| 10 | 158 | S.J.Snooke | South Africa | The Oval | 1912 | Durban[2] | 1922-23 |
| 10 | 48 | J.Langridge | England | Lord's | 1936 | The Oval | 1946 |

*Longest for Australia:*

| | | | | | | | |
|---|---|---|---|---|---|---|---|
| 9 | 305 | R.B.Simpson | Australia | Sydney | 1967-68 | Brisbane[2] | 1977-78 |

*The most matches between appearances is 104 by Younis Ahmed (as above).*

## PLAYERS WHO REPRESENTED TWO COUNTRIES

| Player | Country (Tests) | Seasons | Country (Tests) | Seasons | Total Tests |
|---|---|---|---|---|---|
| Amir Elahi | India (1) | 1947-48 | Pakistan (5) | 1952-53 | 6 |
| J.J.Ferris | Australia (8) | 1886-87 to 1890 | England (1) | 1891-92 | 9 |
| S.C.Guillen | West Indies (5) | 1951-52 | New Zealand (3) | 1955-56 | 8 |
| Gul Mahomed | India (8) | 1946 to 1952-53 | Pakistan (1) | 1956-57 | 9 |
| F.Hearne | England (2) | 1888-89 | South Africa (4) | 1891-92 to 1895-96 | 6 |
| A.H.Kardar | India (3) | 1946 § | Pakistan (23) | 1952-53 to 1957-58 | 26 |
| W.E.Midwinter | Australia (8) | 1876-77 to 1886-87 | England (4) | 1881-82 | 12 |
| F.Mitchell | England (2) | 1898-99 | South Africa (3) | 1912 | 5 |
| W.L.Murdoch | Australia (18) | 1876-77 to 1890 | England (1) | 1891-92 | 19 |
| Nawab of Pataudi, sr | England (3) | 1932-33 to 1934 | India (3) | 1946 | 6 |
| A.J.Traicos | South Africa (3) | 1969-70 | Zimbabwe (4) | 1992-93 | 7 |
| A.E.Trott | Australia (3) | 1894-95 | England (2) | 1898-99 | 5 |
| K.C.Wessels | Australia (24) | 1982-83 to 1985-86 | South Africa (16) | 1991-92 to 1994 | 40 |
| S.M.J.Woods | Australia (3) | 1888 | England (3) | 1895-96 | 6 |

*§ As "Abdul Hafeez".*

## ON THE FIELD THROUGHOUT A MATCH

| | | | | | | Days |
|---|---|---|---|---|---|---|
| Nazar Mohammad | Pakistan | v | India | Lucknow[1] | 1952-53 | 4 |
| D.J.McGlew | South Africa | v | New Zealand | Wellington | 1952-53 | 4 |
| C.A.Milton | England | v | New Zealand | Leeds | 1958 | 5#† |
| J.H.Edrich | England | v | New Zealand | Leeds | 1965 | 5 |

| | | | | | | |
|---|---|---|---|---|---|---|
| D.Lloyd | England | v | India | Birmingham | 1974 | 3 |
| G.Boycott | England | v | Australia | Leeds | 1977 | 4 |
| Taslim Arif | Pakistan | v | Australia | Faisalabad | 1979-80 | 5∇ |
| S.M.Gavaskar | India | v | West Indies | Georgetown | 1982-83 | 5# |
| D.S.B.P.Kuruppu | Sri Lanka | v | New Zealand | Colombo (CCC) | 1986-87 | 5† |
| M.A.Taylor | Australia | v | Pakistan | Sydney | 1989-90 | 6§ |
| M.A.Taylor | Australia | v | South Africa | Melbourne | 1993-94 | 5∇ |
| B.A.Young | New Zealand | v | Sri Lanka | Dunedin | 1996-97 | 5 |

*† In first Test. # Rain prevented play on two days. ∇Rain prevented play on one day. § Rain prevented play on three days.*

## YOUNGEST TEST PLAYERS

| Years | Days | | | | | | |
|---|---|---|---|---|---|---|---|
| 15 | 124 | Mushtaq Mohammad | Pakistan | v | West Indies | Lahore[1] | 1958-59 |
| 16 | 189 | Aaqib Javed | Pakistan | v | New Zealand | Wellington | 1988-89 |
| 16 | 205 | S.R.Tendulkar | India | v | Pakistan | Karachi[1] | 1989-90 |
| 16 | 221 | Aftab Baloch | Pakistan | v | New Zealand | Dacca | 1969-70 |
| 16 | 248 | Nasim-ul-Ghani | Pakistan | v | West Indies | Bridgetown | 1957-58 |
| 16 | 352 | Khalid Hassan | Pakistan | v | England | Nottingham | 1954 |
| 17 | 5 | Zahid Fazal | Pakistan | v | West Indies | Karachi[1] | 1990-91 |
| 17 | 69 | Ataur Rehmann | Pakistan | v | England | Birmingham | 1992 |
| 17 | 118 | L.Sivaramakrishnan | India | v | West Indies | St John's | 1982-83 |
| 17 | 122 | J.E.D.Sealy | West Indies | v | England | Bridgetown | 1929-30 |
| 17 | 129 | Fazl-e-Akbar | Pakistan | v | South Africa | Durban[2] | 1997-98 |
| 17 | 189 | C.D.U.S.Weerasinghe | Sri Lanka | v | India | Colombo (PSS) | 1985-86 |
| 17 | 193 | Maninder Singh | India | v | Pakistan | Karachi[1] | 1932-83 |
| 17 | 239 | I.D.Craig | Australia | v | South Africa | Melbourne | 1952-53 |
| 17 | 245 | G.S.Sobers | West Indies | v | England | Kingston | 1953-54 |
| 17 | 265 | V.L.Mehra | India | v | New Zealand | Bombay[2] | 1955-56 |
| 17 | 266 | Harbhajan Singh | India | v | Australia | Bangalore | 1997-98 |
| 17 | 300 | Hanif Mohammad | Pakistan | v | India | Delhi | 1952-53 |
| 17 | 341 | Intikhab Alam | Pakistan | v | Australia | Karachi[1] | 1959-60 |
| 17 | 364 | Waqar Younis | Pakistan | v | India | Karachi[1] | 1989-90 |
| 18 | 1 | M.S.Atapattu | Sri Lanka | v | India | Chandigarh | 1990-91 |
| 18 | 10 | D.L.Vettori | New Zealand | v | England | Wellington | 1996-97 |
| 18 | 13 | A.G.Milkha Singh | India | v | Australia | Madras[2] | 1959-60 |
| 18 | 26 | Majid Khan | Pakistan | v | Australia | Karachi[1] | 1964-65 |
| 18 | 31 | M.R.Bynoe | West Indies | v | Pakistan | Lahore[1] | 1958-59 |
| 18 | 41 | Salahuddin | Pakistan | v | New Zealand | Rawalpindi[1] | 1964-65 |
| 18 | 44 | Khalid Wazir | Pakistan | v | England | Lord's | 1954 |
| 18 | 78 | A.Ranatunga | Sri Lanka | v | England | Colombo (PSS) | 1981-82 |
| 18 | 81 | B.R.Jurangpathy | Sri Lanka | v | India | Kandy | 1985-86 |
| 18 | 105 | J.B.Stollmeyer | West Indies | v | England | Lord's | 1939 |
| 18 | 136 | Ijaz Ahmed | Pakistan | v | India | Madras[1] | 1986-87 |
| 18 | 147 | C.M.Bandara | Sri Lanka | v | New Zealand | Colombo (PIS) | 1997-98 |
| 18 | 149 | D.B.Close | England | v | New Zealand | Manchester | 1949 |
| 18 | 173 | A.T.Roberts | West Indies | v | New Zealand | Auckland | 1955-56 |
| 18 | 186 | Haseeb Ahsan | Pakistan | v | West Indies | Bridgetown | 1957-58 |
| 18 | 190 | Imran Khan | Pakistan | v | England | Birmingham | 1971 |
| 18 | 197 | D.L.Freeman | New Zealand | v | England | Christchurch | 1932-33 |
| 18 | 212 | H.K.Olonga | Zimbabwe | v | Pakistan | Harare | 1994-95 |
| 18 | 232 | T.W.Garrett | Australia | v | England | Melbourne | 1876-77 |
| 18 | 236 | Wasim Akram | Pakistan | v | New Zealand | Auckland | 1984-85 |
| 18 | 242 | A.P.H.Scott | West Indies | v | India | Kingston | 1952-53 |
| 18 | 249 | B.S.Chandrasekhar | India | v | England | Bombay[2] | 1963-64 |
| 18 | 255 | Saqlain Mushtaq | Pakistan | v | Sri Lanka | Peshawar[2] | 1995-96 |
| 18 | 257 | Shadab Kabir | Pakistan | v | England | Lord's | 1996 |
| 18 | 260 | Mohammad Ilyas | Pakistan | v | Australia | Melbourne | 1964-65 |
| 18 | 267 | H.G.Vivian | New Zealand | v | England | The Oval | 1931 |
| 18 | 270 | R.J.Shastri | India | v | New Zealand | Wellington | 1980-81 |

| | | | | | | | |
|---|---|---|---|---|---|---|---|
| 18 | 288 | C.Sharma | India | v | Pakistan | Lahore[2] | 1984-85 |
| 18 | 295 | R.O.Collinge | New Zealand | v | Pakistan | Wellington | 1964-65 |
| 18 | 299 | D.N.T.Zoysa | Sri Lanka | v | New Zealand | Dunedin | 1996-97 |
| 18 | 311 | P.A.De Silva | Sri Lanka | v | England | Lord's | 1984 |
| 18 | 312 | S.Venkataraghavan | India | v | New Zealand | Madras[2] | 1964-65 |
| 18 | 316 | B.P.Bracewell | New Zealand | v | England | The Oval | 1978 |
| 18 | 318 | Shahid Nazir | Pakistan | v | Zimbabwe | Sheikhupura | 1996-97 |
| 18 | 323 | Saleem Malik | Pakistan | v | Sri Lanka | Karachi[1] | 1981-82 |
| 18 | 340 | P.R.Adams | South Africa | v | England | Port Elizabeth | 1995-96 |

*Hasan Raza (Pakistan), allegedly born 11 March 1982, made his debut in 1996-97 v Zimbabwe at Faisalabad on 24 October 1996 which would make him 14 years 227 days old on his debut. However, medical tests organized by the PCB, showed that he was born in circa 1981 and was at least 15 years of age.*

## OLDEST PLAYERS ON TEST DEBUT

| Years | Days | | | | | | |
|---|---|---|---|---|---|---|---|
| 49 | 119 | J.Southerton | England | v | Australia | Melbourne | 1876-77 |
| 47 | 284 | Miran Bux | Pakistan | v | India | Lahore[1] | 1954-55 |
| 46 | 253 | D.D.Blackie | Australia | v | England | Sydney | 1928-29 |
| 46 | 237 | H.Ironmonger | Australia | v | England | Brisbane[2] | 1928-29 |
| 45 | 154 | A.J.Traicos # | Zimbabwe | v | India | Harare | 1992-93 |
| 42 | 242 | N.Betancourt | West Indies | v | England | Port-of-Spain | 1929-30 |
| 41 | 337 | E.R.Wilson | England | v | Australia | Sydney | 1920-21 |
| 41 | 27 | R.J.D.Jamshedji | India | v | England | Bombay[1] | 1933-34 |
| 40 | 345 | C.A.Wiles | West Indies | v | England | Manchester | 1933 |
| 40 | 295 | O.Henry | South Africa | v | India | Durban[2] | 1992-93 |
| 40 | 216 | S.Kinneir | England | v | Australia | Sydney | 1911-12 |
| 40 | 110 | H.W.Lee | England | v | South Africa | Johannesburg[1] | 1930-31 |
| 40 | 56 | G.W.A.Chubb | South Africa | v | England | Nottingham | 1951 |
| 40 | 37 | C.Ramaswami | India | v | England | Manchester | 1936 |

*# Traicos had previously played three Tests for South Africa in 1969-70.*
*The oldest player to make his debut for New Zealand was H.M.McGirr who was 38 years 101 days old when he appeared against England at Auckland in 1929-30; and for Sri Lanka D.S.De Silva who was 39 years 251 days old when he made his debut in his country's inaugural Test against England at Colombo (PSS) in 1981-82.*

## OLDEST TEST PLAYERS *(Age on final day of their last Test match)*

| Years | Days | | | | | | |
|---|---|---|---|---|---|---|---|
| 52 | 165 | W.Rhodes | England | v | West Indies | Kingston | 1929-30 |
| 50 | 327 | H.Ironmonger | Australia | v | England | Sydney | 1932-33 |
| 50 | 320 | W.G.Grace | England | v | Australia | Nottingham | 1899 |
| 50 | 303 | G.Gunn | England | v | West Indies | Kingston | 1929-30 |
| 49 | 139 | J.Southerton | England | v | Australia | Melbourne | 1876-77 |
| 47 | 302 | Miran Bux | Pakistan | v | India | Peshawar[1] | 1954-55 |
| 47 | 249 | J.B.Hobbs | England | v | Australia | The Oval | 1930 |
| 47 | 87 | F.E.Woolley | England | v | Australia | The Oval | 1934 |
| 46 | 309 | D.D.Blackie | Australia | v | England | Adelaide | 1928-29 |
| 46 | 206 | A.W.Nourse | South Africa | v | England | The Oval | 1924 |
| 46 | 202 | H.Strudwick | England | v | Australia | The Oval | 1926 |
| 46 | 41 | E.H.Hendren | England | v | West Indies | Kingston | 1934-35 |
| 45 | 305 | A.J.Traicos | Zimbabwe | v | India | Delhi | 1992-93 |
| 45 | 245 | G.O.B.Allen | England | v | West Indies | Kingston | 1947-48 |
| 45 | 215 | P.Holmes | England | v | India | Lord's | 1932 |
| 45 | 140 | D.B.Close | England | v | West Indies | Manchester | 1976 |
| 44 | 341 | E.G.Wynyard | England | v | South Africa | Johannesburg[1] | 1905-06 |
| 44 | 317 | J.M.M.Commaille | South Africa | v | England | Cape Town | 1927-28 |
| 44 | 238 | R.Abel | England | v | Australia | Manchester | 1902 |
| 44 | 236 | G.A.Headley | West Indies | v | England | Kingston | 1953-54 |
| 44 | 105 | Amir Elahi | Pakistan | v | India | Calcutta | 1952-53 |

## Umpires

### MOST TEST MATCHES

| Tests | | Country | From | To |
|---|---|---|---|---|
| 66 | H.D.Bird | England | 1973 | 1996 |
| 48 | F.Chester | England | 1924 | 1955 |
| 42 | C.S.Elliott | England | 1957 | 1974 |
| 36 | D.J.Constant | England | 1971 | 1988 |
| 41 † | D.R.Shepherd | England | 1985 | 1998 |
| 37 † | S.A.Bucknor | West Indies | 1988-89 | 1997 |
| 36 | D.J.Constant | England | 1971 | 1988 |
| 36 † | S.G.Randell | Australia | 1984-85 | 1997-98 |
| 34 † | Khizer Hayat | Pakistan | 1979-80 | 1996-97 |
| 33 | J.S.Buller | England | 1956 | 1969 |
| 33 | A.R.Crafter | Australia | 1978-79 | 1991-92 |
| 32 | R.W.Crockett | Australia | 1901-02 | 1924-25 |
| 31 | D.Sang Hue | West Indies | 1961-62 | 1980-81 |
| 29 | J.Phillips | England | 1893 | 1905-06 |
| 29 | F.S.Lee | England | 1949 | 1962 |
| 29 | C.J.Egar | Australia | 1960-61 | 1968-69 |
| 29 † | L.H.Barker | West Indies | 1983-84 | 1996-97 |
| 39 † | R.S.Dunne | New Zealand | 1988-89 | 1998 |
| 28 | D.M.Archer | West Indies | 1980-81 | 1991-92 |
| 27 | R.C.Bailhache | Australia | 1974-75 | 1988-89 |
| 27 † | Mahboob Shah | Pakistan | 1974-75 | 1995-96 |
| 26 | B.J.Meyer | England | 1978 | 1993 |
| 26 | B.L.Aldridge | New Zealand | 1985-86 | 1995-96 |
| 26 † | S.Venkataraghavan | India | 1992-93 | 1997-98 |
| 25 | L.P.Rowan | Australia | 1962-63 | 1970-71 |
| 25 | R.Gosein | West Indies | 1964-65 | 1977-78 |
| 25 | D.B.Hair | Australia | 1991-92 | 1998 |

Most for other countries:

| Tests | | Country | From | To |
|---|---|---|---|---|
| 24 † | C.J.Mitchley | South Africa | 1992-93 | 1997-98 |
| 22 † | K.T.Francis | Sri Lanka | 1981-82 | 1997-98 |
| 18 † | I.D.Robinson | Zimbabwe | 1992-93 | 1997-98 |

† current Test umpire.

*C.J.Egar & L.P.Rowan stood together in 19 Tests, four more than the partnership of R.Gosein & D.Sang Hue.*

## Individual Career Records

These career records for all players appearing in official Test matches are complete to 10 August 1998. (* not out)

| AUSTRALIA | | | | BATTING AND FIELDING | | | | | | | | BOWLING | | | | | |
|---|---|---|---|---|---|---|---|---|---|---|---|---|---|---|---|---|---|
| | Tests | I | N | Runs | HS | Avge | 100 | 50 | 0's | c/s | Balls | Runs | Wks | Avge | 5w | 10w | BB |
| a'Beckett,EL | 4 | 7 | 0 | 143 | 41 | 20.42 | 0 | 0 | 0 | 4 | 1062 | 317 | 3 | 105.66 | 0 | 0 | 1/41 |
| Alderman,TM | 41 | 53 | 22 | 203 | 26* | 6.54 | 0 | 0 | 13 | 27 | 10181 | 4616 | 170 | 27.15 | 14 | 1 | 6/47 |
| Alexander,G | 2 | 4 | 0 | 52 | 33 | 13.00 | 0 | 0 | 0 | 2 | 168 | 93 | 2 | 46.50 | 0 | 0 | 2/69 |
| Alexander,HH | 1 | 2 | 1 | 17 | 17* | 17.00 | 0 | 0 | 1 | 0 | 276 | 154 | 1 | 154.00 | 0 | 0 | 1/129 |
| Allan,FE | 1 | 1 | 0 | 5 | 5 | 5.00 | 0 | 0 | 0 | 0 | 180 | 80 | 4 | 20.00 | 0 | 0 | 2/30 |
| Allan,PJ | 1 | | | | | | 0 | 0 | 0 | 0 | 192 | 83 | 2 | 41.50 | 0 | 0 | 2/58 |
| Allen,RC | 1 | 2 | 0 | 44 | 30 | 22.00 | 0 | 0 | 0 | 2 | | | | | | | |
| Andrews,TJE | 16 | 23 | 1 | 592 | 94 | 26.90 | 0 | 4 | 0 | 12 | 156 | 116 | 1 | 116.00 | 0 | 0 | 1/23 |
| Angel,J | 4 | 7 | 1 | 35 | 11 | 5.83 | 0 | 0 | 2 | 1 | 748 | 463 | 10 | 46.30 | 0 | 0 | 3/54 |
| Archer,KA | 5 | 9 | 0 | 234 | 48 | 26.00 | 0 | 0 | 1 | 0 | | | | | | | |
| Archer,RG | 19 | 30 | 1 | 713 | 128 | 24.58 | 1 | 2 | 4 | 20 | 3576 | 1318 | 48 | 27.45 | 1 | 0 | 5/53 |
| Armstrong,WW | 50 | 84 | 10 | 2863 | 159* | 38.68 | 6 | 8 | 6 | 44 | 8022 | 2923 | 87 | 33.59 | 3 | 0 | 6/35 |
| Badcock,CL | 7 | 12 | 1 | 160 | 118 | 14.54 | 1 | 0 | 4 | 3 | | | | | | | |
| Bannerman,AC | 28 | 50 | 2 | 1108 | 94 | 23.08 | 0 | 8 | 3 | 21 | 292 | 163 | 4 | 40.75 | 0 | 0 | 3/111 |
| Bannerman,C | 3 | 6 | 2 | 239 | 165* | 59.75 | 1 | 0 | 0 | 0 | | | | | | | |
| Bardsley,W | 41 | 66 | 5 | 2469 | 193* | 40.47 | 6 | 14 | 6 | 12 | | | | | | | |
| Barnes,SG | 13 | 19 | 2 | 1072 | 234 | 63.05 | 3 | 5 | 1 | 14 | 594 | 218 | 4 | 54.50 | 0 | 0 | 2/25 |
| Barnett,BA | 4 | 8 | 1 | 195 | 57 | 27.85 | 0 | 1 | 0 | 3/2 | | | | | | | |
| Barrett,JE | 2 | 4 | 1 | 80 | 67* | 26.66 | 0 | 1 | 1 | 1 | | | | | | | |
| Beard,GR | 3 | 5 | 0 | 114 | 49 | 22.80 | 0 | 0 | 0 | 0 | 259 | 109 | 1 | 109.00 | 0 | 0 | 1/26 |
| Benaud,J | 3 | 5 | 0 | 223 | 142 | 44.60 | 1 | 0 | 0 | 0 | 24 | 12 | 2 | 6.00 | 0 | 0 | 2/12 |
| Benaud,R | 63 | 97 | 7 | 2201 | 122 | 24.45 | 3 | 9 | 8 | 65 | 19108 | 6704 | 248 | 27.03 | 16 | 1 | 7/72 |
| Bennett,MJ | 3 | 5 | 2 | 71 | 23 | 23.66 | 0 | 0 | 0 | 5 | 665 | 325 | 6 | 54.16 | 0 | 0 | 3/79 |
| Bevan,MG | 18 | 30 | 3 | 785 | 91 | 29.07 | 0 | 6 | 4 | 8 | 1285 | 703 | 29 | 24.24 | 1 | 1 | 6/82 |
| Bichel,AJ | 3 | 5 | 0 | 47 | 18 | 9.40 | 0 | 0 | 1 | 1 | 519 | 297 | 2 | 148.50 | 0 | 0 | 1/31 |
| Blackham,JM | 35 | 62 | 11 | 800 | 74* | 15.68 | 0 | 4 | 6 | 37/24 | | | | | | | |
| Blackie,DD | 3 | 6 | 3 | 24 | 11* | 8.00 | 0 | 0 | 2 | 2 | 1260 | 444 | 14 | 31.71 | 1 | 0 | 6/94 |
| Blewett,GS | 31 | 53 | 2 | 1843 | 214 | 36.13 | 4 | 10 | 4 | 36 | 1070 | 520 | 9 | 57.77 | 0 | 0 | 2/25 |
| Bonnor,GJ | 17 | 30 | 0 | 512 | 128 | 17.06 | 1 | 2 | 5 | 16 | 164 | 84 | 2 | 42.00 | 0 | 0 | 1/5 |
| Boon,DC | 107 | 190 | 20 | 7422 | 200 | 43.65 | 21 | 32 | 16 | 99 | 36 | 14 | 0 | - | 0 | 0 | 0/0 |
| Booth,BC | 29 | 48 | 6 | 1773 | 169 | 42.21 | 5 | 10 | 5 | 17 | 436 | 146 | 3 | 48.66 | 0 | 0 | 2/33 |
| Border,AR | 156 | 265 | 44 | 11174 | 205 | 50.56 | 27 | 63 | 11 | 156 | 4009 | 1525 | 39 | 39.10 | 2 | 1 | 7/46 |
| Boyle,HF | 12 | 16 | 4 | 153 | 36* | 12.75 | 0 | 0 | 2 | 10 | 1744 | 641 | 32 | 20.03 | 1 | 0 | 6/42 |
| Bradman,DG | 52 | 80 | 10 | 6996 | 334 | 99.94 | 29 | 13 | 7 | 32 | 160 | 72 | 2 | 36.00 | 0 | 0 | 1/8 |
| Bright,RJ | 25 | 39 | 8 | 445 | 33 | 14.35 | 0 | 0 | 6 | 13 | 5541 | 2180 | 53 | 41.13 | 4 | 1 | 7/87 |
| Bromley,EH | 2 | 4 | 0 | 38 | 26 | 9.50 | 0 | 0 | 0 | 2 | 60 | 19 | 0 | - | 0 | 0 | 0/19 |
| Brown,WA | 22 | 35 | 1 | 1592 | 206* | 46.82 | 4 | 9 | 1 | 14 | | | | | | | |
| Bruce,W | 14 | 26 | 2 | 702 | 80 | 29.25 | 0 | 5 | 1 | 12 | 988 | 440 | 12 | 36.66 | 0 | 0 | 3/88 |
| Burge,PJP | 42 | 68 | 8 | 2290 | 181 | 38.16 | 4 | 12 | 5 | 23 | | | | | | | |
| Burke,JW | 24 | 44 | 7 | 1280 | 189 | 34.59 | 3 | 5 | 0 | 18 | 814 | 230 | 8 | 28.75 | 0 | 0 | 4/37 |
| Burn,EJK | 2 | 4 | 0 | 41 | 19 | 10.25 | 0 | 0 | 1 | 0 | | | | | | | |
| Burton,FJ | 2 | 4 | 2 | 4 | 2* | 2.00 | 0 | 0 | 0 | 1/1 | | | | | | | |
| Callaway,ST | 3 | 6 | 1 | 87 | 41 | 17.40 | 0 | 0 | 1 | 0 | 471 | 142 | 6 | 23.66 | 1 | 0 | 5/37 |
| Callen,IW | 1 | 2 | 2 | 26 | 22* | 0 | 0 | 0 | 0 | 1 | 440 | 191 | 6 | 31.83 | 0 | 0 | 3/83 |
| Campbell,GD | 4 | 4 | 0 | 10 | 6 | 2.50 | 0 | 0 | 2 | 1 | 951 | 503 | 13 | 38.69 | 0 | 0 | 3/79 |
| Carkeek,W | 6 | 5 | 2 | 16 | 6* | 5.33 | 0 | 0 | 0 | 6/0 | | | | | | | |
| Carlson,PH | 2 | 4 | 0 | 23 | 21 | 5.75 | 0 | 0 | 2 | 2 | 368 | 99 | 2 | 49.50 | 0 | 0 | 2/41 |
| Carter,H | 28 | 47 | 9 | 873 | 72 | 22.97 | 0 | 4 | 4 | 44/21 | | | | | | | |
| Chappell,GS | 87 | 151 | 19 | 7110 | 247* | 53.86 | 24 | 31 | 12 | 122 | 5327 | 1913 | 47 | 40.70 | 1 | 0 | 5/61 |
| Chappell,IM | 75 | 136 | 10 | 5345 | 196 | 42.42 | 14 | 26 | 11 | 105 | 2873 | 1316 | 20 | 65.80 | 0 | 0 | 2/21 |
| Chappell,TM | 3 | 6 | 1 | 79 | 27 | 15.80 | 0 | 0 | 0 | 2 | | | | | | | |
| Charlton,PC | 2 | 4 | 0 | 29 | 11 | 7.25 | 0 | 0 | 0 | 0 | 45 | 24 | 3 | 8.00 | 0 | 0 | 3/18 |
| Chipperfield,AG | 14 | 20 | 3 | 552 | 109 | 32.47 | 1 | 2 | 1 | 15 | 924 | 437 | 5 | 87.40 | 0 | 0 | 3/91 |
| Clark,WM | 10 | 19 | 2 | 98 | 33 | 5.76 | 0 | 0 | 8 | 6 | 2793 | 1265 | 44 | 28.75 | 0 | 0 | 4/46 |

| **AUSTRALIA** (cont.) | | | | **BATTING AND FIELDING** | | | | | | | | **BOWLING** | | | | | |
|---|---|---|---|---|---|---|---|---|---|---|---|---|---|---|---|---|---|
| | Tests | I | N | Runs | HS | Avge | 100 | 50 | 0's | c/s | Balls | Runs | Wks | Avge | 5w | 10w | BB |
| Colley,DJ | 3 | 4 | 0 | 84 | 54 | 21.00 | 0 | 1 | 0 | 1 | 729 | 312 | 6 | 52.00 | 0 | 0 | 3/83 |
| Collins,HL | 19 | 31 | 1 | 1352 | 203 | 45.06 | 4 | 6 | 0 | 13 | 654 | 252 | 4 | 63.00 | 0 | 0 | 2/47 |
| Coningham,A | 1 | 2 | 0 | 13 | 10 | 6.50 | 0 | 0 | 0 | 0 | 186 | 76 | 2 | 38.00 | 0 | 0 | 2/17 |
| Connolly,AN | 29 | 45 | 20 | 260 | 37 | 10.40 | 0 | 0 | 10 | 17 | 7818 | 2981 | 102 | 29.22 | 4 | 0 | 6/47 |
| Cook,SH | 2 | 2 | 2 | 3 | 3* | - | 0 | 0 | 0 | 0 | 224 | 142 | 7 | 20.28 | 1 | 0 | 5/39 |
| Cooper,BB | 1 | 2 | 0 | 18 | 15 | 9.00 | 0 | 0 | 0 | 2 | | | | | | | |
| Cooper,WH | 2 | 3 | 1 | 13 | 7 | 6.50 | 0 | 0 | 0 | 1 | 466 | 226 | 9 | 25.11 | 1 | 0 | 6/120 |
| Corling,GE | 5 | 4 | 1 | 5 | 3 | 1.66 | 0 | 0 | 2 | 0 | 1159 | 447 | 12 | 37.25 | 0 | 0 | 4/60 |
| Cosier,GJ | 18 | 32 | 1 | 897 | 168 | 28.93 | 2 | 3 | 3 | 14 | 899 | 341 | 5 | 68.20 | 0 | 0 | 2/26 |
| Cottam,JT | 1 | 2 | 0 | 4 | 3 | 2.00 | 0 | 0 | 0 | 1 | | | | | | | |
| Cotter,A | 21 | 37 | 2 | 457 | 45 | 13.05 | 0 | 0 | 6 | 8 | 4633 | 2549 | 89 | 28.64 | 7 | 0 | 7/148 |
| Coulthard,G | 1 | 1 | 1 | 6 | 6* | - | 0 | 0 | 0 | 0 | | | | | | | |
| Cowper,RM | 27 | 46 | 2 | 2061 | 307 | 46.84 | 5 | 10 | 3 | 21 | 3005 | 1139 | 36 | 31.63 | 0 | 0 | 4/48 |
| Craig,ID | 11 | 18 | 0 | 358 | 53 | 19.88 | 0 | 2 | 3 | 2 | | | | | | | |
| Crawford,WPA | 4 | 5 | 2 | 53 | 34 | 17.66 | 0 | 0 | 1 | 1 | 437 | 107 | 7 | 15.28 | 0 | 0 | 3/28 |
| Dale,AC | 1 | 1 | 0 | 5 | 5 | 5.00 | 0 | 0 | 0 | 0 | 168 | 92 | 3 | 30.66 | 0 | 0 | 3/71 |
| Darling,J | 34 | 60 | 2 | 1657 | 178 | 28.56 | 3 | 8 | 8 | 27 | | | | | | | |
| Darling,LS | 12 | 18 | 1 | 474 | 85 | 27.88 | 0 | 3 | 2 | 8 | 162 | 65 | 0 | - | 0 | 0 | 0/3 |
| Darling,WM | 14 | 27 | 1 | 697 | 91 | 26.80 | 0 | 6 | 1 | 5 | | | | | | | |
| Davidson,AK | 44 | 61 | 7 | 1328 | 80 | 24.59 | 0 | 5 | 1 | 42 | 11587 | 3819 | 186 | 20.53 | 14 | 2 | 7/93 |
| Davis,IC | 15 | 27 | 1 | 692 | 105 | 26.61 | 1 | 4 | 9 | 3 | | | | | | | |
| Davis,SP | 1 | 1 | 0 | 0 | 0 | 0.00 | 0 | 0 | 0 | 1 | 150 | 70 | 0 | - | 0 | 0 | 0/70 |
| De Courcy,JH | 3 | 6 | 1 | 81 | 41 | 16.20 | 0 | 0 | 3 | 0 | | | | | | | |
| Dell,AR | 2 | 2 | 2 | 6 | 3* | - | 0 | 0 | 0 | 0 | 559 | 160 | 6 | 26.66 | 0 | 0 | 3/65 |
| Dodemaide,AIC | 10 | 15 | 6 | 202 | 50 | 22.44 | 0 | 1 | 6 | 0 | 2184 | 963 | 34 | 28.32 | 1 | 0 | 6/58 |
| Donnan,H | 5 | 10 | 1 | 75 | 15 | 8.33 | 0 | | 10 | 1 | 54 | 22 | 0 | - | 0 | 0 | 0/22 |
| Dooland,B | 3 | 5 | 1 | 76 | 29 | 19.00 | 0 | | 00 | 3 | 880 | 419 | 9 | 46.55 | 0 | 0 | 4/69 |
| Duff,RA | 22 | 40 | 3 | 1317 | 146 | 35.59 | 2 | | 06 | 14 | 180 | 85 | 4 | 21.25 | 0 | 0 | 2/43 |
| Duncan,JRF | 1 | 1 | 0 | 3 | 3 | 3.00 | 0 | | 00 | 0 | 112 | 30 | 0 | - | 0 | 0 | 0/30 |
| Dyer,GC | 6 | 6 | 0 | 131 | 60 | 21.83 | 0 | 1 | 1 | 22/2 | | | | | | | |
| Dymock,G | 21 | 32 | 7 | 236 | 31* | 9.44 | 0 | 0 | 7 | 1 | 5545 | 2116 | 78 | 27.12 | 5 | 1 | 7/67 |
| Dyson,J | 30 | 58 | 7 | 1359 | 127* | 26.64 | 2 | 5 | 4 | 10 | | | | | | | |
| Eady,CJ | 2 | 4 | 1 | 20 | 10* | 6.66 | 0 | 0 | 0 | 2 | 223 | 112 | 7 | 16.00 | 0 | 0 | 3/30 |
| Eastwood,KH | 1 | 2 | 0 | 5 | 5 | 2.50 | 0 | 0 | 1 | 0 | 40 | 21 | 1 | 21.00 | 0 | 0 | 1/21 |
| Ebeling,HI | 1 | 2 | 0 | 43 | 41 | 21.50 | 0 | 0 | 0 | 0 | 186 | 89 | 3 | 29.66 | 0 | 0 | 3/74 |
| Edwards,JD | 3 | 6 | 1 | 48 | 26 | 9.60 | 0 | 0 | 3 | 1 | | | | | | | |
| Edwards,R | 20 | 32 | 3 | 1171 | 170* | 40.37 | 2 | 9 | 4 | 7 | 12 | 20 | 0 | - | 0 | 0 | 0/20 |
| Edwards,WJ | 3 | 6 | 0 | 68 | 30 | 11.33 | 0 | 0 | 2 | 0 | | | | | | | |
| Elliott,MTG | 17 | 28 | 1 | 1102 | 199 | 40.81 | 3 | 4 | 1 | 11 | 12 | 4 | 0 | - | 0 | 0 | 0/0 |
| Emery,PA | 1 | 1 | 1 | 8 | 8* | - | 0 | 0 | 0 | 5/1 | | | | | | | |
| Emery,SH | 4 | 2 | 0 | 6 | 5 | 3.00 | 0 | 0 | 0 | 2 | 462 | 249 | 5 | 49.80 | 0 | 0 | 2/46 |
| Evans,E | 6 | 10 | 2 | 82 | 33 | 10.25 | 0 | 0 | 3 | 5 | 1247 | 332 | 7 | 47.42 | 0 | 0 | 3/64 |
| Fairfax,AG | 10 | 12 | 4 | 410 | 65 | 51.25 | 0 | 4 | 0 | 15 | 1520 | 645 | 21 | 30.71 | 0 | 0 | 4/31 |
| Favell,LE | 19 | 31 | 3 | 757 | 101 | 27.03 | 1 | 5 | 2 | 9 | | | | | | | |
| Ferris,JJ | 8 | 16 | 4 | 98 | 20* | 8.16 | 0 | 0 | 1 | 4 | 2030 | 684 | 48 | 14.25 | 4 | 0 | 5/26 |
| Fingleton,JHW | 18 | 29 | 1 | 1189 | 136 | 42.46 | 5 | 3 | 3 | 13 | | | | | | | |
| Fleetwood-Smith,LO | 10 | 11 | 5 | 54 | 16* | 9.00 | 0 | 0 | 2 | 0 | 3093 | 1570 | 42 | 37.38 | 2 | 1 | 6/110 |
| Fleming,DW | 4 | 4 | 0 | 40 | 24 | 10.00 | 0 | 0 | 2 | 2 | 902 | 435 | 17 | 25.58 | 0 | 0 | 4/75 |
| Francis,BC | 3 | 5 | 0 | 52 | 27 | 10.40 | 0 | 0 | 1 | 1 | | | | | | | |
| Freeman,EW | 11 | 18 | 0 | 345 | 76 | 19.16 | 0 | 2 | 0 | 5 | 2183 | 1128 | 34 | 33.17 | 0 | 0 | 4/52 |
| Freer,FW | 1 | 1 | 1 | 28 | 28* | - | 0 | 0 | 0 | 0 | 160 | 74 | 3 | 24.66 | 0 | 0 | 2/49 |
| Gannon,JB | 3 | 5 | 4 | 3 | 3* | 3.00 | 0 | 0 | 1 | 3 | 726 | 361 | 11 | 32.81 | 0 | 0 | 4/77 |
| Garrett,TW | 19 | 33 | 6 | 339 | 51* | 12.55 | 0 | 1 | 5 | 7 | 2708 | 970 | 36 | 26.94 | 2 | 0 | 6/78 |
| Gaunt,RA | 3 | 4 | 2 | 6 | 3 | 3.00 | 0 | 0 | 0 | 1 | 716 | 310 | 7 | 44.28 | 0 | 0 | 3/53 |
| Gehrs,DRA | 6 | 11 | 0 | 221 | 67 | 20.09 | 0 | 2 | 1 | 6 | 6 | 4 | 0 | - | 0 | 0 | 0/4 |
| Giffen,G | 31 | 53 | 0 | 1238 | 161 | 23.35 | 1 | 6 | 5 | 24 | 6391 | 2791 | 103 | 27.09 | 7 | 1 | 7/117 |
| Giffen,WF | 3 | 6 | 0 | 11 | 3 | 1.83 | 0 | 0 | 1 | 1 | | | | | | | |

| AUSTRALIA (cont.) | | | | BATTING AND FIELDING | | | | | | | | | | BOWLING | | | |
|---|---|---|---|---|---|---|---|---|---|---|---|---|---|---|---|---|---|
| | Tests | I | N | Runs | HS | Avge | 100 | 50 | 0's | c/s | Balls | Runs | Wks | Avge | 5w | 10w | BB |
| Gilbert,DR | 9 | 12 | 4 | 57 | 15 | 7.12 | 0 | 0 | 1 | 0 | 1647 | 843 | 16 | 52.68 | 0 | 0 | 3/48 |
| Gillespie,JN | 9 | 14 | 7 | 86 | 28* | 12.28 | 0 | 0 | 2 | 3 | 1370 | 713 | 32 | 22.28 | 2 | 0 | 7/37 |
| Gilmour,GJ | 15 | 22 | 1 | 483 | 101 | 23.00 | 1 | 3 | 3 | 8 | 2661 | 1406 | 54 | 26.03 | 3 | 0 | 6/85 |
| Gleeson,JW | 29 | 46 | 8 | 395 | 45 | 10.39 | 0 | 0 | 11 | 17 | 8857 | 3367 | 93 | 36.20 | 3 | 0 | 5/61 |
| Graham,H | 6 | 10 | 0 | 301 | 107 | 30.10 | 2 | 0 | 2 | 3 | | | | | | | |
| Gregory,DW | 3 | 5 | 2 | 60 | 43 | 20.00 | 0 | 0 | 0 | 0 | 20 | 9 | 0 | - | 0 | 0 | 0/9 |
| Gregory,EJ | 1 | 2 | 0 | 11 | 11 | 5.50 | 0 | 0 | 1 | 1 | | | | | | | |
| Gregory,JM | 24 | 34 | 3 | 1146 | 119 | 36.96 | 2 | 7 | 3 | 37 | 5582 | 2648 | 85 | 31.15 | 4 | 0 | 7/69 |
| Gregory,RG | 2 | 3 | 0 | 153 | 80 | 51.00 | 0 | 2 | 0 | 1 | 24 | 14 | 0 | - | 0 | 0 | 0/14 |
| Gregory,SE | 58 | 100 | 7 | 2282 | 201 | 24.53 | 4 | 8 | 12 | 25 | 30 | 33 | 0 | - | 0 | 0 | 0/4 |
| Grimmett,CV | 37 | 50 | 10 | 557 | 50 | 13.92 | 0 | 1 | 7 | 17 | 14513 | 5231 | 216 | 24.21 | 21 | 7 | 7/40 |
| Groube,TU | 1 | 2 | 0 | 11 | 11 | 5.50 | 0 | 0 | 1 | 0 | | | | | | | |
| Grout,ATW | 51 | 67 | 8 | 890 | 74 | 15.08 | 0 | 3 | 11 | 163/24 | | | | | | | |
| Guest,CEJ | 1 | 1 | 0 | 11 | 11 | 11.00 | 0 | 0 | 0 | 0 | 144 | 59 | 0 | - | 0 | 0 | 0/8 |
| Hamence,RA | 3 | 4 | 1 | 81 | 30* | 27.00 | 0 | 0 | 0 | 1 | | | | | | | |
| Hammond,JR | 5 | 5 | 2 | 28 | 19 | 9.33 | 0 | 0 | 1 | 2 | 1031 | 488 | 15 | 32.53 | 0 | 0 | 4/38 |
| Harry,J | 1 | 2 | 0 | 8 | 6 | 4.00 | 0 | 0 | 0 | 1 | | | | | | | |
| Hartigan,RJ | 2 | 4 | 0 | 170 | 116 | 42.50 | 1 | 0 | 0 | 1 | 12 | 7 | 0 | - | 0 | 0 | 0/7 |
| Hartkopf,AEV | 1 | 2 | 0 | 80 | 80 | 40.00 | 0 | 1 | 1 | 0 | 240 | 134 | 1 | 134.00 | 0 | 0 | 1/120 |
| Harvey,MR | 1 | 2 | 0 | 43 | 31 | 21.50 | 0 | 0 | 0 | 0 | | | | | | | |
| Harvey,RN | 79 | 137 | 10 | 6149 | 205 | 48.41 | 21 | 24 | 7 | 64 | 414 | 120 | 3 | 40.00 | 0 | 0 | 1/8 |
| Hassett,AL | 43 | 69 | 3 | 3073 | 198* | 46.56 | 10 | 11 | 1 | 30 | 111 | 78 | 0 | - | 0 | 0 | 0/1 |
| Hawke,NJN | 27 | 37 | 15 | 365 | 45* | 16.59 | 0 | 0 | 6 | 9 | 6974 | 2677 | 91 | 29.41 | 6 | 1 | 7/105 |
| Hayden,ML | 7 | 12 | 0 | 261 | 125 | 21.75 | 1 | 0 | 4 | 8 | | | | | | | |
| Hazlitt,GR | 9 | 12 | 4 | 89 | 34* | 11.12 | 0 | 0 | 2 | 4 | 1563 | 623 | 23 | 27.08 | 1 | 0 | 7/25 |
| Healy,IA | 103 | 157 | 21 | 3906 | 161* | 28.72 | 3 | 21 | 15 | 328/25 | | | | | | | |
| Hendry,HSTL | 11 | 18 | 2 | 335 | 112 | 20.93 | 1 | 0 | 1 | 10 | 1706 | 640 | 16 | 40.00 | 0 | 0 | 3/36 |
| Hibbert,PA | 1 | 2 | 0 | 15 | 13 | 7.50 | 0 | 0 | 0 | 1 | | | | | | | |
| Higgs,JD | 22 | 36 | 16 | 111 | 16 | 5.55 | 0 | 0 | 5 | 3 | 4752 | 2057 | 66 | 31.16 | 2 | 0 | 7/143 |
| Hilditch,AMJ | 18 | 34 | 0 | 1073 | 119 | 31.55 | 2 | 6 | 3 | 13 | | | | | | | |
| Hill,C | 49 | 89 | 2 | 3412 | 191 | 39.21 | 7 | 19 | 9 | 33 | | | | | | | |
| Hill,JC | 3 | 6 | 3 | 21 | 8* | 7.00 | 0 | 0 | 1 | 2 | 606 | 273 | 8 | 34.12 | 0 | 0 | 3/35 |
| Hoare,DE | 1 | 2 | 0 | 35 | 35 | 17.50 | 0 | 0 | 1 | 2 | 232 | 156 | 2 | 78.00 | 0 | 0 | 2/68 |
| Hodges,JR | 2 | 4 | 1 | 10 | 8 | 3.33 | 0 | 0 | 1 | 0 | 136 | 84 | 6 | 14.00 | 0 | 0 | 2/7 |
| Hogan,TG | 7 | 12 | 1 | 205 | 42* | 18.63 | 0 | 0 | 1 | 2 | 1436 | 706 | 15 | 47.06 | 1 | 0 | 5/66 |
| Hogg,RM | 38 | 58 | 13 | 439 | 52 | 9.75 | 0 | 1 | 14 | 7 | 7633 | 3503 | 123 | 28.47 | 6 | 2 | 6/74 |
| Hohns,TV | 7 | 7 | 1 | 136 | 40 | 22.66 | 0 | 0 | 1 | 3 | 1528 | 581 | 17 | 34.11 | 0 | 0 | 3/59 |
| Hole,GB | 18 | 33 | 2 | 789 | 66 | 25.45 | 0 | 6 | 2 | 21 | 398 | 126 | 3 | 42.00 | 0 | 0 | 1/9 |
| Holland,RG | 11 | 15 | 4 | 35 | 10 | 3.18 | 0 | 0 | 7 | 5 | 2889 | 1352 | 34 | 39.76 | 3 | 2 | 6/54 |
| Hookes,DW | 23 | 41 | 3 | 1306 | 143* | 34.36 | 1 | 8 | 4 | 12 | 96 | 41 | 1 | 41.00 | 0 | 0 | 1/4 |
| Hopkins,AJY | 20 | 33 | 2 | 509 | 43 | 25.45 | 0 | 0 | 4 | 11 | 1327 | 696 | 26 | 26.76 | 0 | 0 | 4/81 |
| Horan,TP | 15 | 27 | 2 | 471 | 124 | 18.84 | 1 | 1 | 3 | 6 | 373 | 143 | 11 | 13.00 | 1 | 0 | 6/40 |
| Hordern,HV | 7 | 13 | 2 | 254 | 50 | 23.09 | 0 | 1 | 1 | 6 | 2148 | 1075 | 46 | 23.36 | 5 | 2 | 7/90 |
| Hornibrook,PM | 6 | 7 | 1 | 60 | 26 | 10.00 | 0 | 0 | 1 | 7 | 1579 | 664 | 17 | 39.05 | 1 | 0 | 7/92 |
| Howell,WP | 18 | 27 | 6 | 158 | 35 | 7.52 | 0 | 0 | 8 | 12 | 3892 | 1407 | 49 | 28.71 | 1 | 0 | 5/81 |
| Hughes,KJ | 70 | 124 | 6 | 4415 | 213 | 37.41 | 9 | 22 | 10 | 50 | 85 | 28 | 0 | - | 0 | 0 | 0/0 |
| Hughes,MG | 53 | 70 | 8 | 1032 | 72* | 16.64 | 0 | 2 | 10 | 23 | 12285 | 6017 | 212 | 28.38 | 7 | 1 | 8/87 |
| Hunt,WA | 1 | 1 | 0 | 0 | 0 | 0.00 | 0 | 0 | 1 | 1 | 96 | 39 | 0 | - | 0 | 0 | 0/4 |
| Hurst,AG | 12 | 20 | 3 | 102 | 26 | 6.00 | 0 | 0 | 10 | 3 | 3054 | 1200 | 43 | 27.90 | 2 | 0 | 5/28 |
| Hurwood,A | 2 | 2 | 0 | 5 | 5 | 2.50 | 0 | 0 | 1 | 2 | 517 | 170 | 11 | 15.45 | 0 | 0 | 4/22 |
| Inverarity,RJ | 6 | 11 | 1 | 174 | 56 | 17.40 | 0 | 1 | 1 | 4 | 372 | 93 | 4 | 23.25 | 0 | 0 | 3/26 |
| Iredale,FA | 14 | 23 | 1 | 807 | 140 | 36.68 | 2 | 4 | 2 | 16 | 12 | 3 | 0 | - | 0 | 0 | 0/3 |
| Ironmonger,H | 14 | 21 | 5 | 42 | 12 | 2.62 | 0 | 0 | 6 | 3 | 4695 | 1330 | 74 | 17.97 | 4 | 2 | 7/23 |
| Iverson,JB | 5 | 7 | 3 | 3 | 1* | 0.75 | 0 | 0 | 2 | 2 | 1108 | 320 | 21 | 15.23 | 1 | 0 | 6/27 |
| Jackson,A | 8 | 11 | 1 | 474 | 164 | 47.40 | 1 | 2 | 1 | 7 | | | | | | | |
| Jarman,BN | 19 | 30 | 3 | 400 | 78 | 14.81 | 0 | 2 | 5 | 50/4 | | | | | | | |
| Jarvis,AH | 11 | 21 | 3 | 303 | 82 | 16.83 | 0 | 1 | 1 | 9/9 | | | | | | | |

| **AUSTRALIA** (cont.) | | | | **BATTING AND FIELDING** | | | | | | | | | | **BOWLING** | | | |
|---|---|---|---|---|---|---|---|---|---|---|---|---|---|---|---|---|---|
| | Tests | I | N | Runs | HS | Avge | 100 | 50 | 0's | c/s | Balls | Runs | Wks | Avge | 5w | 10w | BB |
| Jenner,TJ | 9 | 14 | 5 | 208 | 74 | 23.11 | 0 | 1 | 1 | 5 | 1881 | 749 | 24 | 31.20 | 1 | 0 | 5/90 |
| Jennings,CB | 6 | 8 | 2 | 107 | 32 | 17.83 | 0 | 0 | 2 | 5 | | | | | | | |
| Johnson,IW | 45 | 66 | 12 | 1000 | 77 | 18.51 | 0 | 6 | 10 | 30 | 8780 | 3182 | 109 | 29.19 | 3 | 0 | 7/44 |
| Johnson,LJ | 1 | 1 | 1 | 25 | 25* | 0 | 0 | 0 | 0 | 2 | 282 | 74 | 6 | 12.33 | 0 | 0 | 3/8 |
| Johnston,WA | 40 | 49 | 25 | 273 | 29 | 11.37 | 0 | 0 | 7 | 16 | 11048 | 3826 | 160 | 23.91 | 7 | 0 | 6/44 |
| Jones,DM | 52 | 89 | 11 | 3631 | 216 | 46.55 | 11 | 14 | 11 | 34 | 198 | 64 | 1 | 64.00 | 0 | 0 | 1/5 |
| Jones,E | 19 | 26 | 1 | 126 | 20 | 5.04 | 0 | 0 | 5 | 21 | 3748 | 1857 | 64 | 29.01 | 3 | 1 | 7/88 |
| Jones,SP | 12 | 24 | 4 | 432 | 87 | 21.60 | 0 | 1 | 3 | 12 | 262 | 112 | 6 | 18.66 | 0 | 0 | 4/47 |
| Joslin,LR | 1 | 2 | 0 | 9 | 7 | 4.50 | 0 | 0 | 0 | 0 | | | | | | | |
| Julian,BP | 7 | 9 | 1 | 128 | 56* | 16.00 | 0 | 1 | 3 | 4 | 1098 | 599 | 15 | 39.93 | 0 | 0 | 4/36 |
| Kasprowicz,MS | 13 | 17 | 2 | 180 | 25 | 12.00 | 0 | 0 | 3 | 3 | 2558 | 1234 | 36 | 34.27 | 2 | 0 | 7/36 |
| Kelleway,C | 26 | 42 | 4 | 1422 | 147 | 37.42 | 3 | 6 | 1 | 24 | 4363 | 1683 | 52 | 32.36 | 1 | 0 | 5/33 |
| Kelly,JJ | 36 | 56 | 17 | 664 | 46* | 17.02 | 0 | 0 | 7 | 43/20 | | | | | | | |
| Kelly,TJD | 2 | 3 | 0 | 64 | 35 | 21.33 | 0 | 0 | 0 | 1 | | | | | | | |
| Kendall,TK | 2 | 4 | 1 | 39 | 17* | 13.00 | 0 | 0 | 0 | 2 | 563 | 215 | 14 | 15.35 | 1 | 0 | 7/55 |
| Kent,MF | 3 | 6 | 0 | 171 | 54 | 28.50 | 0 | 2 | 0 | 6 | | | | | | | |
| Kerr,RB | 2 | 4 | 0 | 31 | 17 | 7.75 | 0 | 0 | 1 | 1 | | | | | | | |
| Kippax,AF | 22 | 34 | 1 | 1192 | 146 | 36.12 | 2 | 8 | 1 | 13 | 72 | 19 | 0 | - | 0 | 0 | 0/2 |
| Kline,LF | 13 | 16 | 9 | 58 | 15* | 8.28 | 0 | 0 | 3 | 9 | 2373 | 776 | 34 | 22.82 | 1 | 0 | 7/75 |
| Laird,BM | 21 | 40 | 2 | 1341 | 92 | 35.28 | 0 | 11 | 2 | 16 | 18 | 12 | 0 | - | 0 | 0 | 0/3 |
| Langer,JL | 8 | 12 | 0 | 272 | 69 | 22.66 | 0 | 3 | 3 | 2 | | | | | | | |
| Langley,GRA | 26 | 37 | 12 | 374 | 53 | 14.96 | 0 | 1 | 3 | 83/15 | | | | | | | |
| Laughlin,TJ | 3 | 5 | 0 | 87 | 35 | 17.40 | 0 | 0 | 0 | 3 | 516 | 262 | 6 | 43.66 | 1 | 0 | 5/101 |
| Laver,FJ | 15 | 23 | 6 | 196 | 45 | 11.52 | 0 | 0 | 4 | 8 | 2361 | 964 | 37 | 26.05 | 2 | 0 | 8/31 |
| Law,SG | 1 | 1 | 1 | 54 | 54 | - | 0 | 1 | 0 | 1 | 18 | 9 | 0 | - | 0 | 0 | 0/9 |
| Lawry,WM | 67 | 123 | 12 | 5234 | 210 | 47.15 | 13 | 27 | 6 | 30 | 14 | 6 | 0 | - | 0 | 0 | 0/0 |
| Lawson,GF | 46 | 68 | 12 | 894 | 74 | 15.96 | 0 | 4 | 6 | 10 | 11118 | 5501 | 180 | 30.56 | 11 | 2 | 8/112 |
| Lee,PK | 2 | 3 | 0 | 57 | 42 | 19.00 | 0 | 0 | 1 | 1 | 436 | 212 | 5 | 42.40 | 0 | 0 | 4/111 |
| Lehmann,DS | 1 | 1 | 0 | 52 | 52 | 52.00 | 0 | 1 | 0 | 2 | 42 | 27 | 1 | 27.00 | 0 | 0 | 1/27 |
| Lillee,DK | 70 | 90 | 24 | 905 | 73* | 13.71 | 0 | 1 | 10 | 23 | 18467 | 8493 | 355 | 23.92 | 23 | 7 | 7/83 |
| Lindwall,RR | 61 | 84 | 13 | 1502 | 118 | 21.15 | 2 | 5 | 9 | 26 | 13650 | 5251 | 228 | 23.03 | 12 | 0 | 7/38 |
| Love,HSB | 1 | 2 | 0 | 8 | 5 | 4.00 | 0 | 0 | 0 | 3 | | | | | | | |
| Loxton,SJE | 12 | 15 | 0 | 554 | 101 | 36.93 | 1 | 3 | 1 | 7 | 906 | 349 | 8 | 43.62 | 0 | 0 | 3/55 |
| Lyons,JJ | 14 | 27 | 0 | 731 | 134 | 27.07 | 1 | 3 | 1 | 3 | 316 | 149 | 6 | 24.83 | 1 | 0 | 5/30 |
| McAlister,PA | 8 | 16 | 1 | 252 | 41 | 16.80 | 0 | 0 | 0 | 10 | | | | | | | |
| Macartney,CG | 35 | 55 | 4 | 2131 | 170 | 41.78 | 7 | 9 | 1 | 17 | 3561 | 1240 | 45 | 27.55 | 2 | 1 | 7/58 |
| McCabe,SJ | 39 | 62 | 5 | 2748 | 232 | 48.21 | 6 | 13 | 4 | 41 | 3746 | 1543 | 36 | 42.86 | 0 | 0 | 4/13 |
| McCool,CL | 14 | 17 | 4 | 459 | 104* | 35.30 | 1 | 1 | 0 | 14 | 2504 | 958 | 36 | 26.61 | 3 | 0 | 5/41 |
| McCormick,EL | 12 | 14 | 5 | 54 | 17* | 6.00 | 0 | 0 | 3 | 8 | 2107 | 1079 | 36 | 29.97 | 0 | 0 | 4/101 |
| McCosker,RB | 25 | 46 | 5 | 1622 | 127 | 39.56 | 4 | 9 | 5 | 21 | | | | | | | |
| McDermott,CJ | 71 | 90 | 13 | 940 | 42* | 12.20 | 0 | 0 | 13 | 19 | 16586 | 8332 | 291 | 28.63 | 14 | 2 | 8/97 |
| McDonald,CC | 47 | 83 | 4 | 3107 | 170 | 39.32 | 5 | 17 | 2 | 14 | 8 | 3 | 0 | - | 0 | 0 | 0/3 |
| McDonald,EA | 11 | 12 | 5 | 116 | 36 | 16.57 | 0 | 0 | 1 | 3 | 2885 | 1431 | 43 | 33.27 | 2 | 0 | 5/32 |
| McDonnell,PS | 19 | 34 | 1 | 950 | 147 | 28.78 | 3 | 2 | 6 | 6 | 52 | 53 | 0 | - | 0 | 0 | 0/11 |
| MacGill,SCG | 1 | 1 | 0 | 10 | 10 | 10.00 | 0 | 0 | 0 | 1 | 216 | 134 | 5 | 26.80 | 0 | 0 | 3/22 |
| McGrath,GD | 37 | 44 | 14 | 144 | 24 | 4.80 | 0 | 0 | 14 | 8 | 8849 | 3900 | 166 | 23.49 | 9 | 0 | 8/38 |
| McIlwraith,J | 1 | 2 | 0 | 9 | 7 | 4.50 | 0 | 0 | 0 | 1 | | | | | | | |
| McIntyre,PE | 1 | 2 | 0 | 0 | 0 | 0.00 | 0 | 0 | 2 | 0 | 165 | 87 | 2 | 43.50 | 0 | 0 | 2/51 |
| Mackay,KD | 37 | 52 | 7 | 1507 | 89 | 33.48 | 0 | 13 | 6 | 16 | 5792 | 1721 | 50 | 34.42 | 2 | 0 | 6/42 |
| McKenzie,GD | 60 | 89 | 12 | 945 | 76 | 12.27 | 0 | 2 | 15 | 34 | 17681 | 7328 | 246 | 29.78 | 16 | 3 | 8/71 |
| McKibbin,TR | 5 | 8 | 2 | 88 | 28* | 14.66 | 0 | 0 | 2 | 4 | 1032 | 496 | 17 | 29.17 | 0 | 0 | 3/35 |
| McLaren,JW | 1 | 2 | 2 | 0 | 0* | - | 0 | 0 | 0 | 0 | 144 | 70 | 1 | 70.00 | 0 | 0 | 1/23 |
| Maclean,JA | 4 | 8 | 1 | 79 | 33* | 11.28 | 0 | 0 | 2 | 18/0 | | | | | | | |
| McLeod,CE | 17 | 29 | 5 | 573 | 112 | 23.87 | 1 | 4 | 5 | 9 | 3374 | 1325 | 33 | 40.15 | 2 | 0 | 5/65 |
| McLeod,RW | 6 | 11 | 0 | 146 | 31 | 13.27 | 0 | 0 | 0 | 3 | 1089 | 384 | 12 | 32.00 | 1 | 0 | 5/55 |
| McShane,PG | 3 | 6 | 1 | 26 | 12* | 5.20 | 0 | 0 | 3 | 2 | 108 | 48 | 1 | 48.00 | 0 | 0 | 1/39 |
| Maddocks,LV | 7 | 12 | 2 | 177 | 69 | 17.70 | 0 | 1 | 3 | 18/1 | | | | | | | |

| AUSTRALIA (cont.) | BATTING AND FIELDING | | | | | | | | | | BOWLING | | | | | | |
|---|---|---|---|---|---|---|---|---|---|---|---|---|---|---|---|---|---|
| | Tests | I | N | Runs | HS | Avge | 100 | 50 | 0's | c/s | Balls | Runs | Wks | Avge | 5w | 10w | BB |
| Maguire,JN | 3 | 5 | 1 | 28 | 15* | 7.00 | 0 | 0 | 2 | 2 | 616 | 323 | 10 | 32.30 | 0 | 0 | 4/57 |
| Mailey,AA | 21 | 29 | 9 | 222 | 46* | 11.10 | 0 | 0 | 3 | 14 | 6119 | 3358 | 99 | 33.91 | 6 | 2 | 9/121 |
| Mallett,AA | 38 | 50 | 13 | 430 | 43* | 11.62 | 0 | 0 | 10 | 30 | 9990 | 3940 | 132 | 29.84 | 6 | 1 | 8/59 |
| Malone,MF | 1 | 1 | 0 | 46 | 46 | 46.00 | 0 | 0 | 0 | 0 | 342 | 77 | 6 | 12.83 | 1 | 0 | 5/63 |
| Mann,AL | 4 | 8 | 0 | 189 | 105 | 23.62 | 1 | 0 | 2 | 2 | 552 | 316 | 4 | 79.00 | 0 | 0 | 3/12 |
| Marr,AP | 1 | 2 | 0 | 5 | 5 | 2.50 | 0 | 0 | 1 | 0 | 48 | 14 | 0 | - | 0 | 0 | 0/3 |
| Marsh,GR | 50 | 93 | 7 | 2854 | 138 | 33.18 | 4 | 15 | 3 | 38 | | | | | | | |
| Marsh,RW | 96 | 150 | 13 | 3633 | 132 | 26.51 | 3 | 16 | 12 | 343/12 | 72 | 54 | 0 | - | 0 | 0 | 0/3 |
| Martin,JW | 8 | 13 | 1 | 214 | 55 | 17.83 | 0 | 1 | 3 | 5 | 1846 | 832 | 17 | 48.94 | 0 | 0 | 3/56 |
| Martyn,DR | 7 | 12 | 1 | 317 | 74 | 28.81 | 0 | 3 | 1 | 1 | 6 | 0 | 0 | - | 0 | 0 | 0/0 |
| Massie,HH | 9 | 16 | 0 | 249 | 55 | 15.56 | 0 | 1 | 2 | 5 | | | | | | | |
| Massie,RAL | 6 | 8 | 1 | 78 | 42 | 11.14 | 0 | 0 | 3 | 1 | 1739 | 647 | 31 | 20.87 | 2 | 1 | 8/53 |
| Matthews,CD | 3 | 5 | 0 | 54 | 32 | 10.80 | 0 | 0 | 1 | 1 | 570 | 313 | 6 | 52.16 | 0 | 0 | 3/95 |
| Matthews,GRJ | 33 | 53 | 8 | 1849 | 130 | 41.08 | 4 | 12 | 2 | 17 | 6271 | 2942 | 61 | 48.22 | 2 | 1 | 5/103 |
| Matthews,TJ | 8 | 10 | 1 | 153 | 53 | 17.00 | 0 | 1 | 1 | 7 | 1081 | 419 | 16 | 26.18 | 0 | 0 | 4/29 |
| May,TBA | 24 | 28 | 12 | 225 | 42* | 14.06 | 0 | 0 | 3 | 6 | 6577 | 2606 | 75 | 34.74 | 3 | 0 | 5/9 |
| Mayne,LC | 6 | 11 | 3 | 76 | 13 | 9.50 | 0 | 0 | 0 | 3 | 1251 | 628 | 19 | 33.05 | 0 | 0 | 4/33 |
| Mayne,RE | 4 | 4 | 1 | 64 | 25* | 21.33 | 0 | 0 | 1 | 2 | 6 | 1 | 0 | - | 0 | 0 | 0/1 |
| Meckiff,I | 18 | 20 | 7 | 154 | 45* | 11.84 | 0 | 0 | 2 | 9 | 3734 | 1423 | 45 | 31.62 | 2 | 0 | 6/38 |
| Meuleman,KD | 1 | 1 | 0 | 0 | 0 | 0.00 | 0 | 0 | 1 | 1 | | | | | | | |
| Midwinter,WE | 8 | 14 | 1 | 174 | 37 | 13.38 | 0 | 0 | 1 | 5 | 949 | 333 | 14 | 23.78 | 1 | 0 | 5/78 |
| Miller,KR | 55 | 87 | 7 | 2958 | 147 | 36.97 | 7 | 13 | 5 | 38 | 10461 | 3906 | 170 | 22.97 | 7 | 1 | 7/60 |
| Minnett,RB | 9 | 15 | 0 | 391 | 90 | 26.06 | 0 | 3 | 3 | 0 | 589 | 290 | 11 | 26.36 | 0 | 0 | 4/34 |
| Misson,FM | 5 | 5 | 3 | 38 | 25* | 19.00 | 0 | 0 | 1 | 6 | 1197 | 616 | 16 | 38.50 | 0 | 0 | 4/58 |
| Moody,TM | 8 | 14 | 0 | 456 | 106 | 32.57 | 2 | 3 | 1 | 9 | 432 | 147 | 2 | 73.50 | 0 | 0 | 1/17 |
| Moroney,J | 7 | 12 | 1 | 383 | 118 | 34.81 | 2 | 1 | 3 | 0 | | | | | | | |
| Morris,AR | 46 | 79 | 3 | 3533 | 206 | 46.48 | 12 | 12 | 4 | 15 | 111 | 50 | 2 | 25.00 | 0 | 0 | 1/5 |
| Morris,S | 1 | 2 | 1 | 14 | 10* | 14.00 | 0 | 0 | 0 | 0 | 136 | 73 | 2 | 36.50 | 0 | 0 | 2/73 |
| Moses,H | 6 | 10 | 0 | 198 | 33 | 19.80 | 0 | 0 | 0 | 1 | | | | | | | |
| Moss,JK | 1 | 2 | 1 | 60 | 38* | 60.00 | 0 | 0 | 0 | 0 | | | | | | | |
| Moule,WH | 1 | 2 | 0 | 40 | 34 | 20.00 | 0 | 0 | 0 | 1 | 51 | 23 | 3 | 7.66 | 0 | 0 | 3/23 |
| Murdoch,WL | 18 | 33 | 5 | 896 | 211 | 32.00 | 2 | 1 | 3 | 13/1 | | | | | | | |
| Musgrove,H | 1 | 2 | 0 | 13 | 9 | 6.50 | 0 | 0 | 0 | 0 | | | | | | | |
| Nagel,LE | 1 | 2 | 1 | 21 | 21* | 21.00 | 0 | 0 | 1 | 0 | 262 | 110 | 2 | 55.00 | 0 | 0 | 2/110 |
| Nash,LJ | 2 | 2 | 0 | 30 | 17 | 15.00 | 0 | 0 | 0 | 6 | 311 | 126 | 10 | 12.60 | 0 | 0 | 4/18 |
| Nitschke,HC | 2 | 2 | 0 | 53 | 47 | 26.50 | 0 | 0 | 0 | 3 | | | | | | | |
| Noble,MA | 42 | 73 | 7 | 1997 | 133 | 30.25 | 1 | 16 | 4 | 26 | 7159 | 3025 | 121 | 25.00 | 9 | 2 | 7/17 |
| Noblet,G | 3 | 4 | 1 | 22 | 13* | 7.33 | 0 | 0 | 1 | 1 | 774 | 183 | 7 | 26.14 | 0 | 0 | 3/21 |
| Nothling,OE | 1 | 2 | 0 | 52 | 44 | 26.00 | 0 | 0 | 0 | 0 | 276 | 72 | 0 | - | 0 | 0 | 0/12 |
| O'Brien,LPJ | 5 | 8 | 0 | 211 | 61 | 26.37 | 0 | 2 | 1 | 3 | | | | | | | |
| O'Connor,JDA | 4 | 8 | 1 | 86 | 20 | 12.28 | 0 | 0 | 0 | 3 | 692 | 340 | 13 | 26.15 | 1 | 0 | 5/40 |
| O'Donnell,SP | 6 | 10 | 3 | 206 | 48 | 29.42 | 0 | 0 | 1 | 4 | 940 | 504 | 6 | 84.00 | 0 | 0 | 3/37 |
| Ogilvie,AD | 5 | 10 | 0 | 178 | 47 | 17.80 | 0 | 0 | 3 | 5 | | | | | | | |
| O'Keeffe,KJ | 24 | 34 | 9 | 644 | 85 | 25.76 | 0 | 1 | 3 | 15 | 5384 | 2018 | 53 | 38.07 | 1 | 0 | 5/101 |
| Oldfield,WAS | 54 | 80 | 17 | 1427 | 65* | 22.65 | 0 | 4 | 9 | 78/52 | | | | | | | |
| O'Neill,NC | 42 | 69 | 8 | 2779 | 181 | 45.55 | 6 | 15 | 6 | 21 | 1392 | 667 | 17 | 39.23 | 0 | 0 | 4/41 |
| O'Reilly,WJ | 27 | 39 | 7 | 410 | 56* | 12.81 | 0 | 1 | 6 | 7 | 10024 | 3254 | 144 | 22.59 | 11 | 3 | 7/54 |
| Oxenham,RK | 7 | 10 | 0 | 151 | 48 | 15.10 | 0 | 0 | 2 | 4 | 1802 | 522 | 14 | 37.28 | 0 | 0 | 4/39 |
| Palmer,GE | 17 | 25 | 4 | 296 | 48 | 14.09 | 0 | 0 | 3 | 13 | 4517 | 1678 | 78 | 21.51 | 6 | 2 | 7/65 |
| Park,RL | 1 | 1 | 0 | 0 | 0 | 0.00 | 0 | 0 | 1 | 0 | 6 | 9 | 0 | - | 0 | 0 | 0/9 |
| Pascoe,LS | 14 | 19 | 9 | 106 | 30* | 10.60 | 0 | 0 | 3 | 2 | 3403 | 1668 | 64 | 26.06 | 1 | 0 | 5/59 |
| Pellew,CE | 10 | 14 | 1 | 484 | 116 | 37.23 | 2 | 1 | 0 | 4 | 78 | 34 | 0 | - | 0 | 0 | 0/3 |
| Phillips,WB | 27 | 48 | 2 | 1485 | 159 | 32.28 | 2 | 7 | 1 | 52/0 | | | | | | | |
| Phillips,WN | 1 | 2 | 0 | 22 | 14 | 11.00 | 0 | 0 | 0 | 0 | | | | | | | |
| Philpott,PI | 8 | 10 | 1 | 93 | 22 | 10.33 | 0 | 0 | 0 | 5 | 2262 | 1000 | 26 | 38.46 | 1 | 0 | 5/90 |
| Ponsford,WH | 29 | 48 | 4 | 2122 | 266 | 48.22 | 7 | 6 | 1 | 21 | | | | | | | |
| Ponting,RT | 18 | 29 | 1 | 1043 | 127 | 37.25 | 2 | 6 | 0 | 17 | 35 | 8 | 2 | 4.00 | 0 | 0 | 1/0 |

| **AUSTRALIA** (cont.) | | | | **BATTING AND FIELDING** | | | | | | | | **BOWLING** | | | | | |
|---|---|---|---|---|---|---|---|---|---|---|---|---|---|---|---|---|---|
| | Tests | I | N | Runs | HS | Avge | 100 | 50 | 0's | c/s | Balls | Runs | Wks | Avge | 5w | 10w | BB |
| Reiffel,PR | 35 | 50 | 14 | 955 | 79* | 26.52 | 0 | 6 | 5 | 15 | 6403 | 2804 | 104 | 26.96 | 5 | 0 | 6/71 |
| Pope,RJ | 1 | 2 | 0 | 3 | 3 | 1.50 | 0 | 0 | 1 | 0 | | | | | | | |
| Rackemann,CG | 11 | 12 | 4 | 43 | 15* | 5.37 | 0 | 0 | 5 | 2 | 2546 | 1028 | 39 | 26.35 | 3 | 1 | 6/86 |
| Ransford,VS | 20 | 38 | 6 | 1211 | 143* | 37.84 | 1 | 7 | 2 | 10 | 43 | 28 | 1 | 28.00 | 0 | 0 | 1/9 |
| Redpath,IR | 66 | 120 | 11 | 4737 | 171 | 43.45 | 8 | 31 | 9 | 83 | 64 | 41 | 0 | - | 0 | 0 | 0/0 |
| Reedman,JC | 1 | 2 | 0 | 21 | 17 | 10.50 | 0 | 0 | 0 | 1 | 57 | 24 | 1 | 24.00 | 0 | 0 | 1/12 |
| Reid,BA | 27 | 34 | 14 | 93 | 13 | 4.65 | 0 | 0 | 6 | 5 | 6244 | 2784 | 113 | 24.63 | 5 | 2 | 7/51 |
| Reiffel,PR | 29 | 41 | 12 | 648 | 56 | 22.34 | 0 | 3 | 4 | 14 | 5293 | 2401 | 91 | 26.38 | 5 | 0 | 6/71 |
| Renneberg,DA | 8 | 13 | 7 | 22 | 9 | 3.66 | 0 | 0 | 3 | 2 | 1598 | 830 | 23 | 36.08 | 2 | 0 | 5/39 |
| Richardson,AJ | 9 | 13 | 0 | 403 | 100 | 31.00 | 1 | 2 | 1 | 1 | 1812 | 521 | 12 | 43.41 | 0 | 0 | 2/20 |
| Richardson,VY | 19 | 30 | 0 | 706 | 138 | 23.53 | 1 | 1 | 5 | 24 | | | | | | | |
| Rigg,KE | 8 | 12 | 0 | 401 | 127 | 33.41 | 1 | 1 | 0 | 5 | | | | | | | |
| Ring,DT | 13 | 21 | 2 | 426 | 67 | 22.42 | 0 | 4 | 2 | 5 | 3024 | 1305 | 35 | 37.28 | 2 | 0 | 6/72 |
| Ritchie,GM | 30 | 53 | 5 | 1690 | 146 | 35.20 | 3 | 7 | 1 | 14 | 6 | 10 | 0 | - | 0 | 0 | 0/10 |
| Rixon,SJ | 13 | 24 | 3 | 394 | 54 | 18.76 | 0 | 2 | 4 | 42/5 | | | | | | | |
| Robertson,GR | 3 | 5 | 0 | 90 | 57 | 18.00 | 0 | 1 | 2 | 1 | 670 | 413 | 12 | 34.41 | 0 | 0 | 4/72 |
| Robertson,WR | 1 | 2 | 0 | 2 | 2 | 1.00 | 0 | 0 | 1 | 0 | 44 | 24 | 0 | - | 0 | 0 | 0/24 |
| Robinson,RD | 3 | 6 | 0 | 100 | 34 | 16.66 | 0 | 0 | 0 | 4 | | | | | | | |
| Robinson,RH | 1 | 2 | 0 | 5 | 3 | 2.50 | 0 | 0 | 0 | 1 | | | | | | | |
| Rorke,GF | 4 | 4 | 2 | 9 | 7 | 4.50 | 0 | 0 | 1 | 1 | 703 | 203 | 10 | 20.30 | 0 | 0 | 3/23 |
| Rutherford,JW | 1 | 1 | 0 | 30 | 30 | 30.00 | 0 | 0 | 0 | 0 | 36 | 15 | 1 | 15.00 | 0 | 0 | 1/11 |
| Ryder,J | 20 | 32 | 5 | 1394 | 201* | 51.62 | 3 | 9 | 1 | 17 | 1897 | 743 | 17 | 43.70 | 0 | 0 | 2/20 |
| Saggers,RA | 6 | 5 | 2 | 30 | 14 | 10.00 | 0 | 0 | 0 | 16/8 | | | | | | | |
| Saunders,JV | 14 | 23 | 6 | 39 | 11* | 2.29 | 0 | 0 | 8 | 5 | 3565 | 1796 | 79 | 22.73 | 6 | 0 | 7/34 |
| Scott,HJH | 8 | 14 | 1 | 359 | 102 | 27.61 | 1 | 1 | 0 | 8 | 28 | 26 | 0 | - | 0 | 0 | 0/9 |
| Sellers,RHD | 1 | 1 | 0 | 0 | 0 | 0.00 | 0 | 0 | 1 | 1 | 30 | 17 | 0 | - | 0 | 0 | 0/17 |
| Serjeant,CS | 12 | 23 | 1 | 522 | 124 | 23.72 | 1 | 2 | 4 | 13 | | | | | | | |
| Sheahan,AP | 31 | 53 | 6 | 1594 | 127 | 33.91 | 2 | 7 | 3 | 17 | | | | | | | |
| Shepherd,BK | 9 | 14 | 2 | 502 | 96 | 41.93 | 0 | 5 | 1 | 2 | 26 | 9 | 0 | - | 0 | 0 | 0/3 |
| Sievers,MW | 3 | 6 | 1 | 67 | 25* | 13.40 | 0 | 0 | 0 | 4 | 602 | 161 | 9 | 17.88 | 1 | 0 | 5/21 |
| Simpson,RB | 62 | 111 | 7 | 4869 | 311 | 46.81 | 10 | 27 | 8 | 110 | 6881 | 3001 | 71 | 42.26 | 2 | 0 | 5/57 |
| Sincock,DJ | 3 | 4 | 1 | 80 | 29 | 26.66 | 0 | 0 | 0 | 2 | 724 | 410 | 8 | 51.25 | 0 | 0 | 3/67 |
| Slater,KN | 1 | 1 | 1 | 1 | 1* | - | 0 | 0 | 0 | 0 | 256 | 101 | 2 | 50.50 | 0 | 0 | 2/40 |
| Slater,MJ | 37 | 65 | 3 | 2817 | 219 | 45.43 | 7 | 11 | 5 | 11 | 7 | 4 | 1 | 4.00 | 0 | 0 | 1/4 |
| Sleep,PR | 14 | 21 | 1 | 483 | 90 | 24.15 | 0 | 3 | 4 | 4 | 2982 | 1397 | 31 | 45.06 | 1 | 0 | 5/72 |
| Slight,J | 1 | 2 | 0 | 11 | 11 | 5.50 | 0 | 0 | 1 | 0 | | | | | | | |
| Smith,DBM | 2 | 3 | 1 | 30 | 24* | 15.00 | 0 | 0 | 1 | 0 | | | | | | | |
| Smith,SB | 3 | 5 | 0 | 41 | 12 | 8.20 | 0 | 0 | 0 | 1 | | | | | | | |
| Spofforth,FR | 18 | 29 | 6 | 217 | 50 | 9.43 | 0 | 1 | 6 | 11 | 4185 | 1731 | 94 | 18.41 | 7 | 4 | 7/44 |
| Stackpole,KR | 43 | 80 | 5 | 2807 | 207 | 37.42 | 7 | 14 | 5 | 47 | 2321 | 1001 | 15 | 66.73 | 0 | 0 | 2/33 |
| Stevens,GB | 4 | 7 | 0 | 112 | 28 | 16.00 | 0 | 0 | 0 | 2 | | | | | | | |
| Taber,HB | 16 | 27 | 5 | 353 | 48 | 16.04 | 0 | 0 | 3 | 56/4 | | | | | | | |
| Tallon,D | 21 | 26 | 3 | 394 | 92 | 17.13 | 0 | 2 | 3 | 50/8 | | | | | | | |
| Taylor,JM | 20 | 28 | 0 | 997 | 108 | 35.60 | 1 | 8 | 1 | 11 | 114 | 45 | 1 | 45.00 | 0 | 0 | 1/25 |
| Taylor,MA | 96 | 171 | 12 | 6784 | 219 | 42.66 | 18 | 36 | 4 | 144 | 42 | 26 | 1 | 26.00 | 0 | 0 | 1/11 |
| Taylor,PL | 13 | 19 | 3 | 431 | 87 | 26.93 | 0 | 2 | 1 | 10 | 2227 | 1068 | 27 | 39.55 | 1 | 0 | 6/78 |
| Thomas,G | 8 | 12 | 1 | 325 | 61 | 29.54 | 0 | 3 | 0 | 3 | | | | | | | |
| Thoms,GR | 1 | 2 | 0 | 44 | 28 | 22.00 | 0 | 0 | 0 | 0 | | | | | | | |
| Thomson,AL | 4 | 5 | 4 | 22 | 12* | 22.00 | 0 | 0 | 1 | 0 | 1519 | 654 | 12 | 54.50 | 0 | 0 | 3/79 |
| Thomson,JR | 51 | 73 | 20 | 679 | 49 | 12.81 | 0 | 0 | 14 | 20 | 10535 | 5601 | 200 | 28.00 | 8 | 0 | 6/46 |
| Thomson,NFD | 2 | 4 | 0 | 67 | 41 | 16.75 | 0 | 0 | 0 | 3 | 112 | 31 | 1 | 31.00 | 0 | 0 | 1/14 |
| Thurlow,HM | 1 | 1 | 0 | 0 | 0 | 0.00 | 0 | 0 | 1 | 0 | 234 | 86 | 0 | - | 0 | 0 | 0/33 |
| Toohey,PM | 15 | 29 | 1 | 893 | 122 | 31.89 | 1 | 7 | 3 | 9 | 2 | 4 | 0 | - | 0 | 0 | 0/4 |
| Toshack,ERH | 12 | 11 | 6 | 73 | 20* | 14.60 | 0 | 0 | 1 | 4 | 3140 | 989 | 47 | 21.04 | 4 | 1 | 6/29 |
| Travers,JPF | 1 | 2 | 0 | 10 | 9 | 5.00 | 0 | 0 | 0 | 1 | 48 | 14 | 1 | 14.00 | 0 | 0 | 1/14 |
| Tribe,GE | 3 | 3 | 1 | 35 | 25* | 17.50 | 0 | 0 | 0 | 0 | 760 | 330 | 2 | 165.00 | 0 | 0 | 2/48 |
| Trott,AE | 3 | 5 | 3 | 205 | 85* | 102.50 | 0 | 2 | 1 | 4 | 474 | 192 | 9 | 21.33 | 1 | 0 | 8/43 |

| **AUSTRALIA** (cont.) | Tests | I | N | Batting Runs | HS | Avge | 100 | 50 | 0's | c/s | Balls | Bowling Runs | Wks | Bowling Avge | 5w | 10w | BB |
|---|---|---|---|---|---|---|---|---|---|---|---|---|---|---|---|---|---|
| Trott,GHS | 24 | 42 | 0 | 921 | 143 | 21.92 | 1 | 4 | 7 | 21 | 1890 | 1019 | 29 | 35.13 | 0 | 0 | 4/71 |
| Trumble,H | 32 | 57 | 14 | 851 | 70 | 19.79 | 0 | 4 | 7 | 45 | 8099 | 3072 | 141 | 21.78 | 9 | 3 | 8/65 |
| Trumble,JW | 7 | 13 | 1 | 243 | 59 | 20.25 | 0 | 1 | 1 | 3 | 600 | 222 | 10 | 22.20 | 0 | 0 | 3/29 |
| Trumper,VT | 48 | 48 | 8 | 3163 | 214* | 39.04 | 8 | 13 | 7 | 31 | 546 | 317 | 8 | 39.62 | 0 | 0 | 3/60 |
| Turner,A | 14 | 27 | 1 | 768 | 136 | 29.53 | 1 | 3 | 2 | 15 | | | | | | | |
| Turner,CTB | 17 | 32 | 4 | 323 | 29 | 11.53 | 0 | 0 | 6 | 8 | 5179 | 1670 | 101 | 16.53 | 11 | 2 | 7/43 |
| Veivers,TR | 21 | 30 | 4 | 813 | 88 | 31.26 | 0 | 7 | 3 | 7 | 4191 | 1375 | 33 | 41.66 | 0 | 0 | 4/68 |
| Veletta,MRJ | 8 | 11 | 0 | 207 | 39 | 18.81 | 0 | 0 | 0 | 12 | | | | | | | |
| Waite,MG | 2 | 3 | 0 | 11 | 8 | 3.66 | 0 | 0 | 1 | 1 | 552 | 190 | 1 | 190.00 | 0 | 0 | 1/150 |
| Walker,MHN | 34 | 43 | 13 | 586 | 78* | 19.53 | 0 | 1 | 5 | 12 | 10094 | 3792 | 138 | 27.47 | 6 | 0 | 8/143 |
| Wall,TW | 18 | 24 | 5 | 121 | 20 | 6.36 | 0 | 0 | 5 | 11 | 4812 | 2010 | 56 | 35.89 | 3 | 0 | 5/14 |
| Walters,FH | 1 | 2 | 0 | 12 | 7 | 6.00 | 0 | 0 | 0 | 2 | | | | | | | |
| Walters,KD | 74 | 125 | 14 | 5357 | 250 | 48.26 | 15 | 33 | 4 | 43 | 3295 | 1425 | 49 | 29.08 | 1 | 0 | 5/66 |
| Ward,FA | 4 | 8 | 5 | 36 | 18 | 6.00 | 0 | 0 | 2 | 1 | 1268 | 574 | 11 | 52.18 | 1 | 0 | 6/102 |
| Warne,SK | 67 | 93 | 10 | 1230 | 74* | 14.81 | 0 | 2 | 16 | 46 | 19791 | 7756 | 313 | 24.77 | 14 | 4 | 8/71 |
| Watkins,JR | 1 | 2 | 1 | 39 | 36 | 39.00 | 0 | 0 | 0 | 1 | 48 | 21 | 0 | - | 0 | 0 | 0/21 |
| Watson,GD | 5 | 9 | 0 | 97 | 50 | 10.77 | 0 | 1 | 3 | 1 | 552 | 254 | 6 | 42.33 | 0 | 0 | 2/67 |
| Watson,WJ | 4 | 7 | 1 | 106 | 30 | 17.66 | 0 | 0 | 1 | 2 | 6 | 5 | 0 | - | 0 | 0 | 0/5 |
| Waugh,ME | 78 | 128 | 7 | 5219 | 153* | 43.13 | 14 | 32 | 10 | 87 | 3774 | 1805 | 45 | 40.11 | 1 | 0 | 5/40 |
| Waugh,SR | 103 | 162 | 29 | 6480 | 200 | 48.72 | 14 | 38 | 15 | 77 | 6863 | 3036 | 86 | 35.30 | 3 | 0 | 5/28 |
| Wellham,DM | 6 | 11 | 0 | 257 | 103 | 23.36 | 1 | 0 | 0 | 5 | | | | | | | |
| Wessels,KC | 24 | 42 | 1 | 1761 | 179 | 42.95 | 4 | 9 | 3 | 19 | 90 | 42 | 0 | - | 0 | 0 | 0/2 |
| Whatmore,DF | 7 | 13 | 0 | 293 | 77 | 22.53 | 0 | 2 | 1 | 13 | 30 | 11 | 0 | - | 0 | 0 | 0/11 |
| Whitney,MR | 12 | 19 | 8 | 68 | 13 | 6.18 | 0 | 0 | 4 | 2 | 2672 | 1325 | 39 | 33.95 | 2 | 1 | 7/27 |
| Whitty,WJ | 14 | 19 | 7 | 161 | 39* | 13.41 | 0 | 0 | 3 | 4 | 3357 | 1373 | 65 | 21.12 | 3 | 0 | 6/17 |
| Wiener,JM | 6 | 11 | 0 | 281 | 93 | 25.54 | 0 | 2 | 0 | 4 | 78 | 41 | 0 | - | 0 | 0 | 0/19 |
| Wilson,JW | 1 | | | | | | 0 | 0 | 0 | 0 | 216 | 64 | 1 | 64.00 | 0 | 0 | 1/25 |
| Wilson,P | 1 | 2 | 2 | 0 | 0* | - | 0 | 0 | 0 | 0 | 72 | 50 | 0 | - | 0 | 0 | 0/50 |
| Wood,GM | 59 | 112 | 6 | 3374 | 172 | 31.83 | 9 | 13 | 9 | 41 | | | | | | | |
| Woodcock,AJ | 1 | 1 | 0 | 27 | 27 | 27.00 | 0 | 0 | 0 | 1 | | | | | | | |
| Woodfull,WM | 35 | 54 | 4 | 2300 | 161 | 46.00 | 7 | 13 | 6 | 7 | | | | | | | |
| Woods,SMJ | 3 | 6 | 0 | 32 | 18 | 5.33 | 0 | 0 | 2 | 1 | 217 | 121 | 5 | 24.20 | 0 | 0 | 2/35 |
| Woolley,RD | 2 | 2 | 0 | 21 | 13 | 10.50 | 0 | 0 | 0 | 7/0 | | | | | | | |
| Worrall,J | 11 | 22 | 3 | 478 | 76 | 25.15 | 0 | 5 | 2 | 13 | 255 | 127 | 1 | 127.00 | 0 | 0 | 1/97 |
| Wright,KJ | 10 | 18 | 5 | 219 | 55* | 16.84 | 0 | 4 | 2 | 31/4 | | | | | | | |
| Yallop,GN | 39 | 70 | 3 | 2756 | 268 | 41.13 | 8 | 9 | 3 | 23 | 192 | 116 | 1 | 116.00 | 0 | 0 | 1/21 |
| Yardley,B | 33 | 54 | 4 | 978 | 74 | 19.56 | 0 | 4 | 8 | 31 | 8909 | 3986 | 126 | 31.63 | 6 | 1 | 7/98 |
| Young,S | 1 | 2 | 1 | 4 | 4* | 4.00 | 0 | 0 | 1 | 0 | 48 | 13 | 0 | - | 0 | 0 | 0/5 |
| Zoehrer,TJ | 10 | 14 | 2 | 246 | 52* | 20.50 | 0 | 1 | 0 | 18/1 | | | | | | | |

| **ENGLAND** | Tests | I | N | Batting Runs | HS | Avge | 100 | 50 | 0's | c/s | Balls | Bowling Runs | Wks | Bowling Avge | 5w | 10w | BB |
|---|---|---|---|---|---|---|---|---|---|---|---|---|---|---|---|---|---|
| Abel,R | 13 | 22 | 2 | 744 | 132* | 37.20 | 2 | 2 | 1 | 13 | | | | | | | |
| Absolom,CA | 1 | 2 | 0 | 58 | 52 | 29.00 | 0 | 1 | 0 | 0 | | | | | | | |
| Agnew,JP | 3 | 4 | 3 | 10 | 5 | 10.00 | 0 | 0 | 0 | 0 | 552 | 373 | 4 | 93.25 | 0 | 0 | 2/51 |
| Allen,DA | 39 | 51 | 15 | 918 | 88 | 25.50 | 0 | 5 | 4 | 10 | 11297 | 3779 | 122 | 30.97 | 4 | 0 | 5/30 |
| Allen,GOB | 25 | 33 | 2 | 750 | 122 | 24.19 | 1 | 3 | 1 | 20 | 4386 | 2379 | 81 | 29.37 | 5 | 1 | 7/80 |
| Allom,MJC | 5 | 3 | 2 | 14 | 8* | 14.00 | 0 | 0 | 0 | 0 | 817 | 265 | 14 | 18.92 | 1 | 0 | 5/38 |
| Allott,PJW | 13 | 18 | 3 | 213 | 52* | 14.20 | 0 | 1 | 2 | 4 | 2225 | 1084 | 26 | 41.69 | 1 | 0 | 6/61 |
| Ames,LEG | 47 | 72 | 12 | 2434 | 149 | 40.56 | 8 | 7 | 5 | 74/23 | | | | | | | |
| Amiss,DL | 50 | 88 | 10 | 3612 | 262* | 46.30 | 11 | 11 | 10 | 24 | | | | | | | |
| Andrew,KV | 2 | 4 | 1 | 29 | 15 | 9.66 | 0 | 0 | 0 | 1/0 | | | | | | | |
| Appleyard,R | 9 | 9 | 6 | 51 | 19* | 17.00 | 0 | 0 | 0 | 4 | 1596 | 554 | 31 | 17.87 | 1 | 0 | 5/51 |
| Archer,AG | 1 | 2 | 1 | 31 | 24* | 31.00 | 0 | 0 | 0 | 0 | | | | | | | |
| Armitage,T | 2 | 3 | 0 | 33 | 21 | 11.00 | 0 | 0 | 0 | 0 | 12 | 15 | 0 | - | 0 | 0 | 0/15 |
| Arnold,EG | 10 | 15 | 3 | 160 | 40 | 13.33 | 0 | 0 | 5 | 8 | 1683 | 788 | 31 | 25.41 | 1 | 0 | 5/37 |

| **ENGLAND** (cont.) | | | | **BATTING AND FIELDING** | | | | | | | | **BOWLING** | | | | | |
|---|---|---|---|---|---|---|---|---|---|---|---|---|---|---|---|---|---|
| | Tests | I | N | Runs | HS | Avge | 100 | 50 | 0's | c/s | Balls | Runs | Wks | Avge | 5w | 10w | BB |
| Arnold,GG | 34 | 46 | 11 | 421 | 59 | 12.02 | 0 | 1 | 5 | 9 | 7650 | 3254 | 115 | 28.29 | 6 | 0 | 6/45 |
| Arnold,J | 1 | 2 | 0 | 34 | 34 | 17.00 | 0 | 0 | 1 | 0 | | | | | | | |
| Astill,WE | 9 | 15 | 0 | 190 | 40 | 12.66 | 0 | 0 | 2 | 7 | 2182 | 856 | 25 | 34.24 | 0 | 0 | 4/58 |
| Atherton,MA | 84 | 155 | 6 | 5935 | 185 | 39.83 | 12 | 37 | 14 | 56 | 408 | 302 | 2 | 151.00 | 0 | 0 | 1/20 |
| Athey,CWJ | 23 | 41 | 1 | 919 | 123 | 22.97 | 1 | 4 | 2 | 13 | | | | | | | |
| Attewell,W | 10 | 15 | 6 | 150 | 43* | 16.66 | 0 | 0 | 4 | 9 | 2850 | 626 | 28 | 22.35 | 0 | 0 | 4/42 |
| Bailey,RJ | 4 | 8 | 0 | 119 | 43 | 14.87 | 0 | 0 | 2 | 0 | | | | | | | |
| Bailey,TE | 61 | 91 | 14 | 2290 | 134* | 29.74 | 1 | 10 | 7 | 32 | 9712 | 3856 | 132 | 29.21 | 5 | 1 | 7/34 |
| Bairstow,DL | 4 | 7 | 1 | 125 | 59 | 20.83 | 0 | 1 | 1 | 12/1 | | | | | | | |
| Bakewell,AH | 6 | 9 | 0 | 409 | 107 | 45.44 | 1 | 3 | 0 | 3 | 18 | 8 | 0 | - | 0 | 0 | 0/8 |
| Balderstone,JC | 2 | 4 | 0 | 39 | 35 | 9.75 | 0 | 0 | 2 | 1 | 96 | 80 | 1 | 80.00 | 0 | 0 | 1/80 |
| Barber,RW | 28 | 45 | 3 | 1495 | 185 | 35.59 | 1 | 9 | 1 | 21 | 3426 | 1806 | 42 | 43.00 | 0 | 0 | 4/132 |
| Barber,W | 2 | 4 | 0 | 83 | 44 | 20.75 | 0 | 0 | 0 | 1 | 2 | 0 | 1 | 0.00 | 0 | 0 | 1/0 |
| Barlow,GD | 3 | 5 | 1 | 17 | 7* | 4.25 | 0 | 0 | 1 | 0 | | | | | | | |
| Barlow,RG | 17 | 30 | 4 | 591 | 62 | 22.73 | 0 | 2 | 3 | 14 | 2456 | 767 | 34 | 22.55 | 3 | 0 | 7/40 |
| Barnes,SF | 27 | 39 | 9 | 242 | 38* | 8.06 | 0 | 0 | 8 | 12 | 7873 | 3106 | 189 | 16.43 | 24 | 7 | 9/103 |
| Barnes,W | 21 | 33 | 2 | 725 | 134 | 23.38 | 1 | 5 | 3 | 19 | 2289 | 793 | 51 | 15.54 | 3 | 0 | 6/28 |
| Barnett,CJ | 20 | 35 | 4 | 1098 | 129 | 35.41 | 2 | 5 | 1 | 14 | 256 | 93 | 0 | - | 0 | 0 | 0/1 |
| Barnett,KJ | 4 | 7 | 0 | 207 | 80 | 29.57 | 0 | 2 | 1 | 1 | 36 | 32 | 0 | - | 0 | 0 | 0/32 |
| Barratt,F | 5 | 4 | 1 | 28 | 17 | 9.33 | 0 | 0 | 0 | 2 | 750 | 235 | 5 | 47.00 | 0 | 0 | 1/8 |
| Barrington,KF | 82 | 131 | 15 | 6806 | 256 | 58.67 | 20 | 35 | 5 | 58 | 2715 | 1300 | 29 | 44.85 | 0 | 0 | 3/4 |
| Barton,VA | 1 | 1 | 0 | 23 | 23 | 23.00 | 0 | 0 | 0 | 0 | | | | | | | |
| Bates,W | 15 | 26 | 2 | 656 | 64 | 27.33 | 0 | 5 | 0 | 9 | 2364 | 821 | 50 | 16.42 | 4 | 1 | 7/28 |
| Bean,G | 3 | 5 | 0 | 92 | 50 | 18.40 | 0 | 1 | 0 | 4 | | | | | | | |
| Bedser,AV | 51 | 71 | 15 | 714 | 79 | 12.75 | 0 | 1 | 11 | 26 | 15918 | 5876 | 236 | 24.89 | 15 | 5 | 7/44 |
| Benjamin,JE | 1 | 1 | 0 | 0 | 0 | 0.00 | 0 | 0 | 1 | 0 | 168 | 80 | 4 | 20.00 | 0 | 0 | 4/42 |
| Benson,MR | 1 | 2 | 0 | 51 | 30 | 25.50 | 0 | 0 | 0 | 0 | | | | | | | |
| Berry,R | 2 | 4 | 2 | 6 | 4* | 3.00 | 0 | 0 | 1 | 2 | 653 | 228 | 9 | 25.33 | 1 | 0 | 5/63 |
| Bicknell,MP | 2 | 4 | 0 | 26 | 14 | 6.25 | 0 | 0 | 2 | 0 | 522 | 263 | 4 | 65.75 | 0 | 0 | 3/99 |
| Binks,JG | 2 | 4 | 0 | 91 | 55 | 22.75 | 0 | 1 | 0 | 8 | | | | | | | |
| Bird,MC | 10 | 16 | 1 | 280 | 61 | 18.66 | 0 | 2 | 2 | 5 | 264 | 120 | 8 | 15.00 | 0 | 0 | 3/11 |
| Birkenshaw,J | 5 | 7 | 0 | 148 | 64 | 21.14 | 0 | 1 | 1 | 3 | 1017 | 469 | 13 | 36.07 | 1 | 0 | 5/57 |
| Blakey,RJ | 2 | 4 | 0 | 7 | 6 | 1.75 | 0 | 0 | 2 | 2 | | | | | | | |
| Bligh,Hon.IFW | 4 | 7 | 1 | 62 | 19 | 10.33 | 0 | 0 | 2 | 7 | | | | | | | |
| Blythe,C | 19 | 31 | 12 | 183 | 27 | 9.63 | 0 | 0 | 4 | 6 | 4546 | 1863 | 100 | 18.63 | 9 | 4 | 8/59 |
| Board,JH | 6 | 12 | 2 | 108 | 29 | 10.80 | 0 | 0 | 3 | 8/3 | | | | | | | |
| Bolus,JB | 7 | 12 | 0 | 496 | 88 | 41.33 | 0 | 4 | 0 | 2 | 18 | 16 | 0 | - | 0 | 0 | 0/16 |
| Booth,MW | 2 | 2 | 0 | 46 | 32 | 23.00 | 0 | 0 | 0 | 0 | 312 | 130 | 7 | 18.57 | 0 | 0 | 4/49 |
| Bosanquet,BJT | 7 | 14 | 3 | 147 | 27 | 13.36 | 0 | 0 | 0 | 9 | 970 | 604 | 25 | 24.16 | 2 | 0 | 8/107 |
| Botham,IT | 102 | 161 | 6 | 5200 | 208 | 33.54 | 14 | 22 | 15 | 120 | 21815 | 10878 | 383 | 28.40 | 27 | 4 | 8/34 |
| Bowden,MP | 2 | 2 | 0 | 25 | 25 | 12.50 | 0 | 0 | 1 | 1 | | | | | | | |
| Bowes,WE | 15 | 11 | 5 | 28 | 10* | 4.66 | 0 | 0 | 2 | 2 | 3655 | 1519 | 68 | 22.33 | 6 | 0 | 6/33 |
| Bowley,EH | 5 | 7 | 0 | 252 | 109 | 36.00 | 1 | 0 | 0 | 2 | 252 | 116 | 0 | - | 0 | 0 | 0/7 |
| Boycott,G | 108 | 193 | 23 | 8114 | 246* | 47.72 | 22 | 42 | 10 | 33 | 944 | 382 | 7 | 54.57 | 0 | 0 | 3/47 |
| Bradley,WM | 2 | 2 | 1 | 23 | 23* | 23.00 | 0 | 0 | 1 | 0 | 625 | 233 | 6 | 38.83 | 1 | 0 | 5/67 |
| Braund,LC | 23 | 41 | 3 | 987 | 104 | 25.97 | 3 | 2 | 7 | 39 | 3803 | 1810 | 47 | 38.51 | 3 | 0 | 8/81 |
| Brearley,JM | 39 | 66 | 3 | 1442 | 91 | 22.88 | 0 | 9 | 6 | 52 | | | | | | | |
| Brearley,W | 4 | 5 | 2 | 21 | 11* | 7.00 | 0 | 0 | 2 | 0 | 705 | 359 | 17 | 21.11 | 1 | 0 | 5/110 |
| Brennan,DV | 2 | 2 | 0 | 16 | 16 | 8.00 | 0 | 0 | 1 | 0 | | | | | | | |
| Briggs,J | 33 | 50 | 5 | 815 | 121 | 18.11 | 1 | 2 | 10 | 12 | 5332 | 2094 | 118 | 17.74 | 9 | 4 | 8/11 |
| Broad,BC | 25 | 44 | 2 | 1661 | 162 | 39.54 | 6 | 6 | 3 | 10 | 6 | 4 | 0 | - | 0 | 0 | 0/4 |
| Brockwell,W | 7 | 12 | 0 | 202 | 49 | 16.83 | 0 | 0 | 1 | 6 | 582 | 309 | 5 | 61.80 | 0 | 0 | 3/33 |
| Bromley-Davenport,HR | 4 | 6 | 0 | 128 | 84 | 21.33 | 0 | 1 | 1 | 1 | 155 | 98 | 4 | 24.50 | 0 | 0 | 2/46 |
| Brookes,D | 1 | 2 | 0 | 17 | 10 | 8.50 | 0 | 0 | 0 | 1 | | | | | | | |
| Brown,A | 2 | 1 | 1 | 3 | 3* | 0 | 0 | 0 | 0 | 1 | 323 | 150 | 3 | 50.00 | 0 | 0 | 3/27 |
| Brown,DJ | 26 | 34 | 5 | 342 | 44* | 11.79 | 0 | 0 | 6 | 7 | 5098 | 2237 | 79 | 28.31 | 2 | 0 | 5/42 |
| Brown,FR | 22 | 30 | 1 | 734 | 79 | 25.31 | 0 | 5 | 1 | 22 | 3260 | 1398 | 45 | 31.06 | 1 | 0 | 5/49 |

| **ENGLAND** (cont.) | | | | **BATTING AND FIELDING** | | | | | | | **BOWLING** | | | | | | |
|---|---|---|---|---|---|---|---|---|---|---|---|---|---|---|---|---|---|
| | Tests | I | N | Runs | HS | Avge | 100 | 50 | 0's | c/s | Balls | Runs | Wks | Avge | 5w | 10w | BB |
| Brown,G | 7 | 12 | 2 | 229 | 84 | 29.90 | 0 | 2 | 2 | 9/3 | | | | | | | |
| Brown,JT | 8 | 16 | 3 | 470 | 140 | 36.15 | 1 | 1 | 2 | 7 | 35 | 22 | 0 | - | 0 | 0 | 0/22 |
| Brown,SJE | 1 | 2 | 1 | 11 | 10* | 11.00 | 0 | 0 | 0 | 1 | 198 | 138 | 2 | 69.00 | 0 | 0 | 1/60 |
| Buckenham,CP | 4 | 7 | 0 | 43 | 17 | 6.14 | 0 | 0 | 1 | 2 | 1182 | 593 | 21 | 28.23 | 1 | 0 | 5/115 |
| Butcher,AR | 1 | 2 | 0 | 34 | 20 | 17.00 | 0 | 0 | 0 | 0 | 12 | 9 | 0 | - | 0 | 0 | 0/9 |
| Butcher,MA | 13 | 25 | 1 | 717 | 116 | 29.87 | 1 | 4 | 3 | 13 | 96 | 67 | 0 | - | 0 | 0 | 0/1 |
| Butcher,RO | 3 | 5 | 0 | 71 | 32 | 14.20 | 0 | 0 | 1 | 3 | | | | | | | |
| Butler,HJ | 2 | 2 | 1 | 15 | 15* | 15.00 | 0 | 0 | 1 | 1 | 552 | 215 | 12 | 17.91 | 0 | 0 | 4/34 |
| Butt,HR | 3 | 4 | 1 | 22 | 13 | 7.33 | 0 | 0 | 1 | 1/1 | | | | | | | |
| Caddick,AR | 21 | 33 | 4 | 291 | 29* | 10.03 | 0 | 0 | 7 | 8 | 4610 | 2394 | 74 | 32.35 | 5 | 0 | 6/65 |
| Calthorpe,Hon.FSG | 4 | 7 | 0 | 129 | 49 | 18.42 | 0 | 0 | 1 | 3 | 204 | 91 | 1 | 91.00 | 0 | 0 | 1/38 |
| Capel,DJ | 15 | 25 | 1 | 374 | 98 | 15.58 | 0 | 2 | 4 | 6 | 2000 | 1064 | 21 | 50.66 | 0 | 0 | 3/88 |
| Carr,AW | 11 | 13 | 1 | 237 | 62 | 19.75 | 0 | 1 | 0 | 3 | | | | | | | |
| Carr,DB | 2 | 4 | 0 | 135 | 76 | 33.75 | 0 | 1 | 0 | 0 | 210 | 140 | 2 | 70.00 | 0 | 0 | 2/84 |
| Carr,DW | 1 | 1 | 0 | 0 | 0 | 0.00 | 0 | 0 | 1 | 0 | 414 | 282 | 7 | 40.28 | 1 | 0 | 5/146 |
| Cartwright,TW | 5 | 7 | 2 | 26 | 9 | 5.20 | 0 | 0 | 2 | 2 | 1611 | 544 | 15 | 36.26 | 1 | 0 | 6/94 |
| Chapman,APF | 26 | 36 | 4 | 925 | 121 | 28.90 | 1 | 5 | 2 | 32 | 40 | 20 | 0 | - | 0 | 0 | 0/10 |
| Charlwood,HRJ | 2 | 4 | 0 | 63 | 36 | 15.75 | 0 | 0 | 1 | 0 | | | | | | | |
| Chatterton,W | 1 | 1 | 0 | 48 | 48 | 48.00 | 0 | 0 | 0 | 0 | | | | | | | |
| Childs,JH | 2 | 4 | 4 | 2 | 2* | 0 | 0 | 0 | 0 | 1 | 516 | 183 | 3 | 61.00 | 0 | 0 | 1/13 |
| Christopherson,S | 1 | 1 | 0 | 17 | 17 | 17.00 | 0 | 0 | 0 | 0 | 136 | 69 | 1 | 69.00 | 0 | 0 | 1/52 |
| Clark,EW | 8 | 9 | 5 | 36 | 10 | 9.00 | 0 | 0 | 1 | 0 | 1931 | 899 | 32 | 28.09 | 1 | 0 | 5/98 |
| Clay,JC | 1 | | | | | | 0 | 0 | 0 | 1 | 192 | 75 | 0 | - | 0 | 0 | 0/30 |
| Close,DB | 22 | 37 | 2 | 887 | 70 | 25.34 | 0 | 4 | 3 | 24 | 1212 | 532 | 18 | 29.55 | 0 | 0 | 4/35 |
| Coldwell,LJ | 7 | 7 | 5 | 9 | 6* | 4.50 | 0 | 0 | 1 | 1 | 1668 | 610 | 22 | 27.72 | 1 | 0 | 6/85 |
| Compton,DCS | 78 | 131 | 15 | 5807 | 278 | 50.06 | 17 | 28 | 10 | 49 | 2716 | 1410 | 25 | 56.40 | 1 | 0 | 5/70 |
| Cook,C | 1 | 2 | 0 | 4 | 4 | 2.00 | 0 | 0 | 1 | 0 | 180 | 127 | 0 | - | 0 | 0 | 0/40 |
| Cook,G | 7 | 13 | 0 | 203 | 66 | 15.61 | 0 | 2 | 1 | 9 | 42 | 27 | 0 | - | 0 | 0 | 0/2 |
| Cook,NGB | 15 | 25 | 4 | 179 | 31 | 8.52 | 0 | 0 | 2 | 5 | 4174 | 1689 | 52 | 32.48 | 4 | 1 | 6/65 |
| Cope,GA | 3 | 3 | 0 | 40 | 22 | 13.33 | 0 | 0 | 1 | 1 | 864 | 277 | 8 | 34.62 | 0 | 0 | 3/102 |
| Copson,WH | 3 | 1 | 0 | 6 | 6 | 6.00 | 0 | 0 | 0 | 1 | 762 | 297 | 15 | 19.80 | 1 | 0 | 5/85 |
| Cork,DG | 24 | 36 | 5 | 581 | 59 | 18.74 | 0 | 2 | 2 | 11 | 5393 | 2822 | 92 | 30.67 | 5 | 0 | 7/43 |
| Cornford,WL | 4 | 4 | 0 | 36 | 18 | 9.00 | 0 | 0 | 0 | 5/3 | | | | | | | |
| Cottam,RMH | 4 | 5 | 1 | 27 | 13 | 6.75 | 0 | 0 | 0 | 2 | 903 | 327 | 14 | 23.35 | 0 | 0 | 4/50 |
| Coventry,Hon.CJ | 2 | 2 | 1 | 13 | 12 | 13.00 | 0 | 0 | 0 | 0 | | | | | | | |
| Cowans,NG | 19 | 29 | 7 | 175 | 36 | 7.95 | 0 | 0 | 5 | 9 | 3452 | 2003 | 51 | 39.27 | 2 | 0 | 6/77 |
| Cowdrey,CS | 6 | 8 | 1 | 101 | 38 | 14.42 | 0 | 0 | 1 | 5 | 399 | 309 | 4 | 77.25 | 0 | 0 | 2/65 |
| Cowdrey,MC | 114 | 188 | 15 | 7624 | 182 | 44.06 | 22 | 38 | 9 | 120 | 119 | 104 | 0 | - | 0 | 0 | 0/1 |
| Coxon,A | 1 | 2 | 0 | 19 | 19 | 9.50 | 0 | 0 | 1 | 0 | 378 | 172 | 3 | 57.33 | 0 | 0 | 2/90 |
| Cranston,J | 1 | 2 | 0 | 31 | 16 | 15.50 | 0 | 0 | 0 | 1 | | | | | | | |
| Cranston,K | 8 | 14 | 0 | 209 | 45 | 14.92 | 0 | 0 | 2 | 3 | 1010 | 461 | 18 | 25.61 | 0 | 0 | 4/12 |
| Crapp,JF | 7 | 13 | 2 | 319 | 56 | 29.00 | 0 | 3 | 1 | 7 | | | | | | | |
| Crawford,JN | 12 | 23 | 2 | 469 | 74 | 22.33 | 0 | 2 | 1 | 13 | 2203 | 1150 | 39 | 29.48 | 3 | 0 | 5/48 |
| Crawley,JP | 25 | 39 | 4 | 1073 | 112 | 30.65 | 2 | 7 | 3 | 22 | | | | | | | |
| Croft,RDB | 14 | 22 | 5 | 268 | 37* | 15.76 | 0 | 0 | 1 | 8 | 3221 | 1254 | 34 | 36.88 | 1 | 0 | 5/95 |
| Curtis,TS | 5 | 9 | 0 | 140 | 41 | 15.55 | 0 | 0 | 1 | 3 | 18 | 7 | 0 | - | 0 | 0 | 0/7 |
| Cuttell,WR | 2 | 4 | 0 | 65 | 21 | 16.25 | 0 | 0 | 0 | 2 | 285 | 73 | 6 | 12.16 | 0 | 0 | 3/17 |
| Dawson,EW | 5 | 9 | 0 | 175 | 55 | 19.44 | 0 | 1 | 0 | 0 | | | | | | | |
| Dean,H | 3 | 4 | 2 | 10 | 8 | 5.00 | 0 | 0 | 1 | 2 | 447 | 153 | 11 | 13.90 | 0 | 0 | 4/19 |
| DeFreitas,PAJ | 44 | 68 | 5 | 934 | 88 | 14.82 | 0 | 4 | 10 | 14 | 9838 | 4700 | 140 | 33.57 | 4 | 0 | 7/70 |
| Denness,MH | 28 | 45 | 3 | 1667 | 188 | 39.69 | 4 | 7 | 2 | 28 | | | | | | | |
| Denton,D | 11 | 22 | 1 | 424 | 104 | 20.19 | 1 | 1 | 4 | 8 | | | | | | | |
| Dewes,JG | 5 | 10 | 0 | 121 | 67 | 12.10 | 0 | 1 | 1 | 0 | | | | | | | |
| Dexter,ER | 62 | 102 | 8 | 4502 | 205 | 47.89 | 9 | 27 | 6 | 29 | 5317 | 2306 | 66 | 34.93 | 0 | 0 | 4/10 |
| Dilley,GR | 41 | 58 | 19 | 521 | 56 | 13.35 | 0 | 2 | 10 | 10 | 8192 | 4107 | 138 | 29.76 | 6 | 0 | 6/38 |
| Dipper,AE | 1 | 2 | 0 | 51 | 40 | 25.50 | 0 | 0 | 0 | 0/0 | | | | | | | |
| Doggart,GHG | 2 | 4 | 0 | 76 | 29 | 19.00 | 0 | 0 | 1 | 3 | | | | | | | |

| ENGLAND (cont.) | | | | BATTING AND FIELDING | | | | | | | | | | BOWLING | | | |
|---|---|---|---|---|---|---|---|---|---|---|---|---|---|---|---|---|---|
| | Tests | I | N | Runs | HS | Avge | 100 | 50 | 0's | c/s | Balls | Runs | Wks | Avge | 5w | 10w | BB |
| D'Oliveira,BL | 44 | 70 | | 8 | | 2484 | 158 | | | 40.06 | 5 | 15 | 4 | | 29 | | 5706 |
| 1859 47 | 39.55 | 0 | | 0 | | 3/46 | | | | | | | | | | | |
| Dollery,HE | 4 | 7 | 0 | 72 | 37 | 10.28 | 0 | 0 | 2 | 1 | | | | | | | |
| Dolphin,A | 1 | 2 | 0 | 1 | 1 | 0.50 | 0 | 0 | 1 | 1/0 | | | | | | | |
| Douglas,JWHT | 23 | 35 | 2 | 962 | 119 | 29.15 | 1 | 6 | 3 | 9 | 2812 | 1496 | 45 | 33.02 | 1 | 0 | 5/46 |
| Downton,PR | 30 | 48 | 8 | 785 | 74 | 19.62 | 0 | 4 | 4 | 70/5 | | | | | | | |
| Druce,NF | 5 | 9 | 0 | 252 | 64 | 28.00 | 0 | 1 | 0 | 5 | | | | | | | |
| Ducat,A | 1 | 2 | 0 | 5 | 3 | 2.50 | 0 | 0 | 0 | 1 | | | | | | | |
| Duckworth,G | 24 | 28 | 12 | 234 | 39* | 14.62 | 0 | 0 | 2 | 45/15 | | | | | | | |
| Duleepsinhji,KS | 12 | 19 | 2 | 995 | 173 | 58.52 | 3 | 5 | 0 | 10 | 6 | 7 | 0 | - | 0 | 0 | 0/7 |
| Durston,FJ | 1 | 2 | 1 | 8 | 6* | 8.00 | 0 | 0 | 0 | 0 | 202 | 136 | 5 | 27.20 | 0 | 0 | 4/102 |
| Ealham,MA | 8 | 13 | 3 | 210 | 53* | 21.00 | 0 | 2 | 0 | 4 | 1060 | 488 | 17 | 28.70 | 0 | 0 | 4/21 |
| Edmonds,PH | 51 | 65 | 15 | 875 | 64 | 17.50 | 0 | 2 | 5 | 42 | 12028 | 4273 | 125 | 34.18 | 2 | 0 | 7/66 |
| Edrich,JH | 77 | 127 | 9 | 5138 | 310* | 43.54 | 12 | 24 | 6 | 43 | 30 | 23 | 0 | - | 0 | 0 | 0/6 |
| Edrich,WJ | 39 | 63 | 2 | 2440 | 219 | 40.00 | 6 | 13 | 3 | 39 | 3234 | 1693 | 41 | 41.29 | 0 | 0 | 4/68 |
| Elliott,H | 4 | 5 | 1 | 61 | 37* | 15.25 | 0 | 0 | 0 | 8/3 | | | | | | | |
| Ellison,RM | 11 | 16 | 1 | 202 | 41 | 13.46 | 0 | 0 | 1 | 2 | 2264 | 1048 | 35 | 29.94 | 3 | 1 | 6/77 |
| Emburey,JE | 65 | 97 | 20 | 1721 | 75 | 22.35 | 0 | 10 | 16 | 35 | 15571 | 5728 | 147 | 38.96 | 6 | 0 | 7/78 |
| Emmett,GM | 1 | 2 | 0 | 10 | 10 | 5.00 | 0 | 0 | 1 | 0 | | | | | | | |
| Emmett,T | 7 | 13 | 1 | 160 | 48 | 13.33 | 0 | 0 | 1 | 9 | 728 | 284 | 9 | 31.55 | 1 | 0 | 7/68 |
| Evans,AJ | 1 | 2 | 0 | 18 | 14 | 9.00 | 0 | 0 | 0 | 0 | | | | | | | |
| Evans,TG | 91 | 133 | 14 | 2439 | 104 | 20.49 | 2 | 8 | 17 | 173/46 | | | | | | | |
| Fagg,AE | 5 | 8 | 0 | 150 | 39 | 18.75 | 0 | 0 | 0 | 5 | | | | | | | |
| Fairbrother,NH | 10 | 15 | 1 | 219 | 83 | 15.64 | 0 | 1 | 1 | 4 | 12 | 9 | 0 | - | 0 | 0 | 0/9 |
| Fane,FL | 14 | 27 | 1 | 682 | 143 | 26.23 | 1 | 3 | 3 | 6 | | | | | | | |
| Farnes,K | 15 | 17 | 5 | 58 | 20 | 4.83 | 0 | 0 | 4 | 1 | 3932 | 1719 | 60 | 28.65 | 3 | 1 | 6/96 |
| Farrimond,W | 4 | 7 | 0 | 116 | 35 | 16.57 | 0 | 0 | 0 | 5/2 | | | | | | | |
| Fender,PGH | 13 | 21 | 1 | 380 | 60 | 19.00 | 0 | 2 | 3 | 14 | 2178 | 1185 | 29 | 40.86 | 2 | 0 | 5/90 |
| Ferris,JJ | 1 | 1 | 0 | 16 | 16 | 16.00 | 0 | 0 | 0 | 0 | 272 | 91 | 13 | 7.00 | 2 | 1 | 7/37 |
| Fielder,A | 6 | 12 | 5 | 78 | 20 | 11.14 | 0 | 0 | 0 | 4 | 1491 | 711 | 26 | 27.34 | 1 | 0 | 6/82 |
| Fishlock,LB | 4 | 5 | 1 | 47 | 19* | 11.75 | 0 | 0 | 1 | 1 | | | | | | | |
| Flavell,JA | 4 | 6 | 2 | 31 | 14 | 7.75 | 0 | 0 | 0 | 0 | 792 | 367 | 7 | 52.42 | 0 | 0 | 2/65 |
| Fletcher,KWR | 59 | 96 | 14 | 3272 | 216 | 39.90 | 7 | 19 | 6 | 54 | 285 | 193 | 2 | 96.50 | 0 | 0 | 1/6 |
| Flintoff,A | 2 | 3 | 0 | 17 | 17 | 5.66 | 0 | 0 | 2 | 1 | 210 | 122 | 1 | 112.00 | 0 | 0 | 1/52 |
| Flowers,W | 8 | 14 | 0 | 254 | 56 | 18.14 | 0 | 1 | 0 | 2 | 858 | 296 | 14 | 21.14 | 1 | 0 | 5/46 |
| Ford,FGJ | 5 | 9 | 0 | 168 | 48 | 18.66 | 0 | 0 | 1 | 5 | 210 | 129 | 1 | 129.00 | 0 | 0 | 1/47 |
| Foster,FR | 11 | 15 | 1 | 330 | 71 | 23.57 | 0 | 3 | 1 | 11 | 2447 | 926 | 45 | 20.57 | 4 | 0 | 6/91 |
| Foster,NA | 29 | 45 | 7 | 446 | 39 | 11.73 | 0 | 0 | 9 | 7 | 6261 | 2891 | 88 | 32.85 | 5 | 1 | 8/107 |
| Foster,RE | 8 | 14 | 1 | 602 | 287 | 46.30 | 1 | 1 | 1 | 13 | | | | | | | |
| Fothergill,AJ | 2 | 2 | 0 | 33 | 32 | 16.50 | 0 | 0 | 0 | 0 | 321 | 90 | 8 | 11.25 | 0 | 0 | 4/19 |
| Fowler,G | 21 | 37 | 0 | 1307 | 201 | 35.32 | 3 | 8 | 3 | 10 | 18 | 11 | 0 | - | 0 | 0 | 0/0 |
| Fraser,ARC | 43 | 62 | 12 | 348 | 29 | 6.96 | 0 | 0 | 9 | 8 | 10312 | 4493 | 170 | 26.42 | 13 | 2 | 8/53 |
| Freeman,AP | 12 | 16 | 5 | 154 | 50* | 14.00 | 0 | 1 | 2 | 4 | 3732 | 1707 | 66 | 25.86 | 5 | 3 | 7/71 |
| French,BN | 16 | 21 | 4 | 308 | 59 | 18.11 | 0 | 1 | 2 | 38/1 | | | | | | | |
| Fry,CB | 26 | 41 | 3 | 1223 | 144 | 32.18 | 2 | 7 | 3 | 17 | 10 | 3 | 0 | - | 0 | 0 | 0/3 |
| Gallian,JER | 3 | 6 | 0 | 74 | 28 | 12.33 | 0 | 0 | 2 | 1 | 84 | 62 | 0 | - | 0 | 0 | 0/6 |
| Gatting,MW | 79 | 138 | 14 | 4409 | 207 | 35.55 | 10 | 21 | 16 | 59 | 752 | 317 | 4 | 79.25 | 0 | 0 | 1/14 |
| Gay,LH | 1 | 2 | 0 | 37 | 33 | 18.50 | 0 | 0 | 0 | 3/1 | | | | | | | |
| Geary,G | 14 | 20 | 4 | 249 | 66 | 15.56 | 0 | 2 | 3 | 13 | 3810 | 1353 | 46 | 29.41 | 4 | 1 | 7/70 |
| Gibb,PA | 8 | 13 | 0 | 581 | 120 | 44.69 | 2 | 3 | 1 | 3/1 | | | | | | | |
| Gifford,N | 15 | 20 | 9 | 179 | 25* | 16.27 | 0 | 0 | 1 | 8 | 3084 | 1026 | 33 | 31.09 | 1 | 0 | 5/55 |
| Giles,AF | 1 | 2 | 1 | 17 | 16* | 17.00 | 0 | 0 | 0 | 0 | 216 | 106 | 1 | 106.00 | 0 | 0 | 1/106 |
| Gilligan,AER | 11 | 16 | 3 | 209 | 39* | 16.07 | 0 | 0 | 2 | 3 | 2404 | 1046 | 36 | 29.05 | 2 | 1 | 6/7 |
| Gilligan,AHH | 4 | 4 | 0 | 71 | 32 | 17.75 | 0 | 0 | 0 | 0 | | | | | | | |
| Gimblett,H | 3 | 5 | 1 | 129 | 67* | 32.25 | 0 | 1 | 0 | 1 | | | | | | | |
| Gladwin,C | 8 | 11 | 5 | 170 | 51* | 28.33 | 0 | 1 | 0 | 2 | 2129 | 571 | 15 | 38.06 | 0 | 0 | 3/21 |
| Goddard,TWJ | 8 | 5 | 3 | 13 | 8 | 6.50 | 0 | 0 | 1 | 3 | 1563 | 588 | 22 | 26.72 | 1 | 0 | 6/29 |
| Gooch,GA | 118 | 215 | 6 | 8900 | 333 | 42.58 | 20 | 46 | 13 | 103 | 2655 | 1069 | 23 | 46.47 | 0 | 0 | 3/39 |
| Gough,D | 25 | 36 | 5 | 406 | 65 | 13.09 | 0 | 2 | 7 | 8 | 5307 | 2789 | 102 | 27.34 | 4 | 0 | 6/42 |
| Gover,AR | 4 | 1 | 1 | 2 | 2* | 0 | 0 | 0 | 0 | 1 | 816 | 359 | 8 | 44.87 | 0 | 0 | 3/85 |

| ENGLAND (cont.) | BATTING AND FIELDING | | | | | | | | | | BOWLING | | | | | | |
|---|---|---|---|---|---|---|---|---|---|---|---|---|---|---|---|---|---|
| | Tests | I | N | Runs | HS | Avge | 100 | 50 | 0's | c/s | Balls | Runs | Wks | Avge | 5w | 10w | BB |
| Gower,DI | 117 | 204 | 18 | 8231 | 215 | 44.25 | 18 | 39 | 7 | 74 | 36 | 20 | 1 | 20.00 | 0 | 0 | 1/1 |
| Grace,EM | 1 | 2 | 0 | 36 | 36 | 18.00 | 0 | 0 | 1 | 1 | | | | | | | |
| Grace,GF | 1 | 2 | 0 | 0 | 0 | 0.00 | 0 | 0 | 2 | 2 | | | | | | | |
| Grace,WG | 22 | 36 | 2 | 1098 | 170 | 32.29 | 2 | 5 | 2 | 39 | 666 | 236 | 9 | 26.22 | 0 | 0 | 2/12 |
| Graveney,TW | 79 | 123 | 13 | 4882 | 258 | 44.38 | 11 | 20 | 8 | 80 | 260 | 167 | 1 | 167.00 | 0 | 0 | 1/34 |
| Greenhough,T | 4 | 4 | 1 | 4 | 2 | 1.33 | 0 | 0 | 1 | 1 | 1129 | 357 | 16 | 22.31 | 1 | 0 | 5/35 |
| Greenwood,A | 2 | 4 | 0 | 77 | 49 | 19.25 | 0 | 0 | 0 | 2 | | | | | | | |
| Greig,AW | 58 | 93 | 4 | 3599 | 148 | 40.43 | 8 | 20 | 5 | 87 | 9802 | 4541 | 141 | 32.20 | 6 | 2 | 8/86 |
| Greig,IA | 2 | 4 | 0 | 26 | 14 | 6.50 | 0 | 0 | 0 | 0 | 188 | 114 | 4 | 28.50 | 0 | 0 | 4/53 |
| Grieve,BAF | 2 | 3 | 2 | 40 | 14* | 40.00 | 0 | 0 | 0 | 0 | | | | | | | |
| Griffith,SC | 3 | 5 | 0 | 157 | 140 | 31.40 | 1 | 0 | 1 | 5/0 | | | | | | | |
| Gunn,G | 15 | 29 | 1 | 1120 | 122* | 40.00 | 2 | 7 | 3 | 15 | 12 | 8 | 0 | - | 0 | 0 | 0/8 |
| Gunn,JR | 6 | 10 | 2 | 85 | 24 | 10.62 | 0 | 0 | 1 | 3 | 999 | 387 | 18 | 21.50 | 1 | 0 | 5/76 |
| Gunn,W | 11 | 20 | 2 | 392 | 102* | 21.77 | 1 | 1 | 1 | 5 | | | | | | | |
| Haig,NE | 5 | 9 | 0 | 126 | 47 | 14.00 | 0 | 0 | 2 | 4 | 1026 | 448 | 13 | 34.46 | 0 | 0 | 3/73 |
| Haigh,S | 11 | 18 | 3 | 113 | 25 | 7.53 | 0 | 0 | 4 | 8 | 1294 | 622 | 24 | 25.91 | 1 | 0 | 6/11 |
| Hallows,C | 2 | 2 | 1 | 42 | 26 | 42.00 | 0 | 0 | 0 | 0 | | | | | | | |
| Hammond,WR | 85 | 140 | 16 | 7249 | 336* | 58.45 | 22 | 24 | 4 | 110 | 7969 | 3138 | 83 | 37.80 | 2 | 0 | 5/36 |
| Hampshire,JH | 8 | 16 | 1 | 403 | 107 | 26.86 | 1 | 2 | 2 | 9 | | | | | | | |
| Hardinge,HTW | 1 | 2 | 0 | 30 | 25 | 15.00 | 0 | 0 | 0 | 0 | | | | | | | |
| Hardstaff,J jr | 23 | 38 | 3 | 1636 | 205* | 46.74 | 4 | 10 | 4 | 9 | | | | | | | |
| Hardstaff,J sr | 5 | 10 | 0 | 311 | 72 | 31.10 | 0 | 3 | 0 | 1 | | | | | | | |
| Harris,Lord | 4 | 6 | 1 | 145 | 52 | 29.00 | 0 | 1 | 0 | 2 | 32 | 29 | 0 | - | 0 | 0 | 0/14 |
| Hartley,JC | 2 | 4 | 0 | 15 | 9 | 3.75 | 0 | 0 | 2 | 2 | 192 | 115 | 1 | 115.00 | 0 | 0 | 1/62 |
| Hawke,Lord | 5 | 8 | 1 | 55 | 30 | 7.85 | 0 | 0 | 2 | 3 | | | | | | | |
| Hayes,EG | 5 | 9 | 1 | 86 | 35 | 10.75 | 0 | 0 | 2 | 2 | 90 | 52 | 1 | 52.00 | 0 | 0 | 1/28 |
| Hayes,FC | 9 | 17 | 1 | 244 | 106* | 15.25 | 1 | 0 | 6 | 7 | | | | | | | |
| Hayward,TW | 35 | 60 | 2 | 1999 | 137 | 34.46 | 3 | 12 | 7 | 19 | 887 | 514 | 14 | 36.71 | 0 | 0 | 4/22 |
| Headley,DW | 10 | 17 | 4 | 111 | 31 | 8.53 | 0 | 0 | 2 | 5 | 1949 | 1059 | 37 | 28.62 | 0 | 0 | 4/72 |
| Hearne,A | 1 | 1 | 0 | 9 | 9 | 9.00 | 0 | 0 | 0 | 1 | | | | | | | |
| Hearne,F | 2 | 2 | 0 | 47 | 27 | 23.50 | 0 | 0 | 0 | 1 | | | | | | | |
| Hearne,GG | 1 | 1 | 0 | 0 | 0 | 0.00 | 0 | 0 | 1 | 0 | | | | | | | |
| Hearne,JT | 12 | 18 | 4 | 126 | 40 | 9.00 | 0 | 0 | 3 | 4 | 2976 | 1082 | 49 | 22.08 | 4 | 1 | 6/41 |
| Hearne,JW | 24 | 36 | 5 | 806 | 114 | 26.00 | 1 | 2 | 3 | 13 | 2926 | 1462 | 30 | 48.73 | 1 | 0 | 5/49 |
| Hemmings,EE | 16 | 21 | 4 | 383 | 95 | 22.52 | 0 | 2 | 5 | 5 | 4437 | 1825 | 43 | 42.44 | 1 | 0 | 6/58 |
| Hendren,EH | 51 | 83 | 9 | 3525 | 205* | 47.63 | 7 | 21 | 4 | 33 | 47 | 31 | 1 | 31.00 | 0 | 0 | 1/27 |
| Hendrick,M | 30 | 35 | 15 | 128 | 15 | 6.40 | 0 | 0 | 8 | 25 | 6208 | 2248 | 87 | 25.83 | 0 | 0 | 4/28 |
| Heseltine,C | 2 | 2 | 0 | 18 | 18 | 9.00 | 0 | 0 | 1 | 3 | 157 | 84 | 5 | 16.80 | 1 | 0 | 5/38 |
| Hick,GA | 48 | 83 | 6 | 2681 | 178 | 34.81 | 4 | 15 | 3 | 65 | 2973 | 1247 | 22 | 56.68 | 0 | 0 | 4/126 |
| Higgs,K | 15 | 19 | 3 | 185 | 63 | 11.56 | 0 | 1 | 2 | 4 | 4112 | 1473 | 71 | 20.74 | 2 | 0 | 6/91 |
| Hill,A | 2 | 4 | 2 | 101 | 49 | 50.50 | 0 | 0 | 1 | 1 | 340 | 130 | 7 | 18.57 | 0 | 0 | 4/27 |
| Hill,AJL | 3 | 4 | 0 | 251 | 124 | 62.75 | 1 | 1 | 0 | 1 | 40 | 8 | 4 | 2.00 | 0 | 0 | 4/8 |
| Hilton,MJ | 4 | 6 | 1 | 37 | 15 | 7.40 | 0 | 0 | 2 | 1 | 1244 | 477 | 14 | 34.07 | 1 | 0 | 5/61 |
| Hirst,GH | 24 | 38 | 3 | 790 | 85 | 22.57 | 0 | 5 | 5 | 18 | 3967 | 1770 | 59 | 30.00 | 3 | 0 | 5/48 |
| Hitch,JW | 7 | 10 | 3 | 103 | 51* | 14.71 | 0 | 1 | 1 | 4 | 462 | 325 | 7 | 46.42 | 0 | 0 | 2/31 |
| Hobbs,JB | 61 | 102 | 7 | 5410 | 211 | 56.94 | 15 | 28 | 4 | 17 | 376 | 165 | 1 | 165.00 | 0 | 0 | 1/19 |
| Hobbs,RNS | 7 | 8 | 3 | 34 | 15* | 6.80 | 0 | 0 | 1 | 8 | 1291 | 481 | 12 | 40.08 | 0 | 0 | 3/25 |
| Hollies,WE | 13 | 15 | 8 | 37 | 18* | 5.28 | 0 | 0 | 4 | 2 | 3554 | 1332 | 44 | 30.27 | 5 | 0 | 7/50 |
| Hollioake,AJ | 4 | 6 | 0 | 65 | 45 | 10.83 | 0 | 0 | 1 | 4 | 144 | 67 | 2 | 33.50 | 0 | 0 | 2/31 |
| Hollioake,BC | 1 | 2 | 0 | 30 | 28 | 15.00 | 0 | 0 | 0 | 1 | 90 | 83 | 2 | 41.50 | 0 | 0 | 1/26 |
| Holmes,ERT | 5 | 9 | 2 | 114 | 85* | 16.28 | 0 | 1 | 2 | 4 | 108 | 76 | 2 | 38.00 | 0 | 0 | 1/10 |
| Holmes,P | 7 | 14 | 1 | 357 | 88 | 27.46 | 0 | 4 | 3 | 3 | | | | | | | |
| Hone,L | 1 | 2 | 0 | 13 | 7 | 6.50 | 0 | 0 | 0 | 2/0 | | | | | | | |
| Hopwood,JL | 2 | 3 | 1 | 12 | 8 | 6.00 | 0 | 0 | 0 | 0 | 462 | 155 | 0 | - | 0 | 0 | 0/16 |
| Hornby,AN | 3 | 6 | 0 | 21 | 9 | 3.50 | 0 | 0 | 1 | 0 | 28 | 0 | 1 | 0.00 | 0 | 0 | 1/0 |
| Horton,MJ | 2 | 2 | 0 | 60 | 58 | 30.00 | 0 | 1 | 0 | 2 | 238 | 59 | 2 | 29.50 | 0 | 0 | 2/24 |
| Howard,ND | 4 | 6 | 1 | 86 | 23 | 17.20 | 0 | 0 | 0 | 4 | | | | | | | |

| ENGLAND (cont.) | | | | BATTING AND FIELDING | | | | | | | | | | BOWLING | | | |
|---|---|---|---|---|---|---|---|---|---|---|---|---|---|---|---|---|---|
| | Tests | I | N | Runs | HS | Avge | 100 | 50 | 0's | c/s | Balls | Runs | Wks | Avge | 5w | 10w | BB |
| Howell,H | 5 | 8 | 6 | 15 | 5 | 7.50 | 0 | 0 | 0 | 0 | 918 | 559 | 7 | 79.85 | 0 | 0 | 4/115 |
| Howorth,R | 5 | 10 | 2 | 145 | 45* | 18.12 | 0 | 0 | 0 | 2 | 1536 | 635 | 19 | 33.42 | 1 | 0 | 6/124 |
| Humphries,J | 3 | 6 | 1 | 44 | 16 | 8.80 | 0 | 0 | 0 | 7 | | | | | | | |
| Hunter,J | 5 | 7 | 2 | 93 | 39* | 18.60 | 0 | 0 | 0 | 8/3 | | | | | | | |
| Hussain,N | 34 | 61 | 5 | 2033 | 207 | 36.30 | 7 | 6 | 8 | 27 | | | | | | | |
| Hutchings,KL | 7 | 12 | 0 | 341 | 126 | 28.41 | 1 | 1 | 1 | 9 | 90 | 81 | 1 | 81.00 | 0 | 0 | 1/5 |
| Hutton,L | 79 | 138 | 15 | 6971 | 364 | 56.67 | 19 | 33 | 5 | 57 | 260 | 232 | 3 | 77.33 | 0 | 0 | 1/2 |
| Hutton,RA | 5 | 8 | 2 | 219 | 81 | 36.50 | 0 | 2 | 1 | 9 | 738 | 257 | 9 | 28.55 | 0 | 0 | 3/72 |
| Iddon,J | 5 | 7 | 1 | 170 | 73 | 28.33 | 0 | 2 | 3 | 0 | 66 | 27 | 0 | - | 0 | 0 | 0/3 |
| Igglesden,AP | 3 | 5 | 3 | 6 | 3* | 3.00 | 0 | 0 | 2 | 1 | 555 | 329 | 6 | 54.83 | 0 | 0 | 2/91 |
| Ikin,JT | 18 | 31 | 2 | 606 | 60 | 20.89 | 0 | 3 | 4 | 31 | 572 | 354 | 3 | 118.00 | 0 | 0 | 1/38 |
| Illingworth,R | 61 | 90 | 11 | 1836 | 113 | 23.24 | 2 | 5 | 7 | 45 | 11934 | 3807 | 122 | 31.20 | 3 | 0 | 6/29 |
| Illingworth,RK | 9 | 14 | 7 | 128 | 28 | 18.28 | 0 | 0 | 3 | 5 | 1485 | 615 | 19 | 32.36 | 0 | 0 | 4/96 |
| Ilott,MC | 5 | 6 | 2 | 28 | 15 | 7.00 | 0 | 0 | 0 | 0 | 1042 | 542 | 12 | 45.16 | 0 | 0 | 3/48 |
| Insole,DJ | 9 | 17 | 2 | 408 | 110* | 27.20 | 1 | 1 | 2 | 8 | | | | | | | |
| Irani,RC | 2 | 3 | 0 | 76 | 41 | 25.33 | 0 | 0 | 0 | 0 | 126 | 74 | 2 | 37.00 | 0 | 0 | 1/22 |
| Jackman,RD | 4 | 6 | 0 | 42 | 17 | 7.00 | 0 | 0 | 2 | 0 | 1070 | 445 | 14 | 31.78 | 0 | 0 | 4/110 |
| Jackson,Hon.FS | 20 | 33 | 4 | 1415 | 144* | 48.79 | 5 | 6 | 3 | 10 | 1587 | 799 | 24 | 33.29 | 1 | 0 | 5/52 |
| Jackson,HL | 2 | 2 | 1 | 15 | 8 | 15.00 | 0 | 0 | 0 | 1 | 498 | 155 | 7 | 22.14 | 0 | 0 | 2/26 |
| James,SP | 1 | 2 | 0 | 10 | 10 | 5.00 | 0 | 0 | 1 | 0 | | | | | | | |
| Jameson,JA | 4 | 8 | 0 | 214 | 82 | 26.75 | 0 | 1 | 0 | 0 | 42 | 17 | 1 | 17.00 | 0 | 0 | 1/17 |
| Jardine,DR | 22 | 33 | 6 | 1296 | 127 | 48.00 | 1 | 10 | 2 | 26 | 6 | 10 | 0 | - | 0 | 0 | 0/10 |
| Jarvis,PW | 9 | 15 | 2 | 132 | 29* | 10.15 | 0 | 0 | 1 | 2 | 1912 | 965 | 21 | 45.95 | 0 | 0 | 4/107 |
| Jenkins,RO | 9 | 12 | 1 | 198 | 39 | 18.00 | 0 | 0 | 0 | 4 | 2118 | 1098 | 32 | 34.31 | 1 | 0 | 5/116 |
| Jessop,GL | 18 | 26 | 0 | 569 | 104 | 21.88 | 1 | 3 | 3 | 11 | 742 | 354 | 10 | 35.40 | 0 | 0 | 4/68 |
| Jones,AO | 12 | 21 | 0 | 291 | 34 | 13.85 | 0 | 0 | 2 | 15 | 228 | 133 | 3 | 44.33 | 0 | 0 | 3/73 |
| Jones,IJ | 15 | 17 | 9 | 38 | 16 | 4.75 | 0 | 0 | 2 | 4 | 3546 | 1769 | 44 | 40.20 | 1 | 0 | 6/118 |
| Jupp,H | 2 | 4 | 0 | 68 | 63 | 17.00 | 0 | 1 | 1 | 2/0 | | | | | | | |
| Jupp,VWC | 8 | 13 | 1 | 208 | 38 | 17.33 | 0 | 0 | 0 | 5 | 1301 | 616 | 28 | 22.00 | 0 | 0 | 4/37 |
| Keeton,WW | 2 | 4 | 0 | 57 | 25 | 14.25 | 0 | 0 | 1 | 0 | | | | | | | |
| Kennedy,AS | 5 | 8 | 2 | 93 | 41* | 15.50 | 0 | 0 | 1 | 5 | 1683 | 599 | 31 | 19.32 | 2 | 0 | 5/76 |
| Kenyon,D | 8 | 15 | 0 | 192 | 87 | 12.80 | 0 | 1 | 1 | 5 | | | | | | | |
| Killick,ET | 2 | 4 | 0 | 81 | 31 | 20.25 | 0 | 0 | 0 | 2 | | | | | | | |
| Kilner,R | 9 | 8 | 1 | 233 | 74 | 33.28 | 0 | 2 | 0 | 6 | 2368 | 734 | 24 | 30.58 | 0 | 0 | 4/51 |
| King,JH | 1 | 2 | 0 | 64 | 60 | 32.00 | 0 | 1 | 0 | 0 | 162 | 99 | 1 | 99.00 | 0 | 0 | 1/99 |
| Kinneir,S | 1 | 2 | 0 | 52 | 30 | 26.00 | 0 | 0 | 0 | 0 | | | | | | | |
| Knight,AE | 12 | 21 | 0 | 585 | 113 | 27.85 | 1 | 4 | 0 | 21 | | | | | | | |
| Knight,BR | 29 | 38 | 7 | 812 | 127 | 26.19 | 2 | 0 | 2 | 14 | 5377 | 2223 | 70 | 31.75 | 0 | 0 | 4/38 |
| Knight,DJ | 2 | 4 | 0 | 54 | 38 | 13.50 | 0 | 0 | 0 | 1 | | | | | | | |
| Knight,NV | 11 | 19 | 0 | 573 | 113 | 30.15 | 1 | 4 | 0 | 21 | | | | | | | |
| Knott,APE | 95 | 149 | 15 | 4389 | 135 | 32.75 | 5 | 30 | 8 | 250/19 | | | | | | | |
| Knox,NA | 2 | 4 | 1 | 24 | 8* | 8.00 | 0 | 0 | 0 | 0 | 126 | 105 | 3 | 35.00 | 0 | 0 | 2/39 |
| Laker,JC | 46 | 63 | 15 | 676 | 63 | 14.08 | 0 | 2 | 6 | 12 | 12027 | 4101 | 193 | 21.24 | 9 | 3 | 10/53 |
| Lamb,AJ | 79 | 139 | 10 | 4656 | 142 | 36.09 | 14 | 18 | 9 | 75 | 30 | 23 | 1 | 23.00 | 0 | 0 | 1/6 |
| Langridge,J | 8 | 9 | 0 | 242 | 70 | 26.88 | 0 | 1 | 0 | 6 | 1074 | 413 | 19 | 21.73 | 2 | 0 | 7/56 |
| Larkins,W | 13 | 25 | 1 | 493 | 64 | 20.54 | 0 | 3 | 6 | 8 | | | | | | | |
| Larter,JDF | 10 | 7 | 2 | 16 | 10 | 3.20 | 0 | 0 | 2 | 5 | 2172 | 941 | 37 | 25.43 | 2 | 0 | 5/57 |
| Larwood,H | 21 | 28 | 3 | 485 | 98 | 19.40 | 0 | 2 | 4 | 15 | 4969 | 2212 | 78 | 28.35 | 4 | 1 | 6/32 |
| Lathwell,MN | 2 | 4 | 0 | 78 | 33 | 19.50 | 0 | 0 | 1 | 0 | | | | | | | |
| Lawrence,DV | 5 | 6 | 0 | 60 | 34 | 10.00 | 0 | 0 | 0 | 0 | 1089 | 676 | 18 | 37.55 | 1 | 0 | 5/106 |
| Leadbeater,E | 2 | 2 | 0 | 40 | 38 | 20.00 | 0 | 0 | 0 | 3 | 289 | 218 | 2 | 109.00 | 0 | 0 | 1/38 |
| Lee,HW | 1 | 2 | 0 | 19 | 18 | 9.50 | 0 | 0 | 0 | 0 | | | | | | | |
| Lees,WS | 5 | 9 | 3 | 66 | 25* | 11.00 | 0 | 0 | 0 | 2 | 1256 | 467 | 26 | 17.96 | 2 | 0 | 6/78 |
| Legge,GB | 5 | 7 | 1 | 299 | 196 | 49.83 | 1 | 0 | 2 | 1 | 30 | 34 | 0 | - | 0 | 0 | 0/34 |
| Leslie,CFH | 4 | 7 | 0 | 106 | 54 | 15.14 | 0 | 1 | 1 | 1 | 96 | 44 | 4 | 11.00 | 0 | 0 | 3/31 |
| Lever,JK | 21 | 31 | 5 | 306 | 53 | 11.76 | 0 | 1 | 2 | 11 | 4433 | 1951 | 73 | 26.72 | 3 | 1 | 7/46 |
| Lever,P | 17 | 18 | 2 | 350 | 88* | 21.87 | 0 | 2 | 1 | 11 | 3571 | 1509 | 41 | 36.80 | 2 | 0 | 6/38 |

| ENGLAND (cont.) | BATTING AND FIELDING | | | | | | | | | | BOWLING | | | | | | |
|---|---|---|---|---|---|---|---|---|---|---|---|---|---|---|---|---|---|
| | Tests | I | N | Runs | HS | Avge | 100 | 50 | 0's | c/s | Balls | Runs | Wks | Avge | 5w | 10w | BB |
| Leveson Gower,HDG | 3 | 6 | 2 | 95 | 31 | 23.75 | 0 | 0 | 0 | 1 | | | | | | | |
| Levett,WHV | 1 | 2 | 1 | 7 | 5 | 7.00 | 0 | 0 | 0 | 3/0 | | | | | | | |
| Lewis,AR | 9 | 16 | 2 | 457 | 125 | 32.64 | 1 | 3 | 2 | 0 | | | | | | | |
| Lewis,CC | 32 | 51 | 3 | 1105 | 117 | 23.02 | 1 | 4 | 6 | 25 | 6864 | 3479 | 93 | 37.40 | 3 | 0 | 6/111 |
| Leyland,M | 41 | 65 | 5 | 2764 | 187 | 46.06 | 9 | 10 | 6 | 13 | 1103 | 585 | 6 | 97.50 | 0 | 0 | 3/91 |
| Lilley,AFA | 35 | 52 | 8 | 903 | 84 | 20.52 | 0 | 4 | 10 | 70/22 | 25 | 23 | 1 | 23.00 | 0 | 0 | 1/23 |
| Lillywhite,J | 2 | 3 | 1 | 16 | 10 | 8.00 | 0 | 0 | 0 | 1 | 340 | 126 | 8 | 15.75 | 0 | 0 | 4/70 |
| Lloyd,D | 9 | 15 | 2 | 552 | 214* | 42.46 | 1 | 0 | 0 | 11 | 24 | 17 | 0 | - | 0 | 0 | 0/4 |
| Lloyd,TA | 1 | 1 | 1 | 10 | 10* | - | 0 | 0 | 0 | 0 | | | | | | | |
| Loader,PJ | 13 | 19 | 6 | 76 | 17 | 5.84 | 0 | 0 | 3 | 2 | 2662 | 878 | 39 | 22.51 | 1 | 0 | 6/36 |
| Lock,GAR | 49 | 63 | 9 | 742 | 89 | 13.74 | 0 | 3 | 8 | 59 | 13147 | 4451 | 174 | 25.58 | 9 | 3 | 7/35 |
| Lockwood,WH | 12 | 16 | 3 | 231 | 52* | 17.76 | 0 | 1 | 3 | 4 | 1970 | 884 | 43 | 20.55 | 5 | 1 | 7/71 |
| Lohmann,GA | 18 | 26 | 2 | 213 | 62* | 8.87 | 0 | 1 | 7 | 28 | 3821 | 1205 | 112 | 10.75 | 9 | 5 | 9/28 |
| Lowson,FA | 7 | 13 | 0 | 245 | 68 | 18.84 | 0 | 2 | 2 | 5 | | | | | | | |
| Lucas,AP | 5 | 9 | 1 | 157 | 55 | 19.62 | 0 | 1 | 0 | 1 | 120 | 54 | 0 | - | 0 | 0 | 0/23 |
| Luckhurst,BW | 21 | 41 | 5 | 1298 | 131 | 36.05 | 4 | 5 | 4 | 14 | 57 | 32 | 1 | 32.00 | 0 | 0 | 1/9 |
| Lyttelton,Hon.A | 4 | 7 | 1 | 94 | 31 | 15.66 | 0 | 0 | 0 | 2/0 | 48 | 19 | 4 | 4.75 | 0 | 0 | 4/19 |
| Macaulay,GG | 8 | 10 | 4 | 112 | 76 | 18.66 | 0 | 1 | 1 | 5 | 1701 | 662 | 24 | 27.58 | 1 | 0 | 5/64 |
| MacBryan,JCW | 1 | | | | | | 0 | 0 | 0 | 0 | | | | | | | |
| McCague,MJ | 3 | 5 | 0 | 21 | 11 | 4.20 | 0 | 0 | 2 | 1 | 593 | 385 | 6 | 64.16 | 0 | 0 | 4/121 |
| McConnon,JE | 2 | 3 | 1 | 18 | 11 | 9.00 | 0 | 0 | 0 | 4 | 216 | 74 | 4 | 18.50 | 0 | 0 | 3/19 |
| McGahey,CP | 2 | 4 | 0 | 38 | 18 | 9.50 | 0 | 0 | 1 | 1 | | | | | | | |
| MacGregor,G | 8 | 11 | 3 | 96 | 31 | 12.00 | 0 | 0 | 1 | 14/3 | | | | | | | |
| McIntyre,AJW | 3 | 6 | 0 | 19 | 7 | 3.16 | 0 | 0 | 1 | 8/0 | | | | | | | |
| MacKinnon,FA | 1 | 2 | 0 | 5 | 5 | 2.50 | 0 | 0 | 1 | 0 | | | | | | | |
| MacLaren,AC | 35 | 61 | 4 | 1931 | 140 | 33.87 | 5 | 8 | 4 | 29 | | | | | | | |
| McMaster,JEP | 1 | 1 | 0 | 0 | 0 | 0.00 | 0 | 0 | 1 | 0 | | | | | | | |
| Makepeace,JWH | 4 | 8 | 0 | 279 | 117 | 34.87 | 1 | 2 | 0 | 0 | | | | | | | |
| Malcolm,DE | 40 | 58 | 19 | 236 | 29 | 6.05 | 0 | 0 | 16 | 7 | 8468 | 4748 | 128 | 37.09 | 5 | 2 | 9/57 |
| Mallender,NA | 2 | 3 | 0 | 8 | 4 | 2.66 | 0 | 0 | 0 | 0 | 449 | 215 | 10 | 21.50 | 1 | 0 | 5/50 |
| Mann,FG | 7 | 12 | 2 | 376 | 136* | 37.60 | 1 | 0 | 0 | 3 | | | | | | | |
| Mann,FT | 5 | 9 | 1 | 281 | 84 | 35.12 | 0 | 2 | 0 | 4 | | | | | | | |
| Marks,VJ | 6 | 10 | 1 | 249 | 83 | 27.66 | 0 | 3 | 0 | 0 | 1082 | 484 | 11 | 44.00 | 0 | 0 | 3/78 |
| Marriott,CS | 1 | 1 | 0 | 0 | 0 | 0.00 | 0 | 0 | 1 | 1 | 247 | 96 | 11 | 8.72 | 2 | 1 | 6/59 |
| Martin,F | 2 | 2 | 0 | 14 | 13 | 7.00 | 0 | 0 | 0 | 2 | 410 | 141 | 14 | 10.07 | 2 | 1 | 6/50 |
| Martin,JW | 1 | 2 | 0 | 26 | 26 | 13.00 | 0 | 0 | 1 | 0 | 270 | 129 | 1 | 129.00 | 0 | 0 | 1/111 |
| Martin,PJ | 8 | 13 | 0 | 115 | 29 | 8.84 | 0 | 0 | 2 | 6 | 1452 | 580 | 17 | 34.11 | 0 | 0 | 4/60 |
| Mason,JR | 5 | 10 | 0 | 129 | 32 | 12.90 | 0 | 0 | 1 | 3 | 324 | 149 | 2 | 74.50 | 0 | 0 | 1/8 |
| Matthews,ADG | 1 | 1 | 1 | 2 | 2* | 0 | 0 | 0 | 0 | 1 | 180 | 65 | 2 | 32.50 | 0 | 0 | 1/13 |
| May,PBH | 66 | 106 | 9 | 4537 | 285* | 46.77 | 13 | 22 | 8 | 42 | | | | | | | |
| Maynard,MP | 4 | 8 | 0 | 87 | 35 | 10.87 | 0 | 0 | 2 | 3 | | | | | | | |
| Mead,CP | 17 | 26 | 2 | 1185 | 182* | 49.37 | 4 | 3 | 3 | 4 | | | | | | | |
| Mead,W | 1 | 2 | 0 | 7 | 7 | 3.50 | 0 | 0 | 1 | 1 | 265 | 91 | 1 | 91.00 | 0 | 0 | 1/91 |
| Midwinter,WE | 4 | 7 | 0 | 95 | 36 | 13.57 | 0 | 0 | 1 | 5/0 | 776 | 272 | 10 | 27.20 | 0 | 0 | 4/81 |
| Milburn,C | 9 | 16 | 2 | 654 | 139 | 46.71 | 2 | 2 | 0 | 7 | | | | | | | |
| Miller,AM | 1 | 2 | 2 | 24 | 20* | - | 0 | 0 | 0 | 0 | | | | | | | |
| Miller,G | 34 | 51 | 4 | 1213 | 98* | 25.80 | 0 | 7 | 5 | 17 | 5149 | 1859 | 60 | 30.98 | 1 | 0 | 5/44 |
| Milligan,FW | 2 | 4 | 0 | 58 | 38 | 14.50 | 0 | 0 | 0 | 1 | 45 | 29 | 0 | - | 0 | 0 | 0/0 |
| Millman,G | 6 | 7 | 2 | 60 | 32* | 12.00 | 0 | 0 | 2 | 13/2 | | | | | | | |
| Milton,CA | 6 | 9 | 1 | 204 | 104* | 25.50 | 1 | 0 | 0 | 5 | 24 | 12 | 0 | - | 0 | 0 | 0/12 |
| Mitchell,A | 6 | 10 | 0 | 298 | 72 | 29.80 | 0 | 2 | 1 | 9 | 6 | 4 | 0 | - | 0 | 0 | 0/4 |
| Mitchell,F | 2 | 4 | 0 | 88 | 41 | 22.00 | 0 | 0 | 0 | 2 | | | | | | | |
| Mitchell,TB | 5 | 6 | 2 | 20 | 9 | 5.00 | 0 | 0 | 1 | 1 | 894 | 498 | 8 | 62.25 | 0 | 0 | 2/49 |
| Mitchell-Innes,NS | 1 | 1 | 0 | 5 | 5 | 5.00 | 0 | 0 | 0 | 0 | | | | | | | |
| Mold,AW | 3 | 3 | 1 | 0 | 0* | 0.00 | 0 | 0 | 2 | 1 | 491 | 234 | 7 | 33.42 | 0 | 0 | 3/44 |
| Moon,LJ | 4 | 8 | 0 | 182 | 36 | 22.75 | 0 | 0 | 1 | 4 | | | | | | | |
| Morley,F | 4 | 6 | 2 | 6 | 2* | 1.50 | 0 | 0 | 2 | 4 | 972 | 296 | 16 | 18.50 | 1 | 0 | 5/56 |

| ENGLAND (cont.) | | | | BATTING AND FIELDING | | | | | | | | BOWLING | | | | | |
|---|---|---|---|---|---|---|---|---|---|---|---|---|---|---|---|---|---|
| | Tests | I | N | Runs | HS | Avge | 100 | 50 | 0's | c/s | Balls | Runs | Wks | Avge | 5w | 10w | BB |
| Morris,H | 3 | 6 | 0 | 115 | 44 | 19.16 | 0 | 0 | 0 | 3 | | | | | | | |
| Morris,JE | 3 | 5 | 2 | 71 | 32 | 23.66 | 0 | 0 | 0 | 3 | | | | | | | |
| Mortimore,JB | 9 | 12 | 2 | 243 | 73* | 24.30 | 0 | 1 | 1 | 3 | 2162 | 733 | 13 | 56.38 | 0 | 0 | 3/36 |
| Moss,AE | 9 | 7 | 1 | 61 | 26 | 10.16 | 0 | 0 | 1 | 1 | 1657 | 626 | 21 | 29.80 | 0 | 0 | 4/35 |
| Moxon,MD | 10 | 17 | 1 | 455 | 99 | 28.43 | 0 | 3 | 2 | 10 | 48 | 30 | 0 | - | 0 | 0 | 0/3 |
| Mullally,AD | 9 | 12 | 4 | 79 | 24 | 9.87 | 0 | 0 | 3 | 1 | 2379 | 927 | 28 | 33.10 | 0 | 0 | 3/44 |
| Munton,TA | 2 | 2 | 1 | 25 | 25* | 25.00 | 0 | 0 | 1 | 0 | 405 | 200 | 4 | 50.00 | 0 | 0 | 2/22 |
| Murdoch,WL | 1 | 1 | 0 | 12 | 12 | 12.00 | 0 | 0 | 0 | 0/1 | | | | | | | |
| Murray,JT | 21 | 28 | 5 | 506 | 112 | 22.00 | 1 | 2 | 3 | 52/3 | | | | | | | |
| Newham,W | 1 | 2 | 0 | 26 | 17 | 13.00 | 0 | 0 | 0 | 0 | | | | | | | |
| Newport,PJ | 3 | 5 | 1 | 110 | 40* | 27.50 | 0 | 0 | 1 | 1 | 669 | 417 | 10 | 41.70 | 0 | 0 | 4/87 |
| Nichols,MS | 14 | 19 | 7 | 355 | 78* | 29.58 | 0 | 2 | 0 | 11 | 2565 | 1152 | 41 | 28.09 | 2 | 0 | 6/35 |
| Oakman,ASM | 2 | 2 | 0 | 14 | 10 | 7.00 | 0 | 0 | 0 | 7 | 48 | 21 | 0 | - | 0 | 0 | 0/21 |
| O'Brien,TC | 5 | 8 | 0 | 59 | 20 | 7.37 | 0 | 0 | 3 | 4 | | | | | | | |
| O'Connor,J | 4 | 7 | 0 | 153 | 51 | 21.85 | 0 | 1 | 1 | 2 | 162 | 72 | 1 | 72.00 | 0 | 0 | 1/31 |
| Old,CM | 46 | 66 | 9 | 845 | 65 | 14.82 | 0 | 2 | 10 | 22 | 8858 | 4020 | 143 | 28.11 | 4 | 0 | 7/50 |
| Oldfield,N | 1 | 2 | 0 | 99 | 80 | 49.50 | 0 | 1 | 0 | 0 | | | | | | | |
| Padgett,DEV | 2 | 4 | 0 | 51 | 31 | 12.75 | 0 | 0 | 0 | 0 | 12 | 8 | 0 | - | 0 | 0 | 0/8 |
| Paine,GAE | 4 | 7 | 1 | 97 | 49 | 16.16 | 0 | 0 | 1 | 5 | 1044 | 467 | 17 | 27.47 | 1 | 0 | 5/168 |
| Palairet,LCH | 2 | 4 | 0 | 49 | 20 | 12.25 | 0 | 0 | 0 | 2 | | | | | | | |
| Palmer,CH | 1 | 2 | 0 | 22 | 22 | 11.00 | 0 | 0 | 1 | 0 | 30 | 15 | 0 | - | 0 | 0 | 0/15 |
| Palmer,KE | 1 | 1 | 0 | 10 | 10 | 10.00 | 0 | 0 | 0 | 0 | 378 | 189 | 1 | 189.00 | 0 | 0 | 1/113 |
| Parfitt,PH | 37 | 52 | 6 | 1882 | 131* | 40.91 | 7 | 6 | 5 | 42 | 1326 | 574 | 12 | 47.83 | 0 | 0 | 2/5 |
| Parker,CWL | 1 | 1 | 1 | 3 | 3* | - | 0 | 0 | 0 | 0 | 168 | 32 | 2 | 16.00 | 0 | 0 | 2/32 |
| Parker,PWG | 1 | 2 | 0 | 13 | 13 | 6.50 | 0 | 0 | 1 | 0 | | | | | | | |
| Parkhouse,WGA | 7 | 13 | 0 | 373 | 78 | 28.69 | 0 | 2 | 1 | 3 | | | | | | | |
| Parkin,CH | 10 | 16 | 3 | 160 | 36 | 12.30 | 0 | 0 | 1 | 3 | 2095 | 1128 | 32 | 35.25 | 2 | 0 | 5/38 |
| Parks,JH | 1 | 2 | 0 | 29 | 22 | 14.50 | 0 | 0 | 0 | 0 | 126 | 36 | 3 | 12.00 | 0 | 0 | 2/26 |
| Parks,JM | 46 | 68 | 7 | 1962 | 108* | 32.16 | 2 | 9 | 5 | 103/11 | 54 | 51 | 1 | 51.00 | 0 | 0 | 1/43 |
| Pataudi,Nawab of, sr | 3 | 5 | 0 | 144 | 102 | 28.80 | 1 | 0 | 0 | 0 | | | | | | | |
| Patel,MM | 2 | 2 | 0 | 45 | 27 | 22.50 | 0 | 0 | 0 | 2 | 276 | 180 | 1 | 180.00 | 0 | 0 | 1/101 |
| Paynter,E | 20 | 31 | 5 | 1540 | 243 | 59.23 | 4 | 7 | 3 | 7 | | | | | | | |
| Peate,E | 9 | 14 | 8 | 70 | 13 | 11.66 | 0 | 0 | 1 | 2 | 2096 | 682 | 31 | 22.00 | 2 | 0 | 6/85 |
| Peebles,IAR | 13 | 17 | 8 | 98 | 26 | 10.88 | 0 | 0 | 3 | 5 | 2882 | 1391 | 45 | 30.91 | 3 | 0 | 6/63 |
| Peel,R | 20 | 33 | 4 | 427 | 83 | 14.72 | 0 | 3 | 8 | 17 | 5216 | 1715 | 101 | 16.98 | 5 | 1 | 7/31 |
| Penn,F | 1 | 2 | 1 | 50 | 27* | 50.00 | 0 | 0 | 0 | 0 | 12 | 2 | 0 | - | 0 | 0 | 0/2 |
| Perks,RTD | 2 | 2 | 2 | 3 | 2* | 0 | 0 | 0 | 0 | 1 | 829 | 355 | 11 | 32.27 | 2 | 0 | 5/100 |
| Philipson,H | 5 | 8 | 1 | 63 | 30 | 9.00 | 0 | 0 | 0 | 8/3 | | | | | | | |
| Pigott,ACS | 1 | 2 | 1 | 12 | 8* | 12.00 | 0 | 0 | 0 | 0 | 102 | 75 | 2 | 37.50 | 0 | 0 | 2/75 |
| Pilling,R | 8 | 13 | 1 | 91 | 23 | 7.58 | 0 | 0 | 1 | 10/4 | | | | | | | |
| Place,W | 3 | 6 | 1 | 144 | 107 | 28.80 | 1 | 0 | 0 | 0 | | | | | | | |
| Pocock,PI | 25 | 37 | 4 | 206 | 33 | 6.24 | 0 | 0 | 10 | 15 | 6650 | 2976 | 67 | 44.41 | 3 | 0 | 6/79 |
| Pollard,R | 4 | 3 | 2 | 13 | 10* | 13.00 | 0 | 0 | 0 | 3 | 1102 | 378 | 15 | 25.20 | 1 | 0 | 5/24 |
| Poole,CJ | 3 | 5 | 1 | 161 | 69* | 40.25 | 0 | 2 | 0 | 1 | 30 | 9 | 0 | - | 0 | 0 | 0/9 |
| Pope,GH | 1 | 1 | 1 | 8 | 8* | - | 0 | 0 | 0 | 0 | 218 | 85 | 1 | 85.00 | 0 | 0 | 1/49 |
| Pougher,AD | 1 | 1 | 0 | 17 | 17 | 17.00 | 0 | 0 | 0 | 2 | 105 | 26 | 3 | 8.66 | 0 | 0 | 3/26 |
| Price,JSE | 15 | 15 | 6 | 66 | 32 | 7.33 | 0 | 0 | 5 | 7 | 2724 | 1401 | 40 | 35.02 | 1 | 0 | 5/73 |
| Price,WFF | 1 | 2 | 0 | 6 | 6 | 3.00 | 0 | 0 | 1 | 2/0 | | | | | | | |
| Prideaux,RM | 3 | 6 | 1 | 102 | 64 | 20.40 | 0 | 1 | 0 | 0 | 12 | 0 | 0 | - | | | 0/0 |
| Pringle,DR | 30 | 50 | 4 | 695 | 53 | 15.10 | 0 | 1 | 6 | 10 | 5287 | 2518 | 70 | 35.97 | 3 | 0 | 5/95 |
| Pullar,G | 28 | 49 | 4 | 1974 | 175 | 43.86 | 4 | 12 | 3 | 2 | 66 | 37 | 1 | 37.00 | 0 | 0 | 1/1 |
| Quaife,WG | 7 | 13 | 1 | 228 | 68 | 19.00 | 0 | 1 | 1 | 4 | 15 | 6 | 0 | - | 0 | 0 | 0/6 |
| Radford,NV | 3 | 4 | 1 | 21 | 12* | 7.00 | 0 | 0 | 1 | 0 | 678 | 351 | 4 | 87.75 | 0 | 0 | 2/131 |
| Radley,CT | 8 | 10 | 0 | 481 | 158 | 48.10 | 2 | 2 | 1 | 4 | | | | | | | |
| Ramprakash,MR | 28 | 49 | 3 | 1100 | 154 | 23.91 | 1 | 4 | 8 | 20 | 541 | 284 | 3 | 94.66 | 0 | 0 | 1/2 |
| Randall,DW | 47 | 79 | 5 | 2470 | 174 | 33.37 | 7 | 12 | 14 | 31 | 16 | 3 | 0 | - | 0 | 0 | 0/1 |
| Ranjitsinhji,KS | 15 | 26 | 4 | 989 | 175 | 44.95 | 2 | 6 | 2 | 13 | 97 | 39 | 1 | 39.00 | 0 | 0 | 1/23 |

| ENGLAND (cont.) | | | | BATTING AND FIELDING | | | | | | | | BOWLING | | | | | |
|---|---|---|---|---|---|---|---|---|---|---|---|---|---|---|---|---|---|
| | Tests | I | N | Runs | HS | Avge | 100 | 50 | 0's | c/s | Balls | Runs | Wks | Avge | 5w | 10w | BB |
| Read,HD | 1 | | | | | | 0 | 0 | 0 | 0 | 270 | 200 | 6 | 33.33 | 0 | 0 | 4/136 |
| Read,JM | 17 | 29 | 2 | 463 | 57 | 17.14 | 0 | 2 | 3 | 8 | | | | | | | |
| Read,WW | 18 | 27 | 1 | 720 | 117 | 27.69 | 1 | 5 | 0 | 16 | 60 | 63 | 0 | - | 0 | 0 | 0/27 |
| Reeve,DA | 3 | 5 | 0 | 124 | 59 | 24.80 | 0 | 1 | 1 | 1 | 149 | 60 | 2 | 30.00 | 0 | 0 | 1/4 |
| Relf,AE | 13 | 21 | 3 | 416 | 63 | 23.11 | 0 | 1 | 1 | 14 | 1764 | 624 | 25 | 24.96 | 1 | 0 | 5/85 |
| Rhodes,HJ | 2 | 1 | 1 | 0 | 0* | - | 0 | 0 | 0 | 0 | 449 | 244 | 9 | 27.11 | 0 | 0 | 4/50 |
| Rhodes,SJ | 11 | 17 | 5 | 294 | 65* | 24.50 | 0 | 1 | 1 | 46/2 | | | | | | | |
| Rhodes,W | 58 | 98 | 21 | 2325 | 179 | 30.19 | 2 | 11 | 6 | 60 | 8231 | 3425 | 127 | 26.96 | 6 | 1 | 8/68 |
| Richards,CJ | 8 | 13 | 0 | 285 | 133 | 21.92 | 1 | 0 | 2 | 20/1 | | | | | | | |
| Richardson,DW | 1 | 1 | 0 | 33 | 33 | 33.00 | 0 | 0 | 0 | 1 | | | | | | | |
| Richardson,PE | 34 | 56 | 1 | 2061 | 126 | 37.47 | 5 | 9 | 1 | 6 | 120 | 48 | 3 | 16.00 | 0 | 0 | 2/10 |
| Richardson,T | 14 | 24 | 8 | 177 | 25* | 11.06 | 0 | 0 | 3 | 5 | 4497 | 2220 | 88 | 25.22 | 11 | 4 | 8/94 |
| Richmond,TL | 1 | 2 | 0 | 6 | 4 | 3.00 | 0 | 0 | 0 | 0 | 114 | 86 | 2 | 43.00 | 0 | 0 | 2/69 |
| Ridgway,F | 5 | 6 | 0 | 49 | 24 | 8.16 | 0 | 0 | 2 | 3 | 793 | 379 | 7 | 54.14 | 0 | 0 | 4/83 |
| Robertson,JDB | 11 | 21 | 2 | 881 | 133 | 46.36 | 2 | 6 | 0 | 6 | 138 | 58 | 2 | 29.00 | 0 | 0 | 2/17 |
| Robins,RWV | 19 | 27 | 4 | 612 | 108 | 26.60 | 1 | 4 | 4 | 12 | 3318 | 1758 | 64 | 27.46 | 1 | 0 | 6/32 |
| Robinson,RT | 29 | 49 | 5 | 1601 | 175 | 36.38 | 4 | 6 | 5 | 8 | 6 | 0 | 0 | - | 0 | 0 | 0/0 |
| Roope,GRJ | 21 | 32 | 4 | 860 | 77 | 30.71 | 0 | 7 | 3 | 35 | 172 | 76 | 0 | - | 0 | 0 | 0/2 |
| Root,CF | 3 | | | | | | 0 | 0 | 0 | 0 | 642 | 194 | 8 | 24.25 | 0 | 0 | 4/84 |
| Rose,BC | 9 | 16 | 2 | 358 | 70 | 25.57 | 0 | 2 | 0 | 4 | | | | | | | |
| Royle,VPFA | 1 | 2 | 0 | 21 | 18 | 10.50 | 0 | 0 | 0 | 2 | 16 | 6 | 0 | - | 0 | 0 | 0/6 |
| Rumsey,FE | 5 | 5 | 3 | 30 | 21* | 15.00 | 0 | 0 | 0 | 0 | 1145 | 461 | 17 | 27.11 | 0 | 0 | 4/25 |
| Russell,CAG | 10 | 18 | 2 | 910 | 140 | 56.87 | 5 | 2 | 2 | 8 | | | | | | | |
| Russell,RC | 54 | 86 | 16 | 1897 | 128* | 27.10 | 2 | 6 | 8 | 153/12 | | | | | | | |
| Russell,WE | 10 | 18 | 1 | 362 | 70 | 23.27 | 0 | 2 | 2 | 4 | 144 | 44 | 0 | - | 0 | 0 | 0/19 |
| Salisbury,IDK | 11 | 20 | 2 | 282 | 50 | 15.66 | 0 | 1 | 3 | 5 | 1923 | 1260 | 18 | 70.00 | 0 | 0 | 4/163 |
| Sandham,A | 14 | 23 | 0 | 879 | 325 | 38.21 | 2 | 3 | 3 | 4 | | | | | | | |
| Schultz,SS | 1 | 2 | 1 | 20 | 20 | 20.00 | 0 | 0 | 0 | 0 | 35 | 26 | 1 | 26.00 | 0 | 0 | 1/16 |
| Scotton,WH | 15 | 25 | 2 | 510 | 90 | 22.17 | 0 | 3 | 2 | 4 | 20 | 20 | 0 | - | 0 | 0 | 0/20 |
| Selby,J | 6 | 12 | 1 | 256 | 70 | 23.27 | 0 | 2 | 0 | 1/0 | | | | | | | |
| Selvey,MWW | 3 | 5 | 3 | 15 | 5* | 7.50 | 0 | 0 | 1 | 1 | 492 | 343 | 6 | 57.16 | 0 | 0 | 4/41 |
| Shackleton,D | 7 | 13 | 7 | 113 | 42 | 18.83 | 0 | 0 | 0 | 1 | 2078 | 768 | 18 | 42.66 | 0 | 0 | 4/72 |
| Sharp,J | 3 | 6 | 2 | 188 | 105 | 47.00 | 1 | 1 | 0 | 1 | 183 | 111 | 3 | 37.00 | 0 | 0 | 3/67 |
| Sharpe,JW | 3 | 6 | 4 | 44 | 26 | 22.00 | 0 | 0 | 0 | 0 | 975 | 305 | 11 | 27.72 | 1 | 0 | 6/84 |
| Sharpe,PJ | 12 | 21 | 4 | 786 | 111 | 46.23 | 1 | 4 | 1 | 17 | | | | | | | |
| Shaw,A | 7 | 12 | 1 | 111 | 40 | 10.09 | 0 | 0 | 1 | 4 | 1099 | 285 | 12 | 23.75 | 1 | 0 | 5/38 |
| Sheppard,Rev.DS | 22 | 33 | 2 | 1172 | 119 | 37.80 | 3 | 6 | 2 | 12 | | | | | | | |
| Sherwin,M | 3 | 6 | 4 | 30 | 21* | 15.00 | 0 | 0 | 1 | 5/2 | | | | | | | |
| Shrewsbury,A | 23 | 40 | 4 | 1277 | 164 | 35.47 | 3 | 4 | 1 | 29 | 12 | 2 | 0 | - | 0 | 0 | 0/2 |
| Shuter,J | 1 | 1 | 0 | 28 | 28 | 28.00 | 0 | 0 | 0 | 0 | | | | | | | |
| Shuttleworth,K | 5 | 6 | 0 | 46 | 21 | 7.66 | 0 | 0 | 1 | 1 | 1071 | 427 | 12 | 35.58 | 1 | 0 | 5/47 |
| Sidebottom,A | 1 | 1 | 0 | 2 | 2 | 2.00 | 0 | 0 | 0 | 0 | 112 | 65 | 1 | 65.00 | 0 | 0 | 1/65 |
| Silverwood,CEW | 1 | 1 | 0 | 0 | 0 | 0.00 | 0 | 0 | 1 | 1 | 150 | 71 | 4 | 17.75 | 0 | 0 | 3/63 |
| Simpson,RT | 27 | 45 | 3 | 1401 | 156* | 33.35 | 4 | 6 | 6 | 5 | 45 | 22 | 2 | 11.00 | 0 | 0 | 2/4 |
| Simpson-Hayward,GHT | 5 | 8 | 1 | 105 | 29* | 15.00 | 0 | 0 | 1 | 1 | 898 | 420 | 23 | 18.26 | 2 | 0 | 6/43 |
| Sims,JM | 4 | 4 | 0 | 16 | 12 | 4.00 | 0 | 0 | 1 | 6 | 887 | 480 | 11 | 43.63 | 1 | 0 | 5/73 |
| Sinfield,RA | 1 | 1 | 0 | 6 | 6 | 6.00 | 0 | 0 | 0 | 0 | 378 | 123 | 2 | 61.50 | 0 | 0 | 1/51 |
| Slack,WN | 3 | 6 | 0 | 81 | 52 | 13.50 | 0 | 1 | 2 | 3 | | | | | | | |
| Smailes,TF | 1 | 1 | 0 | 25 | 25 | 25.00 | 0 | 0 | 0 | 0 | 120 | 62 | 3 | 20.66 | 0 | 0 | 3/44 |
| Small,GC | 17 | 24 | 7 | 263 | 59 | 15.47 | 0 | 1 | 4 | 9 | 3921 | 1871 | 55 | 34.01 | 2 | 0 | 5/48 |
| Smith,AC | 6 | 7 | 3 | 118 | 69* | 29.50 | 0 | 1 | 0 | 20/0 | | | | | | | |
| Smith,AM | 1 | 2 | 1 | 4 | 4* | 4.00 | 0 | 0 | 1 | 0 | 138 | 89 | 0 | - | 0 | 0 | 0/89 |
| Smith,CA | 1 | 1 | 0 | 3 | 3 | 3.00 | 0 | 0 | 0 | 0 | 154 | 61 | 7 | 8.71 | 1 | 0 | 5/19 |
| Smith,CIJ | 5 | 10 | 0 | 102 | 27 | 10.20 | 0 | 0 | 2 | 1 | 930 | 393 | 15 | 26.20 | 1 | 0 | 5/16 |
| Smith,CL | 8 | 14 | 1 | 392 | 91 | 30.15 | 0 | 2 | 1 | 5 | 102 | 39 | 3 | 13.00 | 0 | 0 | 2/31 |
| Smith,D | 2 | 4 | 0 | 128 | 57 | 32.00 | 0 | 1 | 1 | 1 | | | | | | | |
| Smith,DM | 2 | 4 | 0 | 80 | 47 | 20.00 | 0 | 0 | 1 | 0 | | | | | | | |

| ENGLAND (cont.) | | | | BATTING AND FIELDING | | | | | | | | | | BOWLING | | | |
|---|---|---|---|---|---|---|---|---|---|---|---|---|---|---|---|---|---|
| | Tests | I | N | Runs | HS | Avge | 100 | 50 | 0's | c/s | Balls | Runs | Wks | Avge | 5w | 10w | BB |
| Smith,DR | 5 | 5 | 1 | 38 | 34 | 9.50 | 0 | 0 | 2 | 2 | 972 | 359 | 6 | 59.83 | 0 | 0 | 2/60 |
| Smith,DV | 3 | 4 | 1 | 25 | 16* | 8.33 | 0 | 0 | 1 | 0 | 270 | 97 | 1 | 97.00 | 0 | 0 | 1/12 |
| Smith,EJ | 11 | 14 | 1 | 113 | 22 | 8.69 | 0 | 0 | 2 | 17/3 | | | | | | | |
| Smith,H | 1 | 1 | 0 | 7 | 7 | 7.00 | 0 | 0 | 0 | 1 | | | | | | | |
| Smith,MJK | 50 | 78 | 6 | 2278 | 121 | 31.63 | 3 | 11 | 11 | 53 | 214 | 128 | 1 | 128.00 | 0 | 0 | 1/10 |
| Smith,RA | 62 | 112 | 15 | 4236 | 175 | 43.67 | 9 | 28 | 8 | 39 | 24 | 6 | 0 | - | 0 | 0 | 0/6 |
| Smith,TPB | 4 | 5 | 0 | 33 | 24 | 6.60 | 0 | 0 | 0 | 1 | 538 | 319 | 3 | 106.33 | 0 | 0 | 2/172 |
| Smithson,GA | 2 | 3 | 0 | 70 | 35 | 23.33 | 0 | 0 | 1 | 0 | | | | | | | |
| Snow,JA | 49 | 71 | 14 | 772 | 73 | 13.54 | 0 | 2 | 17 | 16 | 12021 | 5387 | 202 | 26.66 | 8 | 1 | 7/40 |
| Southerton,J | 2 | 3 | 1 | 7 | 6 | 3.50 | 0 | 0 | 1 | 2 | 263 | 107 | 7 | 15.28 | 0 | 0 | 4/46 |
| Spooner,RH | 10 | 15 | 0 | 481 | 119 | 32.06 | 1 | 4 | 2 | 4 | | | | | | | |
| Spooner,RT | 7 | 14 | 1 | 354 | 92 | 27.23 | 0 | 3 | 3 | 10/2 | | | | | | | |
| Stanyforth,RT | 4 | 6 | 1 | 13 | 6* | 2.60 | 0 | 0 | 1 | 7/2 | | | | | | | |
| Staples,SJ | 3 | 5 | 0 | 65 | 39 | 13.00 | 0 | 0 | 0 | 0 | 1149 | 435 | 15 | 29.00 | 0 | 0 | 3/50 |
| Statham,JB | 70 | 87 | 28 | 675 | 38 | 11.44 | 0 | 0 | 13 | 28 | 16056 | 6261 | 252 | 24.84 | 9 | 1 | 7/39 |
| Steel,AG | 13 | 20 | 3 | 600 | 148 | 35.29 | 2 | 0 | 1 | 5 | 1364 | 605 | 29 | 20.86 | 0 | 0 | 3/27 |
| Steele,DS | 8 | 16 | 0 | 673 | 106 | 42.06 | 1 | 5 | 1 | 7 | 88 | 39 | 2 | 19.50 | 0 | 0 | 1/1 |
| Stephenson,JP | 1 | 2 | 0 | 36 | 25 | 18.00 | 0 | 0 | 0 | 0 | | | | | | | |
| Stevens,GTS | 10 | 17 | 0 | 263 | 69 | 15.47 | 0 | 1 | 2 | 9 | 1186 | 648 | 20 | 32.40 | 2 | 1 | 5/90 |
| Stevenson,GB | 2 | 2 | 1 | 28 | 27* | 28.00 | 0 | 0 | 0 | 0 | 312 | 183 | 5 | 36.60 | 0 | 0 | 3/111 |
| Stewart,AJ | 80 | 144 | 10 | 5618 | 190 | 41.92 | 11 | 28 | 4 | 139/7 | 20 | 13 | 0 | - | 0 | 0 | 0/5 |
| Stewart,MJ | 8 | 12 | 1 | 385 | 87 | 35.00 | 0 | 2 | 1 | 6 | | | | | | | |
| Stoddart,AE | 16 | 30 | 2 | 996 | 173 | 35.57 | 2 | 3 | 3 | 6 | 162 | 94 | 2 | 47.00 | 0 | 0 | 1/10 |
| Storer,W | 6 | 11 | 0 | 215 | 51 | 19.54 | 0 | 1 | 0 | 11/0 | 168 | 108 | 2 | 54.00 | 0 | 0 | 1/24 |
| Street,GB | 1 | 2 | 1 | 11 | 7* | 11.00 | 0 | 0 | 0 | 0/1 | | | | | | | |
| Strudwick,H | 28 | 42 | 13 | 230 | 24 | 7.93 | 0 | 0 | 5 | 60/12 | | | | | | | |
| Studd,CT | 5 | 9 | 1 | 160 | 48 | 20.00 | 0 | 0 | 2 | 5 | 384 | 98 | 3 | 32.66 | 0 | 0 | 2/35 |
| Studd,GB | 4 | 7 | 0 | 31 | 9 | 4.42 | 0 | 0 | 1 | 8 | | | | | | | |
| Subba Row,R | 13 | 22 | 1 | 984 | 137 | 46.85 | 3 | 4 | 0 | 6 | 6 | 2 | 0 | - | 0 | 0 | 0/2 |
| Such,PM | 8 | 11 | 4 | 65 | 14* | 9.28 | 0 | 0 | 0 | 28 | 2177 | 803 | 22 | 36.50 | 1 | 0 | 6/67 |
| Sugg,FH | 2 | 2 | 0 | 55 | 31 | 27.50 | 0 | 0 | 0 | 0 | | | | | | | |
| Sutcliffe,H | 54 | 84 | 9 | 4555 | 194 | 60.73 | 16 | 23 | 2 | 23 | | | | | | | |
| Swetman,R | 11 | 17 | 2 | 254 | 65 | 16.93 | 0 | 1 | 2 | 24/2 | | | | | | | |
| Tate,FW | 1 | 2 | 1 | 9 | 5* | 9.00 | 0 | 0 | 0 | 2 | 96 | 51 | 2 | 25.50 | 0 | 0 | 2/7 |
| Tate,MW | 39 | 52 | 5 | 1198 | 100* | 25.48 | 1 | 5 | 5 | 11 | 12523 | 4055 | 155 | 26.16 | 7 | 1 | 6/42 |
| Tattersall,R | 16 | 17 | 7 | 50 | 10* | 5.00 | 0 | 0 | 1 | 8 | 4228 | 1513 | 58 | 26.08 | 4 | 1 | 7/52 |
| Tavare,CJ | 31 | 56 | 2 | 1755 | 149 | 32.50 | 2 | 12 | 5 | 20 | 30 | 11 | 0 | - | 0 | 0 | 0/0 |
| Taylor,JP | 2 | 4 | 2 | 34 | 17* | 17.00 | 0 | 0 | 1 | 0 | 288 | 156 | 3 | 52.00 | 0 | 0 | 1/18 |
| Taylor,K | 3 | 5 | 0 | 57 | 24 | 11.40 | 0 | 0 | 0 | 1 | 12 | 6 | 0 | - | 0 | 0 | 0/6 |
| Taylor,LB | 2 | 1 | 1 | 1 | 1* | 0 | 0 | 0 | 0 | 1 | 381 | 178 | 4 | 44.50 | 0 | 0 | 2/34 |
| Taylor,RW | 57 | 83 | 12 | 1156 | 97 | 16.28 | 0 | 3 | 10 | 167/7 | 12 | 6 | 0 | - | 0 | 0 | 0/6 |
| Tennyson,Hon.LH | 9 | 12 | 1 | 345 | 74* | 31.36 | 0 | 4 | 1 | 6 | 6 | 1 | 0 | - | 0 | 0 | 0/1 |
| Terry,VP | 2 | 3 | 0 | 16 | 8 | 5.33 | 0 | 0 | 0 | 2 | | | | | | | |
| Thomas,JG | 5 | 10 | 4 | 83 | 31* | 13.83 | 0 | 0 | 3 | 0 | 774 | 504 | 10 | 50.40 | 0 | 0 | 4/70 |
| Thompson,GJ | 6 | 10 | 1 | 273 | 63 | 30.33 | 0 | 2 | 0 | 5 | 1367 | 638 | 23 | 27.73 | 0 | 0 | 4/50 |
| Thomson,NI | 5 | 4 | 1 | 69 | 39 | 23.00 | 0 | 0 | 1 | 3 | 1488 | 568 | 9 | 63.11 | 0 | 0 | 2/55 |
| Thorpe,GP | 52 | 95 | 11 | 3366 | 138 | 40.07 | 6 | 23 | 8 | 48 | 138 | 37 | 0 | - | 0 | 0 | 0/0 |
| Titmus,FJ | 53 | 76 | 11 | 1449 | 84* | 22.29 | 0 | 10 | 4 | 35 | 15118 | 4931 | 153 | 32.22 | 7 | 0 | 7/79 |
| Tolchard,RW | 4 | 7 | 2 | 129 | 67 | 25.80 | 0 | 1 | 1 | 5 | | | | | | | |
| Townsend,CL | 2 | 3 | 0 | 51 | 38 | 17.00 | 0 | 0 | 0 | 0 | 140 | 75 | 3 | 25.00 | 0 | 0 | 3/50 |
| Townsend,DCH | 3 | 6 | 0 | 77 | 36 | 12.83 | 0 | 0 | 0 | 1 | 6 | 9 | 0 | - | 0 | 0 | 0/9 |
| Townsend,LF | 4 | 6 | 0 | 97 | 40 | 16.16 | 0 | 0 | 0 | 2 | 399 | 205 | 6 | 34.16 | 0 | 0 | 2/22 |
| Tremlett,MF | 3 | 5 | 2 | 20 | 18* | 6.66 | 0 | 0 | 2 | 0 | 492 | 226 | 4 | 56.50 | 0 | 0 | 2/98 |
| Trott,AE | 2 | 4 | 0 | 23 | 16 | 5.75 | 0 | 0 | 1 | 0 | 474 | 198 | 17 | 11.64 | 1 | 0 | 5/49 |
| Trueman,FS | 67 | 85 | 14 | 981 | 39* | 13.81 | 0 | 0 | 11 | 64 | 15178 | 6625 | 307 | 21.57 | 17 | 3 | 8/31 |
| Tufnell,NC | 1 | 1 | 0 | 14 | 14 | 14.00 | 0 | 0 | 0 | 0/1 | | | | | | | |
| Tufnell,PCR | 34 | 47 | 23 | 123 | 22* | 5.12 | 0 | 0 | 13 | 12 | 9230 | 3636 | 100 | 36.36 | 5 | 2 | 7/47 |

| ENGLAND (cont.) | | | | BATTING AND FIELDING | | | | | | | | BOWLING | | | | | |
|---|---|---|---|---|---|---|---|---|---|---|---|---|---|---|---|---|---|
| | Tests | I | N | Runs | HS | Avge | 100 | 50 | 0's | c/s | Balls | Runs | Wks | Avge | 5w | 10w | BB |
| Turnbull,MJL | 9 | 13 | 2 | 224 | 61 | 20.36 | 0 | 1 | 1 | 1 | | | | | | | |
| Tyldesley,GE | 14 | 20 | 2 | 990 | 122 | 55.00 | 3 | 6 | 2 | 2 | 3 | 2 | 0 | - | 0 | 0 | 0/2 |
| Tyldesley,JT | 31 | 55 | 1 | 1661 | 138 | 30.75 | 4 | 9 | 4 | 16 | | | | | | | |
| Tyldesley,RK | 7 | 7 | 1 | 47 | 29 | 7.83 | 0 | 0 | 1 | 1 | 1615 | 619 | 19 | 32.57 | 0 | 0 | 3/50 |
| Tylecote,EFS | 6 | 9 | 1 | 152 | 66 | 19.00 | 0 | 1 | 4 | 5/5 | | | | | | | |
| Tyler,EJ | 1 | 1 | 0 | 0 | 0 | 0.00 | 0 | 0 | 1 | 0 | 145 | 65 | 4 | 16.25 | 0 | 0 | 3/49 |
| Tyson,FH | 17 | 24 | 3 | 230 | 37* | 10.95 | 0 | 0 | 3 | 4 | 3452 | 1411 | 76 | 18.56 | 4 | 1 | 7/27 |
| Ulyett,G | 25 | 39 | 0 | 949 | 149 | 24.33 | 1 | 7 | 6 | 19 | 2627 | 1020 | 50 | 20.40 | 1 | 0 | 7/36 |
| Underwood,DL | 86 | 116 | 35 | 937 | 45* | 11.56 | 0 | 0 | 19 | 44 | 21862 | 7674 | 297 | 25.83 | 17 | 6 | 8/51 |
| Valentine,BH | 7 | 9 | 2 | 454 | 136 | 64.85 | 2 | 1 | 0 | 2 | | | | | | | |
| Verity,H | 40 | 44 | 12 | 669 | 66* | 20.90 | 0 | 3 | 4 | 30 | 11173 | 3510 | 144 | 24.37 | 5 | 2 | 8/43 |
| Vernon,GF | 1 | 2 | 1 | 14 | 11* | 14.00 | 0 | 0 | 0 | 0 | | | | | | | |
| Vine,J | 2 | 3 | 2 | 46 | 36 | 46.00 | 0 | 0 | 0 | 0 | | | | | | | |
| Voce,W | 27 | 38 | 15 | 308 | 66 | 13.39 | 0 | 1 | 6 | 15 | 6360 | 2733 | 98 | 27.88 | 3 | 2 | 7/70 |
| Waddington,A | 2 | 4 | 0 | 16 | 7 | 4.00 | 0 | 0 | 1 | 1 | 276 | 119 | 1 | 119.00 | 0 | 0 | 1/35 |
| Wainwright,E | 5 | 9 | 0 | 132 | 49 | 14.66 | 0 | 0 | 0 | 2 | 127 | 73 | 0 | - | 0 | 0 | 0/11 |
| Walker,PM | 3 | 4 | 0 | 128 | 52 | 32.00 | 0 | 1 | 0 | 5 | 78 | 34 | 0 | - | 0 | 0 | 0/8 |
| Walters,CF | 11 | 18 | 3 | 784 | 102 | 52.26 | 1 | 7 | 0 | 6 | | | | | | | |
| Ward,Alan | 5 | 6 | 1 | 40 | 21 | 8.00 | 0 | 0 | 4 | 3 | 761 | 453 | 14 | 32.35 | 0 | 0 | 4/61 |
| Ward,Albert | 7 | 13 | 0 | 487 | 117 | 37.46 | 1 | 3 | 1 | 1 | | | | | | | |
| Wardle,JH | 28 | 41 | 8 | 653 | 66 | 19.78 | 0 | 2 | 5 | 12 | 6597 | 2080 | 102 | 20.39 | 5 | 1 | 7/36 |
| Warner,PF | 15 | 28 | 2 | 622 | 132* | 23.92 | 1 | 3 | 4 | 3 | | | | | | | |
| Warr,JJ | 2 | 4 | 0 | 4 | 4 | 1.00 | 0 | 0 | 3 | 0 | 584 | 281 | 1 | 281.00 | 0 | 0 | 1/76 |
| Warren,A | 1 | 1 | 0 | 7 | 7 | 7.00 | 0 | 0 | 0 | 1 | 236 | 113 | 6 | 18.83 | 1 | 0 | 5/57 |
| Washbrook,C | 37 | 66 | 6 | 2569 | 195 | 42.81 | 6 | 12 | 2 | 12 | 36 | 33 | 1 | 33.00 | 0 | 0 | 1/25 |
| Watkin,SL | 3 | 5 | 0 | 25 | 13 | 5.00 | 0 | 0 | 1 | 1 | 534 | 305 | 11 | 27.72 | 0 | 0 | 4/65 |
| Watkins,AJ | 15 | 24 | 4 | 810 | 137* | 40.50 | 2 | 4 | 2 | 17 | 1364 | 554 | 11 | 50.36 | 0 | 0 | 3/20 |
| Watkinson,M | 4 | 6 | 1 | 167 | 82* | 33.40 | 0 | 1 | 1 | 1 | 672 | 348 | 10 | 34.80 | 0 | 0 | 3/64 |
| Watson,W | 23 | 37 | 3 | 879 | 116 | 25.85 | 2 | 3 | 3 | 8 | | | | | | | |
| Webbe,AJ | 1 | 2 | 0 | 4 | 4 | 2.00 | 0 | 0 | 1 | 2 | | | | | | | |
| Wellard,AW | 2 | 4 | 0 | 47 | 38 | 11.75 | 0 | 0 | 1 | 2 | 456 | 237 | 7 | 33.85 | 0 | 0 | 4/81 |
| Wells,AP | 1 | 2 | 1 | 3 | 3* | 3.00 | 0 | 0 | 0 | 0 | | | | | | | |
| Wharton,A | 1 | 2 | 0 | 20 | 13 | 10.00 | 0 | 0 | 0 | 0 | | | | | | | |
| Whitaker,JJ | 1 | 1 | 0 | 11 | 11 | 11.00 | 0 | 0 | 0 | 1 | | | | | | | |
| White,C | 8 | 12 | 0 | 166 | 51 | 13.83 | 0 | 1 | 2 | 3 | 811 | 452 | 11 | 41.09 | 0 | 0 | 3/18 |
| White,DW | 2 | 2 | 0 | 0 | 0 | 0.00 | 0 | 0 | 2 | 0 | 220 | 119 | 4 | 29.75 | 0 | 0 | 3/65 |
| White,JC | 15 | 22 | 9 | 239 | 29 | 18.38 | 0 | 0 | 1 | 6 | 4801 | 1581 | 49 | 32.26 | 3 | 1 | 8/126 |
| Whysall,WW | 4 | 7 | 0 | 209 | 76 | 29.85 | 0 | 2 | 0 | 7 | 16 | 9 | 0 | - | 0 | 0 | 0/9 |
| Wilkinson,LL | 3 | 2 | 1 | 3 | 2 | 3.00 | 0 | 0 | 0 | 0 | 573 | 271 | 7 | 38.71 | 0 | 0 | 2/12 |
| Willey,P | 26 | 50 | 6 | 1184 | 102* | 26.90 | 2 | 5 | 2 | 3 | 1091 | 456 | 7 | 65.14 | 0 | 0 | 2/73 |
| Williams,NF | 1 | 1 | 0 | 38 | 38 | 38.00 | 0 | 0 | 0 | 0 | 246 | 148 | 2 | 74.00 | 0 | 0 | 2/148 |
| Willis,RGD | 90 | 128 | 55 | 840 | 28* | 11.50 | 0 | 0 | 12 | 39 | 17357 | 8190 | 325 | 25.20 | 16 | 0 | 8/43 |
| Wilson,CEM | 2 | 4 | 1 | 42 | 18 | 14.00 | 0 | 0 | 0 | 0 | | | | | | | |
| Wilson,D | 6 | 7 | 1 | 75 | 42 | 12.50 | 0 | 0 | 0 | 1 | 1472 | 466 | 11 | 42.36 | 0 | 0 | 2/17 |
| Wilson,ER | 1 | 2 | 0 | 10 | 5 | 5.00 | 0 | 0 | 0 | 0 | 123 | 36 | 3 | 12.00 | 0 | 0 | 2/28 |
| Wood,A | 4 | 5 | 1 | 80 | 53 | 20.00 | 0 | 1 | 1 | 10/1 | | | | | | | |
| Wood,B | 12 | 21 | 0 | 454 | 90 | 21.61 | 0 | 2 | 1 | 6 | 98 | 50 | 0 | - | 0 | 0 | 0/2 |
| Wood,GEC | 3 | 2 | 0 | 7 | 6 | 3.50 | 0 | 0 | 0 | 5/1 | | | | | | | |
| Wood,H | 4 | 4 | 1 | 204 | 134* | 68.00 | 1 | 1 | 0 | 2/1 | | | | | | | |
| Wood,R | 1 | 2 | 0 | 6 | 6 | 3.00 | 0 | 0 | 1 | 0 | | | | | | | |
| Woods,SMJ | 3 | 4 | 0 | 122 | 53 | 30.50 | 0 | 1 | 0 | 4 | 195 | 129 | 5 | 25.80 | 0 | 0 | 3/28 |
| Woolley,FE | 64 | 98 | 7 | 3283 | 154 | 36.07 | 5 | 23 | 13 | 64 | 6495 | 2815 | 83 | 33.91 | 4 | 1 | 7/76 |
| Woolmer,RA | 19 | 34 | 2 | 1059 | 149 | 33.09 | 3 | 2 | 4 | 10 | 546 | 299 | 4 | 74.75 | 0 | 0 | 1/8 |
| Worthington,TS | 9 | 11 | 0 | 321 | 128 | 29.18 | 1 | 1 | 4 | 8 | 633 | 316 | 8 | 39.50 | 0 | 0 | 2/19 |
| Wright,CW | 3 | 4 | 0 | 125 | 71 | 31.25 | 0 | 1 | 0 | 0 | | | | | | | |
| Wright,DVP | 34 | 39 | 13 | 289 | 45 | 11.11 | 0 | 0 | 7 | 10 | 8135 | 4224 | 108 | 39.11 | 6 | 1 | 7/105 |
| Wyatt,RES | 40 | 64 | 6 | 1839 | 149 | 31.70 | 2 | 12 | 6 | 16 | 1395 | 642 | 18 | 35.66 | 0 | 0 | 3/4 |

| ENGLAND (cont.) | Tests | I | N | Runs | HS | Avge | 100 | 50 | 0's | c/s | Balls | Runs | Wks | Avge | 5w | 10w | BB |
|---|---|---|---|---|---|---|---|---|---|---|---|---|---|---|---|---|---|
| | | | | BATTING AND FIELDING | | | | | | | | | | BOWLING | | | |
| Wynward,EG | 3 | 6 | 0 | 72 | 30 | 12.00 | 0 | 0 | 2 | 0 | 24 | 17 | 0 | - | 0 | 0 | 0/2 |
| Yardley,NWD | 20 | 34 | 2 | 812 | 99 | 25.37 | 0 | 4 | 2 | 14 | 1662 | 707 | 21 | 33.66 | 0 | 0 | 3/67 |
| Young,HI | 2 | 2 | 0 | 43 | 43 | 21.50 | 0 | 0 | 1 | 1 | 556 | 262 | 12 | 21.83 | 0 | 0 | 4/30 |
| Young,JA | 8 | 10 | 5 | 28 | 10* | 5.60 | 0 | 0 | 3 | 5 | 2368 | 757 | 17 | 44.52 | 0 | 0 | 3/65 |
| Young,RA | 2 | 4 | 0 | 27 | 13 | 6.75 | 0 | 0 | 1 | 6/0 | | | | | | | |

| SOUTH AFRICA | Tests | I | N | Runs | HS | Avge | 100 | 50 | 0's | c/s | Balls | Runs | Wks | Avge | 5w | 10w | BB |
|---|---|---|---|---|---|---|---|---|---|---|---|---|---|---|---|---|---|
| | | | | BATTING AND FIELDING | | | | | | | | | | BOWLING | | | |
| Ackerman,HD | 4 | 8 | 0 | 161 | 59 | 20.12 | 0 | 1 | 0 | 2 | | | | | | | |
| Adams,PR | 19 | 26 | 6 | 100 | 29 | 5.00 | 0 | 0 | 6 | 13 | 4093 | 1834 | 59 | 31.08 | 1 | 0 | 6/55 |
| Adcock,NAT | 26 | 39 | 12 | 146 | 24 | 5.40 | 0 | 0 | 9 | 4 | 6391 | 2195 | 104 | 21.10 | 5 | 0 | 6/43 |
| Anderson,JH | 1 | 2 | 0 | 43 | 32 | 21.50 | 0 | 0 | 0 | 1 | | | | | | | |
| Ashley,WH | 1 | 2 | 0 | 1 | 1 | 0.50 | 0 | 0 | 1 | 0 | 173 | 95 | 7 | 13.57 | 1 | 0 | 7/95 |
| Bacher,A | 12 | 22 | 1 | 679 | 73 | 32.33 | 0 | 6 | 1 | 10 | | | | | | | |
| Bacher,AM | 16 | 28 | 1 | 776 | 96 | 28.74 | 0 | 5 | 3 | 10 | 6 | 4 | 0 | - | 0 | 0 | 0/4 |
| Balaskas,XC | 9 | 13 | 1 | 174 | 122* | 14.50 | 1 | 0 | 5 | 5 | 1572 | 806 | 22 | 36.63 | 1 | 0 | 5/49 |
| Barlow,EJ | 30 | 57 | 2 | 2516 | 201 | 45.74 | 6 | 15 | 3 | 35 | 3021 | 1362 | 40 | 34.05 | 1 | 0 | 5/85 |
| Baumgartner,HV | 1 | 2 | 0 | 19 | 16 | 9.50 | 0 | 0 | 0 | 1 | 166 | 99 | 2 | 49.50 | 0 | 0 | 2/99 |
| Beaumont,R | 5 | 9 | 0 | 70 | 31 | 7.77 | 0 | 0 | 2 | 2 | 6 | 0 | 0 | - | 0 | 0 | 0/0 |
| Begbie,DW | 5 | 7 | 0 | 138 | 48 | 19.71 | 0 | 0 | 0 | 2 | 160 | 130 | 1 | 130.00 | 0 | 0 | 1/38 |
| Bell,AJ | 16 | 23 | 12 | 69 | 26* | 6.27 | 0 | 0 | 6 | 6 | 3342 | 1567 | 48 | 32.64 | 4 | 0 | 6/99 |
| Bissett,GF | 4 | 4 | 2 | 38 | 23 | 19.00 | 0 | 0 | 0 | 0 | 989 | 469 | 25 | 18.76 | 2 | 0 | 7/29 |
| Bisset,M | 3 | 6 | 2 | 103 | 35 | 25.75 | 0 | 0 | 0 | 2/1 | | | | | | | |
| Blanckenberg,JM | 18 | 30 | 7 | 455 | 59 | 19.78 | 0 | 2 | 2 | 9 | 3888 | 1817 | 60 | 30.28 | 4 | 0 | 6/76 |
| Bland,KC | 21 | 39 | 5 | 1669 | 144* | 49.08 | 3 | 9 | 2 | 10 | 394 | 125 | 2 | 62.50 | 0 | 0 | 2/16 |
| Bock,EG | 1 | 2 | 2 | 11 | 9* | - | 0 | 0 | 0 | 0 | 138 | 91 | 0 | - | 0 | 0 | 0/42 |
| Bond,GE | 1 | 1 | 0 | 0 | 0 | 0.00 | 0 | 0 | 1 | 0 | 16 | 16 | 0 | - | 0 | 0 | 0/16 |
| Bosch,T | 1 | 2 | 2 | 5 | 5* | - | 0 | 0 | 0 | 0 | 297 | 104 | 3 | 34.66 | 0 | 0 | 2/61 |
| Botten,JT | 3 | 6 | 0 | 65 | 33 | 10.83 | 0 | 0 | 2 | 1 | 828 | 337 | 8 | 42.12 | 0 | 0 | 2/56 |
| Boucher,MV | 11 | 15 | 0 | 334 | 78 | 22.26 | 0 | 3 | 1 | 55/2 | | | | | | | |
| Brann,WH | 3 | 5 | 0 | 71 | 50 | 14.20 | 0 | 1 | 1 | 2 | | | | | | | |
| Briscoe,AW | 2 | 3 | 0 | 33 | 16 | 11.00 | 0 | 0 | 0 | 1 | | | | | | | |
| Bromfield,HD | 9 | 12 | 7 | 59 | 21 | 11.80 | 0 | 0 | 3 | 13 | 1810 | 599 | 17 | 35.23 | 1 | 0 | 5/88 |
| Brown,LS | 2 | 3 | 0 | 17 | 8 | 5.66 | 0 | 0 | 0 | 0 | 318 | 189 | 3 | 63.00 | 0 | 0 | 1/30 |
| Burger,CGD | 2 | 4 | 1 | 62 | 37* | 20.66 | 0 | 0 | 0 | 1 | | | | | | | |
| Burke,SF | 2 | 4 | 1 | 42 | 20 | 14.00 | 0 | 0 | 1 | 0 | 660 | 257 | 11 | 23.36 | 2 | 1 | 6/128 |
| Buys,ID | 1 | 2 | 1 | 4 | 4* | 4.00 | 0 | 0 | 1 | 0 | 144 | 52 | 0 | - | 0 | 0 | 0/20 |
| Cameron,HB | 26 | 45 | 4 | 1239 | 90 | 30.21 | 0 | 10 | 3 | 39/12 | | | | | | | |
| Campbell,T | 5 | 9 | 3 | 90 | 48 | 15.00 | 0 | 0 | 1 | 7/1 | | | | | | | |
| Carlstein,PR | 8 | 14 | 1 | 190 | 42 | 14.61 | 0 | 0 | 1 | 3 | | | | | | | |
| Carter,CP | 10 | 15 | 5 | 181 | 45 | 18.10 | 0 | 0 | 3 | 2 | 1475 | 694 | 28 | 24.78 | 2 | 0 | 6/50 |
| Catterall,RH | 24 | 43 | 2 | 1555 | 120 | 37.92 | 3 | 11 | 3 | 12 | 342 | 162 | 7 | 23.14 | 0 | 0 | 3/15 |
| Chapman,HW | 2 | 4 | 1 | 39 | 17 | 13.00 | 0 | 0 | 0 | 1 | 126 | 104 | 1 | 104.00 | 0 | 0 | 1/51 |
| Cheetham,JE | 24 | 43 | 6 | 883 | 89 | 23.86 | 0 | 5 | 1 | 13 | 6 | 2 | 0 | - | 0 | 0 | 0/2 |
| Chevalier,GA | 1 | 2 | 1 | 0 | 0* | 0.00 | 0 | 0 | 1 | 1 | 253 | 100 | 5 | 20.00 | 0 | 0 | 3/68 |
| Christy,JAJ | 10 | 18 | 0 | 618 | 103 | 34.33 | 1 | 5 | 1 | 3 | 138 | 92 | 2 | 46.00 | 0 | 0 | 1/15 |
| Chubb,GWA | 5 | 9 | 3 | 63 | 15* | 10.50 | 0 | 0 | 0 | 0 | 1425 | 577 | 21 | 27.47 | 2 | 0 | 6/51 |
| Cochran,JAK | 1 | 1 | 0 | 4 | 4 | 4.00 | 0 | 0 | 0 | 0 | 138 | 47 | 0 | - | 0 | 0 | 0/47 |
| Coen,SK | 2 | 4 | 2 | 101 | 41* | 50.50 | 0 | 0 | 0 | 1 | 12 | 7 | 0 | - | 0 | 0 | 0/7 |
| Commaille,JMM | 12 | 22 | 1 | 355 | 47 | 16.90 | 0 | 0 | 1 | 1 | | | | | | | |
| Commins,JB | 3 | 6 | 1 | 125 | 45 | 25.00 | 0 | 0 | 1 | 2 | | | | | | | |
| Conyngham,DP | 1 | 2 | 2 | 6 | 3* | 0 | 0 | 0 | 0 | 1 | 366 | 103 | 2 | 51.50 | 0 | 0 | 1/40 |
| Cook,FJ | 1 | 2 | 0 | 7 | 7 | 3.50 | 0 | 0 | 1 | 0 | | | | | | | |
| Cook,SJ | 3 | 6 | 0 | 107 | 43 | 17.83 | 0 | 0 | 1 | 0 | | | | | | | |
| Cooper,AHC | 1 | 2 | 0 | 6 | 6 | 3.00 | 0 | 0 | 1 | 1 | | | | | | | |
| Cox,JL | 3 | 6 | 1 | 17 | 12* | 3.40 | 0 | 0 | 3 | 1 | 576 | 245 | 4 | 61.25 | 0 | 0 | 2/74 |

| **SOUTH AFRICA** (cont.) | | | | **BATTING AND FIELDING** | | | | | | | | **BOWLING** | | | | | | |
|---|---|---|---|---|---|---|---|---|---|---|---|---|---|---|---|---|---|---|
| | Tests | I | N | Runs | HS | Avge | 100 | 50 | 0's | c/s | Balls | Runs | Wks | Avge | 5w | 10w | BB |
| Cripps,G | 1 | 2 | 0 | 21 | 18 | 10.50 | 0 | 0 | 0 | 0 | 15 | 23 | 0 | - | 0 | 0 | 0/23 |
| Crisp,RJ | 9 | 13 | 1 | 123 | 35 | 10.25 | 0 | 0 | 5 | 3 | 1428 | 747 | 20 | 37.35 | 1 | 0 | 5/99 |
| Cronje,WJ | 51 | 88 | 9 | 3079 | 135 | 38.97 | 6 | 18 | 7 | 18 | 2941 | 978 | 26 | 37.61 | 0 | 0 | 3/21 |
| Cullinan,DJ | 40 | 68 | 6 | 2403 | 153* | 38.75 | 5 | 15 | 8 | 14 | 18 | 4 | 0 | - | 0 | 0 | 0/1 |
| Curnow,SH | 7 | 14 | 0 | 168 | 47 | 12.00 | 0 | 0 | 0 | 5 | | | | | | | |
| Dalton,EL | 15 | 24 | 2 | 698 | 117 | 31.72 | 2 | 3 | 1 | 5 | 864 | 490 | 12 | 40.83 | 0 | 0 | 4/59 |
| Davies,EQ | 5 | 8 | 3 | 9 | 3 | 1.80 | 0 | 0 | 2 | 0 | 768 | 481 | 7 | 68.71 | 0 | 0 | 4/75 |
| Dawson,OC | 9 | 15 | 1 | 293 | 55 | 20.92 | 0 | 1 | 1 | 10 | 1294 | 578 | 10 | 57.80 | 0 | 0 | 2/57 |
| Deane,HG | 17 | 27 | 2 | 628 | 93 | 25.12 | 0 | 3 | 1 | 8 | | | | | | | |
| de Villiers,PS | 18 | 26 | 7 | 359 | 67* | 18.89 | 0 | 2 | 3 | 11 | 4805 | 2063 | 85 | 24.27 | 5 | 2 | 6/23 |
| Dixon,CD | 1 | 2 | 0 | 0 | 0 | 0.00 | 0 | 0 | 2 | 1 | 240 | 118 | 3 | 39.33 | 0 | 0 | 2/62 |
| Donald,AA | 47 | 63 | 24 | 427 | 33 | 10.94 | 0 | 0 | 10 | 12 | 11005 | 5232 | 237 | 22.07 | 15 | 2 | 8/71 |
| Dower,RR | 1 | 2 | 0 | 9 | 9 | 4.50 | 0 | 0 | 1 | 2 | | | | | | | |
| Draper,RG | 2 | 3 | 0 | 25 | 15 | 8.33 | 0 | 0 | 0 | 0 | | | | | | | |
| Duckworth,CAR | 2 | 4 | 0 | 28 | 13 | 7.00 | 0 | 0 | 0 | 3 | | | | | | | |
| Dumbrill,R | 5 | 10 | 0 | 153 | 36 | 15.30 | 0 | 0 | 0 | 3 | 816 | 336 | 9 | 37.33 | 0 | 0 | 4/30 |
| Duminy,JP | 3 | 6 | 0 | 30 | 12 | 5.00 | 0 | 0 | 1 | 2 | 60 | 39 | 1 | 39.00 | 0 | 0 | 1/17 |
| Dunell,OR | 2 | 4 | 1 | 42 | 26* | 14.00 | 0 | 0 | 1 | 1 | | | | | | | |
| Du Preez,JH | 2 | 2 | 0 | 0 | 0 | 0.00 | 0 | 0 | 2 | 2 | 144 | 51 | 3 | 17.00 | 0 | 0 | 2/22 |
| Du Toit,JF | 1 | 2 | 2 | 2 | 2* | 0 | 0 | 0 | 0 | 1 | 85 | 47 | 1 | 47.00 | 0 | 0 | 1/47 |
| Dyer,DV | 3 | 6 | 0 | 96 | 62 | 16.00 | 0 | 1 | 0 | 0 | | | | | | | |
| Eksteen,CE | 6 | 10 | 2 | 87 | 22 | 10.87 | 0 | 0 | 1 | 4 | 1458 | 447 | 8 | 55.87 | 0 | 0 | 3/12 |
| Elgie,MK | 3 | 6 | 0 | 75 | 56 | 12.50 | 0 | 1 | 2 | 4 | 66 | 46 | 0 | - | 0 | 0 | 0/18 |
| Elworthy,S | 1 | 2 | 0 | 58 | 48 | 29.00 | 0 | 0 | 0 | 0 | 186 | 79 | 1 | 79.00 | 0 | 0 | 1/41 |
| Endean,WR | 28 | 52 | 4 | 1630 | 162* | 33.95 | 3 | 8 | 3 | 41 | | | | | | | |
| Farrer,WS | 6 | 10 | 2 | 221 | 40 | 27.62 | 0 | 0 | 0 | 2 | 0 | | | | | | |
| Faulkner,GA | 25 | 47 | 4 | 1754 | 204 | 40.79 | 4 | 8 | 2 | 20 | 4227 | 2180 | 82 | 26.58 | 4 | 0 | 7/84 |
| Fellows-Smith,JP | 4 | 8 | 2 | 166 | 35 | 27.66 | 0 | 0 | 0 | 2 | 114 | 61 | 0 | - | 0 | 0 | 0/13 |
| Fichardt,CG | 2 | 4 | 0 | 15 | 10 | 3.75 | 0 | 0 | 1 | 2 | | | | | | | |
| Finlason,CE | 1 | 2 | 0 | 6 | 6 | 3.00 | 0 | 0 | 1 | 0 | 12 | 7 | 0 | - | 0 | 0 | 0/7 |
| Floquet,CE | 1 | 2 | 1 | 12 | 11* | 12.00 | 0 | 0 | 0 | 0 | 48 | 24 | 0 | - | 0 | 0 | 0/24 |
| Francis,HH | 2 | 4 | 0 | 39 | 29 | 9.75 | 0 | 0 | 0 | 1 | | | | | | | |
| Francois,CM | 5 | 9 | 1 | 252 | 72 | 31.50 | 0 | 1 | 0 | 5 | 684 | 225 | 6 | 37.50 | 0 | 0 | 3/23 |
| Frank,CN | 3 | 6 | 0 | 236 | 152 | 39.33 | 1 | 0 | 0 | 0 | | | | | | | |
| Frank,WHB | 1 | 2 | 0 | 7 | 5 | 3.50 | 0 | 0 | 0 | 0 | 58 | 52 | 1 | 52.00 | 0 | 0 | 1/52 |
| Fuller,ERH | 7 | 9 | 1 | 64 | 17 | 8.00 | 0 | 0 | 2 | 3 | 1898 | 668 | 22 | 30.36 | 1 | 0 | 5/66 |
| Fullerton,GM | 7 | 13 | 0 | 325 | 88 | 25.00 | 0 | 3 | 1 | 10/2 | | | | | | | |
| Funston,KJ | 18 | 33 | 1 | 824 | 92 | 25.75 | 0 | 5 | 2 | 7 | | | | | | | |
| Gamsy,D | 2 | 3 | 1 | 39 | 30* | 19.50 | 0 | 0 | 0 | 5/0 | | | | | | | |
| Gibbs,HH | 7 | 13 | 0 | 223 | 54 | 17.15 | 0 | 1 | 1 | 3 | | | | | | | |
| Gleeson,RA | 1 | 2 | 1 | 4 | 3 | 4.00 | 0 | 0 | 0 | 2 | | | | | | | |
| Glover,GK | 1 | 2 | 1 | 21 | 18* | 21.00 | 0 | 0 | 0 | 0 | 65 | 28 | 1 | 28.00 | 0 | 0 | 1/28 |
| Goddard,TL | 41 | 78 | 5 | 2516 | 112 | 34.46 | 1 | 18 | 4 | 48 | 11736 | 3226 | 123 | 26.22 | 5 | 0 | 6/53 |
| Gordon,N | 5 | 6 | 2 | 8 | 7* | 2.00 | 0 | 0 | 3 | 1 | 1966 | 807 | 20 | 40.35 | 2 | 0 | 5/103 |
| Graham,R | 2 | 4 | 0 | 6 | 4 | 1.50 | 0 | 0 | 2 | 2 | 240 | 127 | 3 | 42.33 | 0 | 0 | 2/22 |
| Grieveson,RE | 2 | 2 | 0 | 114 | 75 | 57.00 | 0 | 1 | 0 | 7/3 | | | | | | | |
| Griffin,GM | 2 | 4 | 0 | 25 | 14 | 6.25 | 0 | 0 | 1 | 0 | 432 | 192 | 8 | 24.00 | 0 | 0 | 4/87 |
| Hall,AE | 7 | 8 | 2 | 11 | 5 | 1.83 | 0 | 0 | 4 | 4 | 2361 | 886 | 40 | 22.15 | 3 | 1 | 7/63 |
| Hall,GG | 1 | 1 | 0 | 0 | 0 | 0.00 | 0 | 0 | 1 | 0 | 186 | 94 | 1 | 94.00 | 0 | 0 | 1/94 |
| Halliwell,EA | 8 | 15 | 0 | 188 | 57 | 12.53 | 0 | 1 | 3 | 9/2 | | | | | | | |
| Halse,CG | 3 | 3 | 3 | 30 | 19* | 0 | 0 | 0 | 0 | 1 | 587 | 260 | 6 | 43.33 | 0 | 0 | 3/50 |
| Hands,PAM | 7 | 12 | 0 | 300 | 83 | 25.00 | 0 | 2 | 2 | 3 | 37 | 18 | 0 | - | 0 | 0 | 0/1 |
| Hands,RHM | 1 | 2 | 0 | 7 | 7 | 3.50 | 0 | 0 | 1 | 0 | | | | | | | |
| Hanley,MA | 1 | 1 | 0 | 0 | 0 | 0.00 | 0 | 0 | 1 | 0 | 232 | 88 | 1 | 88.00 | 0 | 0 | 1/57 |
| Harris,TA | 3 | 5 | 1 | 100 | 60 | 25.00 | 0 | 1 | 0 | 1 | | | | | | | |
| Hartigan,GPD | 5 | 10 | 0 | 114 | 51 | 11.40 | 0 | 1 | 3 | 0 | 252 | 141 | 1 | 141.00 | 0 | 0 | 1/72 |
| Harvey,RL | 2 | 4 | 0 | 51 | 28 | 12.75 | 0 | 0 | 0 | 0 | | | | | | | |
| Hathorn,CMH | 12 | 20 | 1 | 325 | 102 | 17.10 | 1 | 0 | 1 | 5 | | | | | | | |

| **SOUTH AFRICA** (cont.) | | | | **BATTING AND FIELDING** | | | | | | | | | | **BOWLING** | | | |
|---|---|---|---|---|---|---|---|---|---|---|---|---|---|---|---|---|---|
| | Tests | I | N | Runs | HS | Avge | 100 | 50 | 0's | c/s | Balls | Runs | Wks | Avge | 5w | 10w | BB |
| Hearne,F | 4 | 8 | | 0 | | 121 | 30 | | | 15.12 | 0 | 0 | 2 | 2 | | | 62 |
| 40 2 | 20.00 | 0 | | 0 | | 2/40 | | | | | | | | | | | |
| Hearne,GAL | 3 | 5 | 0 | 59 | 28 | 11.80 | 0 | 0 | 2 | 3 | | | | | | | |
| Heine,PS | 14 | 24 | 3 | 209 | 31 | 9.95 | 0 | 0 | 3 | 8 | 3890 | 1455 | 58 | 25.08 | 4 | 0 | 6/58 |
| Henry,O | 3 | 3 | 0 | 53 | 34 | 17.66 | 0 | 0 | 0 | 2 | 427 | 189 | 3 | 63.00 | 0 | 0 | 2/56 |
| Hime,CFW | 1 | 2 | 0 | 8 | 8 | 4.00 | 0 | 0 | 1 | 0 | 55 | 31 | 1 | 31.00 | 0 | 0 | 1/20 |
| Hudson,AC | 35 | 63 | 3 | 2007 | 163 | 33.45 | 4 | 13 | 7 | 35 | | | | | | | |
| Hutchinson,P | 2 | 4 | 0 | 14 | 11 | 3.50 | 0 | 0 | 2 | 3 | | | | | | | |
| Ironside,DEJ | 3 | 4 | 2 | 37 | 13 | 18.50 | 0 | 0 | 0 | 1 | 985 | 275 | 15 | 18.33 | 1 | 0 | 5/51 |
| Irvine,BL | 4 | 7 | 0 | 353 | 102 | 50.42 | 1 | 2 | 0 | 2 | | | | | | | |
| Jack,SD | 2 | 2 | 0 | 7 | 7 | 3.50 | 0 | 0 | 1 | 1 | 462 | 196 | 8 | 24.50 | 0 | 0 | 4/69 |
| Johnson,CL | 1 | 2 | 0 | 10 | 7 | 5.00 | 0 | 0 | 0 | 1 | 140 | 57 | 0 | - | 0 | 0 | 0/57 |
| Kallis,JH | 19 | 30 | 1 | 842 | 132 | 29.03 | 2 | 3 | 2 | 16 | 2187 | 804 | 24 | 33.50 | 0 | 0 | 4/24 |
| Keith,HJ | 8 | 16 | 1 | 318 | 73 | 21.20 | 0 | 2 | 3 | 9 | 108 | 63 | 0 | - | 0 | 0 | 0/19 |
| Kempis,GA | 1 | 2 | 1 | 0 | 0* | 0.00 | 0 | 0 | 1 | 0 | 168 | 76 | 4 | 19.00 | 0 | 0 | 3/53 |
| Kirsten,G | 45 | 81 | 7 | 2895 | 210 | 39.12 | 7 | 15 | 6 | 37 | 325 | 135 | 2 | 67.5 | 0 | 0 | 1/0 |
| Kirsten,PN | 12 | 22 | 2 | 626 | 104 | 31.30 | 1 | 4 | 2 | 8 | 54 | 30 | 0 | - | 0 | 0 | 0/5 |
| Klusener,L | 16 | 25 | 5 | 573 | 102* | 28.65 | 1 | 2 | 2 | 10 | 2803 | 1397 | 42 | 33.26 | 1 | 0 | 8/64 |
| Kotze,JJ | 3 | 5 | 0 | 2 | 2 | 0.40 | 0 | 0 | 4 | 3 | 413 | 243 | 6 | 40.50 | 0 | 0 | 3/64 |
| Kuiper,AP | 1 | 2 | 0 | 34 | 34 | 17.00 | 0 | 0 | 1 | 1 | | | | | | | |
| Kuys,F | 1 | 2 | 0 | 26 | 26 | 13.00 | 0 | 0 | 1 | 0 | 60 | 31 | 2 | 15.50 | 0 | 0 | 2/31 |
| Lance,HR | 13 | 22 | 1 | 591 | 70 | 28.14 | 0 | 5 | 1 | 7 | 948 | 479 | 12 | 39.91 | 0 | 0 | 3/30 |
| Langton,ABC | 15 | 23 | 4 | 298 | 73* | 15.68 | 0 | 2 | 5 | 8 | 4199 | 1827 | 40 | 45.67 | 1 | 0 | 5/58 |
| Lawrence,GB | 5 | 8 | 0 | 141 | 43 | 17.62 | 0 | 0 | 2 | 2 | 1334 | 512 | 28 | 18.28 | 2 | 0 | 8/53 |
| Le Roux,FL | 1 | 2 | 0 | 1 | 1 | 0.50 | 0 | 0 | 1 | 0 | 54 | 24 | 0 | - | 0 | 0 | 0/5 |
| Lewis,PT | 1 | 2 | 0 | 0 | 0 | 0.00 | 0 | 0 | 2 | 0 | | | | | | | |
| Liebenberg,GFJ | 5 | 8 | 0 | 104 | 45 | 13.00 | 0 | 0 | 2 | 1 | | | | | | | |
| Lindsay,DT | 19 | 31 | 1 | 1130 | 182 | 37.66 | 3 | 5 | 2 | 57/2 | | | | | | | |
| Lindsay,JD | 3 | 5 | 2 | 21 | 9* | 7.00 | 0 | 0 | 2 | 4/1 | | | | | | | |
| Lindsay,NV | 1 | 2 | 0 | 35 | 29 | 17.50 | 0 | 0 | 0 | 1 | | | | | | | |
| Ling,WVS | 6 | 10 | 0 | 168 | 38 | 16.80 | 0 | 0 | 3 | 1 | 18 | 20 | 0 | - | 0 | 0 | 0/20 |
| Llewellyn,CB | 15 | 28 | 1 | 544 | 90 | 20.14 | 0 | 4 | 6 | 7 | 2292 | 1421 | 48 | 29.60 | 4 | 1 | 6/92 |
| Lundie,EB | 1 | 2 | 1 | 1 | 1 | 1.00 | 0 | 0 | 0 | 0 | 286 | 107 | 4 | 26.75 | 0 | 0 | 4/101 |
| Macaulay,MJ | 1 | 2 | 0 | 33 | 21 | 16.50 | 0 | 0 | 0 | 0 | 276 | 73 | 2 | 36.50 | 0 | 0 | 1/10 |
| McCarthy,CN | 15 | 24 | 15 | 28 | 5 | 3.11 | 0 | 0 | 6 | 6 | 3499 | 1510 | 36 | 41.94 | 2 | 0 | 6/43 |
| McGlew,DJ | 34 | 64 | 6 | 2440 | 255* | 42.06 | 7 | 10 | 4 | 18 | 32 | 23 | 0 | - | 0 | 0 | 0/7 |
| McKinnon,AH | 8 | 13 | 7 | 107 | 27 | 17.83 | 0 | 0 | 0 | 1 | 2546 | 925 | 26 | 35.57 | 0 | 0 | 4/128 |
| McLean,RA | 40 | 73 | 3 | 2120 | 142 | 30.28 | 5 | 10 | 11 | 23 | 4 | 1 | 0 | - | 0 | 0 | 0/1 |
| McMillan,BM | 38 | 62 | 12 | 1978 | 113 | 39.56 | 3 | 13 | 2 | 49 | 6048 | 2537 | 75 | 33.82 | 0 | 0 | 4/65 |
| McMillan,Q | 13 | 21 | 4 | 306 | 50* | 18.00 | 0 | 1 | 4 | 8 | 2021 | 1243 | 36 | 34.52 | 2 | 0 | 5/66 |
| Mann,NBF | 19 | 31 | 1 | 400 | 52 | 13.33 | 0 | 1 | 4 | 3 | 5796 | 1920 | 58 | 33.10 | 1 | 0 | 6/59 |
| Mansell,PNF | 13 | 22 | 2 | 355 | 90 | 17.75 | 0 | 2 | 3 | 15 | 1506 | 736 | 11 | 66.90 | 0 | 0 | 3/58 |
| Markham,LA | 1 | 1 | 0 | 20 | 20 | 20.00 | 0 | 0 | 0 | 0 | 104 | 72 | 1 | 72.00 | 0 | 0 | 1/34 |
| Marx,WFE | 3 | 6 | 0 | 125 | 36 | 20.83 | 0 | 0 | 1 | 0 | 228 | 144 | 4 | 36.00 | 0 | 0 | 3/85 |
| Matthews,CR | 18 | 25 | 6 | 348 | 62* | 18.31 | 0 | 1 | 4 | 4 | 3932 | 1502 | 52 | 28.88 | 2 | 0 | 5/42 |
| Meintjes,DJ | 2 | 3 | 0 | 43 | 21 | 14.33 | 0 | 0 | 0 | 3 | 246 | 115 | 6 | 19.16 | 0 | 0 | 3/38 |
| Melle,MG | 7 | 12 | 4 | 68 | 17 | 8.50 | 0 | 0 | 1 | 4 | 1667 | 851 | 26 | 32.73 | 2 | 0 | 6/71 |
| Melville,A | 11 | 19 | 2 | 894 | 189 | 52.58 | 4 | 3 | 2 | 8 | | | | | | | |
| Middleton,J | 6 | 12 | 5 | 52 | 22 | 7.42 | 0 | 0 | 2 | 1 | 1064 | 442 | 24 | 18.41 | 2 | 0 | 5/51 |
| Mills,C | 1 | 2 | 0 | 25 | 21 | 12.50 | 0 | 0 | 0 | 2 | 140 | 83 | 2 | 41.50 | 0 | 0 | 2/83 |
| Milton,WH | 3 | 6 | 0 | 68 | 21 | 11.33 | 0 | 0 | 0 | 1 | 79 | 48 | 2 | 24.00 | 0 | 0 | 1/5 |
| Mitchell,B | 42 | 80 | 9 | 3471 | 189* | 48.88 | 8 | 21 | 3 | 56 | 2519 | 1380 | 27 | 51.11 | 1 | 0 | 5/87 |
| Mitchell,F | 3 | 6 | 0 | 28 | 12 | 4.66 | 0 | 0 | 1 | 0 | | | | | | | |
| Morkel,DPB | 16 | 28 | 1 | 663 | 88 | 24.55 | 0 | 4 | 3 | 13 | 1704 | 821 | 18 | 45.61 | 0 | 0 | 4/93 |
| Murray,ARA | 10 | 14 | 1 | 289 | 109 | 22.23 | 1 | 1 | 1 | 3 | 2374 | 710 | 18 | 39.44 | 0 | 0 | 4/169 |
| Nel,JD | 6 | 11 | 0 | 150 | 38 | 13.63 | 0 | 0 | 1 | 1 | | | | | | | |
| Newberry,C | 4 | 8 | 0 | 62 | 16 | 7.75 | 0 | 0 | 1 | 3 | 558 | 268 | 11 | 24.36 | 0 | 0 | 4/72 |
| Newson,ES | 3 | 5 | 1 | 30 | 16 | 7.50 | 0 | 0 | 0 | 3 | 874 | 265 | 4 | 66.25 | 0 | 0 | 2/58 |

| **SOUTH AFRICA** (cont.) | | | | **BATTING AND FIELDING** | | | | | | | | | | **BOWLING** | | | |
|---|---|---|---|---|---|---|---|---|---|---|---|---|---|---|---|---|---|
| | Tests | I | N | Runs | HS | Avge | 100 | 50 | 0's | c/s | Balls | Runs | Wks | Avge | 5w | 10w | BB |
| Nicholson,F | 4 | 8 | 1 | 76 | 29 | 10.85 | 0 | 0 | 4 | 3/0 | | | | | | | |
| Nicolson,JFW | 3 | 5 | 0 | 179 | 78 | 35.80 | 0 | 1 | 0 | 0 | 24 | 17 | 0 | - | 0 | 0 | 0/5 |
| Norton,NO | 1 | 2 | 0 | 9 | 7 | 4.50 | 0 | 0 | 0 | 0 | 90 | 47 | 4 | 11.75 | 0 | 0 | 4/47 |
| Nourse,AD | 34 | 62 | 7 | 2960 | 231 | 53.81 | 9 | 14 | 3 | 12 | 20 | 9 | 0 | - | 0 | 0 | 0/0 |
| Nourse,AW | 45 | 83 | 8 | 2234 | 111 | 29.78 | 1 | 15 | 3 | 43 | 3234 | 1553 | 41 | 37.87 | 0 | 0 | 4/25 |
| Ntini,M | 4 | 5 | 4 | 9 | 4* | 9.00 | 0 | 0 | 1 | 1 | 752 | 358 | 10 | 35.80 | 0 | 0 | 4/72 |
| Nupen,EP | 17 | 31 | 7 | 348 | 69 | 14.50 | 0 | 2 | 5 | 9 | 4159 | 1788 | 50 | 35.76 | 5 | 1 | 6/46 |
| Osche,AE | 2 | 4 | 0 | 16 | 8 | 4.00 | 0 | 0 | 0 | 0 | | | | | | | |
| Osche,AL | 3 | 4 | 1 | 11 | 4* | 3.66 | 0 | 0 | 0 | 1 | 649 | 362 | 10 | 36.20 | 0 | 0 | 4/79 |
| O'Linn,S | 7 | 12 | 1 | 297 | 98 | 27.00 | 0 | 2 | 0 | 4 | | | | | | | |
| Owen-Smith,HG | 5 | 8 | 2 | 252 | 129 | 42.00 | 1 | 1 | 0 | 4 | 156 | 113 | 0 | - | 0 | 0 | 0/3 |
| Palm,AW | 1 | 2 | 0 | 15 | 13 | 7.50 | 0 | 0 | 0 | 1 | | | | | | | |
| Parker,GM | 2 | 4 | 2 | 3 | 2* | 1.50 | 0 | 0 | 2 | 0 | 366 | 273 | 8 | 34.12 | 1 | 0 | 6/152 |
| Parkin,DC | 1 | 2 | 0 | 6 | 6 | 3.00 | 0 | 0 | 1 | 1 | 130 | 82 | 3 | 270.33 | 0 | 0 | 3/82 |
| Partridge,JT | 11 | 12 | 5 | 73 | 13* | 10.42 | 0 | 0 | 0 | 6 | 3684 | 1373 | 44 | 31.20 | 3 | 0 | 7/91 |
| Pearse,COC | 3 | 6 | 0 | 55 | 31 | 9.16 | 0 | 0 | 2 | 1 | 144 | 106 | 3 | 35.33 | 0 | 0 | 3/56 |
| Pegler,SJ | 16 | 28 | 5 | 356 | 35* | 15.47 | 0 | 0 | 6 | 5 | 2989 | 1572 | 47 | 33.44 | 2 | 0 | 7/65 |
| Pithey,AJ | 17 | 27 | 1 | 819 | 154 | 31.50 | 1 | 4 | 2 | 3 | 12 | 5 | 0 | - | 0 | 0 | 0/5 |
| Pithey,DB | 8 | 12 | 1 | 138 | 55 | 12.54 | 0 | 1 | 1 | 6 | 1424 | 577 | 12 | 48.08 | 1 | 0 | 6/58 |
| Plimsoll,JB | 1 | 2 | 1 | 16 | 8* | 16.00 | 0 | 0 | 0 | 0 | 237 | 143 | 3 | 47.66 | 0 | 0 | 3/128 |
| Pollock,PM | 28 | 41 | 13 | 607 | 75* | 21.67 | 0 | 2 | 3 | 9 | 6522 | 2806 | 116 | 24.18 | 9 | 1 | 6/38 |
| Pollock,RG | 23 | 41 | 4 | 2256 | 274 | 60.97 | 7 | 11 | 1 | 17 | 414 | 204 | 4 | 51.00 | 0 | 0 | 2/50 |
| Pollock,SM | 25 | 39 | 8 | 995 | 92 | 32.09 | 0 | 5 | 2 | 10 | 556 | 2175 | 91 | 23.90 | 5 | 0 | 7.78 |
| Poore,RM | 3 | 6 | 0 | 76 | 20 | 12.66 | 0 | 0 | 0 | 3 | 9 | 4 | 1 | 4.00 | 0 | 0 | 1/4 |
| Pothecary,JE | 3 | 4 | 0 | 26 | 12 | 6.50 | 0 | 0 | 0 | 2 | 828 | 354 | 9 | 39.33 | 0 | 0 | 4/58 |
| Powell,AW | 1 | 2 | 0 | 16 | 11 | 8.00 | 0 | 0 | 0 | 2 | 20 | 10 | 1 | 10.00 | 0 | 0 | 1/10 |
| Prince,CFH | 1 | 2 | 0 | 6 | 5 | 3.00 | 0 | 0 | 0 | 0 | | | | | | | |
| Pringle,MW | 4 | 6 | 2 | 67 | 33 | 16.75 | 0 | 0 | 1 | 0 | 652 | 270 | 5 | 54.00 | 0 | 0 | 2/62 |
| Procter,MJ | 7 | 10 | 1 | 226 | 48 | 25.11 | 0 | 0 | 1 | 4 | 1514 | 616 | 41 | 15.02 | 1 | 0 | 6/73 |
| Promnitz,HLE | 2 | 4 | 0 | 14 | 5 | 3.50 | 0 | 0 | 0 | 2 | 528 | 161 | 8 | 20.12 | 1 | 0 | 5/58 |
| Quinn,NA | 12 | 18 | 3 | 90 | 28 | 6.00 | 0 | 0 | 1 | 1 | 2922 | 1145 | 35 | 32.71 | 1 | 0 | 6/92 |
| Reid,N | 1 | 2 | 0 | 17 | 11 | 8.50 | 0 | 0 | 0 | 0 | 126 | 63 | 2 | 31.50 | 0 | 0 | 2/63 |
| Rhodes,JN | 36 | 57 | 3 | 1670 | 117 | 30.92 | 2 | 9 | 4 | 17 | 12 | 5 | 0 | - | 0 | 0 | 0/0 |
| Richards,AR | 1 | 2 | 0 | 6 | 6 | 3.00 | 0 | 0 | 1 | 0 | | | | | | | |
| Richards,BA | 4 | 7 | 0 | 508 | 140 | 72.57 | 2 | 2 | 0 | 3 | 72 | 26 | 1 | 26.00 | 0 | 0 | 1/12 |
| Richards,WHM | 1 | 2 | 0 | 4 | 4 | 2.00 | 0 | 0 | 1 | 0 | | | | | | | |
| Richardson,DJ | 42 | 64 | 7 | 1359 | 109 | 23.84 | 1 | 9 | 8 | 150/2 | | | | | | | |
| Robertson,JB | 3 | 6 | 1 | 51 | 17 | 10.20 | 0 | 0 | 0 | 2 | 738 | 321 | 6 | 53.50 | 0 | 0 | 3/143 |
| Rose-Innes,A | 2 | 4 | 0 | 14 | 13 | 3.50 | 0 | 0 | 2 | 2 | 128 | 89 | 5 | 17.80 | 1 | 0 | 5/43 |
| Routledge,TW | 4 | 8 | 0 | 72 | 24 | 9.00 | 0 | 0 | 1 | 2 | | | | | | | |
| Rowan,AMB | 15 | 23 | 6 | 290 | 41 | 17.05 | 0 | 0 | 3 | 7 | 5193 | 2084 | 54 | 38.59 | 4 | 0 | 5/68 |
| Rowan,EAB | 26 | 50 | 5 | 1965 | 236 | 43.66 | 3 | 12 | 4 | 14 | 19 | 7 | 0 | - | 0 | 0 | 0/0 |
| Rowe,GA | 5 | 9 | 3 | 26 | 13* | 4.33 | 0 | 0 | 3 | 4 | 998 | 456 | 15 | 30.40 | 1 | 0 | 5/115 |
| Rushmere,MW | 1 | 2 | 0 | 6 | 3 | 3.00 | 0 | 0 | 0 | 0 | | | | | | | |
| Samuelson,SV | 1 | 2 | 0 | 22 | 15 | 11.00 | 0 | 0 | 0 | 1 | 108 | 64 | 0 | - | 0 | 0 | 0/64 |
| Schultz,BN | 9 | 8 | 2 | 9 | 6 | 1.50 | 0 | 0 | 3 | 2 | 1733 | 749 | 37 | 20.24 | 2 | 0 | 5/48 |
| Schwarz,RO | 20 | 35 | 8 | 374 | 61 | 13.85 | 0 | 1 | 6 | 18 | 2639 | 1417 | 55 | 25.76 | 2 | 0 | 6/47 |
| Seccull,AW | 1 | 2 | 1 | 23 | 17* | 23.00 | 0 | 0 | 0 | 1 | 60 | 37 | 2 | 18.50 | 0 | 0 | 2/37 |
| Seymour,MA | 7 | 10 | 3 | 84 | 36 | 12.00 | 0 | 0 | 3 | 2 | 1458 | 588 | 9 | 65.33 | 0 | 0 | 3/80 |
| Shalders,WA | 12 | 23 | 1 | 355 | 42 | 16.13 | 0 | 0 | 4 | 3 | 48 | 6 | 1 | 6.00 | 0 | 0 | 1/6 |
| Shepstone,GH | 2 | 4 | 0 | 38 | 21 | 9.50 | 0 | 0 | 1 | 2 | 115 | 47 | 0 | - | 0 | 0 | 0/8 |
| Sherwell,PW | 13 | 22 | 4 | 427 | 115 | 23.72 | 1 | 1 | 1 | 20/16 | | | | | | | |
| Siedle,IJ | 18 | 34 | 0 | 977 | 141 | 28.73 | 1 | 5 | 3 | 7 | 19 | 7 | 1 | 7.00 | 0 | 0 | 1/7 |
| Sinclair,JH | 25 | 47 | 1 | 1069 | 106 | 23.23 | 3 | 3 | 7 | 9 | 3598 | 1996 | 63 | 31.68 | 1 | 0 | 6/26 |
| Smith,CJE | 3 | 6 | 1 | 106 | 45 | 21.20 | 0 | 0 | 0 | 2 | | | | | | | |
| Smith,FW | 3 | 6 | 1 | 45 | 12 | 9.00 | 0 | 0 | 1 | 2 | | | | | | | |
| Smith,VI | 9 | 16 | 6 | 39 | 11* | 3.90 | 0 | 0 | 4 | 3 | 1655 | 769 | 12 | 64.08 | 0 | 0 | 4/143 |

| **SOUTH AFRICA** (cont.) | | | | **BATTING AND FIELDING** | | | | | | | | **BOWLING** | | | | | |
|---|---|---|---|---|---|---|---|---|---|---|---|---|---|---|---|---|---|
| | Tests | I | N | Runs | HS | Avge | 100 | 50 | 0's | c/s | Balls | Runs | Wks | Avge | 5w | 10w | BB |
| Snell,RP | 5 | 8 | 1 | 95 | 48 | 13.57 | 0 | 0 | 1 | 1 | 1025 | 538 | 19 | 28.31 | 0 | 0 | 4/74 |
| Snooke,SD | 1 | 1 | 0 | 0 | 0 | 0.00 | 0 | 0 | 1 | 2 | | | | | | | |
| Snooke,SJ | 26 | 46 | 1 | 1008 | 103 | 22.40 | 1 | 5 | 1 | 24 | 1620 | 702 | 35 | 20.05 | 1 | 1 | 8/70 |
| Solomon,WRT | 1 | 2 | 0 | 4 | 2 | 2.00 | 0 | 0 | 0 | 1 | | | | | | | |
| Stewart,RB | 1 | 2 | 0 | 13 | 9 | 6.50 | 0 | 0 | 0 | 2 | | | | | | | |
| Steyn,PJR | 3 | 6 | 0 | 127 | 46 | 21.16 | 0 | 0 | 0 | 0 | | | | | | | |
| Stricker,LA | 13 | 24 | 0 | 342 | 48 | 14.25 | 0 | 0 | 5 | 3 | 174 | 105 | 1 | 105.00 | 0 | 0 | 1/36 |
| Susskind,MJ | 5 | 8 | 0 | 268 | 65 | 33.50 | 0 | 4 | 0 | 1 | | | | | | | |
| Symcox,PL | 17 | 23 | 1 | 652 | 108 | 29.63 | 1 | 4 | 1 | 5 | 3207 | 1454 | 34 | 42.76 | 0 | 0 | 4/69 |
| Taberer,HM | 1 | 1 | 0 | 2 | 2 | 2.00 | 0 | 0 | 0 | 0 | 60 | 47 | 1 | 48.00 | 0 | 0 | 1/25 |
| Tancred,AB | 2 | 4 | 1 | 87 | 29 | 29.00 | 0 | 0 | 0 | 2 | | | | | | | |
| Tancred,LJ | 14 | 26 | 1 | 530 | 97 | 21.20 | 0 | 2 | 5 | 3 | | | | | | | |
| Tancred,VM | 1 | 2 | 0 | 25 | 18 | 12.50 | 0 | 0 | 0 | 0 | | | | | | | |
| Tapscott,GL | 1 | 2 | 0 | 5 | 4 | 2.50 | 0 | 0 | 0 | 1 | | | | | | | |
| Tapscott,LE | 2 | 3 | 1 | 58 | 50* | 29.00 | 0 | 1 | 0 | 0 | 12 | 2 | 0 | - | 0 | 0 | 0/2 |
| Tayfield,HJ | 37 | 60 | 9 | 862 | 75 | 16.90 | 0 | 2 | 5 | 26 | 13568 | 4405 | 170 | 25.91 | 14 | 2 | 9/113 |
| Taylor,AI | 1 | 2 | 0 | 18 | 12 | 9.00 | 0 | 0 | 0 | 0 | | | | | | | |
| Taylor,D | 2 | 4 | 0 | 85 | 36 | 21.25 | 0 | 0 | 0 | 0 | | | | | | | |
| Taylor,HW | 42 | 76 | 4 | 2936 | 176 | 40.77 | 7 | 17 | 2 | 19 | 342 | 156 | 5 | 31.20 | 0 | 0 | 3/15 |
| Theunissen,NH | 1 | 2 | 1 | 2 | 2* | 2.00 | 0 | 0 | 1 | 0 | 80 | 51 | 0 | - | 0 | 0 | 0/51 |
| Thornton,PG | 1 | 1 | 1 | 1 | 1* | 0 | 0 | 0 | 0 | 1 | 24 | 20 | 1 | 20.00 | 0 | 0 | 1/20 |
| Tomlinson,DS | 1 | 1 | 0 | 9 | 9 | 9.00 | 0 | 0 | 0 | 0 | 60 | 38 | 0 | - | 0 | 0 | 0/38 |
| Traicos,AJ | 3 | 4 | 2 | 8 | 5* | 4.00 | 0 | 0 | 1 | 4 | 470 | 207 | 4 | 51.75 | 0 | 0 | 2/70 |
| Trimborn,PHJ | 4 | 4 | 2 | 13 | 11* | 6.50 | 0 | 0 | 1 | 7 | 747 | 257 | 11 | 23.36 | 0 | 0 | 3/12 |
| Tuckett,L | 9 | 14 | 3 | 131 | 40* | 11.90 | 0 | 0 | 3 | 9 | 2104 | 980 | 19 | 51.57 | 2 | 0 | 5/68 |
| Tuckett,LR | 1 | 2 | 1 | 0 | 0* | 0.00 | 0 | 0 | 1 | 2 | 120 | 69 | 0 | - | 0 | 0 | 0/24 |
| Twentyman-Jones,PS | 1 | 2 | 0 | 0 | 0 | 0.00 | 0 | 0 | 2 | 0 | | | | | | | |
| Van der Bijl,PGV | 5 | 9 | 0 | 460 | 125 | 41.11 | 1 | 2 | 0 | 1 | | | | | | | |
| Van der Merwe,EA | 2 | 4 | 1 | 27 | 19 | 9.00 | 0 | 0 | 1 | 3/0 | | | | | | | |
| Van der Merwe,PL | 15 | 23 | 2 | 533 | 76 | 25.38 | 0 | 3 | 3 | 11 | 79 | 22 | 1 | 22.00 | 0 | 0 | 1/6 |
| Van Ryneveld,CB | 19 | 33 | 6 | 724 | 83 | 26.81 | 0 | 3 | 2 | 14 | 1554 | 671 | 17 | 39.47 | 0 | 0 | 4/67 |
| Varnals,GD | 3 | 6 | 0 | 97 | 23 | 16.16 | 0 | 0 | 0 | 0 | 12 | 2 | 0 | - | 0 | 0 | 0/2 |
| Viljoen,KG | 27 | 50 | 2 | 1365 | 124 | 28.43 | 2 | 9 | 5 | 5 | 48 | 23 | 0 | - | 0 | 0 | 0/10 |
| Vincent,CL | 25 | 38 | 12 | 526 | 60 | 20.23 | 0 | 2 | 4 | 27 | 5851 | 2631 | 84 | 31.32 | 3 | 0 | 6/51 |
| Vintcent,CH | 3 | 6 | 0 | 26 | 9 | 4.33 | 0 | 0 | 1 | 1 | 369 | 193 | 4 | 48.25 | 0 | 0 | 3/8 |
| Vogler,AEE | 15 | 26 | 6 | 340 | 65 | 17.00 | 0 | 2 | 4 | 20 | 2764 | 1455 | 64 | 22.73 | 5 | 1 | 7/94 |
| Wade,HF | 10 | 18 | 2 | 327 | 40* | 20.43 | 0 | 0 | 4 | 4 | | | | | | | |
| Wade,WW | 11 | 19 | 1 | 511 | 125 | 28.38 | 1 | 3 | 3 | 15/2 | | | | | | | |
| Waite,JHB | 50 | 86 | 7 | 2405 | 134 | 30.44 | 4 | 16 | 9 | 124/17 | | | | | | | |
| Walker,KA | 2 | 3 | 0 | 11 | 10 | 3.66 | 0 | 0 | 1 | 3 | 495 | 197 | 6 | 32.83 | 0 | 0 | 4/63 |
| Ward,TA | 23 | 42 | 9 | 459 | 64 | 13.90 | 0 | 2 | 5 | 19/13 | | | | | | | |
| Watkins,JC | 15 | 27 | 1 | 612 | 92 | 23.53 | 0 | 3 | 2 | 12 | 2805 | 816 | 29 | 28.13 | 0 | 0 | 4/22 |
| Wesley,C | 3 | 5 | 0 | 49 | 35 | 9.80 | 0 | 0 | 2 | 1 | | | | | | | |
| Wessels,KC | 16 | 29 | 2 | 1027 | 118 | 38.03 | 2 | 6 | 2 | 12 | | | | | | | |
| Westcott,RJ | 5 | 9 | 0 | 166 | 62 | 18.44 | 0 | 1 | 2 | 0 | 32 | 22 | 0 | - | 0 | 0 | 0/22 |
| White,GC | 17 | 31 | 2 | 872 | 147 | 30.06 | 2 | 4 | 3 | 10 | 498 | 301 | 9 | 33.44 | 0 | 0 | 4/47 |
| Willoughby,JT | 2 | 4 | 0 | 8 | 5 | 2.00 | 0 | 0 | 2 | 0 | 275 | 159 | 6 | 26.50 | 0 | 0 | 2/37 |
| Wimble,CS | 1 | 2 | 0 | 0 | 0 | 0.00 | 0 | 0 | 2 | 0 | | | | | | | |
| Winslow,PL | 5 | 9 | 0 | 186 | 108 | 20.66 | 1 | 0 | 1 | 1 | | | | | | | |
| Wynne,OE | 6 | 12 | 0 | 219 | 50 | 18.25 | 0 | 1 | 0 | 3 | | | | | | | |
| Zulch,JW | 16 | 32 | 2 | 985 | 150 | 32.83 | 2 | 4 | 0 | 4 | 24 | 28 | 0 | - | 0 | 0 | 0/2 |

| WEST INDIES | | | | BATTING AND FIELDING | | | | | | | | BOWLING | | | | | | |
|---|---|---|---|---|---|---|---|---|---|---|---|---|---|---|---|---|---|---|
| | Tests | I | N | Runs | HS | Avge | 100 | 50 | 0's | c/s | Balls | Runs | Wks | Avge | 5w | 10w | BB |
| Achong,EE | 6 | 11 | 1 | 81 | 22 | 8.10 | 0 | 0 | 2 | 6 | 918 | 378 | 8 | 47.25 | 0 | 0 | 2/64 |
| Adams,JC | 33 | 52 | 11 | 2104 | 208 | 51.31 | 5 | 10 | 2 | 33 | 1323 | 672 | 16 | 42.00 | 1 | 0 | 5/17 |
| Alexander,FCM | 25 | 38 | 6 | 961 | 108 | 30.03 | 1 | 7 | 5 | 85/5 | | | | | | | |
| Ali,Imtiaz | 1 | 1 | 1 | 1 | 1* | - | 0 | 0 | 0 | 0 | 204 | 89 | 2 | 44.50 | 0 | 0 | 2/37 |
| Ali,Inshan | 12 | 18 | 2 | 172 | 25 | 10.75 | 0 | 0 | 3 | 7 | 3718 | 1621 | 34 | 47.67 | 1 | 0 | 5/59 |
| Allan,DW | 5 | 7 | 1 | 75 | 40* | 12.50 | 0 | 0 | 0 | 15/3 | | | | | | | |
| Allen,IBA | 2 | 2 | 2 | 5 | 4* | 0 | 0 | 0 | 0 | 1 | 282 | 180 | 5 | 36.00 | 0 | 0 | 2/69 |
| Ambrose,CEL | 81 | 114 | 24 | 1188 | 53 | 13.20 | 0 | 1 | 18 | 16 | 17953 | 7132 | 337 | 21.16 | 20 | 3 | 8/45 |
| Arthurton,KLT | 33 | 50 | 5 | 1382 | 157* | 30.71 | 2 | 8 | 8 | 21 | 473 | 183 | 1 | 183.00 | 0 | 0 | 1/17 |
| Asgarali,NR | 2 | 4 | 0 | 62 | 29 | 15.50 | 0 | 0 | 1 | 0 | | | | | | | |
| Atkinson,DS | 22 | 35 | 6 | 922 | 219 | 31.79 | 1 | 5 | 4 | 11 | 5201 | 1647 | 47 | 35.04 | 3 | 0 | 7/53 |
| Atkinson,ES | 8 | 9 | 1 | 126 | 37 | 15.75 | 0 | 0 | 3 | 2 | 1634 | 589 | 25 | 23.56 | 1 | 0 | 5/42 |
| Austin,RA | 2 | 2 | 0 | 22 | 20 | 11.00 | 0 | 0 | 0 | 2 | 6 | 5 | 0 | - | 0 | 0 | 0/5 |
| Bacchus,SFAF | 19 | 30 | 0 | 782 | 250 | 26.06 | 1 | 3 | 7 | 17 | 6 | 3 | 0 | - | 0 | 0 | 0/3 |
| Baichan,L | 3 | 6 | 2 | 184 | 105* | 46.00 | 1 | 0 | 0 | 2 | | | | | | | |
| Baptiste,EAE | 10 | 11 | 1 | 233 | 87* | 23.30 | 0 | 1 | 1 | 2 | 1362 | 562 | 16 | 35.12 | 0 | 0 | 3/31 |
| Barrett,AG | 6 | 7 | 1 | 40 | 19 | 6.66 | 0 | 0 | 1 | 0 | 1612 | 603 | 13 | 46.38 | 0 | 0 | 3/43 |
| Barrow,I | 11 | 19 | 2 | 276 | 105 | 16.23 | 1 | 0 | 3 | 17/5 | | | | | | | |
| Bartlett,EL | 5 | 8 | 1 | 131 | 84 | 18.71 | 0 | 1 | 1 | 2 | | | | | | | |
| Benjamin,KCG | 26 | 36 | 9 | 222 | 43* | 8.22 | 0 | 1 | 7 | 2 | 5132 | 2785 | 92 | 30.27 | 4 | 1 | 6/66 |
| Benjamin,WKM | 21 | 26 | 1 | 433 | 85 | 17.32 | 0 | 2 | 5 | 12 | 3711 | 1648 | 61 | 27.01 | 0 | 0 | 4/46 |
| Best,CA | 8 | 13 | 1 | 342 | 164 | 28.50 | 1 | 1 | 1 | 8 | 30 | 21 | 0 | - | 0 | 0 | 0/2 |
| Betancourt,N | 1 | 2 | 0 | 52 | 39 | 26.00 | 0 | 0 | 0 | 0 | | | | | | | |
| Binns,AP | 5 | 8 | 1 | 64 | 27 | 9.14 | 0 | 0 | 3 | 14/3 | | | | | | | |
| Birkett,LS | 4 | 8 | 0 | 136 | 64 | 17.00 | 0 | 1 | 1 | 4 | 126 | 71 | 1 | 71.00 | 0 | 0 | 1/16 |
| Bishop,IR | 42 | 61 | 10 | 623 | 48 | 12.21 | 0 | 0 | 10 | 7 | 8317 | 3842 | 161 | 23.86 | 6 | 0 | 6/40 |
| Boyce,KD | 21 | 30 | 3 | 657 | 95* | 24.33 | 0 | 4 | 4 | 5 | 3501 | 1801 | 60 | 30.01 | 2 | 1 | 6/77 |
| Browne,CO | 13 | 20 | 5 | 250 | 39* | 16.66 | 0 | 0 | 5 | 59/1 | | | | | | | |
| Browne,CR | 4 | 8 | 1 | 176 | 70* | 25.14 | 0 | 1 | 2 | 1 | 840 | 288 | 6 | 48.00 | 0 | 0 | 2/72 |
| Butcher,BF | 44 | 78 | 6 | 3104 | 209* | 43.11 | 7 | 16 | 3 | 15 | 256 | 90 | 5 | 18.00 | 1 | 0 | 5/34 |
| Butler,LS | 1 | 1 | 0 | 16 | 16 | 16.00 | 0 | 0 | 0 | 0 | 240 | 151 | 2 | 75.50 | 0 | 0 | 2/151 |
| Butts,CG | 7 | 8 | 1 | 108 | 38 | 15.42 | 0 | 0 | 1 | 2 | 1554 | 595 | 10 | 59.50 | 0 | 0 | 4/73 |
| Bynoe,MR | 4 | 6 | 0 | 111 | 48 | 18.50 | 0 | 0 | 0 | 4 | 30 | 5 | 1 | 5.00 | 0 | 0 | 1/5 |
| Camacho,GS | 11 | 22 | 0 | 640 | 87 | 29.09 | 0 | 4 | 1 | 4 | 18 | 12 | 0 | - | 0 | 0 | 0/12 |
| Cameron,FJ | 5 | 7 | 1 | 151 | 75* | 25.16 | 0 | 1 | 1 | 0 | 786 | 278 | 3 | 92.66 | 0 | 0 | 2/74 |
| Cameron,JH | 2 | 3 | 0 | 6 | 5 | 2.00 | 0 | 0 | 1 | 0 | 232 | 88 | 3 | 29.33 | 0 | 0 | 3/66 |
| Campbell,SL | 29 | 49 | 2 | 1759 | 208 | 37.42 | 2 | 11 | 3 | 20 | | | | | | | |
| Carew,GM | 4 | 7 | 1 | 170 | 107 | 28.33 | 1 | 0 | 1 | 1 | 18 | 2 | 0 | - | 0 | 0 | 0/2 |
| Carew,MC | 19 | 36 | 3 | 1127 | 109 | 34.15 | 1 | 5 | 1 | 13 | 1174 | 437 | 8 | 54.62 | 0 | 0 | 1/11 |
| Challenor,G | 3 | 6 | 0 | 101 | 46 | 16.83 | 0 | 0 | 2 | 0 | | | | | | | |
| Chanderpaul,S | 29 | 46 | 7 | 1842 | 137* | 47.23 | 2 | 15 | 3 | 13 | 1086 | 522 | 4 | 130.50 | 0 | 0 | 1/2 |
| Chang,HS | 1 | 2 | 0 | 8 | 6 | 4.00 | 0 | 0 | 0 | 0 | | | | | | | |
| Christiani,CM | 4 | 7 | 2 | 98 | 32* | 19.60 | 0 | 0 | 1 | 6/1 | | | | | | | |
| Christiani,RJ | 22 | 37 | 3 | 896 | 107 | 26.35 | 1 | 4 | 0 | 19/2 | 234 | 108 | 3 | 36.00 | 0 | 0 | 3/52 |
| Clarke,CB | 3 | 4 | 1 | 3 | 2 | 1.00 | 0 | 0 | 1 | 0 | 456 | 261 | 6 | 43.50 | 0 | 0 | 3/59 |
| Clarke,ST | 11 | 16 | 5 | 172 | 35* | 15.63 | 0 | 0 | 2 | 2 | 2477 | 1170 | 42 | 27.85 | 1 | 0 | 5/126 |
| Constantine,LN | 18 | 33 | 0 | 635 | 90 | 19.24 | 0 | 4 | 4 | 28 | 3583 | 1746 | 58 | 30.10 | 2 | 0 | 5/75 |
| Croft,CEH | 27 | 37 | 22 | 158 | 33 | 10.53 | 0 | 0 | 6 | 8 | 6165 | 2913 | 125 | 23.30 | 3 | 0 | 8/29 |
| Cuffy,CE | 3 | 5 | 2 | 6 | 3* | 2.00 | 0 | 0 | 1 | 1 | 512 | 306 | 7 | 43.71 | 0 | 0 | 4/80 |
| Cummins,AC | 5 | 6 | 1 | 98 | 50 | 19.60 | 0 | 1 | 1 | 1 | 618 | 342 | 8 | 42.75 | 0 | 0 | 4/54 |
| Da Costa,OC | 5 | 9 | 1 | 153 | 39 | 19.12 | 0 | 0 | 1 | 5 | 372 | 175 | 3 | 58.33 | 0 | 0 | 1/14 |
| Daniel,WW | 10 | 11 | 4 | 46 | 11 | 6.57 | 0 | 0 | 2 | 4 | 1754 | 910 | 36 | 25.27 | 1 | 0 | 5/39 |
| Davis,BA | 4 | 8 | 0 | 245 | 68 | 30.62 | 0 | 3 | 0 | 1 | | | | | | | |
| Davis,CA | 15 | 29 | 5 | 1301 | 183 | 54.20 | 4 | 4 | 1 | 4 | 894 | 330 | 2 | 165.00 | 0 | 0 | 1/27 |
| Davis,WW | 15 | 17 | 4 | 202 | 77 | 15.53 | 0 | 1 | 2 | 10 | 2773 | 1472 | 45 | 32.71 | 0 | 0 | 4/19 |
| De Caires,FI | 3 | 6 | 0 | 232 | 80 | 38.66 | 0 | 2 | 1 | 1 | 12 | 9 | 0 | - | 0 | 0 | 0/9 |
| Depeiza,CC | 5 | 8 | 2 | 187 | 122 | 31.16 | 1 | 0 | 1 | 7/4 | 30 | 15 | 0 | - | 0 | 0 | 0/3 |

| **WEST INDIES** (cont.) | | | | **BATTING AND FIELDING** | | | | | | | | | | **BOWLING** | | | |
|---|---|---|---|---|---|---|---|---|---|---|---|---|---|---|---|---|---|
| | Tests | I | N | Runs | HS | Avge | 100 | 50 | 0's | c/s | Balls | Runs | Wks | Avge | 5w | 10w | BB |
| Dewdney,DT | 9 | 12 | 5 | 17 | 5* | 2.42 | 0 | 0 | 3 | 0 | 1641 | 807 | 21 | 38.42 | 1 | 0 | 5/21 |
| Dhanraj,R | 4 | 4 | 0 | 17 | 9 | 4.25 | 0 | 0 | 0 | 1 | 1087 | 595 | 8 | 74.37 | 0 | 0 | 2/49 |
| Dillon,M | 2 | 3 | 1 | 21 | 21 | 10.50 | 0 | 0 | 1 | 0 | 324 | 148 | 4 | 37.00 | 0 | 0 | 3/92 |
| Dowe,UG | 4 | 3 | 2 | 8 | 5* | 8.00 | 0 | 0 | 0 | 3 | 1014 | 534 | 12 | 44.50 | 0 | 0 | 4/69 |
| Dujon,PJL | 81 | 115 | 11 | 3322 | 139 | 31.94 | 5 | 16 | 8 | 267/5 | | | | | | | |
| Edwards,RM | 5 | 8 | 1 | 65 | 22 | 9.28 | 0 | 0 | 2 | 0 | 1311 | 626 | 18 | 34.77 | 1 | 0 | 5/84 |
| Ferguson,W | 8 | 10 | 3 | 200 | 75 | 28.57 | 0 | 2 | 1 | 11 | 2568 | 1165 | 34 | 34.26 | 3 | 1 | 6/92 |
| Fernandes,MP | 2 | 4 | 0 | 49 | 22 | 12.25 | 0 | 0 | 1 | 0 | | | | | | | |
| Findlay,TM | 10 | 16 | 3 | 212 | 44* | 16.30 | 0 | 0 | 1 | 19/2 | | | | | | | |
| Foster,MLC | 14 | 24 | 5 | 580 | 125 | 30.52 | 1 | 1 | 0 | 3 | 1776 | 600 | 9 | 66.66 | 0 | 0 | 2/41 |
| Francis,GN | 10 | 18 | 4 | 81 | 19* | 5.78 | 0 | 0 | 4 | 7 | 1619 | 763 | 23 | 33.17 | 0 | 0 | 4/40 |
| Frederick,MC | 1 | 2 | 0 | 30 | 30 | 15.00 | 0 | 0 | 1 | 0 | | | | | | | |
| Fredericks,RC | 59 | 109 | 7 | 4334 | 169 | 42.49 | 8 | 26 | 7 | 62 | 1187 | 548 | 7 | 78.28 | 0 | 0 | 1/12 |
| Fuller,RL | 1 | 1 | 0 | 1 | 1 | 1.00 | 0 | 0 | 0 | 0 | 48 | 12 | 0 | - | 0 | 0 | 0/2 |
| Furlonge,HA | 3 | 5 | 0 | 99 | 64 | 19.80 | 0 | 1 | 1 | 0 | | | | | | | |
| Ganteaume,AG | 1 | 1 | 0 | 112 | 112 | 112.00 | 1 | 0 | 0 | 0 | | | | | | | |
| Garner,J | 58 | 68 | 14 | 672 | 60 | 12.44 | 0 | 1 | 17 | 42 | 13169 | 5433 | 259 | 20.97 | 7 | 0 | 6/56 |
| Gaskin,BBM | 2 | 3 | 0 | 17 | 10 | 5.66 | 0 | 0 | 1 | 1 | 474 | 158 | 2 | 79.00 | 0 | 0 | 1/15 |
| Gibbs,GL | 1 | 2 | 0 | 12 | 12 | 6.00 | 0 | 0 | 1 | 1 | 24 | 7 | 0 | - | 0 | 0 | 0/2 |
| Gibbs,LR | 79 | 109 | 39 | 488 | 25 | 6.97 | 0 | 0 | 15 | 52 | 27115 | 8989 | 309 | 29.09 | 18 | 2 | 8/38 |
| Gibson,OD | 1 | 2 | 0 | 43 | 29 | 21.50 | 0 | 0 | 0 | 0 | 204 | 132 | 2 | 66.00 | 0 | 0 | 2/81 |
| Gilchrist,R | 13 | 14 | 3 | 60 | 12 | 5.45 | 0 | 0 | 4 | 4 | 3227 | 1521 | 57 | 26.68 | 1 | 0 | 6/55 |
| Gladstone,G | 1 | 1 | 1 | 12 | 12* | - | 0 | 0 | 0 | 0 | 300 | 189 | 1 | 189.00 | 0 | 0 | 1/139 |
| Goddard,JDC | 27 | 39 | 11 | 859 | 83* | 30.67 | 0 | 4 | 5 | 22 | 2931 | 1050 | 33 | 31.81 | 1 | 0 | 5/31 |
| Gomes,HA | 60 | 91 | 11 | 3171 | 143 | 39.63 | 9 | 13 | 5 | 18 | 2401 | 930 | 15 | 62.00 | 0 | 0 | 2/20 |
| Gomez,GE | 29 | 46 | 5 | 1243 | 101 | 30.31 | 1 | 8 | 5 | 18 | 5236 | 1590 | 58 | 27.41 | 1 | 1 | 7/55 |
| Grant,GC | 12 | 21 | 5 | 413 | 71* | 25.81 | 0 | 3 | 1 | 10 | 24 | 18 | 0 | - | 0 | 0 | 0/1 |
| Grant,RS | 7 | 11 | 1 | 220 | 77 | 22.00 | 0 | 1 | 3 | 13 | 986 | 353 | 11 | 32.06 | 0 | 0 | 3/68 |
| Gray,AH | 5 | 8 | 2 | 48 | 12* | 8.00 | 0 | 0 | 2 | 6 | 888 | 377 | 22 | 17.13 | 0 | 0 | 4/39 |
| Greenidge,AE | 6 | 10 | 0 | 222 | 69 | 22.20 | 0 | 2 | 2 | 5 | | | | | | | |
| Greenidge,CG | 108 | 185 | 16 | 7558 | 226 | 44.72 | 19 | 34 | 11 | 96 | 26 | 4 | 0 | - | 0 | 0 | 0/0 |
| Greenidge,GA | 5 | 9 | 2 | 209 | 50 | 29.85 | 0 | 1 | 1 | 3 | 156 | 75 | 0 | - | 0 | 0 | 0/2 |
| Grell,MG | 1 | 2 | 0 | 34 | 21 | 17.00 | 0 | 0 | 0 | 1 | 30 | 17 | 0 | - | 0 | 0 | 0/7 |
| Griffith,CC | 28 | 42 | 10 | 530 | 54 | 16.56 | 0 | 1 | 5 | 16 | 5631 | 2683 | 94 | 28.54 | 5 | 0 | 6/36 |
| Griffith,HC | 13 | 23 | 5 | 91 | 18 | 5.05 | 0 | 0 | 6 | 4 | 2663 | 1243 | 44 | 28.25 | 2 | 0 | 6/103 |
| Griffiths,AFG | 1 | 2 | 0 | 14 | 13 | 7.00 | 0 | 0 | 0 | 0 | | | | | | | |
| Guillen,SC | 5 | 6 | 2 | 104 | 54 | 26.00 | 0 | 1 | 1 | 9/2 | | | | | | | |
| Hall,WW | 48 | 66 | 14 | 818 | 50* | 15.73 | 0 | 2 | 7 | 11 | 10421 | 5066 | 192 | 26.38 | 9 | 1 | 7/69 |
| Harper,RA | 25 | 32 | 3 | 535 | 74 | 18.44 | 0 | 3 | 5 | 36 | 3615 | 1291 | 46 | 28.06 | 1 | 0 | 6/57 |
| Haynes,DL | 116 | 202 | 25 | 7487 | 184 | 42.29 | 18 | 39 | 10 | 65 | 18 | 8 | 1 | 8.00 | 0 | 0 | 1/2 |
| Headley,GA | 22 | 40 | 4 | 2190 | 270* | 60.83 | 10 | 5 | 2 | 14 | 398 | 230 | 0 | - | 0 | 0 | 0/0 |
| Headley,RGA | 2 | 4 | 0 | 62 | 42 | 15.50 | 0 | 0 | 0 | 2 | | | | | | | |
| Hendriks,JL | 20 | 32 | 8 | 447 | 64 | 18.62 | 0 | 2 | 4 | 42/5 | | | | | | | |
| Hoad,ELG | 4 | 8 | 0 | 98 | 36 | 12.25 | 0 | 0 | 1 | 1 | | | | | | | |
| Holder,RIC | 9 | 12 | 2 | 345 | 91 | 34.50 | 0 | 2 | 0 | 8 | | | | | | | |
| Holder,VA | 40 | 59 | 11 | 682 | 42 | 14.20 | 0 | 0 | 7 | 16 | 9095 | 3627 | 109 | 33.27 | 3 | 0 | 6/28 |
| Holding,MA | 60 | 76 | 10 | 910 | 73 | 13.78 | 0 | 6 | 15 | 22 | 12680 | 5898 | 249 | 23.68 | 13 | 2 | 8/92 |
| Holford,DAJ | 24 | 39 | 5 | 768 | 105* | 22.58 | 1 | 3 | 3 | 18 | 4816 | 2009 | 51 | 39.39 | 1 | 0 | 5/23 |
| Holt,JK | 17 | 31 | 2 | 1066 | 166 | 36.75 | 2 | 5 | 2 | 8 | 30 | 20 | 1 | 20.00 | 0 | 0 | 1/20 |
| Hooper,CL | 72 | 120 | 13 | 3720 | 178* | 34.76 | 8 | 17 | 12 | 78 | 9015 | 3773 | 80 | 47.16 | 4 | 0 | 5/26 |
| Howard,AB | 1 | | | | | | 0 | 0 | 0 | 0 | 372 | 140 | 2 | 70.00 | 0 | 0 | 2/140 |
| Hunte,CC | 44 | 78 | 6 | 3245 | 260 | 45.06 | 8 | 13 | 5 | 16 | 270 | 110 | 2 | 55.00 | 0 | 0 | 1/17 |
| Hunte,EAC | 3 | 6 | 1 | 166 | 58 | 33.20 | 0 | 2 | 0 | 5/0 | | | | | | | |
| Hylton,LG | 6 | 8 | 2 | 70 | 19 | 11.66 | 0 | 0 | 0 | 1 | 965 | 418 | 16 | 26.12 | 0 | 0 | 4/27 |
| Johnson,HHH | 3 | 4 | 0 | 38 | 22 | 9.50 | 0 | 0 | 1 | 0 | 789 | 238 | 13 | 18.30 | 2 | 1 | 5/41 |
| Johnson,TF | 1 | 1 | 1 | 9 | 9* | 0 | 0 | 0 | 0 | 1 | 240 | 129 | 3 | 43.00 | 0 | 0 | 2/53 |
| Jones,CEL | 4 | 7 | 0 | 63 | 19 | 9.00 | 0 | 0 | 0 | 3 | 102 | 11 | 0 | - | 0 | 0 | 0/2 |

| WEST INDIES (cont.) | | | | BATTING AND FIELDING | | | | | | | | | | BOWLING | | | |
|---|---|---|---|---|---|---|---|---|---|---|---|---|---|---|---|---|---|
| | Tests | I | N | Runs | HS | Avge | 100 | 50 | 0's | c/s | Balls | Runs | Wks | Avge | 5w | 10w | BB |
| Jones,PE | 9 | 11 | 2 | 47 | 10* | 5.22 | 0 | 0 | 1 | 4 | 1842 | 751 | 25 | 30.04 | 1 | 0 | 5/85 |
| Julien,BD | 24 | 34 | 6 | 866 | 121 | 30.92 | 2 | 3 | 0 | 14 | 4542 | 1868 | 50 | 37.36 | 1 | 0 | 5/57 |
| Jumadeen,RR | 12 | 14 | 10 | 84 | 56 | 21.00 | 0 | 1 | 2 | 4 | 3140 | 1141 | 29 | 39.34 | 0 | 0 | 4/72 |
| Kallicharran,AI | 66 | 109 | 10 | 4399 | 187 | 44.43 | 12 | 21 | 10 | 51 | 406 | 158 | 4 | 39.50 | 0 | 0 | 2/16 |
| Kanhai,RB | 79 | 137 | 6 | 6227 | 256 | 47.53 | 15 | 28 | 7 | 50/0 | 183 | 85 | 0 | - | 0 | 0 | 0/1 |
| Kentish,ESM | 2 | 2 | 1 | 1 | 1* | 0 | 0 | 0 | 1 | 1 | 540 | 178 | 8 | 22.25 | 1 | 0 | 5/49 |
| King,CL | 9 | 16 | 3 | 418 | 100* | 32.15 | 1 | 2 | 3 | 5 | 582 | 282 | 3 | 94.00 | 0 | 0 | 1/30 |
| King,FM | 14 | 17 | 3 | 116 | 21 | 8.28 | 0 | 0 | 4 | 5 | 2869 | 1159 | 29 | 39.96 | 1 | 0 | 5/74 |
| King,LA | 2 | 4 | 0 | 41 | 20 | 10.25 | 0 | 0 | 1 | 2 | 476 | 154 | 9 | 17.11 | 1 | 0 | 5/46 |
| Lambert,CB | 3 | 5 | 0 | 241 | 104 | 48.20 | 1 | 1 | 0 | 5 | 10 | 5 | 1 | 5.00 | 0 | 0 | 1/4 |
| Lara,BC | 53 | 89 | 3 | 4477 | 375 | 52.05 | 10 | 23 | 4 | 74 | 60 | 28 | 0 | - | 0 | 0 | 0/0 |
| Lashley,PD | 4 | 7 | 0 | 159 | 49 | 22.71 | 0 | 0 | 1 | 4 | 18 | 1 | 1 | 1.00 | 0 | 0 | 1/1 |
| Legall,RA | 4 | 5 | 0 | 50 | 23 | 10.00 | 0 | 0 | 0 | 8/1 | | | | | | | |
| Lewis,DM | 3 | 5 | 2 | 259 | 88 | 86.33 | 0 | 3 | 0 | 8/0 | | | | | | | |
| Lewis,RN | 1 | 2 | 0 | 4 | 4 | 2.00 | 0 | 0 | 1 | 0 | 144 | 93 | 0 | - | 0 | 0 | 0/93 |
| Lloyd,CH | 110 | 175 | 14 | 7515 | 242* | 46.67 | 19 | 39 | 4 | 90 | 1716 | 622 | 10 | 62.20 | 0 | 0 | 2/13 |
| Logie,AL | 52 | 78 | 9 | 2470 | 130 | 35.79 | 2 | 16 | 8 | 57 | 7 | 4 | 0 | - | 0 | 0 | 0/0 |
| McLean,NAM | 4 | 4 | 1 | 22 | 11 | 7.33 | 0 | 0 | 0 | 1 | 468 | 203 | 5 | 40.60 | 0 | 0 | 2/46 |
| McMorris,EDAS | 13 | 21 | 0 | 564 | 125 | 26.85 | 1 | 3 | 1 | 5 | | | | | | | |
| McWatt,CA | 6 | 9 | 2 | 202 | 54 | 28.85 | 0 | 2 | 0 | 9/1 | 24 | 16 | 1 | 16.00 | 0 | 0 | 1/16 |
| Madray,IS | 2 | 3 | 0 | 3 | 2 | 1.00 | 0 | 0 | 1 | 2 | 210 | 108 | 0 | - | 0 | 0 | 0/12 |
| Marshall,MD | 81 | 107 | 11 | 1810 | 92 | 18.85 | 0 | 10 | 15 | 25 | 17585 | 7876 | 376 | 20.94 | 22 | 4 | 7/22 |
| Marshall,NE | 1 | 2 | 0 | 8 | 8 | 4.00 | 0 | 0 | 1 | 0 | 279 | 62 | 2 | 31.00 | 0 | 0 | 1/22 |
| Marshall,RE | 4 | 7 | 0 | 143 | 30 | 20.42 | 0 | 0 | 1 | 1 | 52 | 15 | 0 | - | 0 | 0 | 0/3 |
| Martin,FR | 9 | 18 | 1 | 486 | 123* | 28.58 | 1 | 0 | 1 | 2 | 1346 | 619 | 8 | 77.37 | 0 | 0 | 3/91 |
| Martindale,EA | 10 | 14 | 3 | 58 | 22 | 5.27 | 0 | 0 | 3 | 5 | 1605 | 804 | 37 | 21.72 | 3 | 0 | 5/22 |
| Mattis,EH | 4 | 5 | 0 | 145 | 71 | 29.00 | 0 | 1 | 1 | 3 | 36 | 14 | 0 | - | 0 | 0 | 0/4 |
| Mendonça,IL | 2 | 2 | 0 | 81 | 78 | 40.50 | 0 | 1 | 0 | 8/2 | | | | | | | |
| Merry,CA | 2 | 4 | 0 | 34 | 13 | 8.50 | 0 | 0 | 0 | 1 | | | | | | | |
| Miller,R | 1 | 1 | 0 | 23 | 23 | 23.00 | 0 | 0 | 0 | 0 | 96 | 28 | 0 | - | 0 | 0 | 0/28 |
| Moseley,EA | 2 | 4 | 0 | 36 | 26 | 9.00 | 0 | 0 | 1 | 1 | 522 | 261 | 6 | 43.50 | 0 | 0 | 2/70 |
| Mudie,GH | 1 | 1 | 0 | 5 | 5 | 5.00 | 0 | 0 | 0 | 0 | 174 | 40 | 3 | 13.33 | 0 | 0 | 3/23 |
| Murray,DA | 19 | 31 | 3 | 601 | 84 | 21.46 | 0 | 3 | 3 | 57/5 | | | | | | | |
| Murray,DL | 62 | 96 | 9 | 1993 | 91 | 22.90 | 0 | 11 | 7 | 181/8 | | | | | | | |
| Murray,JR | 29 | 38 | 4 | 852 | 101* | 25.05 | 1 | 3 | 6 | 95/3 | | | | | | | |
| Nanan,R | 1 | 2 | 0 | 16 | 8 | 8.00 | 0 | 0 | 0 | 2 | 216 | 91 | 4 | 22.75 | 0 | 0 | 2/37 |
| Neblett,JM | 1 | 2 | 1 | 16 | 11* | 16.00 | 0 | 0 | 0 | 0 | 216 | 75 | 1 | 75.00 | 0 | 0 | 1/44 |
| Noreiga,JM | 4 | 5 | 2 | 11 | 9 | 30.62 | 0 | 0 | 1 | 2 | 1322 | 493 | 17 | 29.00 | 2 | 0 | 9/95 |
| Nunes,RK | 4 | 8 | 0 | 245 | 92 | 30.62 | 0 | 2 | 1 | 2/0 | | | | | | | |
| Nurse,SM | 29 | 54 | 1 | 2523 | 258 | 47.60 | 6 | 10 | 3 | 21 | 42 | 7 | 0 | - | 0 | 0 | 0/0 |
| Padmore,AL | 2 | 2 | 1 | 8 | 8* | 8.00 | 0 | 0 | 1 | 0 | 474 | 135 | 1 | 135.00 | 0 | 0 | 1/36 |
| Pairaudeau,BH | 13 | 21 | 0 | 454 | 115 | 21.61 | 1 | 3 | 3 | 6 | 6 | 3 | 0 | - | 0 | 0 | 0/3 |
| Parry,DR | 12 | 20 | 3 | 381 | 65 | 22.41 | 0 | 3 | 3 | 4 | 1909 | 936 | 23 | 40.69 | 1 | 0 | 5/15 |
| Passailaigue,CC | 1 | 2 | 1 | 46 | 44 | 46.00 | 0 | 0 | 0 | 3 | 12 | 15 | 0 | - | 0 | 0 | 0/15 |
| Patterson,BP | 28 | 38 | 16 | 145 | 21* | 6.59 | 0 | 0 | 8 | 5 | 4829 | 2875 | 93 | 30.91 | 5 | 0 | 5/24 |
| Payne,TRO | 1 | 1 | 0 | 5 | 5 | 5.00 | 0 | 0 | 0 | 5/0 | | | | | | | |
| Philip,N | 9 | 15 | 5 | 297 | 47 | 29.70 | 0 | 0 | 1 | 5 | 1820 | 1041 | 28 | 37.17 | 0 | 0 | 4/48 |
| Pierre,LR | 1 | | | | | | 0 | 0 | 0 | 0 | 42 | 28 | 0 | - | 0 | 0 | 0/9 |
| Rae,AF | 15 | 24 | 2 | 1016 | 109 | 46.18 | 4 | 4 | 1 | 10 | | | | | | | |
| Ramadhin,S | 43 | 58 | 14 | 361 | 44 | 8.20 | 0 | 0 | 14 | 9 | 13939 | 4579 | 158 | 28.98 | 10 | 1 | 7/49 |
| Ramnarine,D | 2 | 2 | 0 | 19 | 19 | 9.50 | 0 | 0 | 1 | 2 | 546 | 148 | 9 | 16.44 | 0 | 0 | 4/29 |
| Reifer,FL | 2 | 4 | 0 | 48 | 29 | 12.00 | 0 | 0 | 1 | 3 | | | | | | | |
| Richards,IVA | 121 | 182 | 12 | 8540 | 291 | 50.23 | 24 | 45 | 10 | 122 | 5170 | 1964 | 32 | 61.37 | 0 | 0 | 2/17 |
| Richardson,RB | 86 | 146 | 12 | 5949 | 194 | 44.39 | 16 | 27 | 8 | 91 | 66 | 18 | 0 | - | 0 | 0 | 0/0 |
| Rickards,KR | 2 | 3 | 0 | 104 | 67 | 34.66 | 0 | 1 | 0 | 0 | | | | | | | |
| Roach,CA | 16 | 32 | 1 | 952 | 209 | 30.70 | 2 | 6 | 6 | 5 | 222 | 103 | 2 | 51.50 | 0 | 0 | 1/18 |
| Roberts,AME | 47 | 62 | 11 | 762 | 68 | 14.94 | 0 | 3 | 6 | 9 | 11355 | 5174 | 202 | 25.61 | 11 | 2 | 7/54 |

| WEST INDIES (cont.) | | | | BATTING AND FIELDING | | | | | | | | BOWLING | | | | | |
|---|---|---|---|---|---|---|---|---|---|---|---|---|---|---|---|---|---|
| | Tests | I | N | Runs | HS | Avge | 100 | 50 | 0's | c/s | Balls | Runs | Wks | Avge | 5w | 10w | BB |
| Roberts,AT | 1 | 2 | 0 | 28 | 28 | 14.00 | 0 | 0 | 1 | 0 | | | | | | | |
| Rodriguez,WV | 5 | 7 | 0 | 96 | 50 | 13.71 | 0 | 1 | 1 | 3 | 573 | 374 | 7 | 53.42 | 0 | 0 | 3/51 |
| Rose,FA | 9 | 11 | 3 | 79 | 34 | 12.87 | 0 | 0 | 1 | 1 | 1387 | 690 | 27 | 25.55 | 1 | 0 | 6/100 |
| Rowe,LG | 30 | 49 | 2 | 2047 | 302 | 43.55 | 7 | 7 | 2 | 17 | 86 | 44 | 0 | - | 0 | 0 | 0/1 |
| St Hill,EL | 2 | 4 | 0 | 18 | 12 | 4.50 | 0 | 0 | 1 | 0 | 558 | 221 | 3 | 73.66 | 0 | 0 | 2/110 |
| St Hill,WH | 3 | 6 | 0 | 117 | 38 | 19.50 | 0 | 0 | 0 | 1 | 12 | 9 | 0 | - | 0 | 0 | 0/9 |
| Samuels,RG | 6 | 12 | 2 | 372 | 125 | 37.20 | 1 | 1 | 0 | 8 | | | | | | | |
| Scarlett,RO | 3 | 4 | 1 | 54 | 29* | 18.00 | 0 | 0 | 0 | 2 | 804 | 209 | 2 | 104.50 | 0 | 0 | 1/46 |
| Scott,APH | 1 | 1 | 0 | 5 | 5 | 5.00 | 0 | 0 | 0 | 0 | 264 | 140 | 0 | - | 0 | 0 | 0/52 |
| Scott,OC | 8 | 13 | 3 | 171 | 35 | 17.10 | 0 | 0 | 1 | 0 | 1405 | 925 | 22 | 42.04 | 1 | 0 | 5/266 |
| Sealey,BJ | 1 | 2 | 0 | 41 | 29 | 20.50 | 0 | 0 | 0 | 0 | 30 | 10 | 1 | 10.00 | 0 | 0 | 1/10 |
| Sealy,JED | 11 | 19 | 2 | 478 | 92 | 28.11 | 0 | 3 | 2 | 6/1 | 156 | 94 | 3 | 31.33 | 0 | 0 | 2/7 |
| Shepherd,JN | 5 | 8 | 0 | 77 | 32 | 9.62 | 0 | 0 | 2 | 4 | 1445 | 479 | 19 | 25.21 | 1 | 0 | 5/104 |
| Shillingford,GC | 7 | 8 | 1 | 57 | 25 | 8.14 | 0 | 0 | 1 | 2 | 1181 | 537 | 15 | 35.80 | 0 | 0 | 3/63 |
| Shillingford,IT | 4 | 7 | 0 | 218 | 120 | 31.14 | 1 | 0 | 0 | 1 | | | | | | | |
| Shivnarine,S | 8 | 14 | 1 | 379 | 63 | 29.15 | 0 | 4 | 2 | 6 | 336 | 167 | 1 | 167.00 | 0 | 0 | 1/13 |
| Simmons,PV | 26 | 47 | 2 | 1002 | 110 | 22.26 | 1 | 4 | 4 | 26 | 624 | 257 | 4 | 64.25 | 0 | 0 | 2/34 |
| Singh,CK | 2 | 3 | 0 | 11 | 11 | 3.66 | 0 | 0 | 2 | 2 | 506 | 166 | 5 | 33.20 | 0 | 0 | 2/28 |
| Small,JA | 3 | 6 | 0 | 79 | 52 | 13.16 | 0 | 1 | 2 | 3 | 366 | 184 | 3 | 61.33 | 0 | 0 | 2/67 |
| Small,MA | 2 | 1 | 1 | 3 | 3* | - | 0 | 0 | 0 | 0 | 270 | 153 | 4 | 38.25 | 0 | 0 | 3/40 |
| Smith,CW | 5 | 10 | 1 | 222 | 55 | 24.66 | 0 | 1 | 0 | 4/1 | | | | | | | |
| Smith,OG | 26 | 42 | 0 | 1331 | 168 | 31.69 | 4 | 6 | 8 | 9 | 4431 | 1625 | 48 | 33.85 | 1 | 0 | 5/90 |
| Sobers,GS | 93 | 160 | 21 | 8032 | 365* | 57.78 | 26 | 30 | 12 | 109 | 21599 | 7999 | 235 | 34.03 | 6 | 0 | 6/73 |
| Solomon,JS | 27 | 46 | 7 | 1326 | 100* | 34.00 | 1 | 9 | 7 | 13 | 702 | 268 | 4 | 67.00 | 0 | 0 | 1/20 |
| Stayers,SC | 4 | 4 | 1 | 58 | 35* | 19.33 | 0 | 0 | 1 | 0 | 636 | 364 | 9 | 40.44 | 0 | 0 | 3/65 |
| Stollmeyer,JB | 32 | 56 | 5 | 2159 | 160 | 42.33 | 4 | 12 | 2 | 20 | 990 | 507 | 13 | 39.00 | 0 | 0 | 3/32 |
| Stollmeyer,VH | 1 | 1 | 0 | 96 | 96 | 96.00 | 0 | 1 | 0 | 0 | | | | | | | |
| Taylor,J | 3 | 5 | 3 | 4 | 4* | 2.00 | 0 | 0 | 2 | 0 | 672 | 273 | 10 | 27.30 | 1 | 0 | 5/109 |
| Thompson,PIC | 2 | 3 | 1 | 17 | 10* | 8.50 | 0 | 0 | 0 | 0 | 228 | 215 | 5 | 43.00 | 0 | 0 | 2/58 |
| Trim,J | 4 | 5 | 1 | 21 | 12 | 5.25 | 0 | 0 | 2 | 2 | 794 | 291 | 18 | 16.16 | 1 | 0 | 5/34 |
| Valentine,AL | 36 | 51 | 21 | 141 | 14 | 4.70 | 0 | 0 | 12 | 13 | 12953 | 4215 | 139 | 30.32 | 8 | 2 | 8/104 |
| Valentine,VA | 2 | 4 | 1 | 35 | 19* | 11.66 | 0 | 0 | 1 | 0 | 288 | 104 | 1 | 104.00 | 0 | 0 | 1/55 |
| Walcott,CL | 44 | 74 | 7 | 3798 | 220 | 56.68 | 15 | 14 | 1 | 53/11 | 1194 | 408 | 11 | 37.09 | 0 | 0 | 3/50 |
| Walcott,LA | 1 | 2 | 1 | 40 | 24 | 40.00 | 0 | 0 | 0 | 0 | 48 | 32 | 1 | 32.00 | 0 | 0 | 1/17 |
| Wallace,PA | 3 | 5 | 0 | 211 | 92 | 42.20 | 0 | 2 | 0 | 3 | | | | | | | |
| Walsh,CA | 101 | 132 | 43 | 799 | 30* | 8.97 | 0 | 0 | 28 | 23 | 21870 | 8584 | 371 | 23.13 | 15 | 2 | 7/37 |
| Watson,CD | 7 | 6 | 1 | 12 | 5 | 2.40 | 0 | 0 | 2 | 1 | 1458 | 724 | 19 | 38.10 | 0 | 0 | 4/62 |
| Weekes,ED | 48 | 81 | 5 | 4455 | 207 | 58.61 | 15 | 19 | 6 | 49 | 122 | 77 | 1 | 77.00 | 0 | 0 | 1/8 |
| Weekes,KH | 2 | 3 | 0 | 173 | 137 | 57.66 | 1 | 0 | 0 | 0 | | | | | | | |
| White,AW | 2 | 4 | 1 | 71 | 57* | 23.66 | 0 | 1 | 0 | 1 | 491 | 152 | 3 | 50.66 | 0 | 0 | 2/34 |
| Wight,CV | 2 | 4 | 1 | 67 | 23 | 22.33 | 0 | 0 | 0 | 0 | 30 | 6 | 0 | - | 0 | 0 | 0/6 |
| Wight,GL | 1 | 1 | 0 | 21 | 21 | 21.00 | 0 | 0 | 0 | 0 | | | | | | | |
| Wiles,CA | 1 | 2 | 0 | 2 | 2 | 1.00 | 0 | 0 | 1 | 0 | | | | | | | |
| Willett,ET | 5 | 8 | 3 | 74 | 26 | 14.80 | 0 | 0 | 2 | 0 | 1326 | 482 | 11 | 43.81 | 0 | 0 | 3/33 |
| Williams,AB | 7 | 12 | 0 | 469 | 111 | 39.08 | 2 | 1 | 1 | 5 | | | | | | | |
| Williams,D | 10 | 17 | 0 | 218 | 65 | 12.82 | 0 | 1 | 7 | 38/2 | | | | | | | |
| Williams,EAV | 4 | 6 | 0 | 113 | 72 | 18.83 | 0 | 1 | 1 | 2 | 796 | 241 | 9 | 26.77 | 0 | 0 | 3/51 |
| Williams,SC | 25 | 41 | 2 | 956 | 128 | 24.51 | 1 | 2 | 6 | 22 | 18 | 19 | 0 | - | 0 | 0 | 0/19 |
| Wishart,KL | 1 | 2 | 0 | 52 | 52 | 26.00 | 0 | 1 | 1 | 0 | | | | | | | |
| Worrell,FMM | 51 | 87 | 9 | 3860 | 261 | 49.48 | 9 | 22 | 11 | 43 | 7141 | 2672 | 69 | 38.72 | 2 | 0 | 7/70 |

| NEW ZEALAND | | | | BATTING AND FIELDING | | | | | | | | BOWLING | | | | | |
|---|---|---|---|---|---|---|---|---|---|---|---|---|---|---|---|---|---|
| | Tests | I | N | Runs | HS | Avge | 100 | 50 | 0's | c/s | Balls | Runs | Wks | Avge | 5w | 10w | BB |
| Alabaster,JC | 21 | 34 | 6 | 272 | 34 | 9.71 | 0 | 0 | 2 | 7 | 3992 | 1863 | 49 | 38.02 | 0 | 0 | 4/46 |
| Alcott,CFW | 6 | 7 | 2 | 113 | 33 | 22.60 | 0 | 0 | 0 | 3 | 1206 | 541 | 6 | 90.16 | 0 | 0 | 2/102 |
| Allott,GI | 6 | 10 | 3 | 18 | 8* | 2.57 | 0 | 0 | 3 | 1 | 1203 | 667 | 11 | 60.63 | 0 | 0 | 4/74 |
| Anderson,RW | 9 | 18 | 0 | 423 | 92 | 23.50 | 0 | 3 | 1 | 1 | | | | | | | |

| NEW ZEALAND (cont.) | | | | BATTING AND FIELDING | | | | | | | | BOWLING | | | | | | |
|---|---|---|---|---|---|---|---|---|---|---|---|---|---|---|---|---|---|---|
| | Tests | I | N | Runs | HS | Avge | 100 | 50 | 0's | c/s | Balls | Runs | Wks | Avge | 5w | 10w | BB |
| Anderson,WM | 1 | 2 | 0 | 5 | 4 | 2.50 | 0 | 0 | 0 | 1 | | | | | | | |
| Andrews,B | 2 | 3 | 2 | 22 | 17 | 22.00 | 0 | 0 | 0 | 1 | 256 | 154 | 2 | 77.00 | 0 | 0 | 2/40 |
| Astle,NJ | 21 | 39 | 2 | 1194 | 125 | 32.27 | 4 | 4 | 3 | 16 | 1319 | 549 | 12 | 45.75 | 0 | 0 | 2/26 |
| Badcock,FT | 7 | 9 | 2 | 137 | 64 | 19.57 | 0 | 2 | 3 | 1 | 1608 | 610 | 16 | 38.12 | 0 | 0 | 4/80 |
| Barber,RT | 1 | 2 | 0 | 17 | 12 | 8.50 | 0 | 0 | 0 | 1 | | | | | | | |
| Bartlett,GA | 10 | 18 | 1 | 263 | 40 | 15.47 | 0 | 0 | 4 | 8 | 1768 | 792 | 24 | 33.00 | 1 | 0 | 6/38 |
| Barton,PT | 7 | 14 | 0 | 285 | 109 | 20.35 | 1 | 1 | 1 | 4 | | | | | | | |
| Beard,DD | 4 | 7 | 2 | 101 | 31 | 20.20 | 0 | 0 | 0 | 2 | 806 | 302 | 9 | 33.55 | 0 | 0 | 3/22 |
| Beck,JEF | 8 | 15 | 0 | 394 | 99 | 26.26 | 0 | 3 | 1 | 0 | | | | | | | |
| Bell,W | 2 | 3 | 3 | 21 | 21* | 0 | 0 | 0 | 0 | 1 | 491 | 235 | 2 | 117.50 | 0 | 0 | 1/54 |
| Bilby,GP | 2 | 4 | 0 | 55 | 28 | 13.75 | 0 | 0 | 0 | 3 | | | | | | | |
| Blain,TE | 11 | 20 | 3 | 456 | 78 | 26.82 | 0 | 1 | 2 | 19/2 | | | | | | | |
| Blair,RW | 19 | 34 | 6 | 189 | 64* | 6.75 | 0 | 1 | 12 | 5 | 3525 | 1515 | 43 | 35.23 | 0 | 0 | 4/85 |
| Blunt,RC | 9 | 13 | 1 | 330 | 96 | 27.50 | 0 | 1 | 1 | 5 | 936 | 472 | 12 | 39.33 | 0 | 0 | 3/17 |
| Bolton,BA | 2 | 3 | 0 | 59 | 33 | 19.66 | 0 | 0 | 1 | 1 | | | | | | | |
| Boock,SL | 30 | 41 | 8 | 207 | 37 | 6.27 | 0 | 0 | 10 | 14 | 6598 | 2564 | 74 | 34.64 | 4 | 0 | 7/87 |
| Bracewell,BP | 6 | 12 | 2 | 24 | 8 | 2.40 | 0 | 0 | 5 | 1 | 1036 | 585 | 14 | 41.78 | 0 | 0 | 3/110 |
| Bracewell,JG | 41 | 60 | 11 | 1001 | 110 | 20.42 | 1 | 4 | 13 | 31 | 8403 | 3653 | 102 | 35.81 | 4 | 1 | 6/32 |
| Bradburn,GE | 5 | 9 | 2 | 105 | 30* | 15.00 | 0 | 0 | 0 | 4 | 616 | 336 | 5 | 67.20 | 0 | 0 | 3/134 |
| Bradburn,WP | 2 | 4 | 0 | 62 | 32 | 15.50 | 0 | 0 | 0 | 2 | | | | | | | |
| Brown,VR | 2 | 3 | 1 | 51 | 36* | 25.50 | 0 | 0 | 1 | 3 | 342 | 176 | 1 | 176.00 | 0 | 0 | 1/17 |
| Burgess,MG | 50 | 92 | 6 | 2684 | 119* | 31.20 | 5 | 14 | 5 | 34 | 498 | 212 | 6 | 35.33 | 0 | 0 | 3/23 |
| Burke,C | 1 | 2 | 0 | 4 | 3 | 2.00 | 0 | 0 | 0 | 0 | 66 | 30 | 2 | 15.00 | 0 | 0 | 2/30 |
| Burtt,TB | 10 | 15 | 3 | 252 | 42 | 21.00 | 0 | 0 | 1 | 2 | 2593 | 1170 | 33 | 35.45 | 3 | 0 | 6/162 |
| Butterfield,LA | 1 | 2 | 0 | 0 | 0 | 0.00 | 0 | 0 | 2 | 0 | 78 | 24 | 0 | - | 0 | 0 | 0/24 |
| Cairns,BL | 43 | 65 | 8 | 928 | 64 | 16.28 | 0 | 2 | 7 | 30 | 10628 | 4279 | 130 | 32.91 | 6 | 1 | 7/74 |
| Cairns,CL | 33 | 57 | 2 | 1442 | 120 | 26.21 | 1 | 12 | 5 | 11 | 6018 | 3294 | 103 | 31.98 | 5 | 0 | 6/52 |
| Cameron,FJ | 19 | 30 | 20 | 116 | 27* | 11.60 | 0 | 0 | 4 | 2 | 4570 | 1849 | 62 | 29.82 | 3 | 0 | 5/34 |
| Cave,HB | 19 | 31 | 5 | 229 | 22* | 8.80 | 0 | 0 | 5 | 8 | 4074 | 1467 | 34 | 43.14 | 0 | 0 | 4/21 |
| Chapple,ME | 14 | 27 | 1 | 497 | 76 | 19.11 | 0 | 3 | 2 | 10 | 248 | 84 | 1 | 84.00 | 0 | 0 | 1/24 |
| Chatfield,EJ | 43 | 54 | 33 | 180 | 21* | 8.57 | 0 | 0 | 11 | 7 | 10360 | 3958 | 123 | 32.17 | 3 | 1 | 6/73 |
| Cleverley,DC | 2 | 4 | 3 | 19 | 10* | 19.00 | 0 | 0 | 0 | 0 | 222 | 130 | 0 | - | 0 | 0 | 0/51 |
| Collinge,RO | 35 | 50 | 13 | 533 | 68* | 14.40 | 0 | 2 | 9 | 10 | 7689 | 3393 | 116 | 29.25 | 3 | 0 | 6/63 |
| Colquhoun,IA | 2 | 4 | 2 | 1 | 1* | 0.50 | 0 | 0 | 2 | 4/0 | | | | | | | |
| Coney,JV | 52 | 85 | 14 | 2668 | 174* | 37.57 | 3 | 16 | 3 | 64 | 2835 | 966 | 27 | 35.77 | 0 | 0 | 3/28 |
| Congdon,BE | 61 | 114 | 7 | 3448 | 176 | 32.22 | 7 | 19 | 9 | 44 | 5620 | 2154 | 59 | 36.50 | 1 | 0 | 5/65 |
| Cowie,J | 9 | 13 | 4 | 90 | 45 | 10.00 | 0 | 0 | 3 | 3 | 2028 | 969 | 45 | 21.53 | 4 | 1 | 6/40 |
| Cresswell,GF | 3 | 5 | 3 | 14 | 12* | 7.00 | 0 | 0 | 1 | 0 | 650 | 292 | 13 | 22.46 | 1 | 0 | 6/168 |
| Cromb,IB | 5 | 8 | 2 | 123 | 51* | 20.50 | 0 | 1 | 1 | 1 | 960 | 442 | 8 | 55.25 | 0 | 0 | 3/113 |
| Crowe,JJ | 39 | 65 | 4 | 1601 | 128 | 26.24 | 3 | 6 | 6 | 41 | 18 | 9 | 0 | - | 0 | 0 | 0/0 |
| Crowe,MD | 77 | 131 | 11 | 5444 | 299 | 45.36 | 17 | 18 | 9 | 70 | 1377 | 676 | 14 | 48.28 | 0 | 0 | 2/25 |
| Cunis,RS | 20 | 31 | 8 | 295 | 51 | 12.82 | 0 | 1 | 6 | 1 | 4250 | 1887 | 51 | 37.00 | 1 | 0 | 6/76 |
| D'Arcy,JW | 5 | 10 | 0 | 136 | 33 | 13.60 | 0 | 0 | 0 | 0 | | | | | | | |
| Davis,HT | 5 | 7 | 4 | 20 | 8* | 6.66 | 0 | 0 | 0 | 4 | 1010 | 499 | 17 | 29.35 | 1 | 0 | 5/63 |
| de Groen,RP | 5 | 10 | 4 | 45 | 22 | 7.50 | 0 | 0 | 1 | 0 | 1060 | 505 | 11 | 45.90 | 0 | 0 | 3/40 |
| Dempster,CS | 10 | 15 | 4 | 723 | 136 | 65.72 | 2 | 5 | 0 | 2 | 5 | 10 | 0 | - | 0 | 0 | 0/10 |
| Dempster,EW | 5 | 8 | 2 | 106 | 47 | 17.66 | 0 | 0 | 2 | 1 | 544 | 219 | 2 | 109.50 | 0 | 0 | 1/24 |
| Dick,AE | 17 | 30 | 4 | 370 | 50* | 14.23 | 0 | 1 | 4 | 47/4 | | | | | | | |
| Dickinson,GR | 3 | 5 | 0 | 31 | 11 | 6.20 | 0 | 0 | 0 | 3 | 451 | 245 | 8 | 30.62 | 0 | 0 | 3/66 |
| Donnelly,MP | 7 | 12 | 1 | 582 | 206 | 52.90 | 1 | 4 | 2 | 7 | 30 | 20 | 0 | - | 0 | 0 | 0/20 |
| Doull,SB | 24 | 38 | 9 | 383 | 31* | 13.20 | 0 | 0 | 7 | 16 | 4620 | 2255 | 83 | 27.16 | 5 | 0 | 5/46 |
| Dowling,GT | 39 | 77 | 3 | 2306 | 239 | 31.16 | 3 | 11 | 6 | 23 | 36 | 19 | 1 | 19.00 | 0 | 0 | 1/19 |
| Dunning,JA | 4 | 6 | 1 | 38 | 19 | 7.60 | 0 | 0 | 2 | 2 | 830 | 493 | 5 | 98.60 | 0 | 0 | 2/35 |
| Edgar,BA | 39 | 68 | 4 | 1958 | 161 | 30.59 | 3 | 12 | 7 | 14 | 18 | 3 | 0 | - | 0 | 0 | 0/3 |
| Edwards,GN | 8 | 15 | 0 | 377 | 55 | 25.13 | 0 | 3 | 2 | 7 | | | | | | | |
| Emery,RWG | 2 | 4 | 0 | 46 | 28 | 11.50 | 0 | 0 | 0 | 0 | 46 | 52 | 2 | 26.00 | 0 | 0 | 2/52 |
| Fisher,FE | 1 | 2 | 0 | 23 | 14 | 11.50 | 0 | 0 | 0 | 0 | 204 | 78 | 1 | 78.00 | 0 | 0 | 1/78 |

| **NEW ZEALAND** (cont.) | | | | **BATTING AND FIELDING** | | | | | | | | | | **BOWLING** | | | |
|---|---|---|---|---|---|---|---|---|---|---|---|---|---|---|---|---|---|
| | Tests | I | N | Runs | HS | Avge | 100 | 50 | 0's | c/s | Balls | Runs | Wks | Avge | 5w | 10w | BB |
| Fleming,SP | 37 | 65 | 3 | 2349 | 176* | 37.88 | 2 | 18 | 6 | 56 | | | | | | | |
| Foley,H | 1 | 2 | 0 | 4 | 2 | 2.00 | 0 | 0 | 0 | 0 | | | | | | | |
| Franklin,TJ | 21 | 37 | 1 | 828 | 101 | 23.00 | 1 | 4 | 2 | 8 | | | | | | | |
| Freeman,DL | 2 | 2 | 0 | 2 | 1 | 1.00 | 0 | 0 | 0 | 0 | 240 | 169 | 1 | 169.00 | 0 | 0 | 1/91 |
| Gallichan,N | 1 | 2 | 0 | 32 | 30 | 16.00 | 0 | 0 | 0 | 0 | 264 | 113 | 3 | 37.66 | 0 | 0 | 3/99 |
| Gedye,SG | 4 | 8 | 0 | 193 | 55 | 24.12 | 0 | 2 | 0 | 0 | | | | | | | |
| Germon,LK | 12 | 21 | 3 | 381 | 55 | 21.16 | 0 | 1 | 3 | 27/2 | | | | | | | |
| Gillespie,SR | 1 | 1 | 0 | 28 | 28 | 28.00 | 0 | 0 | 0 | 0 | 162 | 79 | 1 | 79.00 | 0 | 0 | 1/79 |
| Gray,EJ | 10 | 16 | 0 | 248 | 50 | 15.50 | 0 | 1 | 0 | 6 | 2076 | 886 | 17 | 52.11 | 0 | 0 | 3/73 |
| Greatbatch,MJ | 41 | 71 | 5 | 2021 | 146* | 30.62 | 3 | 10 | 9 | 27 | 6 | 0 | 0 | - | 0 | 0 | 0/0 |
| Guillen,SC | 3 | 6 | 0 | 98 | 41 | 16.33 | 0 | 0 | 2 | 4/1 | | | | | | | |
| Guy,JW | 12 | 23 | 2 | 440 | 102 | 20.95 | 1 | 3 | 3 | 2 | | | | | | | |
| Hadlee,DR | 26 | 42 | 5 | 530 | 56 | 14.32 | 0 | 1 | 9 | 8 | 4883 | 2389 | 71 | 33.64 | 0 | 0 | 4/30 |
| Hadlee,RJ | 86 | 134 | 19 | 3124 | 151* | 27.16 | 2 | 15 | 12 | 39 | 21918 | 9611 | 431 | 22.29 | 36 | 9 | 9/52 |
| Hadlee,WA | 11 | 19 | 1 | 543 | 116 | 30.16 | 1 | 2 | 1 | 6 | | | | | | | |
| Harford,NS | 8 | 15 | 0 | 229 | 93 | 15.26 | 0 | 2 | 4 | 0 | | | | | | | |
| Harford,RI | 3 | 5 | 2 | 7 | 6 | 2.33 | 0 | 0 | 1 | 11/0 | | | | | | | |
| Harris,CZ | 14 | 28 | 3 | 390 | 71 | 15.60 | 0 | 2 | 6 | 12 | 1348 | 613 | 9 | 68.11 | 0 | 0 | 2/57 |
| Harris,PGZ | 9 | 18 | 1 | 378 | 101 | 22.23 | 1 | 1 | 3 | 6 | 42 | 14 | 0 | - | 0 | 0 | 0/14 |
| Harris,RM | 2 | 3 | 0 | 31 | 13 | 10.33 | 0 | 0 | 0 | 0 | | | | | | | |
| Hart,MN | 14 | 24 | 4 | 353 | 45 | 17.65 | 0 | 0 | 3 | 8 | 3086 | 1438 | 29 | 49.58 | 1 | 0 | 5/77 |
| Hartland,BR | 9 | 18 | 0 | 303 | 52 | 16.83 | 0 | 1 | 3 | 5 | | | | | | | |
| Haslam,MJ | 4 | 2 | 1 | 4 | 3 | 4.00 | 0 | 0 | 0 | 22 | 493 | 245 | 2 | 122.50 | 0 | 0 | 1/33 |
| Hastings,BF | 31 | 56 | 6 | 1510 | 117* | 30.20 | 4 | 7 | 6 | 23 | 22 | 9 | 0 | - | 0 | 0 | 0/3 |
| Hayes,JA | 15 | 22 | 7 | 73 | 19 | 4.86 | 0 | 0 | 4 | 3 | 2675 | 1217 | 30 | 40.56 | 0 | 0 | 4/36 |
| Henderson,M | 1 | 2 | 1 | 8 | 6 | 8.00 | 0 | 0 | 0 | 1 | 90 | 64 | 2 | 32.00 | 0 | 0 | 2/38 |
| Horne,MJ | 11 | 20 | 1 | 691 | 157 | 36.36 | 2 | 1 | 1 | 9 | 60 | 22 | 0 | - | 0 | 0 | 0/0 |
| Horne,PA | 4 | 7 | 0 | 71 | 27 | 10.14 | 0 | 0 | 2 | 3 | | | | | | | |
| Hough,KW | 2 | 3 | 2 | 62 | 31* | 62.00 | 0 | 0 | 0 | 1 | 462 | 175 | 6 | 29.16 | 0 | 0 | 3/79 |
| Howarth,GP | 47 | 83 | 5 | 2531 | 147 | 32.44 | 6 | 11 | 7 | 29 | 614 | 271 | 3 | 90.33 | 0 | 0 | 1/13 |
| Howarth,HJ | 30 | 42 | 18 | 291 | 61 | 12.12 | 0 | 1 | 7 | 33 | 8833 | 3178 | 86 | 36.95 | 2 | 0 | 5/34 |
| James,KC | 11 | 13 | 2 | 52 | 14 | 4.72 | 0 | 0 | 4 | 11/5 | | | | | | | |
| Jarvis,TW | 13 | 22 | 1 | 625 | 182 | 29.76 | 1 | 2 | 6 | 3 | 12 | 3 | 0 | - | 0 | 0 | 0/0 |
| Jones,AH | 39 | 74 | 8 | 2922 | 186 | 44.27 | 7 | 11 | 2 | 25 | 328 | 194 | 1 | 194.00 | 0 | 0 | 1/40 |
| Kennedy,RJ | 4 | 5 | 1 | 28 | 22 | 7.00 | 0 | 0 | 2 | 2 | 636 | 380 | 6 | 63.33 | 0 | 0 | 3/28 |
| Kerr,JL | 7 | 12 | 1 | 212 | 59 | 19.27 | 0 | 1 | 2 | 4 | | | | | | | |
| Kuggeleijn,CM | 2 | 4 | 0 | 7 | 7 | 1.75 | 0 | 0 | 3 | 1 | 97 | 67 | 1 | 67.00 | 0 | 0 | 1/50 |
| Larsen,GR | 8 | 13 | 4 | 127 | 26* | 14.11 | 0 | 0 | 2 | 5 | 1961 | 689 | 24 | 28.70 | 0 | 0 | 3/57 |
| Latham,RT | 4 | 7 | 0 | 219 | 119 | 31.28 | 1 | 0 | 1 | 6 | 18 | 6 | 0 | - | 0 | | 0/6 |
| Lees,WK | 21 | 37 | 4 | 778 | 152 | 23.57 | 1 | 1 | 4 | 52/7 | 5 | 4 | 0 | - | 0 | 0 | 0/4 |
| Leggatt,IB | 1 | 1 | 0 | 0 | 0 | 0.00 | 0 | 0 | 1 | 2 | 24 | 6 | 0 | - | 0 | 0 | 0/6 |
| Leggatt,JG | 9 | 18 | 2 | 351 | 61 | 21.93 | 0 | 2 | 1 | 0 | | | | | | | |
| Lissette,AF | 2 | 4 | 2 | 2 | 1* | 1.00 | 0 | 0 | 2 | 1 | 288 | 124 | 3 | 41.33 | 0 | 0 | 2/73 |
| Loveridge,GR | 1 | 1 | 1 | 4 | 4® | - | 0 | 0 | 0 | 0 | | | | | | | |
| Lowry,TC | 7 | 8 | 0 | 223 | 80 | 27.87 | 0 | 2 | 2 | 8 | 12 | 5 | 0 | - | 0 | 0 | 0/5 |
| McEwan,PE | 4 | 7 | 1 | 96 | 40* | 16.00 | 0 | 0 | 1 | 5 | 36 | 13 | 0 | - | 0 | 0 | 0/6 |
| MacGibbon,AR | 26 | 46 | 5 | 814 | 66 | 19.85 | 0 | 3 | 7 | 13 | 5659 | 2160 | 70 | 30.85 | 1 | 0 | 5/64 |
| McGirr,HM | 2 | 1 | 0 | 51 | 51 | 51.00 | 0 | 1 | 0 | 0 | 180 | 115 | 1 | 115.00 | 0 | 0 | 1/65 |
| McGregor,SN | 25 | 47 | 2 | 892 | 111 | 19.82 | 1 | 3 | 5 | 9 | | | | | | | |
| McLeod,EG | 1 | 2 | 1 | 18 | 16 | 18.00 | 0 | 0 | 0 | 0 | 12 | 5 | 0 | - | 0 | 0 | 0/5 |
| McMahon,TG | 5 | 7 | 4 | 7 | 4* | 2.33 | 0 | 0 | 2 | 7/1 | | | | | | | |
| McMillan,CD | 8 | 14 | 0 | 560 | 142 | 40.00 | 2 | 3 | 2 | 3 | 762 | 209 | 6 | 34.83 | 0 | 0 | 2/27 |
| McRae,DAN | 1 | 2 | 0 | 8 | 8 | 4.00 | 0 | 0 | 1 | 0 | 84 | 44 | 0 | - | 0 | 0 | 0/44 |
| Matheson,AM | 2 | 1 | 0 | 7 | 7 | 7.00 | 0 | 0 | 0 | 2 | 282 | 136 | 2 | 68.00 | 0 | 0 | 2/7 |
| Meale,T | 2 | 4 | 0 | 21 | 10 | 5.25 | 0 | 0 | 0 | 0 | | | | | | | |
| Merritt,WE | 6 | 8 | 1 | 73 | 19 | 10.42 | 0 | 0 | 1 | 2 | 936 | 617 | 12 | 51.41 | 0 | 0 | 4/104 |
| Meuli,EM | 1 | 2 | 0 | 38 | 23 | 19.00 | 0 | 0 | 0 | 0 | | | | | | | |

| NEW ZEALAND (cont.) | BATTING AND FIELDING | | | | | | | | | | BOWLING | | | | | | |
|---|---|---|---|---|---|---|---|---|---|---|---|---|---|---|---|---|---|
| | Tests | I | N | Runs | HS | Avge | 100 | 50 | 0's | c/s | Balls | Runs | Wks | Avge | 5w | 10w | BB |
| Milburn,BD | 3 | 3 | 2 | 8 | 4* | 8.00 | 0 | 0 | 1 | 6/2 | | | | | | | |
| Miller,LSM | 13 | 25 | 0 | 346 | 47 | 13.84 | 0 | 0 | 5 | 1 | 2 | 1 | 0 | - | 0 | 0 | 0/1 |
| Mills,JE | 7 | 10 | 1 | 241 | 117 | 26.77 | 1 | 0 | 2 | 1 | | | | | | | |
| Moir,AM | 17 | 30 | 8 | 327 | 41* | 14.86 | 0 | 0 | 5 | 2 | 2650 | 1418 | 28 | 50.64 | 2 | 0 | 6/155 |
| Moloney,DAR | 3 | 6 | 0 | 156 | 64 | 26.00 | 0 | 1 | 1 | 3 | 12 | 9 | 0 | - | 0 | 0 | 0/9 |
| Mooney,FLH | 14 | 22 | 2 | 343 | 46 | 17.15 | 0 | 0 | 1 | 22/8 | 8 | 0 | 0 | - | 0 | 0 | 0/0 |
| Morgan,RW | 20 | 34 | 1 | 734 | 97 | 22.24 | 0 | 5 | 5 | 12 | 1114 | 609 | 5 | 121.80 | 0 | 0 | 1/16 |
| Morrison,BD | 1 | 2 | 0 | 10 | 10 | 5.00 | 0 | 0 | 1 | 1 | 186 | 129 | 2 | 64.50 | 0 | 0 | 2/129 |
| Morrison,DK | 48 | 71 | 26 | 379 | 42 | 8.42 | 0 | 0 | 24 | 15 | 10064 | 5549 | 160 | 34.68 | 10 | 0 | 7/89 |
| Morrison,JFM | 17 | 29 | 0 | 656 | 117 | 22.62 | 1 | 3 | 4 | 9 | 264 | 71 | 2 | 35.50 | 0 | 0 | 2/52 |
| Motz,RC | 32 | 56 | 3 | 612 | 60 | 11.54 | 0 | 3 | 12 | 9 | 7034 | 3148 | 100 | 31.48 | 5 | 0 | 6/63 |
| Murray,BAG | 13 | 26 | 1 | 598 | 90 | 23.92 | 0 | 5 | 1 | 21 | 6 | 0 | 1 | 0.00 | 0 | 0 | 1/0 |
| Murray,DJ | 8 | 16 | 1 | 303 | 52 | 20.20 | 0 | 1 | 3 | 6 | | | | | | | |
| Nash,DJ | 16 | 23 | 6 | 278 | 56 | 16.35 | 0 | 1 | 3 | 7 | 3078 | 1383 | 51 | 27.11 | 2 | 1 | 6/76 |
| Newman,JA | 3 | 4 | 0 | 33 | 19 | 8.25 | 0 | 0 | 0 | 0 | 425 | 254 | 2 | 127.00 | 0 | 0 | 2/76 |
| O'Connor,SB | 6 | 10 | 5 | 28 | 9 | 5.60 | 0 | 0 | 1 | 4 | 1171 | 637 | 18 | 35.38 | 0 | 0 | 4/52 |
| O'Sullivan,DR | 11 | 21 | 4 | 158 | 23* | 9.29 | 0 | 0 | 2 | 2 | 2744 | 1221 | 18 | 67.83 | 1 | 0 | 5/148 |
| Overton,GWF | 3 | 6 | 1 | 8 | 3* | 1.60 | 0 | 0 | 2 | 1 | 729 | 258 | 9 | 28.66 | 0 | 0 | 3/65 |
| Owens,MB | 8 | 12 | 6 | 16 | 8* | 2.66 | 0 | 0 | 5 | 3 | 1074 | 585 | 17 | 34.41 | 0 | 0 | 4/99 |
| Page,ML | 14 | 20 | 0 | 492 | 104 | 24.60 | 1 | 2 | 1 | 6 | 379 | 231 | 5 | 46.20 | 0 | 0 | 2/21 |
| Parker,JM | 36 | 63 | 2 | 1498 | 121 | 24.55 | 3 | 5 | 4 | 30 | 40 | 24 | 1 | 24.00 | 0 | 0 | 1/24 |
| Parker,NM | 3 | 6 | 0 | 89 | 40 | 14.83 | 0 | 0 | 0 | 2 | | | | | | | |
| Parore,AC | 44 | 77 | 9 | 1905 | 100* | 28.01 | 1 | 11 | 2 | 90/3 | | | | | | | |
| Patel,DN | 37 | 66 | 8 | 1200 | 99 | 20.69 | 0 | 5 | 10 | 16 | 6594 | 3154 | 75 | 42.05 | 3 | 0 | 6/50 |
| Petherick,PJ | 6 | 11 | 4 | 34 | 13 | 4.85 | 0 | 0 | 1 | 4 | 1305 | 685 | 16 | 42.81 | 0 | 0 | 3/90 |
| Petrie,EC | 14 | 25 | 5 | 258 | 55 | 12.90 | 0 | 1 | 2 | 25 | | | | | | | |
| Playle,WR | 8 | 15 | 0 | 151 | 65 | 10.06 | 0 | 1 | 3 | 4 | | | | | | | |
| Pocock,BA | 15 | 29 | 0 | 648 | 85 | 22.34 | 0 | 6 | 4 | 5 | 24 | 20 | 0 | - | 0 | 0 | 0/10 |
| Pollard,V | 32 | 59 | 7 | 1266 | 116 | 24.34 | 2 | 7 | 4 | 19 | 4421 | 1853 | 40 | 46.32 | 0 | 0 | 3/3 |
| Poore,MB | 14 | 24 | 1 | 355 | 45 | 15.43 | 0 | 0 | 6 | 1 | 788 | 367 | 9 | 40.77 | 0 | 0 | 2/28 |
| Priest,MW | 3 | 4 | 0 | 56 | 26 | 14.00 | 0 | 0 | 0 | 0 | 377 | 158 | 3 | 52.66 | 0 | 0 | 2/42 |
| Pringle,C | 14 | 21 | 4 | 175 | 30 | 10.29 | 0 | 0 | 6 | 3 | 2985 | 1389 | 30 | 46.30 | 1 | 1 | 7/52 |
| Puna,N | 3 | 5 | 3 | 31 | 18* | 15.50 | 0 | 0 | 0 | 1 | 480 | 240 | 4 | 60.00 | 0 | 0 | 2/40 |
| Rabone,GO | 12 | 20 | 2 | 562 | 107 | 31.22 | 1 | 2 | 0 | 5 | 1385 | 635 | 16 | 39.68 | 1 | 0 | 6/68 |
| Redmond,RE | 1 | 2 | 0 | 163 | 107 | 81.50 | 1 | 1 | 0 | 0 | | | | | | | |
| Reid,JF | 19 | 31 | 3 | 1296 | 180 | 46.28 | 6 | 2 | 4 | 9 | 18 | 7 | 0 | - | 0 | 0 | 0/0 |
| Reid,JR | 58 | 108 | 5 | 3428 | 142 | 33.28 | 6 | 22 | 5 | 43/1 | 7725 | 2835 | 85 | 33.35 | 1 | 0 | 6/60 |
| Roberts,ADG | 7 | 12 | 1 | 254 | 84* | 23.09 | 0 | 1 | 2 | 4 | 440 | 182 | 4 | 45.50 | 0 | 0 | 1/12 |
| Roberts,AW | 5 | 10 | 1 | 248 | 66* | 27.55 | 0 | 3 | 0 | 4 | 459 | 209 | 7 | 29.85 | 0 | 0 | 4/101 |
| Robertson,GK | 1 | 1 | 0 | 12 | 12 | 12.00 | 0 | 0 | 0 | 0 | 144 | 91 | 1 | 91.00 | 0 | 0 | 1/91 |
| Rowe,CG | 1 | 2 | 0 | 0 | 0 | 0.00 | 0 | 0 | 2 | 1 | | | | | | | |
| Rutherford,KR | 56 | 99 | 8 | 2463 | 107* | 27.06 | 3 | 18 | 17 | 31 | 256 | 161 | 1 | 161.00 | 0 | 0 | 1/38 |
| Scott,RH | 1 | 1 | 0 | 18 | 18 | 18.00 | 0 | 0 | 0 | 0 | 138 | 74 | 1 | 74.00 | 0 | 0 | 1/74 |
| Scott,VJ | 10 | 17 | 1 | 458 | 84 | 28.62 | 0 | 3 | 1 | 7 | 18 | 14 | 0 | - | 0 | 0 | 0/5 |
| Sewell,DG | 1 | 1 | 1 | 1 | 1* | - | 0 | 0 | 0 | 0 | 138 | 90 | 0 | - | 0 | 0 | 0/9 |
| Shrimpton,MJF | 10 | 19 | 0 | 265 | 46 | 13.94 | 0 | 0 | 6 | 2 | 257 | 158 | 5 | 31.60 | 0 | 0 | 3/35 |
| Sinclair,BW | 21 | 40 | 1 | 1148 | 138 | 29.43 | 3 | 3 | 5 | 8 | 60 | 32 | 2 | 16.00 | 0 | 0 | 2/32 |
| Sinclair,IM | 2 | 4 | 1 | 25 | 18* | 8.33 | 0 | 0 | 2 | 1 | 233 | 120 | 1 | 120.00 | 0 | 0 | 1/79 |
| Smith,FB | 4 | 6 | 1 | 237 | 96 | 47.40 | 0 | 2 | 0 | 1 | | | | | | | |
| Smith,HD | 1 | 1 | 0 | 4 | 4 | 4.00 | 0 | 0 | 0 | 0 | 120 | 113 | 1 | 113.00 | 0 | 0 | 1/113 |
| Smith,IDS | 63 | 88 | 17 | 1815 | 173 | 25.56 | 2 | 6 | 7 | 168/8 | 18 | 5 | 0 | - | 0 | 0 | 0/5 |
| Snedden,CA | 1 | | | | | | 0 | 0 | 0 | 0 | 96 | 46 | 0 | - | 0 | 0 | 0/46 |
| Snedden,MC | 25 | 30 | 8 | 327 | 33* | 14.86 | 0 | 0 | 6 | 7 | 4775 | 2199 | 58 | 37.91 | 1 | 0 | 5/68 |
| Sparling,JT | 11 | 20 | 2 | 229 | 50 | 12.72 | 0 | 1 | 2 | 3 | 708 | 327 | 5 | 65.40 | 0 | 0 | 1/9 |
| Spearman,CM | 8 | 16 | 0 | 508 | 112 | 31.75 | 1 | 1 | 2 | 6 | | | | | | | |
| Stirling,DA | 6 | 9 | 2 | 108 | 26 | 15.42 | 0 | 0 | 0 | 1 | 902 | 601 | 13 | 46.23 | 0 | 0 | 4/88 |
| Su'a,ML | 13 | 18 | 5 | 165 | 44 | 12.69 | 0 | 0 | 5 | 8 | 2843 | 1377 | 36 | 38.25 | 2 | 0 | 5/73 |

| NEW ZEALAND (cont.) | | | | BATTING AND FIELDING | | | | | | | | BOWLING | | | | | |
|---|---|---|---|---|---|---|---|---|---|---|---|---|---|---|---|---|---|
| | Tests | I | N | Runs | HS | Avge | 100 | 50 | 0's | c/s | Balls | Runs | Wks | Avge | 5w | 10w | BB |
| Sutcliffe,B | 42 | 76 | 8 | 2727 | 230* | 40.10 | 5 | 15 | 5 | 20 | 538 | 344 | 4 | 86.00 | 0 | 0 | 2/38 |
| Taylor,BR | 30 | 50 | 6 | 898 | 124 | 20.40 | 2 | 2 | 8 | 10 | 6334 | 2953 | 111 | 26.60 | 4 | 0 | 7/74 |
| Taylor,DD | 3 | 5 | 0 | 159 | 77 | 31.80 | 0 | 1 | 0 | 2 | | | | | | | |
| Thomson,K | 2 | 4 | 1 | 94 | 69 | 31.33 | 0 | 1 | 1 | 0 | 21 | 9 | 1 | 9.00 | 0 | 0 | 1/9 |
| Thomson,SA | 19 | 35 | 4 | 958 | 120* | 30.90 | 1 | 5 | 3 | 7 | 1990 | 953 | 19 | 50.15 | 0 | 0 | 3/63 |
| Tindill,EWT | 5 | 9 | 1 | 73 | 37* | 9.12 | 0 | 0 | 1 | 6/1 | | | | | | | |
| Troup,GB | 15 | 18 | 6 | 55 | 13* | 4.58 | 0 | 0 | 7 | 2 | 3183 | 1454 | 39 | 37.28 | 1 | 1 | 6/95 |
| Truscott,PB | 1 | 2 | 0 | 29 | 26 | 14.50 | 0 | 0 | 0 | 1 | | | | | | | |
| Turner,GM | 41 | 73 | 6 | 2991 | 259 | 44.64 | 7 | 14 | 1 | 42 | 12 | 5 | 0 | - | 0 | 0 | 0/5 |
| Twose,RG | 8 | 13 | 1 | 345 | 94 | 28.75 | 0 | 3 | 1 | 1 | 156 | 80 | 3 | 26.66 | 0 | 0 | 2/36 |
| Vance,RH | 4 | 7 | 0 | 207 | 68 | 29.57 | 0 | 1 | 0 | 0 | | | | | | | |
| Vaughan,JTC | 6 | 12 | 1 | 201 | 44 | 18.27 | 0 | 0 | 0 | 4 | 1040 | 450 | 11 | 40.90 | 0 | 0 | 4/27 |
| Vettori,DL | 14 | 23 | 4 | 253 | 90 | 13.31 | 0 | 1 | 5 | 9 | 3797 | 1575 | 52 | 30.28 | 2 | 0 | 6/64 |
| Vivian,GE | 5 | 6 | 0 | 110 | 43 | 18.33 | 0 | 0 | 1 | 3 | 198 | 107 | 1 | 107.00 | 0 | 0 | 1/14 |
| Vivian,HG | 7 | 10 | 0 | 421 | 100 | 42.10 | 1 | 5 | 0 | 4 | 1311 | 633 | 17 | 37.23 | 0 | 0 | 4/85 |
| Wadsworth,KJ | 33 | 51 | 4 | 1010 | 80 | 21.48 | 0 | 5 | 5 | 92/4 | | | | | | | |
| Wallace,WM | 13 | 21 | 0 | 439 | 66 | 20.90 | 0 | 5 | 0 | 5 | 6 | 5 | 0 | - | 0 | 0 | 0/5 |
| Walmsley,KP | 2 | 3 | 0 | 8 | 4 | 2.66 | 0 | 0 | 1 | 0 | 666 | 344 | 7 | 49.14 | 0 | 0 | 3/70 |
| Ward,JT | 8 | 12 | 6 | 75 | 35* | 12.50 | 0 | 0 | 2 | 16/1 | | | | | | | |
| Watson,W | 15 | 18 | 6 | 60 | 11 | 5.00 | 0 | 0 | 3 | 4 | 3486 | 1387 | 40 | 34.67 | 1 | 0 | 6/78 |
| Watt,L | 1 | 2 | 0 | 2 | 2 | 1.00 | 0 | 0 | 1 | 0 | | | | | | | |
| Webb,MG | 3 | 2 | 0 | 12 | 12 | 6.00 | 0 | 0 | 1 | 0 | 732 | 471 | 4 | 117.75 | 0 | 0 | 2/114 |
| Webb,PN | 2 | 3 | 0 | 11 | 5 | 3.66 | 0 | 0 | 0 | 2 | | | | | | | |
| Weir,GL | 11 | 16 | 2 | 416 | 74* | 29.71 | 0 | 3 | 1 | 3 | 342 | 209 | 7 | 29.85 | 0 | 0 | 3/38 |
| White,DJ | 2 | 4 | 0 | 31 | 18 | 7.75 | 0 | 0 | 0 | 0 | 3 | 5 | 0 | - | 0 | 0 | 0/5 |
| Whitelaw,PE | 2 | 4 | 2 | 64 | 30 | 32.00 | 0 | 0 | 0 | 0 | | | | | | | |
| Wiseman,PJ | 3 | 5 | 2 | 32 | 23 | 10.66 | 0 | 0 | 0 | 0 | 677 | 288 | 10 | 28.80 | 1 | 0 | 5/82 |
| Wright,JG | 82 | 148 | 7 | 5334 | 185 | 37.82 | 12 | 23 | 7 | 38 | 30 | 5 | 0 | - | 0 | 0 | 0/1 |
| Young,BA | 33 | 64 | 3 | 1971 | 267* | 32.31 | 2 | 11 | 5 | 53 | | | | | | | |
| Yuile,BW | 17 | 33 | 6 | 481 | 64 | 17.81 | 0 | 1 | 3 | 12 | 2897 | 1213 | 34 | 35.67 | 0 | 0 | 4/43 |

| INDIA | | | | BATTING AND FIELDING | | | | | | | | BOWLING | | | | | |
|---|---|---|---|---|---|---|---|---|---|---|---|---|---|---|---|---|---|
| | Tests | I | N | Runs | HS | Avge | 100 | 50 | 0's | c/s | Balls | Runs | Wks | Avge | 5w | 10w | BB |
| Abid Ali,S | 29 | 53 | 3 | 1018 | 81 | 20.36 | 0 | 6 | 3 | 32 | 4164 | 1980 | 47 | 42.12 | 1 | 0 | 6/55 |
| Adhikari,HR | 21 | 36 | 8 | 872 | 114* | 31.14 | 1 | 4 | 5 | 8 | 170 | 82 | 3 | 27.33 | 0 | 0 | 3/68 |
| Amarnath,M | 69 | 113 | 10 | 4378 | 138 | 42.50 | 11 | 24 | 12 | 47 | 3676 | 1782 | 32 | 55.68 | 0 | 0 | 4/63 |
| Amarnath,NB | 24 | 40 | 4 | 878 | 118 | 24.38 | 1 | 4 | 5 | 13 | 4241 | 1481 | 45 | 32.91 | 2 | 0 | 5/96 |
| Amarnath,S | 10 | 18 | 0 | 550 | 124 | 30.55 | 1 | 3 | 1 | 4 | 11 | 5 | 1 | 5.00 | 0 | 0 | 1/5 |
| Amar Singh,L | 7 | 14 | 1 | 292 | 51 | 22.46 | 0 | 1 | 1 | 3 | 2182 | 858 | 28 | 30.64 | 2 | 0 | 7/86 |
| Amir Elahi | 1 | 2 | 0 | 17 | 13 | 8.50 | 0 | 0 | 0 | 0 | | | | | | | |
| Amre,PK | 11 | 13 | 3 | 425 | 103 | 42.50 | 1 | 3 | 0 | 9 | | | | | | | |
| Ankola,SA | 1 | 1 | 0 | 6 | 6 | 6.00 | 0 | 0 | 0 | 0 | 180 | 128 | 2 | 64.00 | 0 | 0 | 1/35 |
| Apte,AL | 1 | 2 | 0 | 15 | 8 | 7.50 | 0 | 0 | 0 | 0 | | | | | | | |
| Apte,ML | 7 | 13 | 2 | 542 | 163* | 49.27 | 1 | 3 | 1 | 2 | 6 | 3 | 0 | - | 0 | 0 | 0/3 |
| Arshad Ayub | 13 | 19 | 4 | 257 | 57 | 17.13 | 0 | 1 | 1 | 2 | 3662 | 1438 | 41 | 35.07 | 3 | 0 | 5/50 |
| Arun,B | 2 | 2 | 1 | 4 | 2* | 4.00 | 0 | 0 | 0 | 2 | 252 | 116 | 4 | 29.00 | 0 | 0 | 3/76 |
| Arun Lal | 16 | 29 | 1 | 729 | 93 | 26.03 | 0 | 6 | 1 | 13 | 16 | 7 | 0 | - | 0 | 0 | 0/1 |
| Azad,K | 7 | 12 | 0 | 135 | 24 | 11.25 | 0 | 0 | 2 | 3 | 750 | 373 | 3 | 124.33 | 0 | 0 | 2/84 |
| Azharuddin,M | 91 | 132 | 8 | 5697 | 199 | 45.94 | 20 | 19 | 5 | 101 | 13 | 16 | 0 | - | 0 | 0 | 0/4 |
| Baig,AA | 10 | 18 | 0 | 428 | 112 | 23.77 | 1 | 2 | 1 | 6 | 18 | 15 | 0 | - | 0 | 0 | 0/2 |
| Banerjee,S | 1 | 1 | 0 | 3 | 3 | 3.00 | 0 | 0 | 0 | 0 | 108 | 47 | 3 | 15.66 | 0 | 0 | 3/47 |
| Banerjee,SA | 1 | 1 | 0 | 0 | 0 | 0.00 | 0 | 0 | 1 | 3 | 306 | 181 | 5 | 36.20 | 0 | 0 | 4/120 |
| Banerjee,SN | 1 | 2 | 0 | 13 | 8 | 6.50 | 0 | 0 | 0 | 0 | 273 | 127 | 5 | 25.40 | 0 | 0 | 4/54 |
| Baqa Jilani,M | 1 | 2 | 1 | 16 | 12 | 16.00 | 0 | 0 | 0 | 0 | 90 | 55 | 0 | - | 0 | 0 | 0/55 |
| Bedi,BS | 67 | 101 | 28 | 656 | 50* | 8.98 | 0 | 1 | 20 | 26 | 21367 | 7637 | 266 | 28.71 | 14 | 1 | 7/98 |
| Bhandari,P | 3 | 4 | 0 | 77 | 39 | 19.25 | 0 | 0 | 0 | 1 | 78 | 39 | 0 | - | 0 | 0 | 0/12 |
| Bhat,AR | 2 | 3 | 1 | 6 | 6 | 3.00 | 0 | 0 | 1 | 0 | 438 | 151 | 4 | 37.75 | 0 | 0 | 2/65 |

| INDIA (cont.) | | | | BATTING AND FIELDING | | | | | | | | BOWLING | | | | | |
|---|---|---|---|---|---|---|---|---|---|---|---|---|---|---|---|---|---|
| | Tests | I | N | Runs | HS | Avge | 100 | 50 | 0's | c/s | Balls | Runs | Wks | Avge | 5w | 10w | BB |
| Binny,RMH | 27 | 41 | 5 | 830 | 83* | 23.05 | 0 | 5 | 7 | 11 | 2870 | 1534 | 47 | 32.63 | 2 | 0 | 6/65 |
| Borde,CG | 55 | 97 | 11 | 3061 | 177* | 35.59 | 5 | 18 | 13 | 37 | 5695 | 2417 | 52 | 46.48 | 1 | 0 | 5/88 |
| Chandrasekhar,BS | 58 | 80 | 39 | 167 | 22 | 4.07 | 0 | 0 | 23 | 25 | 15963 | 7199 | 242 | 29.74 | 16 | 2 | 8/79 |
| Chauhan,CPS | 40 | 68 | 2 | 2084 | 97 | 31.57 | 0 | 16 | 6 | 38 | 174 | 106 | 2 | 53.00 | 0 | 0 | 1/4 |
| Chauhan,RK | 21 | 17 | 3 | 98 | 23 | 7.00 | 0 | 0 | 1 | 12 | 4857 | 1857 | 47 | 39.51 | 0 | 0 | 4/48 |
| Chowdhury,NR | 2 | 2 | 1 | 3 | 3* | 3.00 | 0 | 0 | 1 | 0 | 516 | 205 | 1 | 205.00 | 0 | 0 | 1/130 |
| Colah,SHM | 2 | 4 | 0 | 69 | 31 | 17.25 | 0 | 0 | 0 | 2 | | | | | | | |
| Contractor,NJ | 31 | 52 | 1 | 1611 | 108 | 31.58 | 1 | 11 | 2 | 18 | 186 | 80 | 1 | 80.00 | 0 | 0 | 1/9 |
| Dani,HT | 1 | | | | | | 0 | 0 | 0 | 1 | 60 | 19 | 1 | 19.00 | 0 | 0 | 1/9 |
| Desai,RB | 28 | 44 | 13 | 418 | 85 | 13.48 | 0 | 1 | 8 | 9 | 5597 | 2761 | 74 | 37.31 | 2 | 0 | 6/56 |
| Dilawar Hussain | 3 | 6 | 0 | 254 | 59 | 42.33 | 0 | 3 | 0 | 6/1 | | | | | | | |
| Divecha,RV | 5 | 5 | 0 | 60 | 26 | 12.00 | 0 | 0 | 0 | 5 | 1044 | 361 | 11 | 32.81 | 0 | 0 | 3/102 |
| Doshi,DR | 33 | 38 | 10 | 129 | 20 | 4.60 | 0 | 0 | 14 | 10 | 9322 | 3502 | 114 | 30.71 | 6 | 0 | 6/102 |
| Dravid,RS | 22 | 35 | 3 | 1643 | 148 | 51.34 | 1 | 15 | 0 | 24 | 18 | 6 | 0 | - | 0 | 0 | 0/2 |
| Durani,SA | 29 | 50 | 2 | 1202 | 104 | 25.04 | 1 | 7 | 4 | 14 | 6446 | 2657 | 75 | 35.42 | 3 | 1 | 6/73 |
| Engineer,FM | 46 | 87 | 3 | 2611 | 121 | 31.08 | 2 | 16 | 7 | 66/16 | | | | | | | |
| Gadkari,CV | 6 | 10 | 4 | 129 | 50* | 21.50 | 0 | 1 | 2 | 6 | 102 | 45 | 0 | - | 0 | 0 | 0/8 |
| Gaekwad,AD | 40 | 70 | 4 | 1985 | 201 | 30.07 | 2 | 10 | 4 | 15 | 334 | 187 | 2 | 93.50 | 0 | 0 | 1/4 |
| Gaekwad,DK | 11 | 20 | 1 | 350 | 52 | 18.42 | 0 | 1 | 3 | 5 | 12 | 12 | 0 | - | 0 | 0 | 0/4 |
| Gaekwad,HG | 1 | 2 | 0 | 22 | 14 | 11.00 | 0 | 0 | 0 | 0 | 222 | 47 | 0 | - | 0 | 0 | 0/47 |
| Gandotra,A | 2 | 4 | 0 | 54 | 18 | 13.50 | 0 | 0 | 0 | 1 | 6 | 5 | 0 | - | 0 | 0 | 0/5 |
| Ganesh,D | 4 | 7 | 3 | 25 | 8 | 6.25 | 0 | 0 | 0 | 0 | 461 | 287 | 5 | 57.40 | 0 | 0 | 2/28 |
| Ganguly,SC | 20 | 31 | 2 | 1483 | 173 | 51.13 | 5 | 5 | 3 | 5 | 837 | 439 | 16 | 27.43 | 0 | 0 | 3/28 |
| Gavaskar,SM | 125 | 214 | 16 | 10122 | 236* | 51.12 | 34 | 45 | 12 | 108 | 380 | 206 | 1 | 206.00 | 0 | 0 | 1/34 |
| Ghavri,KD | 39 | 57 | 14 | 913 | 86 | 21.23 | 0 | 2 | 2 | 16 | 7042 | 3656 | 109 | 33.54 | 4 | 0 | 5/33 |
| Ghorpade,JM | 8 | 15 | 0 | 229 | 41 | 15.26 | 0 | 0 | 3 | 4 | 150 | 131 | 0 | - | 0 | 0 | 0/17 |
| Ghulam Ahmed | 22 | 31 | 9 | 192 | 50 | 8.72 | 0 | 1 | 9 | 11 | 5650 | 2052 | 68 | 30.17 | 4 | 1 | 7/49 |
| Gopalan,MJ | 1 | 2 | 1 | 18 | 11* | 18.00 | 0 | 0 | 0 | 3 | 114 | 39 | 1 | 39.00 | 0 | 0 | 1/39 |
| Gopinath,CD | 8 | 12 | 1 | 242 | 50* | 22.00 | 0 | 1 | 4 | 2 | 48 | 11 | 1 | 11.00 | 0 | 0 | 1/11 |
| Guard,GM | 2 | 2 | 0 | 11 | 7 | 5.50 | 0 | 0 | 0 | 2 | 396 | 182 | 3 | 60.66 | 0 | 0 | 2/69 |
| Guha,S | 4 | 7 | 2 | 17 | 6 | 3.40 | 0 | 0 | 1 | 2 | 674 | 311 | 3 | 103.66 | 0 | 0 | 2/66 |
| Gul Mahomed | 8 | 15 | 0 | 166 | 34 | 11.06 | 0 | 0 | 2 | 3 | 77 | 24 | 2 | 12.00 | 0 | 0 | 2/21 |
| Gupte,BP | 3 | 3 | 2 | 28 | 17* | 28.00 | 0 | 0 | 0 | 0 | 678 | 349 | 3 | 116.33 | 0 | 0 | 1/54 |
| Gupte,SP | 36 | 42 | 13 | 183 | 21 | 6.31 | 0 | 0 | 6 | 14 | 11284 | 4403 | 149 | 29.55 | 12 | 1 | 9/102 |
| Gursharan Singh | 1 | 1 | 0 | 18 | 18 | 18.00 | 0 | 0 | 0 | 2 | | | | | | | |
| Hanumant Singh | 14 | 24 | 2 | 686 | 105 | 31.18 | 1 | 5 | 3 | 11 | 66 | 51 | 0 | - | 0 | 0 | 0/5 |
| Harbhajan Singh | 1 | 2 | 1 | 4 | 4* | 4.00 | 0 | 0 | 1 | 1 | 174 | 136 | 2 | 68.00 | 0 | 0 | 2/112 |
| Hardikar,MS | 2 | 4 | 1 | 56 | 32* | 18.66 | 0 | 0 | 1 | 3 | 108 | 55 | 1 | 55.00 | 0 | 0 | 1/9 |
| Harvinder Singh | 2 | 3 | 1 | 0 | 0* | 0.00 | 0 | 0 | 2 | 0 | 138 | 98 | 2 | 49.00 | 0 | 0 | 1/28 |
| Hazare,VS | 30 | 52 | 6 | 2192 | 164* | 47.65 | 7 | 9 | 4 | 11 | 2840 | 1220 | 20 | 61.00 | 0 | 0 | 4/29 |
| Hindelkar,DD | 4 | 7 | 2 | 71 | 26 | 14.20 | 0 | 0 | 0 | 3/0 | | | | | | | |
| Hirwani,ND | 17 | 22 | 12 | 54 | 17 | 5.40 | 0 | 0 | 5 | 5 | 4298 | 1987 | 66 | 30.10 | 4 | 1 | 8/61 |
| Ibrahim,KC | 4 | 8 | 0 | 169 | 85 | 21.12 | 0 | 1 | 1 | 0 | | | | | | | |
| Indrajitsinhji,KS | 4 | 7 | 1 | 51 | 23 | 8.50 | 0 | 0 | 1 | 6/3 | | | | | | | |
| Irani,JK | 2 | 3 | 2 | 3 | 2* | 3.00 | 0 | 0 | 1 | 2/1 | | | | | | | |
| Jadeja,AD | 11 | 16 | 1 | 473 | 96 | 31.53 | 0 | 4 | 1 | 3 | | | | | | | |
| Jahingir Khan,M | 4 | 7 | 0 | 39 | 13 | 5.57 | 0 | 0 | 1 | 4 | 606 | 255 | 4 | 63.75 | 0 | 0 | 4/60 |
| Jai,LP | 1 | 2 | 0 | 19 | 19 | 9.50 | 0 | 0 | 1 | 0 | | | | | | | |
| Jaisimha,ML | 39 | 71 | 4 | 2056 | 129 | 30.68 | 3 | 12 | 9 | 17 | 2097 | 829 | 9 | 92.11 | 0 | 0 | 2/54 |
| Jamshedji,RJD | 1 | 2 | 2 | 5 | 4* | 0 | 0 | 0 | 0 | 2 | 210 | 137 | 3 | 45.66 | 0 | 0 | 3/137 |
| Jayantilal,K | 1 | 1 | 0 | 5 | 5 | 5.00 | 0 | 0 | 0 | 0 | | | | | | | |
| Johnson,DJ | 2 | 3 | 1 | 8 | 5 | 4.00 | 0 | 0 | 0 | 0 | 240 | 143 | 3 | 47.66 | 0 | 0 | 2/52 |
| Joshi,PG | 12 | 20 | 1 | 207 | 52* | 10.89 | 0 | 1 | 3 | 18/9 | | | | | | | |
| Joshi,SB | 9 | 13 | 1 | 181 | 43 | 15.08 | 0 | 0 | 1 | 3 | 1534 | 667 | 21 | 31.76 | 0 | 0 | 4/43 |
| Kambli,VG | 17 | 21 | 1 | 1084 | 227 | 54.20 | 4 | 3 | 3 | 6 | | | | | | | |
| Kanitkar,HS | 2 | 4 | 0 | 111 | 65 | 27.75 | 0 | 1 | 0 | 0 | | | | | | | |
| Kapil Dev | 131 | 184 | 15 | 5248 | 163 | 31.05 | 8 | 27 | 16 | 64 | 28741 | 12867 | 434 | 29.64 | 23 | 2 | 9/83 |

| INDIA (cont.) | | | | BATTING AND FIELDING | | | | | | | | | | BOWLING | | | |
|---|---|---|---|---|---|---|---|---|---|---|---|---|---|---|---|---|---|
| | Tests | I | N | Runs | HS | Avge | 100 | 50 | 0's | c/s | Balls | Runs | Wks | Avge | 5w | 10w | BB |
| Kapoor,AR | 4 | 6 | 1 | 97 | 42 | 19.40 | 0 | 0 | 0 | 1 | 636 | 255 | 6 | 42.50 | 0 | 0 | 2/19 |
| Kardar,AH | 3 | 5 | 0 | 80 | 43 | 16.00 | 0 | 0 | 1 | 1 | | | | | | | |
| Kenny,RB | 5 | 10 | 1 | 245 | 62 | 27.72 | 0 | 3 | 2 | 1 | | | | | | | |
| Kirmani,SMH | 88 | 124 | 22 | 2759 | 102 | 27.04 | 2 | 12 | 7 | 160/38 | 18 | 13 | 1 | 13.00 | 0 | 0 | 1/9 |
| Kishenchand,G | 5 | 10 | 0 | 89 | 44 | 8.90 | 0 | 0 | 5 | 1 | | | | | | | |
| Kripal Singh,AG | 14 | 20 | 5 | 422 | 100* | 28.13 | 1 | 2 | 4 | 4 | 1518 | 584 | 10 | 58.40 | 0 | 0 | 3/43 |
| Krishnamurthy,P | 5 | 6 | 0 | 33 | 20 | 5.50 | 0 | 0 | 2 | 7/1 | | | | | | | |
| Kulkarni,NM | 2 | 1 | 1 | 1 | 1* | - | 0 | 0 | 0 | 1 | 420 | 195 | 1 | 195.00 | 0 | 0 | 1/195 |
| Kulkarni,RR | 3 | 2 | 0 | 2 | 2 | 1.00 | 0 | 0 | 1 | 1 | 366 | 227 | 5 | 45.40 | 0 | 0 | 3/85 |
| Kulkarni,UN | 4 | 8 | 5 | 13 | 7 | 4.33 | 0 | 0 | 1 | 0 | 448 | 238 | 5 | 47.60 | 0 | 0 | 2/37 |
| Kumar,VV | 2 | 2 | 0 | 6 | 6 | 3.00 | 0 | 0 | 1 | 2 | 605 | 202 | 7 | 28.85 | 1 | 0 | 5/64 |
| Kumble,AR | 46 | 55 | 10 | 830 | 88 | 18.44 | 0 | 3 | 6 | 20 | 13978 | 5598 | 197 | 28.41 | 11 | 1 | 7/59 |
| Kunderan,BK | 18 | 34 | 4 | 981 | 192 | 32.70 | 2 | 3 | 1 | 23/7 | 24 | 13 | 0 | - | 0 | 0 | 0/13 |
| Kuruvilla,A | 10 | 11 | 1 | 66 | 35* | 6.60 | 0 | 0 | 5 | 0 | 1765 | 892 | 25 | 35.68 | 1 | 0 | 5/68 |
| Lall Singh | 1 | 2 | 0 | 44 | 29 | 22.00 | 0 | 0 | 0 | 1 | | | | | | | |
| Lamba,R | 4 | 5 | 0 | 102 | 53 | 20.40 | 0 | 1 | 1 | 5 | | | | | | | |
| Laxman,VVS | 10 | 16 | 2 | 405 | 95 | 28.92 | 0 | 4 | 1 | 9 | 102 | 51 | 0 | - | 0 | 0 | 0/1 |
| Madan Lal,S | 39 | 62 | 16 | 1042 | 74 | 22.65 | 0 | 5 | 7 | 15 | 5997 | 2846 | 71 | 40.08 | 4 | 0 | 5/23 |
| Mahomed Nissar | 6 | 11 | 3 | 55 | 14 | 6.87 | 0 | 0 | 2 | 2 | 1211 | 707 | 25 | 28.28 | 3 | 0 | 5/90 |
| Maka,ES | 2 | 1 | 1 | 2 | 2* | 0 | 0 | 0 | 0 | 2/1 | | | | | | | |
| Malhotra,A | 7 | 10 | 1 | 226 | 72* | 25.11 | 0 | 1 | 2 | 2 | 18 | 3 | 0 | - | 0 | 0 | 0/0 |
| Maninder Singh | 35 | 38 | 12 | 99 | 15 | 3.80 | 0 | 0 | 11 | 9 | 8218 | 3288 | 88 | 37.36 | 3 | 2 | 7/27 |
| Manjrekar,SV | 37 | 61 | 6 | 2043 | 218 | 37.14 | 4 | 9 | 3 | 25/1 | 17 | 15 | 0 | - | 0 | 0 | 0/4 |
| Manjrekar,VL | 55 | 92 | 10 | 3208 | 189* | 39.12 | 7 | 15 | 11 | 19/2 | 204 | 44 | 1 | 44.00 | 0 | 0 | 1/16 |
| Mankad,AV | 22 | 42 | 3 | 991 | 97 | 25.41 | 0 | 6 | 3 | 12 | 41 | 43 | 0 | - | 0 | 0 | 0/0 |
| Mankad,MH | 44 | 72 | 5 | 2109 | 231 | 31.47 | 5 | 6 | 7 | 33 | 14686 | 5236 | 162 | 32.32 | 8 | 2 | 8/52 |
| Mantri,MK | 4 | 8 | 1 | 67 | 39 | 9.57 | 0 | 0 | 2 | 8/1 | | | | | | | |
| Meherhomji,KR | 1 | 1 | 1 | 0 | 0* | 0 | 0 | 0 | 0 | 1/0 | | | | | | | |
| Mehra,VL | 8 | 14 | 1 | 329 | 62 | 25.30 | 0 | 2 | 1 | 1 | 36 | 6 | 0 | - | 0 | 0 | 0/1 |
| Merchant,VM | 10 | 18 | 0 | 859 | 154 | 47.72 | 3 | 3 | 2 | 7 | 54 | 40 | 0 | - | 0 | 0 | 0/17 |
| Mhambrey,PL | 2 | 3 | 1 | 58 | 28 | 29.00 | 0 | 0 | 0 | 1 | 258 | 148 | 2 | 74.00 | 0 | 0 | 1/43 |
| Milka Singh,AG | 4 | 6 | 0 | 92 | 35 | 15.33 | 0 | 0 | 0 | 2 | 6 | 2 | 0 | - | 0 | 0 | 0/2 |
| Modi,RS | 10 | 17 | 1 | 736 | 112 | 46.00 | 1 | 6 | 0 | 3 | 30 | 14 | 0 | - | 0 | 0 | 0/14 |
| Mohanty,DS | 2 | 1 | 1 | 0 | 0* | - | 0 | 0 | 0 | 0 | 430 | 239 | 4 | 59.75 | 0 | 0 | 4/78 |
| Mongia,NR | 33 | 49 | 6 | 1235 | 152 | 28.72 | 1 | 5 | 2 | 74/5 | | | | | | | |
| More,KS | 49 | 64 | 14 | 1285 | 73 | 25.70 | 0 | 7 | 7 | 110/20 | 12 | 12 | 0 | - | 0 | | 0/12 |
| Muddiah,VM | 2 | 3 | 1 | 11 | 11 | 5.50 | 0 | 0 | 1 | 0 | 318 | 134 | 3 | 44.66 | 0 | 0 | 2/40 |
| Mushtaq Ali,S | 11 | 20 | 1 | 612 | 112 | 32.21 | 2 | 3 | 1 | 7 | 378 | 202 | 3 | 67.33 | 0 | 0 | 1/45 |
| Nadkarni,RG | 41 | 67 | 12 | 1414 | 122* | 25.70 | 1 | 7 | 6 | 22 | 9165 | 2559 | 88 | 29.07 | 4 | 1 | 6/43 |
| Naik,SS | 3 | 6 | 0 | 141 | 77 | 23.50 | 0 | 1 | 1 | 0 | | | | | | | |
| Naoomal Jeoomal | 3 | 5 | 1 | 108 | 43 | 27.00 | 0 | 0 | 0 | 0 | 108 | 68 | 2 | 34.00 | 0 | 0 | 1/4 |
| Narasimha Rao,MV | 4 | 6 | 1 | 46 | 20* | 9.20 | 0 | 0 | 0 | 8 | 463 | 227 | 3 | 75.66 | 0 | 0 | 2/46 |
| Navle,JG | 2 | 4 | 0 | 42 | 13 | 10.50 | 0 | 0 | 0 | 1 | | | | | | | |
| Nayak,SV | 2 | 3 | 1 | 19 | 11 | 9.50 | 0 | 0 | 0 | 1 | 231 | 132 | 1 | 132.00 | 0 | 0 | 1/16 |
| Nayudu,CK | 7 | 14 | 0 | 350 | 81 | 25.00 | 0 | 2 | 0 | 4 | 858 | 386 | 9 | 42.88 | 0 | 0 | 3/40 |
| Nayudu,CS | 11 | 19 | 3 | 147 | 36 | 9.18 | 0 | 0 | 3 | 3 | 522 | 359 | 2 | 179.50 | 0 | 0 | 1/19 |
| Nazir Ali,S | 2 | 4 | 0 | 30 | 13 | 7.50 | 0 | 0 | 0 | 0 | 138 | 83 | 4 | 20.75 | 0 | 0 | 4/83 |
| Nyalchand,S | 1 | 2 | 1 | 7 | 6* | 7.00 | 0 | 0 | 0 | 0 | 384 | 97 | 3 | 32.33 | 0 | 0 | 3/97 |
| Pai,AM | 1 | 2 | 0 | 10 | 9 | 5.00 | 0 | 0 | 0 | 0 | 114 | 31 | 2 | 15.50 | 0 | 0 | 2/29 |
| Palia,PE | 2 | 4 | 1 | 29 | 16 | 9.66 | 0 | 0 | 0 | 0 | 42 | 13 | 0 | - | 0 | 0 | 0/2 |
| Pandit,CS | 5 | 8 | 1 | 171 | 39 | 24.42 | 0 | 0 | 0 | 14/2 | | | | | | | |
| Parkar,GA | 1 | 2 | 0 | 7 | 6 | 3.50 | 0 | 0 | 0 | 1 | | | | | | | |
| Parkar,RD | 2 | 4 | 0 | 80 | 35 | 20.00 | 0 | 0 | 0 | 0 | | | | | | | |
| Parsana,DD | 2 | 2 | 0 | 1 | 1 | 0.50 | 0 | 0 | 1 | 0 | 120 | 50 | 1 | 50.00 | 0 | 0 | 1/32 |
| Patankar,CT | 1 | 2 | 1 | 14 | 13 | 14.00 | 0 | 0 | 0 | 3/0 | | | | | | | |
| Pataudi,Nawab of, jr | 46 | 83 | 3 | 2793 | 203* | 34.91 | 6 | 16 | 7 | 27 | 132 | 88 | 1 | 88.00 | 0 | 0 | 1/10 |
| Pataudi,Nawab of, sr | 3 | 5 | 0 | 55 | 22 | 11.00 | 0 | 0 | 0 | 0 | | | | | | | |

| **INDIA** (cont.) | BATTING AND FIELDING | | | | | | | | | | BOWLING | | | | | | |
|---|---|---|---|---|---|---|---|---|---|---|---|---|---|---|---|---|---|
| | Tests | I | N | Runs | HS | Avge | 100 | 50 | 0's | c/s | Balls | Runs | Wks | Avge | 5w | 10w | BB |
| Patel,BP | 21 | 38 | 5 | 972 | 115* | 29.45 | 1 | 5 | 0 | 17 | | | | | | | |
| Patel,JM | 7 | 10 | 1 | 25 | 12 | 2.77 | 0 | 0 | 5 | 2 | 1725 | 637 | 29 | 21.96 | 2 | 1 | 9/69 |
| Patel,RG | 1 | 2 | 0 | 0 | 0 | 0.00 | 0 | 0 | 2 | 1 | 84 | 51 | 0 | - | 0 | 0 | 0/14 |
| Patiala,Yuvaraj of | 1 | 2 | 0 | 84 | 60 | 42.00 | 0 | 1 | 0 | 0 | | | | | | | |
| Patil,SM | 29 | 47 | 4 | 1588 | 174 | 36.93 | 4 | 7 | 4 | 12 | 645 | 240 | 9 | 26.66 | 0 | 0 | 2/28 |
| Patil,SR | 1 | 1 | 1 | 14 | 14* | 0 | 0 | 0 | 0 | 1 | 138 | 51 | 2 | 25.50 | 0 | 0 | 1/15 |
| Phadkar,DG | 31 | 45 | 7 | 1229 | 123 | 32.34 | 2 | 8 | 3 | 21 | 5994 | 2285 | 62 | 36.85 | 3 | 0 | 7/159 |
| Prabhakar,M | 39 | 58 | 9 | 1598 | 120 | 32.61 | 1 | 9 | 3 | 20 | 7481 | 3581 | 96 | 37.30 | 3 | 0 | 6/132 |
| Prasanna,EAS | 49 | 84 | 20 | 735 | 37 | 11.48 | 0 | 0 | 15 | 18 | 14353 | 5742 | 189 | 30.38 | 10 | 2 | 8/76 |
| Punjabi,PH | 5 | 10 | 0 | 164 | 33 | 16.40 | 0 | 0 | 0 | 5 | | | | | | | |
| Rai Singh,K | 1 | 2 | 0 | 26 | 24 | 13.00 | 0 | 0 | 0 | 0 | | | | | | | |
| Rajinder Pal | 1 | 2 | 1 | 6 | 3* | 6.00 | 0 | 0 | 0 | 0 | 78 | 22 | 0 | - | 0 | 0 | 0/3 |
| Rajindernath,V | 1 | | | | | | 0 | 0 | 0 | 0/4 | | | | | | | |
| Rajput,LS | 2 | 4 | 0 | 105 | 61 | 26.25 | 0 | 1 | 1 | 1 | | | | | | | |
| Raman,WV | 11 | 19 | 1 | 448 | 96 | 24.88 | 0 | 4 | 4 | 6 | 348 | 129 | 2 | 64.50 | 0 | 0 | 1/7 |
| Ramaswami,C | 2 | 4 | 1 | 170 | 60 | 56.66 | 0 | 1 | 0 | 0 | | | | | | | |
| Ramchand,GS | 33 | 53 | 5 | 1180 | 109 | 24.58 | 2 | 5 | 6 | 20 | 4976 | 1899 | 41 | 46.31 | 1 | 0 | 6/49 |
| Ramji,L | 1 | 2 | 0 | 1 | 1 | 0.50 | 0 | 0 | 1 | 1 | 138 | 64 | 0 | - | 0 | 0 | 0/64 |
| Rangachari,CR | 4 | 6 | 3 | 8 | 8* | 2.66 | 0 | 0 | 3 | 0 | 846 | 493 | 9 | 54.77 | 1 | 0 | 5/107 |
| Rangnekar,KM | 3 | 6 | 0 | 33 | 18 | 5.50 | 0 | 0 | 2 | 1 | | | | | | | |
| Ranjane,VB | 7 | 9 | 3 | 40 | 16 | 6.66 | 0 | 0 | 1 | 1 | 1265 | 649 | 19 | 34.15 | 0 | 0 | 4/72 |
| Rathore,V | 6 | 10 | 0 | 131 | 44 | 13.10 | 0 | 0 | 1 | 12 | | | | | | | |
| Razdan,V | 2 | 2 | 1 | 6 | 6* | 6.00 | 0 | 0 | 1 | 0 | 240 | 141 | 5 | 28.20 | 1 | 0 | 5/79 |
| Reddy,B | 4 | 5 | 1 | 38 | 21 | 9.50 | 0 | 0 | 7 | 9/2 | | | | | | | |
| Rege,MR | 1 | 2 | 0 | 15 | 15 | 7.50 | 0 | 0 | 1 | 1 | | | | | | | |
| Roy,A | 4 | 7 | 0 | 91 | 48 | 13.00 | 0 | 0 | 2 | 0 | | | | | | | |
| Roy,Pankaj | 43 | 79 | 4 | 2442 | 173 | 32.56 | 5 | 9 | 14 | 13 | 104 | 66 | 1 | 66.00 | 0 | 0 | 1/6 |
| Roy,Pranab | 2 | 3 | 1 | 71 | 60* | 35.50 | 0 | 1 | 0 | 1 | | | | | | | |
| Sandhu,BS | 8 | 11 | 4 | 214 | 71 | 30.57 | 0 | 2 | 1 | 1 | 1020 | 557 | 10 | 55.70 | 0 | 0 | 3/87 |
| Sardesai,DN | 30 | 55 | 4 | 2001 | 212 | 39.23 | 5 | 9 | 4 | 4 | 59 | 45 | 0 | - | 0 | 0 | 0/3 |
| Sarwate,CT | 9 | 17 | 1 | 208 | 37 | 13.00 | 0 | 0 | 4 | 0 | 658 | 374 | 3 | 124.66 | 0 | 0 | 1/16 |
| Saxena,RC | 1 | 2 | 0 | 25 | 16 | 12.50 | 0 | 0 | 0 | 0 | 12 | 11 | 0 | - | 0 | 0 | 0/11 |
| Sekhar,TA | 2 | 1 | 1 | 0 | 0* | - | 0 | 0 | 0 | 0 | 216 | 129 | 0 | - | 0 | 0 | 0/43 |
| Sen,P | 14 | 18 | 4 | 165 | 25 | 11.78 | 0 | 0 | 1 | 20/11 | | | | | | | |
| Sengupta,AK | 1 | 2 | 0 | 9 | 8 | 4.50 | 0 | 0 | 0 | 0 | | | | | | | |
| Sharma,AK | 1 | 2 | 0 | 53 | 30 | 26.50 | 0 | 0 | 0 | 1 | 24 | 9 | 0 | - | 0 | 0 | 0/9 |
| Sharma,C | 23 | 27 | 9 | 396 | 54 | 22.00 | 0 | 1 | 2 | 7 | 3470 | 2163 | 61 | 35.45 | 4 | 1 | 6/58 |
| Sharma,G | 5 | 4 | 1 | 11 | 10* | 3.66 | 0 | 0 | 2 | 2 | 1307 | 418 | 10 | 41.80 | 0 | 0 | 4/88 |
| Sharma,PH | 5 | 10 | 0 | 187 | 54 | 18.70 | 0 | 1 | 0 | 1 | 24 | 8 | 0 | - | 0 | 0 | 0/2 |
| Sharma,SK | 2 | 3 | 1 | 56 | 38 | 28.00 | 0 | 0 | 1 | 1 | 414 | 247 | 6 | 41.16 | 0 | 0 | 3/37 |
| Shastri,RJ | 80 | 121 | 14 | 3830 | 206 | 35.79 | 11 | 12 | 9 | 36 | 15751 | 6187 | 151 | 40.97 | 2 | 0 | 5/75 |
| Shinde,SG | 7 | 11 | 5 | 85 | 14 | 14.16 | 0 | 0 | 0 | 0 | 1515 | 717 | 12 | 59.75 | 1 | 0 | 6/91 |
| Shodhan,RH | 3 | 4 | 1 | 181 | 110 | 60.33 | 1 | 0 | 0 | 1 | 60 | 26 | 0 | - | 0 | 0 | 0/1 |
| Shukla,RC | 1 | | | | | | 0 | 0 | 0 | 0 | 294 | 152 | 2 | 76.00 | 0 | 0 | 2/82 |
| Sidhu,NS | 48 | 72 | 2 | 3148 | 201 | 44.97 | 9 | 15 | 8 | 9 | 6 | 9 | 0 | - | 0 | 0 | 0/9 |
| Shivaramakrishnan,L | 9 | 9 | 1 | 130 | 25 | 16.25 | 0 | 0 | 1 | 9 | 2367 | 1145 | 26 | 44.03 | 3 | 1 | 6/64 |
| Sohoni,SW | 4 | 7 | 2 | 83 | 29* | 16.60 | 0 | 0 | 0 | 2 | 532 | 202 | 2 | 101.00 | 0 | 0 | 1/16 |
| Solkar,ED | 27 | 48 | 6 | 1068 | 102 | 25.42 | 1 | 6 | 1 | 53 | 2265 | 1070 | 18 | 59.44 | 0 | 0 | 3/28 |
| Sood,MM | 1 | 2 | 0 | 3 | 3 | 1.50 | 0 | 0 | 1 | 0 | | | | | | | |
| Srikkanth,K | 43 | 72 | 3 | 2062 | 123 | 29.88 | 2 | 12 | 7 | 40 | 216 | 113 | 0 | - | 0 | 0 | 0/1 |
| Srinath,J | 32 | 43 | 13 | 470 | 60 | 15.66 | 0 | 3 | 4 | 15 | 7224 | 3414 | 109 | 31.32 | 2 | 0 | 6/21 |
| Srinivasan,TE | 1 | 2 | 0 | 48 | 29 | 24.00 | 0 | 0 | 0 | 0 | | | | | | | |
| Subramanya,V | 9 | 15 | 1 | 263 | 75 | 18.78 | 0 | 2 | 1 | 9 | 444 | 201 | 3 | 67.00 | 0 | 0 | 2/32 |
| Sunderam,G | 2 | 1 | 1 | 3 | 3* | - | 0 | 0 | 0 | 0 | 396 | 166 | 3 | 55.33 | 0 | 0 | 2/46 |
| Surendranath,R | 11 | 20 | 7 | 136 | 27 | 10.46 | 0 | 0 | 4 | 4 | 2602 | 1053 | 26 | 40.50 | 2 | 0 | 5/75 |
| Surti,RF | 26 | 48 | 4 | 1263 | 99 | 28.70 | 0 | 9 | 5 | 26 | 3870 | 1962 | 42 | 46.71 | 1 | 0 | 5/74 |
| Swamy,VN | 1 | | | | | | 0 | 0 | 0 | 0 | 108 | 45 | 0 | - | 0 | 0 | 0/15 |

| **INDIA** (cont.) | | | | **BATTING AND FIELDING** | | | | | | | | | | **BOWLING** | | | |
|---|---|---|---|---|---|---|---|---|---|---|---|---|---|---|---|---|---|
| | Tests | I | N | Runs | HS | Avge | 100 | 50 | 0's | c/s | Balls | Runs | Wks | Avge | 5w | 10w | BB |
| Tamhane,NS | 21 | 27 | 5 | 225 | 54* | 10.22 | 0 | 1 | 8 | 35/16 | | | | | | | |
| Tarapore,KK | 1 | 1 | 0 | 2 | 2 | 2.00 | 0 | 0 | 0 | 0 | 114 | 72 | 0 | - | 0 | 0 | 0/72 |
| Tendulkar,SR | 61 | 92 | 9 | 4552 | 179 | 54.84 | 16 | 19 | 4 | 47 | 630 | 296 | 5 | 59.20 | 0 | 0 | 2/10 |
| Umrigar,PR | 59 | 94 | 8 | 3631 | 223 | 42.22 | 12 | 14 | 5 | 33 | 4725 | 1473 | 35 | 42.08 | 2 | 0 | 6/74 |
| Vengsarkar,DB | 116 | 185 | 22 | 6868 | 166 | 42.13 | 17 | 35 | 15 | 78 | 47 | 36 | 0 | - | 0 | 0 | 0/3 |
| Venkatapathy Raju,SL | 27 | 33 | 10 | 236 | 31 | 10.26 | 0 | 0 | 3 | 6 | 356 | 2741 | 92 | 29.79 | 5 | 1 | 6/12 |
| Venkataraghavan,S | 57 | 76 | 12 | 748 | 64 | 11.68 | 0 | 2 | 13 | 44 | 14877 | 5634 | 156 | 36.11 | 3 | 1 | 8/72 |
| Venkatesh Prasad,BK | 18 | 24 | 9 | 72 | 15 | 4.80 | 0 | 0 | 5 | 4 | 140 | 1893 | 58 | 32.63 | 5 | 1 | 6/104 |
| Venkataramana,M | 1 | 2 | 2 | 0 | 0* | 0 | 0 | 0 | 0 | 1 | 70 | 58 | 1 | 58.00 | 0 | 0 | 1/10 |
| Viswanath,GR | 91 | 155 | 10 | 6080 | 222 | 41.93 | 14 | 35 | 10 | 63 | 70 | 46 | 1 | 46.00 | 0 | 0 | 1/11 |
| Viswanath,S | 3 | 5 | 0 | 31 | 20 | 6.20 | 0 | 0 | 2 | 11 | | | | | | | |
| Vizianagaram,Maharaj of | 3 | 6 | 2 | 33 | 19* | 8.25 | 0 | 0 | 0 | 1 | | | | | | | |
| Wadekar,AL | 37 | 71 | 3 | 2113 | 143 | 31.07 | 1 | 14 | 7 | 46 | 61 | 55 | 0 | - | 0 | 0 | 0/4 |
| Wassan,AS | 4 | 5 | 1 | 94 | 53 | 23.50 | 0 | 1 | 1 | 1 | 712 | 504 | 10 | 50.40 | 0 | 0 | 4/108 |
| Wazir Ali,S | 7 | 14 | 0 | 237 | 42 | 12.92 | 0 | 0 | 1 | 1 | 30 | 25 | 0 | - | 0 | 0 | 0/0 |
| Yadav,NS | 35 | 40 | 12 | 404 | 43 | 14.42 | 0 | 0 | 4 | 10 | 8349 | 3580 | 102 | 35.09 | 3 | 0 | 5/76 |
| Yadav,V | 1 | 1 | 0 | 30 | 30 | 30.00 | 0 | 0 | 0 | 1/2 | | | | | | | |
| Yajurvindra Singh | 4 | 7 | 1 | 109 | 43* | 7.16 | 0 | 0 | 0 | 11 | 120 | 50 | 0 | - | 0 | 0 | 0/2 |
| Yashpal Sharma | 37 | 59 | 11 | 1606 | 140 | 33.45 | 2 | 9 | 4 | 16 | 30 | 17 | 1 | 17.00 | 0 | 0 | 1/6 |
| Yograj Singh | 1 | 2 | 0 | 10 | 6 | 5.00 | 0 | 0 | 0 | 0 | 90 | 63 | 1 | 63.00 | 0 | 0 | 1/63 |

| **PAKISTAN** | | | | **BATTING AND FIELDING** | | | | | | | | | | **BOWLING** | | | |
|---|---|---|---|---|---|---|---|---|---|---|---|---|---|---|---|---|---|
| | Tests | I | N | Runs | HS | Avge | 100 | 50 | 0's | c/s | Balls | Runs | Wks | Avge | 5w | 10w | BB |
| Aamer Malik | 14 | 19 | 3 | 565 | 117 | 35.31 | 2 | 3 | 3 | 15 | 156 | 89 | 1 | 89.00 | 0 | 0 | 1/0 |
| Aamer Nazir | 6 | 11 | 6 | 31 | 11 | 6.20 | 0 | 0 | 2 | 2 | 1057 | 597 | 20 | 29.85 | 1 | 0 | 5/46 |
| Aamer Sohail | 41 | 72 | 3 | 2554 | 205 | 37.01 | 4 | 13 | 4 | 32 | 1679 | 751 | 17 | 44.17 | 0 | 0 | 4/54 |
| Aaqib Javed | 21 | 25 | 6 | 100 | 28* | 5.26 | 0 | 0 | 7 | 2 | 3754 | 1786 | 54 | 33.07 | 1 | 0 | 5/84 |
| Abdul Kadir | 4 | 8 | 0 | 272 | 95 | 34.00 | 0 | 2 | 2 | 0/1 | | | | | | | |
| Abdul Qadir | 67 | 77 | 10 | 1029 | 61 | 15.35 | 0 | 3 | 7 | 15 | 17126 | 7742 | 236 | 32.80 | 15 | 5 | 9/56 |
| Afaq Hussain | 2 | 4 | 4 | 66 | 35* | 0 | 0 | 0 | 0 | 2 | 240 | 106 | 1 | 106.00 | 0 | 0 | 1/40 |
| Aftab Baloch | 2 | 3 | 1 | 97 | 69* | 48.50 | 0 | 1 | 0 | 0 | 44 | 17 | 0 | - | 0 | 0 | 0/2 |
| Aftab Gul | 6 | 8 | 0 | 182 | 33 | 22.75 | 0 | 0 | 0 | 3 | 6 | 4 | 0 | - | 0 | 0 | 0/4 |
| Agha Saadat Ali | 1 | 1 | 1 | 8 | 8* | 0 | 0 | 0 | 0 | 3 | | | | | | | |
| Agha Zahid | 1 | 2 | 0 | 15 | 14 | 7.50 | 0 | 0 | 0 | 0 | | | | | | | |
| Akram Raza | 9 | 12 | 2 | 155 | 32 | 15.50 | 0 | 0 | 3 | 8 | 1520 | 732 | 13 | 56.30 | 0 | 0 | 3/46 |
| Ali Hussain Rizvi | 1 | | | | | | 0 | 0 | 0 | 0 | 111 | 72 | 2 | 36.00 | 0 | 0 | 2/72 |
| Ali Naqvi | 5 | 9 | 1 | 242 | 115 | 30.25 | 1 | 0 | 0 | 1 | 12 | 11 | 0 | - | 0 | 0 | 0/11 |
| Alimuddin | 25 | 45 | 2 | 1091 | 109 | 25.37 | 2 | 7 | 6 | 8 | 84 | 75 | 1 | 75.00 | 0 | 0 | 1/17 |
| Amir Elahi | 5 | 7 | 1 | 65 | 47 | 10.83 | 0 | 0 | 1 | 0 | 400 | 248 | 7 | 35.42 | 0 | 0 | 4/134 |
| Anil Dalpat | 9 | 12 | 1 | 167 | 52 | 15.18 | 0 | 1 | 0 | 23/3 | | | | | | | |
| Anwar Hussain | 4 | 6 | 0 | 42 | 17 | 7.00 | 0 | 0 | 0 | 0 | 36 | 29 | 1 | 29.00 | 0 | 0 | 1/25 |
| Anwar Khan | 1 | 2 | 1 | 15 | 12 | 15.00 | 0 | 0 | 0 | 0 | 32 | 12 | 0 | - | 0 | 0 | 0/12 |
| Arif Butt | 3 | 5 | 0 | 59 | 20 | 11.80 | 0 | 0 | 1 | 0 | 666 | 288 | 14 | 20.57 | 1 | 0 | 6/89 |
| Arshad Khan | 1 | 1 | 0 | 4 | 4 | 4.00 | 0 | 0 | 0 | 0 | 60 | 32 | 0 | - | 0 | 0 | 0/14 |
| Ashfaq Ahmed | 1 | 2 | 1 | 1 | 1* | 1.00 | 0 | 0 | 1 | 0 | 138 | 53 | 2 | 26.50 | 0 | 0 | 2/31 |
| Ashraf Ali | 8 | 8 | 3 | 229 | 65 | 45.80 | 0 | 2 | 0 | 17/5 | | | | | | | |
| Asif Iqbal | 58 | 99 | 7 | 3575 | 175 | 38.85 | 11 | 12 | 9 | 36 | 3864 | 1502 | 53 | 28.33 | 2 | 0 | 5/48 |
| Asif Masood | 16 | 19 | 10 | 93 | 30* | 10.33 | 0 | 0 | 5 | 5 | 3038 | 1568 | 38 | 41.26 | 1 | 0 | 5/111 |
| Asif Mujtaba | 25 | 41 | 3 | 928 | 65* | 24.42 | 0 | 8 | 5 | 19 | 666 | 303 | 4 | 75.75 | 0 | 0 | 1/0 |
| Ataur Rehman | 13 | 15 | 6 | 76 | 19 | 8.44 | 0 | 0 | 3 | 2 | 1973 | 1071 | 31 | 34.54 | 0 | 0 | 4/50 |
| Atif Rauf | 1 | 2 | 0 | 25 | 16 | 12.50 | 0 | 0 | 0 | 0 | | | | | | | |
| Azeem Hafeez | 18 | 21 | 5 | 134 | 24 | 8.37 | 0 | 0 | 2 | 1 | 4291 | 2202 | 63 | 34.95 | 4 | 0 | 6/46 |
| Azhar Khan | 1 | 1 | 0 | 14 | 14 | 14.00 | 0 | 0 | 0 | 0 | 18 | 2 | 1 | 2.00 | 0 | 0 | 1/2 |
| Azhar Mahmood | 11 | 16 | 4 | 628 | 136 | 52.33 | 3 | 1 | 1 | 6 | 1804 | 774 | 24 | 32.25 | 0 | 0 | 4/53 |
| Azmat Rana | 1 | 1 | 0 | 49 | 49 | 49.00 | 0 | 0 | 0 | 0 | | | | | | | |
| Basit Ali | 19 | 33 | 1 | 858 | 103 | 26.81 | 1 | 5 | 5 | 6 | 6 | 6 | 0 | - | 0 | 0 | 0/6 |
| D'Souza,A | 6 | 10 | 8 | 76 | 23* | 38.00 | 0 | 0 | 0 | 3 | 1587 | 745 | 17 | 43.82 | 1 | 0 | 5/112 |

| PAKISTAN (cont.) | | | | BATTING AND FIELDING | | | | | | | | BOWLING | | | | | |
|---|---|---|---|---|---|---|---|---|---|---|---|---|---|---|---|---|---|
| | Tests | I | N | Runs | HS | Avge | 100 | 50 | 0's | c/s | Balls | Runs | Wks | Avge | 5w | 10w | BB |
| Ehteshamuddin | 5 | 3 | 1 | 2 | 2 | 1.00 | 0 | 0 | 1 | 2 | 940 | 375 | 16 | 23.43 | 1 | 0 | 5/47 |
| Farooq Hamid | 1 | 2 | 0 | 3 | 3 | 1.50 | 0 | 0 | 1 | 0 | 184 | 107 | 1 | 107.00 | 0 | 0 | 1/82 |
| Farrukh Zaman | 1 | | | | | | 0 | 0 | 0 | 0 | 80 | 15 | 0 | - | 0 | 0 | 0/7 |
| Fazal Mahmood | 34 | 50 | 6 | 620 | 60 | 14.09 | 0 | 1 | 10 | 11 | 9834 | 3434 | 139 | 24.70 | 13 | 4 | 7/42 |
| Fazl-e-Akbar | 1 | 2 | 1 | 0 | 0* | 0.00 | 0 | 0 | 1 | 1 | 78 | 32 | 3 | 10.66 | 0 | 0 | 2/16 |
| Ghazali,MEZ | 2 | 4 | 0 | 32 | 18 | 8.00 | 0 | 0 | 2 | 0 | 48 | 18 | 0 | - | 0 | 0 | 0/18 |
| Ghulam Abbas | 1 | 2 | 0 | 12 | 12 | 6.00 | 0 | 0 | 1 | 0 | | | | | | | |
| Gul Mahomed | 1 | 2 | 1 | 39 | 27* | 39.00 | 0 | 0 | 0 | 0 | | | | | | | |
| Hanif Mohammad | 55 | 97 | 8 | 3915 | 337 | 43.98 | 12 | 15 | 5 | 40/0 | 206 | 95 | 1 | 95.00 | 0 | 0 | 1/1 |
| Haroon Rashid | 23 | 36 | 1 | 1217 | 153 | 34.77 | 3 | 5 | 2 | 16 | 8 | 3 | 0 | - | 0 | 0 | 0/3 |
| Hasan Raza | 1 | 1 | 0 | 27 | 27 | 27.00 | 0 | 0 | 0 | 0 | | | | | | | |
| Haseeb Ahsan | 12 | 16 | 7 | 61 | 14 | 6.77 | 0 | 0 | 3 | 1 | 2835 | 1330 | 27 | 49.25 | 2 | 0 | 6/202 |
| Ijaz Ahmed | 46 | 68 | 3 | 2416 | 151 | 37.16 | 8 | 10 | 4 | 28 | 84 | 36 | 1 | 36.00 | 0 | 0 | 1/9 |
| Ijaz Ahmed jr | 2 | 3 | 0 | 29 | 16 | 9.66 | 0 | 0 | 0 | 3 | 24 | 6 | 0 | - | 0 | 0 | 0/1 |
| Ijaz Butt | 8 | 16 | 2 | 279 | 58 | 19.92 | 0 | 1 | 1 | 5/0 | | | | | | | |
| Ijaz Faqih | 5 | 8 | 1 | 183 | 105 | 26.14 | 1 | 0 | 2 | 0 | 534 | 299 | 4 | 74.75 | 0 | 0 | 1/38 |
| Imran Khan | 88 | 126 | 25 | 3807 | 136 | 37.69 | 6 | 18 | 8 | 28 | 19458 | 8258 | 362 | 22.81 | 23 | 6 | 8/58 |
| Imtiaz Ahmed | 41 | 72 | 1 | 2079 | 209 | 29.28 | 3 | 11 | 9 | 77/16 | 6 | 0 | 0 | - | 0 | 0 | 0/0 |
| Intikhab Alam | 47 | 77 | 10 | 1493 | 138 | 22.28 | 1 | 8 | 10 | 20 | 10474 | 4494 | 125 | 35.92 | 5 | 2 | 7/52 |
| Inzamamul Haq | 46 | 77 | 9 | 2995 | 177 | 44.08 | 6 | 20 | 6 | 44 | 9 | 8 | 0 | - | 0 | 0 | 0/8 |
| Iqbal Qasim | 50 | 57 | 15 | 549 | 56 | 13.07 | 0 | 1 | 10 | 42 | 13019 | 4807 | 171 | 28.11 | 8 | 2 | 7/49 |
| Israr Ali | 4 | 8 | 1 | 33 | 10 | 4.71 | 0 | 0 | 1 | 1 | 318 | 165 | 6 | 27.50 | 0 | 0 | 2/29 |
| Jalaluddin | 6 | 3 | 2 | 3 | 2 | 3.00 | 0 | 0 | 0 | 0 | 1200 | 538 | 11 | 48.90 | 0 | 0 | 3/77 |
| Javed Akhtar | 1 | 2 | 1 | 4 | 2* | 4.00 | 0 | 0 | 0 | 0 | 96 | 52 | 0 | - | 0 | 0 | 0/52 |
| Javed Burki | 25 | 48 | 4 | 1341 | 140 | 30.47 | 3 | 4 | 3 | 7 | 42 | 23 | 0 | - | 0 | 0 | 0/3 |
| Javed Miandad | 124 | 189 | 21 | 8832 | 280* | 52.57 | 23 | 43 | 6 | 93/1 | 1470 | 682 | 17 | 40.11 | 0 | 0 | 3/74 |
| Kabir Khan | 4 | 5 | 2 | 24 | 10 | 8.00 | 0 | 0 | 1 | 1 | 655 | 370 | 9 | 41.11 | 0 | 0 | 3/26 |
| Kardar,AH | 23 | 37 | 3 | 847 | 93 | 24.91 | 0 | 5 | 1 | 15 | 2712 | 954 | 21 | 45.42 | 0 | 0 | 3/35 |
| Khalid Hassan | 1 | 2 | 1 | 17 | 10 | 17.00 | 0 | 0 | 0 | 0 | 126 | 116 | 2 | 58.00 | 0 | 0 | 2/116 |
| Khalid Ibadulla | 4 | 8 | 0 | 253 | 166 | 31.62 | 1 | 0 | 0 | 3 | 336 | 99 | 1 | 99.00 | 0 | 0 | 1/42 |
| Khalid Wazir | 2 | 3 | 1 | 14 | 9* | 7.00 | 0 | 0 | 0 | 0 | | | | | | | |
| Khan Mohammad | 13 | 17 | 7 | 100 | 26* | 10.00 | 0 | 0 | 3 | 4 | 3157 | 1292 | 54 | 23.92 | 4 | 0 | 6/21 |
| Liaquat Ali | 5 | 7 | 3 | 28 | 12 | 7.00 | 0 | 0 | 1 | 1 | 808 | 359 | 6 | 59.83 | 0 | 0 | 3/80 |
| Mahmood Hussain | 27 | 39 | 6 | 336 | 35 | 10.18 | 0 | 0 | 8 | 5 | 5910 | 2628 | 68 | 38.64 | 2 | 0 | 6/67 |
| Majid Khan | 63 | 106 | 5 | 3930 | 167 | 38.91 | 8 | 19 | 9 | 70 | 3584 | 1456 | 27 | 53.92 | 0 | 0 | 4/45 |
| Mansoor Akhtar | 19 | 29 | 3 | 655 | 111 | 25.19 | 1 | 3 | 4 | 9 | | | | | | | |
| Manzoor Elahi | 6 | 10 | 2 | 123 | 52 | 15.37 | 0 | 1 | 3 | 7 | 444 | 194 | 7 | 27.71 | 0 | 0 | 2/38 |
| Maqsood Ahmed | 16 | 27 | 1 | 507 | 99 | 19.50 | 0 | 2 | 2 | 13 | 462 | 191 | 3 | 63.66 | 0 | 0 | 2/12 |
| Masood Anwar | 1 | 2 | 0 | 39 | 37 | 19.50 | 0 | 0 | 0 | 0 | 161 | 102 | 3 | 34.00 | 0 | 0 | 2/59 |
| Mathias,W | 21 | 36 | 3 | 783 | 77 | 23.72 | 0 | 3 | 3 | 22 | 24 | 20 | 0 | - | 0 | 0 | 0/20 |
| Miran Bux | 2 | 3 | 2 | 1 | 1* | 1.00 | 0 | 0 | 1 | 0 | 348 | 115 | 2 | 57.50 | 0 | 0 | 2/82 |
| Mohammad Akram | 6 | 9 | 3 | 8 | 5 | 1.33 | 0 | 0 | 3 | 4 | 1033 | 521 | 10 | 52.10 | 0 | 0 | 3/39 |
| Mohammad Aslam | 1 | 2 | 0 | 34 | 18 | 17.00 | 0 | 0 | 0 | 0 | | | | | | | |
| Mohammad Farooq | 7 | 9 | 4 | 85 | 47 | 17.00 | 0 | 0 | 1 | 1 | 1427 | 682 | 21 | 32.47 | 0 | 0 | 4/70 |
| Mohammad Ilyas | 10 | 19 | 0 | 441 | 126 | 23.21 | 1 | 1 | 1 | 6 | 84 | 63 | 0 | - | 0 | 0 | 0/1 |
| Mohammad Munaf | 4 | 7 | 2 | 63 | 19 | 12.60 | 0 | 0 | 0 | 0 | 769 | 341 | 11 | 31.00 | 0 | 0 | 4/42 |
| Mohammad Nazir | 14 | 18 | 10 | 144 | 29* | 18.00 | 0 | 0 | 3 | 4 | 3262 | 1124 | 34 | 33.05 | 3 | 0 | 7/99 |
| Mohammad Ramzan | 1 | 2 | 0 | 36 | 29 | 18.00 | 0 | 0 | 0 | 1 | | | | | | | |
| Mohammad Wasim | 10 | 14 | 2 | 462 | 192 | 38.50 | 2 | 0 | 1 | 11/2 | | | | | | | |
| Mohammad Zahid | 3 | 3 | 1 | 6 | 6* | 3.00 | 0 | 0 | 2 | 0 | 486 | 278 | 13 | 21.38 | 1 | 1 | 7/66 |
| Mohsin Kamal | 9 | 11 | 7 | 37 | 13* | 9.25 | 0 | 0 | 1 | 4 | 1348 | 822 | 24 | 34.25 | 0 | 0 | 4/116 |
| Mohsin Khan | 48 | 79 | 6 | 2709 | 200 | 37.10 | 7 | 9 | 3 | 34 | 86 | 30 | 0 | - | 0 | 0 | 0/0 |
| Moin Khan | 37 | 54 | 6 | 1485 | 117* | 30.93 | 3 | 8 | 4 | 67/9 | | | | | | | |
| Mudassar Nazar | 76 | 116 | 8 | 4114 | 231 | 38.09 | 10 | 17 | 7 | 48 | 5967 | 2532 | 66 | 38.36 | 1 | 0 | 6/32 |
| Mufasir-ul-Haq | 1 | 1 | 1 | 8 | 8* | 0 | 0 | 0 | 0 | 1 | 222 | 84 | 3 | 28.00 | 0 | 0 | 2/50 |
| Munir Malik | 3 | 4 | 1 | 7 | 4 | 2.33 | 0 | 0 | 1 | 1 | 684 | 358 | 9 | 39.77 | 1 | 0 | 5/128 |
| Mushtaq Ahmed | 38 | 54 | 11 | 518 | 59 | 12.04 | 0 | 2 | 9 | 17 | 9544 | 4427 | 160 | 27.66 | 10 | 3 | 7/56 |

| **PAKISTAN** (cont.) | | | | **BATTING AND FIELDING** | | | | | | | | **BOWLING** | | | | | |
|---|---|---|---|---|---|---|---|---|---|---|---|---|---|---|---|---|---|
| | Tests | I | N | Runs | HS | Avge | 100 | 50 | 0's | c/s | Balls | Runs | Wks | Avge | 5w | 10w | BB |
| Mushtaq Mohammad | 57 | 100 | 7 | 3643 | 201 | 39.17 | 10 | 19 | 4 | 42 | 5260 | 2309 | 79 | 29.22 | 3 | - | 5/28 |
| Nadeem Abbasi | 3 | 2 | 0 | 46 | 36 | 23.00 | 0 | 0 | 0 | 6 | | | | | | | |
| Nadeem Ghauri | 1 | 1 | 0 | 0 | 0 | 0.00 | 0 | 0 | 1 | 0 | 48 | 20 | 0 | - | 0 | 0 | 0/20 |
| Nadeem Khan | 1 | 1 | 0 | 25 | 25 | 25.00 | 0 | 0 | 0 | 0 | 312 | 195 | 2 | 97.50 | 0 | 0 | 2/147 |
| Nasim-ul-Ghani | 29 | 50 | 5 | 747 | 101 | 16.60 | 1 | 2 | 8 | 11 | 4406 | 1959 | 52 | 37.67 | 2 | 0 | 6/76 |
| Naushad Ali | 6 | 11 | 0 | 156 | 39 | 14.18 | 0 | 0 | 0 | 9/0 | | | | | | | |
| Naved Anjum | 2 | 3 | 0 | 44 | 22 | 14.66 | 0 | 0 | 0 | 0 | 342 | 162 | 4 | 40.50 | 0 | 0 | 2/57 |
| Nazar Mohammad | 5 | 8 | 1 | 277 | 124* | 39.57 | 1 | 1 | 1 | 7 | 12 | 4 | 0 | - | 0 | 0 | 0/4 |
| Niaz Ahmed | 2 | 3 | 3 | 17 | 16* | 0 | 0 | 0 | 0 | 1 | 294 | 94 | 3 | 31.33 | 0 | 0 | 2/72 |
| Pervez Sajjad | 19 | 20 | 11 | 123 | 24 | 13.66 | 0 | 0 | 2 | 9 | 4145 | 1410 | 59 | 23.89 | 3 | 0 | 7/74 |
| Qasim Omar | 26 | 43 | 2 | 1502 | 210 | 36.63 | 3 | 5 | 2 | 15 | 6 | 0 | 0 | - | 0 | 0 | 0/0 |
| Rameez Raja | 57 | 94 | 5 | 2833 | 122 | 31.83 | 2 | 22 | 7 | 33 | | | | | | | |
| Rashid Khan | 4 | 6 | 3 | 155 | 59 | 51.66 | 0 | 1 | 1 | 2 | 738 | 360 | 8 | 45.00 | 0 | 0 | 3/129 |
| Rashid Latif | 22 | 35 | 6 | 659 | 68* | 22.72 | 0 | 3 | 3 | 73/8 | 12 | 10 | 0 | - | 0 | 0 | 0/10 |
| Rehman,SF | 1 | 2 | 0 | 10 | 8 | 5.00 | 0 | 0 | 0 | 1 | 204 | 99 | 1 | 99.00 | 0 | 0 | 1/43 |
| Rizwan-uz-Zaman | 11 | 19 | 1 | 345 | 60 | 19.16 | 0 | 3 | 2 | 4 | 132 | 46 | 4 | 11.50 | 0 | 0 | 3/26 |
| Sadiq Mohammad | 41 | 74 | 2 | 2579 | 166 | 35.81 | 5 | 10 | 6 | 28 | 200 | 98 | 0 | - | 0 | 0 | 0/0 |
| Saeed Ahmed | 41 | 78 | 4 | 2991 | 172 | 40.41 | 5 | 16 | 2 | 13 | 1980 | 802 | 22 | 36.45 | 0 | 0 | 4/64 |
| Saeed Anwar | 31 | 54 | 1 | 2261 | 176 | 42.66 | 5 | 16 | 5 | 13 | 48 | 23 | 0 | - | 0 | 0 | 0/0 |
| Salahuddin | 5 | 8 | 2 | 117 | 34* | 19.50 | 0 | 0 | 0 | 3 | 546 | 187 | 7 | 26.71 | 0 | 0 | 2/36 |
| Saleem Elahi | 4 | 7 | 0 | 57 | 17 | 8.14 | 0 | 0 | 2 | 8/1 | | | | | | | |
| Saleem Jaffer | 14 | 14 | 6 | 42 | 10* | 5.25 | 0 | 0 | 4 | 2 | 2471 | 1139 | 36 | 31.63 | 1 | 0 | 5/40 |
| Saleem Malik | 96 | 142 | 21 | 5528 | 237 | 45.68 | 15 | 28 | 11 | 61 | 548 | 322 | 5 | 64.40 | 0 | 0 | 1/3 |
| Saleem Yousuf | 32 | 44 | 5 | 1055 | 91* | 27.05 | 0 | 5 | 29 | 91/13 | | | | | | | |
| Salim Altaf | 21 | 31 | 12 | 276 | 53* | 14.52 | 0 | 1 | 4 | 3 | 4001 | 1710 | 46 | 37.17 | 0 | 0 | 4/11 |
| Saqlain Mushtaq | 15 | 22 | 5 | 306 | 79 | 18.00 | 0 | 2 | 6 | 5 | 4298 | 1958 | 58 | 33.75 | 3 | 0 | 5/54 |
| Sarfraz Nawaz | 55 | 72 | 13 | 1045 | 90 | 17.71 | 0 | 4 | 6 | 26 | 13926 | 5798 | 177 | 32.75 | 4 | 1 | 9/86 |
| Shafiq Ahmed | 6 | 10 | 1 | 99 | 27* | 11.00 | 0 | 0 | 3 | 0 | 8 | 1 | 0 | - | 0 | 0 | 0/1 |
| Shafqat Rana | 5 | 7 | 0 | 221 | 95 | 31.57 | 0 | 2 | 1 | 5 | 36 | 9 | 1 | 9.00 | 0 | 0 | 1/2 |
| Shahid Israr | 1 | 1 | 1 | 7 | 7* | 0 | 0 | 0 | 0 | 2/0 | | | | | | | |
| Shahid Mahboob | 1 | | | | | | 0 | 0 | 0 | 0 | 294 | 131 | 2 | 65.50 | 0 | 0 | 2/131 |
| Shahid Mahmood | 1 | 2 | 0 | 25 | 16 | 12.50 | 0 | 0 | 0 | 0 | 36 | 23 | 0 | - | 0 | 0 | 0/23 |
| Shahid Nazir | 7 | 8 | 2 | 45 | 18 | 7.50 | 0 | 0 | 1 | 2 | 926 | 494 | 16 | 30.87 | 1 | 0 | 5/53 |
| Shahid Saeed | 1 | 1 | 0 | 12 | 12 | 12.00 | 0 | 0 | 0 | 0 | 90 | 43 | 0 | - | 0 | 0 | 0/7 |
| Shakeel Ahmed | 3 | 5 | 0 | 74 | 33 | 14.80 | 0 | 0 | 1 | 4 | | | | | | | |
| Sharpe,D | 3 | 6 | 0 | 134 | 56 | 22.33 | 0 | 1 | 0 | 2 | | | | | | | |
| Shoaib Akhtar | 5 | 7 | 3 | 21 | 7* | 5.25 | 0 | 0 | 1 | 2 | 902 | 475 | 12 | 39.58 | 1 | 0 | 5/43 |
| Shoaib Mohammad | 45 | 68 | 7 | 2705 | 203* | 44.34 | 7 | 13 | 6 | 22 | 396 | 170 | 5 | 34.00 | 0 | 0 | 2/8 |
| Shujauddin | 19 | 32 | 6 | 395 | 47 | 15.19 | 0 | 0 | 3 | 8 | 2313 | 801 | 20 | 40.05 | 0 | 0 | 3/18 |
| Sikander Bakht | 26 | 35 | 12 | 146 | 22* | 6.34 | 0 | 0 | 4 | 7 | 4873 | 2412 | 67 | 36.00 | 3 | 1 | 8/69 |
| Tahir Naqqash | 15 | 19 | 5 | 300 | 57 | 21.42 | 0 | 1 | 1 | 3 | 2800 | 1398 | 34 | 41.11 | 2 | 0 | 5/40 |
| Talat Ali | 10 | 18 | 2 | 370 | 61 | 23.12 | 0 | 2 | 2 | 4 | 20 | 7 | 0 | - | 0 | 0 | 0/1 |
| Taslim Arif | 6 | 10 | 2 | 501 | 201* | 62.62 | 1 | 2 | 1 | 7/2 | 30 | 28 | 1 | 28.00 | 0 | 0 | 1/28 |
| Tauseef Ahmed | 34 | 38 | 20 | 318 | 35* | 17.66 | 0 | 0 | 6 | 9 | 7778 | 2950 | 93 | 31.72 | 3 | 0 | 6/45 |
| Waqar Hassan | 21 | 35 | 1 | 1071 | 189 | 31.50 | 1 | 6 | 0 | 10 | 6 | 10 | 0 | - | 0 | 0 | 0/10 |
| Waqar Younis | 53 | 69 | 12 | 556 | 45 | 9.75 | 0 | 0 | 11 | 7 | 10799 | 5748 | 267 | 21.52 | 21 | 5 | 7/76 |
| Wasim Akram | 79 | 109 | 15 | 2020 | 257* | 21.48 | 2 | 4 | 14 | 30 | 17904 | 7705 | 341 | 22.59 | 21 | 4 | 7/119 |
| Wasim Bari | 81 | 112 | 26 | 1366 | 85 | 15.88 | 0 | 6 | 19 | 201/27 | 8 | 2 | 0 | - | 0 | 0 | 0/2 |
| Wasim Raja | 57 | 92 | 14 | 2821 | 125 | 36.16 | 4 | 18 | 8 | 20 | 4092 | 1826 | 51 | 35.80 | 0 | 0 | 4/50 |
| Wazir Mohammad | 20 | 33 | 4 | 801 | 189 | 27.62 | 2 | 3 | 8 | 5 | 24 | 15 | 0 | - | 0 | 0 | 0/5 |
| Younis Ahmed | 4 | 7 | 1 | 177 | 62 | 29.50 | 0 | 1 | 1 | 0 | 6 | 6 | 0 | - | 0 | 0 | 0/6 |
| Yousuf Youhana | 3 | 6 | 0 | 191 | 64 | 31.83 | 0 | 3 | 0 | 4 | | | | | | | |
| Zaheer Abbas | 78 | 124 | 11 | 5062 | 274 | 44.79 | 12 | 20 | 10 | 34 | 370 | 132 | 3 | 44.00 | 0 | 0 | 2/21 |
| Zahid Fazal | 9 | 16 | 0 | 288 | 78 | 18.00 | 0 | 1 | 0 | 5 | | | | | | | |
| Zahoor Elahi | 2 | 3 | 0 | 30 | 22 | 10.00 | 0 | 0 | 0 | 1 | | | | | | | |
| Zakir Khan | 2 | 2 | 2 | 9 | 9* | 0 | 0 | 0 | 0 | 1 | 444 | 259 | 5 | 51.80 | 0 | 0 | 3/80 |
| Zulfiqar Ahmed | 9 | 10 | 4 | 200 | 63* | 33.33 | 0 | 1 | 1 | 5 | 1285 | 366 | 20 | 18.30 | 2 | 1 | 6/42 |

| PAKISTAN (cont.) | | | | BATTING AND FIELDING | | | | | | | | | | BOWLING | | | |
|---|---|---|---|---|---|---|---|---|---|---|---|---|---|---|---|---|---|
| | Tests | I | N | Runs | HS | Avge | 100 | 50 | 0's | c/s | Balls | Runs | Wks | Avge | 5w | 10w | BB |
| Zulqarnain | 3 | 4 | 0 | 24 | 13 | 6.00 | 0 | 0 | 0 | 8/2 | | | | | | | |

| SRI LANKA | | | | BATTING AND FIELDING | | | | | | | | | | BOWLING | | | |
|---|---|---|---|---|---|---|---|---|---|---|---|---|---|---|---|---|---|
| | Tests | I | N | Runs | HS | Avge | 100 | 50 | 0's | c/s | Balls | Runs | Wks | Avge | 5w | 10w | BB |
| Ahangama,FS | 3 | 3 | 1 | 11 | 11 | 5.50 | 0 | 0 | 1 | 1 | 804 | 348 | 18 | 19.33 | 1 | 0 | 5/52 |
| Amalean,KN | 2 | 3 | 2 | 9 | 7* | 9.00 | 0 | 0 | 0 | 1 | 244 | 156 | 7 | 22.28 | 0 | 0 | 4/97 |
| Amerasinghe,MJG | 2 | 4 | 1 | 54 | 34 | 18.00 | 0 | 0 | 0 | 3 | 300 | 150 | 3 | 50.00 | 0 | 0 | 2/73 |
| Anurasiri,SD | 19 | 24 | 5 | 91 | 24 | 4.78 | 0 | 0 | 3 | 5 | 3973 | 1548 | 41 | 37.75 | 0 | 0 | 4/71 |
| Arnold,RP | 3 | 6 | 0 | 138 | 50 | 23.00 | 0 | 1 | 1 | 4 | 78 | 31 | 0 | - | 0 | 0 | 0/2 |
| Atapattu,MS | 19 | 34 | 1 | 981 | 223 | 29.72 | 2 | 3 | 8 | 11 | 48 | 24 | 1 | 24.00 | 0 | 0 | 1/9 |
| Bandara,CM | 1 | 2 | 1 | 0 | 0* | 0.00 | 0 | 0 | 1 | 1 | 126 | 79 | 0 | - | 0 | 0 | 0/38 |
| Bandaratilleke,MLCN | 3 | 5 | 0 | 52 | 20 | 10.40 | 0 | 0 | 0 | 0 | 960 | 338 | 16 | 21.12 | 1 | 0 | 5/36 |
| Dasanayake,PB | 11 | 17 | 2 | 196 | 36 | 13.06 | 0 | 0 | 3 | 20/5 | | | | | | | |
| de Alwis,RG | 11 | 19 | 0 | 152 | 28 | 8.00 | 0 | 0 | 5 | 21/2 | | | | | | | |
| de Mel,ALF | 17 | 28 | 5 | 326 | 34 | 14.17 | 0 | 0 | 5 | 9 | 3518 | 2180 | 59 | 36.94 | 3 | 0 | 6/109 |
| de Silva,AM | 3 | 3 | 0 | 10 | 9 | 3.33 | 0 | 0 | 1 | 4/1 | | | | | | | |
| de Silva,DS | 12 | 22 | 3 | 406 | 61 | 21.36 | 0 | 2 | 3 | 5 | 3031 | 1424 | 38 | 37.47 | 1 | 0 | 5/59 |
| de Silva,EAR | 10 | 16 | 4 | 185 | 50 | 15.41 | 0 | 1 | 3 | 4 | 2388 | 1032 | 8 | 129.00 | 0 | 0 | 2/67 |
| de Silva,GRA | 4 | 7 | 2 | 41 | 14 | 8.20 | 0 | 0 | 2 | 0 | 956 | 385 | 7 | 55.00 | 0 | 0 | 2/38 |
| de Silva,KSC | 6 | 9 | 5 | 19 | 6 | 4.75 | 0 | 0 | 2 | 2 | 1173 | 636 | 13 | 48.92 | 1 | 0 | 5/85 |
| de Silva,PA | 73 | 127 | 9 | 4977 | 267 | 42.17 | 16 | 18 | 6 | 36 | 1820 | 888 | 24 | 37.00 | 0 | 0 | 3/30 |
| de Silva,SKL | 3 | 4 | 2 | 36 | 20+ | 18.00 | 0 | 0 | 1 | 1/0 | | | | | | | |
| Dharmasena,HDPK | 19 | 34 | 5 | 647 | 62* | 22.31 | 0 | 2 | 3 | 11 | 4524 | 1826 | 50 | 36.52 | 3 | 0 | 6/72 |
| Dias,RL | 20 | 36 | 1 | 1285 | 109 | 36.71 | 3 | 8 | 2 | 9 | 24 | 16 | 0 | - | 0 | 0 | 0/16 |
| Dunusinghe,CI | 5 | 10 | 0 | 160 | 91 | 16.00 | 0 | 1 | 3 | 13/2 | | | | | | | |
| Fernando,ERNS | 5 | 10 | 0 | 112 | 46 | 11.20 | 0 | 0 | 3 | 0 | | | | | | | |
| Goonasekera,Y | 2 | 4 | 0 | 48 | 23 | 12.00 | 0 | 0 | 0 | 6 | | | | | | | |
| Goonatillake,HM | 5 | 10 | 2 | 191 | 56 | 23.87 | 0 | 1 | 1 | 10/3 | | | | | | | |
| Guneratne,RPW | 1 | 2 | 2 | 0 | 0* | - | 0 | 0 | 0 | 0 | 102 | 84 | 0 | - | 0 | 0 | 0/84 |
| Gurusinha,AP | 41 | 70 | 7 | 2452 | 143 | 38.92 | 7 | 8 | 3 | 33 | 1408 | 681 | 20 | 34.05 | 0 | 0 | 2/7 |
| Hathurusingha,UC | 24 | 42 | 1 | 1260 | 83 | 30.73 | 0 | 8 | 1 | 6 | 1704 | 668 | 16 | 41.75 | 0 | 0 | 4/66 |
| Jayasekera,RSA | 1 | 2 | 0 | 2 | 2 | 1.00 | 0 | 0 | 1 | 0 | | | | | | | |
| Jayasuriya,ST | 37 | 62 | 6 | 2375 | 340 | 42.41 | 4 | 14 | 7 | 34 | 2250 | 1077 | 25 | 43.08 | 0 | 0 | 4/53 |
| Jayawardene,DPM | 5 | 8 | 0 | 389 | 167 | 48.62 | 1 | 3 | 0 | 9 | 84 | 45 | 0 | - | 0 | 0 | 0/0 |
| Jeganathan,S | 2 | 4 | 0 | 19 | 8 | 4.75 | 0 | 0 | 1 | 0 | 32 | 12 | 0 | - | 0 | 0 | 0/12 |
| John,VB | 6 | 10 | 5 | 53 | 27* | 10.60 | 0 | 0 | 4 | 2 | 1281 | 614 | 28 | 21.92 | 2 | 0 | 5/60 |
| Jurangpathy,BR | 2 | 4 | 0 | 1 | 1 | 0.25 | 0 | 0 | 3 | 2 | 150 | 93 | 1 | 93.00 | 0 | 0 | 1/69 |
| Kalpage,RS | 10 | 17 | 1 | 292 | 63 | 18.25 | 0 | 2 | 0 | 9 | 1361 | 607 | 8 | 75.87 | 0 | 0 | 2/27 |
| Kaluperuma,LW | 2 | 4 | 1 | 12 | 11* | 4.00 | 0 | 0 | 2 | 2 | 162 | 93 | 0 | - | 0 | 0 | 0/24 |
| Kaluperuma,SMS | 4 | 8 | 0 | 88 | 23 | 11.00 | 0 | 0 | 1 | 6 | 240 | 124 | 3 | 41.33 | 0 | 0 | 2/17 |
| Kaluwitharana,RS | 23 | 38 | 2 | 1166 | 132 | 32.38 | 2 | 7 | 3 | 44/10 | | | | | | | |
| Kuruppu,DSBP | 4 | 7 | 2 | 320 | 201* | 64.00 | 1 | 0 | 0 | 1/0 | | | | | | | |
| Kuruppuarachchi,AK | 2 | 2 | 2 | 0 | 0* | - | 0 | 0 | 0 | 0 | 272 | 152 | 8 | 19.00 | 1 | 0 | 5/44 |
| Labrooy,GF | 9 | 14 | 3 | 158 | 70* | 14.36 | 0 | 1 | 3 | 3 | 2158 | 1194 | 27 | 44.22 | 1 | 0 | 5/133 |
| Liyanage,DK | 8 | 8 | 0 | 66 | 23 | 8.25 | 0 | 0 | 1 | 0 | 1271 | 622 | 17 | 36.58 | 0 | 0 | 4/56 |
| Madugalle,RS | 21 | 39 | 4 | 1029 | 103 | 29.40 | 1 | 7 | 4 | 9 | 84 | 38 | 0 | - | 0 | 0 | 0/0 |
| Madurasinghe,MAWR | 3 | 6 | 1 | 24 | 11 | 4.80 | 0 | 0 | 1 | 0 | 396 | 172 | 3 | 57.33 | 0 | 0 | 3/60 |
| Mahanama,RS | 52 | 89 | 1 | 2576 | 225 | 29.27 | 4 | 11 | 8 | 56 | 36 | 30 | 0 | - | 0 | 0 | 0/3 |
| Mendis,LRD | 24 | 43 | 1 | 1329 | 124 | 31.64 | 4 | 8 | 2 | 9 | | | | | | | |
| Muralidaran,M | 41 | 56 | 24 | 428 | 39 | 13.37 | 0 | 0 | 11 | 22 | 12357 | 5244 | 187 | 28.04 | 14 | 1 | 7/94 |
| Pushpakumara,KR | 18 | 24 | 11 | 93 | 23 | 7.15 | 0 | 0 | 4 | 8 | 2905 | 1837 | 47 | 39.08 | 3 | 0 | 7/116 |
| Ramanayake,CPH | 18 | 24 | 9 | 143 | 34* | 9.53 | 0 | 0 | 7 | 6 | 3654 | 1880 | 44 | 42.72 | 1 | 0 | 5/82 |
| Ranasinghe,AN | 2 | 4 | 0 | 88 | 77 | 22.00 | 0 | 1 | 1 | 0 | 114 | 69 | 1 | 69.00 | 0 | 0 | 1/23 |
| Ranatunga,A | 81 | 137 | 8 | 4544 | 135* | 35.22 | 4 | 32 | 12 | 35 | 2367 | 1027 | 16 | 64.18 | 0 | 0 | 2/17 |
| Ranatunga,D | 2 | 3 | 0 | 87 | 44 | 29.00 | 0 | 0 | 0 | 0 | | | | | | | |
| Ranatunga,S | 9 | 17 | 1 | 531 | 118 | 33.18 | 2 | 2 | 1 | 2 | | | | | | | |

| **SRI LANKA** (cont.) | | | | **BATTING AND FIELDING** | | | | | | | | | | **BOWLING** | | | |
|---|---|---|---|---|---|---|---|---|---|---|---|---|---|---|---|---|---|
| | Tests | I | N | Runs | HS | Avge | 100 | 50 | 0's | c/s | Balls | Runs | Wks | Avge | 5w | 10w | BB |
| Ratnayake,RJ | 23 | 36 | 6 | 433 | 56 | 14.43 | 0 | 2 | 5 | 9 | 4955 | 2563 | 73 | 35.11 | 5 | 0 | 6/66 |
| Ratnayeke,JR | 22 | 38 | 6 | 807 | 93 | 25.21 | 0 | 5 | 5 | 1 | 3833 | 1972 | 56 | 35.21 | 4 | 0 | 8/83 |
| Samarasekera,MAR | 4 | 7 | 0 | 118 | 57 | 16.85 | 0 | 1 | 1 | 3 | 192 | 104 | 3 | 34.66 | 0 | 0 | 2/38 |
| Samaraweera,DP | 7 | 14 | 0 | 211 | 42 | 15.07 | 0 | 0 | 1 | 5 | | | | | | | |
| Senanayake,CP | 3 | 5 | 0 | 97 | 64 | 19.40 | 0 | 1 | 1 | 2 | | | | | | | |
| Silva,KJ | 7 | 4 | 1 | 6 | 6* | 2.00 | 0 | 0 | 3 | 1 | 1533 | 647 | 20 | 32.35 | 0 | 0 | 4/16 |
| Silva,SAR | 9 | 16 | 2 | 353 | 111 | 25.21 | 2 | 0 | 1 | 33/1 | | | | | | | |
| Tillakaratne,HP | 52 | 86 | 13 | 2879 | 126* | 39.43 | 6 | 15 | 7 | 83/0 | 34 | 14 | 0 | - | 0 | 0 | 0/1 |
| Vaas,WPUJC | 26 | 39 | 5 | 580 | 57 | 17.05 | 0 | 2 | 3 | 10 | 5555 | 2409 | 83 | 29.02 | 4 | 1 | 6/87 |
| Warnapura,B | 4 | 8 | 0 | 96 | 38 | 12.00 | 0 | 0 | 1 | 2 | 90 | 46 | 0 | - | 0 | 0 | 0/1 |
| Warnaweera,KPJ | 10 | 12 | 3 | 39 | 20 | 4.33 | 0 | 0 | 3 | 0 | 2359 | 1021 | 32 | 31.90 | 0 | 0 | 4/25 |
| Weerasinghe,CDUS | 1 | 1 | 0 | 3 | 3 | 3.00 | 0 | 0 | 0 | 0 | 114 | 36 | 0 | - | 0 | 0 | 0/8 |
| Wettimuny,MD | 2 | 4 | 0 | 28 | 17 | 7.00 | 0 | 0 | 1 | 2 | | | | | | | |
| Wettimuny,S | 23 | 43 | 1 | 1221 | 190 | 29.07 | 2 | 6 | 5 | 10 | 24 | 37 | 0 | - | 0 | 0 | 0/16 |
| Wickramasinghe,GP | 30 | 49 | 5 | 481 | 51 | 10.93 | 0 | 1 | 10 | 10 | 5323 | 2688 | 58 | 46.34 | 1 | 0 | 5/73 |
| Wickremasinghe,AGD | 3 | 3 | 1 | 17 | 13* | 8.50 | 0 | 0 | 0 | 9/1 | | | | | | | |
| Wijegunawardene,KIW | 2 | 4 | 1 | 14 | 6* | 4.66 | 0 | 0 | 0 | 0 | 364 | 148 | 7 | 21.14 | 0 | 0 | 4/52 |
| Wijesuriya,RGCE | 4 | 7 | 2 | 22 | 8 | 4.40 | 0 | 0 | 2 | 1 | 586 | 294 | 1 | 294.00 | 0 | 0 | 1/68 |
| Wijetunge,PK | 1 | 2 | 0 | 10 | 10 | 5.00 | 0 | 0 | 1 | 0 | 312 | 118 | 2 | 59.00 | 0 | 0 | 1/58 |
| Zoysa,DNT | 4 | 7 | 1 | 57 | 16* | 9.50 | 0 | 0 | 3 | 2 | 628 | 307 | 8 | 38.37 | 0 | 0 | 3/47 |

| **ZIMBABWE** | | | | **BATTING AND FIELDING** | | | | | | | | | | **BOWLING** | | | |
|---|---|---|---|---|---|---|---|---|---|---|---|---|---|---|---|---|---|
| | Tests | I | N | Runs | HS | Avge | 100 | 50 | 0's | c/s | Balls | Runs | Wks | Avge | 5w | 10w | BB |
| Arnott,KJ | 4 | 8 | 1 | 302 | 101* | 43.14 | 1 | 1 | 1 | 3 | | | | | | | |
| Brain,DH | 9 | 12 | 1 | 109 | 28 | 9.90 | 0 | 0 | 4 | 1 | 1810 | 915 | 30 | 30.50 | 1 | 0 | 5/42 |
| Brandes,EA | 9 | 13 | 2 | 111 | 39 | 10.09 | 0 | 0 | 2 | 4 | 1870 | 883 | 22 | 40.13 | 0 | 0 | 3/45 |
| Briant,GA | 1 | 2 | 0 | 17 | 16 | 8.50 | 0 | 0 | 0 | 0 | | | | | | | |
| Bruk-Jackson,GK | 2 | 4 | 0 | 39 | 31 | 9.75 | 0 | 0 | 1 | 0 | | | | | | | |
| Burmester,MG | 3 | 4 | 2 | 54 | 30* | 27.00 | 0 | 0 | 1 | 1 | 436 | 227 | 3 | 75.66 | 0 | 0 | 3/78 |
| Butchart,IP | 1 | 2 | 0 | 23 | 15 | 11.50 | 0 | 0 | 0 | 1 | 18 | 11 | 0 | - | 0 | 0 | 0/11 |
| Campbell,ADR | 30 | 54 | 2 | 1531 | 99 | 29.44 | 0 | 11 | 4 | 29 | 42 | 20 | 0 | - | 0 | 0 | 0/1 |
| Carlisle,SV | 6 | 10 | 1 | 175 | 58 | 19.44 | 0 | 1 | 2 | 10 | | | | | | | |
| Crocker,GJ | 3 | 4 | 1 | 69 | 33 | 23.00 | 0 | 0 | 0 | 0 | 456 | 217 | 3 | 72.33 | 0 | 0 | 2/65 |
| Dekker,MH | 14 | 22 | 1 | 333 | 68* | 15.85 | 0 | 2 | 4 | 12 | 60 | 15 | 0 | - | 0 | 0 | 0/4 |
| Evans,CN | 1 | 2 | 0 | 10 | 9 | 5.00 | 0 | 0 | 0 | 1 | 36 | 27 | 0 | - | 0 | 0 | 0/27 |
| Flower,A | 30 | 53 | 7 | 1942 | 156 | 42.21 | 5 | 12 | 2 | 70/5 | 1 | 0 | 0 | - | 0 | 0 | 0/0 |
| Flower,GW | 30 | 54 | 2 | 1991 | 201* | 38.28 | 5 | 8 | 6 | 15 | 756 | 354 | 3 | 118.00 | 0 | 0 | 1/4 |
| Goodwin,MW | 6 | 12 | 1 | 606 | 166* | 55.09 | 1 | 5 | 1 | 5 | 95 | 53 | 0 | - | 0 | 0 | 0/3 |
| Houghton,DL | 22 | 36 | 2 | 1466 | 266 | 43.11 | 4 | 4 | 0 | 17 | 5 | 0 | 0 | - | 0 | 0 | 0/0 |
| Huckle,AG | 6 | 11 | 2 | 32 | 19 | 3.55 | 0 | 0 | 7 | 2 | 1400 | 771 | 22 | 35.04 | 2 | 1 | 6/111 |
| James,WR | 4 | 4 | 0 | 61 | 33 | 15.25 | 0 | 0 | 0 | 16/0 | | | | | | | |
| Jarvis,MP | 5 | 4 | 2 | 10 | 6* | 5.00 | 0 | 0 | 1 | 1 | 1273 | 393 | 11 | 35.72 | 0 | 0 | 3/30 |
| Lock,ACI | 1 | 2 | 1 | 8 | 8* | 8.00 | 0 | 0 | 1 | 0 | 180 | 105 | 5 | 21.00 | 0 | 0 | 3/68 |
| Madondo,TN | 2 | 3 | 0 | 16 | 14 | 5.33 | 0 | 0 | 1 | 0 | | | | | | | |
| Matambanadzo,E | 2 | 3 | 1 | 6 | 4 | 3.00 | 0 | 0 | 0 | 0 | 198 | 155 | 2 | 77.50 | 0 | 0 | 2/62 |
| Mbangwa,M | 6 | 11 | 2 | 16 | 7 | 1.77 | 0 | 0 | 6 | 1 | 1068 | 417 | 15 | 27.80 | 0 | 0 | 3/56 |
| Olonga,HK | 7 | 9 | 1 | 14 | 7 | 1.75 | 0 | 0 | 5 | 4 | 802 | 487 | 10 | 48.70 | 0 | 0 | 3/90 |
| Peall,SG | 4 | 6 | 1 | 59 | 30 | 11.80 | 0 | 0 | 2 | 1 | 888 | 303 | 4 | 75.75 | 0 | 0 | 2/89 |
| Pycroft,AJ | 3 | 5 | 0 | 152 | 60 | 30.40 | 0 | 1 | 0 | 2 | | | | | | | |
| Ranchod,U | 1 | 2 | 0 | 8 | 7 | 4.00 | 0 | 0 | 0 | 0 | 72 | 45 | 1 | 45.00 | 0 | 0 | 1/45 |
| Rennie,GJ | 7 | 14 | 0 | 341 | 57 | 24.35 | 0 | 4 | 3 | 7 | | | | | | | |
| Rennie,JA | 4 | 6 | 1 | 62 | 22 | 12.40 | 0 | 0 | 1 | 1 | 724 | 293 | 3 | 97.66 | 0 | 0 | 2/22 |
| Shah,AH | 3 | 5 | 0 | 122 | 62 | 24.40 | 0 | 1 | 0 | 0 | 186 | 125 | 1 | 125.00 | 0 | 0 | 1/46 |
| Strang,BC | 13 | 23 | 7 | 223 | 53 | 13.93 | 0 | 1 | 4 | 9 | 2633 | 980 | 32 | 30.62 | 1 | 0 | 5/101 |
| Strang,PA | 20 | 34 | 7 | 747 | 106* | 27.66 | 1 | 2 | 2 | 12 | 4852 | 2153 | 57 | 37.77 | 3 | 0 | 5/106 |
| Streak,HH | 23 | 37 | 8 | 507 | 53 | 17.48 | 0 | 2 | 8 | 7 | 5285 | 2335 | 94 | 24.84 | 3 | 0 | 6/90 |

| ZIMBABWE (cont.) | | | | BATTING AND FIELDING | | | | | | | | | BOWLING | | | | | |
|---|---|---|---|---|---|---|---|---|---|---|---|---|---|---|---|---|---|---|
| | Tests | I | N | Runs | HS | Avge | 100 | 50 | 0's | c/s | Balls | Runs | Wks | Avge | 5w | 10w | BB |
| Traicos,AJ | 4 | 6 | 2 | 11 | 5 | 2.75 | 0 | 0 | 1 | 4 | 1141 | 562 | 14 | 40.14 | 1 | 0 | 5/86 |
| Viljoen,DP | 1 | 2 | 0 | 0 | 0 | 0.00 | 0 | 0 | 2 | 1 | 24 | 15 | 1 | 15.00 | 0 | 0 | 1/15 |
| Waller,AC | 2 | 3 | 0 | 69 | 50 | 23.00 | 0 | 1 | 0 | 1 | | | | | | | |
| Whittall,AR | 8 | 16 | 3 | 93 | 17 | 7.15 | 0 | 0 | 1 | 7 | 1322 | 601 | 6 | 100.16 | 0 | 0 | 3/73 |
| Whittall,GJ | 25 | 43 | 3 | 1045 | 203* | 26.12 | 2 | 4 | 4 | 12 | 3040 | 1314 | 36 | 36.50 | 0 | 0 | 4/18 |
| Wishart,CB | 8 | 16 | 1 | 177 | 51 | 11.80 | 0 | 1 | 3 | 4 | | | | | | | |

**COMPLETE TEST RECORD FOR PLAYERS REPRESENTING TWO COUNTRIES**

| | | | | BATTING AND FIELDING | | | | | | | | | BOWLING | | | | |
|---|---|---|---|---|---|---|---|---|---|---|---|---|---|---|---|---|---|
| | Tests | I | N | Runs | HS | Avge | 100 | 50 | 0's | c/s | Balls | Runs | Wks | Avge | 5w | 10w | BB |
| Amir Elahi (I/P) | 6 | 9 | 1 | 82 | 47 | 10.25 | 0 | 0 | 1 | 0 | 400 | 248 | 7 | 35.42 | 0 | 0 | 4/134 |
| Ferris,JJ (A/E) | 9 | 17 | 4 | 114 | 20* | 8.76 | 0 | 0 | 1 | 4 | 2302 | 775 | 61 | 12.70 | 6 | 1 | 7/37 |
| Guillen,SC (W/N) | 8 | 12 | 2 | 202 | 54 | 20.20 | 0 | 1 | 3 | 13/3 | | | | | | | |
| Gul Mahomed (I/P) | 9 | 17 | 1 | 205 | 34 | 12.81 | 0 | 0 | 2 | 3 | 77 | 24 | 2 | 12.00 | 0 | 0 | 2/21 |
| Hearne,F (E/SA) | 6 | 10 | 0 | 168 | 30 | 16.80 | 0 | 0 | 2 | 3 | 62 | 40 | 2 | 20.00 | 0 | 0 | 2/40 |
| Kardar,AH (I/P) | 26 | 42 | 3 | 927 | 93 | 23.76 | 0 | 5 | 2 | 16 | 2712 | 954 | 21 | 45.42 | 0 | 0 | 3/35 |
| Midwinter,WE (A/E) | 12 | 21 | 1 | 269 | 37 | 13.45 | 0 | 0 | 1 | 10 | 1725 | 605 | 24 | 25.20 | 1 | 0 | 5/78 |
| Mitchell,F (E/SA) | 5 | 10 | 0 | 116 | 41 | 11.60 | 0 | 0 | 1 | 2 | | | | | | | |
| Murdoch,WL (A/E) | 19 | 34 | 5 | 908 | 211 | 31.31 | 2 | 1 | 3 | 13/2 | | | | | | | |
| Pataudi, Nawab of, sr (E/I) | 6 | 10 | 0 | 199 | 102 | 19.90 | 1 | 0 | 0 | 0 | | | | | | | |
| Traicos,AJ (SA/Z) | 7 | 10 | 4 | 19 | 5* | 3.16 | 0 | 0 | 2 | 8 | 1611 | 769 | 18 | 42.72 | 0 | 0 | 3/186 |
| Trott,AE (A/E) | 5 | 9 | 3 | 228 | 85* | 38.00 | 0 | 2 | 2 | 4 | 948 | 390 | 26 | 15.00 | 2 | 0 | 8/43 |
| Wessels,KC (A/SA) | 40 | 71 | 3 | 2788 | 179 | 41.00 | 6 | 15 | 5 | 30 | 90 | 42 | 0 | - | 0 | 0 | 0/2 |
| Woods,SMJ (A/E) | 6 | 10 | 0 | 154 | 53 | 15.40 | 0 | 1 | 2 | 5 | 412 | 250 | 10 | 25.00 | 0 | 0 | 3/28 |